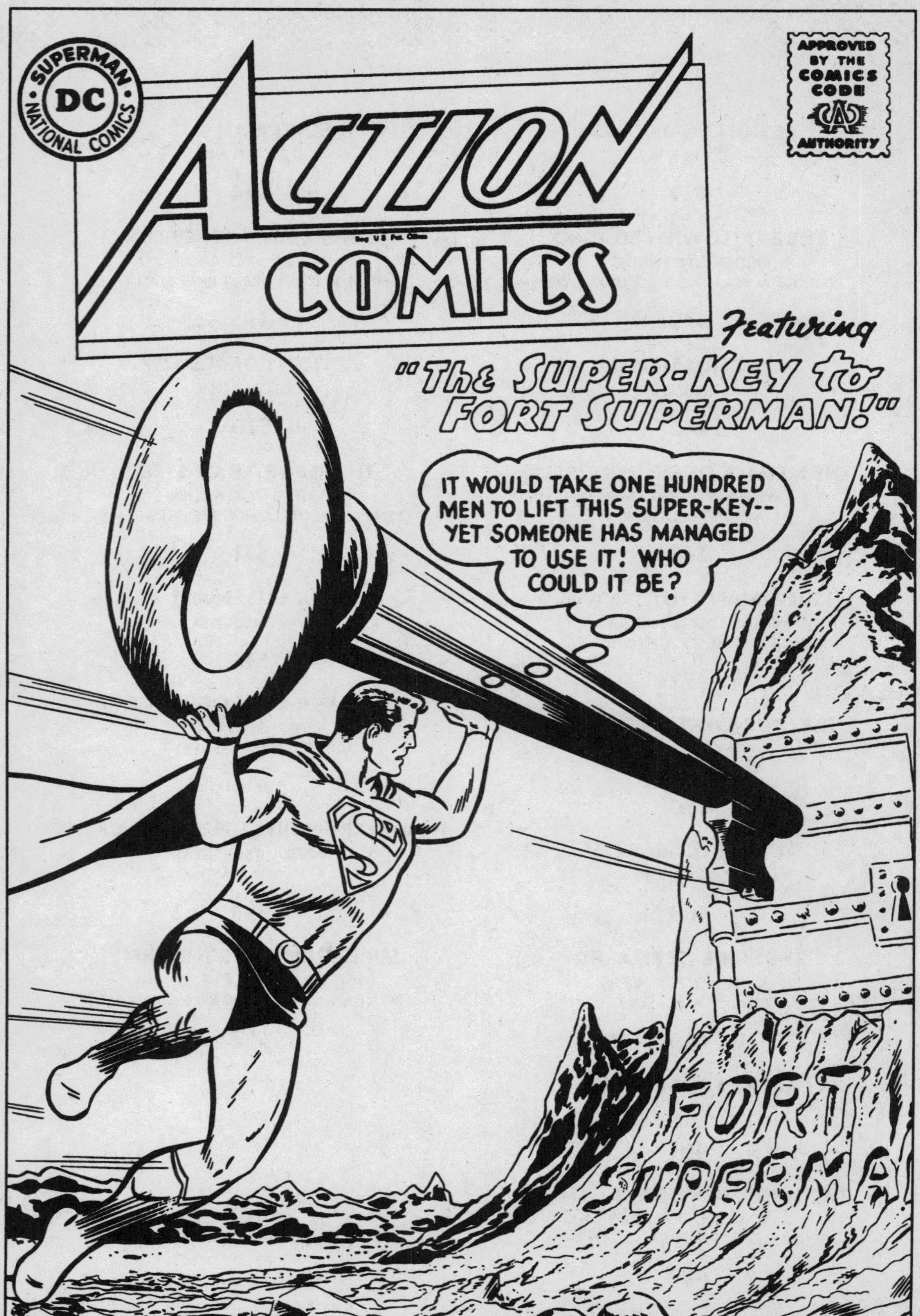
SUPERMAN
DC
NATIONAL COMICS
ACTION
COMICS
APPROVED BY THE COMICS CODE AUTHORITY
Featuring
"The SUPER-KEY to FORT SUPERMAN!"
IT WOULD TAKE ONE HUNDRED MEN TO LIFT THIS SUPER-KEY-- YET SOMEONE HAS MANAGED TO USE IT! WHO COULD IT BE?
FORT

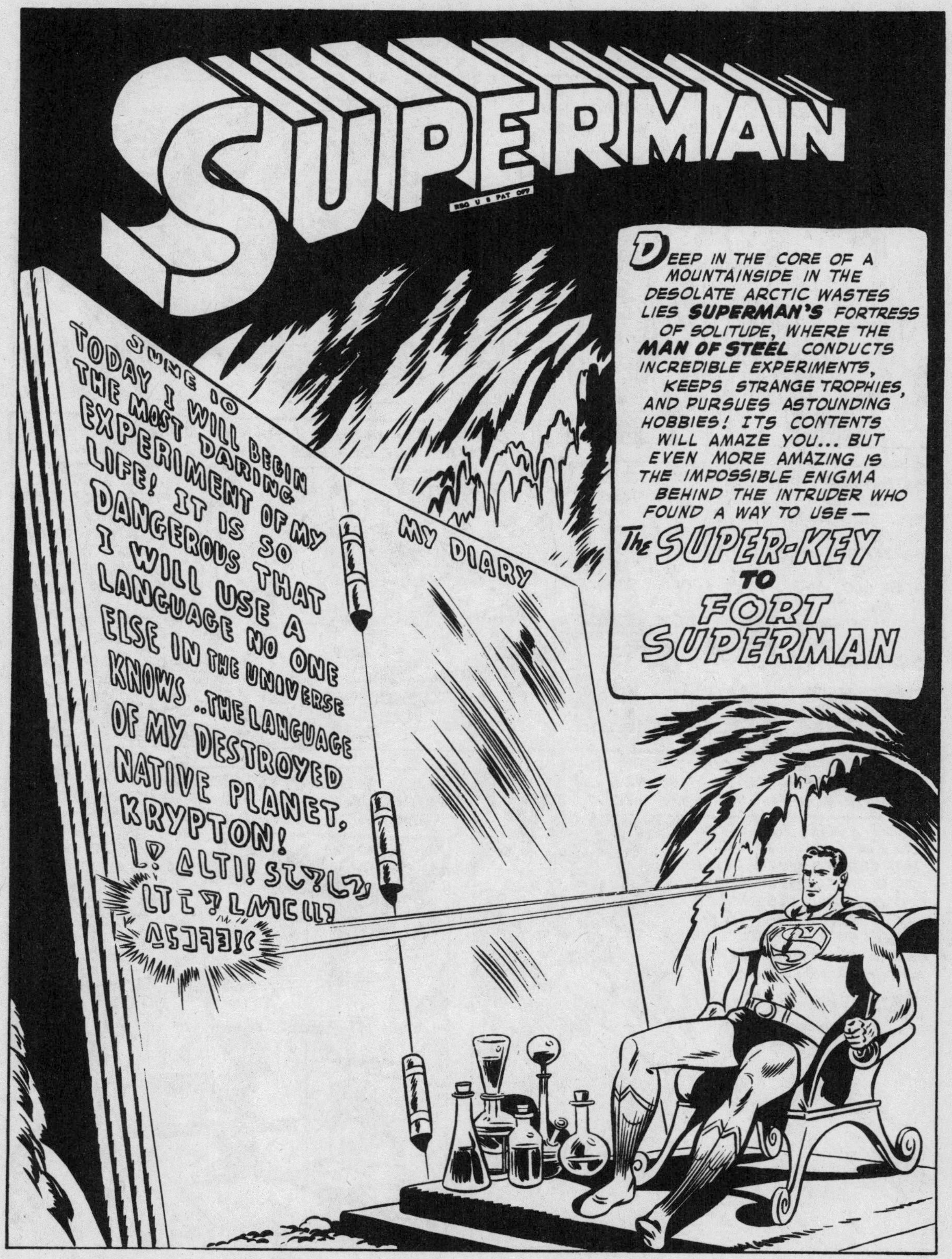
SUPERMAN
JUNE 10
TODAY I WILL BEGIN THE MOST DARING EXPERIMENT OF MY LIFE! IT IS SO DANGEROUS THAT I WILL USE A LANGUAGE NO ONE ELSE IN THE UNIVERSE KNOWS ..THE LANGUAGE OF MY DESTROYED NATIVE PLANET, KRYPTON!
MY DIARY
DEEP IN THE CORE OF A MOUNTAINSIDE IN THE DESOLATE ARCTIC WASTES LIES SUPERMAN'S FORTRESS OF SOLITUDE, WHERE THE MAN OF STEEL CONDUCTS INCREDIBLE EXPERIMENTS, KEEPS STRANGE TROPHIES, AND PURSUES ASTOUNDING HOBBIES! ITS CONTENTS WILL AMAZE YOU... BUT EVEN MORE AMAZING IS THE IMPOSSIBLE ENIGMA BEHIND THE INTRUDER WHO FOUND A WAY TO USE—
The SUPER-KEY TO FORT SUPERMAN

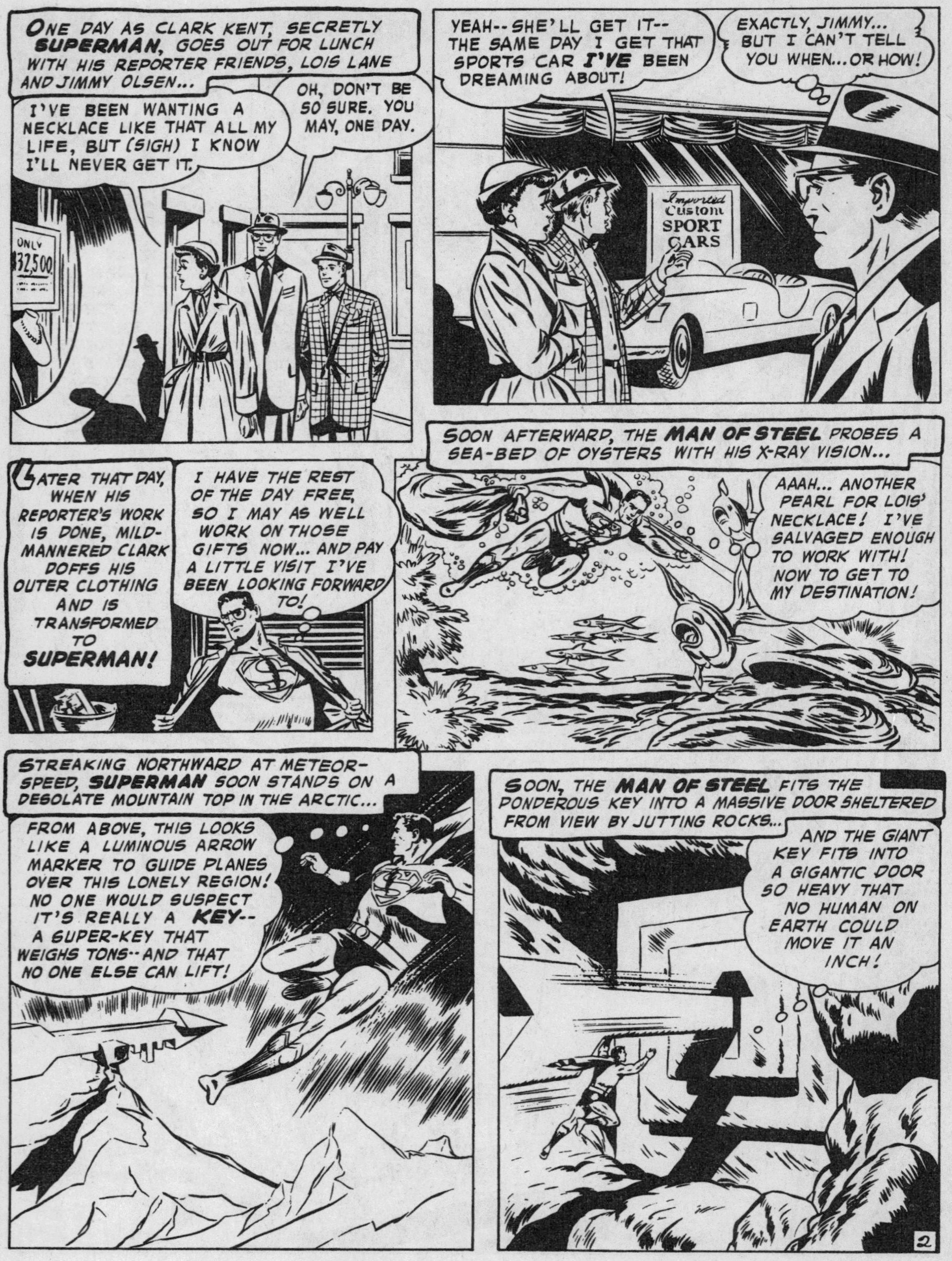
ONE DAY AS CLARK KENT, SECRETLY SUPERMAN, GOES OUT FOR LUNCH WITH HIS REPORTER FRIENDS, LOIS LANE AND JIMMY OLSEN...
I'VE BEEN WANTING A NECKLACE LIKE THAT ALL MY LIFE, BUT (SIGH) I KNOW I'LL NEVER GET IT.
OH, DON'T BE SO SURE. YOU MAY, ONE DAY.
ONLY $32,500
YEAH--SHE'LL GET IT--THE SAME DAY I GET THAT SPORTS CAR I'VE BEEN DREAMING ABOUT!
EXACTLY, JIMMY... BUT I CAN'T TELL YOU WHEN...OR HOW!
Imported Custom SPORT CARS
LATER THAT DAY, WHEN HIS REPORTER'S WORK IS DONE, MILD-MANNERED CLARK DOFFS HIS OUTER CLOTHING AND IS TRANSFORMED TO SUPERMAN!
I HAVE THE REST OF THE DAY FREE, SO I MAY AS WELL WORK ON THOSE GIFTS NOW... AND PAY A LITTLE VISIT I'VE BEEN LOOKING FORWARD TO!
SOON AFTERWARD, THE MAN OF STEEL PROBES A SEA-BED OF OYSTERS WITH HIS X-RAY VISION...
AAAH... ANOTHER PEARL FOR LOIS' NECKLACE! I'VE SALVAGED ENOUGH TO WORK WITH! NOW TO GET TO MY DESTINATION!
STREAKING NORTHWARD AT METEOR-SPEED, SUPERMAN SOON STANDS ON A DESOLATE MOUNTAIN TOP IN THE ARCTIC...
FROM ABOVE, THIS LOOKS LIKE A LUMINOUS ARROW MARKER TO GUIDE PLANES OVER THIS LONELY REGION! NO ONE WOULD SUSPECT IT'S REALLY A KEY--A SUPER-KEY THAT WEIGHS TONS--AND THAT NO ONE ELSE CAN LIFT!
SOON, THE MAN OF STEEL FITS THE PONDEROUS KEY INTO A MASSIVE DOOR SHELTERED FROM VIEW BY JUTTING ROCKS...
AND THE GIANT KEY FITS INTO A GIGANTIC DOOR SO HEAVY THAT NO HUMAN ON EARTH COULD MOVE IT AN INCH!
2

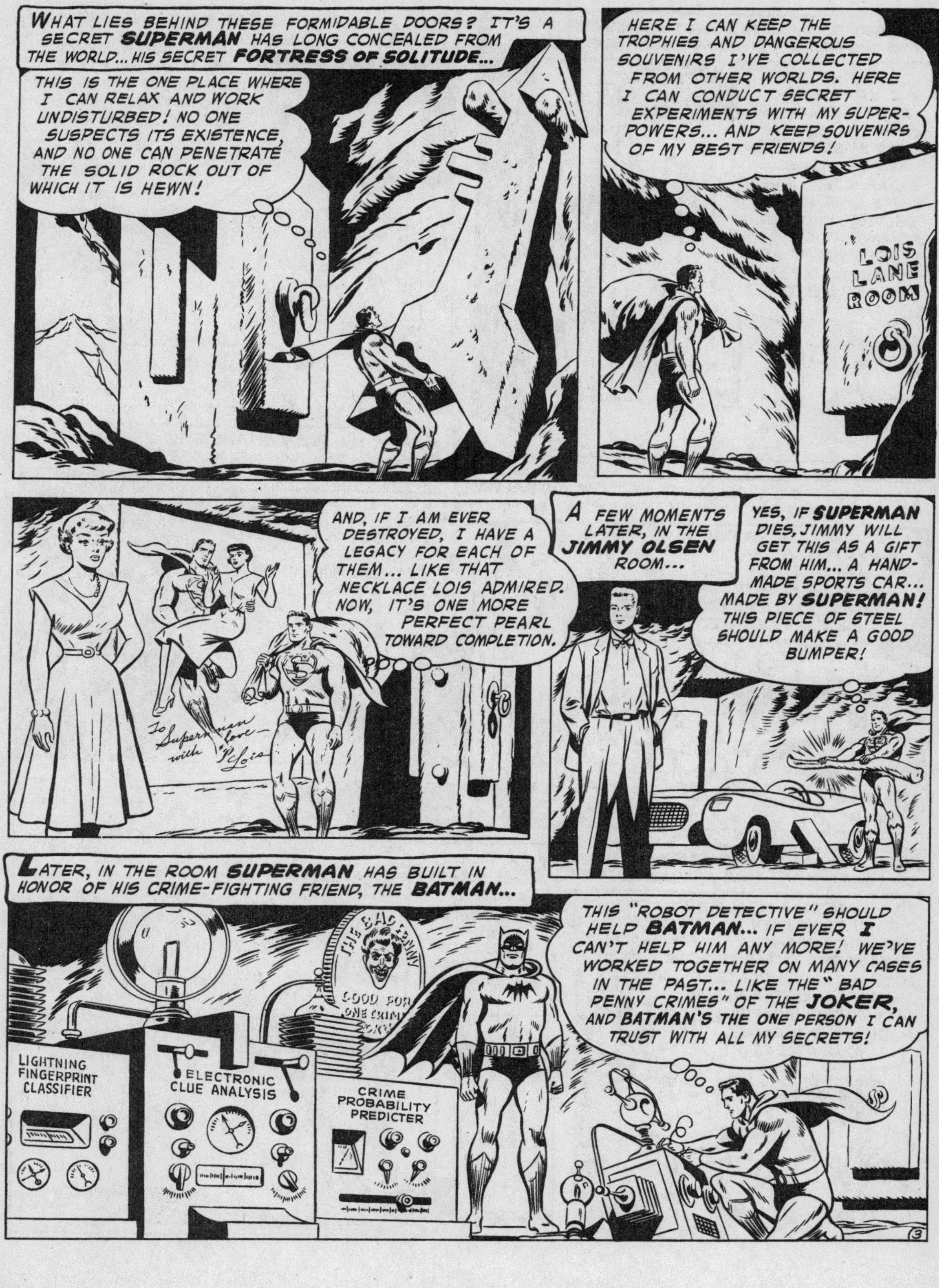
WHAT LIES BEHIND THESE FORMIDABLE DOORS? IT'S A SECRET SUPERMAN HAS LONG CONCEALED FROM THE WORLD... HIS SECRET FORTRESS OF SOLITUDE...
THIS IS THE ONE PLACE WHERE I CAN RELAX AND WORK UNDISTURBED! NO ONE SUSPECTS ITS EXISTENCE, AND NO ONE CAN PENETRATE THE SOLID ROCK OUT OF WHICH IT IS HEWN!
HERE I CAN KEEP THE TROPHIES AND DANGEROUS SOUVENIRS I'VE COLLECTED FROM OTHER WORLDS. HERE I CAN CONDUCT SECRET EXPERIMENTS WITH MY SUPER-POWERS... AND KEEP SOUVENIRS OF MY BEST FRIENDS!
LOIS LANE ROOM
AND, IF I AM EVER DESTROYED, I HAVE A LEGACY FOR EACH OF THEM... LIKE THAT NECKLACE LOIS ADMIRED. NOW, IT'S ONE MORE PERFECT PEARL TOWARD COMPLETION.
To Superman with love — Lois
A FEW MOMENTS LATER, IN THE JIMMY OLSEN ROOM...
YES, IF SUPERMAN DIES, JIMMY WILL GET THIS AS A GIFT FROM HIM... A HAND-MADE SPORTS CAR... MADE BY SUPERMAN! THIS PIECE OF STEEL SHOULD MAKE A GOOD BUMPER!
LATER, IN THE ROOM SUPERMAN HAS BUILT IN HONOR OF HIS CRIME-FIGHTING FRIEND, THE BATMAN...
THIS "ROBOT DETECTIVE" SHOULD HELP BATMAN... IF EVER I CAN'T HELP HIM ANY MORE! WE'VE WORKED TOGETHER ON MANY CASES IN THE PAST... LIKE THE "BAD PENNY CRIMES" OF THE JOKER, AND BATMAN'S THE ONE PERSON I CAN TRUST WITH ALL MY SECRETS!
THE BAD PENNY
GOOD FOR ONE CRIME
LIGHTNING FINGERPRINT CLASSIFIER
ELECTRONIC CLUE ANALYSIS
CRIME PROBABILITY PREDICTER
3

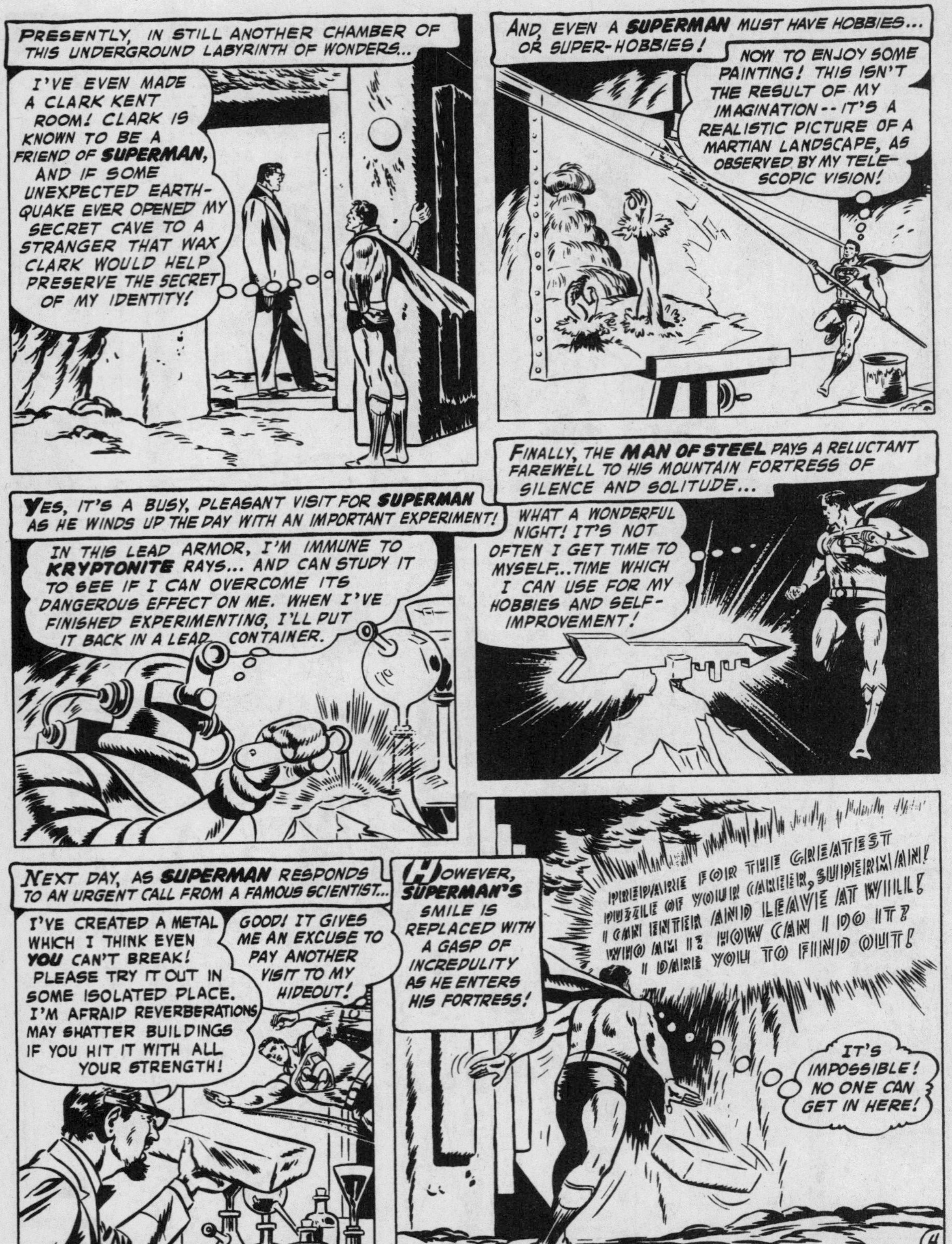
PRESENTLY, IN STILL ANOTHER CHAMBER OF THIS UNDERGROUND LABYRINTH OF WONDERS...
I'VE EVEN MADE A CLARK KENT ROOM! CLARK IS KNOWN TO BE A FRIEND OF SUPERMAN, AND IF SOME UNEXPECTED EARTH-QUAKE EVER OPENED MY SECRET CAVE TO A STRANGER THAT WAX CLARK WOULD HELP PRESERVE THE SECRET OF MY IDENTITY!
AND, EVEN A SUPERMAN MUST HAVE HOBBIES... OR SUPER-HOBBIES!
NOW TO ENJOY SOME PAINTING! THIS ISN'T THE RESULT OF MY IMAGINATION -- IT'S A REALISTIC PICTURE OF A MARTIAN LANDSCAPE, AS OBSERVED BY MY TELE-SCOPIC VISION!
YES, IT'S A BUSY, PLEASANT VISIT FOR SUPERMAN AS HE WINDS UP THE DAY WITH AN IMPORTANT EXPERIMENT!
IN THIS LEAD ARMOR, I'M IMMUNE TO KRYPTONITE RAYS... AND CAN STUDY IT TO SEE IF I CAN OVERCOME ITS DANGEROUS EFFECT ON ME. WHEN I'VE FINISHED EXPERIMENTING, I'LL PUT IT BACK IN A LEAD CONTAINER.
FINALLY, THE MAN OF STEEL PAYS A RELUCTANT FAREWELL TO HIS MOUNTAIN FORTRESS OF SILENCE AND SOLITUDE...
WHAT A WONDERFUL NIGHT! IT'S NOT OFTEN I GET TIME TO MYSELF...TIME WHICH I CAN USE FOR MY HOBBIES AND SELF-IMPROVEMENT!
NEXT DAY, AS SUPERMAN RESPONDS TO AN URGENT CALL FROM A FAMOUS SCIENTIST...
I'VE CREATED A METAL WHICH I THINK EVEN YOU CAN'T BREAK! PLEASE TRY IT OUT IN SOME ISOLATED PLACE. I'M AFRAID REVERBERATIONS MAY SHATTER BUILDINGS IF YOU HIT IT WITH ALL YOUR STRENGTH!
GOOD! IT GIVES ME AN EXCUSE TO PAY ANOTHER VISIT TO MY HIDEOUT!
HOWEVER, SUPERMAN'S SMILE IS REPLACED WITH A GASP OF INCREDULITY AS HE ENTERS HIS FORTRESS!
PREPARE FOR THE GREATEST PUZZLE OF YOUR CAREER, SUPERMAN! I CAN ENTER AND LEAVE AT WILL! WHO AM I? HOW CAN I DO IT? I DARE YOU TO FIND OUT!
IT'S IMPOSSIBLE! NO ONE CAN GET IN HERE!
4

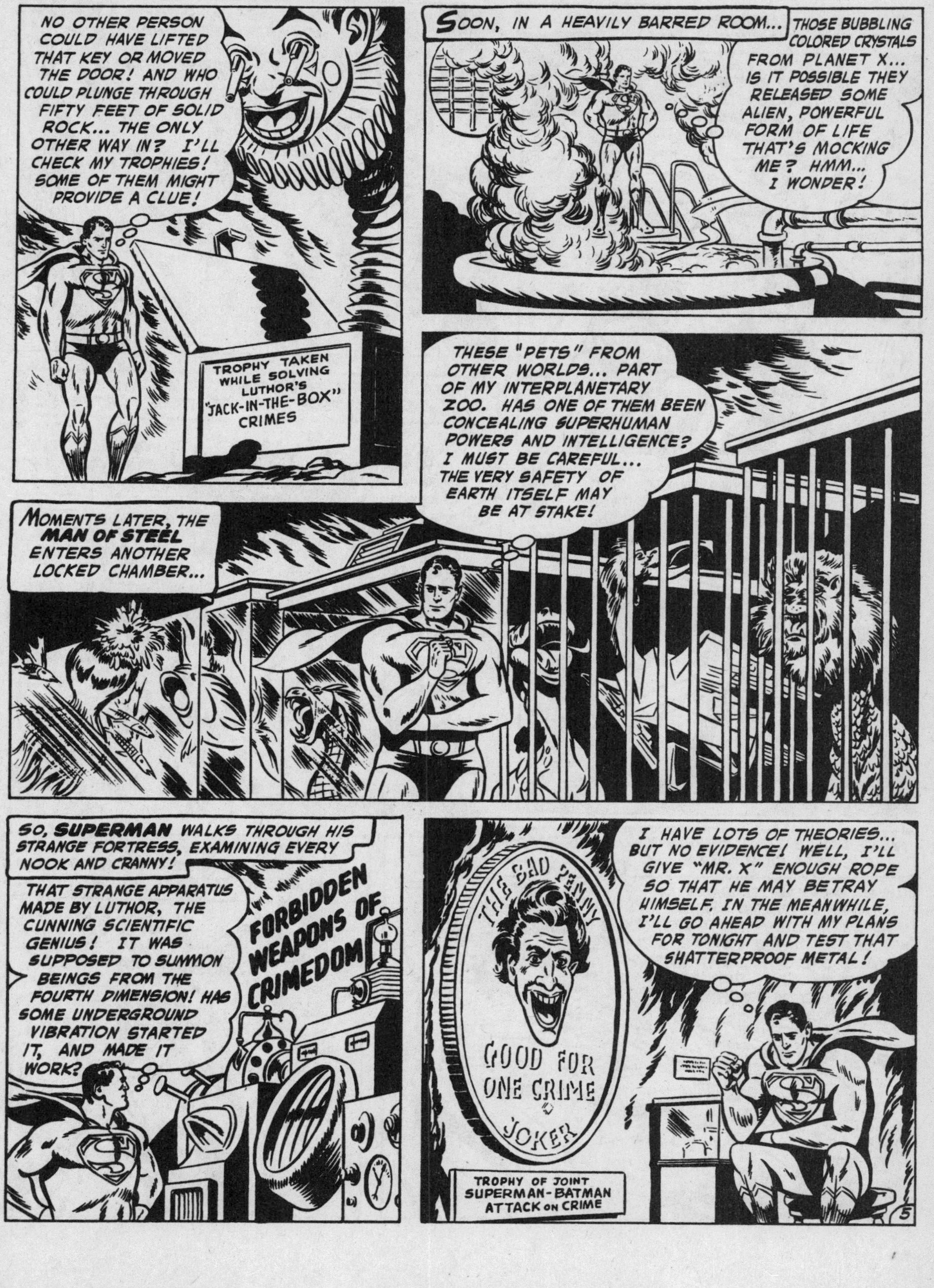
NO OTHER PERSON COULD HAVE LIFTED THAT KEY OR MOVED THE DOOR! AND WHO COULD PLUNGE THROUGH FIFTY FEET OF SOLID ROCK... THE ONLY OTHER WAY IN? I'LL CHECK MY TROPHIES! SOME OF THEM MIGHT PROVIDE A CLUE!
TROPHY TAKEN WHILE SOLVING LUTHOR'S "JACK-IN-THE-BOX" CRIMES
SOON, IN A HEAVILY BARRED ROOM...
THOSE BUBBLING COLORED CRYSTALS FROM PLANET X... IS IT POSSIBLE THEY RELEASED SOME ALIEN, POWERFUL FORM OF LIFE THAT'S MOCKING ME? HMM... I WONDER!
MOMENTS LATER, THE MAN OF STEEL ENTERS ANOTHER LOCKED CHAMBER...
THESE "PETS" FROM OTHER WORLDS... PART OF MY INTERPLANETARY ZOO. HAS ONE OF THEM BEEN CONCEALING SUPERHUMAN POWERS AND INTELLIGENCE? I MUST BE CAREFUL... THE VERY SAFETY OF EARTH ITSELF MAY BE AT STAKE!
SO, SUPERMAN WALKS THROUGH HIS STRANGE FORTRESS, EXAMINING EVERY NOOK AND CRANNY!
THAT STRANGE APPARATUS MADE BY LUTHOR, THE CUNNING SCIENTIFIC GENIUS! IT WAS SUPPOSED TO SUMMON BEINGS FROM THE FOURTH DIMENSION! HAS SOME UNDERGROUND VIBRATION STARTED IT, AND MADE IT WORK?
FORBIDDEN WEAPONS OF CRIMEDOM
I HAVE LOTS OF THEORIES... BUT NO EVIDENCE! WELL, I'LL GIVE "MR. X" ENOUGH ROPE SO THAT HE MAY BETRAY HIMSELF. IN THE MEANWHILE, I'LL GO AHEAD WITH MY PLANS FOR TONIGHT AND TEST THAT SHATTERPROOF METAL!
THE BAD PENNY
GOOD FOR ONE CRIME
JOKER
TROPHY OF JOINT SUPERMAN-BATMAN ATTACK ON CRIME
5

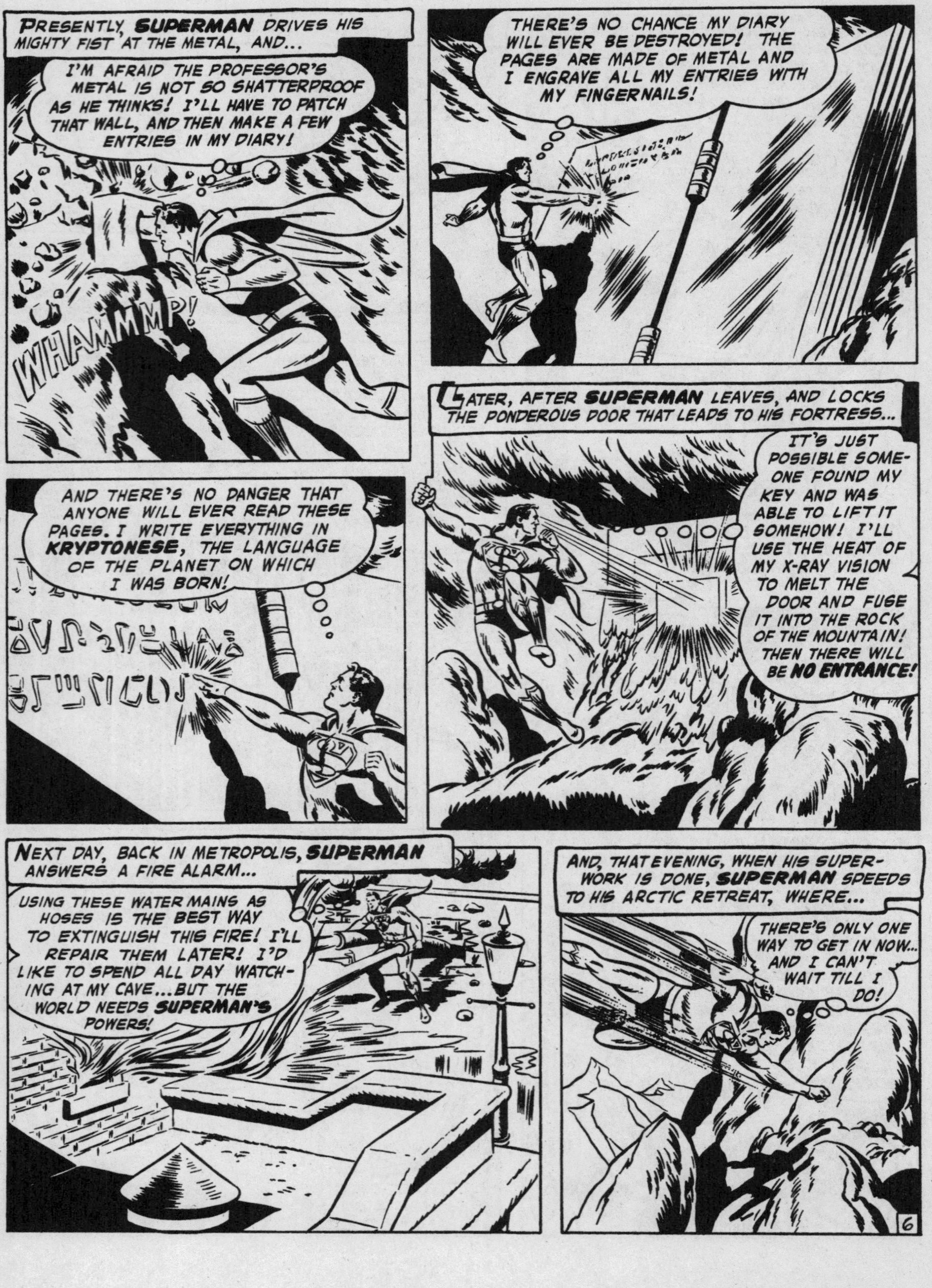
PRESENTLY, SUPERMAN DRIVES HIS MIGHTY FIST AT THE METAL, AND...
I'M AFRAID THE PROFESSOR'S METAL IS NOT SO SHATTERPROOF AS HE THINKS! I'LL HAVE TO PATCH THAT WALL, AND THEN MAKE A FEW ENTRIES IN MY DIARY!
WHAMMMP!
THERE'S NO CHANCE MY DIARY WILL EVER BE DESTROYED! THE PAGES ARE MADE OF METAL AND I ENGRAVE ALL MY ENTRIES WITH MY FINGERNAILS!
AND THERE'S NO DANGER THAT ANYONE WILL EVER READ THESE PAGES. I WRITE EVERYTHING IN KRYPTONESE, THE LANGUAGE OF THE PLANET ON WHICH I WAS BORN!
LATER, AFTER SUPERMAN LEAVES, AND LOCKS THE PONDEROUS DOOR THAT LEADS TO HIS FORTRESS...
IT'S JUST POSSIBLE SOMEONE FOUND MY KEY AND WAS ABLE TO LIFT IT SOMEHOW! I'LL USE THE HEAT OF MY X-RAY VISION TO MELT THE DOOR AND FUSE IT INTO THE ROCK OF THE MOUNTAIN! THEN THERE WILL BE NO ENTRANCE!
NEXT DAY, BACK IN METROPOLIS, SUPERMAN ANSWERS A FIRE ALARM...
USING THESE WATER MAINS AS HOSES IS THE BEST WAY TO EXTINGUISH THIS FIRE! I'LL REPAIR THEM LATER! I'D LIKE TO SPEND ALL DAY WATCHING AT MY CAVE... BUT THE WORLD NEEDS SUPERMAN'S POWERS!
AND, THAT EVENING, WHEN HIS SUPER-WORK IS DONE, SUPERMAN SPEEDS TO HIS ARCTIC RETREAT, WHERE...
THERE'S ONLY ONE WAY TO GET IN NOW... AND I CAN'T WAIT TILL I DO!
6

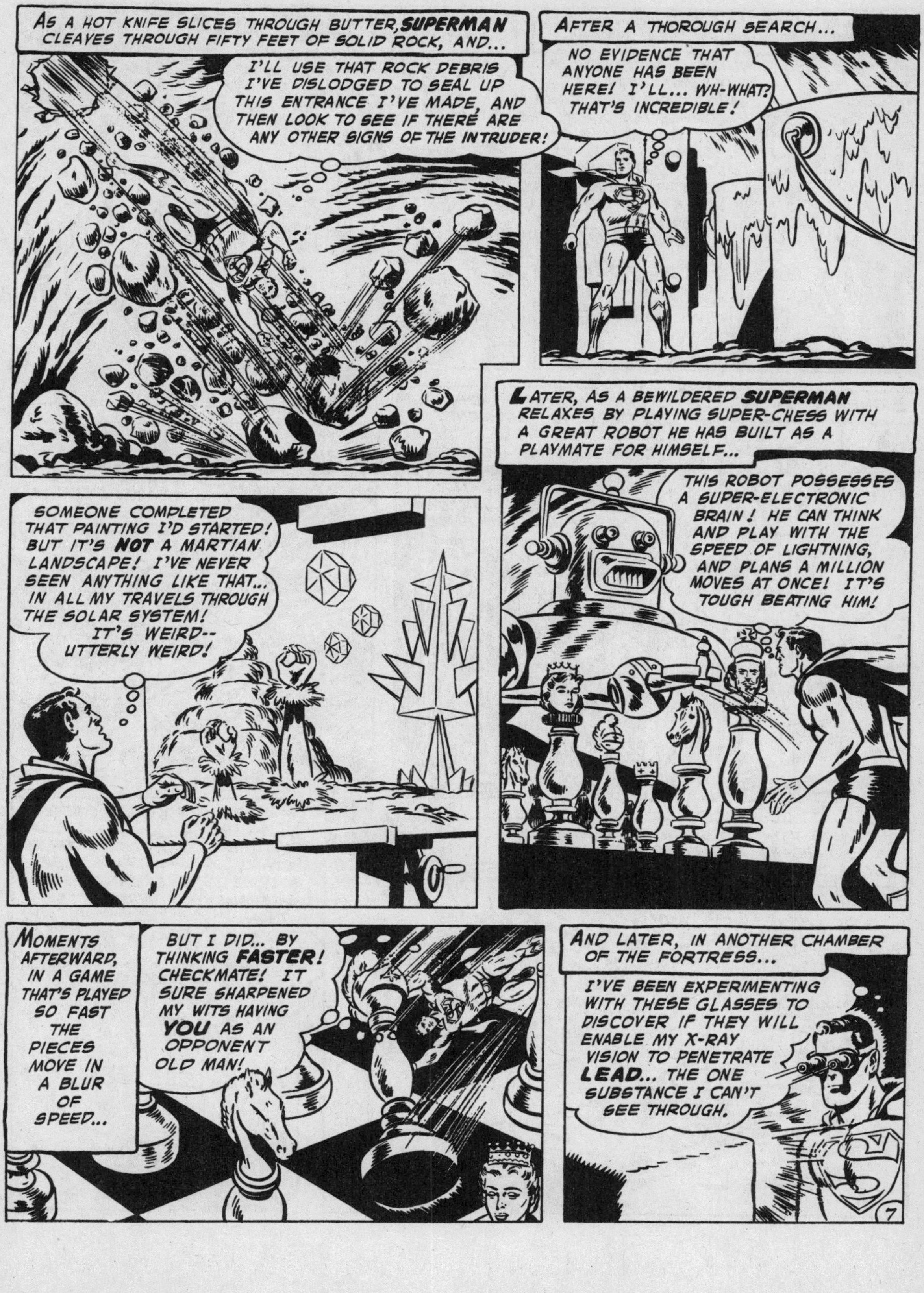
AS A HOT KNIFE SLICES THROUGH BUTTER, SUPERMAN CLEAVES THROUGH FIFTY FEET OF SOLID ROCK, AND...
I'LL USE THAT ROCK DEBRIS I'VE DISLODGED TO SEAL UP THIS ENTRANCE I'VE MADE, AND THEN LOOK TO SEE IF THERE ARE ANY OTHER SIGNS OF THE INTRUDER!
AFTER A THOROUGH SEARCH...
NO EVIDENCE THAT ANYONE HAS BEEN HERE! I'LL... WH-WHAT? THAT'S INCREDIBLE!
SOMEONE COMPLETED THAT PAINTING I'D STARTED! BUT IT'S NOT A MARTIAN LANDSCAPE! I'VE NEVER SEEN ANYTHING LIKE THAT... IN ALL MY TRAVELS THROUGH THE SOLAR SYSTEM! IT'S WEIRD-- UTTERLY WEIRD!
LATER, AS A BEWILDERED SUPERMAN RELAXES BY PLAYING SUPER-CHESS WITH A GREAT ROBOT HE HAS BUILT AS A PLAYMATE FOR HIMSELF...
THIS ROBOT POSSESSES A SUPER-ELECTRONIC BRAIN! HE CAN THINK AND PLAY WITH THE SPEED OF LIGHTNING, AND PLANS A MILLION MOVES AT ONCE! IT'S TOUGH BEATING HIM!
MOMENTS AFTERWARD, IN A GAME THAT'S PLAYED SO FAST THE PIECES MOVE IN A BLUR OF SPEED...
BUT I DID... BY THINKING FASTER! CHECKMATE! IT SURE SHARPENED MY WITS HAVING YOU AS AN OPPONENT OLD MAN!
AND LATER, IN ANOTHER CHAMBER OF THE FORTRESS...
I'VE BEEN EXPERIMENTING WITH THESE GLASSES TO DISCOVER IF THEY WILL ENABLE MY X-RAY VISION TO PENETRATE LEAD... THE ONE SUBSTANCE I CAN'T SEE THROUGH.
7

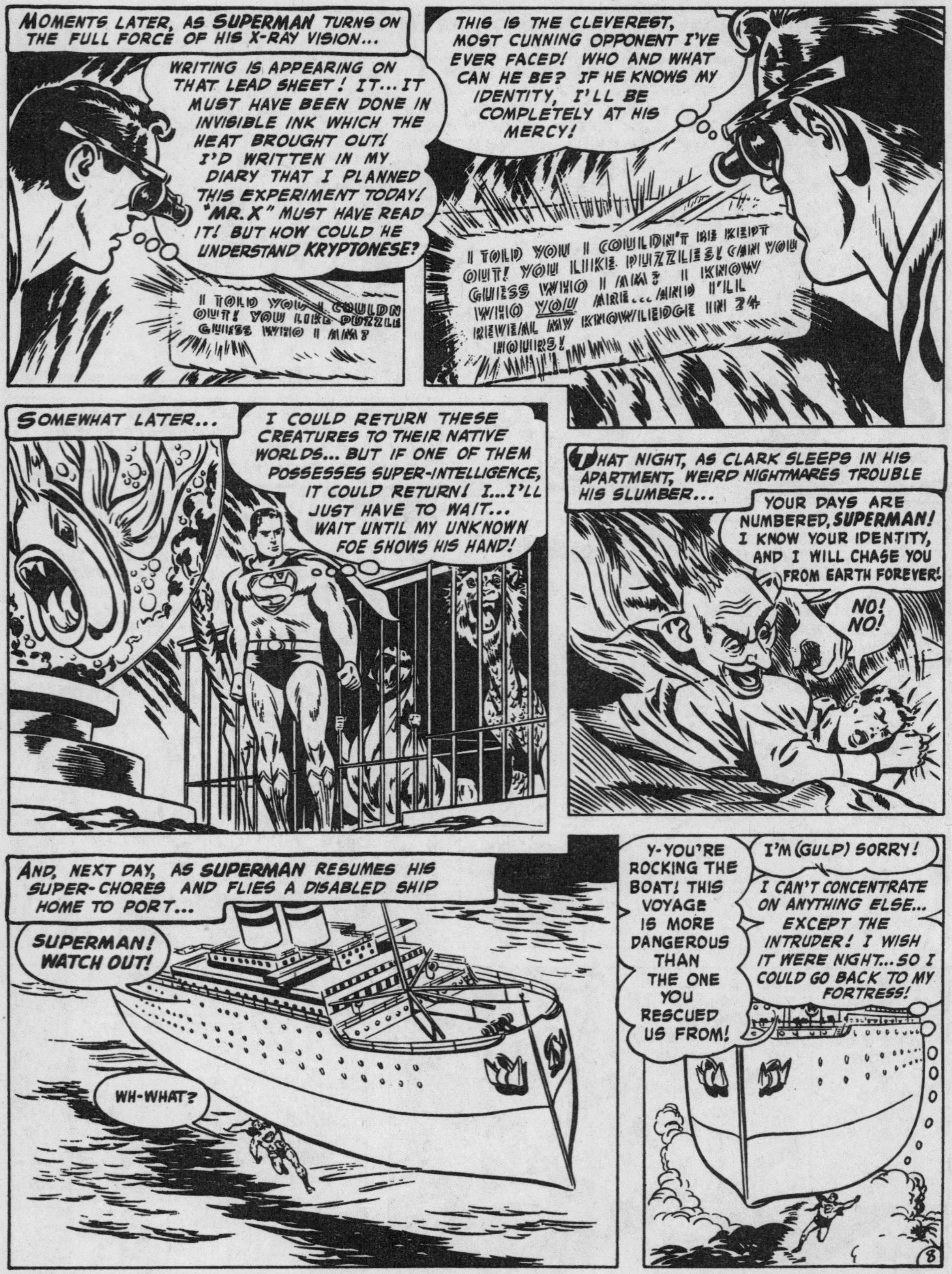
MOMENTS LATER, AS SUPERMAN TURNS ON THE FULL FORCE OF HIS X-RAY VISION...
WRITING IS APPEARING ON THAT LEAD SHEET! IT... IT MUST HAVE BEEN DONE IN INVISIBLE INK WHICH THE HEAT BROUGHT OUT! I'D WRITTEN IN MY DIARY THAT I PLANNED THIS EXPERIMENT TODAY! "MR. X" MUST HAVE READ IT! BUT HOW COULD HE UNDERSTAND KRYPTONESE?
I TOLD YOU I COULDN OUT! YOU LIKE PUZZLE GUESS WHO I AM?
THIS IS THE CLEVEREST, MOST CUNNING OPPONENT I'VE EVER FACED! WHO AND WHAT CAN HE BE? IF HE KNOWS MY IDENTITY, I'LL BE COMPLETELY AT HIS MERCY!
I TOLD YOU I COULDN'T BE KEPT OUT! YOU LIKE PUZZLES! CAN YOU GUESS WHO I AM? I KNOW WHO YOU ARE... AND I'LL REVEAL MY KNOWLEDGE IN 24 HOURS!
SOMEWHAT LATER...
I COULD RETURN THESE CREATURES TO THEIR NATIVE WORLDS... BUT IF ONE OF THEM POSSESSES SUPER-INTELLIGENCE, IT COULD RETURN! I...I'LL JUST HAVE TO WAIT... WAIT UNTIL MY UNKNOWN FOE SHOWS HIS HAND!
THAT NIGHT, AS CLARK SLEEPS IN HIS APARTMENT, WEIRD NIGHTMARES TROUBLE HIS SLUMBER...
YOUR DAYS ARE NUMBERED, SUPERMAN! I KNOW YOUR IDENTITY, AND I WILL CHASE YOU FROM EARTH FOREVER!
NO! NO!
AND, NEXT DAY, AS SUPERMAN RESUMES HIS SUPER-CHORES AND FLIES A DISABLED SHIP HOME TO PORT...
SUPERMAN! WATCH OUT!
WH-WHAT?
Y-YOU'RE ROCKING THE BOAT! THIS VOYAGE IS MORE DANGEROUS THAN THE ONE YOU RESCUED US FROM!
I'M (GULP) SORRY!
I CAN'T CONCENTRATE ON ANYTHING ELSE... EXCEPT THE INTRUDER! I WISH IT WERE NIGHT... SO I COULD GO BACK TO MY FORTRESS!
8

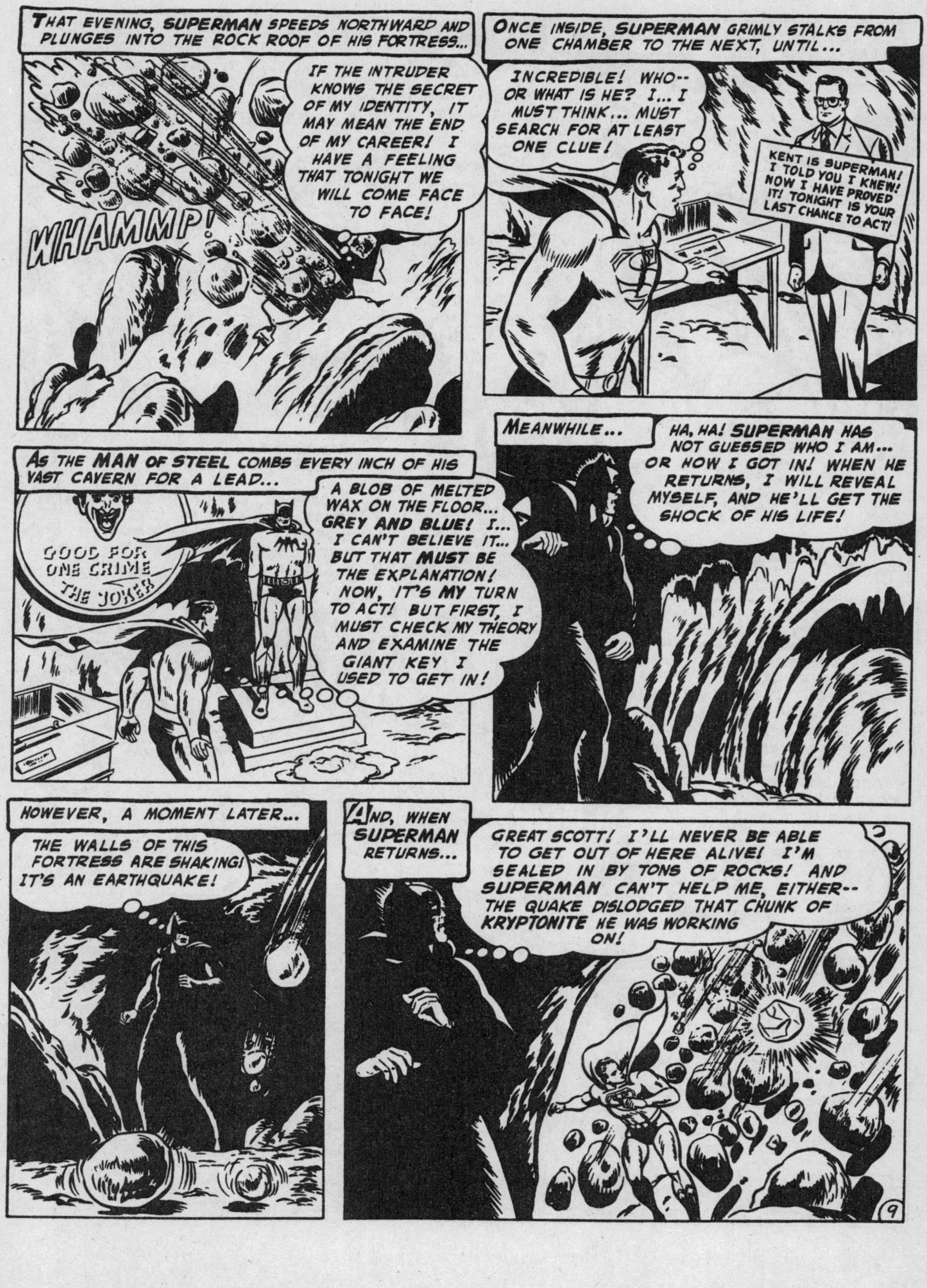
THAT EVENING, SUPERMAN SPEEDS NORTHWARD AND PLUNGES INTO THE ROCK ROOF OF HIS FORTRESS...
IF THE INTRUDER KNOWS THE SECRET OF MY IDENTITY, IT MAY MEAN THE END OF MY CAREER! I HAVE A FEELING THAT TONIGHT WE WILL COME FACE TO FACE!
WHAMMP!
ONCE INSIDE, SUPERMAN GRIMLY STALKS FROM ONE CHAMBER TO THE NEXT, UNTIL...
INCREDIBLE! WHO-- OR WHAT IS HE? I... I MUST THINK... MUST SEARCH FOR AT LEAST ONE CLUE!
KENT IS SUPERMAN! I TOLD YOU I KNEW! NOW I HAVE PROVED IT! TONIGHT IS YOUR LAST CHANCE TO ACT!
AS THE MAN OF STEEL COMBS EVERY INCH OF HIS VAST CAVERN FOR A LEAD...
GOOD FOR ONE CRIME THE JOKER
A BLOB OF MELTED WAX ON THE FLOOR... GREY AND BLUE! I... I CAN'T BELIEVE IT... BUT THAT MUST BE THE EXPLANATION! NOW, IT'S MY TURN TO ACT! BUT FIRST, I MUST CHECK MY THEORY AND EXAMINE THE GIANT KEY I USED TO GET IN!
MEANWHILE...
HA, HA! SUPERMAN HAS NOT GUESSED WHO I AM... OR HOW I GOT IN! WHEN HE RETURNS, I WILL REVEAL MYSELF, AND HE'LL GET THE SHOCK OF HIS LIFE!
HOWEVER, A MOMENT LATER...
THE WALLS OF THIS FORTRESS ARE SHAKING! IT'S AN EARTHQUAKE!
AND, WHEN SUPERMAN RETURNS...
GREAT SCOTT! I'LL NEVER BE ABLE TO GET OUT OF HERE ALIVE! I'M SEALED IN BY TONS OF ROCKS! AND SUPERMAN CAN'T HELP ME, EITHER-- THE QUAKE DISLODGED THAT CHUNK OF KRYPTONITE HE WAS WORKING ON!
9

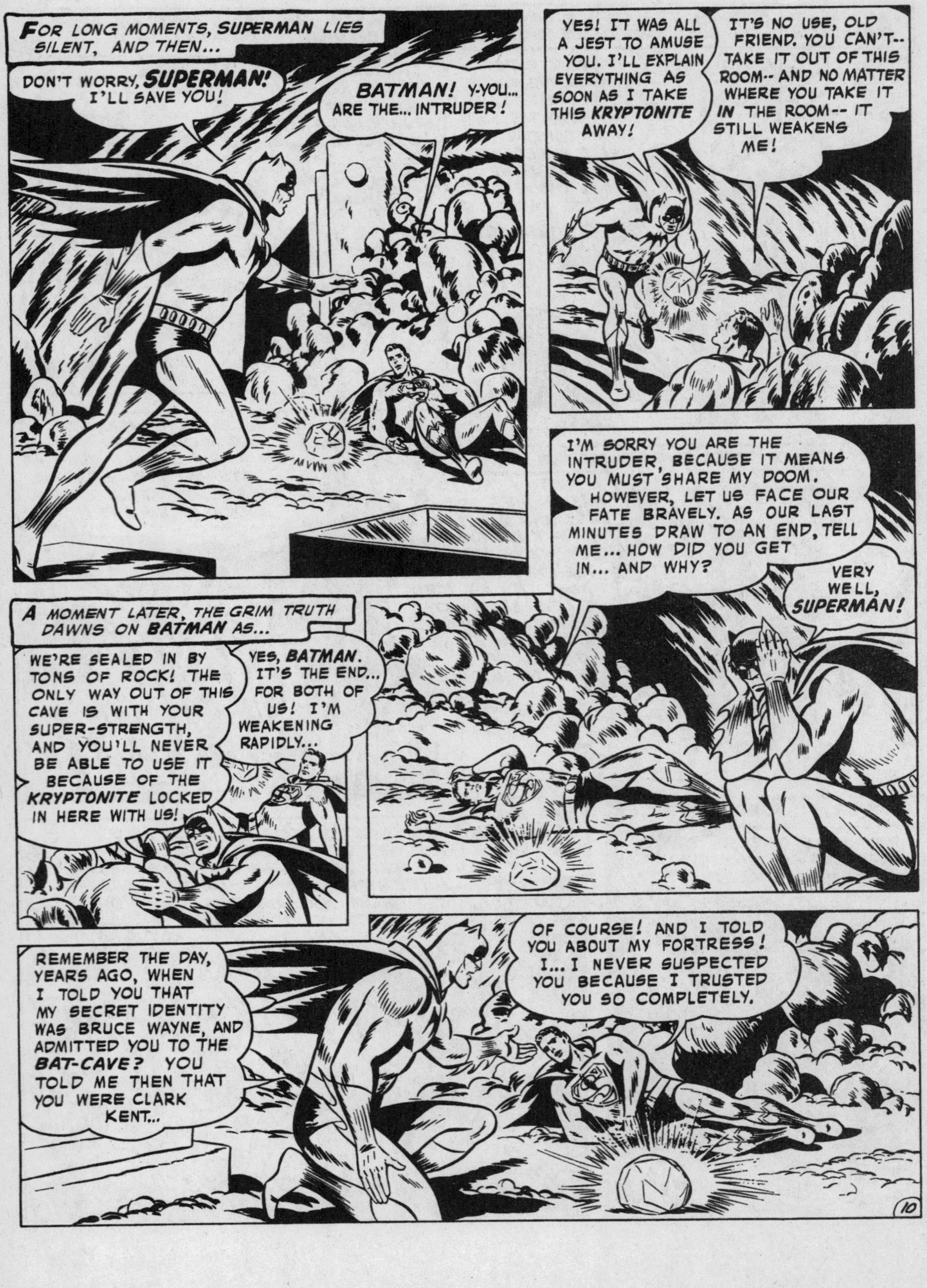
FOR LONG MOMENTS, SUPERMAN LIES SILENT, AND THEN...
DON'T WORRY, SUPERMAN! I'LL SAVE YOU!
BATMAN! Y-YOU... ARE THE... INTRUDER!
YES! IT WAS ALL A JEST TO AMUSE YOU. I'LL EXPLAIN EVERYTHING AS SOON AS I TAKE THIS KRYPTONITE AWAY!
IT'S NO USE, OLD FRIEND. YOU CAN'T-- TAKE IT OUT OF THIS ROOM-- AND NO MATTER WHERE YOU TAKE IT IN THE ROOM-- IT STILL WEAKENS ME!
A MOMENT LATER, THE GRIM TRUTH DAWNS ON BATMAN AS...
WE'RE SEALED IN BY TONS OF ROCK! THE ONLY WAY OUT OF THIS CAVE IS WITH YOUR SUPER-STRENGTH, AND YOU'LL NEVER BE ABLE TO USE IT BECAUSE OF THE KRYPTONITE LOCKED IN HERE WITH US!
YES, BATMAN. IT'S THE END... FOR BOTH OF US! I'M WEAKENING RAPIDLY...
I'M SORRY YOU ARE THE INTRUDER, BECAUSE IT MEANS YOU MUST SHARE MY DOOM. HOWEVER, LET US FACE OUR FATE BRAVELY. AS OUR LAST MINUTES DRAW TO AN END, TELL ME... HOW DID YOU GET IN... AND WHY?
VERY WELL, SUPERMAN!
REMEMBER THE DAY, YEARS AGO, WHEN I TOLD YOU THAT MY SECRET IDENTITY WAS BRUCE WAYNE, AND ADMITTED YOU TO THE BAT-CAVE? YOU TOLD ME THEN THAT YOU WERE CLARK KENT...
OF COURSE! AND I TOLD YOU ABOUT MY FORTRESS! I... I NEVER SUSPECTED YOU BECAUSE I TRUSTED YOU SO COMPLETELY.
10

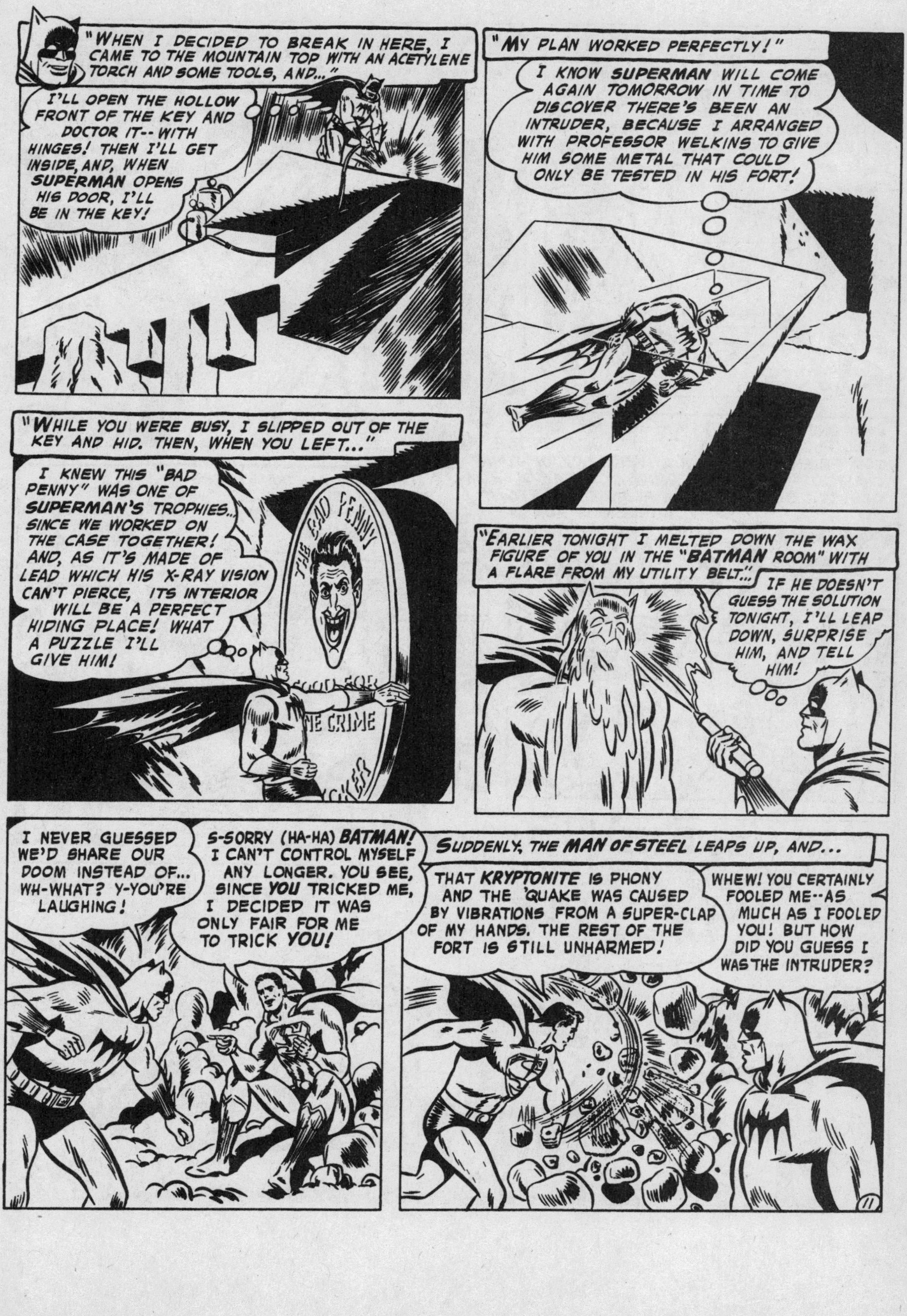
"WHEN I DECIDED TO BREAK IN HERE, I CAME TO THE MOUNTAIN TOP WITH AN ACETYLENE TORCH AND SOME TOOLS, AND..."
I'LL OPEN THE HOLLOW FRONT OF THE KEY AND DOCTOR IT-- WITH HINGES! THEN I'LL GET INSIDE, AND, WHEN SUPERMAN OPENS HIS DOOR, I'LL BE IN THE KEY!
"MY PLAN WORKED PERFECTLY!"
I KNOW SUPERMAN WILL COME AGAIN TOMORROW IN TIME TO DISCOVER THERE'S BEEN AN INTRUDER, BECAUSE I ARRANGED WITH PROFESSOR WELKINS TO GIVE HIM SOME METAL THAT COULD ONLY BE TESTED IN HIS FORT!
"WHILE YOU WERE BUSY, I SLIPPED OUT OF THE KEY AND HID. THEN, WHEN YOU LEFT..."
I KNEW THIS "BAD PENNY" WAS ONE OF SUPERMAN'S TROPHIES... SINCE WE WORKED ON THE CASE TOGETHER! AND, AS IT'S MADE OF LEAD WHICH HIS X-RAY VISION CAN'T PIERCE, ITS INTERIOR WILL BE A PERFECT HIDING PLACE! WHAT A PUZZLE I'LL GIVE HIM!
THE BAD PENNY
CRIME
"EARLIER TONIGHT I MELTED DOWN THE WAX FIGURE OF YOU IN THE "BATMAN ROOM" WITH A FLARE FROM MY UTILITY BELT..."
IF HE DOESN'T GUESS THE SOLUTION TONIGHT, I'LL LEAP DOWN, SURPRISE HIM, AND TELL HIM!
I NEVER GUESSED WE'D SHARE OUR DOOM INSTEAD OF... WH-WHAT? Y-YOU'RE LAUGHING!
S-SORRY (HA-HA) BATMAN! I CAN'T CONTROL MYSELF ANY LONGER. YOU SEE, SINCE YOU TRICKED ME, I DECIDED IT WAS ONLY FAIR FOR ME TO TRICK YOU!
SUDDENLY, THE MAN OF STEEL LEAPS UP, AND...
THAT KRYPTONITE IS PHONY AND THE 'QUAKE WAS CAUSED BY VIBRATIONS FROM A SUPER-CLAP OF MY HANDS. THE REST OF THE FORT IS STILL UNHARMED!
WHEW! YOU CERTAINLY FOOLED ME--AS MUCH AS I FOOLED YOU! BUT HOW DID YOU GUESS I WAS THE INTRUDER?
11

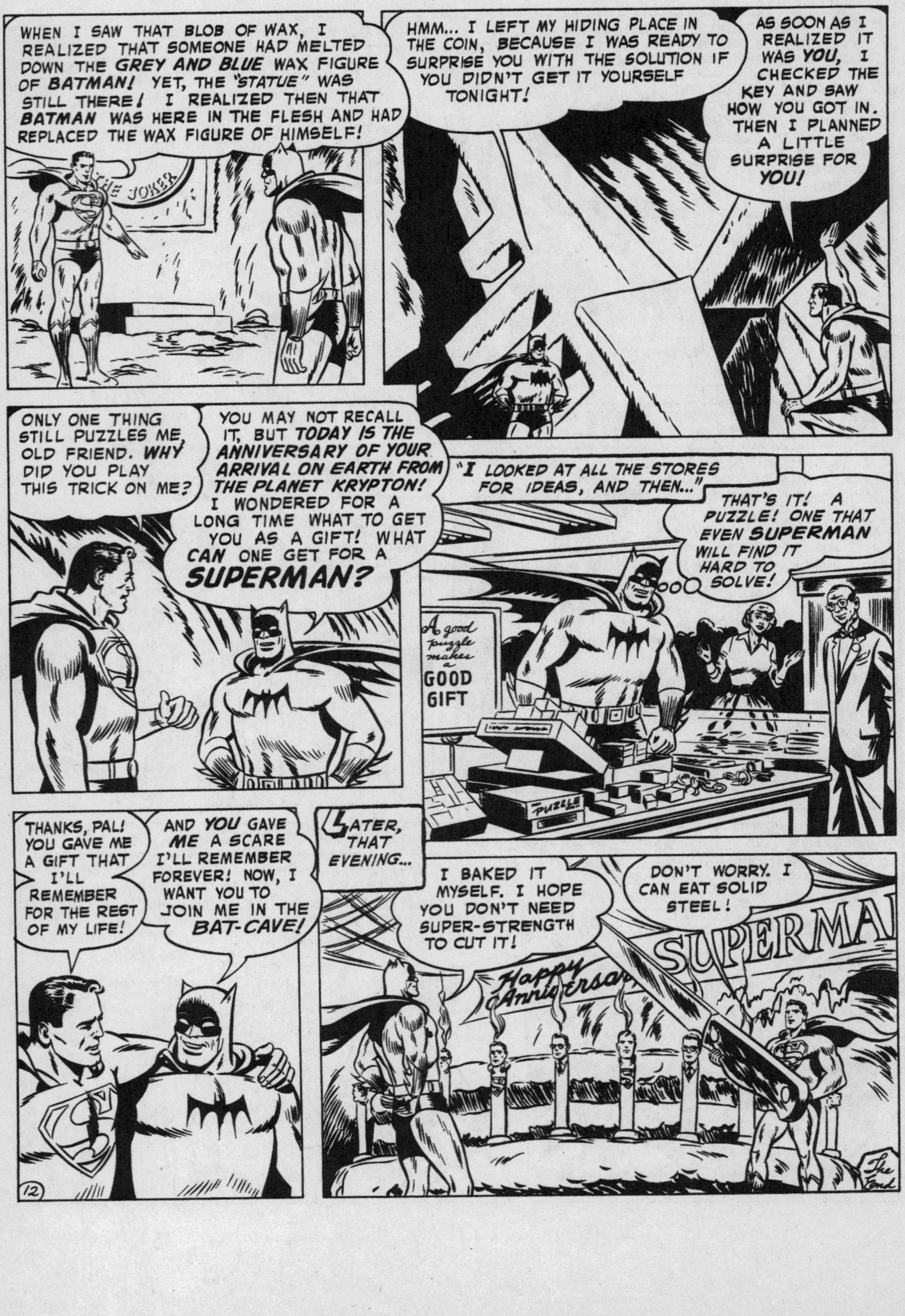
WHEN I SAW THAT BLOB OF WAX, I REALIZED THAT SOMEONE HAD MELTED DOWN THE GREY AND BLUE WAX FIGURE OF BATMAN! YET, THE "STATUE" WAS STILL THERE! I REALIZED THEN THAT BATMAN WAS HERE IN THE FLESH AND HAD REPLACED THE WAX FIGURE OF HIMSELF!
THE JOKER
HMM... I LEFT MY HIDING PLACE IN THE COIN, BECAUSE I WAS READY TO SURPRISE YOU WITH THE SOLUTION IF YOU DIDN'T GET IT YOURSELF TONIGHT!
AS SOON AS I REALIZED IT WAS YOU, I CHECKED THE KEY AND SAW HOW YOU GOT IN. THEN I PLANNED A LITTLE SURPRISE FOR YOU!
ONLY ONE THING STILL PUZZLES ME, OLD FRIEND. WHY DID YOU PLAY THIS TRICK ON ME?
YOU MAY NOT RECALL IT, BUT TODAY IS THE ANNIVERSARY OF YOUR ARRIVAL ON EARTH FROM THE PLANET KRYPTON! I WONDERED FOR A LONG TIME WHAT TO GET YOU AS A GIFT! WHAT CAN ONE GET FOR A SUPERMAN?
"I LOOKED AT ALL THE STORES FOR IDEAS, AND THEN..."
THAT'S IT! A PUZZLE! ONE THAT EVEN SUPERMAN WILL FIND IT HARD TO SOLVE!
A good puzzle makes a GOOD GIFT
PUZZLE
THANKS, PAL! YOU GAVE ME A GIFT THAT I'LL REMEMBER FOR THE REST OF MY LIFE!
AND YOU GAVE ME A SCARE I'LL REMEMBER FOREVER! NOW, I WANT YOU TO JOIN ME IN THE BAT-CAVE!
LATER, THAT EVENING...
I BAKED IT MYSELF. I HOPE YOU DON'T NEED SUPER-STRENGTH TO CUT IT!
DON'T WORRY. I CAN EAT SOLID STEEL!
SUPERMA
Happy Anniversa
12
The End

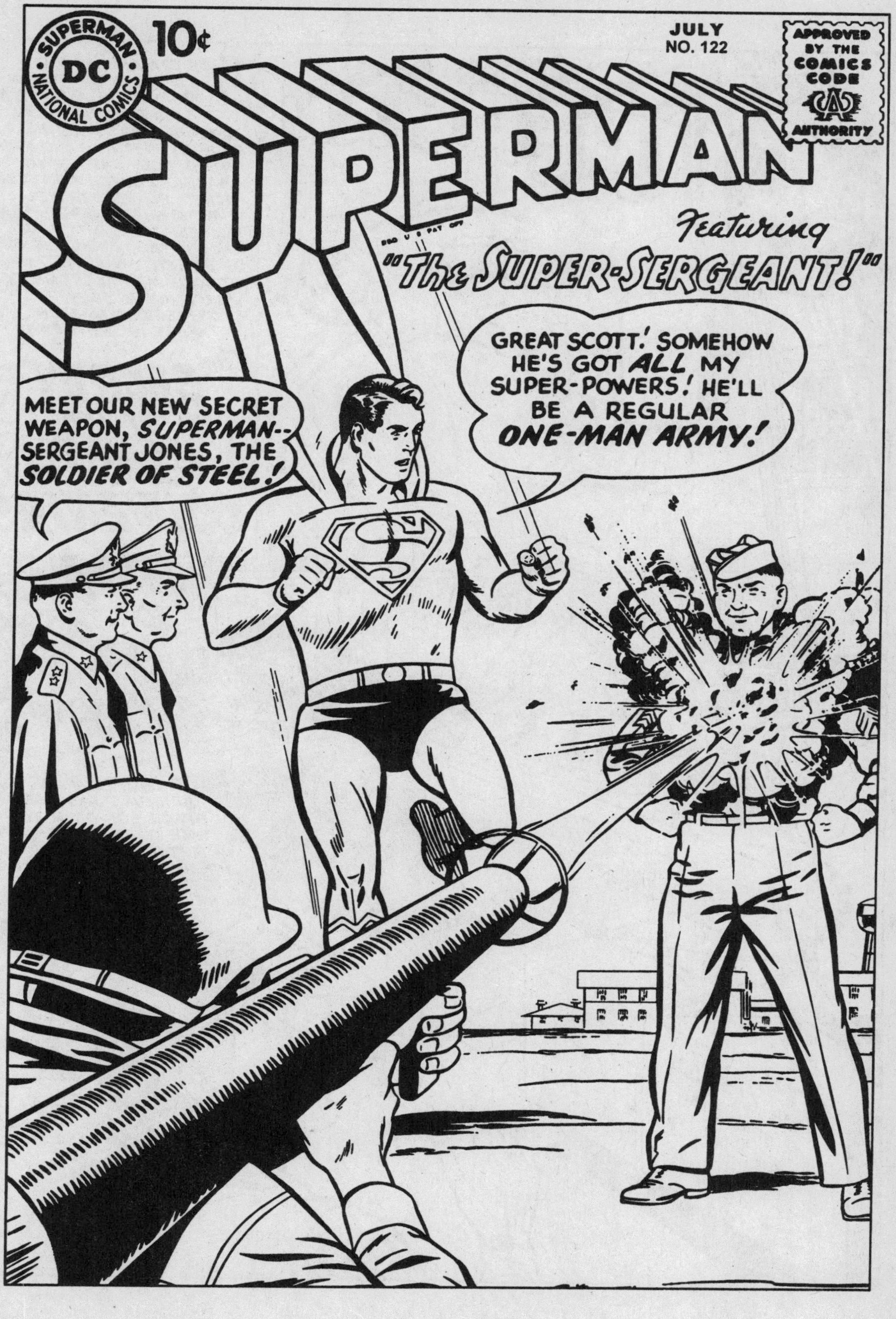
SUPERMAN DC NATIONAL COMICS
10¢
JULY
NO. 122
APPROVED BY THE COMICS CODE AUTHORITY
SUPERMAN
Featuring
"The SUPER-SERGEANT!"
MEET OUR NEW SECRET WEAPON, SUPERMAN--SERGEANT JONES, THE SOLDIER OF STEEL!
GREAT SCOTT! SOMEHOW HE'S GOT ALL MY SUPER-POWERS! HE'LL BE A REGULAR ONE-MAN ARMY!

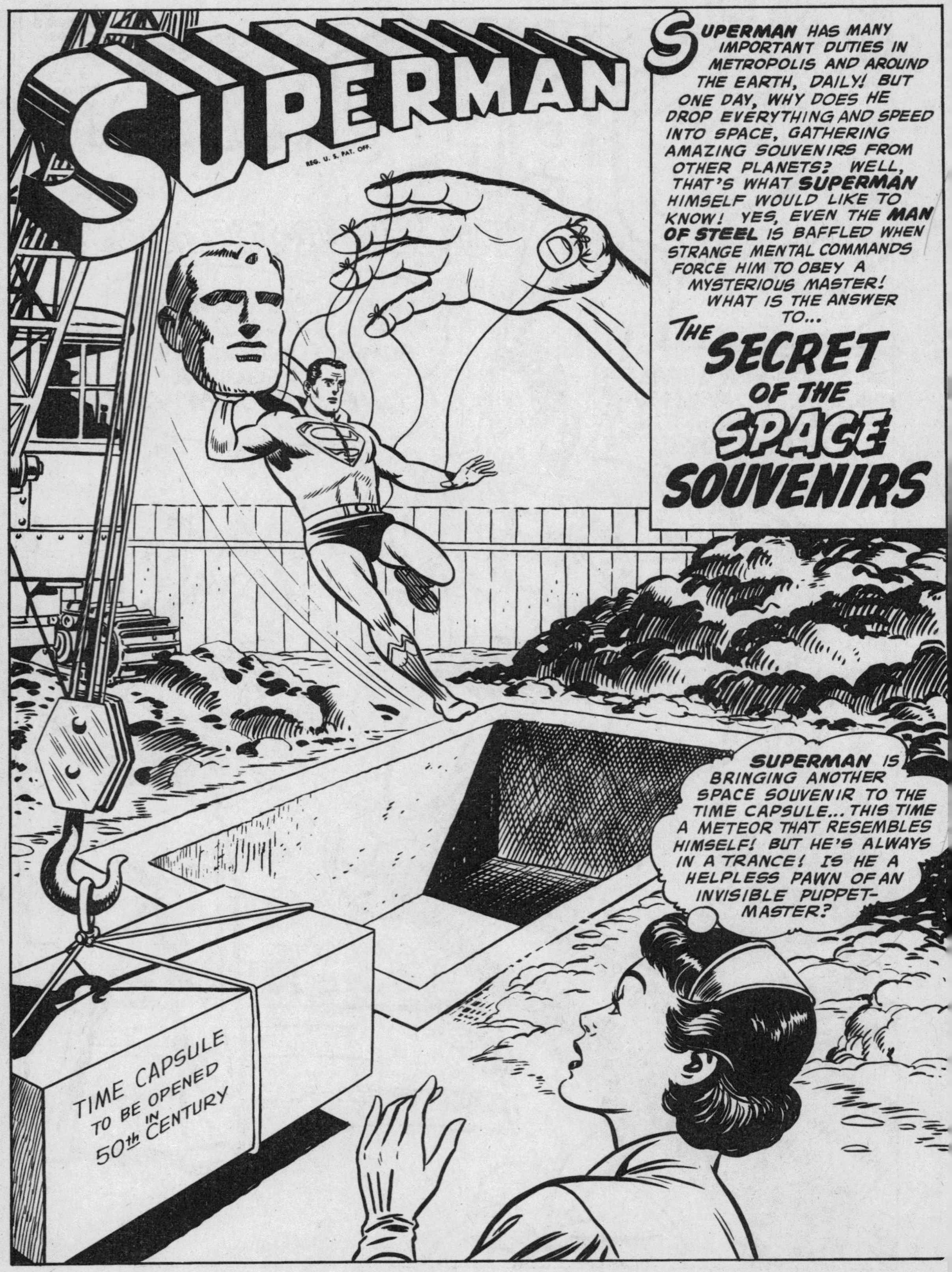
SUPERMAN
REG. U. S. PAT. OFF.
SUPERMAN HAS MANY IMPORTANT DUTIES IN METROPOLIS AND AROUND THE EARTH, DAILY! BUT ONE DAY, WHY DOES HE DROP EVERYTHING AND SPEED INTO SPACE, GATHERING AMAZING SOUVENIRS FROM OTHER PLANETS? WELL, THAT'S WHAT SUPERMAN HIMSELF WOULD LIKE TO KNOW! YES, EVEN THE MAN OF STEEL IS BAFFLED WHEN STRANGE MENTAL COMMANDS FORCE HIM TO OBEY A MYSTERIOUS MASTER! WHAT IS THE ANSWER TO...
THE SECRET OF THE SPACE SOUVENIRS
SUPERMAN IS BRINGING ANOTHER SPACE SOUVENIR TO THE TIME CAPSULE... THIS TIME A METEOR THAT RESEMBLES HIMSELF! BUT HE'S ALWAYS IN A TRANCE! IS HE A HELPLESS PAWN OF AN INVISIBLE PUPPET-MASTER?
TIME CAPSULE TO BE OPENED IN 50th CENTURY

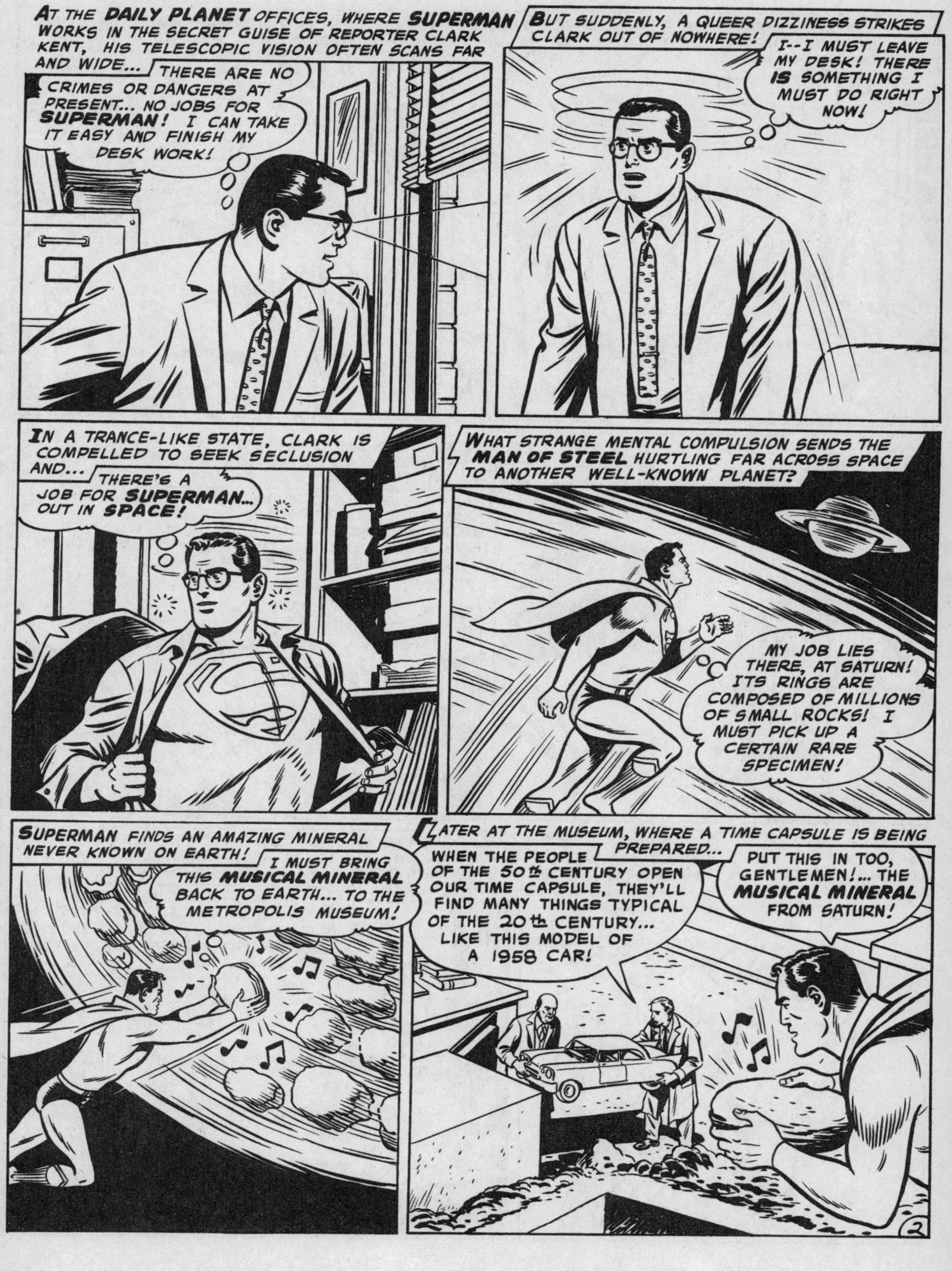
AT THE DAILY PLANET OFFICES, WHERE SUPERMAN WORKS IN THE SECRET GUISE OF REPORTER CLARK KENT, HIS TELESCOPIC VISION OFTEN SCANS FAR AND WIDE...
THERE ARE NO CRIMES OR DANGERS AT PRESENT... NO JOBS FOR SUPERMAN! I CAN TAKE IT EASY AND FINISH MY DESK WORK!
BUT SUDDENLY, A QUEER DIZZINESS STRIKES CLARK OUT OF NOWHERE!
I--I MUST LEAVE MY DESK! THERE IS SOMETHING I MUST DO RIGHT NOW!
IN A TRANCE-LIKE STATE, CLARK IS COMPELLED TO SEEK SECLUSION AND...
THERE'S A JOB FOR SUPERMAN... OUT IN SPACE!
WHAT STRANGE MENTAL COMPULSION SENDS THE MAN OF STEEL HURTLING FAR ACROSS SPACE TO ANOTHER WELL-KNOWN PLANET?
MY JOB LIES THERE, AT SATURN! ITS RINGS ARE COMPOSED OF MILLIONS OF SMALL ROCKS! I MUST PICK UP A CERTAIN RARE SPECIMEN!
SUPERMAN FINDS AN AMAZING MINERAL NEVER KNOWN ON EARTH!
I MUST BRING THIS MUSICAL MINERAL BACK TO EARTH... TO THE METROPOLIS MUSEUM!
LATER AT THE MUSEUM, WHERE A TIME CAPSULE IS BEING PREPARED...
WHEN THE PEOPLE OF THE 50th CENTURY OPEN OUR TIME CAPSULE, THEY'LL FIND MANY THINGS TYPICAL OF THE 20th CENTURY... LIKE THIS MODEL OF A 1958 CAR!
PUT THIS IN TOO, GENTLEMEN!... THE MUSICAL MINERAL FROM SATURN!
2

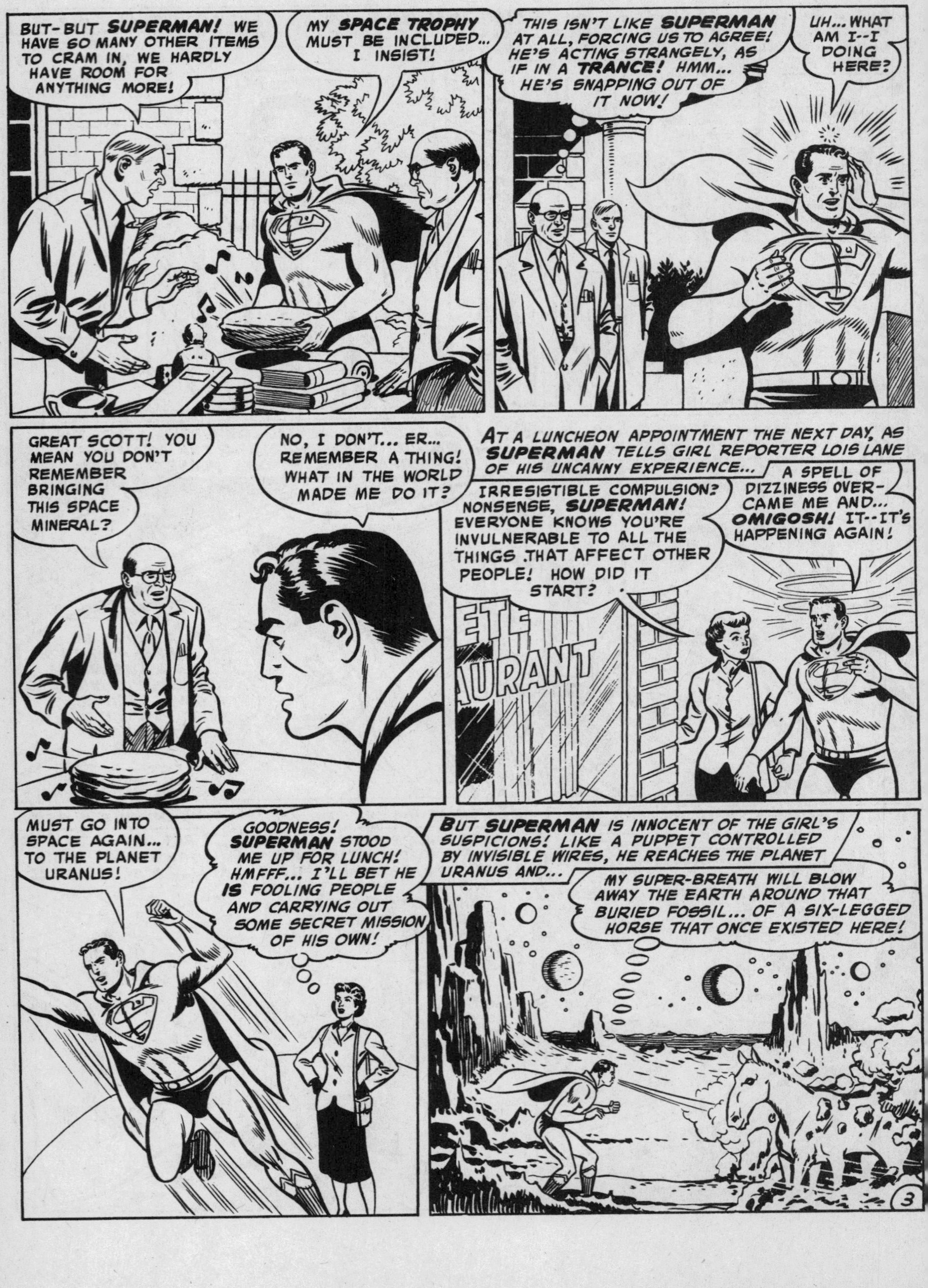
BUT-BUT SUPERMAN! WE HAVE SO MANY OTHER ITEMS TO CRAM IN, WE HARDLY HAVE ROOM FOR ANYTHING MORE!
MY SPACE TROPHY MUST BE INCLUDED... I INSIST!
THIS ISN'T LIKE SUPERMAN AT ALL, FORCING US TO AGREE! HE'S ACTING STRANGELY, AS IF IN A TRANCE! HMM... HE'S SNAPPING OUT OF IT NOW!
UH... WHAT AM I--I DOING HERE?
GREAT SCOTT! YOU MEAN YOU DON'T REMEMBER BRINGING THIS SPACE MINERAL?
NO, I DON'T... ER... REMEMBER A THING! WHAT IN THE WORLD MADE ME DO IT?
AT A LUNCHEON APPOINTMENT THE NEXT DAY, AS SUPERMAN TELLS GIRL REPORTER LOIS LANE OF HIS UNCANNY EXPERIENCE...
A SPELL OF DIZZINESS OVER-CAME ME AND... OMIGOSH! IT--IT'S HAPPENING AGAIN!
IRRESISTIBLE COMPULSION? NONSENSE, SUPERMAN! EVERYONE KNOWS YOU'RE INVULNERABLE TO ALL THE THINGS THAT AFFECT OTHER PEOPLE! HOW DID IT START?
ETE
AURANT
MUST GO INTO SPACE AGAIN... TO THE PLANET URANUS!
GOODNESS! SUPERMAN STOOD ME UP FOR LUNCH! HMFFF... I'LL BET HE IS FOOLING PEOPLE AND CARRYING OUT SOME SECRET MISSION OF HIS OWN!
BUT SUPERMAN IS INNOCENT OF THE GIRL'S SUSPICIONS! LIKE A PUPPET CONTROLLED BY INVISIBLE WIRES, HE REACHES THE PLANET URANUS AND...
MY SUPER-BREATH WILL BLOW AWAY THE EARTH AROUND THAT BURIED FOSSIL... OF A SIX-LEGGED HORSE THAT ONCE EXISTED HERE!
3

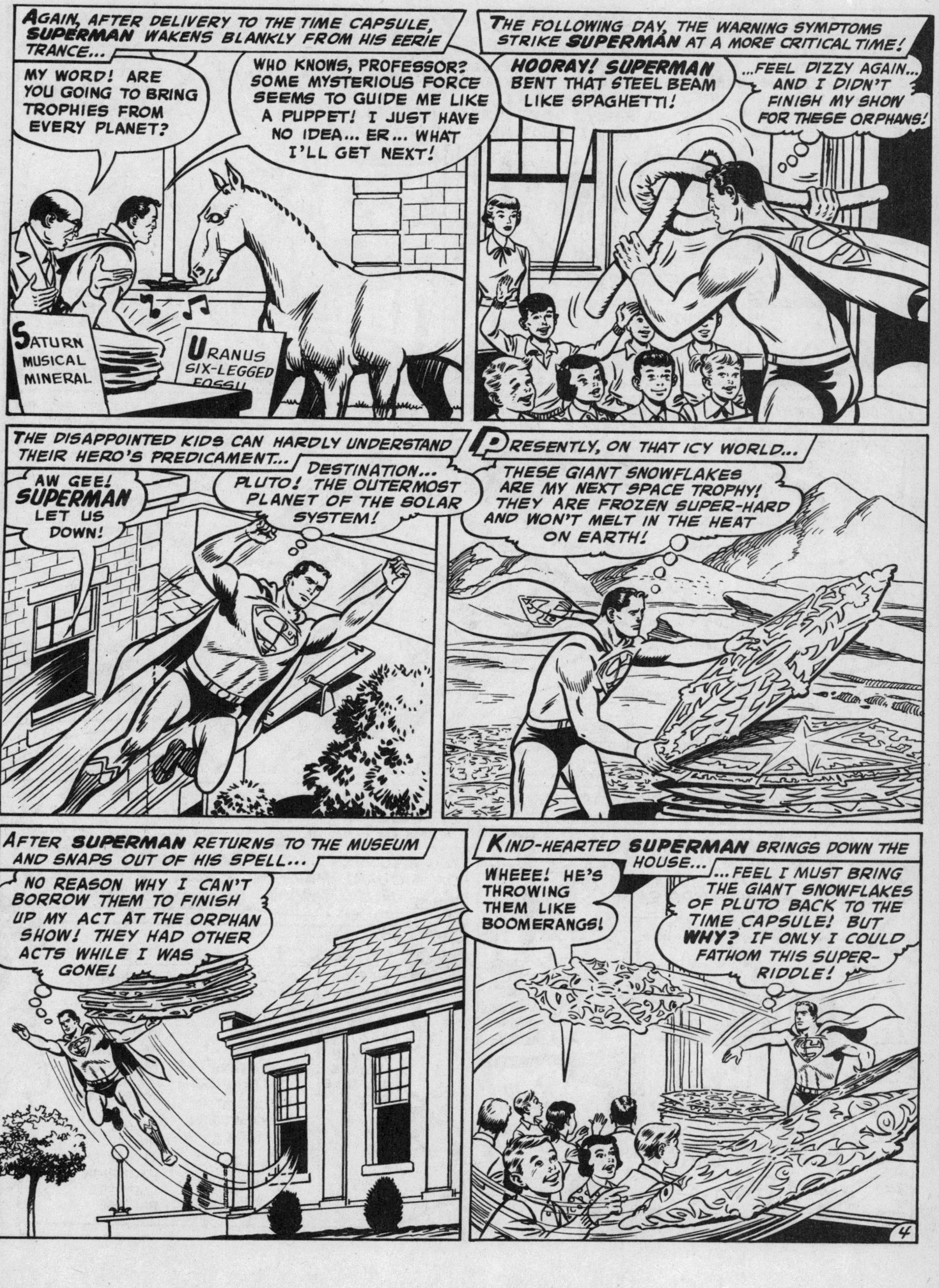
AGAIN, AFTER DELIVERY TO THE TIME CAPSULE, SUPERMAN WAKENS BLANKLY FROM HIS EERIE TRANCE...
MY WORD! ARE YOU GOING TO BRING TROPHIES FROM EVERY PLANET?
WHO KNOWS, PROFESSOR? SOME MYSTERIOUS FORCE SEEMS TO GUIDE ME LIKE A PUPPET! I JUST HAVE NO IDEA... ER... WHAT I'LL GET NEXT!
SATURN MUSICAL MINERAL
URANUS SIX-LEGGED
THE FOLLOWING DAY, THE WARNING SYMPTOMS STRIKE SUPERMAN AT A MORE CRITICAL TIME!
HOORAY! SUPERMAN BENT THAT STEEL BEAM LIKE SPAGHETTI!
...FEEL DIZZY AGAIN... AND I DIDN'T FINISH MY SHOW FOR THESE ORPHANS!
THE DISAPPOINTED KIDS CAN HARDLY UNDERSTAND THEIR HERO'S PREDICAMENT...
AW GEE! SUPERMAN LET US DOWN!
DESTINATION... PLUTO! THE OUTERMOST PLANET OF THE SOLAR SYSTEM!
PRESENTLY, ON THAT ICY WORLD...
THESE GIANT SNOWFLAKES ARE MY NEXT SPACE TROPHY! THEY ARE FROZEN SUPER-HARD AND WON'T MELT IN THE HEAT ON EARTH!
AFTER SUPERMAN RETURNS TO THE MUSEUM AND SNAPS OUT OF HIS SPELL...
NO REASON WHY I CAN'T BORROW THEM TO FINISH UP MY ACT AT THE ORPHAN SHOW! THEY HAD OTHER ACTS WHILE I WAS GONE!
KIND-HEARTED SUPERMAN BRINGS DOWN THE HOUSE...
WHEEE! HE'S THROWING THEM LIKE BOOMERANGS!
...FEEL I MUST BRING THE GIANT SNOWFLAKES OF PLUTO BACK TO THE TIME CAPSULE! BUT WHY? IF ONLY I COULD FATHOM THIS SUPER-RIDDLE!
4

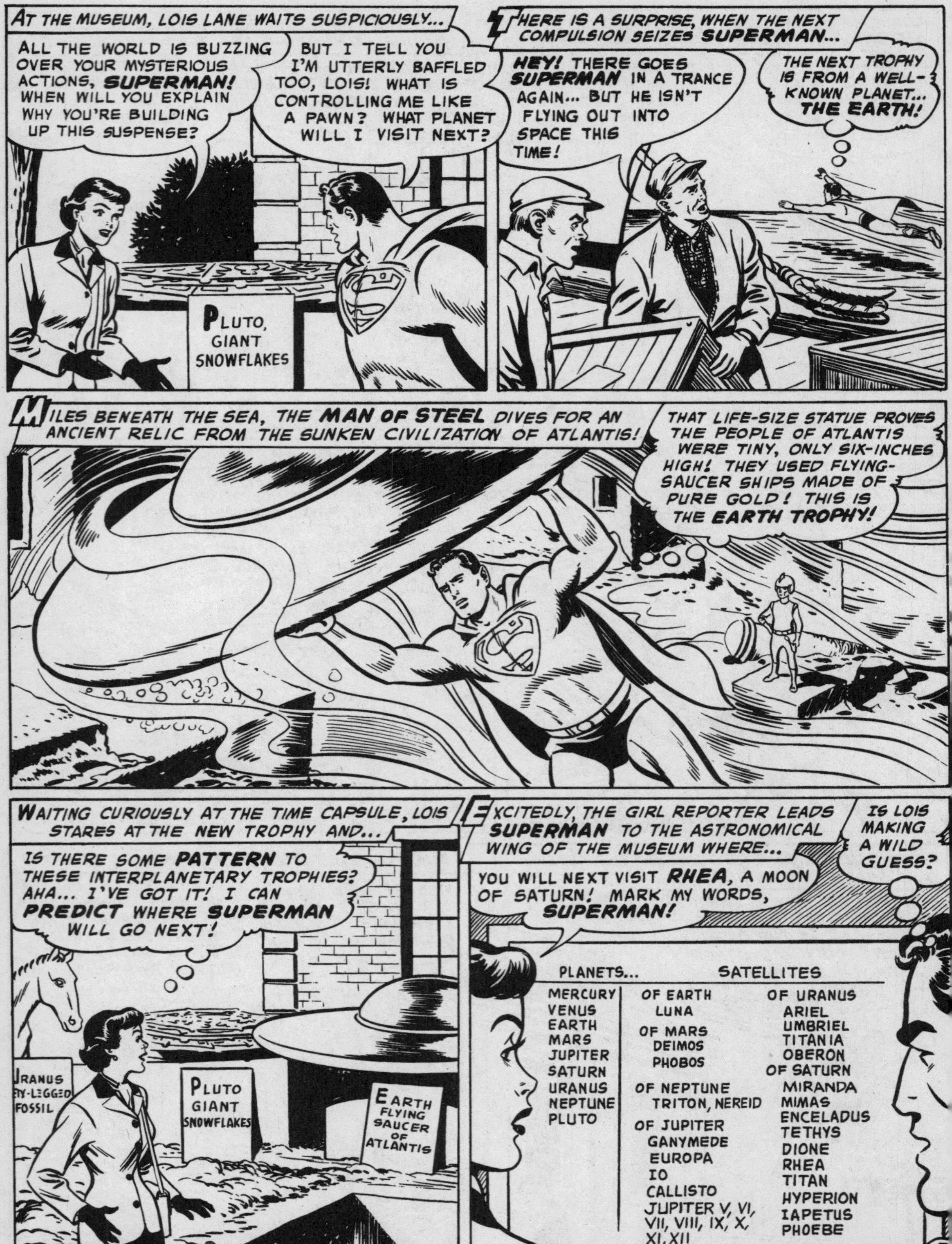
AT THE MUSEUM, LOIS LANE WAITS SUSPICIOUSLY...
ALL THE WORLD IS BUZZING OVER YOUR MYSTERIOUS ACTIONS, SUPERMAN! WHEN WILL YOU EXPLAIN WHY YOU'RE BUILDING UP THIS SUSPENSE?
BUT I TELL YOU I'M UTTERLY BAFFLED TOO, LOIS! WHAT IS CONTROLLING ME LIKE A PAWN? WHAT PLANET WILL I VISIT NEXT?
PLUTO, GIANT SNOWFLAKES
THERE IS A SURPRISE, WHEN THE NEXT COMPULSION SEIZES SUPERMAN...
HEY! THERE GOES SUPERMAN IN A TRANCE AGAIN... BUT HE ISN'T FLYING OUT INTO SPACE THIS TIME!
THE NEXT TROPHY IS FROM A WELL-KNOWN PLANET... THE EARTH!
MILES BENEATH THE SEA, THE MAN OF STEEL DIVES FOR AN ANCIENT RELIC FROM THE SUNKEN CIVILIZATION OF ATLANTIS!
THAT LIFE-SIZE STATUE PROVES THE PEOPLE OF ATLANTIS WERE TINY, ONLY SIX-INCHES HIGH! THEY USED FLYING-SAUCER SHIPS MADE OF PURE GOLD! THIS IS THE EARTH TROPHY!
WAITING CURIOUSLY AT THE TIME CAPSULE, LOIS STARES AT THE NEW TROPHY AND...
IS THERE SOME PATTERN TO THESE INTERPLANETARY TROPHIES? AHA... I'VE GOT IT! I CAN PREDICT WHERE SUPERMAN WILL GO NEXT!
URANUS ...TY-LEGGED FOSSIL
PLUTO GIANT SNOWFLAKES
EARTH FLYING SAUCER OF ATLANTIS
EXCITEDLY, THE GIRL REPORTER LEADS SUPERMAN TO THE ASTRONOMICAL WING OF THE MUSEUM WHERE...
IS LOIS MAKING A WILD GUESS?
YOU WILL NEXT VISIT RHEA, A MOON OF SATURN! MARK MY WORDS, SUPERMAN!
PLANETS... SATELLITES
MERCURY VENUS EARTH MARS JUPITER SATURN URANUS NEPTUNE PLUTO
OF EARTH LUNA
OF MARS DEIMOS PHOBOS
OF NEPTUNE TRITON, NEREID
OF JUPITER GANYMEDE EUROPA IO CALLISTO JUPITER V, VI, VII, VIII, IX, X, XI, XII
OF URANUS ARIEL UMBRIEL TITANIA OBERON
OF SATURN MIRANDA MIMAS ENCELADUS TETHYS DIONE RHEA TITAN HYPERION IAPETUS PHOEBE
5

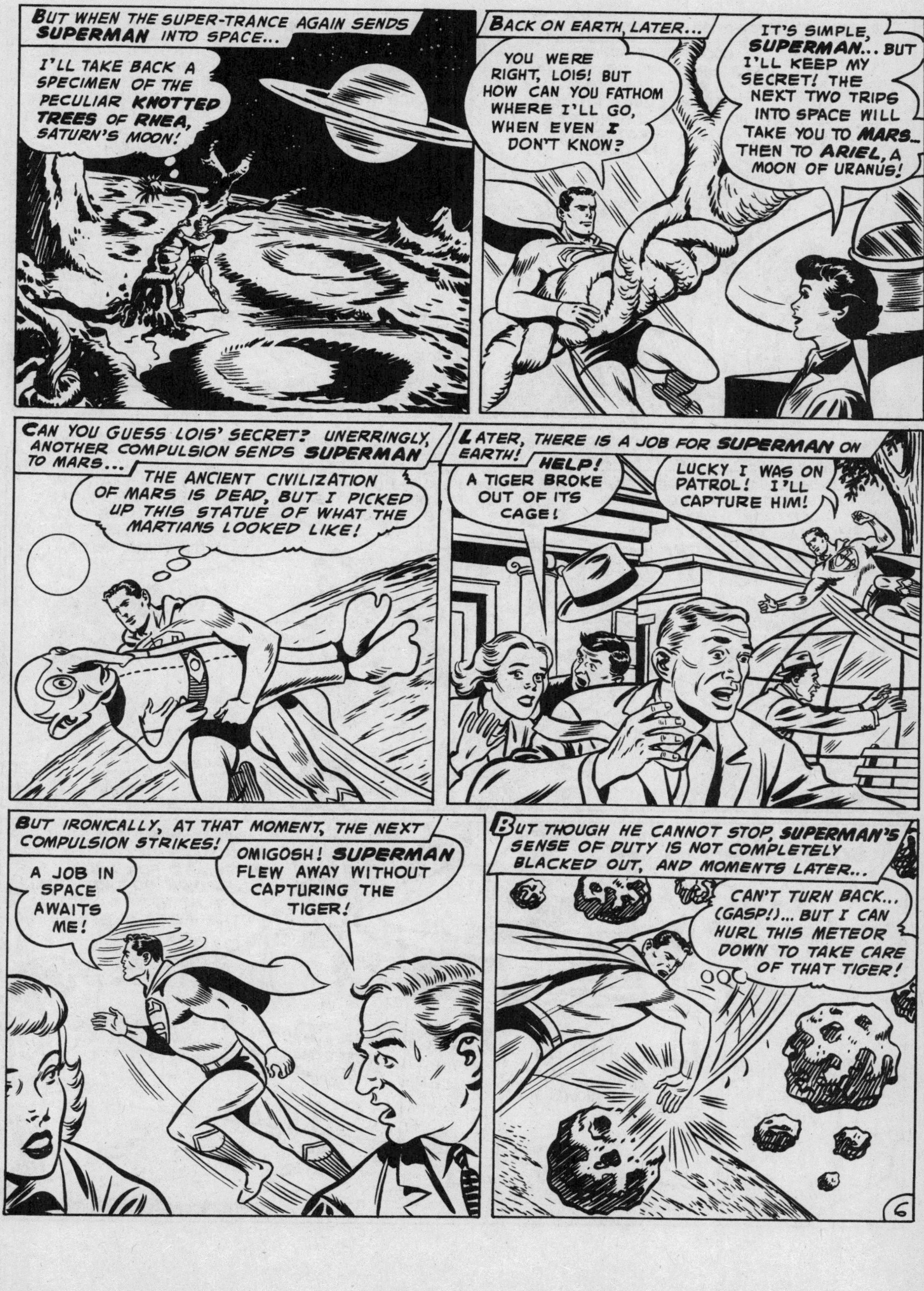
BUT WHEN THE SUPER-TRANCE AGAIN SENDS SUPERMAN INTO SPACE...
I'LL TAKE BACK A SPECIMEN OF THE PECULIAR KNOTTED TREES OF RHEA, SATURN'S MOON!
BACK ON EARTH, LATER...
YOU WERE RIGHT, LOIS! BUT HOW CAN YOU FATHOM WHERE I'LL GO, WHEN EVEN I DON'T KNOW?
IT'S SIMPLE, SUPERMAN... BUT I'LL KEEP MY SECRET! THE NEXT TWO TRIPS INTO SPACE WILL TAKE YOU TO MARS... THEN TO ARIEL, A MOON OF URANUS!
CAN YOU GUESS LOIS' SECRET? UNERRINGLY, ANOTHER COMPULSION SENDS SUPERMAN TO MARS...
THE ANCIENT CIVILIZATION OF MARS IS DEAD, BUT I PICKED UP THIS STATUE OF WHAT THE MARTIANS LOOKED LIKE!
LATER, THERE IS A JOB FOR SUPERMAN ON EARTH!
HELP! A TIGER BROKE OUT OF ITS CAGE!
LUCKY I WAS ON PATROL! I'LL CAPTURE HIM!
BUT IRONICALLY, AT THAT MOMENT, THE NEXT COMPULSION STRIKES!
A JOB IN SPACE AWAITS ME!
OMIGOSH! SUPERMAN FLEW AWAY WITHOUT CAPTURING THE TIGER!
BUT THOUGH HE CANNOT STOP, SUPERMAN'S SENSE OF DUTY IS NOT COMPLETELY BLACKED OUT, AND MOMENTS LATER...
CAN'T TURN BACK... (GASP!)... BUT I CAN HURL THIS METEOR DOWN TO TAKE CARE OF THAT TIGER!
6

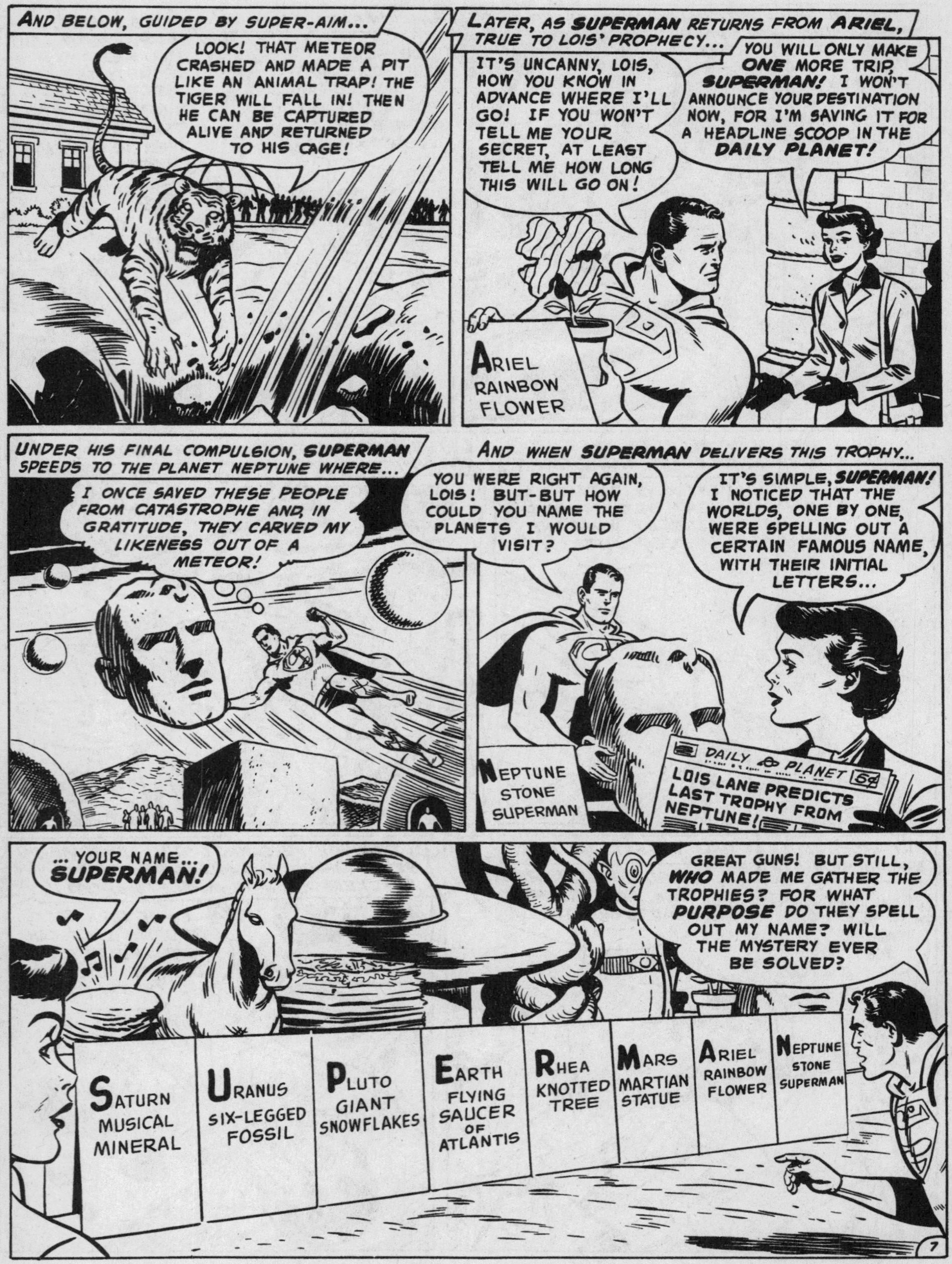
AND BELOW, GUIDED BY SUPER-AIM...
LOOK! THAT METEOR CRASHED AND MADE A PIT LIKE AN ANIMAL TRAP! THE TIGER WILL FALL IN! THEN HE CAN BE CAPTURED ALIVE AND RETURNED TO HIS CAGE!
LATER, AS SUPERMAN RETURNS FROM ARIEL, TRUE TO LOIS' PROPHECY...
IT'S UNCANNY, LOIS, HOW YOU KNOW IN ADVANCE WHERE I'LL GO! IF YOU WON'T TELL ME YOUR SECRET, AT LEAST TELL ME HOW LONG THIS WILL GO ON!
YOU WILL ONLY MAKE ONE MORE TRIP, SUPERMAN! I WON'T ANNOUNCE YOUR DESTINATION NOW, FOR I'M SAVING IT FOR A HEADLINE SCOOP IN THE DAILY PLANET!
ARIEL RAINBOW FLOWER
UNDER HIS FINAL COMPULSION, SUPERMAN SPEEDS TO THE PLANET NEPTUNE WHERE...
I ONCE SAVED THESE PEOPLE FROM CATASTROPHE AND, IN GRATITUDE, THEY CARVED MY LIKENESS OUT OF A METEOR!
AND WHEN SUPERMAN DELIVERS THIS TROPHY...
YOU WERE RIGHT AGAIN, LOIS! BUT-BUT HOW COULD YOU NAME THE PLANETS I WOULD VISIT?
IT'S SIMPLE, SUPERMAN! I NOTICED THAT THE WORLDS, ONE BY ONE, WERE SPELLING OUT A CERTAIN FAMOUS NAME, WITH THEIR INITIAL LETTERS...
NEPTUNE STONE SUPERMAN
DAILY PLANET 5¢
LOIS LANE PREDICTS LAST TROPHY FROM NEPTUNE!
... YOUR NAME... SUPERMAN!
GREAT GUNS! BUT STILL, WHO MADE ME GATHER THE TROPHIES? FOR WHAT PURPOSE DO THEY SPELL OUT MY NAME? WILL THE MYSTERY EVER BE SOLVED?
SATURN MUSICAL MINERAL
URANUS SIX-LEGGED FOSSIL
PLUTO GIANT SNOWFLAKES
EARTH FLYING SAUCER OF ATLANTIS
RHEA KNOTTED TREE
MARS MARTIAN STATUE
ARIEL RAINBOW FLOWER
NEPTUNE STONE SUPERMAN
7

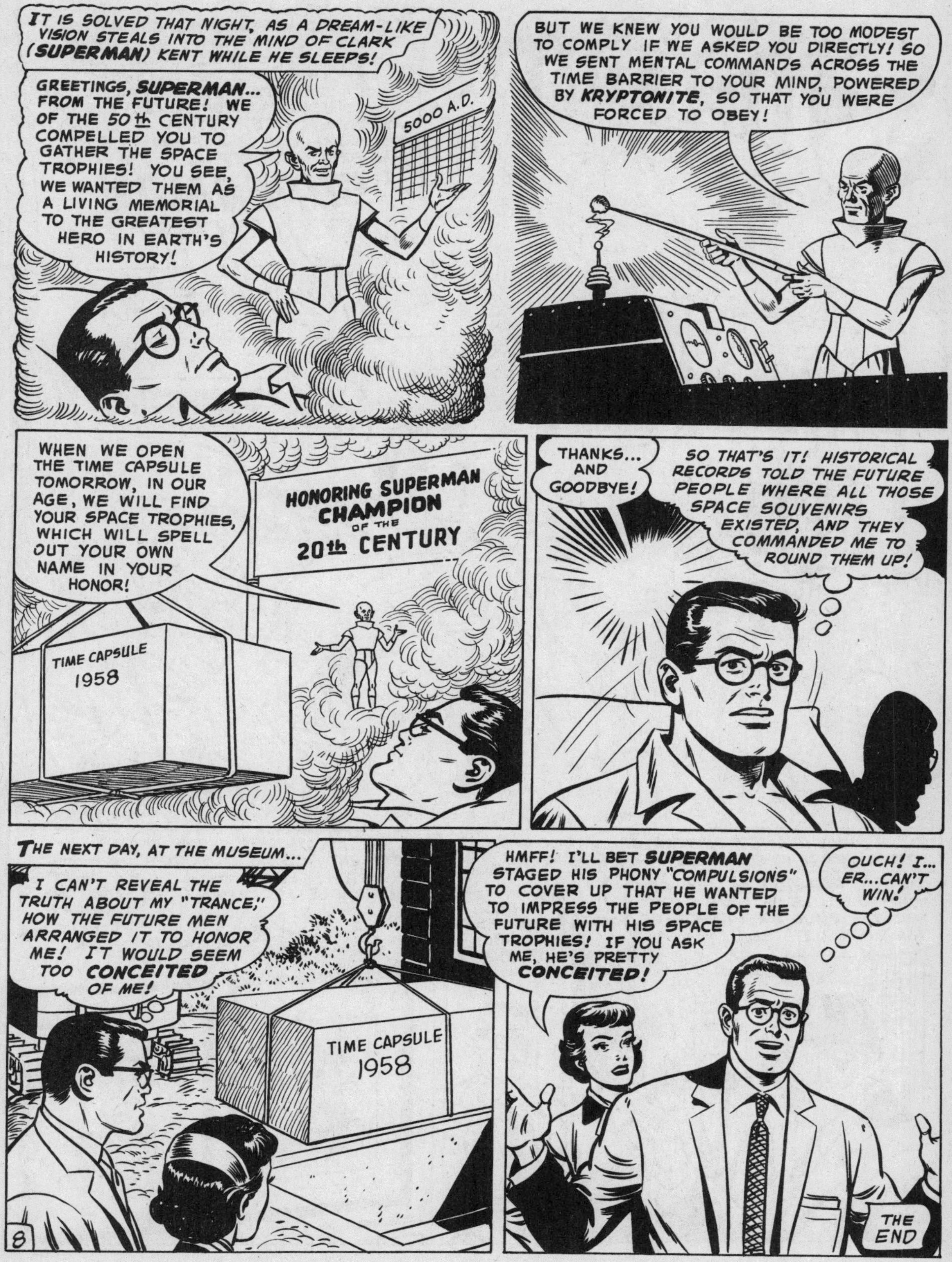
IT IS SOLVED THAT NIGHT, AS A DREAM-LIKE VISION STEALS INTO THE MIND OF CLARK (SUPERMAN) KENT WHILE HE SLEEPS!
GREETINGS, SUPERMAN... FROM THE FUTURE! WE OF THE 50th CENTURY COMPELLED YOU TO GATHER THE SPACE TROPHIES! YOU SEE, WE WANTED THEM AS A LIVING MEMORIAL TO THE GREATEST HERO IN EARTH'S HISTORY!
5000 A.D.
BUT WE KNEW YOU WOULD BE TOO MODEST TO COMPLY IF WE ASKED YOU DIRECTLY! SO WE SENT MENTAL COMMANDS ACROSS THE TIME BARRIER TO YOUR MIND, POWERED BY KRYPTONITE, SO THAT YOU WERE FORCED TO OBEY!
WHEN WE OPEN THE TIME CAPSULE TOMORROW, IN OUR AGE, WE WILL FIND YOUR SPACE TROPHIES, WHICH WILL SPELL OUT YOUR OWN NAME IN YOUR HONOR!
HONORING SUPERMAN CHAMPION OF THE 20th CENTURY
TIME CAPSULE 1958
THANKS... AND GOODBYE!
SO THAT'S IT! HISTORICAL RECORDS TOLD THE FUTURE PEOPLE WHERE ALL THOSE SPACE SOUVENIRS EXISTED, AND THEY COMMANDED ME TO ROUND THEM UP!
THE NEXT DAY, AT THE MUSEUM...
I CAN'T REVEAL THE TRUTH ABOUT MY "TRANCE," HOW THE FUTURE MEN ARRANGED IT TO HONOR ME! IT WOULD SEEM TOO CONCEITED OF ME!
TIME CAPSULE 1958
8
HMFF! I'LL BET SUPERMAN STAGED HIS PHONY "COMPULSIONS" TO COVER UP THAT HE WANTED TO IMPRESS THE PEOPLE OF THE FUTURE WITH HIS SPACE TROPHIES! IF YOU ASK ME, HE'S PRETTY CONCEITED!
OUCH! I... ER...CAN'T WIN!
THE END

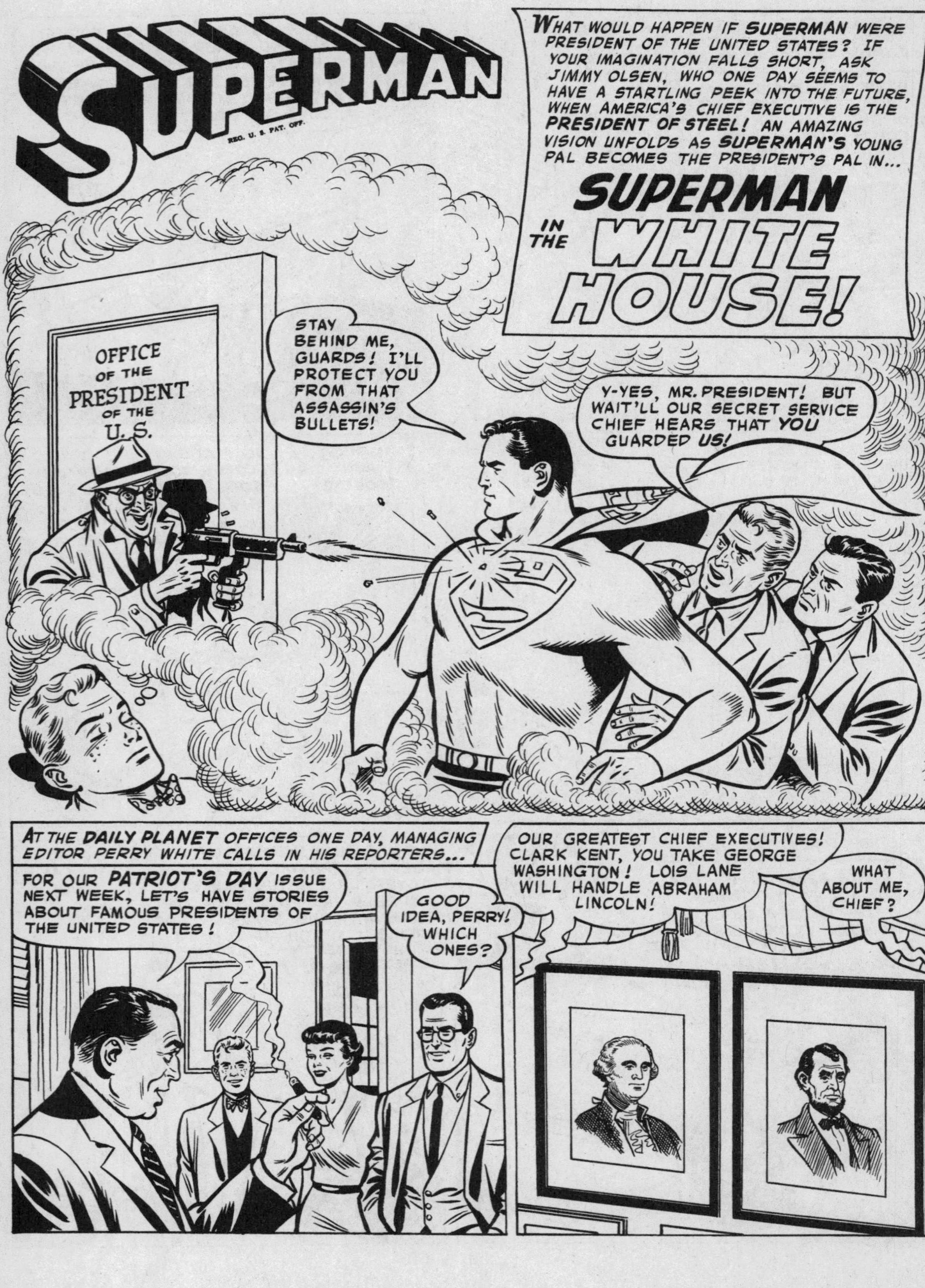
SUPERMAN
REG. U. S. PAT. OFF.
WHAT WOULD HAPPEN IF SUPERMAN WERE PRESIDENT OF THE UNITED STATES? IF YOUR IMAGINATION FALLS SHORT, ASK JIMMY OLSEN, WHO ONE DAY SEEMS TO HAVE A STARTLING PEEK INTO THE FUTURE, WHEN AMERICA'S CHIEF EXECUTIVE IS THE PRESIDENT OF STEEL! AN AMAZING VISION UNFOLDS AS SUPERMAN'S YOUNG PAL BECOMES THE PRESIDENT'S PAL IN...
SUPERMAN IN THE WHITE HOUSE!
OFFICE OF THE PRESIDENT OF THE U.S.
STAY BEHIND ME, GUARDS! I'LL PROTECT YOU FROM THAT ASSASSIN'S BULLETS!
Y-YES, MR. PRESIDENT! BUT WAIT'LL OUR SECRET SERVICE CHIEF HEARS THAT YOU GUARDED US!
AT THE DAILY PLANET OFFICES ONE DAY, MANAGING EDITOR PERRY WHITE CALLS IN HIS REPORTERS...
FOR OUR PATRIOT'S DAY ISSUE NEXT WEEK, LET'S HAVE STORIES ABOUT FAMOUS PRESIDENTS OF THE UNITED STATES!
GOOD IDEA, PERRY! WHICH ONES?
OUR GREATEST CHIEF EXECUTIVES! CLARK KENT, YOU TAKE GEORGE WASHINGTON! LOIS LANE WILL HANDLE ABRAHAM LINCOLN!
WHAT ABOUT ME, CHIEF?

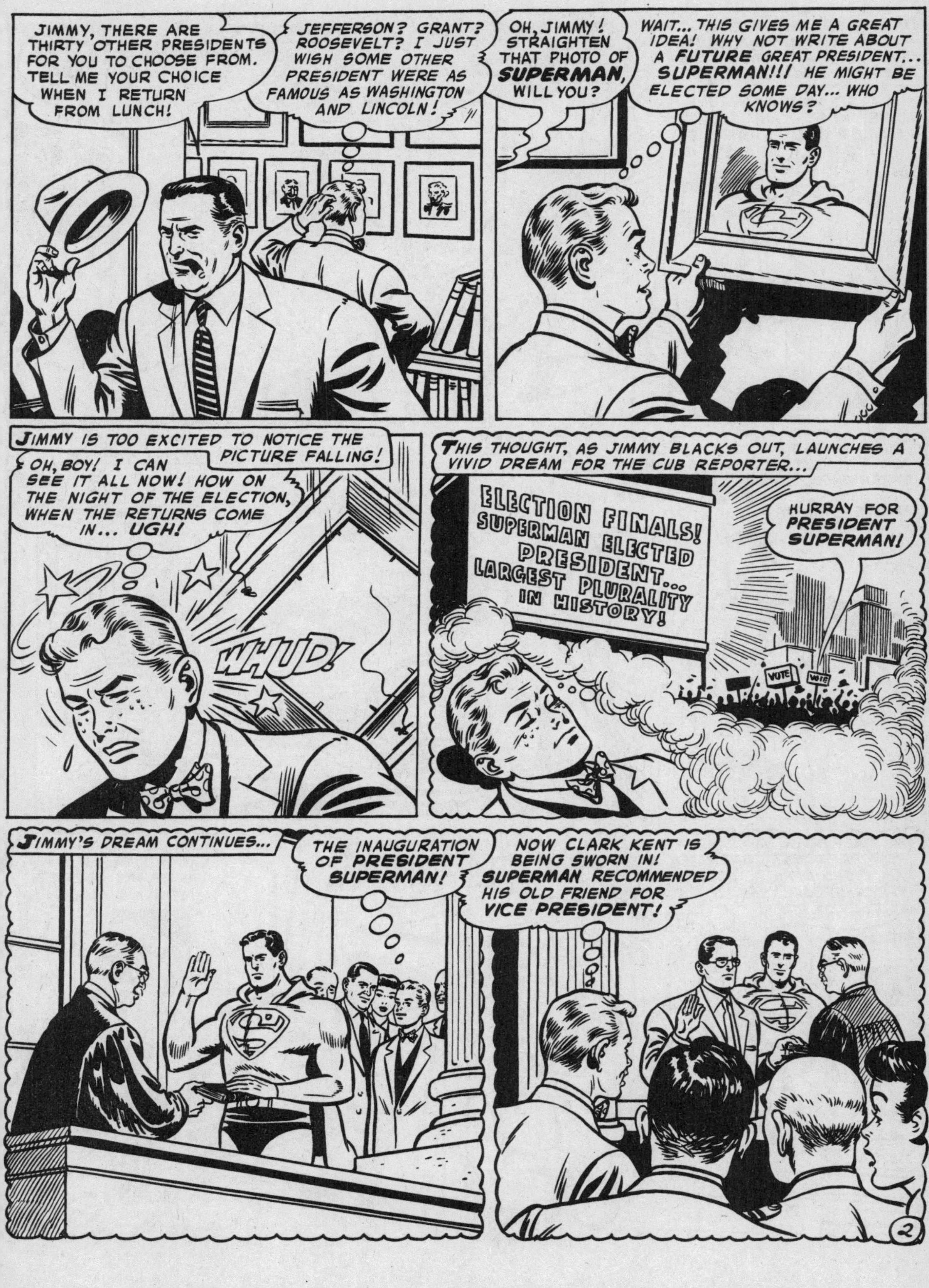
JIMMY, THERE ARE THIRTY OTHER PRESIDENTS FOR YOU TO CHOOSE FROM. TELL ME YOUR CHOICE WHEN I RETURN FROM LUNCH!
JEFFERSON? GRANT? ROOSEVELT? I JUST WISH SOME OTHER PRESIDENT WERE AS FAMOUS AS WASHINGTON AND LINCOLN!
OH, JIMMY! STRAIGHTEN THAT PHOTO OF SUPERMAN, WILL YOU?
WAIT... THIS GIVES ME A GREAT IDEA! WHY NOT WRITE ABOUT A FUTURE GREAT PRESIDENT... SUPERMAN!!! HE MIGHT BE ELECTED SOME DAY... WHO KNOWS?
JIMMY IS TOO EXCITED TO NOTICE THE PICTURE FALLING!
OH, BOY! I CAN SEE IT ALL NOW! HOW ON THE NIGHT OF THE ELECTION, WHEN THE RETURNS COME IN... UGH!
WHUD!
THIS THOUGHT, AS JIMMY BLACKS OUT, LAUNCHES A VIVID DREAM FOR THE CUB REPORTER...
ELECTION FINALS! SUPERMAN ELECTED PRESIDENT... LARGEST PLURALITY IN HISTORY!
HURRAY FOR PRESIDENT SUPERMAN!
VOTE
VOTE
JIMMY'S DREAM CONTINUES...
THE INAUGURATION OF PRESIDENT SUPERMAN!
NOW CLARK KENT IS BEING SWORN IN! SUPERMAN RECOMMENDED HIS OLD FRIEND FOR VICE PRESIDENT!
2

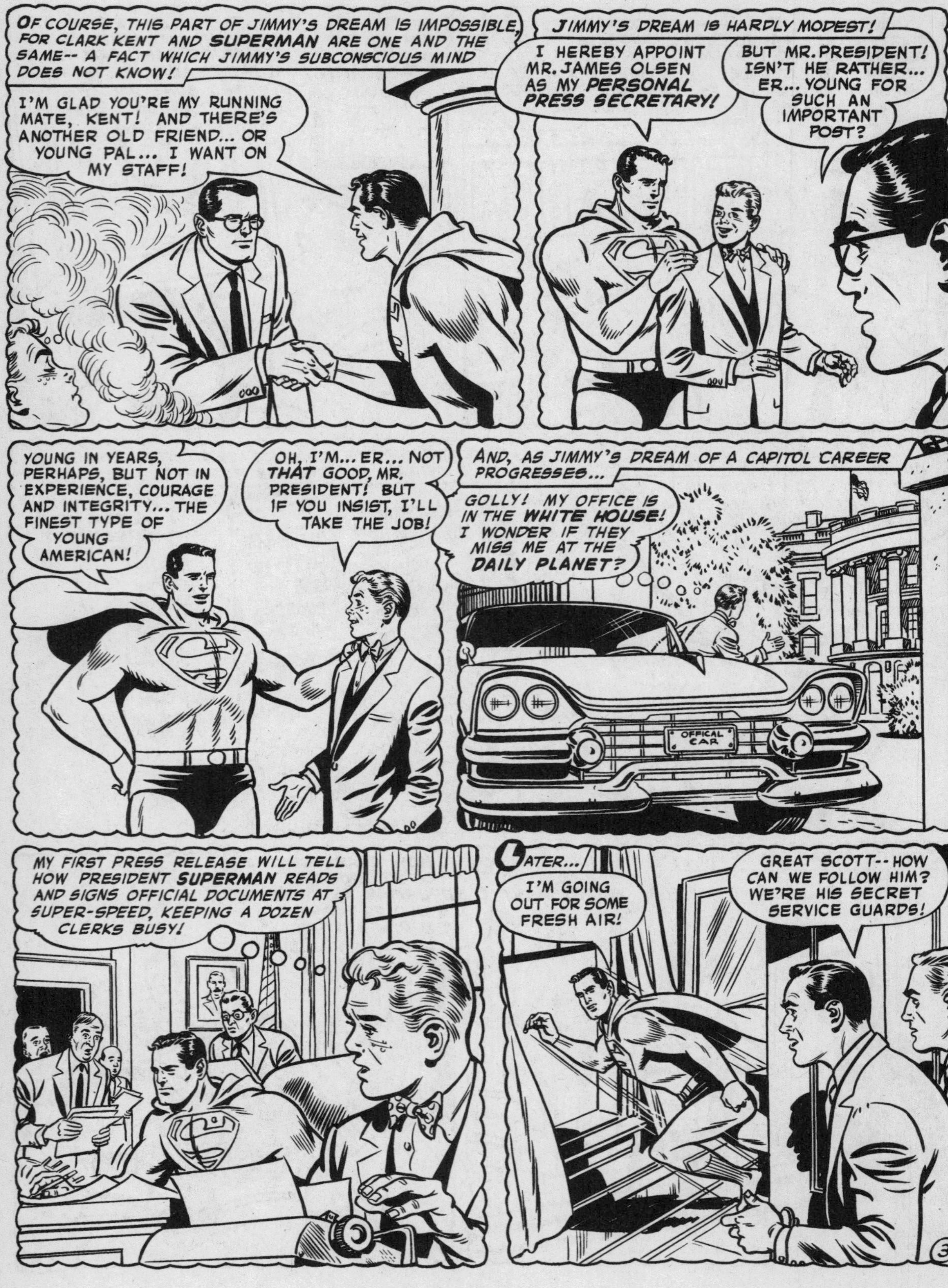
OF COURSE, THIS PART OF JIMMY'S DREAM IS IMPOSSIBLE, FOR CLARK KENT AND SUPERMAN ARE ONE AND THE SAME-- A FACT WHICH JIMMY'S SUBCONSCIOUS MIND DOES NOT KNOW!
I'M GLAD YOU'RE MY RUNNING MATE, KENT! AND THERE'S ANOTHER OLD FRIEND... OR YOUNG PAL... I WANT ON MY STAFF!
JIMMY'S DREAM IS HARDLY MODEST!
I HEREBY APPOINT MR. JAMES OLSEN AS MY PERSONAL PRESS SECRETARY!
BUT MR. PRESIDENT! ISN'T HE RATHER... ER... YOUNG FOR SUCH AN IMPORTANT POST?
YOUNG IN YEARS, PERHAPS, BUT NOT IN EXPERIENCE, COURAGE AND INTEGRITY... THE FINEST TYPE OF YOUNG AMERICAN!
OH, I'M... ER... NOT THAT GOOD, MR. PRESIDENT! BUT IF YOU INSIST, I'LL TAKE THE JOB!
AND, AS JIMMY'S DREAM OF A CAPITOL CAREER PROGRESSES...
GOLLY! MY OFFICE IS IN THE WHITE HOUSE! I WONDER IF THEY MISS ME AT THE DAILY PLANET?
OFFICAL CAR
MY FIRST PRESS RELEASE WILL TELL HOW PRESIDENT SUPERMAN READS AND SIGNS OFFICIAL DOCUMENTS AT SUPER-SPEED, KEEPING A DOZEN CLERKS BUSY!
LATER...
I'M GOING OUT FOR SOME FRESH AIR!
GREAT SCOTT-- HOW CAN WE FOLLOW HIM? WE'RE HIS SECRET SERVICE GUARDS!
3

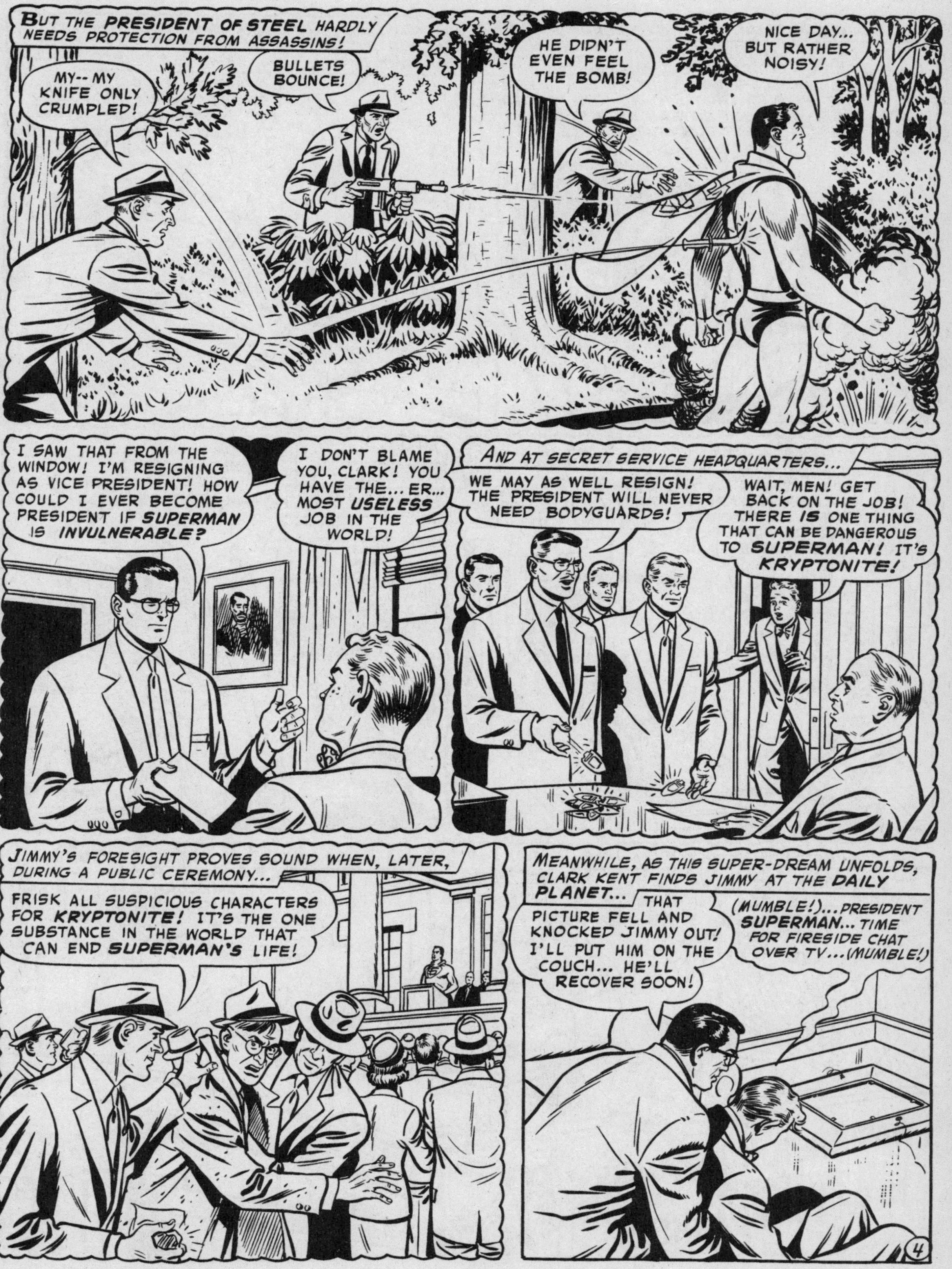
BUT THE PRESIDENT OF STEEL HARDLY NEEDS PROTECTION FROM ASSASSINS!
MY-- MY KNIFE ONLY CRUMPLED!
BULLETS BOUNCE!
HE DIDN'T EVEN FEEL THE BOMB!
NICE DAY... BUT RATHER NOISY!
I SAW THAT FROM THE WINDOW! I'M RESIGNING AS VICE PRESIDENT! HOW COULD I EVER BECOME PRESIDENT IF SUPERMAN IS INVULNERABLE?
I DON'T BLAME YOU, CLARK! YOU HAVE THE... ER... MOST USELESS JOB IN THE WORLD!
AND AT SECRET SERVICE HEADQUARTERS...
WE MAY AS WELL RESIGN! THE PRESIDENT WILL NEVER NEED BODYGUARDS!
WAIT, MEN! GET BACK ON THE JOB! THERE IS ONE THING THAT CAN BE DANGEROUS TO SUPERMAN! IT'S KRYPTONITE!
JIMMY'S FORESIGHT PROVES SOUND WHEN, LATER, DURING A PUBLIC CEREMONY...
FRISK ALL SUSPICIOUS CHARACTERS FOR KRYPTONITE! IT'S THE ONE SUBSTANCE IN THE WORLD THAT CAN END SUPERMAN'S LIFE!
MEANWHILE, AS THIS SUPER-DREAM UNFOLDS, CLARK KENT FINDS JIMMY AT THE DAILY PLANET...
THAT PICTURE FELL AND KNOCKED JIMMY OUT! I'LL PUT HIM ON THE COUCH... HE'LL RECOVER SOON!
(MUMBLE!)... PRESIDENT SUPERMAN... TIME FOR FIRESIDE CHAT OVER TV... (MUMBLE!)
4

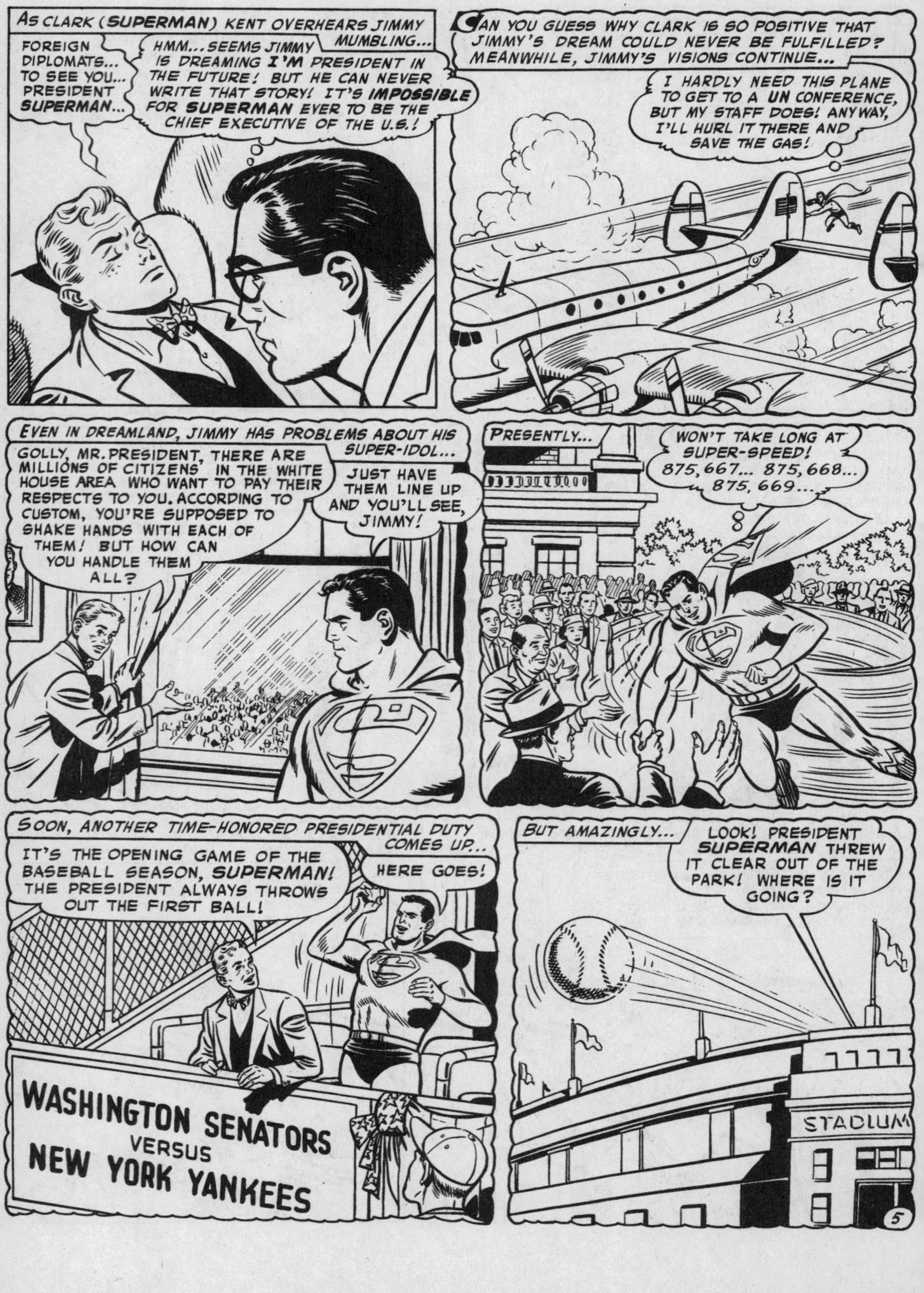
AS CLARK (SUPERMAN) KENT OVERHEARS JIMMY MUMBLING...
FOREIGN DIPLOMATS... TO SEE YOU... PRESIDENT SUPERMAN...
HMM... SEEMS JIMMY IS DREAMING I'M PRESIDENT IN THE FUTURE! BUT HE CAN NEVER WRITE THAT STORY! IT'S IMPOSSIBLE FOR SUPERMAN EVER TO BE THE CHIEF EXECUTIVE OF THE U.S.!
CAN YOU GUESS WHY CLARK IS SO POSITIVE THAT JIMMY'S DREAM COULD NEVER BE FULFILLED? MEANWHILE, JIMMY'S VISIONS CONTINUE...
I HARDLY NEED THIS PLANE TO GET TO A UN CONFERENCE, BUT MY STAFF DOES! ANYWAY, I'LL HURL IT THERE AND SAVE THE GAS!
EVEN IN DREAMLAND, JIMMY HAS PROBLEMS ABOUT HIS SUPER-IDOL...
GOLLY, MR. PRESIDENT, THERE ARE MILLIONS OF CITIZENS IN THE WHITE HOUSE AREA WHO WANT TO PAY THEIR RESPECTS TO YOU. ACCORDING TO CUSTOM, YOU'RE SUPPOSED TO SHAKE HANDS WITH EACH OF THEM! BUT HOW CAN YOU HANDLE THEM ALL?
JUST HAVE THEM LINE UP AND YOU'LL SEE, JIMMY!
PRESENTLY...
WON'T TAKE LONG AT SUPER-SPEED! 875,667... 875,668... 875,669...
SOON, ANOTHER TIME-HONORED PRESIDENTIAL DUTY COMES UP...
IT'S THE OPENING GAME OF THE BASEBALL SEASON, SUPERMAN! THE PRESIDENT ALWAYS THROWS OUT THE FIRST BALL!
HERE GOES!
WASHINGTON SENATORS VERSUS NEW YORK YANKEES
BUT AMAZINGLY...
LOOK! PRESIDENT SUPERMAN THREW IT CLEAR OUT OF THE PARK! WHERE IS IT GOING?
STADIUM
5

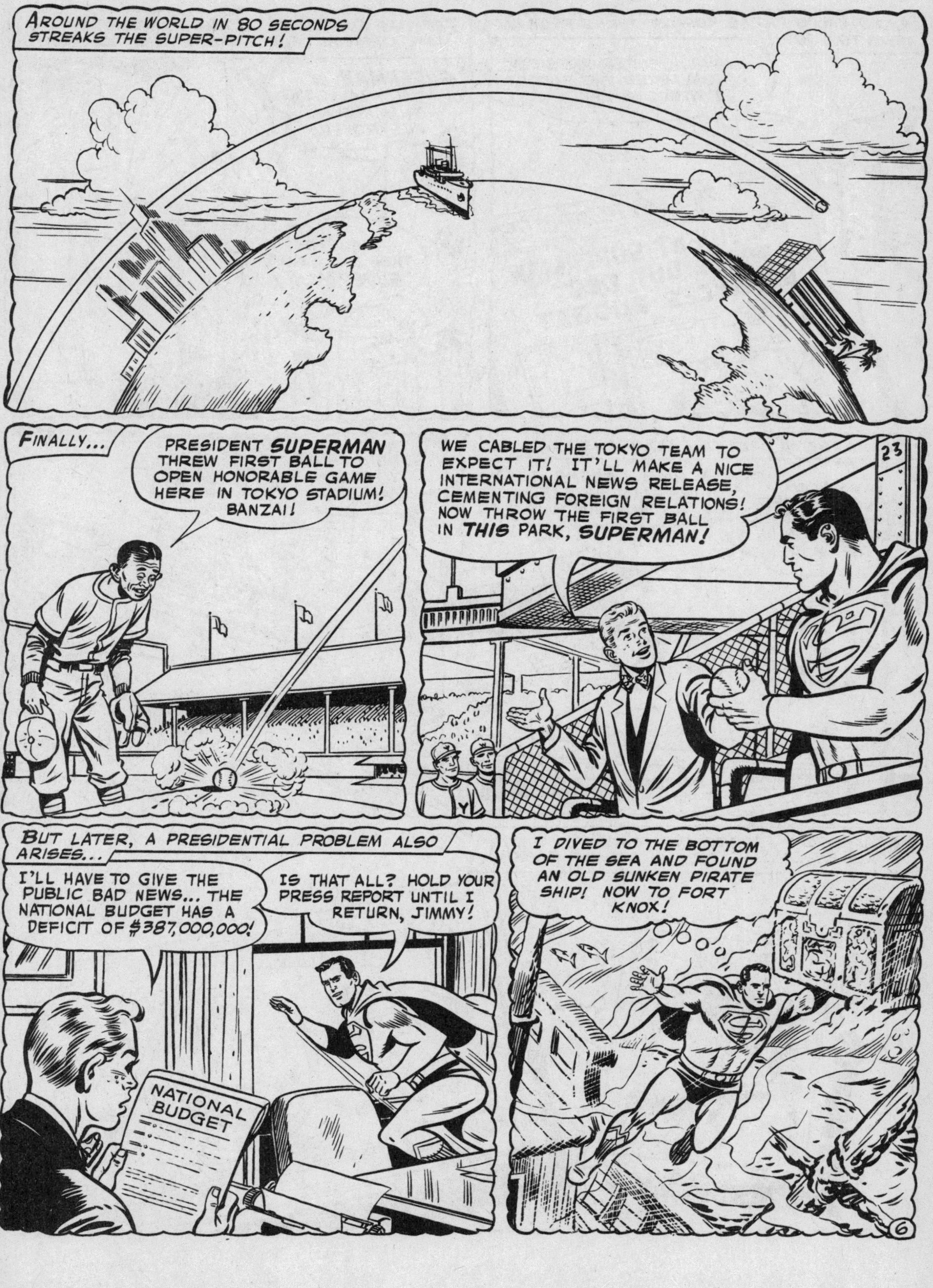
AROUND THE WORLD IN 80 SECONDS STREAKS THE SUPER-PITCH!
FINALLY...
PRESIDENT SUPERMAN THREW FIRST BALL TO OPEN HONORABLE GAME HERE IN TOKYO STADIUM! BANZAI!
WE CABLED THE TOKYO TEAM TO EXPECT IT! IT'LL MAKE A NICE INTERNATIONAL NEWS RELEASE, CEMENTING FOREIGN RELATIONS! NOW THROW THE FIRST BALL IN THIS PARK, SUPERMAN!
23
BUT LATER, A PRESIDENTIAL PROBLEM ALSO ARISES...
I'LL HAVE TO GIVE THE PUBLIC BAD NEWS... THE NATIONAL BUDGET HAS A DEFICIT OF $387,000,000!
IS THAT ALL? HOLD YOUR PRESS REPORT UNTIL I RETURN, JIMMY!
NATIONAL BUDGET
I DIVED TO THE BOTTOM OF THE SEA AND FOUND AN OLD SUNKEN PIRATE SHIP! NOW TO FORT KNOX!
6

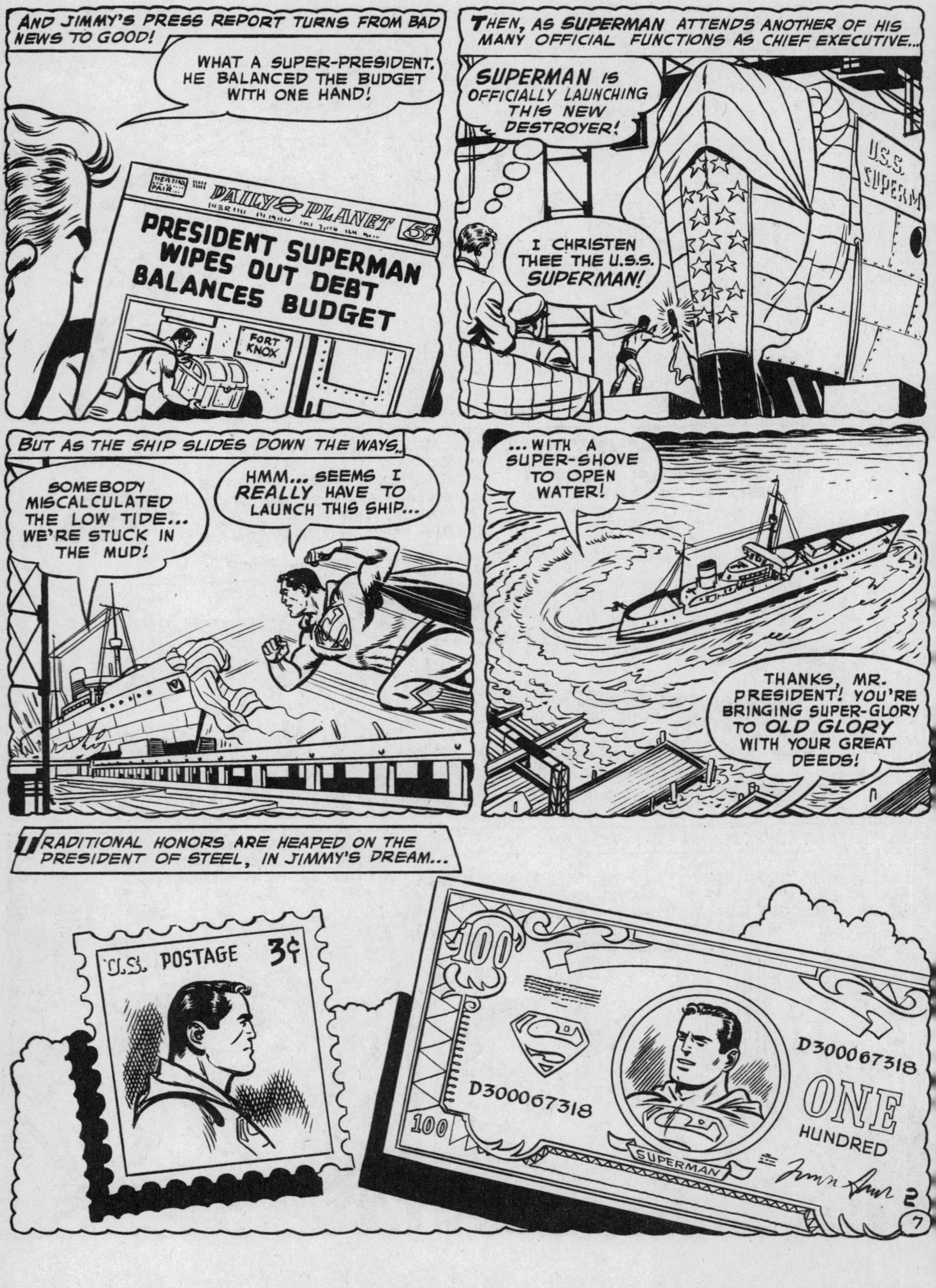
AND JIMMY'S PRESS REPORT TURNS FROM BAD NEWS TO GOOD!
WHAT A SUPER-PRESIDENT. HE BALANCED THE BUDGET WITH ONE HAND!
DAILY PLANET 5¢
PRESIDENT SUPERMAN WIPES OUT DEBT BALANCES BUDGET
FORT KNOX
THEN, AS SUPERMAN ATTENDS ANOTHER OF HIS MANY OFFICIAL FUNCTIONS AS CHIEF EXECUTIVE...
SUPERMAN IS OFFICIALLY LAUNCHING THIS NEW DESTROYER!
I CHRISTEN THEE THE U.S.S. SUPERMAN!
U.S.S. SUPERM
BUT AS THE SHIP SLIDES DOWN THE WAYS..
SOMEBODY MISCALCULATED THE LOW TIDE... WE'RE STUCK IN THE MUD!
HMM... SEEMS I REALLY HAVE TO LAUNCH THIS SHIP...
...WITH A SUPER-SHOVE TO OPEN WATER!
THANKS, MR. PRESIDENT! YOU'RE BRINGING SUPER-GLORY TO OLD GLORY WITH YOUR GREAT DEEDS!
TRADITIONAL HONORS ARE HEAPED ON THE PRESIDENT OF STEEL, IN JIMMY'S DREAM...
U.S. POSTAGE 3¢
100
D300067318
D300067318
ONE HUNDRED
100
SUPERMAN
7

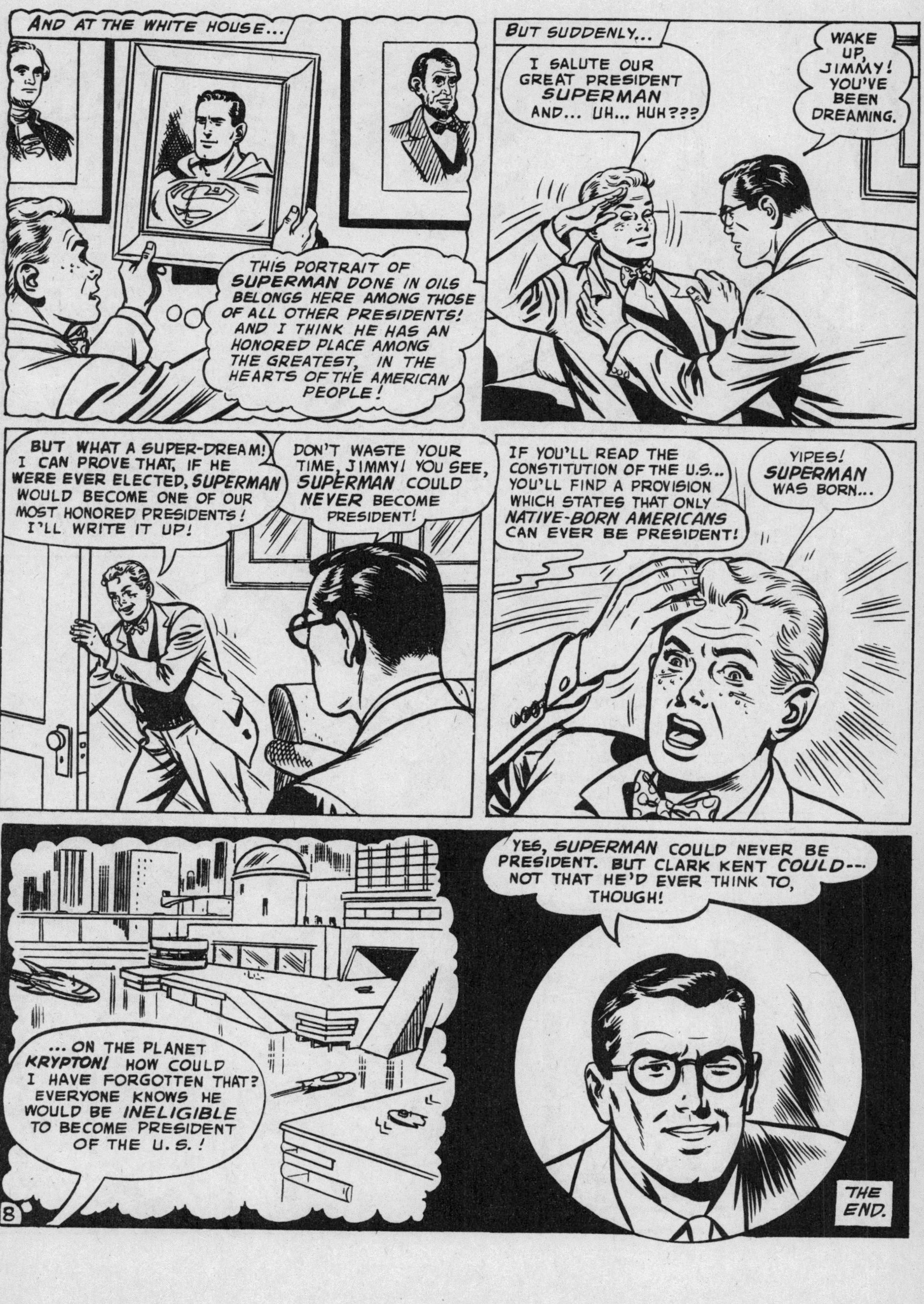
AND AT THE WHITE HOUSE...
THIS PORTRAIT OF SUPERMAN DONE IN OILS BELONGS HERE AMONG THOSE OF ALL OTHER PRESIDENTS! AND I THINK HE HAS AN HONORED PLACE AMONG THE GREATEST, IN THE HEARTS OF THE AMERICAN PEOPLE!
BUT SUDDENLY...
I SALUTE OUR GREAT PRESIDENT SUPERMAN AND... UH... HUH???
WAKE UP, JIMMY! YOU'VE BEEN DREAMING.
BUT WHAT A SUPER-DREAM! I CAN PROVE THAT, IF HE WERE EVER ELECTED, SUPERMAN WOULD BECOME ONE OF OUR MOST HONORED PRESIDENTS! I'LL WRITE IT UP!
DON'T WASTE YOUR TIME, JIMMY! YOU SEE, SUPERMAN COULD NEVER BECOME PRESIDENT!
IF YOU'LL READ THE CONSTITUTION OF THE U.S... YOU'LL FIND A PROVISION WHICH STATES THAT ONLY NATIVE-BORN AMERICANS CAN EVER BE PRESIDENT!
YIPES! SUPERMAN WAS BORN...
...ON THE PLANET KRYPTON! HOW COULD I HAVE FORGOTTEN THAT? EVERYONE KNOWS HE WOULD BE INELIGIBLE TO BECOME PRESIDENT OF THE U.S.!
YES, SUPERMAN COULD NEVER BE PRESIDENT. BUT CLARK KENT COULD--- NOT THAT HE'D EVER THINK TO, THOUGH!
THE END.
8

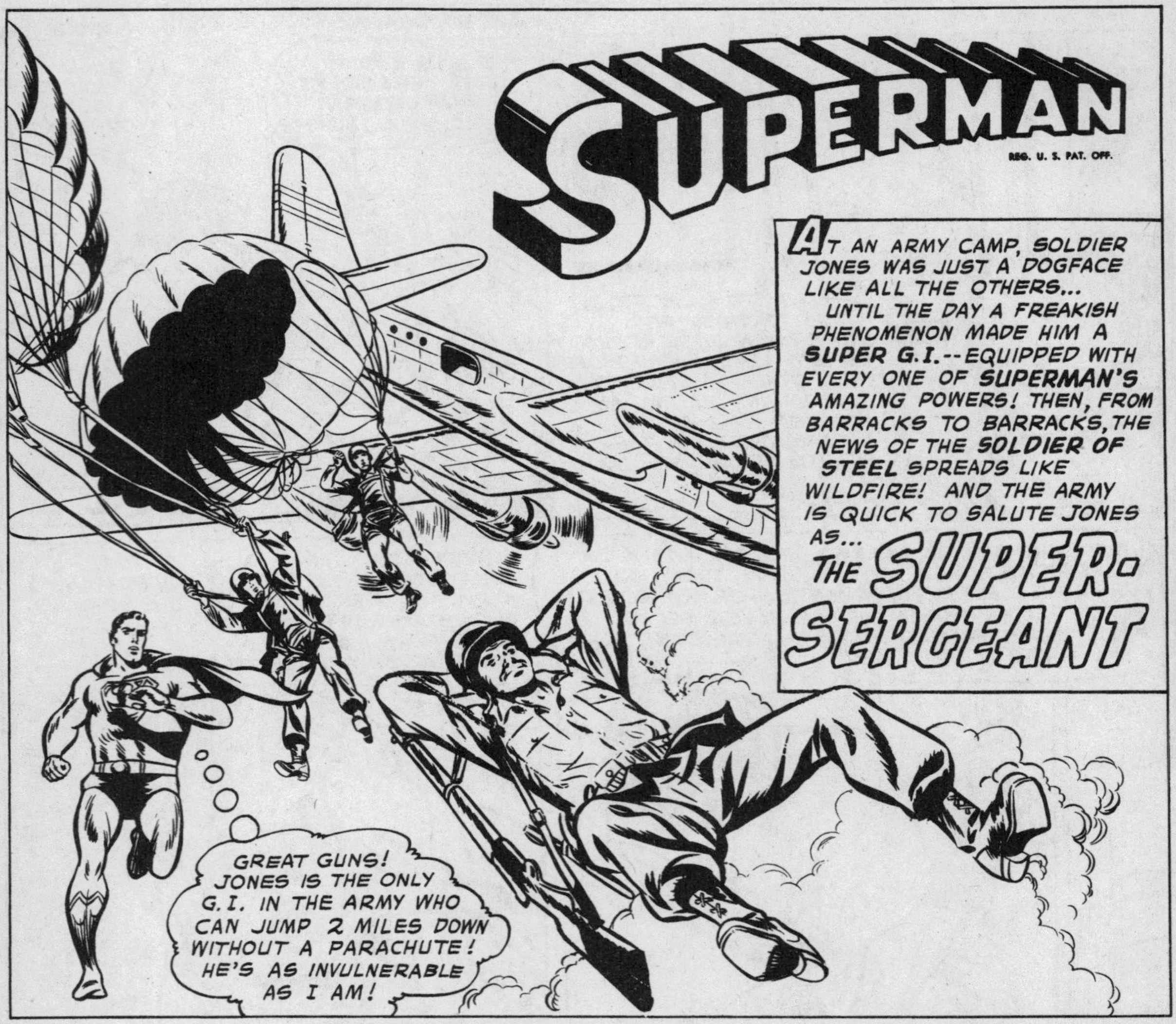
SUPERMAN
REG. U. S. PAT. OFF.
AT AN ARMY CAMP, SOLDIER JONES WAS JUST A DOGFACE LIKE ALL THE OTHERS... UNTIL THE DAY A FREAKISH PHENOMENON MADE HIM A SUPER G.I.--EQUIPPED WITH EVERY ONE OF SUPERMAN'S AMAZING POWERS! THEN, FROM BARRACKS TO BARRACKS, THE NEWS OF THE SOLDIER OF STEEL SPREADS LIKE WILDFIRE! AND THE ARMY IS QUICK TO SALUTE JONES AS...
THE SUPER-SERGEANT
GREAT GUNS! JONES IS THE ONLY G.I. IN THE ARMY WHO CAN JUMP 2 MILES DOWN WITHOUT A PARACHUTE! HE'S AS INVULNERABLE AS I AM!

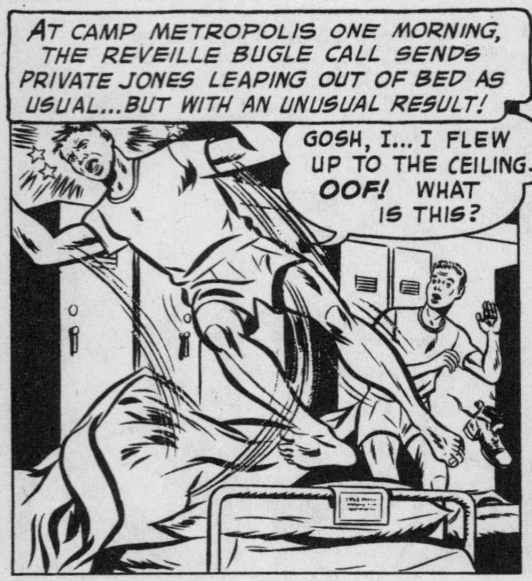
AT CAMP METROPOLIS ONE MORNING, THE REVEILLE BUGLE CALL SENDS PRIVATE JONES LEAPING OUT OF BED AS USUAL...BUT WITH AN UNUSUAL RESULT!
GOSH, I...I FLEW UP TO THE CEILING... OOF! WHAT IS THIS?

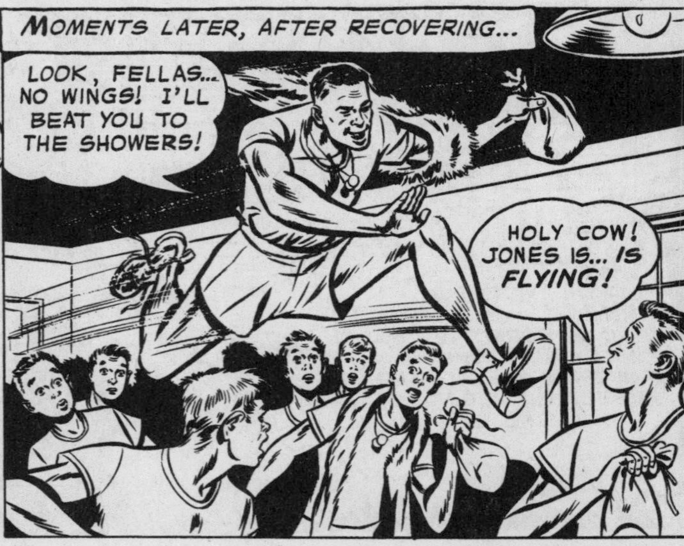
MOMENTS LATER, AFTER RECOVERING...
LOOK, FELLAS... NO WINGS! I'LL BEAT YOU TO THE SHOWERS!
HOLY COW! JONES IS... IS FLYING!

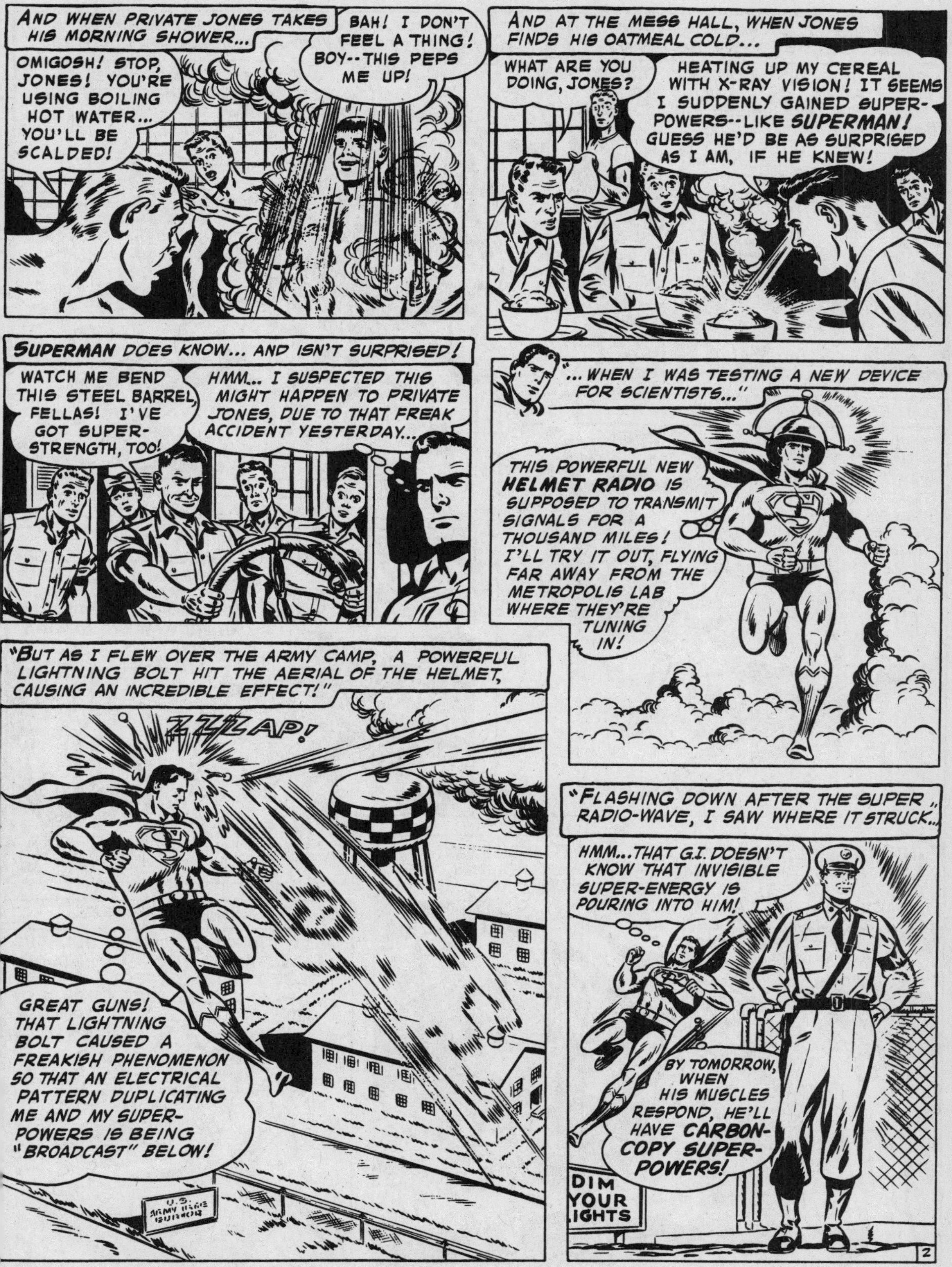
AND WHEN PRIVATE JONES TAKES HIS MORNING SHOWER...
OMIGOSH! STOP, JONES! YOU'RE USING BOILING HOT WATER... YOU'LL BE SCALDED!
BAH! I DON'T FEEL A THING! BOY--THIS PEPS ME UP!
AND AT THE MESS HALL, WHEN JONES FINDS HIS OATMEAL COLD...
WHAT ARE YOU DOING, JONES?
HEATING UP MY CEREAL WITH X-RAY VISION! IT SEEMS I SUDDENLY GAINED SUPER-POWERS--LIKE SUPERMAN! GUESS HE'D BE AS SURPRISED AS I AM, IF HE KNEW!
SUPERMAN DOES KNOW... AND ISN'T SURPRISED!
WATCH ME BEND THIS STEEL BARREL, FELLAS! I'VE GOT SUPER-STRENGTH, TOO!
HMM... I SUSPECTED THIS MIGHT HAPPEN TO PRIVATE JONES, DUE TO THAT FREAK ACCIDENT YESTERDAY...
"...WHEN I WAS TESTING A NEW DEVICE FOR SCIENTISTS..."
THIS POWERFUL NEW HELMET RADIO IS SUPPOSED TO TRANSMIT SIGNALS FOR A THOUSAND MILES! I'LL TRY IT OUT, FLYING FAR AWAY FROM THE METROPOLIS LAB WHERE THEY'RE TUNING IN!
"BUT AS I FLEW OVER THE ARMY CAMP, A POWERFUL LIGHTNING BOLT HIT THE AERIAL OF THE HELMET, CAUSING AN INCREDIBLE EFFECT!"
ZZZAP!
GREAT GUNS! THAT LIGHTNING BOLT CAUSED A FREAKISH PHENOMENON SO THAT AN ELECTRICAL PATTERN DUPLICATING ME AND MY SUPER-POWERS IS BEING "BROADCAST" BELOW!
"FLASHING DOWN AFTER THE SUPER RADIO-WAVE, I SAW WHERE IT STRUCK..."
HMM...THAT G.I. DOESN'T KNOW THAT INVISIBLE SUPER-ENERGY IS POURING INTO HIM!
BY TOMORROW, WHEN HIS MUSCLES RESPOND, HE'LL HAVE CARBON-COPY SUPER-POWERS!
DIM YOUR
2

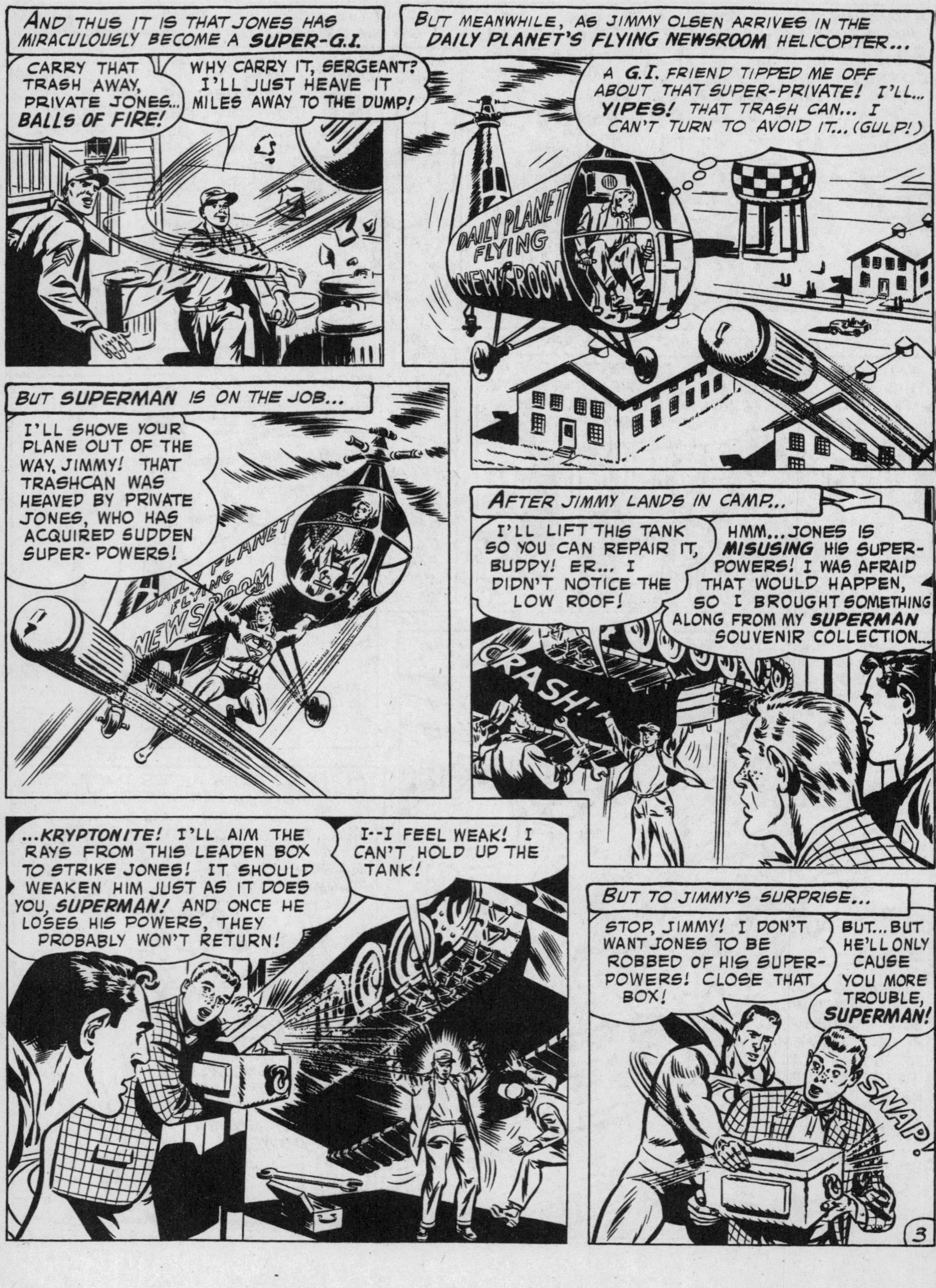
AND THUS IT IS THAT JONES HAS MIRACULOUSLY BECOME A SUPER-G.I.
CARRY THAT TRASH AWAY, PRIVATE JONES... BALLS OF FIRE!
WHY CARRY IT, SERGEANT? I'LL JUST HEAVE IT MILES AWAY TO THE DUMP!
BUT MEANWHILE, AS JIMMY OLSEN ARRIVES IN THE DAILY PLANET'S FLYING NEWSROOM HELICOPTER...
A G.I. FRIEND TIPPED ME OFF ABOUT THAT SUPER-PRIVATE! I'LL... YIPES! THAT TRASH CAN... I CAN'T TURN TO AVOID IT... (GULP!)
DAILY PLANET FLYING NEWSROOM
BUT SUPERMAN IS ON THE JOB...
I'LL SHOVE YOUR PLANE OUT OF THE WAY, JIMMY! THAT TRASHCAN WAS HEAVED BY PRIVATE JONES, WHO HAS ACQUIRED SUDDEN SUPER-POWERS!
DAILY PLANET FLYING NEWSROOM
AFTER JIMMY LANDS IN CAMP...
I'LL LIFT THIS TANK SO YOU CAN REPAIR IT, BUDDY! ER... I DIDN'T NOTICE THE LOW ROOF!
HMM...JONES IS MISUSING HIS SUPER-POWERS! I WAS AFRAID THAT WOULD HAPPEN, SO I BROUGHT SOMETHING ALONG FROM MY SUPERMAN SOUVENIR COLLECTION...
CRASH!
...KRYPTONITE! I'LL AIM THE RAYS FROM THIS LEADEN BOX TO STRIKE JONES! IT SHOULD WEAKEN HIM JUST AS IT DOES YOU, SUPERMAN! AND ONCE HE LOSES HIS POWERS, THEY PROBABLY WON'T RETURN!
I--I FEEL WEAK! I CAN'T HOLD UP THE TANK!
BUT TO JIMMY'S SURPRISE...
STOP, JIMMY! I DON'T WANT JONES TO BE ROBBED OF HIS SUPER-POWERS! CLOSE THAT BOX!
BUT...BUT HE'LL ONLY CAUSE YOU MORE TROUBLE, SUPERMAN!
SNAP!
3

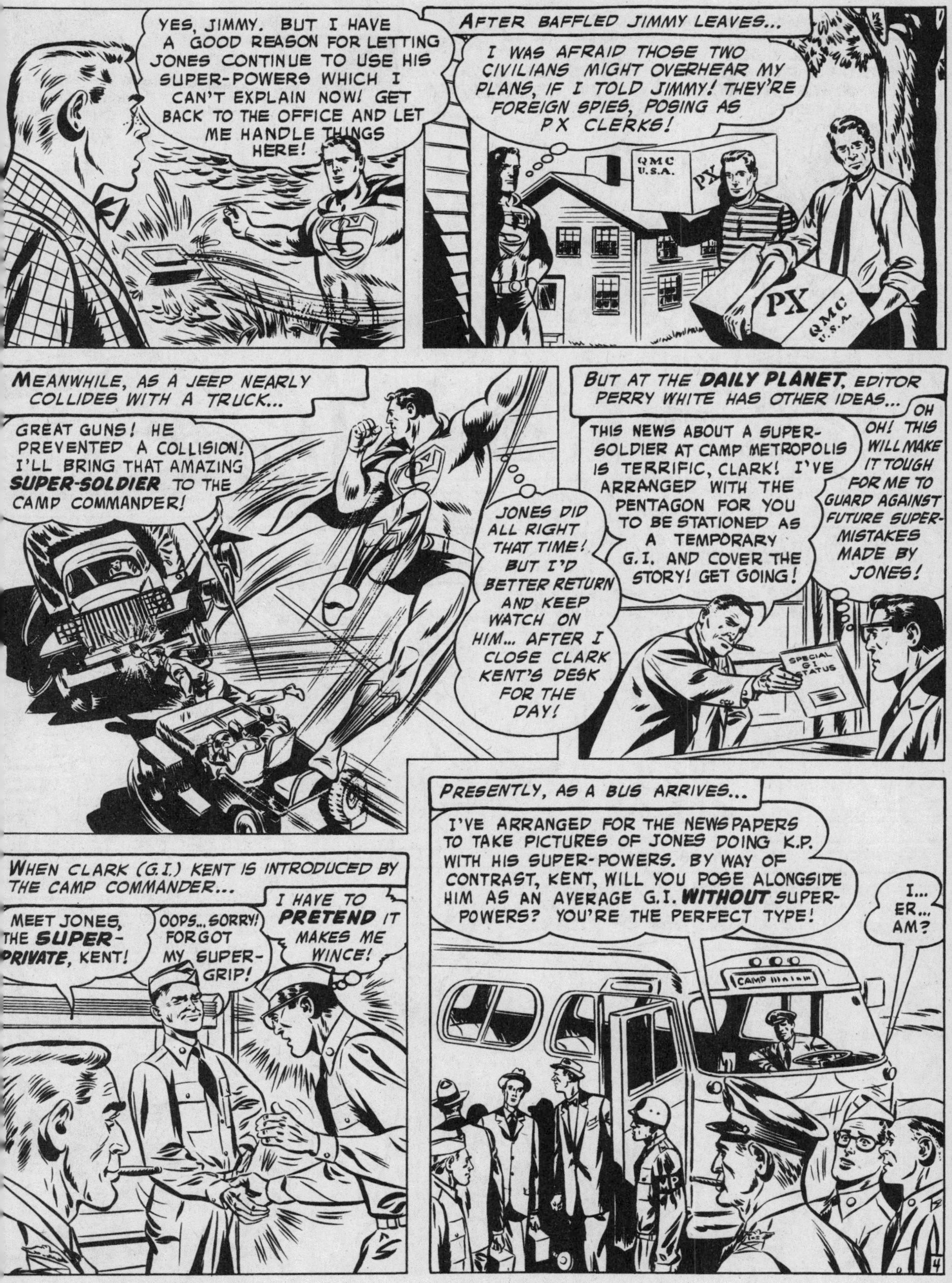
YES, JIMMY. BUT I HAVE A GOOD REASON FOR LETTING JONES CONTINUE TO USE HIS SUPER-POWERS WHICH I CAN'T EXPLAIN NOW! GET BACK TO THE OFFICE AND LET ME HANDLE THINGS HERE!
AFTER BAFFLED JIMMY LEAVES...
I WAS AFRAID THOSE TWO CIVILIANS MIGHT OVERHEAR MY PLANS, IF I TOLD JIMMY! THEY'RE FOREIGN SPIES, POSING AS PX CLERKS!
QMC U.S.A.
PX
PX
QMC U.S.A.
MEANWHILE, AS A JEEP NEARLY COLLIDES WITH A TRUCK...
GREAT GUNS! HE PREVENTED A COLLISION! I'LL BRING THAT AMAZING SUPER-SOLDIER TO THE CAMP COMMANDER!
JONES DID ALL RIGHT THAT TIME! BUT I'D BETTER RETURN AND KEEP WATCH ON HIM... AFTER I CLOSE CLARK KENT'S DESK FOR THE DAY!
BUT AT THE DAILY PLANET, EDITOR PERRY WHITE HAS OTHER IDEAS...
THIS NEWS ABOUT A SUPER-SOLDIER AT CAMP METROPOLIS IS TERRIFIC, CLARK! I'VE ARRANGED WITH THE PENTAGON FOR YOU TO BE STATIONED AS A TEMPORARY G.I. AND COVER THE STORY! GET GOING!
OH OH! THIS WILL MAKE IT TOUGH FOR ME TO GUARD AGAINST FUTURE SUPER-MISTAKES MADE BY JONES!
SPECIAL G.I. STATUS
WHEN CLARK (G.I.) KENT IS INTRODUCED BY THE CAMP COMMANDER...
MEET JONES, THE SUPER-PRIVATE, KENT!
OOPS... SORRY! FORGOT MY SUPER-GRIP!
I HAVE TO PRETEND IT MAKES ME WINCE!
PRESENTLY, AS A BUS ARRIVES...
I'VE ARRANGED FOR THE NEWSPAPERS TO TAKE PICTURES OF JONES DOING K.P. WITH HIS SUPER-POWERS. BY WAY OF CONTRAST, KENT, WILL YOU POSE ALONGSIDE HIM AS AN AVERAGE G.I. WITHOUT SUPER-POWERS? YOU'RE THE PERFECT TYPE!
I... ER... AM?
CAMP
MP
4

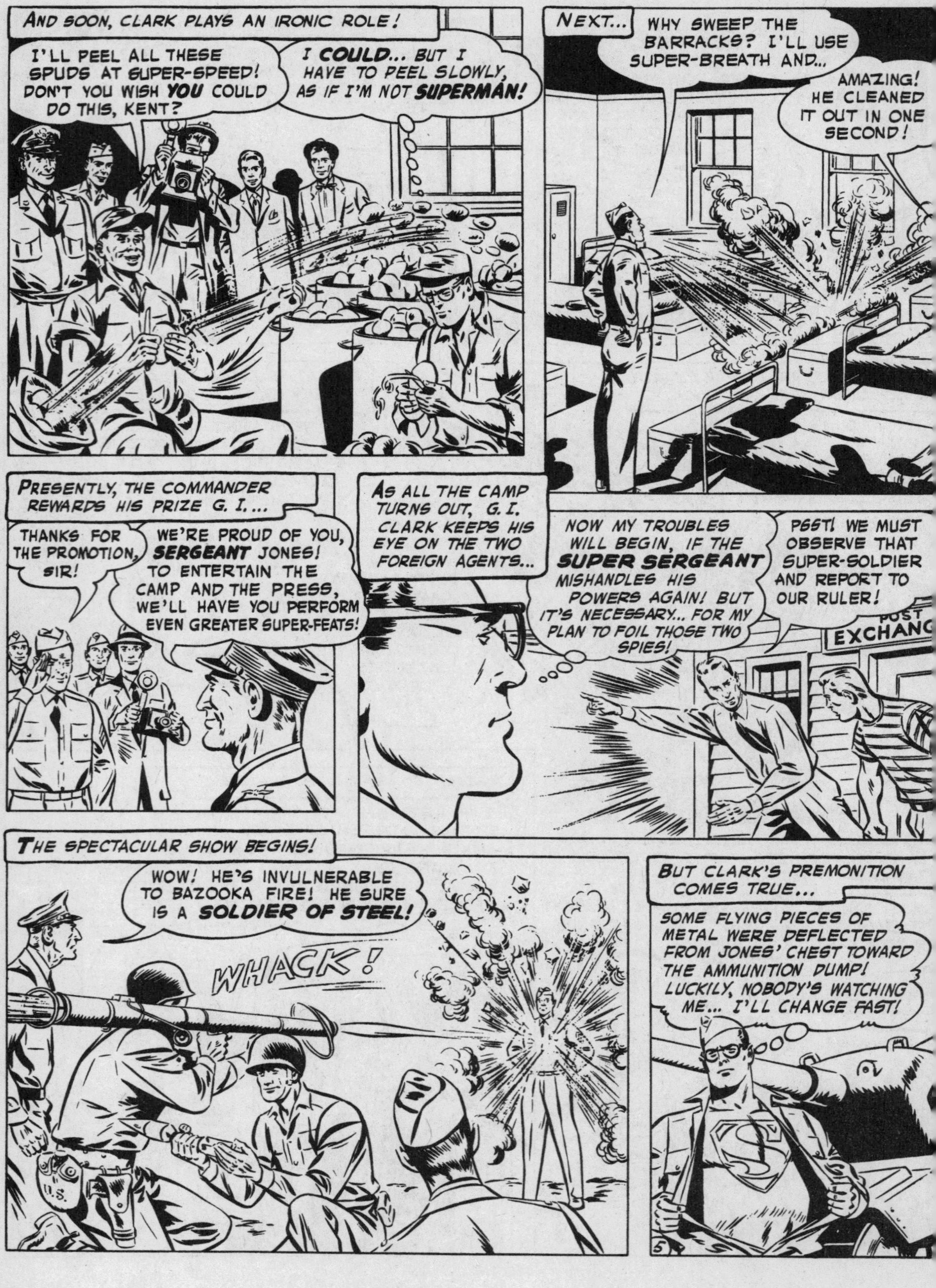
AND SOON, CLARK PLAYS AN IRONIC ROLE!
I'LL PEEL ALL THESE SPUDS AT SUPER-SPEED! DON'T YOU WISH YOU COULD DO THIS, KENT?
I COULD... BUT I HAVE TO PEEL SLOWLY, AS IF I'M NOT SUPERMAN!
NEXT...
WHY SWEEP THE BARRACKS? I'LL USE SUPER-BREATH AND...
AMAZING! HE CLEANED IT OUT IN ONE SECOND!
PRESENTLY, THE COMMANDER REWARDS HIS PRIZE G. I. ...
THANKS FOR THE PROMOTION, SIR!
WE'RE PROUD OF YOU, SERGEANT JONES! TO ENTERTAIN THE CAMP AND THE PRESS, WE'LL HAVE YOU PERFORM EVEN GREATER SUPER-FEATS!
AS ALL THE CAMP TURNS OUT, G. I. CLARK KEEPS HIS EYE ON THE TWO FOREIGN AGENTS...
NOW MY TROUBLES WILL BEGIN, IF THE SUPER SERGEANT MISHANDLES HIS POWERS AGAIN! BUT IT'S NECESSARY... FOR MY PLAN TO FOIL THOSE TWO SPIES!
PSST! WE MUST OBSERVE THAT SUPER-SOLDIER AND REPORT TO OUR RULER!
POST EXCHANG
THE SPECTACULAR SHOW BEGINS!
WOW! HE'S INVULNERABLE TO BAZOOKA FIRE! HE SURE IS A SOLDIER OF STEEL!
WHACK!
U.S.
BUT CLARK'S PREMONITION COMES TRUE...
SOME FLYING PIECES OF METAL WERE DEFLECTED FROM JONES' CHEST TOWARD THE AMMUNITION DUMP! LUCKILY, NOBODY'S WATCHING ME... I'LL CHANGE FAST!
5

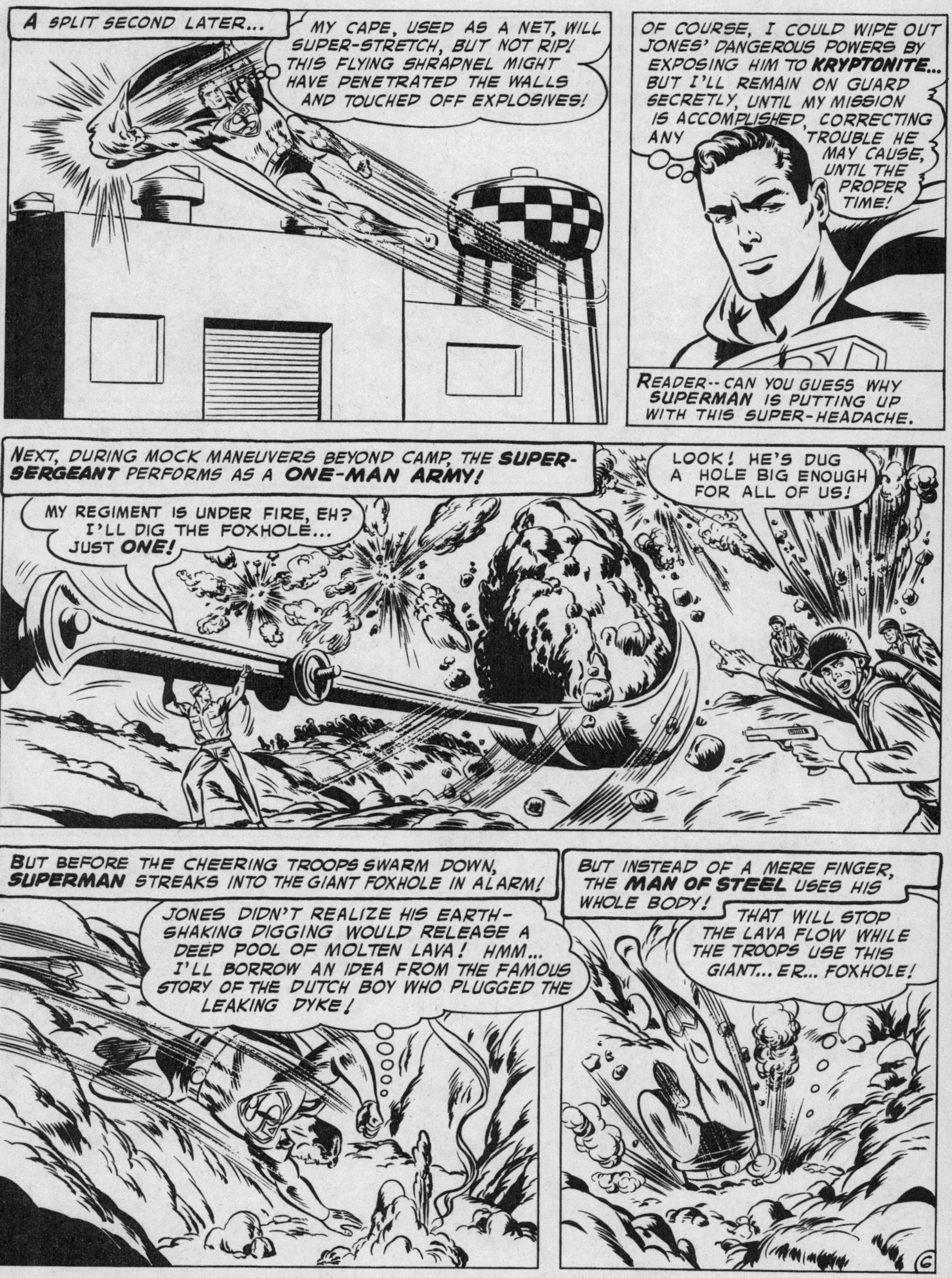
A SPLIT SECOND LATER...
MY CAPE, USED AS A NET, WILL SUPER-STRETCH, BUT NOT RIP! THIS FLYING SHRAPNEL MIGHT HAVE PENETRATED THE WALLS AND TOUCHED OFF EXPLOSIVES!
OF COURSE, I COULD WIPE OUT JONES' DANGEROUS POWERS BY EXPOSING HIM TO KRYPTONITE... BUT I'LL REMAIN ON GUARD SECRETLY, UNTIL MY MISSION IS ACCOMPLISHED, CORRECTING ANY TROUBLE HE MAY CAUSE, UNTIL THE PROPER TIME!
READER--CAN YOU GUESS WHY SUPERMAN IS PUTTING UP WITH THIS SUPER-HEADACHE.
NEXT, DURING MOCK MANEUVERS BEYOND CAMP, THE SUPER-SERGEANT PERFORMS AS A ONE-MAN ARMY!
MY REGIMENT IS UNDER FIRE, EH? I'LL DIG THE FOXHOLE... JUST ONE!
LOOK! HE'S DUG A HOLE BIG ENOUGH FOR ALL OF US!
BUT BEFORE THE CHEERING TROOPS SWARM DOWN, SUPERMAN STREAKS INTO THE GIANT FOXHOLE IN ALARM!
JONES DIDN'T REALIZE HIS EARTH-SHAKING DIGGING WOULD RELEASE A DEEP POOL OF MOLTEN LAVA! HMM... I'LL BORROW AN IDEA FROM THE FAMOUS STORY OF THE DUTCH BOY WHO PLUGGED THE LEAKING DYKE!
BUT INSTEAD OF A MERE FINGER, THE MAN OF STEEL USES HIS WHOLE BODY!
THAT WILL STOP THE LAVA FLOW WHILE THE TROOPS USE THIS GIANT... ER... FOXHOLE!
6

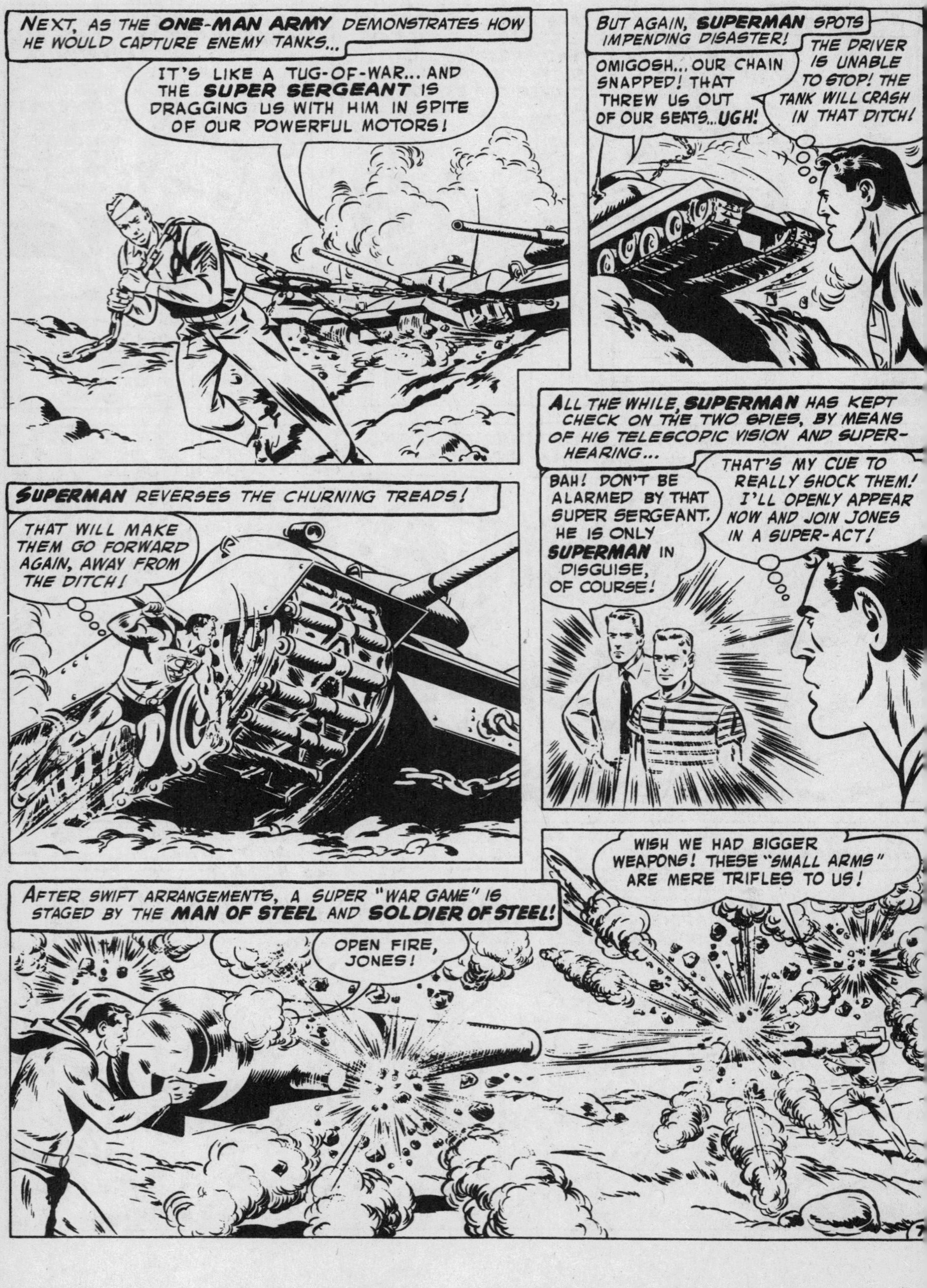
NEXT, AS THE ONE-MAN ARMY DEMONSTRATES HOW HE WOULD CAPTURE ENEMY TANKS...
IT'S LIKE A TUG-OF-WAR... AND THE SUPER SERGEANT IS DRAGGING US WITH HIM IN SPITE OF OUR POWERFUL MOTORS!
BUT AGAIN, SUPERMAN SPOTS IMPENDING DISASTER!
OMIGOSH... OUR CHAIN SNAPPED! THAT THREW US OUT OF OUR SEATS... UGH!
THE DRIVER IS UNABLE TO STOP! THE TANK WILL CRASH IN THAT DITCH!
SUPERMAN REVERSES THE CHURNING TREADS!
THAT WILL MAKE THEM GO FORWARD AGAIN, AWAY FROM THE DITCH!
ALL THE WHILE, SUPERMAN HAS KEPT CHECK ON THE TWO SPIES, BY MEANS OF HIS TELESCOPIC VISION AND SUPER-HEARING...
BAH! DON'T BE ALARMED BY THAT SUPER SERGEANT. HE IS ONLY SUPERMAN IN DISGUISE, OF COURSE!
THAT'S MY CUE TO REALLY SHOCK THEM! I'LL OPENLY APPEAR NOW AND JOIN JONES IN A SUPER-ACT!
AFTER SWIFT ARRANGEMENTS, A SUPER "WAR GAME" IS STAGED BY THE MAN OF STEEL AND SOLDIER OF STEEL!
OPEN FIRE, JONES!
WISH WE HAD BIGGER WEAPONS! THESE "SMALL ARMS" ARE MERE TRIFLES TO US!

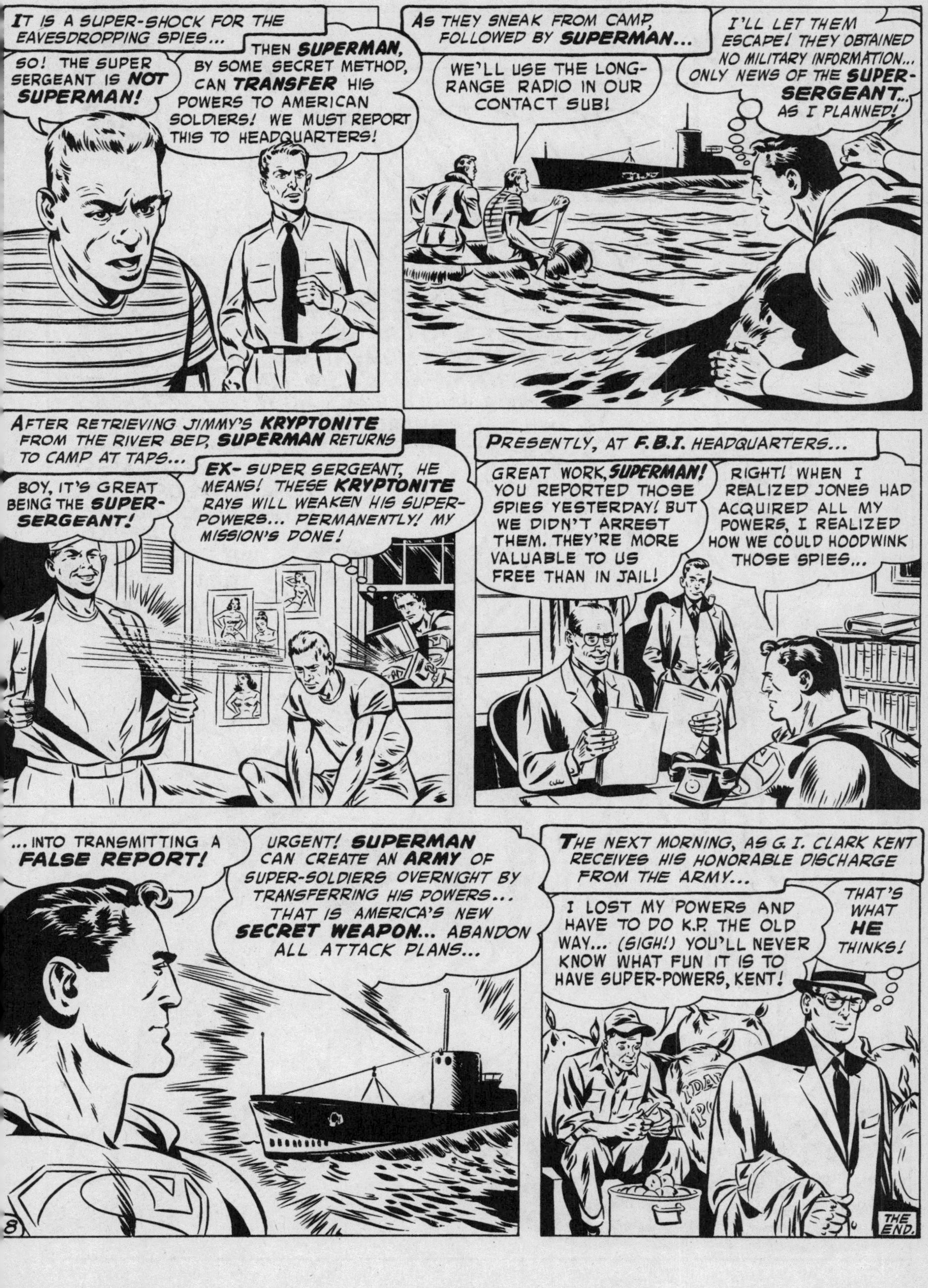
IT IS A SUPER-SHOCK FOR THE EAVESDROPPING SPIES...
SO! THE SUPER SERGEANT IS NOT SUPERMAN!
THEN SUPERMAN, BY SOME SECRET METHOD, CAN TRANSFER HIS POWERS TO AMERICAN SOLDIERS! WE MUST REPORT THIS TO HEADQUARTERS!
AS THEY SNEAK FROM CAMP, FOLLOWED BY SUPERMAN...
WE'LL USE THE LONG-RANGE RADIO IN OUR CONTACT SUB!
I'LL LET THEM ESCAPE! THEY OBTAINED NO MILITARY INFORMATION... ONLY NEWS OF THE SUPER-SERGEANT... AS I PLANNED!
AFTER RETRIEVING JIMMY'S KRYPTONITE FROM THE RIVER BED, SUPERMAN RETURNS TO CAMP AT TAPS...
BOY, IT'S GREAT BEING THE SUPER-SERGEANT!
EX- SUPER SERGEANT, HE MEANS! THESE KRYPTONITE RAYS WILL WEAKEN HIS SUPER-POWERS... PERMANENTLY! MY MISSION'S DONE!
PRESENTLY, AT F.B.I. HEADQUARTERS...
GREAT WORK, SUPERMAN! YOU REPORTED THOSE SPIES YESTERDAY! BUT WE DIDN'T ARREST THEM. THEY'RE MORE VALUABLE TO US FREE THAN IN JAIL!
RIGHT! WHEN I REALIZED JONES HAD ACQUIRED ALL MY POWERS, I REALIZED HOW WE COULD HOODWINK THOSE SPIES...
...INTO TRANSMITTING A FALSE REPORT!
URGENT! SUPERMAN CAN CREATE AN ARMY OF SUPER-SOLDIERS OVERNIGHT BY TRANSFERRING HIS POWERS... THAT IS AMERICA'S NEW SECRET WEAPON... ABANDON ALL ATTACK PLANS...
8
THE NEXT MORNING, AS G.I. CLARK KENT RECEIVES HIS HONORABLE DISCHARGE FROM THE ARMY...
I LOST MY POWERS AND HAVE TO DO K.P. THE OLD WAY... (SIGH!) YOU'LL NEVER KNOW WHAT FUN IT IS TO HAVE SUPER-POWERS, KENT!
THAT'S WHAT HE THINKS!
THE END.

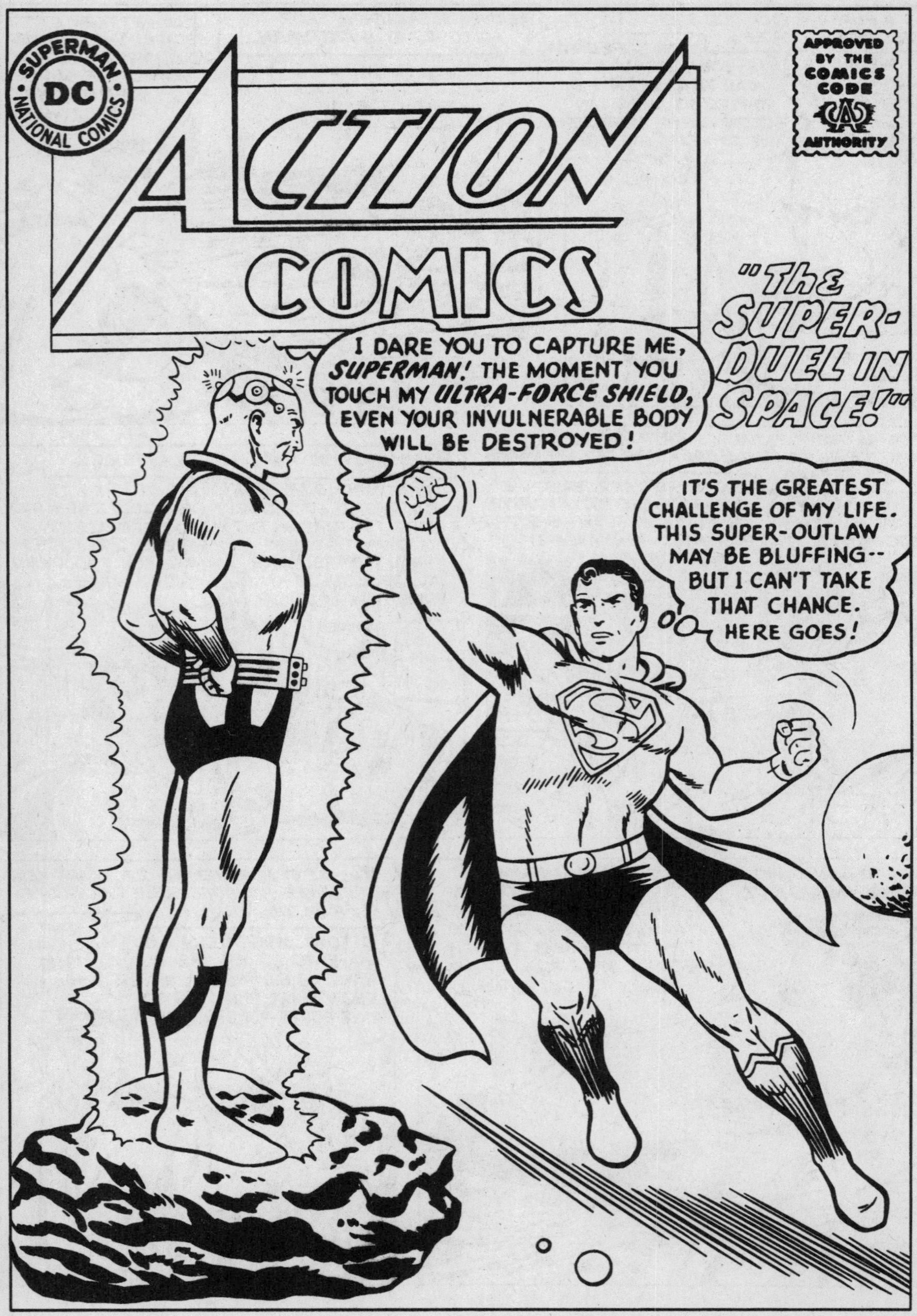
SUPERMAN DC NATIONAL COMICS
APPROVED BY THE COMICS CODE AUTHORITY
ACTION COMICS
"The SUPER-DUEL IN SPACE!"
I DARE YOU TO CAPTURE ME, SUPERMAN! THE MOMENT YOU TOUCH MY ULTRA-FORCE SHIELD, EVEN YOUR INVULNERABLE BODY WILL BE DESTROYED!
IT'S THE GREATEST CHALLENGE OF MY LIFE. THIS SUPER-OUTLAW MAY BE BLUFFING-- BUT I CAN'T TAKE THAT CHANCE. HERE GOES!

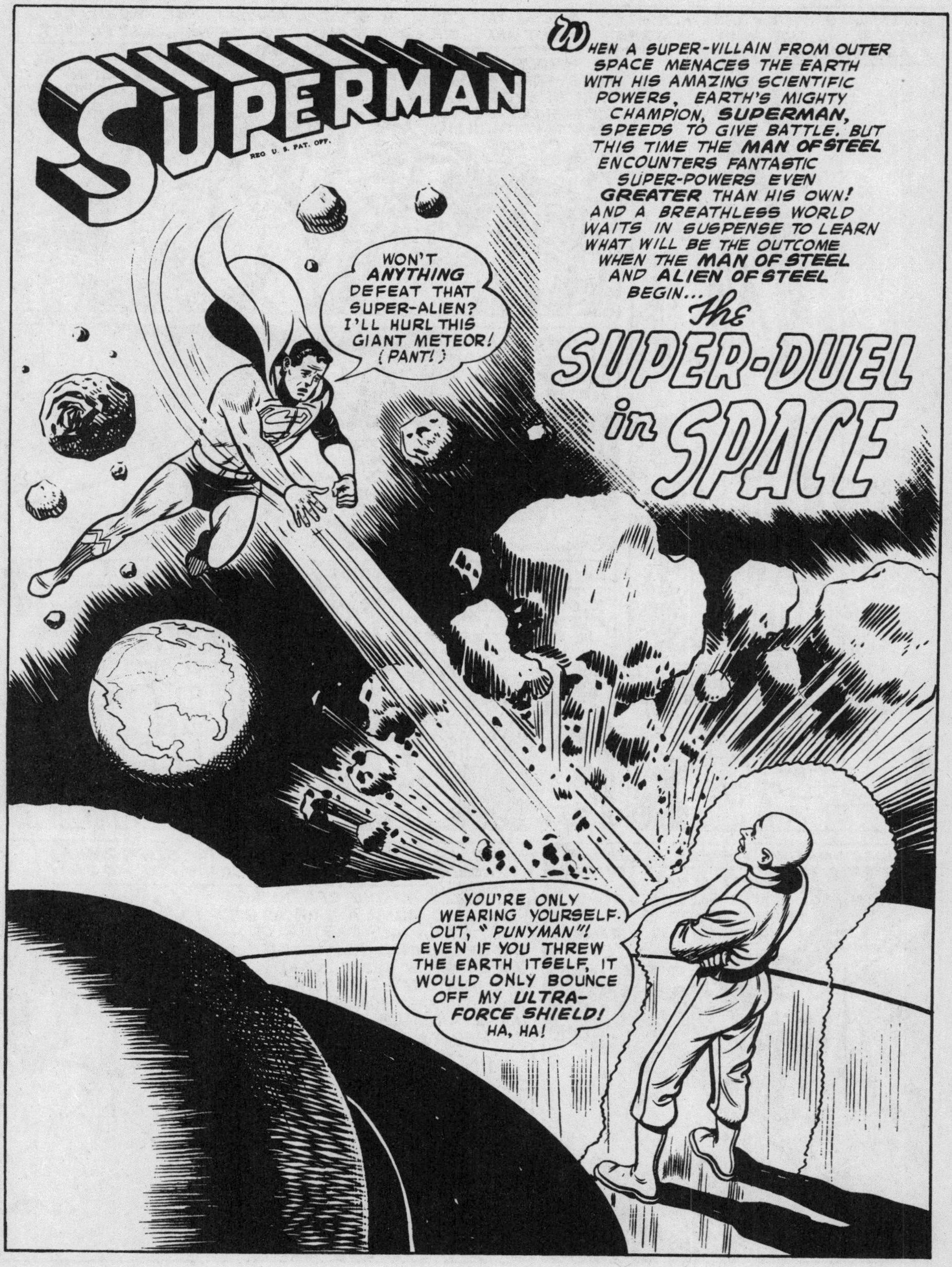
SUPERMAN
REG. U. S. PAT. OFF.
WHEN A SUPER-VILLAIN FROM OUTER SPACE MENACES THE EARTH WITH HIS AMAZING SCIENTIFIC POWERS, EARTH'S MIGHTY CHAMPION, SUPERMAN, SPEEDS TO GIVE BATTLE. BUT THIS TIME THE MAN OF STEEL ENCOUNTERS FANTASTIC SUPER-POWERS EVEN GREATER THAN HIS OWN! AND A BREATHLESS WORLD WAITS IN SUSPENSE TO LEARN WHAT WILL BE THE OUTCOME WHEN THE MAN OF STEEL AND ALIEN OF STEEL BEGIN...
THE SUPER-DUEL IN SPACE
WON'T ANYTHING DEFEAT THAT SUPER-ALIEN? I'LL HURL THIS GIANT METEOR! (PANT!)
YOU'RE ONLY WEARING YOURSELF OUT, "PUNYMAN"! EVEN IF YOU THREW THE EARTH ITSELF, IT WOULD ONLY BOUNCE OFF MY ULTRA-FORCE SHIELD! HA, HA!

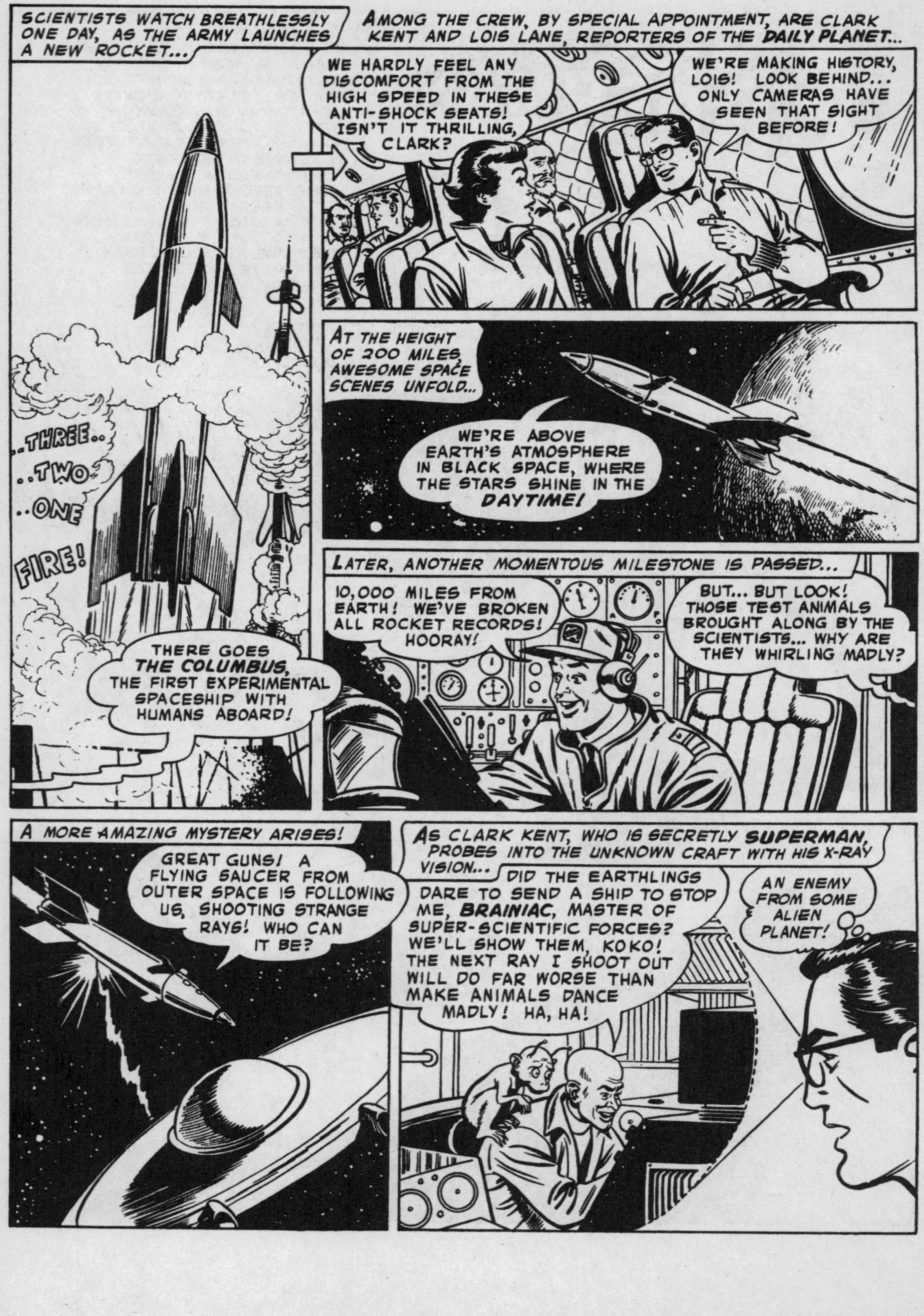
SCIENTISTS WATCH BREATHLESSLY ONE DAY, AS THE ARMY LAUNCHES A NEW ROCKET...
..THREE.. ..TWO.. ..ONE FIRE!
THERE GOES THE COLUMBUS, THE FIRST EXPERIMENTAL SPACESHIP WITH HUMANS ABOARD!
AMONG THE CREW, BY SPECIAL APPOINTMENT, ARE CLARK KENT AND LOIS LANE, REPORTERS OF THE DAILY PLANET...
WE HARDLY FEEL ANY DISCOMFORT FROM THE HIGH SPEED IN THESE ANTI-SHOCK SEATS! ISN'T IT THRILLING, CLARK?
WE'RE MAKING HISTORY, LOIS! LOOK BEHIND... ONLY CAMERAS HAVE SEEN THAT SIGHT BEFORE!
AT THE HEIGHT OF 200 MILES, AWESOME SPACE SCENES UNFOLD...
WE'RE ABOVE EARTH'S ATMOSPHERE IN BLACK SPACE, WHERE THE STARS SHINE IN THE DAYTIME!
LATER, ANOTHER MOMENTOUS MILESTONE IS PASSED...
10,000 MILES FROM EARTH! WE'VE BROKEN ALL ROCKET RECORDS! HOORAY!
BUT... BUT LOOK! THOSE TEST ANIMALS BROUGHT ALONG BY THE SCIENTISTS... WHY ARE THEY WHIRLING MADLY?
A MORE AMAZING MYSTERY ARISES!
GREAT GUNS! A FLYING SAUCER FROM OUTER SPACE IS FOLLOWING US, SHOOTING STRANGE RAYS! WHO CAN IT BE?
AS CLARK KENT, WHO IS SECRETLY SUPERMAN, PROBES INTO THE UNKNOWN CRAFT WITH HIS X-RAY VISION...
DID THE EARTHLINGS DARE TO SEND A SHIP TO STOP ME, BRAINIAC, MASTER OF SUPER-SCIENTIFIC FORCES? WE'LL SHOW THEM, KOKO! THE NEXT RAY I SHOOT OUT WILL DO FAR WORSE THAN MAKE ANIMALS DANCE MADLY! HA, HA!
AN ENEMY FROM SOME ALIEN PLANET!

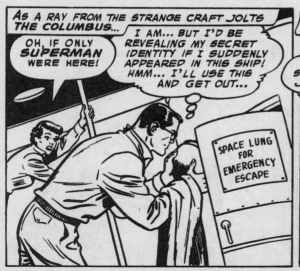

AS A RAY FROM THE STRANGE CRAFT JOLTS THE COLUMBUS...

OH, IF ONLY SUPERMAN WERE HERE!

I AM... BUT I'D BE REVEALING MY SECRET IDENTITY IF I SUDDENLY APPEARED IN THIS SHIP! HMM... I'LL USE THIS AND GET OUT...

SPACE LUNG FOR EMERGENCY ESCAPE

AFTER CLARK DONS THE DEVICE AND EXITS THROUGH THE EMERGENCY ESCAPE HATCH...

POOR CLARK-- HE'S SO AFRAID, HE'S JUMPING BACK TO EARTH!

I'LL PRETEND TO ZOOM BACK TO EARTH, PROPELLED BY THE BUILT-IN SUPERSONIC JETS!

ONCE OUT OF SIGHT, TIMID CLARK CHANGES TO POWERFUL SUPERMAN!

THEY'LL ASSUME CLARK REACHED EARTH AND SENT SUPERMAN TO THE RESCUE. I'LL SPEED BACK AND CAPTURE THAT SINISTER ALIEN!

BUT INCREDIBLY, WHEN SUPERMAN TRIES TO SMASH INTO THE FLYING SAUCER...

OOF! I... I ONLY REBOUNDED FROM AN INVISIBLE WALL!

EARTHLING FOOL! NOTHING IN THE UNIVERSE CAN PENETRATE THE ULTRA-FORCE BARRIER THAT SURROUNDS MY SHIP! HA, HA!

UNABLE TO INVADE THE IMPENETRABLE CRAFT, THE MAN OF STEEL CHANGES TACTICS!

I'LL SHOVE THE EARTH ROCKET AHEAD AT SUPER-SPEED, SO THAT IT WILL BE OUT OF HARM'S WAY! GOT TO GO FASTER... FASTER...!

SUPERMAN WINS THE DEADLY RACE!

WHEW! WE'RE OUT OF RANGE OF HIS DESTRUCTIVE RAYS!

DON'T WORRY ABOUT THEM, KOKO! WE HAVE OTHER BUSINESS TO DO ON EARTH NOW!

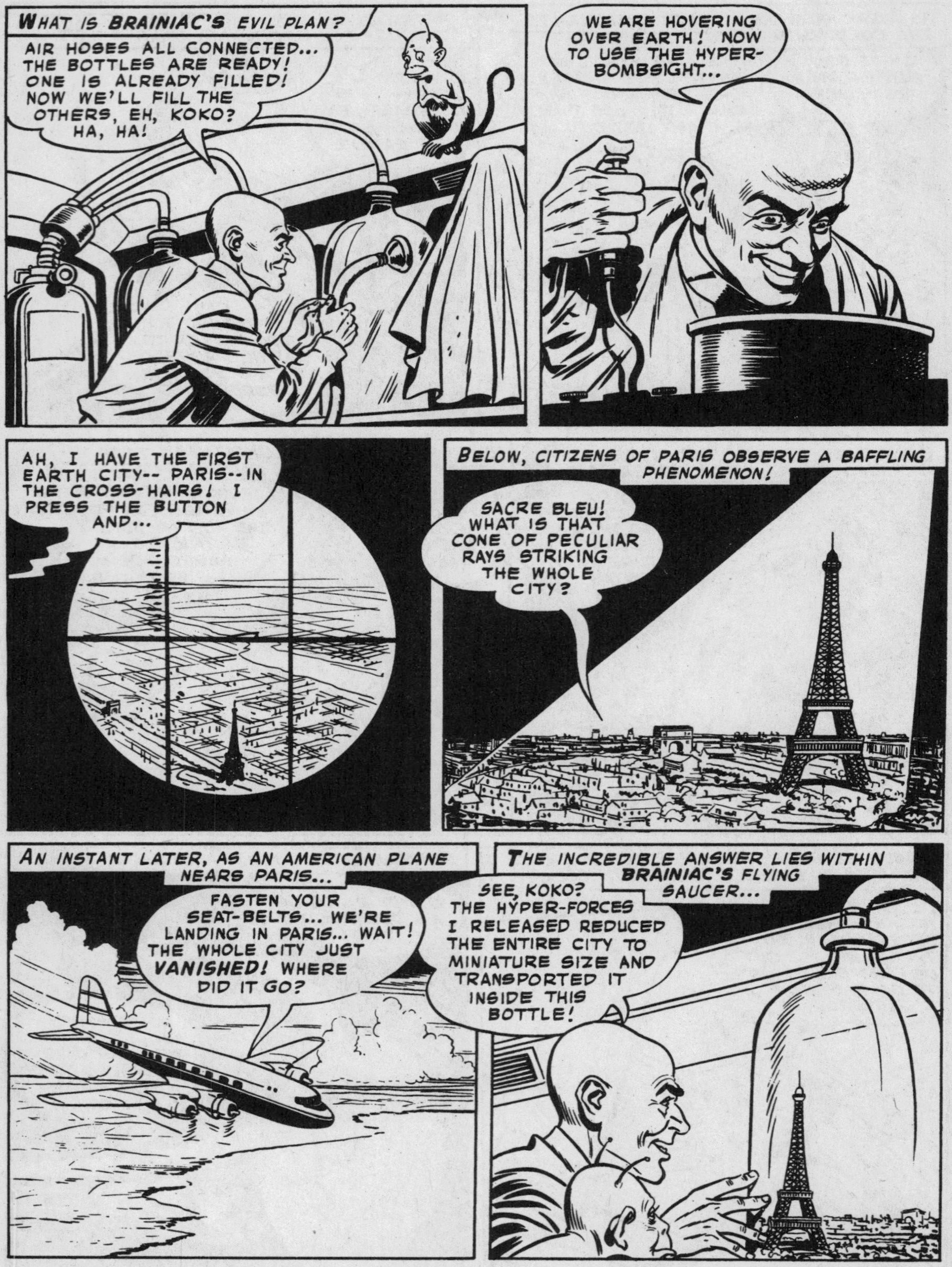
WHAT IS BRAINIAC'S EVIL PLAN?
AIR HOSES ALL CONNECTED... THE BOTTLES ARE READY! ONE IS ALREADY FILLED! NOW WE'LL FILL THE OTHERS, EH, KOKO? HA, HA!
WE ARE HOVERING OVER EARTH! NOW TO USE THE HYPER-BOMBSIGHT...
AH, I HAVE THE FIRST EARTH CITY-- PARIS--IN THE CROSS-HAIRS! I PRESS THE BUTTON AND...
BELOW, CITIZENS OF PARIS OBSERVE A BAFFLING PHENOMENON!
SACRE BLEU! WHAT IS THAT CONE OF PECULIAR RAYS STRIKING THE WHOLE CITY?
AN INSTANT LATER, AS AN AMERICAN PLANE NEARS PARIS...
FASTEN YOUR SEAT-BELTS... WE'RE LANDING IN PARIS... WAIT! THE WHOLE CITY JUST VANISHED! WHERE DID IT GO?
THE INCREDIBLE ANSWER LIES WITHIN BRAINIAC'S FLYING SAUCER...
SEE, KOKO? THE HYPER-FORCES I RELEASED REDUCED THE ENTIRE CITY TO MINIATURE SIZE AND TRANSPORTED IT INSIDE THIS BOTTLE!

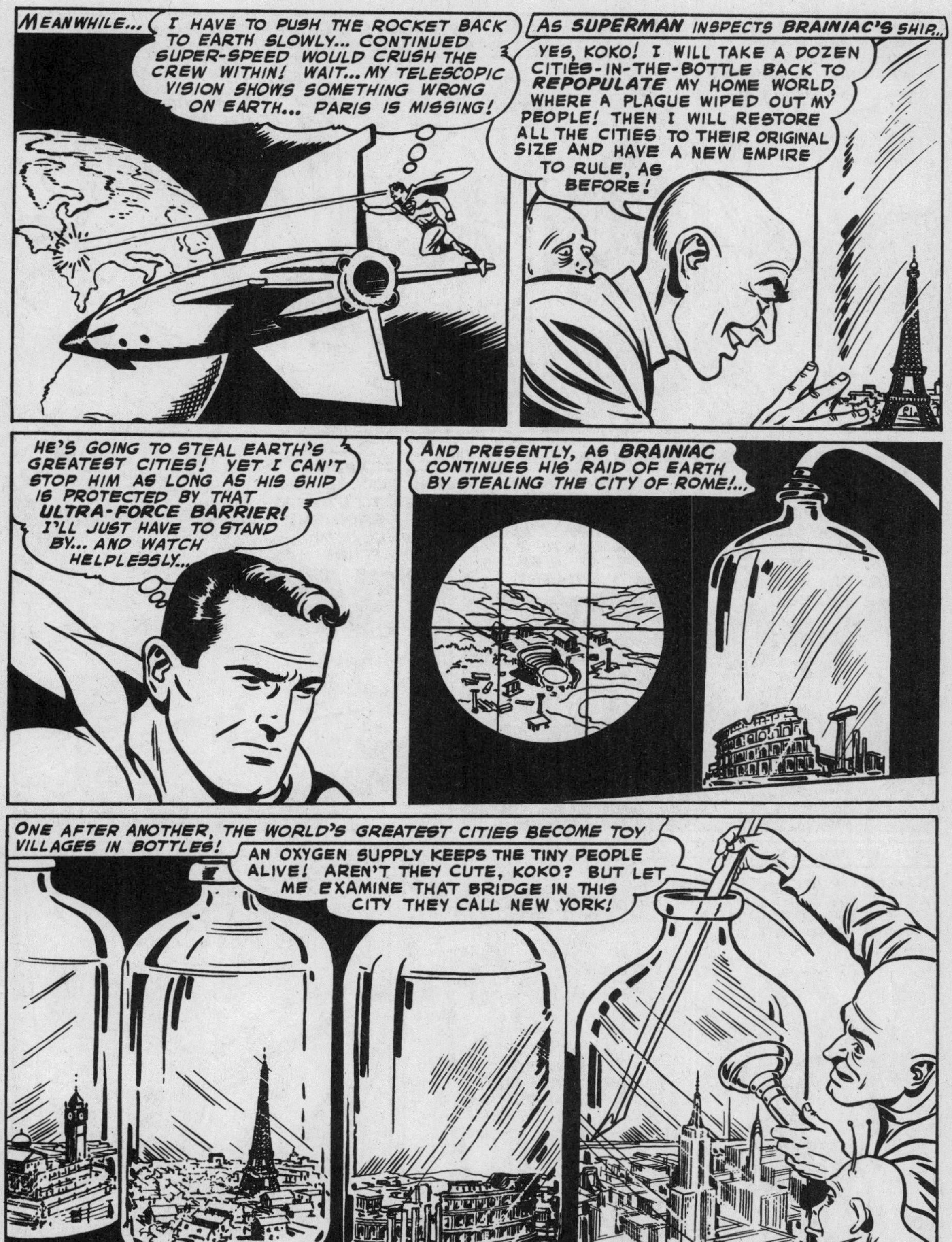
MEANWHILE...
I HAVE TO PUSH THE ROCKET BACK TO EARTH SLOWLY... CONTINUED SUPER-SPEED WOULD CRUSH THE CREW WITHIN! WAIT... MY TELESCOPIC VISION SHOWS SOMETHING WRONG ON EARTH... PARIS IS MISSING!
AS SUPERMAN INSPECTS BRAINIAC'S SHIP...
YES, KOKO! I WILL TAKE A DOZEN CITIES-IN-THE-BOTTLE BACK TO REPOPULATE MY HOME WORLD, WHERE A PLAGUE WIPED OUT MY PEOPLE! THEN I WILL RESTORE ALL THE CITIES TO THEIR ORIGINAL SIZE AND HAVE A NEW EMPIRE TO RULE, AS BEFORE!
HE'S GOING TO STEAL EARTH'S GREATEST CITIES! YET I CAN'T STOP HIM AS LONG AS HIS SHIP IS PROTECTED BY THAT ULTRA-FORCE BARRIER! I'LL JUST HAVE TO STAND BY... AND WATCH HELPLESSLY...
AND PRESENTLY, AS BRAINIAC CONTINUES HIS RAID OF EARTH BY STEALING THE CITY OF ROME!...
ONE AFTER ANOTHER, THE WORLD'S GREATEST CITIES BECOME TOY VILLAGES IN BOTTLES!
AN OXYGEN SUPPLY KEEPS THE TINY PEOPLE ALIVE! AREN'T THEY CUTE, KOKO? BUT LET ME EXAMINE THAT BRIDGE IN THIS CITY THEY CALL NEW YORK!

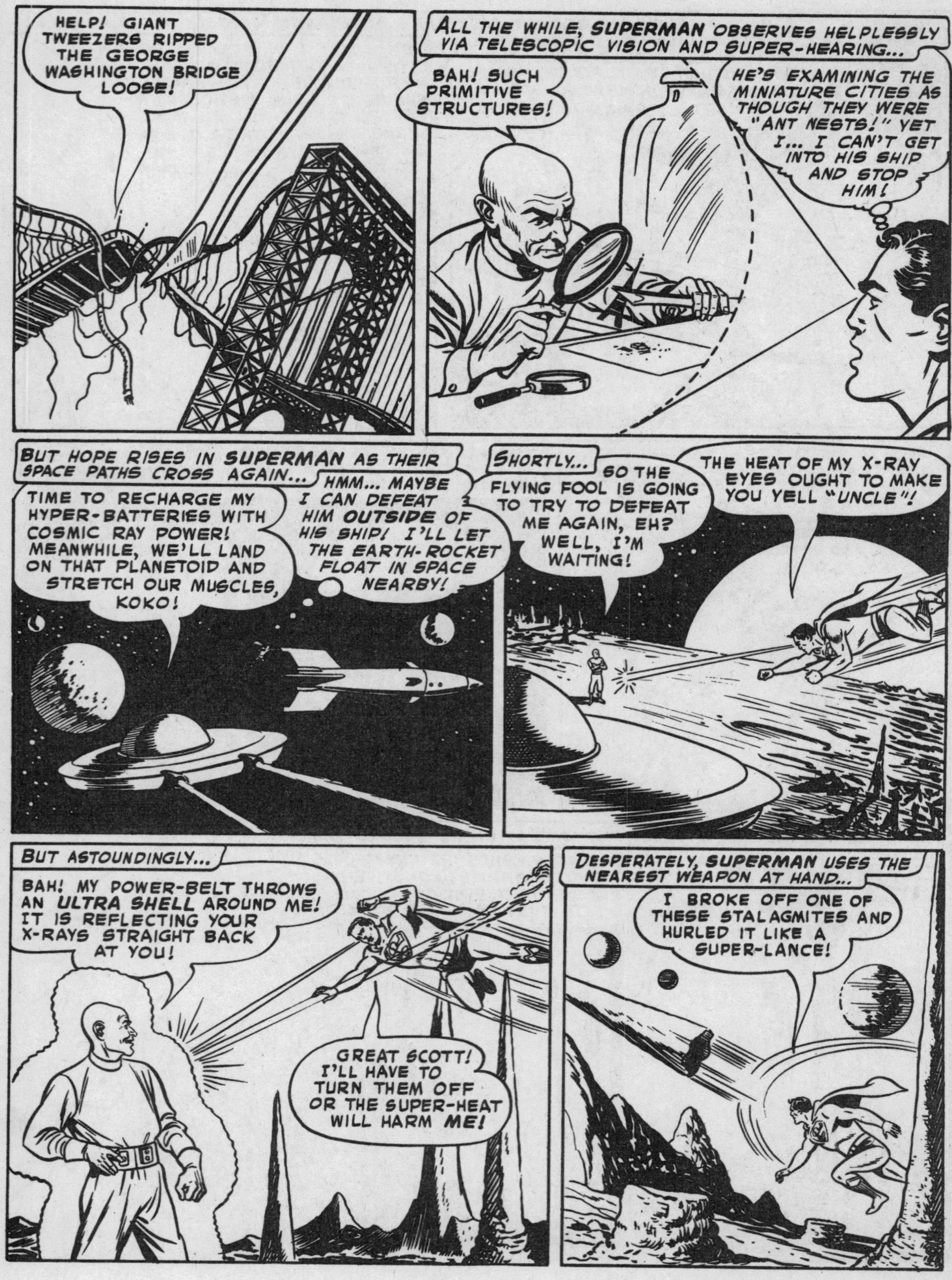
HELP! GIANT TWEEZERS RIPPED THE GEORGE WASHINGTON BRIDGE LOOSE!
ALL THE WHILE, SUPERMAN OBSERVES HELPLESSLY VIA TELESCOPIC VISION AND SUPER-HEARING...
BAH! SUCH PRIMITIVE STRUCTURES!
HE'S EXAMINING THE MINIATURE CITIES AS THOUGH THEY WERE "ANT NESTS!" YET I... I CAN'T GET INTO HIS SHIP AND STOP HIM!
BUT HOPE RISES IN SUPERMAN AS THEIR SPACE PATHS CROSS AGAIN...
TIME TO RECHARGE MY HYPER-BATTERIES WITH COSMIC RAY POWER! MEANWHILE, WE'LL LAND ON THAT PLANETOID AND STRETCH OUR MUSCLES, KOKO!
HMM... MAYBE I CAN DEFEAT HIM OUTSIDE OF HIS SHIP! I'LL LET THE EARTH-ROCKET FLOAT IN SPACE NEARBY!
SHORTLY...
SO THE FLYING FOOL IS GOING TO TRY TO DEFEAT ME AGAIN, EH? WELL, I'M WAITING!
THE HEAT OF MY X-RAY EYES OUGHT TO MAKE YOU YELL "UNCLE"!
BUT ASTOUNDINGLY...
BAH! MY POWER-BELT THROWS AN ULTRA SHELL AROUND ME! IT IS REFLECTING YOUR X-RAYS STRAIGHT BACK AT YOU!
GREAT SCOTT! I'LL HAVE TO TURN THEM OFF OR THE SUPER-HEAT WILL HARM ME!
DESPERATELY, SUPERMAN USES THE NEAREST WEAPON AT HAND...
I BROKE OFF ONE OF THESE STALAGMITES AND HURLED IT LIKE A SUPER-LANCE!

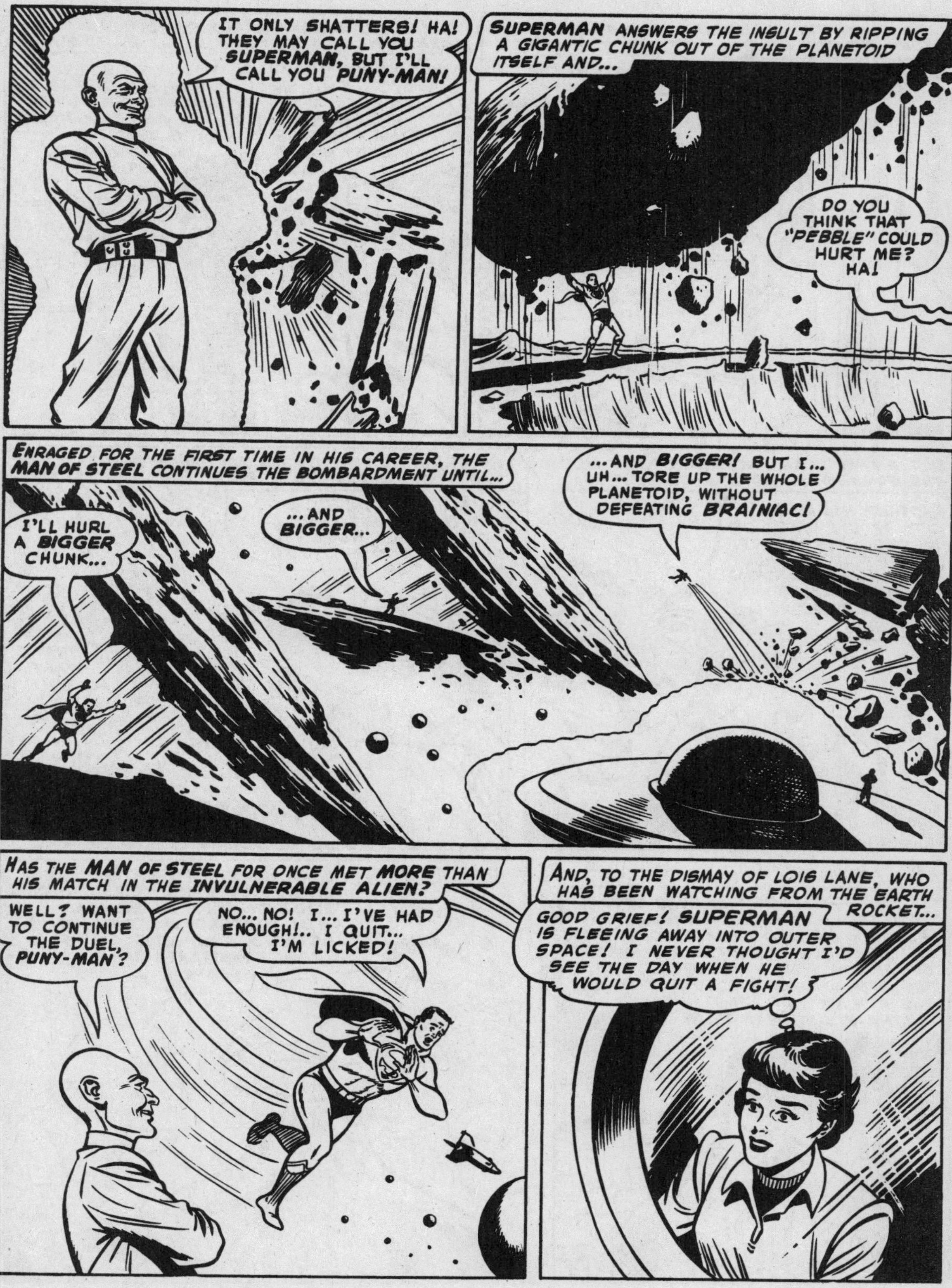
IT ONLY SHATTERS! HA! THEY MAY CALL YOU SUPERMAN, BUT I'LL CALL YOU PUNY-MAN!
SUPERMAN ANSWERS THE INSULT BY RIPPING A GIGANTIC CHUNK OUT OF THE PLANETOID ITSELF AND...
DO YOU THINK THAT "PEBBLE" COULD HURT ME? HA!
ENRAGED FOR THE FIRST TIME IN HIS CAREER, THE MAN OF STEEL CONTINUES THE BOMBARDMENT UNTIL...
I'LL HURL A BIGGER CHUNK...
...AND BIGGER...
...AND BIGGER! BUT I... UH... TORE UP THE WHOLE PLANETOID, WITHOUT DEFEATING BRAINIAC!
HAS THE MAN OF STEEL FOR ONCE MET MORE THAN HIS MATCH IN THE INVULNERABLE ALIEN?
WELL? WANT TO CONTINUE THE DUEL, PUNY-MAN?
NO... NO! I... I'VE HAD ENOUGH!.. I QUIT... I'M LICKED!
AND, TO THE DISMAY OF LOIS LANE, WHO HAS BEEN WATCHING FROM THE EARTH ROCKET...
GOOD GRIEF! SUPERMAN IS FLEEING AWAY INTO OUTER SPACE! I NEVER THOUGHT I'D SEE THE DAY WHEN HE WOULD QUIT A FIGHT!

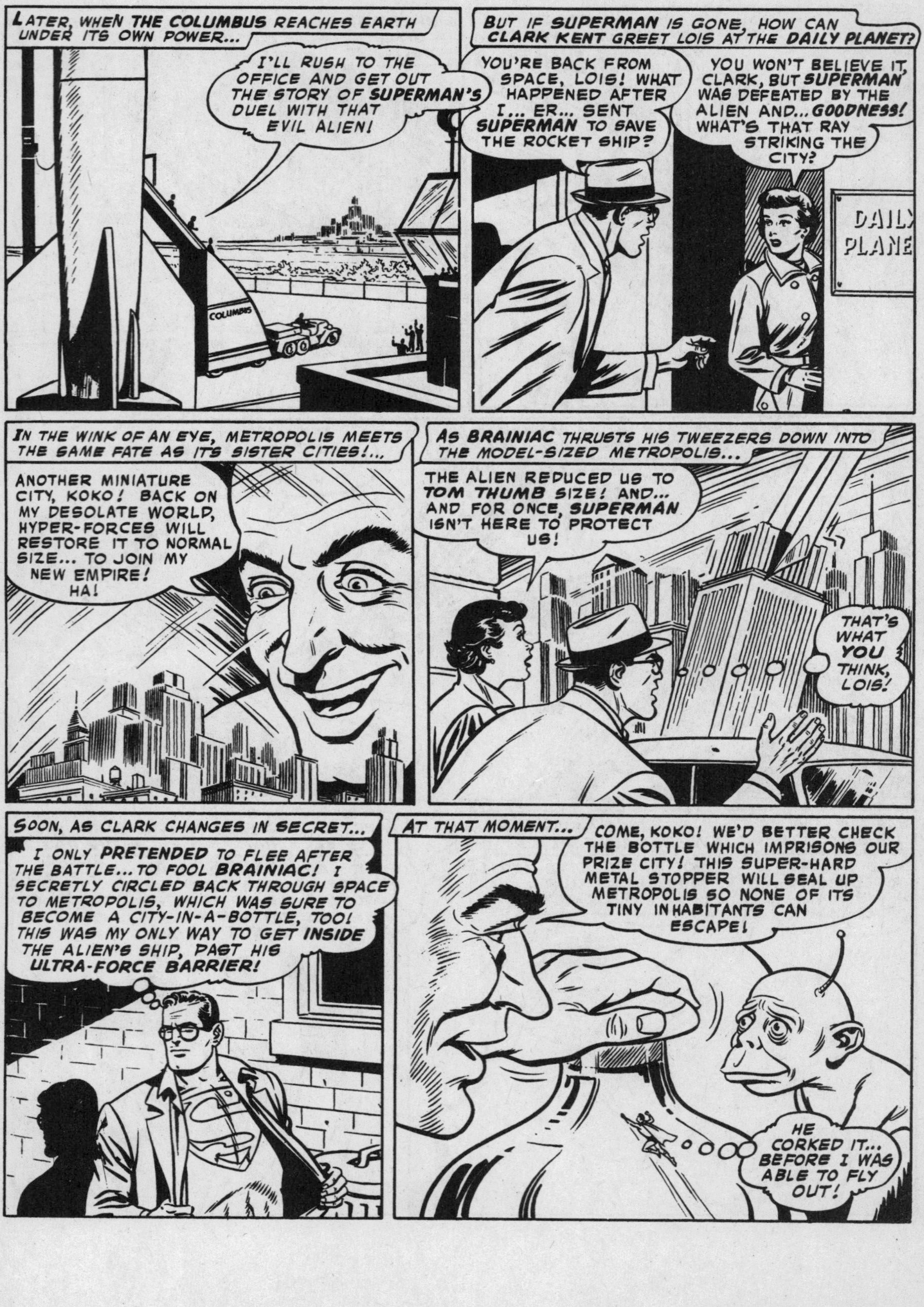
LATER, WHEN THE COLUMBUS REACHES EARTH UNDER ITS OWN POWER...
I'LL RUSH TO THE OFFICE AND GET OUT THE STORY OF SUPERMAN'S DUEL WITH THAT EVIL ALIEN!
COLUMBUS
BUT IF SUPERMAN IS GONE, HOW CAN CLARK KENT GREET LOIS AT THE DAILY PLANET?
YOU'RE BACK FROM SPACE, LOIS! WHAT HAPPENED AFTER I... ER... SENT SUPERMAN TO SAVE THE ROCKET SHIP?
YOU WON'T BELIEVE IT, CLARK, BUT SUPERMAN WAS DEFEATED BY THE ALIEN AND... GOODNESS! WHAT'S THAT RAY STRIKING THE CITY?
DAIL PLANE
IN THE WINK OF AN EYE, METROPOLIS MEETS THE SAME FATE AS ITS SISTER CITIES!...
ANOTHER MINIATURE CITY, KOKO! BACK ON MY DESOLATE WORLD, HYPER-FORCES WILL RESTORE IT TO NORMAL SIZE... TO JOIN MY NEW EMPIRE! HA!
AS BRAINIAC THRUSTS HIS TWEEZERS DOWN INTO THE MODEL-SIZED METROPOLIS...
THE ALIEN REDUCED US TO TOM THUMB SIZE! AND... AND FOR ONCE, SUPERMAN ISN'T HERE TO PROTECT US!
THAT'S WHAT YOU THINK, LOIS!
SOON, AS CLARK CHANGES IN SECRET...
I ONLY PRETENDED TO FLEE AFTER THE BATTLE... TO FOOL BRAINIAC! I SECRETLY CIRCLED BACK THROUGH SPACE TO METROPOLIS, WHICH WAS SURE TO BECOME A CITY-IN-A-BOTTLE, TOO! THIS WAS MY ONLY WAY TO GET INSIDE THE ALIEN'S SHIP, PAST HIS ULTRA-FORCE BARRIER!
AT THAT MOMENT...
COME, KOKO! WE'D BETTER CHECK THE BOTTLE WHICH IMPRISONS OUR PRIZE CITY! THIS SUPER-HARD METAL STOPPER WILL SEAL UP METROPOLIS SO NONE OF ITS TINY INHABITANTS CAN ESCAPE!
HE CORKED IT... BEFORE I WAS ABLE TO FLY OUT!

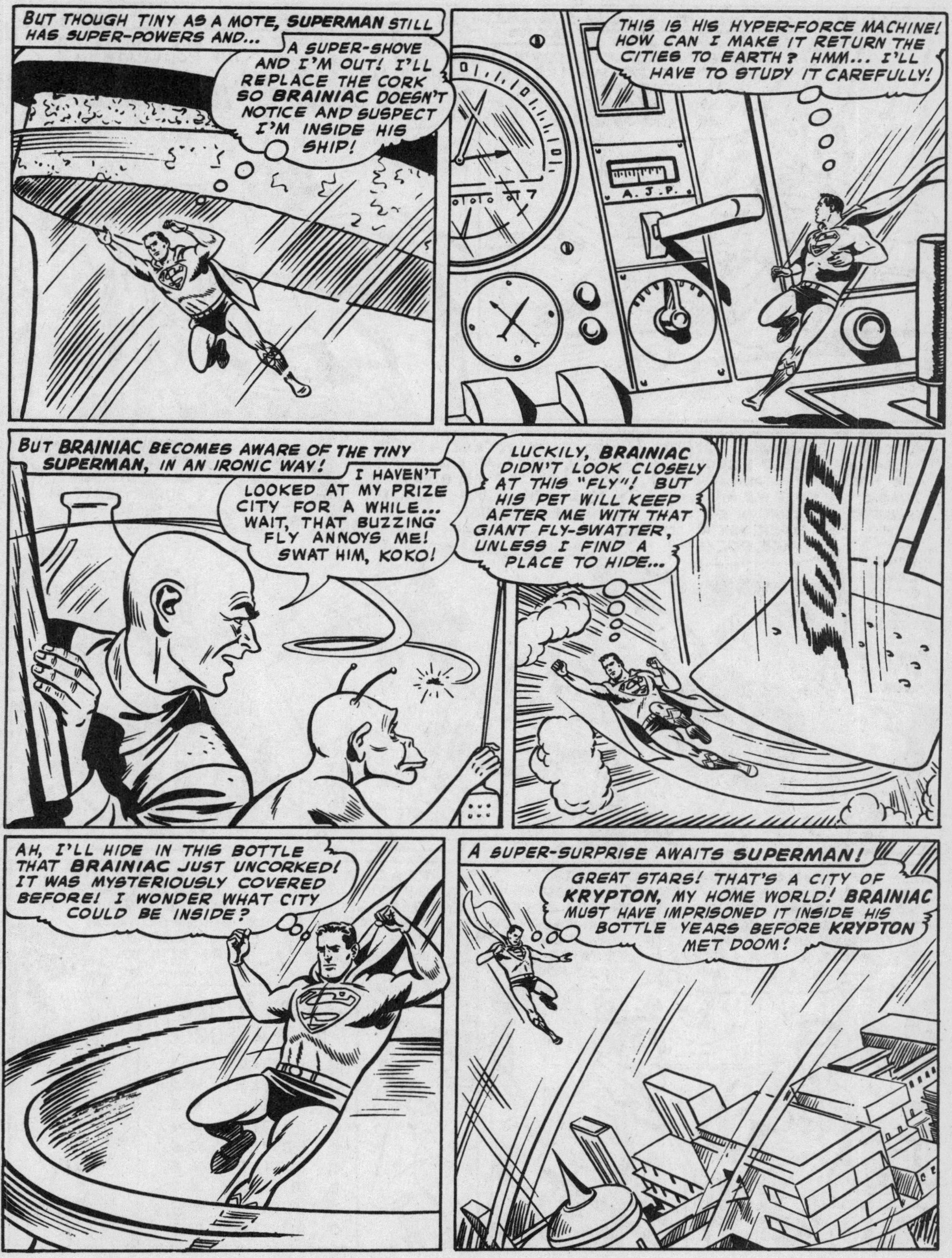
BUT THOUGH TINY AS A MOTE, SUPERMAN STILL HAS SUPER-POWERS AND...
A SUPER-SHOVE AND I'M OUT! I'LL REPLACE THE CORK SO BRAINIAC DOESN'T NOTICE AND SUSPECT I'M INSIDE HIS SHIP!
THIS IS HIS HYPER-FORCE MACHINE! HOW CAN I MAKE IT RETURN THE CITIES TO EARTH? HMM... I'LL HAVE TO STUDY IT CAREFULLY!
A. J. P.
BUT BRAINIAC BECOMES AWARE OF THE TINY SUPERMAN, IN AN IRONIC WAY!
I HAVEN'T LOOKED AT MY PRIZE CITY FOR A WHILE... WAIT, THAT BUZZING FLY ANNOYS ME! SWAT HIM, KOKO!
LUCKILY, BRAINIAC DIDN'T LOOK CLOSELY AT THIS "FLY"! BUT HIS PET WILL KEEP AFTER ME WITH THAT GIANT FLY-SWATTER, UNLESS I FIND A PLACE TO HIDE...
THWT
AH, I'LL HIDE IN THIS BOTTLE THAT BRAINIAC JUST UNCORKED! IT WAS MYSTERIOUSLY COVERED BEFORE! I WONDER WHAT CITY COULD BE INSIDE?
A SUPER-SURPRISE AWAITS SUPERMAN!
GREAT STARS! THAT'S A CITY OF KRYPTON, MY HOME WORLD! BRAINIAC MUST HAVE IMPRISONED IT INSIDE HIS BOTTLE YEARS BEFORE KRYPTON MET DOOM!

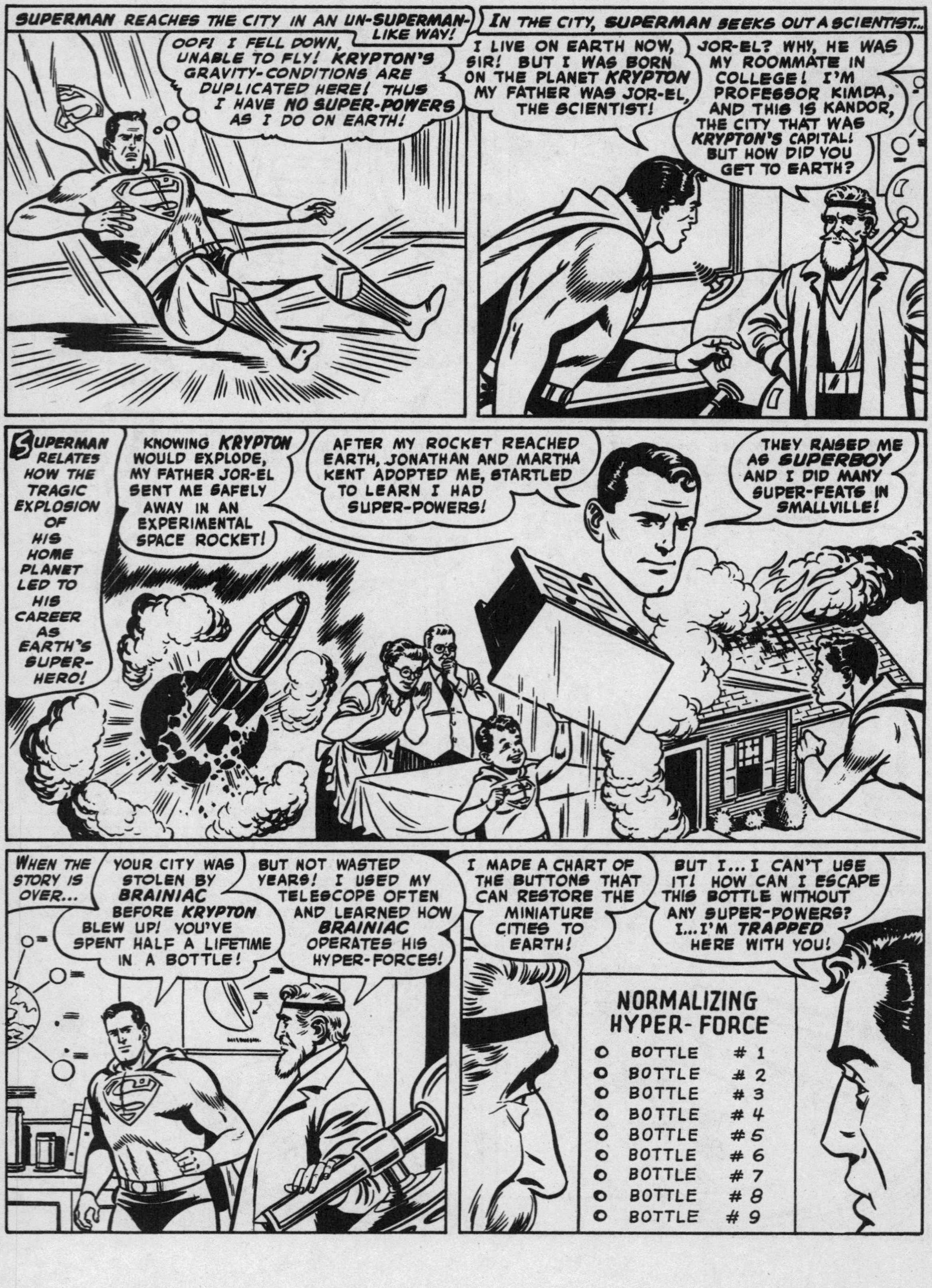
SUPERMAN REACHES THE CITY IN AN UN-SUPERMAN-LIKE WAY!
OOF! I FELL DOWN, UNABLE TO FLY! KRYPTON'S GRAVITY-CONDITIONS ARE DUPLICATED HERE! THUS I HAVE NO SUPER-POWERS AS I DO ON EARTH!
IN THE CITY, SUPERMAN SEEKS OUT A SCIENTIST...
I LIVE ON EARTH NOW, SIR! BUT I WAS BORN ON THE PLANET KRYPTON MY FATHER WAS JOR-EL, THE SCIENTIST!
JOR-EL? WHY, HE WAS MY ROOMMATE IN COLLEGE! I'M PROFESSOR KIMDA, AND THIS IS KANDOR, THE CITY THAT WAS KRYPTON'S CAPITAL! BUT HOW DID YOU GET TO EARTH?
SUPERMAN RELATES HOW THE TRAGIC EXPLOSION OF HIS HOME PLANET LED TO HIS CAREER AS EARTH'S SUPER-HERO!
KNOWING KRYPTON WOULD EXPLODE, MY FATHER JOR-EL SENT ME SAFELY AWAY IN AN EXPERIMENTAL SPACE ROCKET!
AFTER MY ROCKET REACHED EARTH, JONATHAN AND MARTHA KENT ADOPTED ME, STARTLED TO LEARN I HAD SUPER-POWERS!
THEY RAISED ME AS SUPERBOY AND I DID MANY SUPER-FEATS IN SMALLVILLE!
WHEN THE STORY IS OVER...
YOUR CITY WAS STOLEN BY BRAINIAC BEFORE KRYPTON BLEW UP! YOU'VE SPENT HALF A LIFETIME IN A BOTTLE!
BUT NOT WASTED YEARS! I USED MY TELESCOPE OFTEN AND LEARNED HOW BRAINIAC OPERATES HIS HYPER-FORCES!
I MADE A CHART OF THE BUTTONS THAT CAN RESTORE THE MINIATURE CITIES TO EARTH!
BUT I... I CAN'T USE IT! HOW CAN I ESCAPE THIS BOTTLE WITHOUT ANY SUPER-POWERS? I...I'M TRAPPED HERE WITH YOU!
NORMALIZING HYPER-FORCE
BOTTLE # 1
BOTTLE # 2
BOTTLE # 3
BOTTLE # 4
BOTTLE # 5
BOTTLE # 6
BOTTLE # 7
BOTTLE # 8
BOTTLE # 9

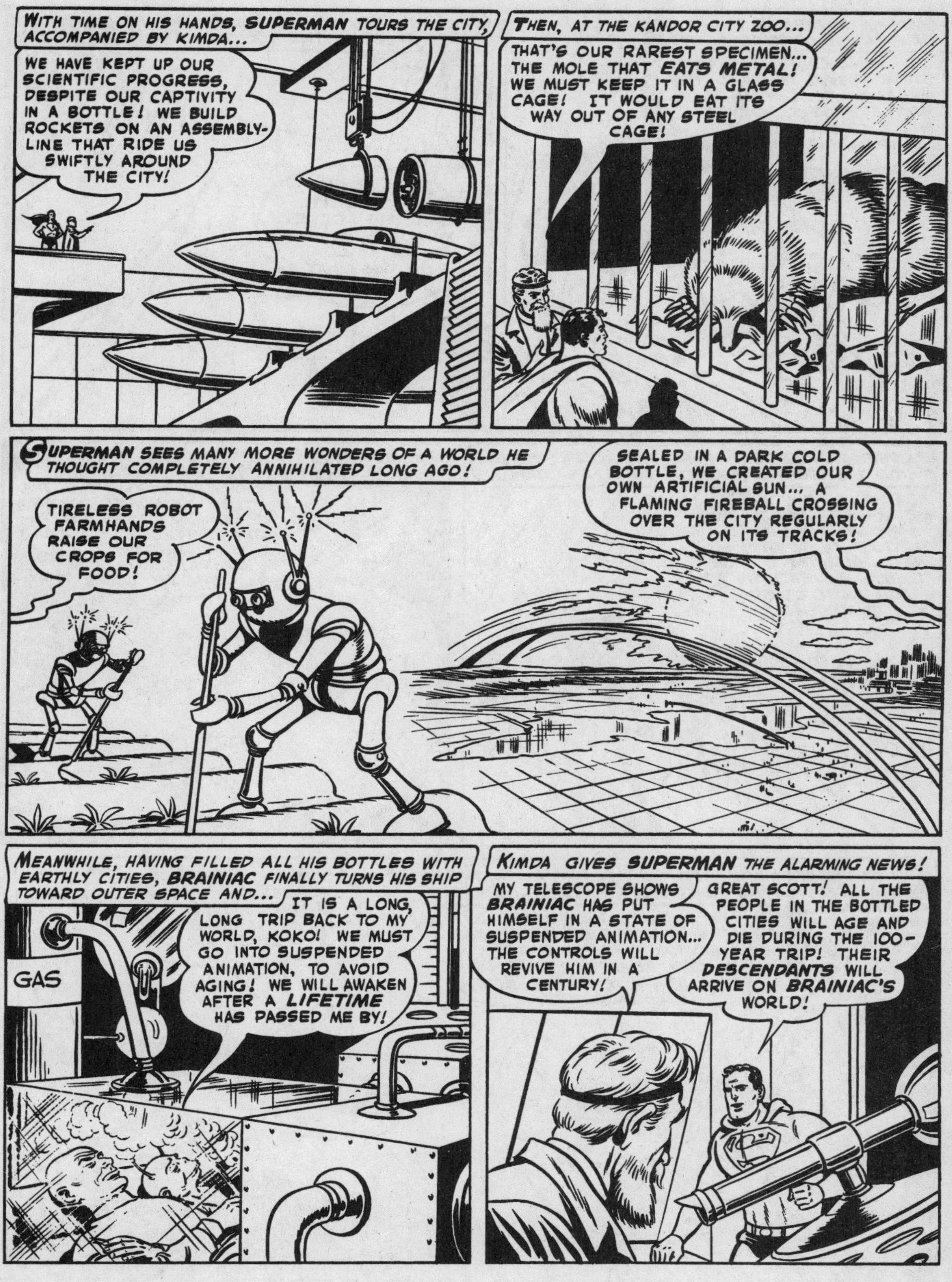
WITH TIME ON HIS HANDS, SUPERMAN TOURS THE CITY, ACCOMPANIED BY KIMDA...
WE HAVE KEPT UP OUR SCIENTIFIC PROGRESS, DESPITE OUR CAPTIVITY IN A BOTTLE! WE BUILD ROCKETS ON AN ASSEMBLY-LINE THAT RIDE US SWIFTLY AROUND THE CITY!
THEN, AT THE KANDOR CITY ZOO...
THAT'S OUR RAREST SPECIMEN... THE MOLE THAT EATS METAL! WE MUST KEEP IT IN A GLASS CAGE! IT WOULD EAT ITS WAY OUT OF ANY STEEL CAGE!
SUPERMAN SEES MANY MORE WONDERS OF A WORLD HE THOUGHT COMPLETELY ANNIHILATED LONG AGO!
TIRELESS ROBOT FARMHANDS RAISE OUR CROPS FOR FOOD!
SEALED IN A DARK COLD BOTTLE, WE CREATED OUR OWN ARTIFICIAL SUN... A FLAMING FIREBALL CROSSING OVER THE CITY REGULARLY ON ITS TRACKS!
MEANWHILE, HAVING FILLED ALL HIS BOTTLES WITH EARTHLY CITIES, BRAINIAC FINALLY TURNS HIS SHIP TOWARD OUTER SPACE AND...
IT IS A LONG, LONG TRIP BACK TO MY WORLD, KOKO! WE MUST GO INTO SUSPENDED ANIMATION, TO AVOID AGING! WE WILL AWAKEN AFTER A LIFETIME HAS PASSED ME BY!
GAS
KIMDA GIVES SUPERMAN THE ALARMING NEWS!
MY TELESCOPE SHOWS BRAINIAC HAS PUT HIMSELF IN A STATE OF SUSPENDED ANIMATION... THE CONTROLS WILL REVIVE HIM IN A CENTURY!
GREAT SCOTT! ALL THE PEOPLE IN THE BOTTLED CITIES WILL AGE AND DIE DURING THE 100-YEAR TRIP! THEIR DESCENDANTS WILL ARRIVE ON BRAINIAC'S WORLD!

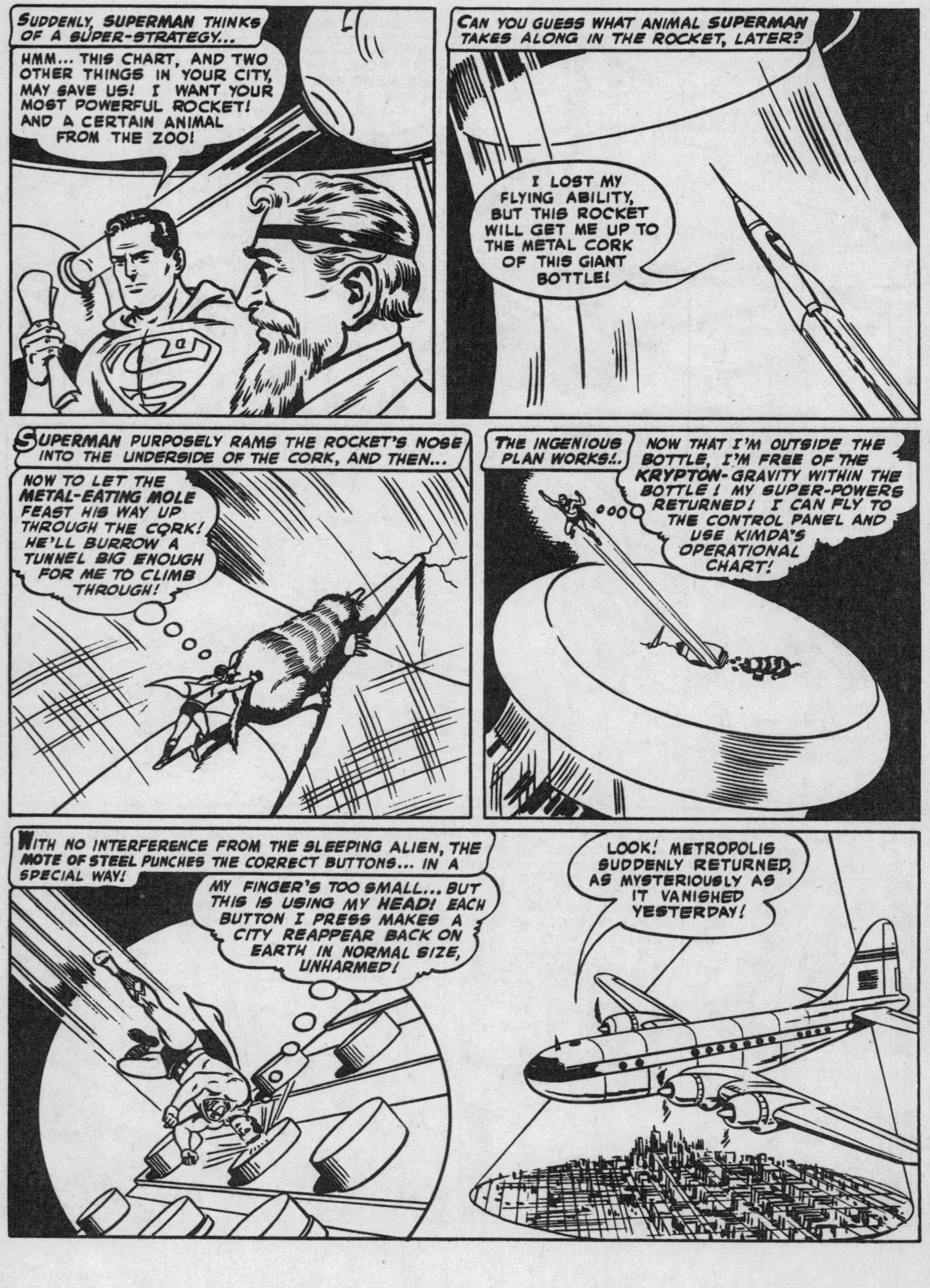
SUDDENLY, SUPERMAN THINKS OF A SUPER-STRATEGY...
HMM... THIS CHART, AND TWO OTHER THINGS IN YOUR CITY, MAY SAVE US! I WANT YOUR MOST POWERFUL ROCKET! AND A CERTAIN ANIMAL FROM THE ZOO!
CAN YOU GUESS WHAT ANIMAL SUPERMAN TAKES ALONG IN THE ROCKET, LATER?
I LOST MY FLYING ABILITY, BUT THIS ROCKET WILL GET ME UP TO THE METAL CORK OF THIS GIANT BOTTLE!
SUPERMAN PURPOSELY RAMS THE ROCKET'S NOSE INTO THE UNDERSIDE OF THE CORK, AND THEN...
NOW TO LET THE METAL-EATING MOLE FEAST HIS WAY UP THROUGH THE CORK! HE'LL BURROW A TUNNEL BIG ENOUGH FOR ME TO CLIMB THROUGH!
THE INGENIOUS PLAN WORKS!..
NOW THAT I'M OUTSIDE THE BOTTLE, I'M FREE OF THE KRYPTON-GRAVITY WITHIN THE BOTTLE! MY SUPER-POWERS RETURNED! I CAN FLY TO THE CONTROL PANEL AND USE KIMDA'S OPERATIONAL CHART!
WITH NO INTERFERENCE FROM THE SLEEPING ALIEN, THE MOTE OF STEEL PUNCHES THE CORRECT BUTTONS... IN A SPECIAL WAY!
MY FINGER'S TOO SMALL... BUT THIS IS USING MY HEAD! EACH BUTTON I PRESS MAKES A CITY REAPPEAR BACK ON EARTH IN NORMAL SIZE, UNHARMED!
LOOK! METROPOLIS SUDDENLY RETURNED, AS MYSTERIOUSLY AS IT VANISHED YESTERDAY!

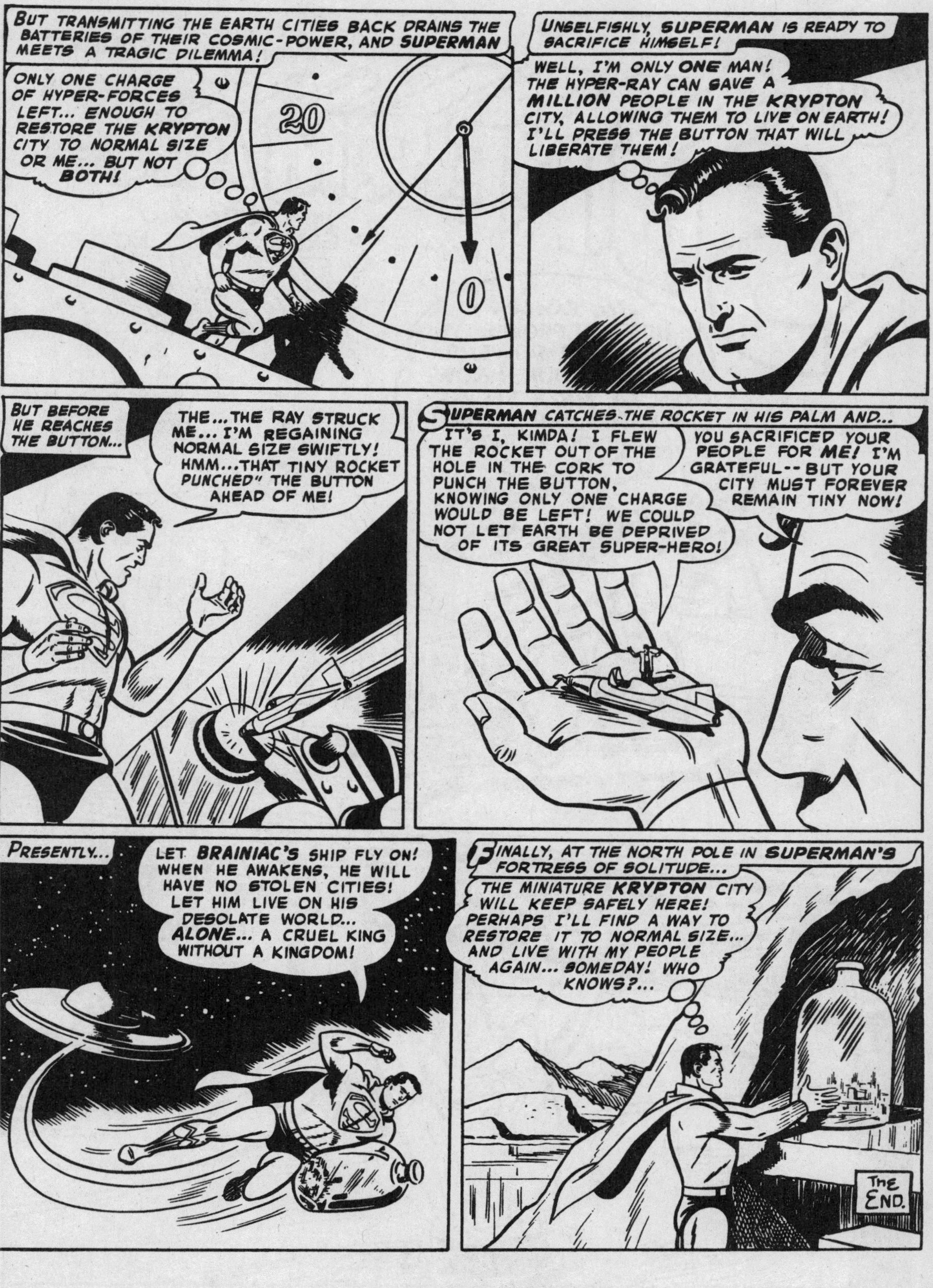
BUT TRANSMITTING THE EARTH CITIES BACK DRAINS THE BATTERIES OF THEIR COSMIC-POWER, AND SUPERMAN MEETS A TRAGIC DILEMMA!
ONLY ONE CHARGE OF HYPER-FORCES LEFT... ENOUGH TO RESTORE THE KRYPTON CITY TO NORMAL SIZE OR ME... BUT NOT BOTH!
20
0
UNSELFISHLY, SUPERMAN IS READY TO SACRIFICE HIMSELF!
WELL, I'M ONLY ONE MAN! THE HYPER-RAY CAN SAVE A MILLION PEOPLE IN THE KRYPTON CITY, ALLOWING THEM TO LIVE ON EARTH! I'LL PRESS THE BUTTON THAT WILL LIBERATE THEM!
BUT BEFORE HE REACHES THE BUTTON...
THE...THE RAY STRUCK ME... I'M REGAINING NORMAL SIZE SWIFTLY! HMM...THAT TINY ROCKET "PUNCHED" THE BUTTON AHEAD OF ME!
SUPERMAN CATCHES THE ROCKET IN HIS PALM AND...
IT'S I, KIMDA! I FLEW THE ROCKET OUT OF THE HOLE IN THE CORK TO PUNCH THE BUTTON, KNOWING ONLY ONE CHARGE WOULD BE LEFT! WE COULD NOT LET EARTH BE DEPRIVED OF ITS GREAT SUPER-HERO!
YOU SACRIFICED YOUR PEOPLE FOR ME! I'M GRATEFUL-- BUT YOUR CITY MUST FOREVER REMAIN TINY NOW!
PRESENTLY...
LET BRAINIAC'S SHIP FLY ON! WHEN HE AWAKENS, HE WILL HAVE NO STOLEN CITIES! LET HIM LIVE ON HIS DESOLATE WORLD... ALONE... A CRUEL KING WITHOUT A KINGDOM!
FINALLY, AT THE NORTH POLE IN SUPERMAN'S FORTRESS OF SOLITUDE...
THE MINIATURE KRYPTON CITY WILL KEEP SAFELY HERE! PERHAPS I'LL FIND A WAY TO RESTORE IT TO NORMAL SIZE... AND LIVE WITH MY PEOPLE AGAIN... SOMEDAY! WHO KNOWS?...
THE END.

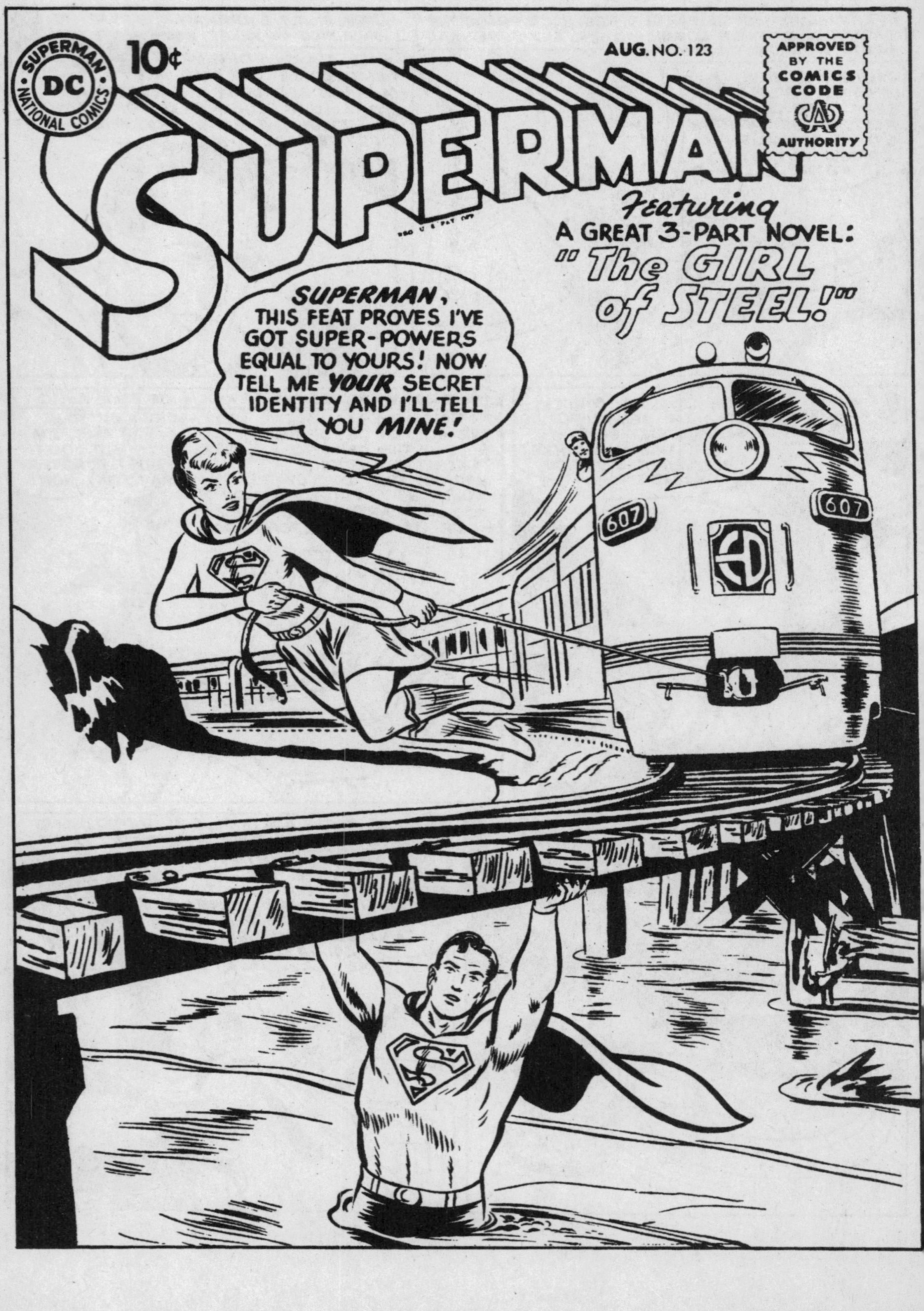

10¢
SUPERMAN DC NATIONAL COMICS
AUG. NO. 123
APPROVED BY THE COMICS CODE AUTHORITY
SUPERMAN
Featuring
A GREAT 3-PART NOVEL:
"The GIRL of STEEL!"
SUPERMAN, THIS FEAT PROVES I'VE GOT SUPER-POWERS EQUAL TO YOURS! NOW TELL ME YOUR SECRET IDENTITY AND I'LL TELL YOU MINE!
607
607

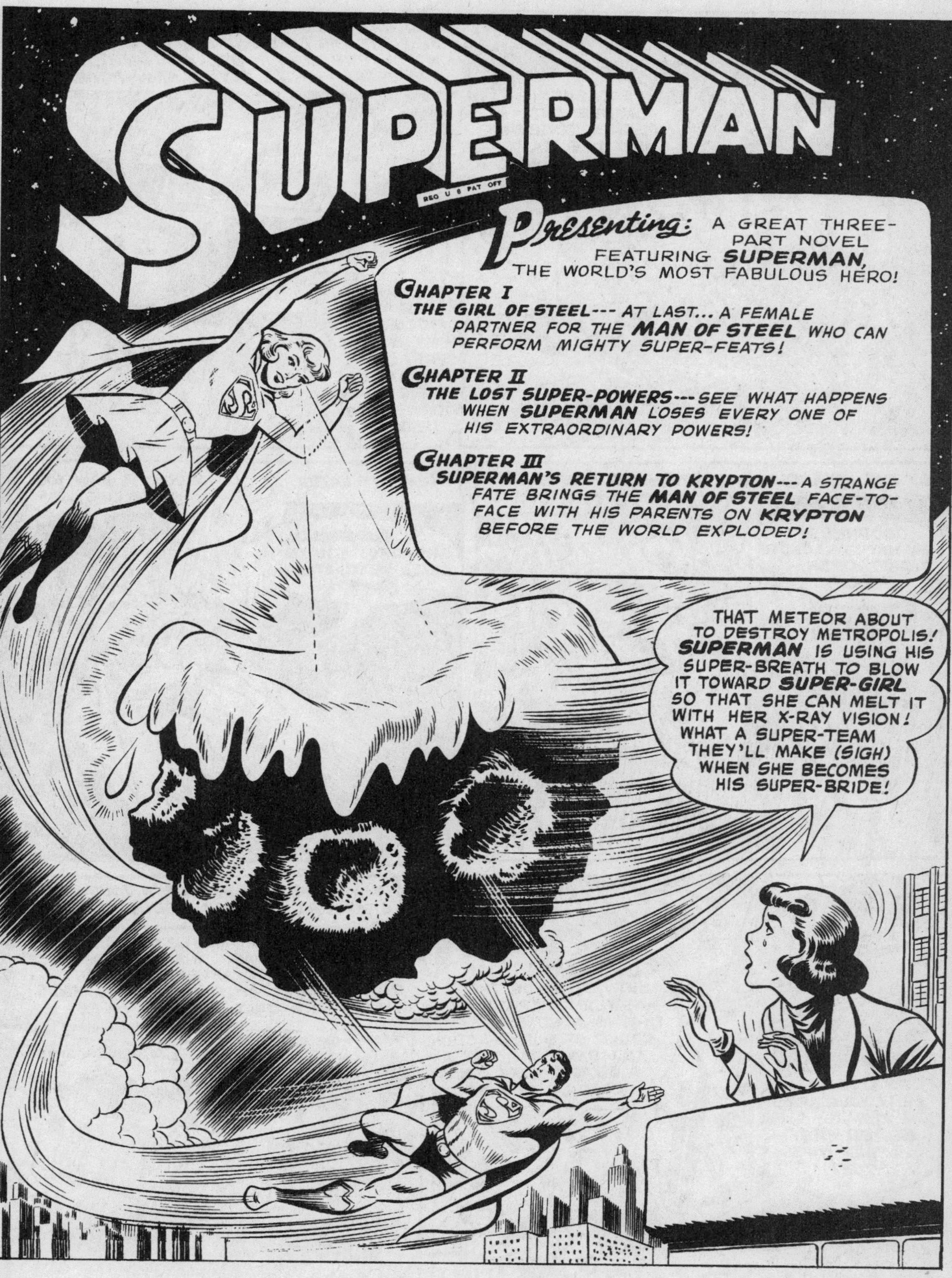
SUPERMAN
REG U S PAT OFF
PRESENTING: A GREAT THREE-PART NOVEL FEATURING SUPERMAN, THE WORLD'S MOST FABULOUS HERO!
CHAPTER I
THE GIRL OF STEEL--- AT LAST... A FEMALE PARTNER FOR THE MAN OF STEEL WHO CAN PERFORM MIGHTY SUPER-FEATS!
CHAPTER II
THE LOST SUPER-POWERS--- SEE WHAT HAPPENS WHEN SUPERMAN LOSES EVERY ONE OF HIS EXTRAORDINARY POWERS!
CHAPTER III
SUPERMAN'S RETURN TO KRYPTON--- A STRANGE FATE BRINGS THE MAN OF STEEL FACE-TO-FACE WITH HIS PARENTS ON KRYPTON BEFORE THE WORLD EXPLODED!
THAT METEOR ABOUT TO DESTROY METROPOLIS! SUPERMAN IS USING HIS SUPER-BREATH TO BLOW IT TOWARD SUPER-GIRL SO THAT SHE CAN MELT IT WITH HER X-RAY VISION! WHAT A SUPER-TEAM THEY'LL MAKE (SIGH) WHEN SHE BECOMES HIS SUPER-BRIDE!

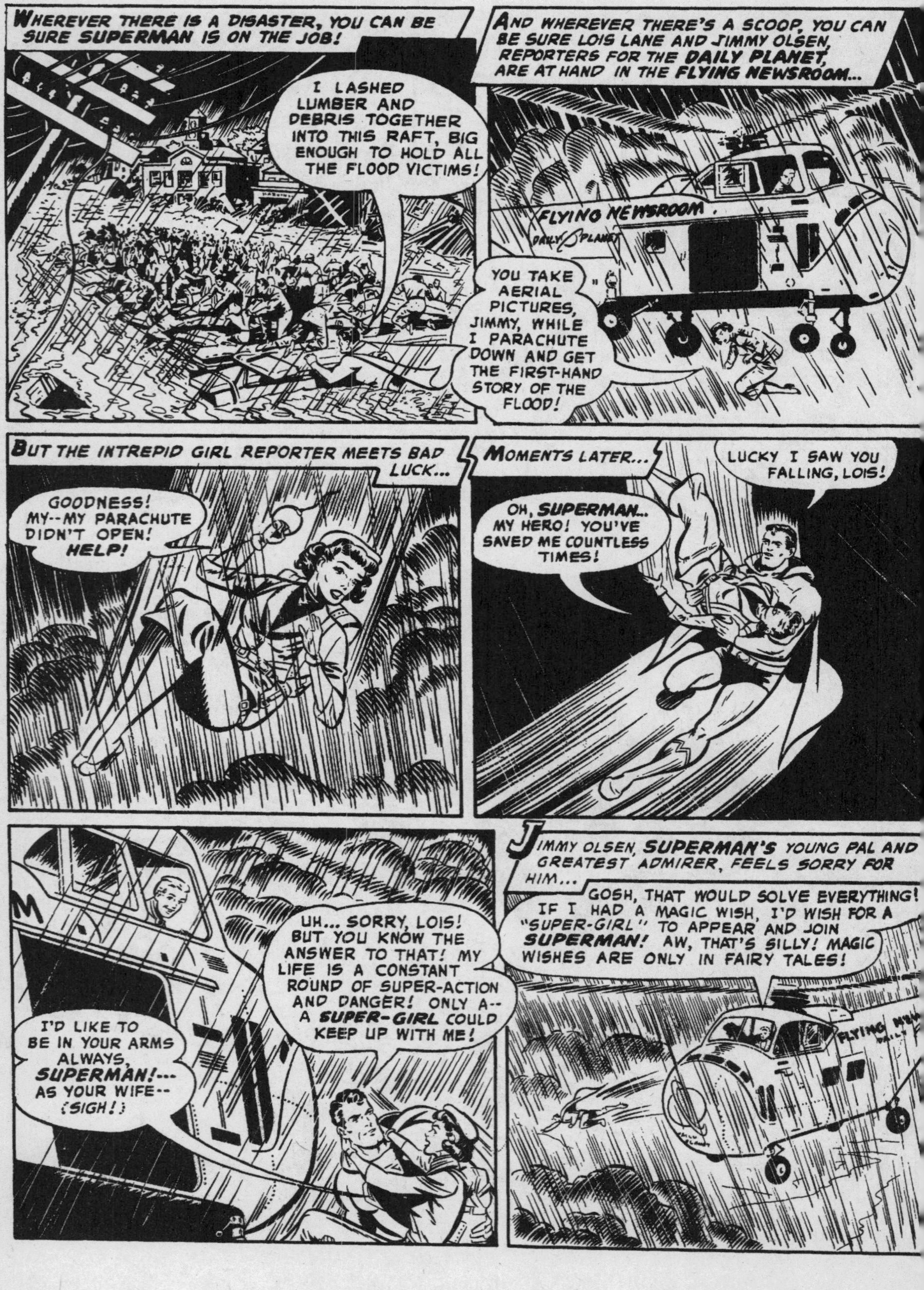
WHEREVER THERE IS A DISASTER, YOU CAN BE SURE SUPERMAN IS ON THE JOB!
I LASHED LUMBER AND DEBRIS TOGETHER INTO THIS RAFT, BIG ENOUGH TO HOLD ALL THE FLOOD VICTIMS!
AND WHEREVER THERE'S A SCOOP, YOU CAN BE SURE LOIS LANE AND JIMMY OLSEN, REPORTERS FOR THE DAILY PLANET, ARE AT HAND IN THE FLYING NEWSROOM...
FLYING NEWSROOM
DAILY PLANET
YOU TAKE AERIAL PICTURES, JIMMY, WHILE I PARACHUTE DOWN AND GET THE FIRST-HAND STORY OF THE FLOOD!
BUT THE INTREPID GIRL REPORTER MEETS BAD LUCK...
GOODNESS! MY--MY PARACHUTE DIDN'T OPEN! HELP!
MOMENTS LATER...
LUCKY I SAW YOU FALLING, LOIS!
OH, SUPERMAN... MY HERO! YOU'VE SAVED ME COUNTLESS TIMES!
I'D LIKE TO BE IN YOUR ARMS ALWAYS, SUPERMAN!--- AS YOUR WIFE-- (SIGH!)
UH... SORRY, LOIS! BUT YOU KNOW THE ANSWER TO THAT! MY LIFE IS A CONSTANT ROUND OF SUPER-ACTION AND DANGER! ONLY A-- A SUPER-GIRL COULD KEEP UP WITH ME!
JIMMY OLSEN, SUPERMAN'S YOUNG PAL AND GREATEST ADMIRER, FEELS SORRY FOR HIM...
GOSH, THAT WOULD SOLVE EVERYTHING! IF I HAD A MAGIC WISH, I'D WISH FOR A "SUPER-GIRL" TO APPEAR AND JOIN SUPERMAN! AW, THAT'S SILLY! MAGIC WISHES ARE ONLY IN FAIRY TALES!

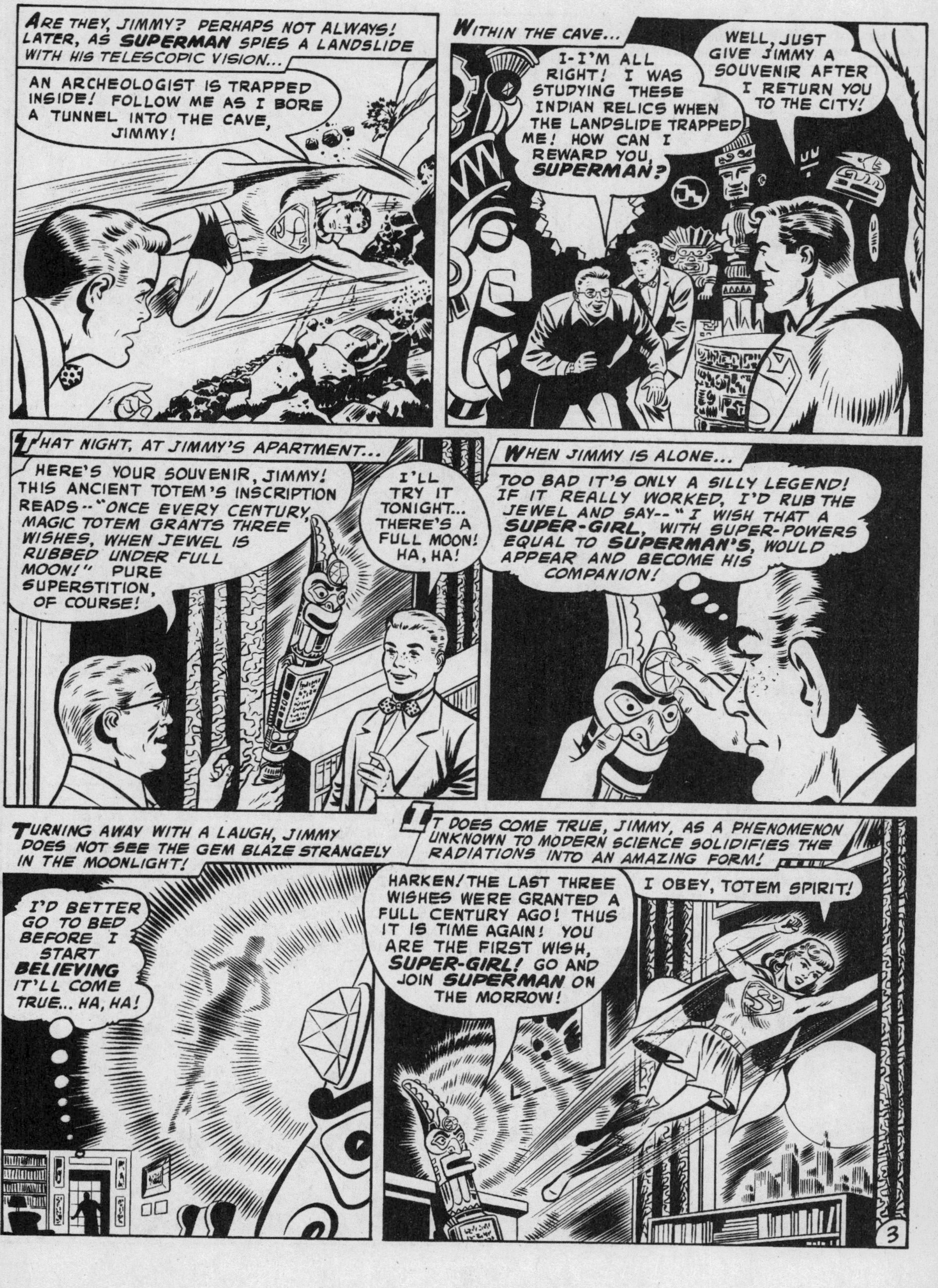
ARE THEY, JIMMY? PERHAPS NOT ALWAYS! LATER, AS SUPERMAN SPIES A LANDSLIDE WITH HIS TELESCOPIC VISION...
AN ARCHEOLOGIST IS TRAPPED INSIDE! FOLLOW ME AS I BORE A TUNNEL INTO THE CAVE, JIMMY!
WITHIN THE CAVE...
I-I'M ALL RIGHT! I WAS STUDYING THESE INDIAN RELICS WHEN THE LANDSLIDE TRAPPED ME! HOW CAN I REWARD YOU, SUPERMAN?
WELL, JUST GIVE JIMMY A SOUVENIR AFTER I RETURN YOU TO THE CITY!
THAT NIGHT, AT JIMMY'S APARTMENT...
HERE'S YOUR SOUVENIR, JIMMY! THIS ANCIENT TOTEM'S INSCRIPTION READS--"ONCE EVERY CENTURY, MAGIC TOTEM GRANTS THREE WISHES, WHEN JEWEL IS RUBBED UNDER FULL MOON!" PURE SUPERSTITION, OF COURSE!
I'LL TRY IT TONIGHT... THERE'S A FULL MOON! HA, HA!
WHEN JIMMY IS ALONE...
TOO BAD IT'S ONLY A SILLY LEGEND! IF IT REALLY WORKED, I'D RUB THE JEWEL AND SAY--"I WISH THAT A SUPER-GIRL, WITH SUPER-POWERS EQUAL TO SUPERMAN'S, WOULD APPEAR AND BECOME HIS COMPANION!
TURNING AWAY WITH A LAUGH, JIMMY DOES NOT SEE THE GEM BLAZE STRANGELY IN THE MOONLIGHT!
I'D BETTER GO TO BED BEFORE I START BELIEVING IT'LL COME TRUE... HA, HA!
IT DOES COME TRUE, JIMMY, AS A PHENOMENON UNKNOWN TO MODERN SCIENCE SOLIDIFIES THE RADIATIONS INTO AN AMAZING FORM!
HARKEN! THE LAST THREE WISHES WERE GRANTED A FULL CENTURY AGO! THUS IT IS TIME AGAIN! YOU ARE THE FIRST WISH, SUPER-GIRL! GO AND JOIN SUPERMAN ON THE MORROW!
I OBEY, TOTEM SPIRIT!
3

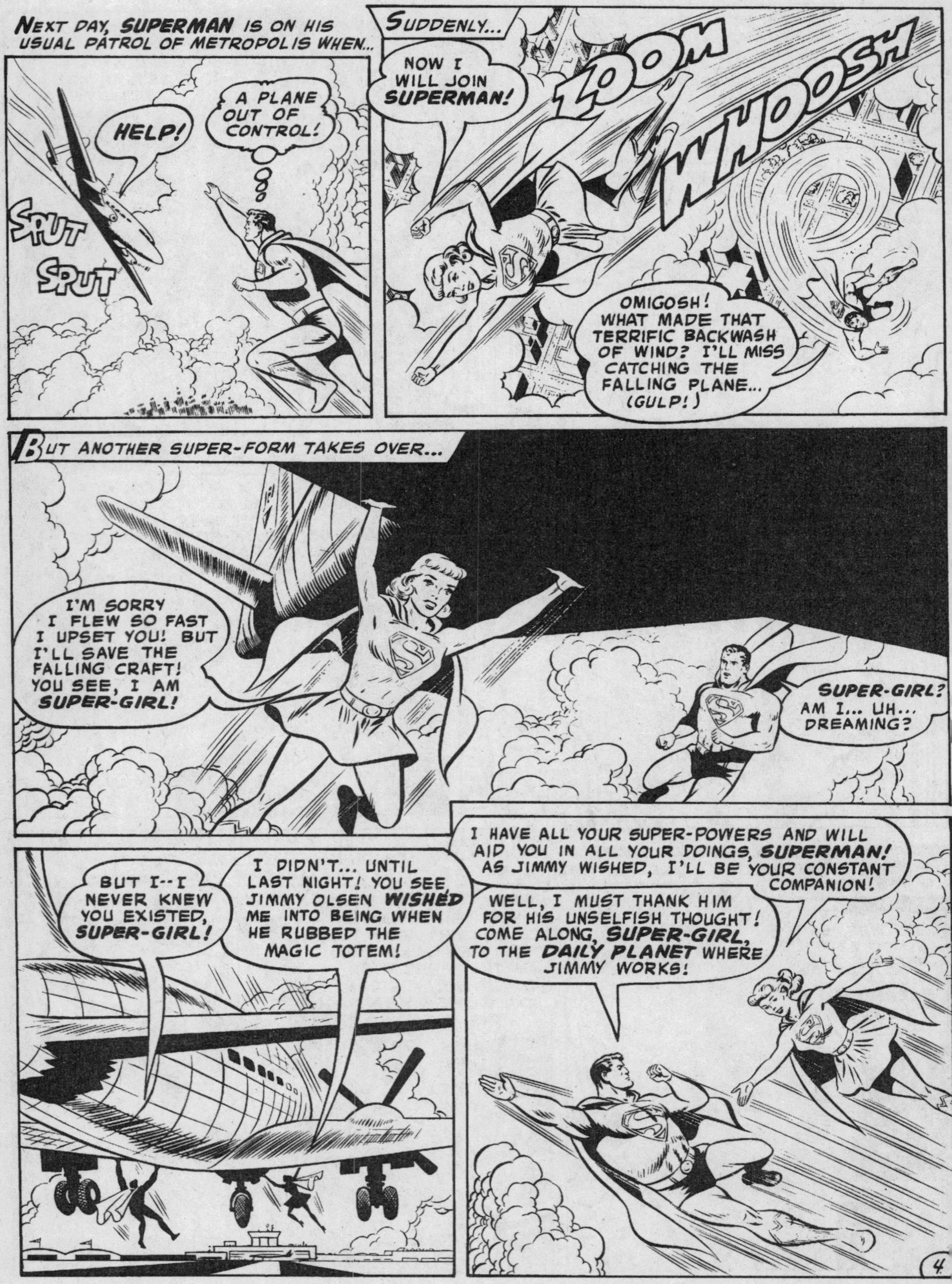
NEXT DAY, SUPERMAN IS ON HIS USUAL PATROL OF METROPOLIS WHEN...
HELP!
A PLANE OUT OF CONTROL!
SPUT
SPUT
SUDDENLY...
NOW I WILL JOIN SUPERMAN!
ZOOM
WHOOSH
OMIGOSH! WHAT MADE THAT TERRIFIC BACKWASH OF WIND? I'LL MISS CATCHING THE FALLING PLANE... (GULP!)
BUT ANOTHER SUPER-FORM TAKES OVER...
I'M SORRY I FLEW SO FAST I UPSET YOU! BUT I'LL SAVE THE FALLING CRAFT! YOU SEE, I AM SUPER-GIRL!
SUPER-GIRL? AM I... UH... DREAMING?
BUT I--I NEVER KNEW YOU EXISTED, SUPER-GIRL!
I DIDN'T... UNTIL LAST NIGHT! YOU SEE, JIMMY OLSEN WISHED ME INTO BEING WHEN HE RUBBED THE MAGIC TOTEM!
I HAVE ALL YOUR SUPER-POWERS AND WILL AID YOU IN ALL YOUR DOINGS, SUPERMAN! AS JIMMY WISHED, I'LL BE YOUR CONSTANT COMPANION!
WELL, I MUST THANK HIM FOR HIS UNSELFISH THOUGHT! COME ALONG, SUPER-GIRL, TO THE DAILY PLANET WHERE JIMMY WORKS!
4

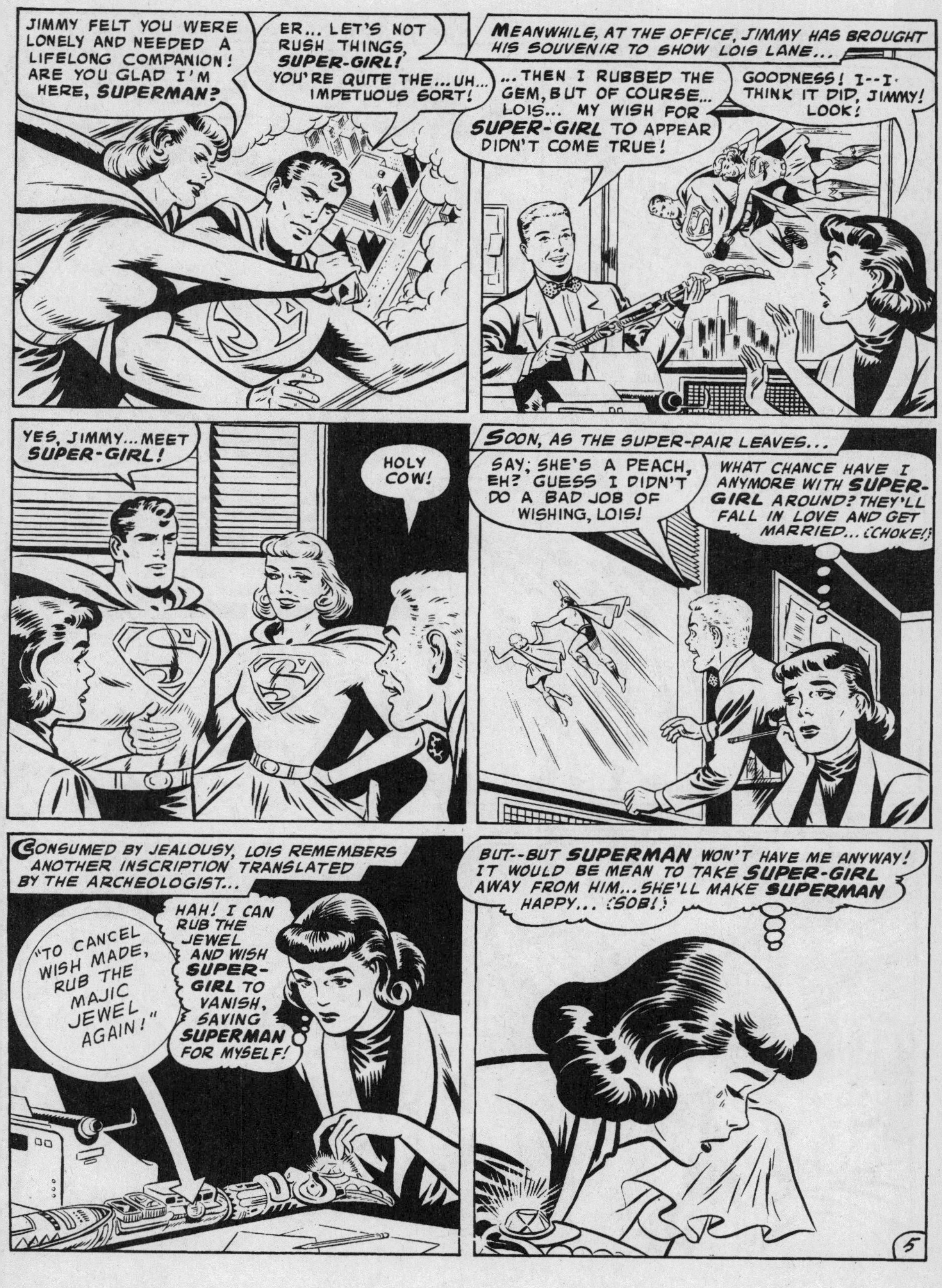
JIMMY FELT YOU WERE LONELY AND NEEDED A LIFELONG COMPANION! ARE YOU GLAD I'M HERE, SUPERMAN?
ER... LET'S NOT RUSH THINGS, SUPER-GIRL! YOU'RE QUITE THE... UH... IMPETUOUS SORT!
MEANWHILE, AT THE OFFICE, JIMMY HAS BROUGHT HIS SOUVENIR TO SHOW LOIS LANE...
...THEN I RUBBED THE GEM, BUT OF COURSE... LOIS... MY WISH FOR SUPER-GIRL TO APPEAR DIDN'T COME TRUE!
GOODNESS! I--I-THINK IT DID, JIMMY! LOOK!
YES, JIMMY... MEET SUPER-GIRL!
HOLY COW!
SOON, AS THE SUPER-PAIR LEAVES...
SAY; SHE'S A PEACH, EH? GUESS I DIDN'T DO A BAD JOB OF WISHING, LOIS!
WHAT CHANCE HAVE I ANYMORE WITH SUPER-GIRL AROUND? THEY'LL FALL IN LOVE AND GET MARRIED... (CHOKE!)
CONSUMED BY JEALOUSY, LOIS REMEMBERS ANOTHER INSCRIPTION TRANSLATED BY THE ARCHEOLOGIST...
"TO CANCEL WISH MADE, RUB THE MAJIC JEWEL AGAIN!"
HAH! I CAN RUB THE JEWEL AND WISH SUPER-GIRL TO VANISH, SAVING SUPERMAN FOR MYSELF!
BUT--BUT SUPERMAN WON'T HAVE ME ANYWAY! IT WOULD BE MEAN TO TAKE SUPER-GIRL AWAY FROM HIM... SHE'LL MAKE SUPERMAN HAPPY... (SOB!)
5

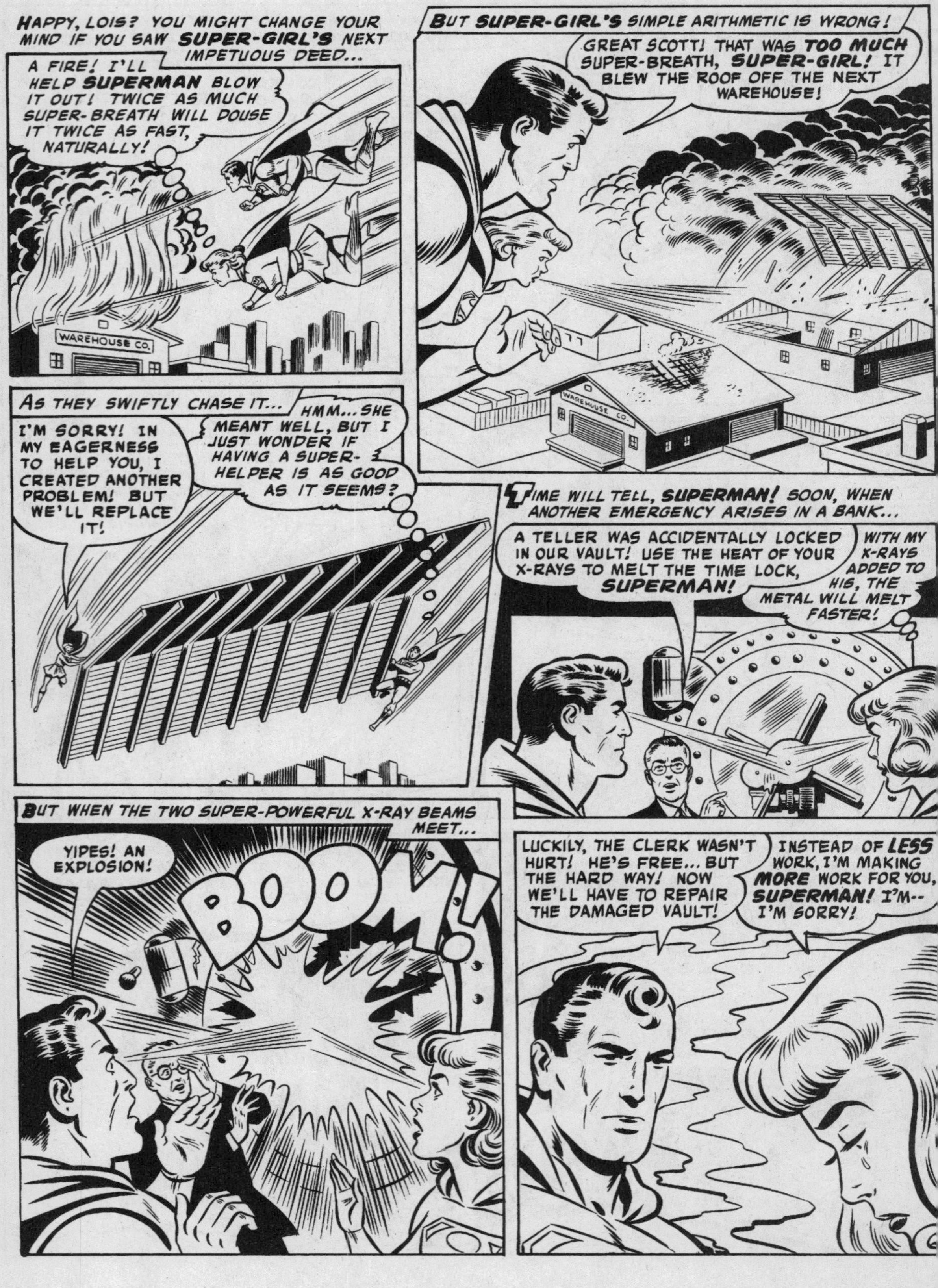
HAPPY, LOIS? YOU MIGHT CHANGE YOUR MIND IF YOU SAW SUPER-GIRL'S NEXT IMPETUOUS DEED...
A FIRE! I'LL HELP SUPERMAN BLOW IT OUT! TWICE AS MUCH SUPER-BREATH WILL DOUSE IT TWICE AS FAST, NATURALLY!
WAREHOUSE CO.
BUT SUPER-GIRL'S SIMPLE ARITHMETIC IS WRONG!
GREAT SCOTT! THAT WAS TOO MUCH SUPER-BREATH, SUPER-GIRL! IT BLEW THE ROOF OFF THE NEXT WAREHOUSE!
WAREHOUSE CO.
AS THEY SWIFTLY CHASE IT...
I'M SORRY! IN MY EAGERNESS TO HELP YOU, I CREATED ANOTHER PROBLEM! BUT WE'LL REPLACE IT!
HMM... SHE MEANT WELL, BUT I JUST WONDER IF HAVING A SUPER-HELPER IS AS GOOD AS IT SEEMS?
TIME WILL TELL, SUPERMAN! SOON, WHEN ANOTHER EMERGENCY ARISES IN A BANK...
A TELLER WAS ACCIDENTALLY LOCKED IN OUR VAULT! USE THE HEAT OF YOUR X-RAYS TO MELT THE TIME LOCK, SUPERMAN!
WITH MY X-RAYS ADDED TO HIS, THE METAL WILL MELT FASTER!
BUT WHEN THE TWO SUPER-POWERFUL X-RAY BEAMS MEET...
YIPES! AN EXPLOSION!
BOOM!
LUCKILY, THE CLERK WASN'T HURT! HE'S FREE... BUT THE HARD WAY! NOW WE'LL HAVE TO REPAIR THE DAMAGED VAULT!
INSTEAD OF LESS WORK, I'M MAKING MORE WORK FOR YOU, SUPERMAN! I'M-- I'M SORRY!

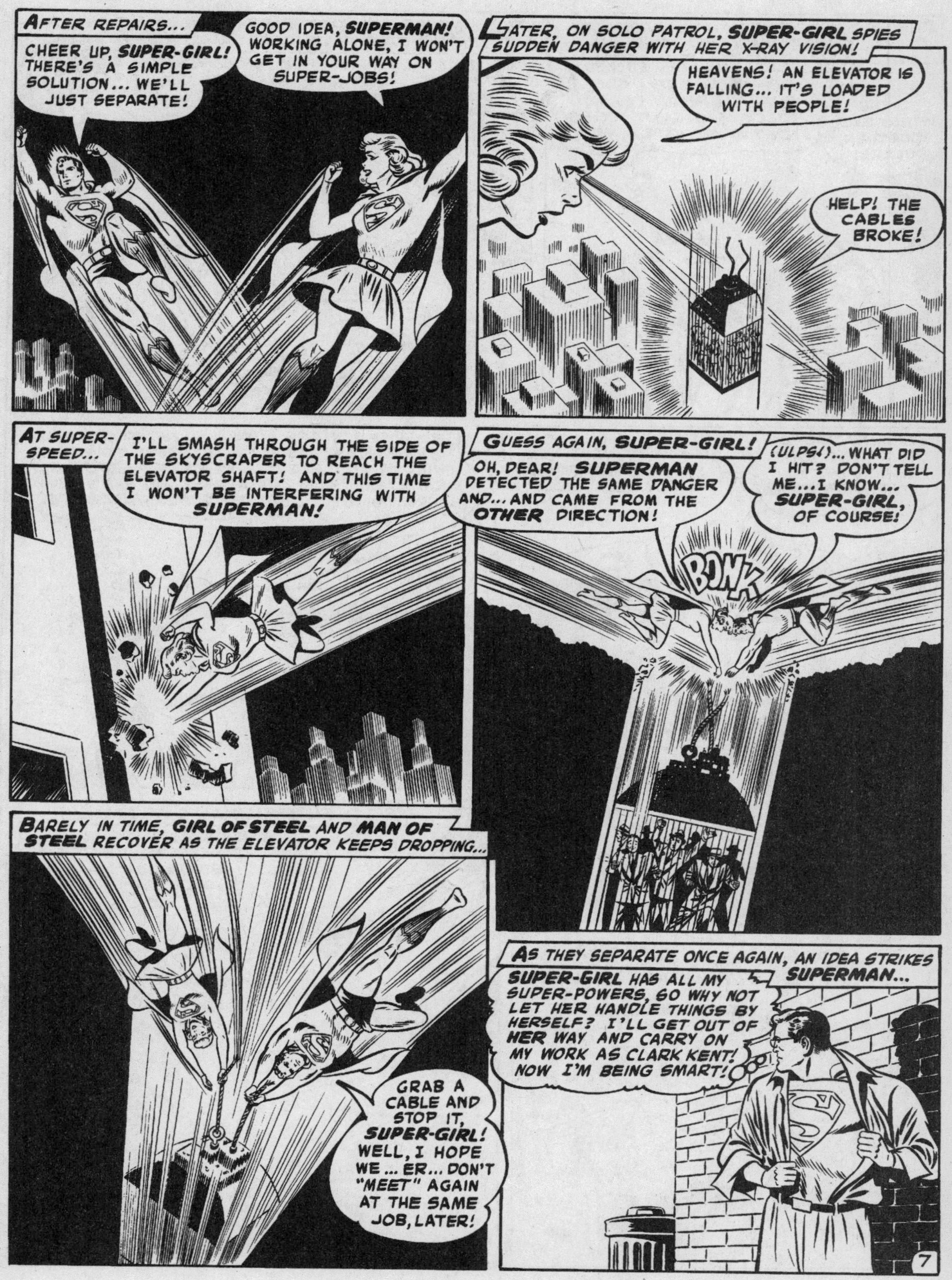
AFTER REPAIRS...
CHEER UP, SUPER-GIRL! THERE'S A SIMPLE SOLUTION... WE'LL JUST SEPARATE!
GOOD IDEA, SUPERMAN! WORKING ALONE, I WON'T GET IN YOUR WAY ON SUPER-JOBS!
LATER, ON SOLO PATROL, SUPER-GIRL SPIES SUDDEN DANGER WITH HER X-RAY VISION!
HEAVENS! AN ELEVATOR IS FALLING... IT'S LOADED WITH PEOPLE!
HELP! THE CABLES BROKE!
AT SUPER-SPEED...
I'LL SMASH THROUGH THE SIDE OF THE SKYSCRAPER TO REACH THE ELEVATOR SHAFT! AND THIS TIME I WON'T BE INTERFERING WITH SUPERMAN!
GUESS AGAIN, SUPER-GIRL!
OH, DEAR! SUPERMAN DETECTED THE SAME DANGER AND... AND CAME FROM THE OTHER DIRECTION!
(ULPS!)... WHAT DID I HIT? DON'T TELL ME... I KNOW... SUPER-GIRL, OF COURSE!
BONK
BARELY IN TIME, GIRL OF STEEL AND MAN OF STEEL RECOVER AS THE ELEVATOR KEEPS DROPPING...
GRAB A CABLE AND STOP IT, SUPER-GIRL! WELL, I HOPE WE ... ER... DON'T "MEET" AGAIN AT THE SAME JOB, LATER!
AS THEY SEPARATE ONCE AGAIN, AN IDEA STRIKES SUPERMAN...
SUPER-GIRL HAS ALL MY SUPER-POWERS, SO WHY NOT LET HER HANDLE THINGS BY HERSELF? I'LL GET OUT OF HER WAY AND CARRY ON MY WORK AS CLARK KENT! NOW I'M BEING SMART!
7

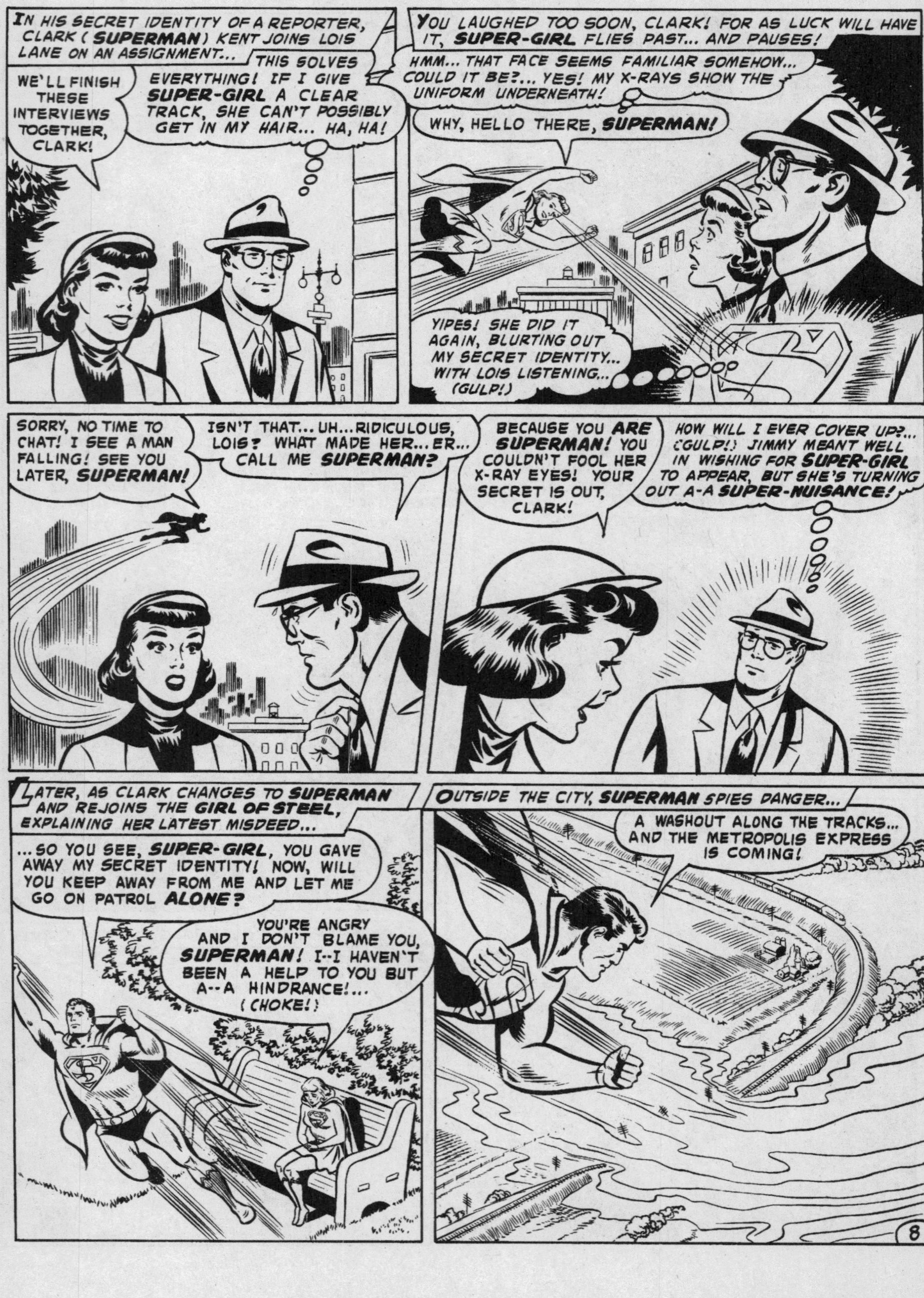
IN HIS SECRET IDENTITY OF A REPORTER, CLARK (SUPERMAN) KENT JOINS LOIS LANE ON AN ASSIGNMENT...
WE'LL FINISH THESE INTERVIEWS TOGETHER, CLARK!
THIS SOLVES EVERYTHING! IF I GIVE SUPER-GIRL A CLEAR TRACK, SHE CAN'T POSSIBLY GET IN MY HAIR... HA, HA!
YOU LAUGHED TOO SOON, CLARK! FOR AS LUCK WILL HAVE IT, SUPER-GIRL FLIES PAST... AND PAUSES!
HMM... THAT FACE SEEMS FAMILIAR SOMEHOW... COULD IT BE?... YES! MY X-RAYS SHOW THE UNIFORM UNDERNEATH!
WHY, HELLO THERE, SUPERMAN!
YIPES! SHE DID IT AGAIN, BLURTING OUT MY SECRET IDENTITY... WITH LOIS LISTENING... (GULP!)
SORRY, NO TIME TO CHAT! I SEE A MAN FALLING! SEE YOU LATER, SUPERMAN!
ISN'T THAT... UH... RIDICULOUS, LOIS? WHAT MADE HER... ER... CALL ME SUPERMAN?
BECAUSE YOU ARE SUPERMAN! YOU COULDN'T FOOL HER X-RAY EYES! YOUR SECRET IS OUT, CLARK!
HOW WILL I EVER COVER UP?... (GULP!) JIMMY MEANT WELL IN WISHING FOR SUPER-GIRL TO APPEAR, BUT SHE'S TURNING OUT A-A SUPER-NUISANCE!
LATER, AS CLARK CHANGES TO SUPERMAN AND REJOINS THE GIRL OF STEEL, EXPLAINING HER LATEST MISDEED...
...SO YOU SEE, SUPER-GIRL, YOU GAVE AWAY MY SECRET IDENTITY! NOW, WILL YOU KEEP AWAY FROM ME AND LET ME GO ON PATROL ALONE?
YOU'RE ANGRY AND I DON'T BLAME YOU, SUPERMAN! I--I HAVEN'T BEEN A HELP TO YOU BUT A--A HINDRANCE!... (CHOKE!)
OUTSIDE THE CITY, SUPERMAN SPIES DANGER...
A WASHOUT ALONG THE TRACKS... AND THE METROPOLIS EXPRESS IS COMING!
8

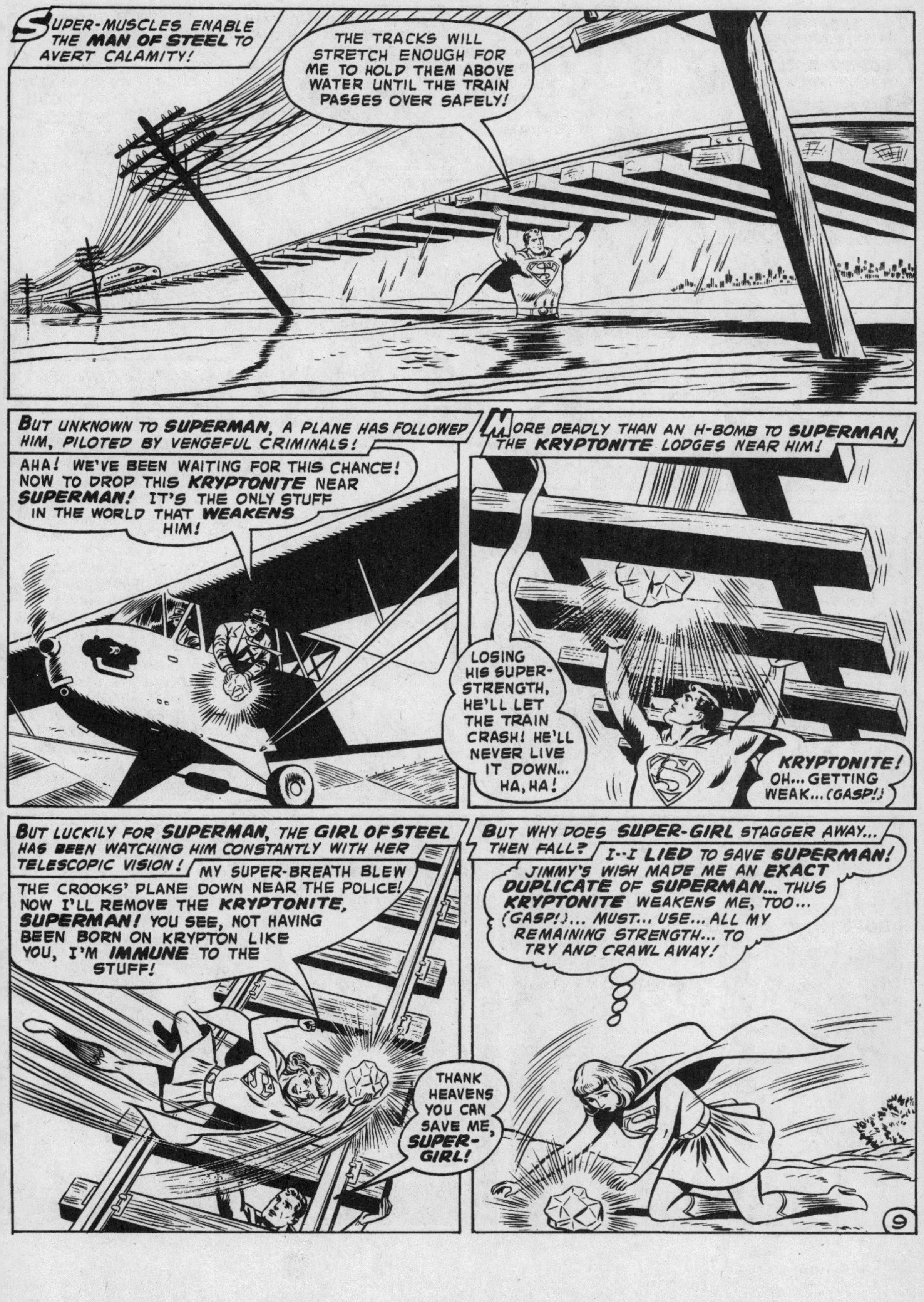
SUPER-MUSCLES ENABLE THE MAN OF STEEL TO AVERT CALAMITY!
THE TRACKS WILL STRETCH ENOUGH FOR ME TO HOLD THEM ABOVE WATER UNTIL THE TRAIN PASSES OVER SAFELY!
BUT UNKNOWN TO SUPERMAN, A PLANE HAS FOLLOWED HIM, PILOTED BY VENGEFUL CRIMINALS!
AHA! WE'VE BEEN WAITING FOR THIS CHANCE! NOW TO DROP THIS KRYPTONITE NEAR SUPERMAN! IT'S THE ONLY STUFF IN THE WORLD THAT WEAKENS HIM!
MORE DEADLY THAN AN H-BOMB TO SUPERMAN, THE KRYPTONITE LODGES NEAR HIM!
LOSING HIS SUPER-STRENGTH, HE'LL LET THE TRAIN CRASH! HE'LL NEVER LIVE IT DOWN... HA, HA!
KRYPTONITE! OH... GETTING WEAK... (GASP!)
BUT LUCKILY FOR SUPERMAN, THE GIRL OF STEEL HAS BEEN WATCHING HIM CONSTANTLY WITH HER TELESCOPIC VISION!
MY SUPER-BREATH BLEW THE CROOKS' PLANE DOWN NEAR THE POLICE! NOW I'LL REMOVE THE KRYPTONITE, SUPERMAN! YOU SEE, NOT HAVING BEEN BORN ON KRYPTON LIKE YOU, I'M IMMUNE TO THE STUFF!
THANK HEAVENS YOU CAN SAVE ME, SUPER-GIRL!
BUT WHY DOES SUPER-GIRL STAGGER AWAY... THEN FALL?
I--I LIED TO SAVE SUPERMAN! JIMMY'S WISH MADE ME AN EXACT DUPLICATE OF SUPERMAN... THUS KRYPTONITE WEAKENS ME, TOO... (GASP!)... MUST... USE... ALL MY REMAINING STRENGTH... TO TRY AND CRAWL AWAY!
9

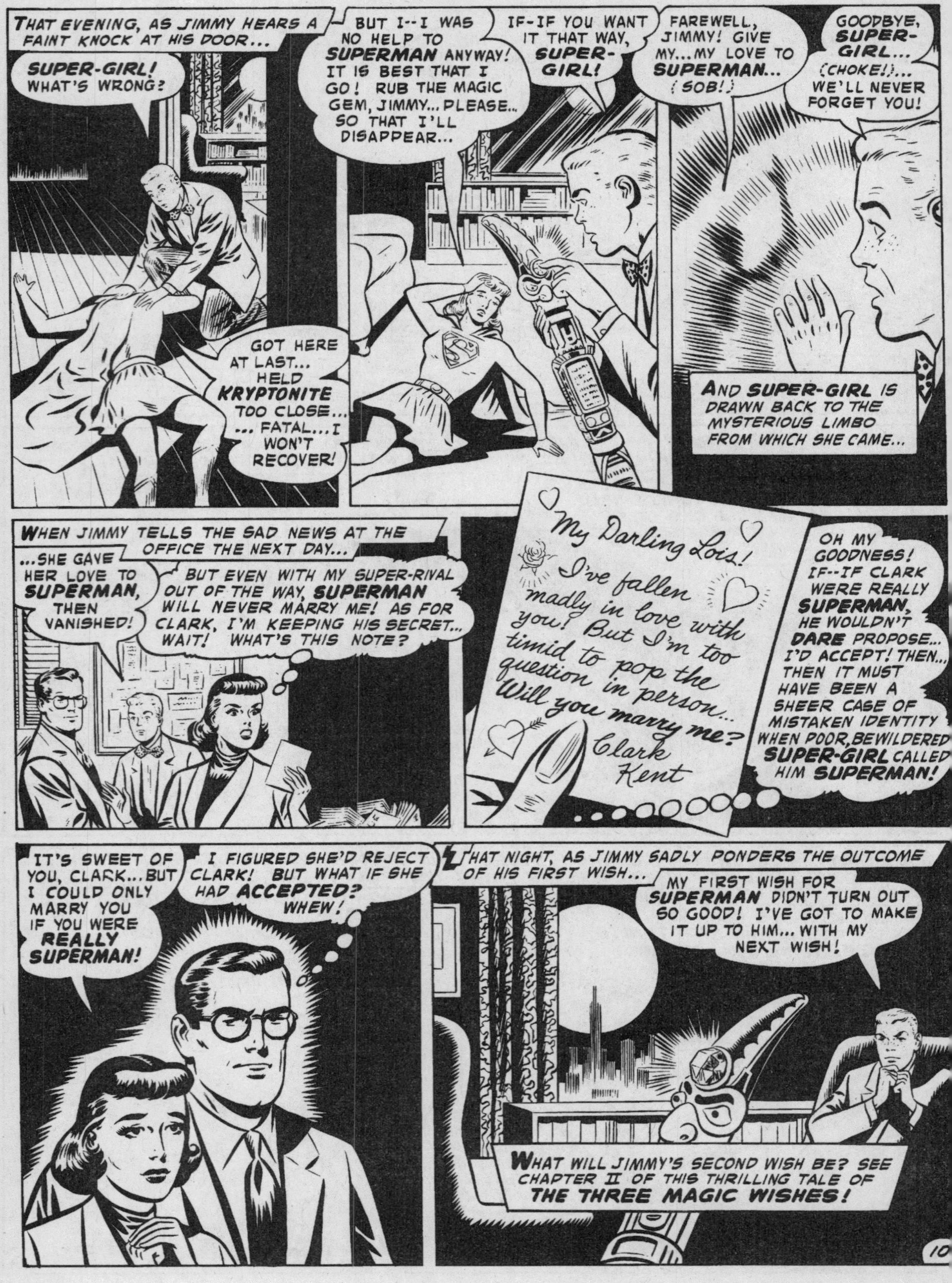
THAT EVENING, AS JIMMY HEARS A FAINT KNOCK AT HIS DOOR...
SUPER-GIRL! WHAT'S WRONG?
GOT HERE AT LAST... HELD KRYPTONITE TOO CLOSE... ...FATAL...I WON'T RECOVER!
BUT I--I WAS NO HELP TO SUPERMAN ANYWAY! IT IS BEST THAT I GO! RUB THE MAGIC GEM, JIMMY...PLEASE.. SO THAT I'LL DISAPPEAR...
IF-IF YOU WANT IT THAT WAY, SUPER-GIRL!
FAREWELL, JIMMY! GIVE MY...MY LOVE TO SUPERMAN... (SOB!)
GOODBYE, SUPER-GIRL... (CHOKE!)... WE'LL NEVER FORGET YOU!
AND SUPER-GIRL IS DRAWN BACK TO THE MYSTERIOUS LIMBO FROM WHICH SHE CAME...
WHEN JIMMY TELLS THE SAD NEWS AT THE OFFICE THE NEXT DAY...
...SHE GAVE HER LOVE TO SUPERMAN, THEN VANISHED!
BUT EVEN WITH MY SUPER-RIVAL OUT OF THE WAY, SUPERMAN WILL NEVER MARRY ME! AS FOR CLARK, I'M KEEPING HIS SECRET... WAIT! WHAT'S THIS NOTE?
My Darling Lois! I've fallen madly in love with you! But I'm too timid to pop the question in person... Will you marry me? Clark Kent
OH MY GOODNESS! IF--IF CLARK WERE REALLY SUPERMAN, HE WOULDN'T DARE PROPOSE... I'D ACCEPT! THEN... THEN IT MUST HAVE BEEN A SHEER CASE OF MISTAKEN IDENTITY WHEN POOR, BEWILDERED SUPER-GIRL CALLED HIM SUPERMAN!
IT'S SWEET OF YOU, CLARK...BUT I COULD ONLY MARRY YOU IF YOU WERE REALLY SUPERMAN!
I FIGURED SHE'D REJECT CLARK! BUT WHAT IF SHE HAD ACCEPTED? WHEW!
THAT NIGHT, AS JIMMY SADLY PONDERS THE OUTCOME OF HIS FIRST WISH...
MY FIRST WISH FOR SUPERMAN DIDN'T TURN OUT SO GOOD! I'VE GOT TO MAKE IT UP TO HIM... WITH MY NEXT WISH!
WHAT WILL JIMMY'S SECOND WISH BE? SEE CHAPTER II OF THIS THRILLING TALE OF THE THREE MAGIC WISHES!
10

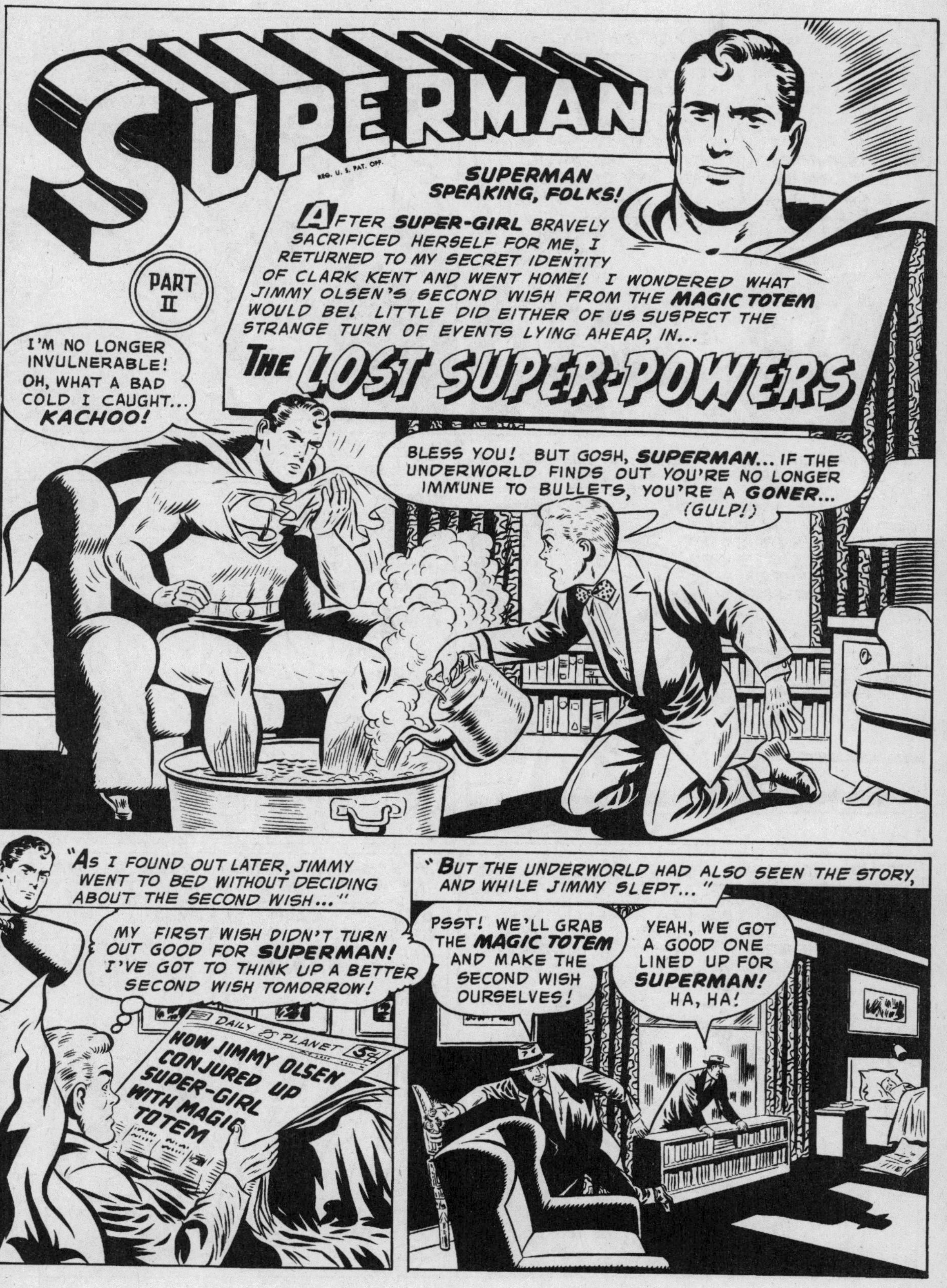
SUPERMAN
REG. U.S. PAT. OFF.
SUPERMAN SPEAKING, FOLKS!
AFTER SUPER-GIRL BRAVELY SACRIFICED HERSELF FOR ME, I RETURNED TO MY SECRET IDENTITY OF CLARK KENT AND WENT HOME! I WONDERED WHAT JIMMY OLSEN'S SECOND WISH FROM THE MAGIC TOTEM WOULD BE! LITTLE DID EITHER OF US SUSPECT THE STRANGE TURN OF EVENTS LYING AHEAD, IN...
THE LOST SUPER-POWERS
PART II
I'M NO LONGER INVULNERABLE! OH, WHAT A BAD COLD I CAUGHT... KACHOO!
BLESS YOU! BUT GOSH, SUPERMAN... IF THE UNDERWORLD FINDS OUT YOU'RE NO LONGER IMMUNE TO BULLETS, YOU'RE A GONER... (GULP!)
"AS I FOUND OUT LATER, JIMMY WENT TO BED WITHOUT DECIDING ABOUT THE SECOND WISH..."
MY FIRST WISH DIDN'T TURN OUT GOOD FOR SUPERMAN! I'VE GOT TO THINK UP A BETTER SECOND WISH TOMORROW!
DAILY PLANET
5¢
HOW JIMMY OLSEN CONJURED UP SUPER-GIRL WITH MAGIC TOTEM
"BUT THE UNDERWORLD HAD ALSO SEEN THE STORY, AND WHILE JIMMY SLEPT..."
PSST! WE'LL GRAB THE MAGIC TOTEM AND MAKE THE SECOND WISH OURSELVES!
YEAH, WE GOT A GOOD ONE LINED UP FOR SUPERMAN! HA, HA!

"*LATER, IN THE BACKYARD OF THE GANG'S HIDEOUT...*"

I RUB THE MAGIC JEWEL UNDER THE FULL MOON AND... *I WISH FOR SUPERMAN TO LOSE ALL HIS SUPER-POWERS!*

NOW WE'LL BURY THE *MAGIC TOTEM!* WITHOUT HIS X-RAY VISION-- *SUPERMAN* WON'T FIND IT... SO HE CAN'T RUB THE MAGIC JEWEL AND CANCEL THE WISH! HA, HA!

BUT WHAT IF ONLY... ER... *GOOD* WISHES COME TRUE, NOT BAD ONES? WILL *SUPERMAN* REALLY LOSE HIS POWERS?

WE'LL MAKE SURE TOMORROW-- BY TAILING *SUPERMAN!*

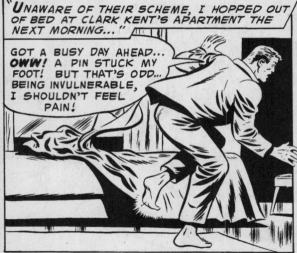

"*UNAWARE OF THEIR SCHEME, I HOPPED OUT OF BED AT CLARK KENT'S APARTMENT THE NEXT MORNING...*"

GOT A BUSY DAY AHEAD... *OWW!* A PIN STUCK MY FOOT! BUT THAT'S ODD... BEING INVULNERABLE, I SHOULDN'T FEEL PAIN!

"*THEN, AS I TOOK MY USUAL BOILING HOT SHOWER THAT WOULD SCALD NORMAL PEOPLE...*"

YIPES! MY SKIN SEEMS ON FIRE! BUT I--I USED TO BE ABLE TO DIVE INTO *MOLTEN LAVA* WITHOUT FEELING IT! WHAT'S WRONG WITH ME TODAY?

"*MY BEWILDERMENT GREW DURING MY SETTING-UP EXERCISES...*"

OOF! I ALWAYS TOSSED THESE AROUND LIKE FEATHERS... BUT NOW I CAN'T BUDGE THEM! WHERE'S MY *SUPER-STRENGTH?*

1000 lb.

"*MOST SHOCKING, WHEN I TRIED TO LEAP FROM THE WINDOW AS USUAL...*"

UGH! I-I CAN'T FLY, EITHER! GREAT SCOTT... THERE'S ONLY ONE ANSWER TO ALL THIS... ONE *HORRIBLE* ANSWER!

CRASH!

2

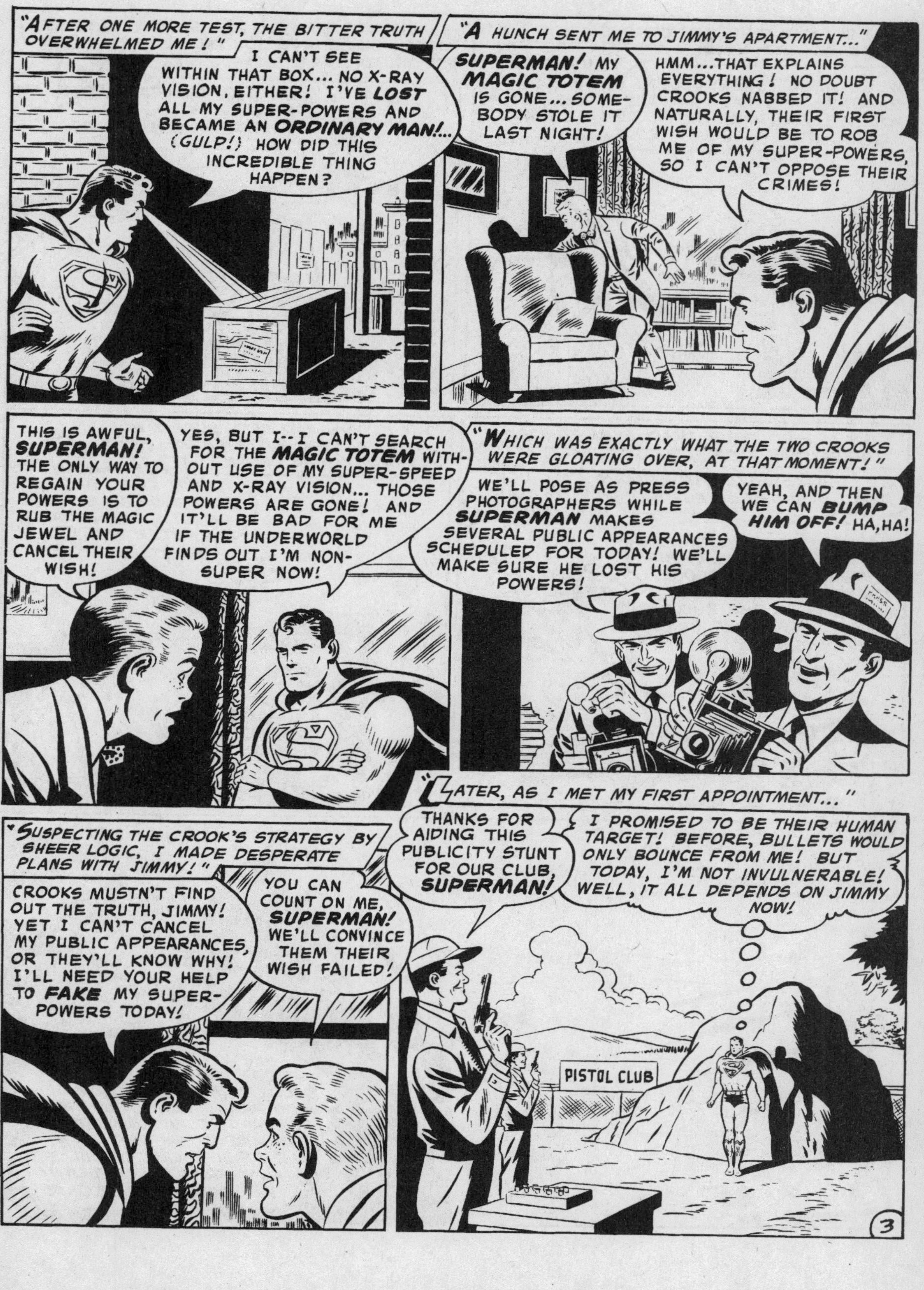
"AFTER ONE MORE TEST, THE BITTER TRUTH OVERWHELMED ME!"
I CAN'T SEE WITHIN THAT BOX... NO X-RAY VISION, EITHER! I'VE **LOST** ALL MY SUPER-POWERS AND BECAME AN **ORDINARY MAN!**... (GULP!) HOW DID THIS INCREDIBLE THING HAPPEN?
"A HUNCH SENT ME TO JIMMY'S APARTMENT..."
SUPERMAN! MY **MAGIC TOTEM** IS GONE... SOMEBODY STOLE IT LAST NIGHT!
HMM...THAT EXPLAINS EVERYTHING! NO DOUBT CROOKS NABBED IT! AND NATURALLY, THEIR FIRST WISH WOULD BE TO ROB ME OF MY SUPER-POWERS, SO I CAN'T OPPOSE THEIR CRIMES!
THIS IS AWFUL, **SUPERMAN!** THE ONLY WAY TO REGAIN YOUR POWERS IS TO RUB THE MAGIC JEWEL AND CANCEL THEIR WISH!
YES, BUT I-- I CAN'T SEARCH FOR THE **MAGIC TOTEM** WITHOUT USE OF MY SUPER-SPEED AND X-RAY VISION... THOSE POWERS ARE GONE! AND IT'LL BE BAD FOR ME IF THE UNDERWORLD FINDS OUT I'M NON-SUPER NOW!
"WHICH WAS EXACTLY WHAT THE TWO CROOKS WERE GLOATING OVER, AT THAT MOMENT!"
WE'LL POSE AS PRESS PHOTOGRAPHERS WHILE **SUPERMAN** MAKES SEVERAL PUBLIC APPEARANCES SCHEDULED FOR TODAY! WE'LL MAKE SURE HE LOST HIS POWERS!
YEAH, AND THEN WE CAN **BUMP HIM OFF!** HA, HA!
"SUSPECTING THE CROOK'S STRATEGY BY SHEER LOGIC, I MADE DESPERATE PLANS WITH JIMMY!"
CROOKS MUSTN'T FIND OUT THE TRUTH, JIMMY! YET I CAN'T CANCEL MY PUBLIC APPEARANCES, OR THEY'LL KNOW WHY! I'LL NEED YOUR HELP TO **FAKE** MY SUPER-POWERS TODAY!
YOU CAN COUNT ON ME, **SUPERMAN!** WE'LL CONVINCE THEM THEIR WISH FAILED!
"LATER, AS I MET MY FIRST APPOINTMENT..."
THANKS FOR AIDING THIS PUBLICITY STUNT FOR OUR CLUB, **SUPERMAN!**
I PROMISED TO BE THEIR HUMAN TARGET! BEFORE, BULLETS WOULD ONLY BOUNCE FROM ME! BUT TODAY, I'M NOT INVULNERABLE! WELL, IT ALL DEPENDS ON JIMMY NOW!
PISTOL CLUB
3

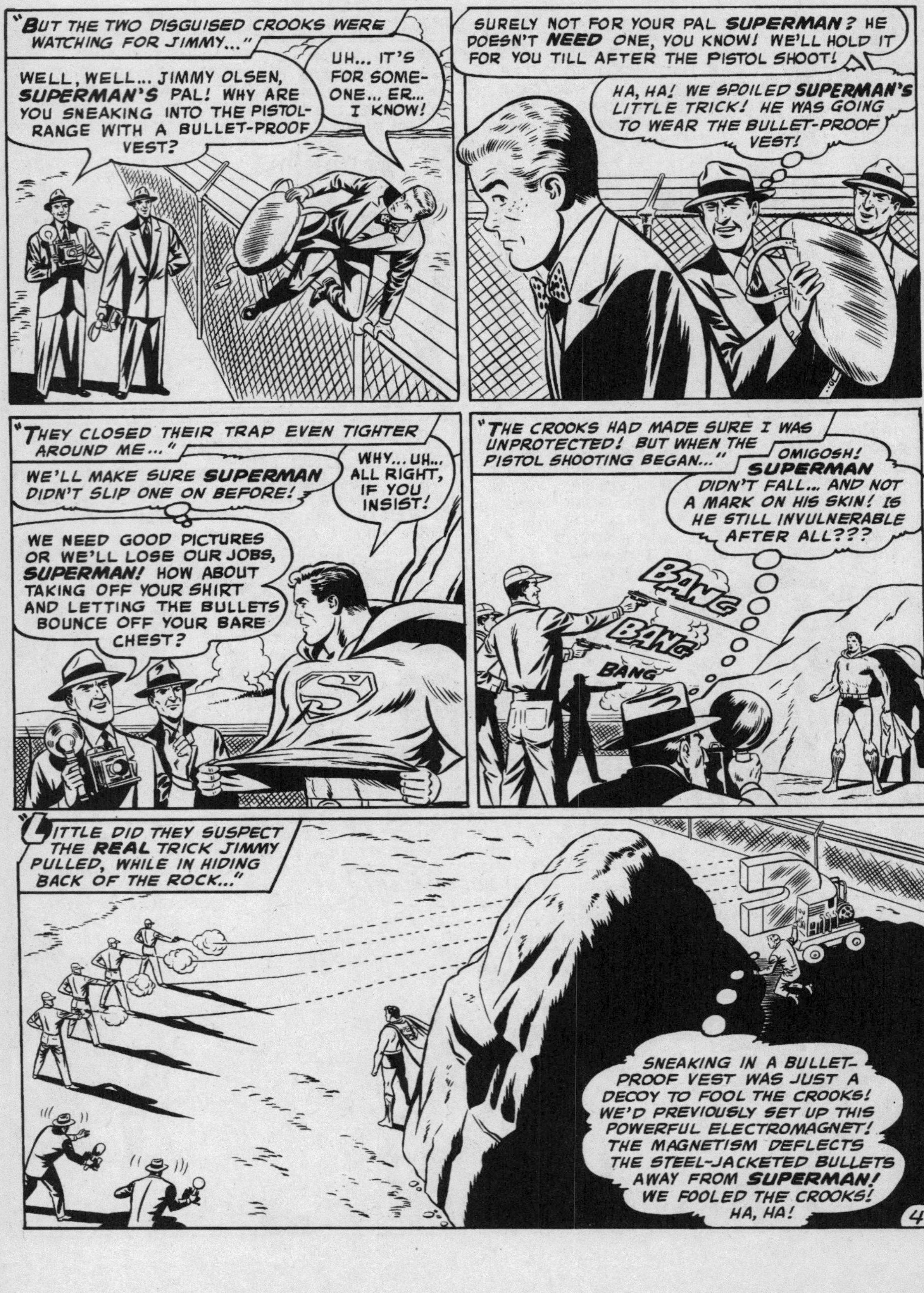
"BUT THE TWO DISGUISED CROOKS WERE WATCHING FOR JIMMY..."
WELL, WELL... JIMMY OLSEN, SUPERMAN'S PAL! WHY ARE YOU SNEAKING INTO THE PISTOL-RANGE WITH A BULLET-PROOF VEST?
UH... IT'S FOR SOME-ONE... ER... I KNOW!
SURELY NOT FOR YOUR PAL SUPERMAN? HE DOESN'T NEED ONE, YOU KNOW! WE'LL HOLD IT FOR YOU TILL AFTER THE PISTOL SHOOT!
HA, HA! WE SPOILED SUPERMAN'S LITTLE TRICK! HE WAS GOING TO WEAR THE BULLET-PROOF VEST!
"THEY CLOSED THEIR TRAP EVEN TIGHTER AROUND ME..."
WE'LL MAKE SURE SUPERMAN DIDN'T SLIP ONE ON BEFORE!
WHY... UH... ALL RIGHT, IF YOU INSIST!
WE NEED GOOD PICTURES OR WE'LL LOSE OUR JOBS, SUPERMAN! HOW ABOUT TAKING OFF YOUR SHIRT AND LETTING THE BULLETS BOUNCE OFF YOUR BARE CHEST?
"THE CROOKS HAD MADE SURE I WAS UNPROTECTED! BUT WHEN THE PISTOL SHOOTING BEGAN..."
OMIGOSH! SUPERMAN DIDN'T FALL... AND NOT A MARK ON HIS SKIN! IS HE STILL INVULNERABLE AFTER ALL???
BANG
BANG
BANG
"LITTLE DID THEY SUSPECT THE REAL TRICK JIMMY PULLED, WHILE IN HIDING BACK OF THE ROCK..."
SNEAKING IN A BULLET-PROOF VEST WAS JUST A DECOY TO FOOL THE CROOKS! WE'D PREVIOUSLY SET UP THIS POWERFUL ELECTROMAGNET! THE MAGNETISM DEFLECTS THE STEEL-JACKETED BULLETS AWAY FROM SUPERMAN! WE FOOLED THE CROOKS! HA, HA!
4

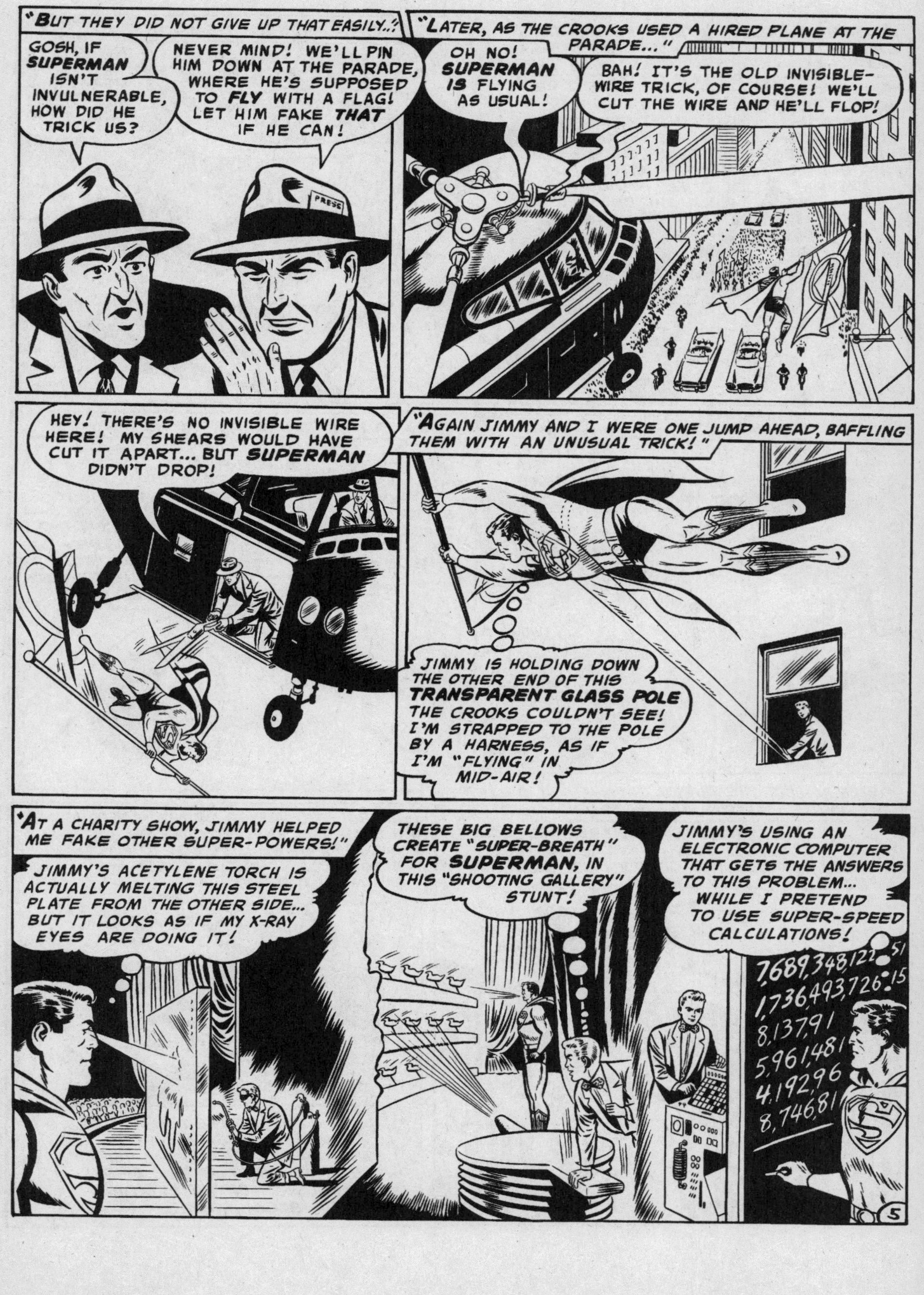
"BUT THEY DID NOT GIVE UP THAT EASILY..!
GOSH, IF SUPERMAN ISN'T INVULNERABLE, HOW DID HE TRICK US?
NEVER MIND! WE'LL PIN HIM DOWN AT THE PARADE, WHERE HE'S SUPPOSED TO FLY WITH A FLAG! LET HIM FAKE THAT IF HE CAN!
PRESS
"LATER, AS THE CROOKS USED A HIRED PLANE AT THE PARADE..."
OH NO! SUPERMAN IS FLYING AS USUAL!
BAH! IT'S THE OLD INVISIBLE-WIRE TRICK, OF COURSE! WE'LL CUT THE WIRE AND HE'LL FLOP!
HEY! THERE'S NO INVISIBLE WIRE HERE! MY SHEARS WOULD HAVE CUT IT APART... BUT SUPERMAN DIDN'T DROP!
"AGAIN JIMMY AND I WERE ONE JUMP AHEAD, BAFFLING THEM WITH AN UNUSUAL TRICK!"
JIMMY IS HOLDING DOWN THE OTHER END OF THIS TRANSPARENT GLASS POLE THE CROOKS COULDN'T SEE! I'M STRAPPED TO THE POLE BY A HARNESS, AS IF I'M "FLYING" IN MID-AIR!
"AT A CHARITY SHOW, JIMMY HELPED ME FAKE OTHER SUPER-POWERS!"
JIMMY'S ACETYLENE TORCH IS ACTUALLY MELTING THIS STEEL PLATE FROM THE OTHER SIDE... BUT IT LOOKS AS IF MY X-RAY EYES ARE DOING IT!
THESE BIG BELLOWS CREATE "SUPER-BREATH" FOR SUPERMAN, IN THIS "SHOOTING GALLERY" STUNT!
JIMMY'S USING AN ELECTRONIC COMPUTER THAT GETS THE ANSWERS TO THIS PROBLEM... WHILE I PRETEND TO USE SUPER-SPEED CALCULATIONS!
7,689,348,122 51
1,736,493,726 15
8,137,91
5,961,481
4,192,96
8,746,81
5

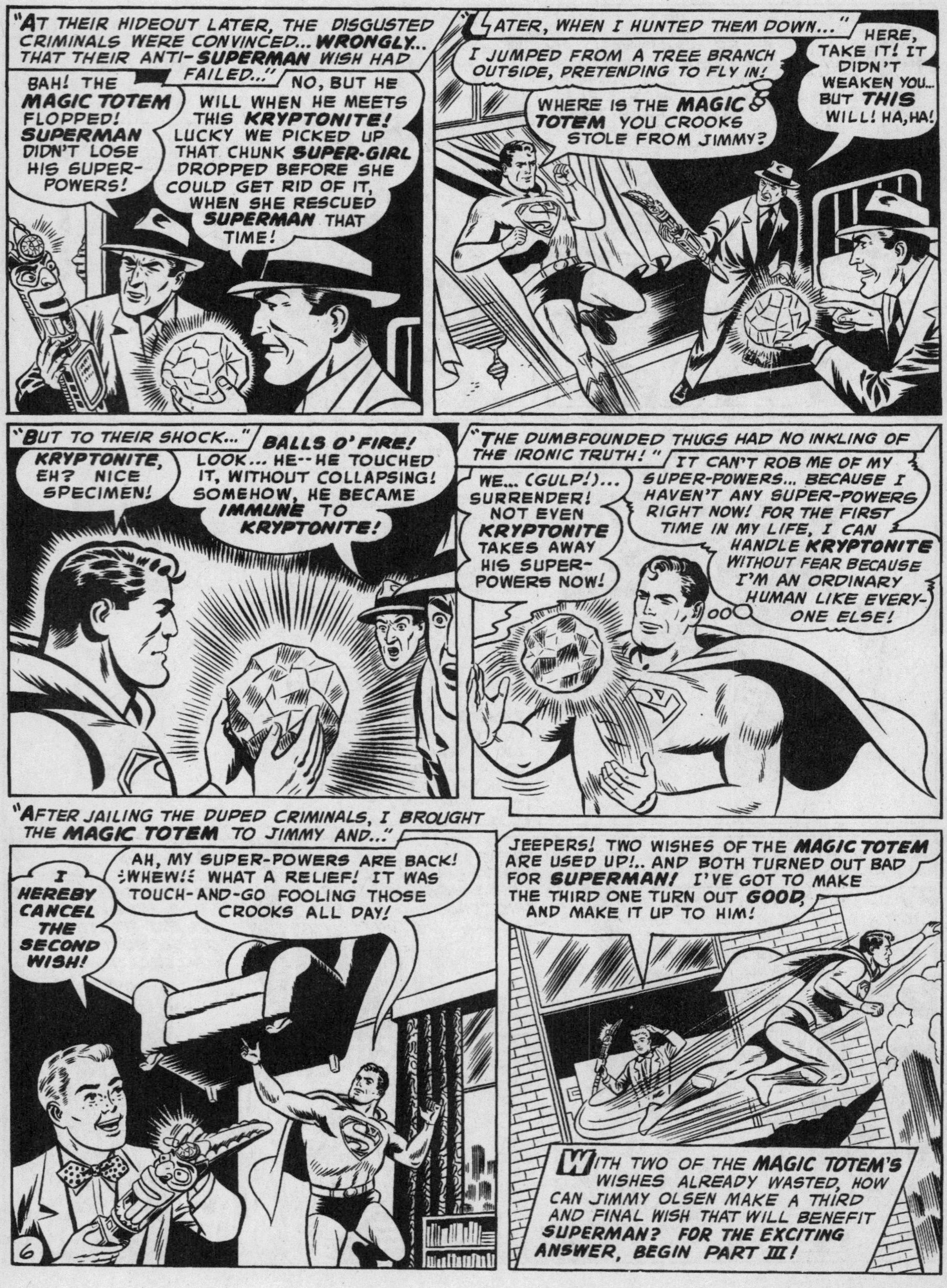
"AT THEIR HIDEOUT LATER, THE DISGUSTED CRIMINALS WERE CONVINCED... WRONGLY... THAT THEIR ANTI-SUPERMAN WISH HAD FAILED..."
BAH! THE MAGIC TOTEM FLOPPED! SUPERMAN DIDN'T LOSE HIS SUPER-POWERS!
NO, BUT HE WILL WHEN HE MEETS THIS KRYPTONITE! LUCKY WE PICKED UP THAT CHUNK SUPER-GIRL DROPPED BEFORE SHE COULD GET RID OF IT, WHEN SHE RESCUED SUPERMAN THAT TIME!
"LATER, WHEN I HUNTED THEM DOWN..."
I JUMPED FROM A TREE BRANCH OUTSIDE, PRETENDING TO FLY IN!
WHERE IS THE MAGIC TOTEM YOU CROOKS STOLE FROM JIMMY?
HERE, TAKE IT! IT DIDN'T WEAKEN YOU... BUT THIS WILL! HA, HA!
"BUT TO THEIR SHOCK..."
KRYPTONITE, EH? NICE SPECIMEN!
BALLS O' FIRE! LOOK... HE--HE TOUCHED IT, WITHOUT COLLAPSING! SOMEHOW, HE BECAME IMMUNE TO KRYPTONITE!
"THE DUMBFOUNDED THUGS HAD NO INKLING OF THE IRONIC TRUTH!"
WE... (GULP!)... SURRENDER! NOT EVEN KRYPTONITE TAKES AWAY HIS SUPER-POWERS NOW!
IT CAN'T ROB ME OF MY SUPER-POWERS... BECAUSE I HAVEN'T ANY SUPER-POWERS RIGHT NOW! FOR THE FIRST TIME IN MY LIFE, I CAN HANDLE KRYPTONITE WITHOUT FEAR BECAUSE I'M AN ORDINARY HUMAN LIKE EVERY-ONE ELSE!
"AFTER JAILING THE DUPED CRIMINALS, I BROUGHT THE MAGIC TOTEM TO JIMMY AND..."
I HEREBY CANCEL THE SECOND WISH!
AH, MY SUPER-POWERS ARE BACK! WHEW! WHAT A RELIEF! IT WAS TOUCH-AND-GO FOOLING THOSE CROOKS ALL DAY!
6
JEEPERS! TWO WISHES OF THE MAGIC TOTEM ARE USED UP!.. AND BOTH TURNED OUT BAD FOR SUPERMAN! I'VE GOT TO MAKE THE THIRD ONE TURN OUT GOOD, AND MAKE IT UP TO HIM!
WITH TWO OF THE MAGIC TOTEM'S WISHES ALREADY WASTED, HOW CAN JIMMY OLSEN MAKE A THIRD AND FINAL WISH THAT WILL BENEFIT SUPERMAN? FOR THE EXCITING ANSWER, BEGIN PART III!

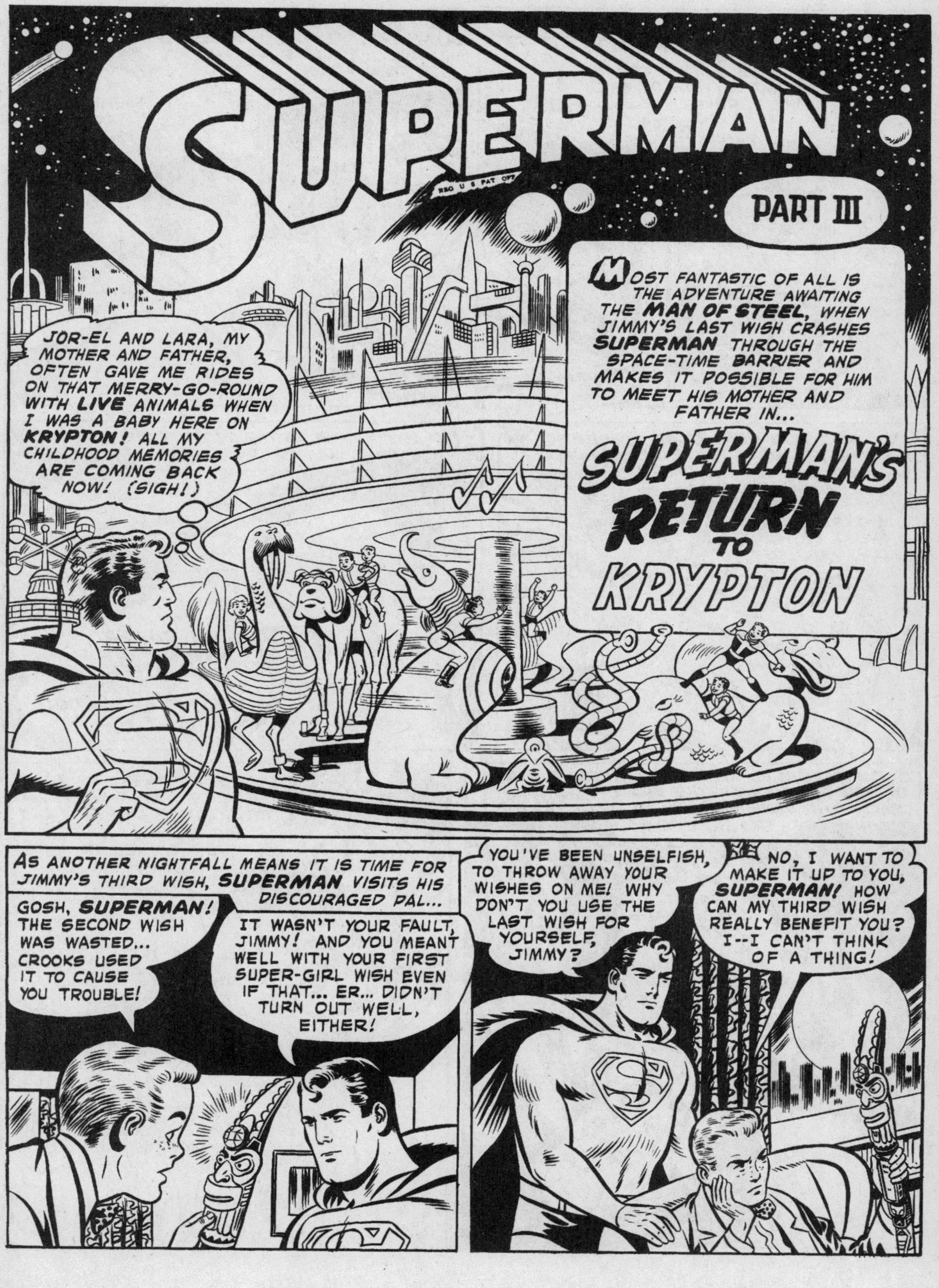
SUPERMAN
REG U S PAT OFF
PART III
MOST FANTASTIC OF ALL IS THE ADVENTURE AWAITING THE MAN OF STEEL, WHEN JIMMY'S LAST WISH CRASHES SUPERMAN THROUGH THE SPACE-TIME BARRIER AND MAKES IT POSSIBLE FOR HIM TO MEET HIS MOTHER AND FATHER IN...
SUPERMAN'S RETURN TO KRYPTON
JOR-EL AND LARA, MY MOTHER AND FATHER, OFTEN GAVE ME RIDES ON THAT MERRY-GO-ROUND WITH LIVE ANIMALS WHEN I WAS A BABY HERE ON KRYPTON! ALL MY CHILDHOOD MEMORIES ARE COMING BACK NOW! (SIGH!)
AS ANOTHER NIGHTFALL MEANS IT IS TIME FOR JIMMY'S THIRD WISH, SUPERMAN VISITS HIS DISCOURAGED PAL...
GOSH, SUPERMAN! THE SECOND WISH WAS WASTED... CROOKS USED IT TO CAUSE YOU TROUBLE!
IT WASN'T YOUR FAULT, JIMMY! AND YOU MEANT WELL WITH YOUR FIRST SUPER-GIRL WISH EVEN IF THAT... ER... DIDN'T TURN OUT WELL, EITHER!
YOU'VE BEEN UNSELFISH, TO THROW AWAY YOUR WISHES ON ME! WHY DON'T YOU USE THE LAST WISH FOR YOURSELF, JIMMY?
NO, I WANT TO MAKE IT UP TO YOU, SUPERMAN! HOW CAN MY THIRD WISH REALLY BENEFIT YOU? I--I CAN'T THINK OF A THING!

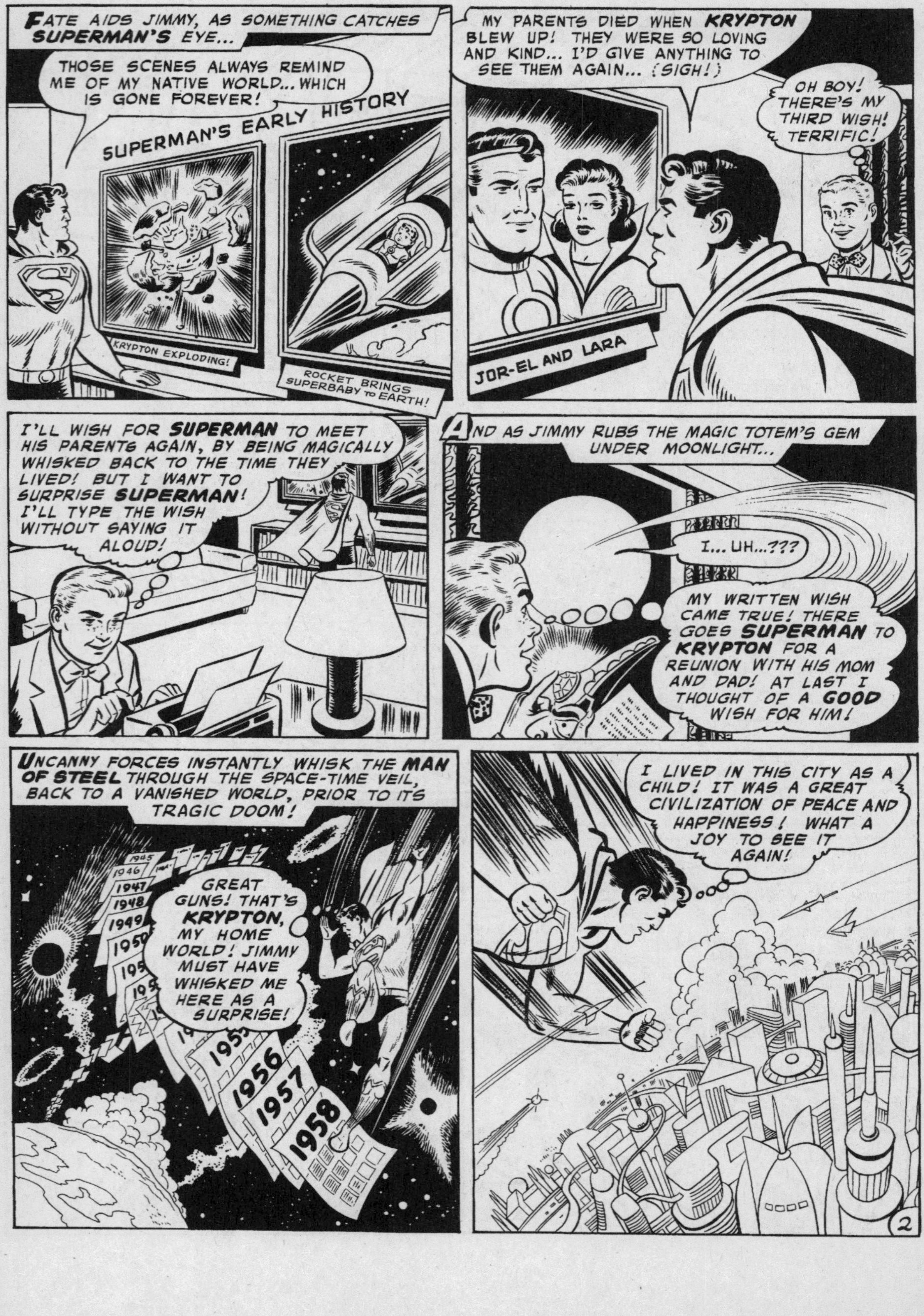
FATE AIDS JIMMY, AS SOMETHING CATCHES SUPERMAN'S EYE...
THOSE SCENES ALWAYS REMIND ME OF MY NATIVE WORLD... WHICH IS GONE FOREVER!
SUPERMAN'S EARLY HISTORY
KRYPTON EXPLODING!
ROCKET BRINGS SUPERBABY TO EARTH!
MY PARENTS DIED WHEN KRYPTON BLEW UP! THEY WERE SO LOVING AND KIND... I'D GIVE ANYTHING TO SEE THEM AGAIN... (SIGH!)
OH BOY! THERE'S MY THIRD WISH! TERRIFIC!
JOR-EL AND LARA
I'LL WISH FOR SUPERMAN TO MEET HIS PARENTS AGAIN, BY BEING MAGICALLY WHISKED BACK TO THE TIME THEY LIVED! BUT I WANT TO SURPRISE SUPERMAN! I'LL TYPE THE WISH WITHOUT SAYING IT ALOUD!
AND AS JIMMY RUBS THE MAGIC TOTEM'S GEM UNDER MOONLIGHT...
I... UH...???
MY WRITTEN WISH CAME TRUE! THERE GOES SUPERMAN TO KRYPTON FOR A REUNION WITH HIS MOM AND DAD! AT LAST I THOUGHT OF A GOOD WISH FOR HIM!
UNCANNY FORCES INSTANTLY WHISK THE MAN OF STEEL THROUGH THE SPACE-TIME VEIL, BACK TO A VANISHED WORLD, PRIOR TO IT'S TRAGIC DOOM!
1945
1946
1947
1948
1949
1950
1956
1957
1958
GREAT GUNS! THAT'S KRYPTON, MY HOME WORLD! JIMMY MUST HAVE WHISKED ME HERE AS A SURPRISE!
I LIVED IN THIS CITY AS A CHILD! IT WAS A GREAT CIVILIZATION OF PEACE AND HAPPINESS! WHAT A JOY TO SEE IT AGAIN!
2

An AWED **SUPERMAN** VIEWS ONCE MORE THE WONDERS AND GLORY OF HIS HOME PLANET!

I REMEMBER THE ZOO AND ITS AMAZING ANIMALS...LIKE THAT **FLAME BEAST!**

HMM...I RECENTLY OPENED THAT VERY **SAME** TIME-CAPSULE ON EARTH! IT MUST HAVE BEEN HURLED THROUGH SPACE WHEN **KRYPTON** BLEW UP!

WHEN RAGING WINDS STRIKE, THE TALLEST SKYSCRAPERS ARE CLEVERLY LOWERED INTO THE GROUND SO THEY WON'T BE BLOWN OVER!

BUT AFTER THE BRIEF STORM, **SUPERMAN** HURRIES EAGERLY TO A CERTAIN STREET...

NOW TO SEE MY PARENTS! THIS WAS OUR HOME...WAIT! HOW CAN **ANOTHER** FAMILY BE LIVING HERE INSTEAD? I--I DON'T UNDERSTAND!

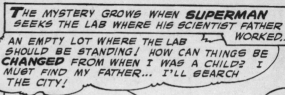

THE MYSTERY GROWS WHEN **SUPERMAN** SEEKS THE LAB WHERE HIS SCIENTIST FATHER WORKED...

AN EMPTY LOT WHERE THE LAB SHOULD BE STANDING! HOW CAN THINGS BE **CHANGED** FROM WHEN I WAS A CHILD? I MUST FIND MY FATHER...I'LL SEARCH THE CITY!

FINALLY...THERE'S MY FATHER, JOR-EL...BUT HE'S A **YOUNG MAN!** SO THAT'S IT! THIS IS THE TIME **BEFORE** HE BECAME A SCIENTIST AND BUILT HIS LAB!

HELLO, JOR-EL

BUT **SUPERMAN** HAS BEEN TOO EXCITED TO NOTICE SOMETHING BEFORE...

OMIGOSH! HE DOESN'T SEEM TO HEAR OR SEE ME...AND HE WALKED **THROUGH** ME! I--I'M ONLY LIKE A PHANTOM, BECAUSE I CAN'T REALLY EXIST HERE BEFORE I WAS BORN!

3

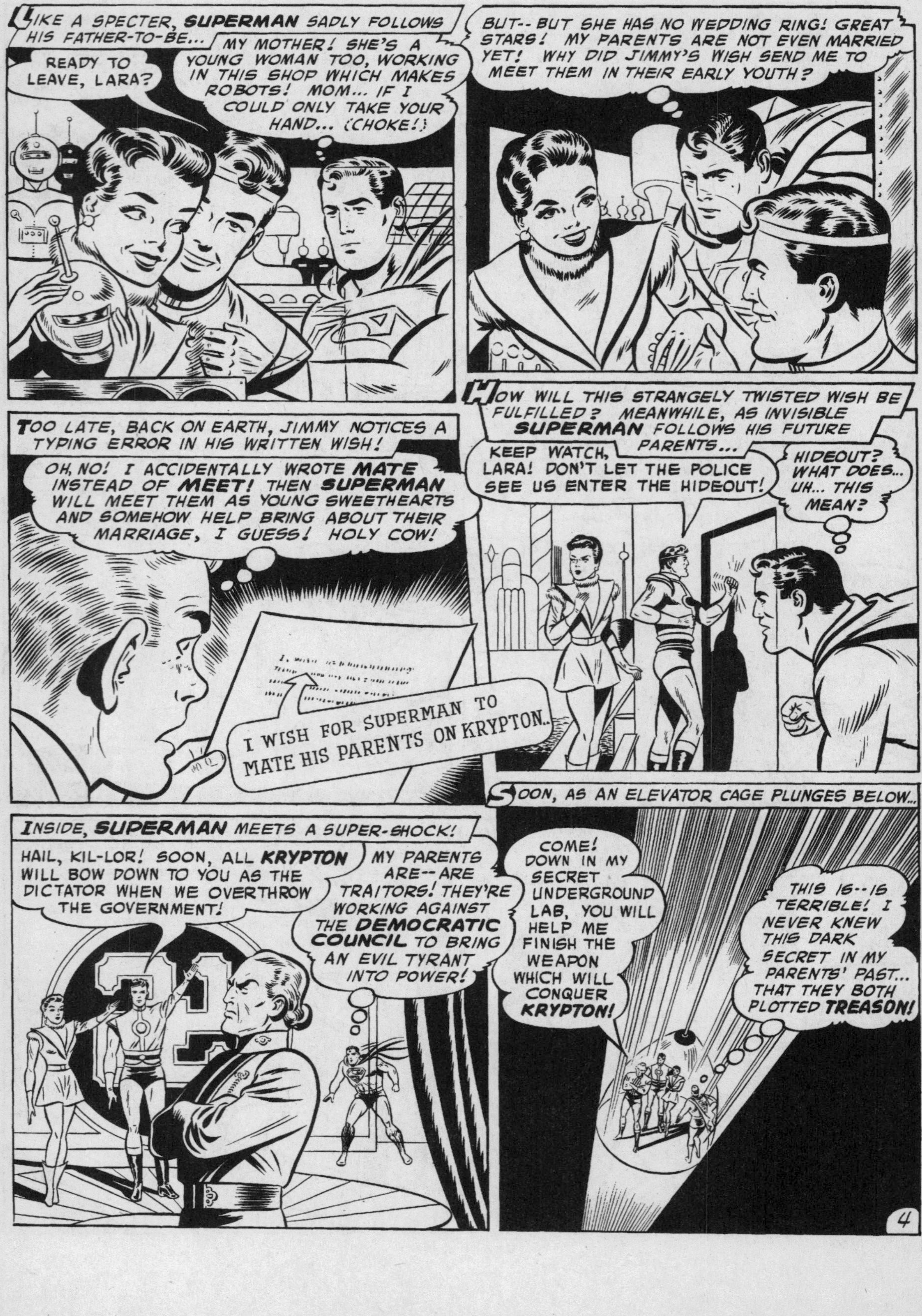
LIKE A SPECTER, SUPERMAN SADLY FOLLOWS HIS FATHER-TO-BE...
READY TO LEAVE, LARA?
MY MOTHER! SHE'S A YOUNG WOMAN TOO, WORKING IN THIS SHOP WHICH MAKES ROBOTS! MOM... IF I COULD ONLY TAKE YOUR HAND... (CHOKE!)
BUT-- BUT SHE HAS NO WEDDING RING! GREAT STARS! MY PARENTS ARE NOT EVEN MARRIED YET! WHY DID JIMMY'S WISH SEND ME TO MEET THEM IN THEIR EARLY YOUTH?
TOO LATE, BACK ON EARTH, JIMMY NOTICES A TYPING ERROR IN HIS WRITTEN WISH!
OH, NO! I ACCIDENTALLY WROTE MATE INSTEAD OF MEET! THEN SUPERMAN WILL MEET THEM AS YOUNG SWEETHEARTS AND SOMEHOW HELP BRING ABOUT THEIR MARRIAGE, I GUESS! HOLY COW!
I WISH FOR SUPERMAN TO MATE HIS PARENTS ON KRYPTON..
HOW WILL THIS STRANGELY TWISTED WISH BE FULFILLED? MEANWHILE, AS INVISIBLE SUPERMAN FOLLOWS HIS FUTURE PARENTS...
KEEP WATCH, LARA! DON'T LET THE POLICE SEE US ENTER THE HIDEOUT!
HIDEOUT? WHAT DOES... UH... THIS MEAN?
INSIDE, SUPERMAN MEETS A SUPER-SHOCK!
HAIL, KIL-LOR! SOON, ALL KRYPTON WILL BOW DOWN TO YOU AS THE DICTATOR WHEN WE OVERTHROW THE GOVERNMENT!
MY PARENTS ARE-- ARE TRAITORS! THEY'RE WORKING AGAINST THE DEMOCRATIC COUNCIL TO BRING AN EVIL TYRANT INTO POWER!
SOON, AS AN ELEVATOR CAGE PLUNGES BELOW...
COME! DOWN IN MY SECRET UNDERGROUND LAB, YOU WILL HELP ME FINISH THE WEAPON WHICH WILL CONQUER KRYPTON!
THIS IS-- IS TERRIBLE! I NEVER KNEW THIS DARK SECRET IN MY PARENTS' PAST... THAT THEY BOTH PLOTTED TREASON!
4

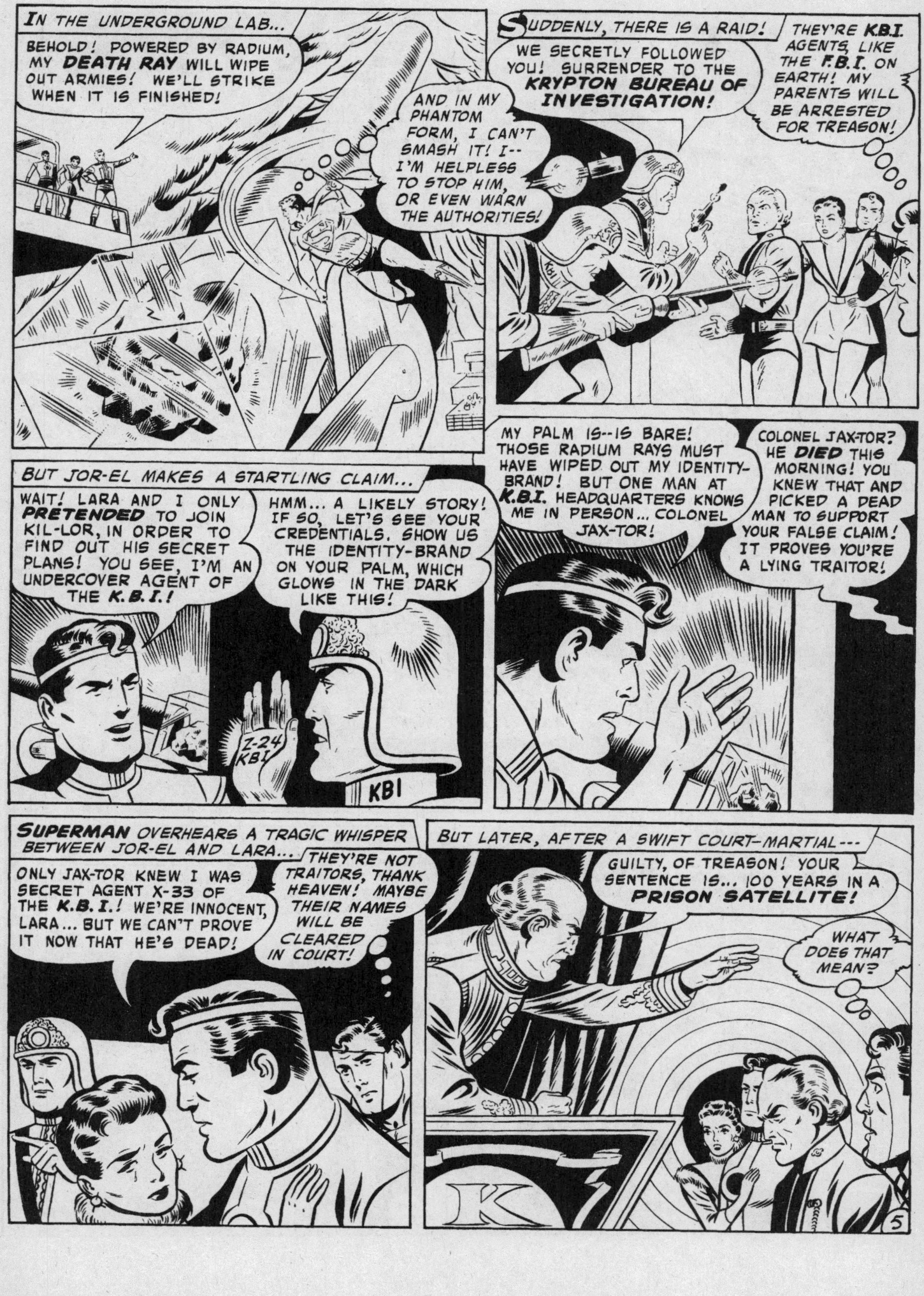
IN THE UNDERGROUND LAB...
BEHOLD! POWERED BY RADIUM, MY DEATH RAY WILL WIPE OUT ARMIES! WE'LL STRIKE WHEN IT IS FINISHED!
AND IN MY PHANTOM FORM, I CAN'T SMASH IT! I-- I'M HELPLESS TO STOP HIM, OR EVEN WARN THE AUTHORITIES!
SUDDENLY, THERE IS A RAID!
WE SECRETLY FOLLOWED YOU! SURRENDER TO THE KRYPTON BUREAU OF INVESTIGATION!
THEY'RE K.B.I. AGENTS, LIKE THE F.B.I. ON EARTH! MY PARENTS WILL BE ARRESTED FOR TREASON!
BUT JOR-EL MAKES A STARTLING CLAIM...
WAIT! LARA AND I ONLY PRETENDED TO JOIN KIL-LOR, IN ORDER TO FIND OUT HIS SECRET PLANS! YOU SEE, I'M AN UNDERCOVER AGENT OF THE K.B.I.!
HMM... A LIKELY STORY! IF SO, LET'S SEE YOUR CREDENTIALS. SHOW US THE IDENTITY-BRAND ON YOUR PALM, WHICH GLOWS IN THE DARK LIKE THIS!
Z-24 KBI
KBI
MY PALM IS--IS BARE! THOSE RADIUM RAYS MUST HAVE WIPED OUT MY IDENTITY-BRAND! BUT ONE MAN AT K.B.I. HEADQUARTERS KNOWS ME IN PERSON... COLONEL JAX-TOR!
COLONEL JAX-TOR? HE DIED THIS MORNING! YOU KNEW THAT AND PICKED A DEAD MAN TO SUPPORT YOUR FALSE CLAIM! IT PROVES YOU'RE A LYING TRAITOR!
SUPERMAN OVERHEARS A TRAGIC WHISPER BETWEEN JOR-EL AND LARA...
ONLY JAX-TOR KNEW I WAS SECRET AGENT X-33 OF THE K.B.I.! WE'RE INNOCENT, LARA... BUT WE CAN'T PROVE IT NOW THAT HE'S DEAD!
THEY'RE NOT TRAITORS, THANK HEAVEN! MAYBE THEIR NAMES WILL BE CLEARED IN COURT!
BUT LATER, AFTER A SWIFT COURT-MARTIAL---
GUILTY, OF TREASON! YOUR SENTENCE IS... 100 YEARS IN A PRISON SATELLITE!
WHAT DOES THAT MEAN?
K
5

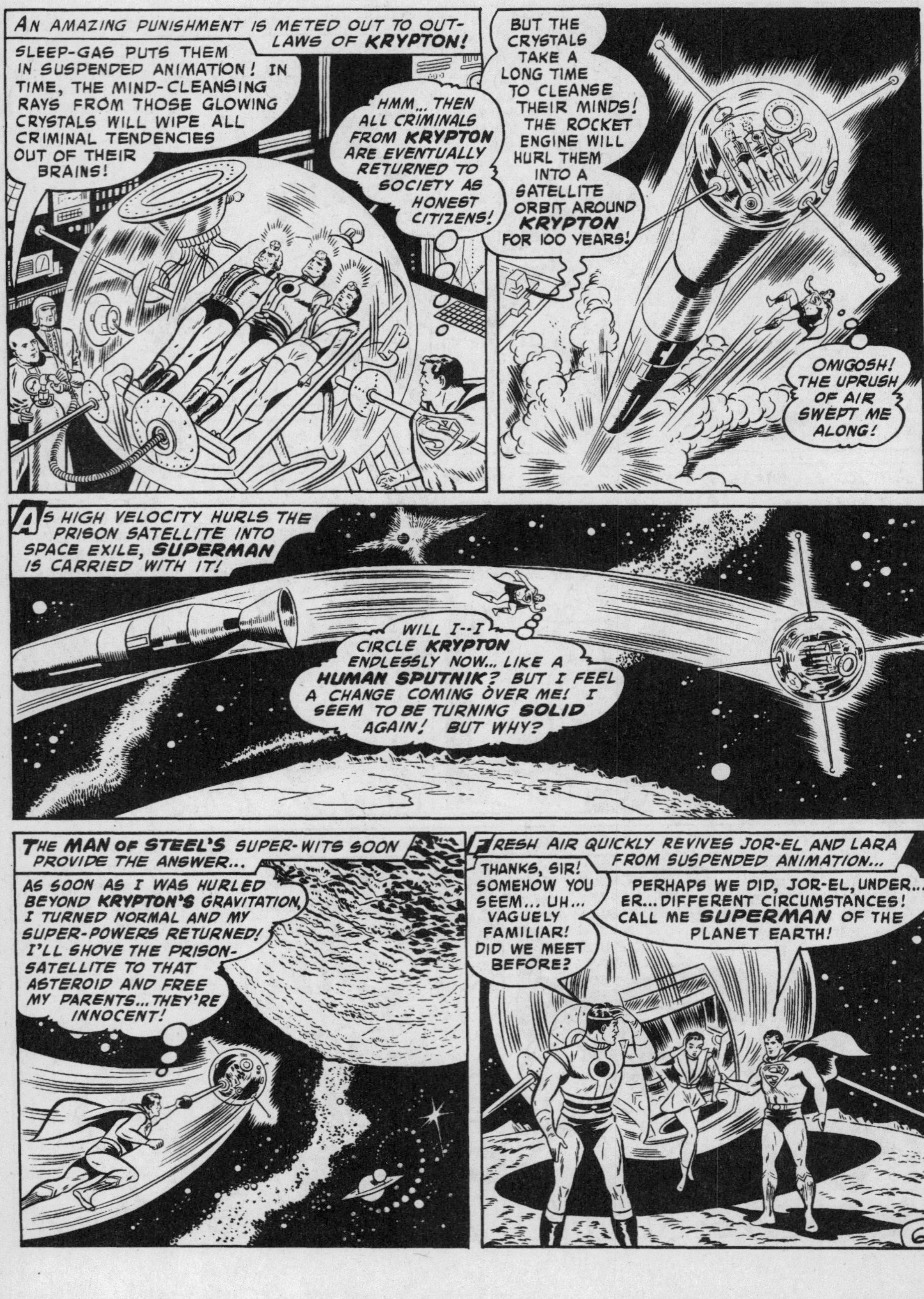
AN AMAZING PUNISHMENT IS METED OUT TO OUT-LAWS OF KRYPTON!
SLEEP-GAS PUTS THEM IN SUSPENDED ANIMATION! IN TIME, THE MIND-CLEANSING RAYS FROM THOSE GLOWING CRYSTALS WILL WIPE ALL CRIMINAL TENDENCIES OUT OF THEIR BRAINS!
HMM... THEN ALL CRIMINALS FROM KRYPTON ARE EVENTUALLY RETURNED TO SOCIETY AS HONEST CITIZENS!
BUT THE CRYSTALS TAKE A LONG TIME TO CLEANSE THEIR MINDS! THE ROCKET ENGINE WILL HURL THEM INTO A SATELLITE ORBIT AROUND KRYPTON FOR 100 YEARS!
OMIGOSH! THE UPRUSH OF AIR SWEPT ME ALONG!
AS HIGH VELOCITY HURLS THE PRISON SATELLITE INTO SPACE EXILE, SUPERMAN IS CARRIED WITH IT!
WILL I--I CIRCLE KRYPTON ENDLESSLY NOW... LIKE A HUMAN SPUTNIK? BUT I FEEL A CHANGE COMING OVER ME! I SEEM TO BE TURNING SOLID AGAIN! BUT WHY?
THE MAN OF STEEL'S SUPER-WITS SOON PROVIDE THE ANSWER...
AS SOON AS I WAS HURLED BEYOND KRYPTON'S GRAVITATION, I TURNED NORMAL AND MY SUPER-POWERS RETURNED! I'LL SHOVE THE PRISON-SATELLITE TO THAT ASTEROID AND FREE MY PARENTS... THEY'RE INNOCENT!
FRESH AIR QUICKLY REVIVES JOR-EL AND LARA FROM SUSPENDED ANIMATION...
THANKS, SIR! SOMEHOW YOU SEEM... UH... VAGUELY FAMILIAR! DID WE MEET BEFORE?
PERHAPS WE DID, JOR-EL, UNDER... ER... DIFFERENT CIRCUMSTANCES! CALL ME SUPERMAN OF THE PLANET EARTH!
6

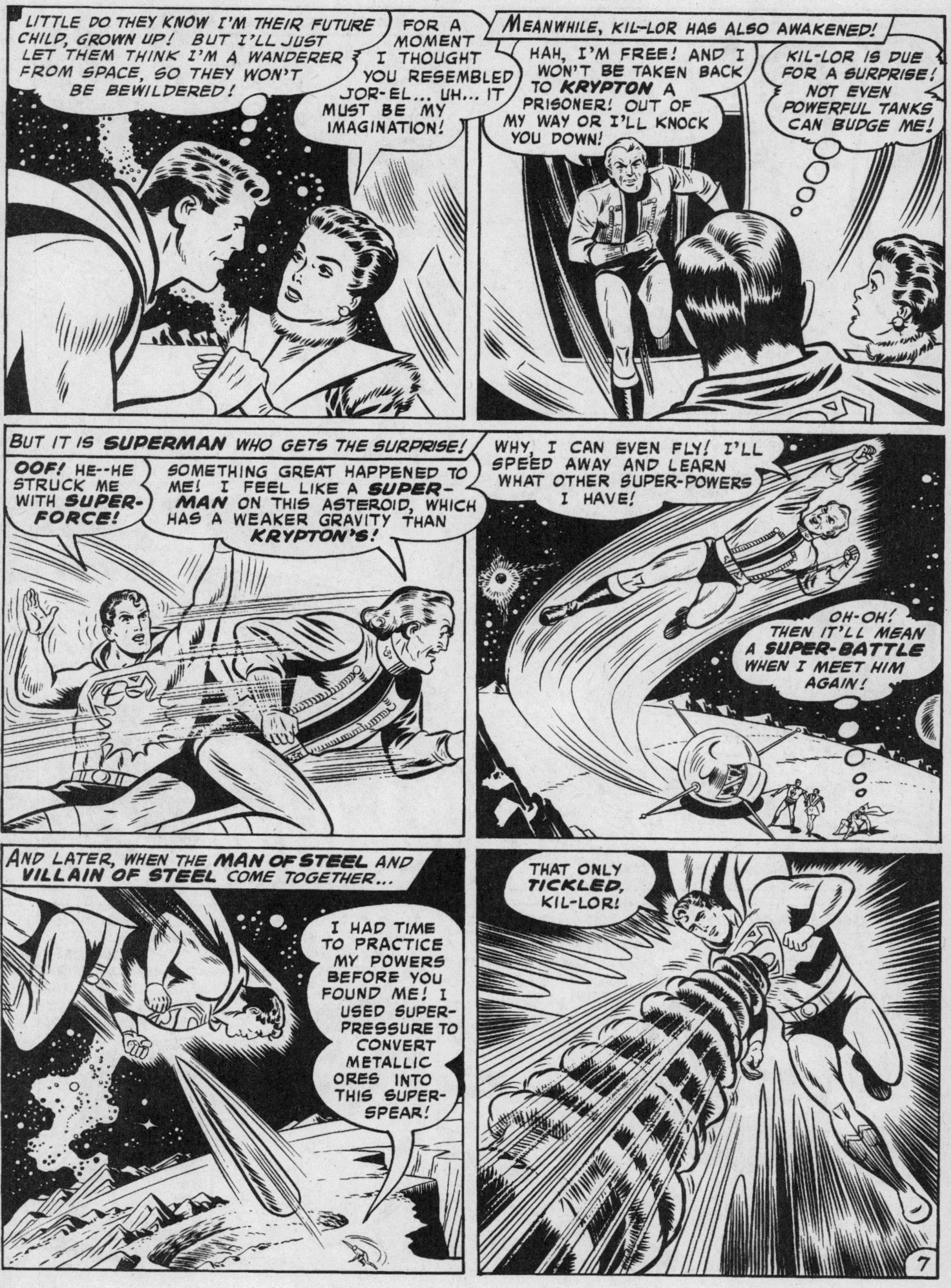
LITTLE DO THEY KNOW I'M THEIR FUTURE CHILD, GROWN UP! BUT I'LL JUST LET THEM THINK I'M A WANDERER FROM SPACE, SO THEY WON'T BE BEWILDERED!
FOR A MOMENT I THOUGHT YOU RESEMBLED JOR-EL... UH... IT MUST BE MY IMAGINATION!
MEANWHILE, KIL-LOR HAS ALSO AWAKENED!
HAH, I'M FREE! AND I WON'T BE TAKEN BACK TO KRYPTON A PRISONER! OUT OF MY WAY OR I'LL KNOCK YOU DOWN!
KIL-LOR IS DUE FOR A SURPRISE! NOT EVEN POWERFUL TANKS CAN BUDGE ME!
BUT IT IS SUPERMAN WHO GETS THE SURPRISE!
OOF! HE--HE STRUCK ME WITH SUPER-FORCE!
SOMETHING GREAT HAPPENED TO ME! I FEEL LIKE A SUPER-MAN ON THIS ASTEROID, WHICH HAS A WEAKER GRAVITY THAN KRYPTON'S!
WHY, I CAN EVEN FLY! I'LL SPEED AWAY AND LEARN WHAT OTHER SUPER-POWERS I HAVE!
OH-OH! THEN IT'LL MEAN A SUPER-BATTLE WHEN I MEET HIM AGAIN!
AND LATER, WHEN THE MAN OF STEEL AND VILLAIN OF STEEL COME TOGETHER...
I HAD TIME TO PRACTICE MY POWERS BEFORE YOU FOUND ME! I USED SUPER-PRESSURE TO CONVERT METALLIC ORES INTO THIS SUPER-SPEAR!
THAT ONLY TICKLED, KIL-LOR!
7

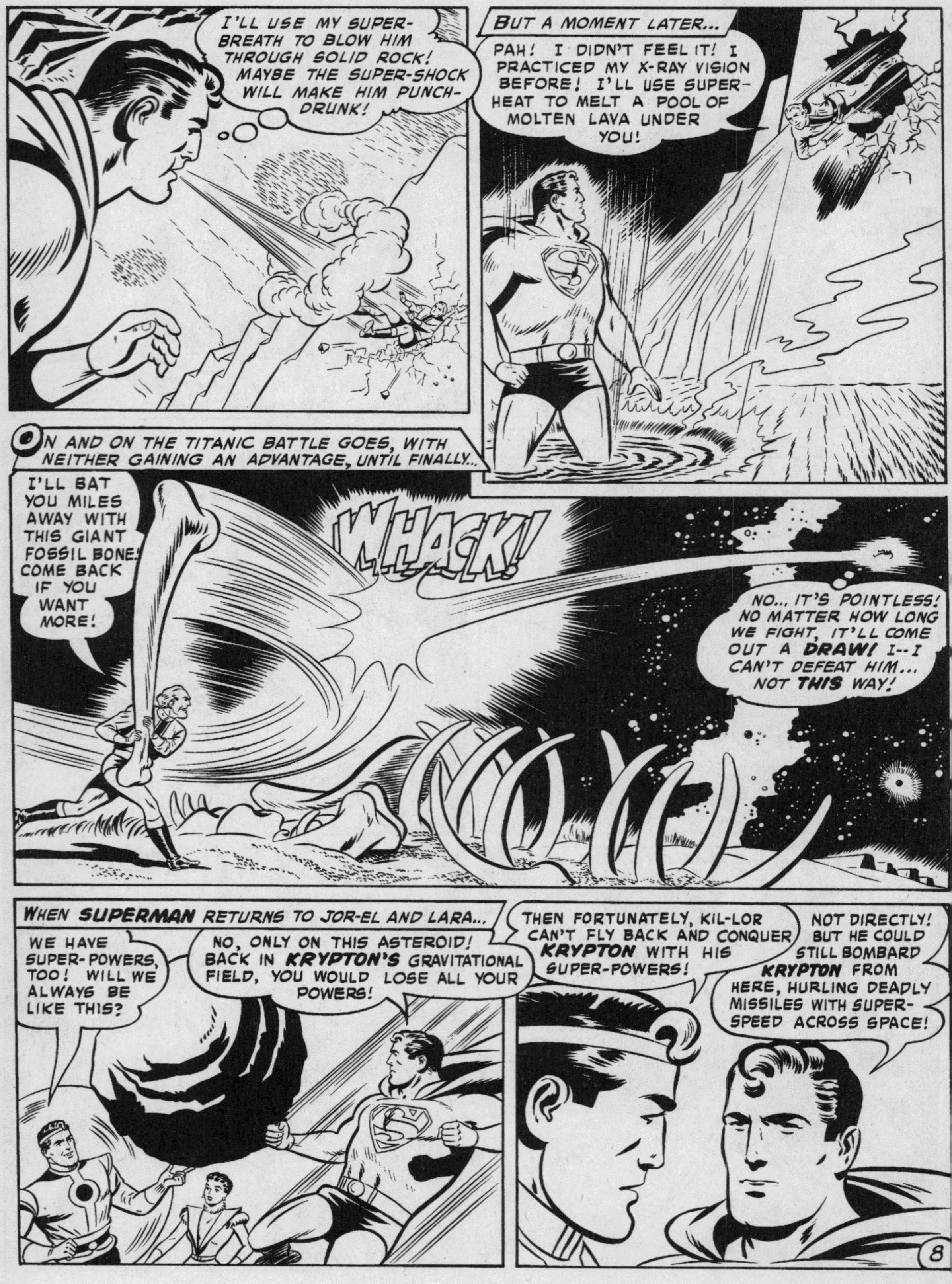
I'LL USE MY SUPER-BREATH TO BLOW HIM THROUGH SOLID ROCK! MAYBE THE SUPER-SHOCK WILL MAKE HIM PUNCH-DRUNK!
BUT A MOMENT LATER...
PAH! I DIDN'T FEEL IT! I PRACTICED MY X-RAY VISION BEFORE! I'LL USE SUPER-HEAT TO MELT A POOL OF MOLTEN LAVA UNDER YOU!
ON AND ON THE TITANIC BATTLE GOES, WITH NEITHER GAINING AN ADVANTAGE, UNTIL FINALLY...
I'LL BAT YOU MILES AWAY WITH THIS GIANT FOSSIL BONE! COME BACK IF YOU WANT MORE!
WHACK!
NO... IT'S POINTLESS! NO MATTER HOW LONG WE FIGHT, IT'LL COME OUT A DRAW! I--I CAN'T DEFEAT HIM... NOT THIS WAY!
WHEN SUPERMAN RETURNS TO JOR-EL AND LARA...
WE HAVE SUPER-POWERS, TOO! WILL WE ALWAYS BE LIKE THIS?
NO, ONLY ON THIS ASTEROID! BACK IN KRYPTON'S GRAVITATIONAL FIELD, YOU WOULD LOSE ALL YOUR POWERS!
THEN FORTUNATELY, KIL-LOR CAN'T FLY BACK AND CONQUER KRYPTON WITH HIS SUPER-POWERS!
NOT DIRECTLY! BUT HE COULD STILL BOMBARD KRYPTON FROM HERE, HURLING DEADLY MISSILES WITH SUPER-SPEED ACROSS SPACE!
8

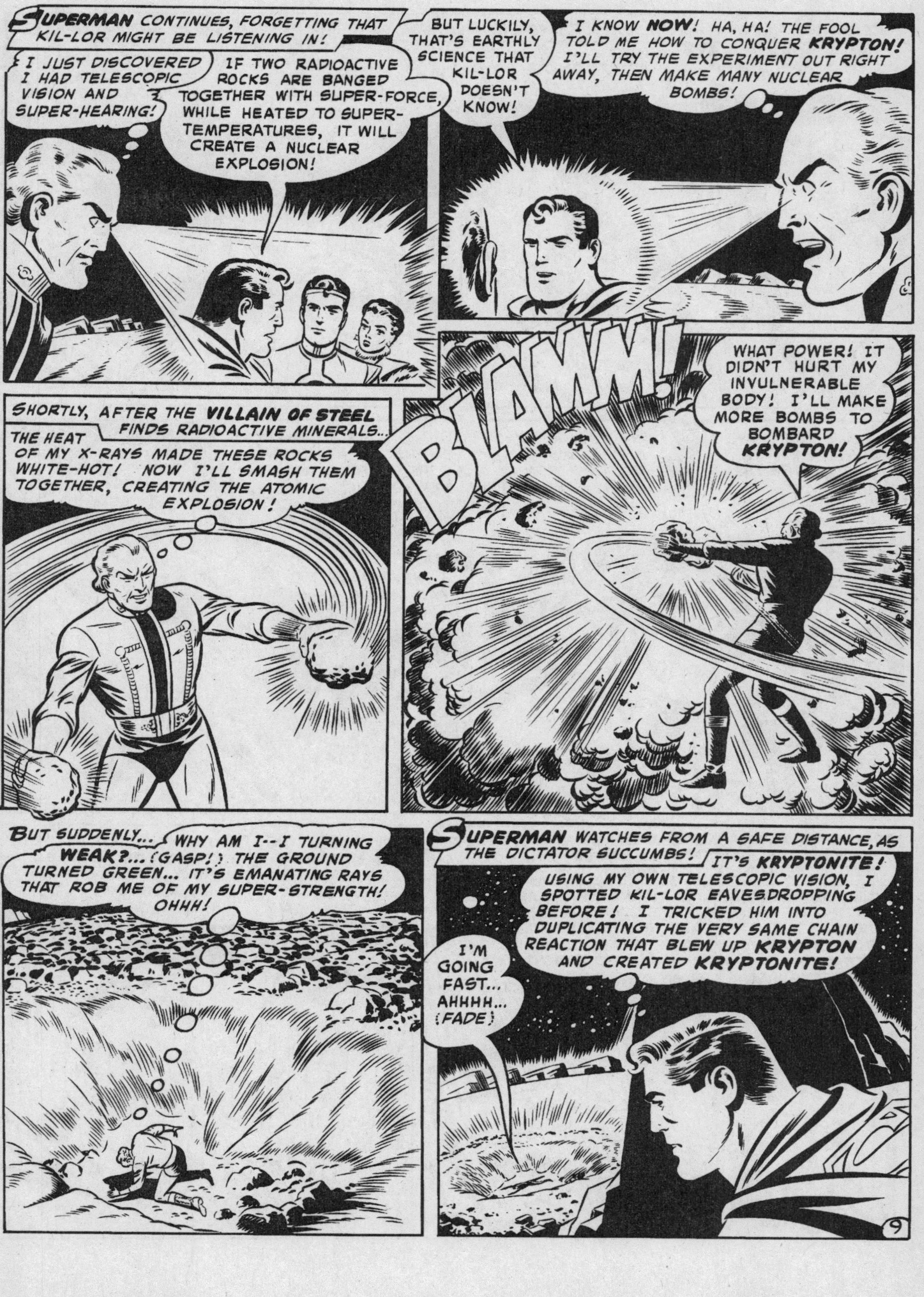
SUPERMAN CONTINUES, FORGETTING THAT KIL-LOR MIGHT BE LISTENING IN!
I JUST DISCOVERED I HAD TELESCOPIC VISION AND SUPER-HEARING!
IF TWO RADIOACTIVE ROCKS ARE BANGED TOGETHER WITH SUPER-FORCE, WHILE HEATED TO SUPER-TEMPERATURES, IT WILL CREATE A NUCLEAR EXPLOSION!
BUT LUCKILY, THAT'S EARTHLY SCIENCE THAT KIL-LOR DOESN'T KNOW!
I KNOW NOW! HA, HA! THE FOOL TOLD ME HOW TO CONQUER KRYPTON! I'LL TRY THE EXPERIMENT OUT RIGHT AWAY, THEN MAKE MANY NUCLEAR BOMBS!
SHORTLY, AFTER THE VILLAIN OF STEEL FINDS RADIOACTIVE MINERALS...
THE HEAT OF MY X-RAYS MADE THESE ROCKS WHITE-HOT! NOW I'LL SMASH THEM TOGETHER, CREATING THE ATOMIC EXPLOSION!
BLAMM!
WHAT POWER! IT DIDN'T HURT MY INVULNERABLE BODY! I'LL MAKE MORE BOMBS TO BOMBARD KRYPTON!
BUT SUDDENLY...
WHY AM I--I TURNING WEAK?... (GASP!) THE GROUND TURNED GREEN... IT'S EMANATING RAYS THAT ROB ME OF MY SUPER-STRENGTH! OHHH!
SUPERMAN WATCHES FROM A SAFE DISTANCE, AS THE DICTATOR SUCCUMBS!
IT'S KRYPTONITE! USING MY OWN TELESCOPIC VISION, I SPOTTED KIL-LOR EAVESDROPPING BEFORE! I TRICKED HIM INTO DUPLICATING THE VERY SAME CHAIN REACTION THAT BLEW UP KRYPTON AND CREATED KRYPTONITE!
I'M GOING FAST... AHHHH... (FADE)
9

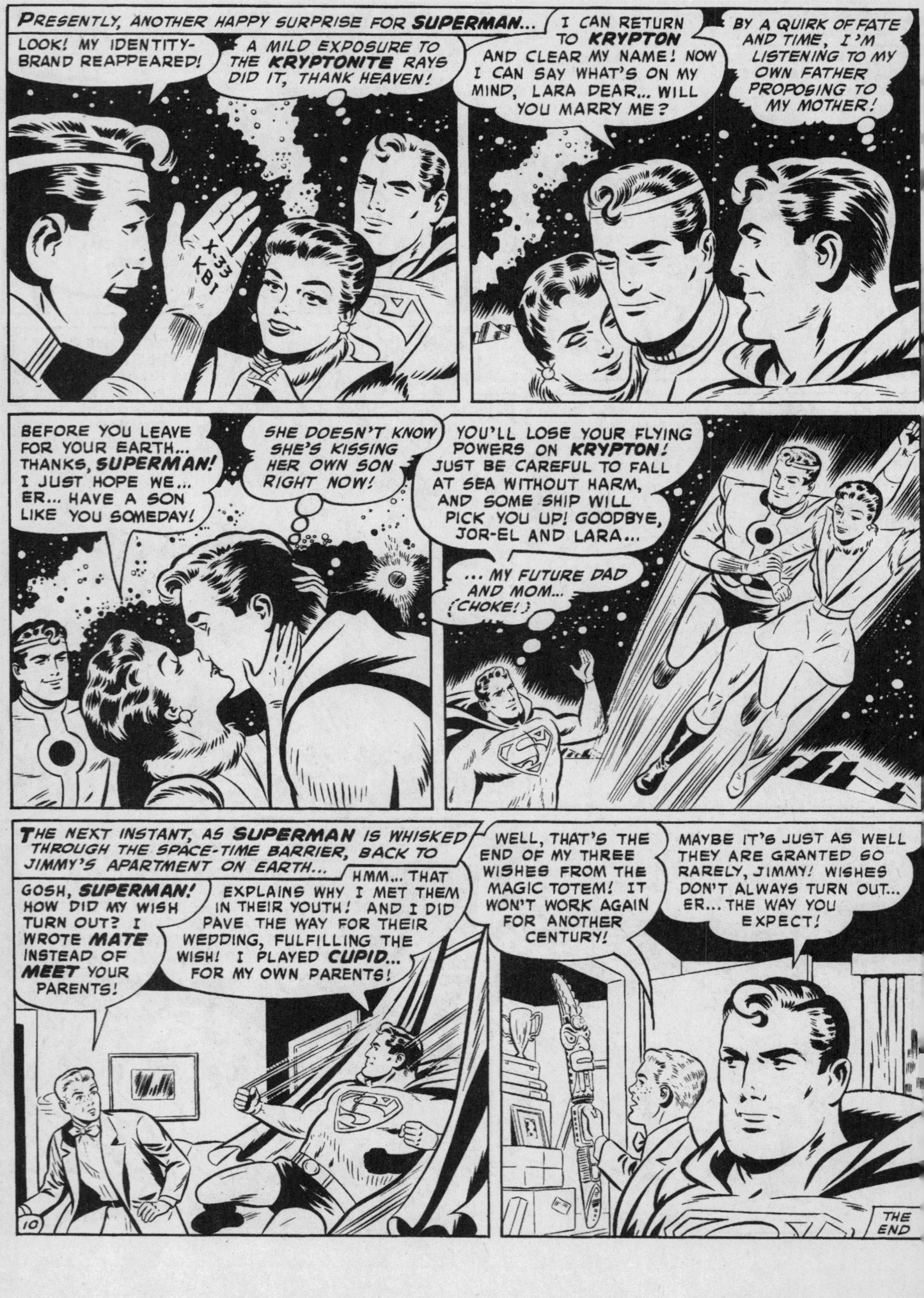
PRESENTLY, ANOTHER HAPPY SURPRISE FOR SUPERMAN...
LOOK! MY IDENTITY-BRAND REAPPEARED!
A MILD EXPOSURE TO THE KRYPTONITE RAYS DID IT, THANK HEAVEN!
X-33 KB1
I CAN RETURN TO KRYPTON AND CLEAR MY NAME! NOW I CAN SAY WHAT'S ON MY MIND, LARA DEAR... WILL YOU MARRY ME?
BY A QUIRK OF FATE AND TIME, I'M LISTENING TO MY OWN FATHER PROPOSING TO MY MOTHER!
BEFORE YOU LEAVE FOR YOUR EARTH... THANKS, SUPERMAN! I JUST HOPE WE... ER... HAVE A SON LIKE YOU SOMEDAY!
SHE DOESN'T KNOW SHE'S KISSING HER OWN SON RIGHT NOW!
YOU'LL LOSE YOUR FLYING POWERS ON KRYPTON! JUST BE CAREFUL TO FALL AT SEA WITHOUT HARM, AND SOME SHIP WILL PICK YOU UP! GOODBYE, JOR-EL AND LARA...
... MY FUTURE DAD AND MOM... (CHOKE!)
THE NEXT INSTANT, AS SUPERMAN IS WHISKED THROUGH THE SPACE-TIME BARRIER, BACK TO JIMMY'S APARTMENT ON EARTH...
GOSH, SUPERMAN! HOW DID MY WISH TURN OUT? I WROTE MATE INSTEAD OF MEET YOUR PARENTS!
HMM... THAT EXPLAINS WHY I MET THEM IN THEIR YOUTH! AND I DID PAVE THE WAY FOR THEIR WEDDING, FULFILLING THE WISH! I PLAYED CUPID... FOR MY OWN PARENTS!
10
WELL, THAT'S THE END OF MY THREE WISHES FROM THE MAGIC TOTEM! IT WON'T WORK AGAIN FOR ANOTHER CENTURY!
MAYBE IT'S JUST AS WELL THEY ARE GRANTED SO RARELY, JIMMY! WISHES DON'T ALWAYS TURN OUT... ER... THE WAY YOU EXPECT!
THE END

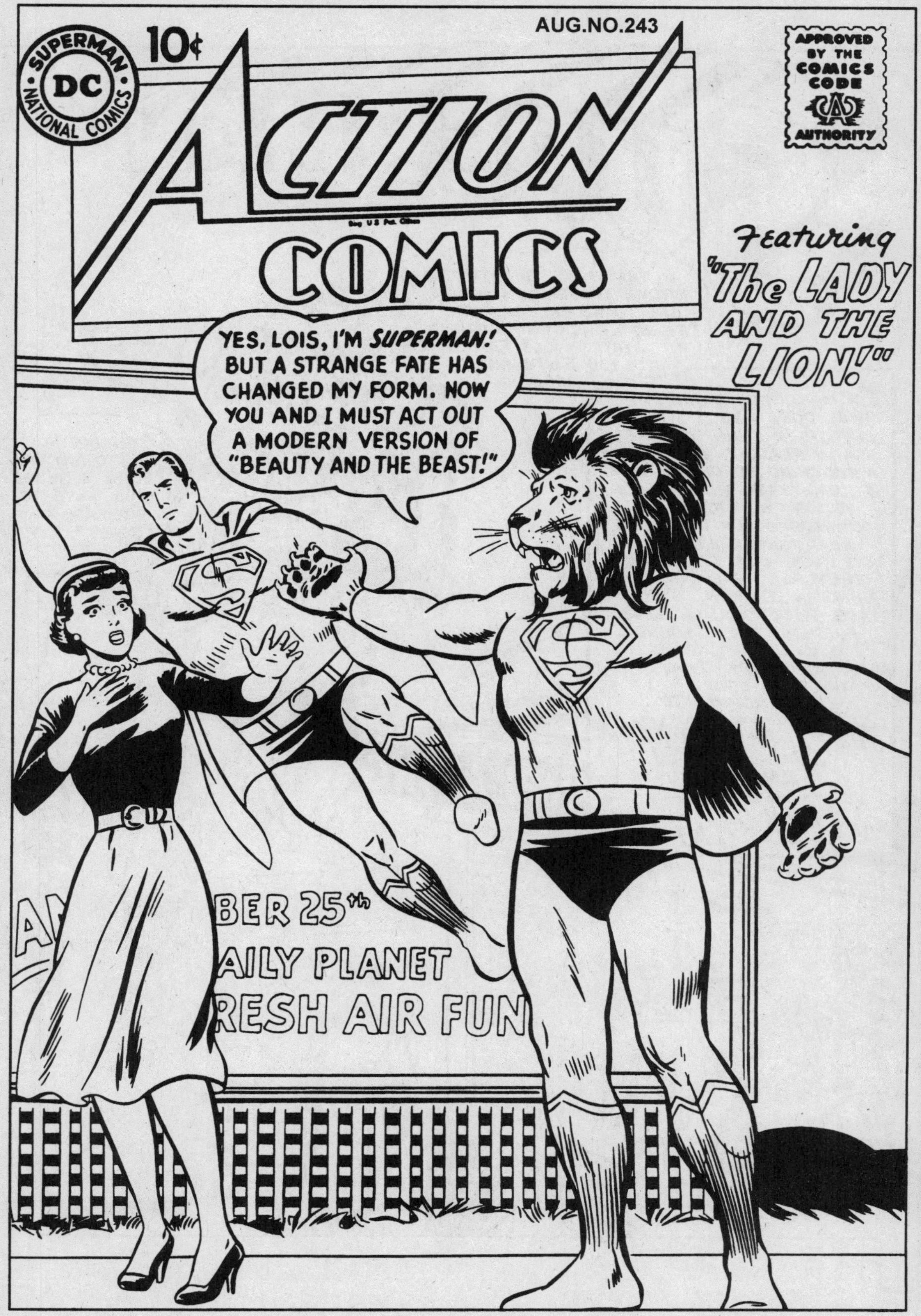
SUPERMAN
DC
NATIONAL COMICS
10¢
AUG. NO. 243
APPROVED BY THE COMICS CODE AUTHORITY
ACTION COMICS
Featuring "The LADY AND THE LION!"
YES, LOIS, I'M SUPERMAN! BUT A STRANGE FATE HAS CHANGED MY FORM. NOW YOU AND I MUST ACT OUT A MODERN VERSION OF "BEAUTY AND THE BEAST!"
BER 25th
AILY PLANET
RESH AIR FUN

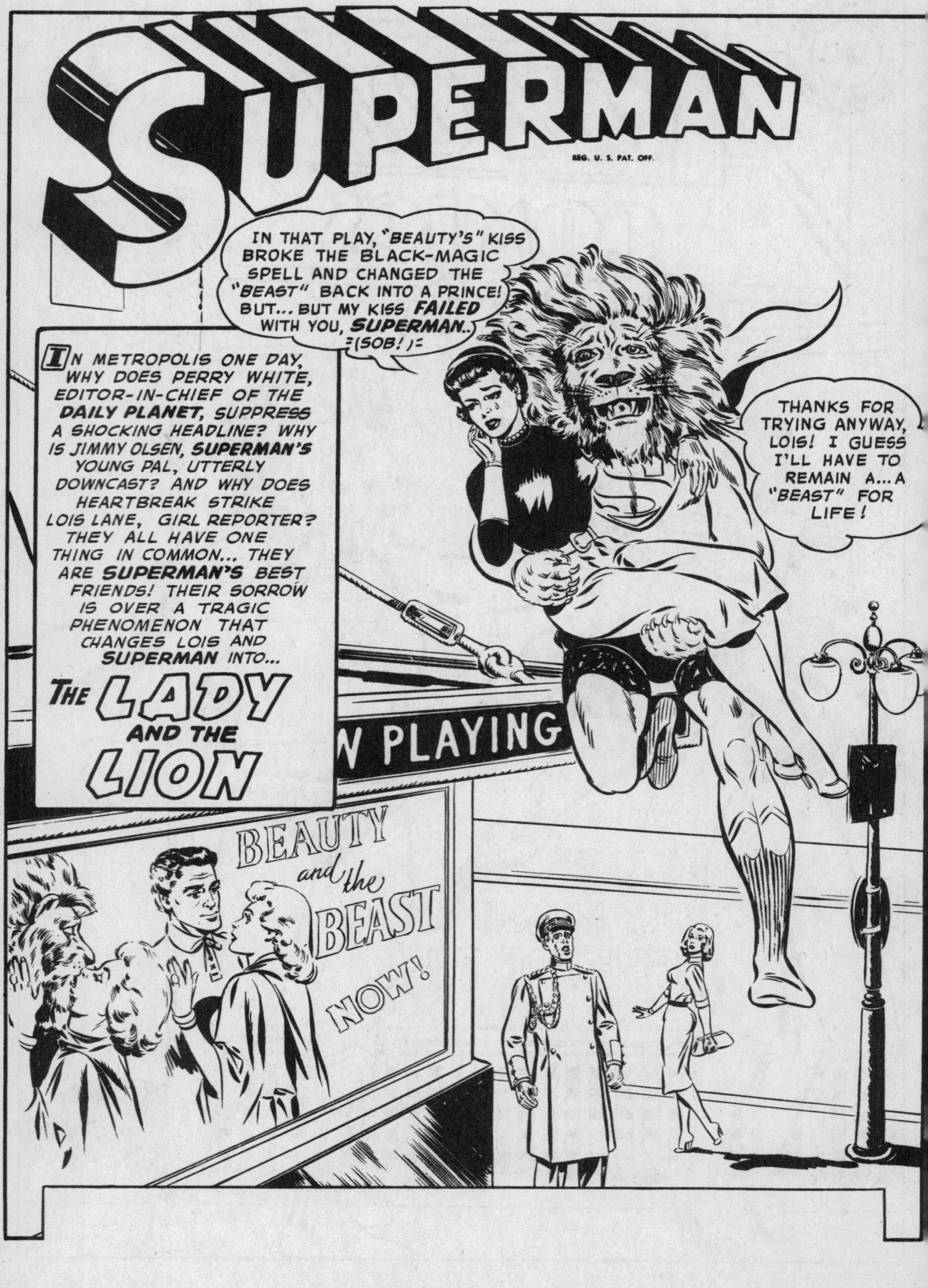
SUPERMAN
REG. U. S. PAT. OFF.
IN THAT PLAY, "BEAUTY'S" KISS BROKE THE BLACK-MAGIC SPELL AND CHANGED THE "BEAST" BACK INTO A PRINCE! BUT... BUT MY KISS FAILED WITH YOU, SUPERMAN.. -(SOB!)-
THANKS FOR TRYING ANYWAY, LOIS! I GUESS I'LL HAVE TO REMAIN A...A "BEAST" FOR LIFE!
IN METROPOLIS ONE DAY, WHY DOES PERRY WHITE, EDITOR-IN-CHIEF OF THE DAILY PLANET, SUPPRESS A SHOCKING HEADLINE? WHY IS JIMMY OLSEN, SUPERMAN'S YOUNG PAL, UTTERLY DOWNCAST? AND WHY DOES HEARTBREAK STRIKE LOIS LANE, GIRL REPORTER? THEY ALL HAVE ONE THING IN COMMON... THEY ARE SUPERMAN'S BEST FRIENDS! THEIR SORROW IS OVER A TRAGIC PHENOMENON THAT CHANGES LOIS AND SUPERMAN INTO...
THE LADY AND THE LION
W PLAYING
BEAUTY and the BEAST
NOW!

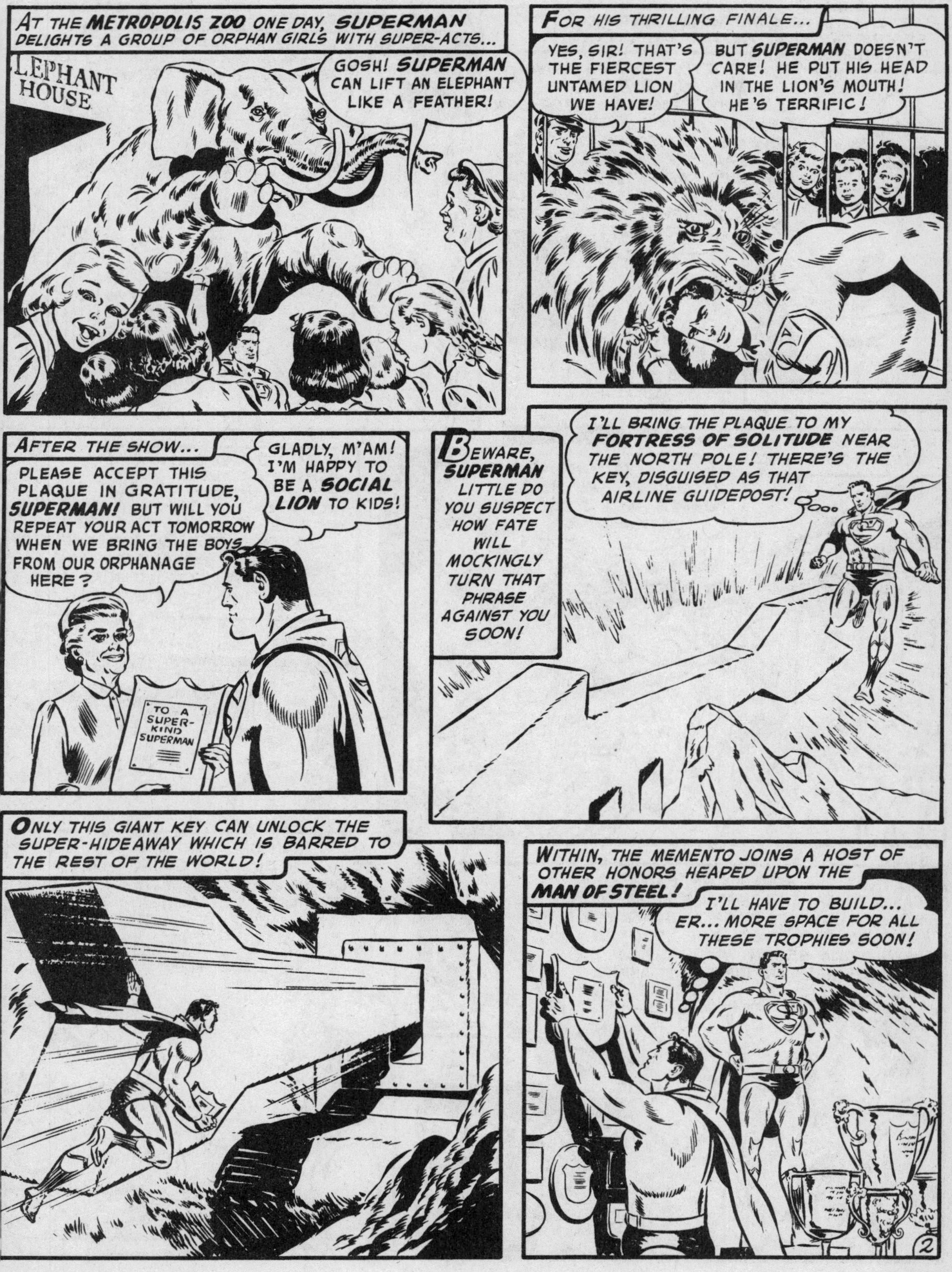
AT THE METROPOLIS ZOO ONE DAY, SUPERMAN DELIGHTS A GROUP OF ORPHAN GIRLS WITH SUPER-ACTS...
LEPHANT HOUSE
GOSH! SUPERMAN CAN LIFT AN ELEPHANT LIKE A FEATHER!
FOR HIS THRILLING FINALE...
YES, SIR! THAT'S THE FIERCEST UNTAMED LION WE HAVE!
BUT SUPERMAN DOESN'T CARE! HE PUT HIS HEAD IN THE LION'S MOUTH! HE'S TERRIFIC!
AFTER THE SHOW...
PLEASE ACCEPT THIS PLAQUE IN GRATITUDE, SUPERMAN! BUT WILL YOU REPEAT YOUR ACT TOMORROW WHEN WE BRING THE BOYS FROM OUR ORPHANAGE HERE?
GLADLY, M'AM! I'M HAPPY TO BE A SOCIAL LION TO KIDS!
TO A SUPER-KIND SUPERMAN
BEWARE, SUPERMAN LITTLE DO YOU SUSPECT HOW FATE WILL MOCKINGLY TURN THAT PHRASE AGAINST YOU SOON!
I'LL BRING THE PLAQUE TO MY FORTRESS OF SOLITUDE NEAR THE NORTH POLE! THERE'S THE KEY, DISGUISED AS THAT AIRLINE GUIDEPOST!
ONLY THIS GIANT KEY CAN UNLOCK THE SUPER-HIDEAWAY WHICH IS BARRED TO THE REST OF THE WORLD!
WITHIN, THE MEMENTO JOINS A HOST OF OTHER HONORS HEAPED UPON THE MAN OF STEEL!
I'LL HAVE TO BUILD... ER... MORE SPACE FOR ALL THESE TROPHIES SOON!
2

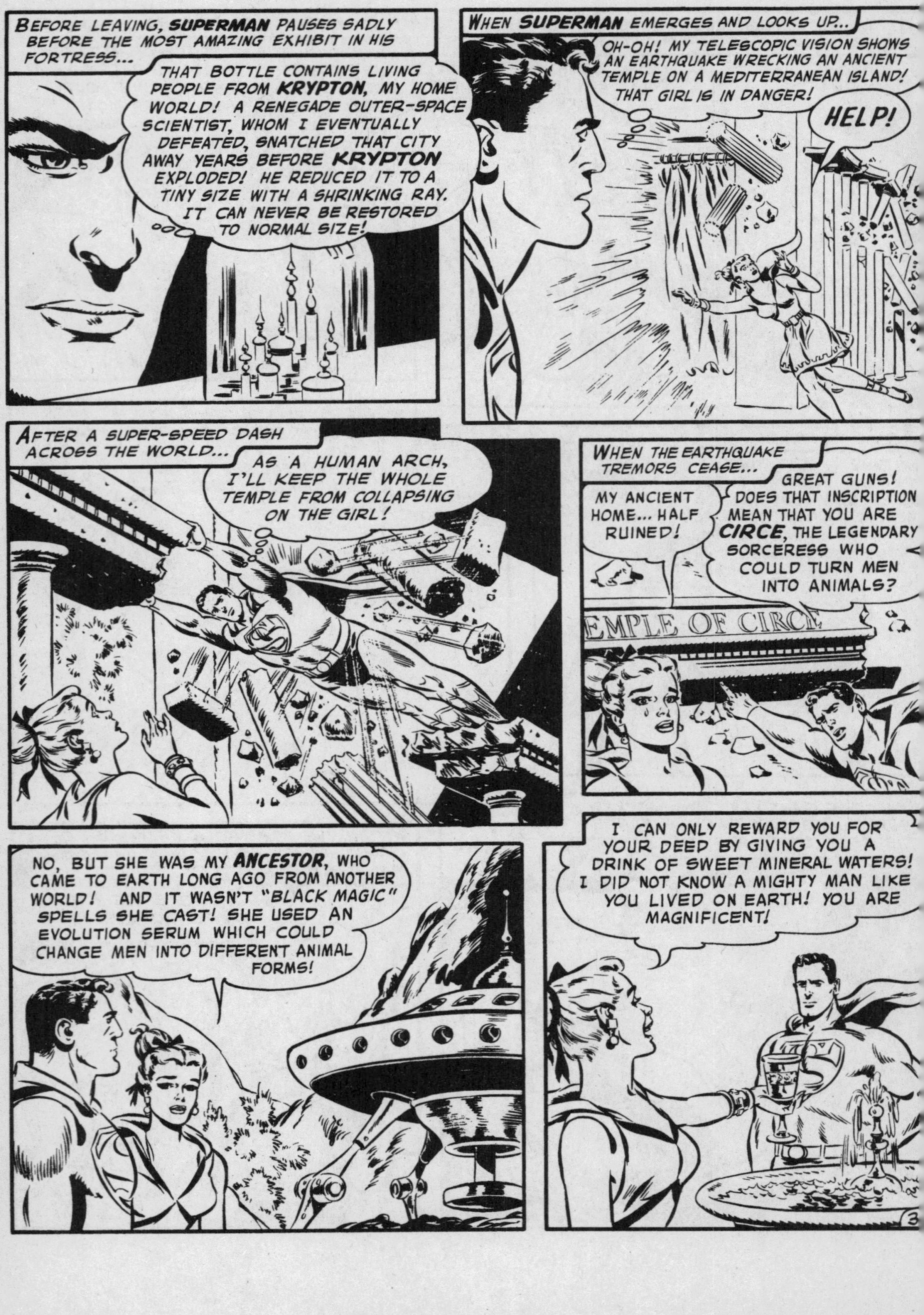
BEFORE LEAVING, SUPERMAN PAUSES SADLY BEFORE THE MOST AMAZING EXHIBIT IN HIS FORTRESS...
THAT BOTTLE CONTAINS LIVING PEOPLE FROM KRYPTON, MY HOME WORLD! A RENEGADE OUTER-SPACE SCIENTIST, WHOM I EVENTUALLY DEFEATED, SNATCHED THAT CITY AWAY YEARS BEFORE KRYPTON EXPLODED! HE REDUCED IT TO A TINY SIZE WITH A SHRINKING RAY. IT CAN NEVER BE RESTORED TO NORMAL SIZE!
WHEN SUPERMAN EMERGES AND LOOKS UP...
OH-OH! MY TELESCOPIC VISION SHOWS AN EARTHQUAKE WRECKING AN ANCIENT TEMPLE ON A MEDITERRANEAN ISLAND! THAT GIRL IS IN DANGER!
HELP!
AFTER A SUPER-SPEED DASH ACROSS THE WORLD...
AS A HUMAN ARCH, I'LL KEEP THE WHOLE TEMPLE FROM COLLAPSING ON THE GIRL!
WHEN THE EARTHQUAKE TREMORS CEASE...
MY ANCIENT HOME... HALF RUINED!
GREAT GUNS! DOES THAT INSCRIPTION MEAN THAT YOU ARE CIRCE, THE LEGENDARY SORCERESS WHO COULD TURN MEN INTO ANIMALS?
EMPLE OF CIRC
NO, BUT SHE WAS MY ANCESTOR, WHO CAME TO EARTH LONG AGO FROM ANOTHER WORLD! AND IT WASN'T "BLACK MAGIC" SPELLS SHE CAST! SHE USED AN EVOLUTION SERUM WHICH COULD CHANGE MEN INTO DIFFERENT ANIMAL FORMS!
I CAN ONLY REWARD YOU FOR YOUR DEED BY GIVING YOU A DRINK OF SWEET MINERAL WATERS! I DID NOT KNOW A MIGHTY MAN LIKE YOU LIVED ON EARTH! YOU ARE MAGNIFICENT!
3

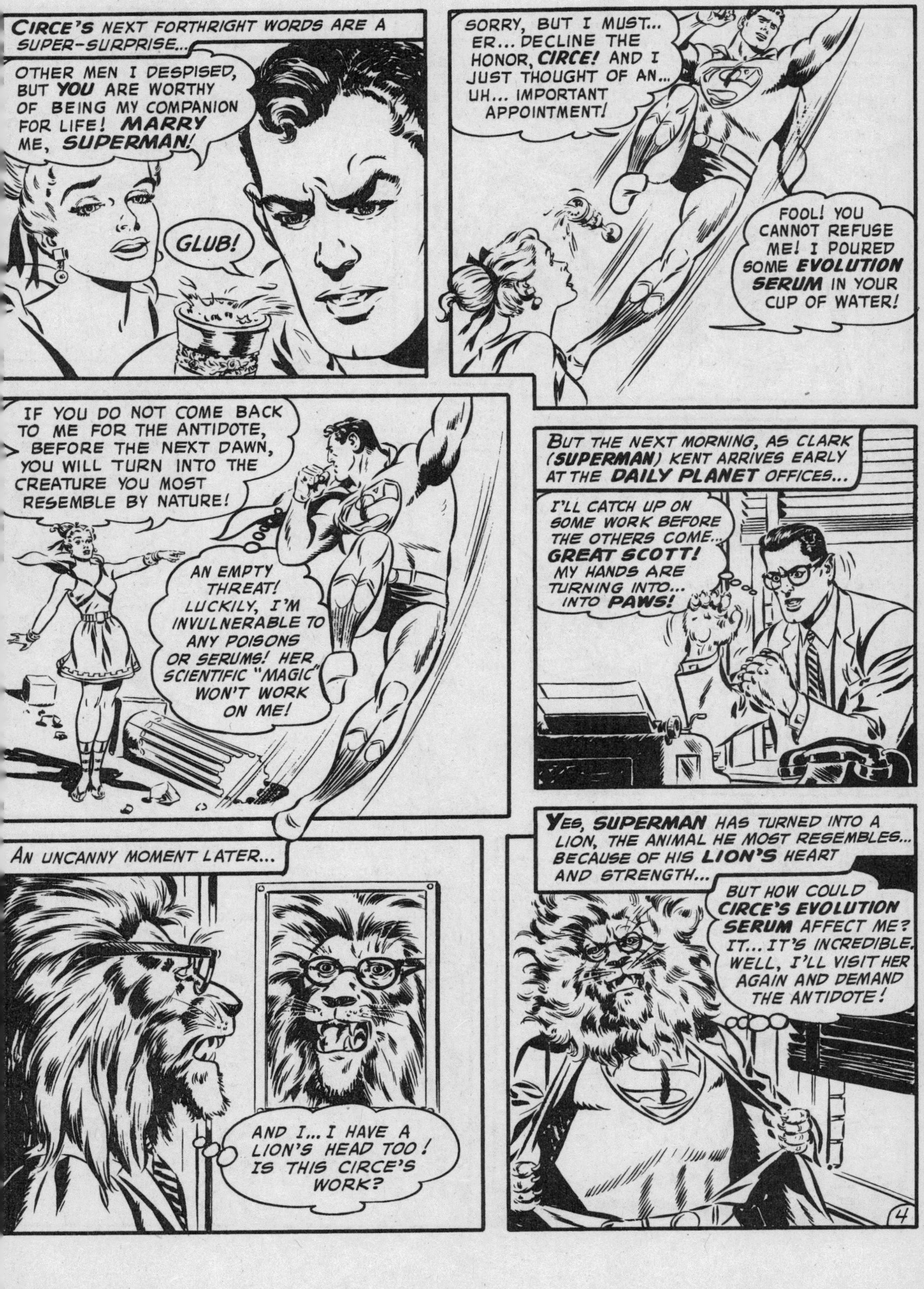
CIRCE'S NEXT FORTHRIGHT WORDS ARE A SUPER-SURPRISE...
OTHER MEN I DESPISED, BUT YOU ARE WORTHY OF BEING MY COMPANION FOR LIFE! MARRY ME, SUPERMAN!
GLUB!
SORRY, BUT I MUST... ER... DECLINE THE HONOR, CIRCE! AND I JUST THOUGHT OF AN... UH... IMPORTANT APPOINTMENT!
FOOL! YOU CANNOT REFUSE ME! I POURED SOME EVOLUTION SERUM IN YOUR CUP OF WATER!
IF YOU DO NOT COME BACK TO ME FOR THE ANTIDOTE, BEFORE THE NEXT DAWN, YOU WILL TURN INTO THE CREATURE YOU MOST RESEMBLE BY NATURE!
AN EMPTY THREAT! LUCKILY, I'M INVULNERABLE TO ANY POISONS OR SERUMS! HER SCIENTIFIC "MAGIC" WON'T WORK ON ME!
BUT THE NEXT MORNING, AS CLARK (SUPERMAN) KENT ARRIVES EARLY AT THE DAILY PLANET OFFICES...
I'LL CATCH UP ON SOME WORK BEFORE THE OTHERS COME... GREAT SCOTT! MY HANDS ARE TURNING INTO... INTO PAWS!
AN UNCANNY MOMENT LATER...
AND I... I HAVE A LION'S HEAD TOO! IS THIS CIRCE'S WORK?
YES, SUPERMAN HAS TURNED INTO A LION, THE ANIMAL HE MOST RESEMBLES... BECAUSE OF HIS LION'S HEART AND STRENGTH...
BUT HOW COULD CIRCE'S EVOLUTION SERUM AFFECT ME? IT... IT'S INCREDIBLE. WELL, I'LL VISIT HER AGAIN AND DEMAND THE ANTIDOTE!
4

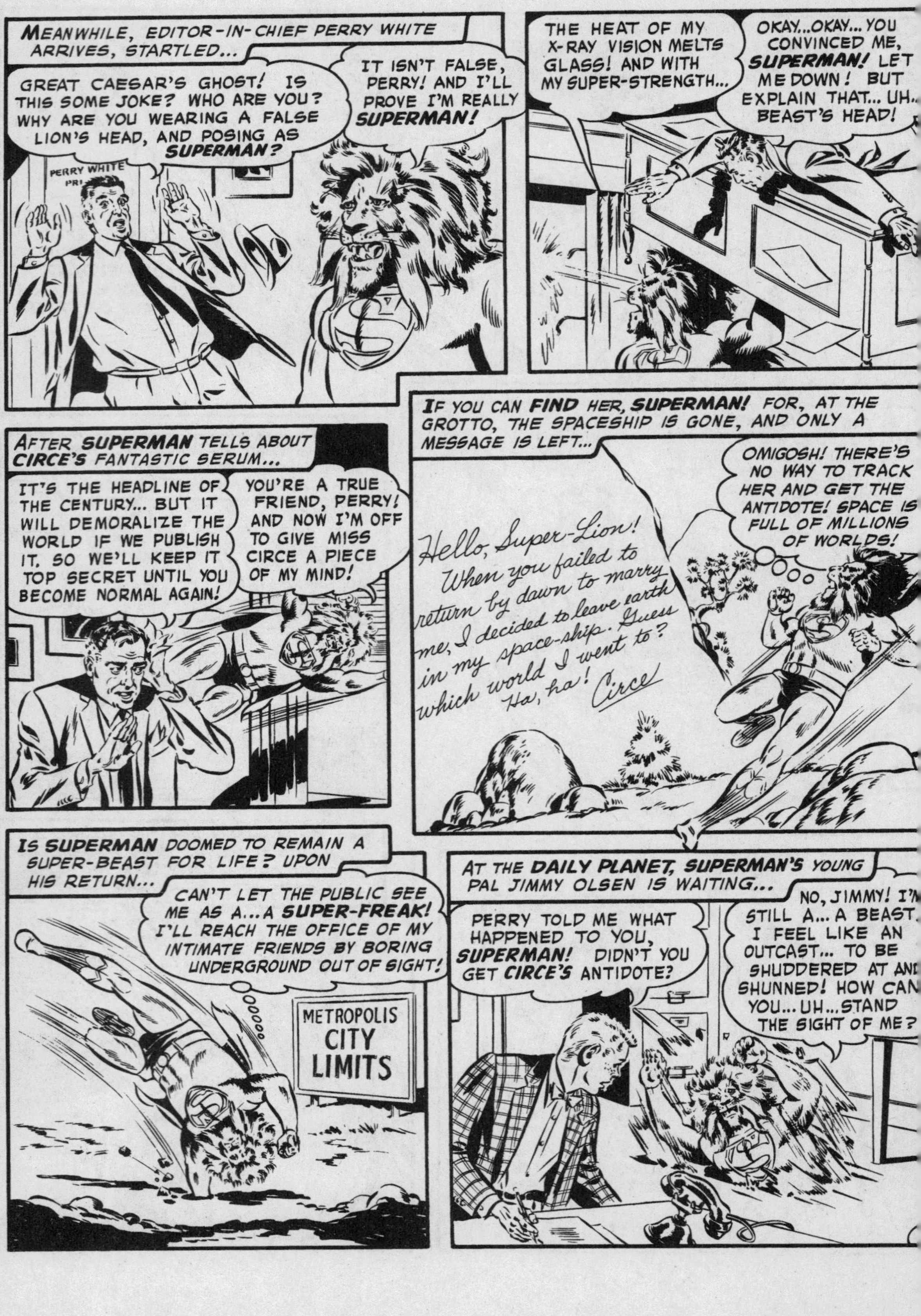
MEANWHILE, EDITOR-IN-CHIEF PERRY WHITE ARRIVES, STARTLED...
GREAT CAESAR'S GHOST! IS THIS SOME JOKE? WHO ARE YOU? WHY ARE YOU WEARING A FALSE LION'S HEAD, AND POSING AS SUPERMAN?
IT ISN'T FALSE, PERRY! AND I'LL PROVE I'M REALLY SUPERMAN!
PERRY WHITE
THE HEAT OF MY X-RAY VISION MELTS GLASS! AND WITH MY SUPER-STRENGTH...
OKAY...OKAY... YOU CONVINCED ME, SUPERMAN! LET ME DOWN! BUT EXPLAIN THAT... UH.. BEAST'S HEAD!
AFTER SUPERMAN TELLS ABOUT CIRCE'S FANTASTIC SERUM...
IT'S THE HEADLINE OF THE CENTURY... BUT IT WILL DEMORALIZE THE WORLD IF WE PUBLISH IT. SO WE'LL KEEP IT TOP SECRET UNTIL YOU BECOME NORMAL AGAIN!
YOU'RE A TRUE FRIEND, PERRY! AND NOW I'M OFF TO GIVE MISS CIRCE A PIECE OF MY MIND!
IF YOU CAN FIND HER, SUPERMAN! FOR, AT THE GROTTO, THE SPACESHIP IS GONE, AND ONLY A MESSAGE IS LEFT...
Hello, Super-Lion! When you failed to return by dawn to marry me, I decided to leave earth in my space-ship. Guess which world I went to? Ha, ha! Circe
OMIGOSH! THERE'S NO WAY TO TRACK HER AND GET THE ANTIDOTE! SPACE IS FULL OF MILLIONS OF WORLDS!
IS SUPERMAN DOOMED TO REMAIN A SUPER-BEAST FOR LIFE? UPON HIS RETURN...
CAN'T LET THE PUBLIC SEE ME AS A...A SUPER-FREAK! I'LL REACH THE OFFICE OF MY INTIMATE FRIENDS BY BORING UNDERGROUND OUT OF SIGHT!
METROPOLIS CITY LIMITS
AT THE DAILY PLANET, SUPERMAN'S YOUNG PAL JIMMY OLSEN IS WAITING...
PERRY TOLD ME WHAT HAPPENED TO YOU, SUPERMAN! DIDN'T YOU GET CIRCE'S ANTIDOTE?
NO, JIMMY! I'M STILL A... A BEAST. I FEEL LIKE AN OUTCAST... TO BE SHUDDERED AT AND SHUNNED! HOW CAN YOU... UH... STAND THE SIGHT OF ME?

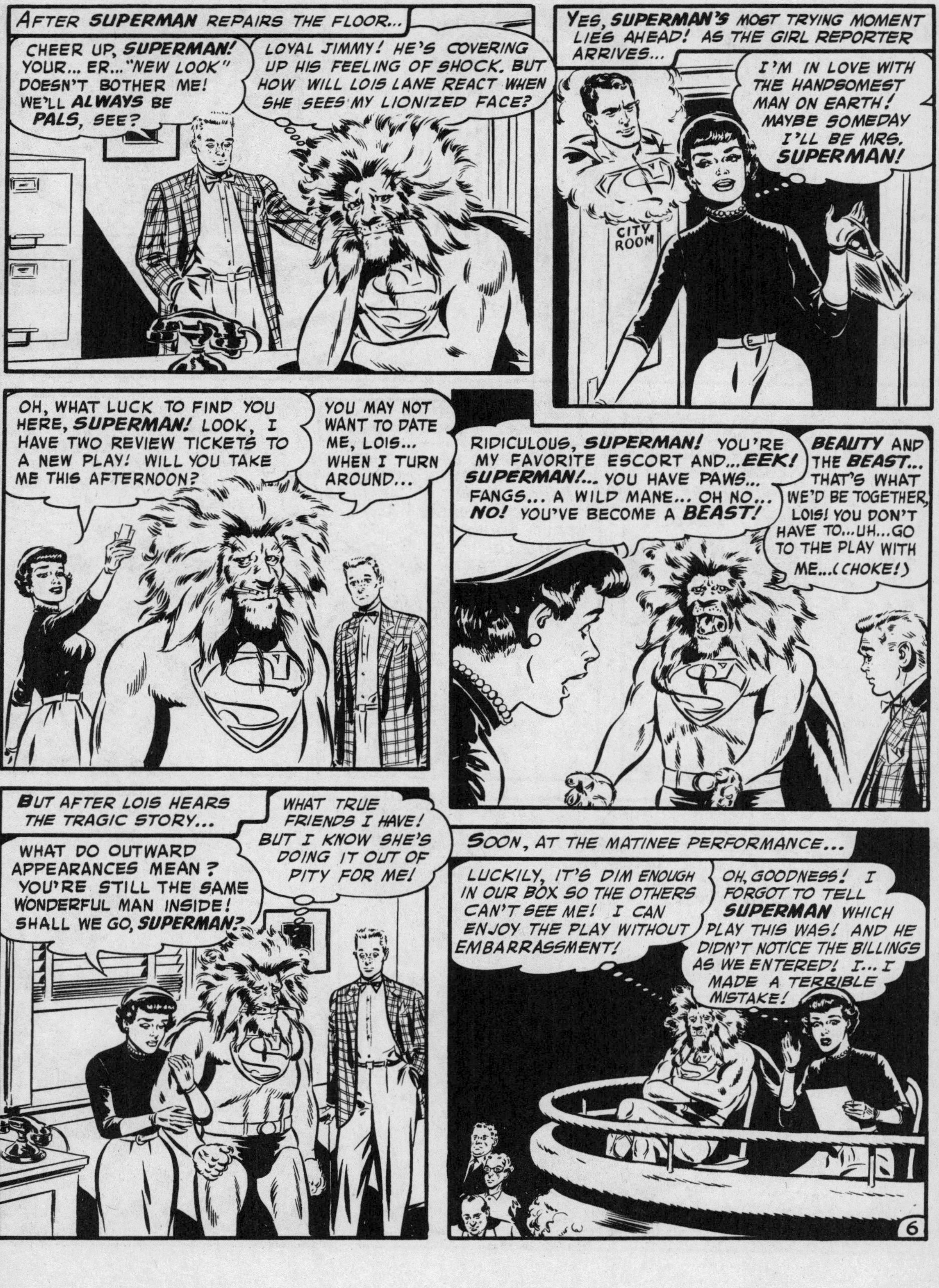
AFTER SUPERMAN REPAIRS THE FLOOR...
CHEER UP, SUPERMAN! YOUR... ER..."NEW LOOK" DOESN'T BOTHER ME! WE'LL ALWAYS BE PALS, SEE?
LOYAL JIMMY! HE'S COVERING UP HIS FEELING OF SHOCK. BUT HOW WILL LOIS LANE REACT WHEN SHE SEES MY LIONIZED FACE?
YES, SUPERMAN'S MOST TRYING MOMENT LIES AHEAD! AS THE GIRL REPORTER ARRIVES...
I'M IN LOVE WITH THE HANDSOMEST MAN ON EARTH! MAYBE SOMEDAY I'LL BE MRS. SUPERMAN!
CITY ROOM
OH, WHAT LUCK TO FIND YOU HERE, SUPERMAN! LOOK, I HAVE TWO REVIEW TICKETS TO A NEW PLAY! WILL YOU TAKE ME THIS AFTERNOON?
YOU MAY NOT WANT TO DATE ME, LOIS... WHEN I TURN AROUND...
RIDICULOUS, SUPERMAN! YOU'RE MY FAVORITE ESCORT AND...EEK! SUPERMAN!... YOU HAVE PAWS... FANGS... A WILD MANE... OH NO... NO! YOU'VE BECOME A BEAST!
BEAUTY AND THE BEAST... THAT'S WHAT WE'D BE TOGETHER, LOIS! YOU DON'T HAVE TO...UH...GO TO THE PLAY WITH ME...(CHOKE!)
BUT AFTER LOIS HEARS THE TRAGIC STORY...
WHAT DO OUTWARD APPEARANCES MEAN? YOU'RE STILL THE SAME WONDERFUL MAN INSIDE! SHALL WE GO, SUPERMAN?
WHAT TRUE FRIENDS I HAVE! BUT I KNOW SHE'S DOING IT OUT OF PITY FOR ME!
SOON, AT THE MATINEE PERFORMANCE...
LUCKILY, IT'S DIM ENOUGH IN OUR BOX SO THE OTHERS CAN'T SEE ME! I CAN ENJOY THE PLAY WITHOUT EMBARRASSMENT!
OH, GOODNESS! I FORGOT TO TELL SUPERMAN WHICH PLAY THIS WAS! AND HE DIDN'T NOTICE THE BILLINGS AS WE ENTERED! I... I MADE A TERRIBLE MISTAKE!
6

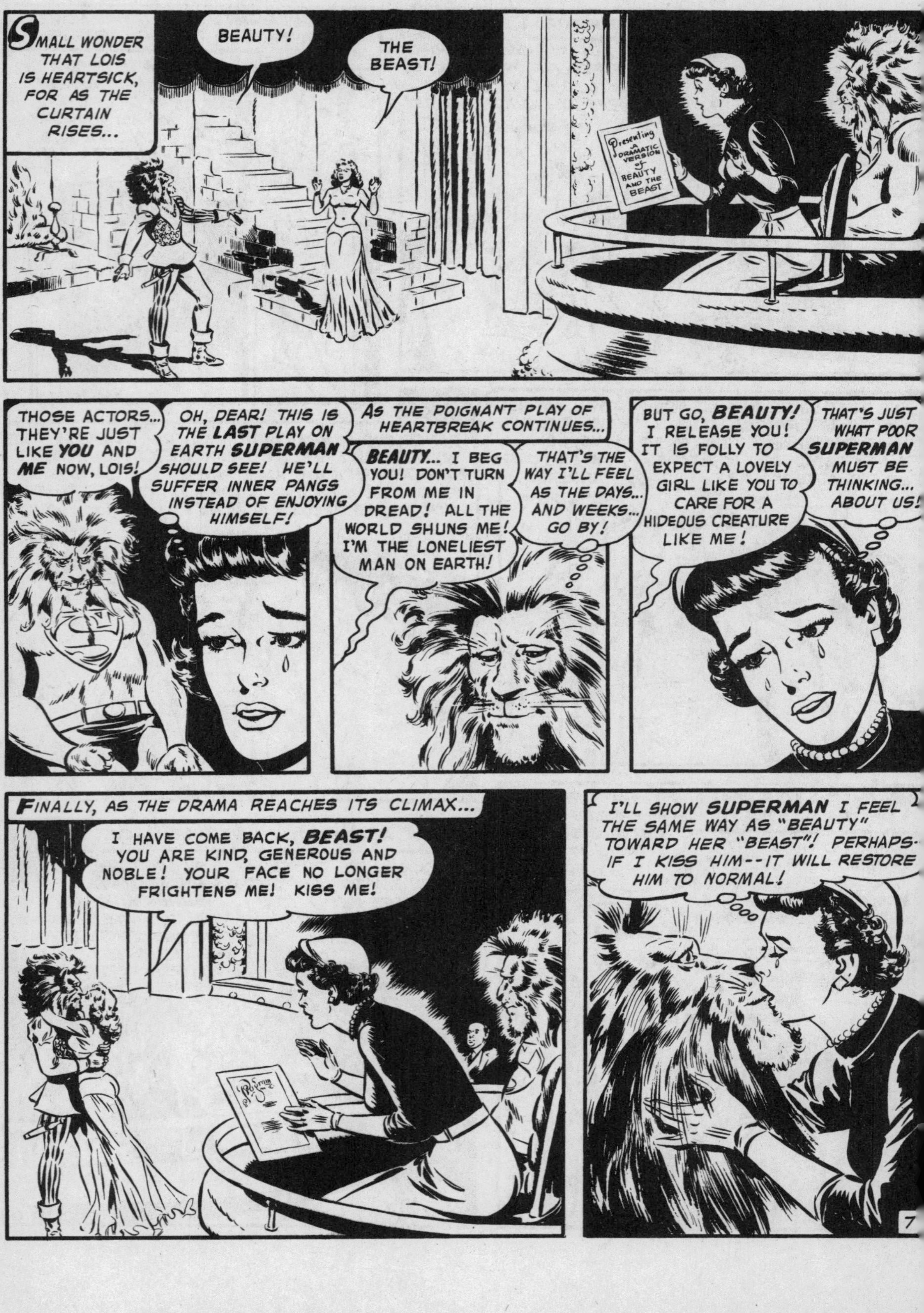
SMALL WONDER THAT LOIS IS HEARTSICK, FOR AS THE CURTAIN RISES...
BEAUTY!
THE BEAST!
Presenting A DRAMATIC VERSION OF BEAUTY AND THE BEAST
THOSE ACTORS... THEY'RE JUST LIKE YOU AND ME NOW, LOIS!
OH, DEAR! THIS IS THE LAST PLAY ON EARTH SUPERMAN SHOULD SEE! HE'LL SUFFER INNER PANGS INSTEAD OF ENJOYING HIMSELF!
AS THE POIGNANT PLAY OF HEARTBREAK CONTINUES...
BEAUTY... I BEG YOU! DON'T TURN FROM ME IN DREAD! ALL THE WORLD SHUNS ME! I'M THE LONELIEST MAN ON EARTH!
THAT'S THE WAY I'LL FEEL AS THE DAYS... AND WEEKS... GO BY!
BUT GO, BEAUTY! I RELEASE YOU! IT IS FOLLY TO EXPECT A LOVELY GIRL LIKE YOU TO CARE FOR A HIDEOUS CREATURE LIKE ME!
THAT'S JUST WHAT POOR SUPERMAN MUST BE THINKING... ABOUT US!
FINALLY, AS THE DRAMA REACHES ITS CLIMAX...
I HAVE COME BACK, BEAST! YOU ARE KIND, GENEROUS AND NOBLE! YOUR FACE NO LONGER FRIGHTENS ME! KISS ME!
I'LL SHOW SUPERMAN I FEEL THE SAME WAY AS "BEAUTY" TOWARD HER "BEAST"! PERHAPS-IF I KISS HIM--IT WILL RESTORE HIM TO NORMAL!
7

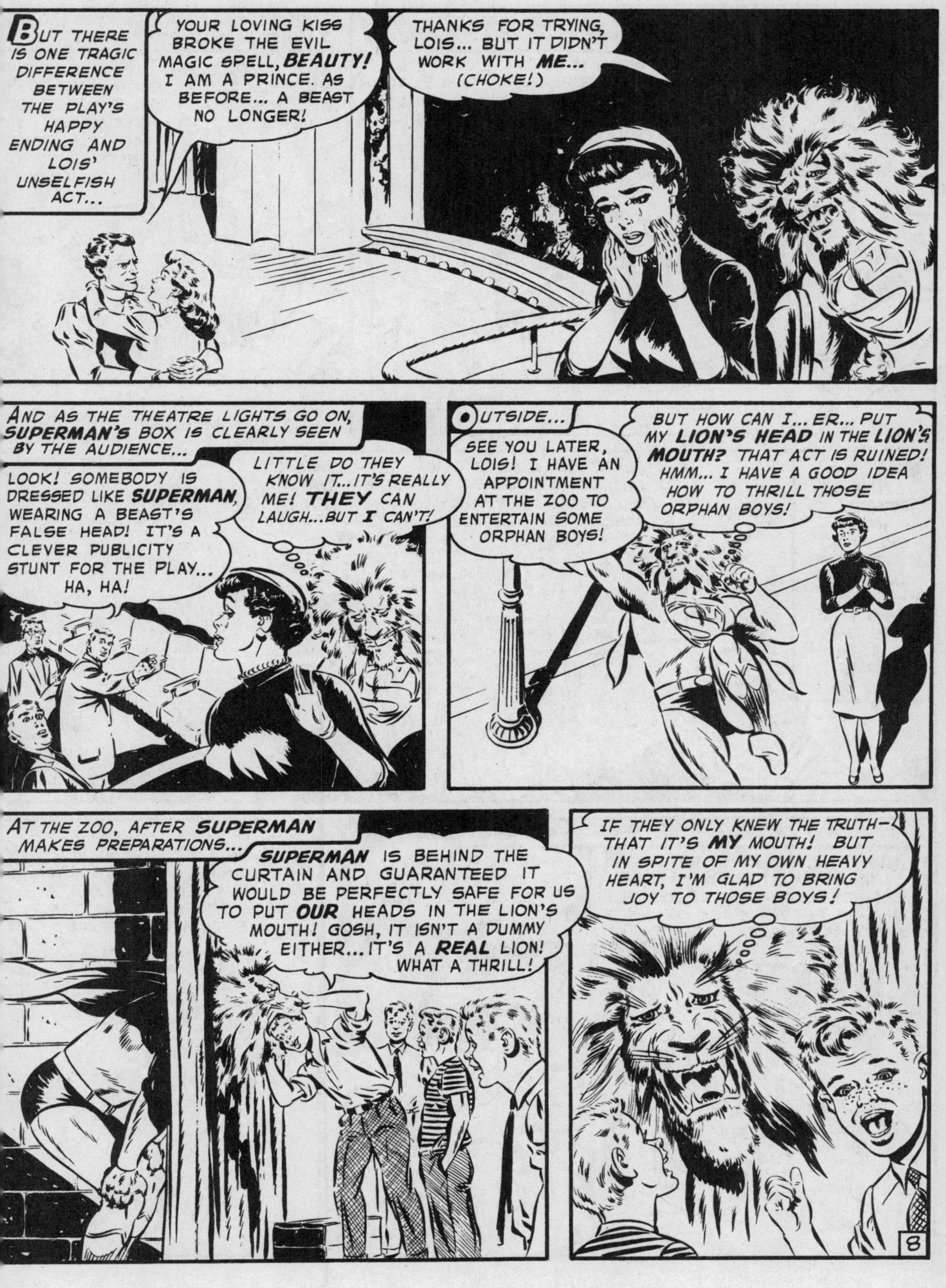
BUT THERE IS ONE TRAGIC DIFFERENCE BETWEEN THE PLAY'S HAPPY ENDING AND LOIS' UNSELFISH ACT...
YOUR LOVING KISS BROKE THE EVIL MAGIC SPELL, BEAUTY! I AM A PRINCE. AS BEFORE... A BEAST NO LONGER!
THANKS FOR TRYING, LOIS... BUT IT DIDN'T WORK WITH ME... (CHOKE!)
AND AS THE THEATRE LIGHTS GO ON, SUPERMAN'S BOX IS CLEARLY SEEN BY THE AUDIENCE...
LOOK! SOMEBODY IS DRESSED LIKE SUPERMAN, WEARING A BEAST'S FALSE HEAD! IT'S A CLEVER PUBLICITY STUNT FOR THE PLAY... HA, HA!
LITTLE DO THEY KNOW IT...IT'S REALLY ME! THEY CAN LAUGH...BUT I CAN'T!
OUTSIDE...
SEE YOU LATER, LOIS! I HAVE AN APPOINTMENT AT THE ZOO TO ENTERTAIN SOME ORPHAN BOYS!
BUT HOW CAN I... ER... PUT MY LION'S HEAD IN THE LION'S MOUTH? THAT ACT IS RUINED! HMM... I HAVE A GOOD IDEA HOW TO THRILL THOSE ORPHAN BOYS!
AT THE ZOO, AFTER SUPERMAN MAKES PREPARATIONS...
SUPERMAN IS BEHIND THE CURTAIN AND GUARANTEED IT WOULD BE PERFECTLY SAFE FOR US TO PUT OUR HEADS IN THE LION'S MOUTH! GOSH, IT ISN'T A DUMMY EITHER... IT'S A REAL LION! WHAT A THRILL!
IF THEY ONLY KNEW THE TRUTH-THAT IT'S MY MOUTH! BUT IN SPITE OF MY OWN HEAVY HEART, I'M GLAD TO BRING JOY TO THOSE BOYS!
8

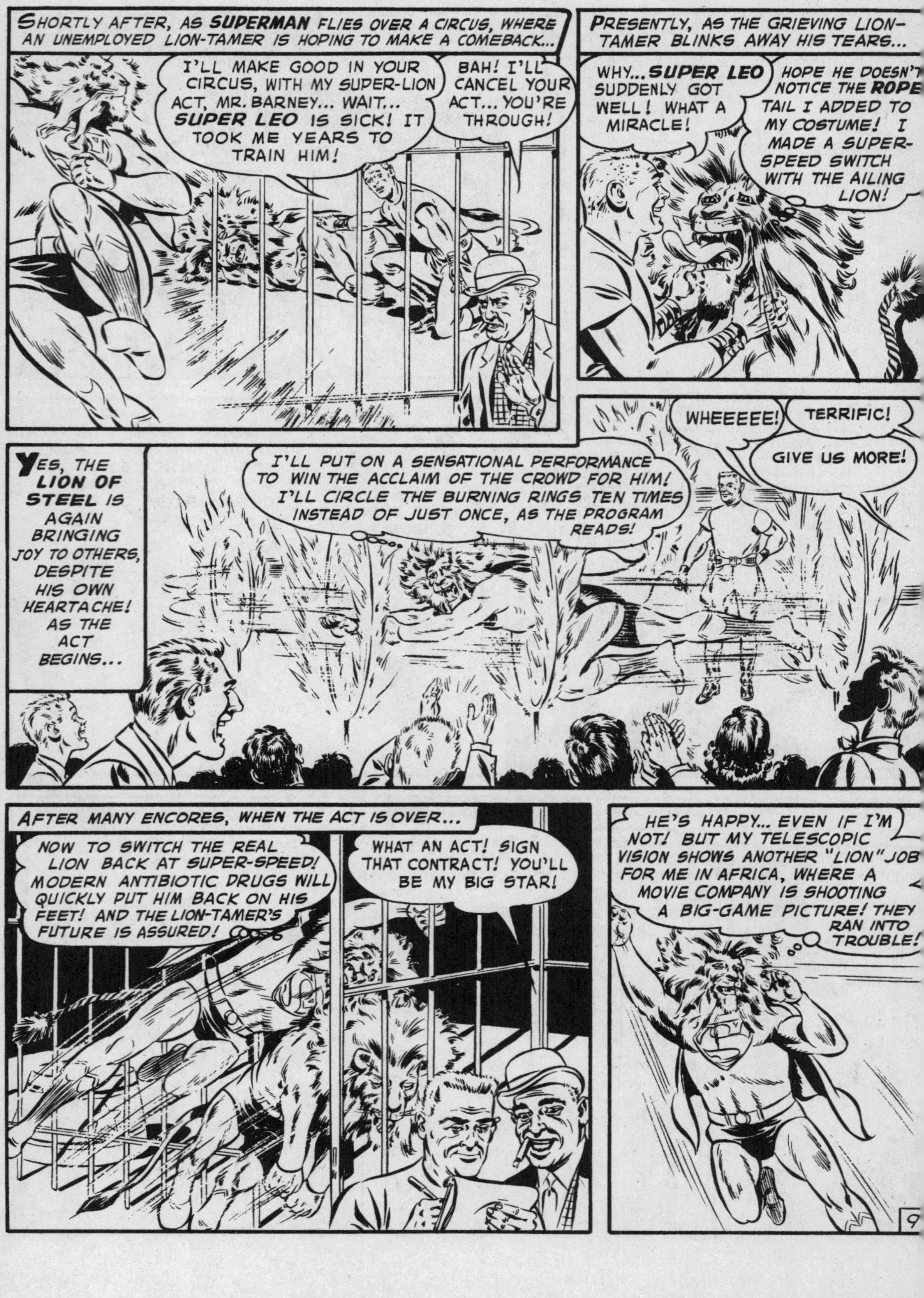
SHORTLY AFTER, AS SUPERMAN FLIES OVER A CIRCUS, WHERE AN UNEMPLOYED LION-TAMER IS HOPING TO MAKE A COMEBACK...
I'LL MAKE GOOD IN YOUR CIRCUS, WITH MY SUPER-LION ACT, MR. BARNEY... WAIT... SUPER LEO IS SICK! IT TOOK ME YEARS TO TRAIN HIM!
BAH! I'LL CANCEL YOUR ACT... YOU'RE THROUGH!
PRESENTLY, AS THE GRIEVING LION-TAMER BLINKS AWAY HIS TEARS...
WHY... SUPER LEO SUDDENLY GOT WELL! WHAT A MIRACLE!
HOPE HE DOESN'T NOTICE THE ROPE TAIL I ADDED TO MY COSTUME! I MADE A SUPER-SPEED SWITCH WITH THE AILING LION!
YES, THE LION OF STEEL IS AGAIN BRINGING JOY TO OTHERS, DESPITE HIS OWN HEARTACHE! AS THE ACT BEGINS...
I'LL PUT ON A SENSATIONAL PERFORMANCE TO WIN THE ACCLAIM OF THE CROWD FOR HIM! I'LL CIRCLE THE BURNING RINGS TEN TIMES INSTEAD OF JUST ONCE, AS THE PROGRAM READS!
WHEEEEE!
TERRIFIC!
GIVE US MORE!
AFTER MANY ENCORES, WHEN THE ACT IS OVER...
NOW TO SWITCH THE REAL LION BACK AT SUPER-SPEED! MODERN ANTIBIOTIC DRUGS WILL QUICKLY PUT HIM BACK ON HIS FEET! AND THE LION-TAMER'S FUTURE IS ASSURED!
WHAT AN ACT! SIGN THAT CONTRACT! YOU'LL BE MY BIG STAR!
HE'S HAPPY... EVEN IF I'M NOT! BUT MY TELESCOPIC VISION SHOWS ANOTHER "LION" JOB FOR ME IN AFRICA, WHERE A MOVIE COMPANY IS SHOOTING A BIG-GAME PICTURE! THEY RAN INTO TROUBLE!
9

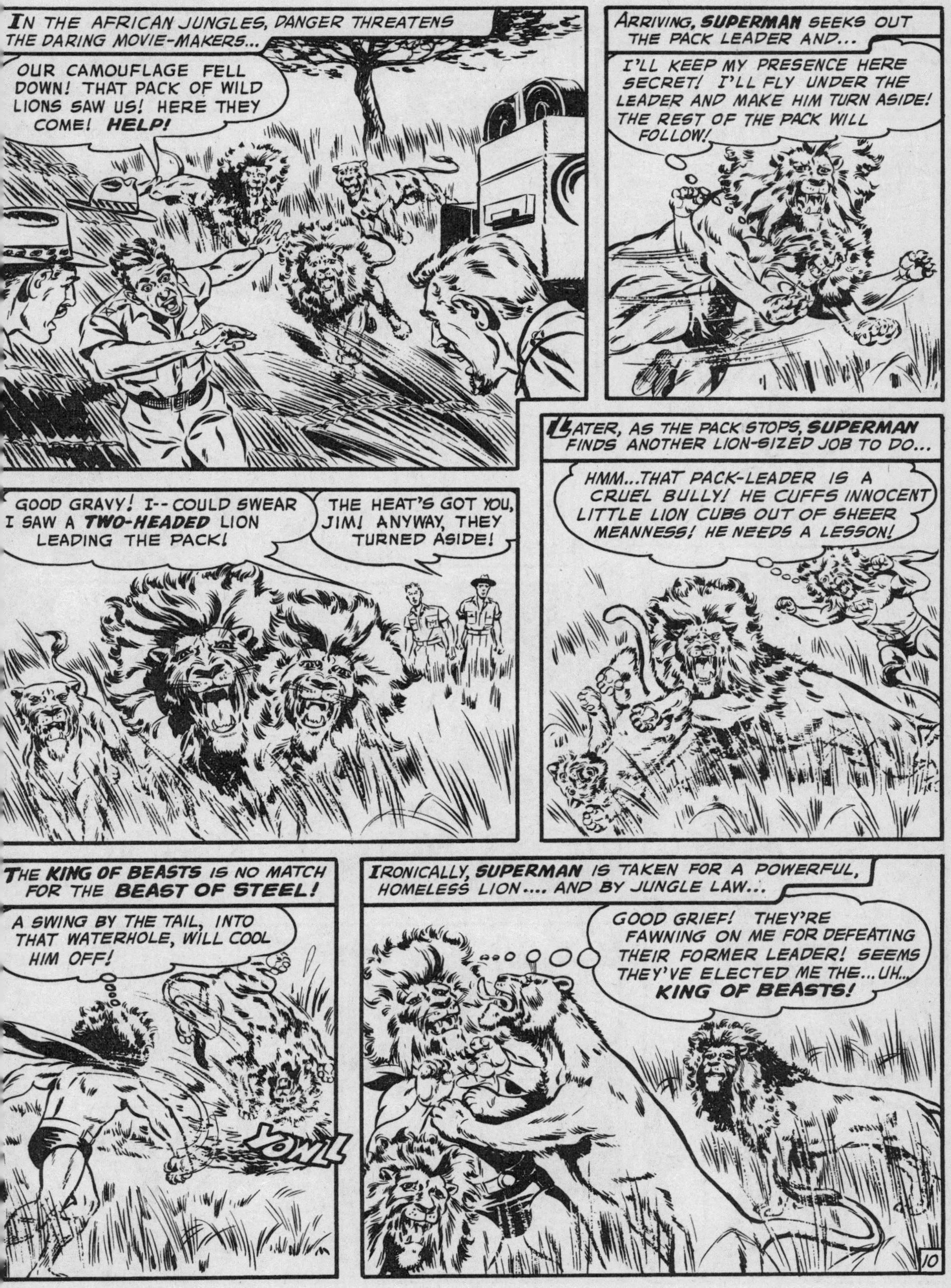
IN THE AFRICAN JUNGLES, DANGER THREATENS THE DARING MOVIE-MAKERS...
OUR CAMOUFLAGE FELL DOWN! THAT PACK OF WILD LIONS SAW US! HERE THEY COME! HELP!
ARRIVING, SUPERMAN SEEKS OUT THE PACK LEADER AND...
I'LL KEEP MY PRESENCE HERE SECRET! I'LL FLY UNDER THE LEADER AND MAKE HIM TURN ASIDE! THE REST OF THE PACK WILL FOLLOW!
GOOD GRAVY! I--COULD SWEAR I SAW A TWO-HEADED LION LEADING THE PACK!
THE HEAT'S GOT YOU, JIM! ANYWAY, THEY TURNED ASIDE!
LATER, AS THE PACK STOPS, SUPERMAN FINDS ANOTHER LION-SIZED JOB TO DO...
HMM...THAT PACK-LEADER IS A CRUEL BULLY! HE CUFFS INNOCENT LITTLE LION CUBS OUT OF SHEER MEANNESS! HE NEEDS A LESSON!
THE KING OF BEASTS IS NO MATCH FOR THE BEAST OF STEEL!
A SWING BY THE TAIL, INTO THAT WATERHOLE, WILL COOL HIM OFF!
YOWL!
IRONICALLY, SUPERMAN IS TAKEN FOR A POWERFUL, HOMELESS LION.... AND BY JUNGLE LAW...
GOOD GRIEF! THEY'RE FAWNING ON ME FOR DEFEATING THEIR FORMER LEADER! SEEMS THEY'VE ELECTED ME THE...UH... KING OF BEASTS!
10

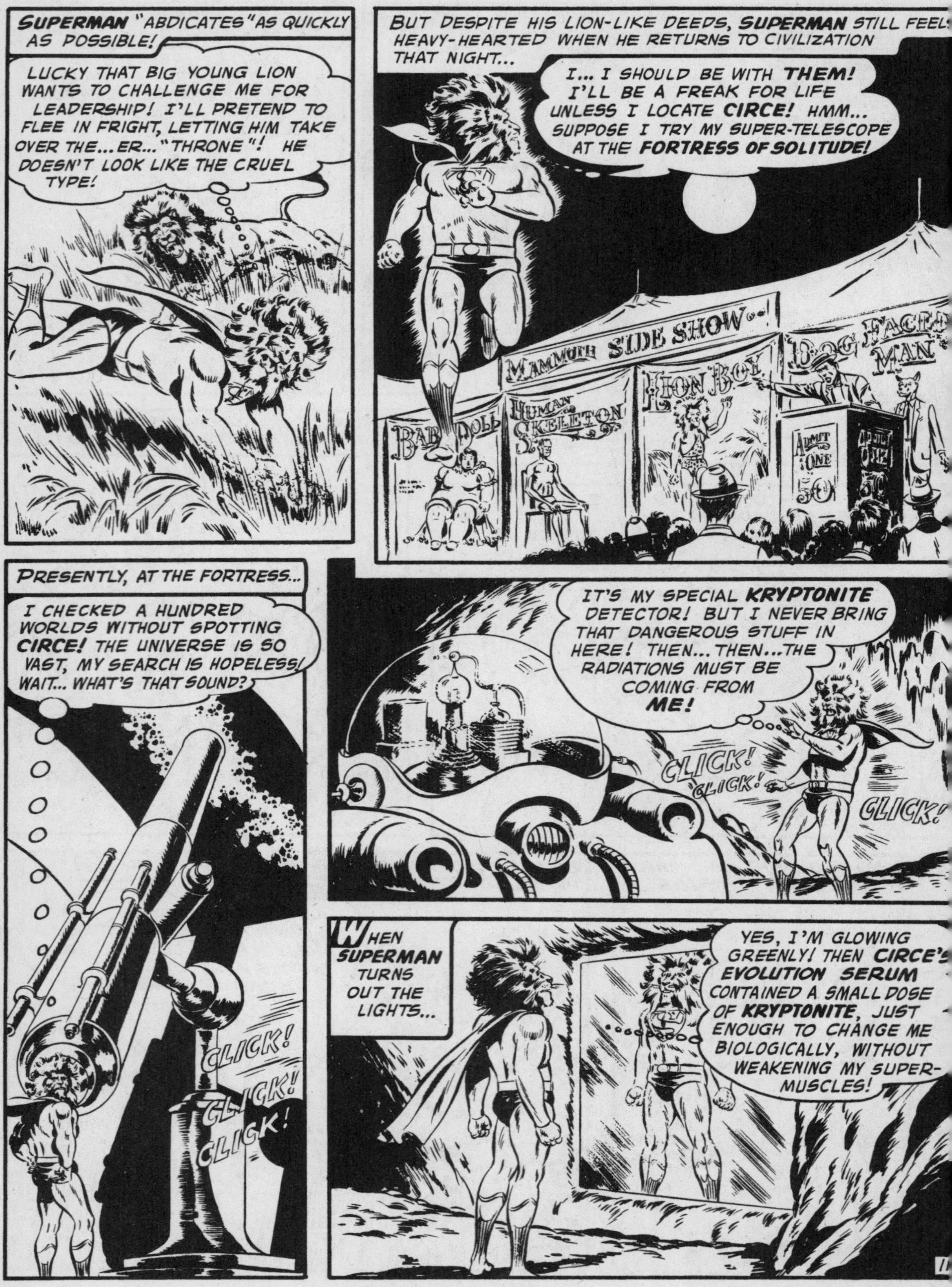
SUPERMAN "ABDICATES" AS QUICKLY AS POSSIBLE!
LUCKY THAT BIG YOUNG LION WANTS TO CHALLENGE ME FOR LEADERSHIP! I'LL PRETEND TO FLEE IN FRIGHT, LETTING HIM TAKE OVER THE...ER..."THRONE"! HE DOESN'T LOOK LIKE THE CRUEL TYPE!
BUT DESPITE HIS LION-LIKE DEEDS, SUPERMAN STILL FEELS HEAVY-HEARTED WHEN HE RETURNS TO CIVILIZATION THAT NIGHT...
I... I SHOULD BE WITH THEM! I'LL BE A FREAK FOR LIFE UNLESS I LOCATE CIRCE! HMM... SUPPOSE I TRY MY SUPER-TELESCOPE AT THE FORTRESS OF SOLITUDE!
MAMMOTH SIDE SHOW
LION BOY
HUMAN SKELETON
BABY DOLL
ADMIT ONE 50
PRESENTLY, AT THE FORTRESS...
I CHECKED A HUNDRED WORLDS WITHOUT SPOTTING CIRCE! THE UNIVERSE IS SO VAST, MY SEARCH IS HOPELESS! WAIT... WHAT'S THAT SOUND?
CLICK!
CLICK!
CLICK!
IT'S MY SPECIAL KRYPTONITE DETECTOR! BUT I NEVER BRING THAT DANGEROUS STUFF IN HERE! THEN...THEN...THE RADIATIONS MUST BE COMING FROM ME!
CLICK!
CLICK!
CLICK!
WHEN SUPERMAN TURNS OUT THE LIGHTS...
YES, I'M GLOWING GREENLY! THEN CIRCE'S EVOLUTION SERUM CONTAINED A SMALL DOSE OF KRYPTONITE, JUST ENOUGH TO CHANGE ME BIOLOGICALLY, WITHOUT WEAKENING MY SUPER-MUSCLES!
11

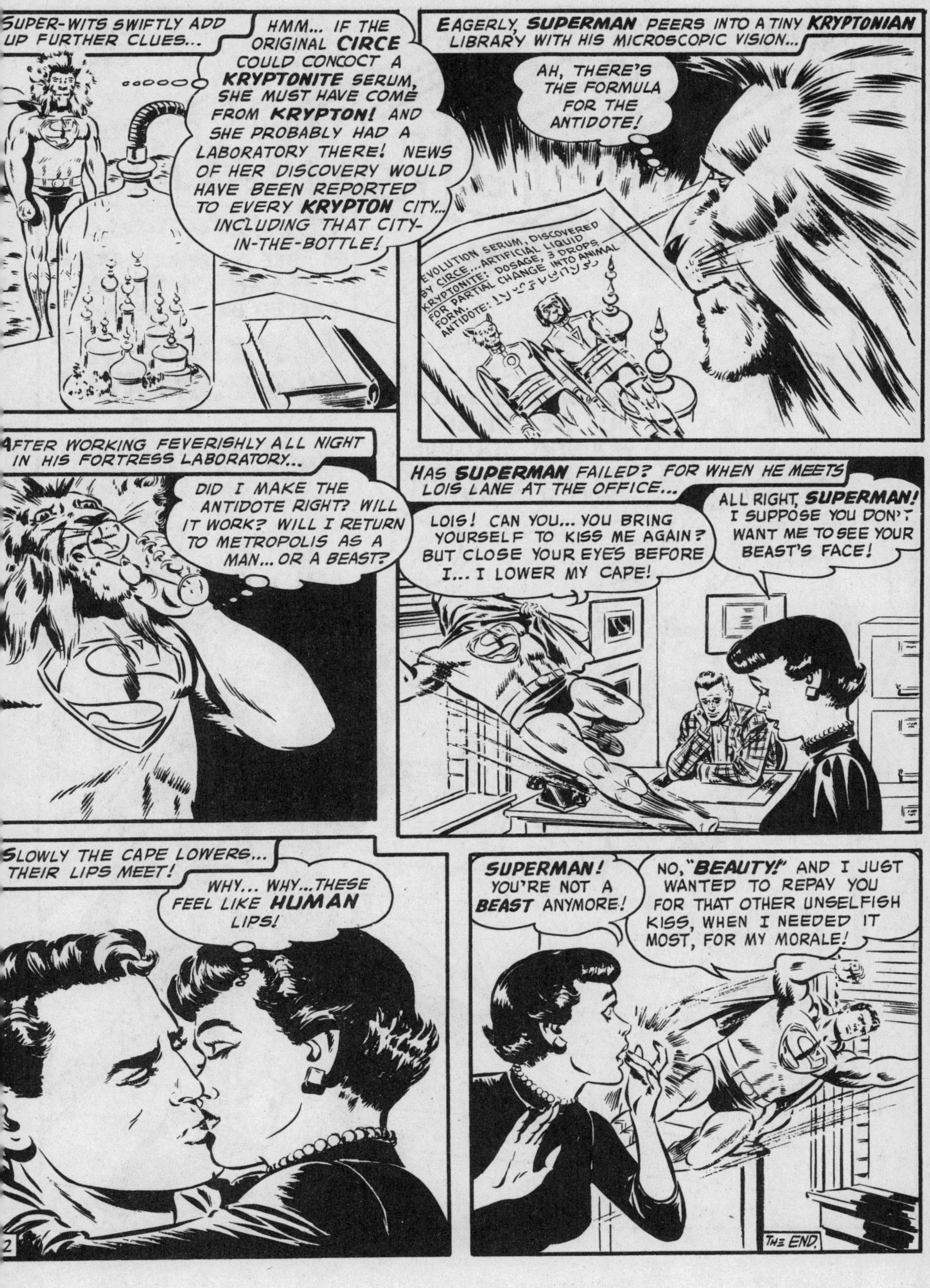
SUPER-WITS SWIFTLY ADD UP FURTHER CLUES...
HMM... IF THE ORIGINAL CIRCE COULD CONCOCT A KRYPTONITE SERUM, SHE MUST HAVE COME FROM KRYPTON! AND SHE PROBABLY HAD A LABORATORY THERE! NEWS OF HER DISCOVERY WOULD HAVE BEEN REPORTED TO EVERY KRYPTON CITY... INCLUDING THAT CITY-IN-THE-BOTTLE!
EAGERLY, SUPERMAN PEERS INTO A TINY KRYPTONIAN LIBRARY WITH HIS MICROSCOPIC VISION...
AH, THERE'S THE FORMULA FOR THE ANTIDOTE!
EVOLUTION SERUM, DISCOVERED BY CIRCE... ARTIFICIAL LIQUID KRYPTONITE: DOSAGE, 3 DROPS FOR PARTIAL CHANGE INTO ANIMAL FORM. ANTIDOTE:
AFTER WORKING FEVERISHLY ALL NIGHT IN HIS FORTRESS LABORATORY...
DID I MAKE THE ANTIDOTE RIGHT? WILL IT WORK? WILL I RETURN TO METROPOLIS AS A MAN... OR A BEAST?
HAS SUPERMAN FAILED? FOR WHEN HE MEETS LOIS LANE AT THE OFFICE...
LOIS! CAN YOU... YOU BRING YOURSELF TO KISS ME AGAIN? BUT CLOSE YOUR EYES BEFORE I... I LOWER MY CAPE!
ALL RIGHT, SUPERMAN! I SUPPOSE YOU DON'T WANT ME TO SEE YOUR BEAST'S FACE!
SLOWLY THE CAPE LOWERS... THEIR LIPS MEET!
WHY... WHY... THESE FEEL LIKE HUMAN LIPS!
SUPERMAN! YOU'RE NOT A BEAST ANYMORE!
NO, "BEAUTY!" AND I JUST WANTED TO REPAY YOU FOR THAT OTHER UNSELFISH KISS, WHEN I NEEDED IT MOST, FOR MY MORALE!
THE END.

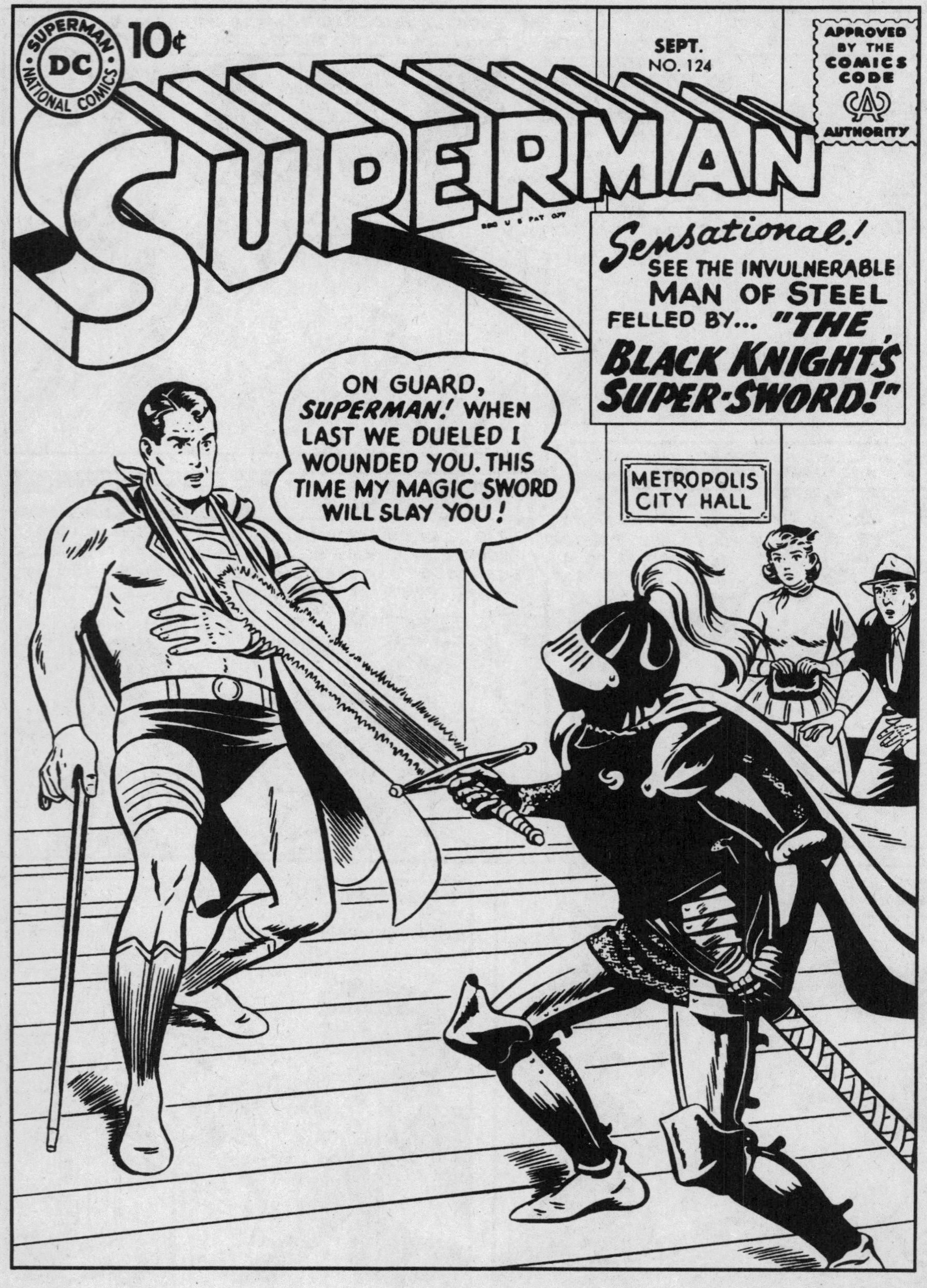
SUPERMAN DC NATIONAL COMICS
10¢
SEPT. NO. 124
APPROVED BY THE COMICS CODE AUTHORITY
SUPERMAN
Sensational! SEE THE INVULNERABLE MAN OF STEEL FELLED BY... "THE BLACK KNIGHT'S SUPER-SWORD!"
ON GUARD, SUPERMAN! WHEN LAST WE DUELED I WOUNDED YOU. THIS TIME MY MAGIC SWORD WILL SLAY YOU!
METROPOLIS CITY HALL

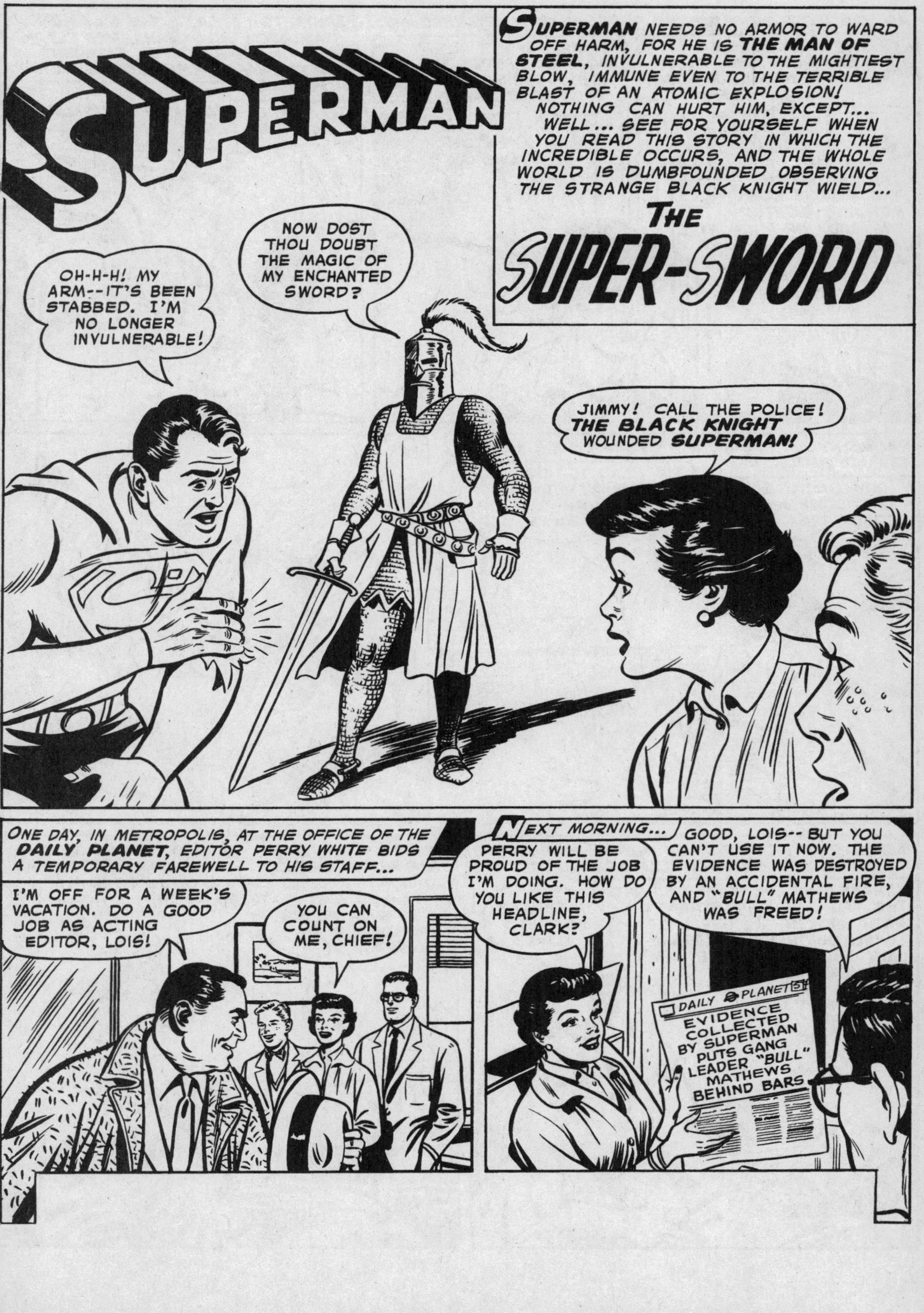
SUPERMAN
SUPERMAN NEEDS NO ARMOR TO WARD OFF HARM, FOR HE IS THE MAN OF STEEL, INVULNERABLE TO THE MIGHTIEST BLOW, IMMUNE EVEN TO THE TERRIBLE BLAST OF AN ATOMIC EXPLOSION! NOTHING CAN HURT HIM, EXCEPT... WELL... SEE FOR YOURSELF WHEN YOU READ THIS STORY IN WHICH THE INCREDIBLE OCCURS, AND THE WHOLE WORLD IS DUMBFOUNDED OBSERVING THE STRANGE BLACK KNIGHT WIELD...
THE SUPER-SWORD
OH-H-H! MY ARM--IT'S BEEN STABBED. I'M NO LONGER INVULNERABLE!
NOW DOST THOU DOUBT THE MAGIC OF MY ENCHANTED SWORD?
JIMMY! CALL THE POLICE! THE BLACK KNIGHT WOUNDED SUPERMAN!
ONE DAY, IN METROPOLIS, AT THE OFFICE OF THE DAILY PLANET, EDITOR PERRY WHITE BIDS A TEMPORARY FAREWELL TO HIS STAFF...
I'M OFF FOR A WEEK'S VACATION. DO A GOOD JOB AS ACTING EDITOR, LOIS!
YOU CAN COUNT ON ME, CHIEF!
NEXT MORNING...
PERRY WILL BE PROUD OF THE JOB I'M DOING. HOW DO YOU LIKE THIS HEADLINE, CLARK?
GOOD, LOIS-- BUT YOU CAN'T USE IT NOW. THE EVIDENCE WAS DESTROYED BY AN ACCIDENTAL FIRE, AND "BULL" MATHEWS WAS FREED!
DAILY PLANET
EVIDENCE COLLECTED BY SUPERMAN PUTS GANG LEADER "BULL" MATHEWS BEHIND BARS

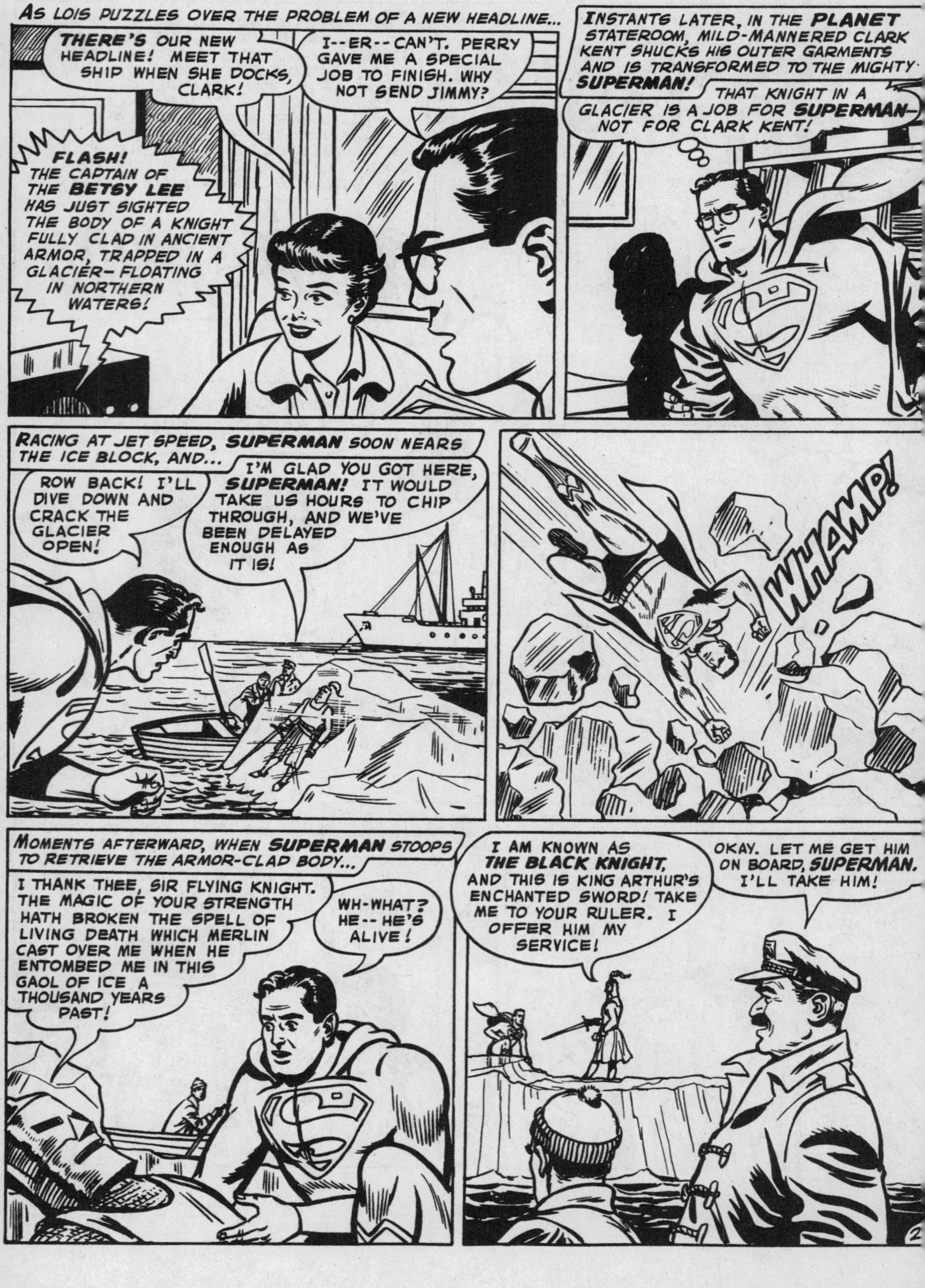
AS LOIS PUZZLES OVER THE PROBLEM OF A NEW HEADLINE...
FLASH! THE CAPTAIN OF THE BETSY LEE HAS JUST SIGHTED THE BODY OF A KNIGHT FULLY CLAD IN ANCIENT ARMOR, TRAPPED IN A GLACIER-- FLOATING IN NORTHERN WATERS!
THERE'S OUR NEW HEADLINE! MEET THAT SHIP WHEN SHE DOCKS, CLARK!
I--ER--CAN'T. PERRY GAVE ME A SPECIAL JOB TO FINISH. WHY NOT SEND JIMMY?
INSTANTS LATER, IN THE PLANET STATEROOM, MILD-MANNERED CLARK KENT SHUCKS HIS OUTER GARMENTS AND IS TRANSFORMED TO THE MIGHTY SUPERMAN!
THAT KNIGHT IN A GLACIER IS A JOB FOR SUPERMAN-- NOT FOR CLARK KENT!
RACING AT JET SPEED, SUPERMAN SOON NEARS THE ICE BLOCK, AND...
ROW BACK! I'LL DIVE DOWN AND CRACK THE GLACIER OPEN!
I'M GLAD YOU GOT HERE, SUPERMAN! IT WOULD TAKE US HOURS TO CHIP THROUGH, AND WE'VE BEEN DELAYED ENOUGH AS IT IS!
WHAMP!
MOMENTS AFTERWARD, WHEN SUPERMAN STOOPS TO RETRIEVE THE ARMOR-CLAD BODY...
I THANK THEE, SIR FLYING KNIGHT. THE MAGIC OF YOUR STRENGTH HATH BROKEN THE SPELL OF LIVING DEATH WHICH MERLIN CAST OVER ME WHEN HE ENTOMBED ME IN THIS GAOL OF ICE A THOUSAND YEARS PAST!
WH-WHAT? HE--HE'S ALIVE!
I AM KNOWN AS THE BLACK KNIGHT, AND THIS IS KING ARTHUR'S ENCHANTED SWORD! TAKE ME TO YOUR RULER. I OFFER HIM MY SERVICE!
OKAY. LET ME GET HIM ON BOARD, SUPERMAN. I'LL TAKE HIM!
2

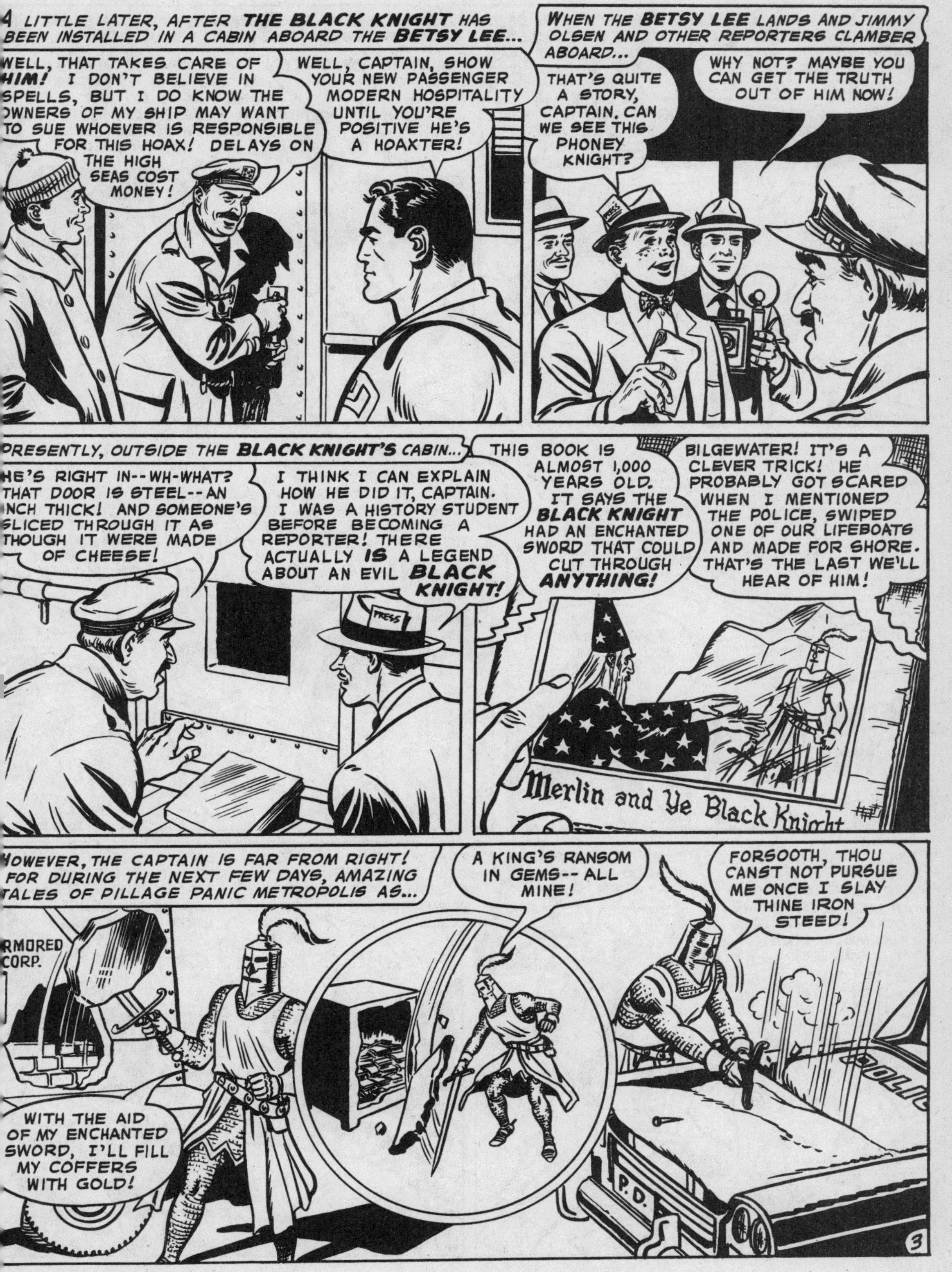
A LITTLE LATER, AFTER THE BLACK KNIGHT HAS BEEN INSTALLED IN A CABIN ABOARD THE BETSY LEE...
WELL, THAT TAKES CARE OF HIM! I DON'T BELIEVE IN SPELLS, BUT I DO KNOW THE OWNERS OF MY SHIP MAY WANT TO SUE WHOEVER IS RESPONSIBLE FOR THIS HOAX! DELAYS ON THE HIGH SEAS COST MONEY!
WELL, CAPTAIN, SHOW YOUR NEW PASSENGER MODERN HOSPITALITY UNTIL YOU'RE POSITIVE HE'S A HOAXTER!
WHEN THE BETSY LEE LANDS AND JIMMY OLSEN AND OTHER REPORTERS CLAMBER ABOARD...
THAT'S QUITE A STORY, CAPTAIN. CAN WE SEE THIS PHONEY KNIGHT?
WHY NOT? MAYBE YOU CAN GET THE TRUTH OUT OF HIM NOW!
PRESS
PRESENTLY, OUTSIDE THE BLACK KNIGHT'S CABIN...
HE'S RIGHT IN--WH-WHAT? THAT DOOR IS STEEL--AN INCH THICK! AND SOMEONE'S SLICED THROUGH IT AS THOUGH IT WERE MADE OF CHEESE!
I THINK I CAN EXPLAIN HOW HE DID IT, CAPTAIN. I WAS A HISTORY STUDENT BEFORE BECOMING A REPORTER! THERE ACTUALLY IS A LEGEND ABOUT AN EVIL BLACK KNIGHT!
PRESS
THIS BOOK IS ALMOST 1,000 YEARS OLD. IT SAYS THE BLACK KNIGHT HAD AN ENCHANTED SWORD THAT COULD CUT THROUGH ANYTHING!
BILGEWATER! IT'S A CLEVER TRICK! HE PROBABLY GOT SCARED WHEN I MENTIONED THE POLICE, SWIPED ONE OF OUR LIFEBOATS AND MADE FOR SHORE. THAT'S THE LAST WE'LL HEAR OF HIM!
Merlin and Ye Black Knight
HOWEVER, THE CAPTAIN IS FAR FROM RIGHT! FOR DURING THE NEXT FEW DAYS, AMAZING TALES OF PILLAGE PANIC METROPOLIS AS...
RMORED CORP.
WITH THE AID OF MY ENCHANTED SWORD, I'LL FILL MY COFFERS WITH GOLD!
A KING'S RANSOM IN GEMS--ALL MINE!
FORSOOTH, THOU CANST NOT PURSUE ME ONCE I SLAY THINE IRON STEED!
P.D.
3

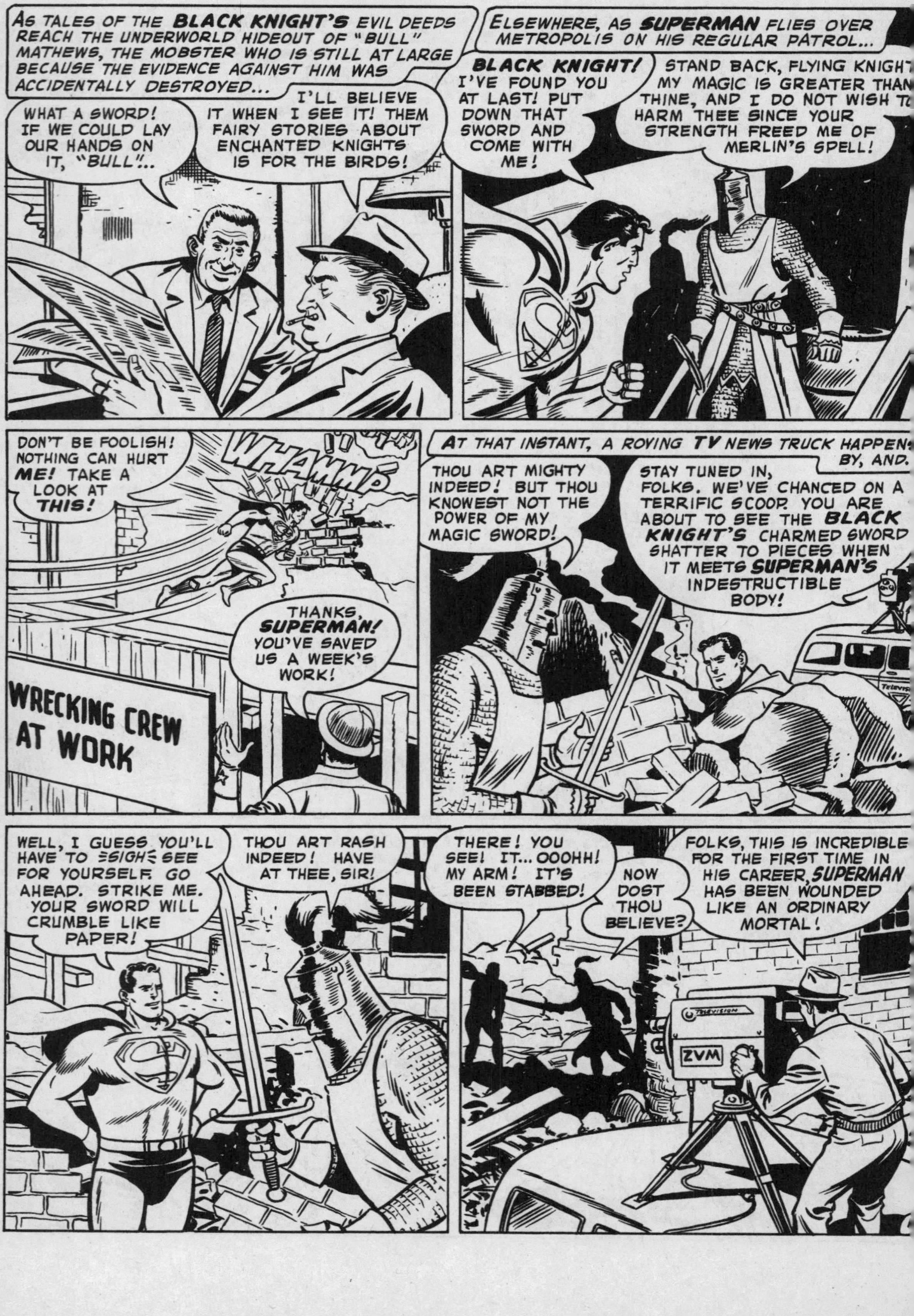
AS TALES OF THE BLACK KNIGHT'S EVIL DEEDS REACH THE UNDERWORLD HIDEOUT OF "BULL" MATHEWS, THE MOBSTER WHO IS STILL AT LARGE BECAUSE THE EVIDENCE AGAINST HIM WAS ACCIDENTALLY DESTROYED...
WHAT A SWORD! IF WE COULD LAY OUR HANDS ON IT, "BULL"...
I'LL BELIEVE IT WHEN I SEE IT! THEM FAIRY STORIES ABOUT ENCHANTED KNIGHTS IS FOR THE BIRDS!
ELSEWHERE, AS SUPERMAN FLIES OVER METROPOLIS ON HIS REGULAR PATROL...
BLACK KNIGHT! I'VE FOUND YOU AT LAST! PUT DOWN THAT SWORD AND COME WITH ME!
STAND BACK, FLYING KNIGHT MY MAGIC IS GREATER THAN THINE, AND I DO NOT WISH TO HARM THEE SINCE YOUR STRENGTH FREED ME OF MERLIN'S SPELL!
DON'T BE FOOLISH! NOTHING CAN HURT ME! TAKE A LOOK AT THIS!
WHAMMP
THANKS, SUPERMAN! YOU'VE SAVED US A WEEK'S WORK!
WRECKING CREW AT WORK
AT THAT INSTANT, A ROYING TV NEWS TRUCK HAPPENS BY, AND.
THOU ART MIGHTY INDEED! BUT THOU KNOWEST NOT THE POWER OF MY MAGIC SWORD!
STAY TUNED IN, FOLKS. WE'VE CHANCED ON A TERRIFIC SCOOP. YOU ARE ABOUT TO SEE THE BLACK KNIGHT'S CHARMED SWORD SHATTER TO PIECES WHEN IT MEETS SUPERMAN'S INDESTRUCTIBLE BODY!
WELL, I GUESS YOU'LL HAVE TO SIGH SEE FOR YOURSELF. GO AHEAD. STRIKE ME. YOUR SWORD WILL CRUMBLE LIKE PAPER!
THOU ART RASH INDEED! HAVE AT THEE, SIR!
THERE! YOU SEE! IT... OOOHH! MY ARM! IT'S BEEN STABBED!
NOW DOST THOU BELIEVE?
FOLKS, THIS IS INCREDIBLE FOR THE FIRST TIME IN HIS CAREER, SUPERMAN HAS BEEN WOUNDED LIKE AN ORDINARY MORTAL!
ZVM

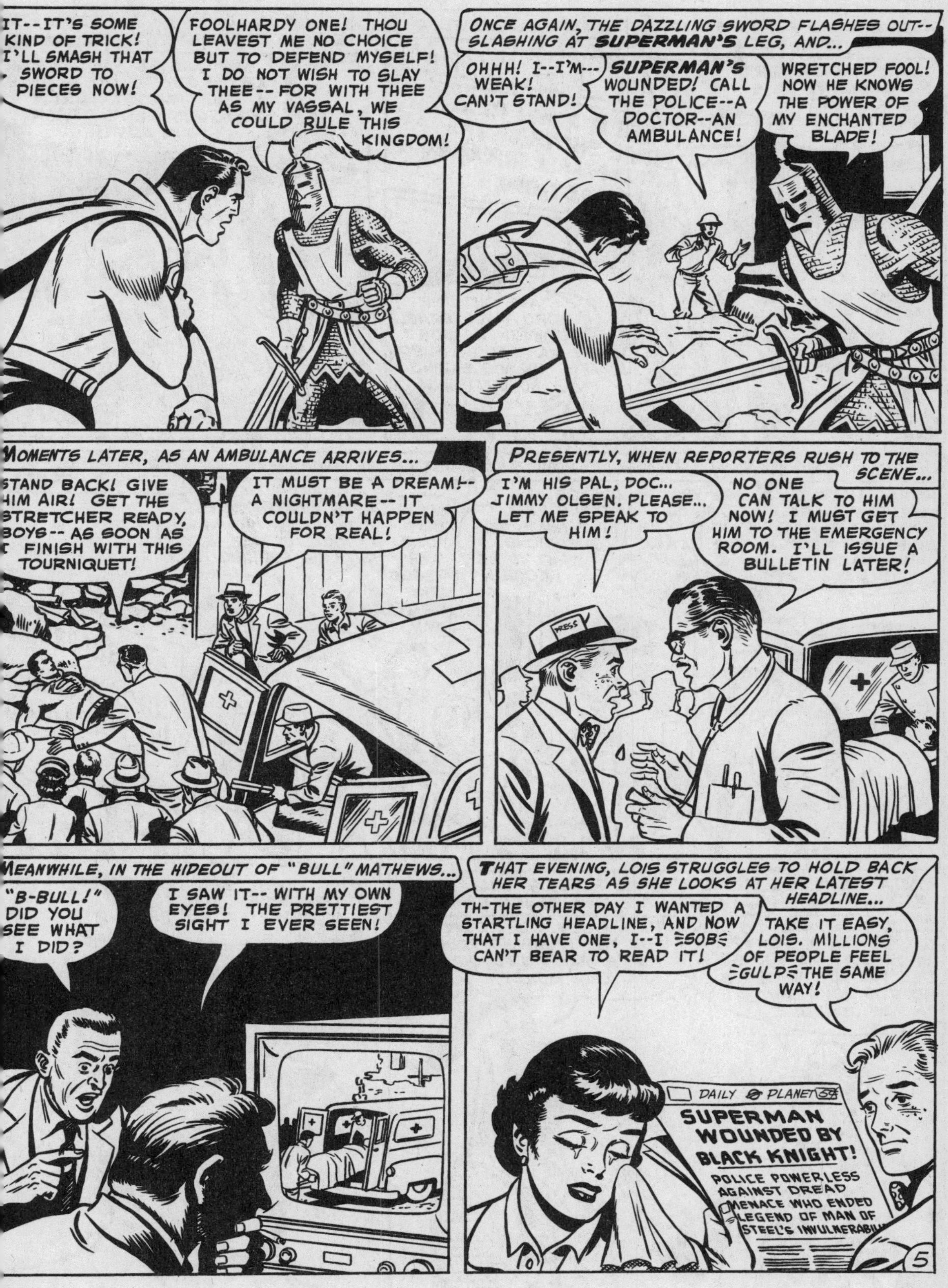
IT--IT'S SOME KIND OF TRICK! I'LL SMASH THAT SWORD TO PIECES NOW!
FOOLHARDY ONE! THOU LEAVEST ME NO CHOICE BUT TO DEFEND MYSELF! I DO NOT WISH TO SLAY THEE--FOR WITH THEE AS MY VASSAL, WE COULD RULE THIS KINGDOM!
ONCE AGAIN, THE DAZZLING SWORD FLASHES OUT--SLASHING AT SUPERMAN'S LEG, AND...
OHHH! I--I'M--- WEAK! CAN'T STAND!
SUPERMAN'S WOUNDED! CALL THE POLICE--A DOCTOR--AN AMBULANCE!
WRETCHED FOOL! NOW HE KNOWS THE POWER OF MY ENCHANTED BLADE!
MOMENTS LATER, AS AN AMBULANCE ARRIVES...
STAND BACK! GIVE HIM AIR! GET THE STRETCHER READY, BOYS--AS SOON AS I FINISH WITH THIS TOURNIQUET!
IT MUST BE A DREAM!--A NIGHTMARE--IT COULDN'T HAPPEN FOR REAL!
PRESENTLY, WHEN REPORTERS RUSH TO THE SCENE...
I'M HIS PAL, DOC... JIMMY OLSEN. PLEASE... LET ME SPEAK TO HIM!
NO ONE CAN TALK TO HIM NOW! I MUST GET HIM TO THE EMERGENCY ROOM. I'LL ISSUE A BULLETIN LATER!
PRESS
MEANWHILE, IN THE HIDEOUT OF "BULL" MATHEWS...
"B-BULL!" DID YOU SEE WHAT I DID?
I SAW IT--WITH MY OWN EYES! THE PRETTIEST SIGHT I EVER SEEN!
THAT EVENING, LOIS STRUGGLES TO HOLD BACK HER TEARS AS SHE LOOKS AT HER LATEST HEADLINE...
TH-THE OTHER DAY I WANTED A STARTLING HEADLINE, AND NOW THAT I HAVE ONE, I--I SOB CAN'T BEAR TO READ IT!
TAKE IT EASY, LOIS. MILLIONS OF PEOPLE FEEL GULP THE SAME WAY!
DAILY PLANET
SUPERMAN WOUNDED BY BLACK KNIGHT!
POLICE POWERLESS AGAINST DREAD MENACE WHO ENDED LEGEND OF MAN OF STEEL'S INVULNERABI
5

AND, AS RADIO AND TV SCATTER THE NEWS TO THE FOUR CORNERS OF AN INCREDULOUS WORLD...

THAT BOUNDER HURT *SUPERMAN!* HE'S A DISGRACE TO BRITISH SOIL!

SEE IT NOW! REAL MOVIE SHOTS OF THE *INVULNERABLE* SUPERMAN IN ACTION!

TAKE OUT THE WORD *"INVULNERABLE,"* JONES! WE DON'T WANT TO BE SUED FOR MISLEADING ADVERTISING!

MEANWHILE, IN OTHER QUARTERS, THE NEWS IS RECEIVED WITH JOY!

WHAT ARE WE WAITING FOR? *LET'S GO!* WE GOTTA MAKE A DEAL WITH THAT *BLACK KNIGHT!* LET'S TRACK HIM DOWN!

DAILY PLANET

THE END OF A LEGEND

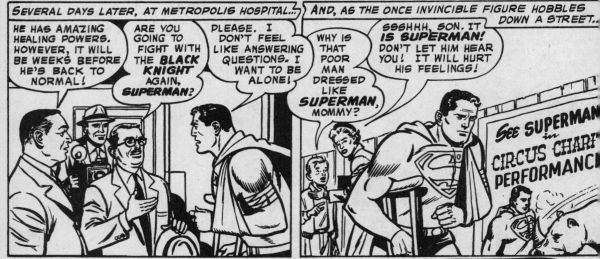

SEVERAL DAYS LATER, AT METROPOLIS HOSPITAL...

HE HAS AMAZING HEALING POWERS. HOWEVER, IT WILL BE WEEKS BEFORE HE'S BACK TO NORMAL!

ARE YOU GOING TO FIGHT WITH THE *BLACK KNIGHT* AGAIN, *SUPERMAN?*

PLEASE. I DON'T FEEL LIKE ANSWERING QUESTIONS. I WANT TO BE ALONE!

AND, AS THE ONCE INVINCIBLE FIGURE HOBBLES DOWN A STREET...

WHY IS THAT POOR MAN DRESSED LIKE *SUPERMAN,* MOMMY?

SSSHHH, SON. IT *IS SUPERMAN!* DON'T LET HIM HEAR YOU! IT WILL HURT HIS FEELINGS!

SEE SUPERMAN IN CIRCUS CHARI'... PERFORMANCE...

AT THAT MOMENT, ELSEWHERE IN METROPOLIS, "BULL" MATHEWS HAS FINALLY CONTACTED *THE BLACK KNIGHT,* AND...

WELL, WHAT DO YOU SAY, *BLACK KNIGHT?* I'M AN OUTLAW LIKE YOURSELF. I'LL PAY ANY PRICE TO BORROW YOUR SWORD A FEW HOURS!

'TIS A FAVOR I'LL GRANT YOU FOR TEN THOUSAND POUNDS-- THAT'S ABOUT $30,000 IN YOUR MONEY!

THAT'S... ER... VERY =GULP= GENEROUS. I'LL PAY YOU RIGHT AFTER I USE IT!

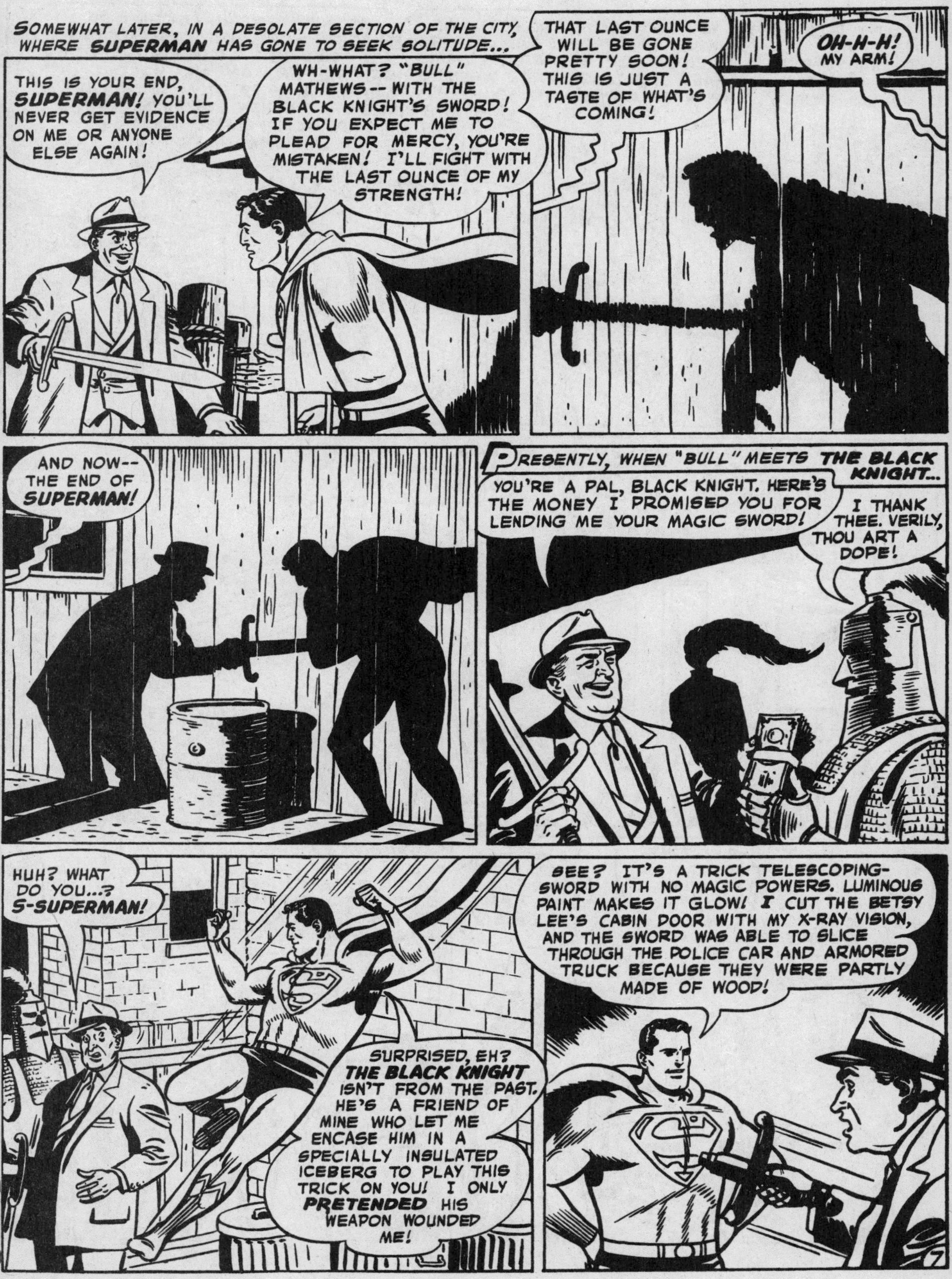
SOMEWHAT LATER, IN A DESOLATE SECTION OF THE CITY, WHERE SUPERMAN HAS GONE TO SEEK SOLITUDE...
THIS IS YOUR END, SUPERMAN! YOU'LL NEVER GET EVIDENCE ON ME OR ANYONE ELSE AGAIN!
WH-WHAT? "BULL" MATHEWS -- WITH THE BLACK KNIGHT'S SWORD! IF YOU EXPECT ME TO PLEAD FOR MERCY, YOU'RE MISTAKEN! I'LL FIGHT WITH THE LAST OUNCE OF MY STRENGTH!
THAT LAST OUNCE WILL BE GONE PRETTY SOON! THIS IS JUST A TASTE OF WHAT'S COMING!
OH-H-H! MY ARM!
AND NOW-- THE END OF SUPERMAN!
PRESENTLY, WHEN "BULL" MEETS THE BLACK KNIGHT...
YOU'RE A PAL, BLACK KNIGHT. HERE'S THE MONEY I PROMISED YOU FOR LENDING ME YOUR MAGIC SWORD!
I THANK THEE. VERILY, THOU ART A DOPE!
HUH? WHAT DO YOU...? S-SUPERMAN!
SURPRISED, EH? THE BLACK KNIGHT ISN'T FROM THE PAST. HE'S A FRIEND OF MINE WHO LET ME ENCASE HIM IN A SPECIALLY INSULATED ICEBERG TO PLAY THIS TRICK ON YOU! I ONLY PRETENDED HIS WEAPON WOUNDED ME!
SEE? IT'S A TRICK TELESCOPING-SWORD WITH NO MAGIC POWERS. LUMINOUS PAINT MAKES IT GLOW! I CUT THE BETSY LEE'S CABIN DOOR WITH MY X-RAY VISION, AND THE SWORD WAS ABLE TO SLICE THROUGH THE POLICE CAR AND ARMORED TRUCK BECAUSE THEY WERE PARTLY MADE OF WOOD!
7

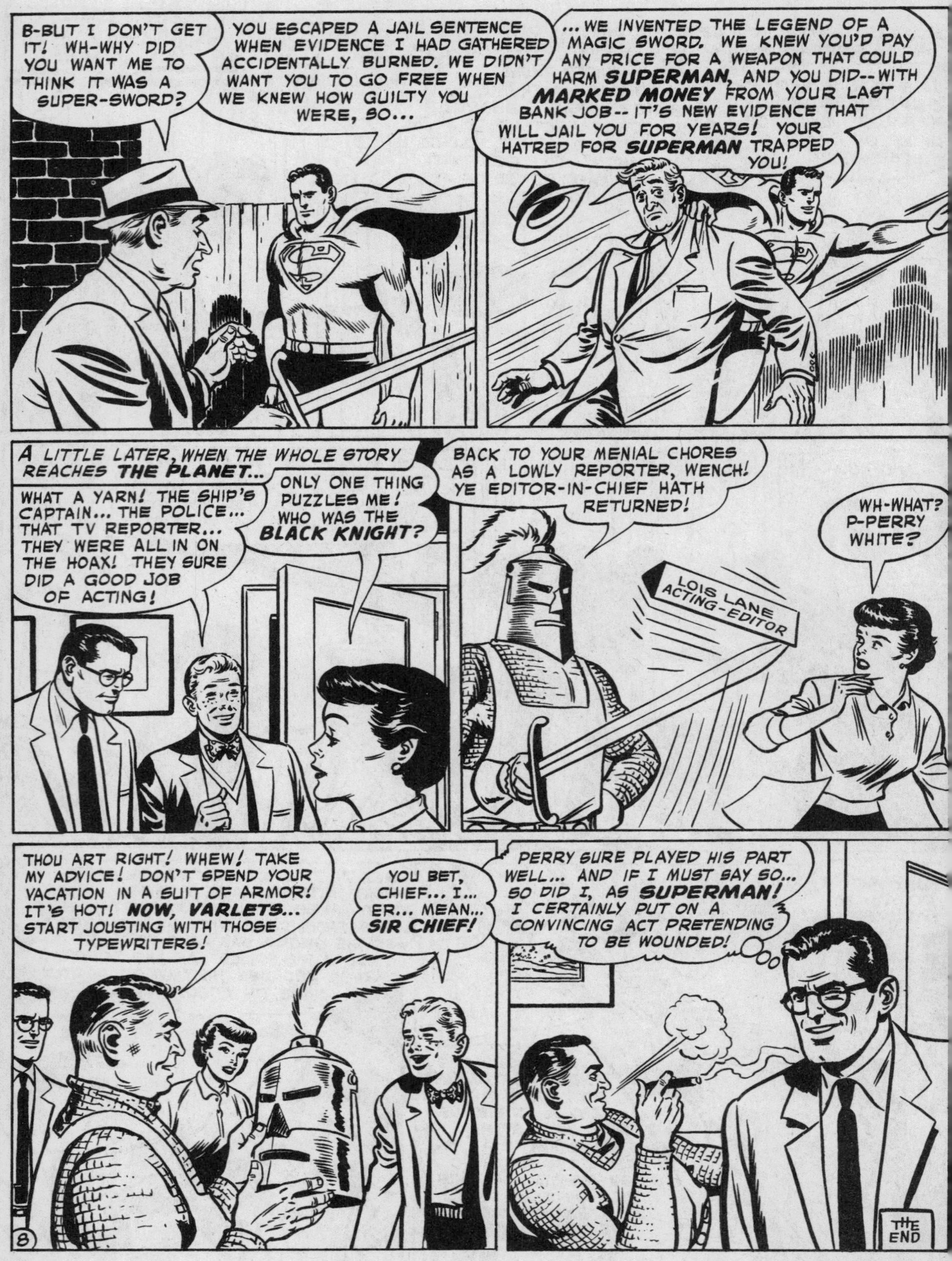
B-BUT I DON'T GET IT! WH-WHY DID YOU WANT ME TO THINK IT WAS A SUPER-SWORD?
YOU ESCAPED A JAIL SENTENCE WHEN EVIDENCE I HAD GATHERED ACCIDENTALLY BURNED. WE DIDN'T WANT YOU TO GO FREE WHEN WE KNEW HOW GUILTY YOU WERE, SO...
...WE INVENTED THE LEGEND OF A MAGIC SWORD. WE KNEW YOU'D PAY ANY PRICE FOR A WEAPON THAT COULD HARM SUPERMAN, AND YOU DID--WITH MARKED MONEY FROM YOUR LAST BANK JOB-- IT'S NEW EVIDENCE THAT WILL JAIL YOU FOR YEARS! YOUR HATRED FOR SUPERMAN TRAPPED YOU!
A LITTLE LATER, WHEN THE WHOLE STORY REACHES THE PLANET...
WHAT A YARN! THE SHIP'S CAPTAIN... THE POLICE... THAT TV REPORTER... THEY WERE ALL IN ON THE HOAX! THEY SURE DID A GOOD JOB OF ACTING!
ONLY ONE THING PUZZLES ME! WHO WAS THE BLACK KNIGHT?
BACK TO YOUR MENIAL CHORES AS A LOWLY REPORTER, WENCH! YE EDITOR-IN-CHIEF HATH RETURNED!
LOIS LANE ACTING-EDITOR
WH-WHAT? P-PERRY WHITE?
THOU ART RIGHT! WHEW! TAKE MY ADVICE! DON'T SPEND YOUR VACATION IN A SUIT OF ARMOR! IT'S HOT! NOW, VARLETS... START JOUSTING WITH THOSE TYPEWRITERS!
YOU BET, CHIEF... I... ER... MEAN... SIR CHIEF!
8
PERRY SURE PLAYED HIS PART WELL... AND IF I MUST SAY SO... SO DID I, AS SUPERMAN! I CERTAINLY PUT ON A CONVINCING ACT PRETENDING TO BE WOUNDED!
THE END

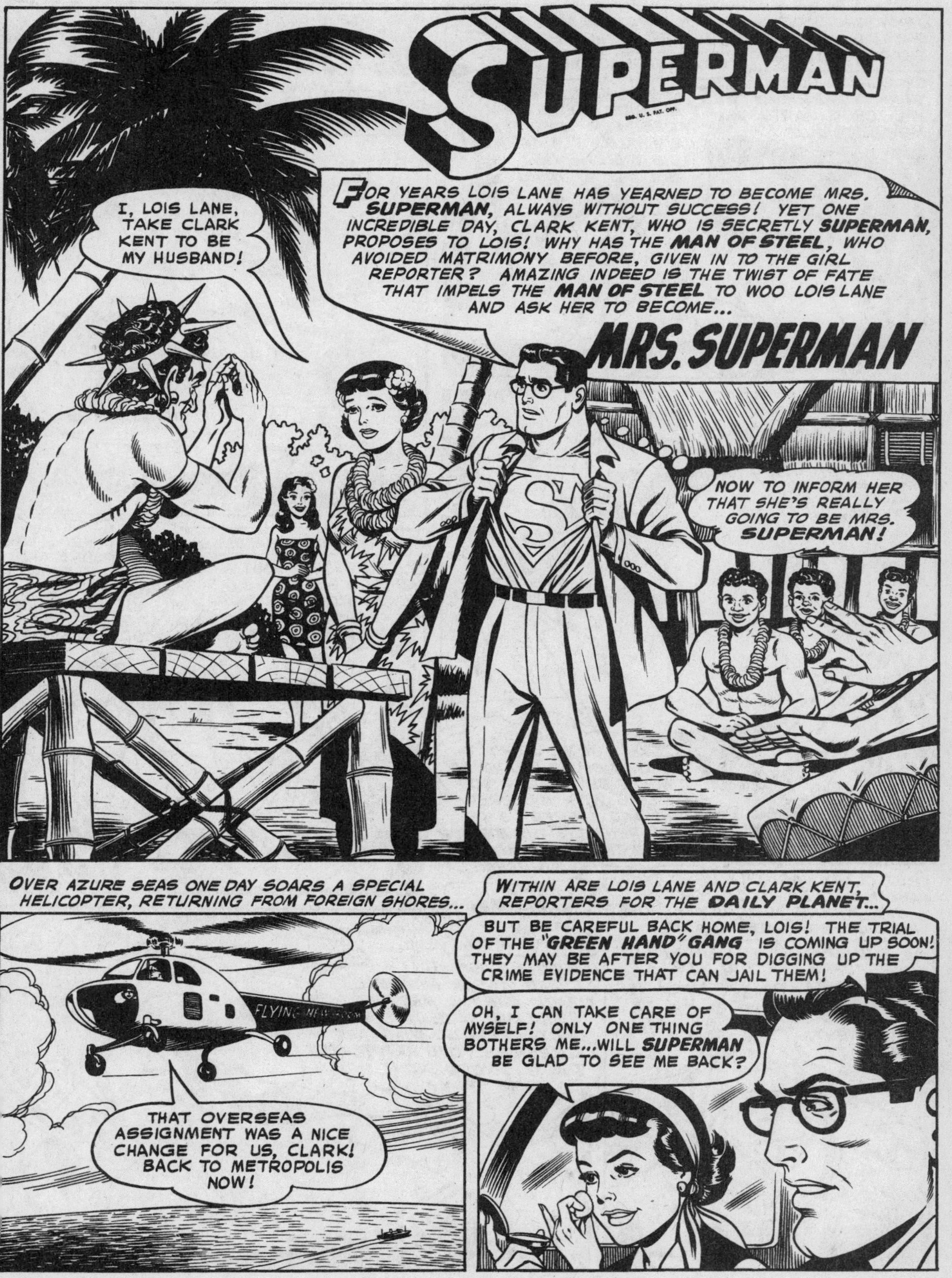
SUPERMAN
I, LOIS LANE, TAKE CLARK KENT TO BE MY HUSBAND!
FOR YEARS LOIS LANE HAS YEARNED TO BECOME MRS. SUPERMAN, ALWAYS WITHOUT SUCCESS! YET ONE INCREDIBLE DAY, CLARK KENT, WHO IS SECRETLY SUPERMAN, PROPOSES TO LOIS! WHY HAS THE MAN OF STEEL, WHO AVOIDED MATRIMONY BEFORE, GIVEN IN TO THE GIRL REPORTER? AMAZING INDEED IS THE TWIST OF FATE THAT IMPELS THE MAN OF STEEL TO WOO LOIS LANE AND ASK HER TO BECOME...
MRS. SUPERMAN
NOW TO INFORM HER THAT SHE'S REALLY GOING TO BE MRS. SUPERMAN!
OVER AZURE SEAS ONE DAY SOARS A SPECIAL HELICOPTER, RETURNING FROM FOREIGN SHORES...
THAT OVERSEAS ASSIGNMENT WAS A NICE CHANGE FOR US, CLARK! BACK TO METROPOLIS NOW!
WITHIN ARE LOIS LANE AND CLARK KENT, REPORTERS FOR THE DAILY PLANET...
BUT BE CAREFUL BACK HOME, LOIS! THE TRIAL OF THE "GREEN HAND" GANG IS COMING UP SOON! THEY MAY BE AFTER YOU FOR DIGGING UP THE CRIME EVIDENCE THAT CAN JAIL THEM!
OH, I CAN TAKE CARE OF MYSELF! ONLY ONE THING BOTHERS ME...WILL SUPERMAN BE GLAD TO SEE ME BACK?

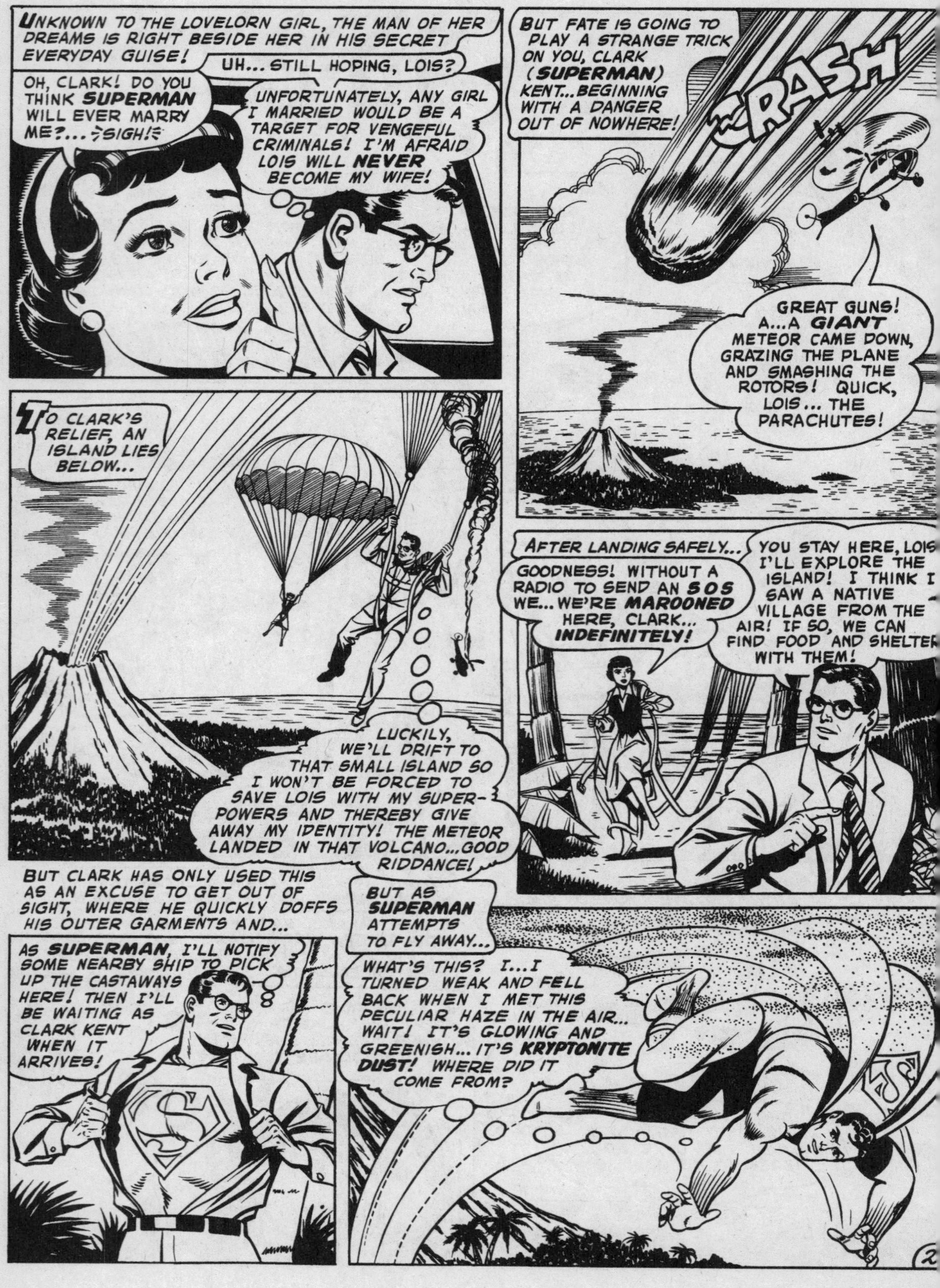
UNKNOWN TO THE LOVELORN GIRL, THE MAN OF HER DREAMS IS RIGHT BESIDE HER IN HIS SECRET EVERYDAY GUISE!
UH... STILL HOPING, LOIS?
OH, CLARK! DO YOU THINK SUPERMAN WILL EVER MARRY ME?... SIGH!
UNFORTUNATELY, ANY GIRL I MARRIED WOULD BE A TARGET FOR VENGEFUL CRIMINALS! I'M AFRAID LOIS WILL NEVER BECOME MY WIFE!
BUT FATE IS GOING TO PLAY A STRANGE TRICK ON YOU, CLARK (SUPERMAN) KENT... BEGINNING WITH A DANGER OUT OF NOWHERE!
CRASH
GREAT GUNS! A...A GIANT METEOR CAME DOWN, GRAZING THE PLANE AND SMASHING THE ROTORS! QUICK, LOIS... THE PARACHUTES!
TO CLARK'S RELIEF, AN ISLAND LIES BELOW...
LUCKILY, WE'LL DRIFT TO THAT SMALL ISLAND SO I WON'T BE FORCED TO SAVE LOIS WITH MY SUPER-POWERS AND THEREBY GIVE AWAY MY IDENTITY! THE METEOR LANDED IN THAT VOLCANO...GOOD RIDDANCE!
AFTER LANDING SAFELY...
GOODNESS! WITHOUT A RADIO TO SEND AN SOS WE...WE'RE MAROONED HERE, CLARK... INDEFINITELY!
YOU STAY HERE, LOIS I'LL EXPLORE THE ISLAND! I THINK I SAW A NATIVE VILLAGE FROM THE AIR! IF SO, WE CAN FIND FOOD AND SHELTER WITH THEM!
BUT CLARK HAS ONLY USED THIS AS AN EXCUSE TO GET OUT OF SIGHT, WHERE HE QUICKLY DOFFS HIS OUTER GARMENTS AND...
AS SUPERMAN, I'LL NOTIFY SOME NEARBY SHIP TO PICK UP THE CASTAWAYS HERE! THEN I'LL BE WAITING AS CLARK KENT WHEN IT ARRIVES!
BUT AS SUPERMAN ATTEMPTS TO FLY AWAY...
WHAT'S THIS? I...I TURNED WEAK AND FELL BACK WHEN I MET THIS PECULIAR HAZE IN THE AIR... WAIT! IT'S GLOWING AND GREENISH... IT'S KRYPTONITE DUST! WHERE DID IT COME FROM?
2

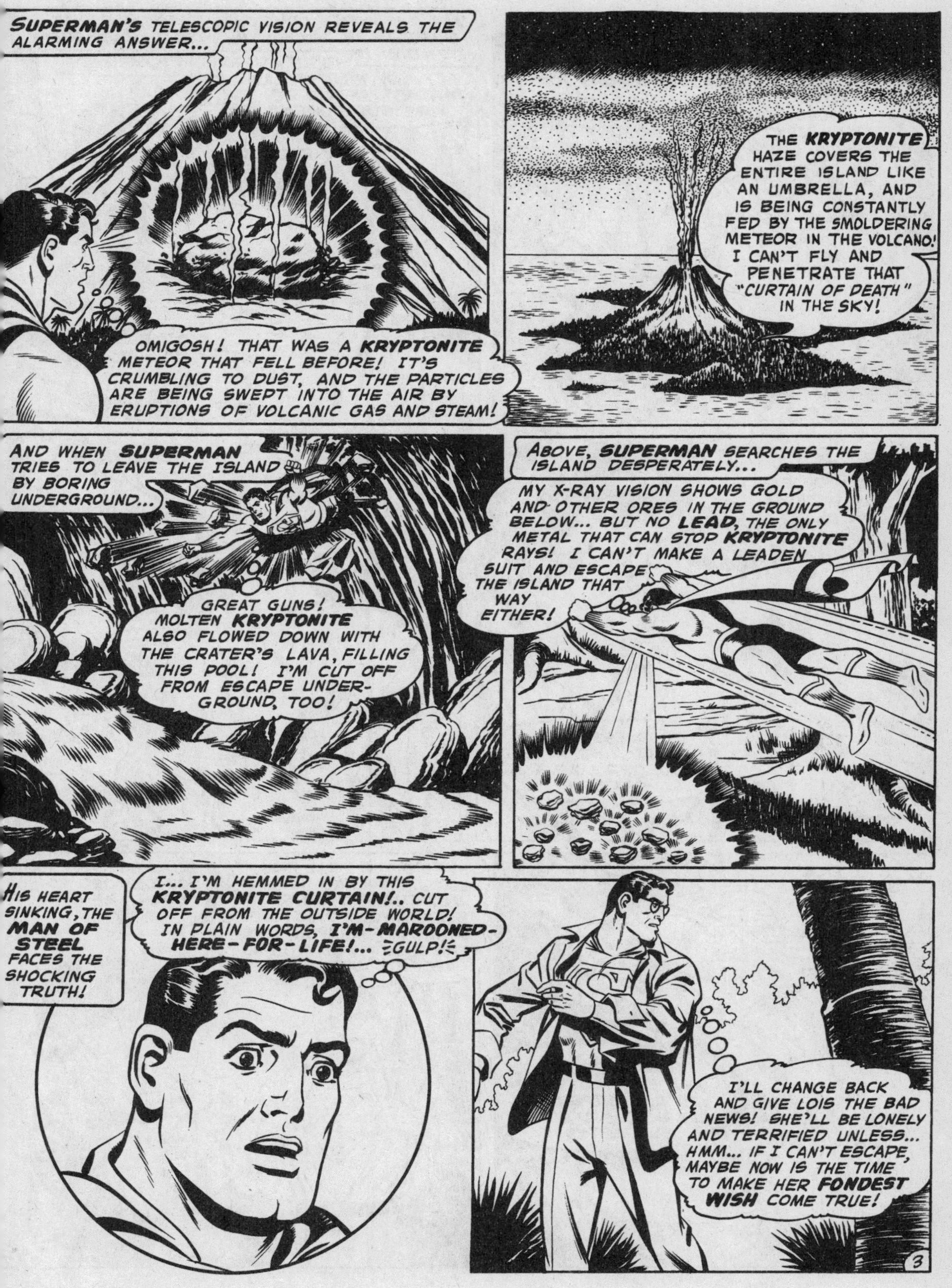
SUPERMAN'S TELESCOPIC VISION REVEALS THE ALARMING ANSWER...
OMIGOSH! THAT WAS A KRYPTONITE METEOR THAT FELL BEFORE! IT'S CRUMBLING TO DUST, AND THE PARTICLES ARE BEING SWEPT INTO THE AIR BY ERUPTIONS OF VOLCANIC GAS AND STEAM!
THE KRYPTONITE HAZE COVERS THE ENTIRE ISLAND LIKE AN UMBRELLA, AND IS BEING CONSTANTLY FED BY THE SMOLDERING METEOR IN THE VOLCANO! I CAN'T FLY AND PENETRATE THAT "CURTAIN OF DEATH" IN THE SKY!
AND WHEN SUPERMAN TRIES TO LEAVE THE ISLAND BY BORING UNDERGROUND...
GREAT GUNS! MOLTEN KRYPTONITE ALSO FLOWED DOWN WITH THE CRATER'S LAVA, FILLING THIS POOL! I'M CUT OFF FROM ESCAPE UNDER-GROUND, TOO!
ABOVE, SUPERMAN SEARCHES THE ISLAND DESPERATELY...
MY X-RAY VISION SHOWS GOLD AND OTHER ORES IN THE GROUND BELOW... BUT NO LEAD, THE ONLY METAL THAT CAN STOP KRYPTONITE RAYS! I CAN'T MAKE A LEADEN SUIT AND ESCAPE THE ISLAND THAT WAY EITHER!
HIS HEART SINKING, THE MAN OF STEEL FACES THE SHOCKING TRUTH!
I... I'M HEMMED IN BY THIS KRYPTONITE CURTAIN!.. CUT OFF FROM THE OUTSIDE WORLD! IN PLAIN WORDS, I'M-MAROONED-HERE-FOR-LIFE!... GULP!
I'LL CHANGE BACK AND GIVE LOIS THE BAD NEWS! SHE'LL BE LONELY AND TERRIFIED UNLESS... HMM... IF I CAN'T ESCAPE, MAYBE NOW IS THE TIME TO MAKE HER FONDEST WISH COME TRUE!
3

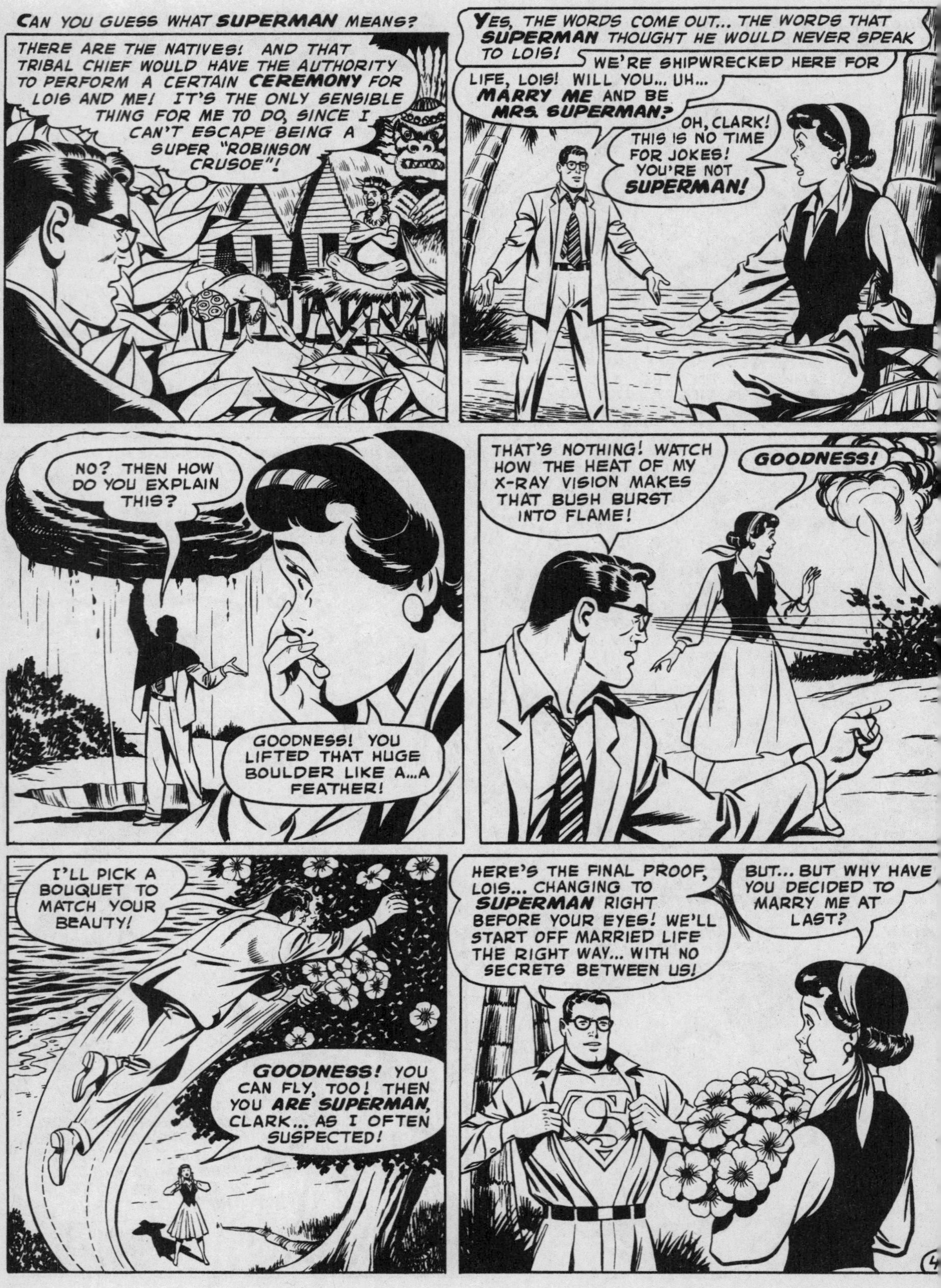
CAN YOU GUESS WHAT SUPERMAN MEANS?
THERE ARE THE NATIVES! AND THAT TRIBAL CHIEF WOULD HAVE THE AUTHORITY TO PERFORM A CERTAIN CEREMONY FOR LOIS AND ME! IT'S THE ONLY SENSIBLE THING FOR ME TO DO, SINCE I CAN'T ESCAPE BEING A SUPER "ROBINSON CRUSOE"!
YES, THE WORDS COME OUT... THE WORDS THAT SUPERMAN THOUGHT HE WOULD NEVER SPEAK TO LOIS!
WE'RE SHIPWRECKED HERE FOR LIFE, LOIS! WILL YOU... UH... MARRY ME AND BE MRS. SUPERMAN?
OH, CLARK! THIS IS NO TIME FOR JOKES! YOU'RE NOT SUPERMAN!
NO? THEN HOW DO YOU EXPLAIN THIS?
GOODNESS! YOU LIFTED THAT HUGE BOULDER LIKE A...A FEATHER!
THAT'S NOTHING! WATCH HOW THE HEAT OF MY X-RAY VISION MAKES THAT BUSH BURST INTO FLAME!
GOODNESS!
I'LL PICK A BOUQUET TO MATCH YOUR BEAUTY!
GOODNESS! YOU CAN FLY, TOO! THEN YOU ARE SUPERMAN, CLARK... AS I OFTEN SUSPECTED!
HERE'S THE FINAL PROOF, LOIS... CHANGING TO SUPERMAN RIGHT BEFORE YOUR EYES! WE'LL START OFF MARRIED LIFE THE RIGHT WAY... WITH NO SECRETS BETWEEN US!
BUT... BUT WHY HAVE YOU DECIDED TO MARRY ME AT LAST?

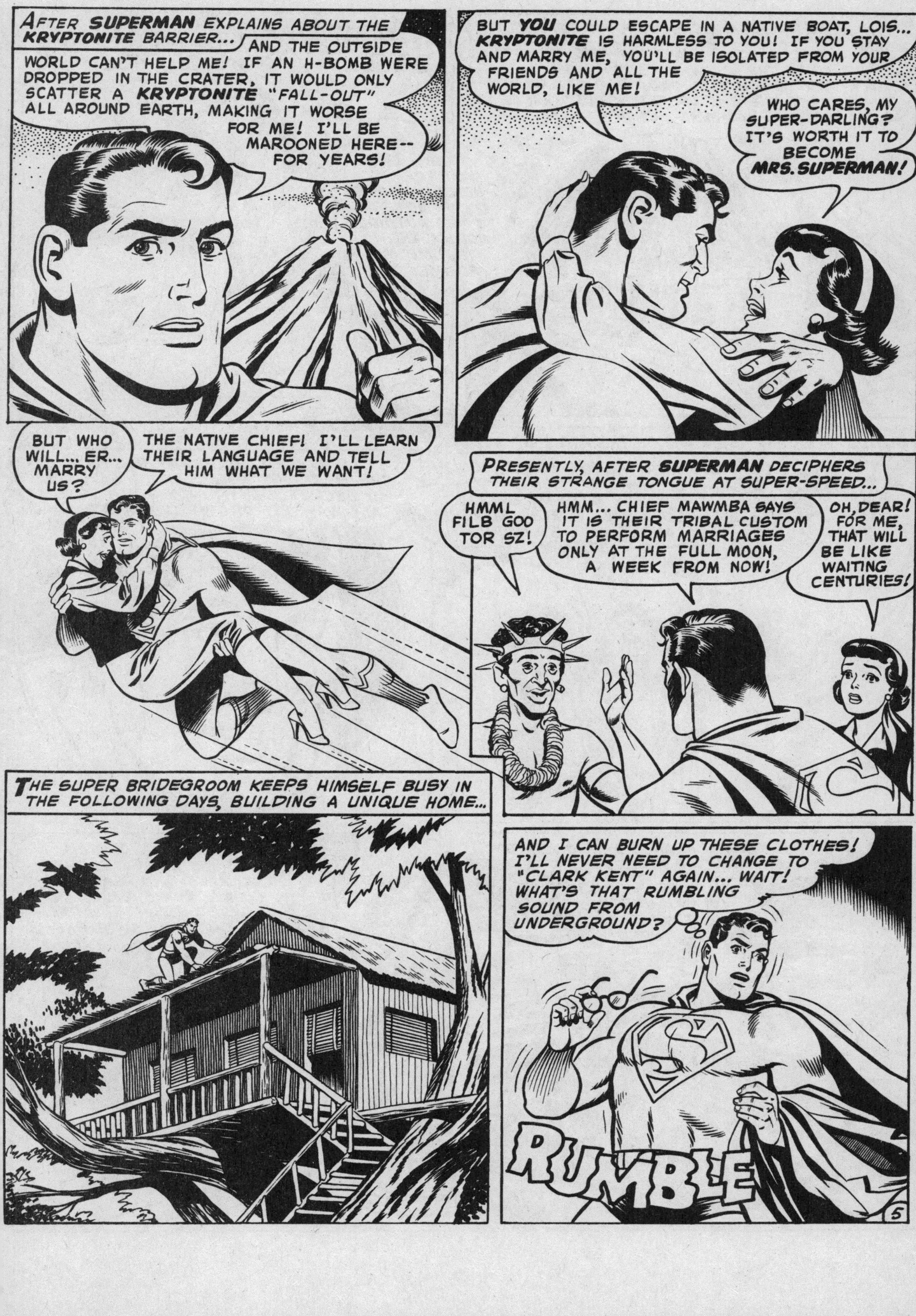
AFTER SUPERMAN EXPLAINS ABOUT THE KRYPTONITE BARRIER...
AND THE OUTSIDE WORLD CAN'T HELP ME! IF AN H-BOMB WERE DROPPED IN THE CRATER, IT WOULD ONLY SCATTER A KRYPTONITE "FALL-OUT" ALL AROUND EARTH, MAKING IT WORSE FOR ME! I'LL BE MAROONED HERE-- FOR YEARS!
BUT YOU COULD ESCAPE IN A NATIVE BOAT, LOIS... KRYPTONITE IS HARMLESS TO YOU! IF YOU STAY AND MARRY ME, YOU'LL BE ISOLATED FROM YOUR FRIENDS AND ALL THE WORLD, LIKE ME!
WHO CARES, MY SUPER-DARLING? IT'S WORTH IT TO BECOME MRS. SUPERMAN!
BUT WHO WILL... ER... MARRY US?
THE NATIVE CHIEF! I'LL LEARN THEIR LANGUAGE AND TELL HIM WHAT WE WANT!
PRESENTLY, AFTER SUPERMAN DECIPHERS THEIR STRANGE TONGUE AT SUPER-SPEED...
HMML FILB GOO TOR SZ!
HMM... CHIEF MAWMBA SAYS IT IS THEIR TRIBAL CUSTOM TO PERFORM MARRIAGES ONLY AT THE FULL MOON, A WEEK FROM NOW!
OH, DEAR! FOR ME, THAT WILL BE LIKE WAITING CENTURIES!
THE SUPER BRIDEGROOM KEEPS HIMSELF BUSY IN THE FOLLOWING DAYS, BUILDING A UNIQUE HOME...
AND I CAN BURN UP THESE CLOTHES! I'LL NEVER NEED TO CHANGE TO "CLARK KENT" AGAIN... WAIT! WHAT'S THAT RUMBLING SOUND FROM UNDERGROUND?
RUMBLE
5

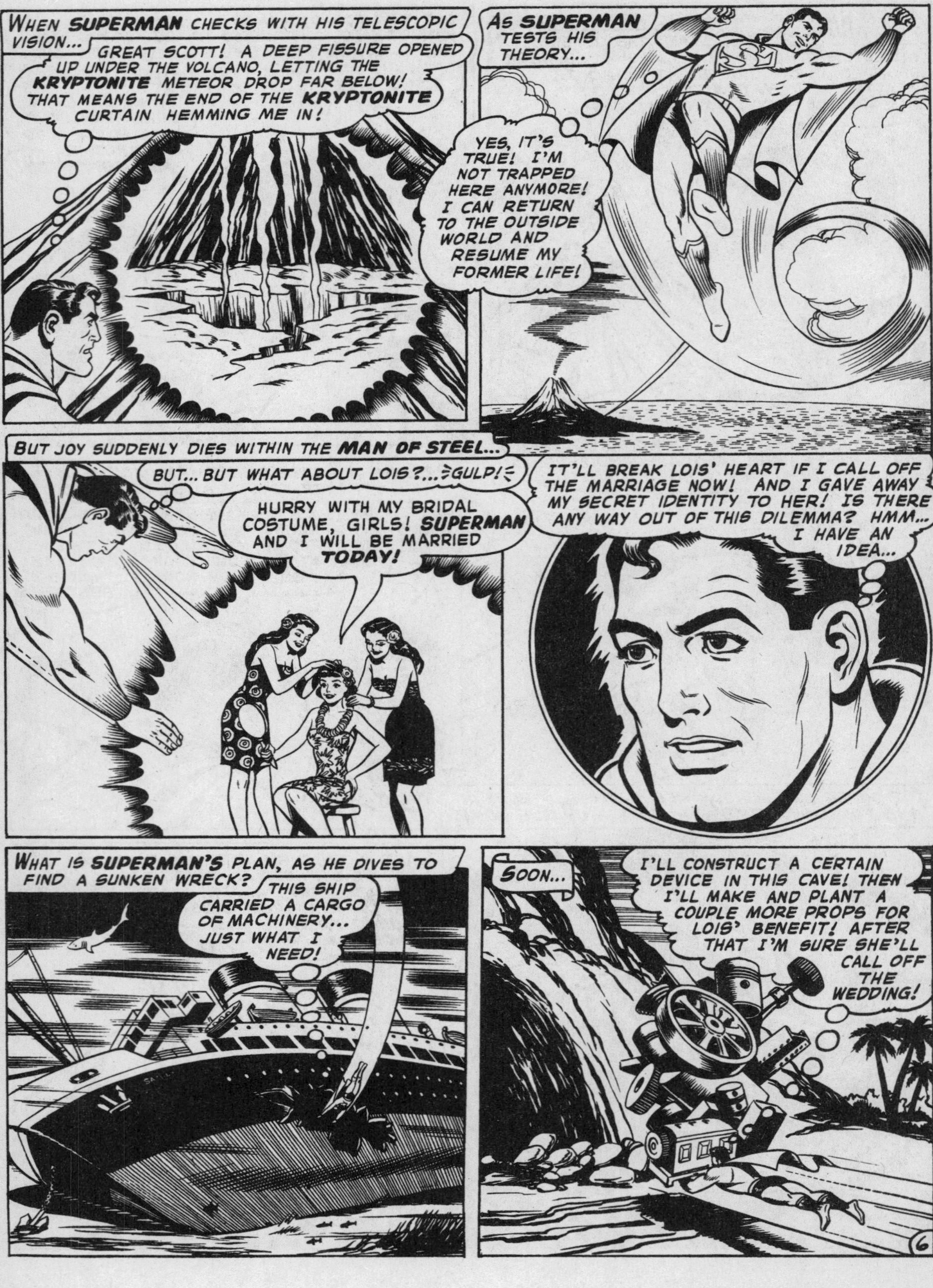
WHEN SUPERMAN CHECKS WITH HIS TELESCOPIC VISION...
GREAT SCOTT! A DEEP FISSURE OPENED UP UNDER THE VOLCANO, LETTING THE KRYPTONITE METEOR DROP FAR BELOW! THAT MEANS THE END OF THE KRYPTONITE CURTAIN HEMMING ME IN!
AS SUPERMAN TESTS HIS THEORY...
YES, IT'S TRUE! I'M NOT TRAPPED HERE ANYMORE! I CAN RETURN TO THE OUTSIDE WORLD AND RESUME MY FORMER LIFE!
BUT JOY SUDDENLY DIES WITHIN THE MAN OF STEEL...
BUT... BUT WHAT ABOUT LOIS?... GULP!
HURRY WITH MY BRIDAL COSTUME, GIRLS! SUPERMAN AND I WILL BE MARRIED TODAY!
IT'LL BREAK LOIS' HEART IF I CALL OFF THE MARRIAGE NOW! AND I GAVE AWAY MY SECRET IDENTITY TO HER! IS THERE ANY WAY OUT OF THIS DILEMMA? HMM... I HAVE AN IDEA...
WHAT IS SUPERMAN'S PLAN, AS HE DIVES TO FIND A SUNKEN WRECK?
THIS SHIP CARRIED A CARGO OF MACHINERY... JUST WHAT I NEED!
SOON...
I'LL CONSTRUCT A CERTAIN DEVICE IN THIS CAVE! THEN I'LL MAKE AND PLANT A COUPLE MORE PROPS FOR LOIS' BENEFIT! AFTER THAT I'M SURE SHE'LL CALL OFF THE WEDDING!
6

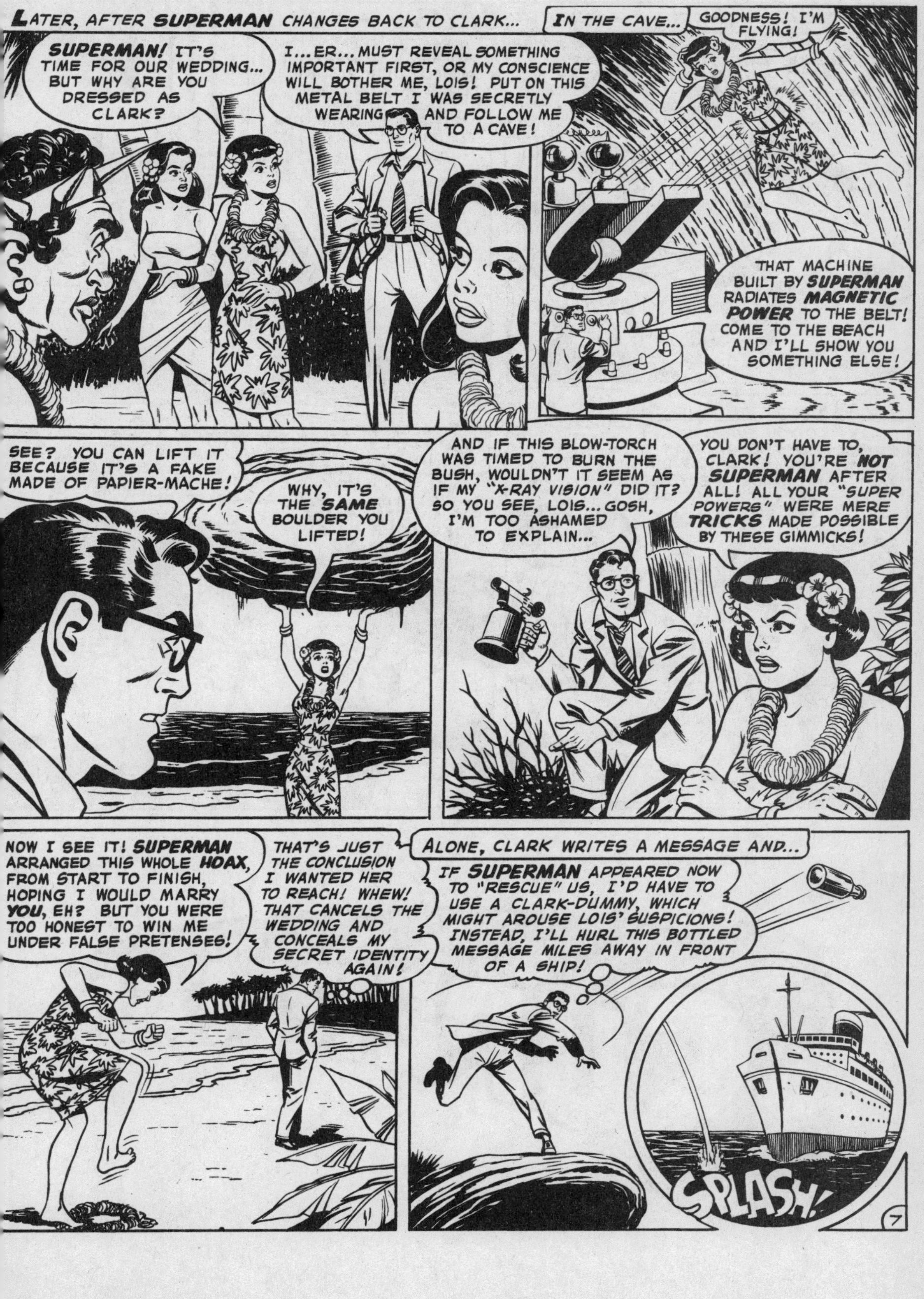
LATER, AFTER SUPERMAN CHANGES BACK TO CLARK...
SUPERMAN! IT'S TIME FOR OUR WEDDING... BUT WHY ARE YOU DRESSED AS CLARK?
I...ER...MUST REVEAL SOMETHING IMPORTANT FIRST, OR MY CONSCIENCE WILL BOTHER ME, LOIS! PUT ON THIS METAL BELT I WAS SECRETLY WEARING AND FOLLOW ME TO A CAVE!
IN THE CAVE...
GOODNESS! I'M FLYING!
THAT MACHINE BUILT BY SUPERMAN RADIATES MAGNETIC POWER TO THE BELT! COME TO THE BEACH AND I'LL SHOW YOU SOMETHING ELSE!
SEE? YOU CAN LIFT IT BECAUSE IT'S A FAKE MADE OF PAPIER-MACHE!
WHY, IT'S THE SAME BOULDER YOU LIFTED!
AND IF THIS BLOW-TORCH WAS TIMED TO BURN THE BUSH, WOULDN'T IT SEEM AS IF MY "X-RAY VISION" DID IT? SO YOU SEE, LOIS... GOSH, I'M TOO ASHAMED TO EXPLAIN...
YOU DON'T HAVE TO, CLARK! YOU'RE NOT SUPERMAN AFTER ALL! ALL YOUR "SUPER POWERS" WERE MERE TRICKS MADE POSSIBLE BY THESE GIMMICKS!
NOW I SEE IT! SUPERMAN ARRANGED THIS WHOLE HOAX, FROM START TO FINISH, HOPING I WOULD MARRY YOU, EH? BUT YOU WERE TOO HONEST TO WIN ME UNDER FALSE PRETENSES!
THAT'S JUST THE CONCLUSION I WANTED HER TO REACH! WHEW! THAT CANCELS THE WEDDING AND CONCEALS MY SECRET IDENTITY AGAIN!
ALONE, CLARK WRITES A MESSAGE AND...
IF SUPERMAN APPEARED NOW TO "RESCUE" US, I'D HAVE TO USE A CLARK-DUMMY, WHICH MIGHT AROUSE LOIS' SUSPICIONS! INSTEAD, I'LL HURL THIS BOTTLED MESSAGE MILES AWAY IN FRONT OF A SHIP!
SPLASH!
7

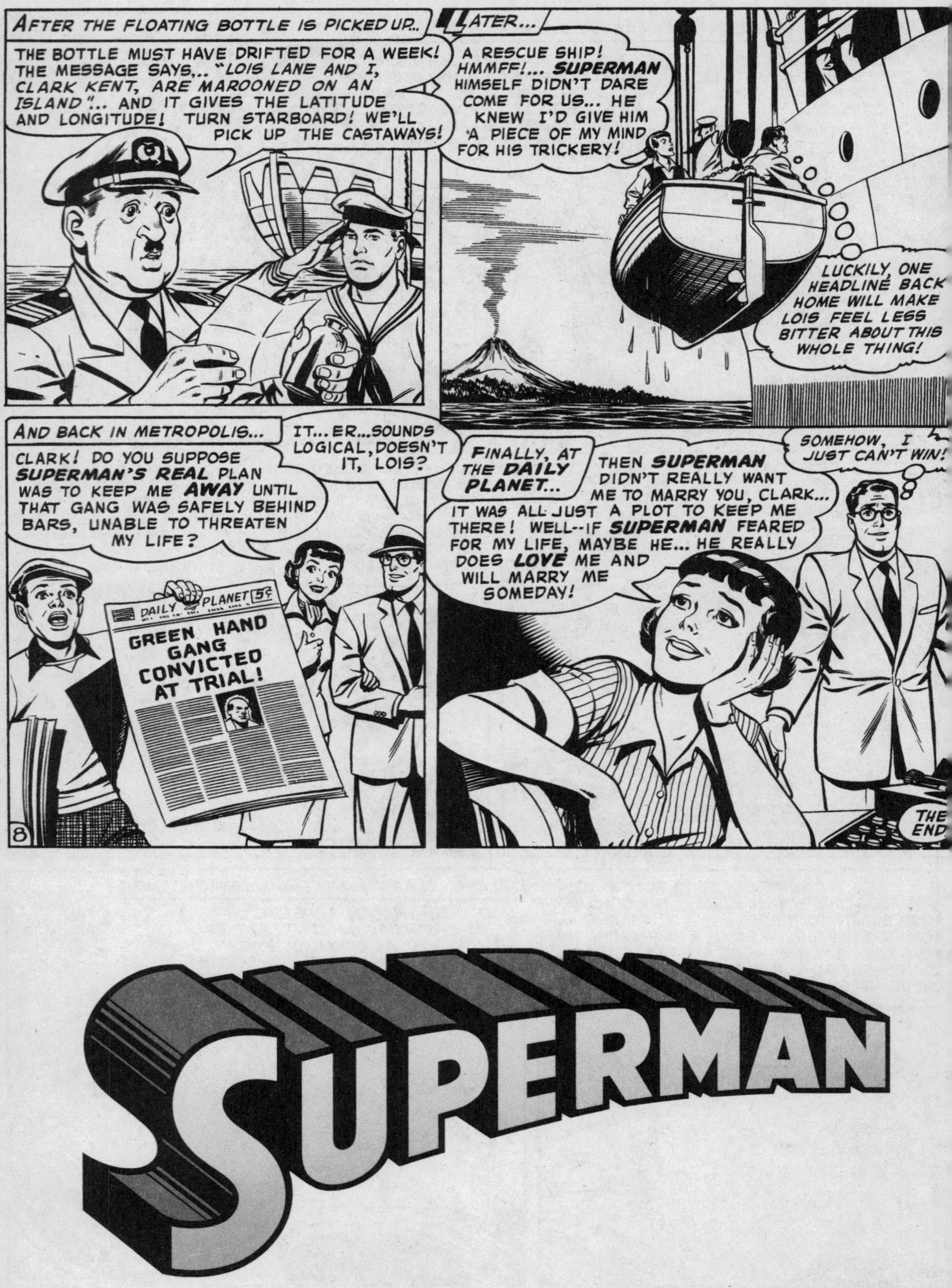
AFTER THE FLOATING BOTTLE IS PICKED UP..
THE BOTTLE MUST HAVE DRIFTED FOR A WEEK! THE MESSAGE SAYS,.. "LOIS LANE AND I, CLARK KENT, ARE MAROONED ON AN ISLAND"... AND IT GIVES THE LATITUDE AND LONGITUDE! TURN STARBOARD! WE'LL PICK UP THE CASTAWAYS!
LATER...
A RESCUE SHIP! HMMFF!... SUPERMAN HIMSELF DIDN'T DARE COME FOR US... HE KNEW I'D GIVE HIM A PIECE OF MY MIND FOR HIS TRICKERY!
LUCKILY, ONE HEADLINE BACK HOME WILL MAKE LOIS FEEL LESS BITTER ABOUT THIS WHOLE THING!
AND BACK IN METROPOLIS...
CLARK! DO YOU SUPPOSE SUPERMAN'S REAL PLAN WAS TO KEEP ME AWAY UNTIL THAT GANG WAS SAFELY BEHIND BARS, UNABLE TO THREATEN MY LIFE?
IT...ER...SOUNDS LOGICAL, DOESN'T IT, LOIS?
DAILY PLANET 5¢
GREEN HAND GANG CONVICTED AT TRIAL!
8
FINALLY, AT THE DAILY PLANET...
THEN SUPERMAN DIDN'T REALLY WANT ME TO MARRY YOU, CLARK... IT WAS ALL JUST A PLOT TO KEEP ME THERE! WELL--IF SUPERMAN FEARED FOR MY LIFE, MAYBE HE... HE REALLY DOES LOVE ME AND WILL MARRY ME SOMEDAY!
SOMEHOW, I JUST CAN'T WIN!
THE END

SUPERMAN

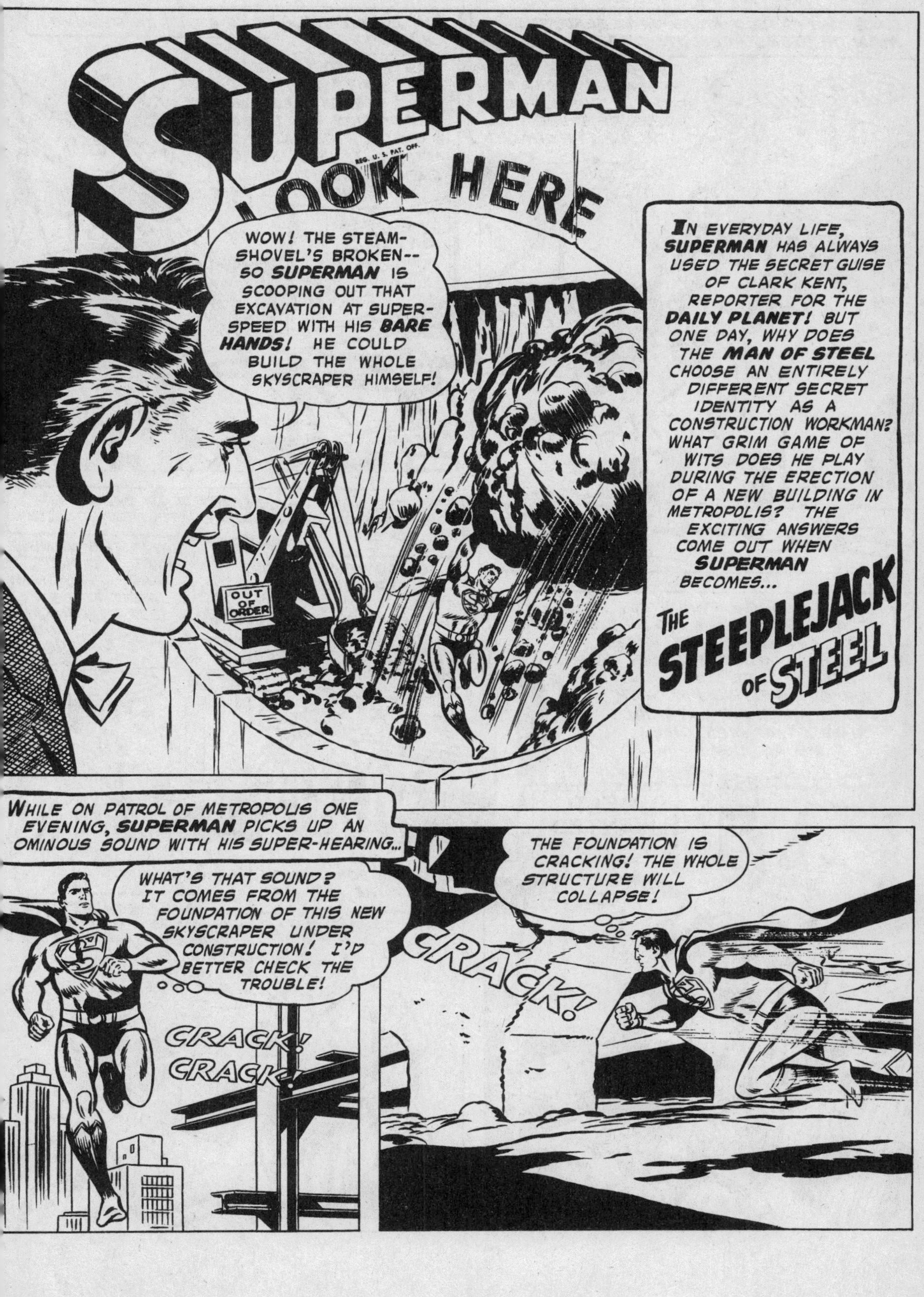
SUPERMAN
REG. U.S. PAT. OFF.
LOOK HERE
WOW! THE STEAM-SHOVEL'S BROKEN-- SO SUPERMAN IS SCOOPING OUT THAT EXCAVATION AT SUPER-SPEED WITH HIS BARE HANDS! HE COULD BUILD THE WHOLE SKYSCRAPER HIMSELF!
OUT OF ORDER
IN EVERYDAY LIFE, SUPERMAN HAS ALWAYS USED THE SECRET GUISE OF CLARK KENT, REPORTER FOR THE DAILY PLANET! BUT ONE DAY, WHY DOES THE MAN OF STEEL CHOOSE AN ENTIRELY DIFFERENT SECRET IDENTITY AS A CONSTRUCTION WORKMAN? WHAT GRIM GAME OF WITS DOES HE PLAY DURING THE ERECTION OF A NEW BUILDING IN METROPOLIS? THE EXCITING ANSWERS COME OUT WHEN SUPERMAN BECOMES...
THE STEEPLEJACK OF STEEL
WHILE ON PATROL OF METROPOLIS ONE EVENING, SUPERMAN PICKS UP AN OMINOUS SOUND WITH HIS SUPER-HEARING...
WHAT'S THAT SOUND? IT COMES FROM THE FOUNDATION OF THIS NEW SKYSCRAPER UNDER CONSTRUCTION! I'D BETTER CHECK THE TROUBLE!
CRACK! CRACK!
THE FOUNDATION IS CRACKING! THE WHOLE STRUCTURE WILL COLLAPSE!
CRACK!

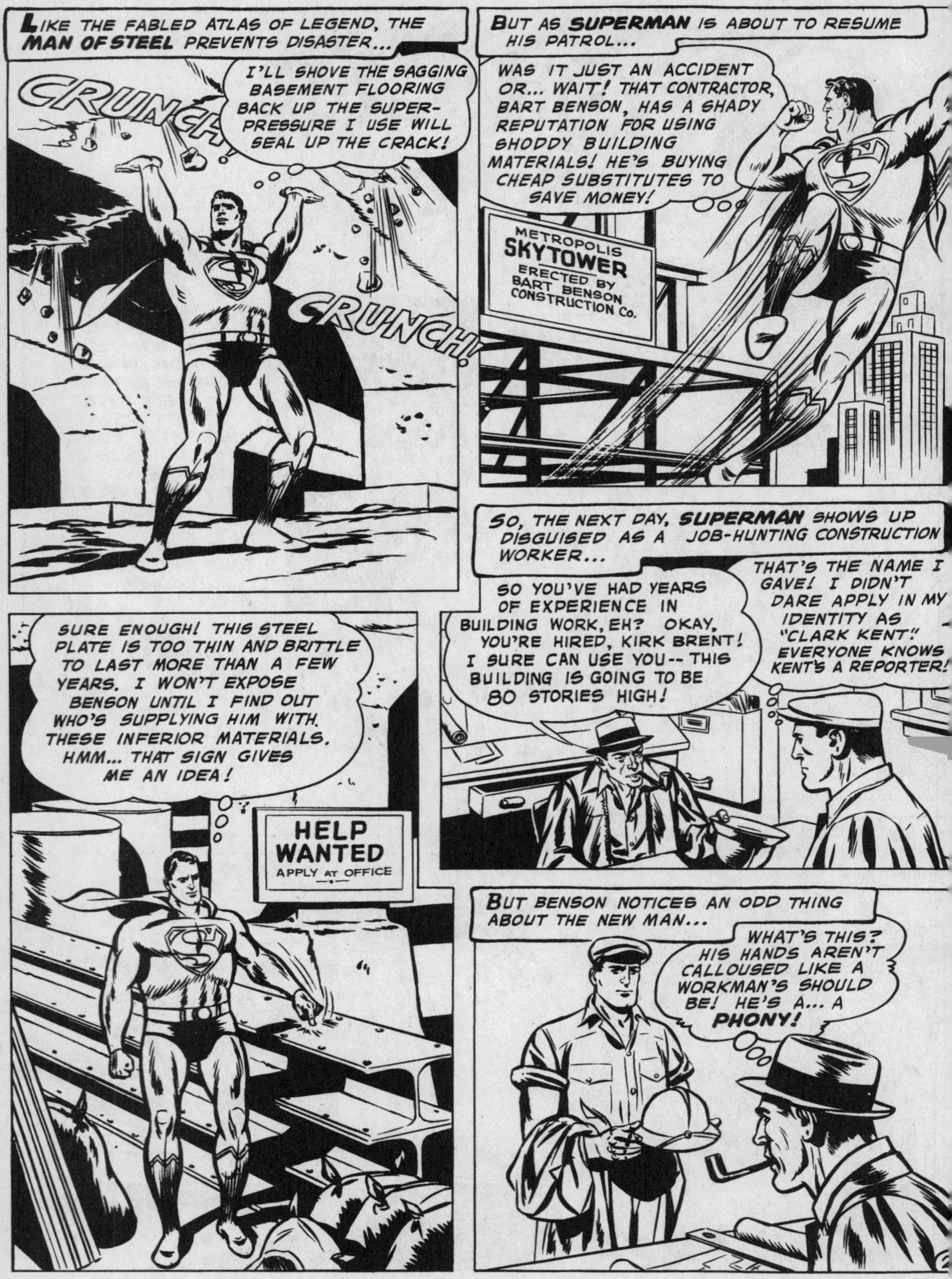
LIKE THE FABLED ATLAS OF LEGEND, THE MAN OF STEEL PREVENTS DISASTER...
I'LL SHOVE THE SAGGING BASEMENT FLOORING BACK UP THE SUPER-PRESSURE I USE WILL SEAL UP THE CRACK!
CRUNCH!
CRUNCH!
BUT AS SUPERMAN IS ABOUT TO RESUME HIS PATROL...
WAS IT JUST AN ACCIDENT OR... WAIT! THAT CONTRACTOR, BART BENSON, HAS A SHADY REPUTATION FOR USING SHODDY BUILDING MATERIALS! HE'S BUYING CHEAP SUBSTITUTES TO SAVE MONEY!
METROPOLIS SKYTOWER ERECTED BY BART BENSON CONSTRUCTION Co.
SURE ENOUGH! THIS STEEL PLATE IS TOO THIN AND BRITTLE TO LAST MORE THAN A FEW YEARS. I WON'T EXPOSE BENSON UNTIL I FIND OUT WHO'S SUPPLYING HIM WITH THESE INFERIOR MATERIALS. HMM... THAT SIGN GIVES ME AN IDEA!
HELP WANTED APPLY AT OFFICE
SO, THE NEXT DAY, SUPERMAN SHOWS UP DISGUISED AS A JOB-HUNTING CONSTRUCTION WORKER...
SO YOU'VE HAD YEARS OF EXPERIENCE IN BUILDING WORK, EH? OKAY, YOU'RE HIRED, KIRK BRENT! I SURE CAN USE YOU -- THIS BUILDING IS GOING TO BE 80 STORIES HIGH!
THAT'S THE NAME I GAVE! I DIDN'T DARE APPLY IN MY IDENTITY AS "CLARK KENT!" EVERYONE KNOWS KENT'S A REPORTER!
BUT BENSON NOTICES AN ODD THING ABOUT THE NEW MAN...
WHAT'S THIS? HIS HANDS AREN'T CALLOUSED LIKE A WORKMAN'S SHOULD BE! HE'S A... A PHONY!

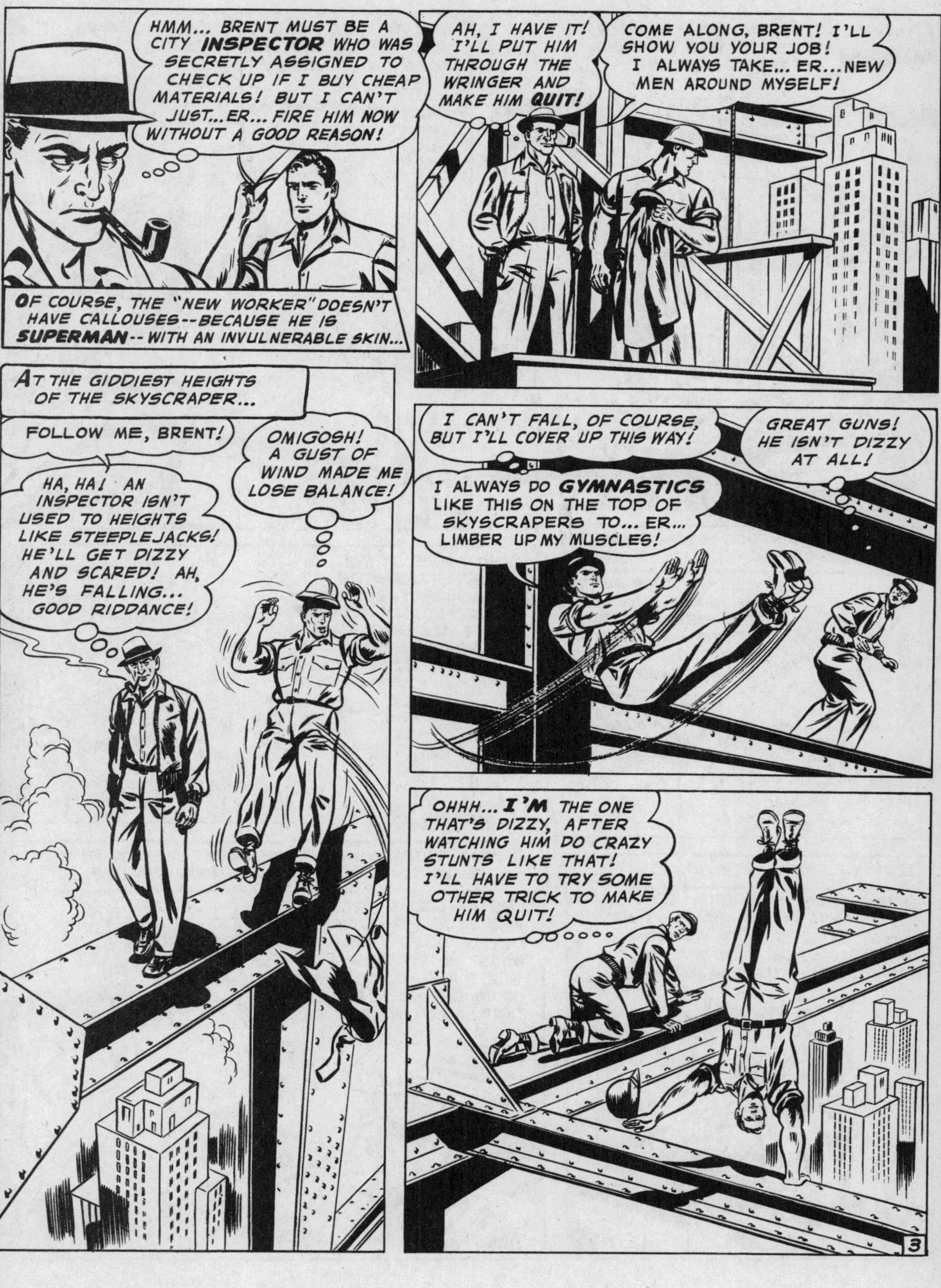
HMM... BRENT MUST BE A CITY INSPECTOR WHO WAS SECRETLY ASSIGNED TO CHECK UP IF I BUY CHEAP MATERIALS! BUT I CAN'T JUST...ER... FIRE HIM NOW WITHOUT A GOOD REASON!
OF COURSE, THE "NEW WORKER" DOESN'T HAVE CALLOUSES--BECAUSE HE IS SUPERMAN-- WITH AN INVULNERABLE SKIN...
AH, I HAVE IT! I'LL PUT HIM THROUGH THE WRINGER AND MAKE HIM QUIT!
COME ALONG, BRENT! I'LL SHOW YOU YOUR JOB! I ALWAYS TAKE... ER... NEW MEN AROUND MYSELF!
AT THE GIDDIEST HEIGHTS OF THE SKYSCRAPER...
FOLLOW ME, BRENT!
HA, HA! AN INSPECTOR ISN'T USED TO HEIGHTS LIKE STEEPLEJACKS! HE'LL GET DIZZY AND SCARED! AH, HE'S FALLING... GOOD RIDDANCE!
OMIGOSH! A GUST OF WIND MADE ME LOSE BALANCE!
I CAN'T FALL, OF COURSE, BUT I'LL COVER UP THIS WAY!
I ALWAYS DO GYMNASTICS LIKE THIS ON THE TOP OF SKYSCRAPERS TO... ER... LIMBER UP MY MUSCLES!
GREAT GUNS! HE ISN'T DIZZY AT ALL!
OHHH... I'M THE ONE THAT'S DIZZY, AFTER WATCHING HIM DO CRAZY STUNTS LIKE THAT! I'LL HAVE TO TRY SOME OTHER TRICK TO MAKE HIM QUIT!
3

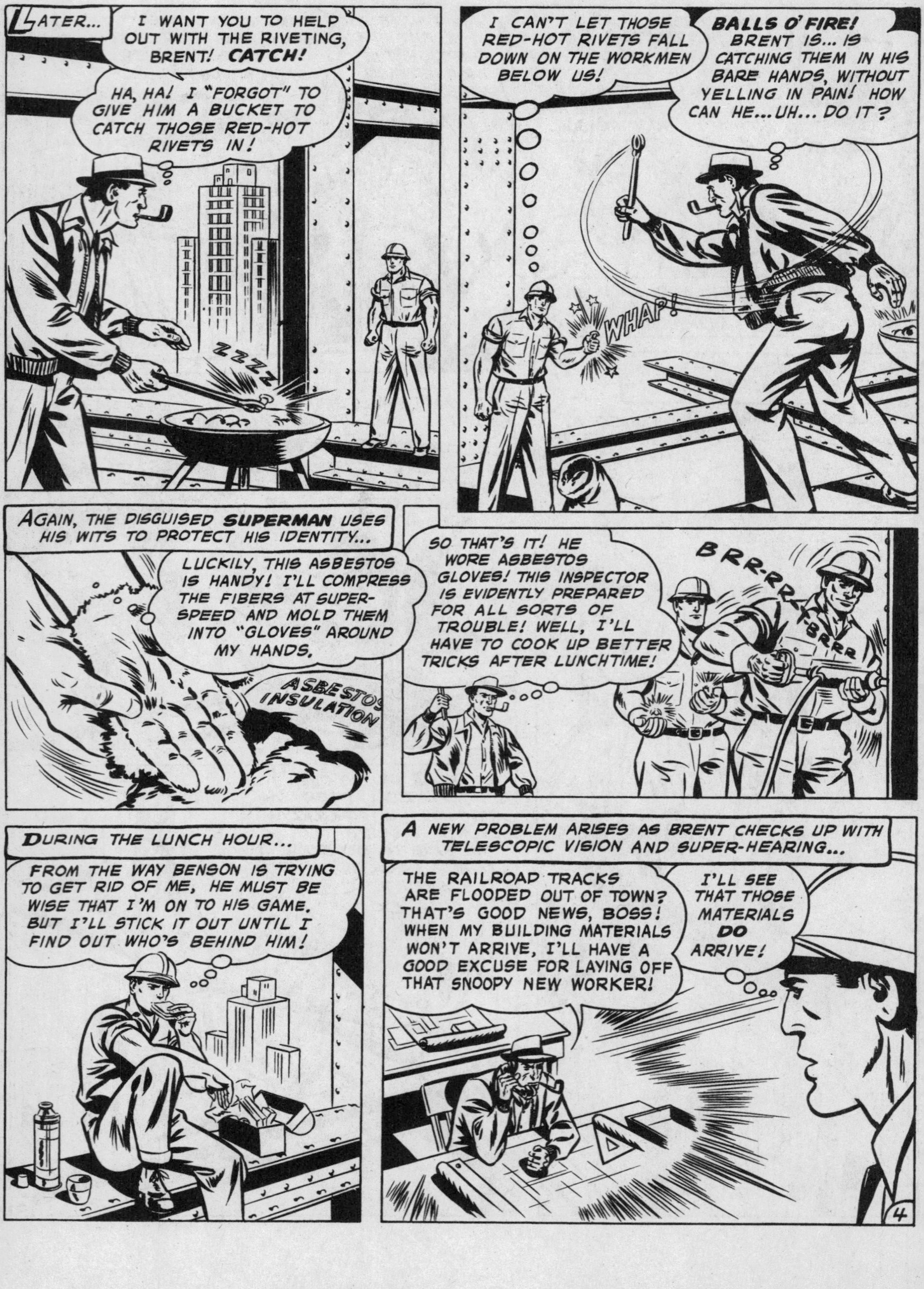
LATER...
I WANT YOU TO HELP OUT WITH THE RIVETING, BRENT! CATCH!
HA, HA! I "FORGOT" TO GIVE HIM A BUCKET TO CATCH THOSE RED-HOT RIVETS IN!
ZZZZ
I CAN'T LET THOSE RED-HOT RIVETS FALL DOWN ON THE WORKMEN BELOW US!
BALLS O' FIRE! BRENT IS... IS CATCHING THEM IN HIS BARE HANDS, WITHOUT YELLING IN PAIN! HOW CAN HE... UH... DO IT?
WHAP!
AGAIN, THE DISGUISED SUPERMAN USES HIS WITS TO PROTECT HIS IDENTITY...
LUCKILY, THIS ASBESTOS IS HANDY! I'LL COMPRESS THE FIBERS AT SUPER-SPEED AND MOLD THEM INTO "GLOVES" AROUND MY HANDS.
ASBESTOS INSULATION
SO THAT'S IT! HE WORE ASBESTOS GLOVES! THIS INSPECTOR IS EVIDENTLY PREPARED FOR ALL SORTS OF TROUBLE! WELL, I'LL HAVE TO COOK UP BETTER TRICKS AFTER LUNCHTIME!
BRRR-RR-BRRR
DURING THE LUNCH HOUR...
FROM THE WAY BENSON IS TRYING TO GET RID OF ME, HE MUST BE WISE THAT I'M ON TO HIS GAME. BUT I'LL STICK IT OUT UNTIL I FIND OUT WHO'S BEHIND HIM!
A NEW PROBLEM ARISES AS BRENT CHECKS UP WITH TELESCOPIC VISION AND SUPER-HEARING...
THE RAILROAD TRACKS ARE FLOODED OUT OF TOWN? THAT'S GOOD NEWS, BOSS! WHEN MY BUILDING MATERIALS WON'T ARRIVE, I'LL HAVE A GOOD EXCUSE FOR LAYING OFF THAT SNOOPY NEW WORKER!
I'LL SEE THAT THOSE MATERIALS DO ARRIVE!
4

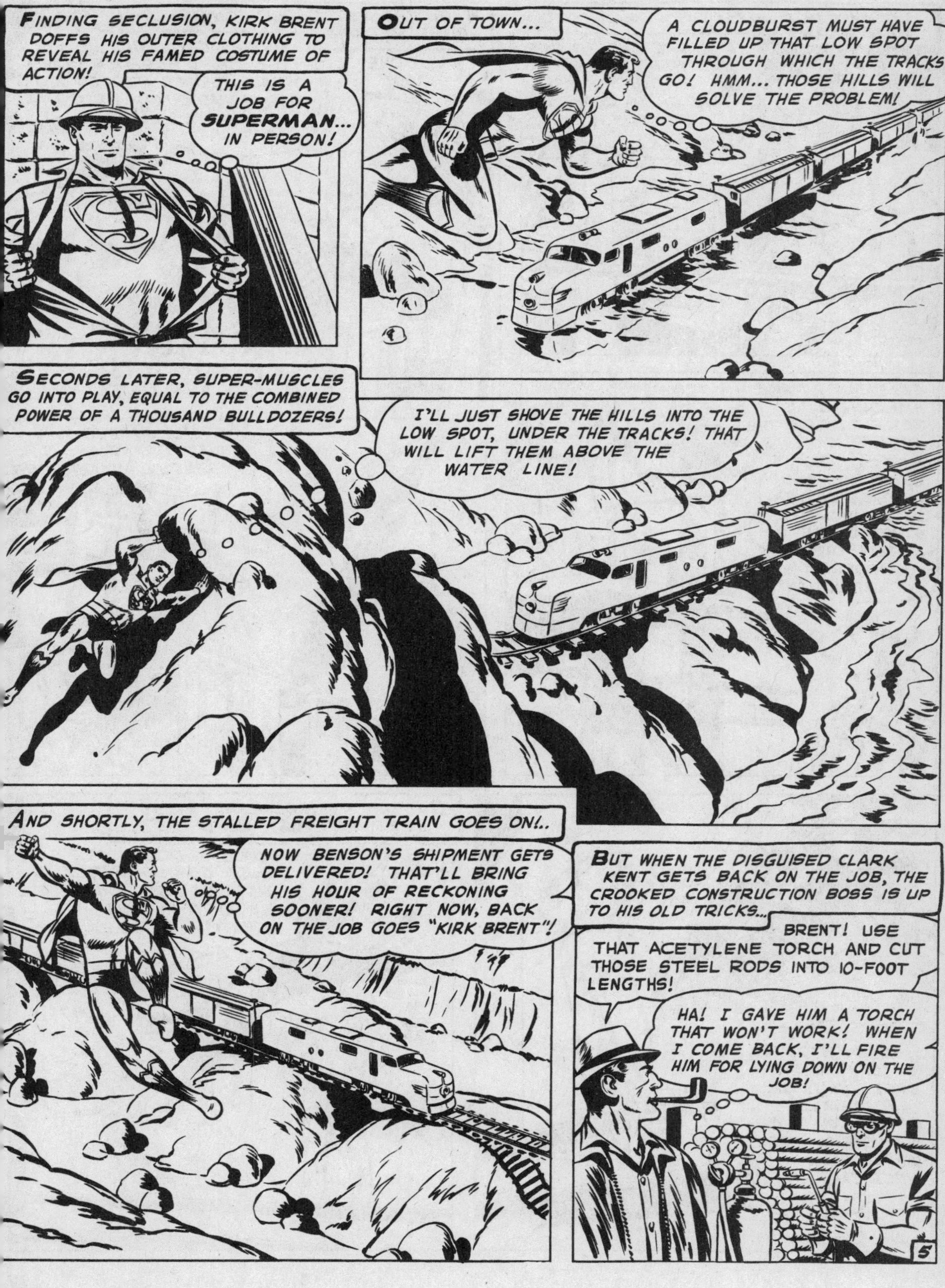
FINDING SECLUSION, KIRK BRENT DOFFS HIS OUTER CLOTHING TO REVEAL HIS FAMED COSTUME OF ACTION!
THIS IS A JOB FOR SUPERMAN... IN PERSON!
OUT OF TOWN...
A CLOUDBURST MUST HAVE FILLED UP THAT LOW SPOT THROUGH WHICH THE TRACKS GO! HMM... THOSE HILLS WILL SOLVE THE PROBLEM!
SECONDS LATER, SUPER-MUSCLES GO INTO PLAY, EQUAL TO THE COMBINED POWER OF A THOUSAND BULLDOZERS!
I'LL JUST SHOVE THE HILLS INTO THE LOW SPOT, UNDER THE TRACKS! THAT WILL LIFT THEM ABOVE THE WATER LINE!
AND SHORTLY, THE STALLED FREIGHT TRAIN GOES ON!..
NOW BENSON'S SHIPMENT GETS DELIVERED! THAT'LL BRING HIS HOUR OF RECKONING SOONER! RIGHT NOW, BACK ON THE JOB GOES "KIRK BRENT"!
BUT WHEN THE DISGUISED CLARK KENT GETS BACK ON THE JOB, THE CROOKED CONSTRUCTION BOSS IS UP TO HIS OLD TRICKS...
BRENT! USE THAT ACETYLENE TORCH AND CUT THOSE STEEL RODS INTO 10-FOOT LENGTHS!
HA! I GAVE HIM A TORCH THAT WON'T WORK! WHEN I COME BACK, I'LL FIRE HIM FOR LYING DOWN ON THE JOB!
5

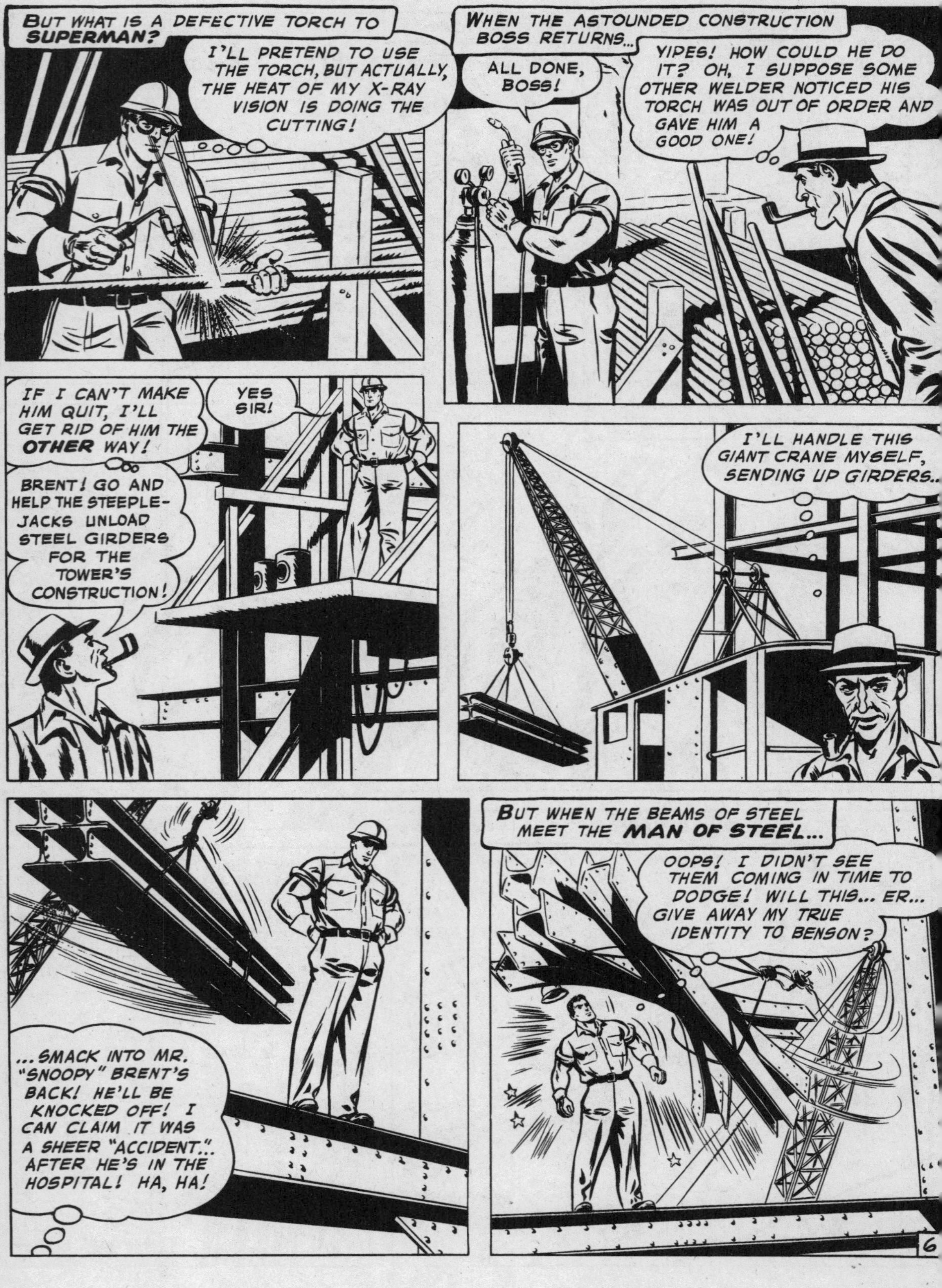
BUT WHAT IS A DEFECTIVE TORCH TO SUPERMAN?
I'LL PRETEND TO USE THE TORCH, BUT ACTUALLY, THE HEAT OF MY X-RAY VISION IS DOING THE CUTTING!
WHEN THE ASTOUNDED CONSTRUCTION BOSS RETURNS...
ALL DONE, BOSS!
YIPES! HOW COULD HE DO IT? OH, I SUPPOSE SOME OTHER WELDER NOTICED HIS TORCH WAS OUT OF ORDER AND GAVE HIM A GOOD ONE!
IF I CAN'T MAKE HIM QUIT, I'LL GET RID OF HIM THE OTHER WAY!
BRENT! GO AND HELP THE STEEPLE-JACKS UNLOAD STEEL GIRDERS FOR THE TOWER'S CONSTRUCTION!
YES SIR!
I'LL HANDLE THIS GIANT CRANE MYSELF, SENDING UP GIRDERS...
...SMACK INTO MR. "SNOOPY" BRENT'S BACK! HE'LL BE KNOCKED OFF! I CAN CLAIM IT WAS A SHEER "ACCIDENT"... AFTER HE'S IN THE HOSPITAL! HA, HA!
BUT WHEN THE BEAMS OF STEEL MEET THE MAN OF STEEL...
OOPS! I DIDN'T SEE THEM COMING IN TIME TO DODGE! WILL THIS... ER... GIVE AWAY MY TRUE IDENTITY TO BENSON?
6

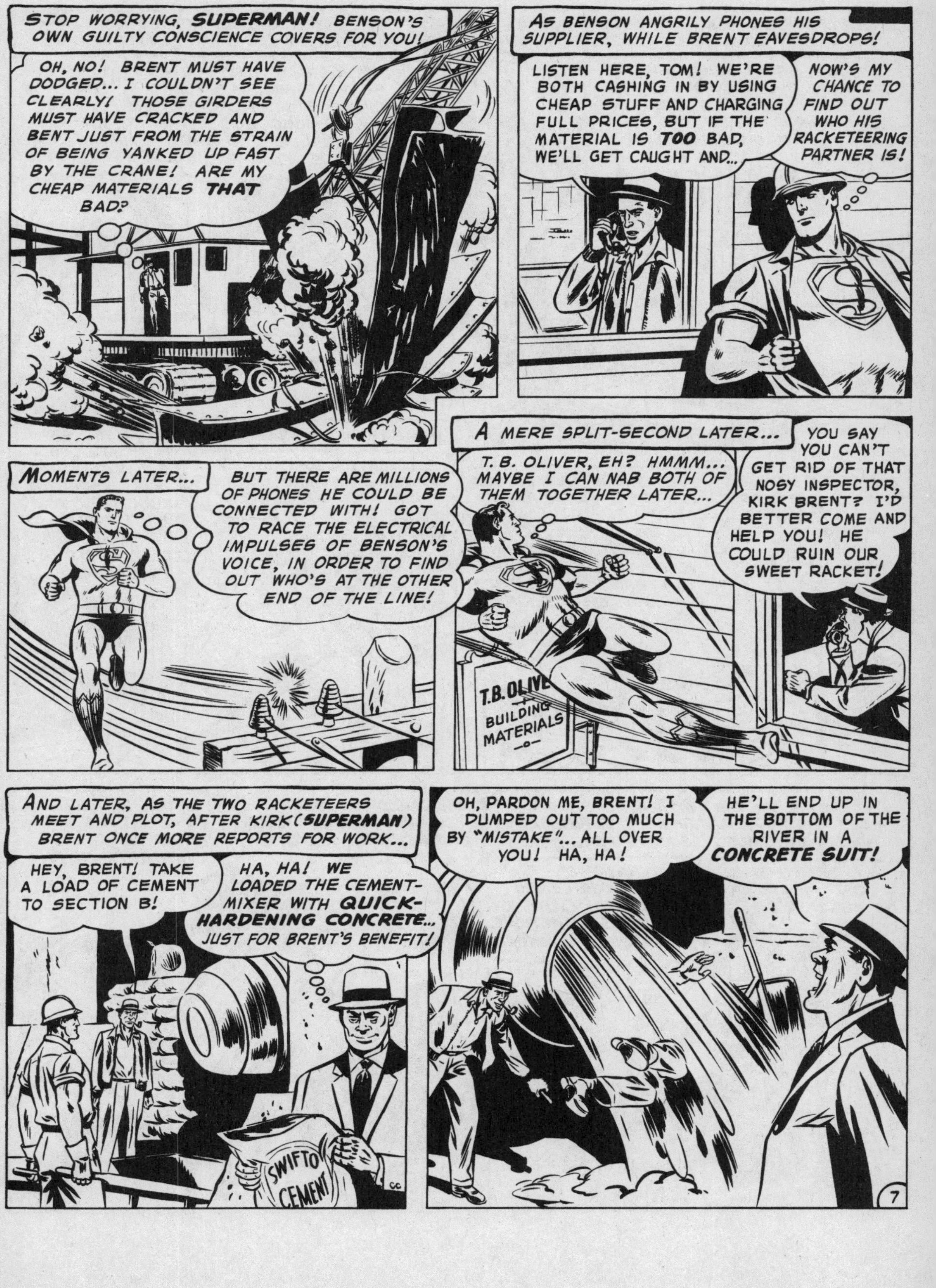
STOP WORRYING, SUPERMAN! BENSON'S OWN GUILTY CONSCIENCE COVERS FOR YOU!
OH, NO! BRENT MUST HAVE DODGED... I COULDN'T SEE CLEARLY! THOSE GIRDERS MUST HAVE CRACKED AND BENT JUST FROM THE STRAIN OF BEING YANKED UP FAST BY THE CRANE! ARE MY CHEAP MATERIALS THAT BAD?
AS BENSON ANGRILY PHONES HIS SUPPLIER, WHILE BRENT EAVESDROPS!
LISTEN HERE, TOM! WE'RE BOTH CASHING IN BY USING CHEAP STUFF AND CHARGING FULL PRICES, BUT IF THE MATERIAL IS TOO BAD, WE'LL GET CAUGHT AND...
NOW'S MY CHANCE TO FIND OUT WHO HIS RACKETEERING PARTNER IS!
MOMENTS LATER...
BUT THERE ARE MILLIONS OF PHONES HE COULD BE CONNECTED WITH! GOT TO RACE THE ELECTRICAL IMPULSES OF BENSON'S VOICE, IN ORDER TO FIND OUT WHO'S AT THE OTHER END OF THE LINE!
A MERE SPLIT-SECOND LATER...
T. B. OLIVER, EH? HMMM... MAYBE I CAN NAB BOTH OF THEM TOGETHER LATER...
YOU SAY YOU CAN'T GET RID OF THAT NOSY INSPECTOR, KIRK BRENT? I'D BETTER COME AND HELP YOU! HE COULD RUIN OUR SWEET RACKET!
T.B. OLIVE
BUILDING MATERIALS
AND LATER, AS THE TWO RACKETEERS MEET AND PLOT, AFTER KIRK (SUPERMAN) BRENT ONCE MORE REPORTS FOR WORK...
HEY, BRENT! TAKE A LOAD OF CEMENT TO SECTION B!
HA, HA! WE LOADED THE CEMENT-MIXER WITH QUICK-HARDENING CONCRETE... JUST FOR BRENT'S BENEFIT!
SWIFTO CEMENT
OH, PARDON ME, BRENT! I DUMPED OUT TOO MUCH BY "MISTAKE"... ALL OVER YOU! HA, HA!
HE'LL END UP IN THE BOTTOM OF THE RIVER IN A CONCRETE SUIT!
7

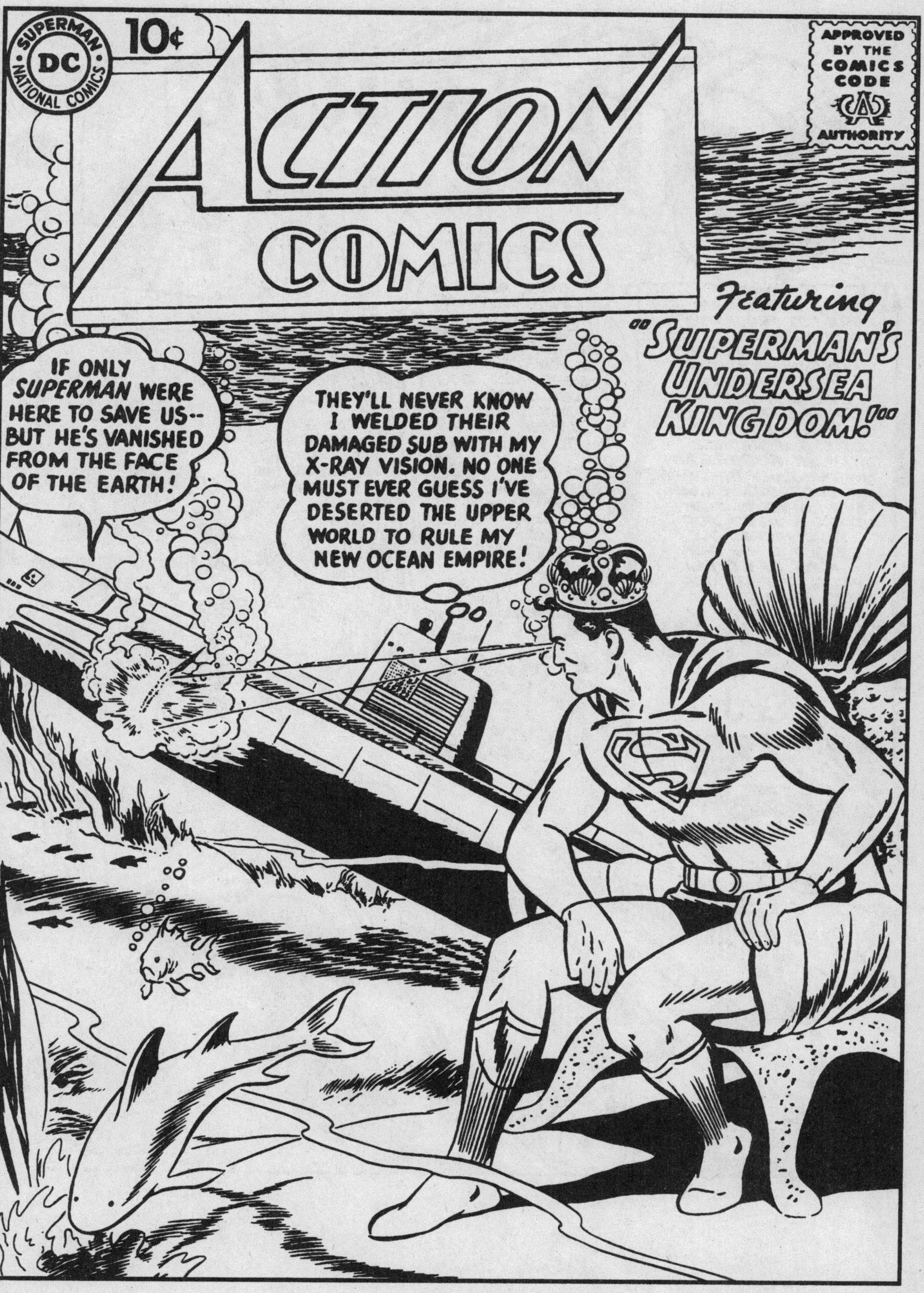
SUPERMAN DC NATIONAL COMICS
10¢
ACTION COMICS
APPROVED BY THE COMICS CODE AUTHORITY
Featuring "SUPERMAN'S UNDERSEA KINGDOM!"
IF ONLY SUPERMAN WERE HERE TO SAVE US-- BUT HE'S VANISHED FROM THE FACE OF THE EARTH!
THEY'LL NEVER KNOW I WELDED THEIR DAMAGED SUB WITH MY X-RAY VISION. NO ONE MUST EVER GUESS I'VE DESERTED THE UPPER WORLD TO RULE MY NEW OCEAN EMPIRE!

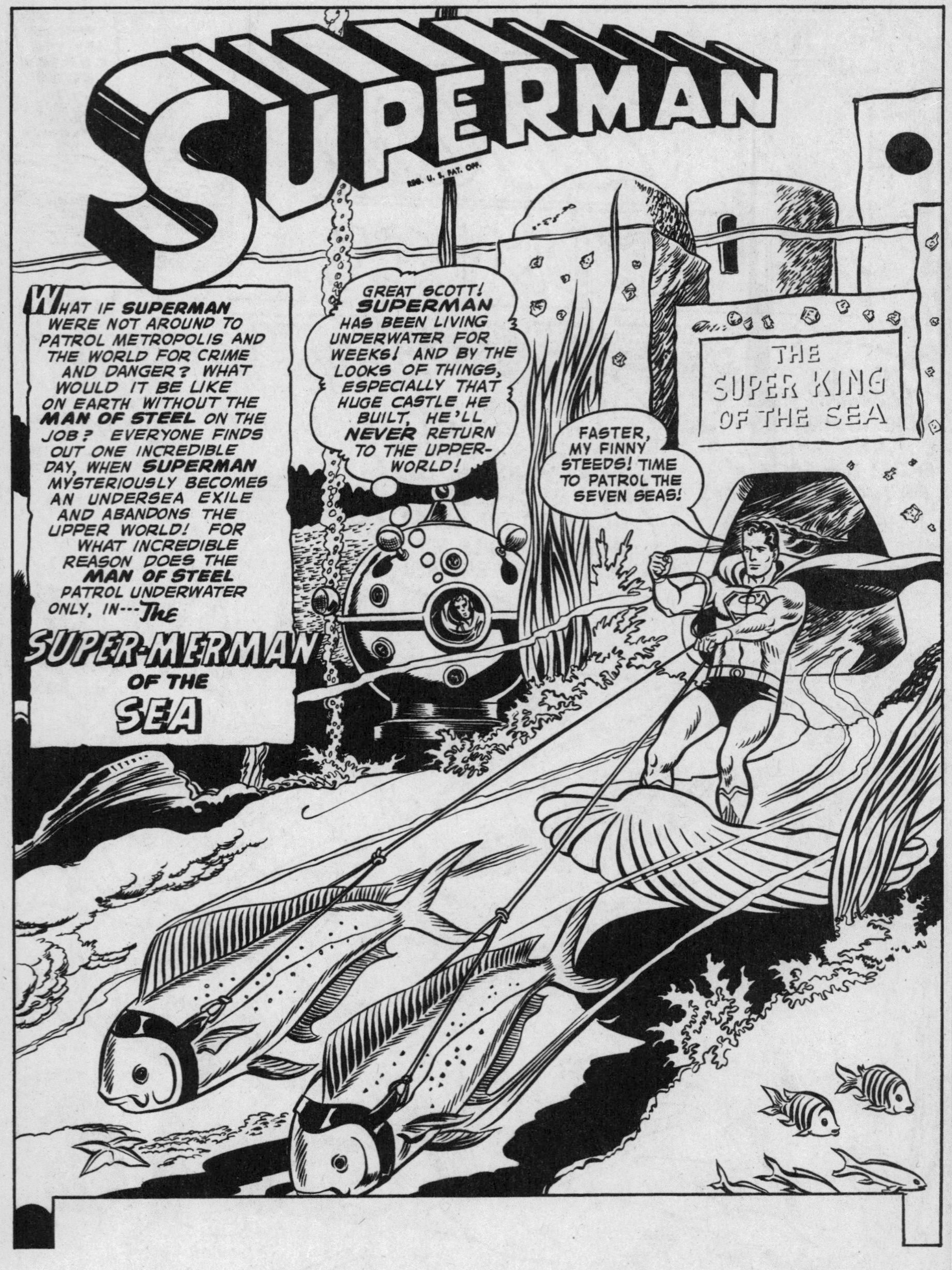
SUPERMAN
REG. U. S. PAT. OFF.
WHAT IF SUPERMAN WERE NOT AROUND TO PATROL METROPOLIS AND THE WORLD FOR CRIME AND DANGER? WHAT WOULD IT BE LIKE ON EARTH WITHOUT THE MAN OF STEEL ON THE JOB? EVERYONE FINDS OUT ONE INCREDIBLE DAY, WHEN SUPERMAN MYSTERIOUSLY BECOMES AN UNDERSEA EXILE AND ABANDONS THE UPPER WORLD! FOR WHAT INCREDIBLE REASON DOES THE MAN OF STEEL PATROL UNDERWATER ONLY, IN---The
SUPER-MERMAN OF THE SEA
GREAT SCOTT! SUPERMAN HAS BEEN LIVING UNDERWATER FOR WEEKS! AND BY THE LOOKS OF THINGS, ESPECIALLY THAT HUGE CASTLE HE BUILT, HE'LL NEVER RETURN TO THE UPPER-WORLD!
THE SUPER KING OF THE SEA
FASTER, MY FINNY STEEDS! TIME TO PATROL THE SEVEN SEAS!

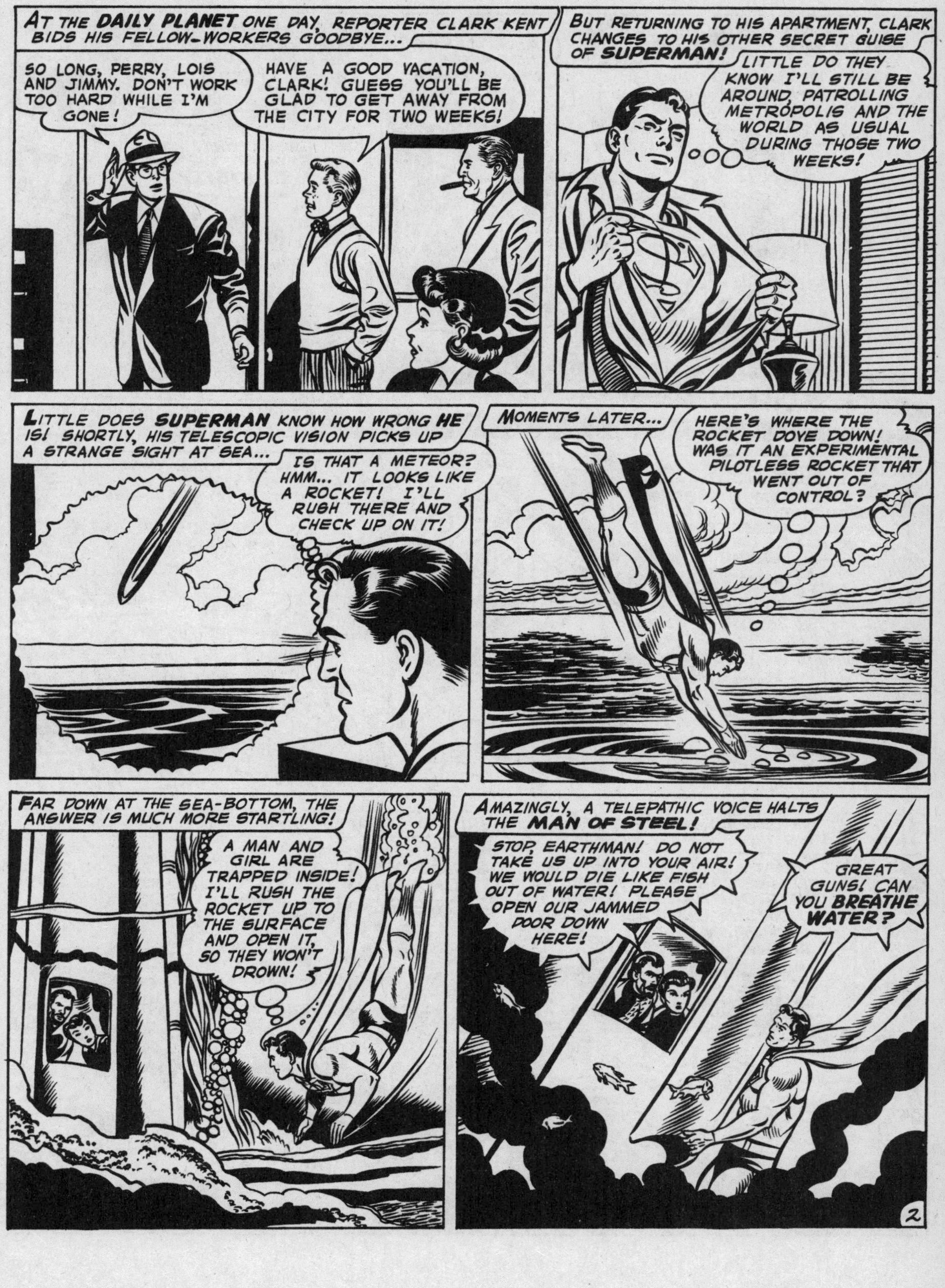
AT THE DAILY PLANET ONE DAY, REPORTER CLARK KENT BIDS HIS FELLOW-WORKERS GOODBYE...
SO LONG, PERRY, LOIS AND JIMMY. DON'T WORK TOO HARD WHILE I'M GONE!
HAVE A GOOD VACATION, CLARK! GUESS YOU'LL BE GLAD TO GET AWAY FROM THE CITY FOR TWO WEEKS!
BUT RETURNING TO HIS APARTMENT, CLARK CHANGES TO HIS OTHER SECRET GUISE OF SUPERMAN!
LITTLE DO THEY KNOW I'LL STILL BE AROUND, PATROLLING METROPOLIS AND THE WORLD AS USUAL DURING THOSE TWO WEEKS!
LITTLE DOES SUPERMAN KNOW HOW WRONG HE IS! SHORTLY, HIS TELESCOPIC VISION PICKS UP A STRANGE SIGHT AT SEA...
IS THAT A METEOR? HMM... IT LOOKS LIKE A ROCKET! I'LL RUSH THERE AND CHECK UP ON IT!
MOMENTS LATER...
HERE'S WHERE THE ROCKET DOVE DOWN! WAS IT AN EXPERIMENTAL PILOTLESS ROCKET THAT WENT OUT OF CONTROL?
FAR DOWN AT THE SEA-BOTTOM, THE ANSWER IS MUCH MORE STARTLING!
A MAN AND GIRL ARE TRAPPED INSIDE! I'LL RUSH THE ROCKET UP TO THE SURFACE AND OPEN IT, SO THEY WON'T DROWN!
AMAZINGLY, A TELEPATHIC VOICE HALTS THE MAN OF STEEL!
STOP, EARTHMAN! DO NOT TAKE US UP INTO YOUR AIR! WE WOULD DIE LIKE FISH OUT OF WATER! PLEASE OPEN OUR JAMMED DOOR DOWN HERE!
GREAT GUNS! CAN YOU BREATHE WATER?
2

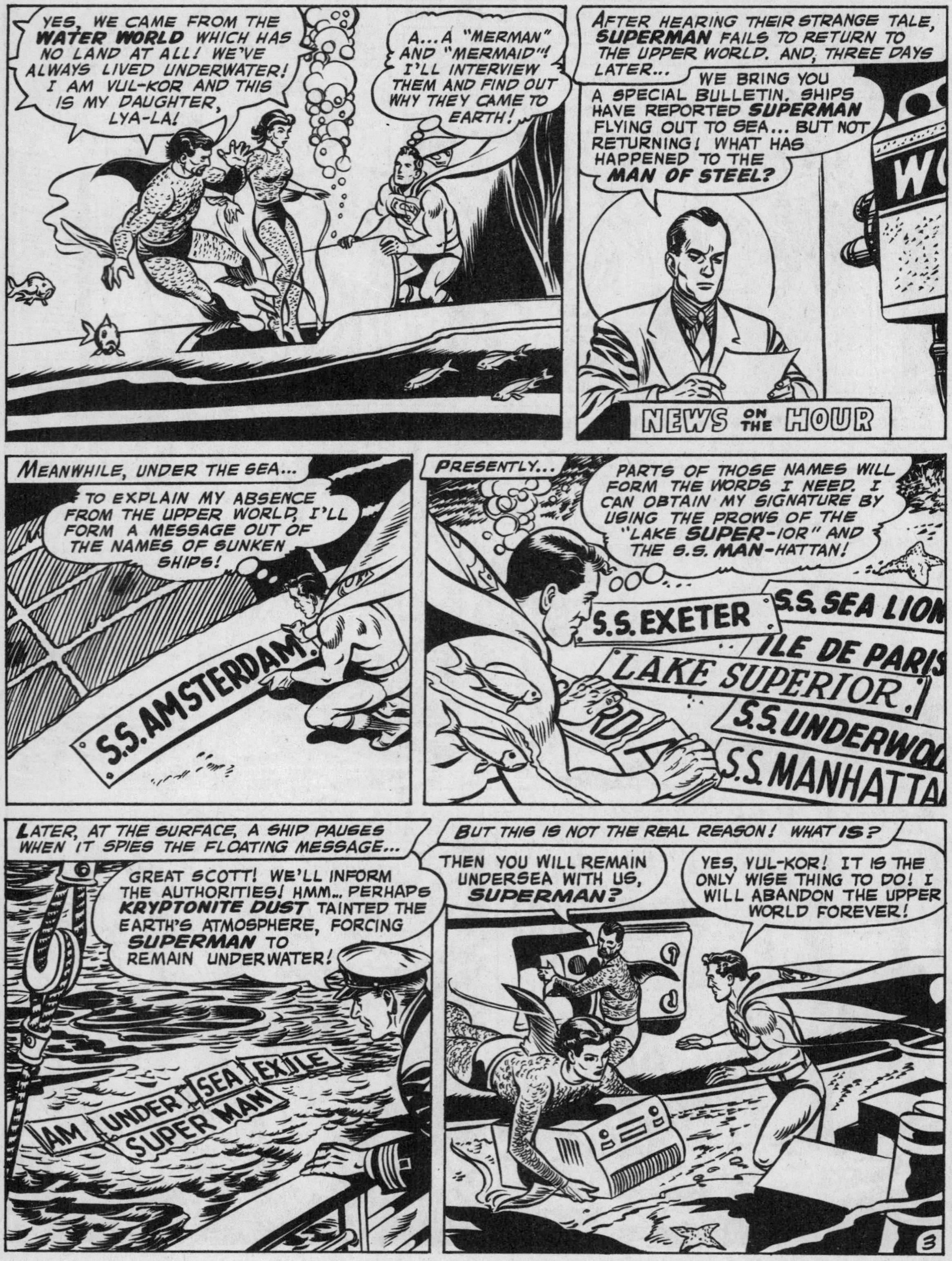
YES, WE CAME FROM THE WATER WORLD WHICH HAS NO LAND AT ALL! WE'VE ALWAYS LIVED UNDERWATER! I AM VUL-KOR AND THIS IS MY DAUGHTER, LYA-LA!
A... A "MERMAN" AND "MERMAID"! I'LL INTERVIEW THEM AND FIND OUT WHY THEY CAME TO EARTH!
AFTER HEARING THEIR STRANGE TALE, SUPERMAN FAILS TO RETURN TO THE UPPER WORLD. AND, THREE DAYS LATER...
WE BRING YOU A SPECIAL BULLETIN. SHIPS HAVE REPORTED SUPERMAN FLYING OUT TO SEA... BUT NOT RETURNING! WHAT HAS HAPPENED TO THE MAN OF STEEL?
NEWS ON THE HOUR
MEANWHILE, UNDER THE SEA...
TO EXPLAIN MY ABSENCE FROM THE UPPER WORLD, I'LL FORM A MESSAGE OUT OF THE NAMES OF SUNKEN SHIPS!
S.S. AMSTERDAM
PRESENTLY...
PARTS OF THOSE NAMES WILL FORM THE WORDS I NEED. I CAN OBTAIN MY SIGNATURE BY USING THE PROWS OF THE "LAKE SUPER-IOR" AND THE S.S. MAN-HATTAN!
S.S. EXETER
S.S. SEA LION
ILE DE PARIS
LAKE SUPERIOR
S.S. UNDERWOO
S.S. MANHATTA
LATER, AT THE SURFACE, A SHIP PAUSES WHEN IT SPIES THE FLOATING MESSAGE...
GREAT SCOTT! WE'LL INFORM THE AUTHORITIES! HMM... PERHAPS KRYPTONITE DUST TAINTED THE EARTH'S ATMOSPHERE, FORCING SUPERMAN TO REMAIN UNDERWATER!
AM UNDER SEA EXILE SUPER MAN
BUT THIS IS NOT THE REAL REASON! WHAT IS?
THEN YOU WILL REMAIN UNDERSEA WITH US, SUPERMAN?
YES, VUL-KOR! IT IS THE ONLY WISE THING TO DO! I WILL ABANDON THE UPPER WORLD FOREVER!
3

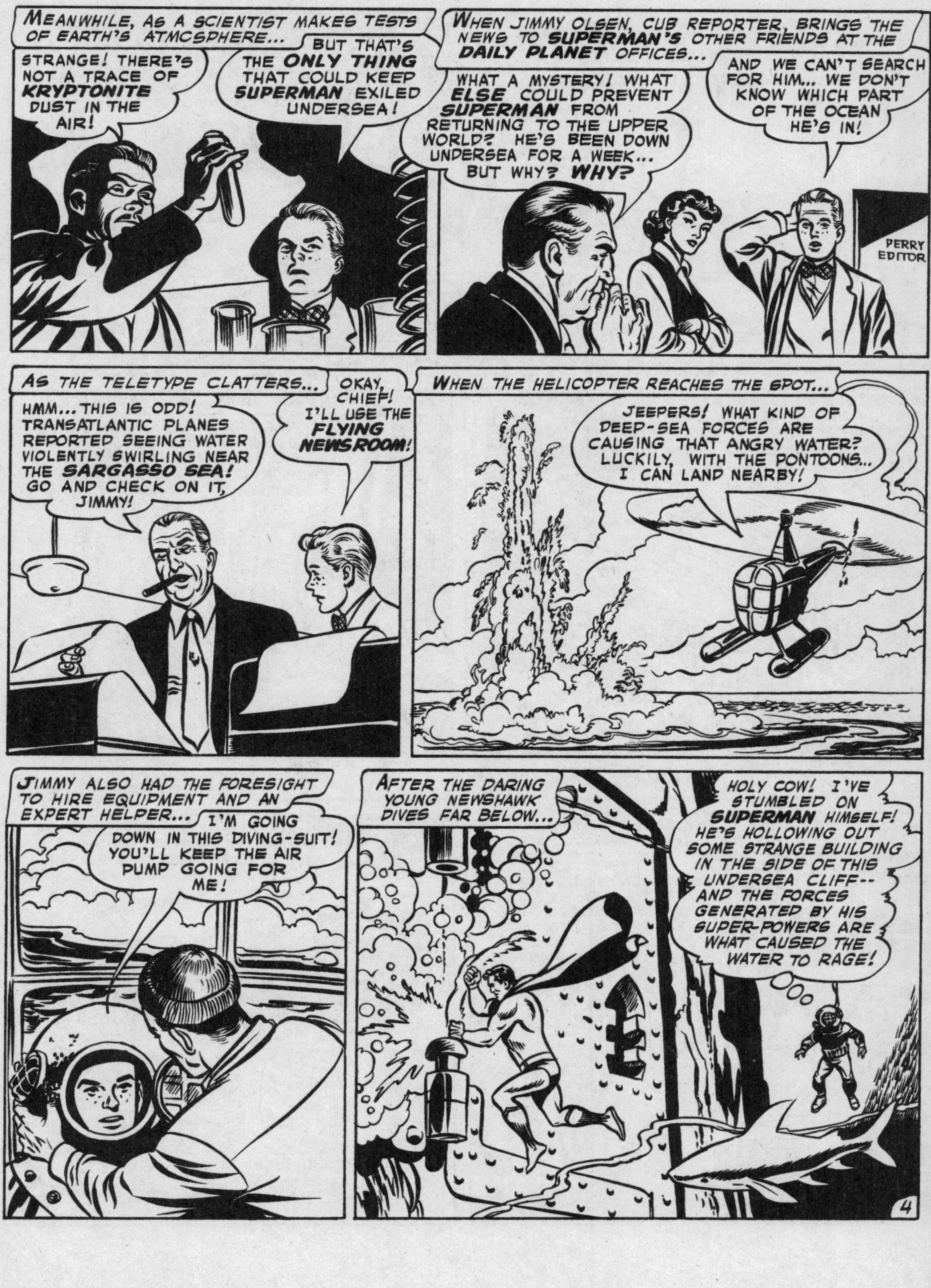
MEANWHILE, AS A SCIENTIST MAKES TESTS OF EARTH'S ATMOSPHERE...
STRANGE! THERE'S NOT A TRACE OF KRYPTONITE DUST IN THE AIR!
BUT THAT'S THE ONLY THING THAT COULD KEEP SUPERMAN EXILED UNDERSEA!
WHEN JIMMY OLSEN, CUB REPORTER, BRINGS THE NEWS TO SUPERMAN'S OTHER FRIENDS AT THE DAILY PLANET OFFICES...
WHAT A MYSTERY! WHAT ELSE COULD PREVENT SUPERMAN FROM RETURNING TO THE UPPER WORLD? HE'S BEEN DOWN UNDERSEA FOR A WEEK... BUT WHY? WHY?
AND WE CAN'T SEARCH FOR HIM... WE DON'T KNOW WHICH PART OF THE OCEAN HE'S IN!
PERRY EDITOR
AS THE TELETYPE CLATTERS...
HMM... THIS IS ODD! TRANSATLANTIC PLANES REPORTED SEEING WATER VIOLENTLY SWIRLING NEAR THE SARGASSO SEA! GO AND CHECK ON IT, JIMMY!
OKAY, CHIEF! I'LL USE THE FLYING NEWSROOM!
WHEN THE HELICOPTER REACHES THE SPOT...
JEEPERS! WHAT KIND OF DEEP-SEA FORCES ARE CAUSING THAT ANGRY WATER? LUCKILY, WITH THE PONTOONS... I CAN LAND NEARBY!
JIMMY ALSO HAD THE FORESIGHT TO HIRE EQUIPMENT AND AN EXPERT HELPER...
I'M GOING DOWN IN THIS DIVING-SUIT! YOU'LL KEEP THE AIR PUMP GOING FOR ME!
AFTER THE DARING YOUNG NEWSHAWK DIVES FAR BELOW...
HOLY COW! I'VE STUMBLED ON SUPERMAN HIMSELF! HE'S HOLLOWING OUT SOME STRANGE BUILDING IN THE SIDE OF THIS UNDERSEA CLIFF-- AND THE FORCES GENERATED BY HIS SUPER-POWERS ARE WHAT CAUSED THE WATER TO RAGE!
4

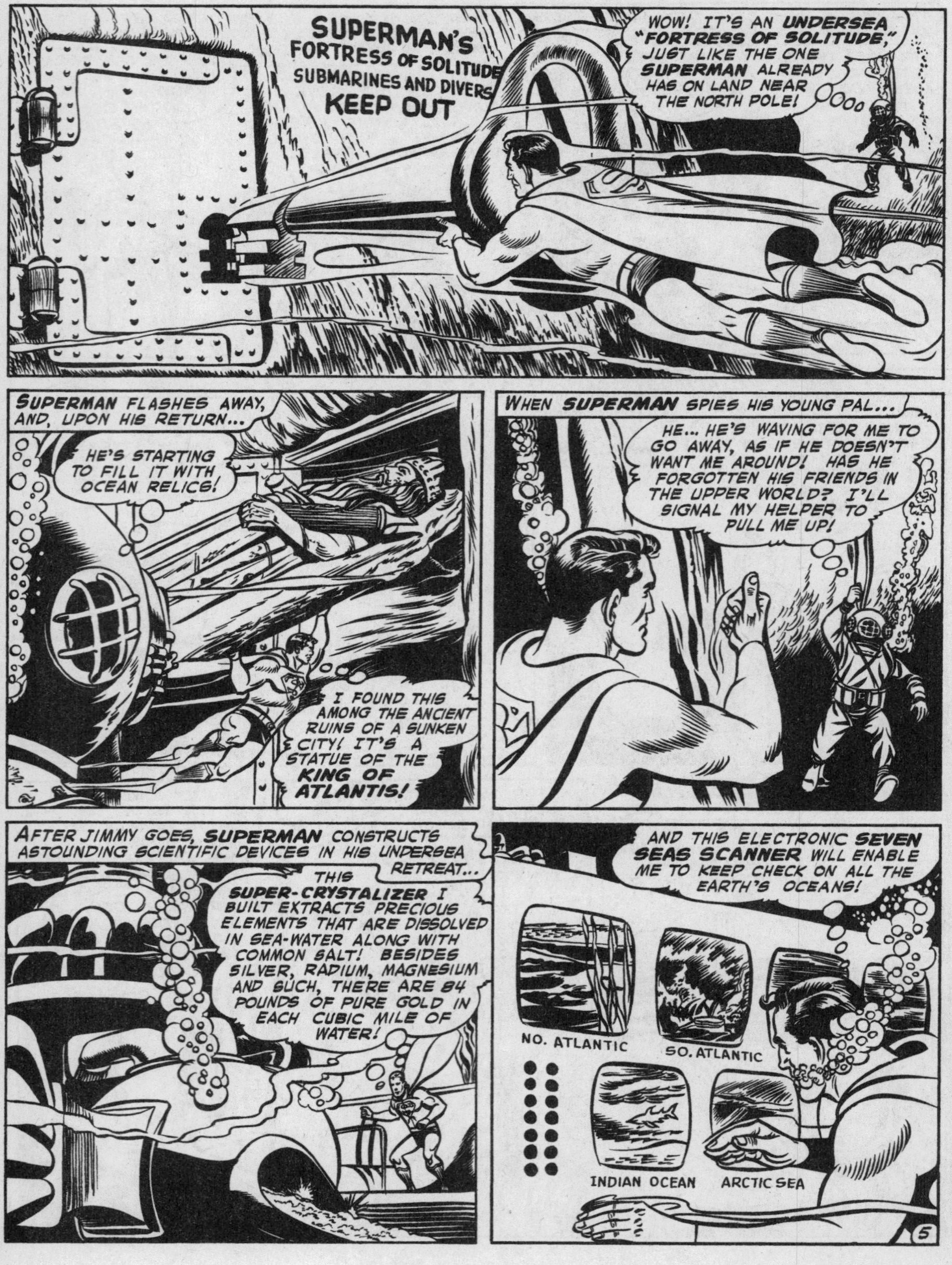
SUPERMAN's FORTRESS OF SOLITUDE
SUBMARINES AND DIVERS KEEP OUT
WOW! IT'S AN UNDERSEA "FORTRESS OF SOLITUDE," JUST LIKE THE ONE SUPERMAN ALREADY HAS ON LAND NEAR THE NORTH POLE!
SUPERMAN FLASHES AWAY, AND, UPON HIS RETURN...
HE'S STARTING TO FILL IT WITH OCEAN RELICS!
I FOUND THIS AMONG THE ANCIENT RUINS OF A SUNKEN CITY! IT'S A STATUE OF THE KING OF ATLANTIS!
WHEN SUPERMAN SPIES HIS YOUNG PAL...
HE... HE'S WAVING FOR ME TO GO AWAY, AS IF HE DOESN'T WANT ME AROUND! HAS HE FORGOTTEN HIS FRIENDS IN THE UPPER WORLD? I'LL SIGNAL MY HELPER TO PULL ME UP!
AFTER JIMMY GOES, SUPERMAN CONSTRUCTS ASTOUNDING SCIENTIFIC DEVICES IN HIS UNDERSEA RETREAT...
THIS SUPER-CRYSTALIZER I BUILT EXTRACTS PRECIOUS ELEMENTS THAT ARE DISSOLVED IN SEA-WATER ALONG WITH COMMON SALT! BESIDES SILVER, RADIUM, MAGNESIUM AND SUCH, THERE ARE 84 POUNDS OF PURE GOLD IN EACH CUBIC MILE OF WATER!
AND THIS ELECTRONIC SEVEN SEAS SCANNER WILL ENABLE ME TO KEEP CHECK ON ALL THE EARTH'S OCEANS!
NO. ATLANTIC
SO. ATLANTIC
INDIAN OCEAN
ARCTIC SEA
5

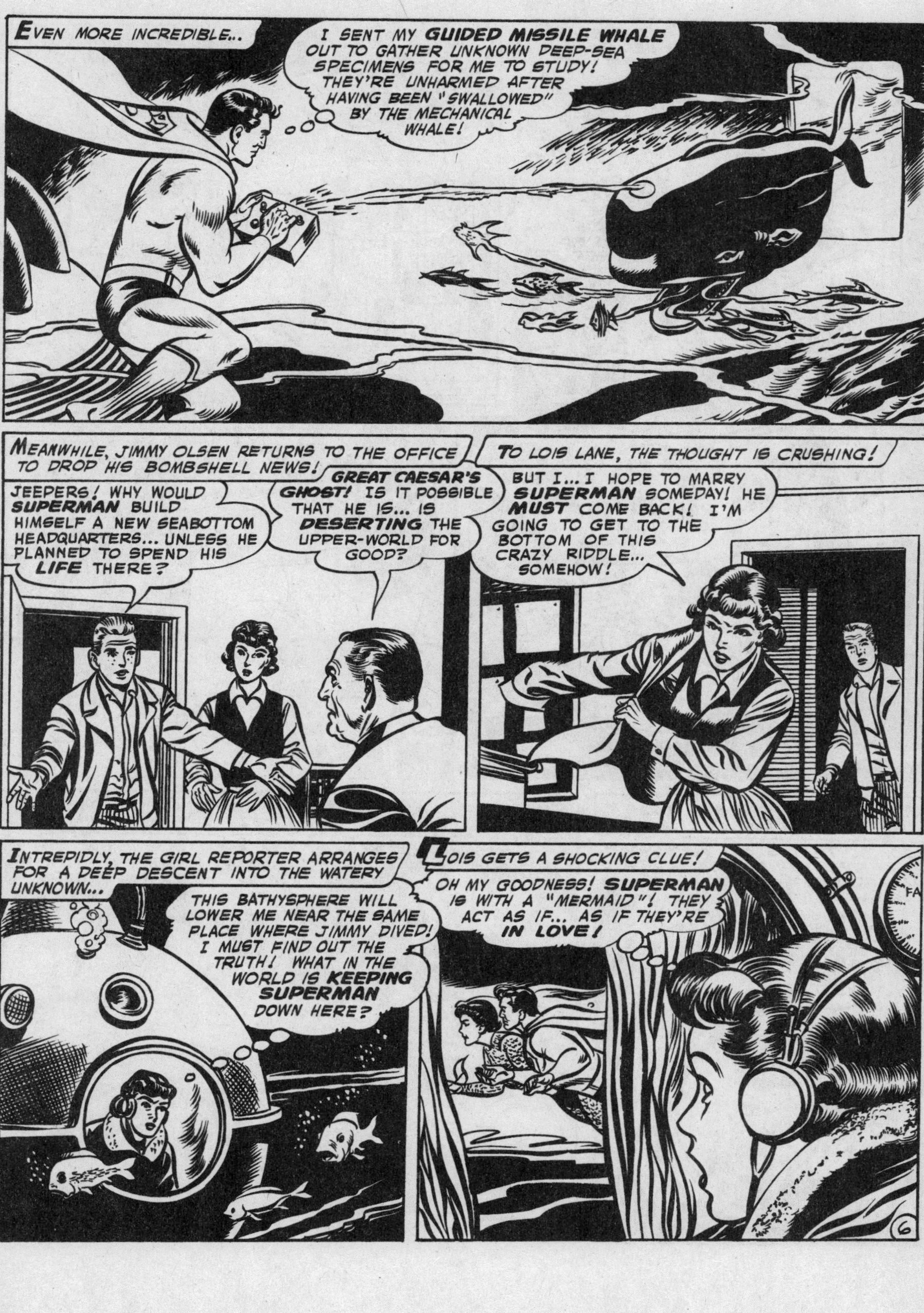
EVEN MORE INCREDIBLE...
I SENT MY GUIDED MISSILE WHALE OUT TO GATHER UNKNOWN DEEP-SEA SPECIMENS FOR ME TO STUDY! THEY'RE UNHARMED AFTER HAVING BEEN "SWALLOWED" BY THE MECHANICAL WHALE!
MEANWHILE, JIMMY OLSEN RETURNS TO THE OFFICE TO DROP HIS BOMBSHELL NEWS!
JEEPERS! WHY WOULD SUPERMAN BUILD HIMSELF A NEW SEABOTTOM HEADQUARTERS... UNLESS HE PLANNED TO SPEND HIS LIFE THERE?
GREAT CAESAR'S GHOST! IS IT POSSIBLE THAT HE IS... IS DESERTING THE UPPER-WORLD FOR GOOD?
TO LOIS LANE, THE THOUGHT IS CRUSHING!
BUT I... I HOPE TO MARRY SUPERMAN SOMEDAY! HE MUST COME BACK! I'M GOING TO GET TO THE BOTTOM OF THIS CRAZY RIDDLE... SOMEHOW!
INTREPIDLY, THE GIRL REPORTER ARRANGES FOR A DEEP DESCENT INTO THE WATERY UNKNOWN...
THIS BATHYSPHERE WILL LOWER ME NEAR THE SAME PLACE WHERE JIMMY DIVED! I MUST FIND OUT THE TRUTH! WHAT IN THE WORLD IS KEEPING SUPERMAN DOWN HERE?
LOIS GETS A SHOCKING CLUE!
OH MY GOODNESS! SUPERMAN IS WITH A "MERMAID"! THEY ACT AS IF... AS IF THEY'RE IN LOVE!
6

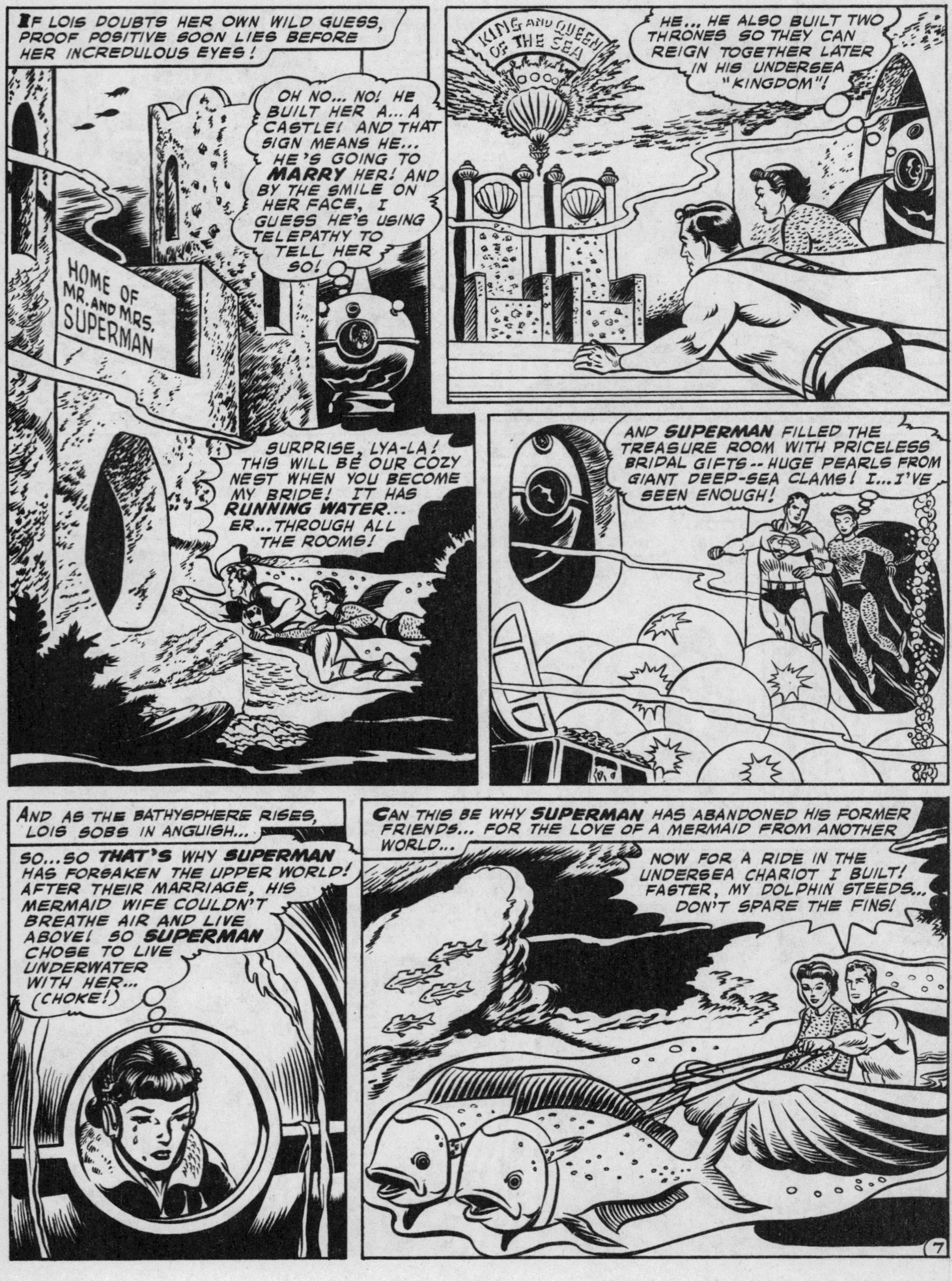
IF LOIS DOUBTS HER OWN WILD GUESS, PROOF POSITIVE SOON LIES BEFORE HER INCREDULOUS EYES!
OH NO... NO! HE BUILT HER A... A CASTLE! AND THAT SIGN MEANS HE... HE'S GOING TO MARRY HER! AND BY THE SMILE ON HER FACE, I GUESS HE'S USING TELEPATHY TO TELL HER SO!
HOME OF MR. AND MRS. SUPERMAN
SURPRISE, LYA-LA! THIS WILL BE OUR COZY NEST WHEN YOU BECOME MY BRIDE! IT HAS RUNNING WATER... ER... THROUGH ALL THE ROOMS!
KING AND QUEEN OF THE SEA
HE... HE ALSO BUILT TWO THRONES SO THEY CAN REIGN TOGETHER LATER IN HIS UNDERSEA "KINGDOM"!
AND SUPERMAN FILLED THE TREASURE ROOM WITH PRICELESS BRIDAL GIFTS -- HUGE PEARLS FROM GIANT DEEP-SEA CLAMS! I... I'VE SEEN ENOUGH!
AND AS THE BATHYSPHERE RISES, LOIS SOBS IN ANGUISH...
SO... SO THAT'S WHY SUPERMAN HAS FORSAKEN THE UPPER WORLD! AFTER THEIR MARRIAGE, HIS MERMAID WIFE COULDN'T BREATHE AIR AND LIVE ABOVE! SO SUPERMAN CHOSE TO LIVE UNDERWATER WITH HER... (CHOKE!)
CAN THIS BE WHY SUPERMAN HAS ABANDONED HIS FORMER FRIENDS... FOR THE LOVE OF A MERMAID FROM ANOTHER WORLD...
NOW FOR A RIDE IN THE UNDERSEA CHARIOT I BUILT! FASTER, MY DOLPHIN STEEDS... DON'T SPARE THE FINS!
7

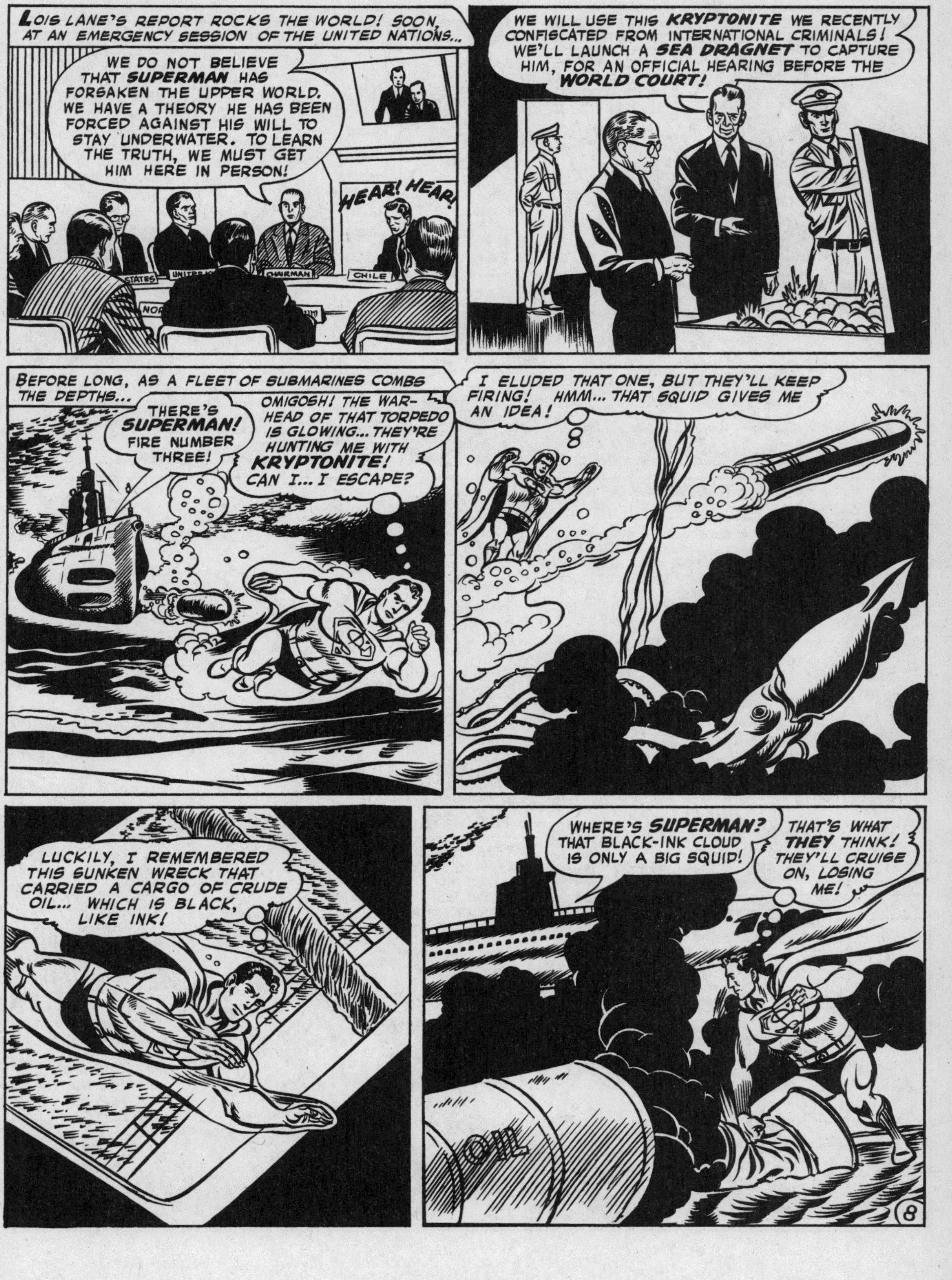
LOIS LANE'S REPORT ROCKS THE WORLD! SOON, AT AN EMERGENCY SESSION OF THE UNITED NATIONS...
WE DO NOT BELIEVE THAT SUPERMAN HAS FORSAKEN THE UPPER WORLD. WE HAVE A THEORY HE HAS BEEN FORCED AGAINST HIS WILL TO STAY UNDERWATER. TO LEARN THE TRUTH, WE MUST GET HIM HERE IN PERSON!
HEAR! HEAR!
STATES
CHAIRMAN
CHILE
WE WILL USE THIS KRYPTONITE WE RECENTLY CONFISCATED FROM INTERNATIONAL CRIMINALS! WE'LL LAUNCH A SEA DRAGNET TO CAPTURE HIM, FOR AN OFFICIAL HEARING BEFORE THE WORLD COURT!
BEFORE LONG, AS A FLEET OF SUBMARINES COMBS THE DEPTHS...
THERE'S SUPERMAN! FIRE NUMBER THREE!
OMIGOSH! THE WAR-HEAD OF THAT TORPEDO IS GLOWING... THEY'RE HUNTING ME WITH KRYPTONITE! CAN I... I ESCAPE?
I ELUDED THAT ONE, BUT THEY'LL KEEP FIRING! HMM... THAT SQUID GIVES ME AN IDEA!
LUCKILY, I REMEMBERED THIS SUNKEN WRECK THAT CARRIED A CARGO OF CRUDE OIL... WHICH IS BLACK, LIKE INK!
WHERE'S SUPERMAN? THAT BLACK-INK CLOUD IS ONLY A BIG SQUID!
THAT'S WHAT THEY THINK! THEY'LL CRUISE ON, LOSING ME!
OIL
8

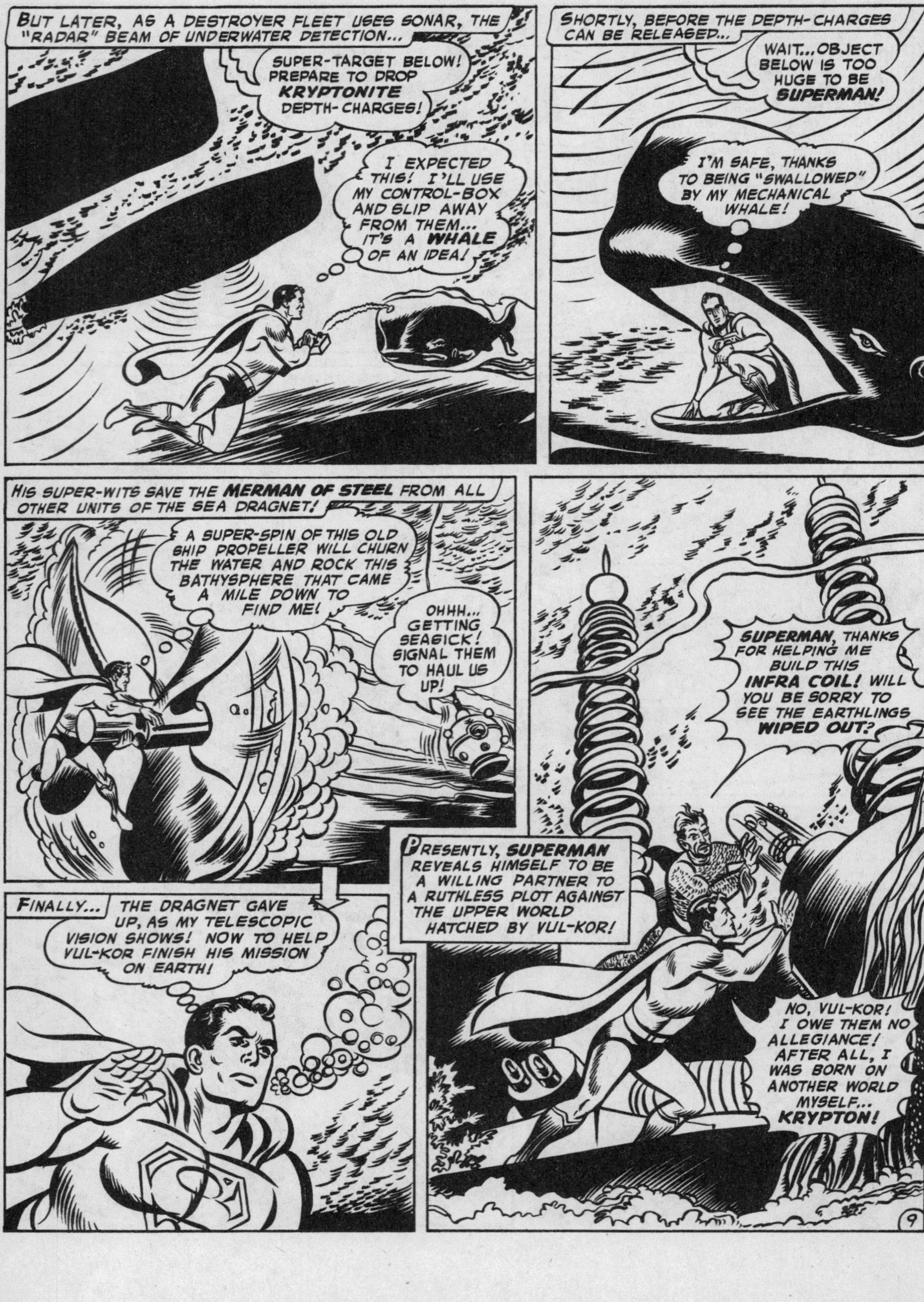

BUT LATER, AS A DESTROYER FLEET USES SONAR, THE "RADAR" BEAM OF UNDERWATER DETECTION...
SUPER-TARGET BELOW! PREPARE TO DROP KRYPTONITE DEPTH-CHARGES!
I EXPECTED THIS! I'LL USE MY CONTROL-BOX AND SLIP AWAY FROM THEM... IT'S A WHALE OF AN IDEA!
SHORTLY, BEFORE THE DEPTH-CHARGES CAN BE RELEASED...
WAIT...OBJECT BELOW IS TOO HUGE TO BE SUPERMAN!
I'M SAFE, THANKS TO BEING "SWALLOWED" BY MY MECHANICAL WHALE!
HIS SUPER-WITS SAVE THE MERMAN OF STEEL FROM ALL OTHER UNITS OF THE SEA DRAGNET!
A SUPER-SPIN OF THIS OLD SHIP PROPELLER WILL CHURN THE WATER AND ROCK THIS BATHYSPHERE THAT CAME A MILE DOWN TO FIND ME!
OHHH... GETTING SEASICK! SIGNAL THEM TO HAUL US UP!
FINALLY...
THE DRAGNET GAVE UP, AS MY TELESCOPIC VISION SHOWS! NOW TO HELP VUL-KOR FINISH HIS MISSION ON EARTH!
PRESENTLY, SUPERMAN REVEALS HIMSELF TO BE A WILLING PARTNER TO A RUTHLESS PLOT AGAINST THE UPPER WORLD HATCHED BY VUL-KOR!
SUPERMAN, THANKS FOR HELPING ME BUILD THIS INFRA COIL! WILL YOU BE SORRY TO SEE THE EARTHLINGS WIPED OUT?
NO, VUL-KOR! I OWE THEM NO ALLEGIANCE! AFTER ALL, I WAS BORN ON ANOTHER WORLD MYSELF... KRYPTON!
9

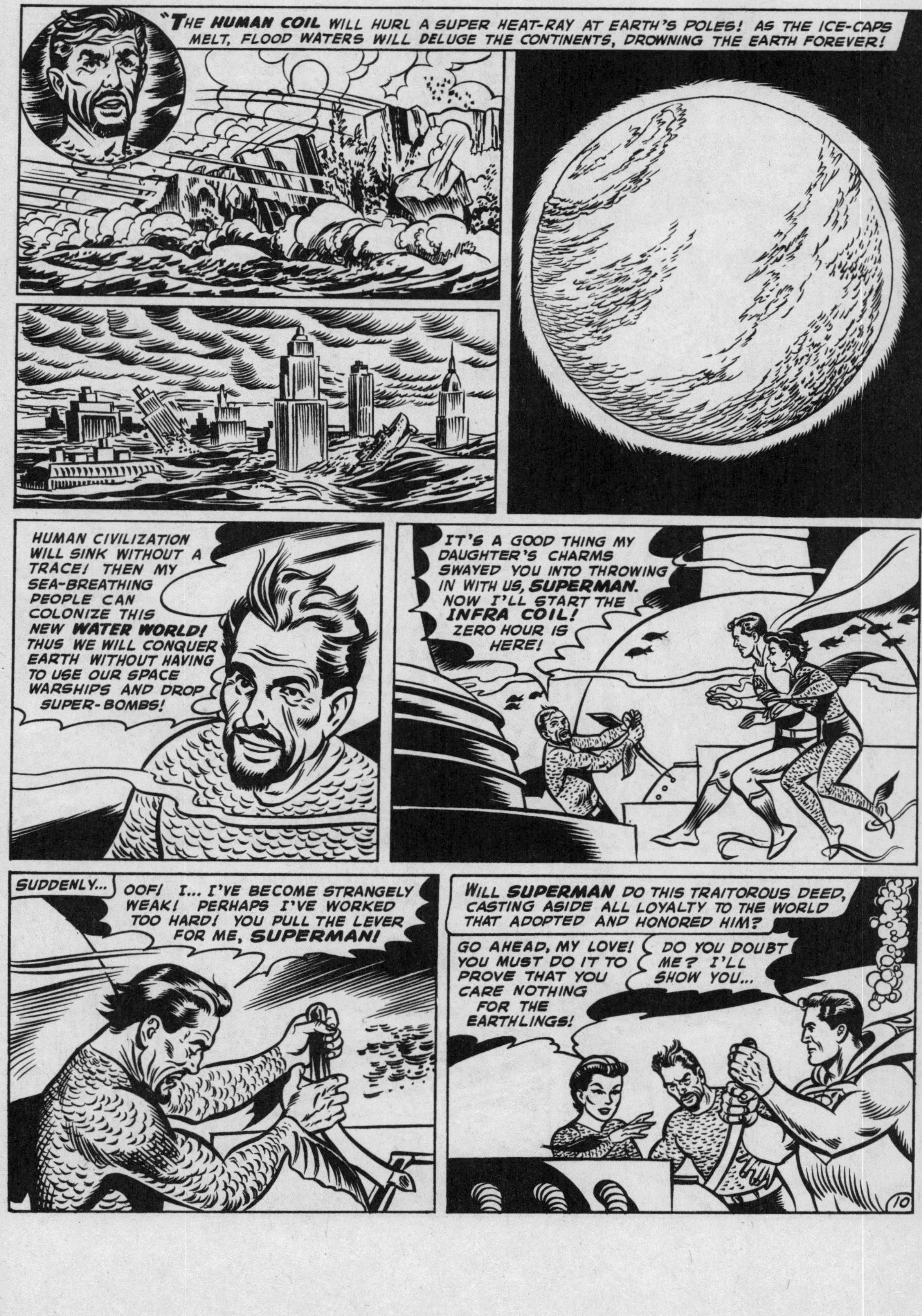
"THE HUMAN COIL WILL HURL A SUPER HEAT-RAY AT EARTH'S POLES! AS THE ICE-CAPS MELT, FLOOD WATERS WILL DELUGE THE CONTINENTS, DROWNING THE EARTH FOREVER!
HUMAN CIVILIZATION WILL SINK WITHOUT A TRACE! THEN MY SEA-BREATHING PEOPLE CAN COLONIZE THIS NEW WATER WORLD! THUS WE WILL CONQUER EARTH WITHOUT HAVING TO USE OUR SPACE WARSHIPS AND DROP SUPER-BOMBS!
IT'S A GOOD THING MY DAUGHTER'S CHARMS SWAYED YOU INTO THROWING IN WITH US, SUPERMAN. NOW I'LL START THE INFRA COIL! ZERO HOUR IS HERE!
SUDDENLY...
OOF! I... I'VE BECOME STRANGELY WEAK! PERHAPS I'VE WORKED TOO HARD! YOU PULL THE LEVER FOR ME, SUPERMAN!
WILL SUPERMAN DO THIS TRAITOROUS DEED, CASTING ASIDE ALL LOYALTY TO THE WORLD THAT ADOPTED AND HONORED HIM?
GO AHEAD, MY LOVE! YOU MUST DO IT TO PROVE THAT YOU CARE NOTHING FOR THE EARTHLINGS!
DO YOU DOUBT ME? I'LL SHOW YOU...
10

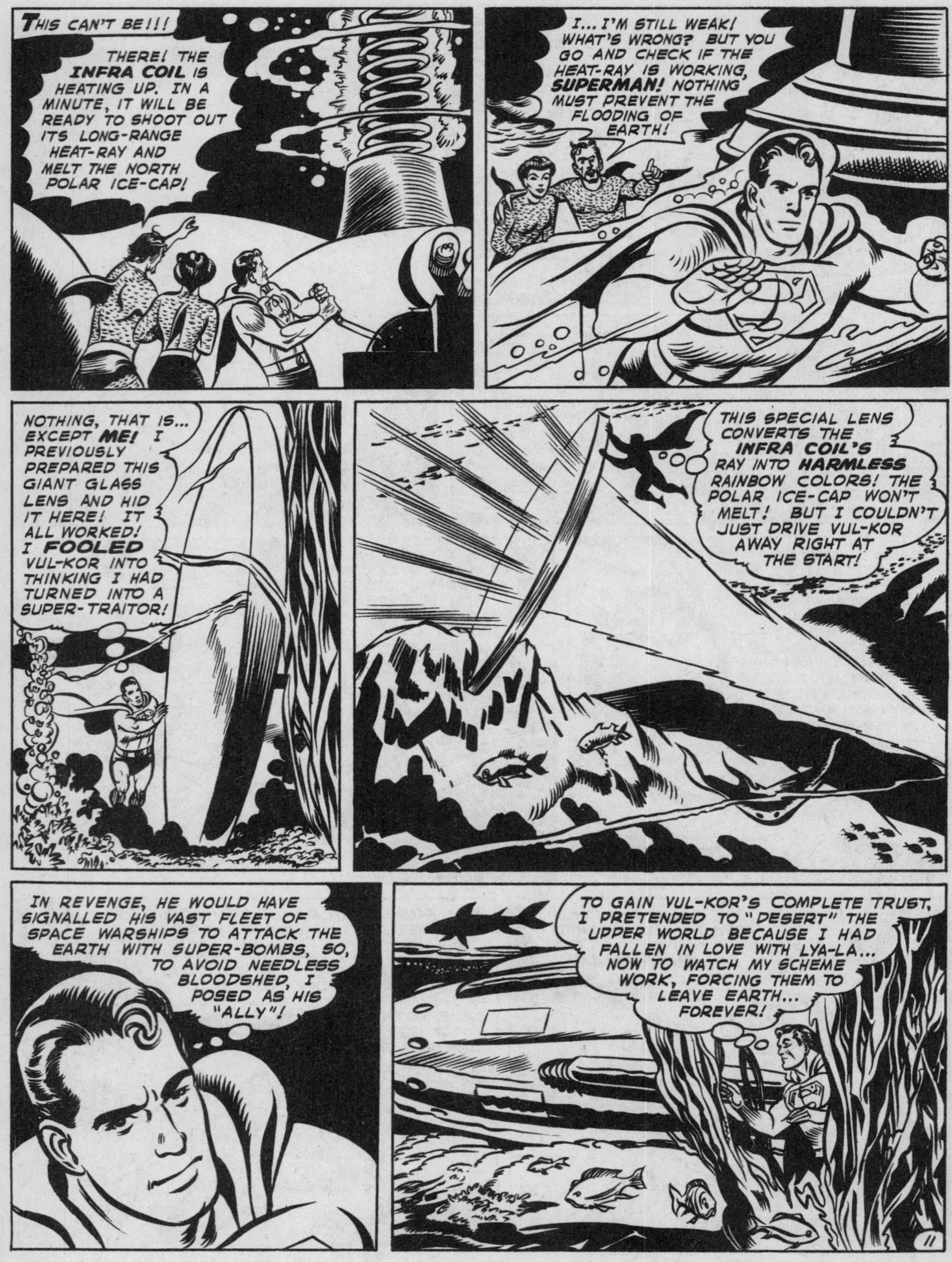
THIS CAN'T BE!!!
THERE! THE INFRA COIL IS HEATING UP. IN A MINUTE, IT WILL BE READY TO SHOOT OUT ITS LONG-RANGE HEAT-RAY AND MELT THE NORTH POLAR ICE-CAP!
I... I'M STILL WEAK! WHAT'S WRONG? BUT YOU GO AND CHECK IF THE HEAT-RAY IS WORKING, SUPERMAN! NOTHING MUST PREVENT THE FLOODING OF EARTH!
NOTHING, THAT IS... EXCEPT ME! I PREVIOUSLY PREPARED THIS GIANT GLASS LENS AND HID IT HERE! IT ALL WORKED! I FOOLED VUL-KOR INTO THINKING I HAD TURNED INTO A SUPER-TRAITOR!
THIS SPECIAL LENS CONVERTS THE INFRA COIL'S RAY INTO HARMLESS RAINBOW COLORS! THE POLAR ICE-CAP WON'T MELT! BUT I COULDN'T JUST DRIVE VUL-KOR AWAY RIGHT AT THE START!
IN REVENGE, HE WOULD HAVE SIGNALLED HIS VAST FLEET OF SPACE WARSHIPS TO ATTACK THE EARTH WITH SUPER-BOMBS, SO, TO AVOID NEEDLESS BLOODSHED, I POSED AS HIS "ALLY"!
TO GAIN VUL-KOR'S COMPLETE TRUST, I PRETENDED TO "DESERT" THE UPPER WORLD BECAUSE I HAD FALLEN IN LOVE WITH LYA-LA... NOW TO WATCH MY SCHEME WORK, FORCING THEM TO LEAVE EARTH... FOREVER!
11

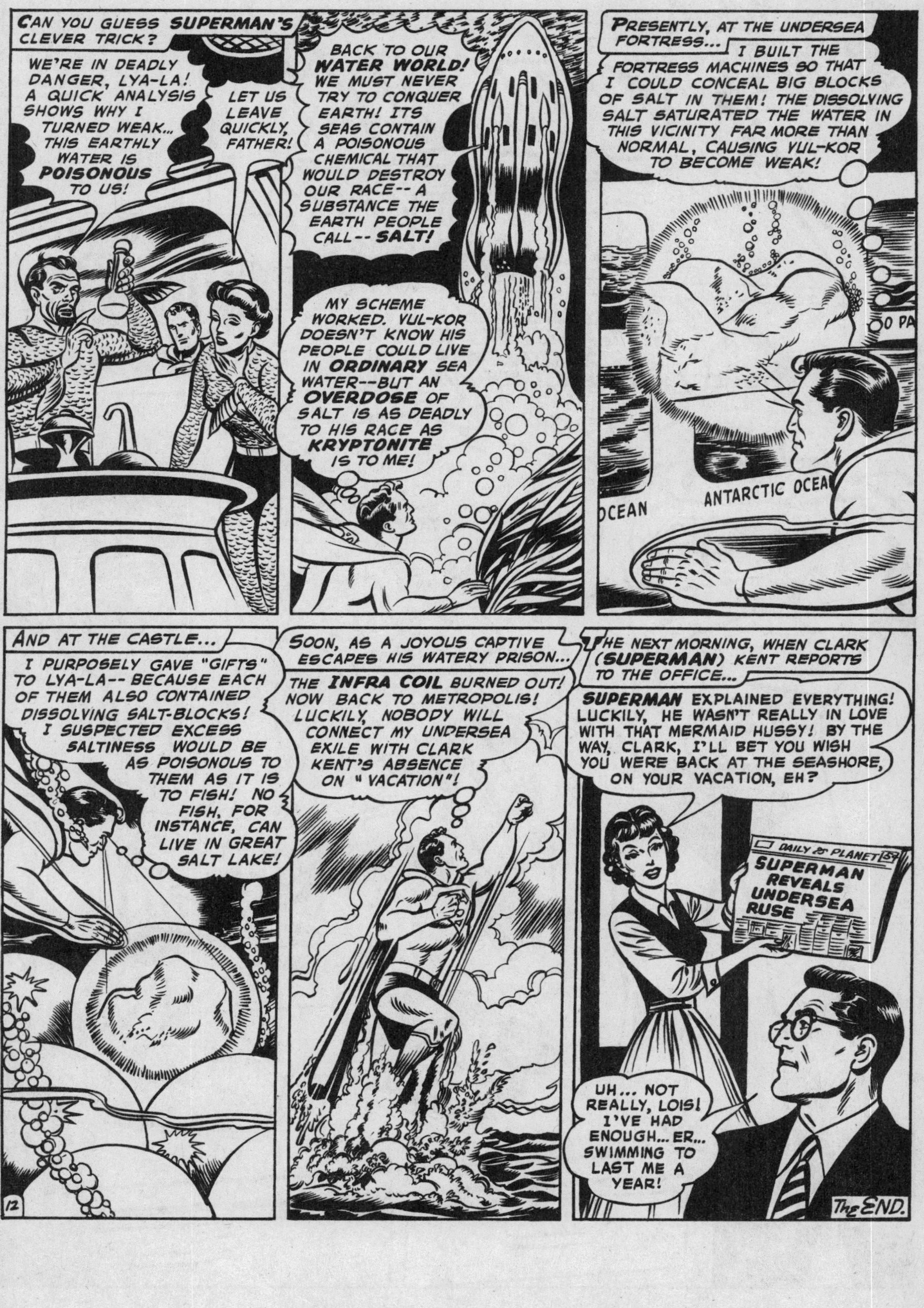
CAN YOU GUESS SUPERMAN'S CLEVER TRICK?
WE'RE IN DEADLY DANGER, LYA-LA! A QUICK ANALYSIS SHOWS WHY I TURNED WEAK... THIS EARTHLY WATER IS POISONOUS TO US!
LET US LEAVE QUICKLY, FATHER!
BACK TO OUR WATER WORLD! WE MUST NEVER TRY TO CONQUER EARTH! ITS SEAS CONTAIN A POISONOUS CHEMICAL THAT WOULD DESTROY OUR RACE-- A SUBSTANCE THE EARTH PEOPLE CALL-- SALT!
MY SCHEME WORKED. YUL-KOR DOESN'T KNOW HIS PEOPLE COULD LIVE IN ORDINARY SEA WATER--BUT AN OVERDOSE OF SALT IS AS DEADLY TO HIS RACE AS KRYPTONITE IS TO ME!
PRESENTLY, AT THE UNDERSEA FORTRESS...
I BUILT THE FORTRESS MACHINES SO THAT I COULD CONCEAL BIG BLOCKS OF SALT IN THEM! THE DISSOLVING SALT SATURATED THE WATER IN THIS VICINITY FAR MORE THAN NORMAL, CAUSING YUL-KOR TO BECOME WEAK!
0 PA
OCEAN
ANTARCTIC OCEA
AND AT THE CASTLE...
I PURPOSELY GAVE "GIFTS" TO LYA-LA-- BECAUSE EACH OF THEM ALSO CONTAINED DISSOLVING SALT-BLOCKS! I SUSPECTED EXCESS SALTINESS WOULD BE AS POISONOUS TO THEM AS IT IS TO FISH! NO FISH, FOR INSTANCE, CAN LIVE IN GREAT SALT LAKE!
12
SOON, AS A JOYOUS CAPTIVE ESCAPES HIS WATERY PRISON...
THE INFRA COIL BURNED OUT! NOW BACK TO METROPOLIS! LUCKILY, NOBODY WILL CONNECT MY UNDERSEA EXILE WITH CLARK KENT'S ABSENCE ON "VACATION"!
THE NEXT MORNING, WHEN CLARK (SUPERMAN) KENT REPORTS TO THE OFFICE...
SUPERMAN EXPLAINED EVERYTHING! LUCKILY, HE WASN'T REALLY IN LOVE WITH THAT MERMAID HUSSY! BY THE WAY, CLARK, I'LL BET YOU WISH YOU WERE BACK AT THE SEASHORE, ON YOUR VACATION, EH?
DAILY PLANET 5¢
SUPERMAN REVEALS UNDERSEA RUSE
UH... NOT REALLY, LOIS! I'VE HAD ENOUGH... ER... SWIMMING TO LAST ME A YEAR!
THE END.

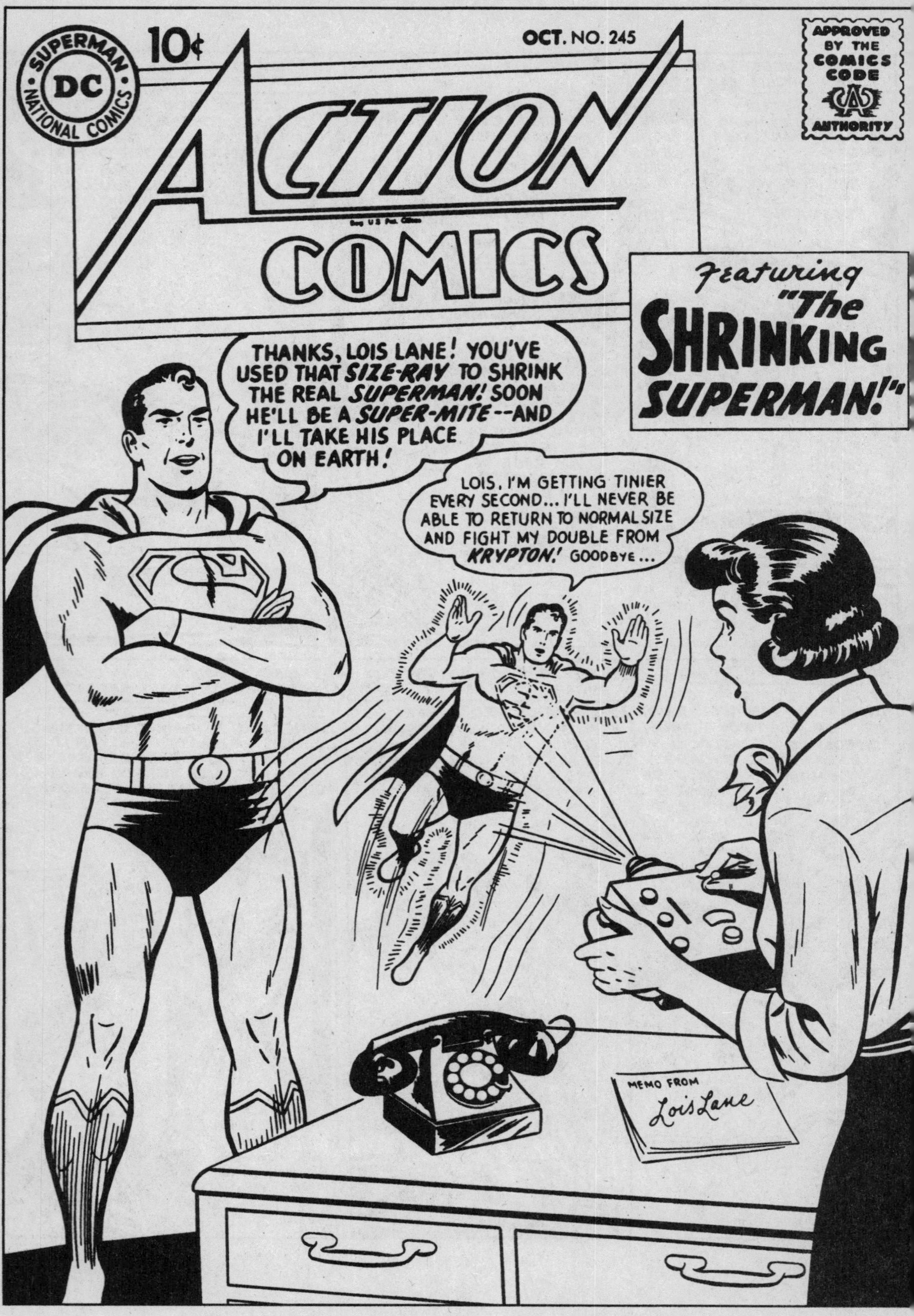
SUPERMAN DC NATIONAL COMICS
10¢
OCT. NO. 245
APPROVED BY THE COMICS CODE AUTHORITY
ACTION COMICS
Featuring "The SHRINKING SUPERMAN!"
THANKS, LOIS LANE! YOU'VE USED THAT SIZE-RAY TO SHRINK THE REAL SUPERMAN! SOON HE'LL BE A SUPER-MITE--AND I'LL TAKE HIS PLACE ON EARTH!
LOIS, I'M GETTING TINIER EVERY SECOND... I'LL NEVER BE ABLE TO RETURN TO NORMAL SIZE AND FIGHT MY DOUBLE FROM KRYPTON! GOODBYE...
MEMO FROM
Lois Lane

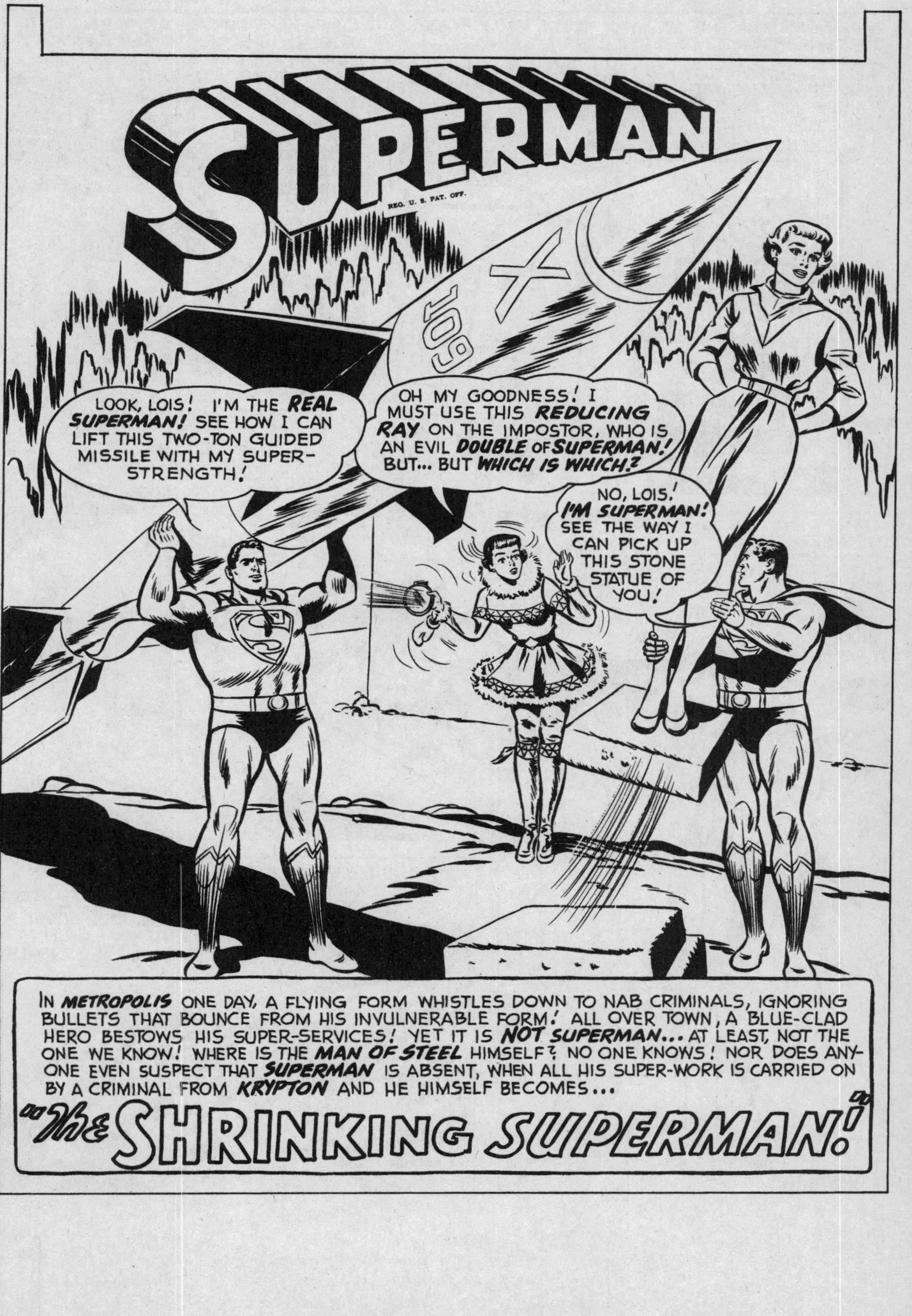
SUPERMAN
REG. U. S. PAT. OFF.
X 109
LOOK, LOIS! I'M THE REAL SUPERMAN! SEE HOW I CAN LIFT THIS TWO-TON GUIDED MISSILE WITH MY SUPER-STRENGTH!
OH MY GOODNESS! I MUST USE THIS REDUCING RAY ON THE IMPOSTOR, WHO IS AN EVIL DOUBLE OF SUPERMAN! BUT... BUT WHICH IS WHICH?
NO, LOIS! I'M SUPERMAN! SEE THE WAY I CAN PICK UP THIS STONE STATUE OF YOU!
IN METROPOLIS ONE DAY, A FLYING FORM WHISTLES DOWN TO NAB CRIMINALS, IGNORING BULLETS THAT BOUNCE FROM HIS INVULNERABLE FORM! ALL OVER TOWN, A BLUE-CLAD HERO BESTOWS HIS SUPER-SERVICES! YET IT IS NOT SUPERMAN... AT LEAST, NOT THE ONE WE KNOW! WHERE IS THE MAN OF STEEL HIMSELF? NO ONE KNOWS! NOR DOES ANYONE EVEN SUSPECT THAT SUPERMAN IS ABSENT, WHEN ALL HIS SUPER-WORK IS CARRIED ON BY A CRIMINAL FROM KRYPTON AND HE HIMSELF BECOMES...
"The SHRINKING SUPERMAN!"

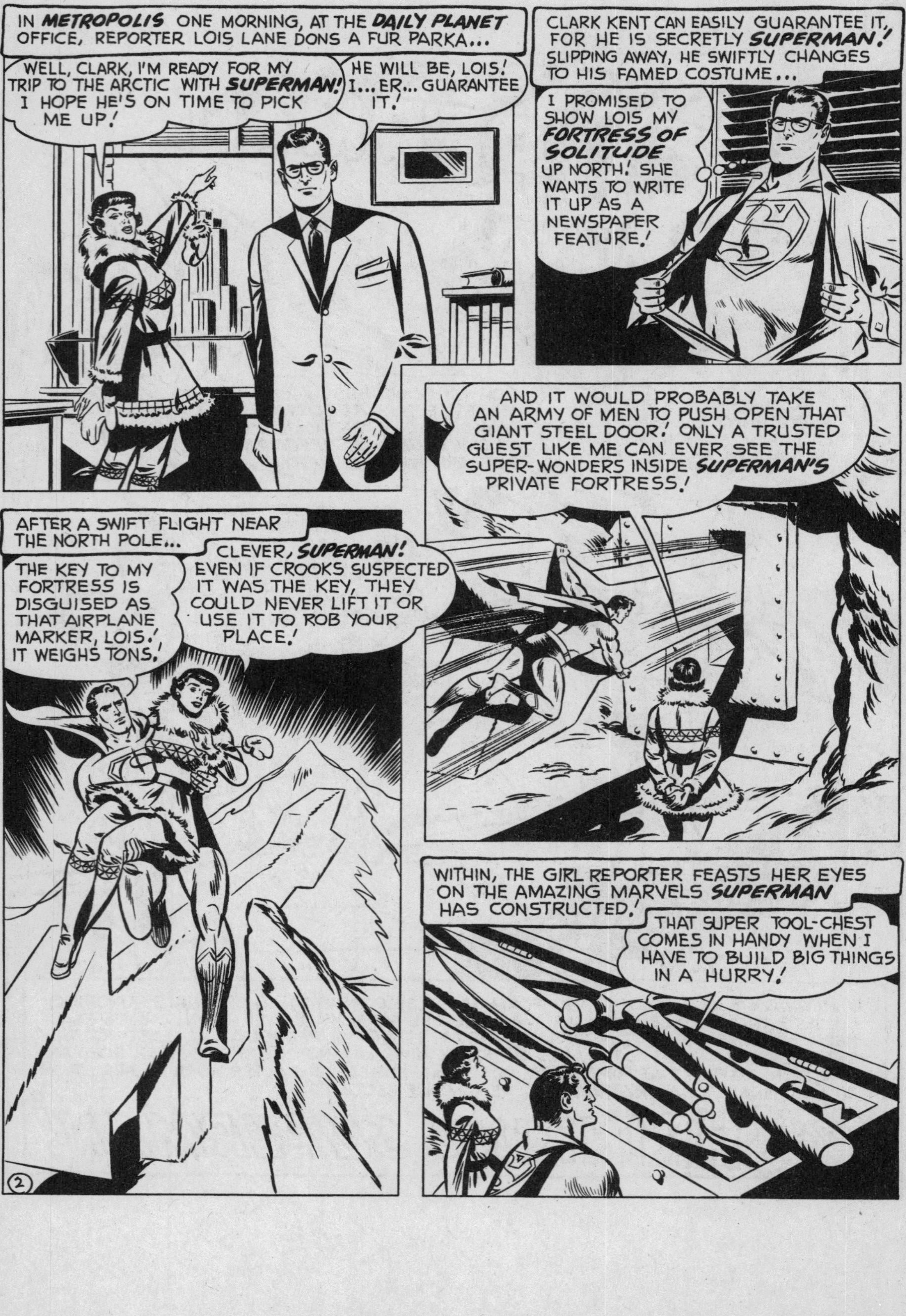
IN METROPOLIS ONE MORNING, AT THE DAILY PLANET OFFICE, REPORTER LOIS LANE DONS A FUR PARKA...
WELL, CLARK, I'M READY FOR MY TRIP TO THE ARCTIC WITH SUPERMAN! I HOPE HE'S ON TIME TO PICK ME UP!
HE WILL BE, LOIS! I... ER... GUARANTEE IT!
CLARK KENT CAN EASILY GUARANTEE IT, FOR HE IS SECRETLY SUPERMAN! SLIPPING AWAY, HE SWIFTLY CHANGES TO HIS FAMED COSTUME...
I PROMISED TO SHOW LOIS MY FORTRESS OF SOLITUDE UP NORTH! SHE WANTS TO WRITE IT UP AS A NEWSPAPER FEATURE!
AFTER A SWIFT FLIGHT NEAR THE NORTH POLE...
THE KEY TO MY FORTRESS IS DISGUISED AS THAT AIRPLANE MARKER, LOIS! IT WEIGHS TONS!
CLEVER, SUPERMAN! EVEN IF CROOKS SUSPECTED IT WAS THE KEY, THEY COULD NEVER LIFT IT OR USE IT TO ROB YOUR PLACE!
2
AND IT WOULD PROBABLY TAKE AN ARMY OF MEN TO PUSH OPEN THAT GIANT STEEL DOOR! ONLY A TRUSTED GUEST LIKE ME CAN EVER SEE THE SUPER-WONDERS INSIDE SUPERMAN'S PRIVATE FORTRESS!
WITHIN, THE GIRL REPORTER FEASTS HER EYES ON THE AMAZING MARVELS SUPERMAN HAS CONSTRUCTED!
THAT SUPER TOOL-CHEST COMES IN HANDY WHEN I HAVE TO BUILD BIG THINGS IN A HURRY!

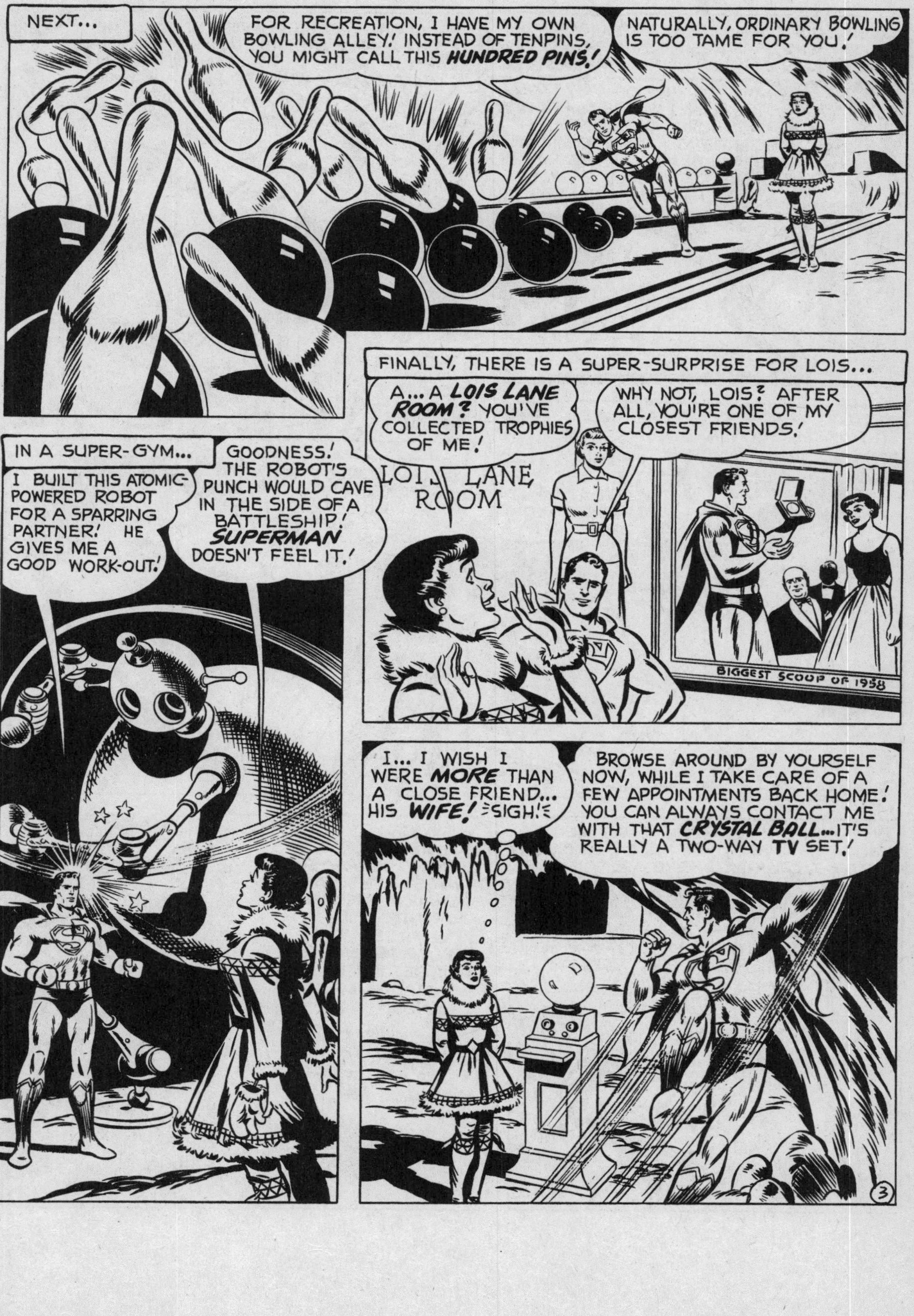
NEXT...
FOR RECREATION, I HAVE MY OWN BOWLING ALLEY! INSTEAD OF TENPINS, YOU MIGHT CALL THIS HUNDRED PINS!
NATURALLY, ORDINARY BOWLING IS TOO TAME FOR YOU!
IN A SUPER-GYM...
I BUILT THIS ATOMIC-POWERED ROBOT FOR A SPARRING PARTNER! HE GIVES ME A GOOD WORK-OUT!
GOODNESS! THE ROBOT'S PUNCH WOULD CAVE IN THE SIDE OF A BATTLESHIP! SUPERMAN DOESN'T FEEL IT!
FINALLY, THERE IS A SUPER-SURPRISE FOR LOIS...
A... A LOIS LANE ROOM? YOU'VE COLLECTED TROPHIES OF ME!
WHY NOT, LOIS? AFTER ALL, YOU'RE ONE OF MY CLOSEST FRIENDS!
LOIS LANE ROOM
BIGGEST SCOOP OF 1958
I... I WISH I WERE MORE THAN A CLOSE FRIEND... HIS WIFE! SIGH!
BROWSE AROUND BY YOURSELF NOW, WHILE I TAKE CARE OF A FEW APPOINTMENTS BACK HOME! YOU CAN ALWAYS CONTACT ME WITH THAT CRYSTAL BALL... IT'S REALLY A TWO-WAY TV SET!
3

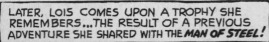

LATER, LOIS COMES UPON A TROPHY SHE REMEMBERS...THE RESULT OF A PREVIOUS ADVENTURE SHE SHARED WITH THE *MAN OF STEEL!*

THAT'S A CITY OF *KRYPTON,* THE PLANET WHERE *SUPERMAN* WAS BORN! AN EVIL SPACE SCIENTIST SHRUNK IT TO MINIATURE SIZE WITH A REDUCING RAY BEFORE THAT WORLD BLEW UP! THEN HE SEALED IT IN A BOTTLE!

AIR HAS TO BE PUMPED IN, FOR THE TINY PEOPLE ARE STILL ALIVE AND GOING ABOUT THEIR DAILY BUSINESS! SOME DAY *SUPERMAN* HOPES TO FIND A WAY TO ENLARGE THEM TO NORMAL SIZE!

BUT LOIS BENDS TOO CLOSE OVER THE MIDGET CITY AND...

OOPS!... I KNOCKED IT TO THE FLOOR BY ACCIDENT! OH, DEAR! I HOPE I DIDN'T SMASH IT!

NO... LUCKILY, IT ONLY CRACKED A BIT! THE AIR WILL LEAK OUT SLOWLY! *SUPERMAN* WILL REPAIR IT WHEN HE RETURNS! NO HARM DONE!

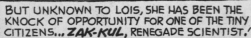

BUT UNKNOWN TO LOIS, SHE HAS BEEN THE KNOCK OF OPPORTUNITY FOR ONE OF THE TINY CITIZENS...*ZAK-KUL,* RENEGADE SCIENTIST!

WHAT LUCK! MY CHANCE TO SQUEEZE OUT OF THIS GIANT CRACK AND ESCAPE FROM THE BOTTLE! LET THE POLICE OF *KRYPTON* WONDER WHERE I LEFT! HA, HA!

PREVIOUSLY, I ISOLATED THE RARE ELEMENT *ILLIUM-349,* WHOSE RAYS CAN CHANGE THE SIZE OF THE BODY! I'LL PRESS THE *ENLARGER BUTTON* AND RETURN TO NORMAL HUMAN SIZE!

4

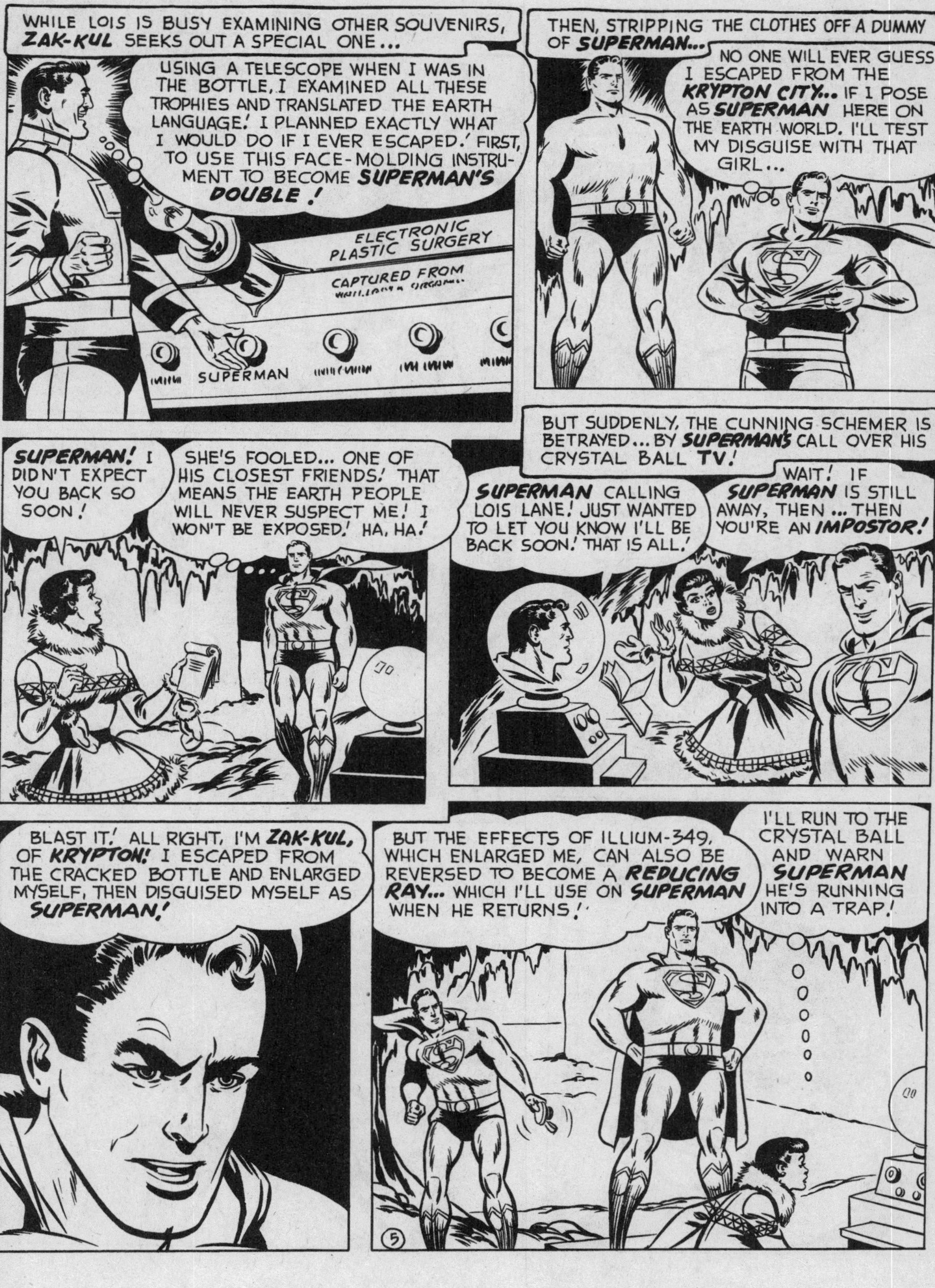
WHILE LOIS IS BUSY EXAMINING OTHER SOUVENIRS, ZAK-KUL SEEKS OUT A SPECIAL ONE...
USING A TELESCOPE WHEN I WAS IN THE BOTTLE, I EXAMINED ALL THESE TROPHIES AND TRANSLATED THE EARTH LANGUAGE! I PLANNED EXACTLY WHAT I WOULD DO IF I EVER ESCAPED! FIRST, TO USE THIS FACE-MOLDING INSTRUMENT TO BECOME SUPERMAN'S DOUBLE!
ELECTRONIC PLASTIC SURGERY
CAPTURED FROM
SUPERMAN
THEN, STRIPPING THE CLOTHES OFF A DUMMY OF SUPERMAN...
NO ONE WILL EVER GUESS I ESCAPED FROM THE KRYPTON CITY... IF I POSE AS SUPERMAN HERE ON THE EARTH WORLD. I'LL TEST MY DISGUISE WITH THAT GIRL...
SUPERMAN! I DIDN'T EXPECT YOU BACK SO SOON!
SHE'S FOOLED... ONE OF HIS CLOSEST FRIENDS! THAT MEANS THE EARTH PEOPLE WILL NEVER SUSPECT ME! I WON'T BE EXPOSED! HA, HA!
BUT SUDDENLY, THE CUNNING SCHEMER IS BETRAYED... BY SUPERMAN'S CALL OVER HIS CRYSTAL BALL TV!
SUPERMAN CALLING LOIS LANE! JUST WANTED TO LET YOU KNOW I'LL BE BACK SOON! THAT IS ALL!
WAIT! IF SUPERMAN IS STILL AWAY, THEN ... THEN YOU'RE AN IMPOSTOR!
BLAST IT! ALL RIGHT, I'M ZAK-KUL, OF KRYPTON! I ESCAPED FROM THE CRACKED BOTTLE AND ENLARGED MYSELF, THEN DISGUISED MYSELF AS SUPERMAN!
BUT THE EFFECTS OF ILLIUM-349, WHICH ENLARGED ME, CAN ALSO BE REVERSED TO BECOME A REDUCING RAY... WHICH I'LL USE ON SUPERMAN WHEN HE RETURNS!
I'LL RUN TO THE CRYSTAL BALL AND WARN SUPERMAN HE'S RUNNING INTO A TRAP!
5

FOOL! YOU FORGOT THAT, SINCE I CAME FROM *KRYPTON,* I HAVE THE SAME *SUPER-POWERS* AS *SUPERMAN* ON YOUR EARTH! THE HEAT OF MY X-RAY VISION MELTS THAT STATUE'S NECK... THE FALLING HEAD WILL KNOCK YOU OUT!

OHHHHH...

WHEN LOIS' SENSES RETURN, SHE MEETS A BEWILDERING SIGHT!

OH MY GOODNESS! THE REAL *SUPERMAN* JUST CAME BACK... I SEE TWO OF THEM, EXACTLY ALIKE!

BUT LUCKILY, *ZAK-KUL* DIDN'T HAVE TIME TO PICK UP HIS RAY DEVICE BEFORE *SUPERMAN* ARRIVED! I'LL SNATCH IT AND REDUCE THE FALSE *SUPERMAN* TO TINY SIZE AGAIN!

USE IT ON THAT IMPOSTOR, LOIS! I'M THE *REAL SUPERMAN,* OF COURSE!

NO, LOIS... HE'S LYING! *I'M* THE GENUINE *SUPERMAN!*

OH MY GOODNESS! WHICH IS... (GULP!) *WHICH*?

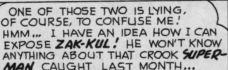

ONE OF THOSE TWO IS LYING, OF COURSE, TO CONFUSE ME! HMM... I HAVE AN IDEA HOW I CAN EXPOSE *ZAK-KUL!* HE WON'T KNOW ANYTHING ABOUT THAT CROOK *SUPERMAN* CAUGHT LAST MONTH...

YOU!... IF YOU'RE REALLY *SUPERMAN,* DESCRIBE THAT CROOK YOU CAPTURED, "GUNNER" GATES! WELL?

"GUNNER" WEARS AN EYE-PATCH!

WHY...UH... OH, I NAB SO *MANY* CROOKS, LOIS! HOW CAN I REMEMBER THAT PARTICULAR ONE?

HAH! PRETTY THIN, MR. *FAKE* SUPERMAN! YOU CAN'T REMEMBER BECAUSE YOU'RE *ZAK-KUL,* THAT'S WHY!

QUICK THINKING, LOIS! YOU SMOKED HIM OUT! USE THE *REDUCING RAY* ON THAT IMPOSTOR UNTIL HE'S TINY SIZE AGAIN!

SHORTLY...

BACK IN THE BOTTLE, YOU ROGUE! YOUR PLOT FAILED AND YOU'LL LOSE YOUR SUPER-POWERS BACK IN THE *KRYPTON CITY!*

NOW THE HEAT OF MY X-RAY VISION WILL FUSE THE CRACKS! *ZAK-KUL* WILL NEVER ESCAPE AGAIN!

TOO BAD THE OTHER TINY INHABITANTS CAN'T BE ENLARGED... THAT WAS THE LAST CHARGE OF ILLIUM-349!

PRESENTLY...

WE LOCKED THE FORTRESS... BACK TO *METROPOLIS!* GOSH, I'M GLAD THAT FALSE *SUPERMAN* ISN'T AT LARGE!

BUT *I* AM THE FALSE *SUPERMAN!* THE *REAL SUPERMAN* SOMEHOW FUMBLED HER QUESTION AND WAS SEALED IN THE BOTTLE IN *MY* PLACE! NOW I'LL TAKE *HIS* PLACE! HA, HA!

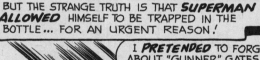

BUT THE STRANGE TRUTH IS THAT SUPERMAN *ALLOWED* HIMSELF TO BE TRAPPED IN THE BOTTLE... FOR AN URGENT REASON!

I *PRETENDED* TO FORGET ABOUT "GUNNER" GATES... FOR LOIS' SAKE! IF *ZAK-KUL* HAD BEEN EXPOSED, HE WOULD HAVE DESPERATELY STARTED A *SUPER-FIGHT* WITH ME! IT MIGHT HAVE WRECKED THE FORTRESS, KILLING LOIS... ALSO SMASHING THE BOTTLE! I... I COULDN'T RISK THAT DANGER!

WHEN I TRY TO SMASH THE GLASS IT ONLY HURTS MY HAND! WITHIN THIS BOTTLE, WHERE *KRYPTON'S* NON-EARTHLY GRAVITY CONDITIONS ARE IN FORCE, I HAVE NO SUPER-POWERS! I... I'M JUST AN *ORDINARY MAN!*

7

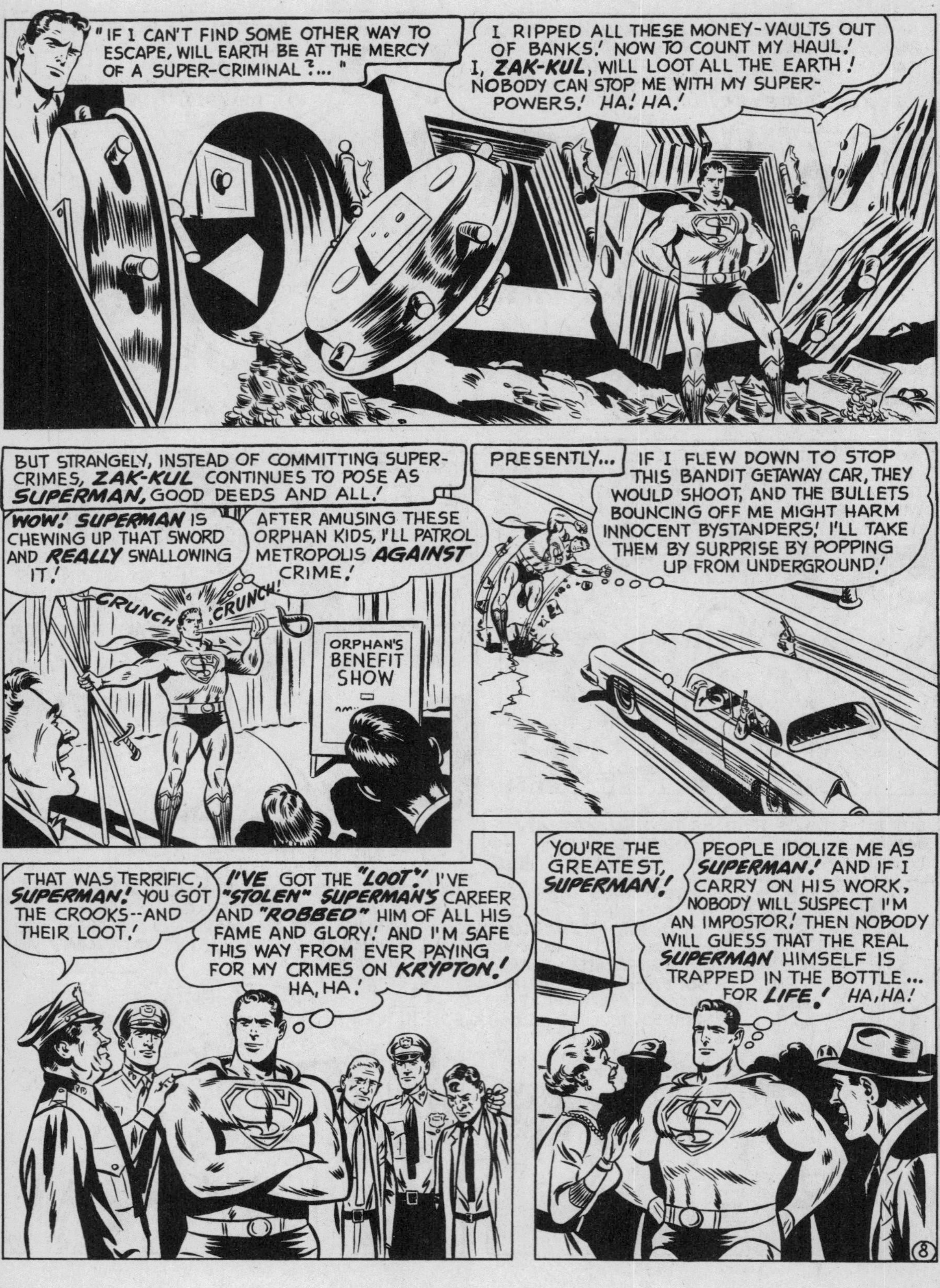
"IF I CAN'T FIND SOME OTHER WAY TO ESCAPE, WILL EARTH BE AT THE MERCY OF A SUPER-CRIMINAL?..."
I RIPPED ALL THESE MONEY-VAULTS OUT OF BANKS! NOW TO COUNT MY HAUL! I, ZAK-KUL, WILL LOOT ALL THE EARTH! NOBODY CAN STOP ME WITH MY SUPER-POWERS! HA! HA!
BUT STRANGELY, INSTEAD OF COMMITTING SUPER-CRIMES, ZAK-KUL CONTINUES TO POSE AS SUPERMAN, GOOD DEEDS AND ALL!
WOW! SUPERMAN IS CHEWING UP THAT SWORD AND REALLY SWALLOWING IT!
AFTER AMUSING THESE ORPHAN KIDS, I'LL PATROL METROPOLIS AGAINST CRIME!
CRUNCH
CRUNCH!
ORPHAN'S BENEFIT SHOW
PRESENTLY...
IF I FLEW DOWN TO STOP THIS BANDIT GETAWAY CAR, THEY WOULD SHOOT, AND THE BULLETS BOUNCING OFF ME MIGHT HARM INNOCENT BYSTANDERS! I'LL TAKE THEM BY SURPRISE BY POPPING UP FROM UNDERGROUND!
THAT WAS TERRIFIC, SUPERMAN! YOU GOT THE CROOKS--AND THEIR LOOT!
I'VE GOT THE "LOOT"! I'VE "STOLEN" SUPERMAN'S CAREER AND "ROBBED" HIM OF ALL HIS FAME AND GLORY! AND I'M SAFE THIS WAY FROM EVER PAYING FOR MY CRIMES ON KRYPTON! HA, HA!
YOU'RE THE GREATEST, SUPERMAN!
PEOPLE IDOLIZE ME AS SUPERMAN! AND IF I CARRY ON HIS WORK, NOBODY WILL SUSPECT I'M AN IMPOSTOR! THEN NOBODY WILL GUESS THAT THE REAL SUPERMAN HIMSELF IS TRAPPED IN THE BOTTLE... FOR LIFE! HA, HA!
8

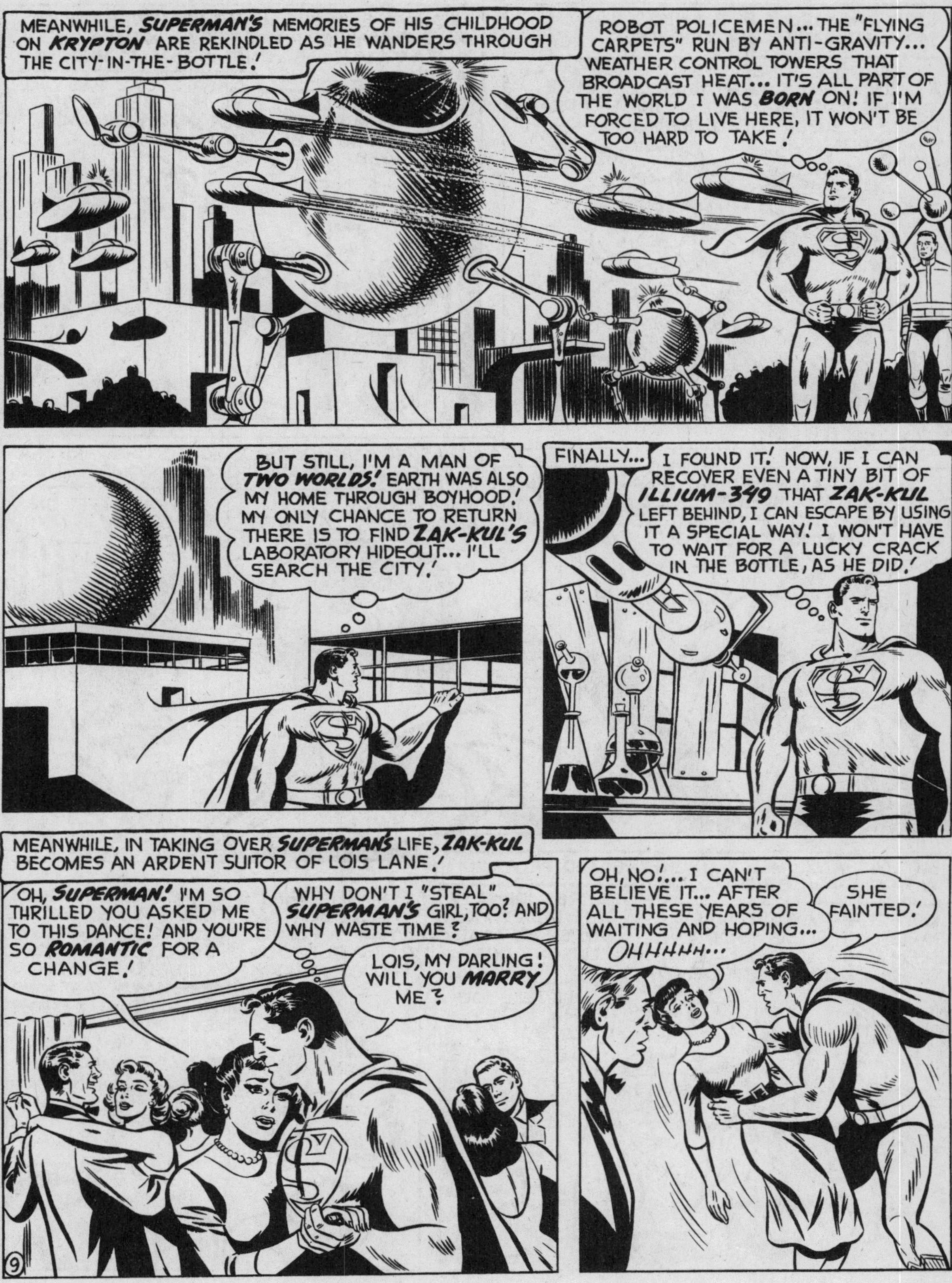
MEANWHILE, SUPERMAN'S MEMORIES OF HIS CHILDHOOD ON KRYPTON ARE REKINDLED AS HE WANDERS THROUGH THE CITY-IN-THE-BOTTLE!
ROBOT POLICEMEN... THE "FLYING CARPETS" RUN BY ANTI-GRAVITY... WEATHER CONTROL TOWERS THAT BROADCAST HEAT... IT'S ALL PART OF THE WORLD I WAS BORN ON! IF I'M FORCED TO LIVE HERE, IT WON'T BE TOO HARD TO TAKE!
BUT STILL, I'M A MAN OF TWO WORLDS! EARTH WAS ALSO MY HOME THROUGH BOYHOOD! MY ONLY CHANCE TO RETURN THERE IS TO FIND ZAK-KUL'S LABORATORY HIDEOUT... I'LL SEARCH THE CITY!
FINALLY...
I FOUND IT! NOW, IF I CAN RECOVER EVEN A TINY BIT OF ILLIUM-349 THAT ZAK-KUL LEFT BEHIND, I CAN ESCAPE BY USING IT A SPECIAL WAY! I WON'T HAVE TO WAIT FOR A LUCKY CRACK IN THE BOTTLE, AS HE DID!
MEANWHILE, IN TAKING OVER SUPERMAN'S LIFE, ZAK-KUL BECOMES AN ARDENT SUITOR OF LOIS LANE!
OH, SUPERMAN! I'M SO THRILLED YOU ASKED ME TO THIS DANCE! AND YOU'RE SO ROMANTIC FOR A CHANGE!
WHY DON'T I "STEAL" SUPERMAN'S GIRL, TOO? AND WHY WASTE TIME?
LOIS, MY DARLING! WILL YOU MARRY ME?
9
OH, NO!... I CAN'T BELIEVE IT... AFTER ALL THESE YEARS OF WAITING AND HOPING... OHHHHH...
SHE FAINTED!

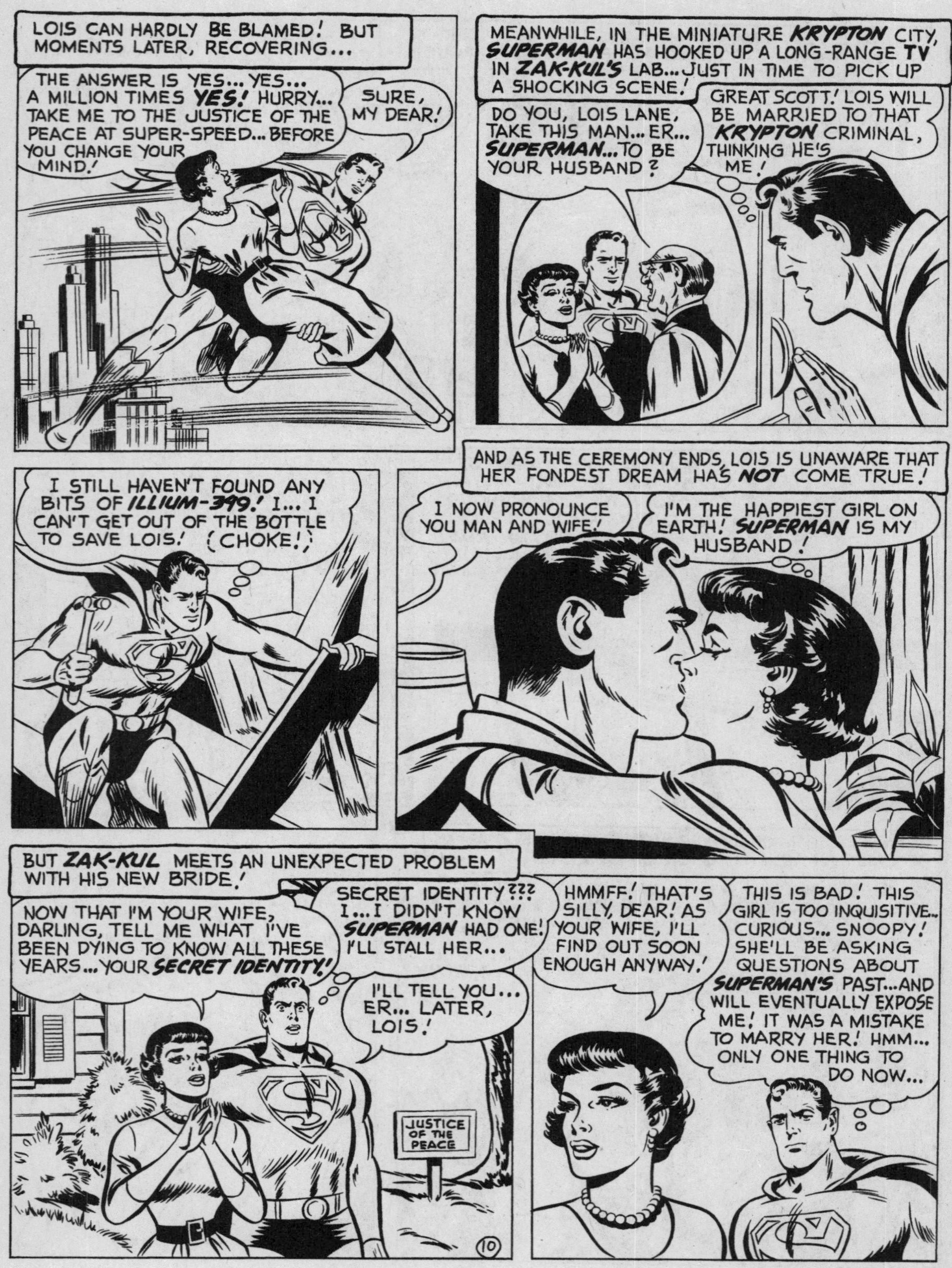
LOIS CAN HARDLY BE BLAMED! BUT MOMENTS LATER, RECOVERING...
THE ANSWER IS YES... YES... A MILLION TIMES YES! HURRY... TAKE ME TO THE JUSTICE OF THE PEACE AT SUPER-SPEED... BEFORE YOU CHANGE YOUR MIND!
SURE, MY DEAR!
MEANWHILE, IN THE MINIATURE KRYPTON CITY, SUPERMAN HAS HOOKED UP A LONG-RANGE TV IN ZAK-KUL'S LAB... JUST IN TIME TO PICK UP A SHOCKING SCENE!
DO YOU, LOIS LANE, TAKE THIS MAN... ER... SUPERMAN... TO BE YOUR HUSBAND?
GREAT SCOTT! LOIS WILL BE MARRIED TO THAT KRYPTON CRIMINAL, THINKING HE'S ME!
I STILL HAVEN'T FOUND ANY BITS OF ILLIUM-399! I... I CAN'T GET OUT OF THE BOTTLE TO SAVE LOIS! (CHOKE!)
AND AS THE CEREMONY ENDS, LOIS IS UNAWARE THAT HER FONDEST DREAM HAS NOT COME TRUE!
I NOW PRONOUNCE YOU MAN AND WIFE!
I'M THE HAPPIEST GIRL ON EARTH! SUPERMAN IS MY HUSBAND!
BUT ZAK-KUL MEETS AN UNEXPECTED PROBLEM WITH HIS NEW BRIDE!
NOW THAT I'M YOUR WIFE, DARLING, TELL ME WHAT I'VE BEEN DYING TO KNOW ALL THESE YEARS... YOUR SECRET IDENTITY!
SECRET IDENTITY??? I... I DIDN'T KNOW SUPERMAN HAD ONE! I'LL STALL HER...
I'LL TELL YOU... ER... LATER, LOIS!
JUSTICE OF THE PEACE
10
HMMFF! THAT'S SILLY, DEAR! AS YOUR WIFE, I'LL FIND OUT SOON ENOUGH ANYWAY!
THIS IS BAD! THIS GIRL IS TOO INQUISITIVE... CURIOUS... SNOOPY! SHE'LL BE ASKING QUESTIONS ABOUT SUPERMAN'S PAST... AND WILL EVENTUALLY EXPOSE ME! IT WAS A MISTAKE TO MARRY HER! HMM... ONLY ONE THING TO DO NOW...

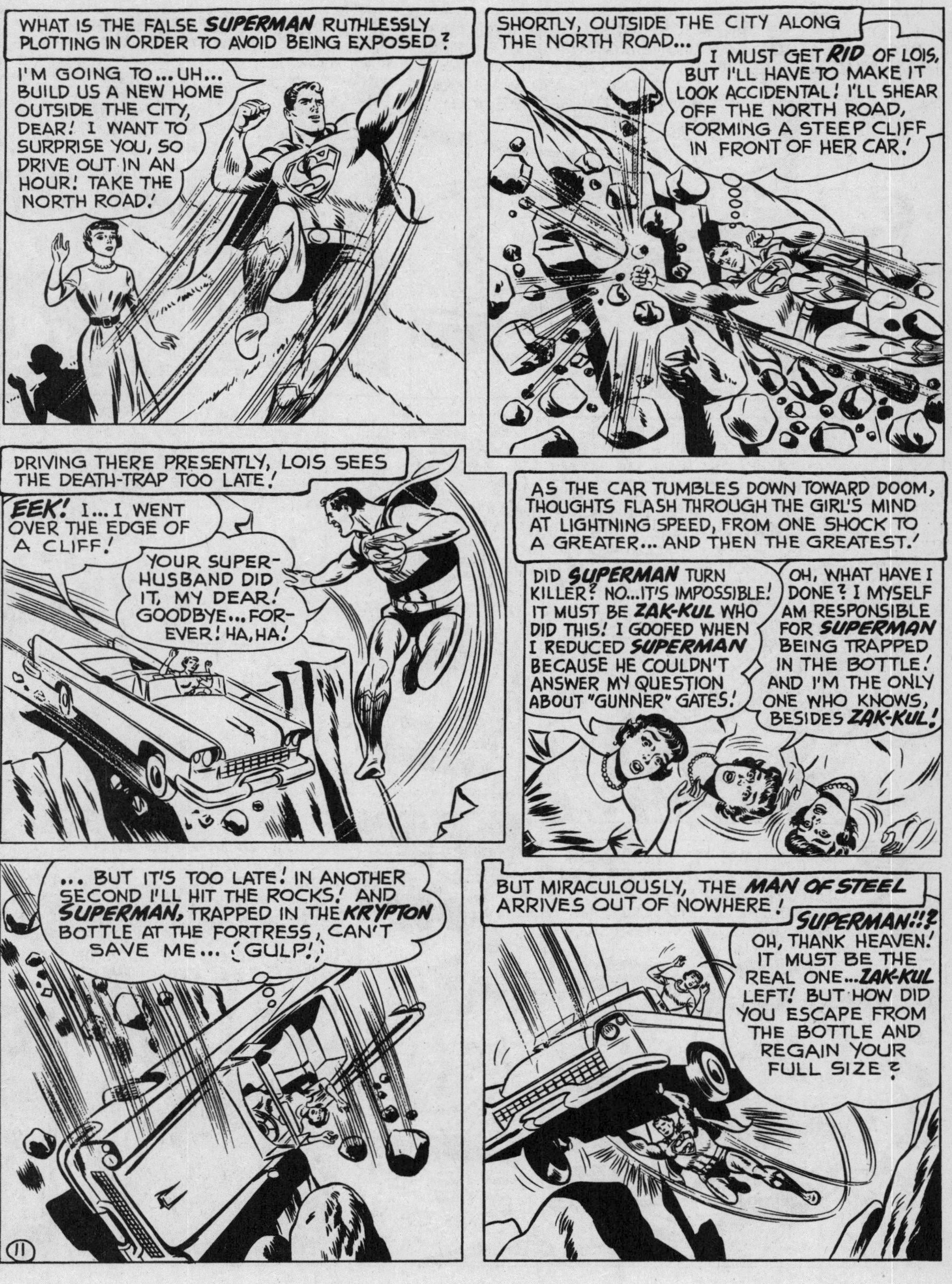
WHAT IS THE FALSE SUPERMAN RUTHLESSLY PLOTTING IN ORDER TO AVOID BEING EXPOSED?
I'M GOING TO... UH... BUILD US A NEW HOME OUTSIDE THE CITY, DEAR! I WANT TO SURPRISE YOU, SO DRIVE OUT IN AN HOUR! TAKE THE NORTH ROAD!
SHORTLY, OUTSIDE THE CITY ALONG THE NORTH ROAD...
I MUST GET RID OF LOIS, BUT I'LL HAVE TO MAKE IT LOOK ACCIDENTAL! I'LL SHEAR OFF THE NORTH ROAD, FORMING A STEEP CLIFF IN FRONT OF HER CAR!
DRIVING THERE PRESENTLY, LOIS SEES THE DEATH-TRAP TOO LATE!
EEK! I... I WENT OVER THE EDGE OF A CLIFF!
YOUR SUPER-HUSBAND DID IT, MY DEAR! GOODBYE... FOR-EVER! HA, HA!
AS THE CAR TUMBLES DOWN TOWARD DOOM, THOUGHTS FLASH THROUGH THE GIRL'S MIND AT LIGHTNING SPEED, FROM ONE SHOCK TO A GREATER... AND THEN THE GREATEST!
DID SUPERMAN TURN KILLER? NO...IT'S IMPOSSIBLE! IT MUST BE ZAK-KUL WHO DID THIS! I GOOFED WHEN I REDUCED SUPERMAN BECAUSE HE COULDN'T ANSWER MY QUESTION ABOUT "GUNNER" GATES!
OH, WHAT HAVE I DONE? I MYSELF AM RESPONSIBLE FOR SUPERMAN BEING TRAPPED IN THE BOTTLE! AND I'M THE ONLY ONE WHO KNOWS, BESIDES ZAK-KUL!
... BUT IT'S TOO LATE! IN ANOTHER SECOND I'LL HIT THE ROCKS! AND SUPERMAN, TRAPPED IN THE KRYPTON BOTTLE AT THE FORTRESS, CAN'T SAVE ME... (GULP!)
11
BUT MIRACULOUSLY, THE MAN OF STEEL ARRIVES OUT OF NOWHERE!
SUPERMAN!!? OH, THANK HEAVEN! IT MUST BE THE REAL ONE...ZAK-KUL LEFT! BUT HOW DID YOU ESCAPE FROM THE BOTTLE AND REGAIN YOUR FULL SIZE?

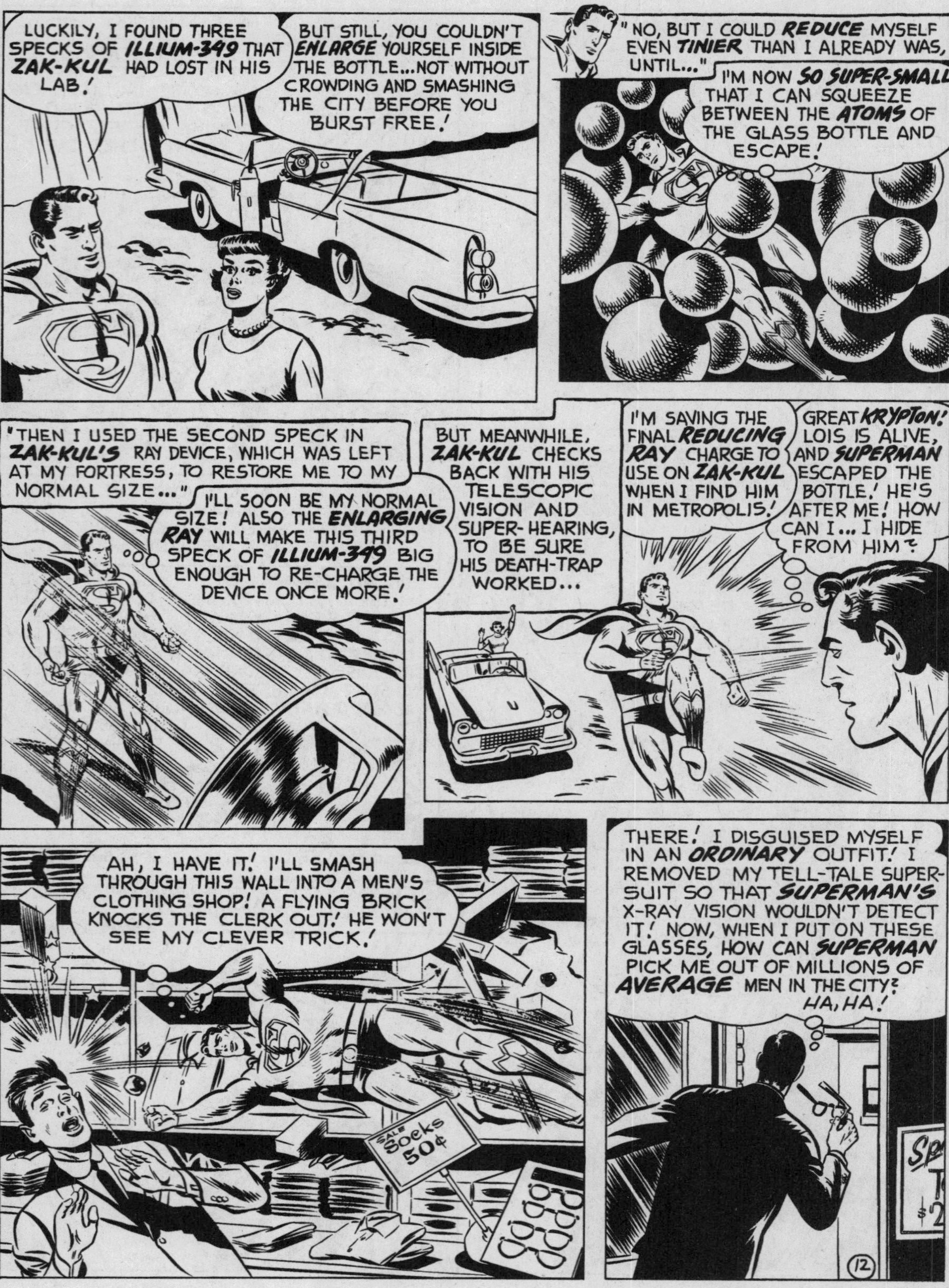
LUCKILY, I FOUND THREE SPECKS OF ILLIUM-349 THAT ZAK-KUL HAD LOST IN HIS LAB!
BUT STILL, YOU COULDN'T ENLARGE YOURSELF INSIDE THE BOTTLE...NOT WITHOUT CROWDING AND SMASHING THE CITY BEFORE YOU BURST FREE!
"NO, BUT I COULD REDUCE MYSELF EVEN TINIER THAN I ALREADY WAS, UNTIL..."
I'M NOW SO SUPER-SMALL THAT I CAN SQUEEZE BETWEEN THE ATOMS OF THE GLASS BOTTLE AND ESCAPE!
"THEN I USED THE SECOND SPECK IN ZAK-KUL'S RAY DEVICE, WHICH WAS LEFT AT MY FORTRESS, TO RESTORE ME TO MY NORMAL SIZE..."
I'LL SOON BE MY NORMAL SIZE! ALSO THE ENLARGING RAY WILL MAKE THIS THIRD SPECK OF ILLIUM-349 BIG ENOUGH TO RE-CHARGE THE DEVICE ONCE MORE!
BUT MEANWHILE, ZAK-KUL CHECKS BACK WITH HIS TELESCOPIC VISION AND SUPER-HEARING, TO BE SURE HIS DEATH-TRAP WORKED...
I'M SAVING THE FINAL REDUCING RAY CHARGE TO USE ON ZAK-KUL WHEN I FIND HIM IN METROPOLIS!
GREAT KRYPTON! LOIS IS ALIVE, AND SUPERMAN ESCAPED THE BOTTLE! HE'S AFTER ME! HOW CAN I... I HIDE FROM HIM?
AH, I HAVE IT! I'LL SMASH THROUGH THIS WALL INTO A MEN'S CLOTHING SHOP! A FLYING BRICK KNOCKS THE CLERK OUT! HE WON'T SEE MY CLEVER TRICK!
SALE Socks 50¢
THERE! I DISGUISED MYSELF IN AN ORDINARY OUTFIT! I REMOVED MY TELL-TALE SUPER-SUIT SO THAT SUPERMAN'S X-RAY VISION WOULDN'T DETECT IT! NOW, WHEN I PUT ON THESE GLASSES, HOW CAN SUPERMAN PICK ME OUT OF MILLIONS OF AVERAGE MEN IN THE CITY? HA, HA!
12

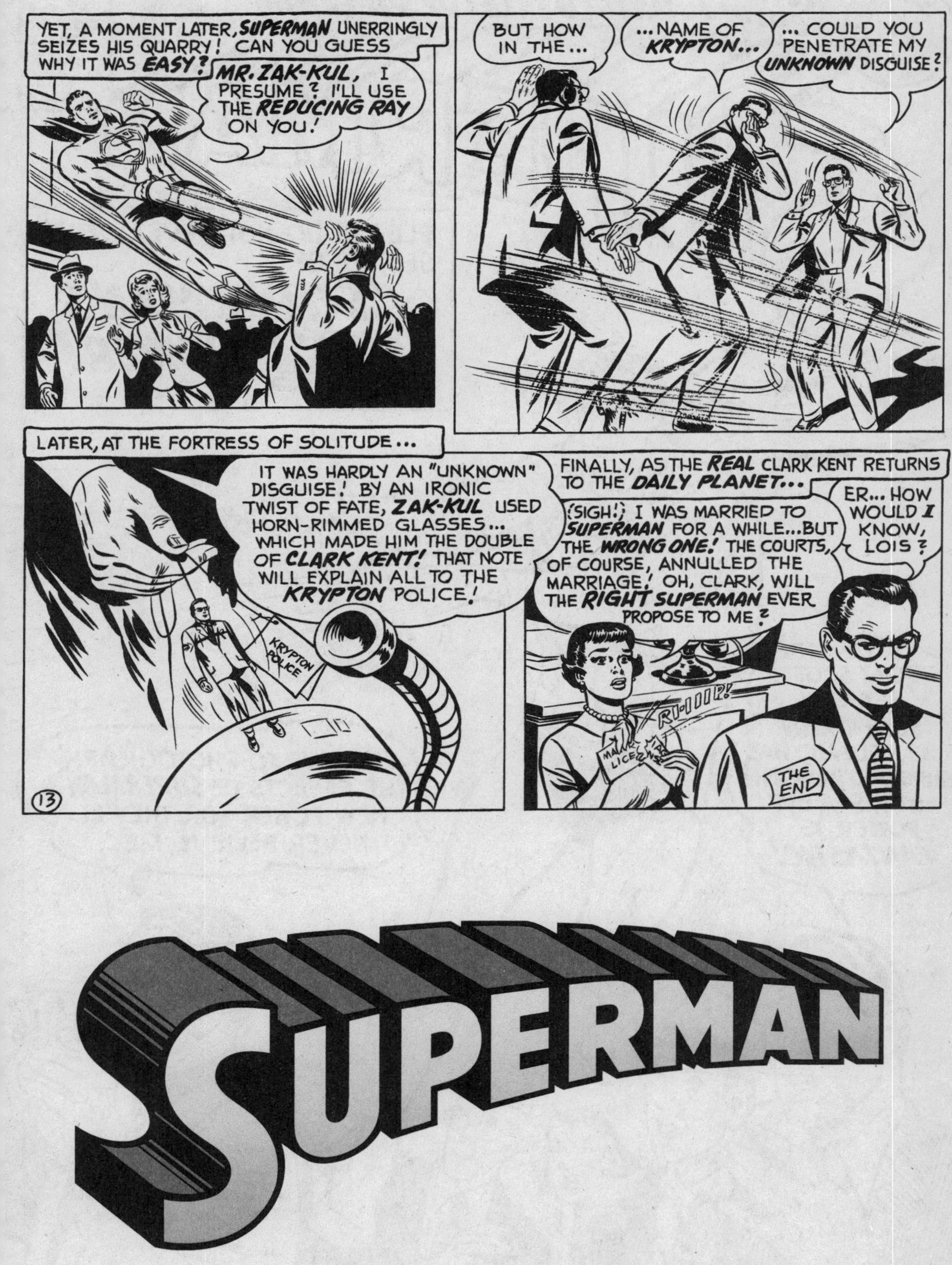
YET, A MOMENT LATER, SUPERMAN UNERRINGLY SEIZES HIS QUARRY! CAN YOU GUESS WHY IT WAS EASY?
MR. ZAK-KUL, I PRESUME? I'LL USE THE REDUCING RAY ON YOU!
BUT HOW IN THE...
...NAME OF KRYPTON...
...COULD YOU PENETRATE MY UNKNOWN DISGUISE?
LATER, AT THE FORTRESS OF SOLITUDE...
IT WAS HARDLY AN "UNKNOWN" DISGUISE! BY AN IRONIC TWIST OF FATE, ZAK-KUL USED HORN-RIMMED GLASSES... WHICH MADE HIM THE DOUBLE OF CLARK KENT! THAT NOTE WILL EXPLAIN ALL TO THE KRYPTON POLICE!
KRYPTON POLICE
13
FINALLY, AS THE REAL CLARK KENT RETURNS TO THE DAILY PLANET...
(SIGH!) I WAS MARRIED TO SUPERMAN FOR A WHILE...BUT THE WRONG ONE! THE COURTS, OF COURSE, ANNULLED THE MARRIAGE! OH, CLARK, WILL THE RIGHT SUPERMAN EVER PROPOSE TO ME?
ER... HOW WOULD I KNOW, LOIS?
RI-IIIP!
THE END

SUPERMAN

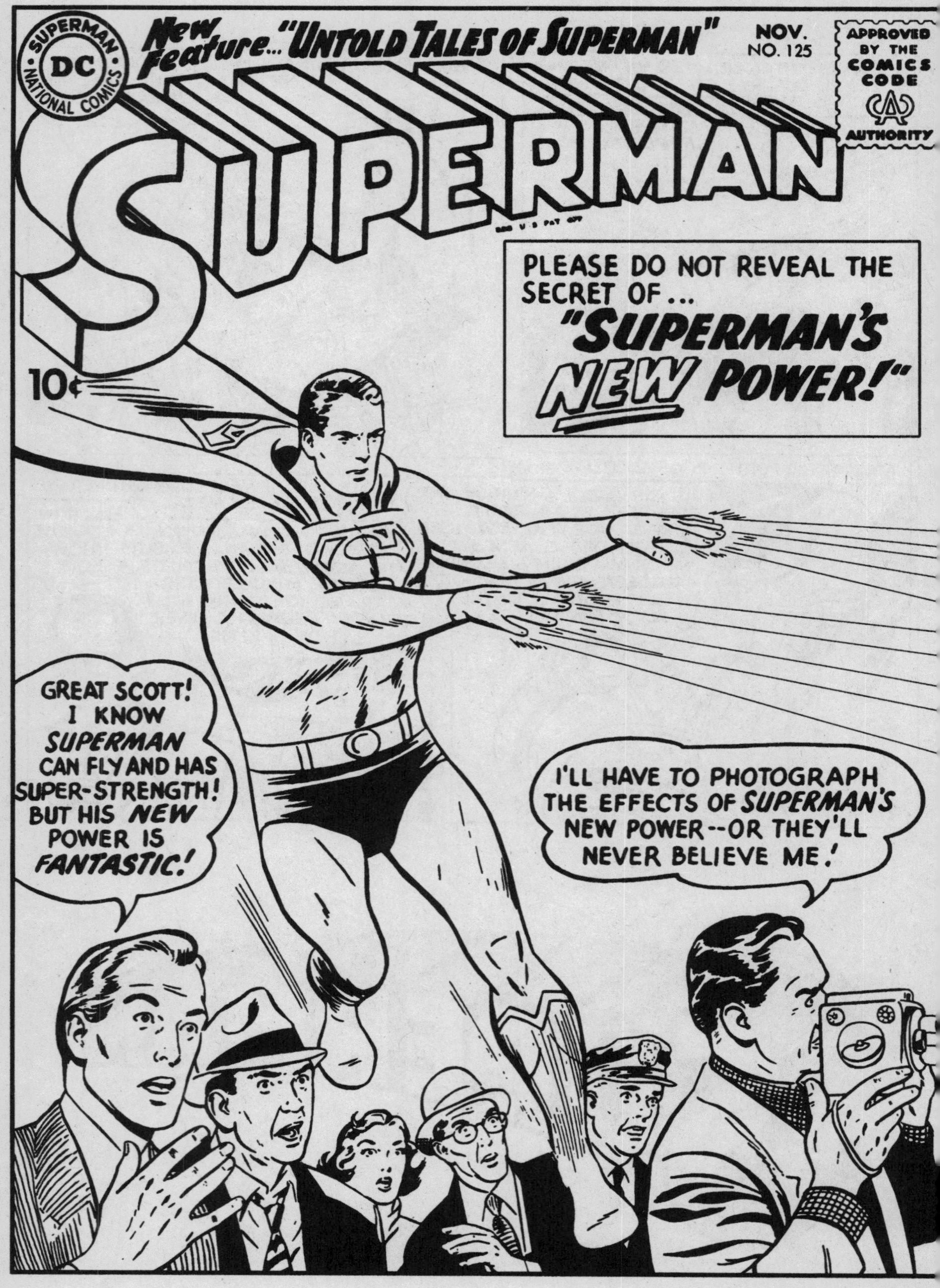
New Feature... "UNTOLD TALES OF SUPERMAN"
NOV. NO. 125
APPROVED BY THE COMICS CODE AUTHORITY
SUPERMAN DC NATIONAL COMICS
SUPERMAN
10¢
PLEASE DO NOT REVEAL THE SECRET OF ... "SUPERMAN'S NEW POWER!"
GREAT SCOTT! I KNOW SUPERMAN CAN FLY AND HAS SUPER-STRENGTH! BUT HIS NEW POWER IS FANTASTIC!
I'LL HAVE TO PHOTOGRAPH THE EFFECTS OF SUPERMAN'S NEW POWER--OR THEY'LL NEVER BELIEVE ME!

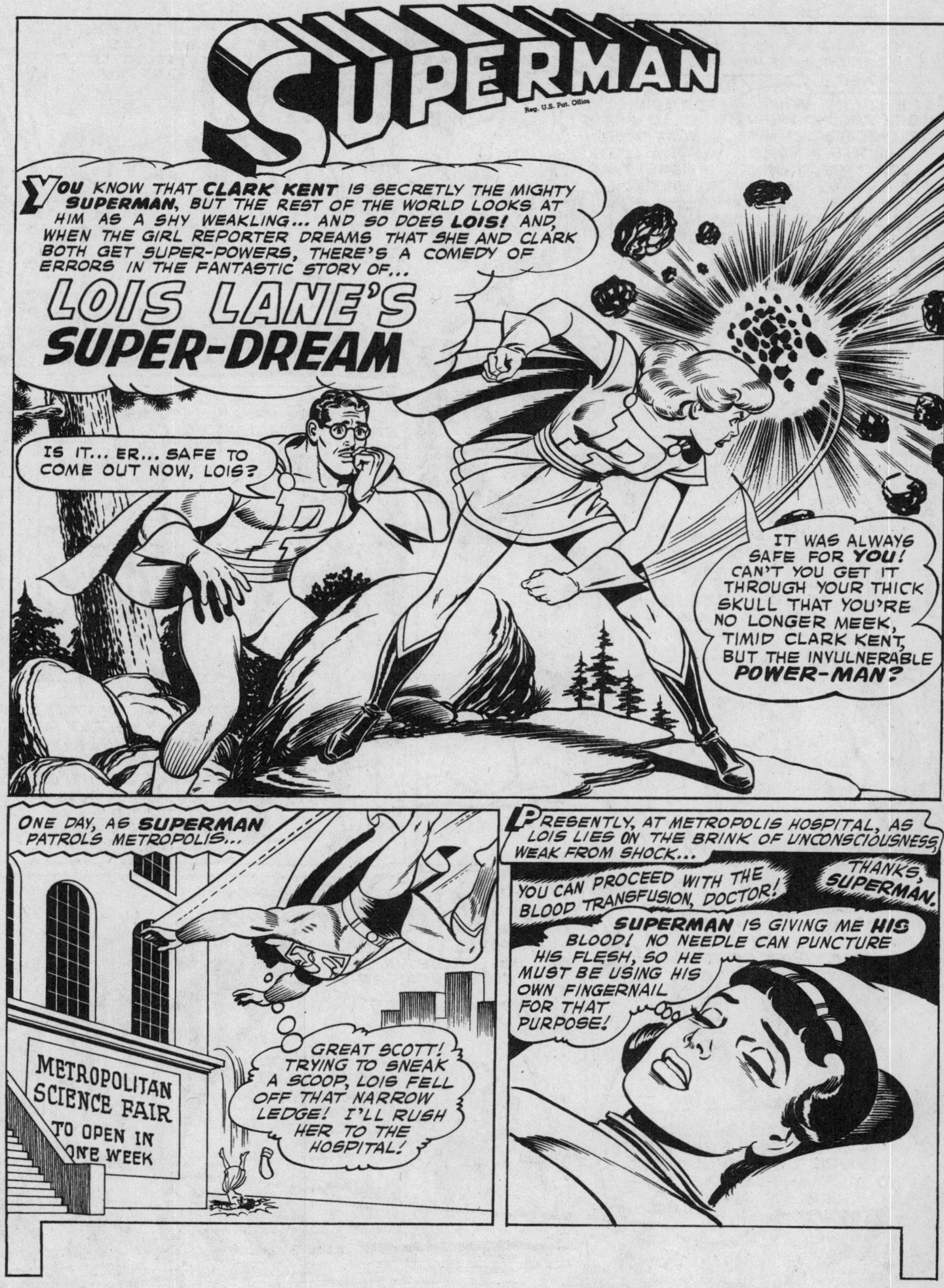
SUPERMAN
Reg. U.S. Pat. Office
YOU KNOW THAT CLARK KENT IS SECRETLY THE MIGHTY SUPERMAN, BUT THE REST OF THE WORLD LOOKS AT HIM AS A SHY WEAKLING... AND SO DOES LOIS! AND, WHEN THE GIRL REPORTER DREAMS THAT SHE AND CLARK BOTH GET SUPER-POWERS, THERE'S A COMEDY OF ERRORS IN THE FANTASTIC STORY OF...
LOIS LANE'S SUPER-DREAM
IS IT... ER... SAFE TO COME OUT NOW, LOIS?
IT WAS ALWAYS SAFE FOR YOU! CAN'T YOU GET IT THROUGH YOUR THICK SKULL THAT YOU'RE NO LONGER MEEK, TIMID CLARK KENT, BUT THE INVULNERABLE POWER-MAN?
ONE DAY, AS SUPERMAN PATROLS METROPOLIS...
METROPOLITAN SCIENCE FAIR TO OPEN IN ONE WEEK
GREAT SCOTT! TRYING TO SNEAK A SCOOP, LOIS FELL OFF THAT NARROW LEDGE! I'LL RUSH HER TO THE HOSPITAL!
PRESENTLY, AT METROPOLIS HOSPITAL, AS LOIS LIES ON THE BRINK OF UNCONSCIOUSNESS, WEAK FROM SHOCK...
YOU CAN PROCEED WITH THE BLOOD TRANSFUSION, DOCTOR!
THANKS, SUPERMAN.
SUPERMAN IS GIVING ME HIS BLOOD! NO NEEDLE CAN PUNCTURE HIS FLESH, SO HE MUST BE USING HIS OWN FINGERNAIL FOR THAT PURPOSE!

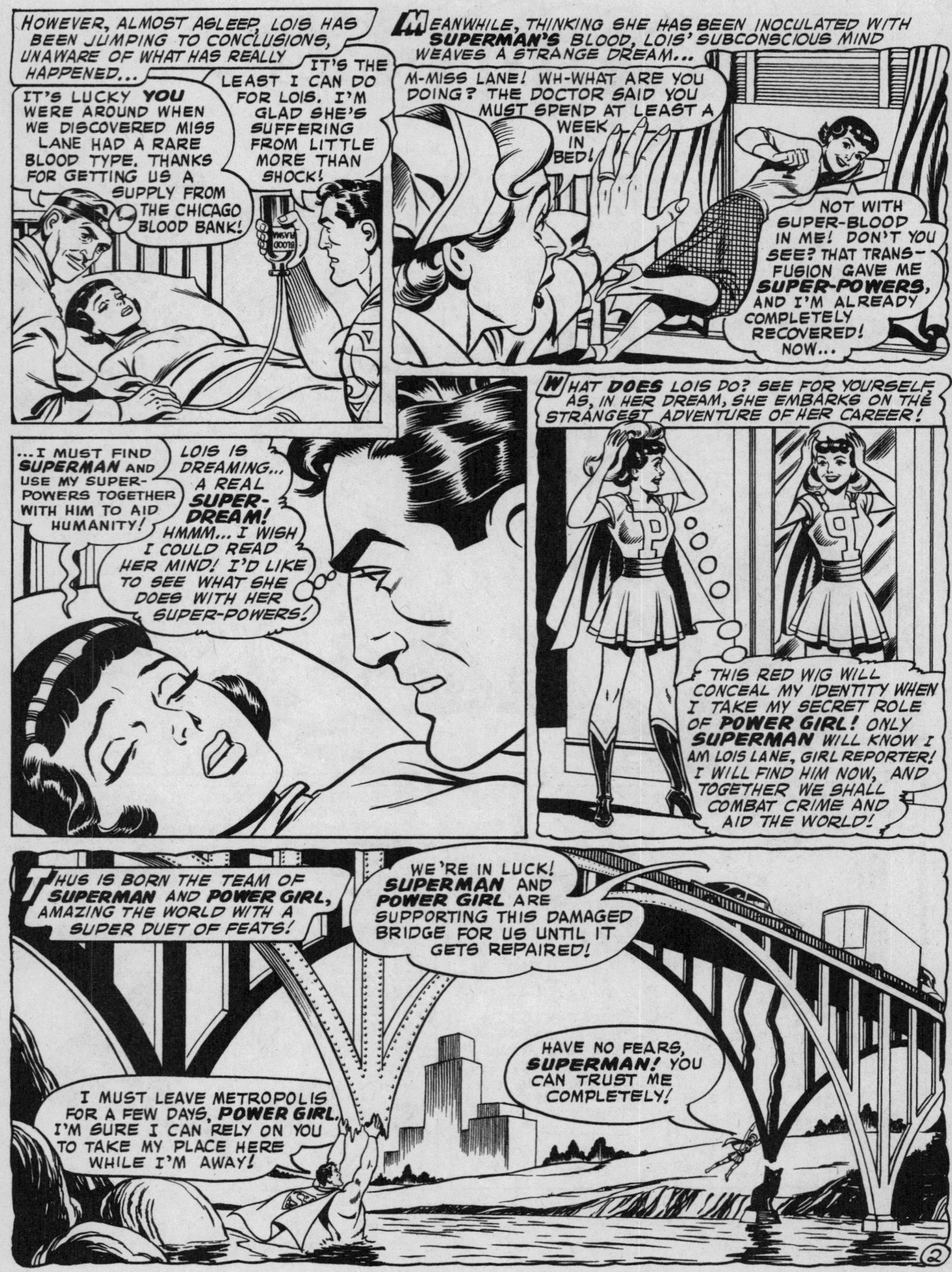

HOWEVER, ALMOST ASLEEP, LOIS HAS BEEN JUMPING TO CONCLUSIONS, UNAWARE OF WHAT HAS REALLY HAPPENED...
IT'S LUCKY YOU WERE AROUND WHEN WE DISCOVERED MISS LANE HAD A RARE BLOOD TYPE. THANKS FOR GETTING US A SUPPLY FROM THE CHICAGO BLOOD BANK!
IT'S THE LEAST I CAN DO FOR LOIS. I'M GLAD SHE'S SUFFERING FROM LITTLE MORE THAN SHOCK!
BLOOD PLASMA
MEANWHILE, THINKING SHE HAS BEEN INOCULATED WITH SUPERMAN'S BLOOD, LOIS' SUBCONSCIOUS MIND WEAVES A STRANGE DREAM...
M-MISS LANE! WH-WHAT ARE YOU DOING? THE DOCTOR SAID YOU MUST SPEND AT LEAST A WEEK IN BED!
NOT WITH SUPER-BLOOD IN ME! DON'T YOU SEE? THAT TRANS-FUSION GAVE ME SUPER-POWERS, AND I'M ALREADY COMPLETELY RECOVERED! NOW...
...I MUST FIND SUPERMAN AND USE MY SUPER-POWERS TOGETHER WITH HIM TO AID HUMANITY!
LOIS IS DREAMING... A REAL SUPER-DREAM! HMMM... I WISH I COULD READ HER MIND! I'D LIKE TO SEE WHAT SHE DOES WITH HER SUPER-POWERS!
WHAT DOES LOIS DO? SEE FOR YOURSELF AS, IN HER DREAM, SHE EMBARKS ON THE STRANGEST ADVENTURE OF HER CAREER!
THIS RED WIG WILL CONCEAL MY IDENTITY WHEN I TAKE MY SECRET ROLE OF POWER GIRL! ONLY SUPERMAN WILL KNOW I AM LOIS LANE, GIRL REPORTER! I WILL FIND HIM NOW, AND TOGETHER WE SHALL COMBAT CRIME AND AID THE WORLD!
THUS IS BORN THE TEAM OF SUPERMAN AND POWER GIRL, AMAZING THE WORLD WITH A SUPER DUET OF FEATS!
WE'RE IN LUCK! SUPERMAN AND POWER GIRL ARE SUPPORTING THIS DAMAGED BRIDGE FOR US UNTIL IT GETS REPAIRED!
I MUST LEAVE METROPOLIS FOR A FEW DAYS, POWER GIRL. I'M SURE I CAN RELY ON YOU TO TAKE MY PLACE HERE WHILE I'M AWAY!
HAVE NO FEARS, SUPERMAN! YOU CAN TRUST ME COMPLETELY!
2

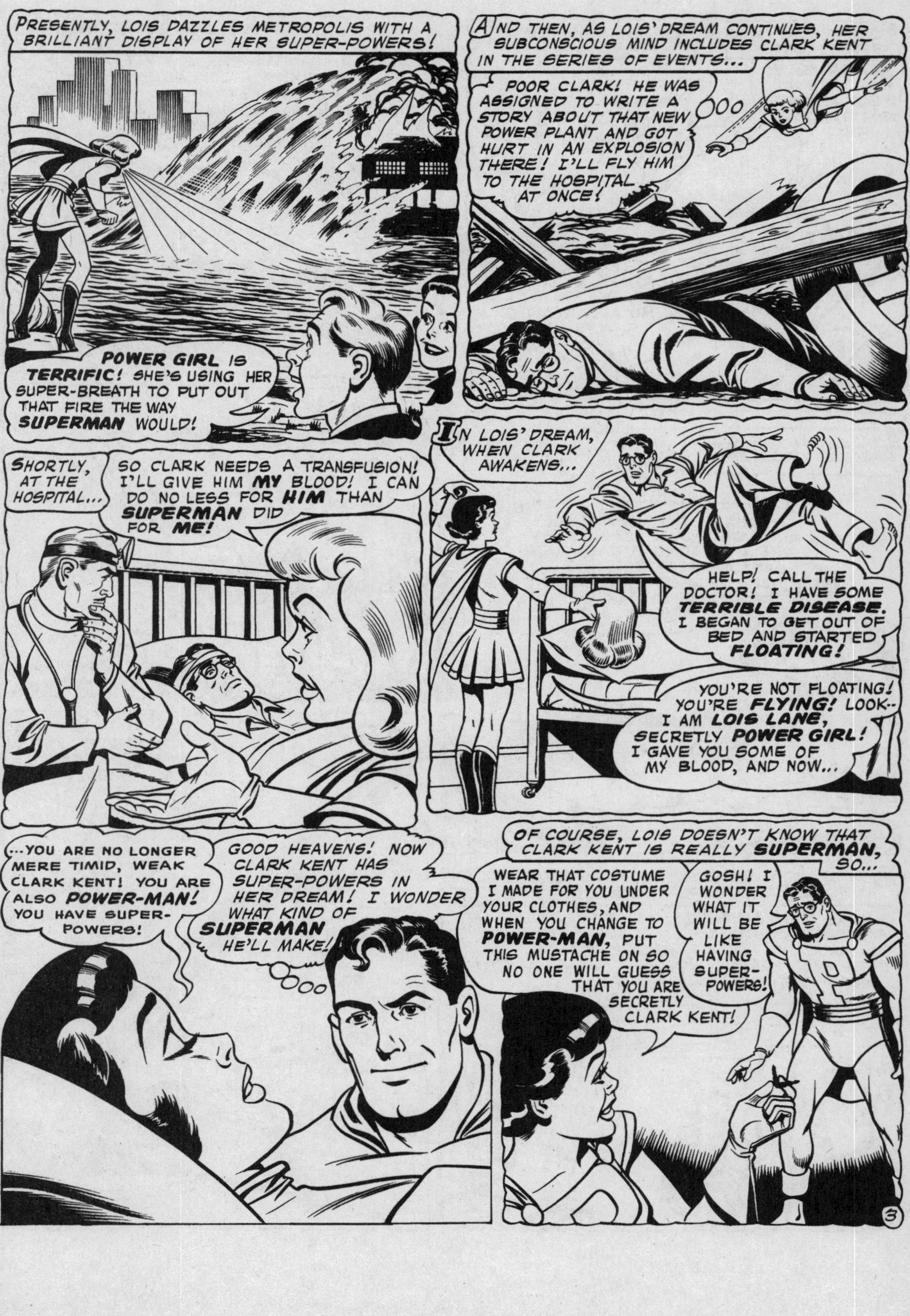
PRESENTLY, LOIS DAZZLES METROPOLIS WITH A BRILLIANT DISPLAY OF HER SUPER-POWERS!
POWER GIRL IS TERRIFIC! SHE'S USING HER SUPER-BREATH TO PUT OUT THAT FIRE THE WAY SUPERMAN WOULD!
AND THEN, AS LOIS' DREAM CONTINUES, HER SUBCONSCIOUS MIND INCLUDES CLARK KENT IN THE SERIES OF EVENTS...
POOR CLARK! HE WAS ASSIGNED TO WRITE A STORY ABOUT THAT NEW POWER PLANT AND GOT HURT IN AN EXPLOSION THERE! I'LL FLY HIM TO THE HOSPITAL AT ONCE!
SHORTLY, AT THE HOSPITAL...
SO CLARK NEEDS A TRANSFUSION! I'LL GIVE HIM MY BLOOD! I CAN DO NO LESS FOR HIM THAN SUPERMAN DID FOR ME!
IN LOIS' DREAM, WHEN CLARK AWAKENS...
HELP! CALL THE DOCTOR! I HAVE SOME TERRIBLE DISEASE. I BEGAN TO GET OUT OF BED AND STARTED FLOATING!
YOU'RE NOT FLOATING! YOU'RE FLYING! LOOK-- I AM LOIS LANE, SECRETLY POWER GIRL! I GAVE YOU SOME OF MY BLOOD, AND NOW...
...YOU ARE NO LONGER MERE TIMID, WEAK CLARK KENT! YOU ARE ALSO POWER-MAN! YOU HAVE SUPER-POWERS!
GOOD HEAVENS! NOW CLARK KENT HAS SUPER-POWERS IN HER DREAM! I WONDER WHAT KIND OF SUPERMAN HE'LL MAKE!
OF COURSE, LOIS DOESN'T KNOW THAT CLARK KENT IS REALLY SUPERMAN, SO...
WEAR THAT COSTUME I MADE FOR YOU UNDER YOUR CLOTHES, AND WHEN YOU CHANGE TO POWER-MAN, PUT THIS MUSTACHE ON SO NO ONE WILL GUESS THAT YOU ARE SECRETLY CLARK KENT!
GOSH! I WONDER WHAT IT WILL BE LIKE HAVING SUPER-POWERS!
3

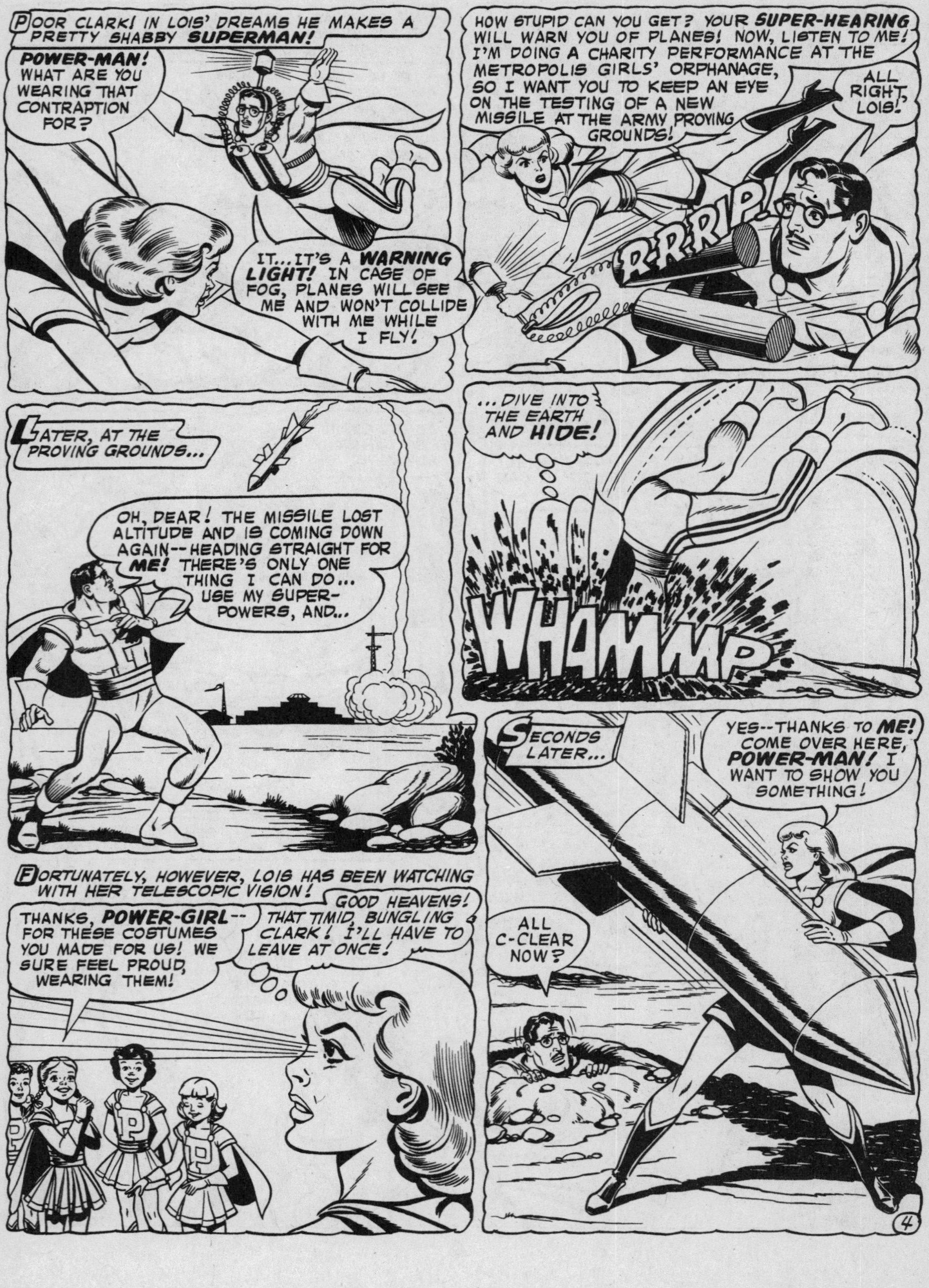
POOR CLARK! IN LOIS' DREAMS HE MAKES A PRETTY SHABBY SUPERMAN!
POWER-MAN! WHAT ARE YOU WEARING THAT CONTRAPTION FOR?
IT... IT'S A WARNING LIGHT! IN CASE OF FOG, PLANES WILL SEE ME AND WON'T COLLIDE WITH ME WHILE I FLY!
HOW STUPID CAN YOU GET? YOUR SUPER-HEARING WILL WARN YOU OF PLANES! NOW, LISTEN TO ME! I'M DOING A CHARITY PERFORMANCE AT THE METROPOLIS GIRLS' ORPHANAGE, SO I WANT YOU TO KEEP AN EYE ON THE TESTING OF A NEW MISSILE AT THE ARMY PROVING GROUNDS!
ALL RIGHT, LOIS!
R-R-RIP!
LATER, AT THE PROVING GROUNDS...
OH, DEAR! THE MISSILE LOST ALTITUDE AND IS COMING DOWN AGAIN--HEADING STRAIGHT FOR ME! THERE'S ONLY ONE THING I CAN DO... USE MY SUPER-POWERS, AND...
... DIVE INTO THE EARTH AND HIDE!
WHAMMMP!
FORTUNATELY, HOWEVER, LOIS HAS BEEN WATCHING WITH HER TELESCOPIC VISION!
THANKS, POWER-GIRL-- FOR THESE COSTUMES YOU MADE FOR US! WE SURE FEEL PROUD, WEARING THEM!
GOOD HEAVENS! THAT TIMID, BUNGLING CLARK! I'LL HAVE TO LEAVE AT ONCE!
SECONDS LATER...
YES--THANKS TO ME! COME OVER HERE, POWER-MAN! I WANT TO SHOW YOU SOMETHING!
ALL C-CLEAR NOW?
4

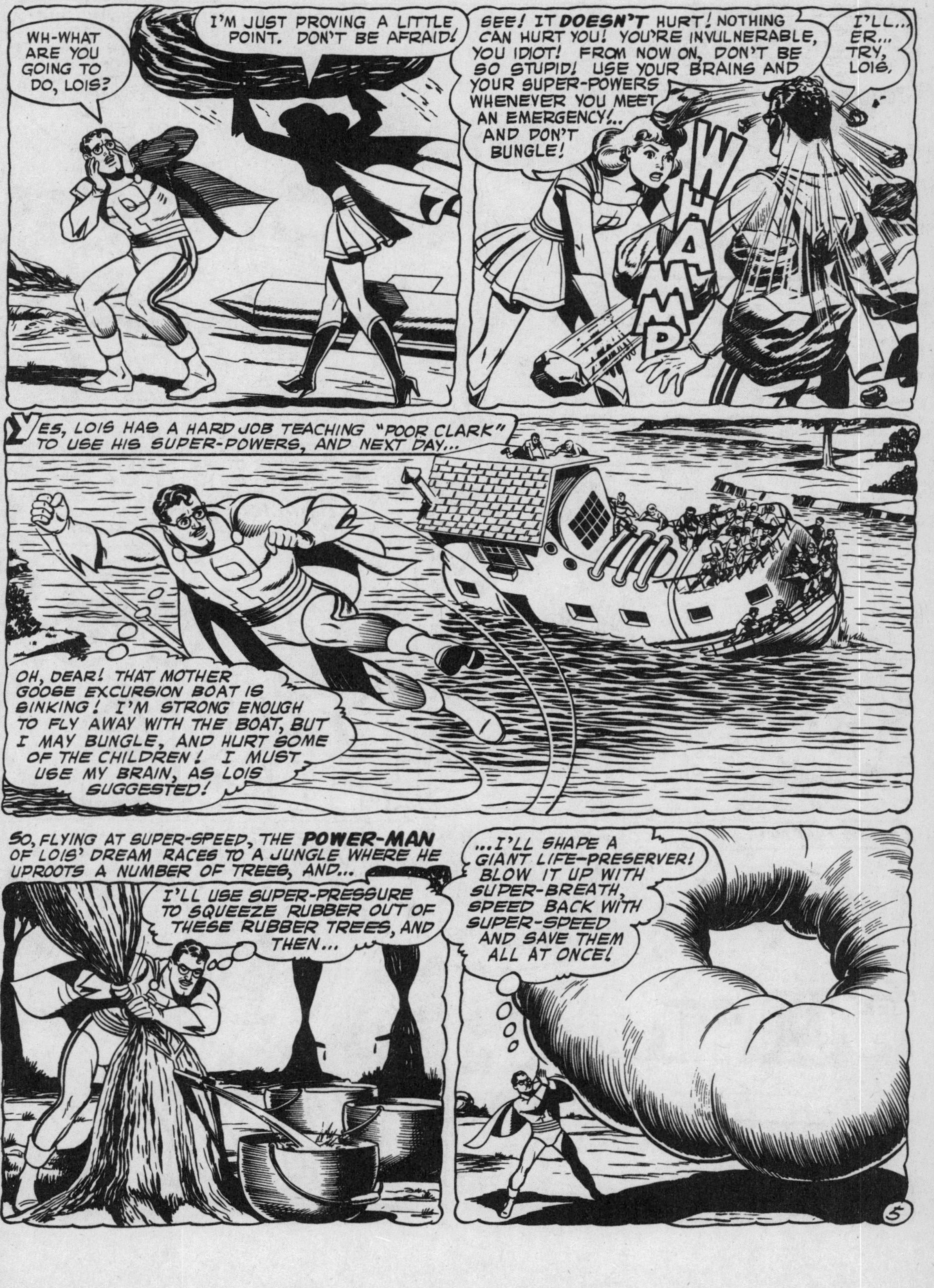
WH-WHAT ARE YOU GOING TO DO, LOIS?
I'M JUST PROVING A LITTLE POINT. DON'T BE AFRAID!
SEE! IT DOESN'T HURT! NOTHING CAN HURT YOU! YOU'RE INVULNERABLE, YOU IDIOT! FROM NOW ON, DON'T BE SO STUPID! USE YOUR BRAINS AND YOUR SUPER-POWERS WHENEVER YOU MEET AN EMERGENCY!.. AND DON'T BUNGLE!
I'LL... ER... TRY, LOIS.
WHAMMP
YES, LOIS HAS A HARD JOB TEACHING "POOR CLARK" TO USE HIS SUPER-POWERS, AND NEXT DAY...
OH, DEAR! THAT MOTHER GOOSE EXCURSION BOAT IS SINKING! I'M STRONG ENOUGH TO FLY AWAY WITH THE BOAT, BUT I MAY BUNGLE, AND HURT SOME OF THE CHILDREN! I MUST USE MY BRAIN, AS LOIS SUGGESTED!
SO, FLYING AT SUPER-SPEED, THE POWER-MAN OF LOIS' DREAM RACES TO A JUNGLE WHERE HE UPROOTS A NUMBER OF TREES, AND...
I'LL USE SUPER-PRESSURE TO SQUEEZE RUBBER OUT OF THESE RUBBER TREES, AND THEN...
...I'LL SHAPE A GIANT LIFE-PRESERVER! BLOW IT UP WITH SUPER-BREATH, SPEED BACK WITH SUPER-SPEED AND SAVE THEM ALL AT ONCE!
5

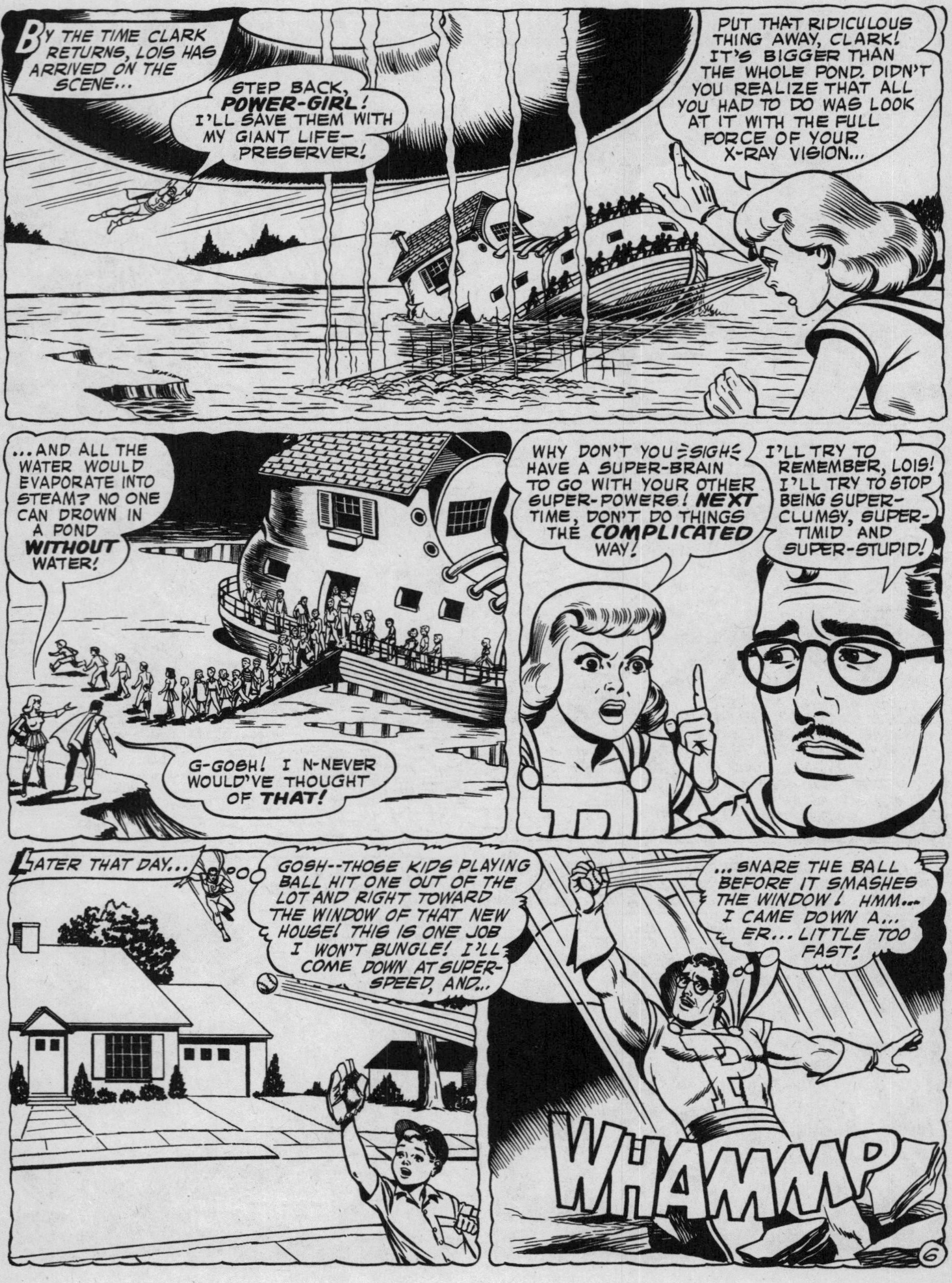
BY THE TIME CLARK RETURNS, LOIS HAS ARRIVED ON THE SCENE...
STEP BACK, POWER-GIRL! I'LL SAVE THEM WITH MY GIANT LIFE-PRESERVER!
PUT THAT RIDICULOUS THING AWAY, CLARK! IT'S BIGGER THAN THE WHOLE POND. DIDN'T YOU REALIZE THAT ALL YOU HAD TO DO WAS LOOK AT IT WITH THE FULL FORCE OF YOUR X-RAY VISION...
...AND ALL THE WATER WOULD EVAPORATE INTO STEAM? NO ONE CAN DROWN IN A POND WITHOUT WATER!
G-GOSH! I N-NEVER WOULD'VE THOUGHT OF THAT!
WHY DON'T YOU -SIGH- HAVE A SUPER-BRAIN TO GO WITH YOUR OTHER SUPER-POWERS! NEXT TIME, DON'T DO THINGS THE COMPLICATED WAY!
I'LL TRY TO REMEMBER, LOIS! I'LL TRY TO STOP BEING SUPER-CLUMSY, SUPER-TIMID AND SUPER-STUPID!
LATER THAT DAY...
GOSH--THOSE KIDS PLAYING BALL HIT ONE OUT OF THE LOT AND RIGHT TOWARD THE WINDOW OF THAT NEW HOUSE! THIS IS ONE JOB I WON'T BUNGLE! I'LL COME DOWN AT SUPER-SPEED, AND...
...SNARE THE BALL BEFORE IT SMASHES THE WINDOW! HMM... I CAME DOWN A... ER... LITTLE TOO FAST!
WHAMMP
6

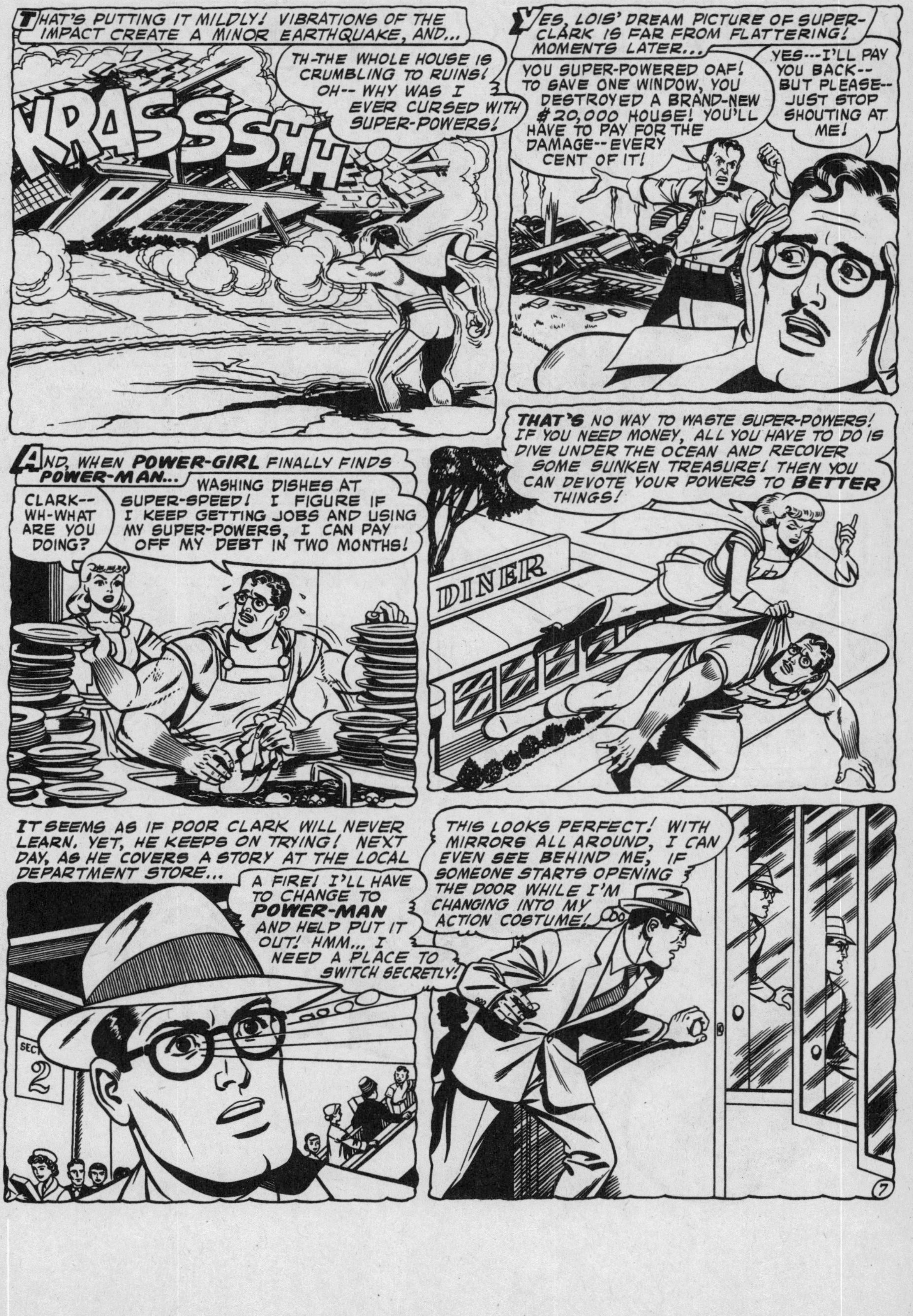
THAT'S PUTTING IT MILDLY! VIBRATIONS OF THE IMPACT CREATE A MINOR EARTHQUAKE, AND...
TH-THE WHOLE HOUSE IS CRUMBLING TO RUINS! OH-- WHY WAS I EVER CURSED WITH SUPER-POWERS!
KRASSSHH
YES, LOIS' DREAM PICTURE OF SUPER-CLARK IS FAR FROM FLATTERING! MOMENTS LATER...
YOU SUPER-POWERED OAF! TO SAVE ONE WINDOW, YOU DESTROYED A BRAND-NEW $20,000 HOUSE! YOU'LL HAVE TO PAY FOR THE DAMAGE-- EVERY CENT OF IT!
YES---I'LL PAY YOU BACK-- BUT PLEASE-- JUST STOP SHOUTING AT ME!
AND, WHEN POWER-GIRL FINALLY FINDS POWER-MAN...
CLARK-- WH-WHAT ARE YOU DOING?
WASHING DISHES AT SUPER-SPEED! I FIGURE IF I KEEP GETTING JOBS AND USING MY SUPER-POWERS, I CAN PAY OFF MY DEBT IN TWO MONTHS!
THAT'S NO WAY TO WASTE SUPER-POWERS! IF YOU NEED MONEY, ALL YOU HAVE TO DO IS DIVE UNDER THE OCEAN AND RECOVER SOME SUNKEN TREASURE! THEN YOU CAN DEVOTE YOUR POWERS TO BETTER THINGS!
DINER
IT SEEMS AS IF POOR CLARK WILL NEVER LEARN. YET, HE KEEPS ON TRYING! NEXT DAY, AS HE COVERS A STORY AT THE LOCAL DEPARTMENT STORE...
A FIRE! I'LL HAVE TO CHANGE TO POWER-MAN AND HELP PUT IT OUT! HMM... I NEED A PLACE TO SWITCH SECRETLY!
SECT
2
THIS LOOKS PERFECT! WITH MIRRORS ALL AROUND, I CAN EVEN SEE BEHIND ME, IF SOMEONE STARTS OPENING THE DOOR WHILE I'M CHANGING INTO MY ACTION COSTUME!
7

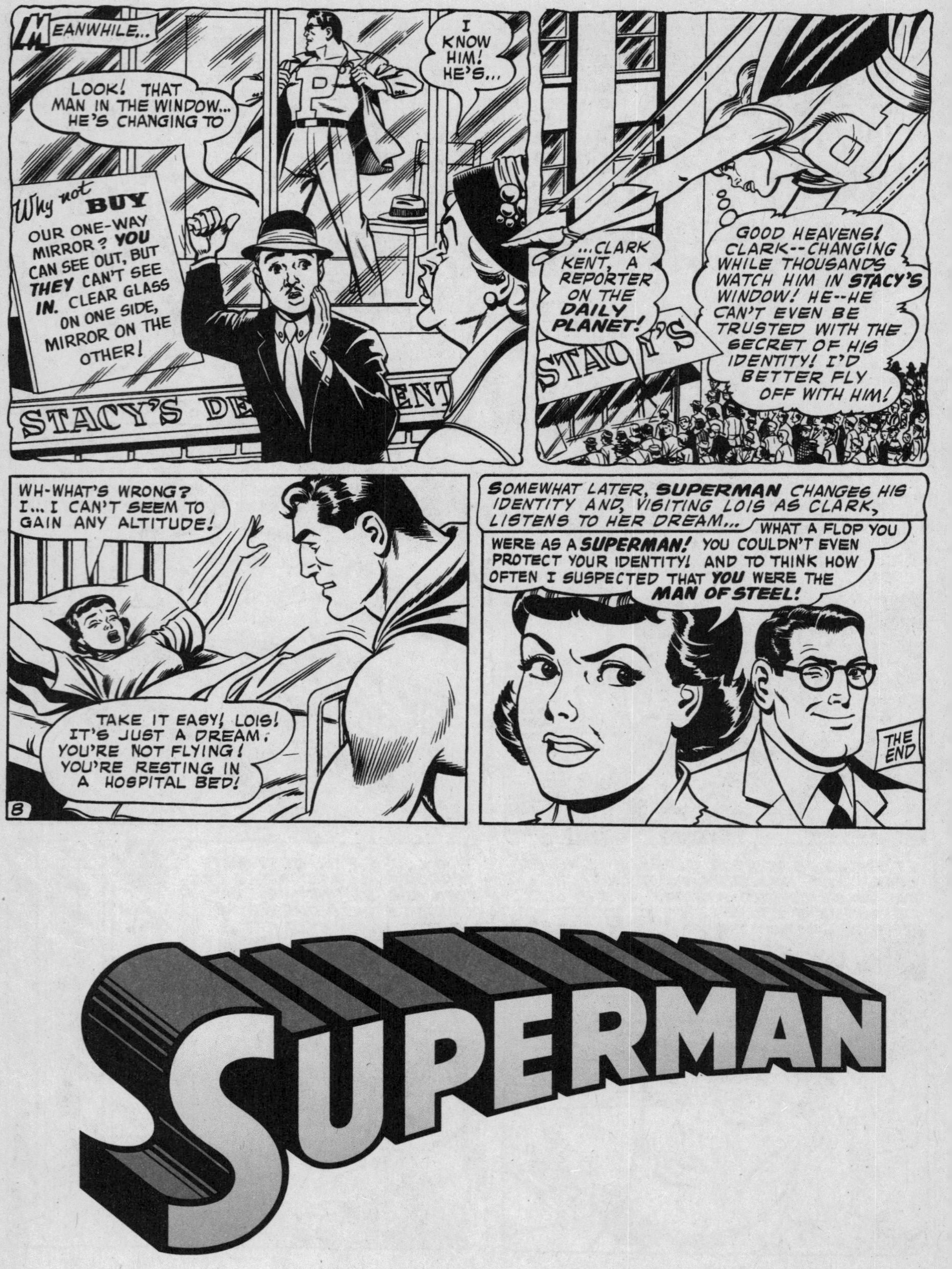
MEANWHILE...
LOOK! THAT MAN IN THE WINDOW... HE'S CHANGING TO
I KNOW HIM! HE'S...
Why not BUY OUR ONE-WAY MIRROR? YOU CAN SEE OUT, BUT THEY CAN'T SEE IN. CLEAR GLASS ON ONE SIDE, MIRROR ON THE OTHER!
STACY'S DE ENT
...CLARK KENT, A REPORTER ON THE DAILY PLANET!
GOOD HEAVENS! CLARK--CHANGING WHILE THOUSANDS WATCH HIM IN STACY'S WINDOW! HE--HE CAN'T EVEN BE TRUSTED WITH THE SECRET OF HIS IDENTITY! I'D BETTER FLY OFF WITH HIM!
STACY'S
WH-WHAT'S WRONG? I... I CAN'T SEEM TO GAIN ANY ALTITUDE!
TAKE IT EASY, LOIS! IT'S JUST A DREAM; YOU'RE NOT FLYING! YOU'RE RESTING IN A HOSPITAL BED!
8
SOMEWHAT LATER, SUPERMAN CHANGES HIS IDENTITY AND, VISITING LOIS AS CLARK, LISTENS TO HER DREAM...
WHAT A FLOP YOU WERE AS A SUPERMAN! YOU COULDN'T EVEN PROTECT YOUR IDENTITY! AND TO THINK HOW OFTEN I SUSPECTED THAT YOU WERE THE MAN OF STEEL!
THE END

SUPERMAN

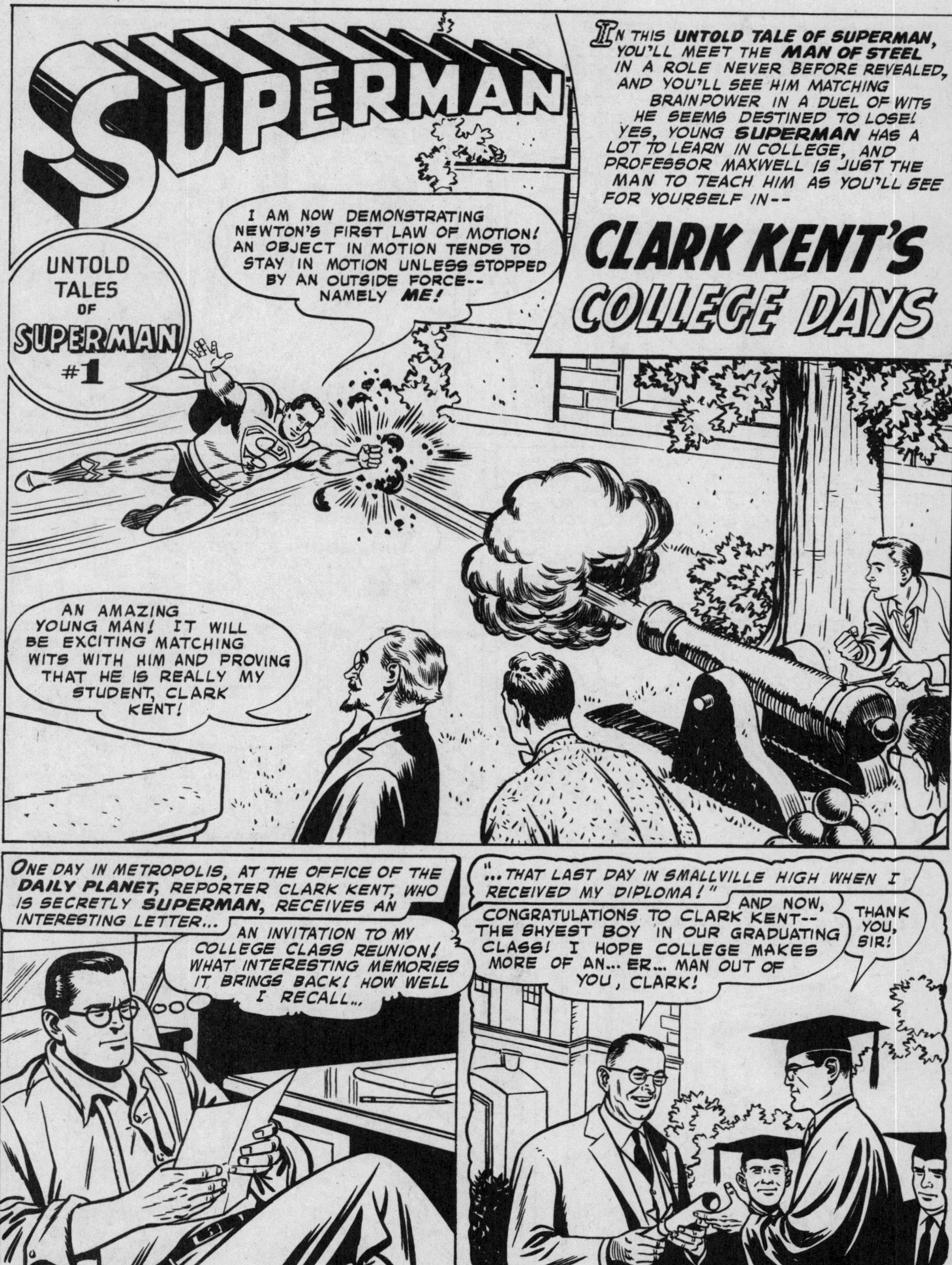
SUPERMAN
UNTOLD TALES OF SUPERMAN #1
IN THIS UNTOLD TALE OF SUPERMAN, YOU'LL MEET THE MAN OF STEEL IN A ROLE NEVER BEFORE REVEALED, AND YOU'LL SEE HIM MATCHING BRAINPOWER IN A DUEL OF WITS HE SEEMS DESTINED TO LOSE! YES, YOUNG SUPERMAN HAS A LOT TO LEARN IN COLLEGE, AND PROFESSOR MAXWELL IS JUST THE MAN TO TEACH HIM AS YOU'LL SEE FOR YOURSELF IN--
CLARK KENT'S COLLEGE DAYS
I AM NOW DEMONSTRATING NEWTON'S FIRST LAW OF MOTION! AN OBJECT IN MOTION TENDS TO STAY IN MOTION UNLESS STOPPED BY AN OUTSIDE FORCE-- NAMELY ME!
AN AMAZING YOUNG MAN! IT WILL BE EXCITING MATCHING WITS WITH HIM AND PROVING THAT HE IS REALLY MY STUDENT, CLARK KENT!
ONE DAY IN METROPOLIS, AT THE OFFICE OF THE DAILY PLANET, REPORTER CLARK KENT, WHO IS SECRETLY SUPERMAN, RECEIVES AN INTERESTING LETTER...
AN INVITATION TO MY COLLEGE CLASS REUNION! WHAT INTERESTING MEMORIES IT BRINGS BACK! HOW WELL I RECALL...
"...THAT LAST DAY IN SMALLVILLE HIGH WHEN I RECEIVED MY DIPLOMA!"
AND NOW, CONGRATULATIONS TO CLARK KENT-- THE SHYEST BOY IN OUR GRADUATING CLASS! I HOPE COLLEGE MAKES MORE OF AN... ER... MAN OUT OF YOU, CLARK!
THANK YOU, SIR!

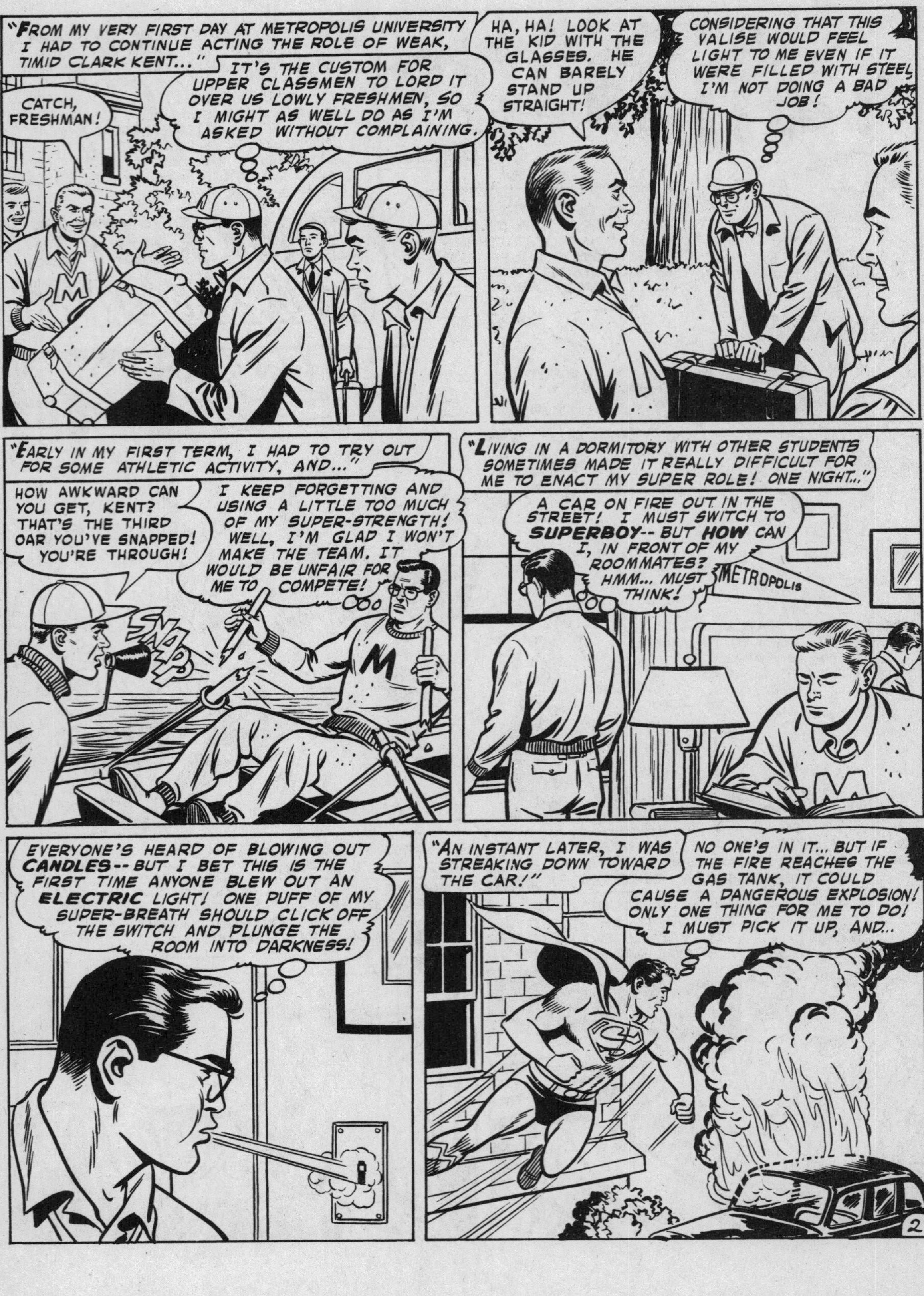

"FROM MY VERY FIRST DAY AT METROPOLIS UNIVERSITY I HAD TO CONTINUE ACTING THE ROLE OF WEAK, TIMID CLARK KENT..."
CATCH, FRESHMAN!
IT'S THE CUSTOM FOR UPPER CLASSMEN TO LORD IT OVER US LOWLY FRESHMEN, SO I MIGHT AS WELL DO AS I'M ASKED WITHOUT COMPLAINING.
HA, HA! LOOK AT THE KID WITH THE GLASSES. HE CAN BARELY STAND UP STRAIGHT!
CONSIDERING THAT THIS VALISE WOULD FEEL LIGHT TO ME EVEN IF IT WERE FILLED WITH STEEL, I'M NOT DOING A BAD JOB!
"EARLY IN MY FIRST TERM, I HAD TO TRY OUT FOR SOME ATHLETIC ACTIVITY, AND..."
HOW AWKWARD CAN YOU GET, KENT? THAT'S THE THIRD OAR YOU'VE SNAPPED! YOU'RE THROUGH!
I KEEP FORGETTING AND USING A LITTLE TOO MUCH OF MY SUPER-STRENGTH! WELL, I'M GLAD I WON'T MAKE THE TEAM. IT WOULD BE UNFAIR FOR ME TO COMPETE!
SNAP
"LIVING IN A DORMITORY WITH OTHER STUDENTS SOMETIMES MADE IT REALLY DIFFICULT FOR ME TO ENACT MY SUPER ROLE! ONE NIGHT..."
A CAR ON FIRE OUT IN THE STREET! I MUST SWITCH TO SUPERBOY-- BUT HOW CAN I, IN FRONT OF MY ROOMMATES? HMM... MUST THINK!
METROPOLIS
EVERYONE'S HEARD OF BLOWING OUT CANDLES-- BUT I BET THIS IS THE FIRST TIME ANYONE BLEW OUT AN ELECTRIC LIGHT! ONE PUFF OF MY SUPER-BREATH SHOULD CLICK OFF THE SWITCH AND PLUNGE THE ROOM INTO DARKNESS!
"AN INSTANT LATER, I WAS STREAKING DOWN TOWARD THE CAR!"
NO ONE'S IN IT... BUT IF THE FIRE REACHES THE GAS TANK, IT COULD CAUSE A DANGEROUS EXPLOSION! ONLY ONE THING FOR ME TO DO! I MUST PICK IT UP, AND...
2

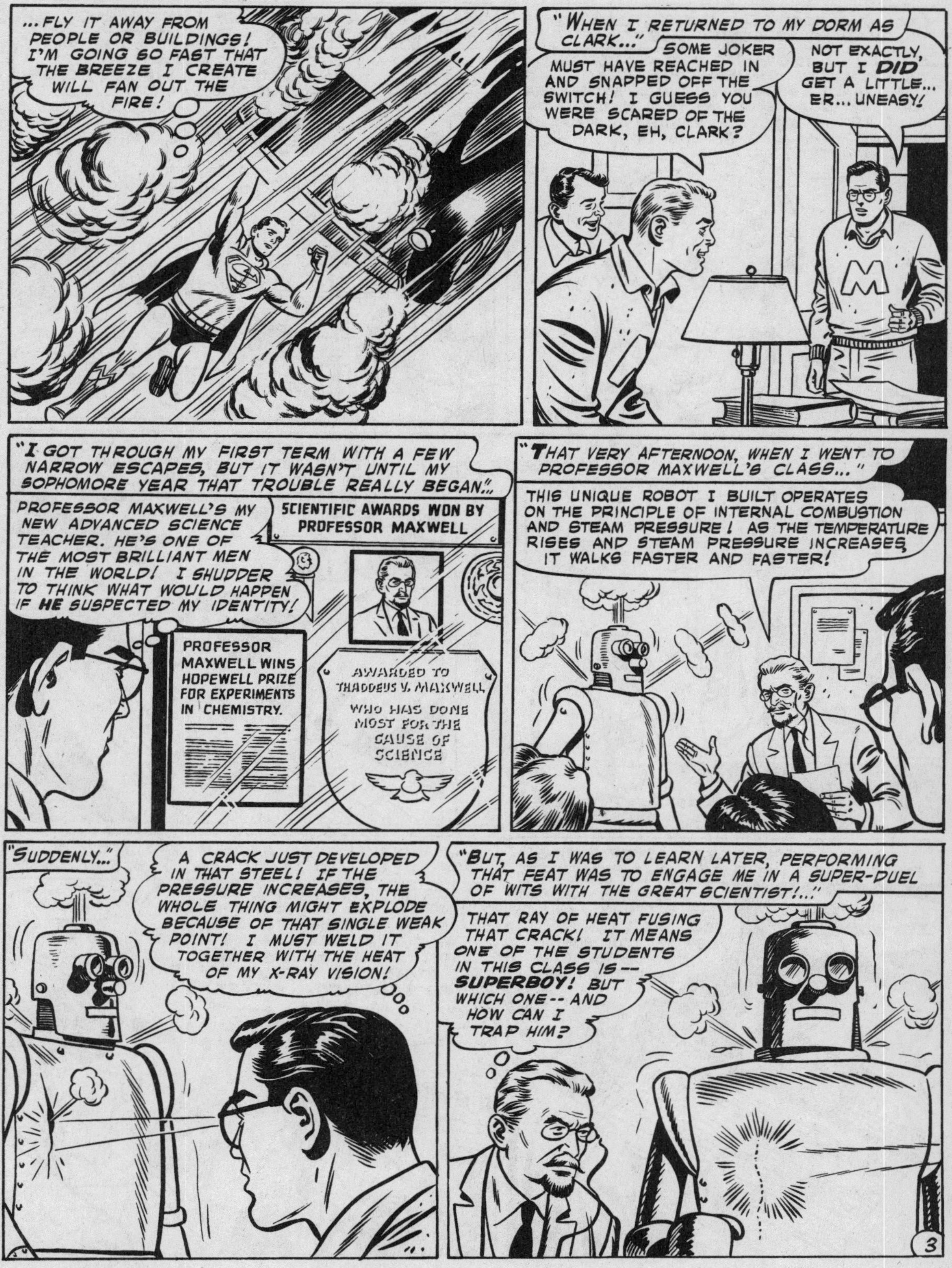
...FLY IT AWAY FROM PEOPLE OR BUILDINGS! I'M GOING SO FAST THAT THE BREEZE I CREATE WILL FAN OUT THE FIRE!
"WHEN I RETURNED TO MY DORM AS CLARK..."
SOME JOKER MUST HAVE REACHED IN AND SNAPPED OFF THE SWITCH! I GUESS YOU WERE SCARED OF THE DARK, EH, CLARK?
NOT EXACTLY, BUT I DID GET A LITTLE... ER... UNEASY!
"I GOT THROUGH MY FIRST TERM WITH A FEW NARROW ESCAPES, BUT IT WASN'T UNTIL MY SOPHOMORE YEAR THAT TROUBLE REALLY BEGAN!..."
PROFESSOR MAXWELL'S MY NEW ADVANCED SCIENCE TEACHER. HE'S ONE OF THE MOST BRILLIANT MEN IN THE WORLD! I SHUDDER TO THINK WHAT WOULD HAPPEN IF HE SUSPECTED MY IDENTITY!
SCIENTIFIC AWARDS WON BY PROFESSOR MAXWELL
PROFESSOR MAXWELL WINS HOPEWELL PRIZE FOR EXPERIMENTS IN CHEMISTRY.
AWARDED TO THADDEUS V. MAXWELL WHO HAS DONE MOST FOR THE CAUSE OF SCIENCE
"THAT VERY AFTERNOON, WHEN I WENT TO PROFESSOR MAXWELL'S CLASS..."
THIS UNIQUE ROBOT I BUILT OPERATES ON THE PRINCIPLE OF INTERNAL COMBUSTION AND STEAM PRESSURE! AS THE TEMPERATURE RISES AND STEAM PRESSURE INCREASES, IT WALKS FASTER AND FASTER!
"SUDDENLY..."
A CRACK JUST DEVELOPED IN THAT STEEL! IF THE PRESSURE INCREASES, THE WHOLE THING MIGHT EXPLODE BECAUSE OF THAT SINGLE WEAK POINT! I MUST WELD IT TOGETHER WITH THE HEAT OF MY X-RAY VISION!
"BUT, AS I WAS TO LEARN LATER, PERFORMING THAT FEAT WAS TO ENGAGE ME IN A SUPER-DUEL OF WITS WITH THE GREAT SCIENTIST!..."
THAT RAY OF HEAT FUSING THAT CRACK! IT MEANS ONE OF THE STUDENTS IN THIS CLASS IS -- SUPERBOY! BUT WHICH ONE -- AND HOW CAN I TRAP HIM?
3

"I COULD ALMOST READ THE PROFESSOR'S THOUGHTS AS HE STARED SILENTLY AT THE CLASS..."

NO ONE HAS EVER PENETRATED THE SECRET OF *SUPERBOY'S* IDENTITY, AND I HAVE NEVER FAILED IN AN EXPERIMENT. NOW THAT I AM SURE HE IS A MEMBER OF MY CLASS IT WILL BE INTRIGUING TO SOLVE HIS SECRET-- JUST FOR MY OWN SATISFACTION!

"NEXT DAY IN CLASS, I KNEW I HAD GUESSED WHAT HE WAS THINKING WHEN..."

TODAY WE WILL PERFORM A FEW EXPERIMENTS TO DEMONSTRATE HOW A *LIE DETECTOR* WORKS! *FRED HOLLAND*, PLEASE STEP UP HERE. I SHALL ASK YOU A QUESTION WHICH YOU MAY ANSWER EITHER WITH THE TRUTH OR A FALSEHOOD!

FRED, ARE *YOU SUPERBOY?*

ME, *SUPERBOY?* HA, HA! OF COURSE NOT, PROFESSOR MAXWELL!

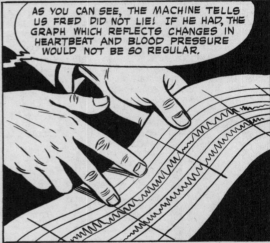

AS YOU CAN SEE, THE MACHINE TELLS US FRED DID NOT LIE! IF HE HAD, THE GRAPH WHICH REFLECTS CHANGES IN HEARTBEAT AND BLOOD PRESSURE WOULD NOT BE SO REGULAR.

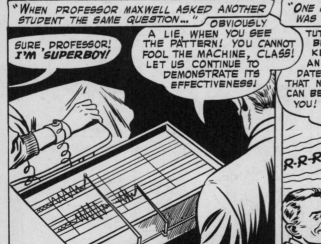

"WHEN PROFESSOR MAXWELL ASKED ANOTHER STUDENT THE SAME QUESTION..."

SURE, PROFESSOR! *I'M SUPERBOY!*

OBVIOUSLY A LIE, WHEN YOU SEE THE PATTERN! YOU CANNOT FOOL THE MACHINE, CLASS! LET US CONTINUE TO DEMONSTRATE ITS EFFECTIVENESS!

"ONE AFTER ANOTHER, EACH MEMBER OF THE CLASS WAS CALLED. AND FINALLY, WHEN IT WAS *MY* TURN..."

TUT-TUT! THE PERIOD ENDED BEFORE YOU HAD *YOUR* CHANCE, KENT! HOWEVER, I'LL GIVE YOU AN OPPORTUNITY AT SOME FUTURE DATE! ANYWAY, WE NOW *KNOW* THAT NO ONE ELSE IN THIS CLASS CAN BE *SUPERBOY*-- EXCEPT YOU! HA, HA-- THAT'S A JOKE!

SAVED BY THE BELL-- SO FAR!

R-R-RIN-N-G

4

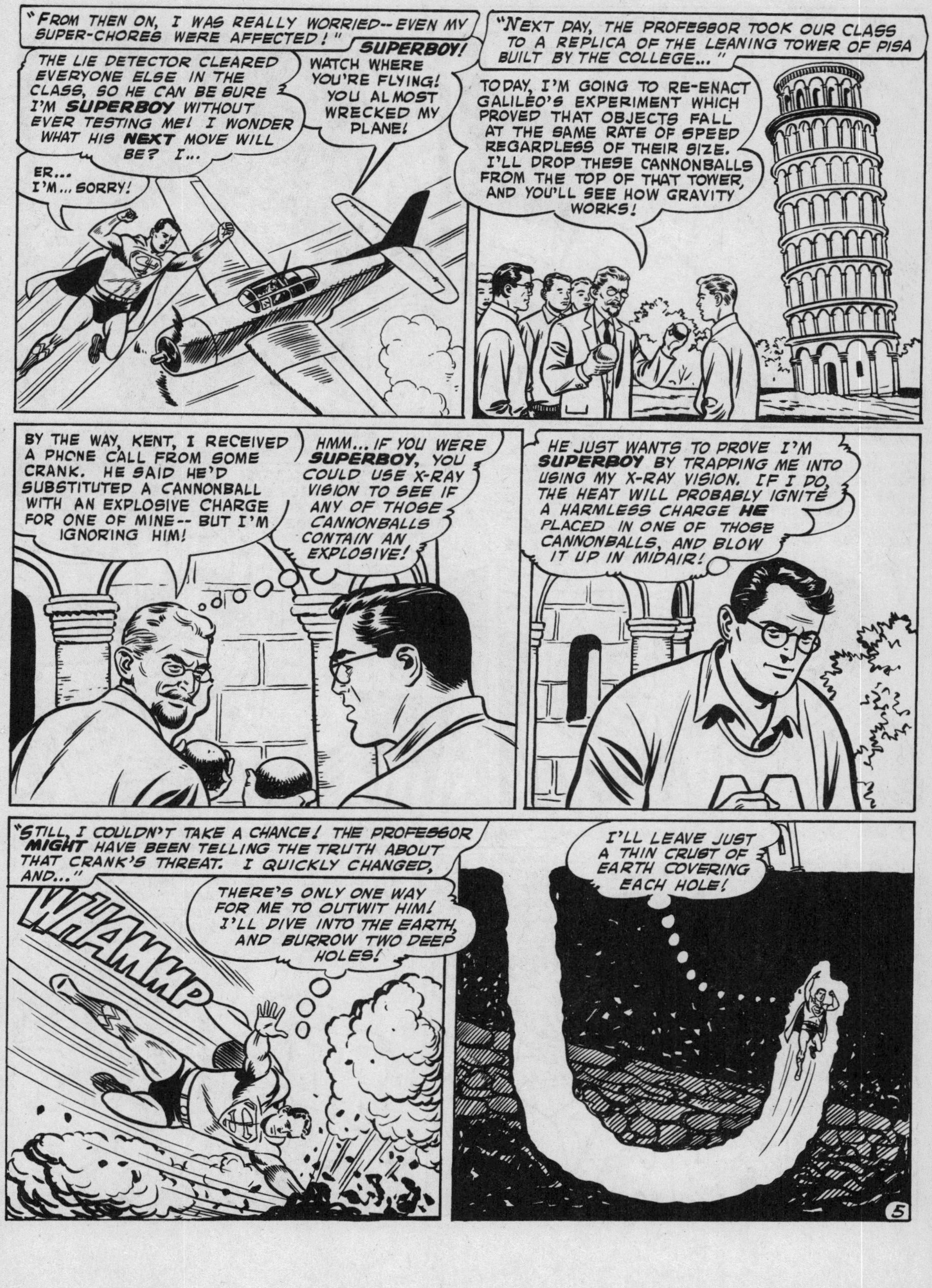
"FROM THEN ON, I WAS REALLY WORRIED-- EVEN MY SUPER-CHORES WERE AFFECTED!"
THE LIE DETECTOR CLEARED EVERYONE ELSE IN THE CLASS, SO HE CAN BE SURE I'M SUPERBOY WITHOUT EVER TESTING ME! I WONDER WHAT HIS NEXT MOVE WILL BE? I...
SUPERBOY! WATCH WHERE YOU'RE FLYING! YOU ALMOST WRECKED MY PLANE!
ER... I'M... SORRY!
"NEXT DAY, THE PROFESSOR TOOK OUR CLASS TO A REPLICA OF THE LEANING TOWER OF PISA BUILT BY THE COLLEGE..."
TODAY, I'M GOING TO RE-ENACT GALILEO'S EXPERIMENT WHICH PROVED THAT OBJECTS FALL AT THE SAME RATE OF SPEED REGARDLESS OF THEIR SIZE. I'LL DROP THESE CANNONBALLS FROM THE TOP OF THAT TOWER, AND YOU'LL SEE HOW GRAVITY WORKS!
BY THE WAY, KENT, I RECEIVED A PHONE CALL FROM SOME CRANK. HE SAID HE'D SUBSTITUTED A CANNONBALL WITH AN EXPLOSIVE CHARGE FOR ONE OF MINE-- BUT I'M IGNORING HIM!
HMM... IF YOU WERE SUPERBOY, YOU COULD USE X-RAY VISION TO SEE IF ANY OF THOSE CANNONBALLS CONTAIN AN EXPLOSIVE!
HE JUST WANTS TO PROVE I'M SUPERBOY BY TRAPPING ME INTO USING MY X-RAY VISION. IF I DO, THE HEAT WILL PROBABLY IGNITE A HARMLESS CHARGE HE PLACED IN ONE OF THOSE CANNONBALLS, AND BLOW IT UP IN MIDAIR!
"STILL, I COULDN'T TAKE A CHANCE! THE PROFESSOR MIGHT HAVE BEEN TELLING THE TRUTH ABOUT THAT CRANK'S THREAT. I QUICKLY CHANGED, AND..."
WHAMMP
THERE'S ONLY ONE WAY FOR ME TO OUTWIT HIM! I'LL DIVE INTO THE EARTH, AND BURROW TWO DEEP HOLES!
I'LL LEAVE JUST A THIN CRUST OF EARTH COVERING EACH HOLE!
5

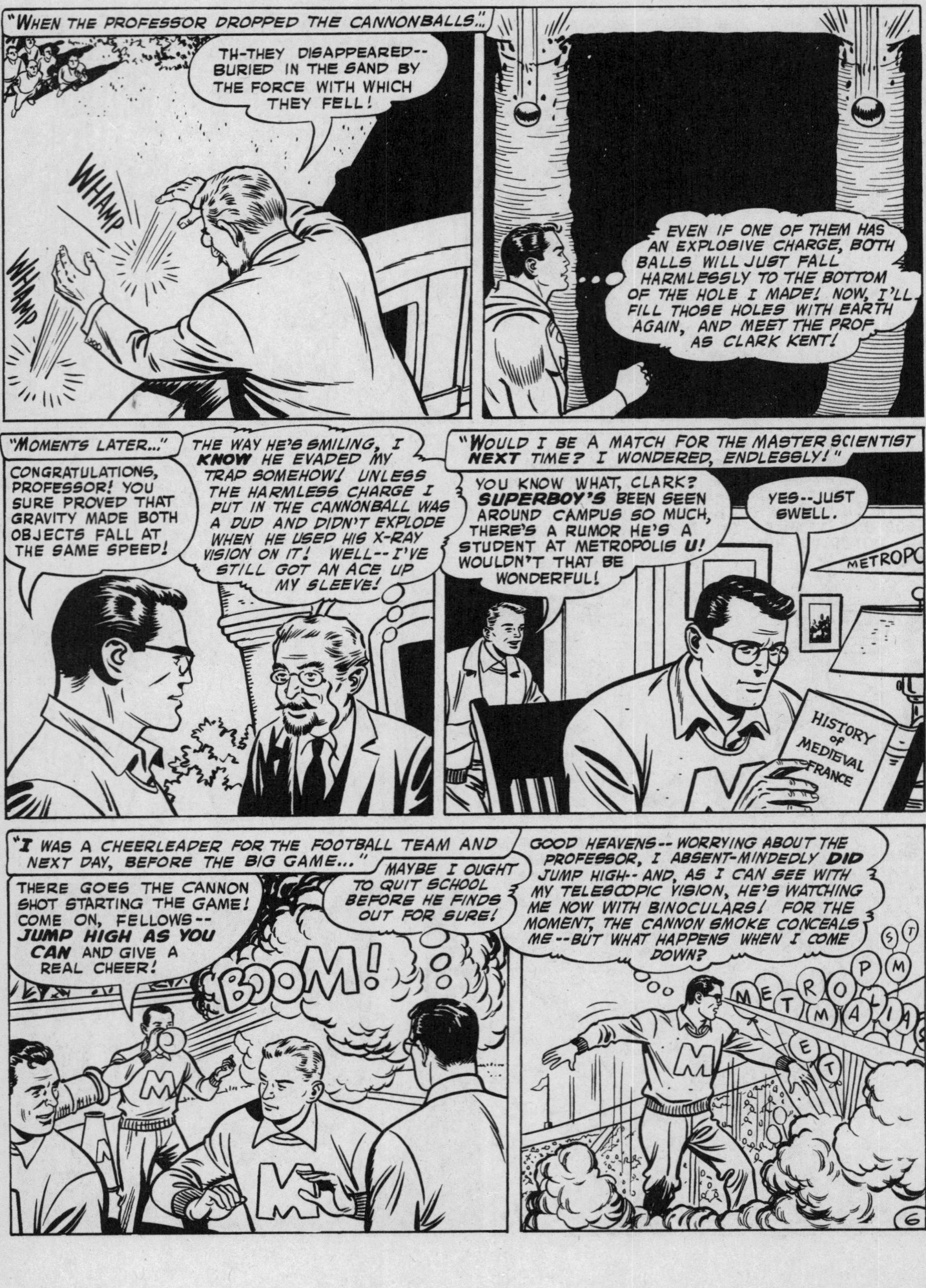
"WHEN THE PROFESSOR DROPPED THE CANNONBALLS..."
TH-THEY DISAPPEARED--BURIED IN THE SAND BY THE FORCE WITH WHICH THEY FELL!
WHAMP
WHAMP
EVEN IF ONE OF THEM HAS AN EXPLOSIVE CHARGE, BOTH BALLS WILL JUST FALL HARMLESSLY TO THE BOTTOM OF THE HOLE I MADE! NOW, I'LL FILL THOSE HOLES WITH EARTH AGAIN, AND MEET THE PROF AS CLARK KENT!
"MOMENTS LATER..."
CONGRATULATIONS, PROFESSOR! YOU SURE PROVED THAT GRAVITY MADE BOTH OBJECTS FALL AT THE SAME SPEED!
THE WAY HE'S SMILING, I KNOW HE EVADED MY TRAP SOMEHOW! UNLESS THE HARMLESS CHARGE I PUT IN THE CANNONBALL WAS A DUD AND DIDN'T EXPLODE WHEN HE USED HIS X-RAY VISION ON IT! WELL--I'VE STILL GOT AN ACE UP MY SLEEVE!
"WOULD I BE A MATCH FOR THE MASTER SCIENTIST NEXT TIME? I WONDERED, ENDLESSLY!"
YOU KNOW WHAT, CLARK? SUPERBOY'S BEEN SEEN AROUND CAMPUS SO MUCH, THERE'S A RUMOR HE'S A STUDENT AT METROPOLIS U! WOULDN'T THAT BE WONDERFUL!
YES--JUST SWELL.
METROPO
HISTORY of MEDIEVAL FRANCE
"I WAS A CHEERLEADER FOR THE FOOTBALL TEAM AND NEXT DAY, BEFORE THE BIG GAME..."
THERE GOES THE CANNON SHOT STARTING THE GAME! COME ON, FELLOWS--JUMP HIGH AS YOU CAN AND GIVE A REAL CHEER!
MAYBE I OUGHT TO QUIT SCHOOL BEFORE HE FINDS OUT FOR SURE!
BOOM!
GOOD HEAVENS--WORRYING ABOUT THE PROFESSOR, I ABSENT-MINDEDLY DID JUMP HIGH--AND, AS I CAN SEE WITH MY TELESCOPIC VISION, HE'S WATCHING ME NOW WITH BINOCULARS! FOR THE MOMENT, THE CANNON SMOKE CONCEALS ME--BUT WHAT HAPPENS WHEN I COME DOWN?
6

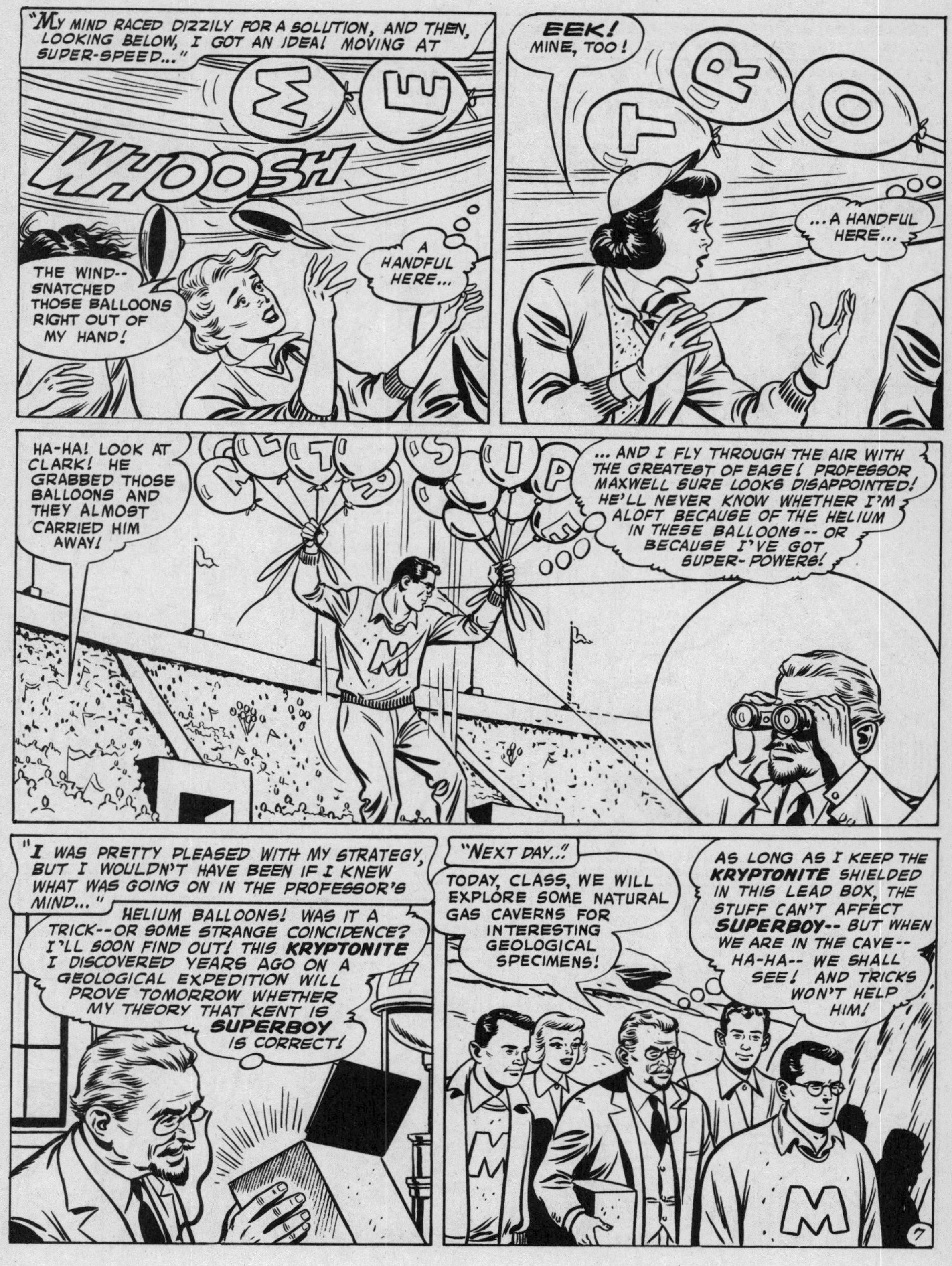
"MY MIND RACED DIZZILY FOR A SOLUTION, AND THEN, LOOKING BELOW, I GOT AN IDEA! MOVING AT SUPER-SPEED..."
WHOOSH
THE WIND--SNATCHED THOSE BALLOONS RIGHT OUT OF MY HAND!
A HANDFUL HERE...
EEK! MINE, TOO!
...A HANDFUL HERE...
HA-HA! LOOK AT CLARK! HE GRABBED THOSE BALLOONS AND THEY ALMOST CARRIED HIM AWAY!
... AND I FLY THROUGH THE AIR WITH THE GREATEST OF EASE! PROFESSOR MAXWELL SURE LOOKS DISAPPOINTED! HE'LL NEVER KNOW WHETHER I'M ALOFT BECAUSE OF THE HELIUM IN THESE BALLOONS -- OR BECAUSE I'VE GOT SUPER-POWERS!
"I WAS PRETTY PLEASED WITH MY STRATEGY, BUT I WOULDN'T HAVE BEEN IF I KNEW WHAT WAS GOING ON IN THE PROFESSOR'S MIND..."
HELIUM BALLOONS! WAS IT A TRICK--OR SOME STRANGE COINCIDENCE? I'LL SOON FIND OUT! THIS KRYPTONITE I DISCOVERED YEARS AGO ON A GEOLOGICAL EXPEDITION WILL PROVE TOMORROW WHETHER MY THEORY THAT KENT IS SUPERBOY IS CORRECT!
"NEXT DAY..."
TODAY, CLASS, WE WILL EXPLORE SOME NATURAL GAS CAVERNS FOR INTERESTING GEOLOGICAL SPECIMENS!
AS LONG AS I KEEP THE KRYPTONITE SHIELDED IN THIS LEAD BOX, THE STUFF CAN'T AFFECT SUPERBOY-- BUT WHEN WE ARE IN THE CAVE-- HA-HA-- WE SHALL SEE! AND TRICKS WON'T HELP HIM!
7

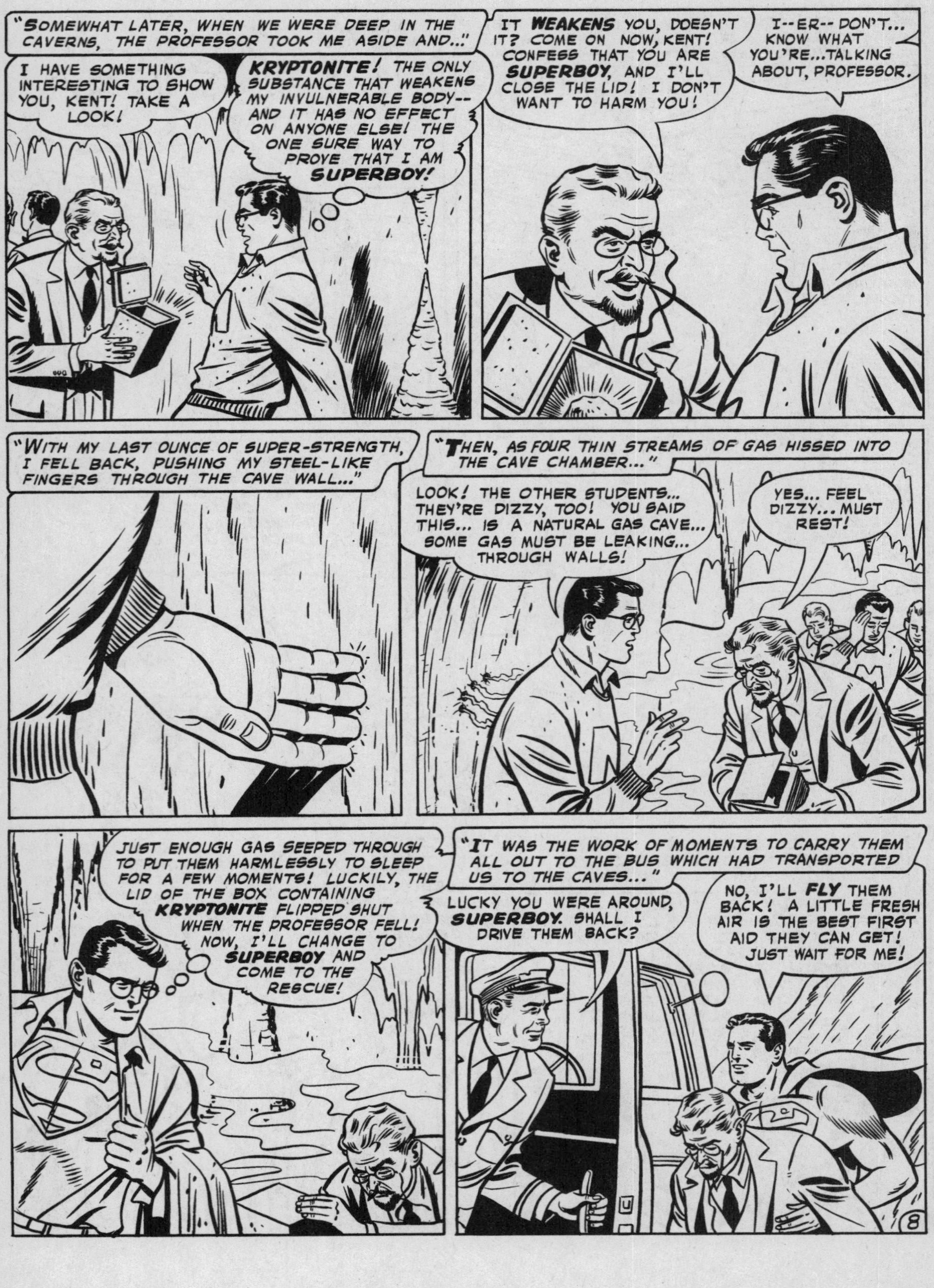
"SOMEWHAT LATER, WHEN WE WERE DEEP IN THE CAVERNS, THE PROFESSOR TOOK ME ASIDE AND..."
I HAVE SOMETHING INTERESTING TO SHOW YOU, KENT! TAKE A LOOK!
KRYPTONITE! THE ONLY SUBSTANCE THAT WEAKENS MY INVULNERABLE BODY--AND IT HAS NO EFFECT ON ANYONE ELSE! THE ONE SURE WAY TO PROVE THAT I AM SUPERBOY!
IT WEAKENS YOU, DOESN'T IT? COME ON NOW, KENT! CONFESS THAT YOU ARE SUPERBOY, AND I'LL CLOSE THE LID! I DON'T WANT TO HARM YOU!
I--ER--DON'T... KNOW WHAT YOU'RE...TALKING ABOUT, PROFESSOR.
"WITH MY LAST OUNCE OF SUPER-STRENGTH, I FELL BACK, PUSHING MY STEEL-LIKE FINGERS THROUGH THE CAVE WALL..."
"THEN, AS FOUR THIN STREAMS OF GAS HISSED INTO THE CAVE CHAMBER..."
LOOK! THE OTHER STUDENTS... THEY'RE DIZZY, TOO! YOU SAID THIS... IS A NATURAL GAS CAVE... SOME GAS MUST BE LEAKING... THROUGH WALLS!
YES... FEEL DIZZY... MUST REST!
JUST ENOUGH GAS SEEPED THROUGH TO PUT THEM HARMLESSLY TO SLEEP FOR A FEW MOMENTS! LUCKILY, THE LID OF THE BOX CONTAINING KRYPTONITE FLIPPED SHUT WHEN THE PROFESSOR FELL! NOW, I'LL CHANGE TO SUPERBOY AND COME TO THE RESCUE!
"IT WAS THE WORK OF MOMENTS TO CARRY THEM ALL OUT TO THE BUS WHICH HAD TRANSPORTED US TO THE CAVES..."
LUCKY YOU WERE AROUND, SUPERBOY. SHALL I DRIVE THEM BACK?
NO, I'LL FLY THEM BACK! A LITTLE FRESH AIR IS THE BEST FIRST AID THEY CAN GET! JUST WAIT FOR ME!
8

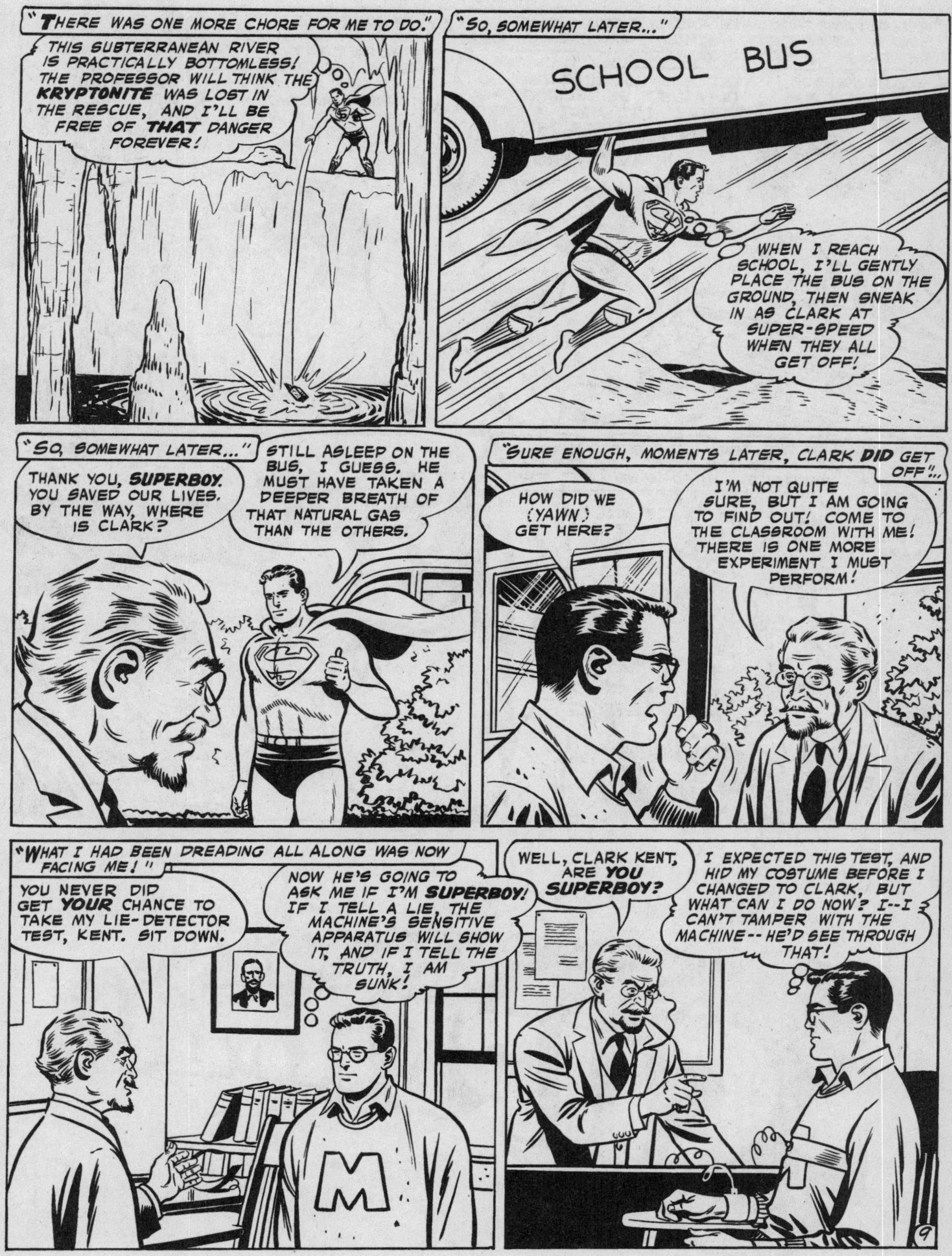
"THERE WAS ONE MORE CHORE FOR ME TO DO."
THIS SUBTERRANEAN RIVER IS PRACTICALLY BOTTOMLESS! THE PROFESSOR WILL THINK THE KRYPTONITE WAS LOST IN THE RESCUE, AND I'LL BE FREE OF THAT DANGER FOREVER!
"SO, SOMEWHAT LATER..."
SCHOOL BUS
WHEN I REACH SCHOOL, I'LL GENTLY PLACE THE BUS ON THE GROUND, THEN SNEAK IN AS CLARK AT SUPER-SPEED WHEN THEY ALL GET OFF!
"SO, SOMEWHAT LATER..."
THANK YOU, SUPERBOY. YOU SAVED OUR LIVES. BY THE WAY, WHERE IS CLARK?
STILL ASLEEP ON THE BUS, I GUESS. HE MUST HAVE TAKEN A DEEPER BREATH OF THAT NATURAL GAS THAN THE OTHERS.
"SURE ENOUGH, MOMENTS LATER, CLARK DID GET OFF!"...
HOW DID WE (YAWN) GET HERE?
I'M NOT QUITE SURE, BUT I AM GOING TO FIND OUT! COME TO THE CLASSROOM WITH ME! THERE IS ONE MORE EXPERIMENT I MUST PERFORM!
"WHAT I HAD BEEN DREADING ALL ALONG WAS NOW FACING ME!"
YOU NEVER DID GET YOUR CHANCE TO TAKE MY LIE-DETECTOR TEST, KENT. SIT DOWN.
NOW HE'S GOING TO ASK ME IF I'M SUPERBOY! IF I TELL A LIE, THE MACHINE'S SENSITIVE APPARATUS WILL SHOW IT, AND IF I TELL THE TRUTH, I AM SUNK!
WELL, CLARK KENT, ARE YOU SUPERBOY?
I EXPECTED THIS TEST, AND HID MY COSTUME BEFORE I CHANGED TO CLARK, BUT WHAT CAN I DO NOW? I--I CAN'T TAMPER WITH THE MACHINE--HE'D SEE THROUGH THAT!
9

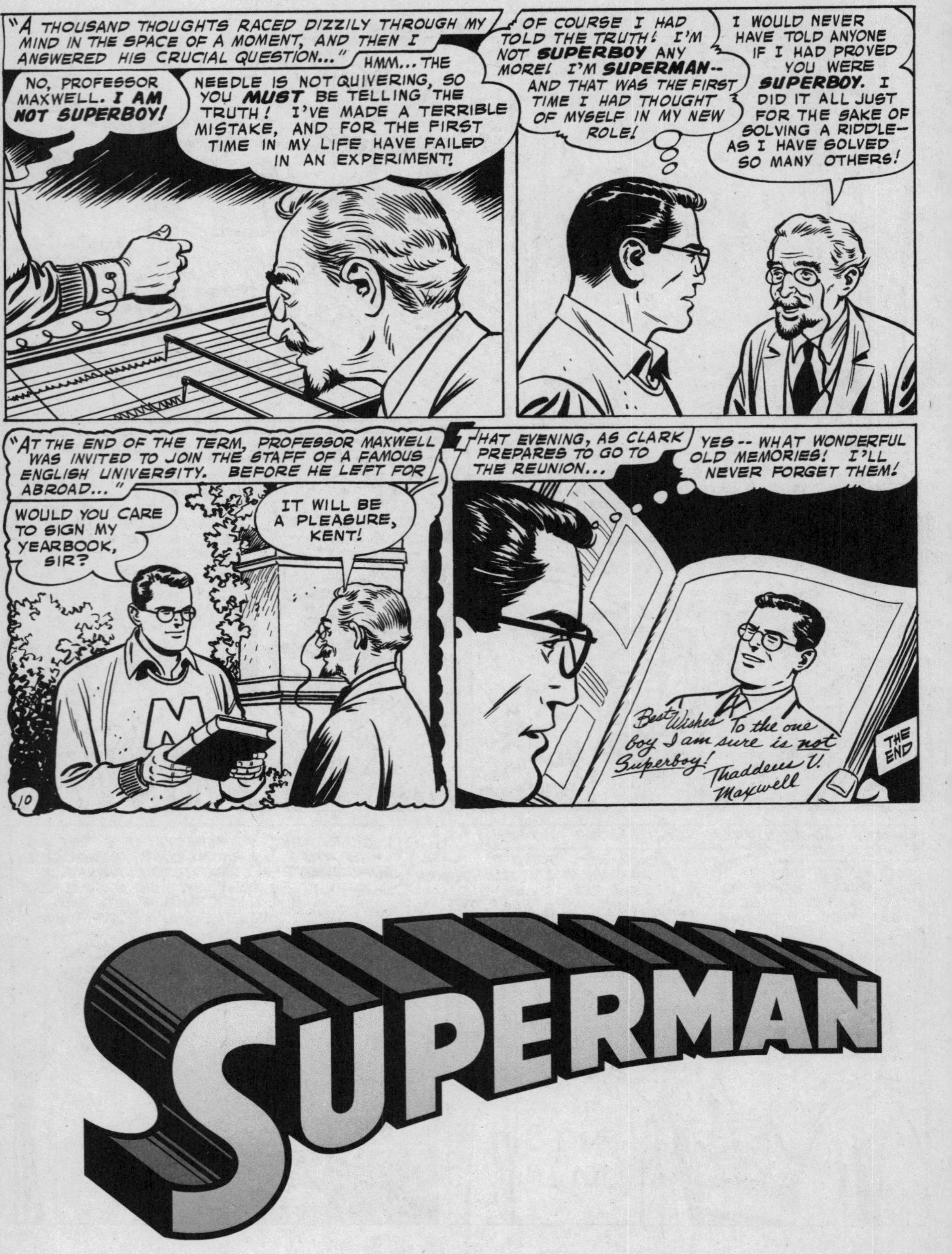
"A THOUSAND THOUGHTS RACED DIZZILY THROUGH MY MIND IN THE SPACE OF A MOMENT, AND THEN I ANSWERED HIS CRUCIAL QUESTION..."
NO, PROFESSOR MAXWELL. I AM NOT SUPERBOY!
HMM... THE NEEDLE IS NOT QUIVERING, SO YOU MUST BE TELLING THE TRUTH! I'VE MADE A TERRIBLE MISTAKE, AND FOR THE FIRST TIME IN MY LIFE HAVE FAILED IN AN EXPERIMENT!
OF COURSE I HAD TOLD THE TRUTH! I'M NOT SUPERBOY ANY MORE! I'M SUPERMAN-- AND THAT WAS THE FIRST TIME I HAD THOUGHT OF MYSELF IN MY NEW ROLE!
I WOULD NEVER HAVE TOLD ANYONE IF I HAD PROVED YOU WERE SUPERBOY. I DID IT ALL JUST FOR THE SAKE OF SOLVING A RIDDLE-- AS I HAVE SOLVED SO MANY OTHERS!
"AT THE END OF THE TERM, PROFESSOR MAXWELL WAS INVITED TO JOIN THE STAFF OF A FAMOUS ENGLISH UNIVERSITY. BEFORE HE LEFT FOR ABROAD..."
WOULD YOU CARE TO SIGN MY YEARBOOK, SIR?
IT WILL BE A PLEASURE, KENT!
10
THAT EVENING, AS CLARK PREPARES TO GO TO THE REUNION...
YES -- WHAT WONDERFUL OLD MEMORIES! I'LL NEVER FORGET THEM!
Best Wishes To the one boy I am sure is not Superboy! Thaddeus V. Maxwell
THE END

SUPERMAN

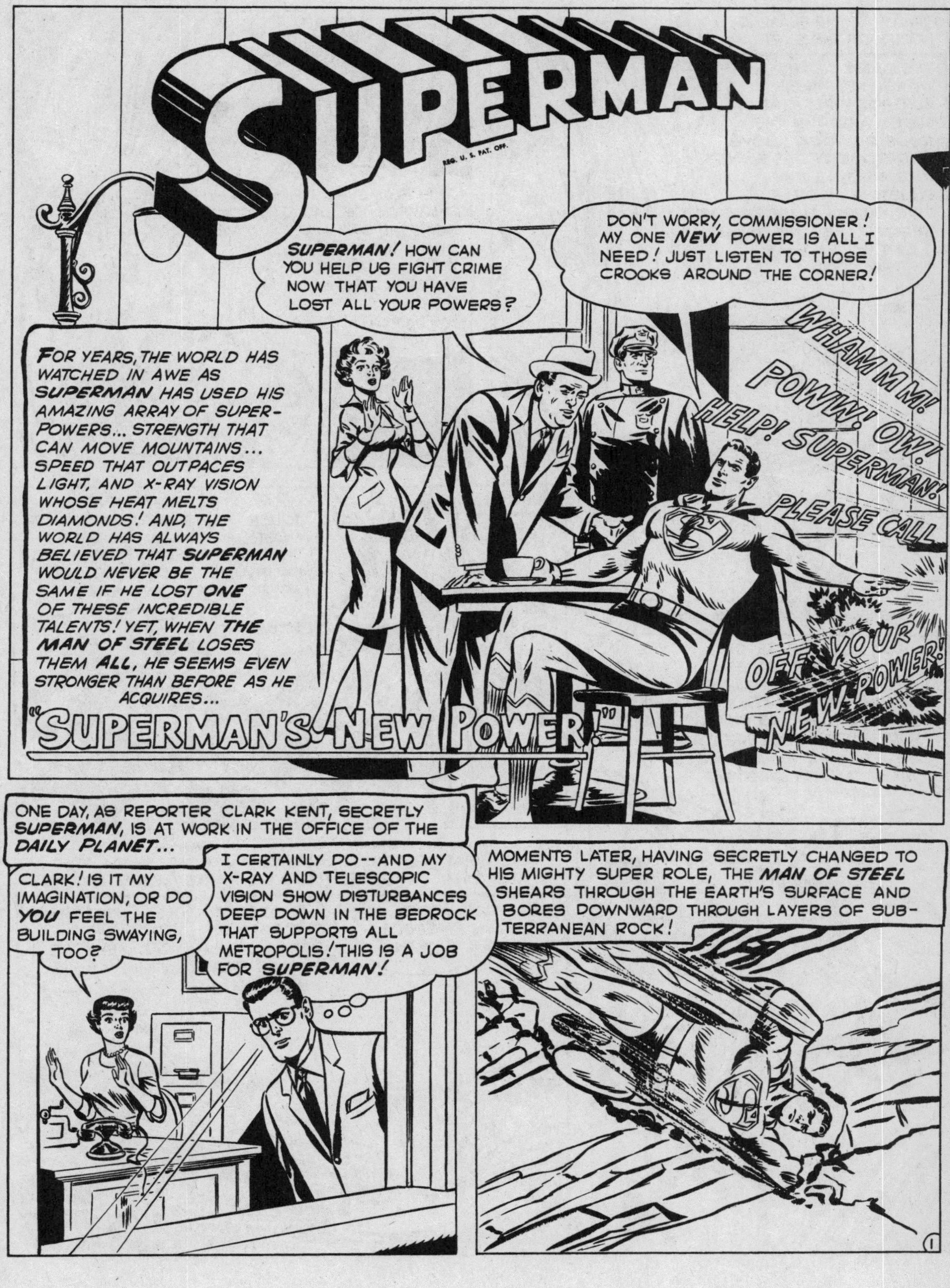
SUPERMAN
REG. U. S. PAT. OFF.
SUPERMAN! HOW CAN YOU HELP US FIGHT CRIME NOW THAT YOU HAVE LOST ALL YOUR POWERS?
DON'T WORRY, COMMISSIONER! MY ONE NEW POWER IS ALL I NEED! JUST LISTEN TO THOSE CROOKS AROUND THE CORNER!
WHAMMMM! POWW! OW! HELP! SUPERMAN! PLEASE CALL OFF YOUR NEW POWER!
FOR YEARS, THE WORLD HAS WATCHED IN AWE AS SUPERMAN HAS USED HIS AMAZING ARRAY OF SUPER-POWERS... STRENGTH THAT CAN MOVE MOUNTAINS... SPEED THAT OUTPACES LIGHT, AND X-RAY VISION WHOSE HEAT MELTS DIAMONDS! AND, THE WORLD HAS ALWAYS BELIEVED THAT SUPERMAN WOULD NEVER BE THE SAME IF HE LOST ONE OF THESE INCREDIBLE TALENTS! YET, WHEN THE MAN OF STEEL LOSES THEM ALL, HE SEEMS EVEN STRONGER THAN BEFORE AS HE ACQUIRES...
"SUPERMAN'S NEW POWER!"
ONE DAY, AS REPORTER CLARK KENT, SECRETLY SUPERMAN, IS AT WORK IN THE OFFICE OF THE DAILY PLANET...
CLARK! IS IT MY IMAGINATION, OR DO YOU FEEL THE BUILDING SWAYING, TOO?
I CERTAINLY DO--AND MY X-RAY AND TELESCOPIC VISION SHOW DISTURBANCES DEEP DOWN IN THE BEDROCK THAT SUPPORTS ALL METROPOLIS! THIS IS A JOB FOR SUPERMAN!
MOMENTS LATER, HAVING SECRETLY CHANGED TO HIS MIGHTY SUPER ROLE, THE MAN OF STEEL SHEARS THROUGH THE EARTH'S SURFACE AND BORES DOWNWARD THROUGH LAYERS OF SUB-TERRANEAN ROCK!
1

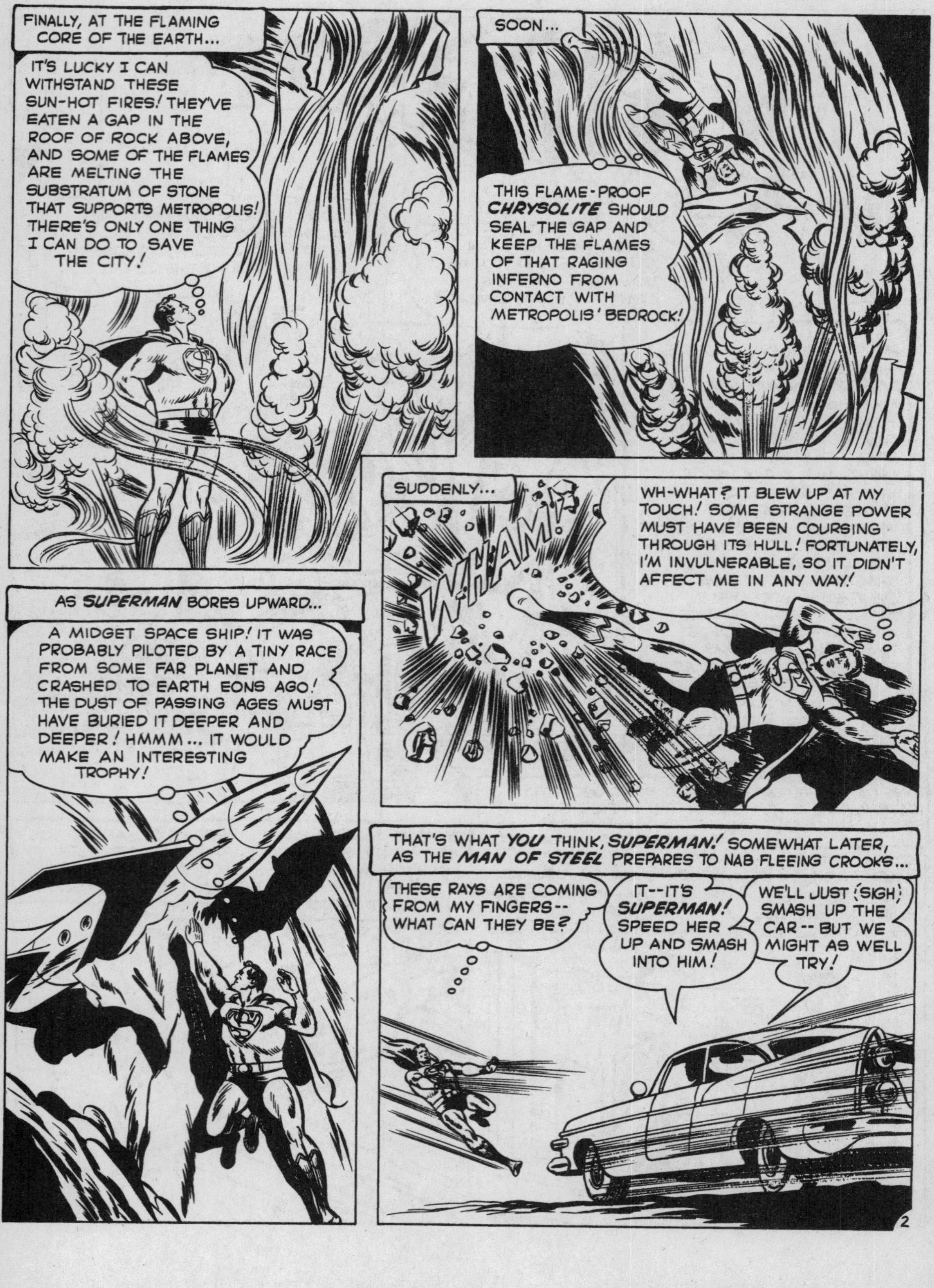
FINALLY, AT THE FLAMING CORE OF THE EARTH...
IT'S LUCKY I CAN WITHSTAND THESE SUN-HOT FIRES! THEY'VE EATEN A GAP IN THE ROOF OF ROCK ABOVE, AND SOME OF THE FLAMES ARE MELTING THE SUBSTRATUM OF STONE THAT SUPPORTS METROPOLIS! THERE'S ONLY ONE THING I CAN DO TO SAVE THE CITY!
SOON...
THIS FLAME-PROOF CHRYSOLITE SHOULD SEAL THE GAP AND KEEP THE FLAMES OF THAT RAGING INFERNO FROM CONTACT WITH METROPOLIS' BEDROCK!
AS SUPERMAN BORES UPWARD...
A MIDGET SPACE SHIP! IT WAS PROBABLY PILOTED BY A TINY RACE FROM SOME FAR PLANET AND CRASHED TO EARTH EONS AGO! THE DUST OF PASSING AGES MUST HAVE BURIED IT DEEPER AND DEEPER! HMMM... IT WOULD MAKE AN INTERESTING TROPHY!
SUDDENLY...
WHAM!
WH-WHAT? IT BLEW UP AT MY TOUCH! SOME STRANGE POWER MUST HAVE BEEN COURSING THROUGH ITS HULL! FORTUNATELY, I'M INVULNERABLE, SO IT DIDN'T AFFECT ME IN ANY WAY!
THAT'S WHAT YOU THINK, SUPERMAN! SOMEWHAT LATER, AS THE MAN OF STEEL PREPARES TO NAB FLEEING CROOKS...
THESE RAYS ARE COMING FROM MY FINGERS-- WHAT CAN THEY BE?
IT--IT'S SUPERMAN! SPEED HER UP AND SMASH INTO HIM!
WE'LL JUST (SIGH) SMASH UP THE CAR -- BUT WE MIGHT AS WELL TRY!

2

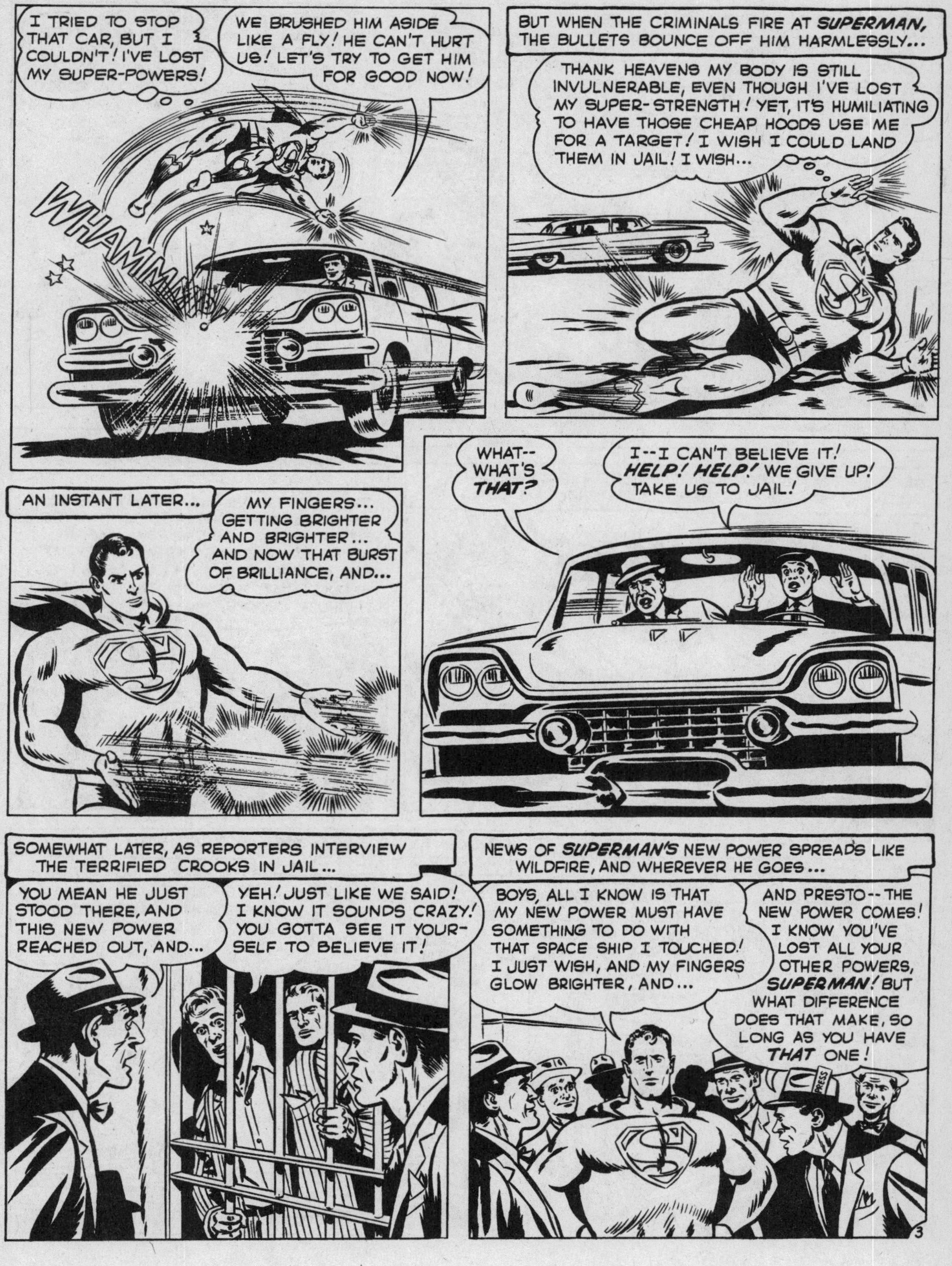
I TRIED TO STOP THAT CAR, BUT I COULDN'T! I'VE LOST MY SUPER-POWERS!
WE BRUSHED HIM ASIDE LIKE A FLY! HE CAN'T HURT US! LET'S TRY TO GET HIM FOR GOOD NOW!
WHAMM
BUT WHEN THE CRIMINALS FIRE AT SUPERMAN, THE BULLETS BOUNCE OFF HIM HARMLESSLY...
THANK HEAVENS MY BODY IS STILL INVULNERABLE, EVEN THOUGH I'VE LOST MY SUPER-STRENGTH! YET, IT'S HUMILIATING TO HAVE THOSE CHEAP HOODS USE ME FOR A TARGET! I WISH I COULD LAND THEM IN JAIL! I WISH...
AN INSTANT LATER...
MY FINGERS... GETTING BRIGHTER AND BRIGHTER... AND NOW THAT BURST OF BRILLIANCE, AND...
WHAT-- WHAT'S THAT?
I--I CAN'T BELIEVE IT! HELP! HELP! WE GIVE UP! TAKE US TO JAIL!
SOMEWHAT LATER, AS REPORTERS INTERVIEW THE TERRIFIED CROOKS IN JAIL...
YOU MEAN HE JUST STOOD THERE, AND THIS NEW POWER REACHED OUT, AND...
YEH! JUST LIKE WE SAID! I KNOW IT SOUNDS CRAZY! YOU GOTTA SEE IT YOURSELF TO BELIEVE IT!
NEWS OF SUPERMAN'S NEW POWER SPREADS LIKE WILDFIRE, AND WHEREVER HE GOES...
BOYS, ALL I KNOW IS THAT MY NEW POWER MUST HAVE SOMETHING TO DO WITH THAT SPACE SHIP I TOUCHED! I JUST WISH, AND MY FINGERS GLOW BRIGHTER, AND...
AND PRESTO--THE NEW POWER COMES! I KNOW YOU'VE LOST ALL YOUR OTHER POWERS, SUPERMAN! BUT WHAT DIFFERENCE DOES THAT MAKE, SO LONG AS YOU HAVE THAT ONE!
PRESS
3

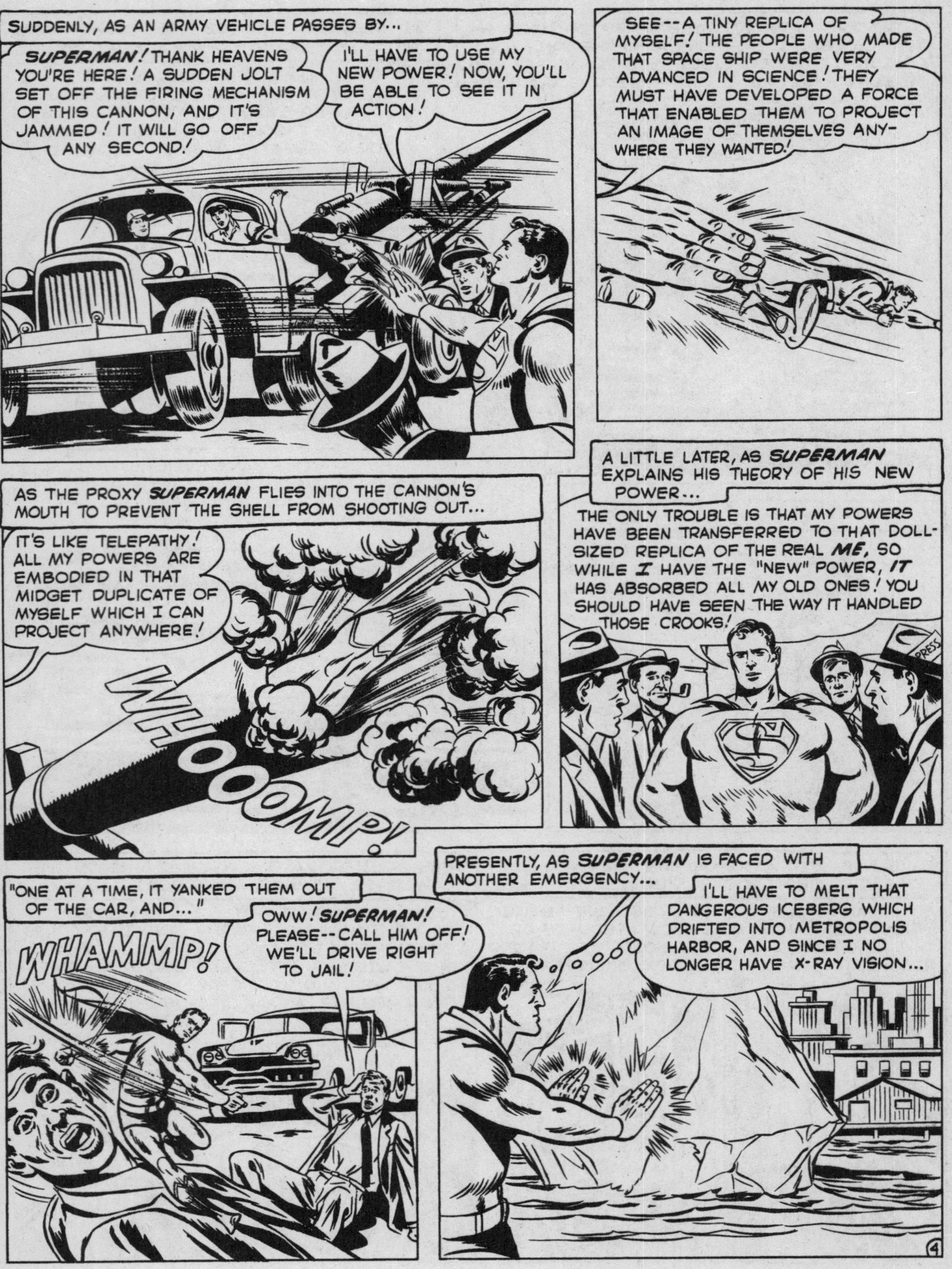
SUDDENLY, AS AN ARMY VEHICLE PASSES BY...
SUPERMAN! THANK HEAVENS YOU'RE HERE! A SUDDEN JOLT SET OFF THE FIRING MECHANISM OF THIS CANNON, AND IT'S JAMMED! IT WILL GO OFF ANY SECOND!
I'LL HAVE TO USE MY NEW POWER! NOW, YOU'LL BE ABLE TO SEE IT IN ACTION!
SEE--A TINY REPLICA OF MYSELF! THE PEOPLE WHO MADE THAT SPACE SHIP WERE VERY ADVANCED IN SCIENCE! THEY MUST HAVE DEVELOPED A FORCE THAT ENABLED THEM TO PROJECT AN IMAGE OF THEMSELVES ANY-WHERE THEY WANTED!
AS THE PROXY SUPERMAN FLIES INTO THE CANNON'S MOUTH TO PREVENT THE SHELL FROM SHOOTING OUT...
IT'S LIKE TELEPATHY! ALL MY POWERS ARE EMBODIED IN THAT MIDGET DUPLICATE OF MYSELF WHICH I CAN PROJECT ANYWHERE!
WHOOOOMP!
A LITTLE LATER, AS SUPERMAN EXPLAINS HIS THEORY OF HIS NEW POWER...
THE ONLY TROUBLE IS THAT MY POWERS HAVE BEEN TRANSFERRED TO THAT DOLL-SIZED REPLICA OF THE REAL ME, SO WHILE I HAVE THE "NEW" POWER, IT HAS ABSORBED ALL MY OLD ONES! YOU SHOULD HAVE SEEN THE WAY IT HANDLED THOSE CROOKS!
PRESS
"ONE AT A TIME, IT YANKED THEM OUT OF THE CAR, AND..."
WHAMMP!
OWW! SUPERMAN! PLEASE--CALL HIM OFF! WE'LL DRIVE RIGHT TO JAIL!
PRESENTLY, AS SUPERMAN IS FACED WITH ANOTHER EMERGENCY...
I'LL HAVE TO MELT THAT DANGEROUS ICEBERG WHICH DRIFTED INTO METROPOLIS HARBOR, AND SINCE I NO LONGER HAVE X-RAY VISION...
4

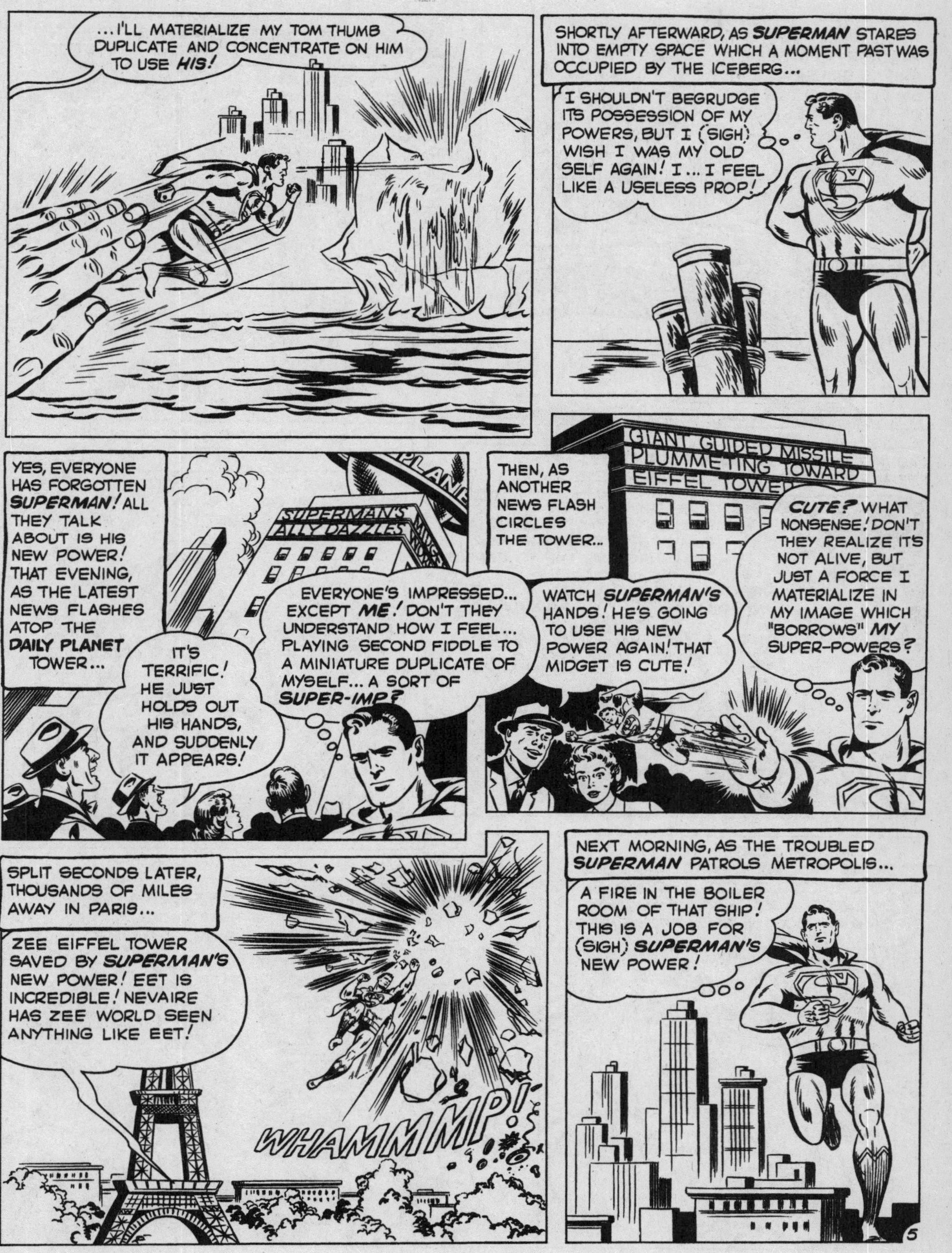
...I'LL MATERIALIZE MY TOM THUMB DUPLICATE AND CONCENTRATE ON HIM TO USE HIS!
SHORTLY AFTERWARD, AS SUPERMAN STARES INTO EMPTY SPACE WHICH A MOMENT PAST WAS OCCUPIED BY THE ICEBERG...
I SHOULDN'T BEGRUDGE ITS POSSESSION OF MY POWERS, BUT I (SIGH) WISH I WAS MY OLD SELF AGAIN! I... I FEEL LIKE A USELESS PROP!
YES, EVERYONE HAS FORGOTTEN SUPERMAN! ALL THEY TALK ABOUT IS HIS NEW POWER! THAT EVENING, AS THE LATEST NEWS FLASHES ATOP THE DAILY PLANET TOWER...
SUPERMAN'S ALLY DAZZLES
IT'S TERRIFIC! HE JUST HOLDS OUT HIS HANDS, AND SUDDENLY IT APPEARS!
EVERYONE'S IMPRESSED... EXCEPT ME! DON'T THEY UNDERSTAND HOW I FEEL... PLAYING SECOND FIDDLE TO A MINIATURE DUPLICATE OF MYSELF... A SORT OF SUPER-IMP?
THEN, AS ANOTHER NEWS FLASH CIRCLES THE TOWER...
GIANT GUIDED MISSILE PLUMMETING TOWARD EIFFEL TOWE
WATCH SUPERMAN'S HANDS! HE'S GOING TO USE HIS NEW POWER AGAIN! THAT MIDGET IS CUTE!
CUTE? WHAT NONSENSE! DON'T THEY REALIZE IT'S NOT ALIVE, BUT JUST A FORCE I MATERIALIZE IN MY IMAGE WHICH "BORROWS" MY SUPER-POWERS?
SPLIT SECONDS LATER, THOUSANDS OF MILES AWAY IN PARIS...
ZEE EIFFEL TOWER SAVED BY SUPERMAN'S NEW POWER! EET IS INCREDIBLE! NEVAIRE HAS ZEE WORLD SEEN ANYTHING LIKE EET!
WHAMMMMP!
NEXT MORNING, AS THE TROUBLED SUPERMAN PATROLS METROPOLIS...
A FIRE IN THE BOILER ROOM OF THAT SHIP! THIS IS A JOB FOR (SIGH) SUPERMAN'S NEW POWER!
5

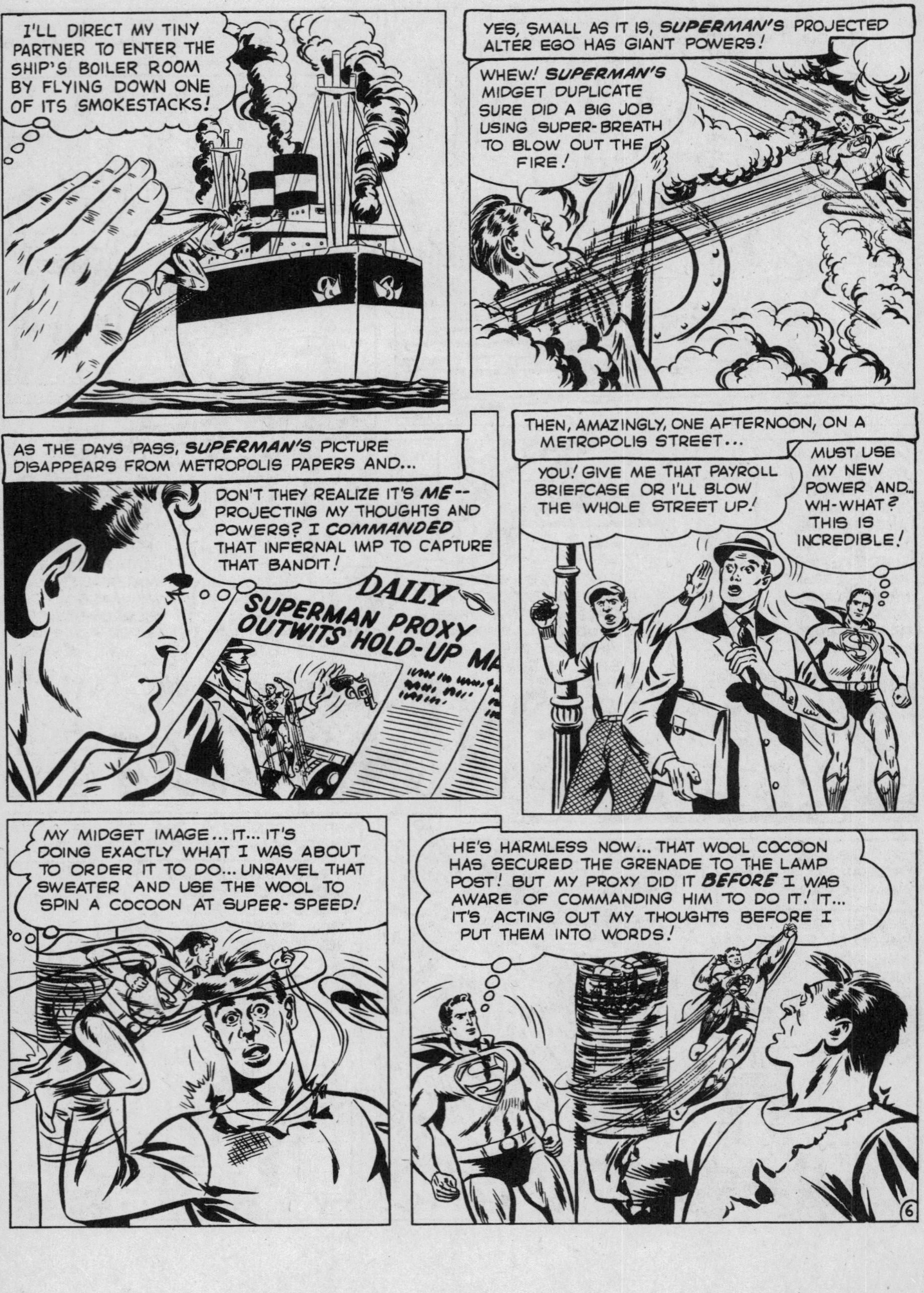
I'LL DIRECT MY TINY PARTNER TO ENTER THE SHIP'S BOILER ROOM BY FLYING DOWN ONE OF ITS SMOKESTACKS!
YES, SMALL AS IT IS, SUPERMAN'S PROJECTED ALTER EGO HAS GIANT POWERS!
WHEW! SUPERMAN'S MIDGET DUPLICATE SURE DID A BIG JOB USING SUPER-BREATH TO BLOW OUT THE FIRE!
AS THE DAYS PASS, SUPERMAN'S PICTURE DISAPPEARS FROM METROPOLIS PAPERS AND...
DON'T THEY REALIZE IT'S ME-- PROJECTING MY THOUGHTS AND POWERS? I COMMANDED THAT INFERNAL IMP TO CAPTURE THAT BANDIT!
DAILY
SUPERMAN PROXY OUTWITS HOLD-UP MA
THEN, AMAZINGLY, ONE AFTERNOON, ON A METROPOLIS STREET...
YOU! GIVE ME THAT PAYROLL BRIEFCASE OR I'LL BLOW THE WHOLE STREET UP!
MUST USE MY NEW POWER AND... WH-WHAT? THIS IS INCREDIBLE!
MY MIDGET IMAGE... IT... IT'S DOING EXACTLY WHAT I WAS ABOUT TO ORDER IT TO DO... UNRAVEL THAT SWEATER AND USE THE WOOL TO SPIN A COCOON AT SUPER-SPEED!
HE'S HARMLESS NOW... THAT WOOL COCOON HAS SECURED THE GRENADE TO THE LAMP POST! BUT MY PROXY DID IT BEFORE I WAS AWARE OF COMMANDING HIM TO DO IT! IT... IT'S ACTING OUT MY THOUGHTS BEFORE I PUT THEM INTO WORDS!
6

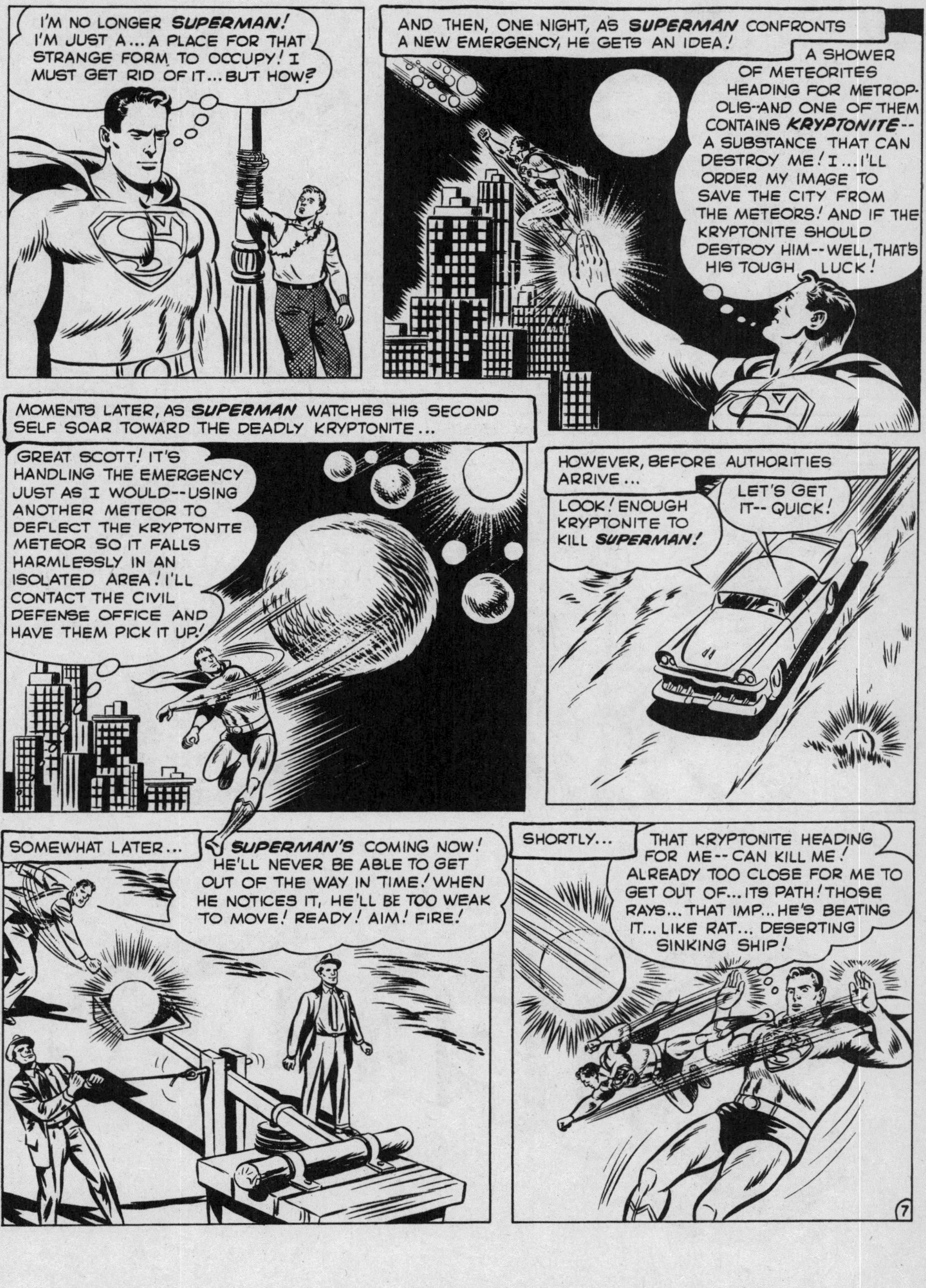
I'M NO LONGER SUPERMAN! I'M JUST A... A PLACE FOR THAT STRANGE FORM TO OCCUPY! I MUST GET RID OF IT... BUT HOW?
AND THEN, ONE NIGHT, AS SUPERMAN CONFRONTS A NEW EMERGENCY, HE GETS AN IDEA!
A SHOWER OF METEORITES HEADING FOR METROPOLIS--AND ONE OF THEM CONTAINS KRYPTONITE-- A SUBSTANCE THAT CAN DESTROY ME! I...I'LL ORDER MY IMAGE TO SAVE THE CITY FROM THE METEORS! AND IF THE KRYPTONITE SHOULD DESTROY HIM--WELL, THAT'S HIS TOUGH LUCK!
MOMENTS LATER, AS SUPERMAN WATCHES HIS SECOND SELF SOAR TOWARD THE DEADLY KRYPTONITE...
GREAT SCOTT! IT'S HANDLING THE EMERGENCY JUST AS I WOULD--USING ANOTHER METEOR TO DEFLECT THE KRYPTONITE METEOR SO IT FALLS HARMLESSLY IN AN ISOLATED AREA! I'LL CONTACT THE CIVIL DEFENSE OFFICE AND HAVE THEM PICK IT UP!
HOWEVER, BEFORE AUTHORITIES ARRIVE...
LOOK! ENOUGH KRYPTONITE TO KILL SUPERMAN!
LET'S GET IT-- QUICK!
SOMEWHAT LATER...
SUPERMAN'S COMING NOW! HE'LL NEVER BE ABLE TO GET OUT OF THE WAY IN TIME! WHEN HE NOTICES IT, HE'LL BE TOO WEAK TO MOVE! READY! AIM! FIRE!
SHORTLY...
THAT KRYPTONITE HEADING FOR ME--CAN KILL ME! ALREADY TOO CLOSE FOR ME TO GET OUT OF... ITS PATH! THOSE RAYS... THAT IMP... HE'S BEATING IT... LIKE RAT... DESERTING SINKING SHIP!
7

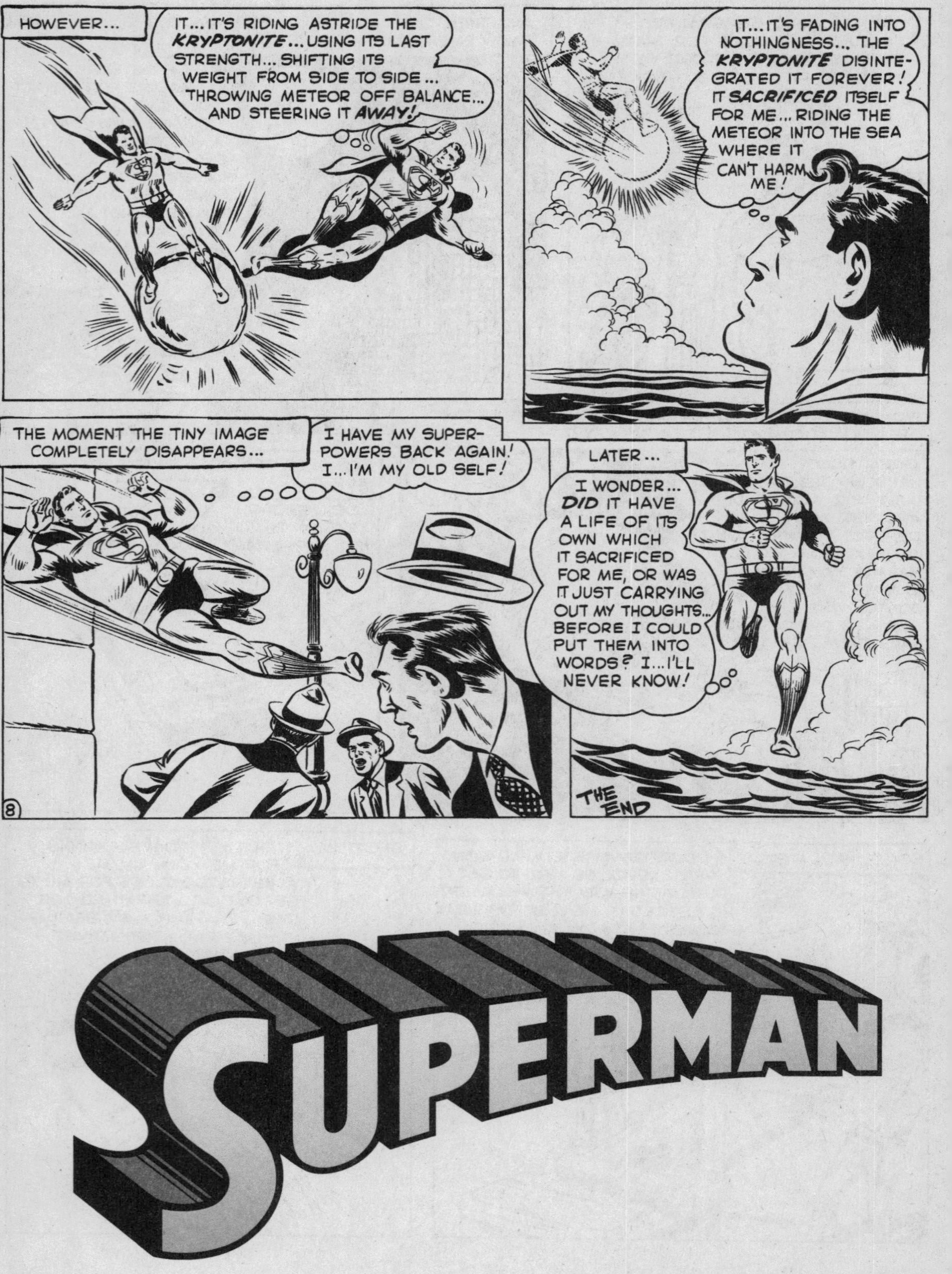
HOWEVER...
IT... IT'S RIDING ASTRIDE THE KRYPTONITE... USING ITS LAST STRENGTH... SHIFTING ITS WEIGHT FROM SIDE TO SIDE... THROWING METEOR OFF BALANCE... AND STEERING IT AWAY!
IT... IT'S FADING INTO NOTHINGNESS... THE KRYPTONITE DISINTEGRATED IT FOREVER! IT SACRIFICED ITSELF FOR ME... RIDING THE METEOR INTO THE SEA WHERE IT CAN'T HARM ME!
THE MOMENT THE TINY IMAGE COMPLETELY DISAPPEARS...
I HAVE MY SUPER-POWERS BACK AGAIN! I... I'M MY OLD SELF!
8
LATER...
I WONDER... DID IT HAVE A LIFE OF ITS OWN WHICH IT SACRIFICED FOR ME, OR WAS IT JUST CARRYING OUT MY THOUGHTS... BEFORE I COULD PUT THEM INTO WORDS? I... I'LL NEVER KNOW!
THE END

SUPERMAN

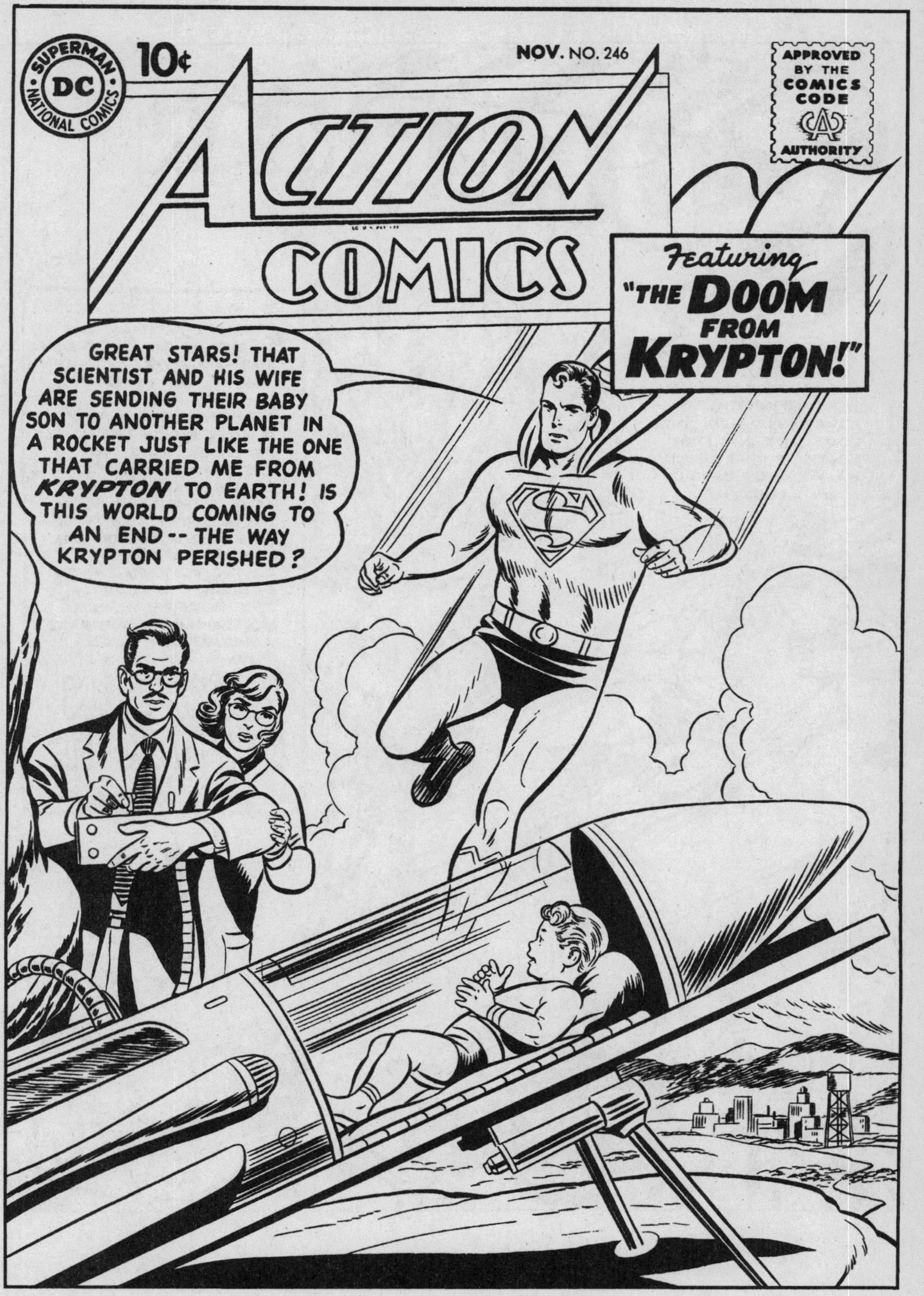
SUPERMAN
DC
NATIONAL COMICS
10¢
NOV. NO. 246
APPROVED BY THE COMICS CODE AUTHORITY
ACTION
COMICS
Featuring "THE DOOM FROM KRYPTON!"
GREAT STARS! THAT SCIENTIST AND HIS WIFE ARE SENDING THEIR BABY SON TO ANOTHER PLANET IN A ROCKET JUST LIKE THE ONE THAT CARRIED ME FROM KRYPTON TO EARTH! IS THIS WORLD COMING TO AN END -- THE WAY KRYPTON PERISHED?

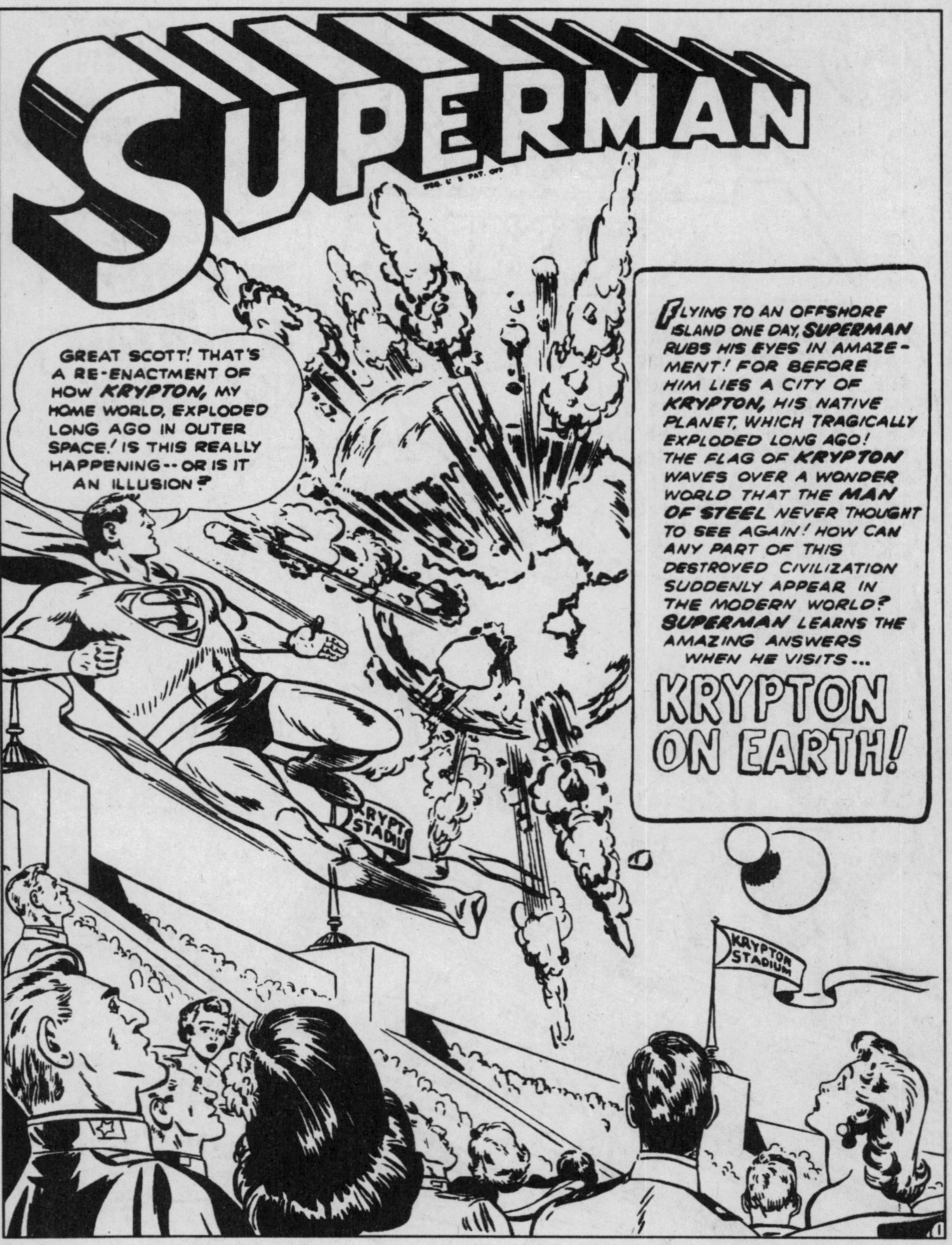
SUPERMAN
GREAT SCOTT! THAT'S A RE-ENACTMENT OF HOW KRYPTON, MY HOME WORLD, EXPLODED LONG AGO IN OUTER SPACE! IS THIS REALLY HAPPENING--OR IS IT AN ILLUSION?
FLYING TO AN OFFSHORE ISLAND ONE DAY, SUPERMAN RUBS HIS EYES IN AMAZEMENT! FOR BEFORE HIM LIES A CITY OF KRYPTON, HIS NATIVE PLANET, WHICH TRAGICALLY EXPLODED LONG AGO! THE FLAG OF KRYPTON WAVES OVER A WONDER WORLD THAT THE MAN OF STEEL NEVER THOUGHT TO SEE AGAIN! HOW CAN ANY PART OF THIS DESTROYED CIVILIZATION SUDDENLY APPEAR IN THE MODERN WORLD? SUPERMAN LEARNS THE AMAZING ANSWERS WHEN HE VISITS...
KRYPTON ON EARTH!
KRYPTON STADIUM

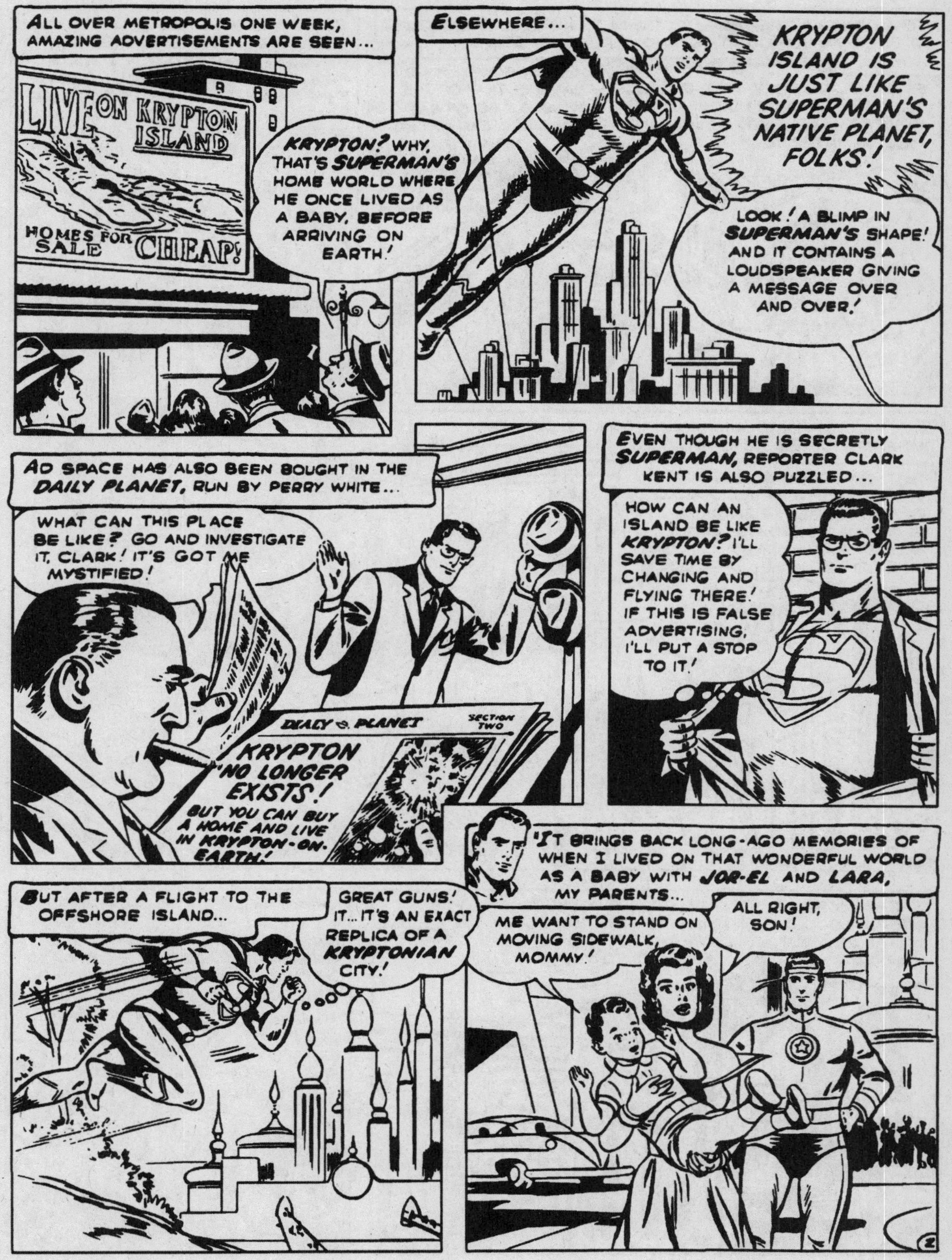

ALL OVER METROPOLIS ONE WEEK, AMAZING ADVERTISEMENTS ARE SEEN...
LIVE ON KRYPTON ISLAND
HOMES FOR SALE CHEAP!
KRYPTON? WHY, THAT'S SUPERMAN'S HOME WORLD WHERE HE ONCE LIVED AS A BABY, BEFORE ARRIVING ON EARTH!
ELSEWHERE...
KRYPTON ISLAND IS JUST LIKE SUPERMAN'S NATIVE PLANET, FOLKS!
LOOK! A BLIMP IN SUPERMAN'S SHAPE! AND IT CONTAINS A LOUDSPEAKER GIVING A MESSAGE OVER AND OVER!
AD SPACE HAS ALSO BEEN BOUGHT IN THE DAILY PLANET, RUN BY PERRY WHITE...
WHAT CAN THIS PLACE BE LIKE? GO AND INVESTIGATE IT, CLARK! IT'S GOT ME MYSTIFIED!
DAILY PLANET
SECTION TWO
KRYPTON NO LONGER EXISTS! BUT YOU CAN BUY A HOME AND LIVE IN KRYPTON-ON-EARTH!
EVEN THOUGH HE IS SECRETLY SUPERMAN, REPORTER CLARK KENT IS ALSO PUZZLED...
HOW CAN AN ISLAND BE LIKE KRYPTON? I'LL SAVE TIME BY CHANGING AND FLYING THERE! IF THIS IS FALSE ADVERTISING, I'LL PUT A STOP TO IT!
BUT AFTER A FLIGHT TO THE OFFSHORE ISLAND...
GREAT GUNS! IT... IT'S AN EXACT REPLICA OF A KRYPTONIAN CITY!
"IT BRINGS BACK LONG-AGO MEMORIES OF WHEN I LIVED ON THAT WONDERFUL WORLD AS A BABY WITH JOR-EL AND LARA, MY PARENTS...
ME WANT TO STAND ON MOVING SIDEWALK, MOMMY!
ALL RIGHT, SON!
2

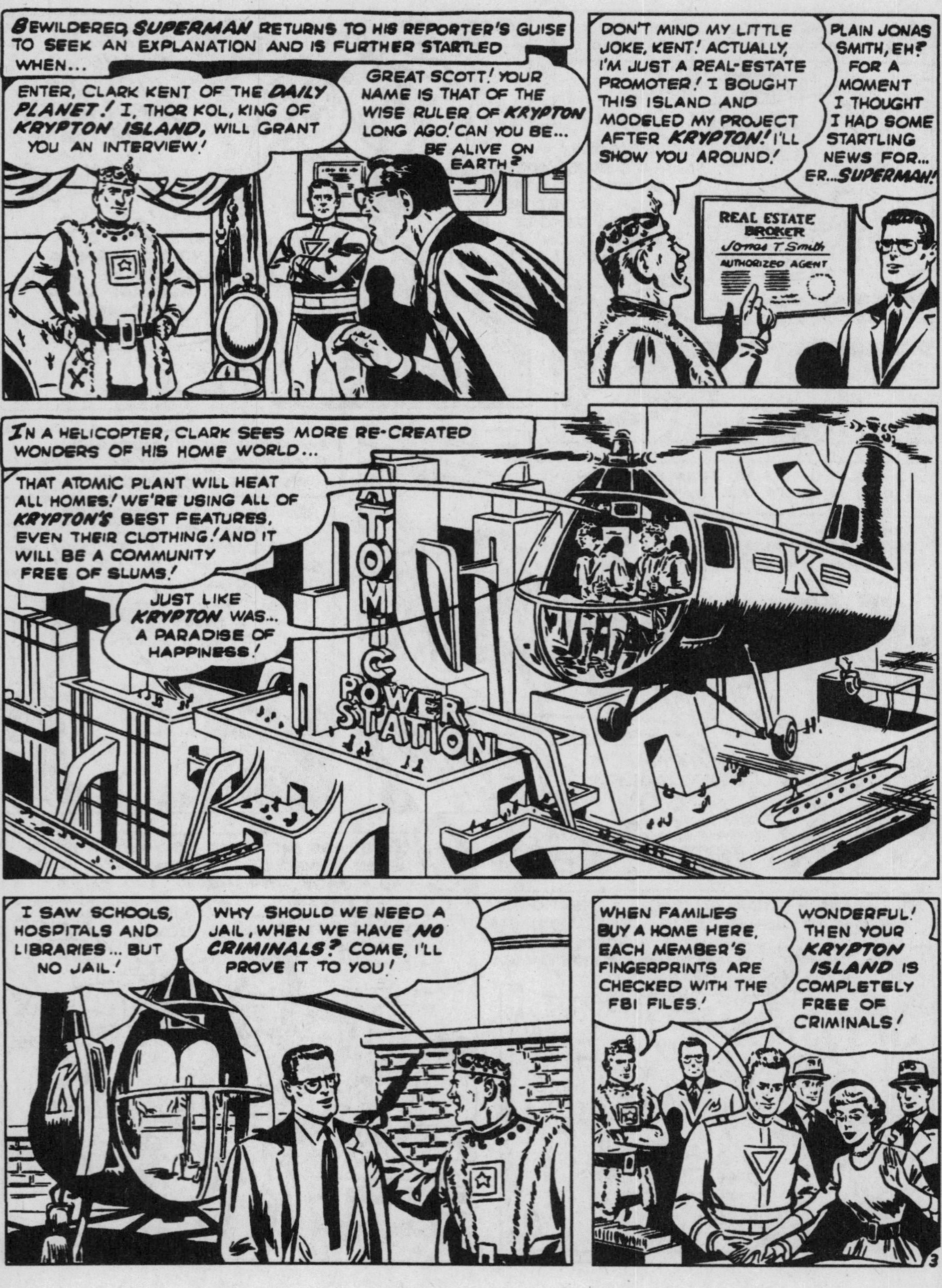
BEWILDERED, SUPERMAN RETURNS TO HIS REPORTER'S GUISE TO SEEK AN EXPLANATION AND IS FURTHER STARTLED WHEN...
ENTER, CLARK KENT OF THE DAILY PLANET! I, THOR KOL, KING OF KRYPTON ISLAND, WILL GRANT YOU AN INTERVIEW!
GREAT SCOTT! YOUR NAME IS THAT OF THE WISE RULER OF KRYPTON LONG AGO! CAN YOU BE... BE ALIVE ON EARTH?
DON'T MIND MY LITTLE JOKE, KENT! ACTUALLY, I'M JUST A REAL-ESTATE PROMOTER! I BOUGHT THIS ISLAND AND MODELED MY PROJECT AFTER KRYPTON! I'LL SHOW YOU AROUND!
PLAIN JONAS SMITH, EH? FOR A MOMENT I THOUGHT I HAD SOME STARTLING NEWS FOR... ER...SUPERMAN!
REAL ESTATE BROKER
Jonas T Smith
AUTHORIZED AGENT
IN A HELICOPTER, CLARK SEES MORE RE-CREATED WONDERS OF HIS HOME WORLD...
THAT ATOMIC PLANT WILL HEAT ALL HOMES! WE'RE USING ALL OF KRYPTON'S BEST FEATURES, EVEN THEIR CLOTHING! AND IT WILL BE A COMMUNITY FREE OF SLUMS!
JUST LIKE KRYPTON WAS... A PARADISE OF HAPPINESS!
ATOMIC POWER STATION
K
I SAW SCHOOLS, HOSPITALS AND LIBRARIES ... BUT NO JAIL!
WHY SHOULD WE NEED A JAIL, WHEN WE HAVE NO CRIMINALS? COME, I'LL PROVE IT TO YOU!
WHEN FAMILIES BUY A HOME HERE, EACH MEMBER'S FINGERPRINTS ARE CHECKED WITH THE FBI FILES!
WONDERFUL! THEN YOUR KRYPTON ISLAND IS COMPLETELY FREE OF CRIMINALS!
3

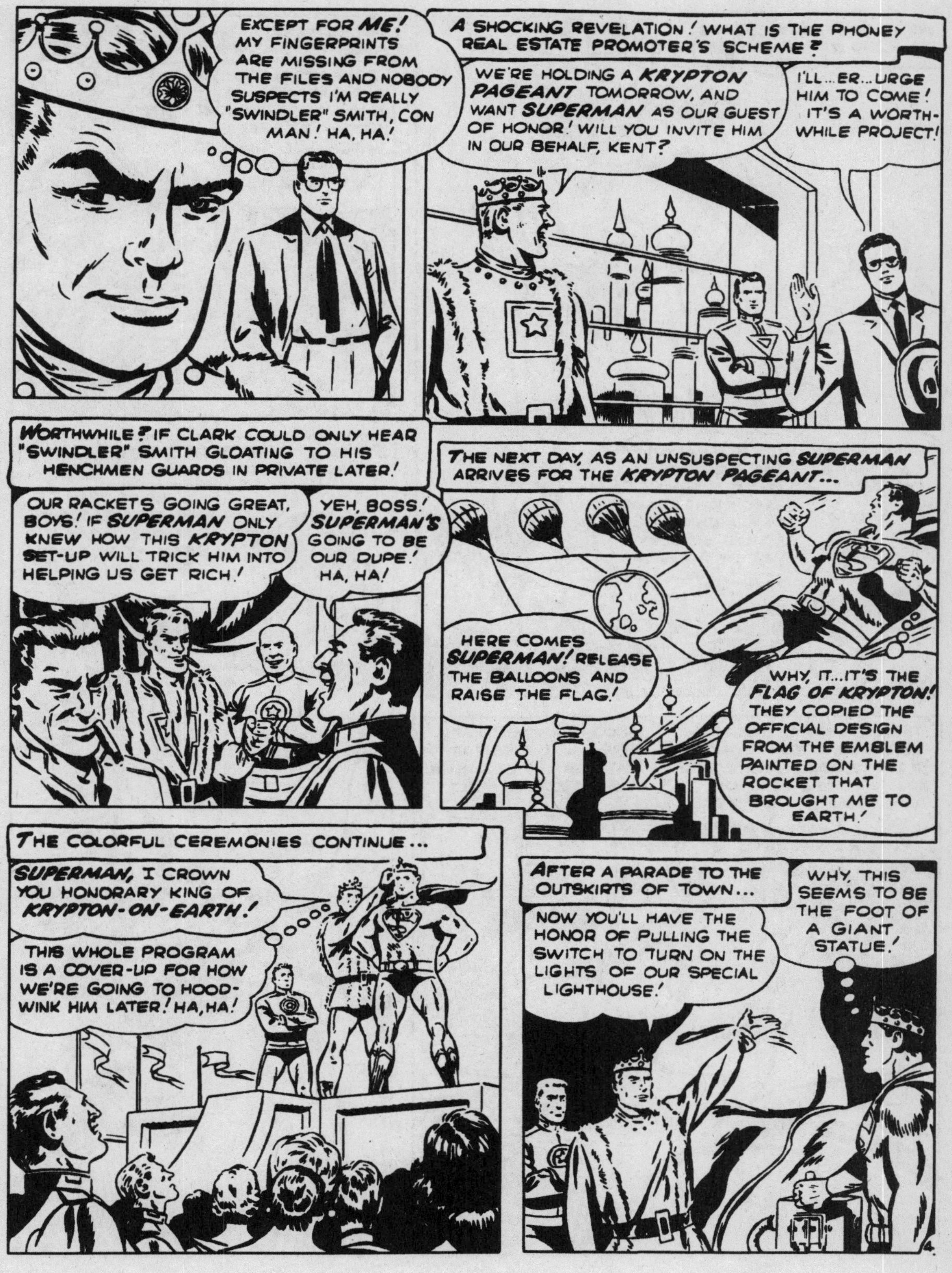
EXCEPT FOR ME! MY FINGERPRINTS ARE MISSING FROM THE FILES AND NOBODY SUSPECTS I'M REALLY "SWINDLER" SMITH, CON MAN! HA, HA!
A SHOCKING REVELATION! WHAT IS THE PHONEY REAL ESTATE PROMOTER'S SCHEME?
WE'RE HOLDING A KRYPTON PAGEANT TOMORROW, AND WANT SUPERMAN AS OUR GUEST OF HONOR! WILL YOU INVITE HIM IN OUR BEHALF, KENT?
I'LL...ER...URGE HIM TO COME! IT'S A WORTH-WHILE PROJECT!
WORTHWHILE? IF CLARK COULD ONLY HEAR "SWINDLER" SMITH GLOATING TO HIS HENCHMEN GUARDS IN PRIVATE LATER!
OUR RACKET'S GOING GREAT, BOYS! IF SUPERMAN ONLY KNEW HOW THIS KRYPTON SET-UP WILL TRICK HIM INTO HELPING US GET RICH!
YEH, BOSS! SUPERMAN'S GOING TO BE OUR DUPE! HA, HA!
THE NEXT DAY, AS AN UNSUSPECTING SUPERMAN ARRIVES FOR THE KRYPTON PAGEANT...
HERE COMES SUPERMAN! RELEASE THE BALLOONS AND RAISE THE FLAG!
WHY, IT...IT'S THE FLAG OF KRYPTON! THEY COPIED THE OFFICIAL DESIGN FROM THE EMBLEM PAINTED ON THE ROCKET THAT BROUGHT ME TO EARTH!
THE COLORFUL CEREMONIES CONTINUE...
SUPERMAN, I CROWN YOU HONORARY KING OF KRYPTON-ON-EARTH!
THIS WHOLE PROGRAM IS A COVER-UP FOR HOW WE'RE GOING TO HOOD-WINK HIM LATER! HA, HA!
AFTER A PARADE TO THE OUTSKIRTS OF TOWN...
NOW YOU'LL HAVE THE HONOR OF PULLING THE SWITCH TO TURN ON THE LIGHTS OF OUR SPECIAL LIGHTHOUSE!
WHY, THIS SEEMS TO BE THE FOOT OF A GIANT STATUE!
4

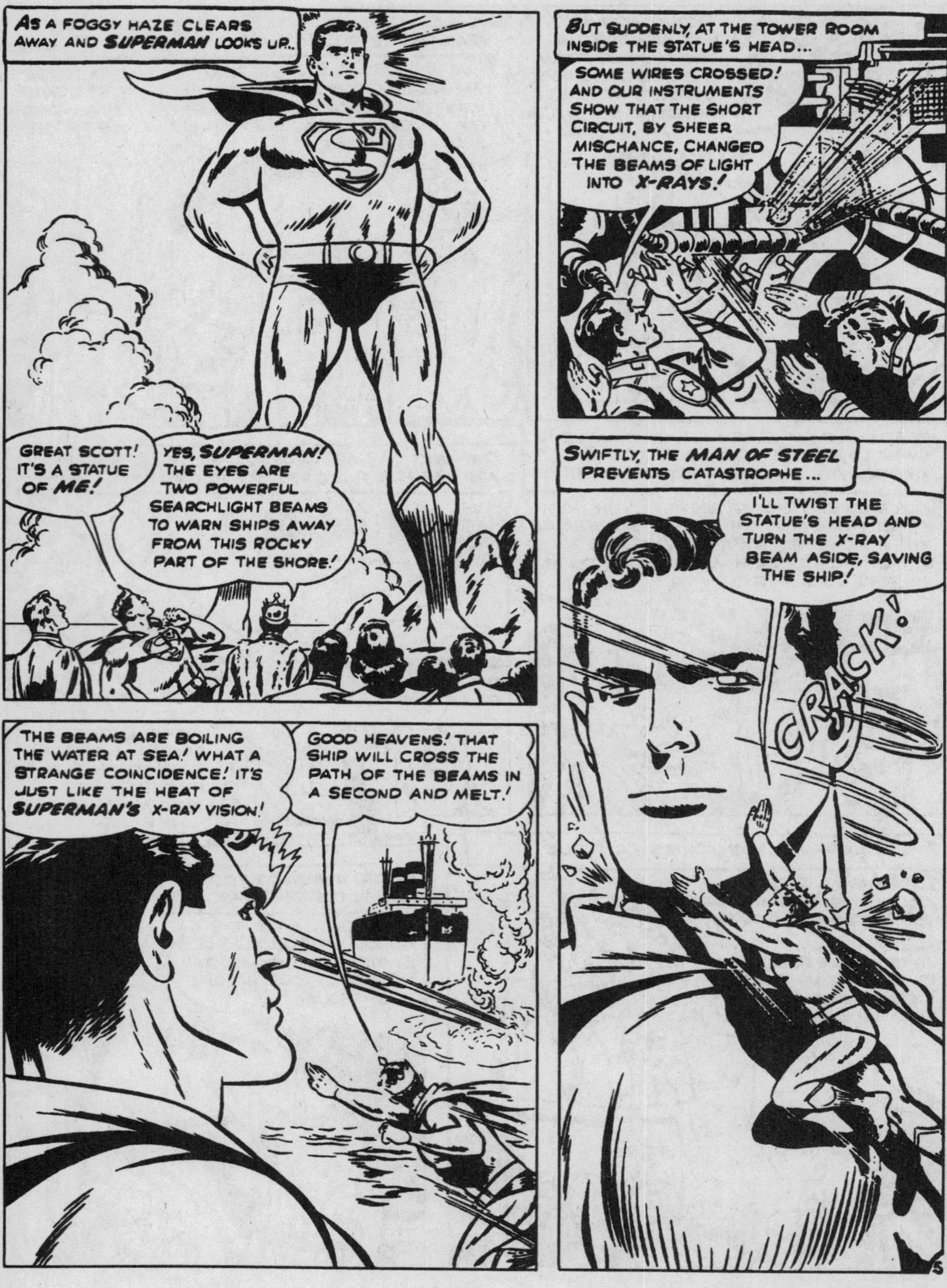
AS A FOGGY HAZE CLEARS AWAY AND SUPERMAN LOOKS UP..
GREAT SCOTT! IT'S A STATUE OF ME!
YES, SUPERMAN! THE EYES ARE TWO POWERFUL SEARCHLIGHT BEAMS TO WARN SHIPS AWAY FROM THIS ROCKY PART OF THE SHORE!
THE BEAMS ARE BOILING THE WATER AT SEA! WHAT A STRANGE COINCIDENCE! IT'S JUST LIKE THE HEAT OF SUPERMAN'S X-RAY VISION!
GOOD HEAVENS! THAT SHIP WILL CROSS THE PATH OF THE BEAMS IN A SECOND AND MELT!
BUT SUDDENLY, AT THE TOWER ROOM INSIDE THE STATUE'S HEAD...
SOME WIRES CROSSED! AND OUR INSTRUMENTS SHOW THAT THE SHORT CIRCUIT, BY SHEER MISCHANCE, CHANGED THE BEAMS OF LIGHT INTO X-RAYS!
SWIFTLY, THE MAN OF STEEL PREVENTS CATASTROPHE...
I'LL TWIST THE STATUE'S HEAD AND TURN THE X-RAY BEAM ASIDE, SAVING THE SHIP!
CRACK!
5

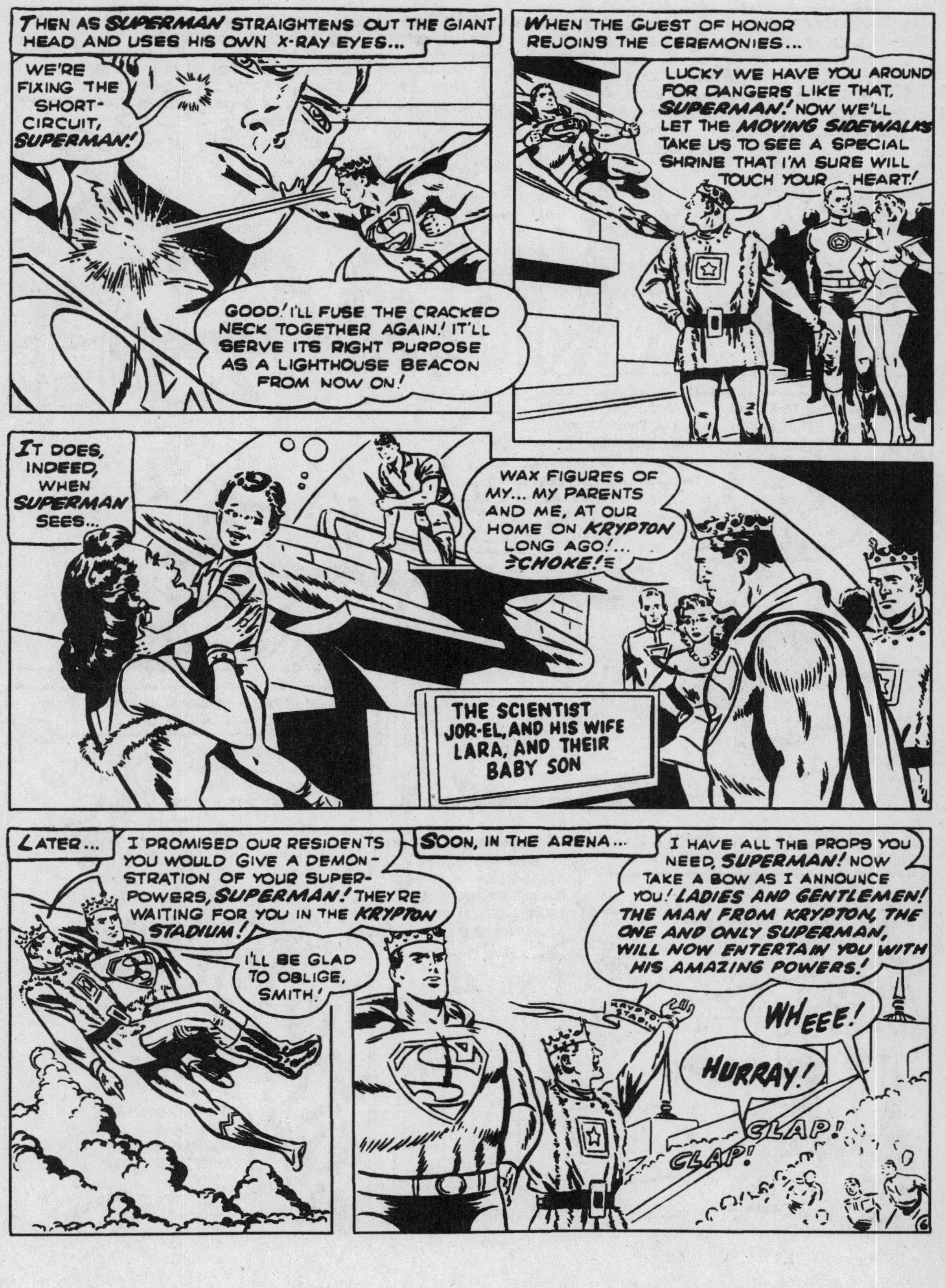
THEN AS SUPERMAN STRAIGHTENS OUT THE GIANT HEAD AND USES HIS OWN X-RAY EYES...
WE'RE FIXING THE SHORT-CIRCUIT, SUPERMAN!
GOOD! I'LL FUSE THE CRACKED NECK TOGETHER AGAIN! IT'LL SERVE ITS RIGHT PURPOSE AS A LIGHTHOUSE BEACON FROM NOW ON!
WHEN THE GUEST OF HONOR REJOINS THE CEREMONIES...
LUCKY WE HAVE YOU AROUND FOR DANGERS LIKE THAT, SUPERMAN! NOW WE'LL LET THE MOVING SIDEWALKS TAKE US TO SEE A SPECIAL SHRINE THAT I'M SURE WILL TOUCH YOUR HEART!
IT DOES, INDEED, WHEN SUPERMAN SEES...
WAX FIGURES OF MY... MY PARENTS AND ME, AT OUR HOME ON KRYPTON LONG AGO!... CHOKE!
THE SCIENTIST JOR-EL, AND HIS WIFE LARA, AND THEIR BABY SON
LATER...
I PROMISED OUR RESIDENTS YOU WOULD GIVE A DEMON-STRATION OF YOUR SUPER-POWERS, SUPERMAN! THEY'RE WAITING FOR YOU IN THE KRYPTON STADIUM!
I'LL BE GLAD TO OBLIGE, SMITH!
SOON, IN THE ARENA...
I HAVE ALL THE PROPS YOU NEED, SUPERMAN! NOW TAKE A BOW AS I ANNOUNCE YOU! LADIES AND GENTLEMEN! THE MAN FROM KRYPTON, THE ONE AND ONLY SUPERMAN, WILL NOW ENTERTAIN YOU WITH HIS AMAZING POWERS!
WHEEE!
HURRAY!
CLAP!
CLAP!
6

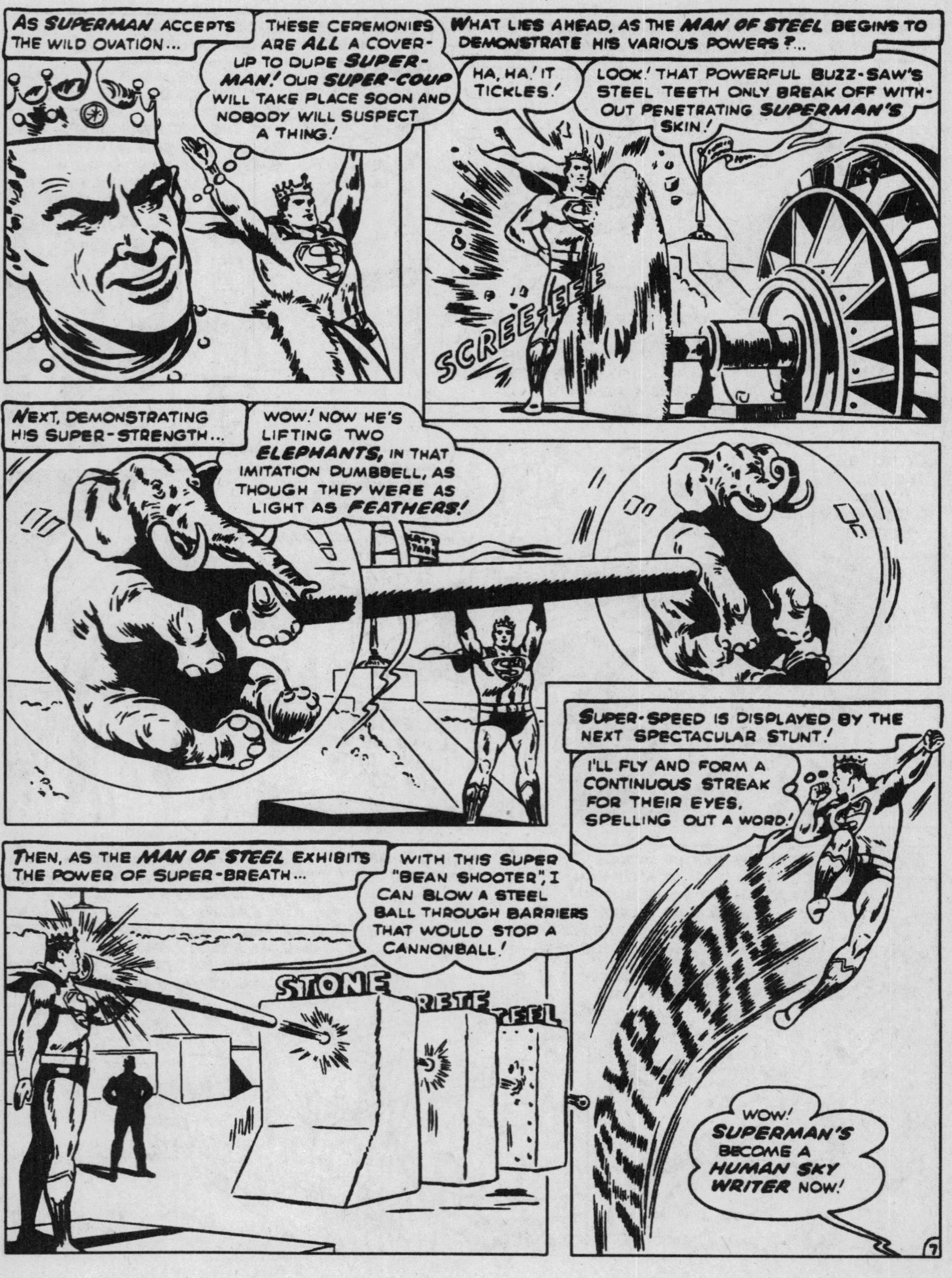
AS SUPERMAN ACCEPTS THE WILD OVATION...
THESE CEREMONIES ARE ALL A COVER-UP TO DUPE SUPERMAN! OUR SUPER-COUP WILL TAKE PLACE SOON AND NOBODY WILL SUSPECT A THING!
WHAT LIES AHEAD, AS THE MAN OF STEEL BEGINS TO DEMONSTRATE HIS VARIOUS POWERS?...
HA, HA! IT TICKLES!
LOOK! THAT POWERFUL BUZZ-SAW'S STEEL TEETH ONLY BREAK OFF WITHOUT PENETRATING SUPERMAN'S SKIN!
SCREE-EEE
NEXT, DEMONSTRATING HIS SUPER-STRENGTH...
WOW! NOW HE'S LIFTING TWO ELEPHANTS, IN THAT IMITATION DUMBBELL, AS THOUGH THEY WERE AS LIGHT AS FEATHERS!
SUPER-SPEED IS DISPLAYED BY THE NEXT SPECTACULAR STUNT!
I'LL FLY AND FORM A CONTINUOUS STREAK FOR THEIR EYES, SPELLING OUT A WORD!
THEN, AS THE MAN OF STEEL EXHIBITS THE POWER OF SUPER-BREATH...
WITH THIS SUPER "BEAN SHOOTER", I CAN BLOW A STEEL BALL THROUGH BARRIERS THAT WOULD STOP A CANNONBALL!
STONE
WOW! SUPERMAN'S BECOME A HUMAN SKY WRITER NOW!
7

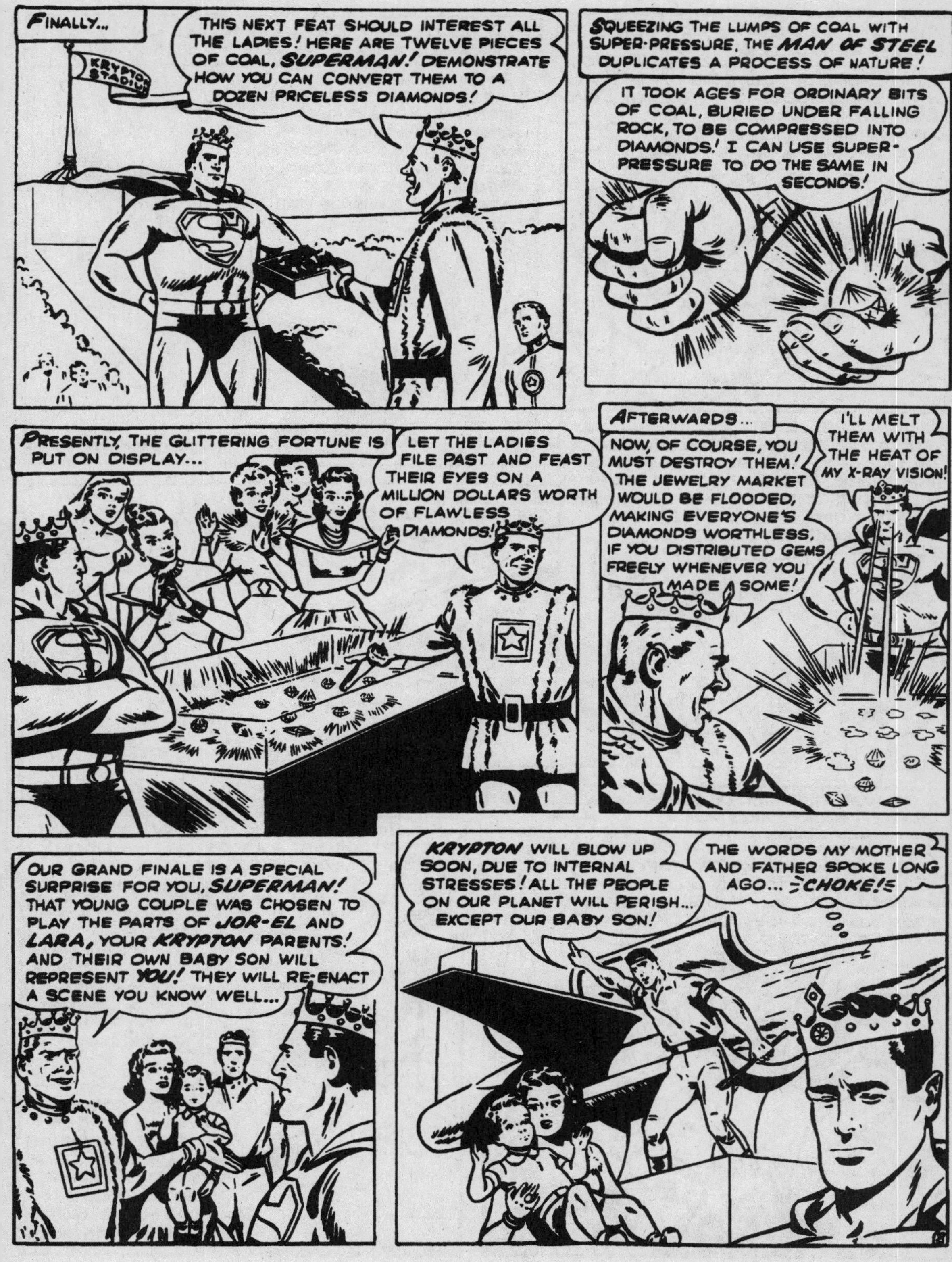
FINALLY...
THIS NEXT FEAT SHOULD INTEREST ALL THE LADIES! HERE ARE TWELVE PIECES OF COAL, SUPERMAN! DEMONSTRATE HOW YOU CAN CONVERT THEM TO A DOZEN PRICELESS DIAMONDS!
KRYPTON STADIUM
SQUEEZING THE LUMPS OF COAL WITH SUPER-PRESSURE, THE MAN OF STEEL DUPLICATES A PROCESS OF NATURE!
IT TOOK AGES FOR ORDINARY BITS OF COAL, BURIED UNDER FALLING ROCK, TO BE COMPRESSED INTO DIAMONDS! I CAN USE SUPER-PRESSURE TO DO THE SAME IN SECONDS!
PRESENTLY, THE GLITTERING FORTUNE IS PUT ON DISPLAY...
LET THE LADIES FILE PAST AND FEAST THEIR EYES ON A MILLION DOLLARS WORTH OF FLAWLESS DIAMONDS!
AFTERWARDS...
NOW, OF COURSE, YOU MUST DESTROY THEM! THE JEWELRY MARKET WOULD BE FLOODED, MAKING EVERYONE'S DIAMONDS WORTHLESS, IF YOU DISTRIBUTED GEMS FREELY WHENEVER YOU MADE SOME!
I'LL MELT THEM WITH THE HEAT OF MY X-RAY VISION!
OUR GRAND FINALE IS A SPECIAL SURPRISE FOR YOU, SUPERMAN! THAT YOUNG COUPLE WAS CHOSEN TO PLAY THE PARTS OF JOR-EL AND LARA, YOUR KRYPTON PARENTS! AND THEIR OWN BABY SON WILL REPRESENT YOU! THEY WILL RE-ENACT A SCENE YOU KNOW WELL...
KRYPTON WILL BLOW UP SOON, DUE TO INTERNAL STRESSES! ALL THE PEOPLE ON OUR PLANET WILL PERISH... EXCEPT OUR BABY SON!
THE WORDS MY MOTHER AND FATHER SPOKE LONG AGO... CHOKE!

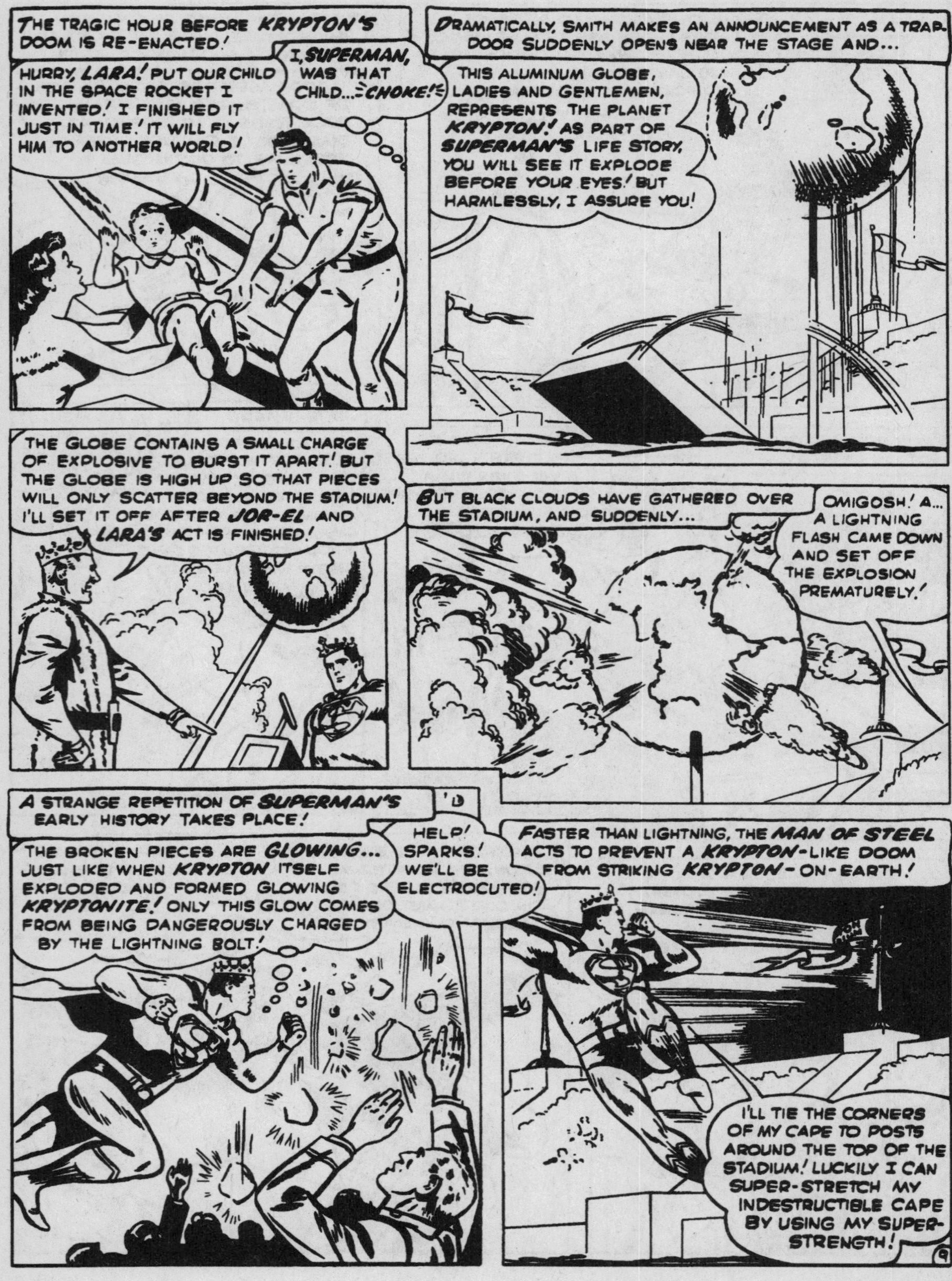
THE TRAGIC HOUR BEFORE KRYPTON'S DOOM IS RE-ENACTED!
HURRY, LARA! PUT OUR CHILD IN THE SPACE ROCKET I INVENTED! I FINISHED IT JUST IN TIME! IT WILL FLY HIM TO ANOTHER WORLD!
I, SUPERMAN, WAS THAT CHILD... CHOKE!
DRAMATICALLY, SMITH MAKES AN ANNOUNCEMENT AS A TRAP-DOOR SUDDENLY OPENS NEAR THE STAGE AND...
THIS ALUMINUM GLOBE, LADIES AND GENTLEMEN, REPRESENTS THE PLANET KRYPTON! AS PART OF SUPERMAN'S LIFE STORY, YOU WILL SEE IT EXPLODE BEFORE YOUR EYES! BUT HARMLESSLY, I ASSURE YOU!
THE GLOBE CONTAINS A SMALL CHARGE OF EXPLOSIVE TO BURST IT APART! BUT THE GLOBE IS HIGH UP SO THAT PIECES WILL ONLY SCATTER BEYOND THE STADIUM! I'LL SET IT OFF AFTER JOR-EL AND LARA'S ACT IS FINISHED!
BUT BLACK CLOUDS HAVE GATHERED OVER THE STADIUM, AND SUDDENLY...
OMIGOSH! A... A LIGHTNING FLASH CAME DOWN AND SET OFF THE EXPLOSION PREMATURELY!
A STRANGE REPETITION OF SUPERMAN'S EARLY HISTORY TAKES PLACE!
THE BROKEN PIECES ARE GLOWING... JUST LIKE WHEN KRYPTON ITSELF EXPLODED AND FORMED GLOWING KRYPTONITE! ONLY THIS GLOW COMES FROM BEING DANGEROUSLY CHARGED BY THE LIGHTNING BOLT!
HELP! SPARKS! WE'LL BE ELECTROCUTED!
FASTER THAN LIGHTNING, THE MAN OF STEEL ACTS TO PREVENT A KRYPTON-LIKE DOOM FROM STRIKING KRYPTON-ON-EARTH!
I'LL TIE THE CORNERS OF MY CAPE TO POSTS AROUND THE TOP OF THE STADIUM! LUCKILY I CAN SUPER-STRETCH MY INDESTRUCTIBLE CAPE BY USING MY SUPER-STRENGTH!
9

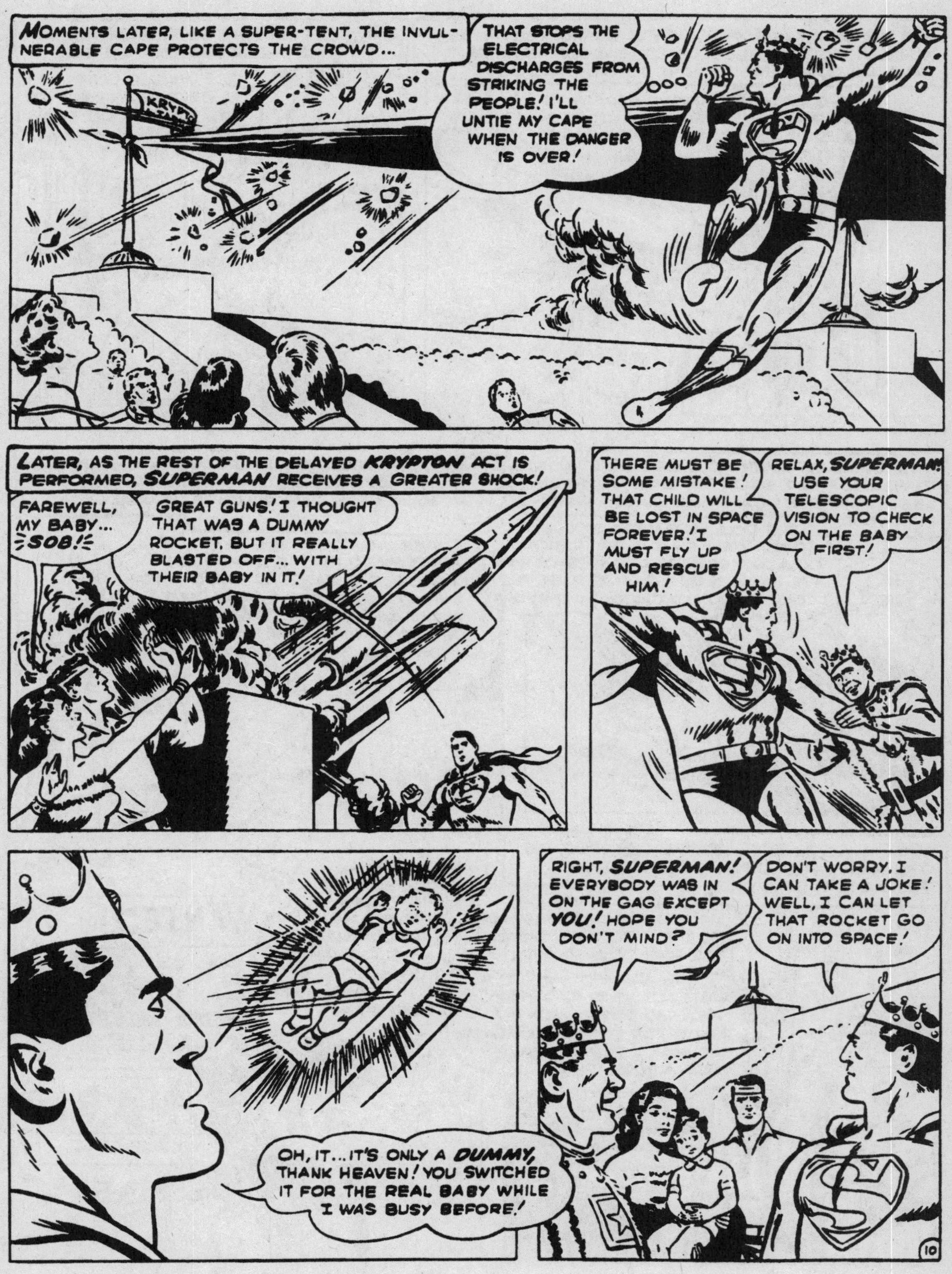
MOMENTS LATER, LIKE A SUPER-TENT, THE INVULNERABLE CAPE PROTECTS THE CROWD...
THAT STOPS THE ELECTRICAL DISCHARGES FROM STRIKING THE PEOPLE! I'LL UNTIE MY CAPE WHEN THE DANGER IS OVER!
LATER, AS THE REST OF THE DELAYED KRYPTON ACT IS PERFORMED, SUPERMAN RECEIVES A GREATER SHOCK!
FAREWELL, MY BABY... SOB!
GREAT GUNS! I THOUGHT THAT WAS A DUMMY ROCKET, BUT IT REALLY BLASTED OFF... WITH THEIR BABY IN IT!
THERE MUST BE SOME MISTAKE! THAT CHILD WILL BE LOST IN SPACE FOREVER! I MUST FLY UP AND RESCUE HIM!
RELAX, SUPERMAN! USE YOUR TELESCOPIC VISION TO CHECK ON THE BABY FIRST!
OH, IT...IT'S ONLY A DUMMY, THANK HEAVEN! YOU SWITCHED IT FOR THE REAL BABY WHILE I WAS BUSY BEFORE!
RIGHT, SUPERMAN! EVERYBODY WAS IN ON THE GAG EXCEPT YOU! HOPE YOU DON'T MIND?
DON'T WORRY, I CAN TAKE A JOKE! WELL, I CAN LET THAT ROCKET GO ON INTO SPACE!
10

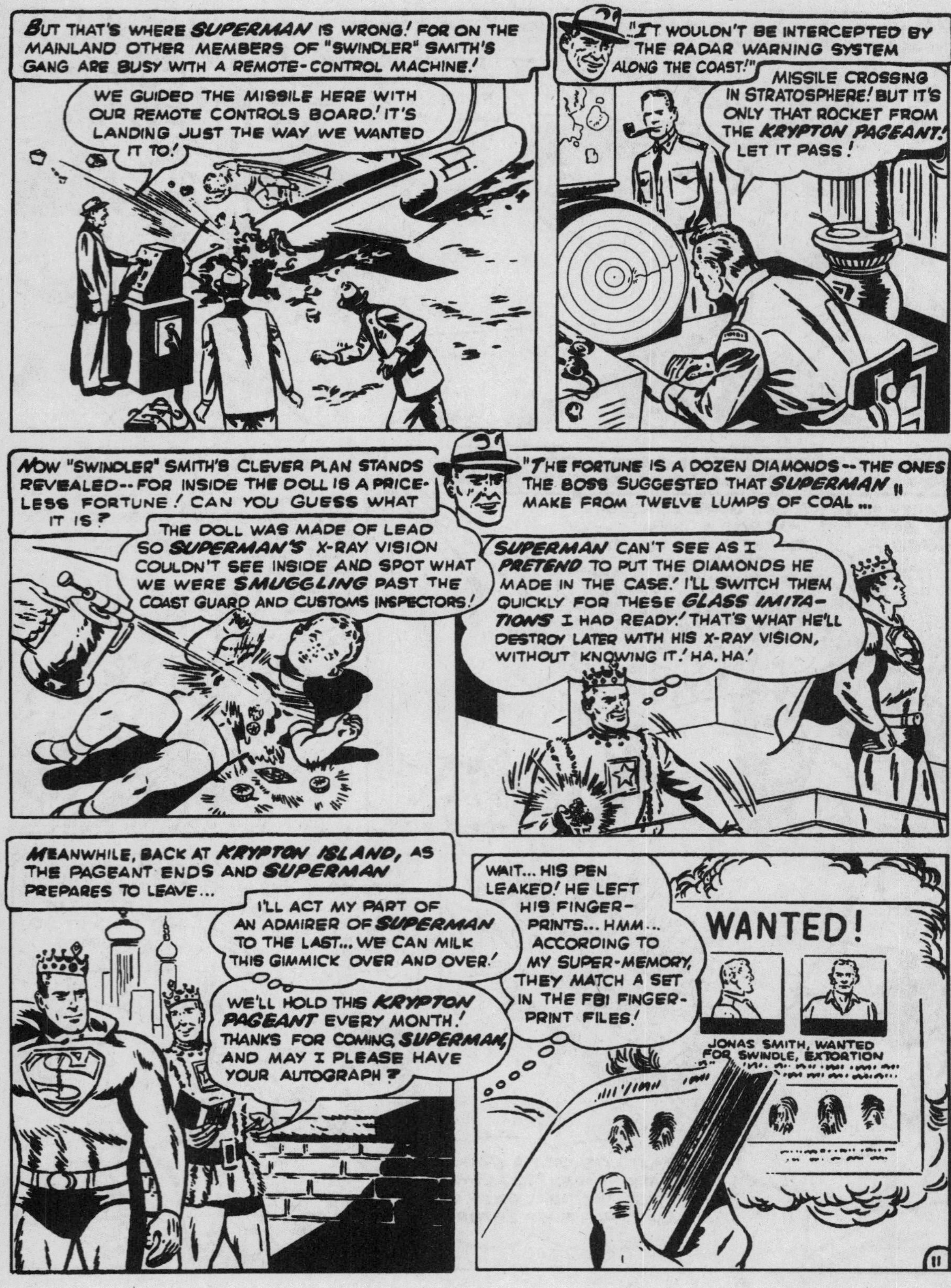
BUT THAT'S WHERE SUPERMAN IS WRONG! FOR ON THE MAINLAND OTHER MEMBERS OF "SWINDLER" SMITH'S GANG ARE BUSY WITH A REMOTE-CONTROL MACHINE!
WE GUIDED THE MISSILE HERE WITH OUR REMOTE CONTROLS BOARD! IT'S LANDING JUST THE WAY WE WANTED IT TO!
..."IT WOULDN'T BE INTERCEPTED BY THE RADAR WARNING SYSTEM ALONG THE COAST!"
MISSILE CROSSING IN STRATOSPHERE! BUT IT'S ONLY THAT ROCKET FROM THE KRYPTON PAGEANT! LET IT PASS!
NOW "SWINDLER" SMITH'S CLEVER PLAN STANDS REVEALED--FOR INSIDE THE DOLL IS A PRICELESS FORTUNE! CAN YOU GUESS WHAT IT IS?
THE DOLL WAS MADE OF LEAD SO SUPERMAN'S X-RAY VISION COULDN'T SEE INSIDE AND SPOT WHAT WE WERE SMUGGLING PAST THE COAST GUARD AND CUSTOMS INSPECTORS!
"THE FORTUNE IS A DOZEN DIAMONDS--THE ONES THE BOSS SUGGESTED THAT SUPERMAN MAKE FROM TWELVE LUMPS OF COAL..."
SUPERMAN CAN'T SEE AS I PRETEND TO PUT THE DIAMONDS HE MADE IN THE CASE! I'LL SWITCH THEM QUICKLY FOR THESE GLASS IMITATIONS I HAD READY! THAT'S WHAT HE'LL DESTROY LATER WITH HIS X-RAY VISION, WITHOUT KNOWING IT! HA, HA!
MEANWHILE, BACK AT KRYPTON ISLAND, AS THE PAGEANT ENDS AND SUPERMAN PREPARES TO LEAVE...
I'LL ACT MY PART OF AN ADMIRER OF SUPERMAN TO THE LAST... WE CAN MILK THIS GIMMICK OVER AND OVER!
WE'LL HOLD THIS KRYPTON PAGEANT EVERY MONTH! THANKS FOR COMING, SUPERMAN, AND MAY I PLEASE HAVE YOUR AUTOGRAPH?
WAIT... HIS PEN LEAKED! HE LEFT HIS FINGERPRINTS... HMM... ACCORDING TO MY SUPER-MEMORY, THEY MATCH A SET IN THE FBI FINGERPRINT FILES!
WANTED!
JONAS SMITH, WANTED FOR SWINDLE, EXTORTION
11

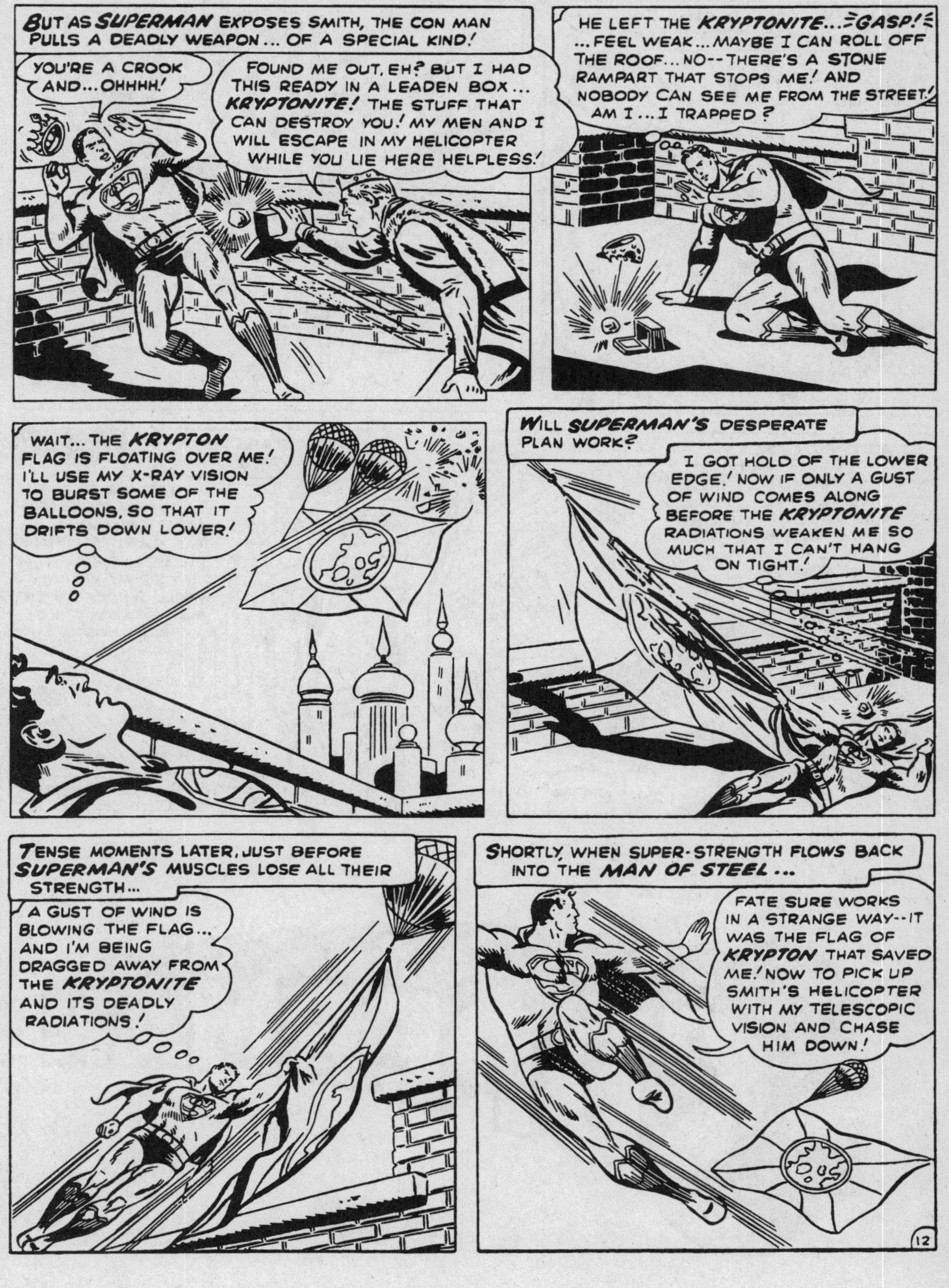
BUT AS SUPERMAN EXPOSES SMITH, THE CON MAN PULLS A DEADLY WEAPON ... OF A SPECIAL KIND!
YOU'RE A CROOK AND... OHHHH!
FOUND ME OUT, EH? BUT I HAD THIS READY IN A LEADEN BOX ... KRYPTONITE! THE STUFF THAT CAN DESTROY YOU! MY MEN AND I WILL ESCAPE IN MY HELICOPTER WHILE YOU LIE HERE HELPLESS!
HE LEFT THE KRYPTONITE... GASP! ... FEEL WEAK ... MAYBE I CAN ROLL OFF THE ROOF... NO--THERE'S A STONE RAMPART THAT STOPS ME! AND NOBODY CAN SEE ME FROM THE STREET! AM I ... I TRAPPED?
WAIT... THE KRYPTON FLAG IS FLOATING OVER ME! I'LL USE MY X-RAY VISION TO BURST SOME OF THE BALLOONS, SO THAT IT DRIFTS DOWN LOWER!
WILL SUPERMAN'S DESPERATE PLAN WORK?
I GOT HOLD OF THE LOWER EDGE! NOW IF ONLY A GUST OF WIND COMES ALONG BEFORE THE KRYPTONITE RADIATIONS WEAKEN ME SO MUCH THAT I CAN'T HANG ON TIGHT!
TENSE MOMENTS LATER, JUST BEFORE SUPERMAN'S MUSCLES LOSE ALL THEIR STRENGTH...
A GUST OF WIND IS BLOWING THE FLAG... AND I'M BEING DRAGGED AWAY FROM THE KRYPTONITE AND ITS DEADLY RADIATIONS!
SHORTLY, WHEN SUPER-STRENGTH FLOWS BACK INTO THE MAN OF STEEL ...
FATE SURE WORKS IN A STRANGE WAY--IT WAS THE FLAG OF KRYPTON THAT SAVED ME! NOW TO PICK UP SMITH'S HELICOPTER WITH MY TELESCOPIC VISION AND CHASE HIM DOWN!
12

ELSEWHERE, AS "SWINDLER" SMITH MEETS HIS HENCHMEN ON THE MAINLAND...
WE'LL SORT THE DIAMONDS HERE AND... YIPES! THEY'RE MELTING!
I'M ONLY FINISHING THE JOB I MEANT TO DO BEFORE!
YOUR RACKET "EXPLODED"... LIKE KRYPTON DID! HAVE A ROCKET RIDE TO THE NEXT "WORLD" YOU'LL LIVE IN... JAIL!
AT KRYPTON ISLAND, THE NEXT DAY...
SURE, SUPERMAN! I'LL CARRY ON THE DEVELOPMENT OF KRYPTON ISLAND AS A NEW COMMUNITY OF HOMES!
Metropolis REAL ESTATE CO.
GOOD! THEN THOSE WHO BOUGHT HOMES HERE ALREADY WON'T BE CHEATED!
13
LATER, AS CLARK RETURNS TO THE DAILY PLANET...
WHENEVER I'M FREE OF DUTY IN METROPOLIS, I CAN SPEND TIME IN KRYPTONOPOLIS! IT'LL BE LIKE RE-VISITING MY NATIVE WORLD WHERE I SPENT MANY HAPPY CHILDHOOD HOURS!
DAILY PLANET
NEW COMMUNITY ADOPTS OFFICIAL NAME OF KRYPTONOPOLIS
THE END

SUPERMAN

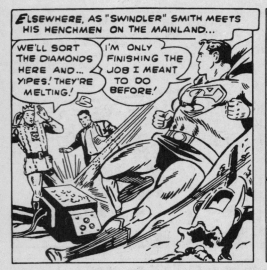

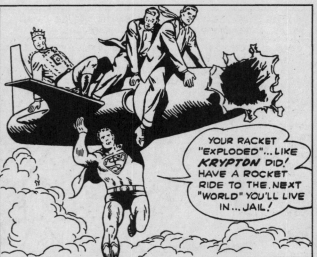

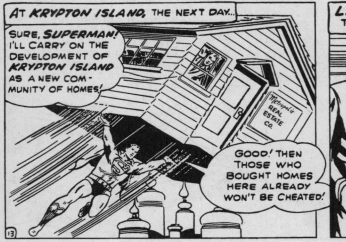

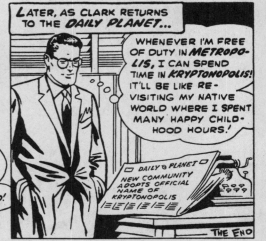

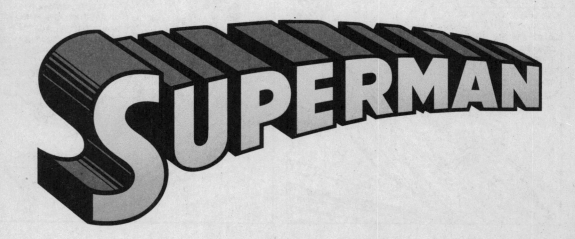

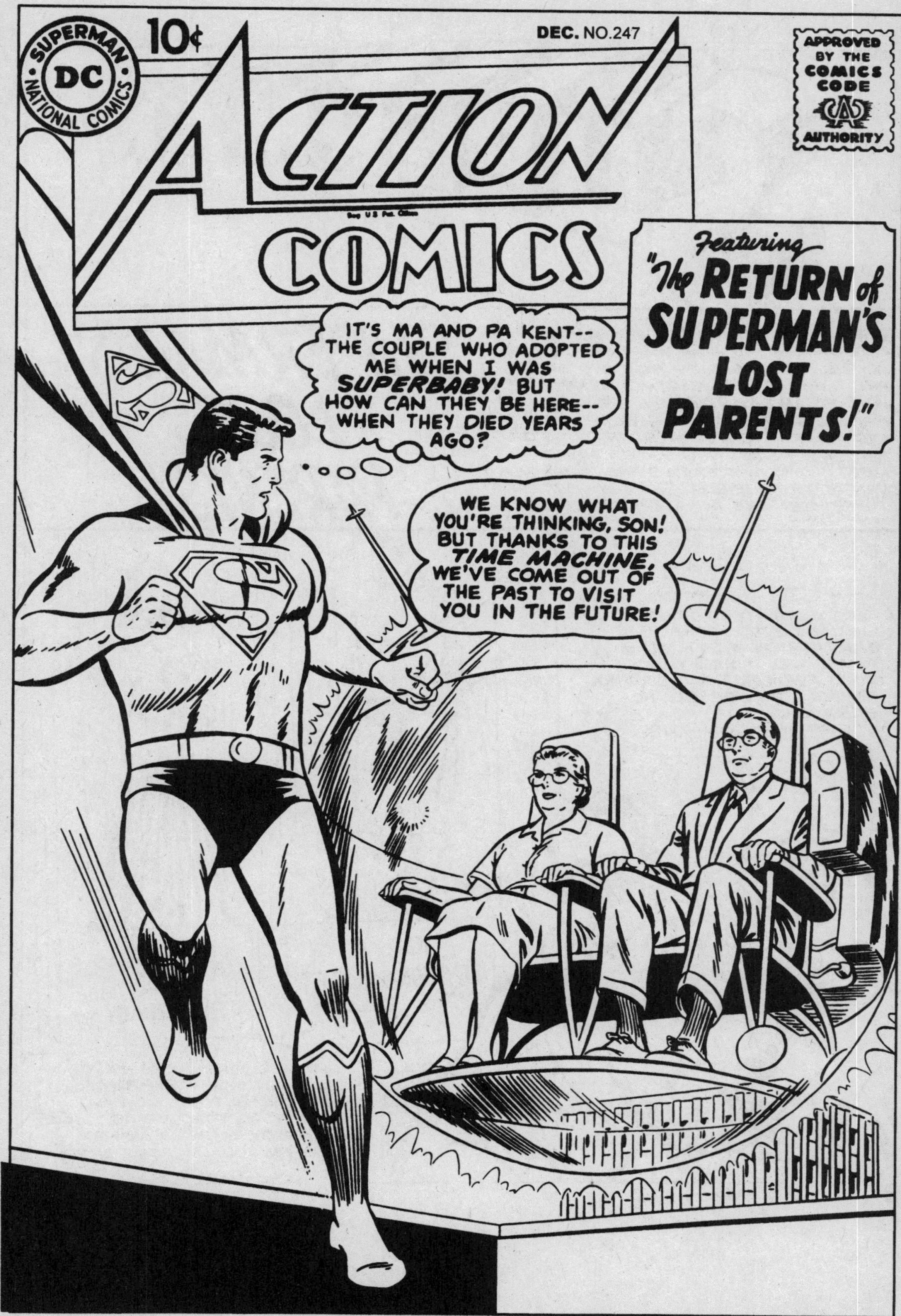
10¢
SUPERMAN DC NATIONAL COMICS
DEC. NO.247
ACTION COMICS
APPROVED BY THE COMICS CODE AUTHORITY
Featuring "The RETURN of SUPERMAN'S LOST PARENTS!"
IT'S MA AND PA KENT-- THE COUPLE WHO ADOPTED ME WHEN I WAS SUPERBABY! BUT HOW CAN THEY BE HERE-- WHEN THEY DIED YEARS AGO?
WE KNOW WHAT YOU'RE THINKING, SON! BUT THANKS TO THIS TIME MACHINE, WE'VE COME OUT OF THE PAST TO VISIT YOU IN THE FUTURE!

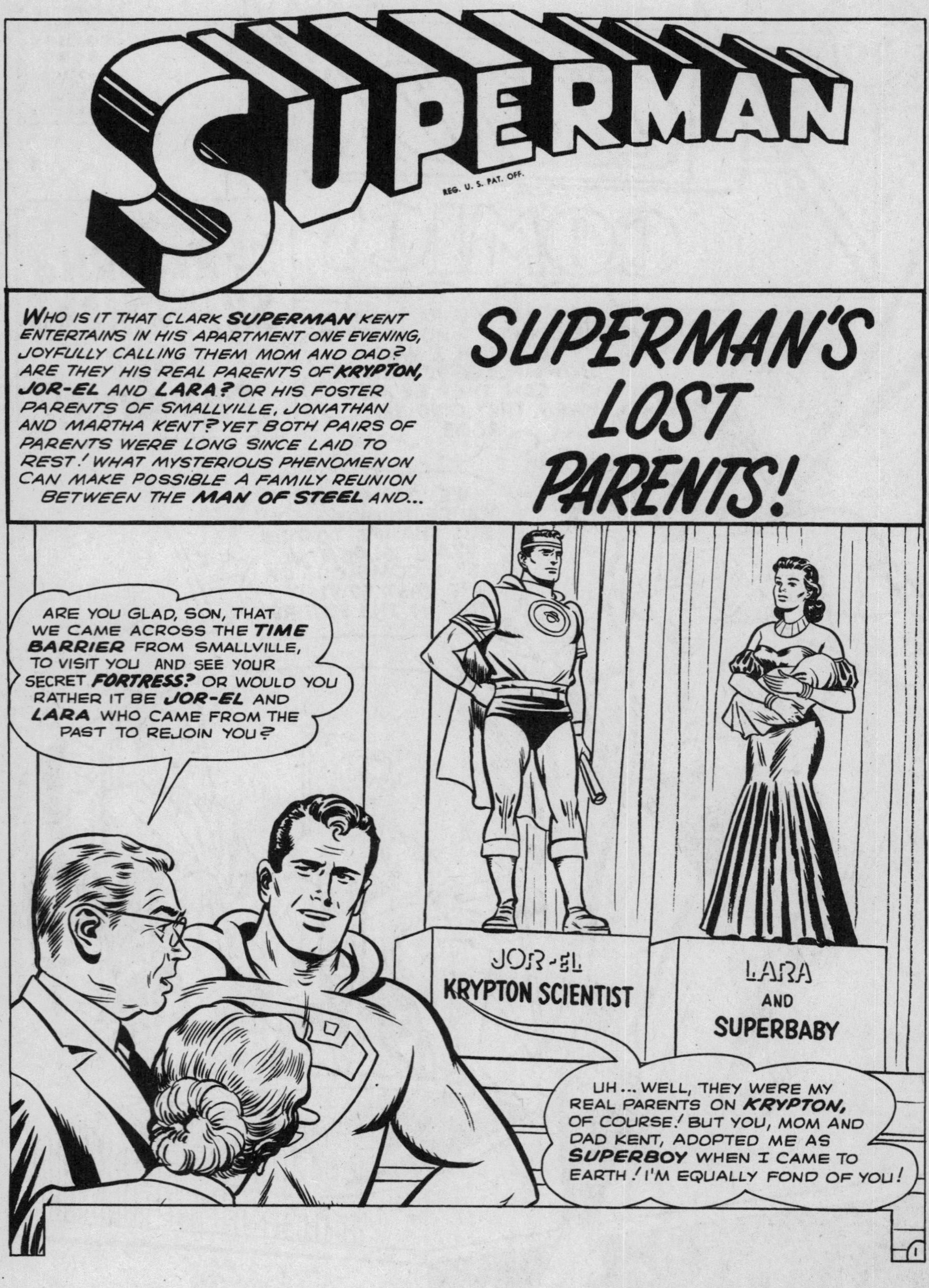
SUPERMAN
REG. U. S. PAT. OFF.
WHO IS IT THAT CLARK SUPERMAN KENT ENTERTAINS IN HIS APARTMENT ONE EVENING, JOYFULLY CALLING THEM MOM AND DAD? ARE THEY HIS REAL PARENTS OF KRYPTON, JOR-EL AND LARA? OR HIS FOSTER PARENTS OF SMALLVILLE, JONATHAN AND MARTHA KENT? YET BOTH PAIRS OF PARENTS WERE LONG SINCE LAID TO REST! WHAT MYSTERIOUS PHENOMENON CAN MAKE POSSIBLE A FAMILY REUNION BETWEEN THE MAN OF STEEL AND...
SUPERMAN'S LOST PARENTS!
ARE YOU GLAD, SON, THAT WE CAME ACROSS THE TIME BARRIER FROM SMALLVILLE, TO VISIT YOU AND SEE YOUR SECRET FORTRESS? OR WOULD YOU RATHER IT BE JOR-EL AND LARA WHO CAME FROM THE PAST TO REJOIN YOU?
JOR-EL KRYPTON SCIENTIST
LARA AND SUPERBABY
UH... WELL, THEY WERE MY REAL PARENTS ON KRYPTON, OF COURSE! BUT YOU, MOM AND DAD KENT, ADOPTED ME AS SUPERBOY WHEN I CAME TO EARTH! I'M EQUALLY FOND OF YOU!
1

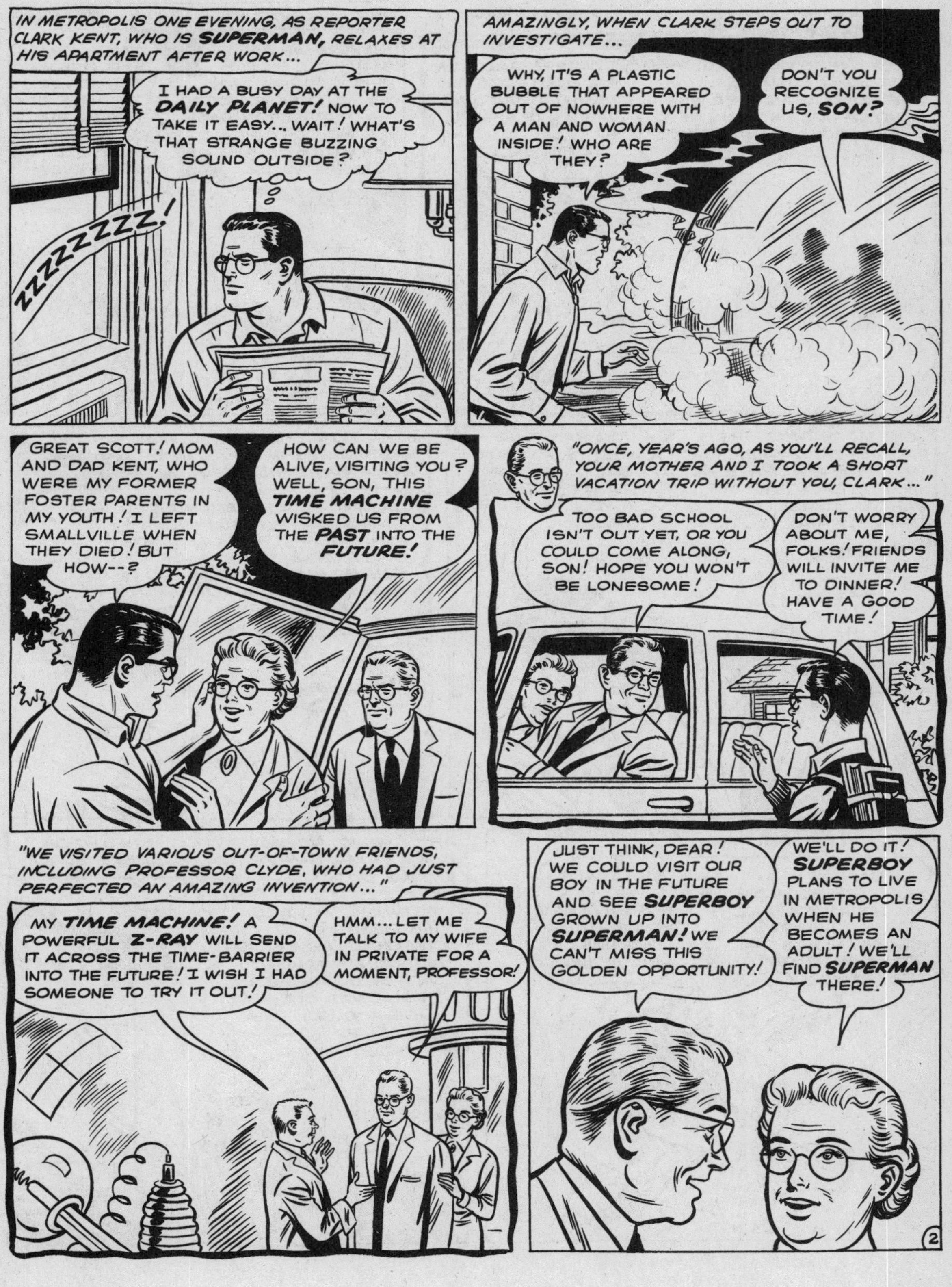
IN METROPOLIS ONE EVENING, AS REPORTER CLARK KENT, WHO IS SUPERMAN, RELAXES AT HIS APARTMENT AFTER WORK...
I HAD A BUSY DAY AT THE DAILY PLANET! NOW TO TAKE IT EASY... WAIT! WHAT'S THAT STRANGE BUZZING SOUND OUTSIDE?
ZZZZZZZZZ!
AMAZINGLY, WHEN CLARK STEPS OUT TO INVESTIGATE...
WHY, IT'S A PLASTIC BUBBLE THAT APPEARED OUT OF NOWHERE WITH A MAN AND WOMAN INSIDE! WHO ARE THEY?
DON'T YOU RECOGNIZE US, SON?
GREAT SCOTT! MOM AND DAD KENT, WHO WERE MY FORMER FOSTER PARENTS IN MY YOUTH! I LEFT SMALLVILLE WHEN THEY DIED! BUT HOW--?
HOW CAN WE BE ALIVE, VISITING YOU? WELL, SON, THIS TIME MACHINE WISKED US FROM THE PAST INTO THE FUTURE!
"ONCE, YEAR'S AGO, AS YOU'LL RECALL, YOUR MOTHER AND I TOOK A SHORT VACATION TRIP WITHOUT YOU, CLARK..."
TOO BAD SCHOOL ISN'T OUT YET, OR YOU COULD COME ALONG, SON! HOPE YOU WON'T BE LONESOME!
DON'T WORRY ABOUT ME, FOLKS! FRIENDS WILL INVITE ME TO DINNER! HAVE A GOOD TIME!
"WE VISITED VARIOUS OUT-OF-TOWN FRIENDS, INCLUDING PROFESSOR CLYDE, WHO HAD JUST PERFECTED AN AMAZING INVENTION..."
MY TIME MACHINE! A POWERFUL Z-RAY WILL SEND IT ACROSS THE TIME-BARRIER INTO THE FUTURE! I WISH I HAD SOMEONE TO TRY IT OUT!
HMM... LET ME TALK TO MY WIFE IN PRIVATE FOR A MOMENT, PROFESSOR!
JUST THINK, DEAR! WE COULD VISIT OUR BOY IN THE FUTURE AND SEE SUPERBOY GROWN UP INTO SUPERMAN! WE CAN'T MISS THIS GOLDEN OPPORTUNITY!
WE'LL DO IT! SUPERBOY PLANS TO LIVE IN METROPOLIS WHEN HE BECOMES AN ADULT! WE'LL FIND SUPERMAN THERE!
2

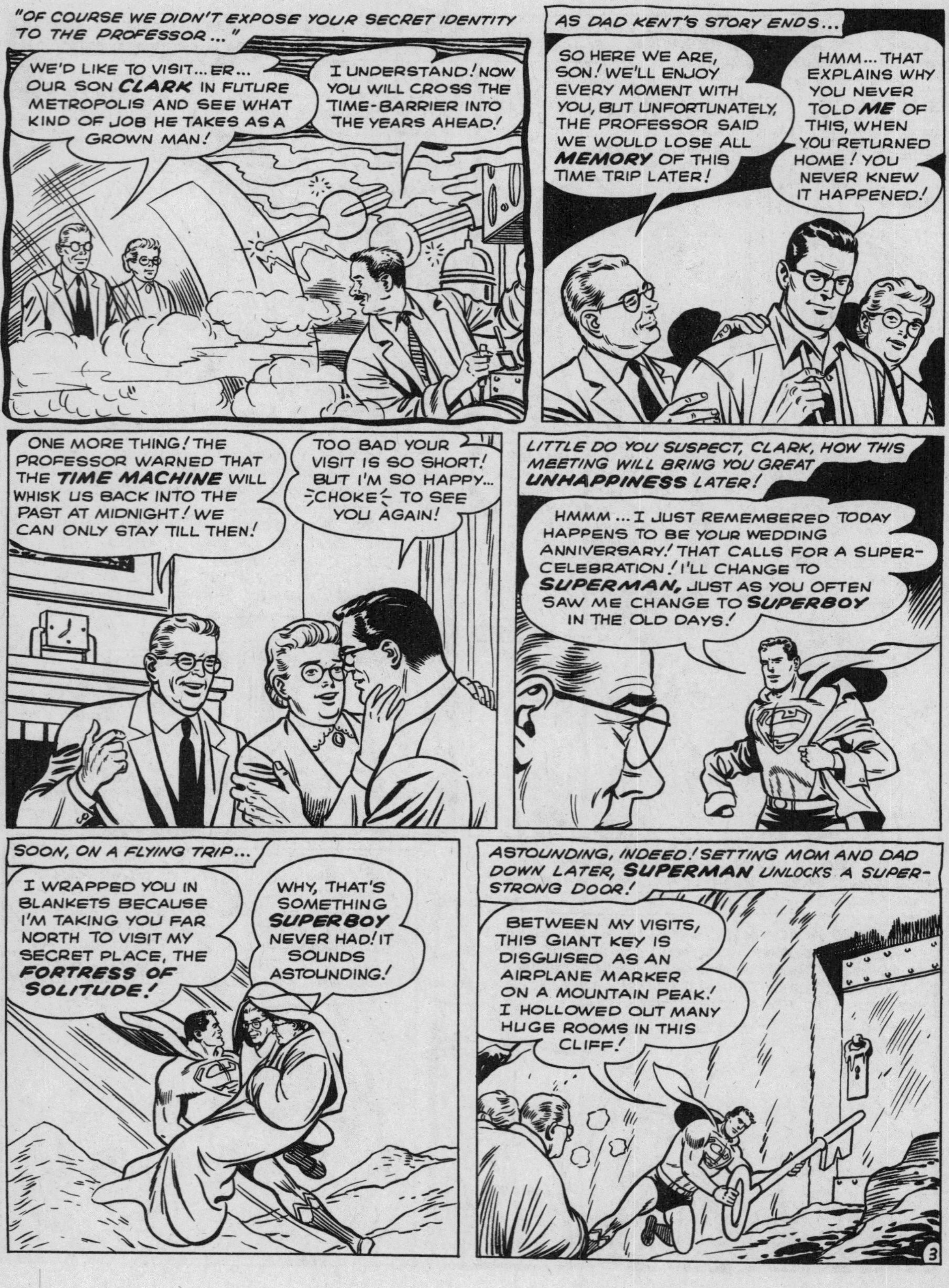
"OF COURSE WE DIDN'T EXPOSE YOUR SECRET IDENTITY TO THE PROFESSOR ..."
WE'D LIKE TO VISIT... ER... OUR SON CLARK IN FUTURE METROPOLIS AND SEE WHAT KIND OF JOB HE TAKES AS A GROWN MAN!
I UNDERSTAND! NOW YOU WILL CROSS THE TIME-BARRIER INTO THE YEARS AHEAD!
AS DAD KENT'S STORY ENDS...
SO HERE WE ARE, SON! WE'LL ENJOY EVERY MOMENT WITH YOU, BUT UNFORTUNATELY, THE PROFESSOR SAID WE WOULD LOSE ALL MEMORY OF THIS TIME TRIP LATER!
HMM... THAT EXPLAINS WHY YOU NEVER TOLD ME OF THIS, WHEN YOU RETURNED HOME! YOU NEVER KNEW IT HAPPENED!
ONE MORE THING! THE PROFESSOR WARNED THAT THE TIME MACHINE WILL WHISK US BACK INTO THE PAST AT MIDNIGHT! WE CAN ONLY STAY TILL THEN!
TOO BAD YOUR VISIT IS SO SHORT! BUT I'M SO HAPPY... CHOKE TO SEE YOU AGAIN!
LITTLE DO YOU SUSPECT, CLARK, HOW THIS MEETING WILL BRING YOU GREAT UNHAPPINESS LATER!
HMMM ... I JUST REMEMBERED TODAY HAPPENS TO BE YOUR WEDDING ANNIVERSARY! THAT CALLS FOR A SUPER-CELEBRATION! I'LL CHANGE TO SUPERMAN, JUST AS YOU OFTEN SAW ME CHANGE TO SUPERBOY IN THE OLD DAYS!
SOON, ON A FLYING TRIP...
I WRAPPED YOU IN BLANKETS BECAUSE I'M TAKING YOU FAR NORTH TO VISIT MY SECRET PLACE, THE FORTRESS OF SOLITUDE!
WHY, THAT'S SOMETHING SUPERBOY NEVER HAD! IT SOUNDS ASTOUNDING!
ASTOUNDING, INDEED! SETTING MOM AND DAD DOWN LATER, SUPERMAN UNLOCKS A SUPER-STRONG DOOR!
BETWEEN MY VISITS, THIS GIANT KEY IS DISGUISED AS AN AIRPLANE MARKER ON A MOUNTAIN PEAK! I HOLLOWED OUT MANY HUGE ROOMS IN THIS CLIFF!
3

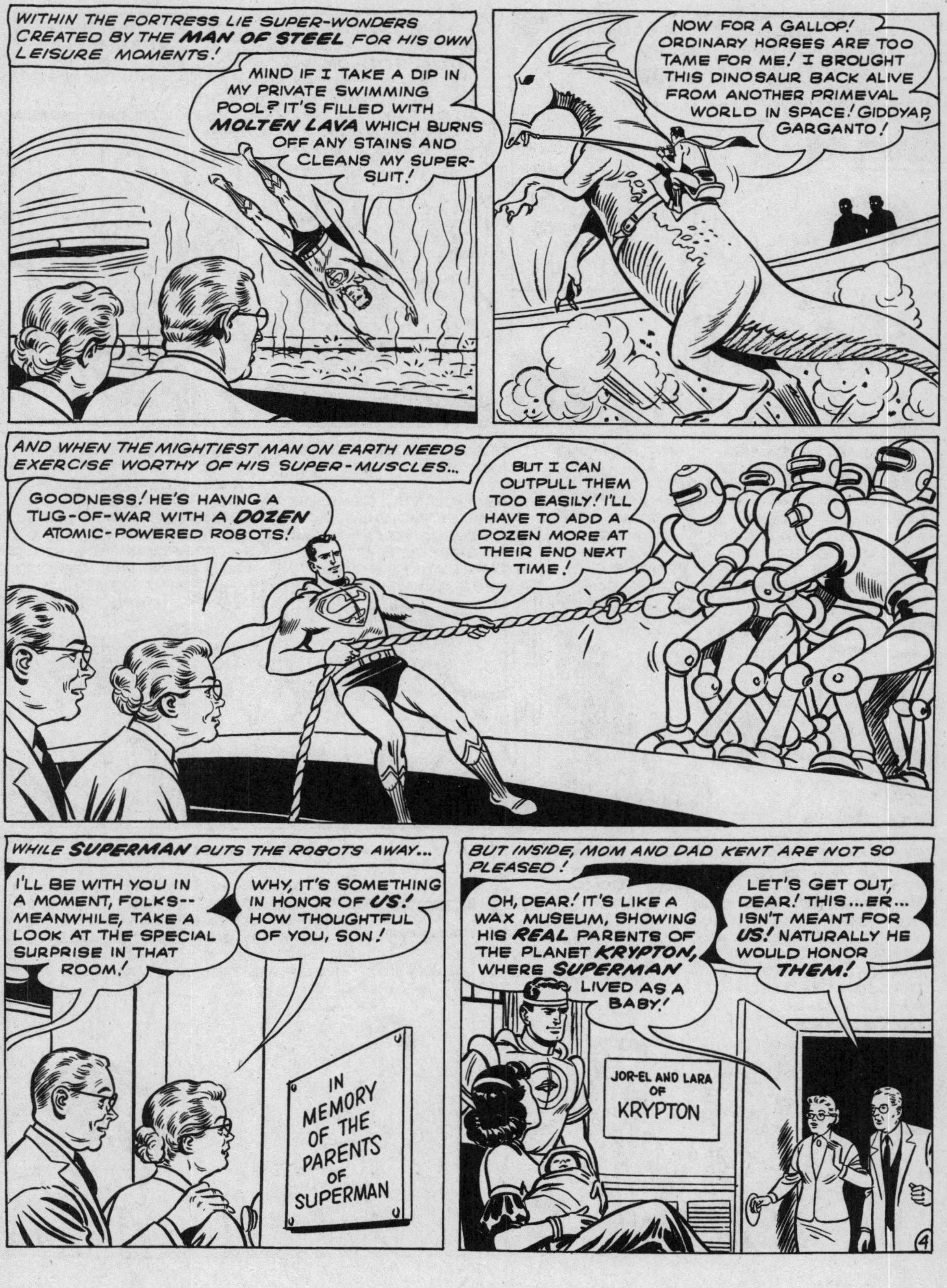
WITHIN THE FORTRESS LIE SUPER-WONDERS CREATED BY THE MAN OF STEEL FOR HIS OWN LEISURE MOMENTS!
MIND IF I TAKE A DIP IN MY PRIVATE SWIMMING POOL? IT'S FILLED WITH MOLTEN LAVA WHICH BURNS OFF ANY STAINS AND CLEANS MY SUPER-SUIT!
NOW FOR A GALLOP! ORDINARY HORSES ARE TOO TAME FOR ME! I BROUGHT THIS DINOSAUR BACK ALIVE FROM ANOTHER PRIMEVAL WORLD IN SPACE! GIDDYAP, GARGANTO!
AND WHEN THE MIGHTIEST MAN ON EARTH NEEDS EXERCISE WORTHY OF HIS SUPER-MUSCLES...
GOODNESS! HE'S HAVING A TUG-OF-WAR WITH A DOZEN ATOMIC-POWERED ROBOTS!
BUT I CAN OUTPULL THEM TOO EASILY! I'LL HAVE TO ADD A DOZEN MORE AT THEIR END NEXT TIME!
WHILE SUPERMAN PUTS THE ROBOTS AWAY...
I'LL BE WITH YOU IN A MOMENT, FOLKS-- MEANWHILE, TAKE A LOOK AT THE SPECIAL SURPRISE IN THAT ROOM!
WHY, IT'S SOMETHING IN HONOR OF US! HOW THOUGHTFUL OF YOU, SON!
IN MEMORY OF THE PARENTS OF SUPERMAN
BUT INSIDE, MOM AND DAD KENT ARE NOT SO PLEASED!
OH, DEAR! IT'S LIKE A WAX MUSEUM, SHOWING HIS REAL PARENTS OF THE PLANET KRYPTON, WHERE SUPERMAN LIVED AS A BABY!
LET'S GET OUT, DEAR! THIS...ER... ISN'T MEANT FOR US! NATURALLY HE WOULD HONOR THEM!
JOR-EL AND LARA OF KRYPTON
4

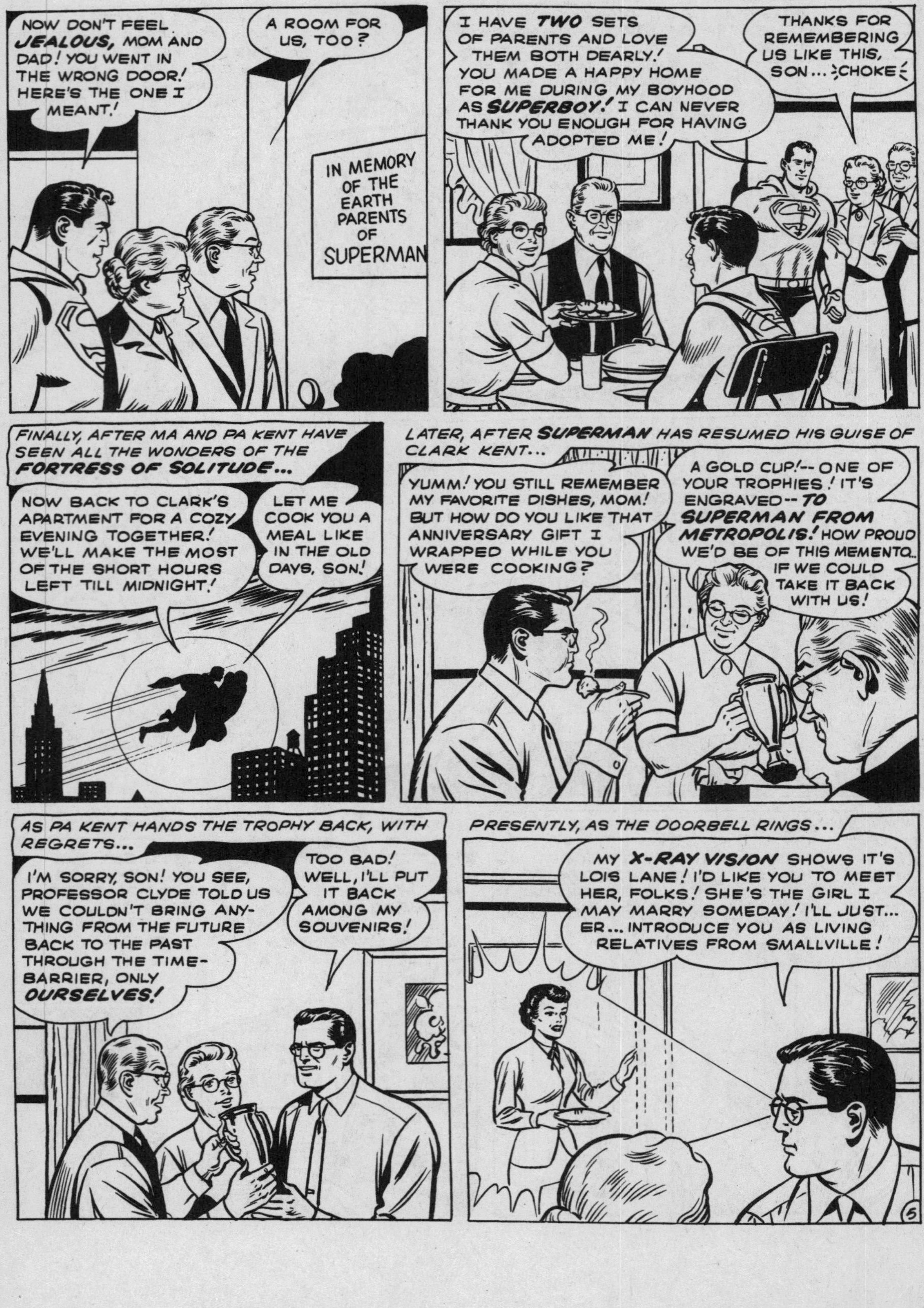
NOW DON'T FEEL JEALOUS, MOM AND DAD! YOU WENT IN THE WRONG DOOR! HERE'S THE ONE I MEANT!
A ROOM FOR US, TOO?
IN MEMORY OF THE EARTH PARENTS OF SUPERMAN
I HAVE TWO SETS OF PARENTS AND LOVE THEM BOTH DEARLY! YOU MADE A HAPPY HOME FOR ME DURING MY BOYHOOD AS SUPERBOY! I CAN NEVER THANK YOU ENOUGH FOR HAVING ADOPTED ME!
THANKS FOR REMEMBERING US LIKE THIS, SON... CHOKE
FINALLY, AFTER MA AND PA KENT HAVE SEEN ALL THE WONDERS OF THE FORTRESS OF SOLITUDE...
NOW BACK TO CLARK'S APARTMENT FOR A COZY EVENING TOGETHER! WE'LL MAKE THE MOST OF THE SHORT HOURS LEFT TILL MIDNIGHT!
LET ME COOK YOU A MEAL LIKE IN THE OLD DAYS, SON!
LATER, AFTER SUPERMAN HAS RESUMED HIS GUISE OF CLARK KENT...
YUMM! YOU STILL REMEMBER MY FAVORITE DISHES, MOM! BUT HOW DO YOU LIKE THAT ANNIVERSARY GIFT I WRAPPED WHILE YOU WERE COOKING?
A GOLD CUP!-- ONE OF YOUR TROPHIES! IT'S ENGRAVED-- TO SUPERMAN FROM METROPOLIS! HOW PROUD WE'D BE OF THIS MEMENTO... IF WE COULD TAKE IT BACK WITH US!
AS PA KENT HANDS THE TROPHY BACK, WITH REGRETS...
I'M SORRY, SON! YOU SEE, PROFESSOR CLYDE TOLD US WE COULDN'T BRING ANYTHING FROM THE FUTURE BACK TO THE PAST THROUGH THE TIME-BARRIER, ONLY OURSELVES!
TOO BAD! WELL, I'LL PUT IT BACK AMONG MY SOUVENIRS!
PRESENTLY, AS THE DOORBELL RINGS...
MY X-RAY VISION SHOWS IT'S LOIS LANE! I'D LIKE YOU TO MEET HER, FOLKS! SHE'S THE GIRL I MAY MARRY SOMEDAY! I'LL JUST... ER... INTRODUCE YOU AS LIVING RELATIVES FROM SMALLVILLE!
5

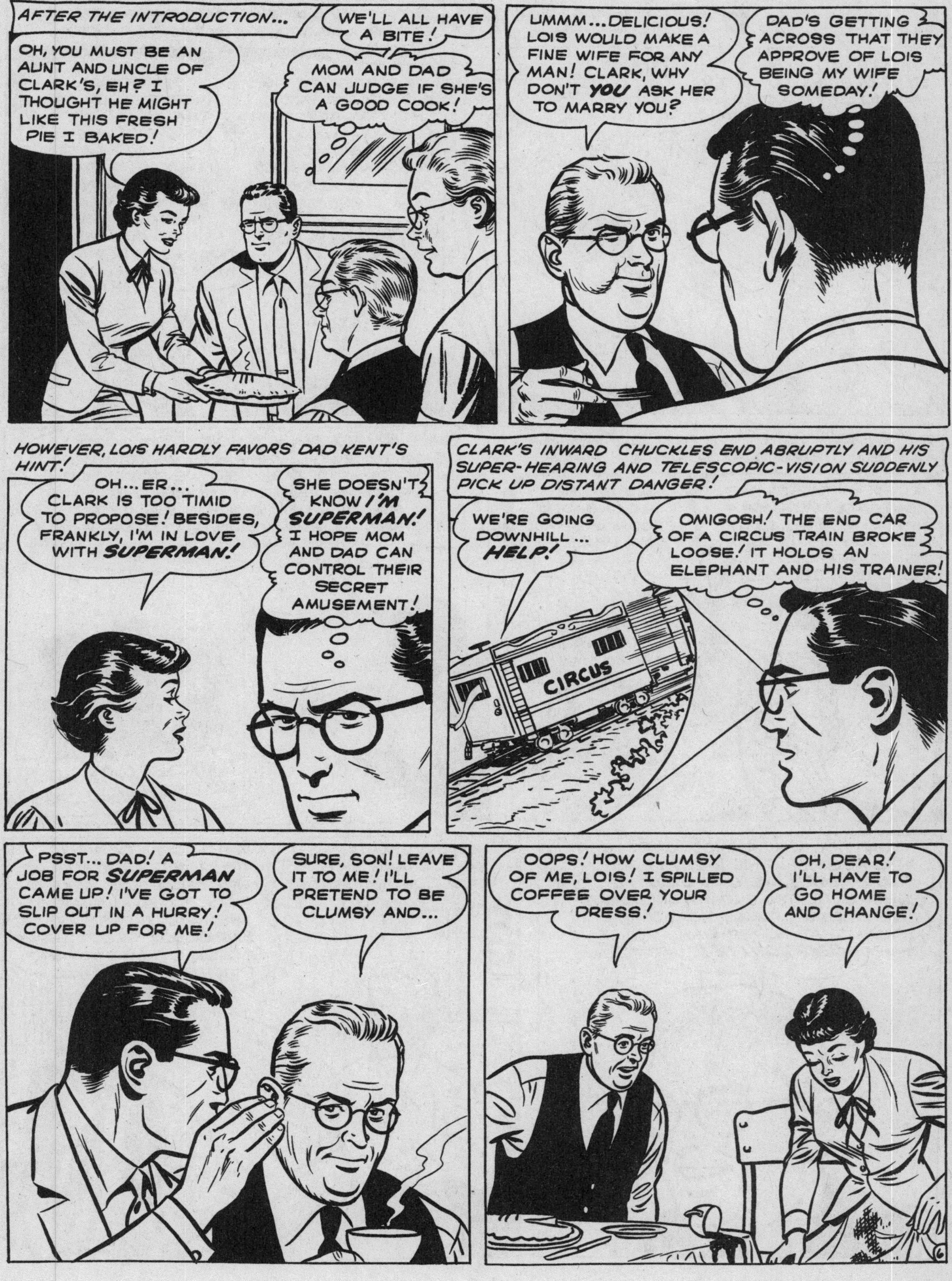
AFTER THE INTRODUCTION...
OH, YOU MUST BE AN AUNT AND UNCLE OF CLARK'S, EH? I THOUGHT HE MIGHT LIKE THIS FRESH PIE I BAKED!
WE'LL ALL HAVE A BITE!
MOM AND DAD CAN JUDGE IF SHE'S A GOOD COOK!
UMMM... DELICIOUS! LOIS WOULD MAKE A FINE WIFE FOR ANY MAN! CLARK, WHY DON'T YOU ASK HER TO MARRY YOU?
DAD'S GETTING ACROSS THAT THEY APPROVE OF LOIS BEING MY WIFE SOMEDAY!
HOWEVER, LOIS HARDLY FAVORS DAD KENT'S HINT!
OH... ER... CLARK IS TOO TIMID TO PROPOSE! BESIDES, FRANKLY, I'M IN LOVE WITH SUPERMAN!
SHE DOESN'T KNOW I'M SUPERMAN! I HOPE MOM AND DAD CAN CONTROL THEIR SECRET AMUSEMENT!
CLARK'S INWARD CHUCKLES END ABRUPTLY AND HIS SUPER-HEARING AND TELESCOPIC-VISION SUDDENLY PICK UP DISTANT DANGER!
WE'RE GOING DOWNHILL ... HELP!
OMIGOSH! THE END CAR OF A CIRCUS TRAIN BROKE LOOSE! IT HOLDS AN ELEPHANT AND HIS TRAINER!
CIRCUS
PSST... DAD! A JOB FOR SUPERMAN CAME UP! I'VE GOT TO SLIP OUT IN A HURRY! COVER UP FOR ME!
SURE, SON! LEAVE IT TO ME! I'LL PRETEND TO BE CLUMSY AND...
OOPS! HOW CLUMSY OF ME, LOIS! I SPILLED COFFEE OVER YOUR DRESS!
OH, DEAR! I'LL HAVE TO GO HOME AND CHANGE!
6

WITH LOIS GONE, CLARK SWIFTLY SHEDS HIS OUTER GARMENTS AND IS ON HIS WAY!

THANKS, DAD! WHEN I WAS *SUPERBOY,* YOU OFTEN HAD TO GET RID OF SNOOPY LANA LANG THAT WAY! NOW, YOU ALSO KEPT LOIS LANE FROM SUSPECTING MY SECRET IDENTITY!

BUT AFTER *SUPERMAN* LEAVES, STRANGE WORDS ARE SPOKEN BY THE PAIR LEFT BEHIND...

WE PROTECTED HIS BIG SECRET FROM THAT GIRL REPORTER... BUT MEANWHILE, *SUPERMAN* SPILLED THE BEANS TO *US!* OUR PLAN WORKED, MILLICENT!

YES, CEDRIC! HE NEVER TUMBLED THAT OUR "TIME MACHINE" WAS A PROP FROM A SCIENCE-FICTION MOVIE AND THAT WE WERE MR. AND MRS. CARSON OF METROPOLIS, PLAYING OUR GREATEST ROLES AS MR. AND MRS. KENT OF SMALLVILLE! ⹂HA, HA⹂

THE SHOCKING TRUTH IS THAT *SUPERMAN* HAS BEEN HOAXED BY SCHEMING ACTORS!

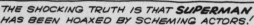

I'LL FIX MY FALSE NOSE TIGHTER! *SUPERMAN* NEVER THOUGHT TO USE HIS X-RAY VISION AND PENETRATE OUR DISGUISES, BECAUSE WE TALKED SO *CONVINCINGLY* ABOUT HIS BOYHOOD!

AND AFTER CHECKING OLD RECORDS OF ALL SMALLVILLE FAMILIES, WE CHOSE THE RIGHT ONES AS THE MOST LIKELY TO BE *SUPERBOY'S* FOSTER PARENTS... THE KENTS!

WHILE *SUPERMAN'S* GONE, IT'S A GOOD TIME TO REVIEW ALL THE FACTS WE GATHERED ABOUT THE KENT FAMILY, SO WE DON'T SLIP UP BEFORE WE LEAVE AT MIDNIGHT! THIS FALSE FOUNTAIN PEN, WHICH IS REALLY A DISGUISED MICROFILM PROJECTOR, SURE COMES IN HANDY!

CLARK'S NEXT DOOR NEIGHBORS PROFESSOR LANG AND LANA

NOW THAT WE TRICKED CLARK KENT INTO REVEALING HIS IDENTITY AS *SUPERMAN,* WE CAN SELL THE SECRET TO THE UNDERWORLD! BUT WE STILL WANT ONE MORE THING FROM THAT SUPER-SAP... *KRYPTONITE!*

CEDRIC, COULDN'T WE STILL TAKE THIS GOLD CUP ALONG... UH...!

WANT TO TIP OFF OUR HOAX, MILLICENT? IF WE PRETENDED TO TAKE IT BACK TO SMALLVILLE, THEN WHY DIDN'T *SUPERBOY* SEE IT THERE? FORGET IT! WE'LL REAP PLENTY *MORE!*

7

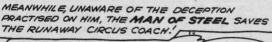

MEANWHILE, UNAWARE OF THE DECEPTION PRACTISED ON HIM, THE *MAN OF STEEL* SAVES THE RUNAWAY CIRCUS COACH.'

JOLTING THE CAR TO A STOP MIGHT FRIGHTEN THE ELEPHANT INTO SMASHING OUT! THIS'LL STOP IT SMOOTHLY, IF I USE MY HANDS ON ONE WHEEL LIKE A SUPER- *BRAKE!*

WHEN *SUPERMAN* RETURNS TO HIS PHONEY PARENTS, TELLING THEM OF HIS FEAT...

MAGNIFICENT, SON, JUST LIKE THE SUPER-DEEDS YOU DID AS *SUPERBOY!* BUT TELL ME, DO YOU STILL USE ROBOT SUBSTITUTES FOR EMERGENCIES AS YOU DID IN SMALLVILLE?

SURE, DAD! I KEEP THEM IN THIS SECRET CLOSET!

WITHIN THE CLOSET ARE *"MEN OF STEEL"* USED IN SPECIAL CASES!

EACH IS DESIGNED TO USE ONE OF MY SUPER-POWERS WHEN NEEDED! I SEND OUT THE ROBOTS WHEN CLARK'S ABSENCE WOULD BE SUSPICIOUS! OR WHEN I SUSPECT THAT CRIMINALS ARE WAITING TO USE *KRYPTONITE* AGAINST ME!

SUPER-STRENGTH

X-RAY VISION

FLYING

SUPER-BREATH

HMMM... THAT REMINDS ME, SON! PROFESSOR CLYDE SAID HE HAD A THEORY HOW TO MAKE A *KRYPTONITE ANTIDOTE!* IF YOU COULD ROUND UP *KRYPTONITE* FOR US TO TAKE BACK TO HIM FOR THE EXPERIMENT, WE'LL PROJECT THE ANTIDOTE TO YOU ACROSS THE TIME-BARRIER!

THE EXPERIMENT MAY NOT SUCCEED, BUT IT'S WORTH A TRY! I'LL FIND SOME *KRYPTONITE* NOW!

HA, HA! JUST WHAT WE WANT! *SUPERMAN* HIMSELF WILL BRING US *KRYPTONITE* WHICH WE'LL USE *AGAINST* HIM LATER!

8

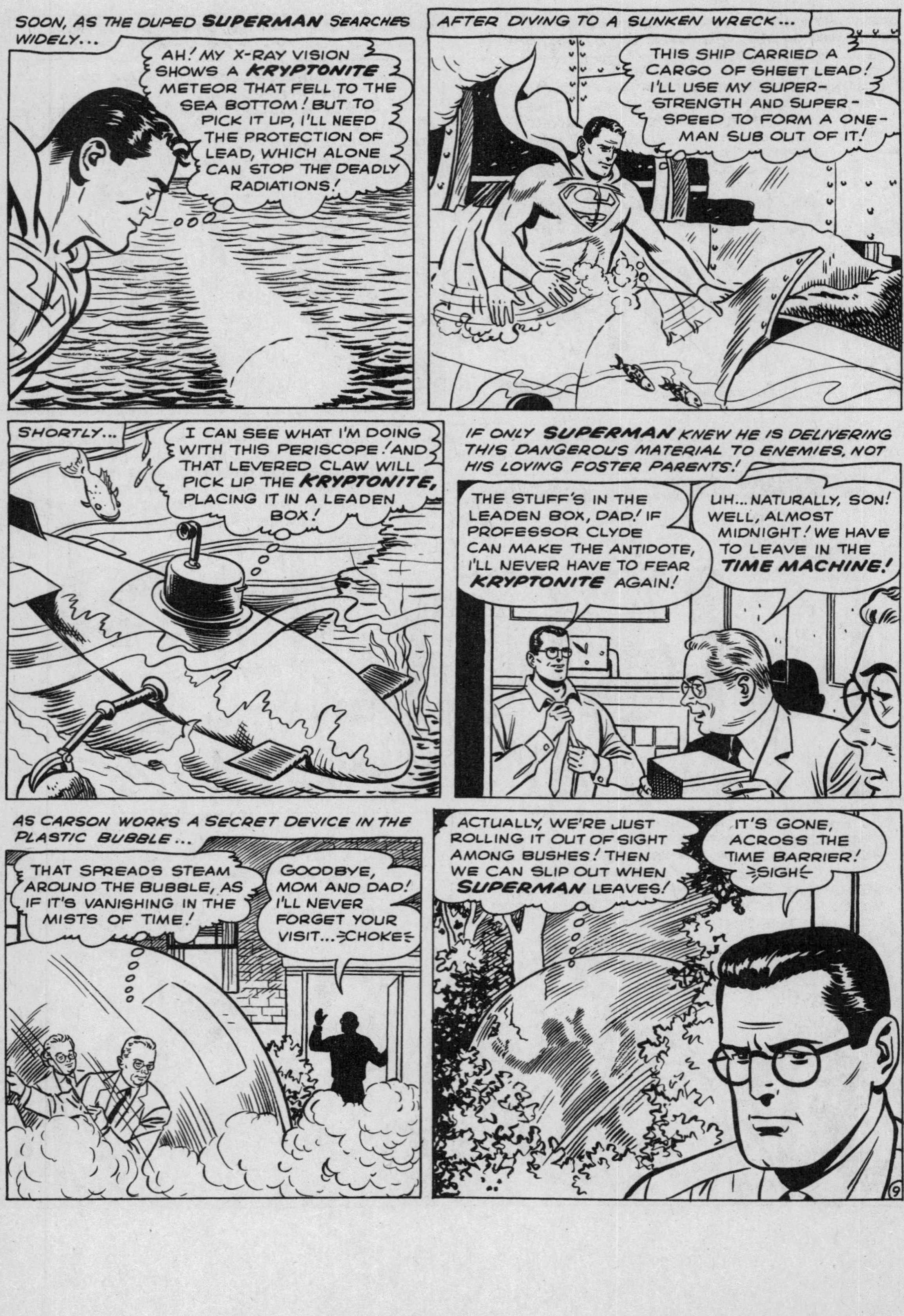
SOON, AS THE DUPED SUPERMAN SEARCHES WIDELY...
AH! MY X-RAY VISION SHOWS A KRYPTONITE METEOR THAT FELL TO THE SEA BOTTOM! BUT TO PICK IT UP, I'LL NEED THE PROTECTION OF LEAD, WHICH ALONE CAN STOP THE DEADLY RADIATIONS!
AFTER DIVING TO A SUNKEN WRECK...
THIS SHIP CARRIED A CARGO OF SHEET LEAD! I'LL USE MY SUPER-STRENGTH AND SUPER-SPEED TO FORM A ONE-MAN SUB OUT OF IT!
SHORTLY...
I CAN SEE WHAT I'M DOING WITH THIS PERISCOPE! AND THAT LEVERED CLAW WILL PICK UP THE KRYPTONITE, PLACING IT IN A LEADEN BOX!
IF ONLY SUPERMAN KNEW HE IS DELIVERING THIS DANGEROUS MATERIAL TO ENEMIES, NOT HIS LOVING FOSTER PARENTS!
THE STUFF'S IN THE LEADEN BOX, DAD! IF PROFESSOR CLYDE CAN MAKE THE ANTIDOTE, I'LL NEVER HAVE TO FEAR KRYPTONITE AGAIN!
UH... NATURALLY, SON! WELL, ALMOST MIDNIGHT! WE HAVE TO LEAVE IN THE TIME MACHINE!
AS CARSON WORKS A SECRET DEVICE IN THE PLASTIC BUBBLE...
THAT SPREADS STEAM AROUND THE BUBBLE, AS IF IT'S VANISHING IN THE MISTS OF TIME!
GOODBYE, MOM AND DAD! I'LL NEVER FORGET YOUR VISIT... CHOKE
ACTUALLY, WE'RE JUST ROLLING IT OUT OF SIGHT AMONG BUSHES! THEN WE CAN SLIP OUT WHEN SUPERMAN LEAVES!
IT'S GONE, ACROSS THE TIME BARRIER! SIGH
9

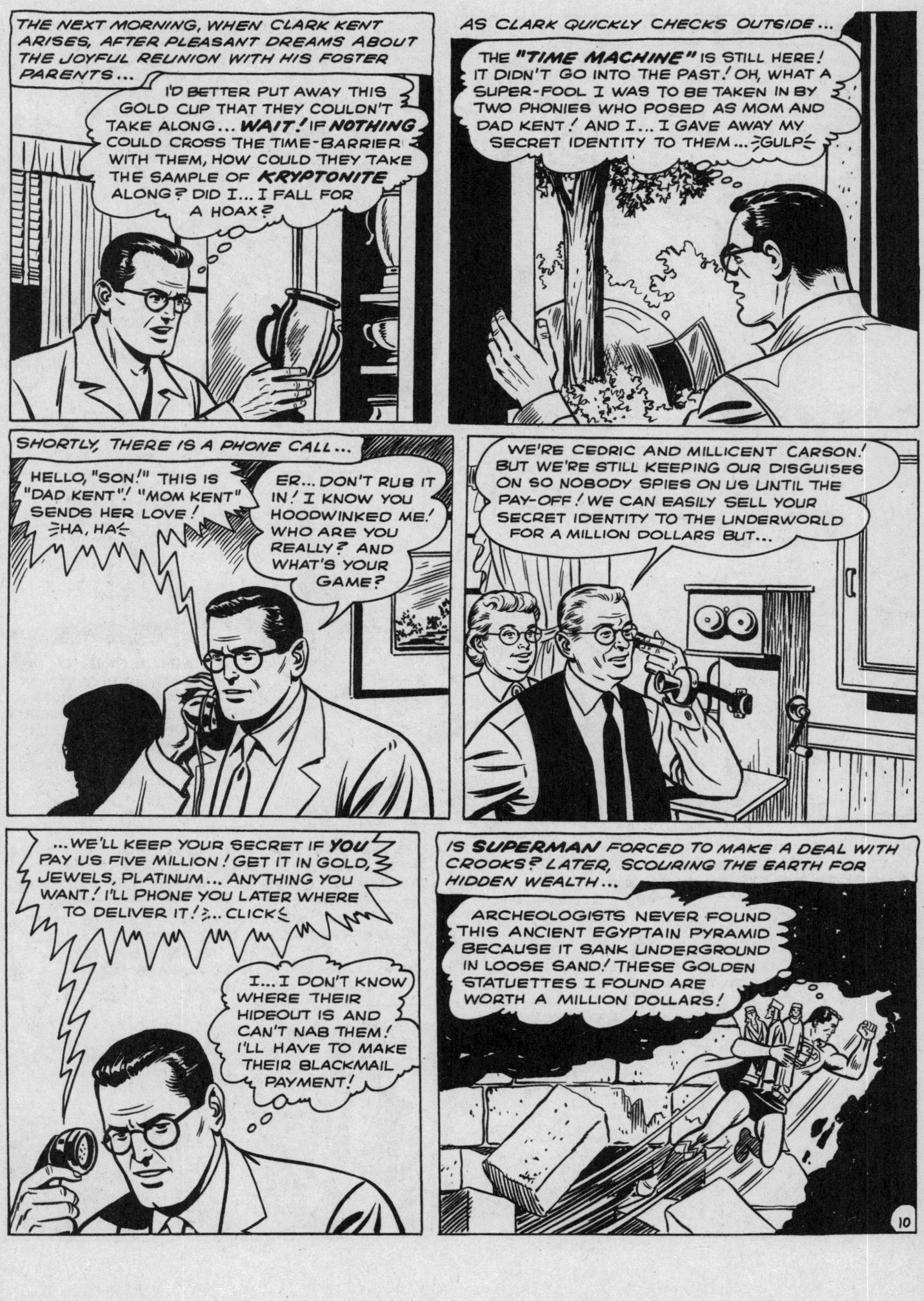
THE NEXT MORNING, WHEN CLARK KENT ARISES, AFTER PLEASANT DREAMS ABOUT THE JOYFUL REUNION WITH HIS FOSTER PARENTS...
I'D BETTER PUT AWAY THIS GOLD CUP THAT THEY COULDN'T TAKE ALONG... WAIT! IF NOTHING COULD CROSS THE TIME-BARRIER WITH THEM, HOW COULD THEY TAKE THE SAMPLE OF KRYPTONITE ALONG? DID I... I FALL FOR A HOAX?
AS CLARK QUICKLY CHECKS OUTSIDE...
THE "TIME MACHINE" IS STILL HERE! IT DIDN'T GO INTO THE PAST! OH, WHAT A SUPER-FOOL I WAS TO BE TAKEN IN BY TWO PHONIES WHO POSED AS MOM AND DAD KENT! AND I... I GAVE AWAY MY SECRET IDENTITY TO THEM... GULP
SHORTLY, THERE IS A PHONE CALL...
HELLO, "SON!" THIS IS "DAD KENT"! "MOM KENT" SENDS HER LOVE! HA, HA
ER... DON'T RUB IT IN! I KNOW YOU HOODWINKED ME! WHO ARE YOU REALLY? AND WHAT'S YOUR GAME?
WE'RE CEDRIC AND MILLICENT CARSON! BUT WE'RE STILL KEEPING OUR DISGUISES ON SO NOBODY SPIES ON US UNTIL THE PAY-OFF! WE CAN EASILY SELL YOUR SECRET IDENTITY TO THE UNDERWORLD FOR A MILLION DOLLARS BUT...
...WE'LL KEEP YOUR SECRET IF YOU PAY US FIVE MILLION! GET IT IN GOLD, JEWELS, PLATINUM... ANYTHING YOU WANT! I'LL PHONE YOU LATER WHERE TO DELIVER IT! ... CLICK
I... I DON'T KNOW WHERE THEIR HIDEOUT IS AND CAN'T NAB THEM! I'LL HAVE TO MAKE THEIR BLACKMAIL PAYMENT!
IS SUPERMAN FORCED TO MAKE A DEAL WITH CROOKS? LATER, SCOURING THE EARTH FOR HIDDEN WEALTH...
ARCHEOLOGISTS NEVER FOUND THIS ANCIENT EGYPTAIN PYRAMID BECAUSE IT SANK UNDERGROUND IN LOOSE SAND! THESE GOLDEN STATUETTES I FOUND ARE WORTH A MILLION DOLLARS!
10

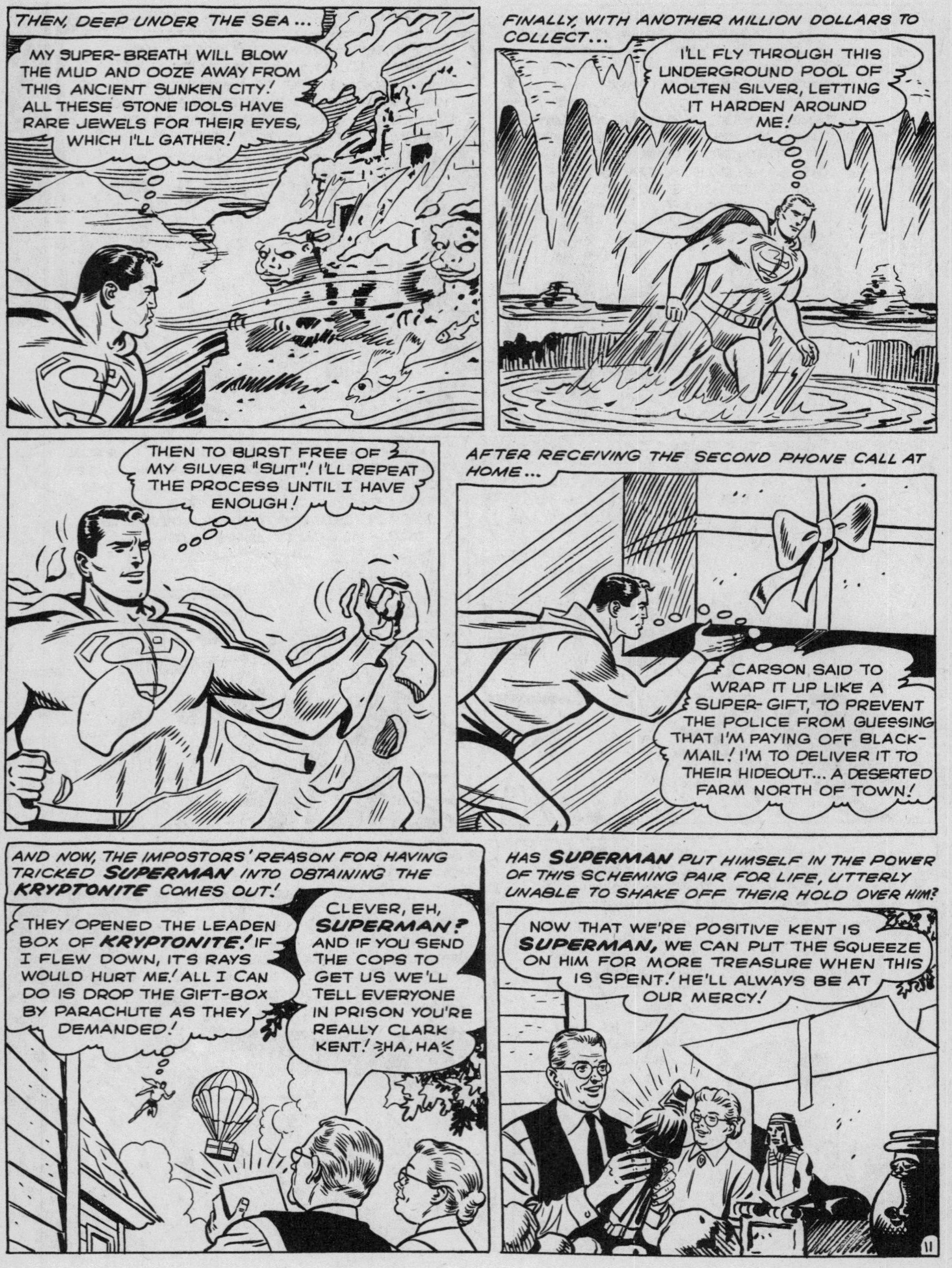
THEN, DEEP UNDER THE SEA...
MY SUPER-BREATH WILL BLOW THE MUD AND OOZE AWAY FROM THIS ANCIENT SUNKEN CITY! ALL THESE STONE IDOLS HAVE RARE JEWELS FOR THEIR EYES, WHICH I'LL GATHER!
FINALLY, WITH ANOTHER MILLION DOLLARS TO COLLECT...
I'LL FLY THROUGH THIS UNDERGROUND POOL OF MOLTEN SILVER, LETTING IT HARDEN AROUND ME!
THEN TO BURST FREE OF MY SILVER "SUIT"! I'LL REPEAT THE PROCESS UNTIL I HAVE ENOUGH!
AFTER RECEIVING THE SECOND PHONE CALL AT HOME...
CARSON SAID TO WRAP IT UP LIKE A SUPER-GIFT, TO PREVENT THE POLICE FROM GUESSING THAT I'M PAYING OFF BLACK-MAIL! I'M TO DELIVER IT TO THEIR HIDEOUT... A DESERTED FARM NORTH OF TOWN!
AND NOW, THE IMPOSTORS' REASON FOR HAVING TRICKED SUPERMAN INTO OBTAINING THE KRYPTONITE COMES OUT!
THEY OPENED THE LEADEN BOX OF KRYPTONITE! IF I FLEW DOWN, IT'S RAYS WOULD HURT ME! ALL I CAN DO IS DROP THE GIFT-BOX BY PARACHUTE AS THEY DEMANDED!
CLEVER, EH, SUPERMAN? AND IF YOU SEND THE COPS TO GET US WE'LL TELL EVERYONE IN PRISON YOU'RE REALLY CLARK KENT! HA, HA
HAS SUPERMAN PUT HIMSELF IN THE POWER OF THIS SCHEMING PAIR FOR LIFE, UTTERLY UNABLE TO SHAKE OFF THEIR HOLD OVER HIM?
NOW THAT WE'RE POSITIVE KENT IS SUPERMAN, WE CAN PUT THE SQUEEZE ON HIM FOR MORE TREASURE WHEN THIS IS SPENT! HE'LL ALWAYS BE AT OUR MERCY!
11

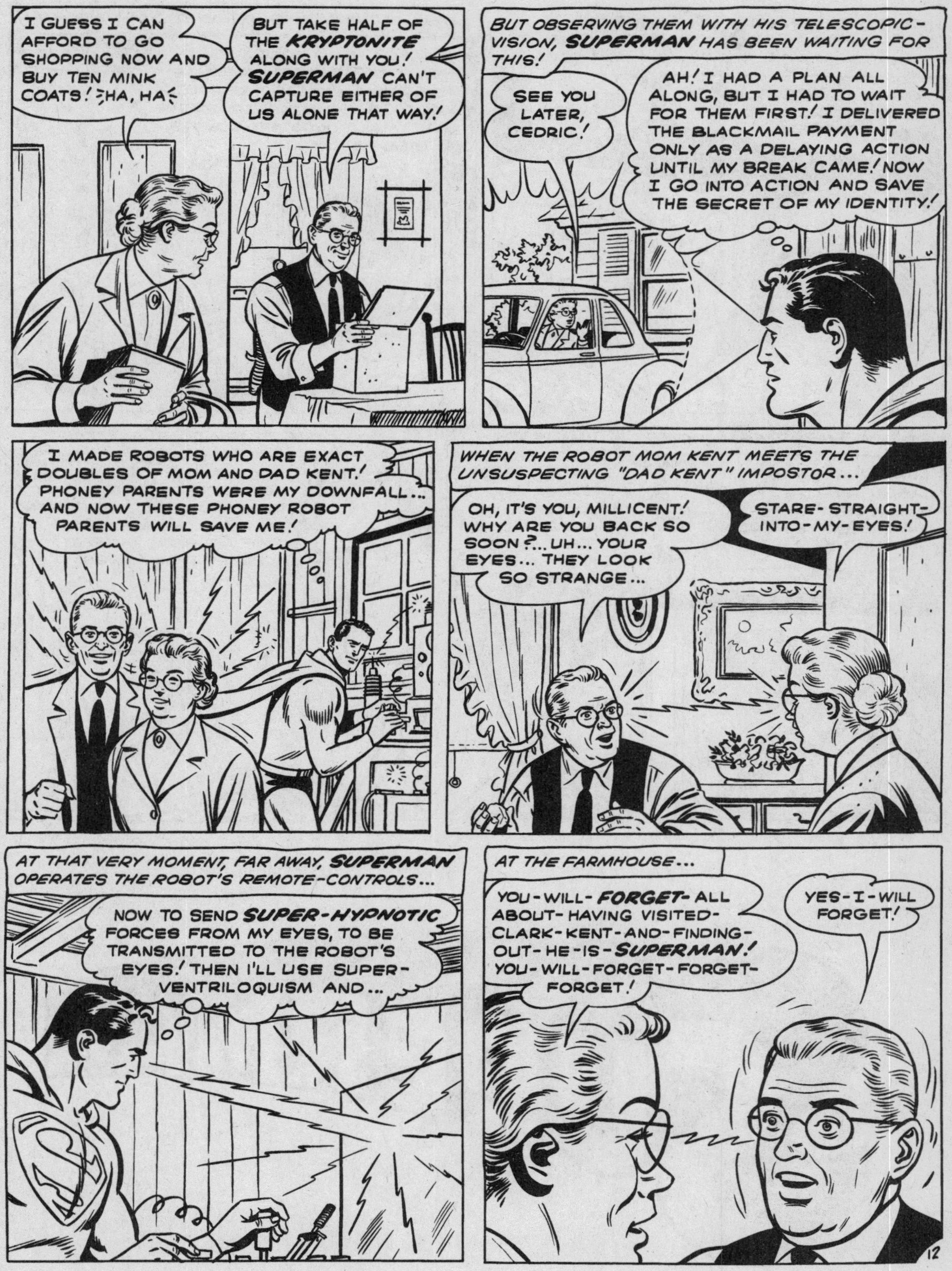
I GUESS I CAN AFFORD TO GO SHOPPING NOW AND BUY TEN MINK COATS! HA, HA
BUT TAKE HALF OF THE KRYPTONITE ALONG WITH YOU! SUPERMAN CAN'T CAPTURE EITHER OF US ALONE THAT WAY!
BUT OBSERVING THEM WITH HIS TELESCOPIC-VISION, SUPERMAN HAS BEEN WAITING FOR THIS!
SEE YOU LATER, CEDRIC!
AH! I HAD A PLAN ALL ALONG, BUT I HAD TO WAIT FOR THEM FIRST! I DELIVERED THE BLACKMAIL PAYMENT ONLY AS A DELAYING ACTION UNTIL MY BREAK CAME! NOW I GO INTO ACTION AND SAVE THE SECRET OF MY IDENTITY!
I MADE ROBOTS WHO ARE EXACT DOUBLES OF MOM AND DAD KENT! PHONEY PARENTS WERE MY DOWNFALL... AND NOW THESE PHONEY ROBOT PARENTS WILL SAVE ME!
WHEN THE ROBOT MOM KENT MEETS THE UNSUSPECTING "DAD KENT" IMPOSTOR...
OH, IT'S YOU, MILLICENT! WHY ARE YOU BACK SO SOON?... UH... YOUR EYES... THEY LOOK SO STRANGE...
STARE-STRAIGHT-INTO-MY-EYES!
AT THAT VERY MOMENT, FAR AWAY, SUPERMAN OPERATES THE ROBOT'S REMOTE-CONTROLS...
NOW TO SEND SUPER-HYPNOTIC FORCES FROM MY EYES, TO BE TRANSMITTED TO THE ROBOT'S EYES! THEN I'LL USE SUPER-VENTRILOQUISM AND...
AT THE FARMHOUSE...
YOU-WILL-FORGET-ALL ABOUT-HAVING VISITED-CLARK-KENT-AND-FINDING-OUT-HE-IS-SUPERMAN! YOU-WILL-FORGET-FORGET-FORGET!
YES-I-WILL FORGET!
12

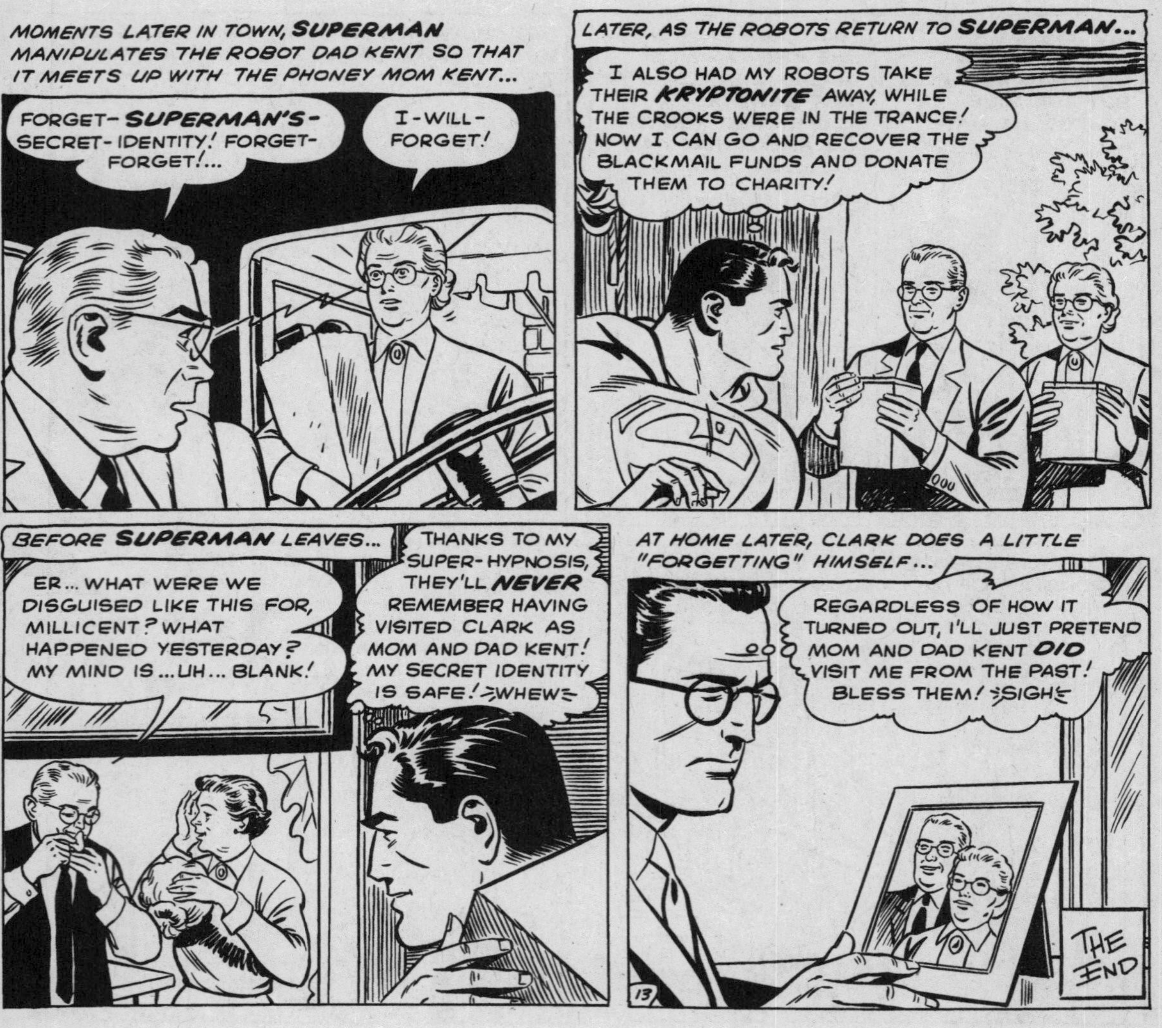
MOMENTS LATER IN TOWN, SUPERMAN MANIPULATES THE ROBOT DAD KENT SO THAT IT MEETS UP WITH THE PHONEY MOM KENT...
FORGET- SUPERMAN'S- SECRET- IDENTITY! FORGET- FORGET!...
I- WILL- FORGET!
LATER, AS THE ROBOTS RETURN TO SUPERMAN...
I ALSO HAD MY ROBOTS TAKE THEIR KRYPTONITE AWAY, WHILE THE CROOKS WERE IN THE TRANCE! NOW I CAN GO AND RECOVER THE BLACKMAIL FUNDS AND DONATE THEM TO CHARITY!
BEFORE SUPERMAN LEAVES...
ER... WHAT WERE WE DISGUISED LIKE THIS FOR, MILLICENT? WHAT HAPPENED YESTERDAY? MY MIND IS ...UH... BLANK!
THANKS TO MY SUPER- HYPNOSIS, THEY'LL NEVER REMEMBER HAVING VISITED CLARK AS MOM AND DAD KENT! MY SECRET IDENTITY IS SAFE! WHEW
AT HOME LATER, CLARK DOES A LITTLE "FORGETTING" HIMSELF...
REGARDLESS OF HOW IT TURNED OUT, I'LL JUST PRETEND MOM AND DAD KENT DID VISIT ME FROM THE PAST! BLESS THEM! SIGH
13
THE END

SUPERMAN

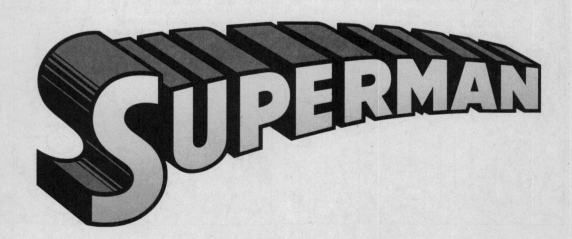

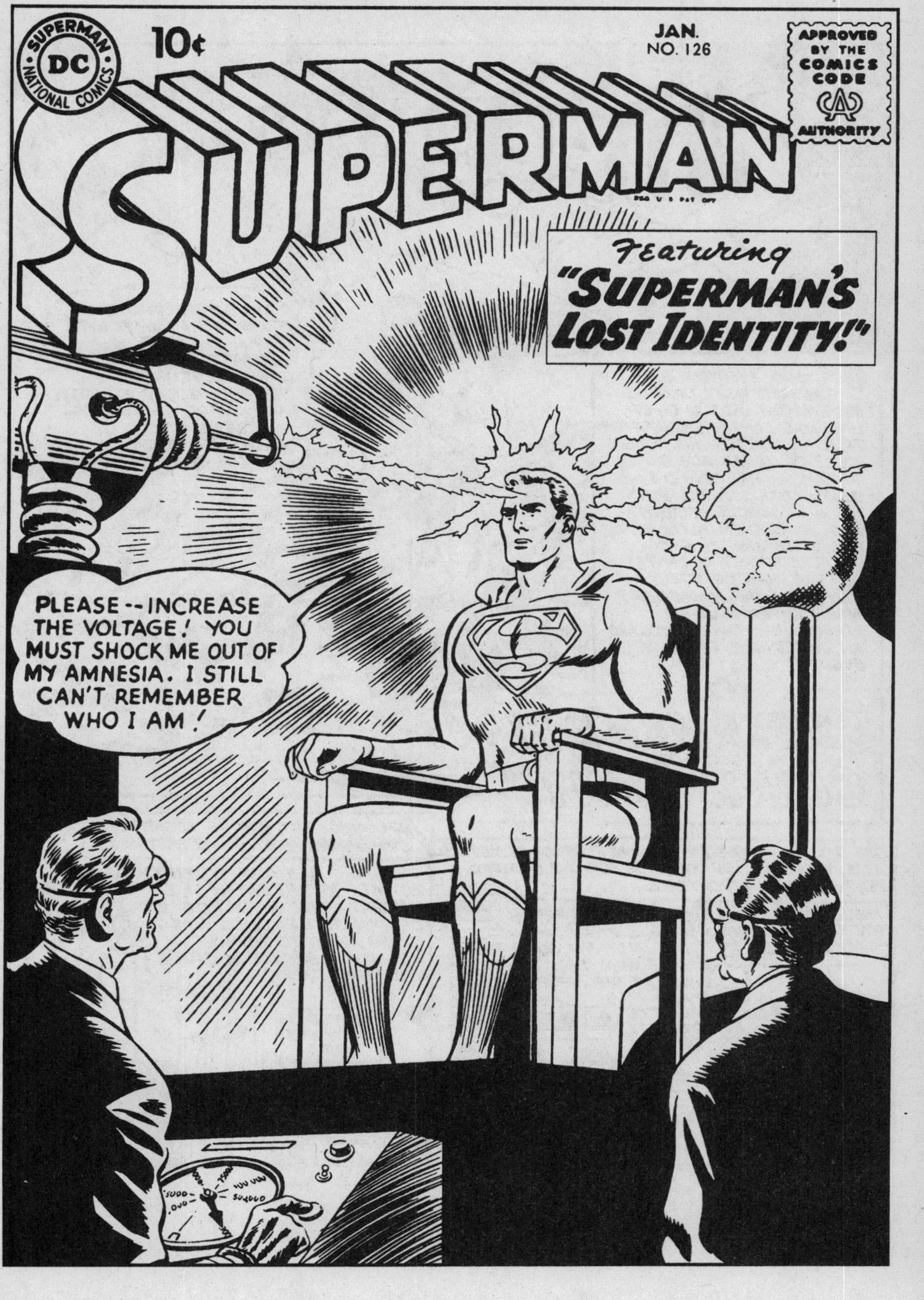
SUPERMAN DC NATIONAL COMICS
10¢
JAN.
NO. 126
APPROVED BY THE COMICS CODE AUTHORITY
SUPERMAN
Featuring "SUPERMAN'S LOST IDENTITY!"
PLEASE--INCREASE THE VOLTAGE! YOU MUST SHOCK ME OUT OF MY AMNESIA. I STILL CAN'T REMEMBER WHO I AM!

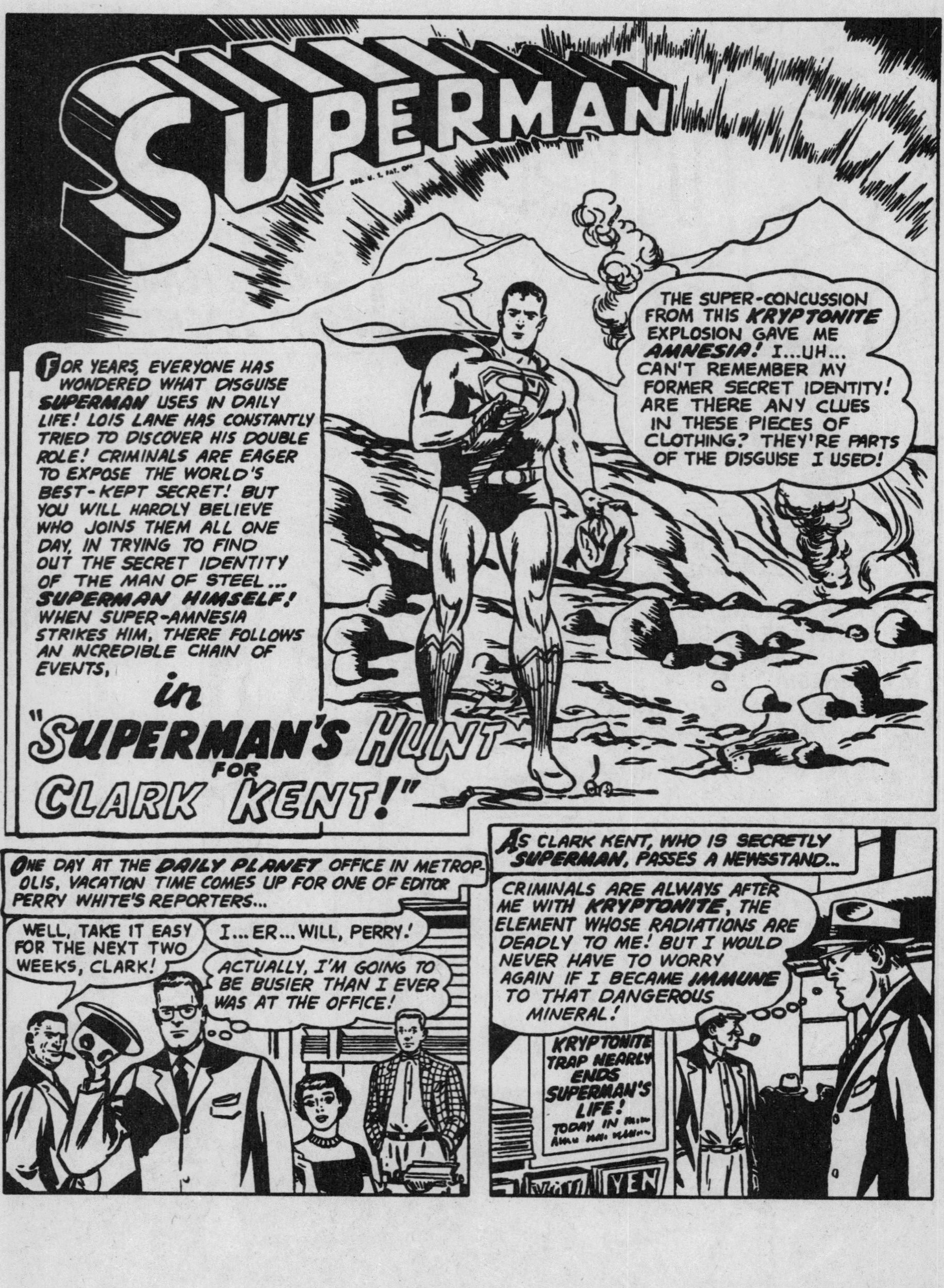
SUPERMAN
FOR YEARS, EVERYONE HAS WONDERED WHAT DISGUISE SUPERMAN USES IN DAILY LIFE! LOIS LANE HAS CONSTANTLY TRIED TO DISCOVER HIS DOUBLE ROLE! CRIMINALS ARE EAGER TO EXPOSE THE WORLD'S BEST-KEPT SECRET! BUT YOU WILL HARDLY BELIEVE WHO JOINS THEM ALL ONE DAY, IN TRYING TO FIND OUT THE SECRET IDENTITY OF THE MAN OF STEEL... SUPERMAN HIMSELF! WHEN SUPER-AMNESIA STRIKES HIM, THERE FOLLOWS AN INCREDIBLE CHAIN OF EVENTS,
in "SUPERMAN'S HUNT FOR CLARK KENT!"
THE SUPER-CONCUSSION FROM THIS KRYPTONITE EXPLOSION GAVE ME AMNESIA! I...UH... CAN'T REMEMBER MY FORMER SECRET IDENTITY! ARE THERE ANY CLUES IN THESE PIECES OF CLOTHING? THEY'RE PARTS OF THE DISGUISE I USED!
ONE DAY AT THE DAILY PLANET OFFICE IN METROPOLIS, VACATION TIME COMES UP FOR ONE OF EDITOR PERRY WHITE'S REPORTERS...
WELL, TAKE IT EASY FOR THE NEXT TWO WEEKS, CLARK!
I...ER...WILL, PERRY!
ACTUALLY, I'M GOING TO BE BUSIER THAN I EVER WAS AT THE OFFICE!
AS CLARK KENT, WHO IS SECRETLY SUPERMAN, PASSES A NEWSSTAND...
CRIMINALS ARE ALWAYS AFTER ME WITH KRYPTONITE, THE ELEMENT WHOSE RADIATIONS ARE DEADLY TO ME! BUT I WOULD NEVER HAVE TO WORRY AGAIN IF I BECAME IMMUNE TO THAT DANGEROUS MINERAL!
KRYPTONITE TRAP NEARLY ENDS SUPERMAN'S LIFE!
TODAY IN
YEN

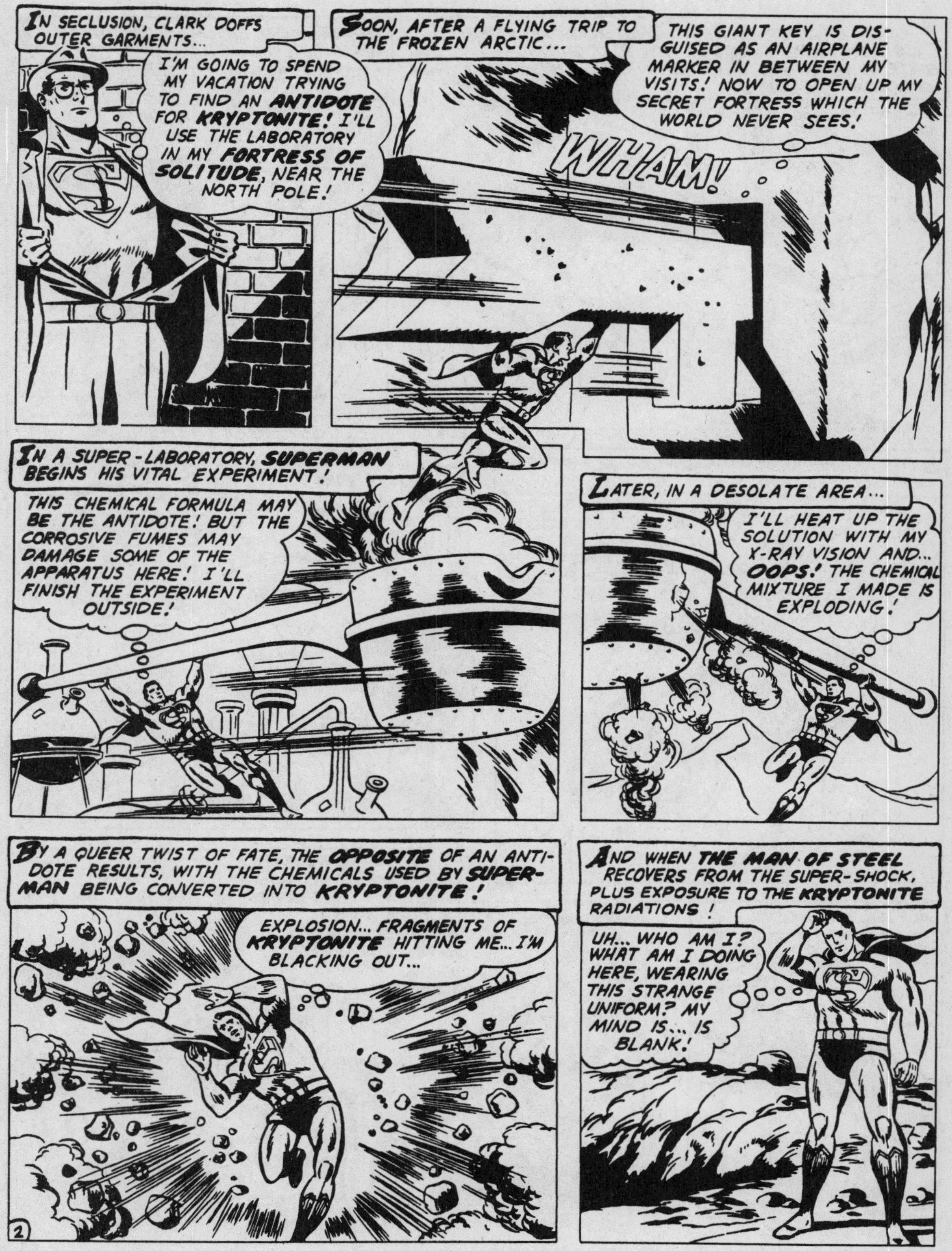
IN SECLUSION, CLARK DOFFS OUTER GARMENTS...
I'M GOING TO SPEND MY VACATION TRYING TO FIND AN ANTIDOTE FOR KRYPTONITE! I'LL USE THE LABORATORY IN MY FORTRESS OF SOLITUDE, NEAR THE NORTH POLE!
SOON, AFTER A FLYING TRIP TO THE FROZEN ARCTIC...
THIS GIANT KEY IS DISGUISED AS AN AIRPLANE MARKER IN BETWEEN MY VISITS! NOW TO OPEN UP MY SECRET FORTRESS WHICH THE WORLD NEVER SEES!
WHAM!
IN A SUPER-LABORATORY, SUPERMAN BEGINS HIS VITAL EXPERIMENT!
THIS CHEMICAL FORMULA MAY BE THE ANTIDOTE! BUT THE CORROSIVE FUMES MAY DAMAGE SOME OF THE APPARATUS HERE! I'LL FINISH THE EXPERIMENT OUTSIDE!
LATER, IN A DESOLATE AREA...
I'LL HEAT UP THE SOLUTION WITH MY X-RAY VISION AND... OOPS! THE CHEMICAL MIXTURE I MADE IS EXPLODING!
BY A QUEER TWIST OF FATE, THE OPPOSITE OF AN ANTIDOTE RESULTS, WITH THE CHEMICALS USED BY SUPERMAN BEING CONVERTED INTO KRYPTONITE!
EXPLOSION... FRAGMENTS OF KRYPTONITE HITTING ME... I'M BLACKING OUT...
2
AND WHEN THE MAN OF STEEL RECOVERS FROM THE SUPER-SHOCK, PLUS EXPOSURE TO THE KRYPTONITE RADIATIONS!
UH... WHO AM I? WHAT AM I DOING HERE, WEARING THIS STRANGE UNIFORM? MY MIND IS... IS BLANK!

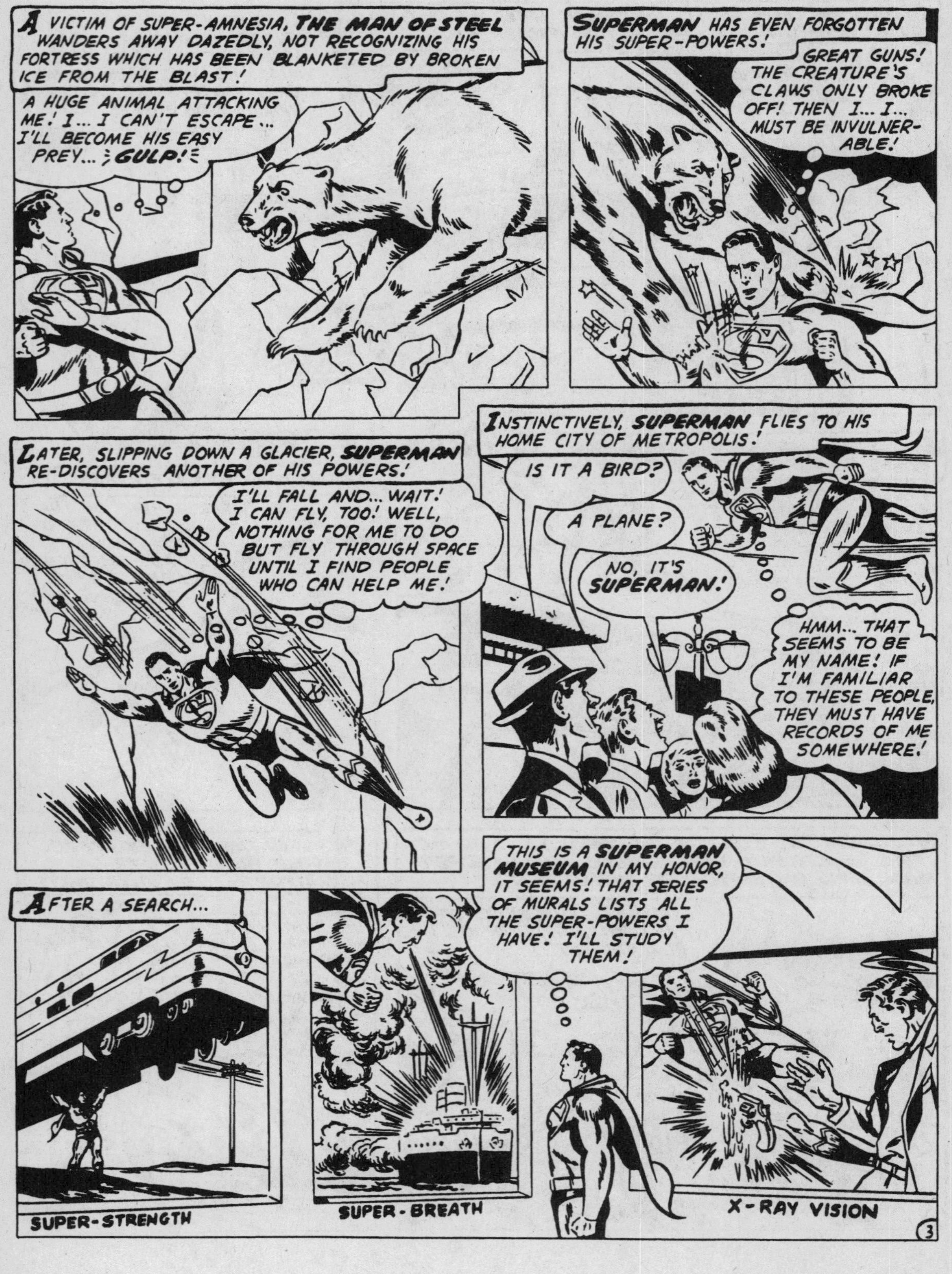
A VICTIM OF SUPER-AMNESIA, THE MAN OF STEEL WANDERS AWAY DAZEDLY, NOT RECOGNIZING HIS FORTRESS WHICH HAS BEEN BLANKETED BY BROKEN ICE FROM THE BLAST!
A HUGE ANIMAL ATTACKING ME! I... I CAN'T ESCAPE... I'LL BECOME HIS EASY PREY... GULP!
SUPERMAN HAS EVEN FORGOTTEN HIS SUPER-POWERS!
GREAT GUNS! THE CREATURE'S CLAWS ONLY BROKE OFF! THEN I... I... MUST BE INVULNERABLE!
LATER, SLIPPING DOWN A GLACIER, SUPERMAN RE-DISCOVERS ANOTHER OF HIS POWERS!
I'LL FALL AND... WAIT! I CAN FLY, TOO! WELL, NOTHING FOR ME TO DO BUT FLY THROUGH SPACE UNTIL I FIND PEOPLE WHO CAN HELP ME!
INSTINCTIVELY, SUPERMAN FLIES TO HIS HOME CITY OF METROPOLIS!
IS IT A BIRD?
A PLANE?
NO, IT'S SUPERMAN!
HMM... THAT SEEMS TO BE MY NAME! IF I'M FAMILIAR TO THESE PEOPLE, THEY MUST HAVE RECORDS OF ME SOMEWHERE!
AFTER A SEARCH...
THIS IS A SUPERMAN MUSEUM IN MY HONOR, IT SEEMS! THAT SERIES OF MURALS LISTS ALL THE SUPER-POWERS I HAVE! I'LL STUDY THEM!
SUPER-STRENGTH
SUPER-BREATH
X-RAY VISION
3

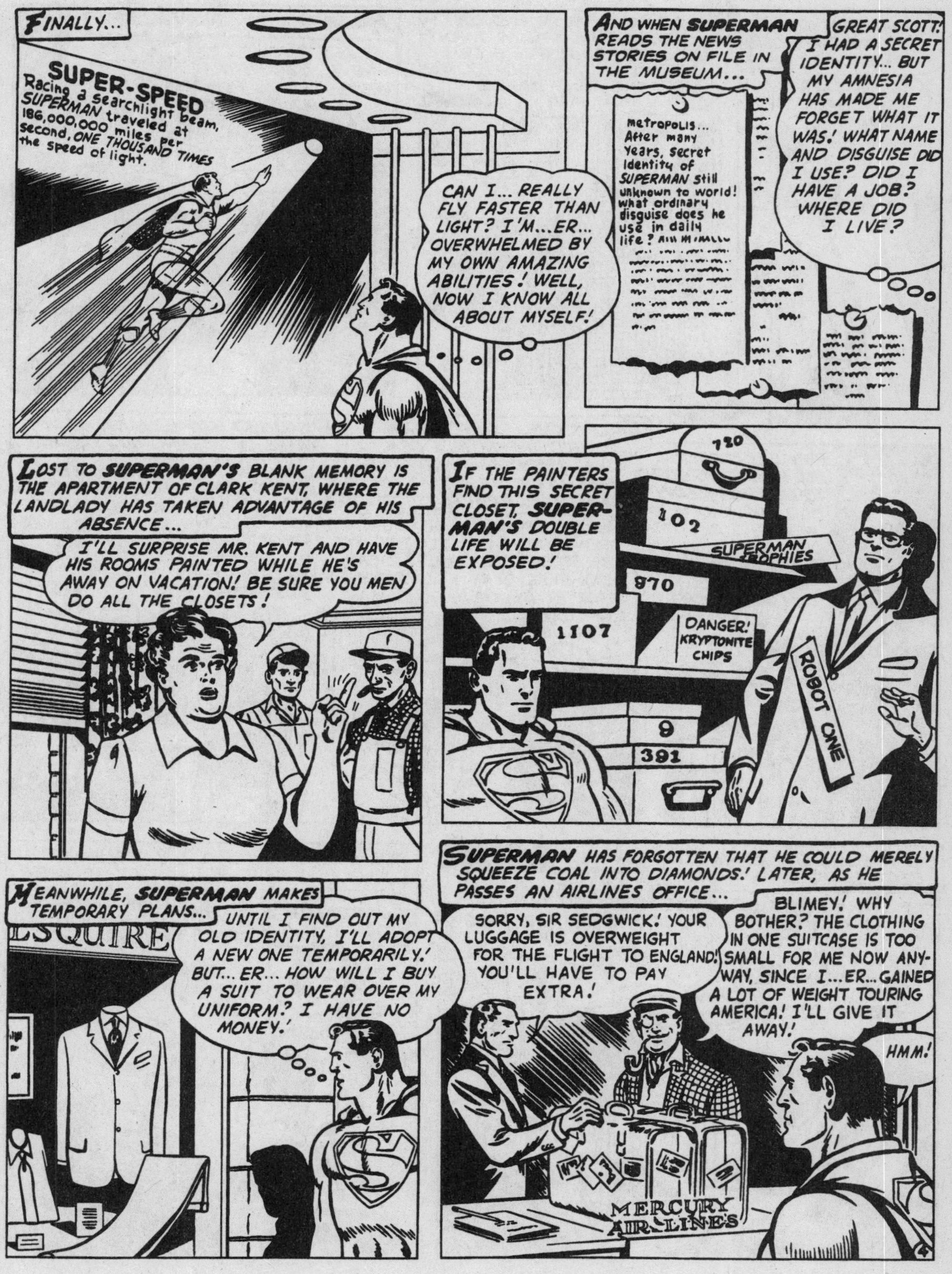
FINALLY...
SUPER-SPEED
Racing a searchlight beam, SUPERMAN traveled at 186,000,000 miles per second, ONE THOUSAND TIMES the speed of light.
CAN I... REALLY FLY FASTER THAN LIGHT? I'M...ER... OVERWHELMED BY MY OWN AMAZING ABILITIES! WELL, NOW I KNOW ALL ABOUT MYSELF!
AND WHEN SUPERMAN READS THE NEWS STORIES ON FILE IN THE MUSEUM...
METROPOLIS... After many years, secret identity of SUPERMAN still unknown to world! what ordinary disguise does he use in daily life?
GREAT SCOTT! I HAD A SECRET IDENTITY... BUT MY AMNESIA HAS MADE ME FORGET WHAT IT WAS! WHAT NAME AND DISGUISE DID I USE? DID I HAVE A JOB? WHERE DID I LIVE?
LOST TO SUPERMAN'S BLANK MEMORY IS THE APARTMENT OF CLARK KENT, WHERE THE LANDLADY HAS TAKEN ADVANTAGE OF HIS ABSENCE...
I'LL SURPRISE MR. KENT AND HAVE HIS ROOMS PAINTED WHILE HE'S AWAY ON VACATION! BE SURE YOU MEN DO ALL THE CLOSETS!
IF THE PAINTERS FIND THIS SECRET CLOSET, SUPERMAN'S DOUBLE LIFE WILL BE EXPOSED!
720
102
SUPERMAN TROPHIES
870
1107
DANGER! KRYPTONITE CHIPS
ROBOT ONE
9
391
MEANWHILE, SUPERMAN MAKES TEMPORARY PLANS...
ESQUIRE
UNTIL I FIND OUT MY OLD IDENTITY, I'LL ADOPT A NEW ONE TEMPORARILY! BUT... ER... HOW WILL I BUY A SUIT TO WEAR OVER MY UNIFORM? I HAVE NO MONEY!
SUPERMAN HAS FORGOTTEN THAT HE COULD MERELY SQUEEZE COAL INTO DIAMONDS! LATER, AS HE PASSES AN AIRLINES OFFICE...
SORRY, SIR SEDGWICK! YOUR LUGGAGE IS OVERWEIGHT FOR THE FLIGHT TO ENGLAND! YOU'LL HAVE TO PAY EXTRA!
BLIMEY! WHY BOTHER? THE CLOTHING IN ONE SUITCASE IS TOO SMALL FOR ME NOW ANYWAY, SINCE I...ER...GAINED A LOT OF WEIGHT TOURING AMERICA! I'LL GIVE IT AWAY!
HMM!
MERCURY AIRLINES
4

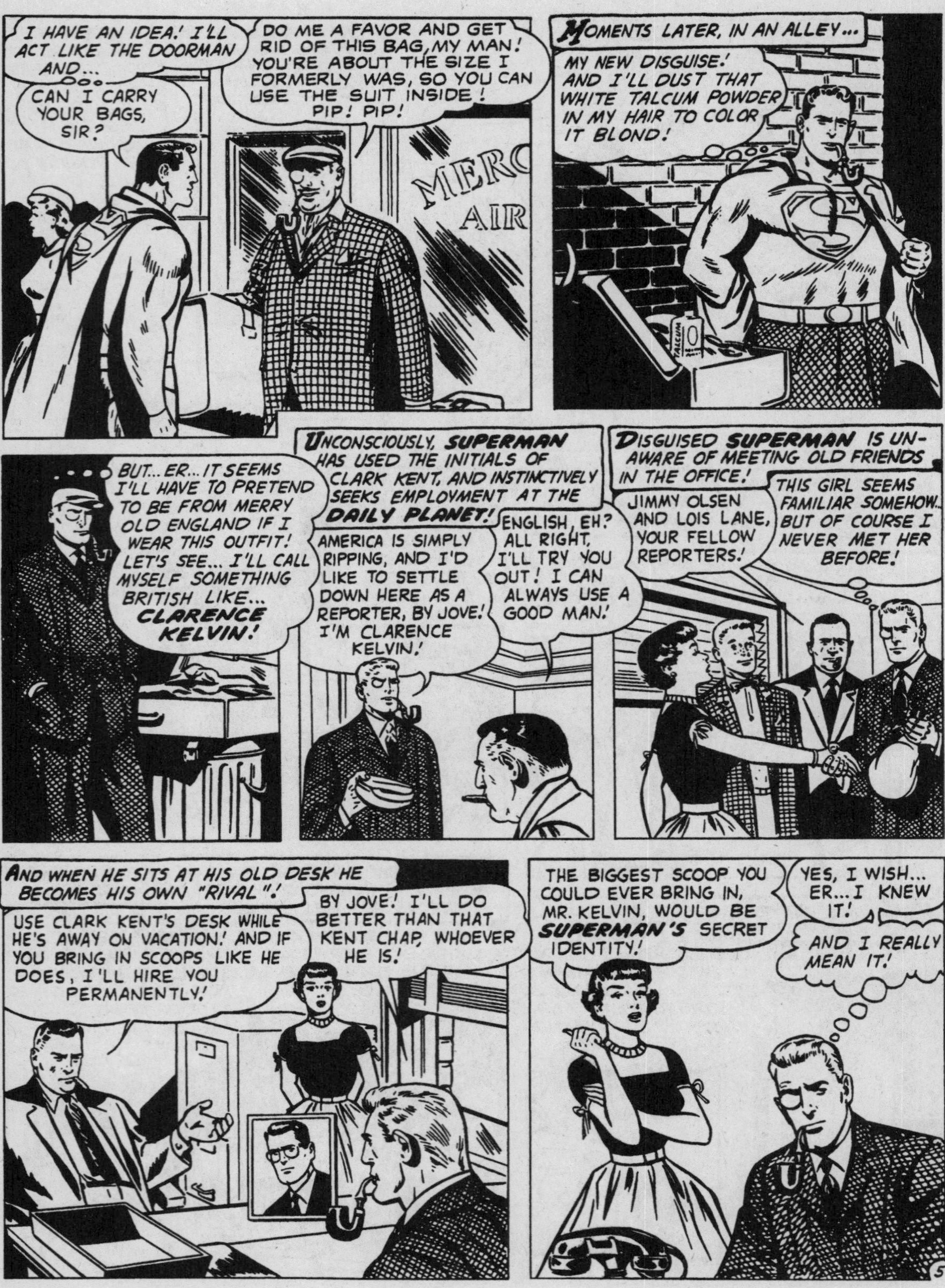
I HAVE AN IDEA! I'LL ACT LIKE THE DOORMAN AND...
CAN I CARRY YOUR BAGS, SIR?
DO ME A FAVOR AND GET RID OF THIS BAG, MY MAN! YOU'RE ABOUT THE SIZE I FORMERLY WAS, SO YOU CAN USE THE SUIT INSIDE! PIP! PIP!
MERC
AIR
MOMENTS LATER, IN AN ALLEY...
MY NEW DISGUISE! AND I'LL DUST THAT WHITE TALCUM POWDER IN MY HAIR TO COLOR IT BLOND!
BUT... ER... IT SEEMS I'LL HAVE TO PRETEND TO BE FROM MERRY OLD ENGLAND IF I WEAR THIS OUTFIT! LET'S SEE... I'LL CALL MYSELF SOMETHING BRITISH LIKE... CLARENCE KELVIN!
UNCONSCIOUSLY, SUPERMAN HAS USED THE INITIALS OF CLARK KENT, AND INSTINCTIVELY SEEKS EMPLOYMENT AT THE DAILY PLANET!
AMERICA IS SIMPLY RIPPING, AND I'D LIKE TO SETTLE DOWN HERE AS A REPORTER, BY JOVE! I'M CLARENCE KELVIN!
ENGLISH, EH? ALL RIGHT, I'LL TRY YOU OUT! I CAN ALWAYS USE A GOOD MAN!
DISGUISED SUPERMAN IS UNAWARE OF MEETING OLD FRIENDS IN THE OFFICE!
JIMMY OLSEN AND LOIS LANE, YOUR FELLOW REPORTERS!
THIS GIRL SEEMS FAMILIAR SOMEHOW... BUT OF COURSE I NEVER MET HER BEFORE!
AND WHEN HE SITS AT HIS OLD DESK HE BECOMES HIS OWN "RIVAL"!
USE CLARK KENT'S DESK WHILE HE'S AWAY ON VACATION! AND IF YOU BRING IN SCOOPS LIKE HE DOES, I'LL HIRE YOU PERMANENTLY!
BY JOVE! I'LL DO BETTER THAN THAT KENT CHAP, WHOEVER HE IS!
THE BIGGEST SCOOP YOU COULD EVER BRING IN, MR. KELVIN, WOULD BE SUPERMAN'S SECRET IDENTITY!
YES, I WISH... ER... I KNEW IT!
AND I REALLY MEAN IT!
5

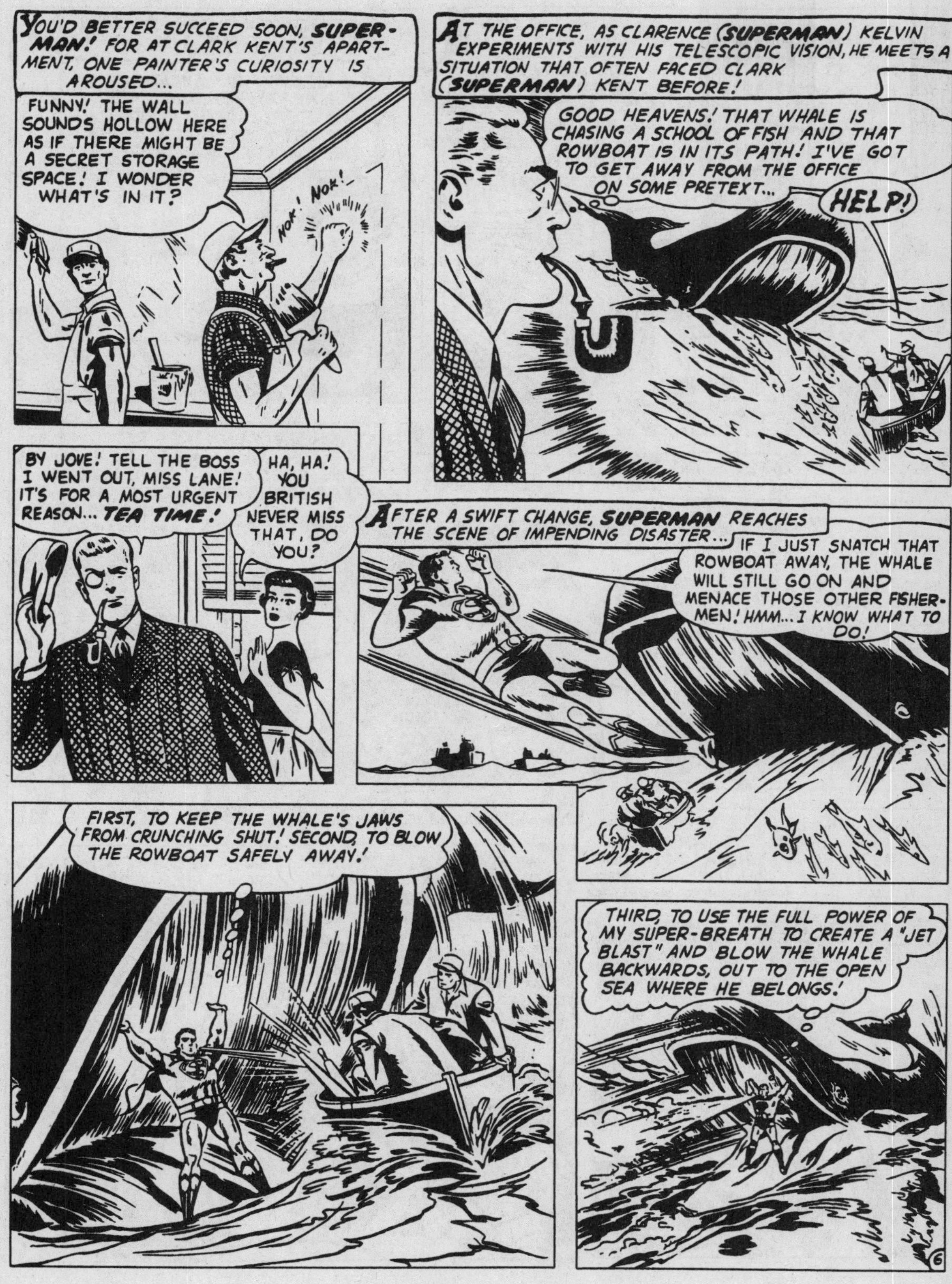
YOU'D BETTER SUCCEED SOON, SUPERMAN! FOR AT CLARK KENT'S APARTMENT, ONE PAINTER'S CURIOSITY IS AROUSED...
FUNNY! THE WALL SOUNDS HOLLOW HERE AS IF THERE MIGHT BE A SECRET STORAGE SPACE! I WONDER WHAT'S IN IT?
NOK! NOK!
AT THE OFFICE, AS CLARENCE (SUPERMAN) KELVIN EXPERIMENTS WITH HIS TELESCOPIC VISION, HE MEETS A SITUATION THAT OFTEN FACED CLARK (SUPERMAN) KENT BEFORE!
GOOD HEAVENS! THAT WHALE IS CHASING A SCHOOL OF FISH AND THAT ROWBOAT IS IN ITS PATH! I'VE GOT TO GET AWAY FROM THE OFFICE ON SOME PRETEXT...
HELP!
BY JOVE! TELL THE BOSS I WENT OUT, MISS LANE! IT'S FOR A MOST URGENT REASON... TEA TIME!
HA, HA! YOU BRITISH NEVER MISS THAT, DO YOU?
AFTER A SWIFT CHANGE, SUPERMAN REACHES THE SCENE OF IMPENDING DISASTER...
IF I JUST SNATCH THAT ROWBOAT AWAY, THE WHALE WILL STILL GO ON AND MENACE THOSE OTHER FISHERMEN! HMM... I KNOW WHAT TO DO!
FIRST, TO KEEP THE WHALE'S JAWS FROM CRUNCHING SHUT! SECOND, TO BLOW THE ROWBOAT SAFELY AWAY!
THIRD, TO USE THE FULL POWER OF MY SUPER-BREATH TO CREATE A "JET BLAST" AND BLOW THE WHALE BACKWARDS, OUT TO THE OPEN SEA WHERE HE BELONGS!
6

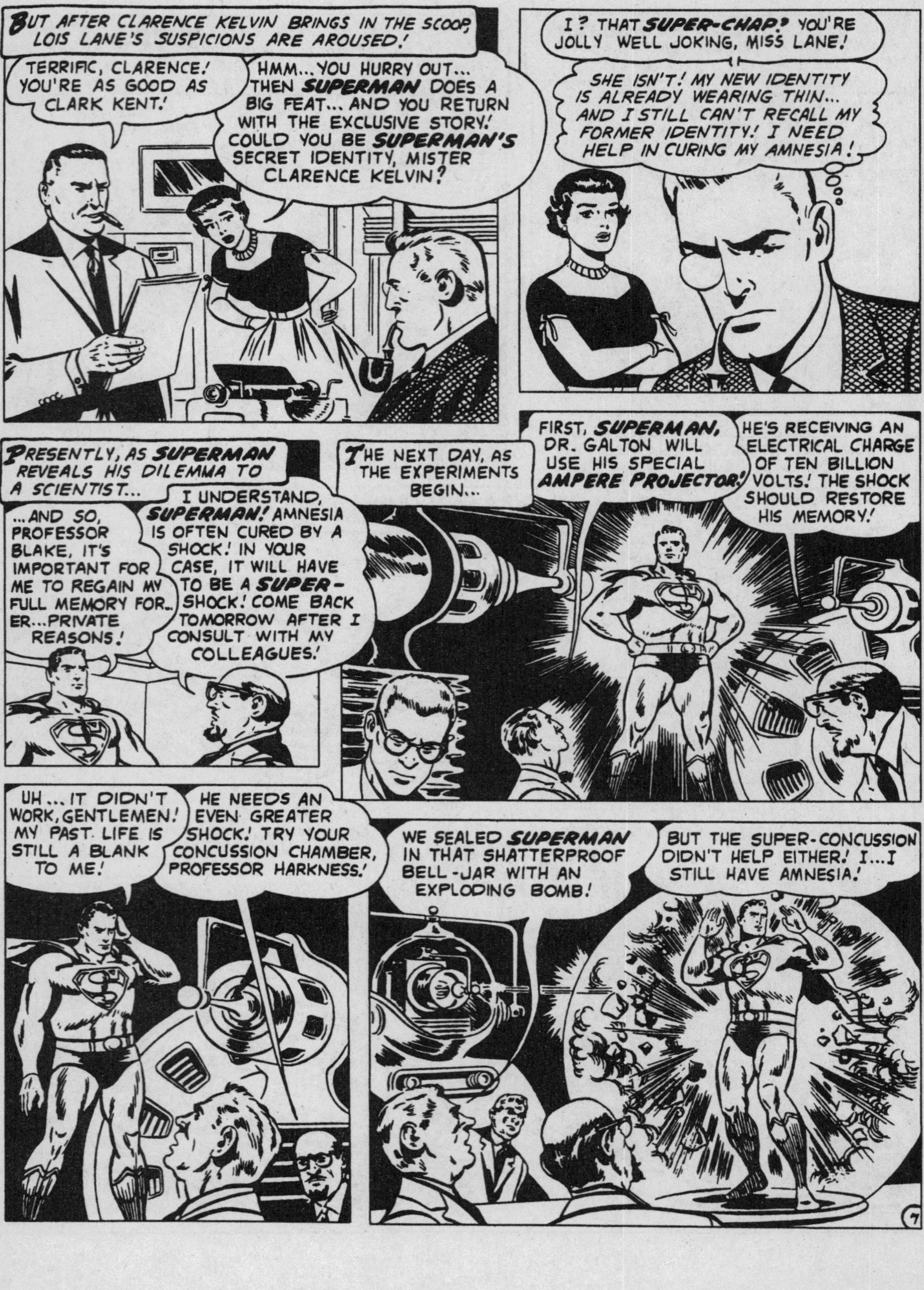
BUT AFTER CLARENCE KELVIN BRINGS IN THE SCOOP, LOIS LANE'S SUSPICIONS ARE AROUSED!
TERRIFIC, CLARENCE! YOU'RE AS GOOD AS CLARK KENT!
HMM... YOU HURRY OUT... THEN SUPERMAN DOES A BIG FEAT... AND YOU RETURN WITH THE EXCLUSIVE STORY! COULD YOU BE SUPERMAN'S SECRET IDENTITY, MISTER CLARENCE KELVIN?
I? THAT SUPER-CHAP? YOU'RE JOLLY WELL JOKING, MISS LANE!
SHE ISN'T! MY NEW IDENTITY IS ALREADY WEARING THIN... AND I STILL CAN'T RECALL MY FORMER IDENTITY! I NEED HELP IN CURING MY AMNESIA!
PRESENTLY, AS SUPERMAN REVEALS HIS DILEMMA TO A SCIENTIST...
...AND SO, PROFESSOR BLAKE, IT'S IMPORTANT FOR ME TO REGAIN MY FULL MEMORY FOR.. ER...PRIVATE REASONS!
I UNDERSTAND, SUPERMAN! AMNESIA IS OFTEN CURED BY A SHOCK! IN YOUR CASE, IT WILL HAVE TO BE A SUPER-SHOCK! COME BACK TOMORROW AFTER I CONSULT WITH MY COLLEAGUES!
THE NEXT DAY, AS THE EXPERIMENTS BEGIN...
FIRST, SUPERMAN, DR. GALTON WILL USE HIS SPECIAL AMPERE PROJECTOR!
HE'S RECEIVING AN ELECTRICAL CHARGE OF TEN BILLION VOLTS! THE SHOCK SHOULD RESTORE HIS MEMORY!
UH... IT DIDN'T WORK, GENTLEMEN! MY PAST LIFE IS STILL A BLANK TO ME!
HE NEEDS AN EVEN GREATER SHOCK! TRY YOUR CONCUSSION CHAMBER, PROFESSOR HARKNESS!
WE SEALED SUPERMAN IN THAT SHATTERPROOF BELL-JAR WITH AN EXPLODING BOMB!
BUT THE SUPER-CONCUSSION DIDN'T HELP EITHER! I...I STILL HAVE AMNESIA!
7

METHOD AFTER METHOD IS TRIED TO GIVE THE *MAN OF STEEL* A MENTAL SHOCK!

THAT ATOMIC CANNON SHOT YOU AGAINST A BARRIER OF STEEL ARMOR PLATE! WILL THE BLOW TO YOUR HEAD CURE YOUR AMNESIA?

ER... AFRAID NOT, SIR! TO ME, IT'S NO WORSE THAN AN ACORN FALLING!

WHAM!

CRASH!

THEN...

AND THIS ICE-COLD PLUNGE INTO LIQUEFIED HYDROGEN, AT SUPER-LOW TEMPERATURES, DIDN'T DO THE TRICK EITHER!

FINALLY...

SORRY, *SUPERMAN!* THERE ARE NO GREATER SHOCKS KNOWN TO SCIENCE!

AND I STILL HAVE AMNESIA! WELL, THANKS FOR TRYING, GENTLEMEN! I MAY *NEVER* DISCOVER MY FORMER SECRET IDENTITY!

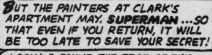

BUT THE PAINTERS AT CLARK'S APARTMENT MAY, *SUPERMAN* ...SO THAT EVEN IF YOU RETURN, IT WILL BE TOO LATE TO SAVE YOUR SECRET!

LOOK! I FOUND THE EDGE OF THIS SECRET CLOSET, BUT I CAN'T PULL IT OPEN WITH MY FINGERS! I SUPPOSE THERE'S SOME SECRET BUTTON THAT OPENS IT! WISH I COULD FIND IT AND SEE WHAT KENT HIDES IN HERE!

MEANWHILE, STILL SEARCHING FOR A CLUE TO HIS IDENTITY, *THE MAN OF STEEL* RETURNS TO THE *SUPERMAN MUSEUM*..

ARE THERE ANY HIDDEN CLUES HERE TO MY SECRET IDENTITY? WAIT...

SUPERBABY'S LANDING ON EARTH BY ROCKET! SUPERMAN DISCOVERED THIS FACT BY OVER-TAKING LIGHTRAYS OF THIS SCENE, WHICH LEFT EARTH YEARS AGO!

8

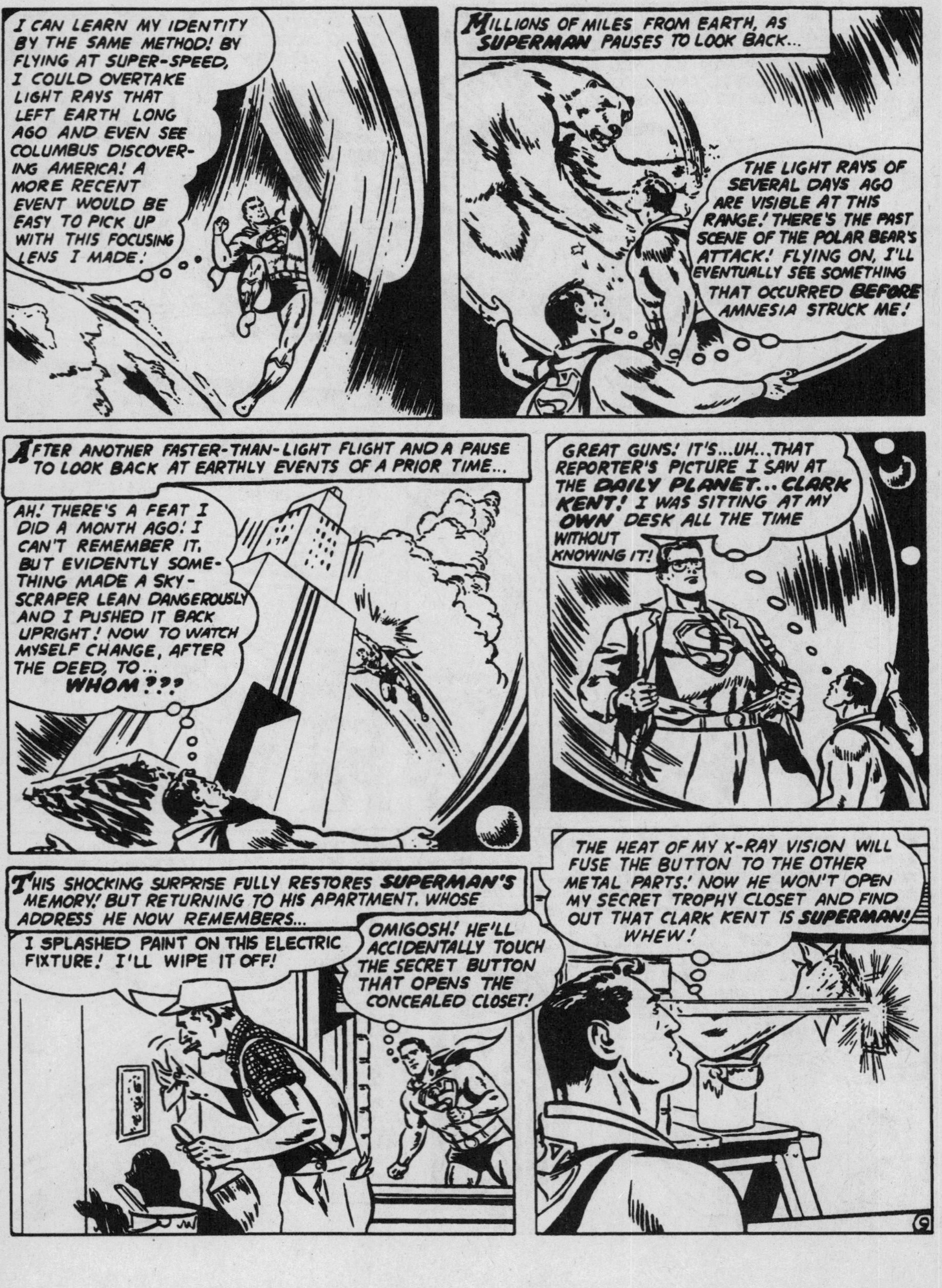
I CAN LEARN MY IDENTITY BY THE SAME METHOD! BY FLYING AT SUPER-SPEED, I COULD OVERTAKE LIGHT RAYS THAT LEFT EARTH LONG AGO AND EVEN SEE COLUMBUS DISCOVERING AMERICA! A MORE RECENT EVENT WOULD BE EASY TO PICK UP WITH THIS FOCUSING LENS I MADE!
MILLIONS OF MILES FROM EARTH, AS SUPERMAN PAUSES TO LOOK BACK...
THE LIGHT RAYS OF SEVERAL DAYS AGO ARE VISIBLE AT THIS RANGE! THERE'S THE PAST SCENE OF THE POLAR BEAR'S ATTACK! FLYING ON, I'LL EVENTUALLY SEE SOMETHING THAT OCCURRED BEFORE AMNESIA STRUCK ME!
AFTER ANOTHER FASTER-THAN-LIGHT FLIGHT AND A PAUSE TO LOOK BACK AT EARTHLY EVENTS OF A PRIOR TIME...
AH! THERE'S A FEAT I DID A MONTH AGO! I CAN'T REMEMBER IT, BUT EVIDENTLY SOMETHING MADE A SKYSCRAPER LEAN DANGEROUSLY AND I PUSHED IT BACK UPRIGHT! NOW TO WATCH MYSELF CHANGE, AFTER THE DEED, TO... WHOM???
GREAT GUNS! IT'S...UH...THAT REPORTER'S PICTURE I SAW AT THE DAILY PLANET...CLARK KENT! I WAS SITTING AT MY OWN DESK ALL THE TIME WITHOUT KNOWING IT!
THIS SHOCKING SURPRISE FULLY RESTORES SUPERMAN'S MEMORY! BUT RETURNING TO HIS APARTMENT, WHOSE ADDRESS HE NOW REMEMBERS...
I SPLASHED PAINT ON THIS ELECTRIC FIXTURE! I'LL WIPE IT OFF!
OMIGOSH! HE'LL ACCIDENTALLY TOUCH THE SECRET BUTTON THAT OPENS THE CONCEALED CLOSET!
THE HEAT OF MY X-RAY VISION WILL FUSE THE BUTTON TO THE OTHER METAL PARTS! NOW HE WON'T OPEN MY SECRET TROPHY CLOSET AND FIND OUT THAT CLARK KENT IS SUPERMAN! WHEW!
9

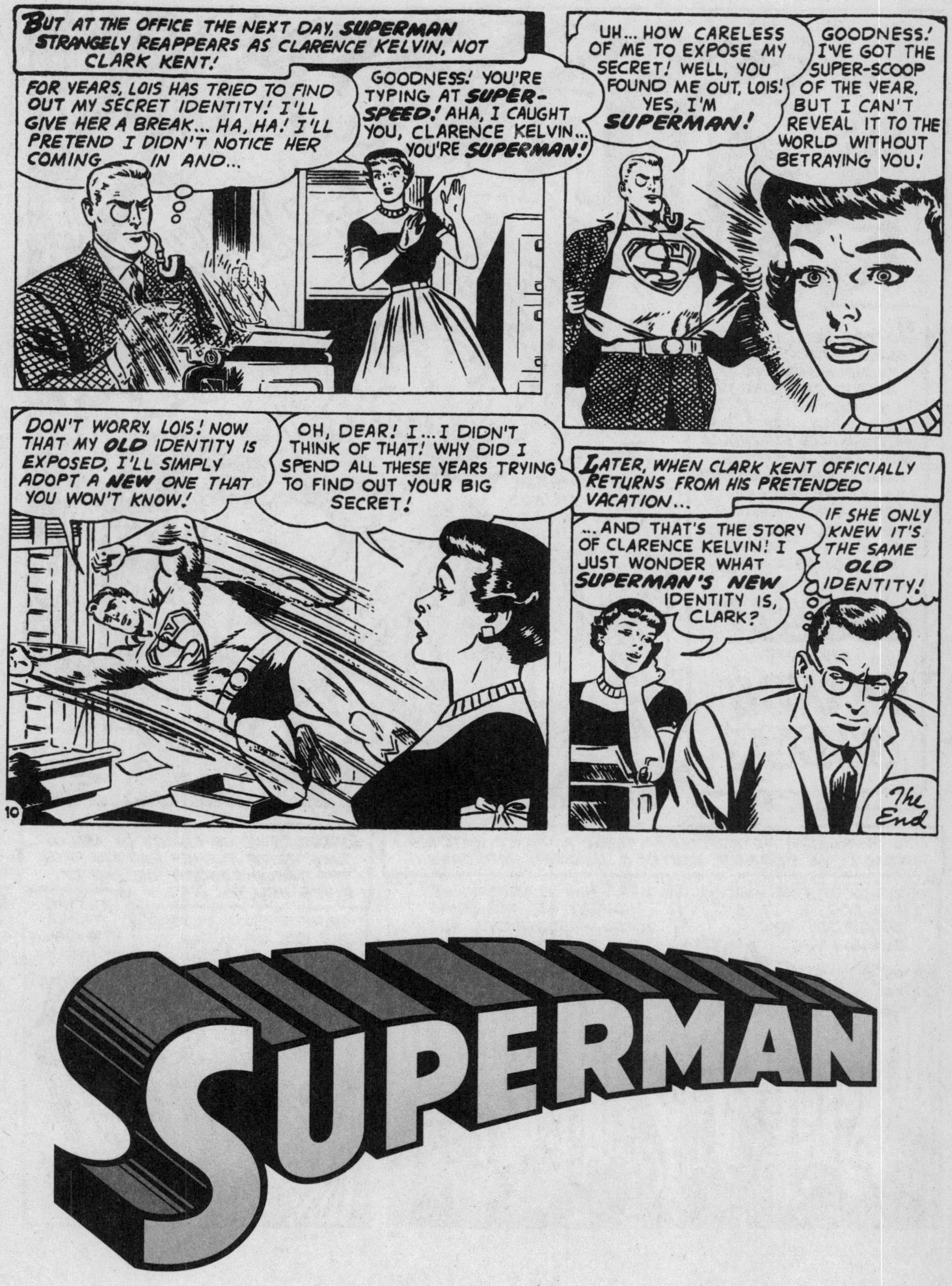
BUT AT THE OFFICE THE NEXT DAY, SUPERMAN STRANGELY REAPPEARS AS CLARENCE KELVIN, NOT CLARK KENT!
FOR YEARS, LOIS HAS TRIED TO FIND OUT MY SECRET IDENTITY! I'LL GIVE HER A BREAK... HA, HA! I'LL PRETEND I DIDN'T NOTICE HER COMING IN AND...
GOODNESS! YOU'RE TYPING AT SUPER-SPEED! AHA, I CAUGHT YOU, CLARENCE KELVIN... YOU'RE SUPERMAN!
UH... HOW CARELESS OF ME TO EXPOSE MY SECRET! WELL, YOU FOUND ME OUT, LOIS! YES, I'M SUPERMAN!
GOODNESS! I'VE GOT THE SUPER-SCOOP OF THE YEAR, BUT I CAN'T REVEAL IT TO THE WORLD WITHOUT BETRAYING YOU!
DON'T WORRY, LOIS! NOW THAT MY OLD IDENTITY IS EXPOSED, I'LL SIMPLY ADOPT A NEW ONE THAT YOU WON'T KNOW!
OH, DEAR! I...I DIDN'T THINK OF THAT! WHY DID I SPEND ALL THESE YEARS TRYING TO FIND OUT YOUR BIG SECRET!
10
LATER, WHEN CLARK KENT OFFICIALLY RETURNS FROM HIS PRETENDED VACATION...
...AND THAT'S THE STORY OF CLARENCE KELVIN! I JUST WONDER WHAT SUPERMAN'S NEW IDENTITY IS, CLARK?
IF SHE ONLY KNEW IT'S THE SAME OLD IDENTITY!
The End

SUPERMAN

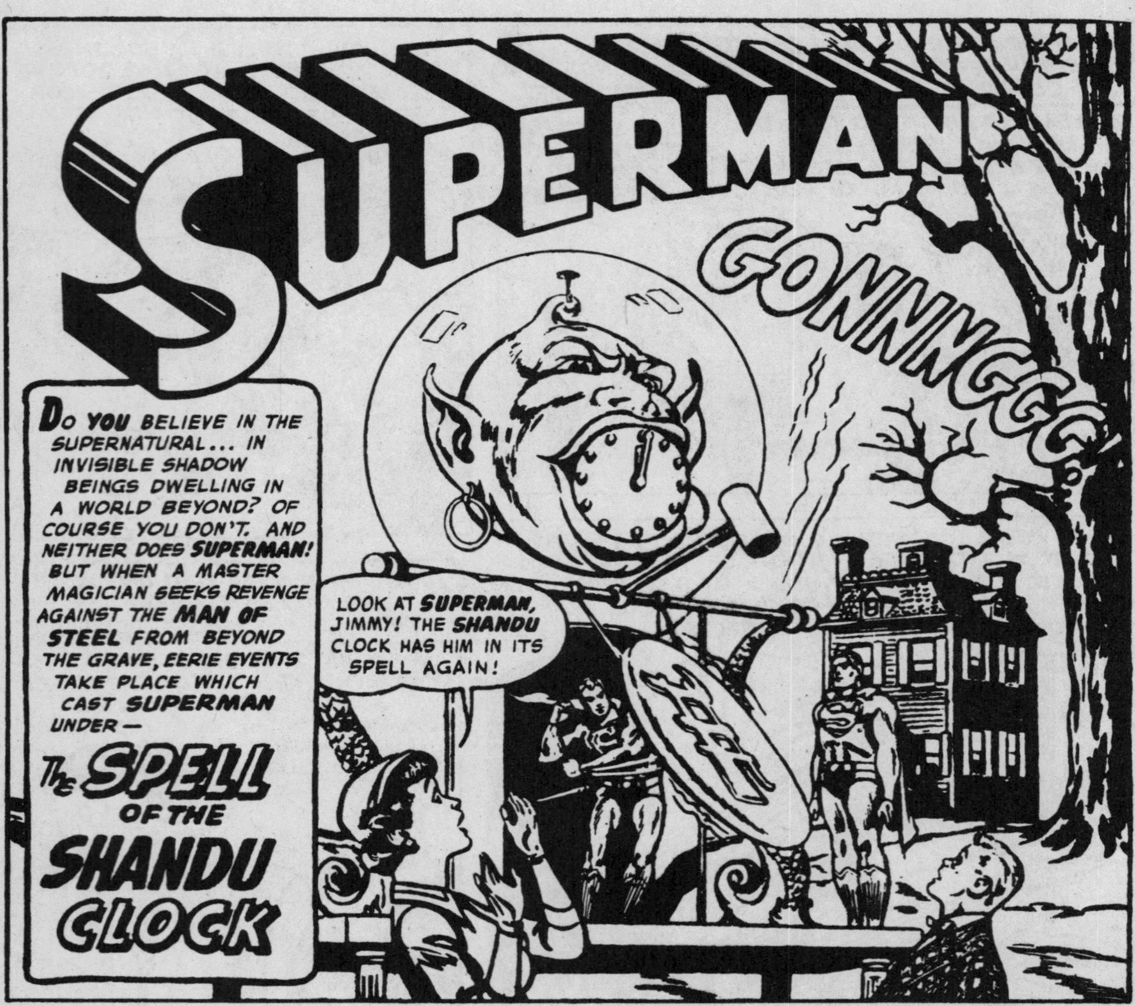
SUPERMAN
GONNNGGG
DO YOU BELIEVE IN THE SUPERNATURAL... IN INVISIBLE SHADOW BEINGS DWELLING IN A WORLD BEYOND? OF COURSE YOU DON'T. AND NEITHER DOES SUPERMAN! BUT WHEN A MASTER MAGICIAN SEEKS REVENGE AGAINST THE MAN OF STEEL FROM BEYOND THE GRAVE, EERIE EVENTS TAKE PLACE WHICH CAST SUPERMAN UNDER —
THE SPELL OF THE SHANDU CLOCK
LOOK AT SUPERMAN, JIMMY! THE SHANDU CLOCK HAS HIM IN ITS SPELL AGAIN!

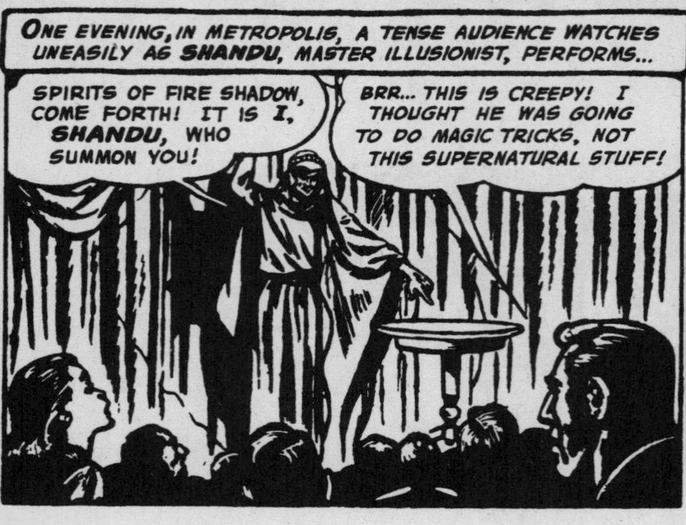
ONE EVENING, IN METROPOLIS, A TENSE AUDIENCE WATCHES UNEASILY AS SHANDU, MASTER ILLUSIONIST, PERFORMS...
SPIRITS OF FIRE SHADOW, COME FORTH! IT IS I, SHANDU, WHO SUMMON YOU!
BRR... THIS IS CREEPY! I THOUGHT HE WAS GOING TO DO MAGIC TRICKS, NOT THIS SUPERNATURAL STUFF!

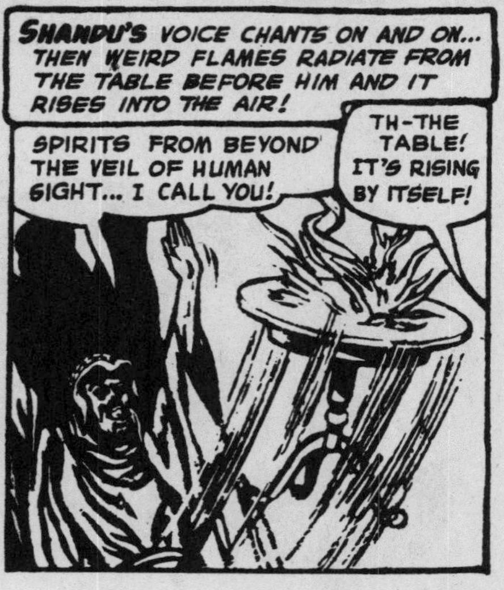
SHANDU'S VOICE CHANTS ON AND ON... THEN WEIRD FLAMES RADIATE FROM THE TABLE BEFORE HIM AND IT RISES INTO THE AIR!
SPIRITS FROM BEYOND THE VEIL OF HUMAN SIGHT... I CALL YOU!
TH-THE TABLE! IT'S RISING BY ITSELF!

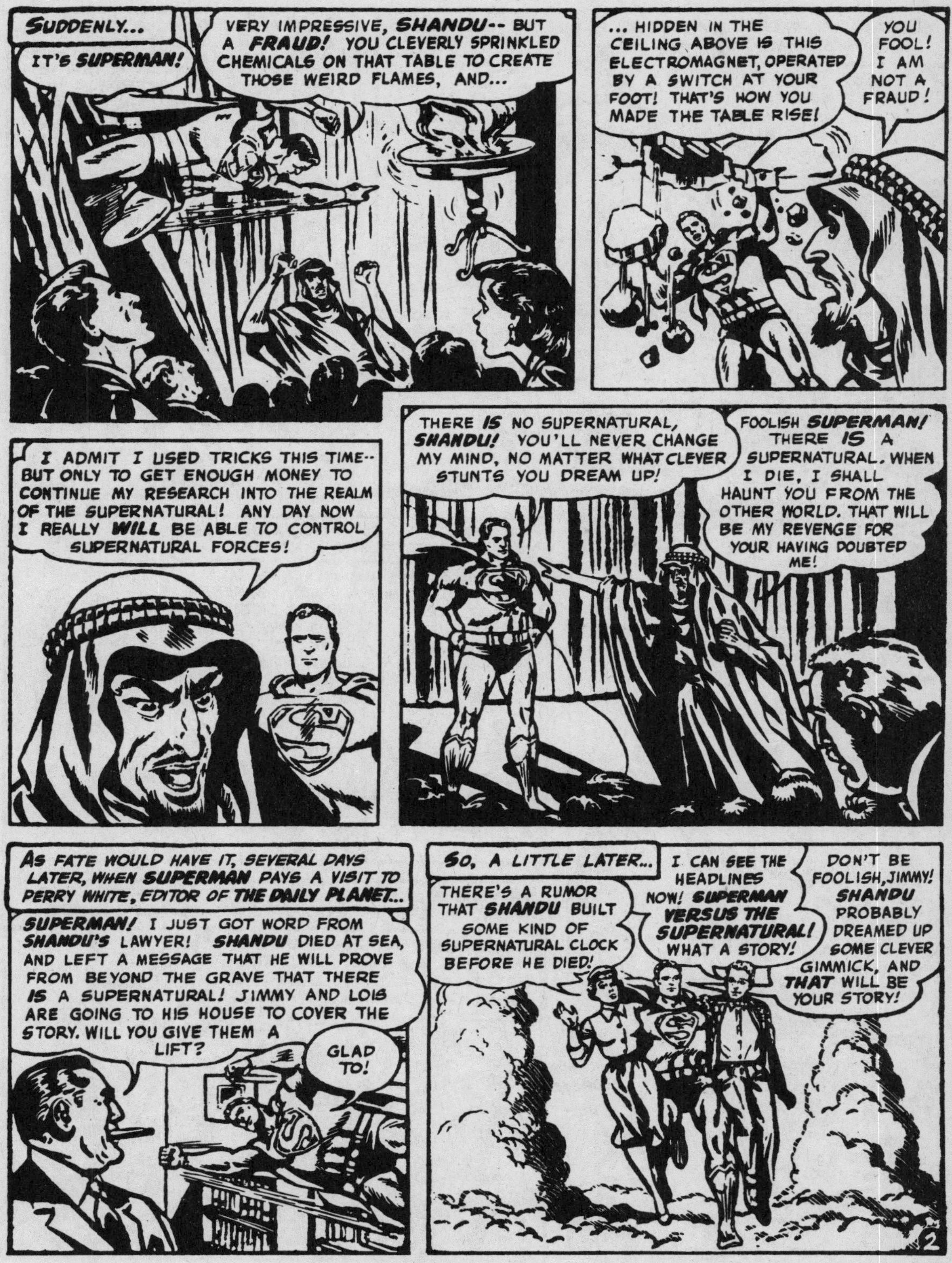
SUDDENLY...
IT'S SUPERMAN!
VERY IMPRESSIVE, SHANDU-- BUT A FRAUD! YOU CLEVERLY SPRINKLED CHEMICALS ON THAT TABLE TO CREATE THOSE WEIRD FLAMES, AND...
... HIDDEN IN THE CEILING ABOVE IS THIS ELECTROMAGNET, OPERATED BY A SWITCH AT YOUR FOOT! THAT'S HOW YOU MADE THE TABLE RISE!
YOU FOOL! I AM NOT A FRAUD!
I ADMIT I USED TRICKS THIS TIME-- BUT ONLY TO GET ENOUGH MONEY TO CONTINUE MY RESEARCH INTO THE REALM OF THE SUPERNATURAL! ANY DAY NOW I REALLY WILL BE ABLE TO CONTROL SUPERNATURAL FORCES!
THERE IS NO SUPERNATURAL, SHANDU! YOU'LL NEVER CHANGE MY MIND, NO MATTER WHAT CLEVER STUNTS YOU DREAM UP!
FOOLISH SUPERMAN! THERE IS A SUPERNATURAL. WHEN I DIE, I SHALL HAUNT YOU FROM THE OTHER WORLD. THAT WILL BE MY REVENGE FOR YOUR HAVING DOUBTED ME!
AS FATE WOULD HAVE IT, SEVERAL DAYS LATER, WHEN SUPERMAN PAYS A VISIT TO PERRY WHITE, EDITOR OF THE DAILY PLANET...
SUPERMAN! I JUST GOT WORD FROM SHANDU'S LAWYER! SHANDU DIED AT SEA, AND LEFT A MESSAGE THAT HE WILL PROVE FROM BEYOND THE GRAVE THAT THERE IS A SUPERNATURAL! JIMMY AND LOIS ARE GOING TO HIS HOUSE TO COVER THE STORY. WILL YOU GIVE THEM A LIFT?
GLAD TO!
SO, A LITTLE LATER...
THERE'S A RUMOR THAT SHANDU BUILT SOME KIND OF SUPERNATURAL CLOCK BEFORE HE DIED!
I CAN SEE THE HEADLINES NOW! SUPERMAN VERSUS THE SUPERNATURAL! WHAT A STORY!
DON'T BE FOOLISH, JIMMY! SHANDU PROBABLY DREAMED UP SOME CLEVER GIMMICK, AND THAT WILL BE YOUR STORY!
2

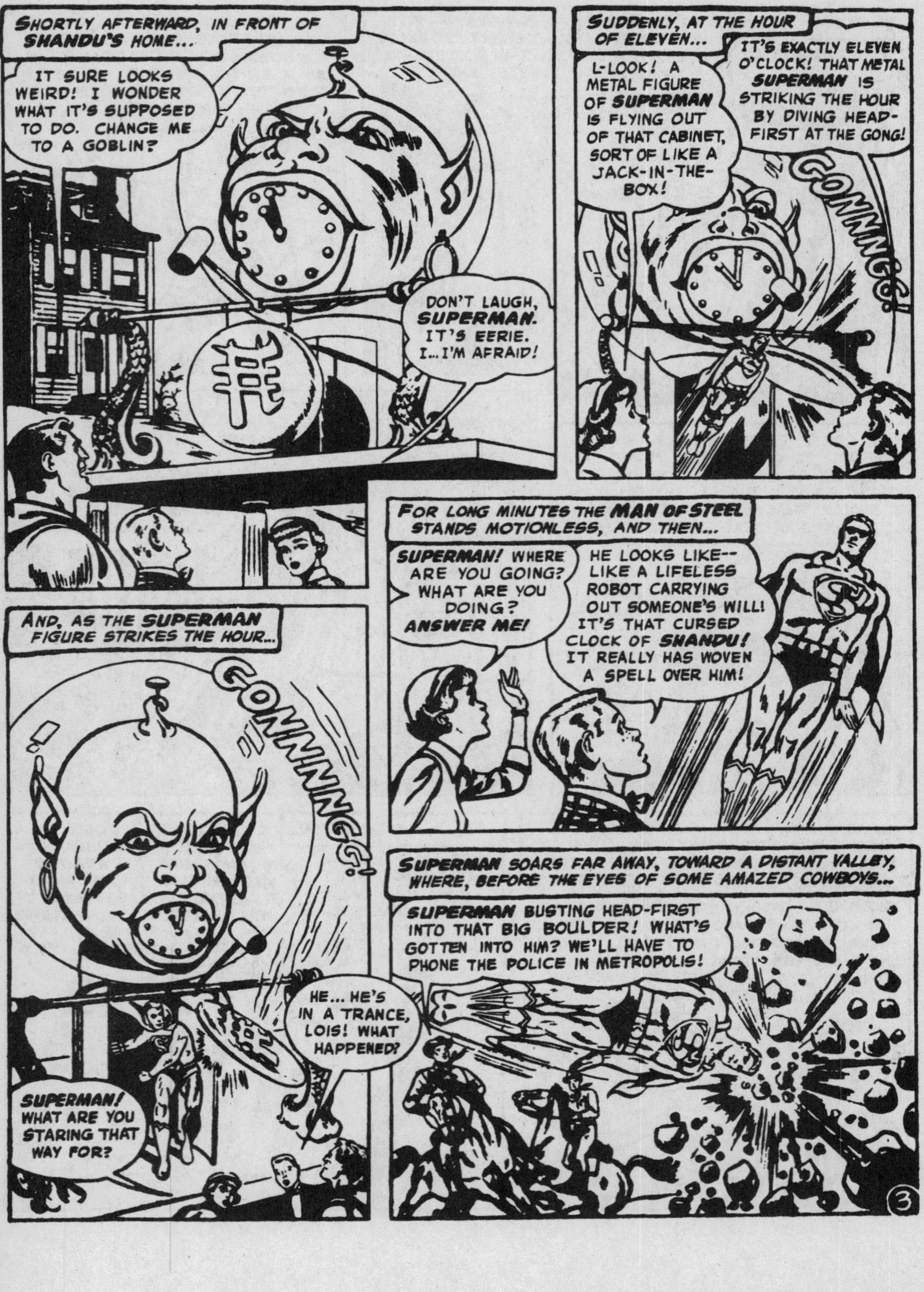
SHORTLY AFTERWARD, IN FRONT OF SHANDU'S HOME...
IT SURE LOOKS WEIRD! I WONDER WHAT IT'S SUPPOSED TO DO. CHANGE ME TO A GOBLIN?
DON'T LAUGH, SUPERMAN. IT'S EERIE. I...I'M AFRAID!
SUDDENLY, AT THE HOUR OF ELEVEN...
L-LOOK! A METAL FIGURE OF SUPERMAN IS FLYING OUT OF THAT CABINET, SORT OF LIKE A JACK-IN-THE-BOX!
IT'S EXACTLY ELEVEN O'CLOCK! THAT METAL SUPERMAN IS STRIKING THE HOUR BY DIVING HEAD-FIRST AT THE GONG!
GONNNG!
AND, AS THE SUPERMAN FIGURE STRIKES THE HOUR...
GONNNNG!
SUPERMAN! WHAT ARE YOU STARING THAT WAY FOR?
HE... HE'S IN A TRANCE, LOIS! WHAT HAPPENED?
FOR LONG MINUTES THE MAN OF STEEL STANDS MOTIONLESS, AND THEN...
SUPERMAN! WHERE ARE YOU GOING? WHAT ARE YOU DOING? ANSWER ME!
HE LOOKS LIKE-- LIKE A LIFELESS ROBOT CARRYING OUT SOMEONE'S WILL! IT'S THAT CURSED CLOCK OF SHANDU! IT REALLY HAS WOVEN A SPELL OVER HIM!
SUPERMAN SOARS FAR AWAY, TOWARD A DISTANT VALLEY, WHERE, BEFORE THE EYES OF SOME AMAZED COWBOYS...
SUPERMAN BUSTING HEAD-FIRST INTO THAT BIG BOULDER! WHAT'S GOTTEN INTO HIM? WE'LL HAVE TO PHONE THE POLICE IN METROPOLIS!
3

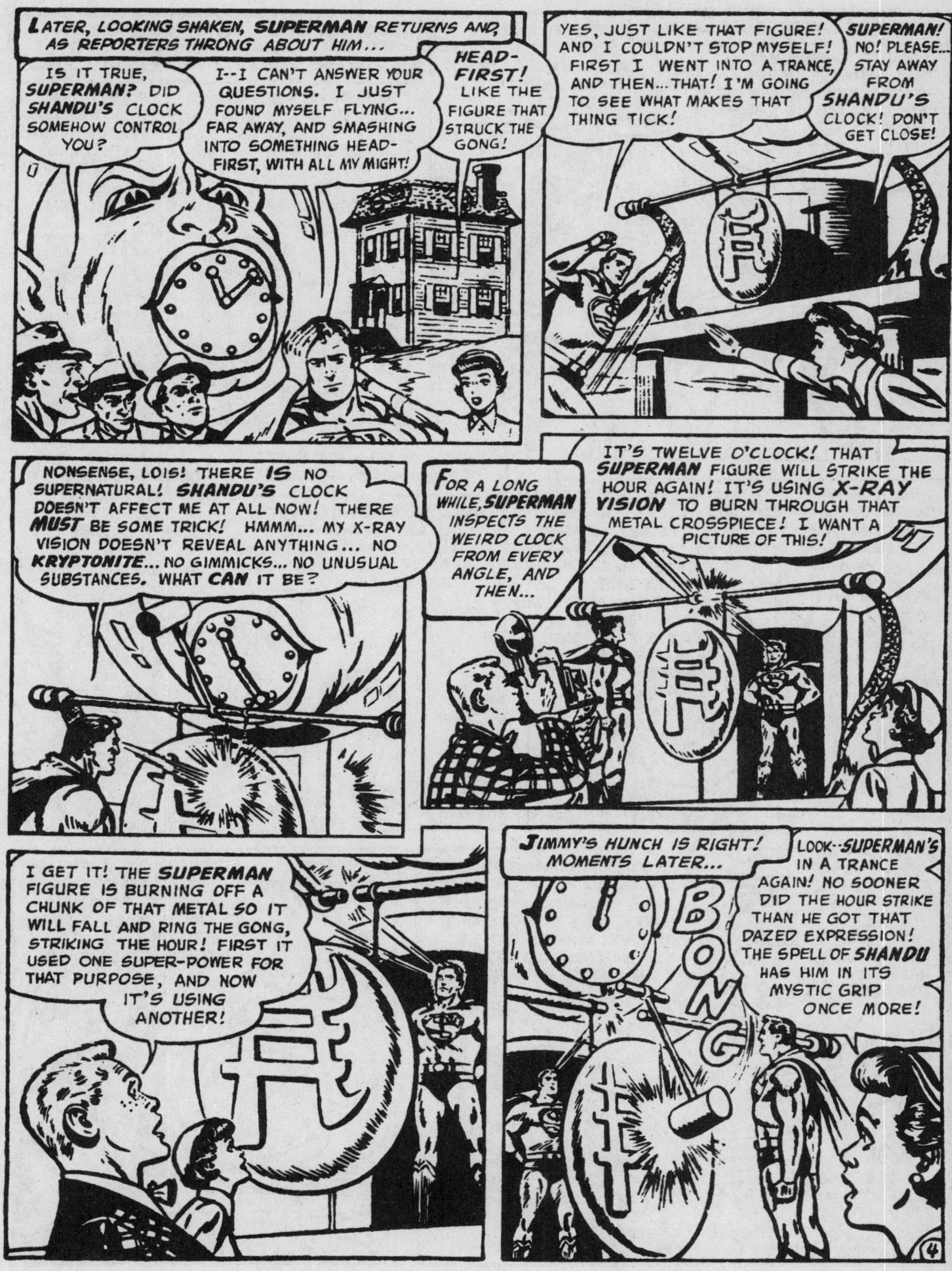
LATER, LOOKING SHAKEN, SUPERMAN RETURNS AND, AS REPORTERS THRONG ABOUT HIM...
IS IT TRUE, SUPERMAN? DID SHANDU'S CLOCK SOMEHOW CONTROL YOU?
I--I CAN'T ANSWER YOUR QUESTIONS. I JUST FOUND MYSELF FLYING... FAR AWAY, AND SMASHING INTO SOMETHING HEAD-FIRST, WITH ALL MY MIGHT!
HEAD-FIRST! LIKE THE FIGURE THAT STRUCK THE GONG!
YES, JUST LIKE THAT FIGURE! AND I COULDN'T STOP MYSELF! FIRST I WENT INTO A TRANCE, AND THEN...THAT! I'M GOING TO SEE WHAT MAKES THAT THING TICK!
SUPERMAN! NO! PLEASE... STAY AWAY FROM SHANDU'S CLOCK! DON'T GET CLOSE!
NONSENSE, LOIS! THERE IS NO SUPERNATURAL! SHANDU'S CLOCK DOESN'T AFFECT ME AT ALL NOW! THERE MUST BE SOME TRICK! HMMM... MY X-RAY VISION DOESN'T REVEAL ANYTHING... NO KRYPTONITE... NO GIMMICKS... NO UNUSUAL SUBSTANCES. WHAT CAN IT BE?
FOR A LONG WHILE, SUPERMAN INSPECTS THE WEIRD CLOCK FROM EVERY ANGLE, AND THEN...
IT'S TWELVE O'CLOCK! THAT SUPERMAN FIGURE WILL STRIKE THE HOUR AGAIN! IT'S USING X-RAY VISION TO BURN THROUGH THAT METAL CROSSPIECE! I WANT A PICTURE OF THIS!
I GET IT! THE SUPERMAN FIGURE IS BURNING OFF A CHUNK OF THAT METAL SO IT WILL FALL AND RING THE GONG, STRIKING THE HOUR! FIRST IT USED ONE SUPER-POWER FOR THAT PURPOSE, AND NOW IT'S USING ANOTHER!
JIMMY'S HUNCH IS RIGHT! MOMENTS LATER...
BONG
LOOK--SUPERMAN'S IN A TRANCE AGAIN! NO SOONER DID THE HOUR STRIKE THAN HE GOT THAT DAZED EXPRESSION! THE SPELL OF SHANDU HAS HIM IN ITS MYSTIC GRIP ONCE MORE!
4

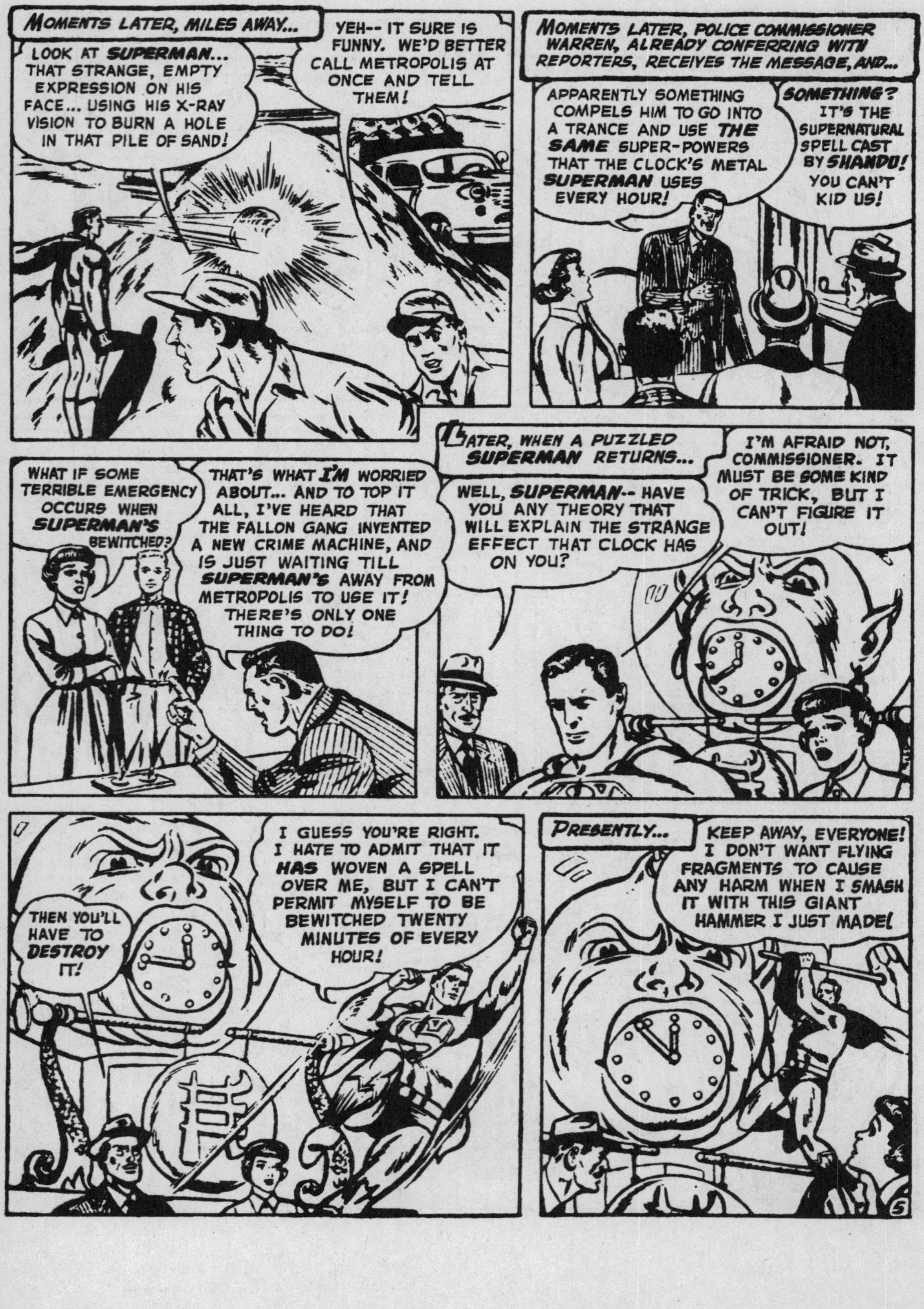
MOMENTS LATER, MILES AWAY...
LOOK AT SUPERMAN... THAT STRANGE, EMPTY EXPRESSION ON HIS FACE... USING HIS X-RAY VISION TO BURN A HOLE IN THAT PILE OF SAND!
YEH-- IT SURE IS FUNNY. WE'D BETTER CALL METROPOLIS AT ONCE AND TELL THEM!
MOMENTS LATER, POLICE COMMISSIONER WARREN, ALREADY CONFERRING WITH REPORTERS, RECEIVES THE MESSAGE, AND...
APPARENTLY SOMETHING COMPELS HIM TO GO INTO A TRANCE AND USE THE SAME SUPER-POWERS THAT THE CLOCK'S METAL SUPERMAN USES EVERY HOUR!
SOMETHING? IT'S THE SUPERNATURAL SPELL CAST BY SHANDU! YOU CAN'T KID US!
WHAT IF SOME TERRIBLE EMERGENCY OCCURS WHEN SUPERMAN'S BEWITCHED?
THAT'S WHAT I'M WORRIED ABOUT... AND TO TOP IT ALL, I'VE HEARD THAT THE FALLON GANG INVENTED A NEW CRIME MACHINE, AND IS JUST WAITING TILL SUPERMAN'S AWAY FROM METROPOLIS TO USE IT! THERE'S ONLY ONE THING TO DO!
LATER, WHEN A PUZZLED SUPERMAN RETURNS...
WELL, SUPERMAN-- HAVE YOU ANY THEORY THAT WILL EXPLAIN THE STRANGE EFFECT THAT CLOCK HAS ON YOU?
I'M AFRAID NOT, COMMISSIONER. IT MUST BE SOME KIND OF TRICK, BUT I CAN'T FIGURE IT OUT!
THEN YOU'LL HAVE TO DESTROY IT!
I GUESS YOU'RE RIGHT. I HATE TO ADMIT THAT IT HAS WOVEN A SPELL OVER ME, BUT I CAN'T PERMIT MYSELF TO BE BEWITCHED TWENTY MINUTES OF EVERY HOUR!
PRESENTLY...
KEEP AWAY, EVERYONE! I DON'T WANT FLYING FRAGMENTS TO CAUSE ANY HARM WHEN I SMASH IT WITH THIS GIANT HAMMER I JUST MADE!
5

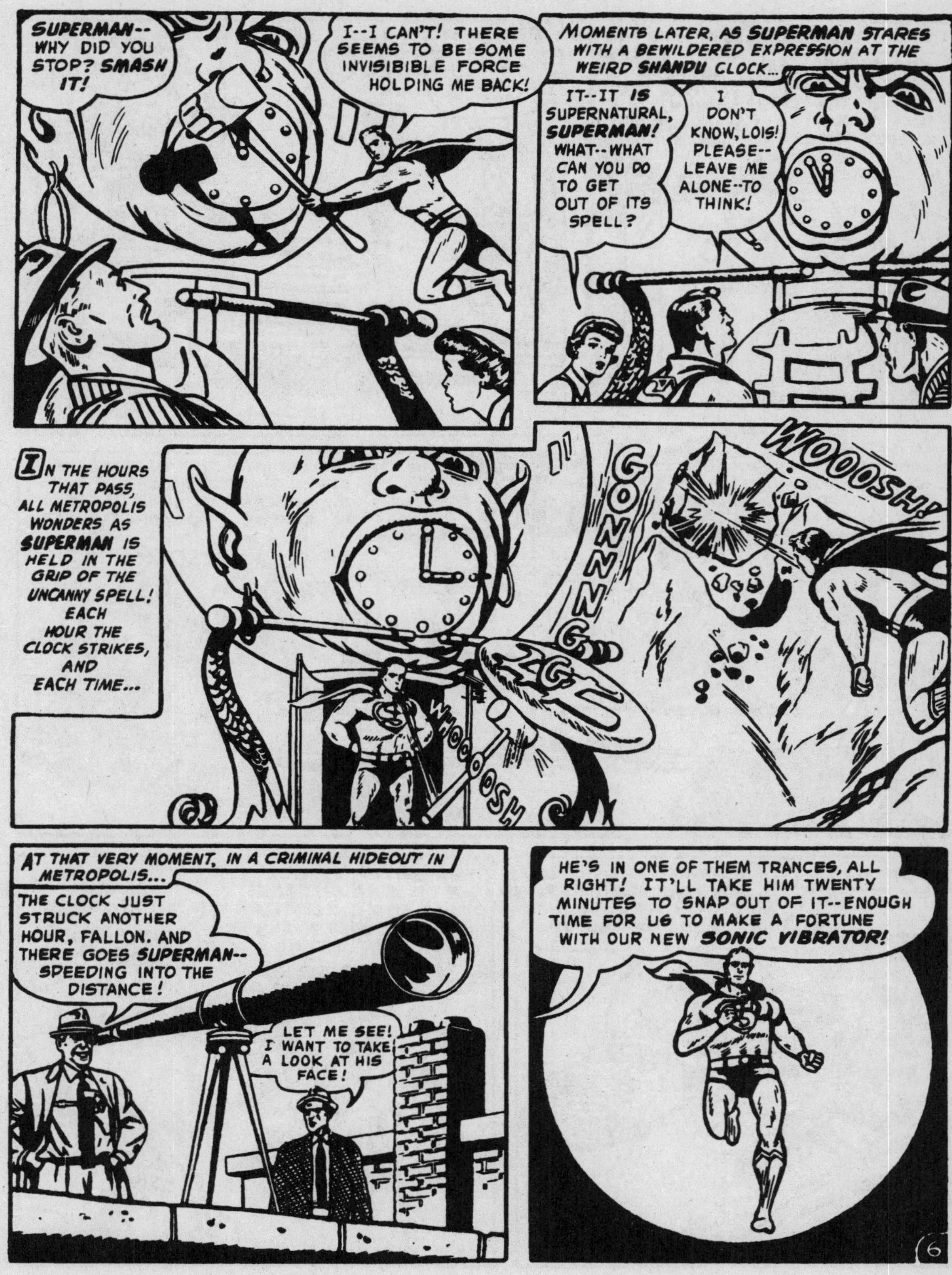
SUPERMAN-- WHY DID YOU STOP? SMASH IT!
I--I CAN'T! THERE SEEMS TO BE SOME INVISIBLE FORCE HOLDING ME BACK!
MOMENTS LATER, AS SUPERMAN STARES WITH A BEWILDERED EXPRESSION AT THE WEIRD SHANDU CLOCK...
IT--IT IS SUPERNATURAL, SUPERMAN! WHAT--WHAT CAN YOU DO TO GET OUT OF ITS SPELL?
I DON'T KNOW, LOIS! PLEASE-- LEAVE ME ALONE--TO THINK!
IN THE HOURS THAT PASS, ALL METROPOLIS WONDERS AS SUPERMAN IS HELD IN THE GRIP OF THE UNCANNY SPELL! EACH HOUR THE CLOCK STRIKES, AND EACH TIME...
GONNNNG
WHOOOOSH
WOOOOSH!
AT THAT VERY MOMENT, IN A CRIMINAL HIDEOUT IN METROPOLIS...
THE CLOCK JUST STRUCK ANOTHER HOUR, FALLON. AND THERE GOES SUPERMAN-- SPEEDING INTO THE DISTANCE!
LET ME SEE! I WANT TO TAKE A LOOK AT HIS FACE!
HE'S IN ONE OF THEM TRANCES, ALL RIGHT! IT'LL TAKE HIM TWENTY MINUTES TO SNAP OUT OF IT--ENOUGH TIME FOR US TO MAKE A FORTUNE WITH OUR NEW SONIC VIBRATOR!
6

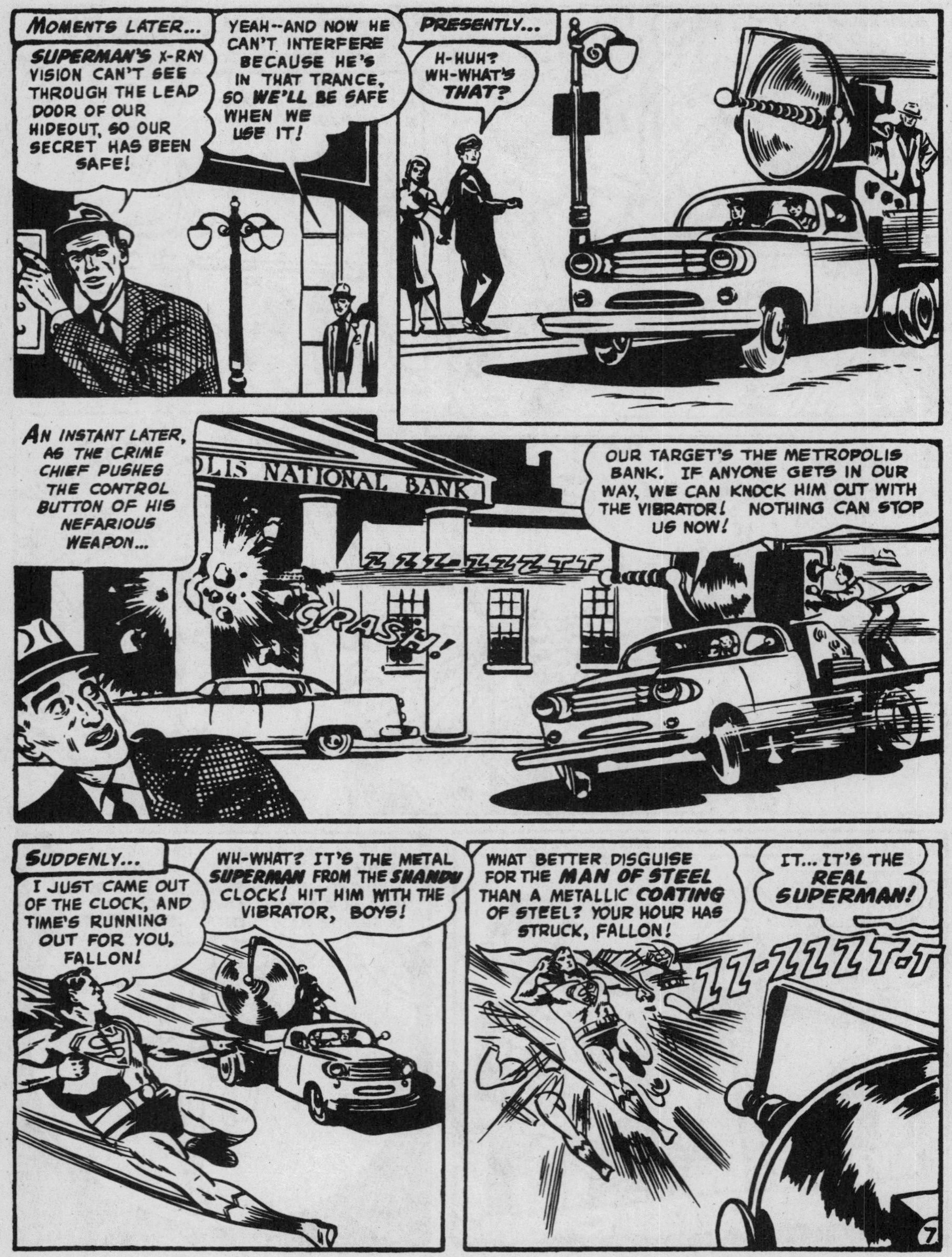
MOMENTS LATER...
SUPERMAN'S X-RAY VISION CAN'T SEE THROUGH THE LEAD DOOR OF OUR HIDEOUT, SO OUR SECRET HAS BEEN SAFE!
YEAH--AND NOW HE CAN'T INTERFERE BECAUSE HE'S IN THAT TRANCE, SO WE'LL BE SAFE WHEN WE USE IT!
PRESENTLY...
H-HUH? WH-WHAT'S THAT?
AN INSTANT LATER, AS THE CRIME CHIEF PUSHES THE CONTROL BUTTON OF HIS NEFARIOUS WEAPON...
OLIS NATIONAL BANK
OUR TARGET'S THE METROPOLIS BANK. IF ANYONE GETS IN OUR WAY, WE CAN KNOCK HIM OUT WITH THE VIBRATOR! NOTHING CAN STOP US NOW!
ZZZ-ZZZZTT
CRASH!
SUDDENLY...
I JUST CAME OUT OF THE CLOCK, AND TIME'S RUNNING OUT FOR YOU, FALLON!
WH-WHAT? IT'S THE METAL SUPERMAN FROM THE SHANDU CLOCK! HIT HIM WITH THE VIBRATOR, BOYS!
WHAT BETTER DISGUISE FOR THE MAN OF STEEL THAN A METALLIC COATING OF STEEL? YOUR HOUR HAS STRUCK, FALLON!
IT... IT'S THE REAL SUPERMAN!
ZZ-ZZZZT-T
7

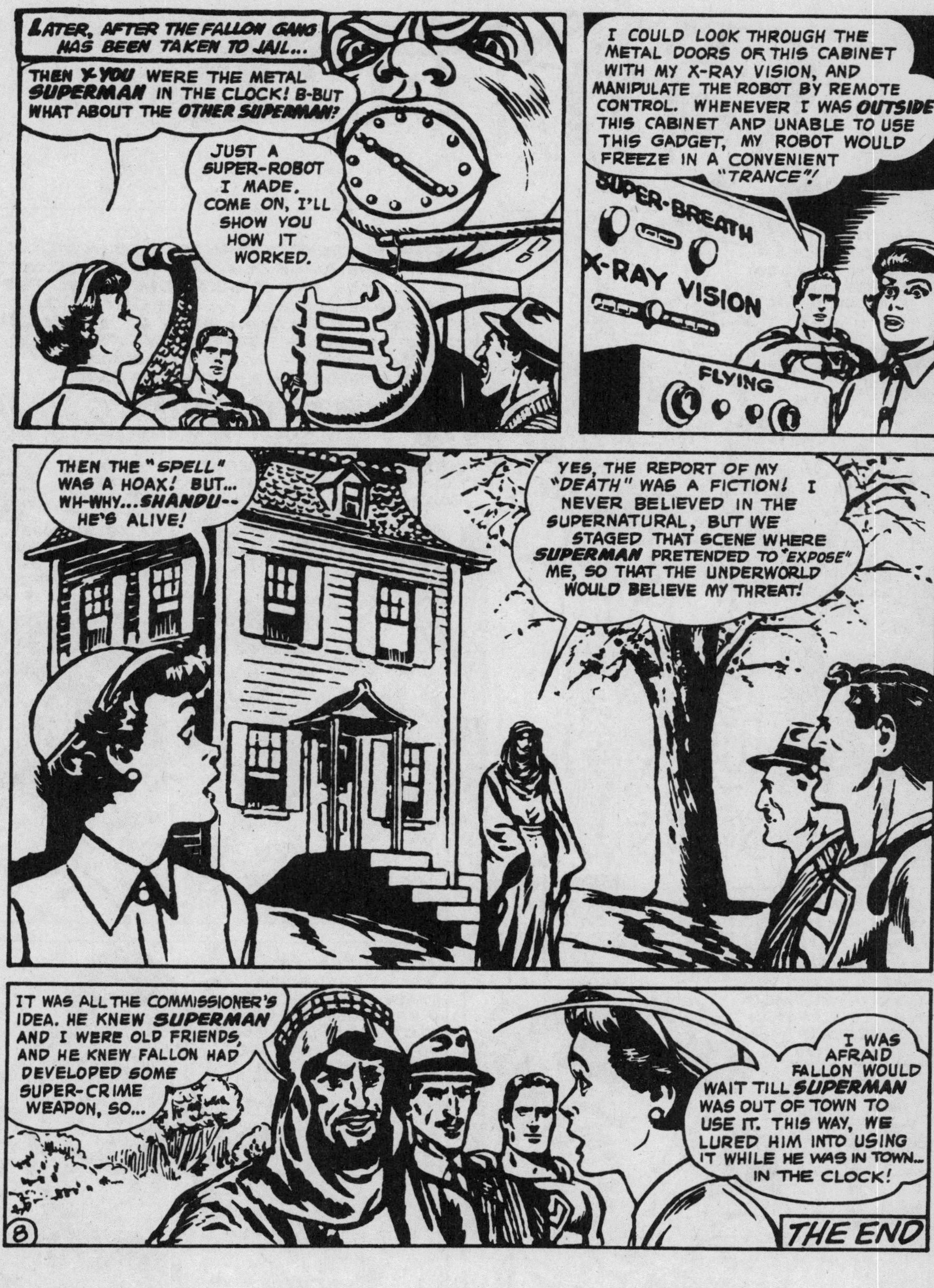
LATER, AFTER THE FALLON GANG HAS BEEN TAKEN TO JAIL...
THEN Y-YOU WERE THE METAL SUPERMAN IN THE CLOCK! B-BUT WHAT ABOUT THE OTHER SUPERMAN?
JUST A SUPER-ROBOT I MADE. COME ON, I'LL SHOW YOU HOW IT WORKED.
I COULD LOOK THROUGH THE METAL DOORS OF THIS CABINET WITH MY X-RAY VISION, AND MANIPULATE THE ROBOT BY REMOTE CONTROL. WHENEVER I WAS OUTSIDE THIS CABINET AND UNABLE TO USE THIS GADGET, MY ROBOT WOULD FREEZE IN A CONVENIENT "TRANCE"!
SUPER-BREATH
X-RAY VISION
FLYING
THEN THE "SPELL" WAS A HOAX! BUT... WH-WHY...SHANDU--HE'S ALIVE!
YES, THE REPORT OF MY "DEATH" WAS A FICTION! I NEVER BELIEVED IN THE SUPERNATURAL, BUT WE STAGED THAT SCENE WHERE SUPERMAN PRETENDED TO "EXPOSE" ME, SO THAT THE UNDERWORLD WOULD BELIEVE MY THREAT!
IT WAS ALL THE COMMISSIONER'S IDEA. HE KNEW SUPERMAN AND I WERE OLD FRIENDS, AND HE KNEW FALLON HAD DEVELOPED SOME SUPER-CRIME WEAPON, SO...
I WAS AFRAID FALLON WOULD WAIT TILL SUPERMAN WAS OUT OF TOWN TO USE IT. THIS WAY, WE LURED HIM INTO USING IT WHILE HE WAS IN TOWN... IN THE CLOCK!
8
THE END

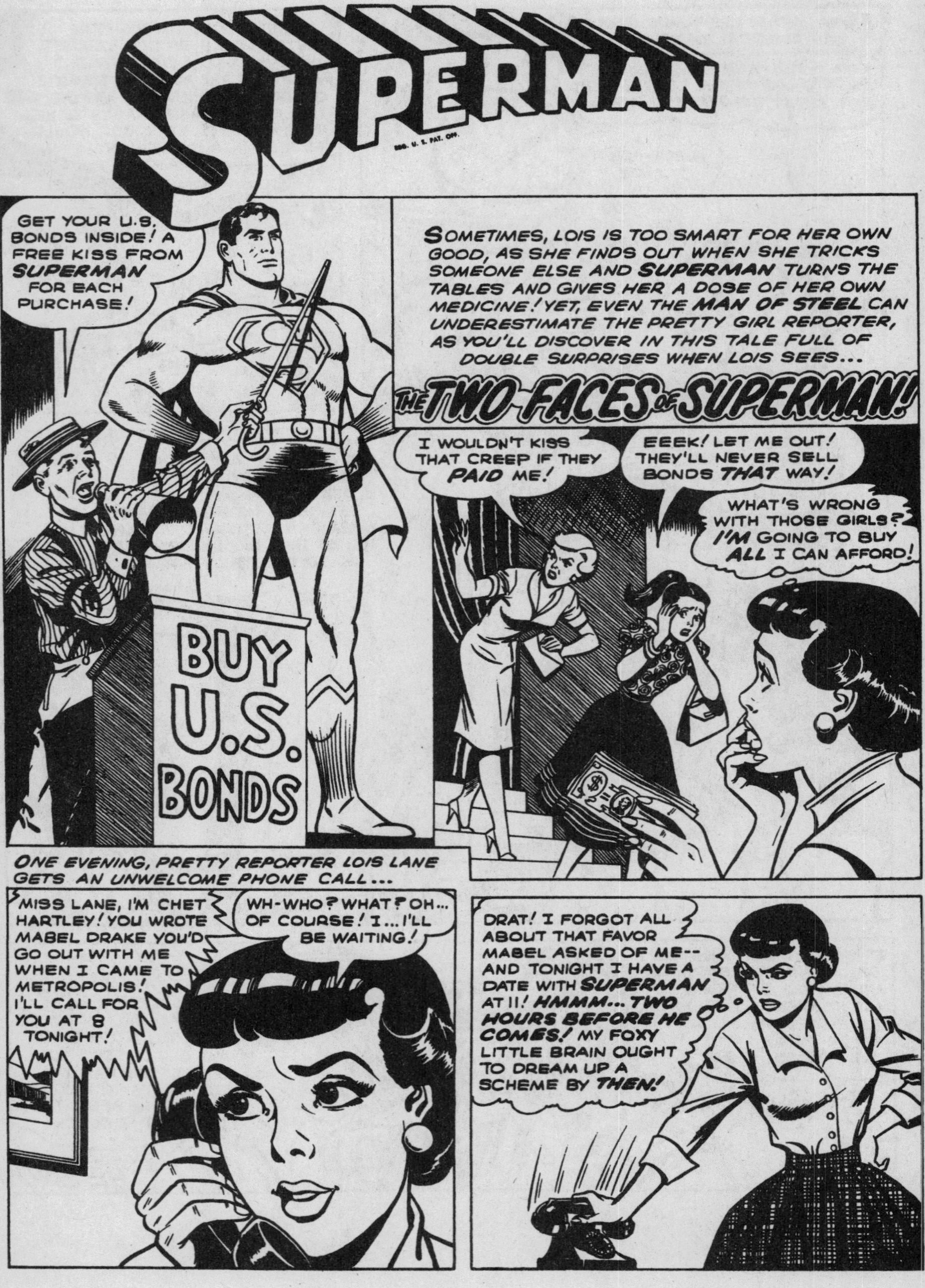
SUPERMAN
REG. U. S. PAT. OFF.
GET YOUR U.S. BONDS INSIDE! A FREE KISS FROM SUPERMAN FOR EACH PURCHASE!
BUY U.S. BONDS
SOMETIMES, LOIS IS TOO SMART FOR HER OWN GOOD, AS SHE FINDS OUT WHEN SHE TRICKS SOMEONE ELSE AND SUPERMAN TURNS THE TABLES AND GIVES HER A DOSE OF HER OWN MEDICINE! YET, EVEN THE MAN OF STEEL CAN UNDERESTIMATE THE PRETTY GIRL REPORTER, AS YOU'LL DISCOVER IN THIS TALE FULL OF DOUBLE SURPRISES WHEN LOIS SEES...
THE TWO FACES OF SUPERMAN!
I WOULDN'T KISS THAT CREEP IF THEY PAID ME!
EEEK! LET ME OUT! THEY'LL NEVER SELL BONDS THAT WAY!
WHAT'S WRONG WITH THOSE GIRLS? I'M GOING TO BUY ALL I CAN AFFORD!
ONE EVENING, PRETTY REPORTER LOIS LANE GETS AN UNWELCOME PHONE CALL...
MISS LANE, I'M CHET HARTLEY! YOU WROTE MABEL DRAKE YOU'D GO OUT WITH ME WHEN I CAME TO METROPOLIS! I'LL CALL FOR YOU AT 8 TONIGHT!
WH-WHO? WHAT? OH... OF COURSE! I...I'LL BE WAITING!
DRAT! I FORGOT ALL ABOUT THAT FAVOR MABEL ASKED OF ME-- AND TONIGHT I HAVE A DATE WITH SUPERMAN AT 11! HMMM... TWO HOURS BEFORE HE COMES! MY FOXY LITTLE BRAIN OUGHT TO DREAM UP A SCHEME BY THEN!

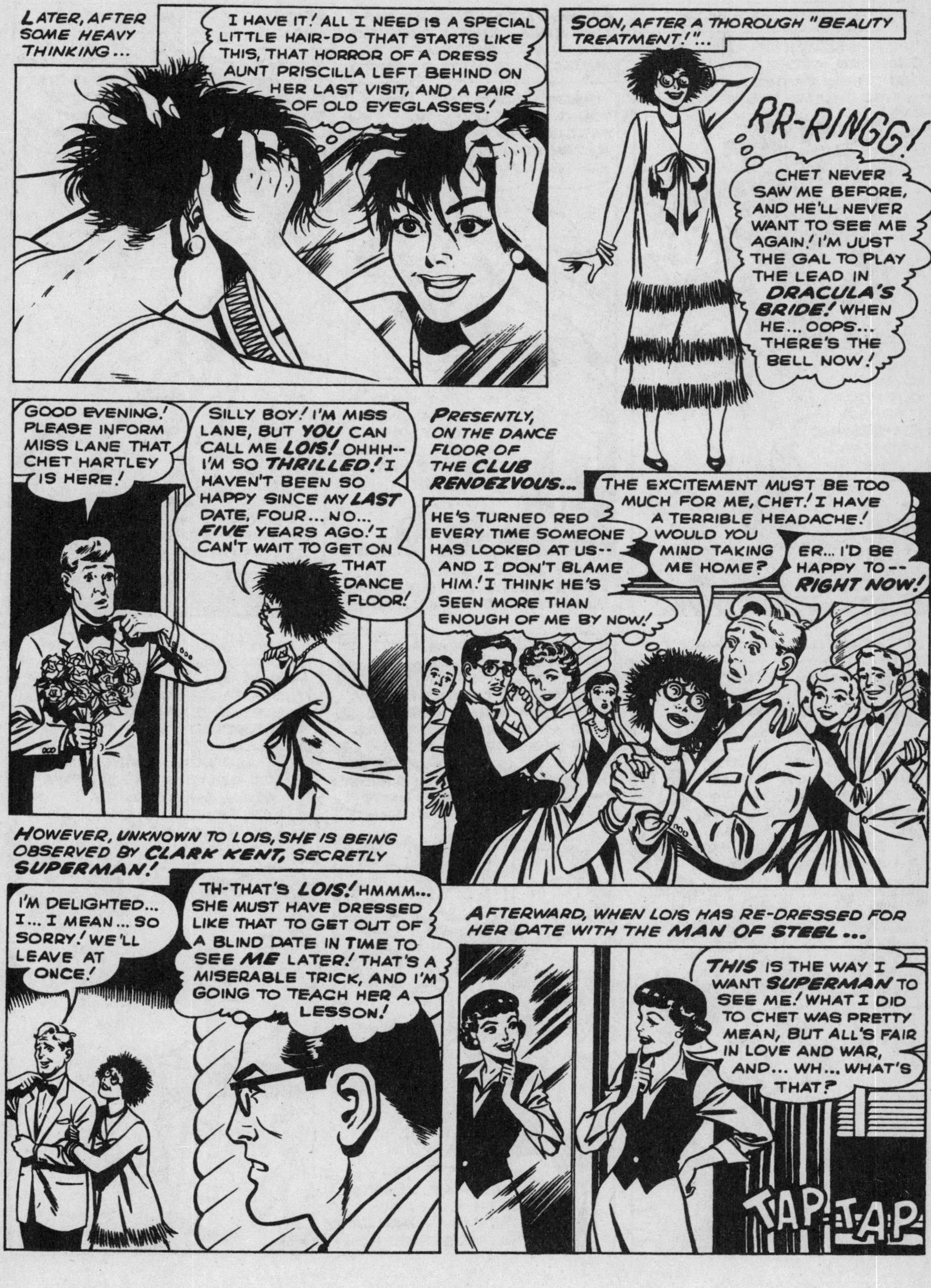
LATER, AFTER SOME HEAVY THINKING...
I HAVE IT! ALL I NEED IS A SPECIAL LITTLE HAIR-DO THAT STARTS LIKE THIS, THAT HORROR OF A DRESS AUNT PRISCILLA LEFT BEHIND ON HER LAST VISIT, AND A PAIR OF OLD EYEGLASSES!
SOON, AFTER A THOROUGH "BEAUTY TREATMENT!"...
RR-RINGG!
CHET NEVER SAW ME BEFORE, AND HE'LL NEVER WANT TO SEE ME AGAIN! I'M JUST THE GAL TO PLAY THE LEAD IN DRACULA'S BRIDE! WHEN HE... OOPS... THERE'S THE BELL NOW!
GOOD EVENING! PLEASE INFORM MISS LANE THAT CHET HARTLEY IS HERE!
SILLY BOY! I'M MISS LANE, BUT YOU CAN CALL ME LOIS! OHHH-- I'M SO THRILLED! I HAVEN'T BEEN SO HAPPY SINCE MY LAST DATE, FOUR... NO... FIVE YEARS AGO! I CAN'T WAIT TO GET ON THAT DANCE FLOOR!
PRESENTLY, ON THE DANCE FLOOR OF THE CLUB RENDEZVOUS...
HE'S TURNED RED EVERY TIME SOMEONE HAS LOOKED AT US-- AND I DON'T BLAME HIM! I THINK HE'S SEEN MORE THAN ENOUGH OF ME BY NOW!
THE EXCITEMENT MUST BE TOO MUCH FOR ME, CHET! I HAVE A TERRIBLE HEADACHE! WOULD YOU MIND TAKING ME HOME?
ER... I'D BE HAPPY TO -- RIGHT NOW!
HOWEVER, UNKNOWN TO LOIS, SHE IS BEING OBSERVED BY CLARK KENT, SECRETLY SUPERMAN!
I'M DELIGHTED... I... I MEAN... SO SORRY! WE'LL LEAVE AT ONCE!
TH-THAT'S LOIS! HMMM... SHE MUST HAVE DRESSED LIKE THAT TO GET OUT OF A BLIND DATE IN TIME TO SEE ME LATER! THAT'S A MISERABLE TRICK, AND I'M GOING TO TEACH HER A LESSON!
AFTERWARD, WHEN LOIS HAS RE-DRESSED FOR HER DATE WITH THE MAN OF STEEL...
THIS IS THE WAY I WANT SUPERMAN TO SEE ME! WHAT I DID TO CHET WAS PRETTY MEAN, BUT ALL'S FAIR IN LOVE AND WAR, AND... WH... WHAT'S THAT?
TAP-TAP

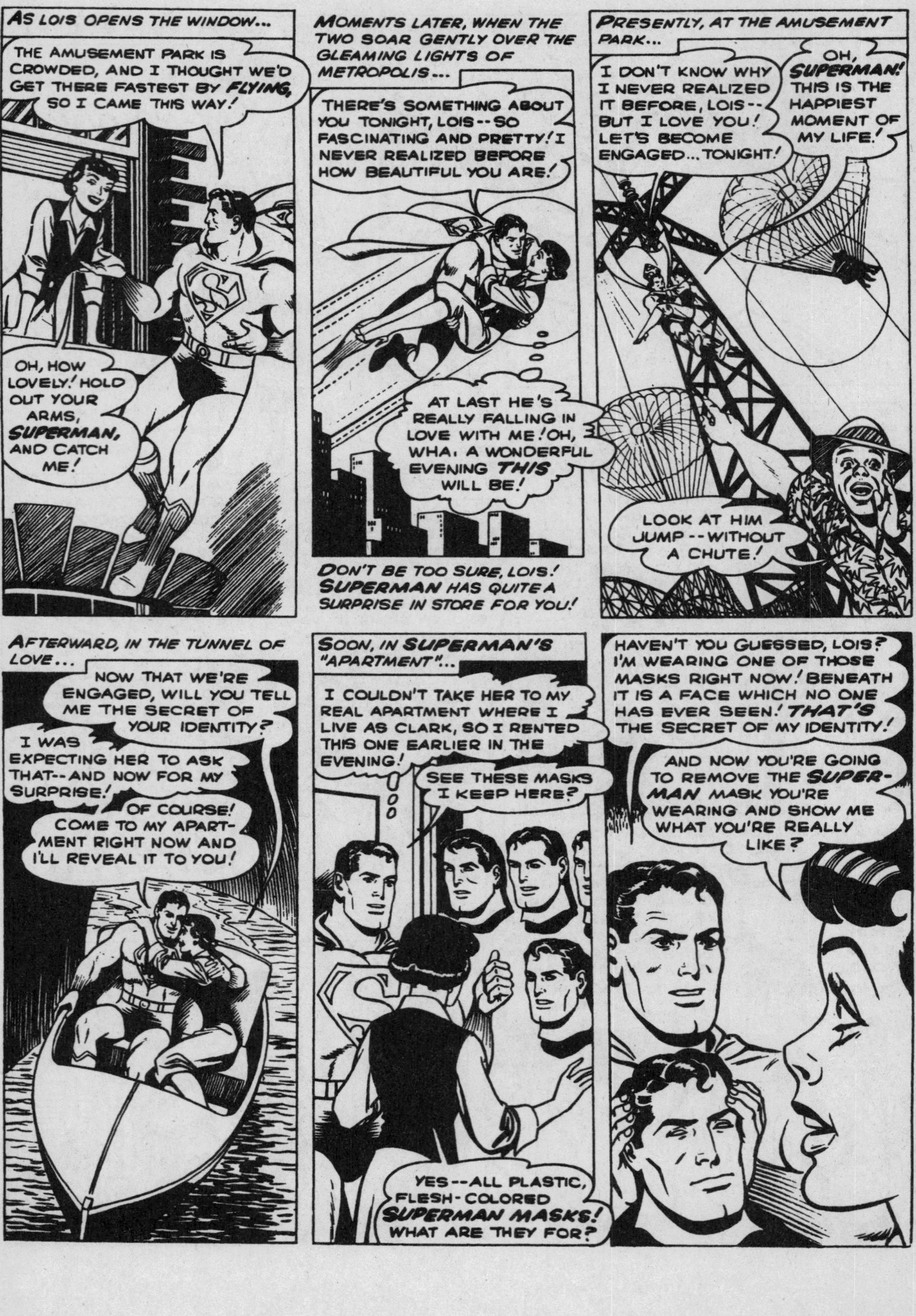
AS LOIS OPENS THE WINDOW...
THE AMUSEMENT PARK IS CROWDED, AND I THOUGHT WE'D GET THERE FASTEST BY FLYING, SO I CAME THIS WAY!
OH, HOW LOVELY! HOLD OUT YOUR ARMS, SUPERMAN, AND CATCH ME!
MOMENTS LATER, WHEN THE TWO SOAR GENTLY OVER THE GLEAMING LIGHTS OF METROPOLIS...
THERE'S SOMETHING ABOUT YOU TONIGHT, LOIS--SO FASCINATING AND PRETTY! I NEVER REALIZED BEFORE HOW BEAUTIFUL YOU ARE!
AT LAST HE'S REALLY FALLING IN LOVE WITH ME! OH, WHA, A WONDERFUL EVENING THIS WILL BE!
DON'T BE TOO SURE, LOIS! SUPERMAN HAS QUITE A SURPRISE IN STORE FOR YOU!
PRESENTLY, AT THE AMUSEMENT PARK...
I DON'T KNOW WHY I NEVER REALIZED IT BEFORE, LOIS--BUT I LOVE YOU! LET'S BECOME ENGAGED...TONIGHT!
OH, SUPERMAN! THIS IS THE HAPPIEST MOMENT OF MY LIFE!
LOOK AT HIM JUMP--WITHOUT A CHUTE!
AFTERWARD, IN THE TUNNEL OF LOVE...
NOW THAT WE'RE ENGAGED, WILL YOU TELL ME THE SECRET OF YOUR IDENTITY?
I WAS EXPECTING HER TO ASK THAT--AND NOW FOR MY SURPRISE!
OF COURSE! COME TO MY APARTMENT RIGHT NOW AND I'LL REVEAL IT TO YOU!
SOON, IN SUPERMAN'S "APARTMENT"...
I COULDN'T TAKE HER TO MY REAL APARTMENT WHERE I LIVE AS CLARK, SO I RENTED THIS ONE EARLIER IN THE EVENING!
SEE THESE MASKS I KEEP HERE?
YES--ALL PLASTIC, FLESH-COLORED SUPERMAN MASKS! WHAT ARE THEY FOR?
HAVEN'T YOU GUESSED, LOIS? I'M WEARING ONE OF THOSE MASKS RIGHT NOW! BENEATH IT IS A FACE WHICH NO ONE HAS EVER SEEN! THAT'S THE SECRET OF MY IDENTITY!
AND NOW YOU'RE GOING TO REMOVE THE SUPERMAN MASK YOU'RE WEARING AND SHOW ME WHAT YOU'RE REALLY LIKE?

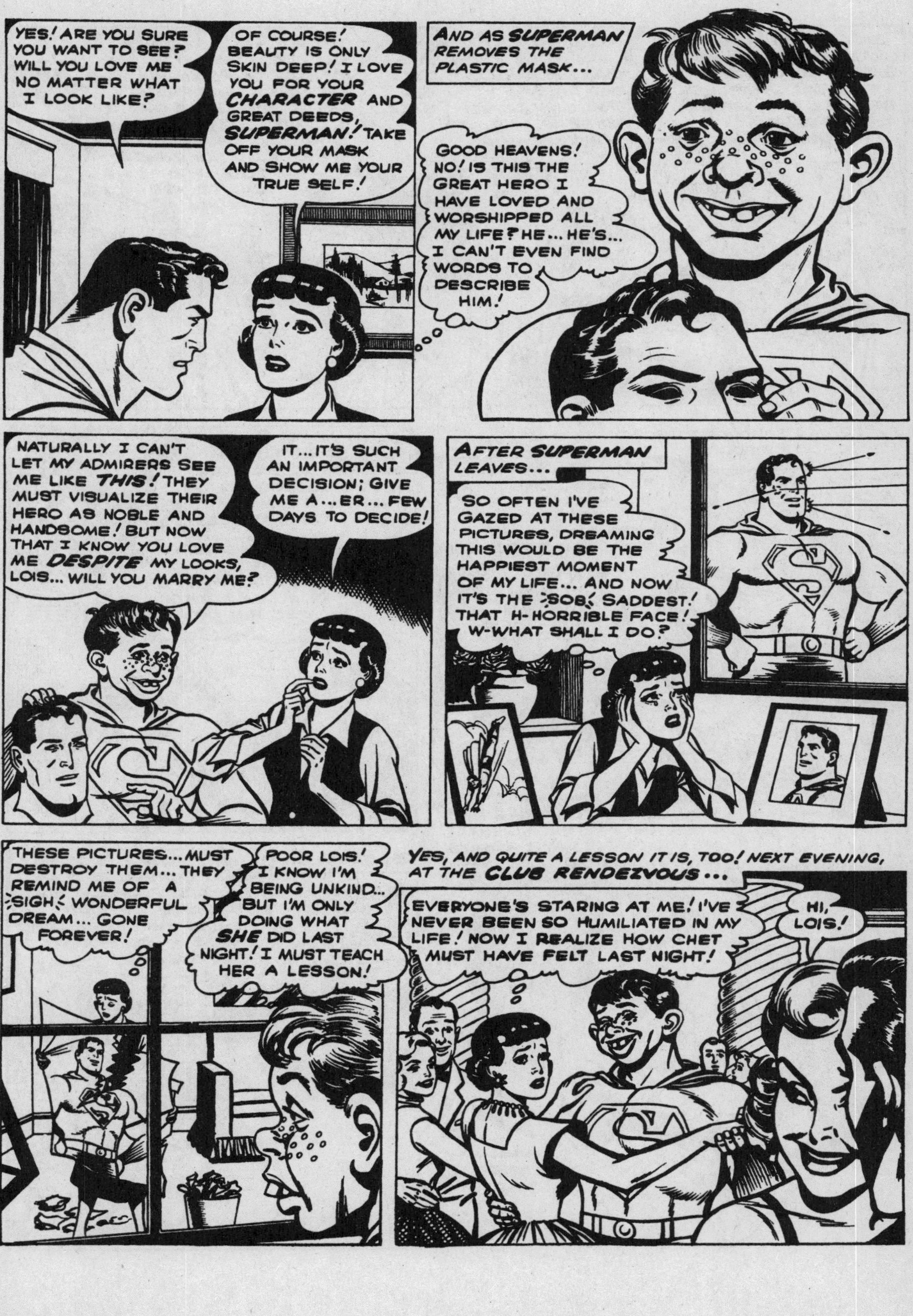
YES! ARE YOU SURE YOU WANT TO SEE? WILL YOU LOVE ME NO MATTER WHAT I LOOK LIKE?
OF COURSE! BEAUTY IS ONLY SKIN DEEP! I LOVE YOU FOR YOUR CHARACTER AND GREAT DEEDS, SUPERMAN! TAKE OFF YOUR MASK AND SHOW ME YOUR TRUE SELF!
AND AS SUPERMAN REMOVES THE PLASTIC MASK...
GOOD HEAVENS! NO! IS THIS THE GREAT HERO I HAVE LOVED AND WORSHIPPED ALL MY LIFE? HE... HE'S... I CAN'T EVEN FIND WORDS TO DESCRIBE HIM!
NATURALLY I CAN'T LET MY ADMIRERS SEE ME LIKE THIS! THEY MUST VISUALIZE THEIR HERO AS NOBLE AND HANDSOME! BUT NOW THAT I KNOW YOU LOVE ME DESPITE MY LOOKS, LOIS... WILL YOU MARRY ME?
IT... IT'S SUCH AN IMPORTANT DECISION; GIVE ME A... ER... FEW DAYS TO DECIDE!
AFTER SUPERMAN LEAVES...
SO OFTEN I'VE GAZED AT THESE PICTURES, DREAMING THIS WOULD BE THE HAPPIEST MOMENT OF MY LIFE... AND NOW IT'S THE -SOB- SADDEST! THAT H-HORRIBLE FACE! W-WHAT SHALL I DO?
THESE PICTURES... MUST DESTROY THEM... THEY REMIND ME OF A -SIGH- WONDERFUL DREAM... GONE FOREVER!
POOR LOIS! I KNOW I'M BEING UNKIND... BUT I'M ONLY DOING WHAT SHE DID LAST NIGHT! I MUST TEACH HER A LESSON!
YES, AND QUITE A LESSON IT IS, TOO! NEXT EVENING, AT THE CLUB RENDEZVOUS...
EVERYONE'S STARING AT ME! I'VE NEVER BEEN SO HUMILIATED IN MY LIFE! NOW I REALIZE HOW CHET MUST HAVE FELT LAST NIGHT!
HI, LOIS!

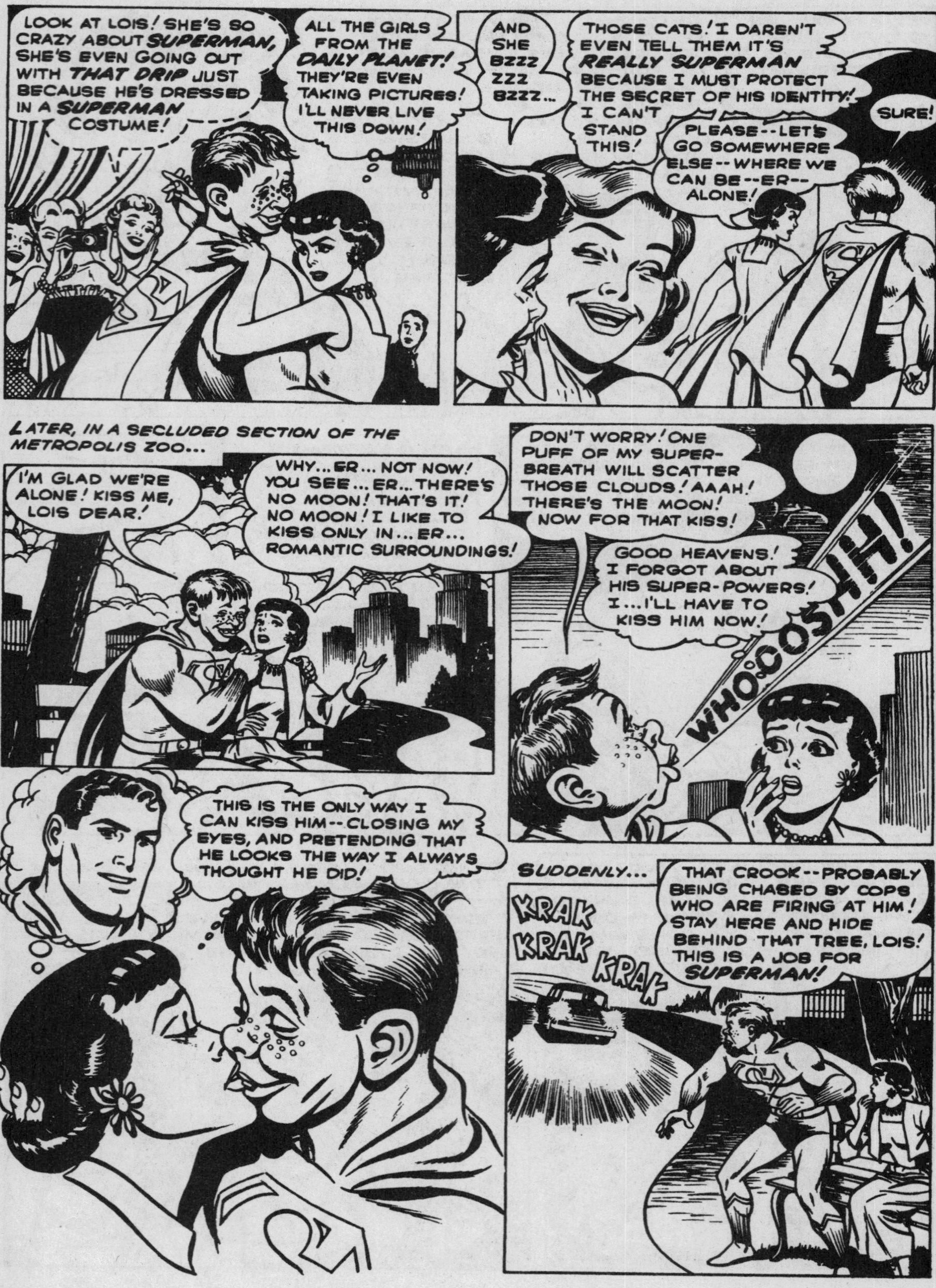
LOOK AT LOIS! SHE'S SO CRAZY ABOUT SUPERMAN, SHE'S EVEN GOING OUT WITH THAT DRIP JUST BECAUSE HE'S DRESSED IN A SUPERMAN COSTUME!
ALL THE GIRLS FROM THE DAILY PLANET! THEY'RE EVEN TAKING PICTURES! I'LL NEVER LIVE THIS DOWN!
AND SHE BZZZ ZZZ BZZZ...
THOSE CATS! I DAREN'T EVEN TELL THEM IT'S REALLY SUPERMAN BECAUSE I MUST PROTECT THE SECRET OF HIS IDENTITY! I CAN'T STAND THIS!
PLEASE--LET'S GO SOMEWHERE ELSE--WHERE WE CAN BE--ER--ALONE!
SURE!
LATER, IN A SECLUDED SECTION OF THE METROPOLIS ZOO...
I'M GLAD WE'RE ALONE! KISS ME, LOIS DEAR!
WHY...ER...NOT NOW! YOU SEE...ER...THERE'S NO MOON! THAT'S IT! NO MOON! I LIKE TO KISS ONLY IN...ER... ROMANTIC SURROUNDINGS!
DON'T WORRY! ONE PUFF OF MY SUPER-BREATH WILL SCATTER THOSE CLOUDS! AAAH! THERE'S THE MOON! NOW FOR THAT KISS!
GOOD HEAVENS! I FORGOT ABOUT HIS SUPER-POWERS! I...I'LL HAVE TO KISS HIM NOW!
WHOOOSHH!
THIS IS THE ONLY WAY I CAN KISS HIM--CLOSING MY EYES, AND PRETENDING THAT HE LOOKS THE WAY I ALWAYS THOUGHT HE DID!
SUDDENLY...
KRAK
KRAK
KRAK
THAT CROOK--PROBABLY BEING CHASED BY COPS WHO ARE FIRING AT HIM! STAY HERE AND HIDE BEHIND THAT TREE, LOIS! THIS IS A JOB FOR SUPERMAN!

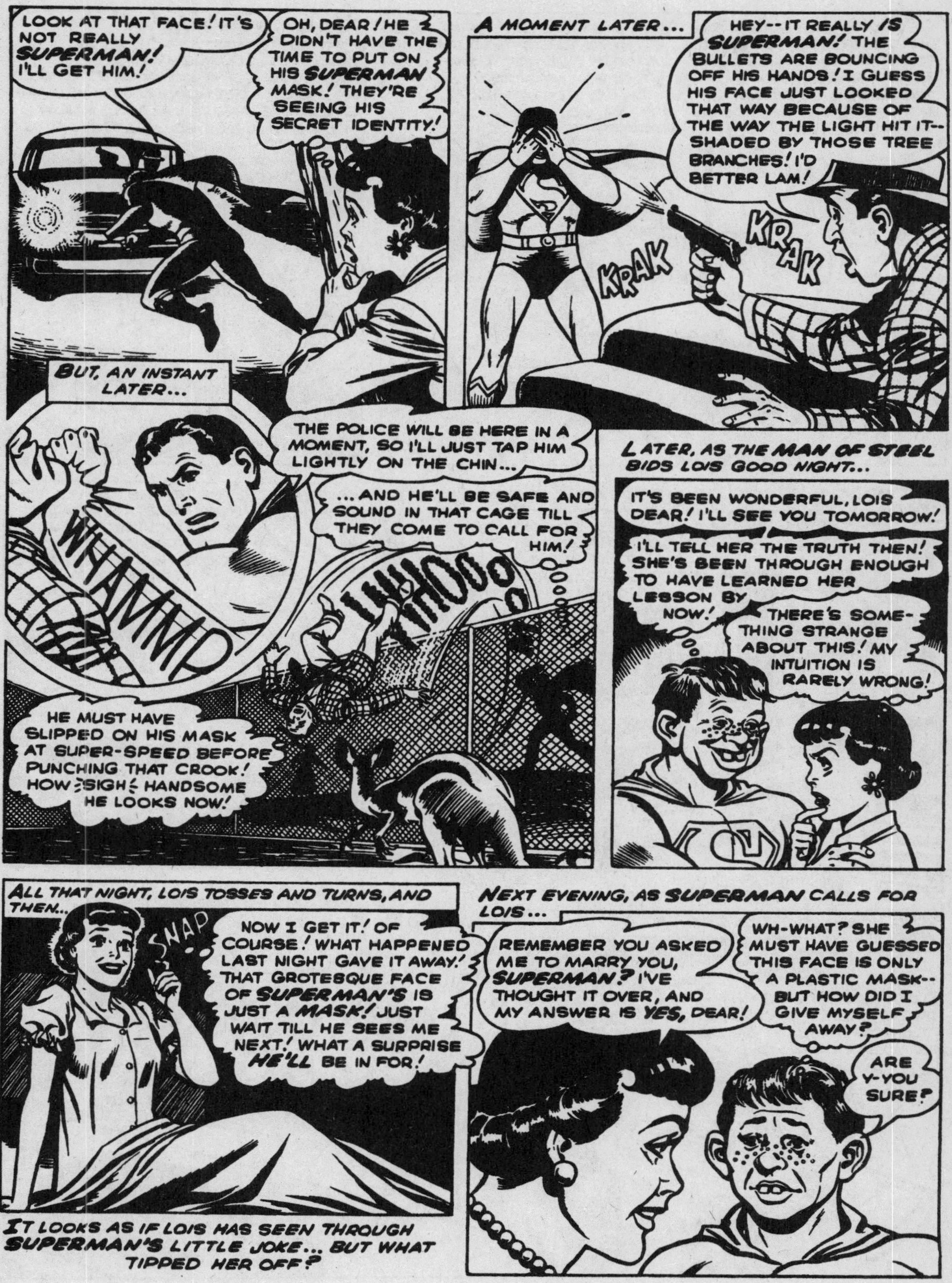
LOOK AT THAT FACE! IT'S NOT REALLY SUPERMAN! I'LL GET HIM!
OH, DEAR! HE DIDN'T HAVE THE TIME TO PUT ON HIS SUPERMAN MASK! THEY'RE SEEING HIS SECRET IDENTITY!
A MOMENT LATER...
HEY--IT REALLY IS SUPERMAN! THE BULLETS ARE BOUNCING OFF HIS HANDS! I GUESS HIS FACE JUST LOOKED THAT WAY BECAUSE OF THE WAY THE LIGHT HIT IT--SHADED BY THOSE TREE BRANCHES! I'D BETTER LAM!
KRAK
KRAK
BUT, AN INSTANT LATER...
THE POLICE WILL BE HERE IN A MOMENT, SO I'LL JUST TAP HIM LIGHTLY ON THE CHIN...
...AND HE'LL BE SAFE AND SOUND IN THAT CAGE TILL THEY COME TO CALL FOR HIM!
WHAMMM
WHOOO
HE MUST HAVE SLIPPED ON HIS MASK AT SUPER-SPEED BEFORE PUNCHING THAT CROOK! HOW -SIGH- HANDSOME HE LOOKS NOW!
LATER, AS THE MAN OF STEEL BIDS LOIS GOOD NIGHT...
IT'S BEEN WONDERFUL, LOIS DEAR! I'LL SEE YOU TOMORROW!
I'LL TELL HER THE TRUTH THEN! SHE'S BEEN THROUGH ENOUGH TO HAVE LEARNED HER LESSON BY NOW!
THERE'S SOMETHING STRANGE ABOUT THIS! MY INTUITION IS RARELY WRONG!
ALL THAT NIGHT, LOIS TOSSES AND TURNS, AND THEN...
SNAP
NOW I GET IT! OF COURSE! WHAT HAPPENED LAST NIGHT GAVE IT AWAY! THAT GROTESQUE FACE OF SUPERMAN'S IS JUST A MASK! JUST WAIT TILL HE SEES ME NEXT! WHAT A SURPRISE HE'LL BE IN FOR!
NEXT EVENING, AS SUPERMAN CALLS FOR LOIS...
REMEMBER YOU ASKED ME TO MARRY YOU, SUPERMAN? I'VE THOUGHT IT OVER, AND MY ANSWER IS YES, DEAR!
WH-WHAT? SHE MUST HAVE GUESSED THIS FACE IS ONLY A PLASTIC MASK--BUT HOW DID I GIVE MYSELF AWAY?
ARE Y-YOU SURE?
IT LOOKS AS IF LOIS HAS SEEN THROUGH SUPERMAN'S LITTLE JOKE... BUT WHAT TIPPED HER OFF?

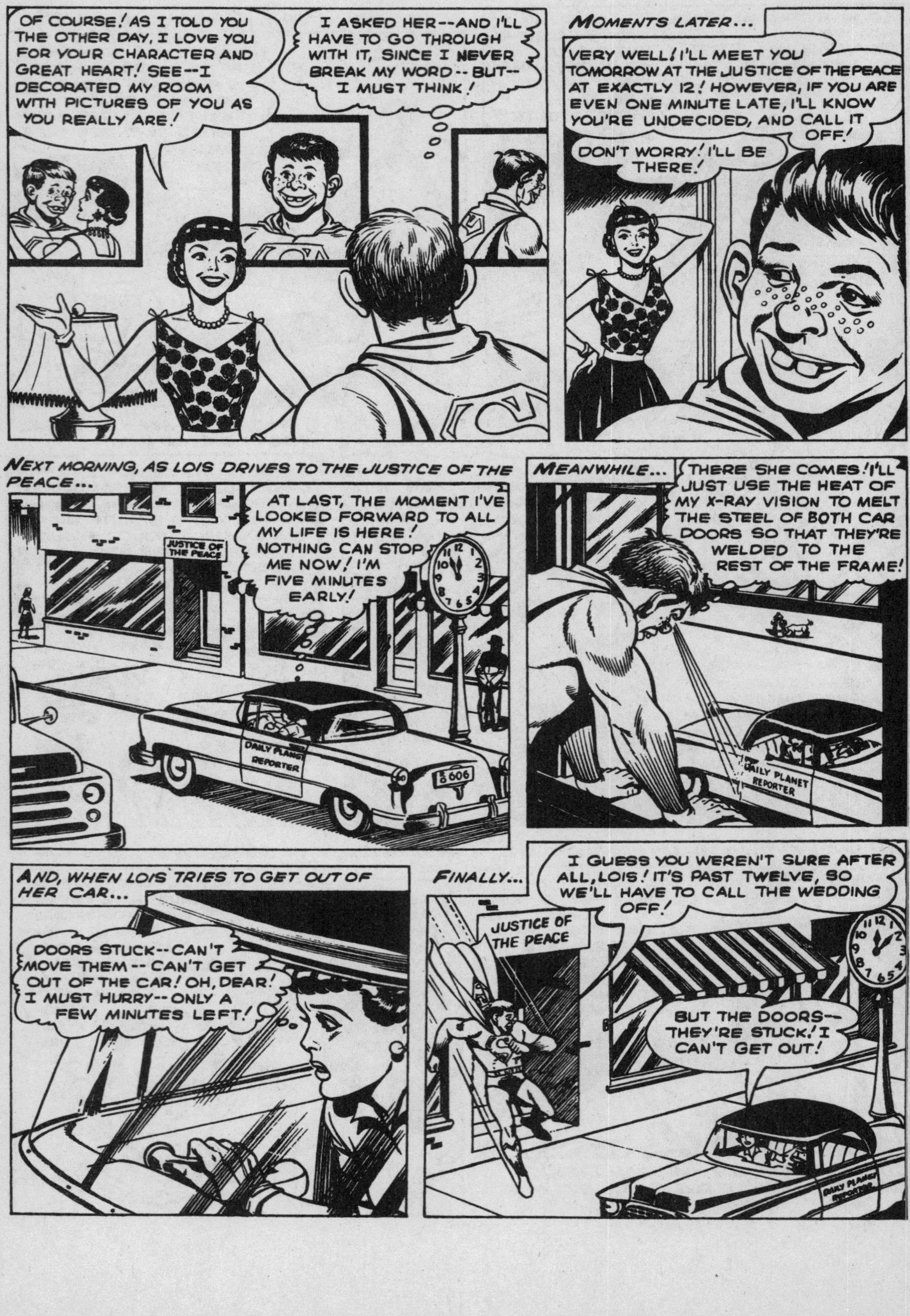
OF COURSE! AS I TOLD YOU THE OTHER DAY, I LOVE YOU FOR YOUR CHARACTER AND GREAT HEART! SEE--I DECORATED MY ROOM WITH PICTURES OF YOU AS YOU REALLY ARE!
I ASKED HER--AND I'LL HAVE TO GO THROUGH WITH IT, SINCE I NEVER BREAK MY WORD -- BUT-- I MUST THINK!
MOMENTS LATER...
VERY WELL! I'LL MEET YOU TOMORROW AT THE JUSTICE OF THE PEACE AT EXACTLY 12! HOWEVER, IF YOU ARE EVEN ONE MINUTE LATE, I'LL KNOW YOU'RE UNDECIDED, AND CALL IT OFF!
DON'T WORRY! I'LL BE THERE!
NEXT MORNING, AS LOIS DRIVES TO THE JUSTICE OF THE PEACE...
JUSTICE OF THE PEACE
AT LAST, THE MOMENT I'VE LOOKED FORWARD TO ALL MY LIFE IS HERE! NOTHING CAN STOP ME NOW! I'M FIVE MINUTES EARLY!
DAILY PLANET REPORTER
MEANWHILE...
THERE SHE COMES! I'LL JUST USE THE HEAT OF MY X-RAY VISION TO MELT THE STEEL OF BOTH CAR DOORS SO THAT THEY'RE WELDED TO THE REST OF THE FRAME!
DAILY PLANET REPORTER
AND, WHEN LOIS TRIES TO GET OUT OF HER CAR...
DOORS STUCK--CAN'T MOVE THEM -- CAN'T GET OUT OF THE CAR! OH, DEAR! I MUST HURRY-- ONLY A FEW MINUTES LEFT!
FINALLY...
I GUESS YOU WEREN'T SURE AFTER ALL, LOIS! IT'S PAST TWELVE, SO WE'LL HAVE TO CALL THE WEDDING OFF!
JUSTICE OF THE PEACE
BUT THE DOORS-- THEY'RE STUCK! I CAN'T GET OUT!

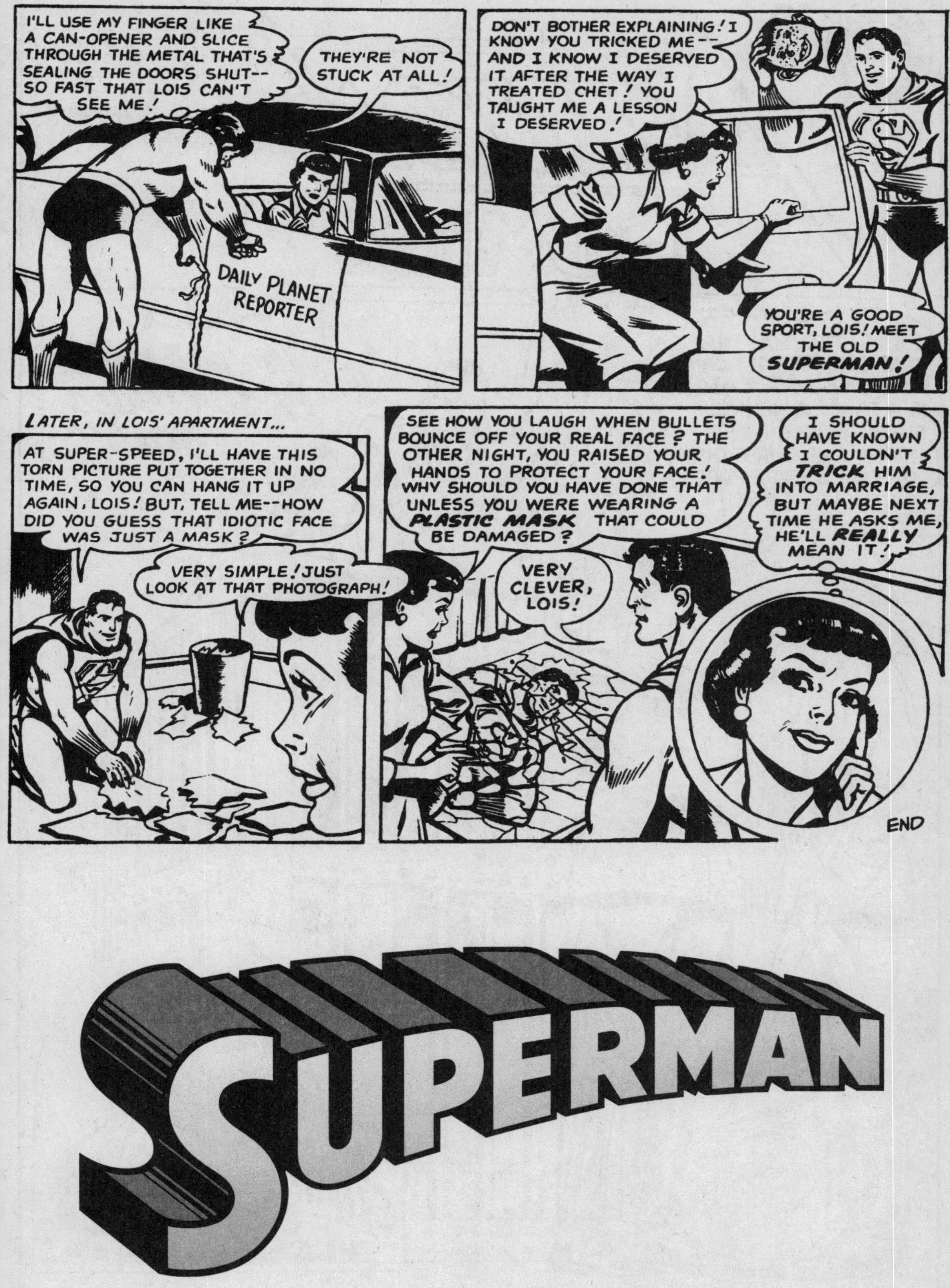
I'LL USE MY FINGER LIKE A CAN-OPENER AND SLICE THROUGH THE METAL THAT'S SEALING THE DOORS SHUT-- SO FAST THAT LOIS CAN'T SEE ME!
THEY'RE NOT STUCK AT ALL!
DAILY PLANET REPORTER
DON'T BOTHER EXPLAINING! I KNOW YOU TRICKED ME-- AND I KNOW I DESERVED IT AFTER THE WAY I TREATED CHET! YOU TAUGHT ME A LESSON I DESERVED!
YOU'RE A GOOD SPORT, LOIS! MEET THE OLD SUPERMAN!
LATER, IN LOIS' APARTMENT...
AT SUPER-SPEED, I'LL HAVE THIS TORN PICTURE PUT TOGETHER IN NO TIME, SO YOU CAN HANG IT UP AGAIN, LOIS! BUT, TELL ME--HOW DID YOU GUESS THAT IDIOTIC FACE WAS JUST A MASK?
VERY SIMPLE! JUST LOOK AT THAT PHOTOGRAPH!
SEE HOW YOU LAUGH WHEN BULLETS BOUNCE OFF YOUR REAL FACE? THE OTHER NIGHT, YOU RAISED YOUR HANDS TO PROTECT YOUR FACE! WHY SHOULD YOU HAVE DONE THAT UNLESS YOU WERE WEARING A PLASTIC MASK THAT COULD BE DAMAGED?
VERY CLEVER, LOIS!
I SHOULD HAVE KNOWN I COULDN'T TRICK HIM INTO MARRIAGE, BUT MAYBE NEXT TIME HE ASKS ME, HE'LL REALLY MEAN IT!
END

SUPERMAN

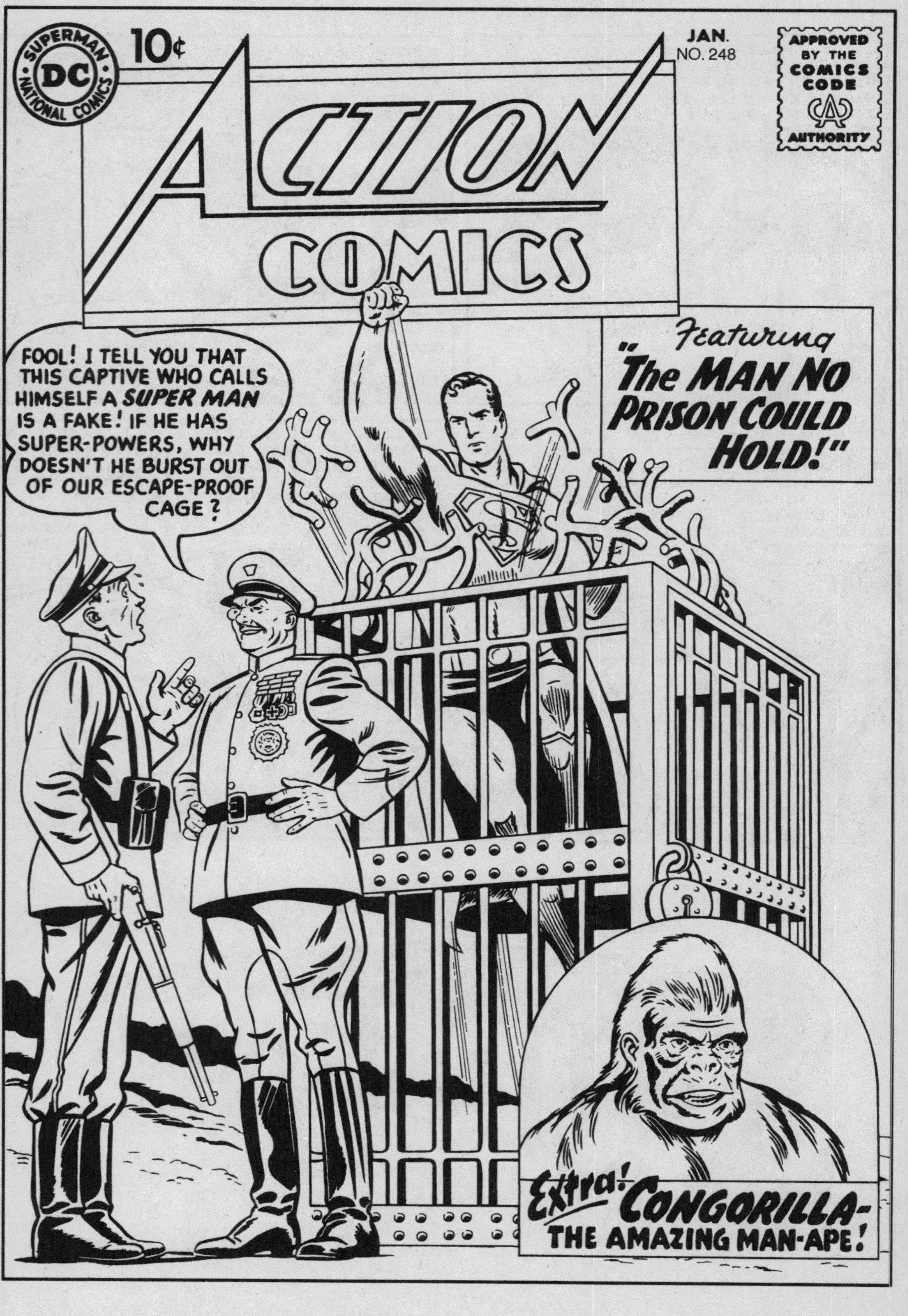
SUPERMAN DC NATIONAL COMICS
10¢
ACTION COMICS
JAN. NO. 248
APPROVED BY THE COMICS CODE AUTHORITY
Featuring "The MAN NO PRISON COULD HOLD!"
FOOL! I TELL YOU THAT THIS CAPTIVE WHO CALLS HIMSELF A SUPER MAN IS A FAKE! IF HE HAS SUPER-POWERS, WHY DOESN'T HE BURST OUT OF OUR ESCAPE-PROOF CAGE?
Extra! CONGORILLA- THE AMAZING MAN-APE!

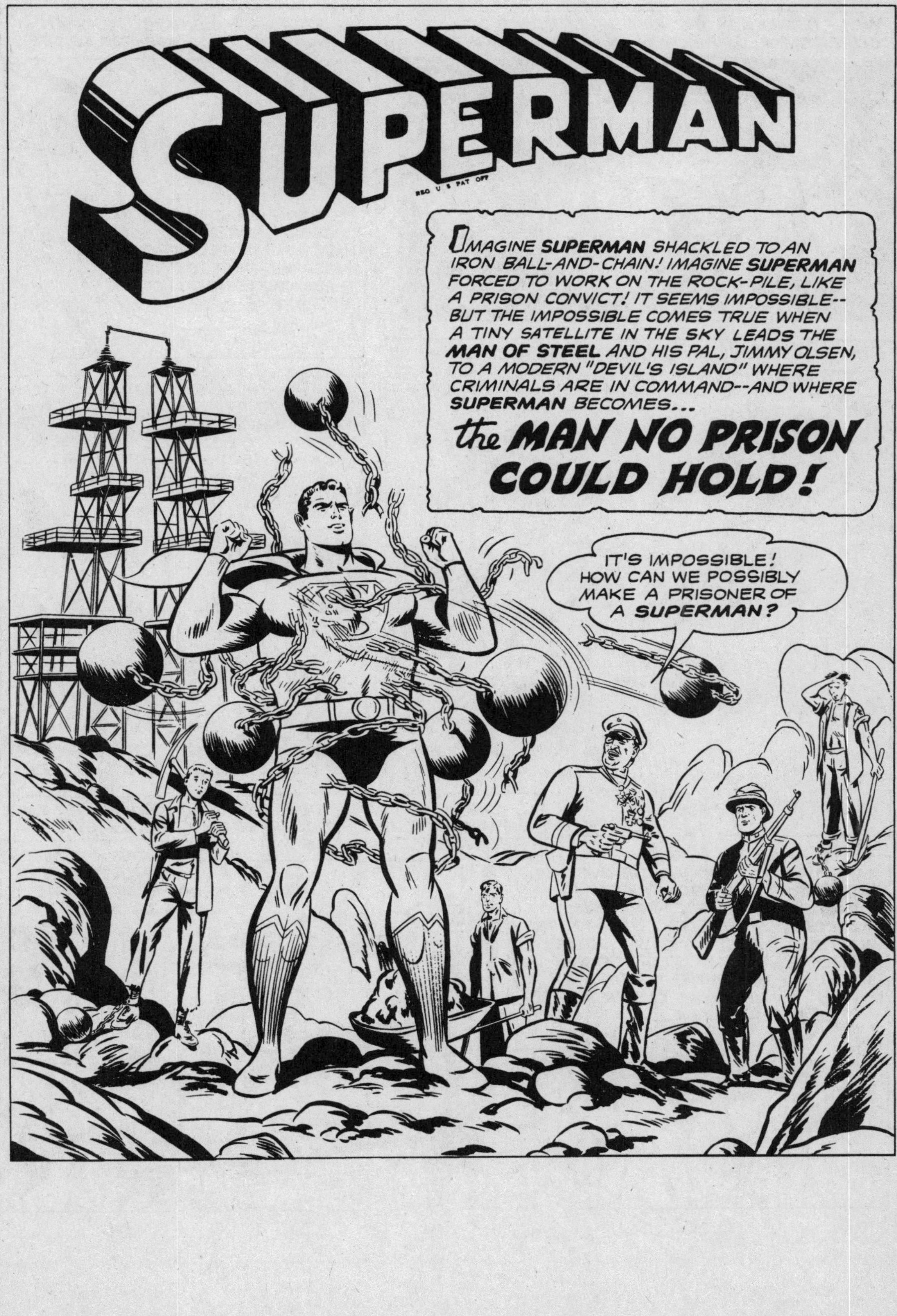
SUPERMAN
REG. U.S. PAT. OFF.
IMAGINE SUPERMAN SHACKLED TO AN IRON BALL-AND-CHAIN! IMAGINE SUPERMAN FORCED TO WORK ON THE ROCK-PILE, LIKE A PRISON CONVICT! IT SEEMS IMPOSSIBLE-- BUT THE IMPOSSIBLE COMES TRUE WHEN A TINY SATELLITE IN THE SKY LEADS THE MAN OF STEEL AND HIS PAL, JIMMY OLSEN, TO A MODERN "DEVIL'S ISLAND" WHERE CRIMINALS ARE IN COMMAND--AND WHERE SUPERMAN BECOMES...
the MAN NO PRISON COULD HOLD!
IT'S IMPOSSIBLE! HOW CAN WE POSSIBLY MAKE A PRISONER OF A SUPERMAN?

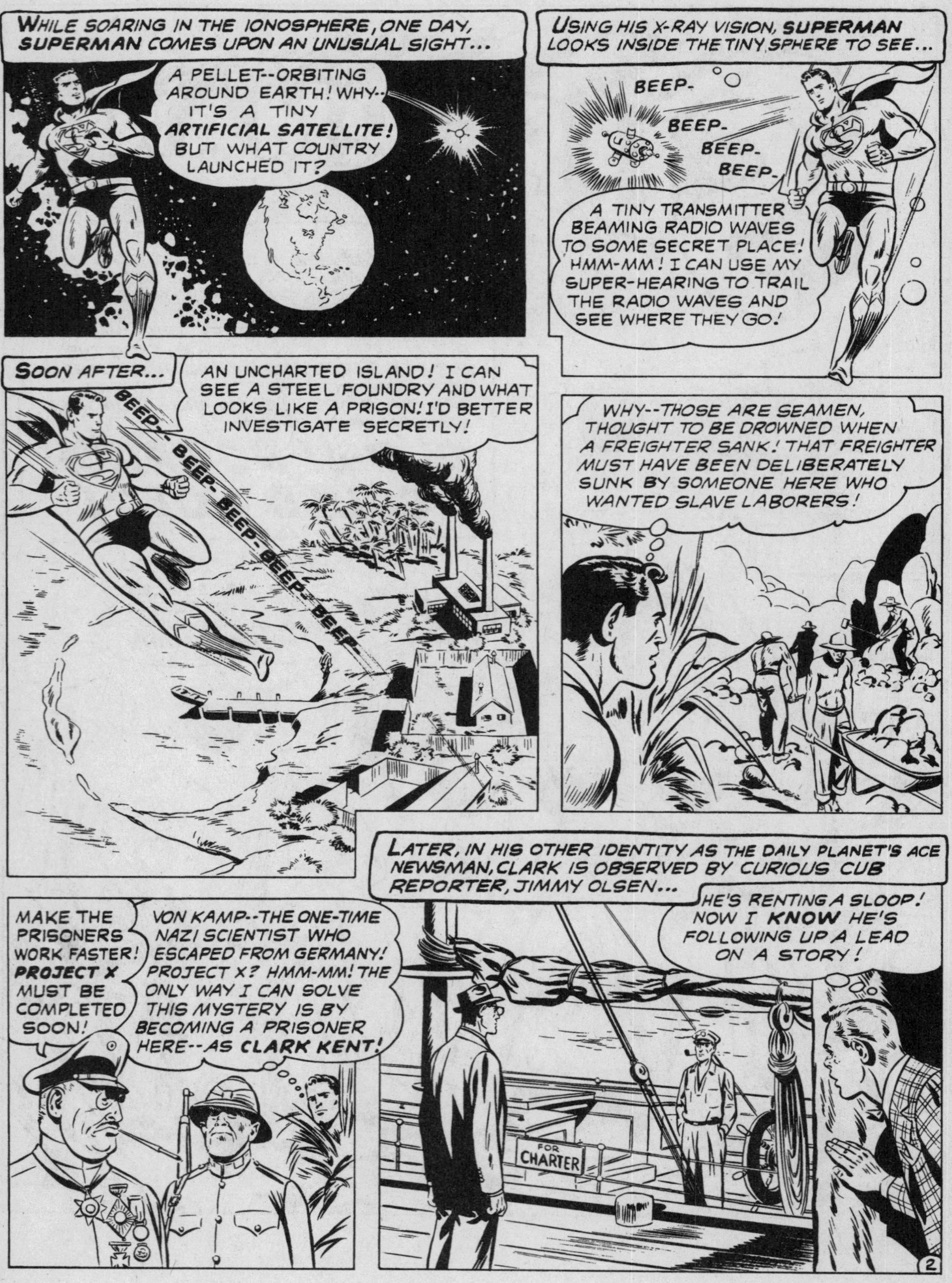
WHILE SOARING IN THE IONOSPHERE, ONE DAY, SUPERMAN COMES UPON AN UNUSUAL SIGHT...
A PELLET--ORBITING AROUND EARTH! WHY-- IT'S A TINY ARTIFICIAL SATELLITE! BUT WHAT COUNTRY LAUNCHED IT?
USING HIS X-RAY VISION, SUPERMAN LOOKS INSIDE THE TINY SPHERE TO SEE...
BEEP- BEEP- BEEP- BEEP-
A TINY TRANSMITTER BEAMING RADIO WAVES TO SOME SECRET PLACE! HMM-MM! I CAN USE MY SUPER-HEARING TO TRAIL THE RADIO WAVES AND SEE WHERE THEY GO!
SOON AFTER...
AN UNCHARTED ISLAND! I CAN SEE A STEEL FOUNDRY AND WHAT LOOKS LIKE A PRISON! I'D BETTER INVESTIGATE SECRETLY!
BEEP-BEEP-BEEP-BEEP-BEEP
WHY--THOSE ARE SEAMEN, THOUGHT TO BE DROWNED WHEN A FREIGHTER SANK! THAT FREIGHTER MUST HAVE BEEN DELIBERATELY SUNK BY SOMEONE HERE WHO WANTED SLAVE LABORERS!
MAKE THE PRISONERS WORK FASTER! PROJECT X MUST BE COMPLETED SOON!
VON KAMP--THE ONE-TIME NAZI SCIENTIST WHO ESCAPED FROM GERMANY! PROJECT X? HMM-MM! THE ONLY WAY I CAN SOLVE THIS MYSTERY IS BY BECOMING A PRISONER HERE--AS CLARK KENT!
LATER, IN HIS OTHER IDENTITY AS THE DAILY PLANET'S ACE NEWSMAN, CLARK IS OBSERVED BY CURIOUS CUB REPORTER, JIMMY OLSEN...
HE'S RENTING A SLOOP! NOW I KNOW HE'S FOLLOWING UP A LEAD ON A STORY!
FOR CHARTER
2

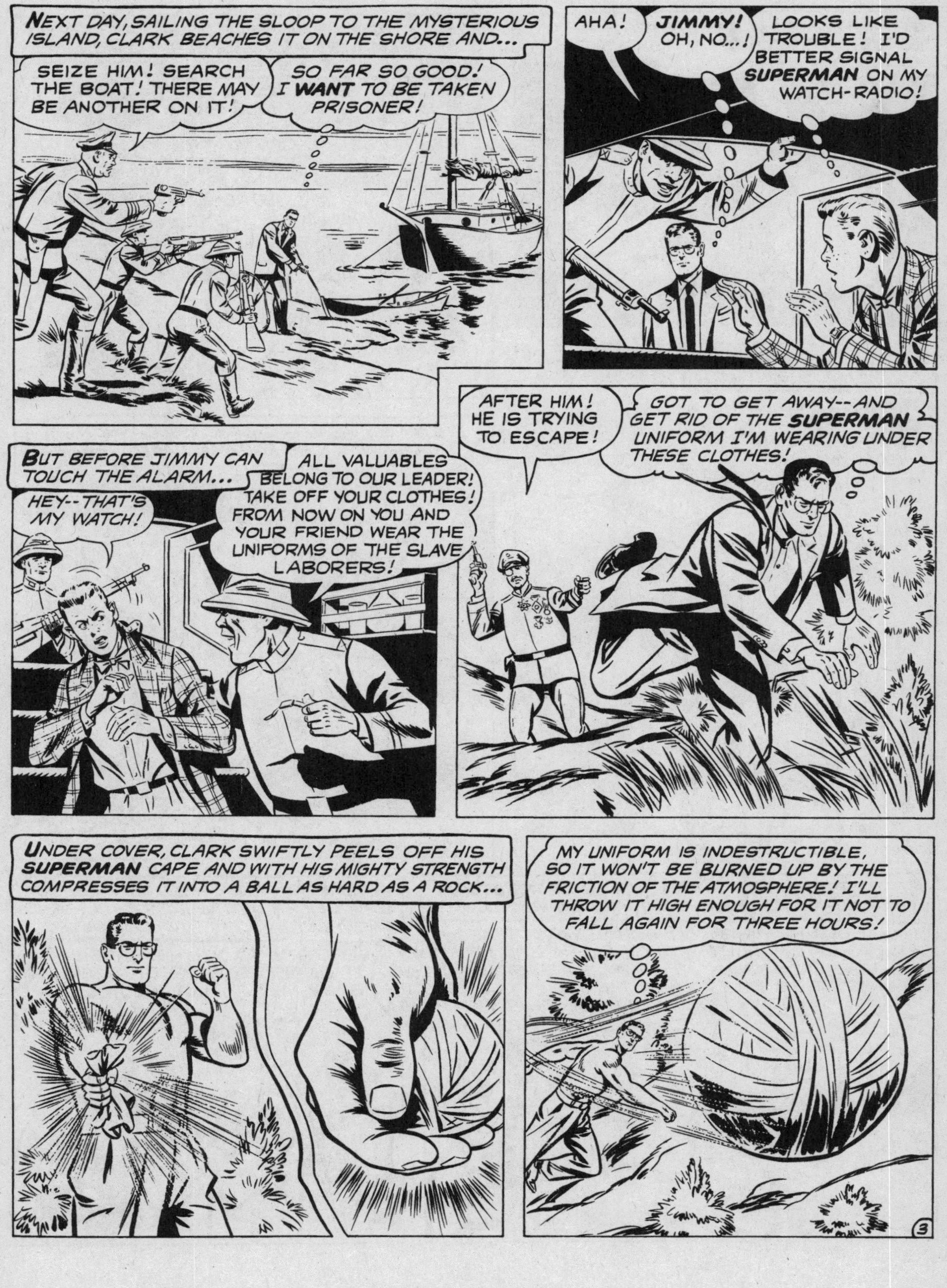
NEXT DAY, SAILING THE SLOOP TO THE MYSTERIOUS ISLAND, CLARK BEACHES IT ON THE SHORE AND...
SEIZE HIM! SEARCH THE BOAT! THERE MAY BE ANOTHER ON IT!
SO FAR SO GOOD! I WANT TO BE TAKEN PRISONER!
AHA!
JIMMY! OH, NO...!
LOOKS LIKE TROUBLE! I'D BETTER SIGNAL SUPERMAN ON MY WATCH-RADIO!
BUT BEFORE JIMMY CAN TOUCH THE ALARM...
HEY--THAT'S MY WATCH!
ALL VALUABLES BELONG TO OUR LEADER! TAKE OFF YOUR CLOTHES! FROM NOW ON YOU AND YOUR FRIEND WEAR THE UNIFORMS OF THE SLAVE LABORERS!
AFTER HIM! HE IS TRYING TO ESCAPE!
GOT TO GET AWAY--AND GET RID OF THE SUPERMAN UNIFORM I'M WEARING UNDER THESE CLOTHES!
UNDER COVER, CLARK SWIFTLY PEELS OFF HIS SUPERMAN CAPE AND WITH HIS MIGHTY STRENGTH COMPRESSES IT INTO A BALL AS HARD AS A ROCK...
MY UNIFORM IS INDESTRUCTIBLE, SO IT WON'T BE BURNED UP BY THE FRICTION OF THE ATMOSPHERE! I'LL THROW IT HIGH ENOUGH FOR IT NOT TO FALL AGAIN FOR THREE HOURS!
3

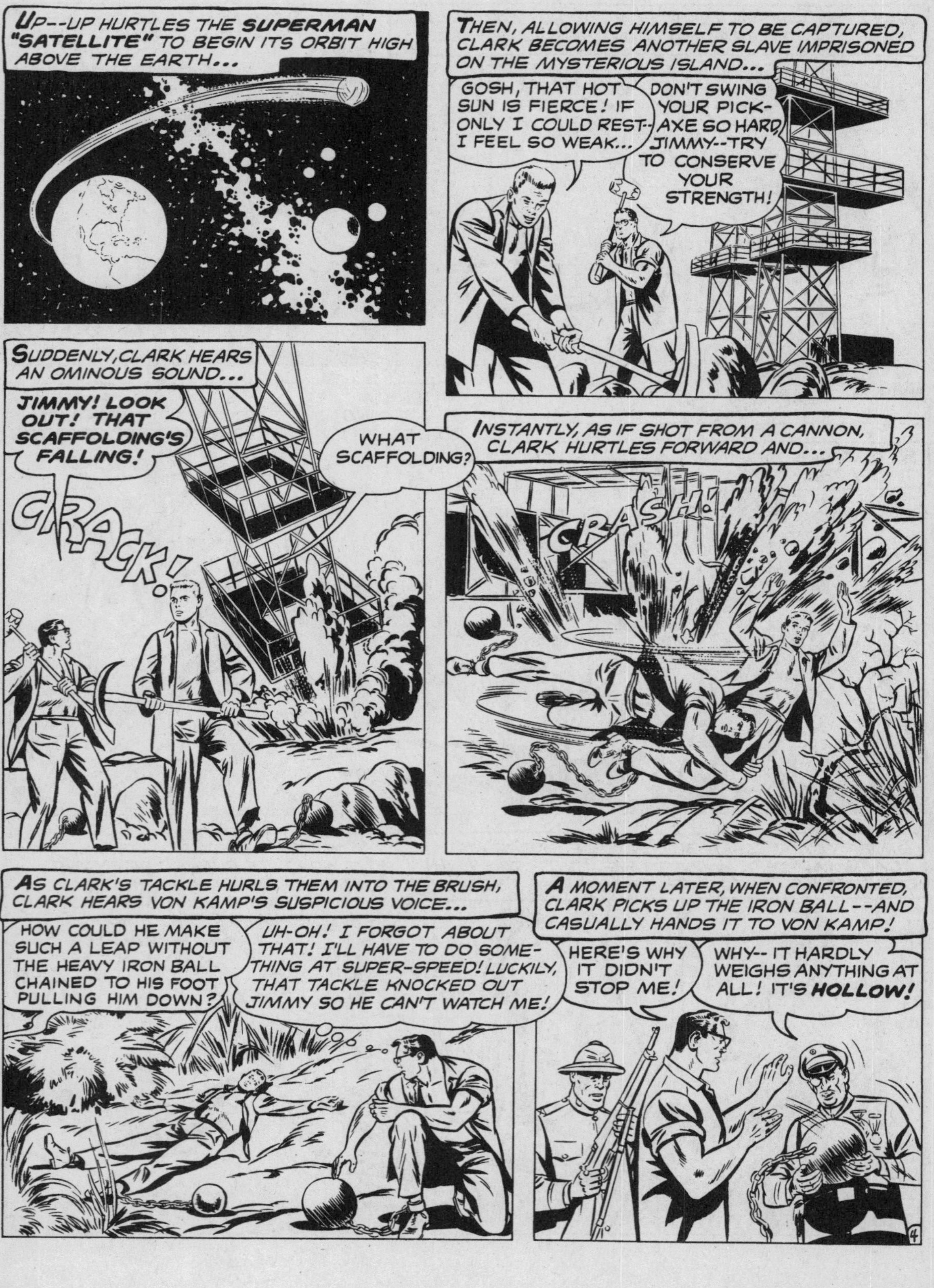
UP--UP HURTLES THE SUPERMAN "SATELLITE" TO BEGIN ITS ORBIT HIGH ABOVE THE EARTH...
THEN, ALLOWING HIMSELF TO BE CAPTURED, CLARK BECOMES ANOTHER SLAVE IMPRISONED ON THE MYSTERIOUS ISLAND...
GOSH, THAT HOT SUN IS FIERCE! IF ONLY I COULD REST-- I FEEL SO WEAK...
DON'T SWING YOUR PICK-AXE SO HARD, JIMMY--TRY TO CONSERVE YOUR STRENGTH!
SUDDENLY, CLARK HEARS AN OMINOUS SOUND...
JIMMY! LOOK OUT! THAT SCAFFOLDING'S FALLING!
WHAT SCAFFOLDING?
CRACK!
INSTANTLY, AS IF SHOT FROM A CANNON, CLARK HURTLES FORWARD AND...
CRASH!
AS CLARK'S TACKLE HURLS THEM INTO THE BRUSH, CLARK HEARS VON KAMP'S SUSPICIOUS VOICE...
HOW COULD HE MAKE SUCH A LEAP WITHOUT THE HEAVY IRON BALL CHAINED TO HIS FOOT PULLING HIM DOWN?
UH-OH! I FORGOT ABOUT THAT! I'LL HAVE TO DO SOMETHING AT SUPER-SPEED! LUCKILY, THAT TACKLE KNOCKED OUT JIMMY SO HE CAN'T WATCH ME!
A MOMENT LATER, WHEN CONFRONTED, CLARK PICKS UP THE IRON BALL--AND CASUALLY HANDS IT TO VON KAMP!
HERE'S WHY IT DIDN'T STOP ME!
WHY-- IT HARDLY WEIGHS ANYTHING AT ALL! IT'S HOLLOW!
4

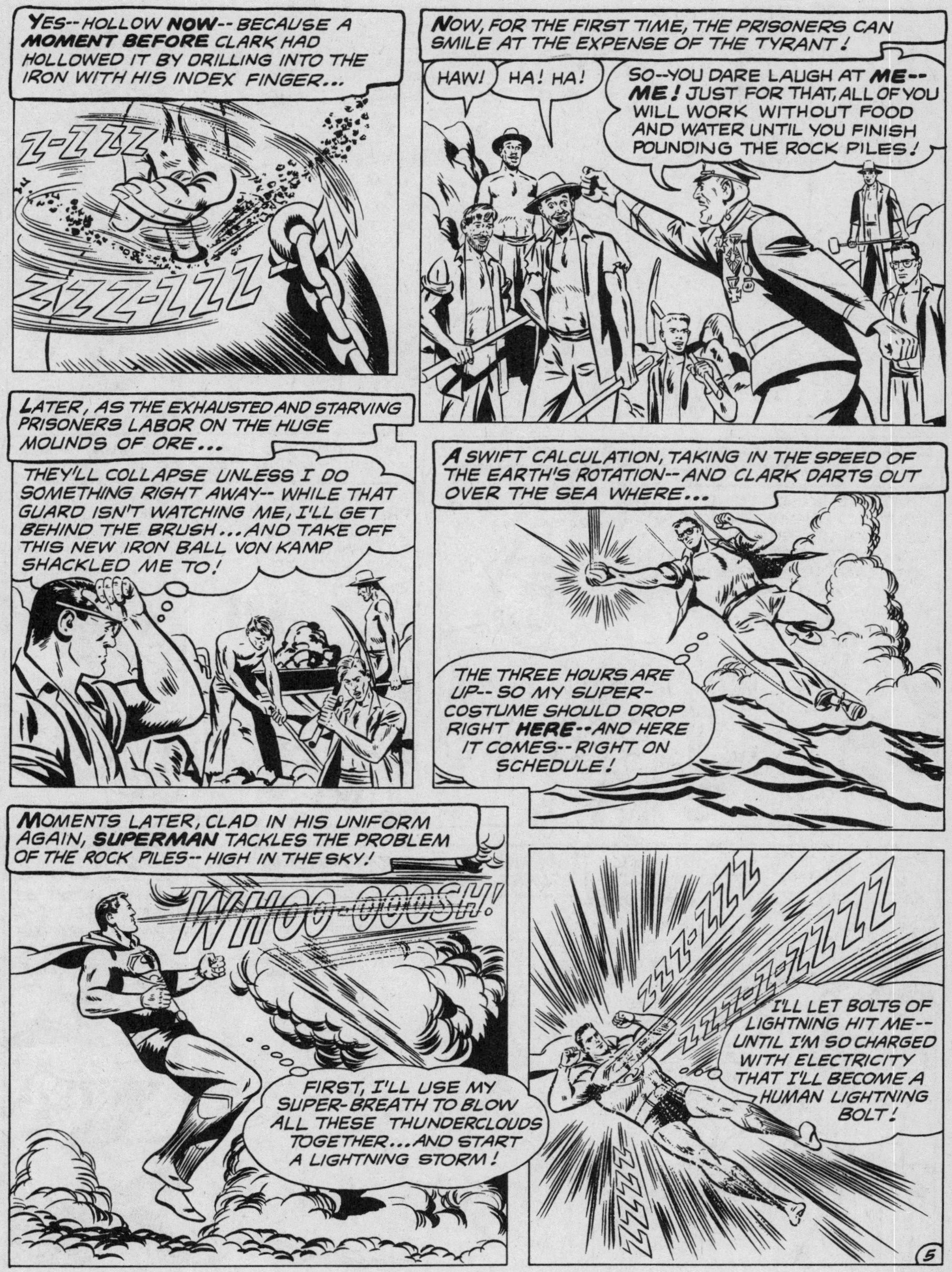
YES-- HOLLOW NOW-- BECAUSE A MOMENT BEFORE CLARK HAD HOLLOWED IT BY DRILLING INTO THE IRON WITH HIS INDEX FINGER...
Z-ZZZZ
ZZZ-ZZZ
NOW, FOR THE FIRST TIME, THE PRISONERS CAN SMILE AT THE EXPENSE OF THE TYRANT!
HAW!
HA! HA!
SO--YOU DARE LAUGH AT ME-- ME! JUST FOR THAT, ALL OF YOU WILL WORK WITHOUT FOOD AND WATER UNTIL YOU FINISH POUNDING THE ROCK PILES!
LATER, AS THE EXHAUSTED AND STARVING PRISONERS LABOR ON THE HUGE MOUNDS OF ORE...
THEY'LL COLLAPSE UNLESS I DO SOMETHING RIGHT AWAY-- WHILE THAT GUARD ISN'T WATCHING ME, I'LL GET BEHIND THE BRUSH... AND TAKE OFF THIS NEW IRON BALL VON KAMP SHACKLED ME TO!
A SWIFT CALCULATION, TAKING IN THE SPEED OF THE EARTH'S ROTATION-- AND CLARK DARTS OUT OVER THE SEA WHERE...
THE THREE HOURS ARE UP-- SO MY SUPER-COSTUME SHOULD DROP RIGHT HERE--AND HERE IT COMES-- RIGHT ON SCHEDULE!
MOMENTS LATER, CLAD IN HIS UNIFORM AGAIN, SUPERMAN TACKLES THE PROBLEM OF THE ROCK PILES-- HIGH IN THE SKY!
WHOO-OOOSH!
FIRST, I'LL USE MY SUPER-BREATH TO BLOW ALL THESE THUNDERCLOUDS TOGETHER... AND START A LIGHTNING STORM!
ZZZZ-ZZZ
ZZZZ-Z-ZZZZ
I'LL LET BOLTS OF LIGHTNING HIT ME-- UNTIL I'M SO CHARGED WITH ELECTRICITY THAT I'LL BECOME A HUMAN LIGHTNING BOLT!
5

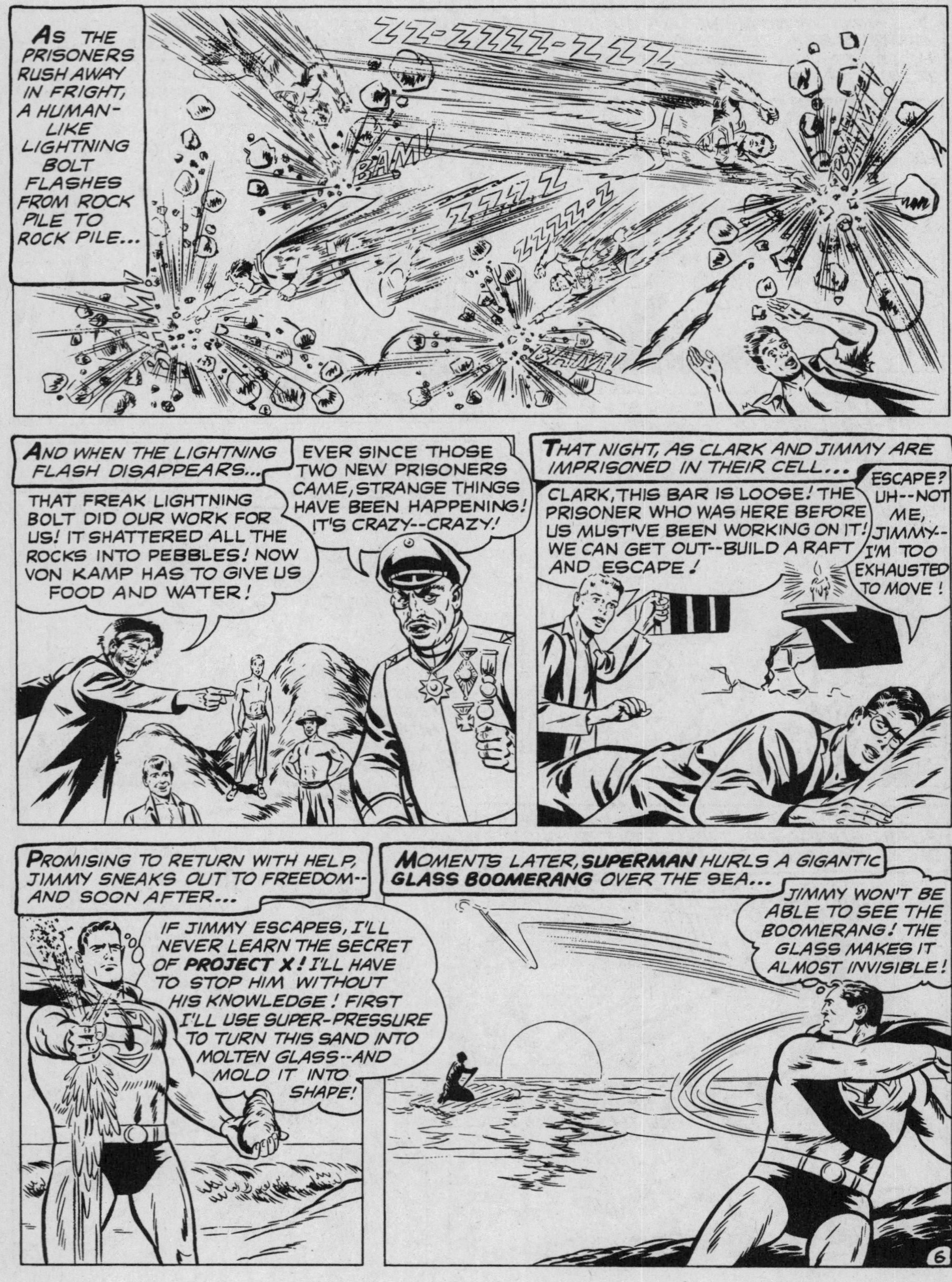
AS THE PRISONERS RUSH AWAY IN FRIGHT, A HUMAN-LIKE LIGHTNING BOLT FLASHES FROM ROCK PILE TO ROCK PILE...
ZZ-ZZZZZ-ZZZ
BAM!
ZZZZZ
ZZZZZ-Z
BAM!
AND WHEN THE LIGHTNING FLASH DISAPPEARS...
THAT FREAK LIGHTNING BOLT DID OUR WORK FOR US! IT SHATTERED ALL THE ROCKS INTO PEBBLES! NOW VON KAMP HAS TO GIVE US FOOD AND WATER!
EVER SINCE THOSE TWO NEW PRISONERS CAME, STRANGE THINGS HAVE BEEN HAPPENING! IT'S CRAZY--CRAZY!
THAT NIGHT, AS CLARK AND JIMMY ARE IMPRISONED IN THEIR CELL...
CLARK, THIS BAR IS LOOSE! THE PRISONER WHO WAS HERE BEFORE US MUST'VE BEEN WORKING ON IT! WE CAN GET OUT--BUILD A RAFT AND ESCAPE!
ESCAPE? UH--NOT ME, JIMMY--I'M TOO EXHAUSTED TO MOVE!
PROMISING TO RETURN WITH HELP, JIMMY SNEAKS OUT TO FREEDOM--AND SOON AFTER...
IF JIMMY ESCAPES, I'LL NEVER LEARN THE SECRET OF PROJECT X! I'LL HAVE TO STOP HIM WITHOUT HIS KNOWLEDGE! FIRST I'LL USE SUPER-PRESSURE TO TURN THIS SAND INTO MOLTEN GLASS--AND MOLD IT INTO SHAPE!
MOMENTS LATER, SUPERMAN HURLS A GIGANTIC GLASS BOOMERANG OVER THE SEA...
JIMMY WON'T BE ABLE TO SEE THE BOOMERANG! THE GLASS MAKES IT ALMOST INVISIBLE!
6

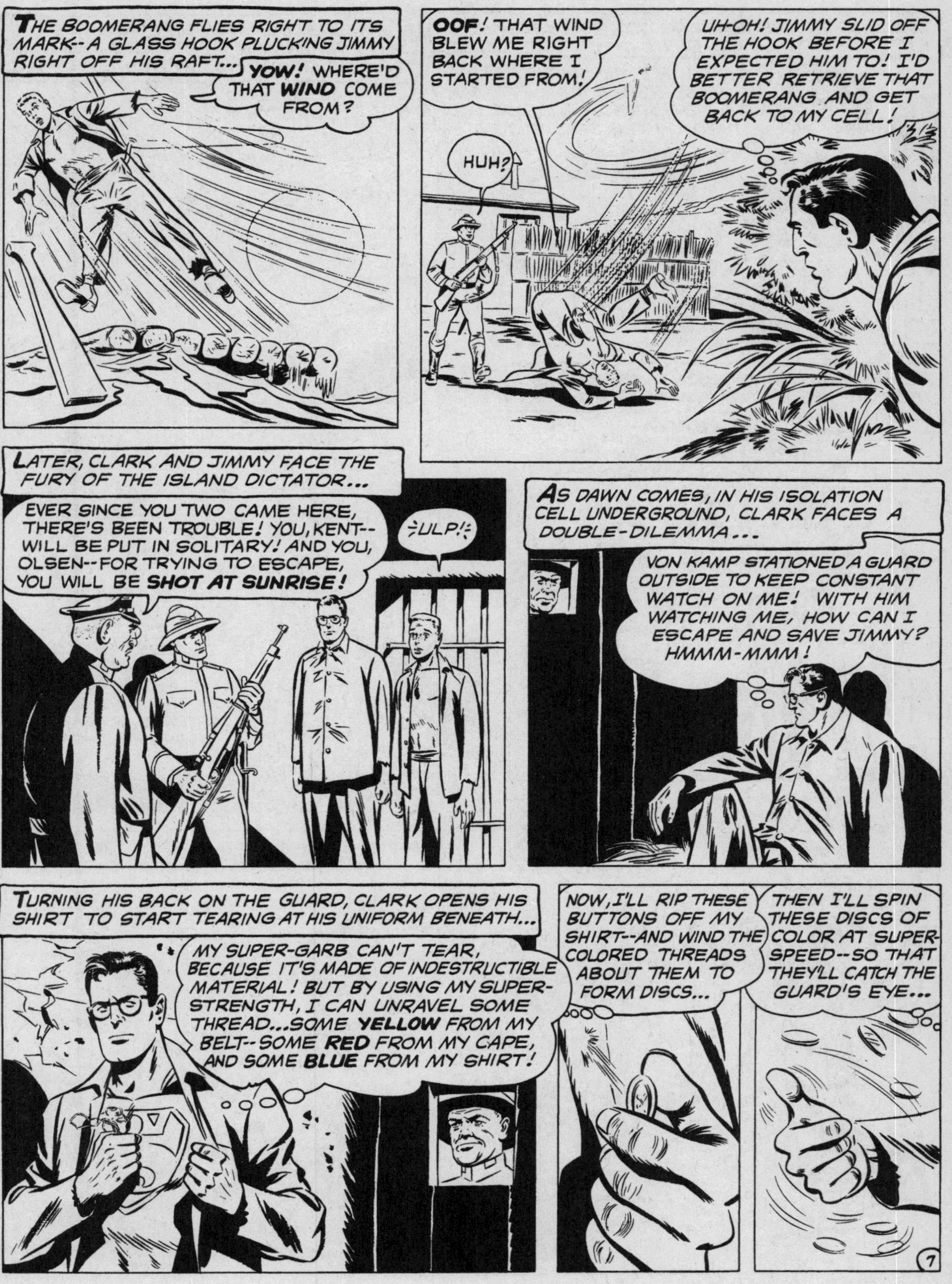

THE BOOMERANG FLIES RIGHT TO ITS MARK-- A GLASS HOOK PLUCKING JIMMY RIGHT OFF HIS RAFT...
YOW! WHERE'D THAT WIND COME FROM?
OOF! THAT WIND BLEW ME RIGHT BACK WHERE I STARTED FROM!
UH-OH! JIMMY SLID OFF THE HOOK BEFORE I EXPECTED HIM TO! I'D BETTER RETRIEVE THAT BOOMERANG AND GET BACK TO MY CELL!
HUH?
LATER, CLARK AND JIMMY FACE THE FURY OF THE ISLAND DICTATOR...
EVER SINCE YOU TWO CAME HERE, THERE'S BEEN TROUBLE! YOU, KENT-- WILL BE PUT IN SOLITARY! AND YOU, OLSEN--FOR TRYING TO ESCAPE, YOU WILL BE SHOT AT SUNRISE!
ULP!
AS DAWN COMES, IN HIS ISOLATION CELL UNDERGROUND, CLARK FACES A DOUBLE-DILEMMA...
VON KAMP STATIONED A GUARD OUTSIDE TO KEEP CONSTANT WATCH ON ME! WITH HIM WATCHING ME, HOW CAN I ESCAPE AND SAVE JIMMY? HMMM-MMM!
TURNING HIS BACK ON THE GUARD, CLARK OPENS HIS SHIRT TO START TEARING AT HIS UNIFORM BENEATH...
MY SUPER-GARB CAN'T TEAR, BECAUSE IT'S MADE OF INDESTRUCTIBLE MATERIAL! BUT BY USING MY SUPER-STRENGTH, I CAN UNRAVEL SOME THREAD...SOME YELLOW FROM MY BELT--SOME RED FROM MY CAPE, AND SOME BLUE FROM MY SHIRT!
NOW, I'LL RIP THESE BUTTONS OFF MY SHIRT--AND WIND THE COLORED THREADS ABOUT THEM TO FORM DISCS...
THEN I'LL SPIN THESE DISCS OF COLOR AT SUPER-SPEED--SO THAT THEY'LL CATCH THE GUARD'S EYE...
7

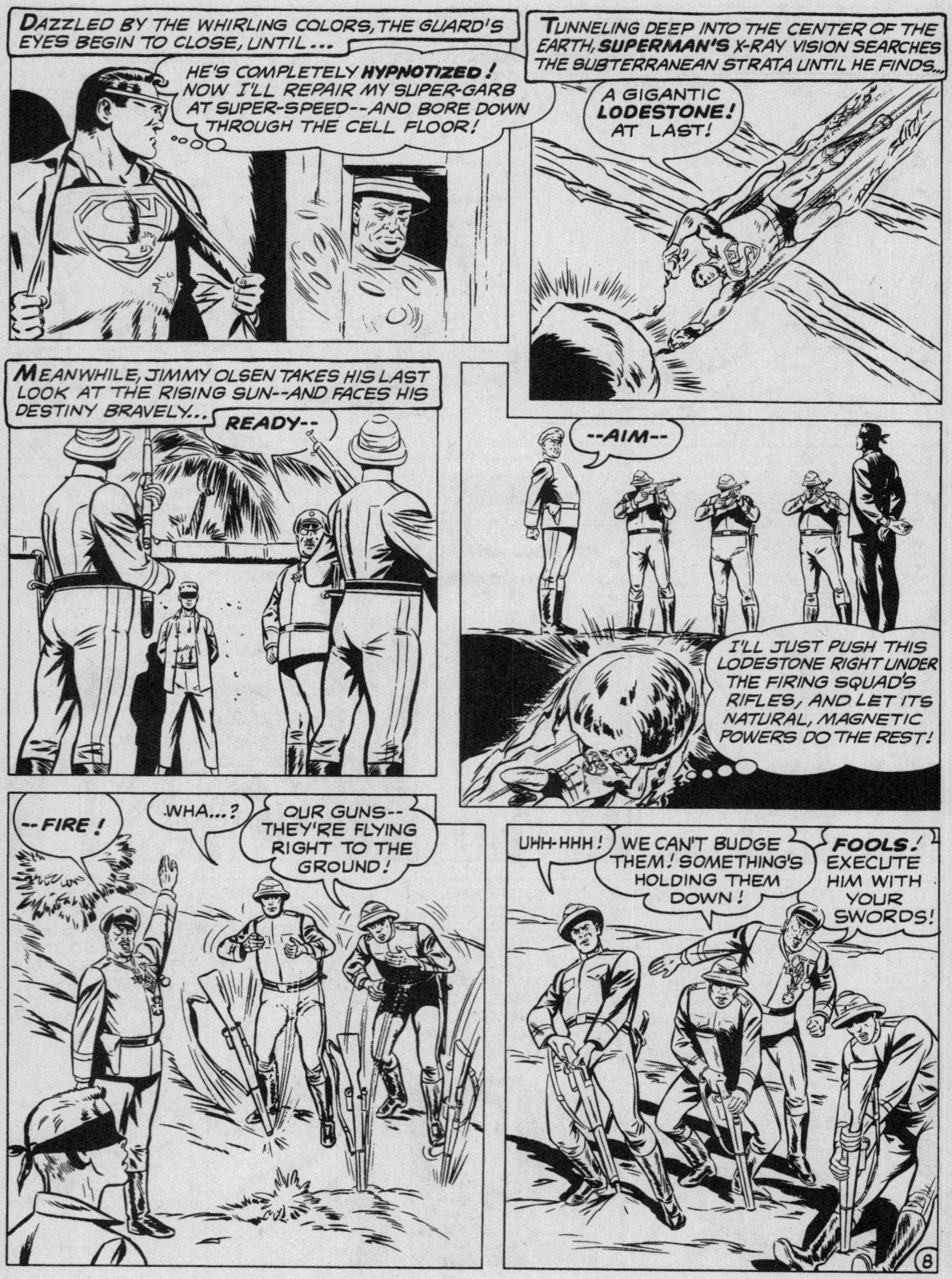
DAZZLED BY THE WHIRLING COLORS, THE GUARD'S EYES BEGIN TO CLOSE, UNTIL...
HE'S COMPLETELY HYPNOTIZED! NOW I'LL REPAIR MY SUPER-GARB AT SUPER-SPEED--AND BORE DOWN THROUGH THE CELL FLOOR!
TUNNELING DEEP INTO THE CENTER OF THE EARTH, SUPERMAN'S X-RAY VISION SEARCHES THE SUBTERRANEAN STRATA UNTIL HE FINDS...
A GIGANTIC LODESTONE! AT LAST!
MEANWHILE, JIMMY OLSEN TAKES HIS LAST LOOK AT THE RISING SUN--AND FACES HIS DESTINY BRAVELY...
READY--
--AIM--
I'LL JUST PUSH THIS LODESTONE RIGHT UNDER THE FIRING SQUAD'S RIFLES, AND LET ITS NATURAL, MAGNETIC POWERS DO THE REST!
--FIRE!
WHA...?
OUR GUNS-- THEY'RE FLYING RIGHT TO THE GROUND!
UHH-HHH!
WE CAN'T BUDGE THEM! SOMETHING'S HOLDING THEM DOWN!
FOOLS! EXECUTE HIM WITH YOUR SWORDS!
8

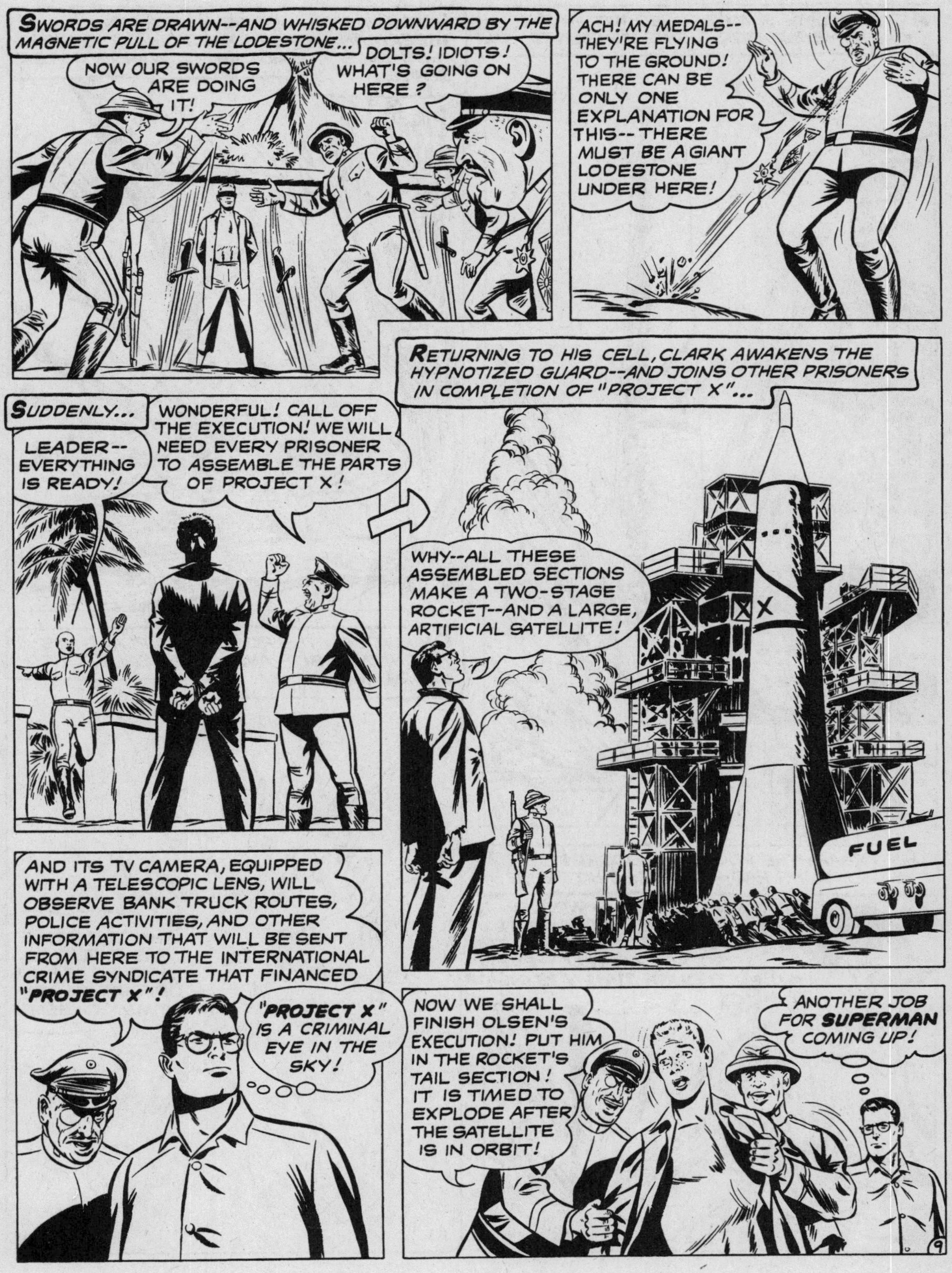
SWORDS ARE DRAWN--AND WHISKED DOWNWARD BY THE MAGNETIC PULL OF THE LODESTONE...
NOW OUR SWORDS ARE DOING IT!
DOLTS! IDIOTS! WHAT'S GOING ON HERE ?
ACH! MY MEDALS-- THEY'RE FLYING TO THE GROUND! THERE CAN BE ONLY ONE EXPLANATION FOR THIS-- THERE MUST BE A GIANT LODESTONE UNDER HERE!
SUDDENLY...
LEADER-- EVERYTHING IS READY!
WONDERFUL! CALL OFF THE EXECUTION! WE WILL NEED EVERY PRISONER TO ASSEMBLE THE PARTS OF PROJECT X!
RETURNING TO HIS CELL, CLARK AWAKENS THE HYPNOTIZED GUARD--AND JOINS OTHER PRISONERS IN COMPLETION OF "PROJECT X"...
WHY--ALL THESE ASSEMBLED SECTIONS MAKE A TWO-STAGE ROCKET--AND A LARGE, ARTIFICIAL SATELLITE!
X
FUEL
AND ITS TV CAMERA, EQUIPPED WITH A TELESCOPIC LENS, WILL OBSERVE BANK TRUCK ROUTES, POLICE ACTIVITIES, AND OTHER INFORMATION THAT WILL BE SENT FROM HERE TO THE INTERNATIONAL CRIME SYNDICATE THAT FINANCED "PROJECT X"!
"PROJECT X" IS A CRIMINAL EYE IN THE SKY!
NOW WE SHALL FINISH OLSEN'S EXECUTION! PUT HIM IN THE ROCKET'S TAIL SECTION! IT IS TIMED TO EXPLODE AFTER THE SATELLITE IS IN ORBIT!
ANOTHER JOB FOR SUPERMAN COMING UP!
9

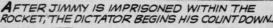

AFTER JIMMY IS IMPRISONED WITHIN THE ROCKET, THE DICTATOR BEGINS HIS COUNT DOWN...

8-7-6-5 4-3-2-1-- FIRE!

STREAKING SO FAST HE IS UNSEEN, **SUPERMAN** GATHERS HIS TITANIC STRENGTH-- AND HURLS THE ROCKET TOWARDS OUTER SPACE!

WOOOOSH!

ON HURTLES THE ROCKET TO PLACE ITS "MOON" IN ORBIT--AND AS THE TAIL SECTION DROPS AWAY...

JETS ROAR--THE ROCKET SHUDDERS ON THE LAUNCHING PAD--BUT DOES NOT RISE!

SOMETHING'S WRONG WITH THE MECHANISM! I'LL HAVE TO LAUNCH THE ROCKET MYSELF--EVEN THOUGH JIMMY IS INSIDE!

BOOM!

AHA! THE ROCKET HAS EXPLODED! THAT IS THE END OF THAT PEST, JIMMY OLSEN!

10

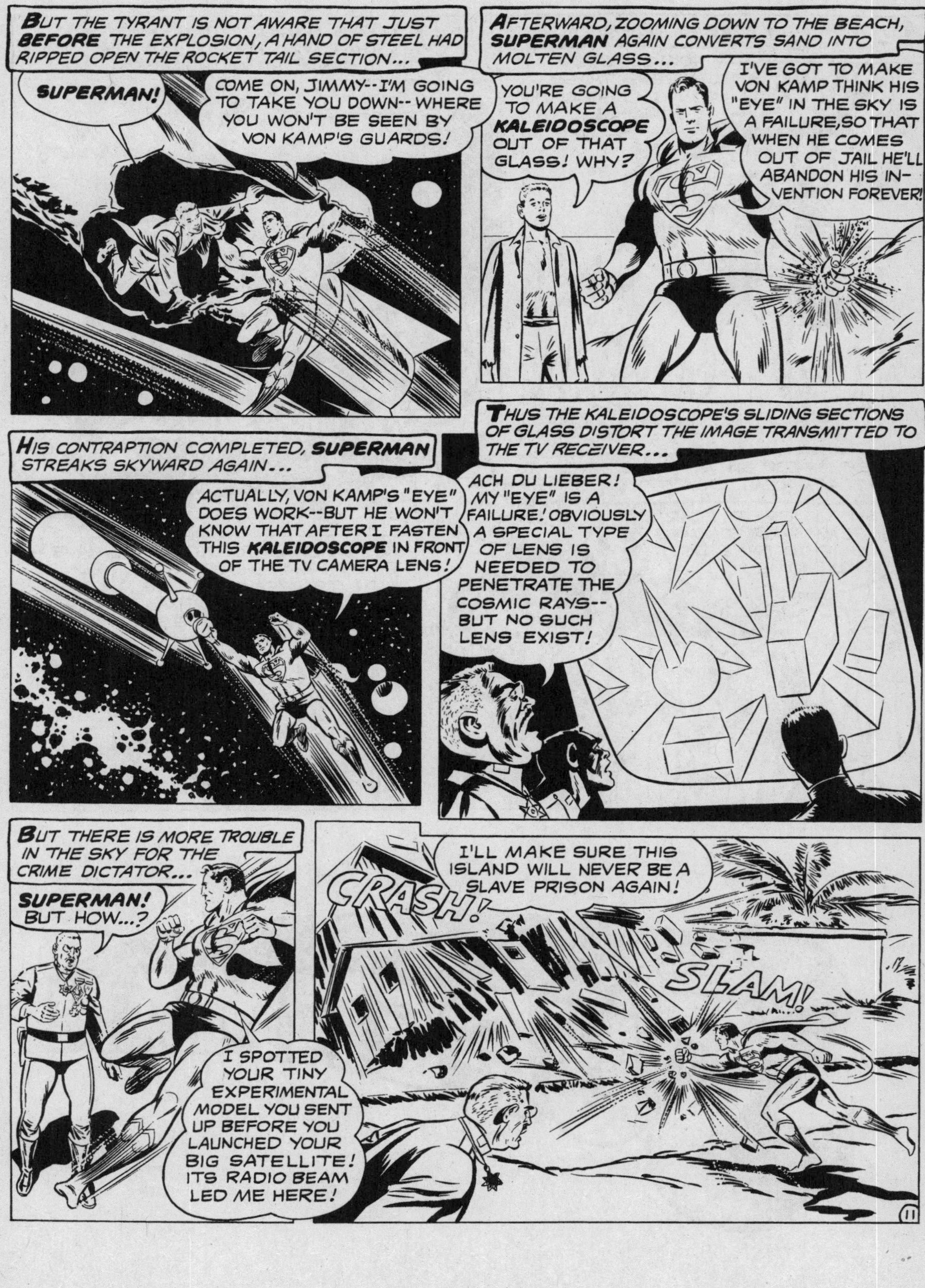
BUT THE TYRANT IS NOT AWARE THAT JUST **BEFORE** THE EXPLOSION, A HAND OF STEEL HAD RIPPED OPEN THE ROCKET TAIL SECTION...
SUPERMAN!
COME ON, JIMMY--I'M GOING TO TAKE YOU DOWN--WHERE YOU WON'T BE SEEN BY VON KAMP'S GUARDS!
AFTERWARD, ZOOMING DOWN TO THE BEACH, **SUPERMAN** AGAIN CONVERTS SAND INTO MOLTEN GLASS...
YOU'RE GOING TO MAKE A **KALEIDOSCOPE** OUT OF THAT GLASS! WHY?
I'VE GOT TO MAKE VON KAMP THINK HIS "EYE" IN THE SKY IS A FAILURE, SO THAT WHEN HE COMES OUT OF JAIL HE'LL ABANDON HIS INVENTION FOREVER!
HIS CONTRAPTION COMPLETED, **SUPERMAN** STREAKS SKYWARD AGAIN...
ACTUALLY, VON KAMP'S "EYE" DOES WORK--BUT HE WON'T KNOW THAT AFTER I FASTEN THIS **KALEIDOSCOPE** IN FRONT OF THE TV CAMERA LENS!
THUS THE KALEIDOSCOPE'S SLIDING SECTIONS OF GLASS DISTORT THE IMAGE TRANSMITTED TO THE TV RECEIVER...
ACH DU LIEBER! MY "EYE" IS A FAILURE! OBVIOUSLY A SPECIAL TYPE OF LENS IS NEEDED TO PENETRATE THE COSMIC RAYS--BUT NO SUCH LENS EXIST!
BUT THERE IS MORE TROUBLE IN THE SKY FOR THE CRIME DICTATOR...
SUPERMAN! BUT HOW...?
I SPOTTED YOUR TINY EXPERIMENTAL MODEL YOU SENT UP BEFORE YOU LAUNCHED YOUR BIG SATELLITE! ITS RADIO BEAM LED ME HERE!
I'LL MAKE SURE THIS ISLAND WILL NEVER BE A SLAVE PRISON AGAIN!
CRASH!
SLAM!
11

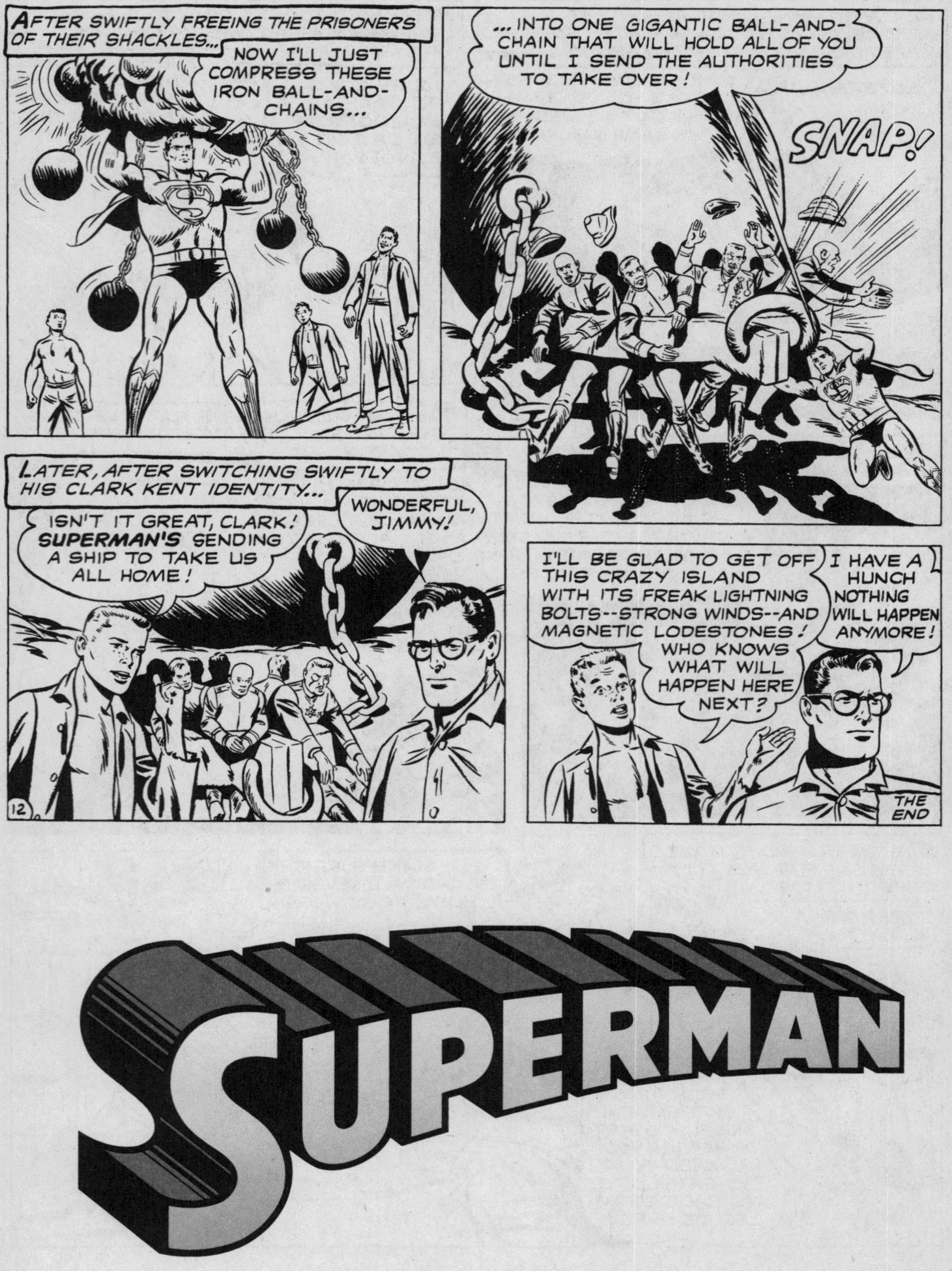
AFTER SWIFTLY FREEING THE PRISONERS OF THEIR SHACKLES...
NOW I'LL JUST COMPRESS THESE IRON BALL-AND-CHAINS...
...INTO ONE GIGANTIC BALL-AND-CHAIN THAT WILL HOLD ALL OF YOU UNTIL I SEND THE AUTHORITIES TO TAKE OVER!
SNAP!
LATER, AFTER SWITCHING SWIFTLY TO HIS CLARK KENT IDENTITY...
ISN'T IT GREAT, CLARK! SUPERMAN'S SENDING A SHIP TO TAKE US ALL HOME!
WONDERFUL, JIMMY!
12
I'LL BE GLAD TO GET OFF THIS CRAZY ISLAND WITH ITS FREAK LIGHTNING BOLTS--STRONG WINDS--AND MAGNETIC LODESTONES! WHO KNOWS WHAT WILL HAPPEN HERE NEXT?
I HAVE A HUNCH NOTHING WILL HAPPEN ANYMORE!
THE END

SUPERMAN

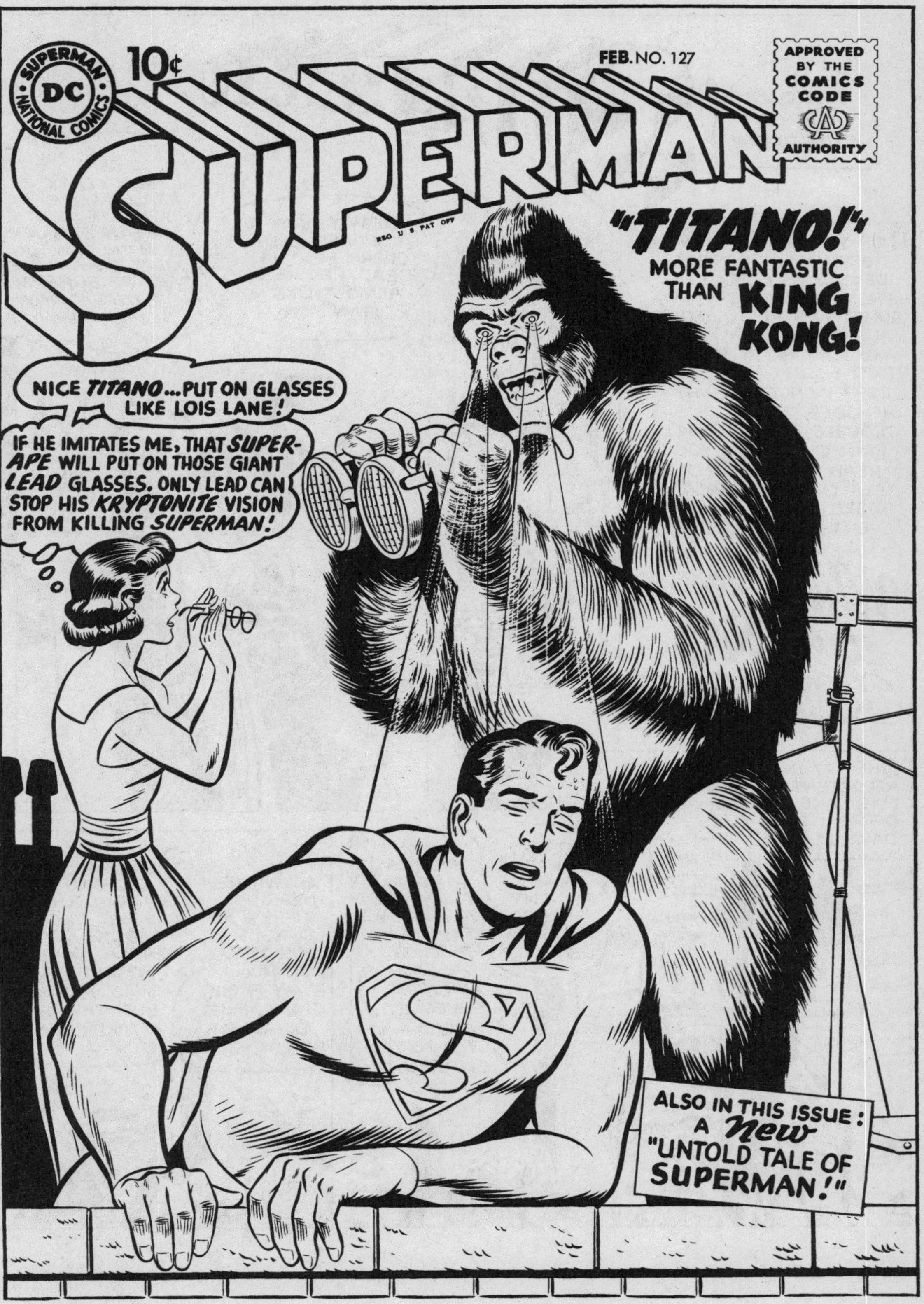
SUPERMAN DC NATIONAL COMICS
10¢
FEB. NO. 127
APPROVED BY THE COMICS CODE AUTHORITY
SUPERMAN
REG. U. S. PAT. OFF.
"TITANO!" MORE FANTASTIC THAN KING KONG!
NICE TITANO...PUT ON GLASSES LIKE LOIS LANE!
IF HE IMITATES ME, THAT SUPER-APE WILL PUT ON THOSE GIANT LEAD GLASSES. ONLY LEAD CAN STOP HIS KRYPTONITE VISION FROM KILLING SUPERMAN!
ALSO IN THIS ISSUE: A New "UNTOLD TALE OF SUPERMAN!"

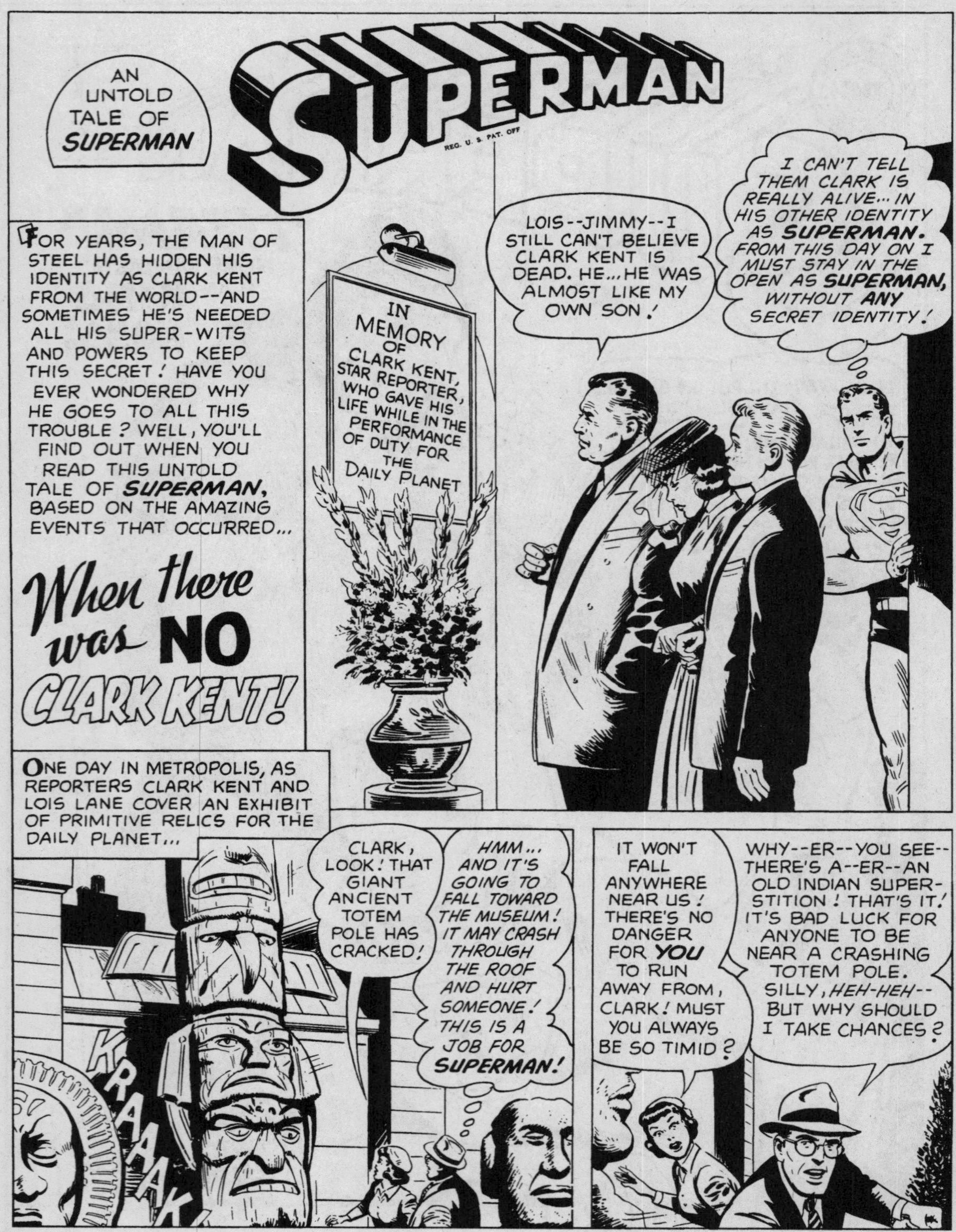

AN UNTOLD TALE OF SUPERMAN
SUPERMAN
REG. U. S. PAT. OFF
FOR YEARS, THE MAN OF STEEL HAS HIDDEN HIS IDENTITY AS CLARK KENT FROM THE WORLD--AND SOMETIMES HE'S NEEDED ALL HIS SUPER-WITS AND POWERS TO KEEP THIS SECRET! HAVE YOU EVER WONDERED WHY HE GOES TO ALL THIS TROUBLE? WELL, YOU'LL FIND OUT WHEN YOU READ THIS UNTOLD TALE OF SUPERMAN, BASED ON THE AMAZING EVENTS THAT OCCURRED...
When there was NO CLARK KENT!
IN MEMORY OF CLARK KENT, STAR REPORTER, WHO GAVE HIS LIFE WHILE IN THE PERFORMANCE OF DUTY FOR THE DAILY PLANET
LOIS--JIMMY--I STILL CAN'T BELIEVE CLARK KENT IS DEAD. HE...HE WAS ALMOST LIKE MY OWN SON!
I CAN'T TELL THEM CLARK IS REALLY ALIVE... IN HIS OTHER IDENTITY AS SUPERMAN. FROM THIS DAY ON I MUST STAY IN THE OPEN AS SUPERMAN, WITHOUT ANY SECRET IDENTITY!
ONE DAY IN METROPOLIS, AS REPORTERS CLARK KENT AND LOIS LANE COVER AN EXHIBIT OF PRIMITIVE RELICS FOR THE DAILY PLANET...
KRAAAK
CLARK, LOOK! THAT GIANT ANCIENT TOTEM POLE HAS CRACKED!
HMM... AND IT'S GOING TO FALL TOWARD THE MUSEUM! IT MAY CRASH THROUGH THE ROOF AND HURT SOMEONE! THIS IS A JOB FOR SUPERMAN!
IT WON'T FALL ANYWHERE NEAR US! THERE'S NO DANGER FOR YOU TO RUN AWAY FROM, CLARK! MUST YOU ALWAYS BE SO TIMID?
WHY--ER--YOU SEE--THERE'S A--ER--AN OLD INDIAN SUPERSTITION! THAT'S IT! IT'S BAD LUCK FOR ANYONE TO BE NEAR A CRASHING TOTEM POLE. SILLY, HEH-HEH--BUT WHY SHOULD I TAKE CHANCES?

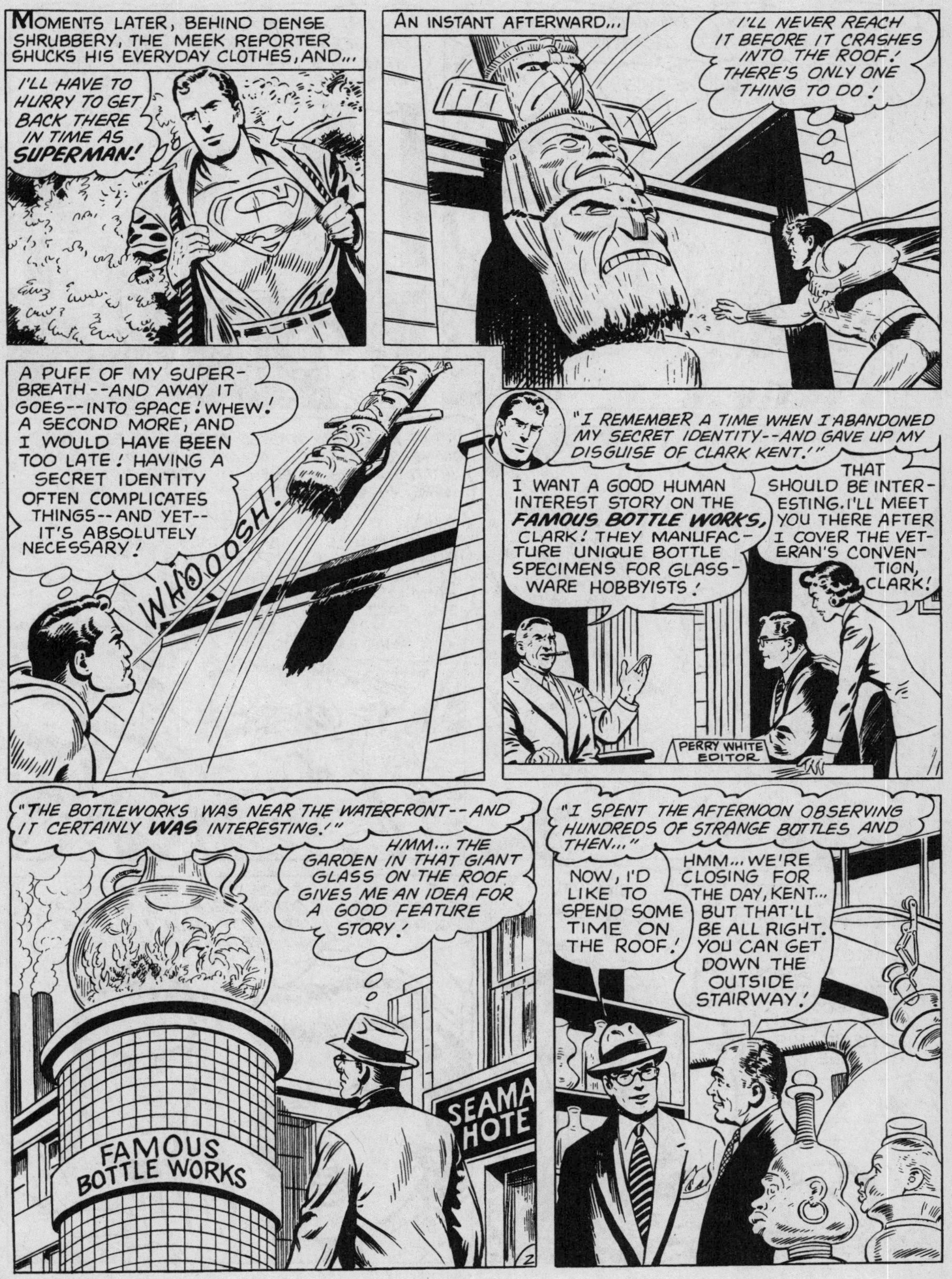
MOMENTS LATER, BEHIND DENSE SHRUBBERY, THE MEEK REPORTER SHUCKS HIS EVERYDAY CLOTHES, AND...
I'LL HAVE TO HURRY TO GET BACK THERE IN TIME AS SUPERMAN!
AN INSTANT AFTERWARD...
I'LL NEVER REACH IT BEFORE IT CRASHES INTO THE ROOF! THERE'S ONLY ONE THING TO DO!
A PUFF OF MY SUPER-BREATH--AND AWAY IT GOES--INTO SPACE! WHEW! A SECOND MORE, AND I WOULD HAVE BEEN TOO LATE! HAVING A SECRET IDENTITY OFTEN COMPLICATES THINGS--AND YET--IT'S ABSOLUTELY NECESSARY!
WHOOOSH!
"I REMEMBER A TIME WHEN I ABANDONED MY SECRET IDENTITY--AND GAVE UP MY DISGUISE OF CLARK KENT!"
I WANT A GOOD HUMAN INTEREST STORY ON THE FAMOUS BOTTLE WORKS, CLARK! THEY MANUFACTURE UNIQUE BOTTLE SPECIMENS FOR GLASSWARE HOBBYISTS!
THAT SHOULD BE INTERESTING. I'LL MEET YOU THERE AFTER I COVER THE VETERAN'S CONVENTION, CLARK!
PERRY WHITE EDITOR
"THE BOTTLEWORKS WAS NEAR THE WATERFRONT--AND IT CERTAINLY WAS INTERESTING!"
HMM... THE GARDEN IN THAT GIANT GLASS ON THE ROOF GIVES ME AN IDEA FOR A GOOD FEATURE STORY!
FAMOUS BOTTLE WORKS
SEAMA HOTE
2
"I SPENT THE AFTERNOON OBSERVING HUNDREDS OF STRANGE BOTTLES AND THEN..."
NOW, I'D LIKE TO SPEND SOME TIME ON THE ROOF!
HMM... WE'RE CLOSING FOR THE DAY, KENT... BUT THAT'LL BE ALL RIGHT. YOU CAN GET DOWN THE OUTSIDE STAIRWAY!

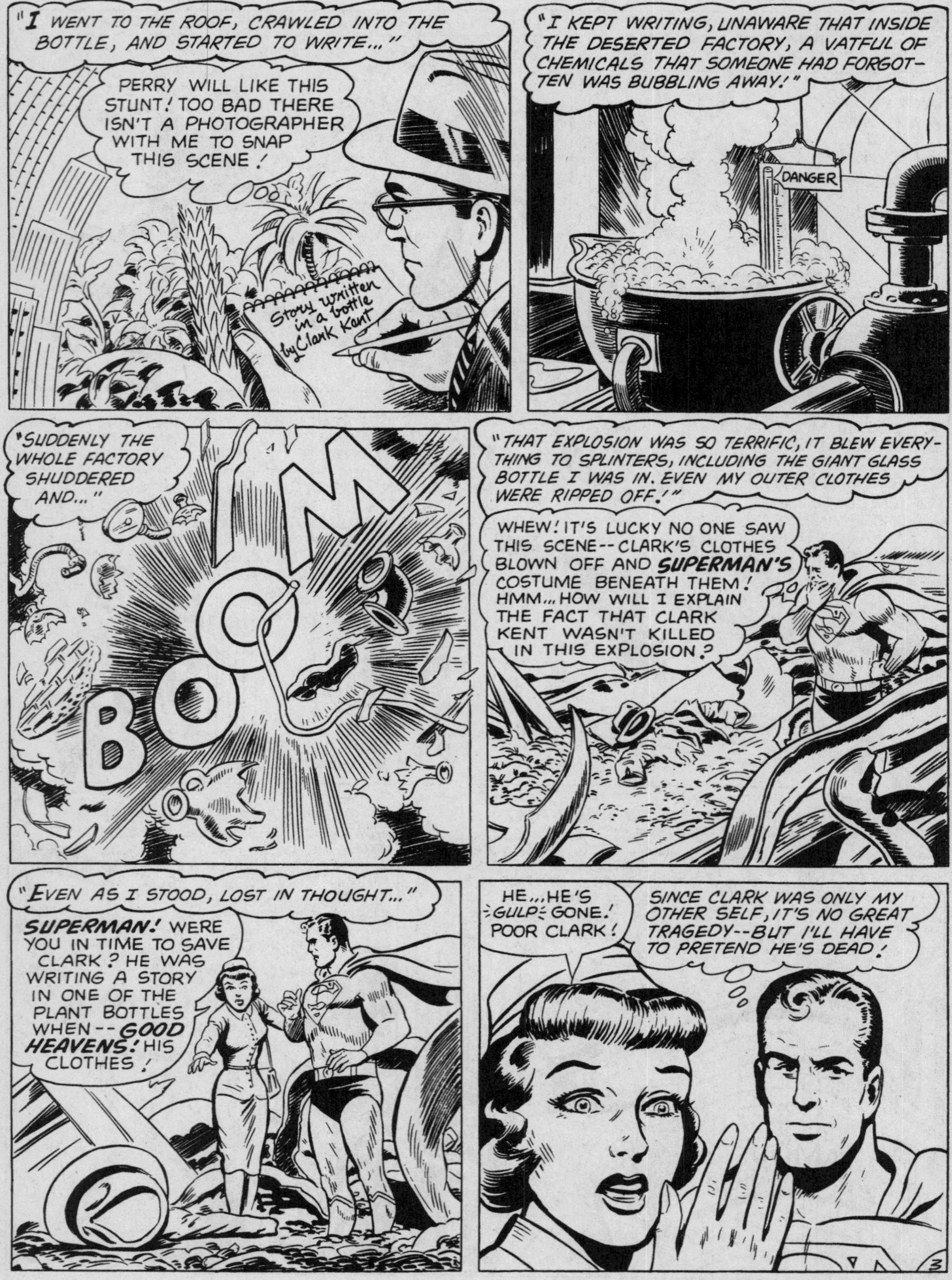
"I WENT TO THE ROOF, CRAWLED INTO THE BOTTLE, AND STARTED TO WRITE..."
PERRY WILL LIKE THIS STUNT! TOO BAD THERE ISN'T A PHOTOGRAPHER WITH ME TO SNAP THIS SCENE!
Story written in a bottle by Clark Kent
"I KEPT WRITING, UNAWARE THAT INSIDE THE DESERTED FACTORY, A VATFUL OF CHEMICALS THAT SOMEONE HAD FORGOTTEN WAS BUBBLING AWAY!"
DANGER
"SUDDENLY THE WHOLE FACTORY SHUDDERED AND..."
BOOM
"THAT EXPLOSION WAS SO TERRIFIC, IT BLEW EVERYTHING TO SPLINTERS, INCLUDING THE GIANT GLASS BOTTLE I WAS IN. EVEN MY OUTER CLOTHES WERE RIPPED OFF!"
WHEW! IT'S LUCKY NO ONE SAW THIS SCENE--CLARK'S CLOTHES BLOWN OFF AND SUPERMAN'S COSTUME BENEATH THEM! HMM... HOW WILL I EXPLAIN THE FACT THAT CLARK KENT WASN'T KILLED IN THIS EXPLOSION?
"EVEN AS I STOOD, LOST IN THOUGHT..."
SUPERMAN! WERE YOU IN TIME TO SAVE CLARK? HE WAS WRITING A STORY IN ONE OF THE PLANT BOTTLES WHEN--GOOD HEAVENS! HIS CLOTHES!
HE...HE'S -GULP- GONE! POOR CLARK!
SINCE CLARK WAS ONLY MY OTHER SELF, IT'S NO GREAT TRAGEDY--BUT I'LL HAVE TO PRETEND HE'S DEAD!
3

"NEXT DAY, AFTER I ATTENDED FUNERAL SERVICES FOR MY POOR SECRET SELF..."

I...I...CAN'T BELIEVE CLARK IS G-GONE! I... I FEEL ≥SOB≤ TERRIBLE!

THERE, THERE, LOIS, TAKE IT EASY! CLARK WOULDN'T WANT YOU TO FEEL LIKE THAT! I--ER--KNOW!

"I TRIED TO CONSOLE LOIS BY TAKING HER TO DINNER, BUT..."

I...I CAN'T EAT A MORSEL, SUPERMAN! SOMEHOW I FEEL THAT CLARK'S HERE WITH US--IN SPIRIT...

WHY, ER--SURE HE IS, LOIS! I'M ABSOLUTELY CERTAIN OF THAT!

HMM...NOW I HAVE THE JOB OF CREATING ANOTHER SECRET IDENTITY TO REPLACE CLARK!

"IT WAS THEN THAT THE IDEA CAME TO ME!"

HMM...MAYBE I SHOULD DO WITHOUT A SECRET IDENTITY FOR ONCE! LEADING A DOUBLE LIFE HAS ALWAYS COMPLICATED MY CAREER AS SUPERMAN! YES! FROM NOW ON, I'LL BE JUST ONE PERSON... SUPERMAN!

"I APPROACHED MY PAL, JIMMY OLSEN, CUB REPORTER FOR THE PLANET, AND..."

NO ONE EVER KNEW IT, JIMMY-- BUT I USED TO LIVE WITH CLARK IN SECRET AT HIS APARTMENT. NOW THAT HE'S GONE, DO YOU MIND IF I LIVE WITH YOU IN YOUR APARTMENT?

MIND? GOSH SUPERMAN... THIS IS THE GREATEST THING THAT EVER HAPPENED TO ME!

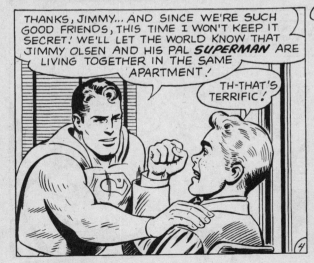

THANKS, JIMMY... AND SINCE WE'RE SUCH GOOD FRIENDS, THIS TIME I WON'T KEEP IT SECRET! WE'LL LET THE WORLD KNOW THAT JIMMY OLSEN AND HIS PAL SUPERMAN ARE LIVING TOGETHER IN THE SAME APARTMENT!

TH-THAT'S TERRIFIC!

"IF I HAD ONLY KNOWN WHAT WAS GOING TO HAPPEN..."

WAIT TILL THE NEIGHBORS TAKE A GANDER AT THIS!

JIMMY OLSEN AND SUPERMAN 4 H

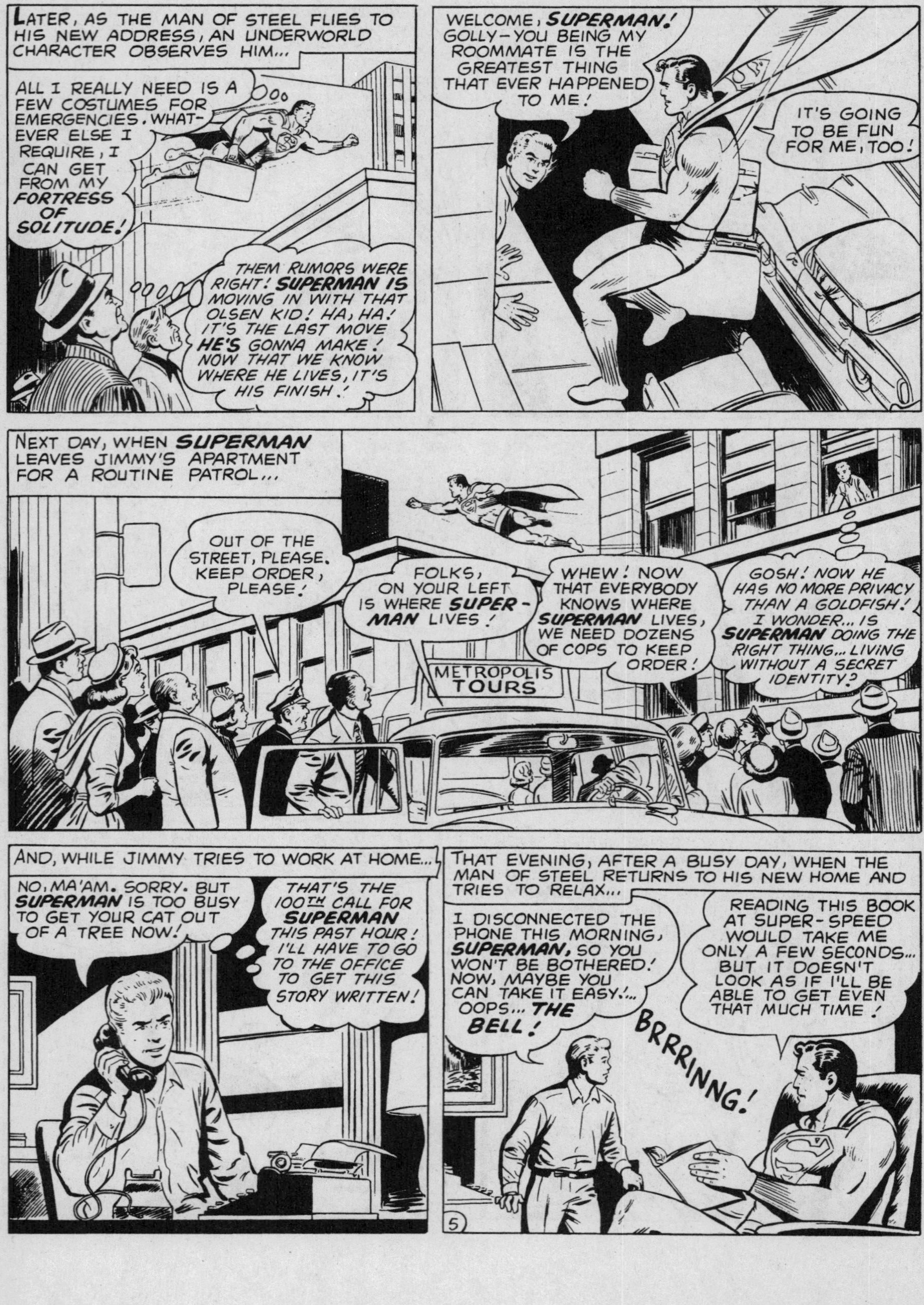
LATER, AS THE MAN OF STEEL FLIES TO HIS NEW ADDRESS, AN UNDERWORLD CHARACTER OBSERVES HIM...
ALL I REALLY NEED IS A FEW COSTUMES FOR EMERGENCIES. WHAT-EVER ELSE I REQUIRE, I CAN GET FROM MY FORTRESS OF SOLITUDE!
THEM RUMORS WERE RIGHT! SUPERMAN IS MOVING IN WITH THAT OLSEN KID! HA, HA! IT'S THE LAST MOVE HE'S GONNA MAKE! NOW THAT WE KNOW WHERE HE LIVES, IT'S HIS FINISH!
WELCOME, SUPERMAN! GOLLY–YOU BEING MY ROOMMATE IS THE GREATEST THING THAT EVER HAPPENED TO ME!
IT'S GOING TO BE FUN FOR ME, TOO!
NEXT DAY, WHEN SUPERMAN LEAVES JIMMY'S APARTMENT FOR A ROUTINE PATROL...
OUT OF THE STREET, PLEASE. KEEP ORDER, PLEASE!
FOLKS, ON YOUR LEFT IS WHERE SUPER-MAN LIVES!
WHEW! NOW THAT EVERYBODY KNOWS WHERE SUPERMAN LIVES, WE NEED DOZENS OF COPS TO KEEP ORDER!
GOSH! NOW HE HAS NO MORE PRIVACY THAN A GOLDFISH! I WONDER... IS SUPERMAN DOING THE RIGHT THING... LIVING WITHOUT A SECRET IDENTITY?
METROPOLIS TOURS
AND, WHILE JIMMY TRIES TO WORK AT HOME...
NO, MA'AM. SORRY. BUT SUPERMAN IS TOO BUSY TO GET YOUR CAT OUT OF A TREE NOW!
THAT'S THE 100TH CALL FOR SUPERMAN THIS PAST HOUR! I'LL HAVE TO GO TO THE OFFICE TO GET THIS STORY WRITTEN!
THAT EVENING, AFTER A BUSY DAY, WHEN THE MAN OF STEEL RETURNS TO HIS NEW HOME AND TRIES TO RELAX...
I DISCONNECTED THE PHONE THIS MORNING, SUPERMAN, SO YOU WON'T BE BOTHERED! NOW, MAYBE YOU CAN TAKE IT EASY!... OOPS... THE BELL!
READING THIS BOOK AT SUPER-SPEED WOULD TAKE ME ONLY A FEW SECONDS... BUT IT DOESN'T LOOK AS IF I'LL BE ABLE TO GET EVEN THAT MUCH TIME!
BRRRINNG!
5

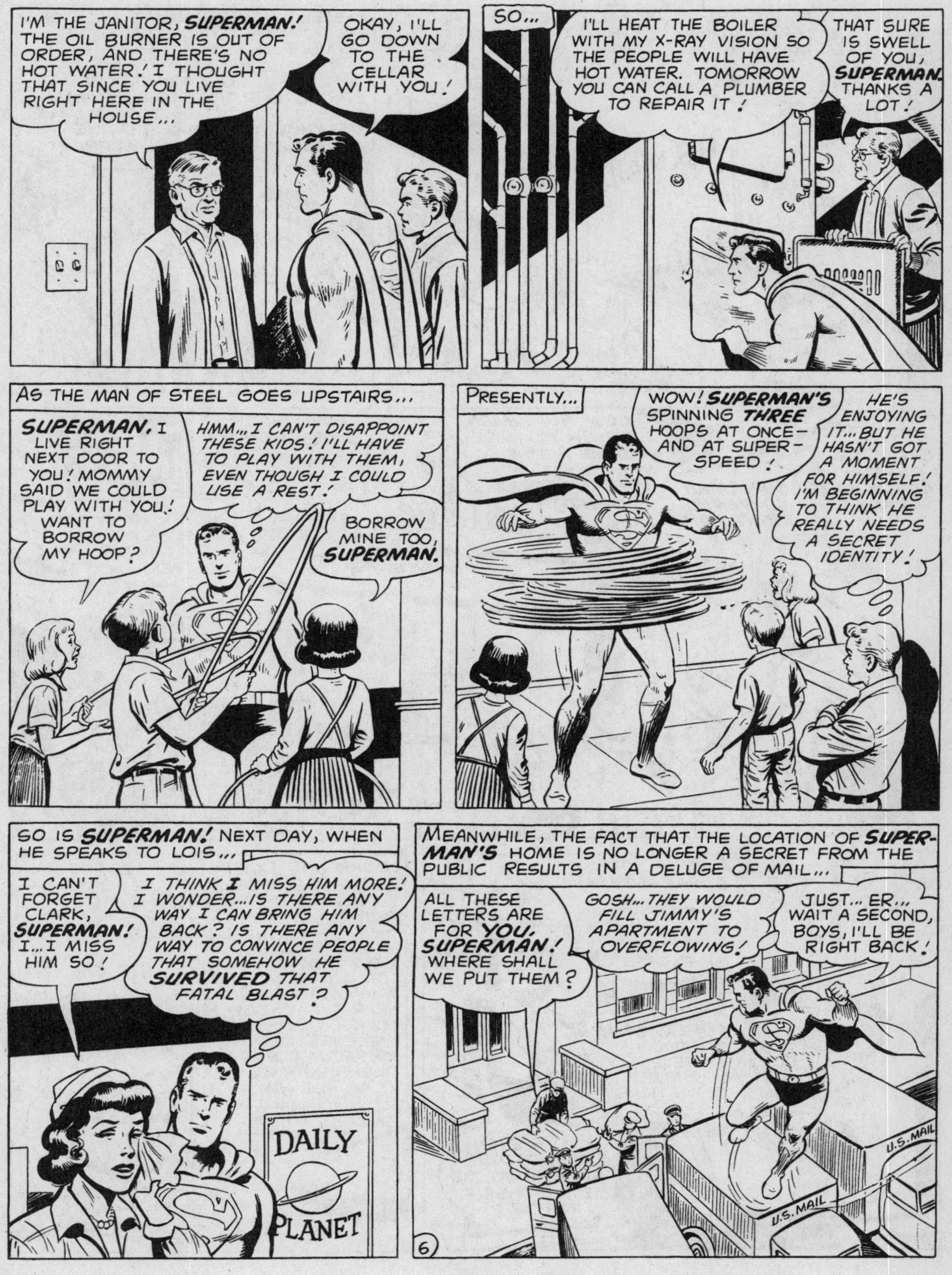
I'M THE JANITOR, SUPERMAN! THE OIL BURNER IS OUT OF ORDER, AND THERE'S NO HOT WATER! I THOUGHT THAT SINCE YOU LIVE RIGHT HERE IN THE HOUSE...
OKAY, I'LL GO DOWN TO THE CELLAR WITH YOU!
SO...
I'LL HEAT THE BOILER WITH MY X-RAY VISION SO THE PEOPLE WILL HAVE HOT WATER. TOMORROW YOU CAN CALL A PLUMBER TO REPAIR IT!
THAT SURE IS SWELL OF YOU, SUPERMAN! THANKS A LOT!
AS THE MAN OF STEEL GOES UPSTAIRS...
SUPERMAN, I LIVE RIGHT NEXT DOOR TO YOU! MOMMY SAID WE COULD PLAY WITH YOU! WANT TO BORROW MY HOOP?
HMM... I CAN'T DISAPPOINT THESE KIDS! I'LL HAVE TO PLAY WITH THEM, EVEN THOUGH I COULD USE A REST!
BORROW MINE TOO, SUPERMAN.
PRESENTLY...
WOW! SUPERMAN'S SPINNING THREE HOOPS AT ONCE--AND AT SUPER-SPEED!
HE'S ENJOYING IT... BUT HE HASN'T GOT A MOMENT FOR HIMSELF! I'M BEGINNING TO THINK HE REALLY NEEDS A SECRET IDENTITY!
SO IS SUPERMAN! NEXT DAY, WHEN HE SPEAKS TO LOIS...
I CAN'T FORGET CLARK, SUPERMAN! I... I MISS HIM SO!
I THINK I MISS HIM MORE! I WONDER... IS THERE ANY WAY I CAN BRING HIM BACK? IS THERE ANY WAY TO CONVINCE PEOPLE THAT SOMEHOW HE SURVIVED THAT FATAL BLAST?
DAILY PLANET
MEANWHILE, THE FACT THAT THE LOCATION OF SUPERMAN'S HOME IS NO LONGER A SECRET FROM THE PUBLIC RESULTS IN A DELUGE OF MAIL...
ALL THESE LETTERS ARE FOR YOU, SUPERMAN! WHERE SHALL WE PUT THEM?
GOSH... THEY WOULD FILL JIMMY'S APARTMENT TO OVERFLOWING!
JUST... ER... WAIT A SECOND, BOYS, I'LL BE RIGHT BACK!
U.S. MAIL
U.S. MAIL
6

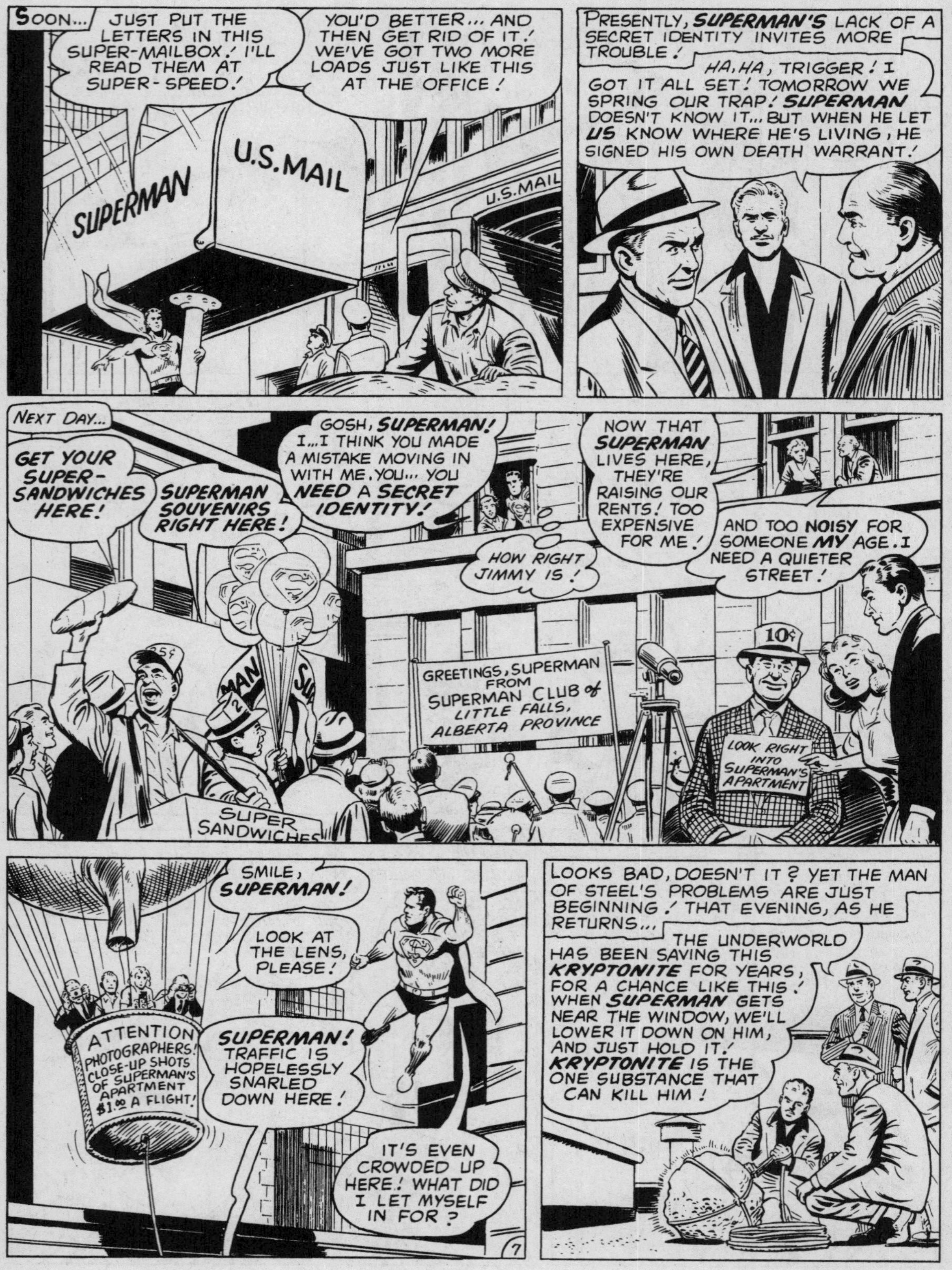
SOON...
JUST PUT THE LETTERS IN THIS SUPER-MAILBOX! I'LL READ THEM AT SUPER-SPEED!
YOU'D BETTER... AND THEN GET RID OF IT! WE'VE GOT TWO MORE LOADS JUST LIKE THIS AT THE OFFICE!
U.S. MAIL
SUPERMAN
U.S. MAIL
PRESENTLY, SUPERMAN'S LACK OF A SECRET IDENTITY INVITES MORE TROUBLE!
HA, HA, TRIGGER! I GOT IT ALL SET! TOMORROW WE SPRING OUR TRAP! SUPERMAN DOESN'T KNOW IT... BUT WHEN HE LET US KNOW WHERE HE'S LIVING, HE SIGNED HIS OWN DEATH WARRANT!
NEXT DAY...
GET YOUR SUPER-SANDWICHES HERE!
SUPERMAN SOUVENIRS RIGHT HERE!
GOSH, SUPERMAN! I... I THINK YOU MADE A MISTAKE MOVING IN WITH ME. YOU... YOU NEED A SECRET IDENTITY!
HOW RIGHT JIMMY IS!
NOW THAT SUPERMAN LIVES HERE, THEY'RE RAISING OUR RENTS! TOO EXPENSIVE FOR ME!
AND TOO NOISY FOR SOMEONE MY AGE. I NEED A QUIETER STREET!
GREETINGS, SUPERMAN FROM SUPERMAN CLUB of LITTLE FALLS, ALBERTA PROVINCE
10¢
LOOK RIGHT INTO SUPERMAN'S APARTMENT
SUPER SANDWICHES
SMILE, SUPERMAN!
LOOK AT THE LENS, PLEASE!
ATTENTION PHOTOGRAPHERS! CLOSE-UP SHOTS OF SUPERMAN'S APARTMENT $1.00 A FLIGHT!
SUPERMAN! TRAFFIC IS HOPELESSLY SNARLED DOWN HERE!
IT'S EVEN CROWDED UP HERE! WHAT DID I LET MYSELF IN FOR?
7
LOOKS BAD, DOESN'T IT? YET THE MAN OF STEEL'S PROBLEMS ARE JUST BEGINNING! THAT EVENING, AS HE RETURNS...
THE UNDERWORLD HAS BEEN SAVING THIS KRYPTONITE FOR YEARS, FOR A CHANCE LIKE THIS! WHEN SUPERMAN GETS NEAR THE WINDOW, WE'LL LOWER IT DOWN ON HIM, AND JUST HOLD IT! KRYPTONITE IS THE ONE SUBSTANCE THAT CAN KILL HIM!

AN INSTANT LATER...

GOOD HEAVENS... *KRYPTONITE*... IT... IT SURE WAS A MISTAKE LETTING THE WORLD KNOW WHERE I LIVED! I... I'M TOO WEAK TO CRAWL INTO THE APARTMENT... TOO WEAK TO CALL FOR HELP! LOOKS... LIKE... THE END!

CAN'T THINK OF A... WAIT... MY *SUPER-HEARING* DETECTS SOMETHING BELOW! IF... I... CAN ONLY HANG ON... FEW SECONDS... MORE... MUST... GET STRENGTH! JUST... FEW MOMENTS... THEN... FALL!

SECONDS LATER...

HE'S ALMOST GONE! ALL I'VE GOTTA DO IS LOWER THAT *KRYPTONITE* SO WHEN HE FALLS IT RESTS RIGHT ON HIM!

JUST AS I HOPED... MY STEEL BODY... CRASHED RIGHT THROUGH THE PAVEMENT!

KRASHHH!

AND, A MOMENT AFTERWARD...

LUCKY I HEARD THIS SUBWAY TRAIN COMING, AND COULD HOLD OUT TILL IT GOT BELOW ME! NOW THAT I'M RIDING OUT OF RANGE OF THE *KRYPTONITE* RAYS, I'LL WATCH THOSE CROOKS WITH MY TELESCOPIC VISION AND HAVE THE POLICE GET THEM AND THEIR *KRYPTONITE!*

EXPRESS

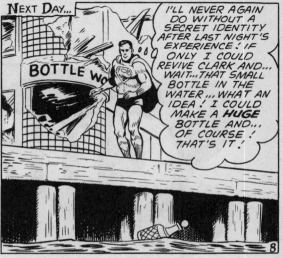

NEXT DAY...

I'LL NEVER AGAIN DO WITHOUT A SECRET IDENTITY AFTER LAST NIGHT'S EXPERIENCE! IF ONLY I COULD REVIVE CLARK AND... WAIT... THAT SMALL BOTTLE IN THE WATER... WHAT AN IDEA! I COULD MAKE A *HUGE* BOTTLE AND... OF COURSE! THAT'S IT!

BOTTLE W

8

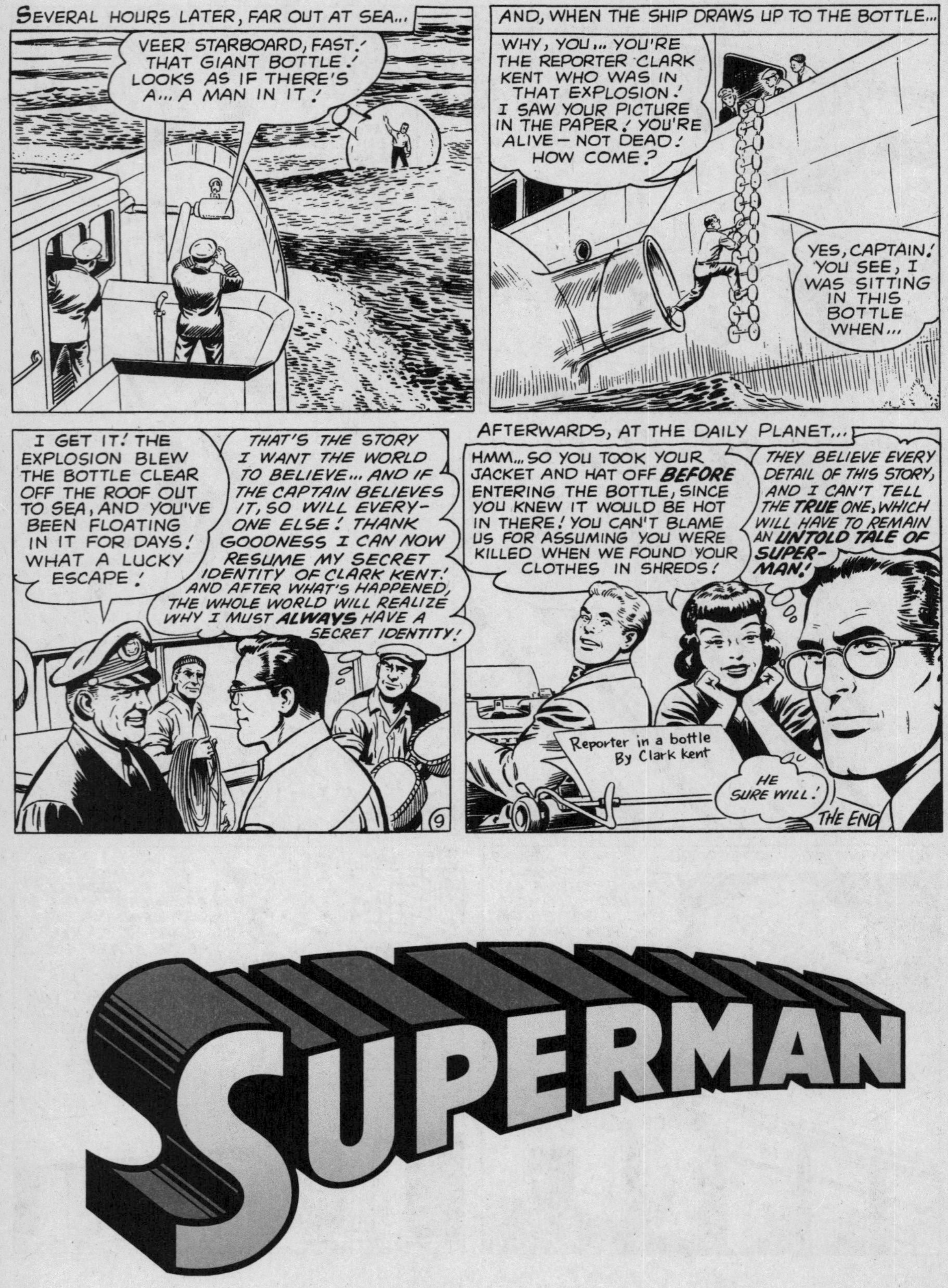
SEVERAL HOURS LATER, FAR OUT AT SEA...
VEER STARBOARD, FAST! THAT GIANT BOTTLE! LOOKS AS IF THERE'S A... A MAN IN IT!
AND, WHEN THE SHIP DRAWS UP TO THE BOTTLE...
WHY, YOU... YOU'RE THE REPORTER CLARK KENT WHO WAS IN THAT EXPLOSION! I SAW YOUR PICTURE IN THE PAPER! YOU'RE ALIVE -- NOT DEAD! HOW COME?
YES, CAPTAIN! YOU SEE, I WAS SITTING IN THIS BOTTLE WHEN...
I GET IT! THE EXPLOSION BLEW THE BOTTLE CLEAR OFF THE ROOF OUT TO SEA, AND YOU'VE BEEN FLOATING IN IT FOR DAYS! WHAT A LUCKY ESCAPE!
THAT'S THE STORY I WANT THE WORLD TO BELIEVE... AND IF THE CAPTAIN BELIEVES IT, SO WILL EVERYONE ELSE! THANK GOODNESS I CAN NOW RESUME MY SECRET IDENTITY OF CLARK KENT! AND AFTER WHAT'S HAPPENED, THE WHOLE WORLD WILL REALIZE WHY I MUST ALWAYS HAVE A SECRET IDENTITY!
9
AFTERWARDS, AT THE DAILY PLANET...
HMM... SO YOU TOOK YOUR JACKET AND HAT OFF BEFORE ENTERING THE BOTTLE, SINCE YOU KNEW IT WOULD BE HOT IN THERE! YOU CAN'T BLAME US FOR ASSUMING YOU WERE KILLED WHEN WE FOUND YOUR CLOTHES IN SHREDS!
THEY BELIEVE EVERY DETAIL OF THIS STORY, AND I CAN'T TELL THE TRUE ONE, WHICH WILL HAVE TO REMAIN AN UNTOLD TALE OF SUPERMAN!
Reporter in a bottle
By Clark kent
HE SURE WILL!
THE END

SUPERMAN

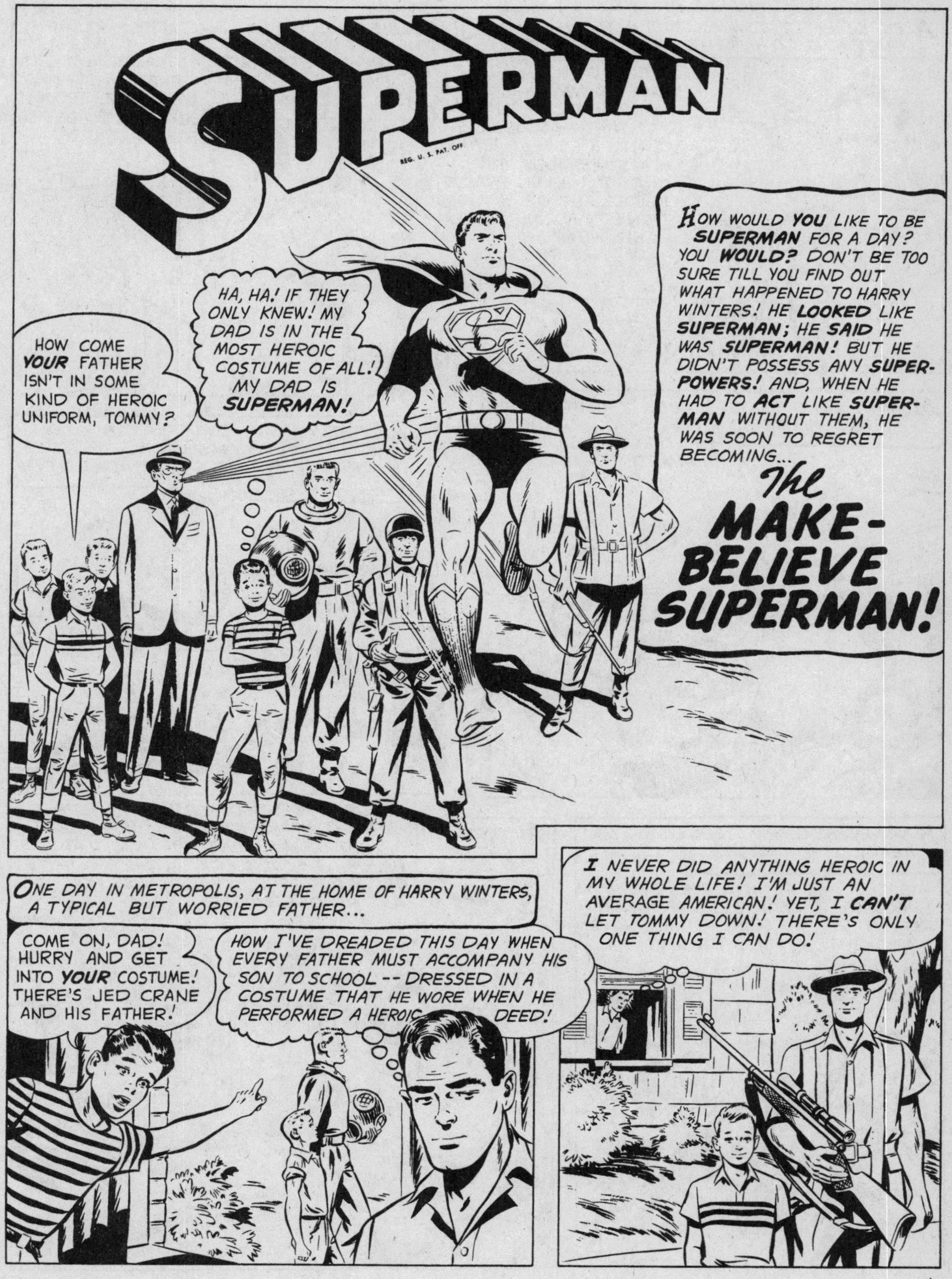
SUPERMAN
REG. U.S. PAT. OFF.
HOW COME YOUR FATHER ISN'T IN SOME KIND OF HEROIC UNIFORM, TOMMY?
HA, HA! IF THEY ONLY KNEW! MY DAD IS IN THE MOST HEROIC COSTUME OF ALL! MY DAD IS SUPERMAN!
HOW WOULD YOU LIKE TO BE SUPERMAN FOR A DAY? YOU WOULD? DON'T BE TOO SURE TILL YOU FIND OUT WHAT HAPPENED TO HARRY WINTERS! HE LOOKED LIKE SUPERMAN; HE SAID HE WAS SUPERMAN! BUT HE DIDN'T POSSESS ANY SUPER-POWERS! AND, WHEN HE HAD TO ACT LIKE SUPER-MAN WITHOUT THEM, HE WAS SOON TO REGRET BECOMING...
The MAKE-BELIEVE SUPERMAN!
ONE DAY IN METROPOLIS, AT THE HOME OF HARRY WINTERS, A TYPICAL BUT WORRIED FATHER...
COME ON, DAD! HURRY AND GET INTO YOUR COSTUME! THERE'S JED CRANE AND HIS FATHER!
HOW I'VE DREADED THIS DAY WHEN EVERY FATHER MUST ACCOMPANY HIS SON TO SCHOOL -- DRESSED IN A COSTUME THAT HE WORE WHEN HE PERFORMED A HEROIC DEED!
I NEVER DID ANYTHING HEROIC IN MY WHOLE LIFE! I'M JUST AN AVERAGE AMERICAN! YET, I CAN'T LET TOMMY DOWN! THERE'S ONLY ONE THING I CAN DO!

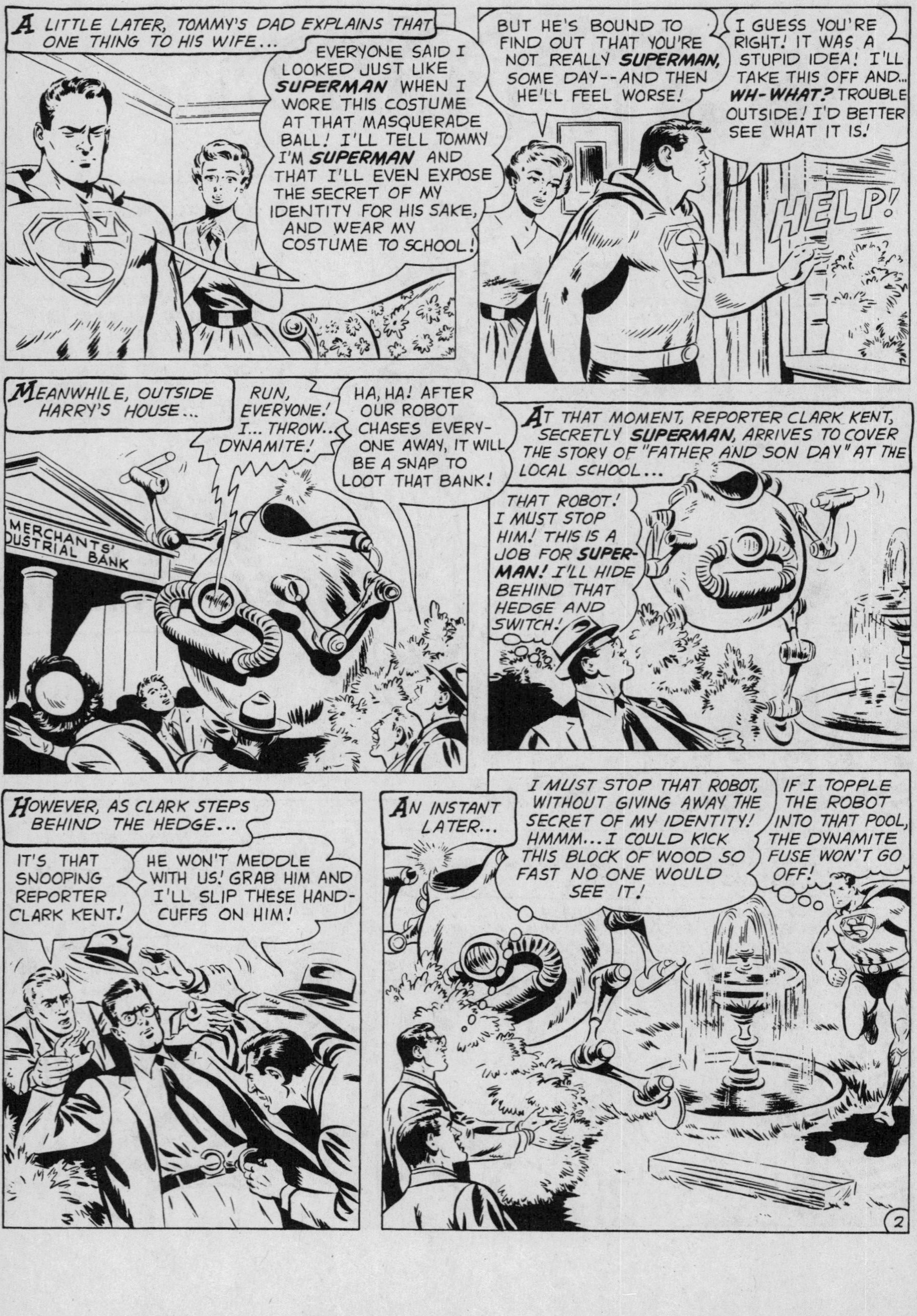
A LITTLE LATER, TOMMY'S DAD EXPLAINS THAT ONE THING TO HIS WIFE...
EVERYONE SAID I LOOKED JUST LIKE SUPERMAN WHEN I WORE THIS COSTUME AT THAT MASQUERADE BALL! I'LL TELL TOMMY I'M SUPERMAN AND THAT I'LL EVEN EXPOSE THE SECRET OF MY IDENTITY FOR HIS SAKE, AND WEAR MY COSTUME TO SCHOOL!
BUT HE'S BOUND TO FIND OUT THAT YOU'RE NOT REALLY SUPERMAN, SOME DAY--AND THEN HE'LL FEEL WORSE!
I GUESS YOU'RE RIGHT! IT WAS A STUPID IDEA! I'LL TAKE THIS OFF AND... WH-WHAT? TROUBLE OUTSIDE! I'D BETTER SEE WHAT IT IS!
HELP!
MEANWHILE, OUTSIDE HARRY'S HOUSE...
RUN, EVERYONE! I... THROW.. DYNAMITE!
HA, HA! AFTER OUR ROBOT CHASES EVERYONE AWAY, IT WILL BE A SNAP TO LOOT THAT BANK!
MERCHANTS' USTRIAL BANK
AT THAT MOMENT, REPORTER CLARK KENT, SECRETLY SUPERMAN, ARRIVES TO COVER THE STORY OF "FATHER AND SON DAY" AT THE LOCAL SCHOOL...
THAT ROBOT! I MUST STOP HIM! THIS IS A JOB FOR SUPERMAN! I'LL HIDE BEHIND THAT HEDGE AND SWITCH!
HOWEVER, AS CLARK STEPS BEHIND THE HEDGE...
IT'S THAT SNOOPING REPORTER CLARK KENT!
HE WON'T MEDDLE WITH US! GRAB HIM AND I'LL SLIP THESE HANDCUFFS ON HIM!
AN INSTANT LATER...
I MUST STOP THAT ROBOT, WITHOUT GIVING AWAY THE SECRET OF MY IDENTITY! HMMM... I COULD KICK THIS BLOCK OF WOOD SO FAST NO ONE WOULD SEE IT!
IF I TOPPLE THE ROBOT INTO THAT POOL, THE DYNAMITE FUSE WON'T GO OFF!
2

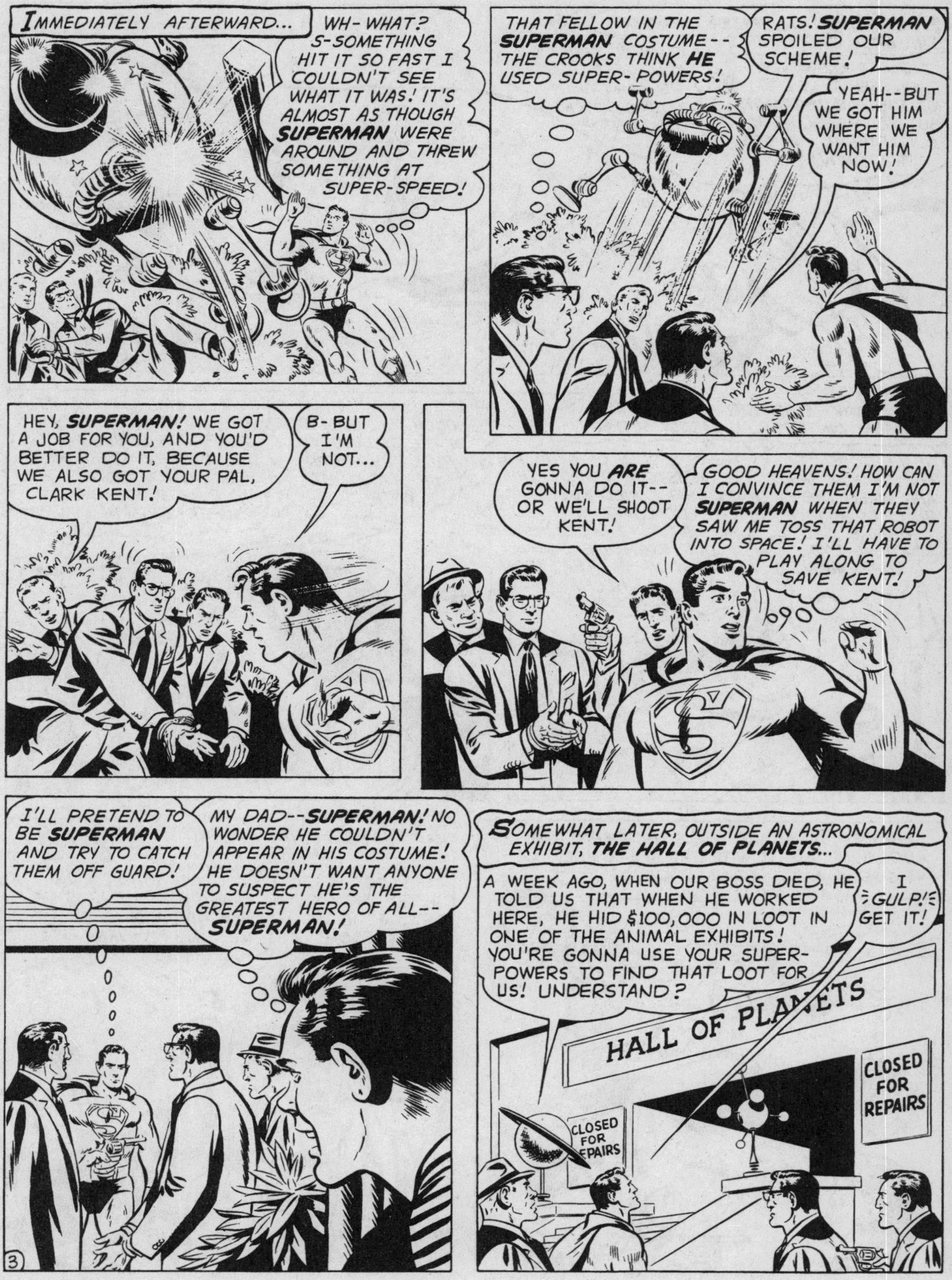
IMMEDIATELY AFTERWARD...
WH-WHAT? S-SOMETHING HIT IT SO FAST I COULDN'T SEE WHAT IT WAS! IT'S ALMOST AS THOUGH SUPERMAN WERE AROUND AND THREW SOMETHING AT SUPER-SPEED!
THAT FELLOW IN THE SUPERMAN COSTUME-- THE CROOKS THINK HE USED SUPER-POWERS!
RATS! SUPERMAN SPOILED OUR SCHEME!
YEAH--BUT WE GOT HIM WHERE WE WANT HIM NOW!
HEY, SUPERMAN! WE GOT A JOB FOR YOU, AND YOU'D BETTER DO IT, BECAUSE WE ALSO GOT YOUR PAL, CLARK KENT!
B-BUT I'M NOT...
YES YOU ARE GONNA DO IT-- OR WE'LL SHOOT KENT!
GOOD HEAVENS! HOW CAN I CONVINCE THEM I'M NOT SUPERMAN WHEN THEY SAW ME TOSS THAT ROBOT INTO SPACE! I'LL HAVE TO PLAY ALONG TO SAVE KENT!
I'LL PRETEND TO BE SUPERMAN AND TRY TO CATCH THEM OFF GUARD!
MY DAD--SUPERMAN! NO WONDER HE COULDN'T APPEAR IN HIS COSTUME! HE DOESN'T WANT ANYONE TO SUSPECT HE'S THE GREATEST HERO OF ALL-- SUPERMAN!
3
SOMEWHAT LATER, OUTSIDE AN ASTRONOMICAL EXHIBIT, THE HALL OF PLANETS...
A WEEK AGO, WHEN OUR BOSS DIED, HE TOLD US THAT WHEN HE WORKED HERE, HE HID $100,000 IN LOOT IN ONE OF THE ANIMAL EXHIBITS! YOU'RE GONNA USE YOUR SUPER-POWERS TO FIND THAT LOOT FOR US! UNDERSTAND?
I GULP! GET IT!
HALL OF PLANETS
CLOSED FOR REPAIRS
CLOSED FOR REPAIRS

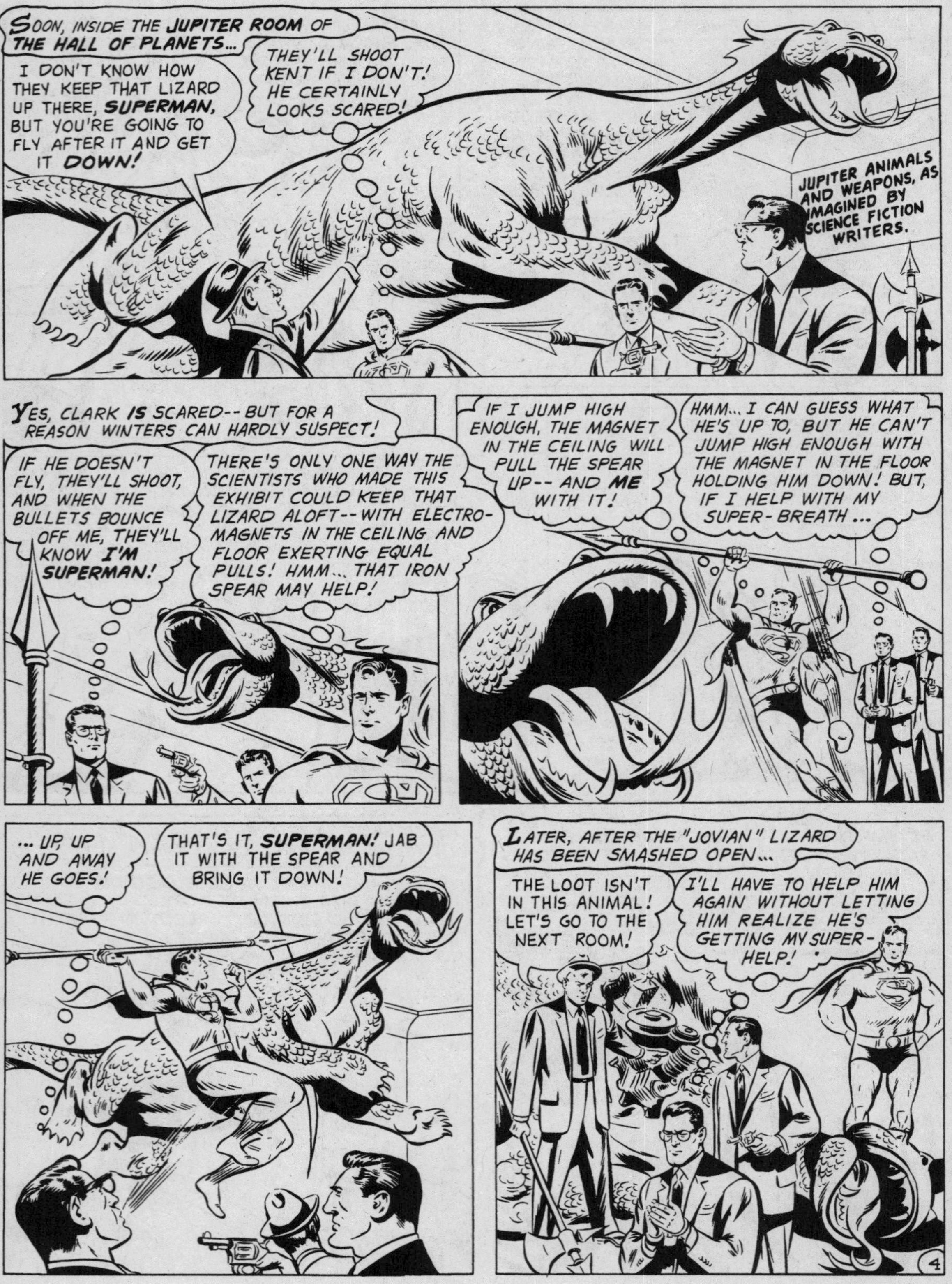
SOON, INSIDE THE JUPITER ROOM OF THE HALL OF PLANETS...
I DON'T KNOW HOW THEY KEEP THAT LIZARD UP THERE, SUPERMAN, BUT YOU'RE GOING TO FLY AFTER IT AND GET IT DOWN!
THEY'LL SHOOT KENT IF I DON'T! HE CERTAINLY LOOKS SCARED!
JUPITER ANIMALS AND WEAPONS, AS IMAGINED BY SCIENCE FICTION WRITERS.
YES, CLARK IS SCARED-- BUT FOR A REASON WINTERS CAN HARDLY SUSPECT!
IF HE DOESN'T FLY, THEY'LL SHOOT, AND WHEN THE BULLETS BOUNCE OFF ME, THEY'LL KNOW I'M SUPERMAN!
THERE'S ONLY ONE WAY THE SCIENTISTS WHO MADE THIS EXHIBIT COULD KEEP THAT LIZARD ALOFT--WITH ELECTRO-MAGNETS IN THE CEILING AND FLOOR EXERTING EQUAL PULLS! HMM... THAT IRON SPEAR MAY HELP!
IF I JUMP HIGH ENOUGH, THE MAGNET IN THE CEILING WILL PULL THE SPEAR UP-- AND ME WITH IT!
HMM... I CAN GUESS WHAT HE'S UP TO, BUT HE CAN'T JUMP HIGH ENOUGH WITH THE MAGNET IN THE FLOOR HOLDING HIM DOWN! BUT, IF I HELP WITH MY SUPER-BREATH...
... UP, UP AND AWAY HE GOES!
THAT'S IT, SUPERMAN! JAB IT WITH THE SPEAR AND BRING IT DOWN!
LATER, AFTER THE "JOVIAN" LIZARD HAS BEEN SMASHED OPEN...
THE LOOT ISN'T IN THIS ANIMAL! LET'S GO TO THE NEXT ROOM!
I'LL HAVE TO HELP HIM AGAIN WITHOUT LETTING HIM REALIZE HE'S GETTING MY SUPER-HELP!
4

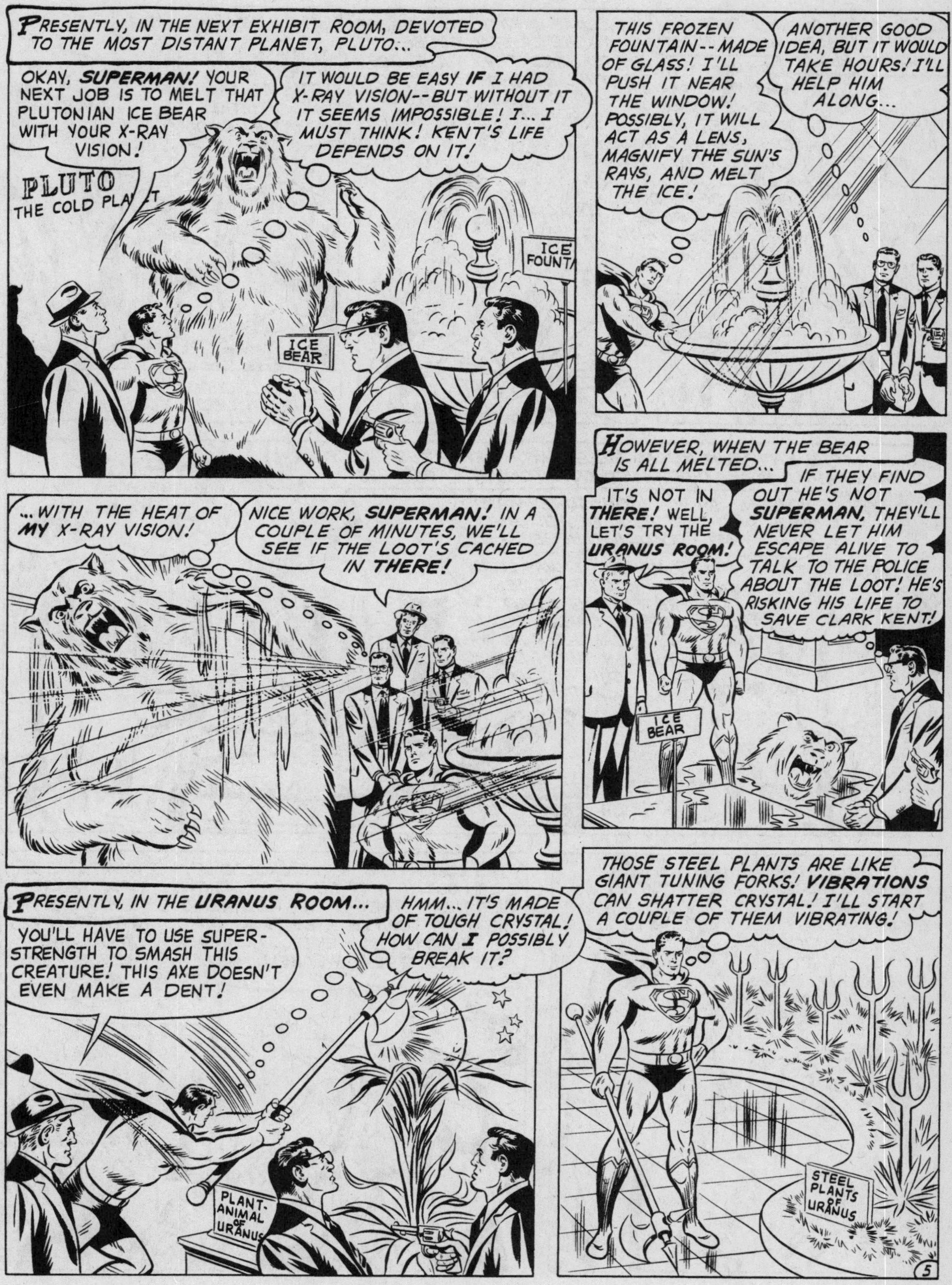
PRESENTLY, IN THE NEXT EXHIBIT ROOM, DEVOTED TO THE MOST DISTANT PLANET, PLUTO...
OKAY, SUPERMAN! YOUR NEXT JOB IS TO MELT THAT PLUTONIAN ICE BEAR WITH YOUR X-RAY VISION!
IT WOULD BE EASY IF I HAD X-RAY VISION--BUT WITHOUT IT IT SEEMS IMPOSSIBLE! I... I MUST THINK! KENT'S LIFE DEPENDS ON IT!
PLUTO
THE COLD PLA T
ICE BEAR
ICE FOUNTA
THIS FROZEN FOUNTAIN--MADE OF GLASS! I'LL PUSH IT NEAR THE WINDOW! POSSIBLY, IT WILL ACT AS A LENS, MAGNIFY THE SUN'S RAYS, AND MELT THE ICE!
ANOTHER GOOD IDEA, BUT IT WOULD TAKE HOURS! I'LL HELP HIM ALONG...
...WITH THE HEAT OF MY X-RAY VISION!
NICE WORK, SUPERMAN! IN A COUPLE OF MINUTES, WE'LL SEE IF THE LOOT'S CACHED IN THERE!
HOWEVER, WHEN THE BEAR IS ALL MELTED...
IT'S NOT IN THERE! WELL, LET'S TRY THE URANUS ROOM!
IF THEY FIND OUT HE'S NOT SUPERMAN, THEY'LL NEVER LET HIM ESCAPE ALIVE TO TALK TO THE POLICE ABOUT THE LOOT! HE'S RISKING HIS LIFE TO SAVE CLARK KENT!
ICE BEAR
PRESENTLY, IN THE URANUS ROOM...
YOU'LL HAVE TO USE SUPER-STRENGTH TO SMASH THIS CREATURE! THIS AXE DOESN'T EVEN MAKE A DENT!
HMM... IT'S MADE OF TOUGH CRYSTAL! HOW CAN I POSSIBLY BREAK IT?
PLANT-ANIMAL OF URANUS
THOSE STEEL PLANTS ARE LIKE GIANT TUNING FORKS! VIBRATIONS CAN SHATTER CRYSTAL! I'LL START A COUPLE OF THEM VIBRATING!
STEEL PLANTS OF URANUS
5

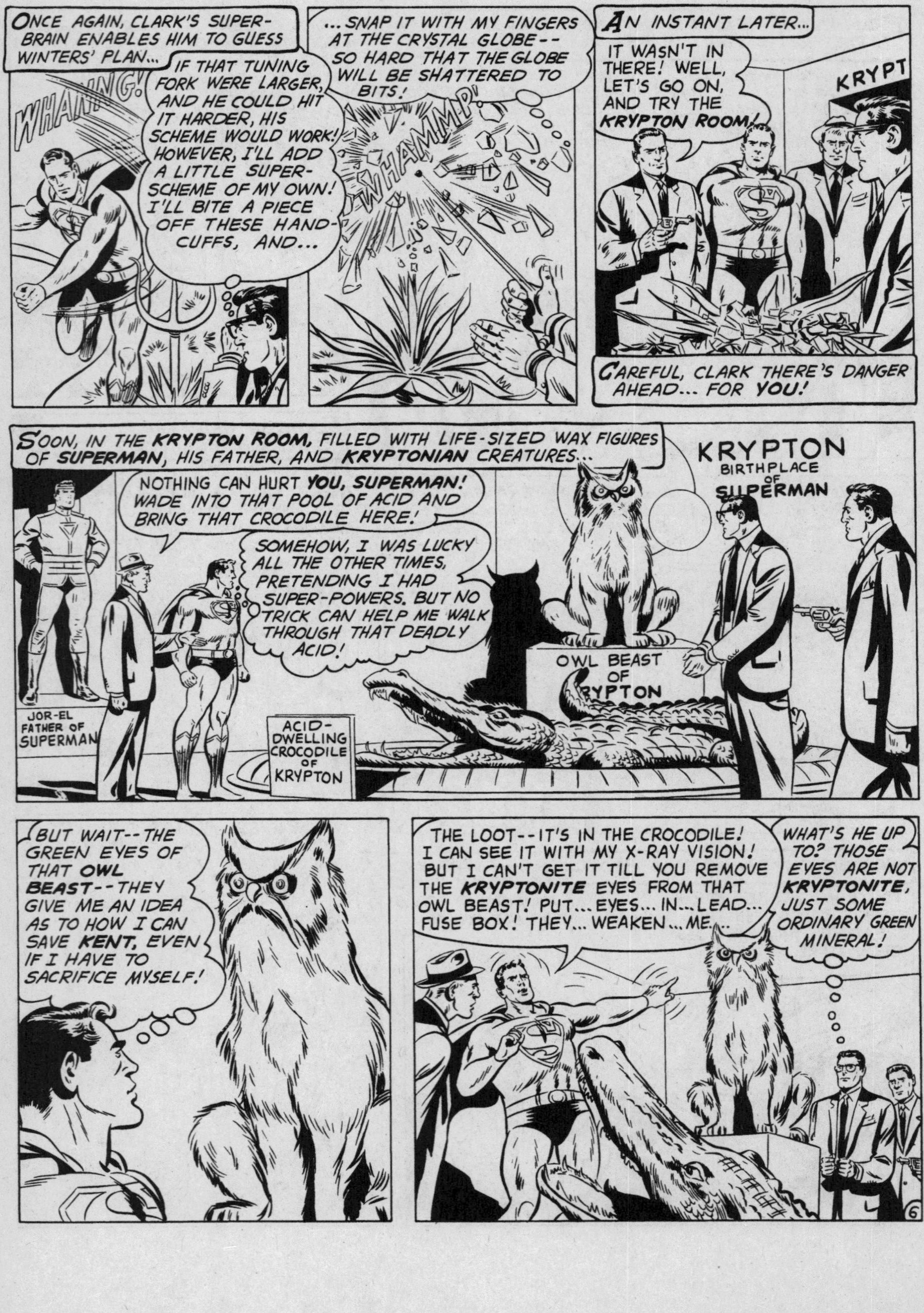
ONCE AGAIN, CLARK'S SUPER-BRAIN ENABLES HIM TO GUESS WINTERS' PLAN...
WHANNG!
IF THAT TUNING FORK WERE LARGER, AND HE COULD HIT IT HARDER, HIS SCHEME WOULD WORK! HOWEVER, I'LL ADD A LITTLE SUPER-SCHEME OF MY OWN! I'LL BITE A PIECE OFF THESE HAND-CUFFS, AND...
...SNAP IT WITH MY FINGERS AT THE CRYSTAL GLOBE-- SO HARD THAT THE GLOBE WILL BE SHATTERED TO BITS!
WHAMMP!
AN INSTANT LATER...
IT WASN'T IN THERE! WELL, LET'S GO ON, AND TRY THE KRYPTON ROOM!
KRYPT
CAREFUL, CLARK THERE'S DANGER AHEAD... FOR YOU!
SOON, IN THE KRYPTON ROOM, FILLED WITH LIFE-SIZED WAX FIGURES OF SUPERMAN, HIS FATHER, AND KRYPTONIAN CREATURES...
NOTHING CAN HURT YOU, SUPERMAN! WADE INTO THAT POOL OF ACID AND BRING THAT CROCODILE HERE!
SOMEHOW, I WAS LUCKY ALL THE OTHER TIMES, PRETENDING I HAD SUPER-POWERS. BUT NO TRICK CAN HELP ME WALK THROUGH THAT DEADLY ACID!
KRYPTON BIRTHPLACE OF SUPERMAN
JOR-EL FATHER OF SUPERMAN
ACID-DWELLING CROCODILE OF KRYPTON
OWL BEAST OF KRYPTON
BUT WAIT--THE GREEN EYES OF THAT OWL BEAST--THEY GIVE ME AN IDEA AS TO HOW I CAN SAVE KENT, EVEN IF I HAVE TO SACRIFICE MYSELF!
THE LOOT--IT'S IN THE CROCODILE! I CAN SEE IT WITH MY X-RAY VISION! BUT I CAN'T GET IT TILL YOU REMOVE THE KRYPTONITE EYES FROM THAT OWL BEAST! PUT... EYES... IN... LEAD... FUSE BOX! THEY... WEAKEN... ME...
WHAT'S HE UP TO? THOSE EYES ARE NOT KRYPTONITE, JUST SOME ORDINARY GREEN MINERAL!
6

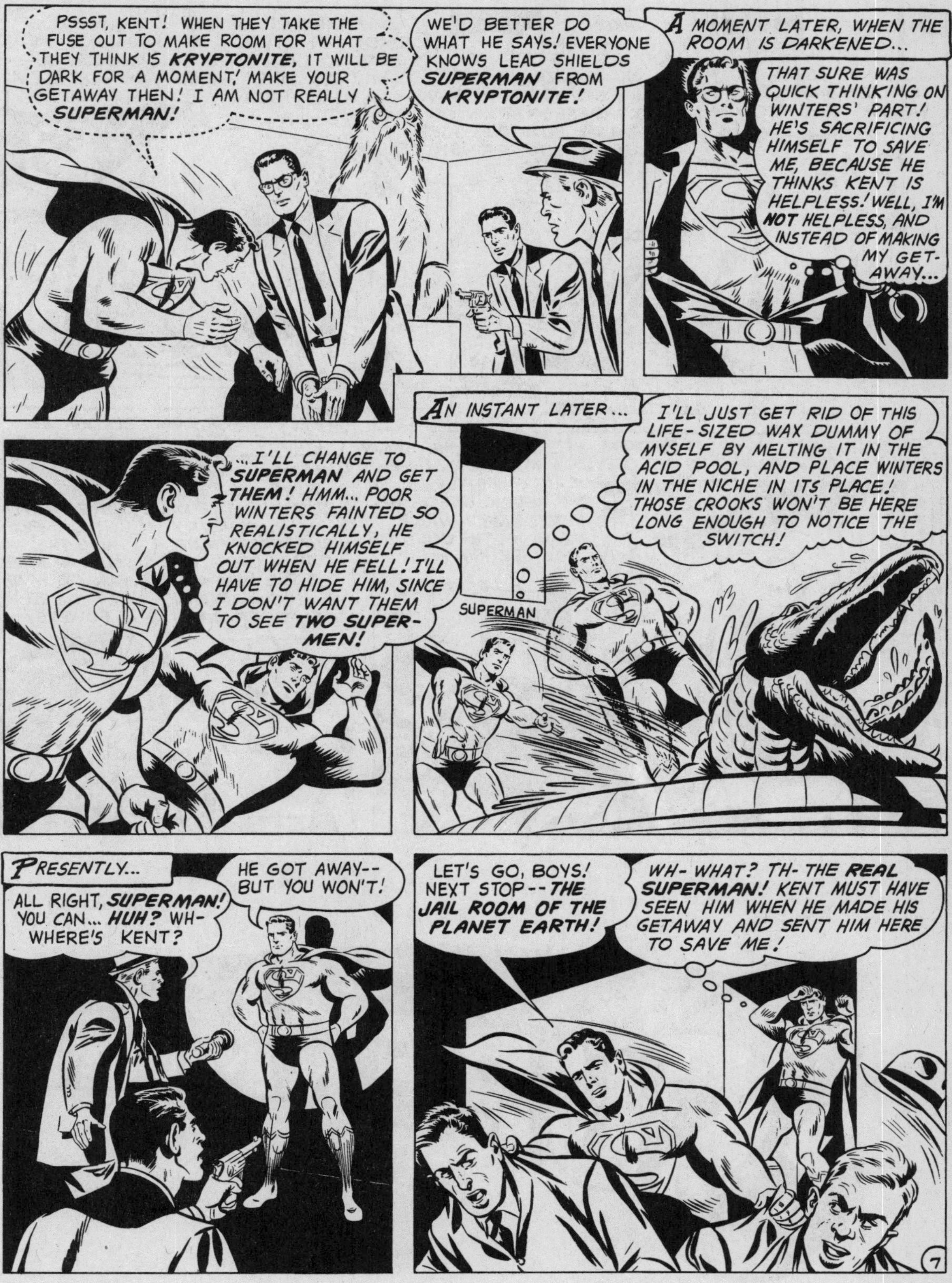
PSSST, KENT! WHEN THEY TAKE THE FUSE OUT TO MAKE ROOM FOR WHAT THEY THINK IS KRYPTONITE, IT WILL BE DARK FOR A MOMENT! MAKE YOUR GETAWAY THEN! I AM NOT REALLY SUPERMAN!
WE'D BETTER DO WHAT HE SAYS! EVERYONE KNOWS LEAD SHIELDS SUPERMAN FROM KRYPTONITE!
A MOMENT LATER, WHEN THE ROOM IS DARKENED...
THAT SURE WAS QUICK THINKING ON WINTERS' PART! HE'S SACRIFICING HIMSELF TO SAVE ME, BECAUSE HE THINKS KENT IS HELPLESS! WELL, I'M NOT HELPLESS, AND INSTEAD OF MAKING MY GET-AWAY...
...I'LL CHANGE TO SUPERMAN AND GET THEM! HMM... POOR WINTERS FAINTED SO REALISTICALLY, HE KNOCKED HIMSELF OUT WHEN HE FELL! I'LL HAVE TO HIDE HIM, SINCE I DON'T WANT THEM TO SEE TWO SUPER-MEN!
AN INSTANT LATER...
I'LL JUST GET RID OF THIS LIFE-SIZED WAX DUMMY OF MYSELF BY MELTING IT IN THE ACID POOL, AND PLACE WINTERS IN THE NICHE IN ITS PLACE! THOSE CROOKS WON'T BE HERE LONG ENOUGH TO NOTICE THE SWITCH!
SUPERMAN
PRESENTLY...
ALL RIGHT, SUPERMAN! YOU CAN... HUH? WH-WHERE'S KENT?
HE GOT AWAY--BUT YOU WON'T!
LET'S GO, BOYS! NEXT STOP--THE JAIL ROOM OF THE PLANET EARTH!
WH-WHAT? TH-THE REAL SUPERMAN! KENT MUST HAVE SEEN HIM WHEN HE MADE HIS GETAWAY AND SENT HIM HERE TO SAVE ME!
7

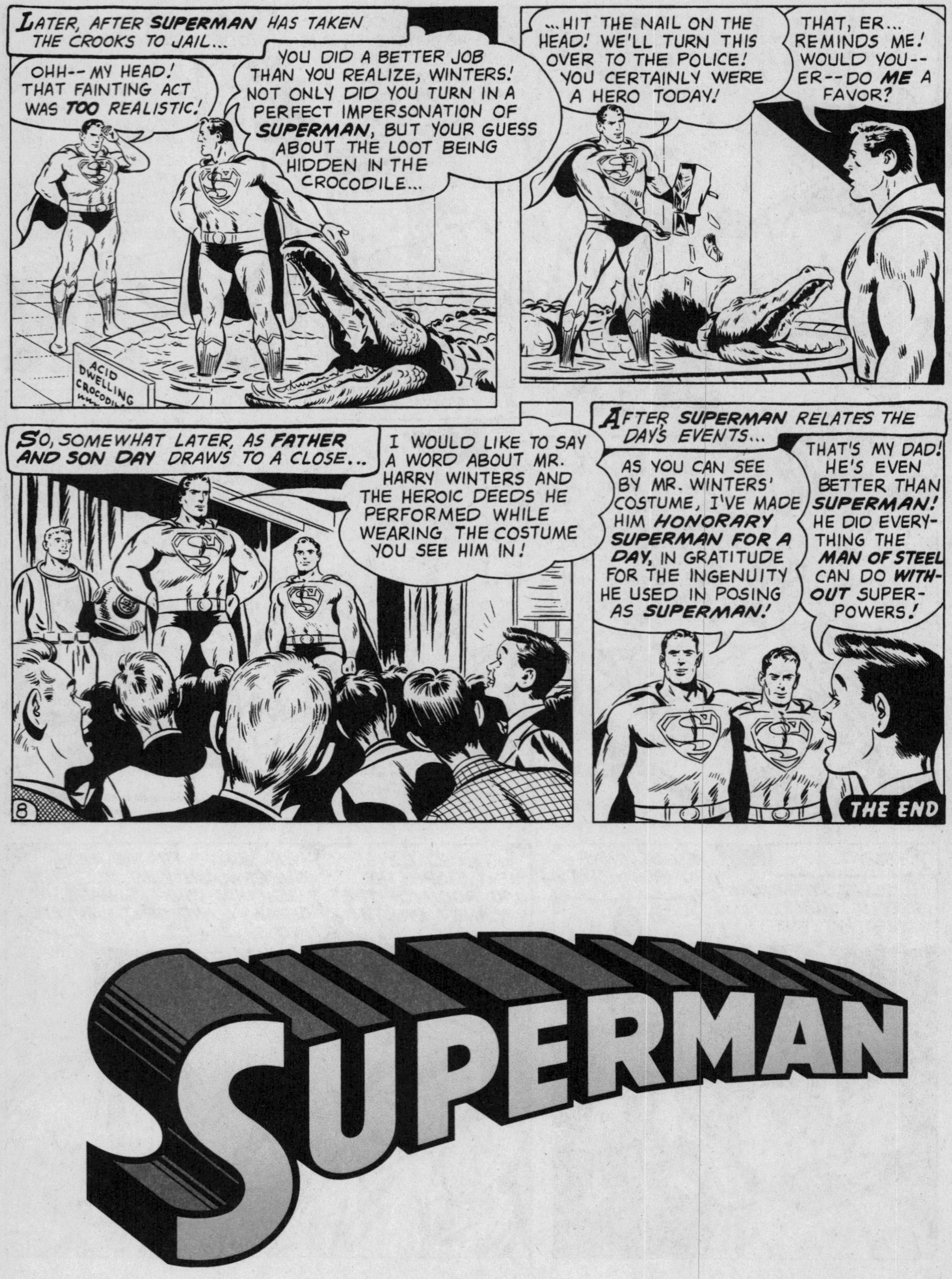
LATER, AFTER SUPERMAN HAS TAKEN THE CROOKS TO JAIL...
OHH-- MY HEAD! THAT FAINTING ACT WAS TOO REALISTIC!
YOU DID A BETTER JOB THAN YOU REALIZE, WINTERS! NOT ONLY DID YOU TURN IN A PERFECT IMPERSONATION OF SUPERMAN, BUT YOUR GUESS ABOUT THE LOOT BEING HIDDEN IN THE CROCODILE...
ACID DWELLING
...HIT THE NAIL ON THE HEAD! WE'LL TURN THIS OVER TO THE POLICE! YOU CERTAINLY WERE A HERO TODAY!
THAT, ER... REMINDS ME! WOULD YOU-- ER--DO ME A FAVOR?
SO, SOMEWHAT LATER, AS FATHER AND SON DAY DRAWS TO A CLOSE...
I WOULD LIKE TO SAY A WORD ABOUT MR. HARRY WINTERS AND THE HEROIC DEEDS HE PERFORMED WHILE WEARING THE COSTUME YOU SEE HIM IN!
8
AFTER SUPERMAN RELATES THE DAY'S EVENTS...
AS YOU CAN SEE BY MR. WINTERS' COSTUME, I'VE MADE HIM HONORARY SUPERMAN FOR A DAY, IN GRATITUDE FOR THE INGENUITY HE USED IN POSING AS SUPERMAN!
THAT'S MY DAD! HE'S EVEN BETTER THAN SUPERMAN! HE DID EVERYTHING THE MAN OF STEEL CAN DO WITHOUT SUPER-POWERS!
THE END

SUPERMAN

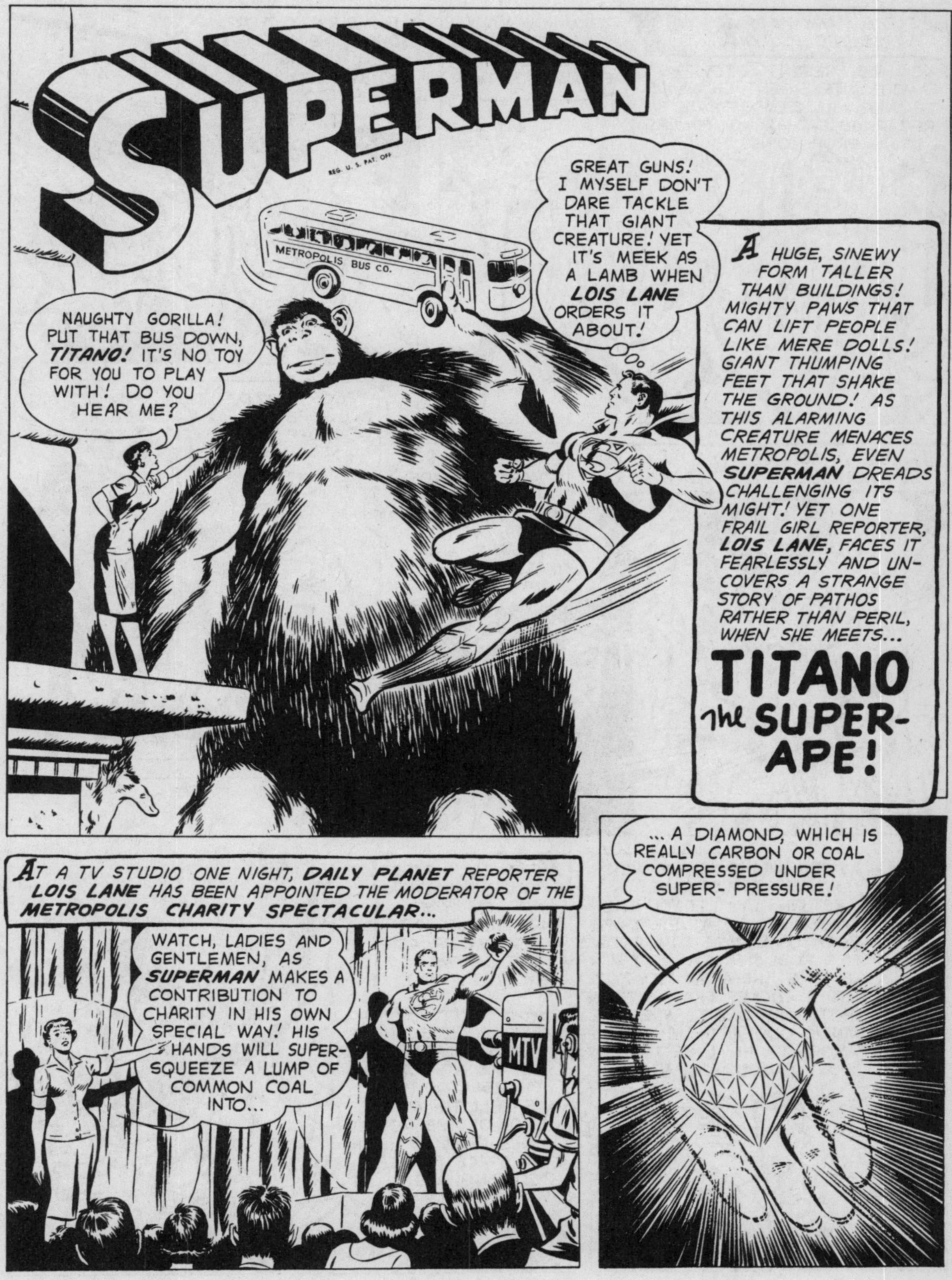
SUPERMAN
REG. U. S. PAT. OFF.
NAUGHTY GORILLA! PUT THAT BUS DOWN, TITANO! IT'S NO TOY FOR YOU TO PLAY WITH! DO YOU HEAR ME?
METROPOLIS BUS CO.
GREAT GUNS! I MYSELF DON'T DARE TACKLE THAT GIANT CREATURE! YET IT'S MEEK AS A LAMB WHEN LOIS LANE ORDERS IT ABOUT!
A HUGE, SINEWY FORM TALLER THAN BUILDINGS! MIGHTY PAWS THAT CAN LIFT PEOPLE LIKE MERE DOLLS! GIANT THUMPING FEET THAT SHAKE THE GROUND! AS THIS ALARMING CREATURE MENACES METROPOLIS, EVEN SUPERMAN DREADS CHALLENGING ITS MIGHT! YET ONE FRAIL GIRL REPORTER, LOIS LANE, FACES IT FEARLESSLY AND UNCOVERS A STRANGE STORY OF PATHOS RATHER THAN PERIL, WHEN SHE MEETS...
TITANO the SUPER-APE!
AT A TV STUDIO ONE NIGHT, DAILY PLANET REPORTER LOIS LANE HAS BEEN APPOINTED THE MODERATOR OF THE METROPOLIS CHARITY SPECTACULAR...
WATCH, LADIES AND GENTLEMEN, AS SUPERMAN MAKES A CONTRIBUTION TO CHARITY IN HIS OWN SPECIAL WAY! HIS HANDS WILL SUPER-SQUEEZE A LUMP OF COMMON COAL INTO...
MTV
... A DIAMOND, WHICH IS REALLY CARBON OR COAL COMPRESSED UNDER SUPER- PRESSURE!

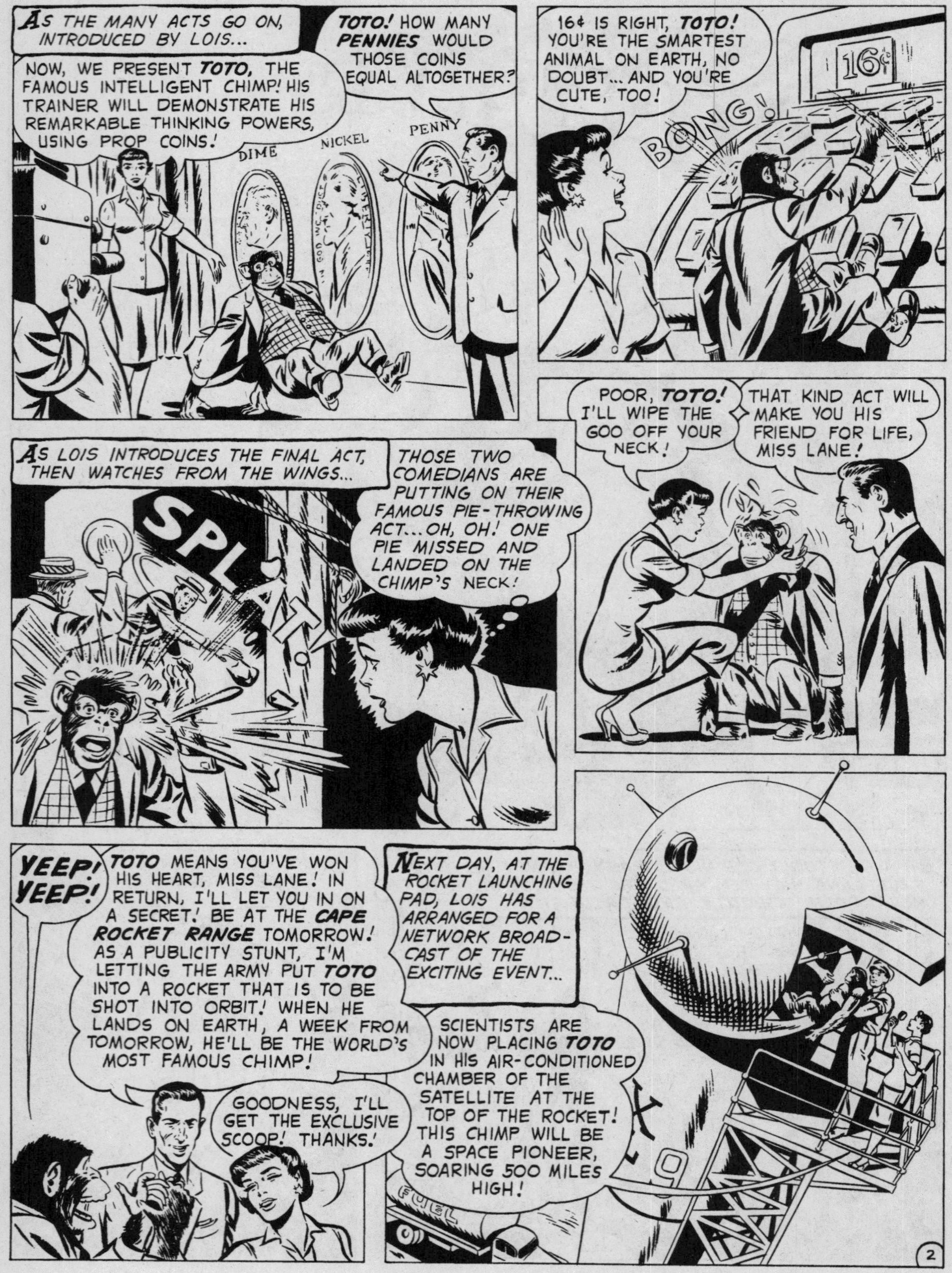
AS THE MANY ACTS GO ON, INTRODUCED BY LOIS...
NOW, WE PRESENT TOTO, THE FAMOUS INTELLIGENT CHIMP! HIS TRAINER WILL DEMONSTRATE HIS REMARKABLE THINKING POWERS, USING PROP COINS!
TOTO! HOW MANY PENNIES WOULD THOSE COINS EQUAL ALTOGETHER?
DIME
NICKEL
PENNY
16¢ IS RIGHT, TOTO! YOU'RE THE SMARTEST ANIMAL ON EARTH, NO DOUBT... AND YOU'RE CUTE, TOO!
BONG!
16¢
AS LOIS INTRODUCES THE FINAL ACT, THEN WATCHES FROM THE WINGS...
THOSE TWO COMEDIANS ARE PUTTING ON THEIR FAMOUS PIE-THROWING ACT...OH, OH! ONE PIE MISSED AND LANDED ON THE CHIMP'S NECK!
SPLAT!
POOR, TOTO! I'LL WIPE THE GOO OFF YOUR NECK!
THAT KIND ACT WILL MAKE YOU HIS FRIEND FOR LIFE, MISS LANE!
YEEP! YEEP!
TOTO MEANS YOU'VE WON HIS HEART, MISS LANE! IN RETURN, I'LL LET YOU IN ON A SECRET! BE AT THE CAPE ROCKET RANGE TOMORROW! AS A PUBLICITY STUNT, I'M LETTING THE ARMY PUT TOTO INTO A ROCKET THAT IS TO BE SHOT INTO ORBIT! WHEN HE LANDS ON EARTH, A WEEK FROM TOMORROW, HE'LL BE THE WORLD'S MOST FAMOUS CHIMP!
GOODNESS, I'LL GET THE EXCLUSIVE SCOOP! THANKS!
NEXT DAY, AT THE ROCKET LAUNCHING PAD, LOIS HAS ARRANGED FOR A NETWORK BROADCAST OF THE EXCITING EVENT...
SCIENTISTS ARE NOW PLACING TOTO IN HIS AIR-CONDITIONED CHAMBER OF THE SATELLITE AT THE TOP OF THE ROCKET! THIS CHIMP WILL BE A SPACE PIONEER, SOARING 500 MILES HIGH!
FUEL
2

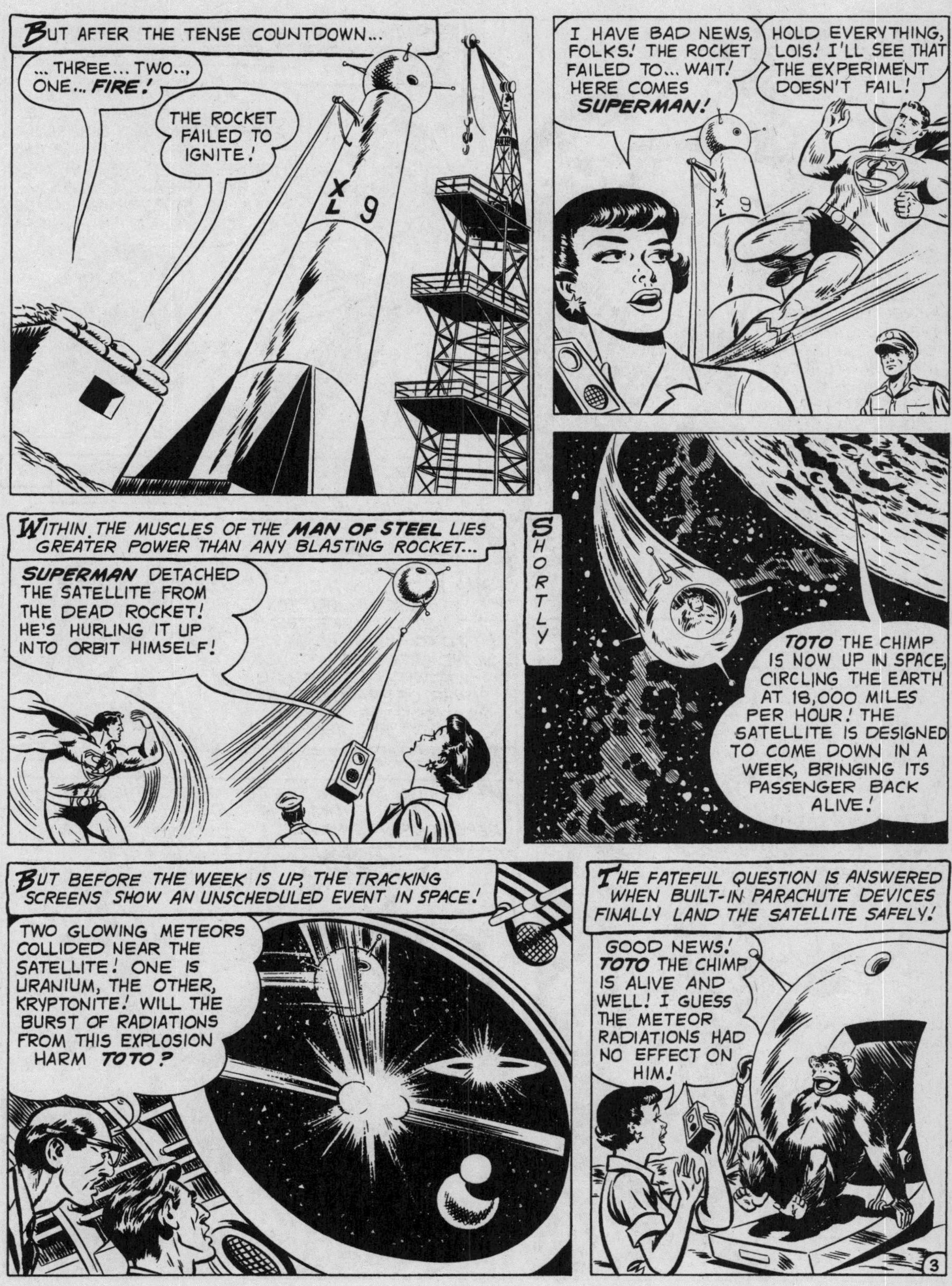
BUT AFTER THE TENSE COUNTDOWN...
... THREE... TWO..., ONE... FIRE!
THE ROCKET FAILED TO IGNITE!
XL 9
I HAVE BAD NEWS, FOLKS! THE ROCKET FAILED TO... WAIT! HERE COMES SUPERMAN!
HOLD EVERYTHING, LOIS! I'LL SEE THAT THE EXPERIMENT DOESN'T FAIL!
WITHIN THE MUSCLES OF THE MAN OF STEEL LIES GREATER POWER THAN ANY BLASTING ROCKET...
SUPERMAN DETACHED THE SATELLITE FROM THE DEAD ROCKET! HE'S HURLING IT UP INTO ORBIT HIMSELF!
SHORTLY
TOTO THE CHIMP IS NOW UP IN SPACE, CIRCLING THE EARTH AT 18,000 MILES PER HOUR! THE SATELLITE IS DESIGNED TO COME DOWN IN A WEEK, BRINGING ITS PASSENGER BACK ALIVE!
BUT BEFORE THE WEEK IS UP, THE TRACKING SCREENS SHOW AN UNSCHEDULED EVENT IN SPACE!
TWO GLOWING METEORS COLLIDED NEAR THE SATELLITE! ONE IS URANIUM, THE OTHER, KRYPTONITE! WILL THE BURST OF RADIATIONS FROM THIS EXPLOSION HARM TOTO?
THE FATEFUL QUESTION IS ANSWERED WHEN BUILT-IN PARACHUTE DEVICES FINALLY LAND THE SATELLITE SAFELY!
GOOD NEWS! TOTO THE CHIMP IS ALIVE AND WELL! I GUESS THE METEOR RADIATIONS HAD NO EFFECT ON HIM!
3

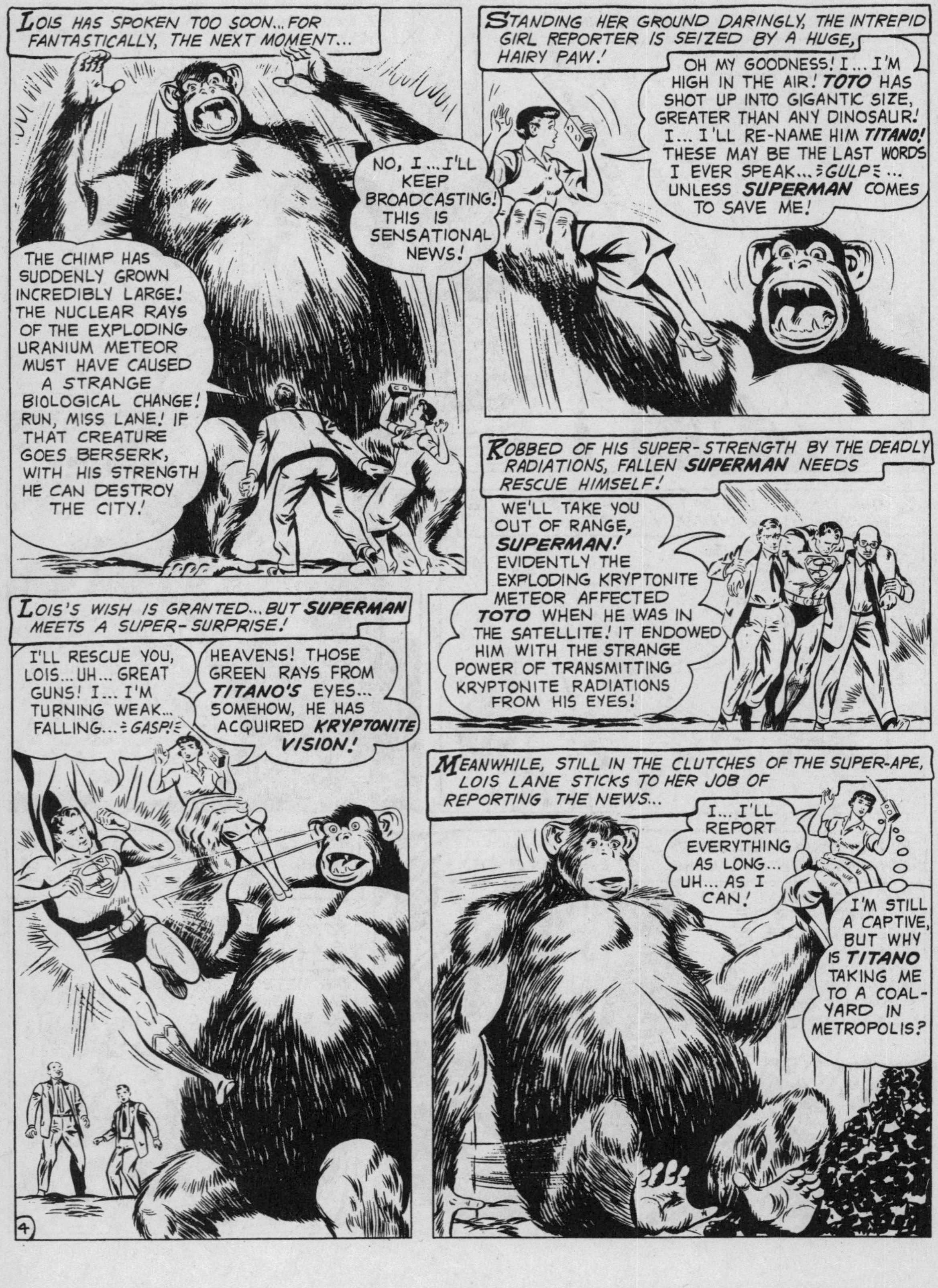
LOIS HAS SPOKEN TOO SOON...FOR FANTASTICALLY, THE NEXT MOMENT...
NO, I...I'LL KEEP BROADCASTING! THIS IS SENSATIONAL NEWS!
THE CHIMP HAS SUDDENLY GROWN INCREDIBLY LARGE! THE NUCLEAR RAYS OF THE EXPLODING URANIUM METEOR MUST HAVE CAUSED A STRANGE BIOLOGICAL CHANGE! RUN, MISS LANE! IF THAT CREATURE GOES BERSERK, WITH HIS STRENGTH HE CAN DESTROY THE CITY!
STANDING HER GROUND DARINGLY, THE INTREPID GIRL REPORTER IS SEIZED BY A HUGE, HAIRY PAW!
OH MY GOODNESS! I... I'M HIGH IN THE AIR! TOTO HAS SHOT UP INTO GIGANTIC SIZE, GREATER THAN ANY DINOSAUR! I... I'LL RE-NAME HIM TITANO! THESE MAY BE THE LAST WORDS I EVER SPEAK...GULP... UNLESS SUPERMAN COMES TO SAVE ME!
LOIS'S WISH IS GRANTED...BUT SUPERMAN MEETS A SUPER-SURPRISE!
I'LL RESCUE YOU, LOIS...UH... GREAT GUNS! I... I'M TURNING WEAK... FALLING... GASP!
HEAVENS! THOSE GREEN RAYS FROM TITANO'S EYES... SOMEHOW, HE HAS ACQUIRED KRYPTONITE VISION!
4
ROBBED OF HIS SUPER-STRENGTH BY THE DEADLY RADIATIONS, FALLEN SUPERMAN NEEDS RESCUE HIMSELF!
WE'LL TAKE YOU OUT OF RANGE, SUPERMAN! EVIDENTLY THE EXPLODING KRYPTONITE METEOR AFFECTED TOTO WHEN HE WAS IN THE SATELLITE! IT ENDOWED HIM WITH THE STRANGE POWER OF TRANSMITTING KRYPTONITE RADIATIONS FROM HIS EYES!
MEANWHILE, STILL IN THE CLUTCHES OF THE SUPER-APE, LOIS LANE STICKS TO HER JOB OF REPORTING THE NEWS...
I... I'LL REPORT EVERYTHING AS LONG... UH... AS I CAN!
I'M STILL A CAPTIVE, BUT WHY IS TITANO TAKING ME TO A COAL-YARD IN METROPOLIS?

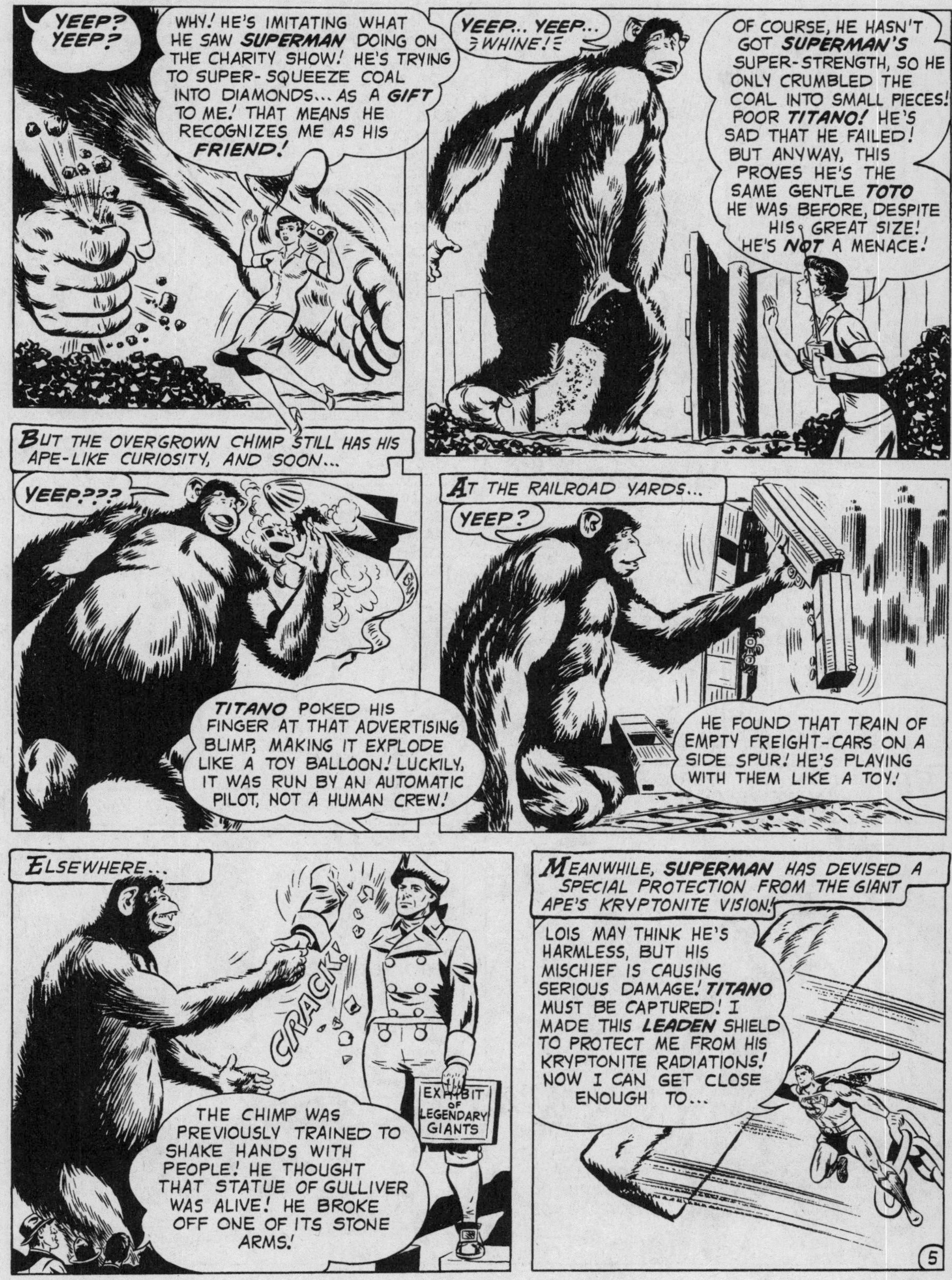
YEEP? YEEP?
WHY! HE'S IMITATING WHAT HE SAW SUPERMAN DOING ON THE CHARITY SHOW! HE'S TRYING TO SUPER-SQUEEZE COAL INTO DIAMONDS... AS A GIFT TO ME! THAT MEANS HE RECOGNIZES ME AS HIS FRIEND!
YEEP... YEEP... WHINE!
OF COURSE, HE HASN'T GOT SUPERMAN'S SUPER-STRENGTH, SO HE ONLY CRUMBLED THE COAL INTO SMALL PIECES! POOR TITANO! HE'S SAD THAT HE FAILED! BUT ANYWAY, THIS PROVES HE'S THE SAME GENTLE TOTO HE WAS BEFORE, DESPITE HIS GREAT SIZE! HE'S NOT A MENACE!
BUT THE OVERGROWN CHIMP STILL HAS HIS APE-LIKE CURIOSITY, AND SOON...
YEEP???
TITANO POKED HIS FINGER AT THAT ADVERTISING BLIMP, MAKING IT EXPLODE LIKE A TOY BALLOON! LUCKILY, IT WAS RUN BY AN AUTOMATIC PILOT, NOT A HUMAN CREW!
AT THE RAILROAD YARDS...
YEEP?
HE FOUND THAT TRAIN OF EMPTY FREIGHT-CARS ON A SIDE SPUR! HE'S PLAYING WITH THEM LIKE A TOY!
ELSEWHERE...
CRACK!
EXHIBIT OF LEGENDARY GIANTS
THE CHIMP WAS PREVIOUSLY TRAINED TO SHAKE HANDS WITH PEOPLE! HE THOUGHT THAT STATUE OF GULLIVER WAS ALIVE! HE BROKE OFF ONE OF ITS STONE ARMS!
MEANWHILE, SUPERMAN HAS DEVISED A SPECIAL PROTECTION FROM THE GIANT APE'S KRYPTONITE VISION!
LOIS MAY THINK HE'S HARMLESS, BUT HIS MISCHIEF IS CAUSING SERIOUS DAMAGE! TITANO MUST BE CAPTURED! I MADE THIS LEADEN SHIELD TO PROTECT ME FROM HIS KRYPTONITE RADIATIONS! NOW I CAN GET CLOSE ENOUGH TO...
5

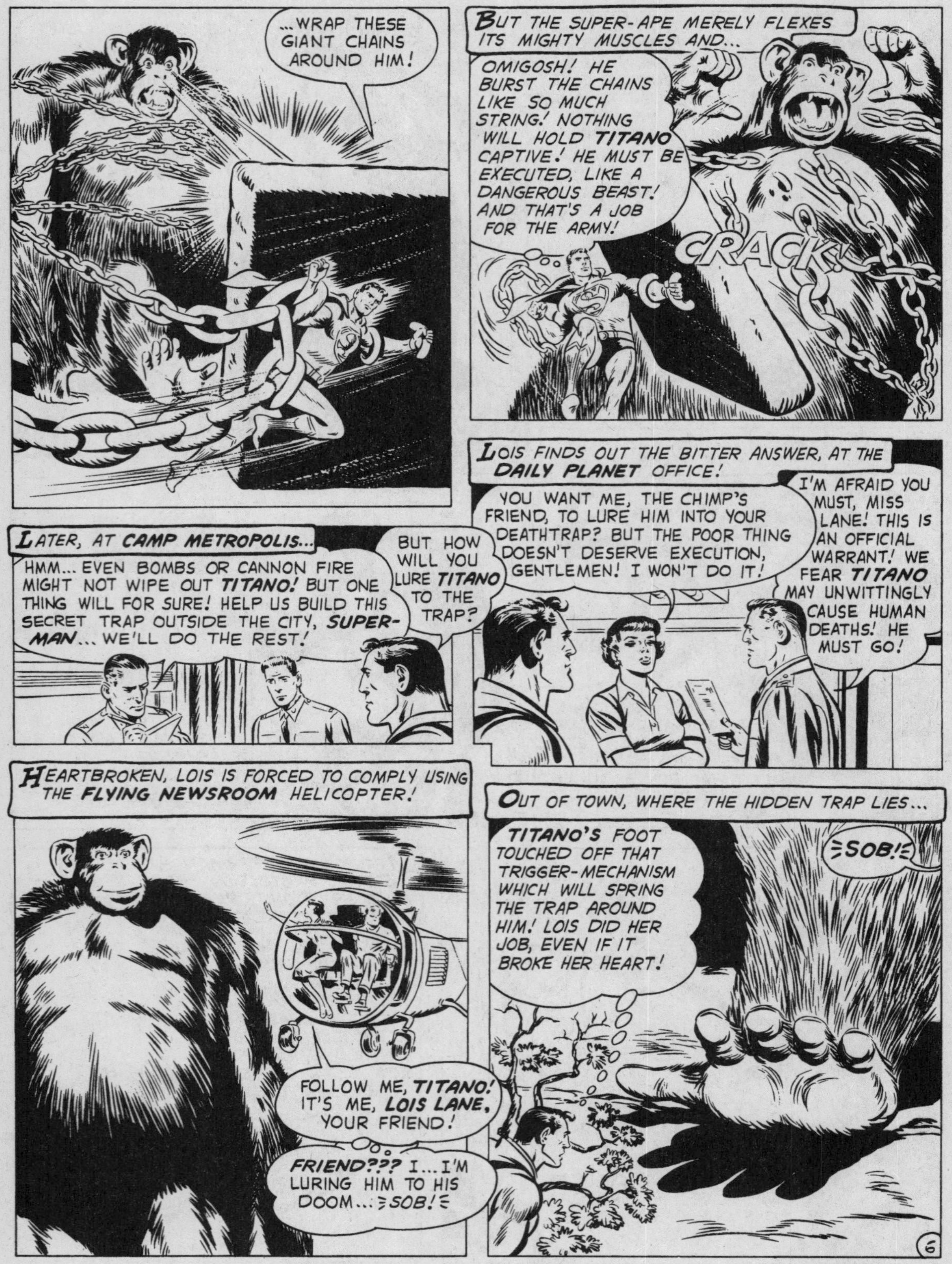
...WRAP THESE GIANT CHAINS AROUND HIM!
BUT THE SUPER-APE MERELY FLEXES ITS MIGHTY MUSCLES AND...
OMIGOSH! HE BURST THE CHAINS LIKE SO MUCH STRING! NOTHING WILL HOLD TITANO CAPTIVE! HE MUST BE EXECUTED, LIKE A DANGEROUS BEAST! AND THAT'S A JOB FOR THE ARMY!
CRACK!
LATER, AT CAMP METROPOLIS...
HMM... EVEN BOMBS OR CANNON FIRE MIGHT NOT WIPE OUT TITANO! BUT ONE THING WILL FOR SURE! HELP US BUILD THIS SECRET TRAP OUTSIDE THE CITY, SUPERMAN... WE'LL DO THE REST!
BUT HOW WILL YOU LURE TITANO TO THE TRAP?
LOIS FINDS OUT THE BITTER ANSWER, AT THE DAILY PLANET OFFICE!
YOU WANT ME, THE CHIMP'S FRIEND, TO LURE HIM INTO YOUR DEATHTRAP? BUT THE POOR THING DOESN'T DESERVE EXECUTION, GENTLEMEN! I WON'T DO IT!
I'M AFRAID YOU MUST, MISS LANE! THIS IS AN OFFICIAL WARRANT! WE FEAR TITANO MAY UNWITTINGLY CAUSE HUMAN DEATHS! HE MUST GO!
HEARTBROKEN, LOIS IS FORCED TO COMPLY USING THE FLYING NEWSROOM HELICOPTER!
FOLLOW ME, TITANO! IT'S ME, LOIS LANE, YOUR FRIEND!
FRIEND??? I...I'M LURING HIM TO HIS DOOM...SOB!
OUT OF TOWN, WHERE THE HIDDEN TRAP LIES...
TITANO'S FOOT TOUCHED OFF THAT TRIGGER-MECHANISM WHICH WILL SPRING THE TRAP AROUND HIM! LOIS DID HER JOB, EVEN IF IT BROKE HER HEART!
SOB!
6

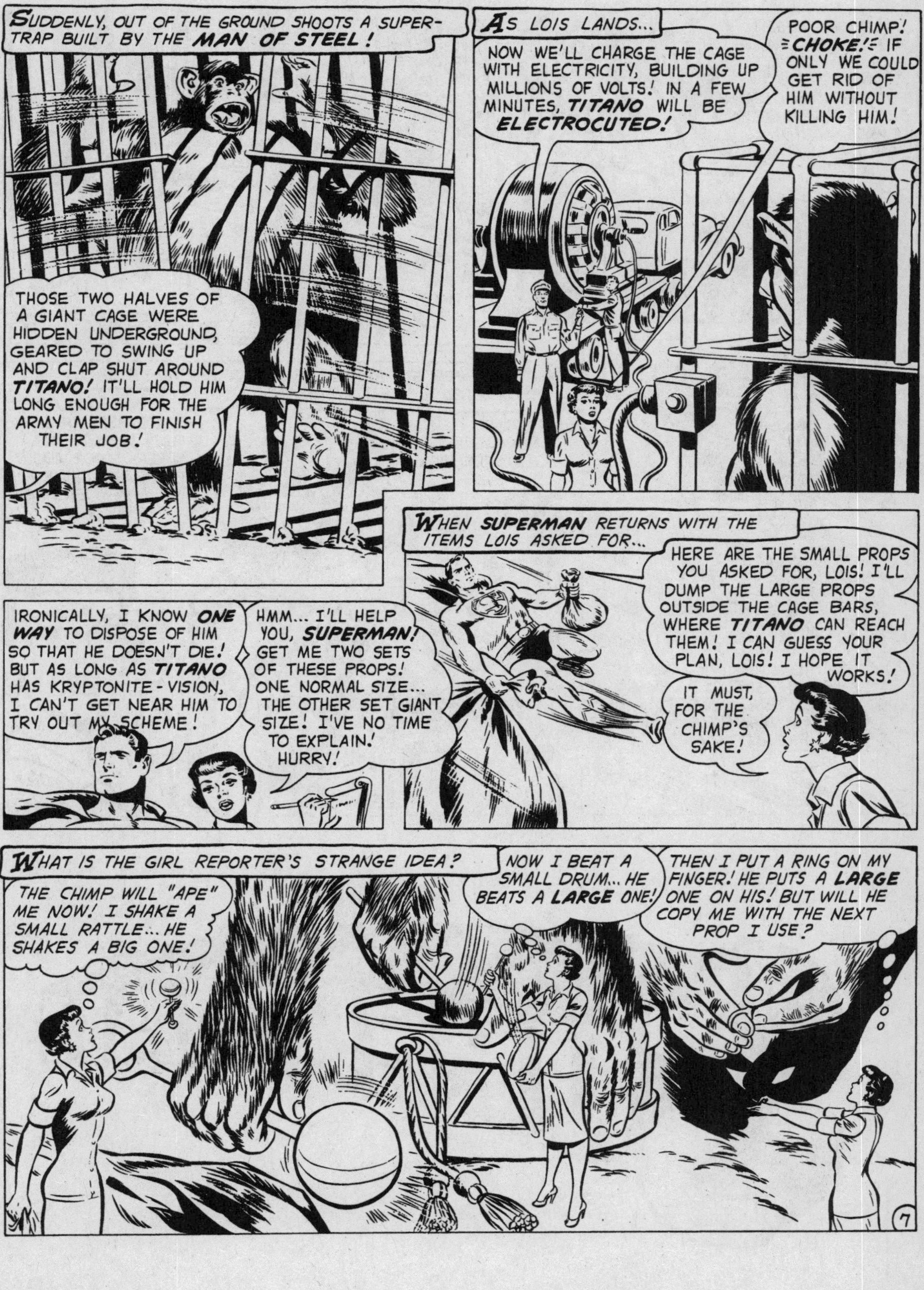
SUDDENLY, OUT OF THE GROUND SHOOTS A SUPER-TRAP BUILT BY THE MAN OF STEEL!
THOSE TWO HALVES OF A GIANT CAGE WERE HIDDEN UNDERGROUND, GEARED TO SWING UP AND CLAP SHUT AROUND TITANO! IT'LL HOLD HIM LONG ENOUGH FOR THE ARMY MEN TO FINISH THEIR JOB!
AS LOIS LANDS...
NOW WE'LL CHARGE THE CAGE WITH ELECTRICITY, BUILDING UP MILLIONS OF VOLTS! IN A FEW MINUTES, TITANO WILL BE ELECTROCUTED!
POOR CHIMP! CHOKE! IF ONLY WE COULD GET RID OF HIM WITHOUT KILLING HIM!
IRONICALLY, I KNOW ONE WAY TO DISPOSE OF HIM SO THAT HE DOESN'T DIE! BUT AS LONG AS TITANO HAS KRYPTONITE-VISION, I CAN'T GET NEAR HIM TO TRY OUT MY SCHEME!
HMM... I'LL HELP YOU, SUPERMAN! GET ME TWO SETS OF THESE PROPS! ONE NORMAL SIZE... THE OTHER SET GIANT SIZE! I'VE NO TIME TO EXPLAIN! HURRY!
WHEN SUPERMAN RETURNS WITH THE ITEMS LOIS ASKED FOR...
HERE ARE THE SMALL PROPS YOU ASKED FOR, LOIS! I'LL DUMP THE LARGE PROPS OUTSIDE THE CAGE BARS, WHERE TITANO CAN REACH THEM! I CAN GUESS YOUR PLAN, LOIS! I HOPE IT WORKS!
IT MUST, FOR THE CHIMP'S SAKE!
WHAT IS THE GIRL REPORTER'S STRANGE IDEA?
THE CHIMP WILL "APE" ME NOW! I SHAKE A SMALL RATTLE... HE SHAKES A BIG ONE!
NOW I BEAT A SMALL DRUM... HE BEATS A LARGE ONE!
THEN I PUT A RING ON MY FINGER! HE PUTS A LARGE ONE ON HIS! BUT WILL HE COPY ME WITH THE NEXT PROP I USE?
7

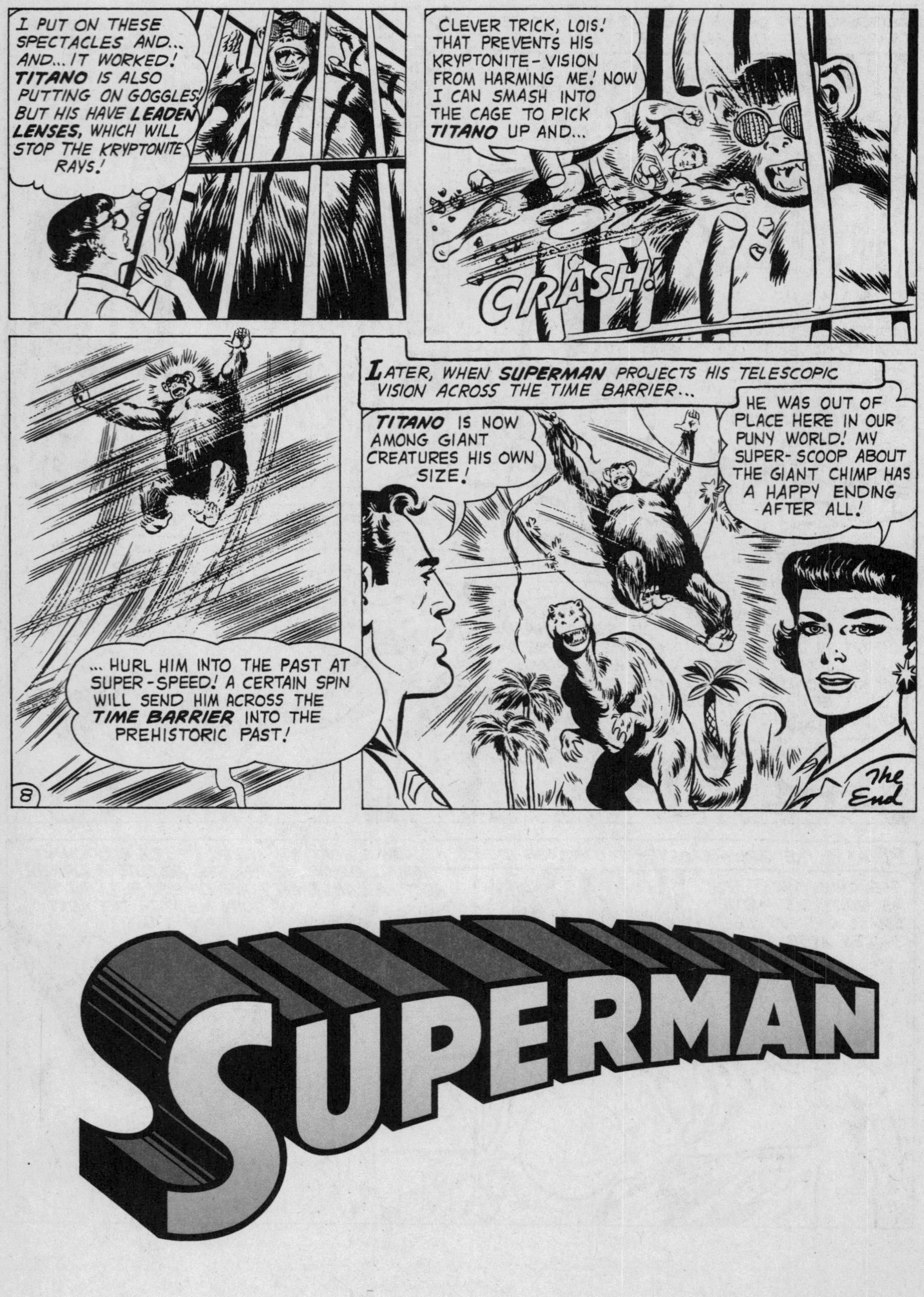
I PUT ON THESE SPECTACLES AND... AND...IT WORKED! TITANO IS ALSO PUTTING ON GOGGLES! BUT HIS HAVE LEADEN LENSES, WHICH WILL STOP THE KRYPTONITE RAYS!
CLEVER TRICK, LOIS! THAT PREVENTS HIS KRYPTONITE-VISION FROM HARMING ME! NOW I CAN SMASH INTO THE CAGE TO PICK TITANO UP AND...
CRASH!
...HURL HIM INTO THE PAST AT SUPER-SPEED! A CERTAIN SPIN WILL SEND HIM ACROSS THE TIME BARRIER INTO THE PREHISTORIC PAST!
8
LATER, WHEN SUPERMAN PROJECTS HIS TELESCOPIC VISION ACROSS THE TIME BARRIER...
TITANO IS NOW AMONG GIANT CREATURES HIS OWN SIZE!
HE WAS OUT OF PLACE HERE IN OUR PUNY WORLD! MY SUPER-SCOOP ABOUT THE GIANT CHIMP HAS A HAPPY ENDING AFTER ALL!
The End

SUPERMAN

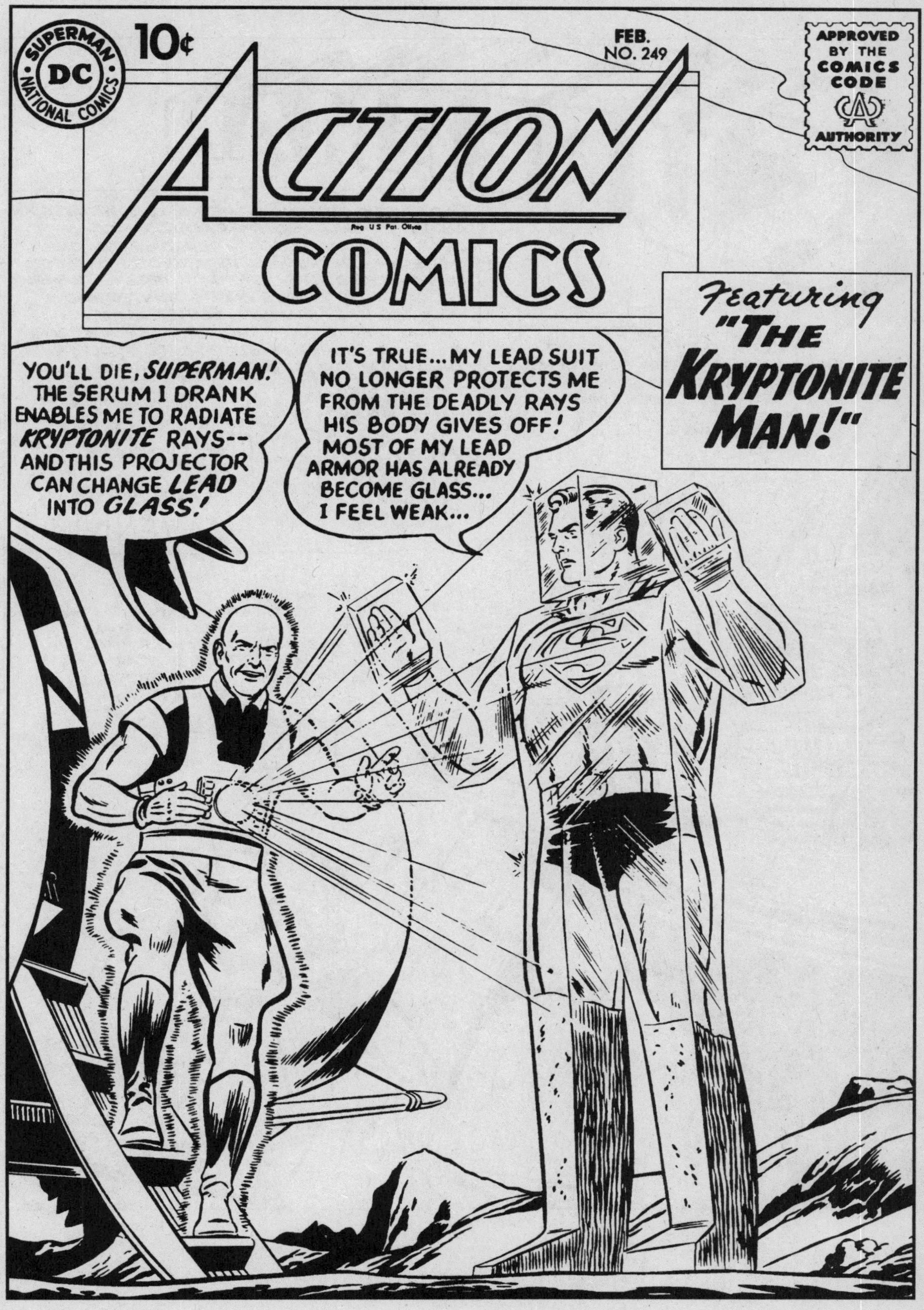
SUPERMAN DC NATIONAL COMICS
10¢
FEB. NO. 249
APPROVED BY THE COMICS CODE AUTHORITY
ACTION
Reg U S Pat Office
COMICS
Featuring "THE KRYPTONITE MAN!"
YOU'LL DIE, SUPERMAN! THE SERUM I DRANK ENABLES ME TO RADIATE KRYPTONITE RAYS--AND THIS PROJECTOR CAN CHANGE LEAD INTO GLASS!
IT'S TRUE... MY LEAD SUIT NO LONGER PROTECTS ME FROM THE DEADLY RAYS HIS BODY GIVES OFF! MOST OF MY LEAD ARMOR HAS ALREADY BECOME GLASS... I FEEL WEAK...

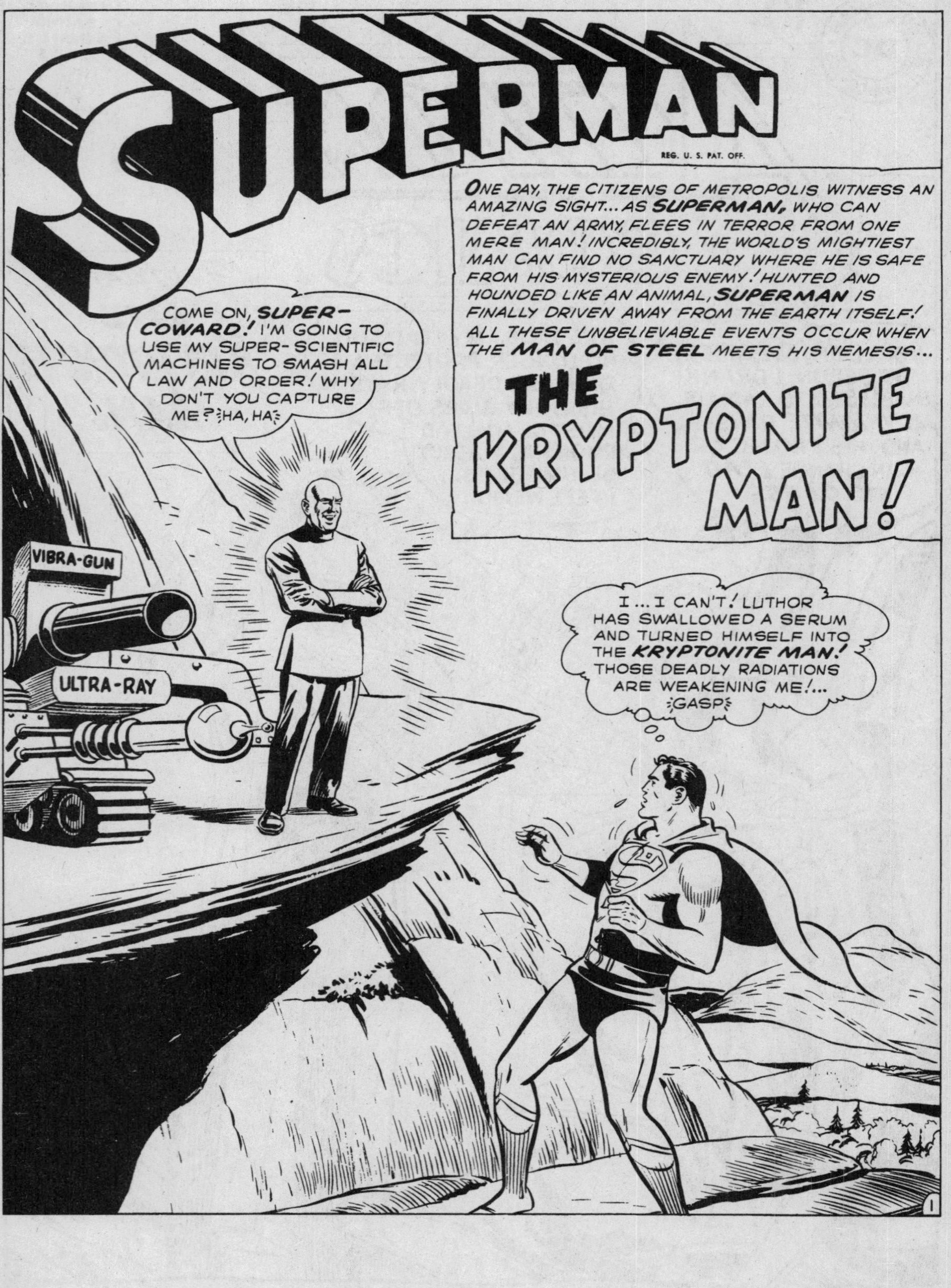
SUPERMAN
REG. U. S. PAT. OFF.
ONE DAY, THE CITIZENS OF METROPOLIS WITNESS AN AMAZING SIGHT... AS SUPERMAN, WHO CAN DEFEAT AN ARMY, FLEES IN TERROR FROM ONE MERE MAN! INCREDIBLY, THE WORLD'S MIGHTIEST MAN CAN FIND NO SANCTUARY WHERE HE IS SAFE FROM HIS MYSTERIOUS ENEMY! HUNTED AND HOUNDED LIKE AN ANIMAL, SUPERMAN IS FINALLY DRIVEN AWAY FROM THE EARTH ITSELF! ALL THESE UNBELIEVABLE EVENTS OCCUR WHEN THE MAN OF STEEL MEETS HIS NEMESIS...
THE KRYPTONITE MAN!
COME ON, SUPER-COWARD! I'M GOING TO USE MY SUPER-SCIENTIFIC MACHINES TO SMASH ALL LAW AND ORDER! WHY DON'T YOU CAPTURE ME? HA, HA
VIBRA-GUN
ULTRA-RAY
I... I CAN'T! LUTHOR HAS SWALLOWED A SERUM AND TURNED HIMSELF INTO THE KRYPTONITE MAN! THOSE DEADLY RADIATIONS ARE WEAKENING ME!... GASP
1

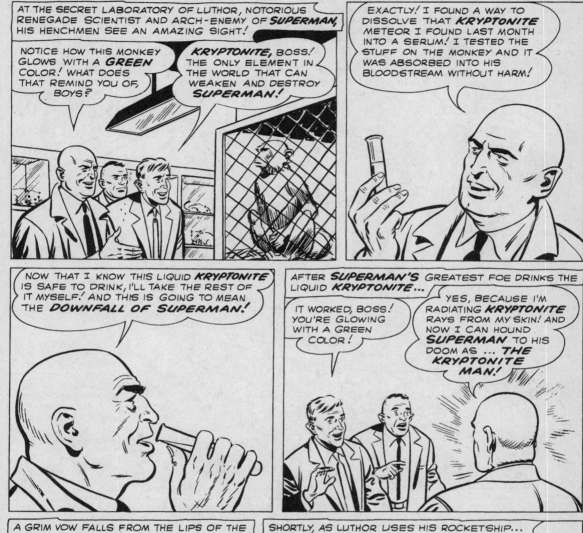

AT THE SECRET LABORATORY OF LUTHOR, NOTORIOUS RENEGADE SCIENTIST AND ARCH-ENEMY OF *SUPERMAN,* HIS HENCHMEN SEE AN AMAZING SIGHT!

NOTICE HOW THIS MONKEY GLOWS WITH A *GREEN* COLOR! WHAT DOES THAT REMIND YOU OF, BOYS?

KRYPTONITE, BOSS! THE ONLY ELEMENT IN THE WORLD THAT CAN WEAKEN AND DESTROY *SUPERMAN!*

EXACTLY! I FOUND A WAY TO DISSOLVE THAT *KRYPTONITE* METEOR I FOUND LAST MONTH INTO A SERUM! I TESTED THE STUFF ON THE MONKEY AND IT WAS ABSORBED INTO HIS BLOODSTREAM WITHOUT HARM!

NOW THAT I KNOW THIS LIQUID *KRYPTONITE* IS SAFE TO DRINK, I'LL TAKE THE REST OF IT MYSELF! AND THIS IS GOING TO MEAN THE *DOWNFALL OF SUPERMAN!*

AFTER *SUPERMAN'S* GREATEST FOE DRINKS THE LIQUID *KRYPTONITE...*

IT WORKED, BOSS! YOU'RE GLOWING WITH A GREEN COLOR!

YES, BECAUSE I'M RADIATING *KRYPTONITE* RAYS FROM MY SKIN! AND NOW I CAN HOUND *SUPERMAN* TO HIS DOOM AS ... *THE KRYPTONITE MAN!*

A GRIM VOW FALLS FROM THE LIPS OF THE CRIMINAL GENIUS!

BUT I'LL MAKE HIM SUFFER FOR ALL THE TIMES HE DEFEATED ME BEFORE! I'LL PLAY WITH HIM LIKE A CAT WITH A MOUSE! I'LL HUMILIATE HIM AGAIN AND AGAIN UNTIL HE BEGS FOR MERCY! THEN I'LL DESTROY HIM! ¿HAHHH¿

SHORTLY, AS LUTHOR USES HIS ROCKETSHIP...

I'LL GO RIGHT TO METROPOLIS, *SUPERMAN'S* BASE OF OPERATIONS! THE AIR FORCE CAN'T SHOOT DOWN MY SPECIAL ARMORED SHIP! AND WHEN *SUPERMAN* AND I MEET, I'LL HAVE THE UPPER HAND AS THE *KRYPTONITE MAN!*

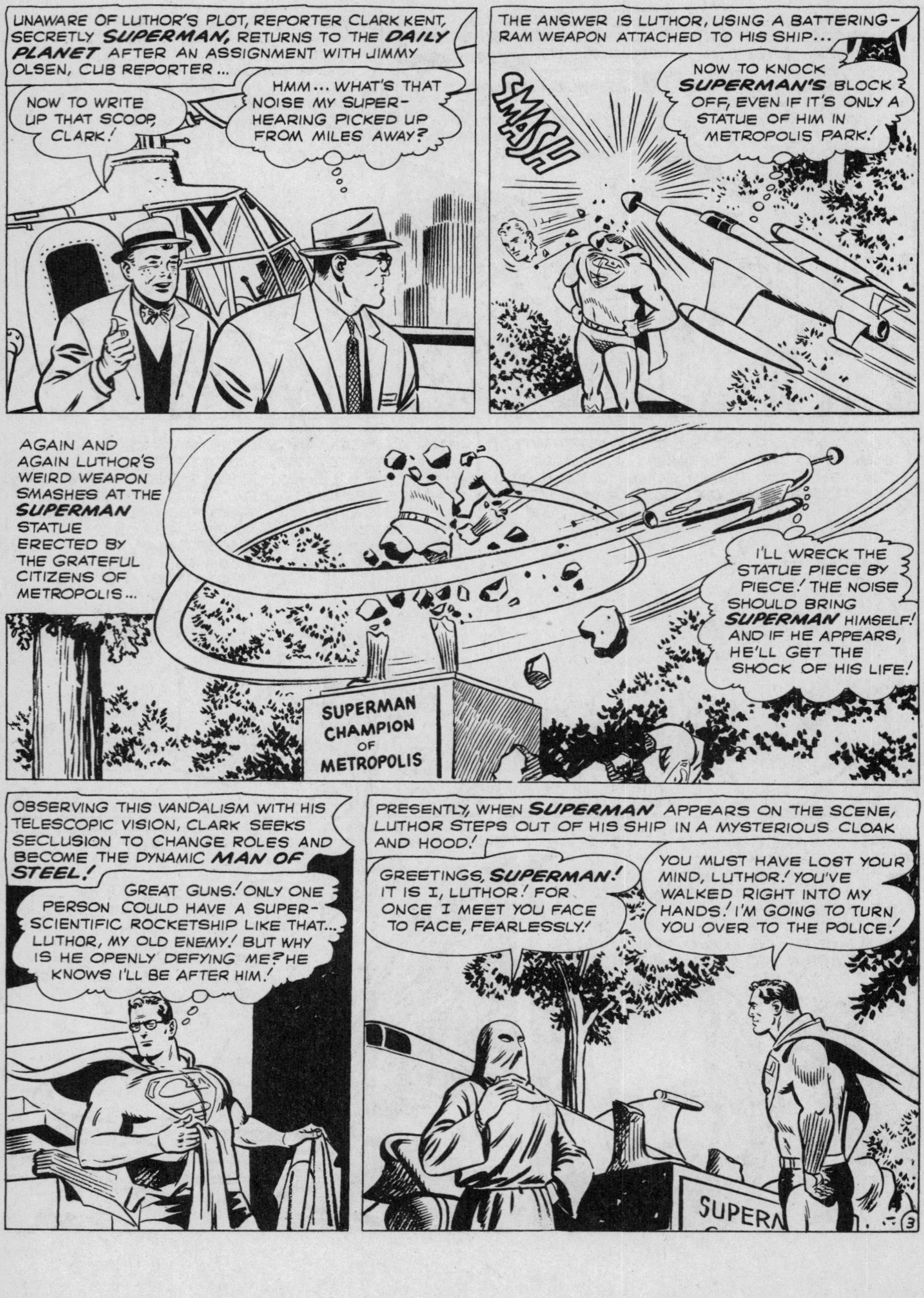
UNAWARE OF LUTHOR'S PLOT, REPORTER CLARK KENT, SECRETLY SUPERMAN, RETURNS TO THE DAILY PLANET AFTER AN ASSIGNMENT WITH JIMMY OLSEN, CUB REPORTER ...
NOW TO WRITE UP THAT SCOOP, CLARK!
HMM... WHAT'S THAT NOISE MY SUPER-HEARING PICKED UP FROM MILES AWAY?
THE ANSWER IS LUTHOR, USING A BATTERING-RAM WEAPON ATTACHED TO HIS SHIP...
SMASH
NOW TO KNOCK SUPERMAN'S BLOCK OFF, EVEN IF IT'S ONLY A STATUE OF HIM IN METROPOLIS PARK!
AGAIN AND AGAIN LUTHOR'S WEIRD WEAPON SMASHES AT THE SUPERMAN STATUE ERECTED BY THE GRATEFUL CITIZENS OF METROPOLIS...
I'LL WRECK THE STATUE PIECE BY PIECE! THE NOISE SHOULD BRING SUPERMAN HIMSELF! AND IF HE APPEARS, HE'LL GET THE SHOCK OF HIS LIFE!
SUPERMAN CHAMPION OF METROPOLIS
OBSERVING THIS VANDALISM WITH HIS TELESCOPIC VISION, CLARK SEEKS SECLUSION TO CHANGE ROLES AND BECOME THE DYNAMIC MAN OF STEEL!
GREAT GUNS! ONLY ONE PERSON COULD HAVE A SUPER-SCIENTIFIC ROCKETSHIP LIKE THAT... LUTHOR, MY OLD ENEMY! BUT WHY IS HE OPENLY DEFYING ME? HE KNOWS I'LL BE AFTER HIM!
PRESENTLY, WHEN SUPERMAN APPEARS ON THE SCENE, LUTHOR STEPS OUT OF HIS SHIP IN A MYSTERIOUS CLOAK AND HOOD!
GREETINGS, SUPERMAN! IT IS I, LUTHOR! FOR ONCE I MEET YOU FACE TO FACE, FEARLESSLY!
YOU MUST HAVE LOST YOUR MIND, LUTHOR! YOU'VE WALKED RIGHT INTO MY HANDS! I'M GOING TO TURN YOU OVER TO THE POLICE!
SUPERM
3

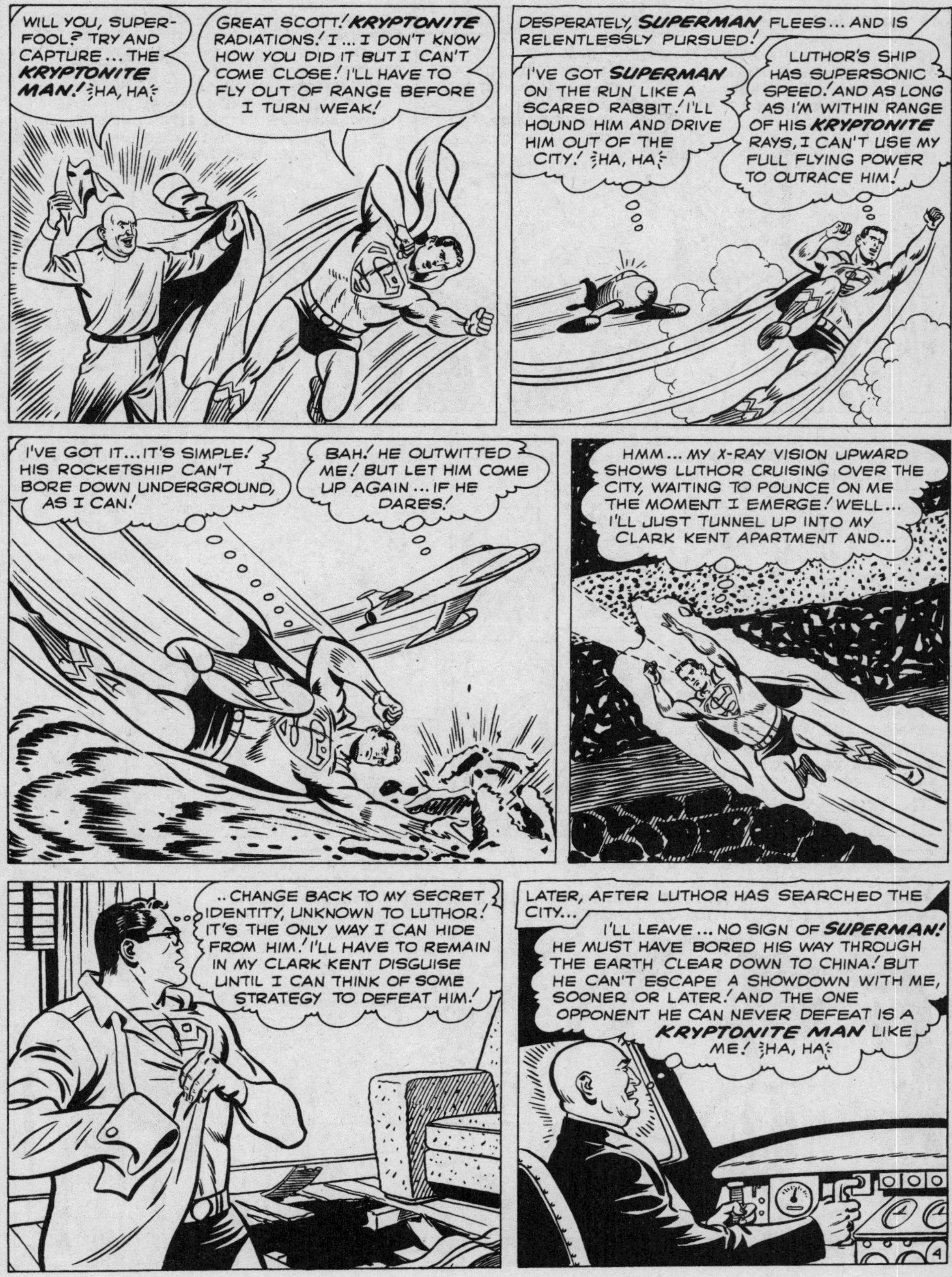
WILL YOU, SUPER-FOOL? TRY AND CAPTURE ... THE KRYPTONITE MAN! HA, HA
GREAT SCOTT! KRYPTONITE RADIATIONS! I ... I DON'T KNOW HOW YOU DID IT BUT I CAN'T COME CLOSE! I'LL HAVE TO FLY OUT OF RANGE BEFORE I TURN WEAK!
DESPERATELY, SUPERMAN FLEES ... AND IS RELENTLESSLY PURSUED!
I'VE GOT SUPERMAN ON THE RUN LIKE A SCARED RABBIT! I'LL HOUND HIM AND DRIVE HIM OUT OF THE CITY! HA, HA
LUTHOR'S SHIP HAS SUPERSONIC SPEED! AND AS LONG AS I'M WITHIN RANGE OF HIS KRYPTONITE RAYS, I CAN'T USE MY FULL FLYING POWER TO OUTRACE HIM!
I'VE GOT IT ... IT'S SIMPLE! HIS ROCKETSHIP CAN'T BORE DOWN UNDERGROUND, AS I CAN!
BAH! HE OUTWITTED ME! BUT LET HIM COME UP AGAIN ... IF HE DARES!
HMM ... MY X-RAY VISION UPWARD SHOWS LUTHOR CRUISING OVER THE CITY, WAITING TO POUNCE ON ME THE MOMENT I EMERGE! WELL ... I'LL JUST TUNNEL UP INTO MY CLARK KENT APARTMENT AND...
.. CHANGE BACK TO MY SECRET IDENTITY, UNKNOWN TO LUTHOR! IT'S THE ONLY WAY I CAN HIDE FROM HIM! I'LL HAVE TO REMAIN IN MY CLARK KENT DISGUISE UNTIL I CAN THINK OF SOME STRATEGY TO DEFEAT HIM!
LATER, AFTER LUTHOR HAS SEARCHED THE CITY...
I'LL LEAVE ... NO SIGN OF SUPERMAN! HE MUST HAVE BORED HIS WAY THROUGH THE EARTH CLEAR DOWN TO CHINA! BUT HE CAN'T ESCAPE A SHOWDOWN WITH ME, SOONER OR LATER! AND THE ONE OPPONENT HE CAN NEVER DEFEAT IS A KRYPTONITE MAN LIKE ME! HA, HA
4

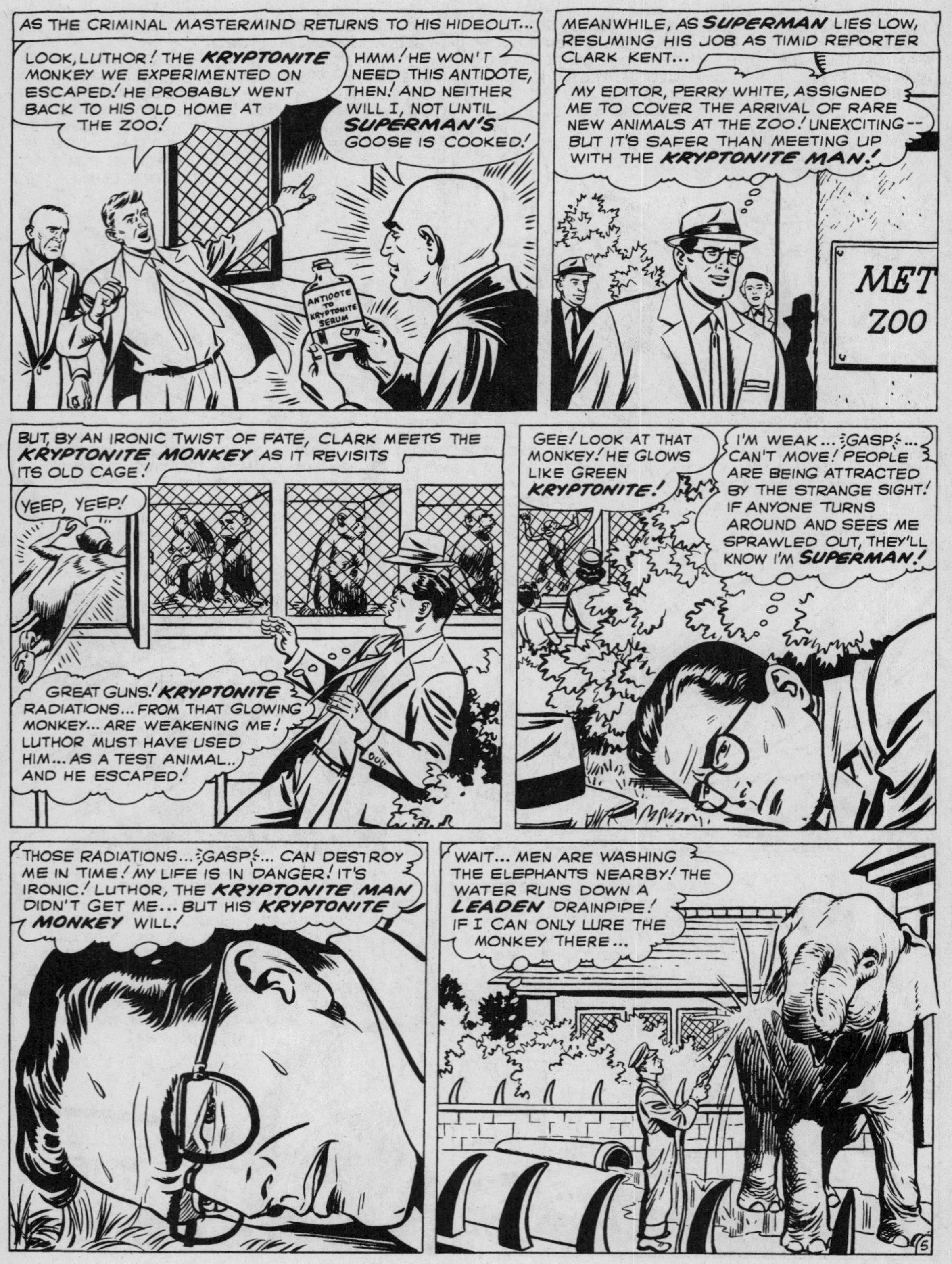
AS THE CRIMINAL MASTERMIND RETURNS TO HIS HIDEOUT...
LOOK, LUTHOR! THE KRYPTONITE MONKEY WE EXPERIMENTED ON ESCAPED! HE PROBABLY WENT BACK TO HIS OLD HOME AT THE ZOO!
HMM! HE WON'T NEED THIS ANTIDOTE, THEN! AND NEITHER WILL I, NOT UNTIL SUPERMAN'S GOOSE IS COOKED!
ANTIDOTE TO KRYPTONITE SERUM
MEANWHILE, AS SUPERMAN LIES LOW, RESUMING HIS JOB AS TIMID REPORTER CLARK KENT...
MY EDITOR, PERRY WHITE, ASSIGNED ME TO COVER THE ARRIVAL OF RARE NEW ANIMALS AT THE ZOO! UNEXCITING-- BUT IT'S SAFER THAN MEETING UP WITH THE KRYPTONITE MAN!
MET ZOO
BUT, BY AN IRONIC TWIST OF FATE, CLARK MEETS THE KRYPTONITE MONKEY AS IT REVISITS ITS OLD CAGE!
YEEP, YEEP!
GREAT GUNS! KRYPTONITE RADIATIONS... FROM THAT GLOWING MONKEY... ARE WEAKENING ME! LUTHOR MUST HAVE USED HIM... AS A TEST ANIMAL.. AND HE ESCAPED!
GEE! LOOK AT THAT MONKEY! HE GLOWS LIKE GREEN KRYPTONITE!
I'M WEAK... GASP... CAN'T MOVE! PEOPLE ARE BEING ATTRACTED BY THE STRANGE SIGHT! IF ANYONE TURNS AROUND AND SEES ME SPRAWLED OUT, THEY'LL KNOW I'M SUPERMAN!
THOSE RADIATIONS... GASP... CAN DESTROY ME IN TIME! MY LIFE IS IN DANGER! IT'S IRONIC! LUTHOR, THE KRYPTONITE MAN DIDN'T GET ME... BUT HIS KRYPTONITE MONKEY WILL!
WAIT... MEN ARE WASHING THE ELEPHANTS NEARBY! THE WATER RUNS DOWN A LEADEN DRAINPIPE! IF I CAN ONLY LURE THE MONKEY THERE...
5

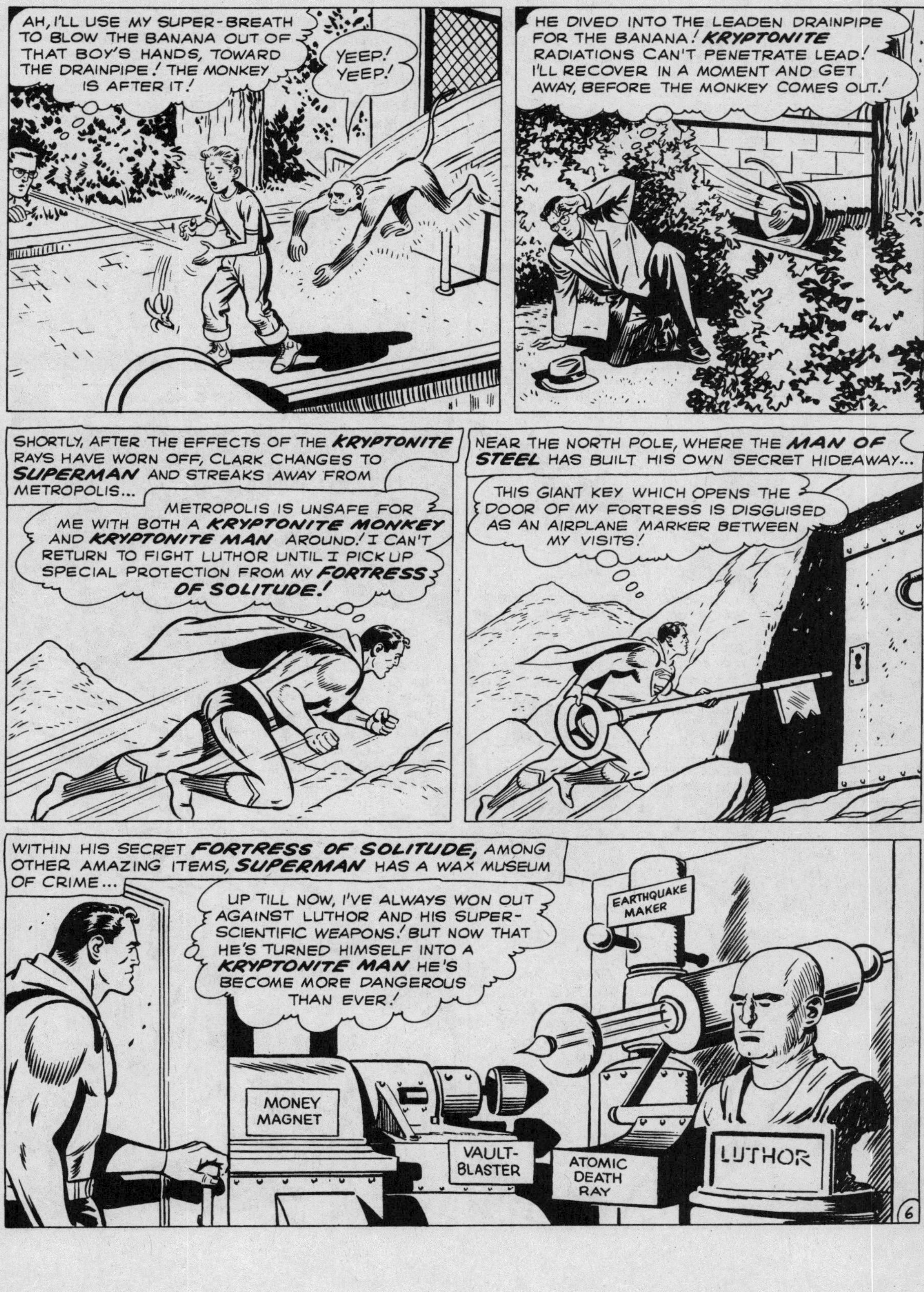
AH, I'LL USE MY SUPER-BREATH TO BLOW THE BANANA OUT OF THAT BOY'S HANDS, TOWARD THE DRAINPIPE! THE MONKEY IS AFTER IT!
YEEP! YEEP!
HE DIVED INTO THE LEADEN DRAINPIPE FOR THE BANANA! KRYPTONITE RADIATIONS CAN'T PENETRATE LEAD! I'LL RECOVER IN A MOMENT AND GET AWAY, BEFORE THE MONKEY COMES OUT!
SHORTLY, AFTER THE EFFECTS OF THE KRYPTONITE RAYS HAVE WORN OFF, CLARK CHANGES TO SUPERMAN AND STREAKS AWAY FROM METROPOLIS...
METROPOLIS IS UNSAFE FOR ME WITH BOTH A KRYPTONITE MONKEY AND KRYPTONITE MAN AROUND! I CAN'T RETURN TO FIGHT LUTHOR UNTIL I PICK UP SPECIAL PROTECTION FROM MY FORTRESS OF SOLITUDE!
NEAR THE NORTH POLE, WHERE THE MAN OF STEEL HAS BUILT HIS OWN SECRET HIDEAWAY...
THIS GIANT KEY WHICH OPENS THE DOOR OF MY FORTRESS IS DISGUISED AS AN AIRPLANE MARKER BETWEEN MY VISITS!
WITHIN HIS SECRET FORTRESS OF SOLITUDE, AMONG OTHER AMAZING ITEMS, SUPERMAN HAS A WAX MUSEUM OF CRIME...
UP TILL NOW, I'VE ALWAYS WON OUT AGAINST LUTHOR AND HIS SUPER-SCIENTIFIC WEAPONS! BUT NOW THAT HE'S TURNED HIMSELF INTO A KRYPTONITE MAN HE'S BECOME MORE DANGEROUS THAN EVER!
EARTHQUAKE MAKER
MONEY MAGNET
VAULT-BLASTER
ATOMIC DEATH RAY
LUTHOR
6

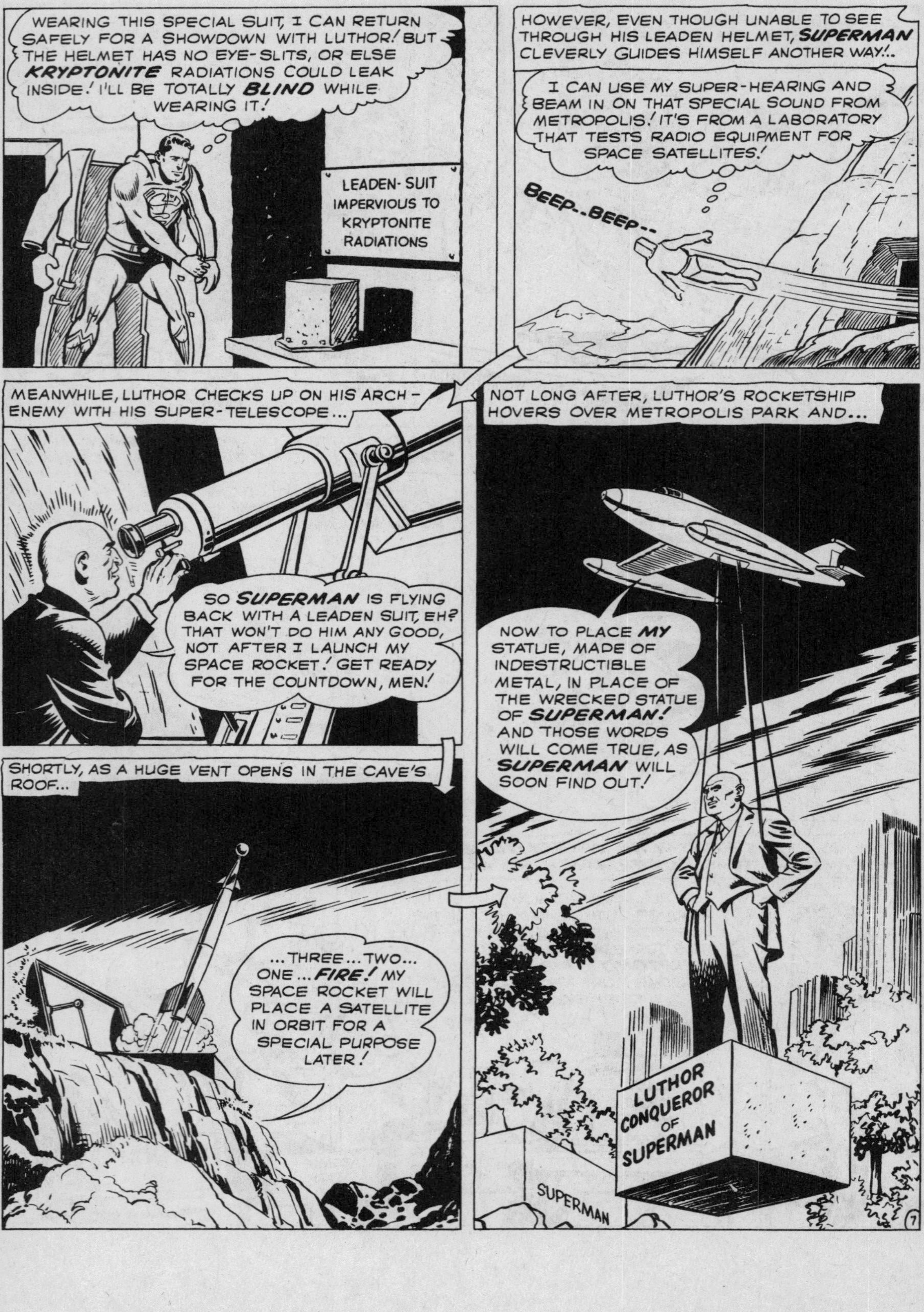
WEARING THIS SPECIAL SUIT, I CAN RETURN SAFELY FOR A SHOWDOWN WITH LUTHOR! BUT THE HELMET HAS NO EYE-SLITS, OR ELSE KRYPTONITE RADIATIONS COULD LEAK INSIDE! I'LL BE TOTALLY BLIND WHILE WEARING IT!
LEADEN-SUIT IMPERVIOUS TO KRYPTONITE RADIATIONS
HOWEVER, EVEN THOUGH UNABLE TO SEE THROUGH HIS LEADEN HELMET, SUPERMAN CLEVERLY GUIDES HIMSELF ANOTHER WAY!..
I CAN USE MY SUPER-HEARING AND BEAM IN ON THAT SPECIAL SOUND FROM METROPOLIS! IT'S FROM A LABORATORY THAT TESTS RADIO EQUIPMENT FOR SPACE SATELLITES!
BEEP..BEEP..
MEANWHILE, LUTHOR CHECKS UP ON HIS ARCH-ENEMY WITH HIS SUPER-TELESCOPE...
SO SUPERMAN IS FLYING BACK WITH A LEADEN SUIT, EH? THAT WON'T DO HIM ANY GOOD, NOT AFTER I LAUNCH MY SPACE ROCKET! GET READY FOR THE COUNTDOWN, MEN!
SHORTLY, AS A HUGE VENT OPENS IN THE CAVE'S ROOF...
...THREE...TWO... ONE...FIRE! MY SPACE ROCKET WILL PLACE A SATELLITE IN ORBIT FOR A SPECIAL PURPOSE LATER!
NOT LONG AFTER, LUTHOR'S ROCKETSHIP HOVERS OVER METROPOLIS PARK AND...
NOW TO PLACE MY STATUE, MADE OF INDESTRUCTIBLE METAL, IN PLACE OF THE WRECKED STATUE OF SUPERMAN! AND THOSE WORDS WILL COME TRUE, AS SUPERMAN WILL SOON FIND OUT!
LUTHOR CONQUEROR OF SUPERMAN
SUPERMAN
7

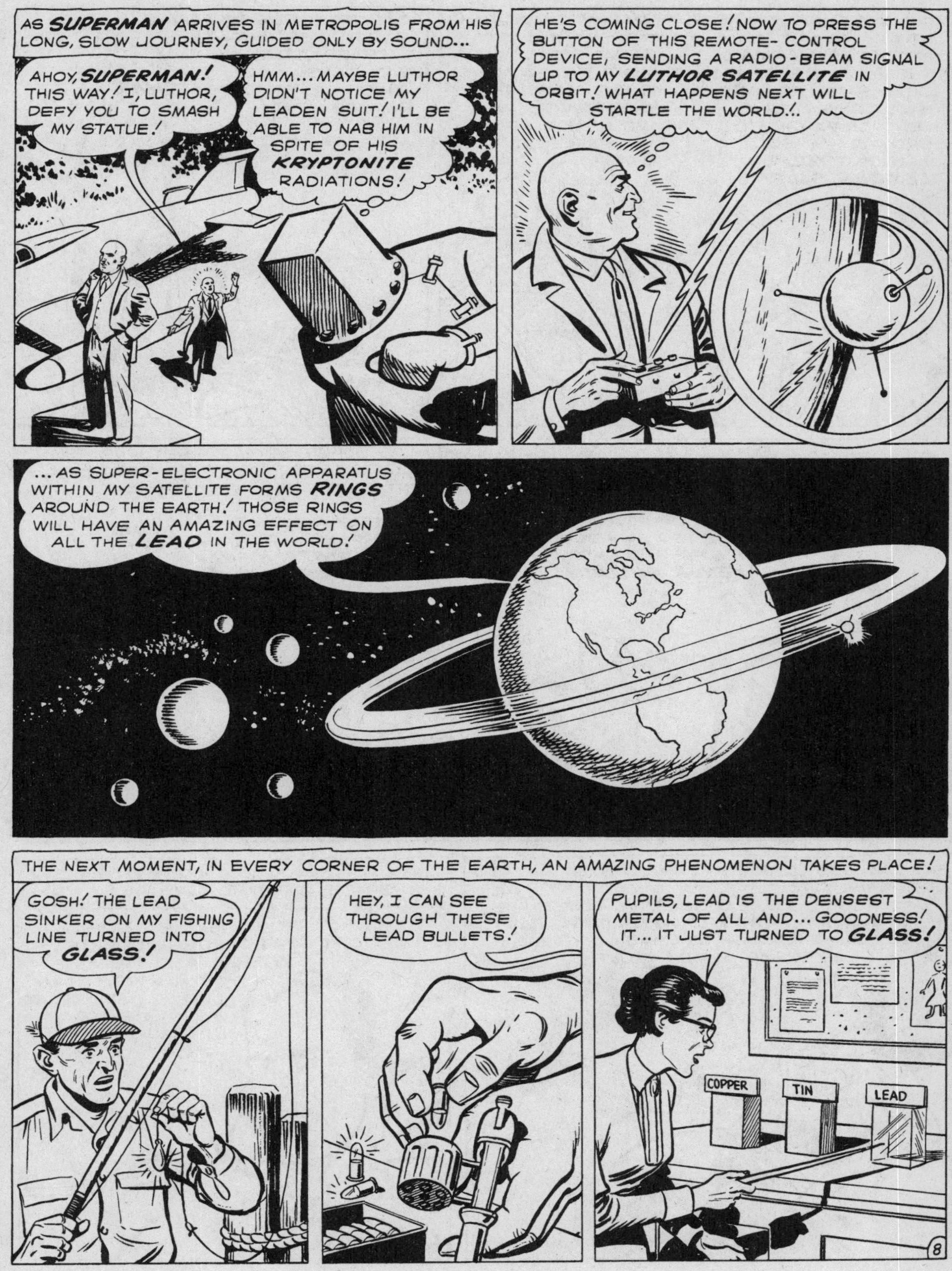
AS SUPERMAN ARRIVES IN METROPOLIS FROM HIS LONG, SLOW JOURNEY, GUIDED ONLY BY SOUND...
AHOY, SUPERMAN! THIS WAY! I, LUTHOR, DEFY YOU TO SMASH MY STATUE!
HMM... MAYBE LUTHOR DIDN'T NOTICE MY LEADEN SUIT! I'LL BE ABLE TO NAB HIM IN SPITE OF HIS KRYPTONITE RADIATIONS!
HE'S COMING CLOSE! NOW TO PRESS THE BUTTON OF THIS REMOTE-CONTROL DEVICE, SENDING A RADIO-BEAM SIGNAL UP TO MY LUTHOR SATELLITE IN ORBIT! WHAT HAPPENS NEXT WILL STARTLE THE WORLD!..
...AS SUPER-ELECTRONIC APPARATUS WITHIN MY SATELLITE FORMS RINGS AROUND THE EARTH! THOSE RINGS WILL HAVE AN AMAZING EFFECT ON ALL THE LEAD IN THE WORLD!
THE NEXT MOMENT, IN EVERY CORNER OF THE EARTH, AN AMAZING PHENOMENON TAKES PLACE!
GOSH! THE LEAD SINKER ON MY FISHING LINE TURNED INTO GLASS!
HEY, I CAN SEE THROUGH THESE LEAD BULLETS!
PUPILS, LEAD IS THE DENSEST METAL OF ALL AND... GOODNESS! IT... IT JUST TURNED TO GLASS!
COPPER
TIN
LEAD
8

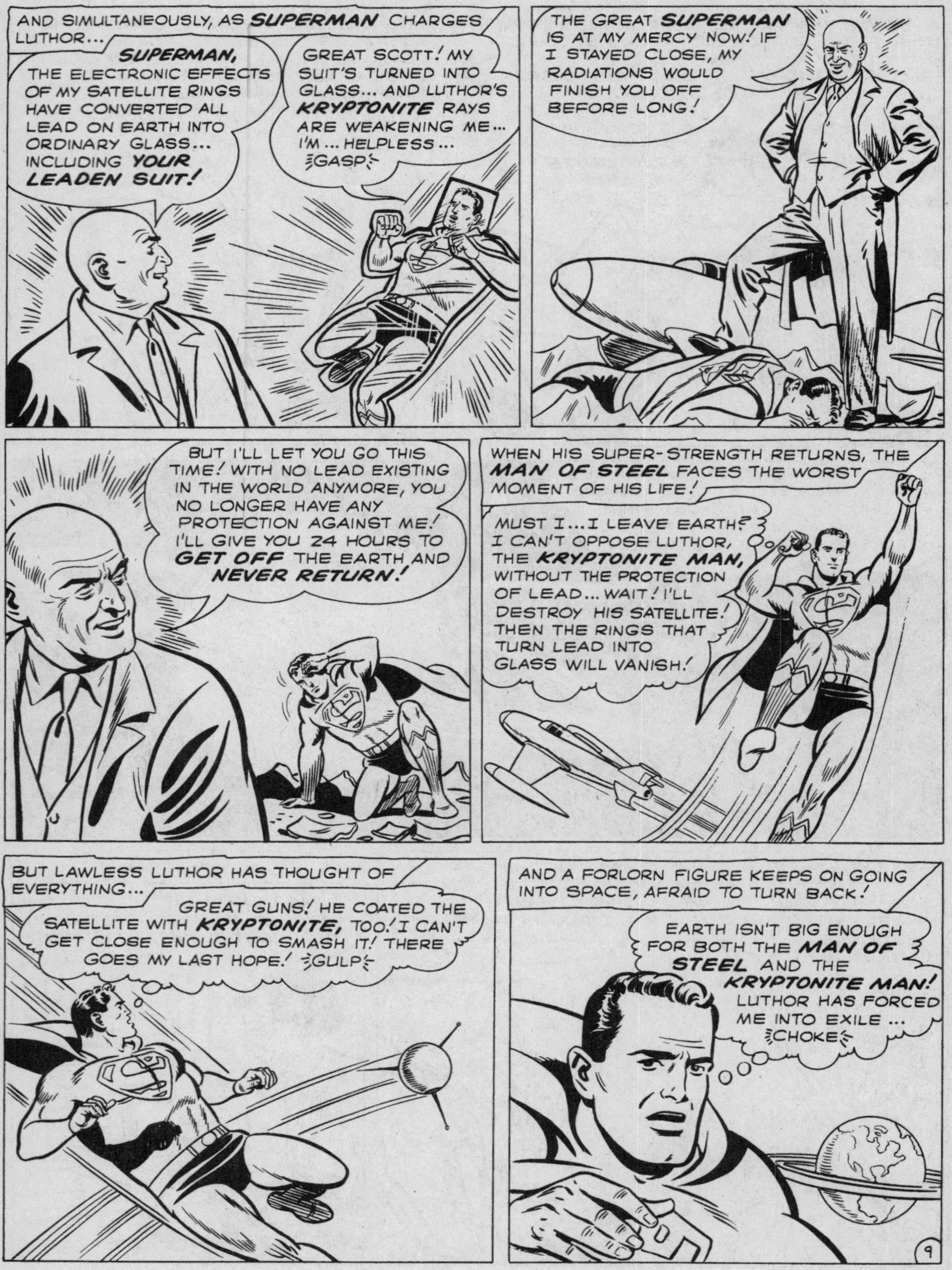
AND SIMULTANEOUSLY, AS SUPERMAN CHARGES LUTHOR...
SUPERMAN, THE ELECTRONIC EFFECTS OF MY SATELLITE RINGS HAVE CONVERTED ALL LEAD ON EARTH INTO ORDINARY GLASS... INCLUDING YOUR LEADEN SUIT!
GREAT SCOTT! MY SUIT'S TURNED INTO GLASS... AND LUTHOR'S KRYPTONITE RAYS ARE WEAKENING ME... I'M ... HELPLESS... GASP
THE GREAT SUPERMAN IS AT MY MERCY NOW! IF I STAYED CLOSE, MY RADIATIONS WOULD FINISH YOU OFF BEFORE LONG!
BUT I'LL LET YOU GO THIS TIME! WITH NO LEAD EXISTING IN THE WORLD ANYMORE, YOU NO LONGER HAVE ANY PROTECTION AGAINST ME! I'LL GIVE YOU 24 HOURS TO GET OFF THE EARTH AND NEVER RETURN!
WHEN HIS SUPER-STRENGTH RETURNS, THE MAN OF STEEL FACES THE WORST MOMENT OF HIS LIFE!
MUST I...I LEAVE EARTH? I CAN'T OPPOSE LUTHOR, THE KRYPTONITE MAN, WITHOUT THE PROTECTION OF LEAD... WAIT! I'LL DESTROY HIS SATELLITE! THEN THE RINGS THAT TURN LEAD INTO GLASS WILL VANISH!
BUT LAWLESS LUTHOR HAS THOUGHT OF EVERYTHING...
GREAT GUNS! HE COATED THE SATELLITE WITH KRYPTONITE, TOO! I CAN'T GET CLOSE ENOUGH TO SMASH IT! THERE GOES MY LAST HOPE! GULP
AND A FORLORN FIGURE KEEPS ON GOING INTO SPACE, AFRAID TO TURN BACK!
EARTH ISN'T BIG ENOUGH FOR BOTH THE MAN OF STEEL AND THE KRYPTONITE MAN! LUTHOR HAS FORCED ME INTO EXILE ... CHOKE
9

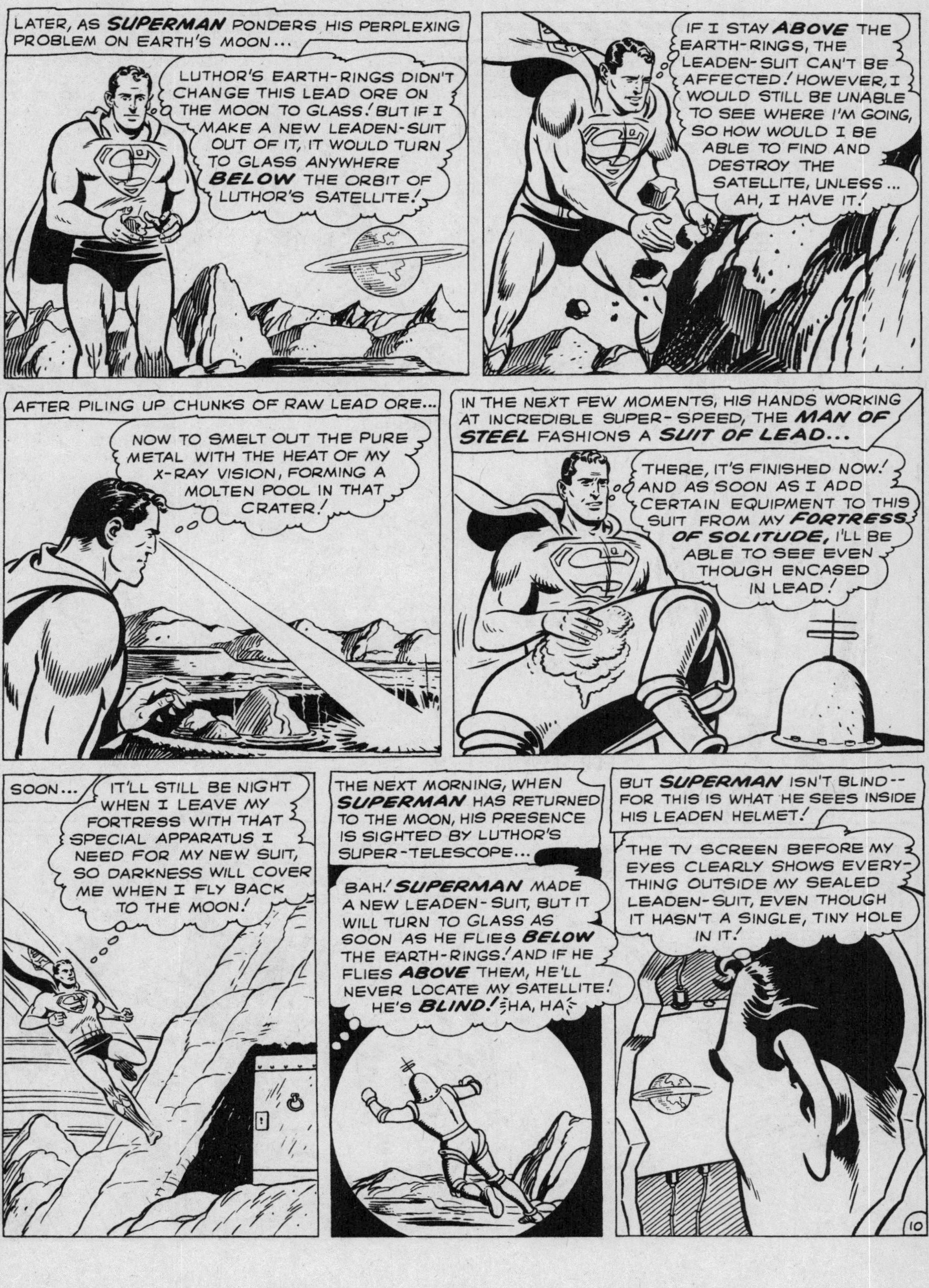
LATER, AS SUPERMAN PONDERS HIS PERPLEXING PROBLEM ON EARTH'S MOON...
LUTHOR'S EARTH-RINGS DIDN'T CHANGE THIS LEAD ORE ON THE MOON TO GLASS! BUT IF I MAKE A NEW LEADEN-SUIT OUT OF IT, IT WOULD TURN TO GLASS ANYWHERE BELOW THE ORBIT OF LUTHOR'S SATELLITE!
IF I STAY ABOVE THE EARTH-RINGS, THE LEADEN-SUIT CAN'T BE AFFECTED! HOWEVER, I WOULD STILL BE UNABLE TO SEE WHERE I'M GOING, SO HOW WOULD I BE ABLE TO FIND AND DESTROY THE SATELLITE, UNLESS... AH, I HAVE IT!
AFTER PILING UP CHUNKS OF RAW LEAD ORE...
NOW TO SMELT OUT THE PURE METAL WITH THE HEAT OF MY X-RAY VISION, FORMING A MOLTEN POOL IN THAT CRATER!
IN THE NEXT FEW MOMENTS, HIS HANDS WORKING AT INCREDIBLE SUPER-SPEED, THE MAN OF STEEL FASHIONS A SUIT OF LEAD...
THERE, IT'S FINISHED NOW! AND AS SOON AS I ADD CERTAIN EQUIPMENT TO THIS SUIT FROM MY FORTRESS OF SOLITUDE, I'LL BE ABLE TO SEE EVEN THOUGH ENCASED IN LEAD!
SOON...
IT'LL STILL BE NIGHT WHEN I LEAVE MY FORTRESS WITH THAT SPECIAL APPARATUS I NEED FOR MY NEW SUIT, SO DARKNESS WILL COVER ME WHEN I FLY BACK TO THE MOON!
THE NEXT MORNING, WHEN SUPERMAN HAS RETURNED TO THE MOON, HIS PRESENCE IS SIGHTED BY LUTHOR'S SUPER-TELESCOPE...
BAH! SUPERMAN MADE A NEW LEADEN-SUIT, BUT IT WILL TURN TO GLASS AS SOON AS HE FLIES BELOW THE EARTH-RINGS! AND IF HE FLIES ABOVE THEM, HE'LL NEVER LOCATE MY SATELLITE! HE'S BLIND! HA, HA
BUT SUPERMAN ISN'T BLIND-- FOR THIS IS WHAT HE SEES INSIDE HIS LEADEN HELMET!
THE TV SCREEN BEFORE MY EYES CLEARLY SHOWS EVERYTHING OUTSIDE MY SEALED LEADEN-SUIT, EVEN THOUGH IT HASN'T A SINGLE, TINY HOLE IN IT!
10

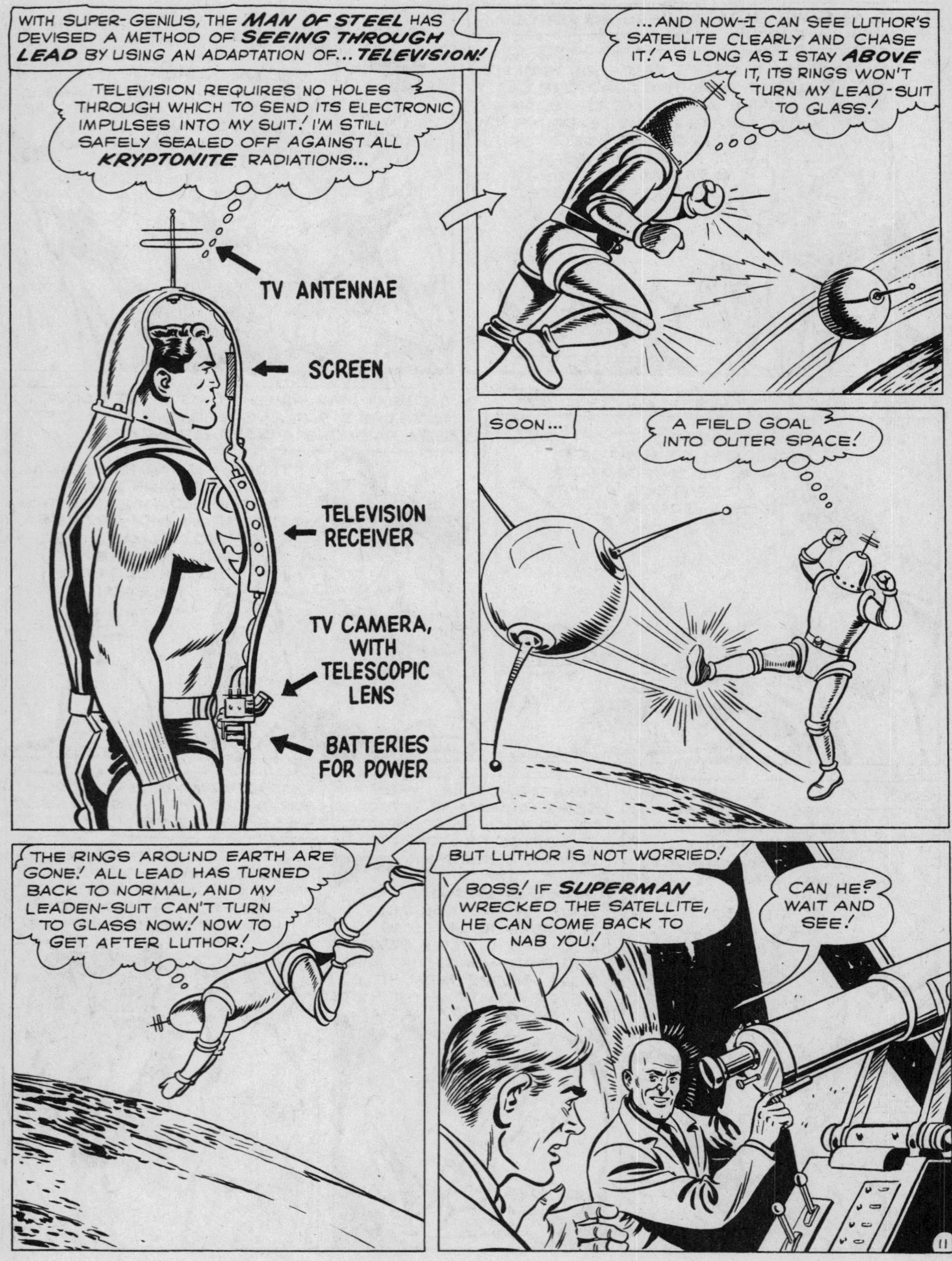
WITH SUPER-GENIUS, THE MAN OF STEEL HAS DEVISED A METHOD OF SEEING THROUGH LEAD BY USING AN ADAPTATION OF... TELEVISION!
TELEVISION REQUIRES NO HOLES THROUGH WHICH TO SEND ITS ELECTRONIC IMPULSES INTO MY SUIT! I'M STILL SAFELY SEALED OFF AGAINST ALL KRYPTONITE RADIATIONS...
TV ANTENNAE
SCREEN
TELEVISION RECEIVER
TV CAMERA, WITH TELESCOPIC LENS
BATTERIES FOR POWER
...AND NOW-I CAN SEE LUTHOR'S SATELLITE CLEARLY AND CHASE IT! AS LONG AS I STAY ABOVE IT, ITS RINGS WON'T TURN MY LEAD-SUIT TO GLASS!
SOON...
A FIELD GOAL INTO OUTER SPACE!
THE RINGS AROUND EARTH ARE GONE! ALL LEAD HAS TURNED BACK TO NORMAL, AND MY LEADEN-SUIT CAN'T TURN TO GLASS NOW! NOW TO GET AFTER LUTHOR!
BUT LUTHOR IS NOT WORRIED!
BOSS! IF SUPERMAN WRECKED THE SATELLITE, HE CAN COME BACK TO NAB YOU!
CAN HE? WAIT AND SEE!
11

AS *SUPERMAN* ARRIVES AFTER SUNSET...

HALT, *SUPERMAN*, OR I'LL BLOW APART YOUR LEADEN-SUIT, EXPOSING YOU TO MY RADIATIONS! YOU FORGET I'M STILL THE *KRYPTONITE MAN*! THAT MEANS YOU'LL HAVE TO WEAR THAT LEADEN-SUIT ALL YOUR LIFE! -HA, HA-

NO, I WON'T, LUTHOR! I'LL PEEL IT OFF RIGHT NOW!

BUT MY RADIATIONS WILL DESTROY YOU... WAIT! WHY AREN'T YOU WEAKENING AND FALLING?

INCREDIBLY, *SUPERMAN* IGNORES THE BARRAGE OF DEADLY RAYS...

GREAT SCOTT! YOU'RE STILL STANDING ... AND EVEN COMING TOWARD ME! FALL! *SUPERMAN*, WHY DON'T YOU FALL DOWN?... -GULP-... THEN YOU MUST HAVE SOMEHOW MADE YOURSELF *IMMUNE* TO *KRYPTONITE*!

LUTHOR IS UNAWARE OF THE TRUTH!

ACTUALLY, I'M TOO WEAK... TO MOVE! INVISIBLE WIRES... ARE HOLDING ME UP... AND MOVING MY FEET, FOOLING LUTHOR!

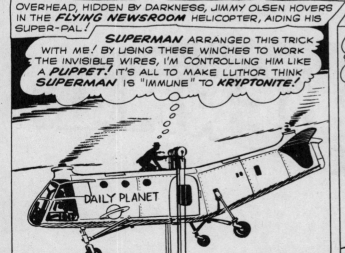

OVERHEAD, HIDDEN BY DARKNESS, JIMMY OLSEN HOVERS IN THE *FLYING NEWSROOM* HELICOPTER, AIDING HIS SUPER-PAL!

SUPERMAN ARRANGED THIS TRICK WITH ME! BY USING THESE WINCHES TO WORK THE INVISIBLE WIRES, I'M CONTROLLING HIM LIKE A *PUPPET*! IT'S ALL TO MAKE LUTHOR THINK *SUPERMAN* IS "IMMUNE" TO *KRYPTONITE*!

DAILY PLANET

COMPLETELY HOODWINKED, LUTHOR SLIPS A VIAL FROM HIS POCKET AND...

MY *KRYPTONITE* RADIATIONS ARE USELESS AGAINST *SUPERMAN* NOW! IN FACT, THIS GREEN GLOW WILL BETRAY ME IN THE DARK! *SUPERMAN* OR THE POLICE WILL EASILY TRAIL ME! I'D BETTER TAKE THE ANTIDOTE!

12

MOMENTS LATER...
MY GLOW DIED! MY SKIN IS NO LONGER GIVING OFF KRYPTONITE RADIATIONS! NOW TO SNEAK AWAY FROM SUPERMAN!
NO YOU DON'T, LUTHOR! YOU FORGOT I CAN SEE IN THE DARK WITH MY X-RAY VISION! AND THANKS FOR TAKING THE ANTIDOTE, ALLOWING ME TO REGAIN MY SUPER-STRENGTH!
LATER, AT JAIL, AFTER LUTHOR HEARS THE STORY...
YOU AND OLSEN TRICKED ME LIKE A BABY, INTO TAKING THE ANTIDOTE! BAH!
POLICE ALSO GAVE THE ANTIDOTE TO YOUR KRYPTONITE MONKEY! IT'S NO LONGER A MENACE TO ME!
13
AFTER CLARK KENT HAS WRITTEN UP THE SCOOP...
THAT HEADLINE TO MY STORY JUST ABOUT SUMS IT ALL UP!
DAILY PLANET
"MAN OF LEAD" DEFEATS "KRYPTONITE MAN"
THE END

SUPERMAN

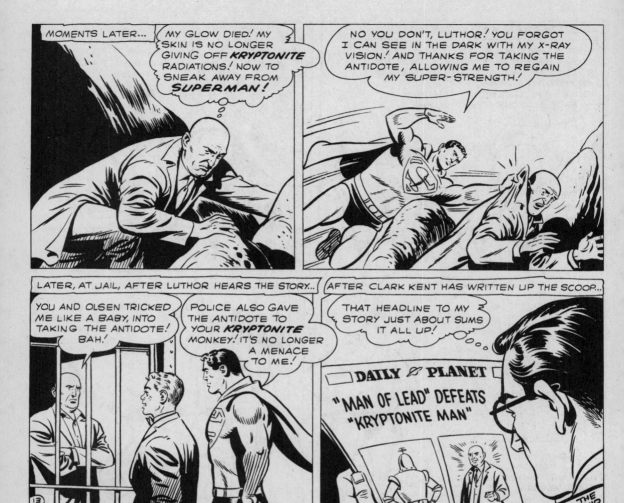

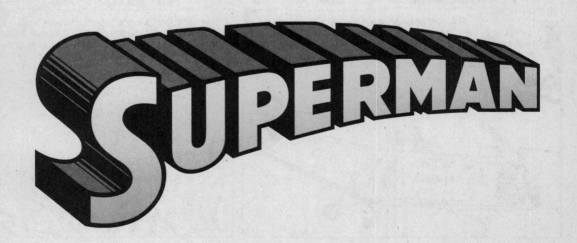

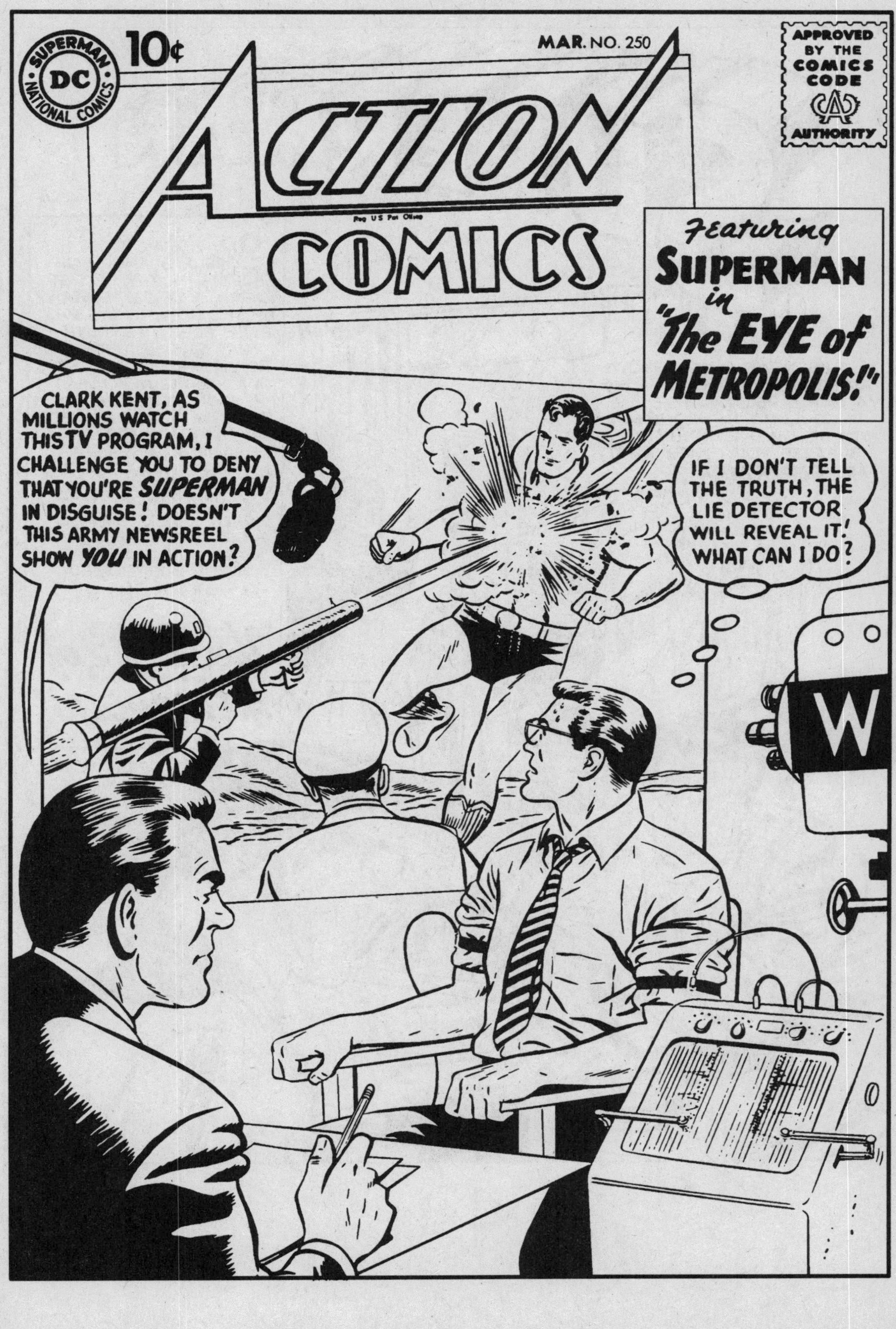
SUPERMAN DC NATIONAL COMICS
10¢
MAR. NO. 250
APPROVED BY THE COMICS CODE AUTHORITY
ACTION COMICS
Reg U S Pat Office
Featuring SUPERMAN in "The EYE of METROPOLIS!"
CLARK KENT, AS MILLIONS WATCH THIS TV PROGRAM, I CHALLENGE YOU TO DENY THAT YOU'RE SUPERMAN IN DISGUISE! DOESN'T THIS ARMY NEWSREEL SHOW YOU IN ACTION?
IF I DON'T TELL THE TRUTH, THE LIE DETECTOR WILL REVEAL IT! WHAT CAN I DO?
W

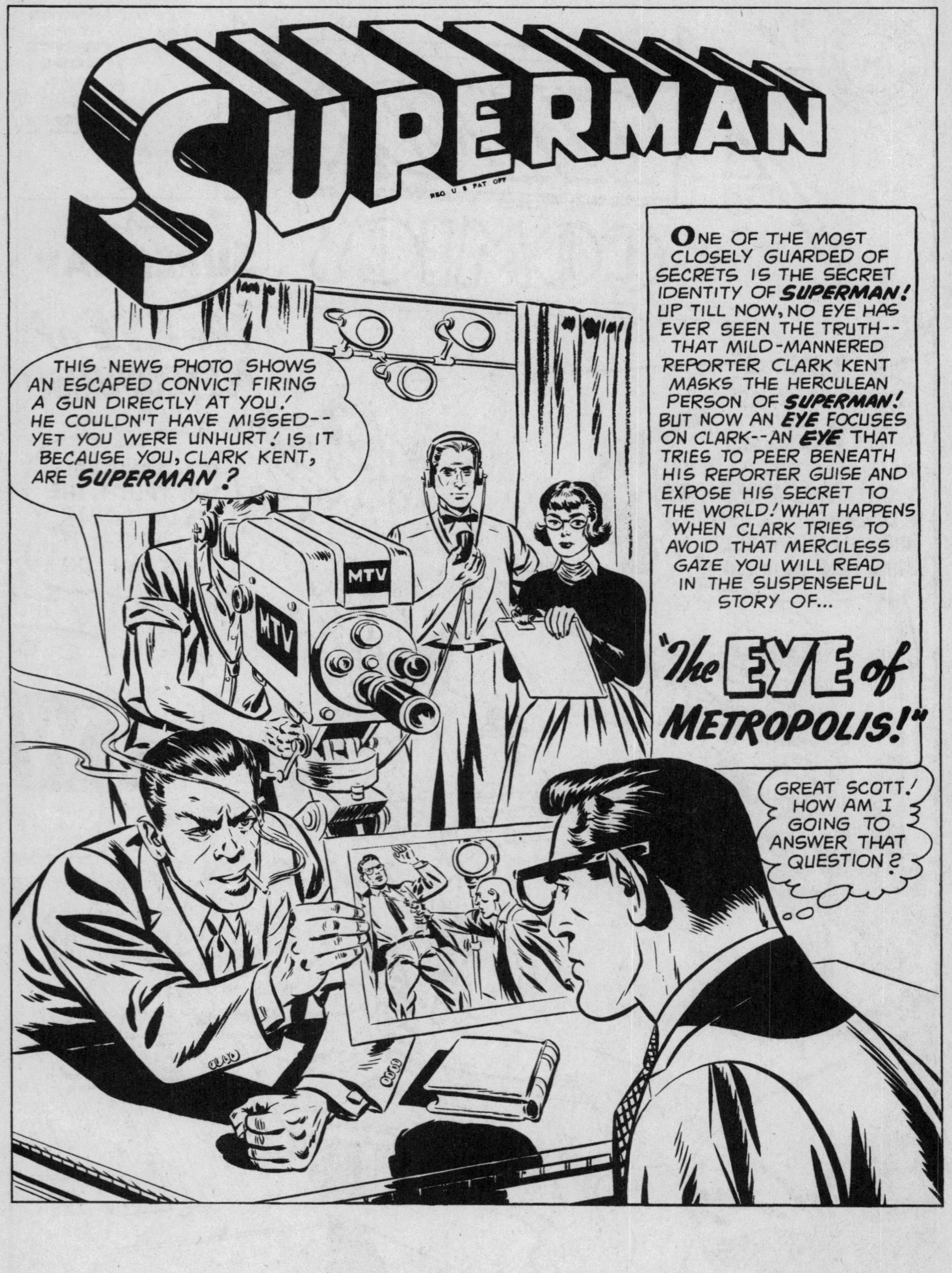
SUPERMAN
REG. U.S. PAT. OFF.
ONE OF THE MOST CLOSELY GUARDED OF SECRETS IS THE SECRET IDENTITY OF SUPERMAN! UP TILL NOW, NO EYE HAS EVER SEEN THE TRUTH-- THAT MILD-MANNERED REPORTER CLARK KENT MASKS THE HERCULEAN PERSON OF SUPERMAN! BUT NOW AN EYE FOCUSES ON CLARK--AN EYE THAT TRIES TO PEER BENEATH HIS REPORTER GUISE AND EXPOSE HIS SECRET TO THE WORLD! WHAT HAPPENS WHEN CLARK TRIES TO AVOID THAT MERCILESS GAZE YOU WILL READ IN THE SUSPENSEFUL STORY OF...
"The EYE of METROPOLIS!"
THIS NEWS PHOTO SHOWS AN ESCAPED CONVICT FIRING A GUN DIRECTLY AT YOU! HE COULDN'T HAVE MISSED-- YET YOU WERE UNHURT! IS IT BECAUSE YOU, CLARK KENT, ARE SUPERMAN?
MTV
MTV
GREAT SCOTT! HOW AM I GOING TO ANSWER THAT QUESTION?

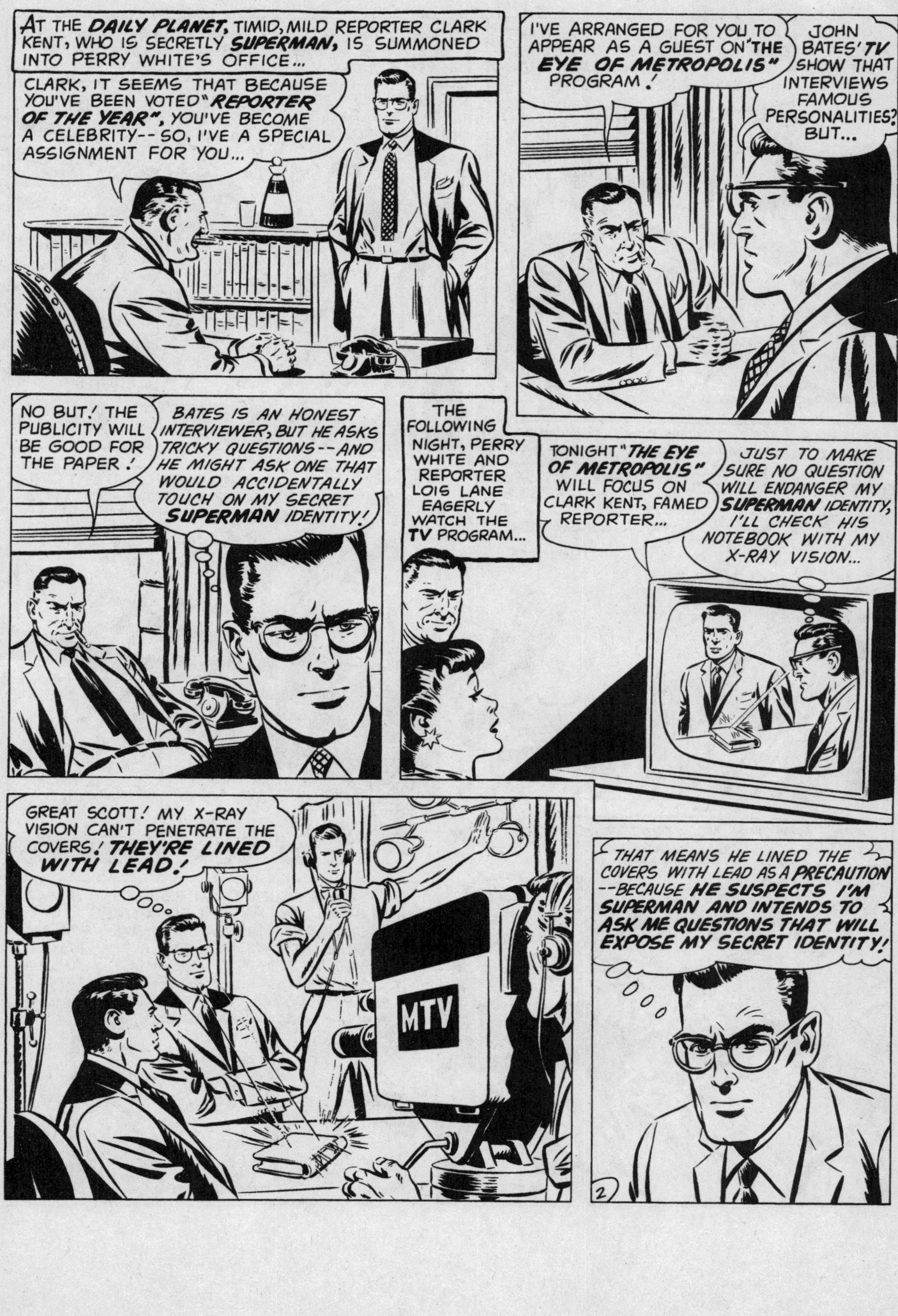
AT THE DAILY PLANET, TIMID, MILD REPORTER CLARK KENT, WHO IS SECRETLY SUPERMAN, IS SUMMONED INTO PERRY WHITE'S OFFICE...
CLARK, IT SEEMS THAT BECAUSE YOU'VE BEEN VOTED "REPORTER OF THE YEAR", YOU'VE BECOME A CELEBRITY-- SO, I'VE A SPECIAL ASSIGNMENT FOR YOU...
I'VE ARRANGED FOR YOU TO APPEAR AS A GUEST ON "THE EYE OF METROPOLIS" PROGRAM!
JOHN BATES' TV SHOW THAT INTERVIEWS FAMOUS PERSONALITIES? BUT...
NO BUT! THE PUBLICITY WILL BE GOOD FOR THE PAPER!
BATES IS AN HONEST INTERVIEWER, BUT HE ASKS TRICKY QUESTIONS--AND HE MIGHT ASK ONE THAT WOULD ACCIDENTALLY TOUCH ON MY SECRET SUPERMAN IDENTITY!
THE FOLLOWING NIGHT, PERRY WHITE AND REPORTER LOIS LANE EAGERLY WATCH THE TV PROGRAM...
TONIGHT "THE EYE OF METROPOLIS" WILL FOCUS ON CLARK KENT, FAMED REPORTER...
JUST TO MAKE SURE NO QUESTION WILL ENDANGER MY SUPERMAN IDENTITY, I'LL CHECK HIS NOTEBOOK WITH MY X-RAY VISION...
GREAT SCOTT! MY X-RAY VISION CAN'T PENETRATE THE COVERS! THEY'RE LINED WITH LEAD!
MTV
THAT MEANS HE LINED THE COVERS WITH LEAD AS A PRECAUTION --BECAUSE HE SUSPECTS I'M SUPERMAN AND INTENDS TO ASK ME QUESTIONS THAT WILL EXPOSE MY SECRET IDENTITY!
2

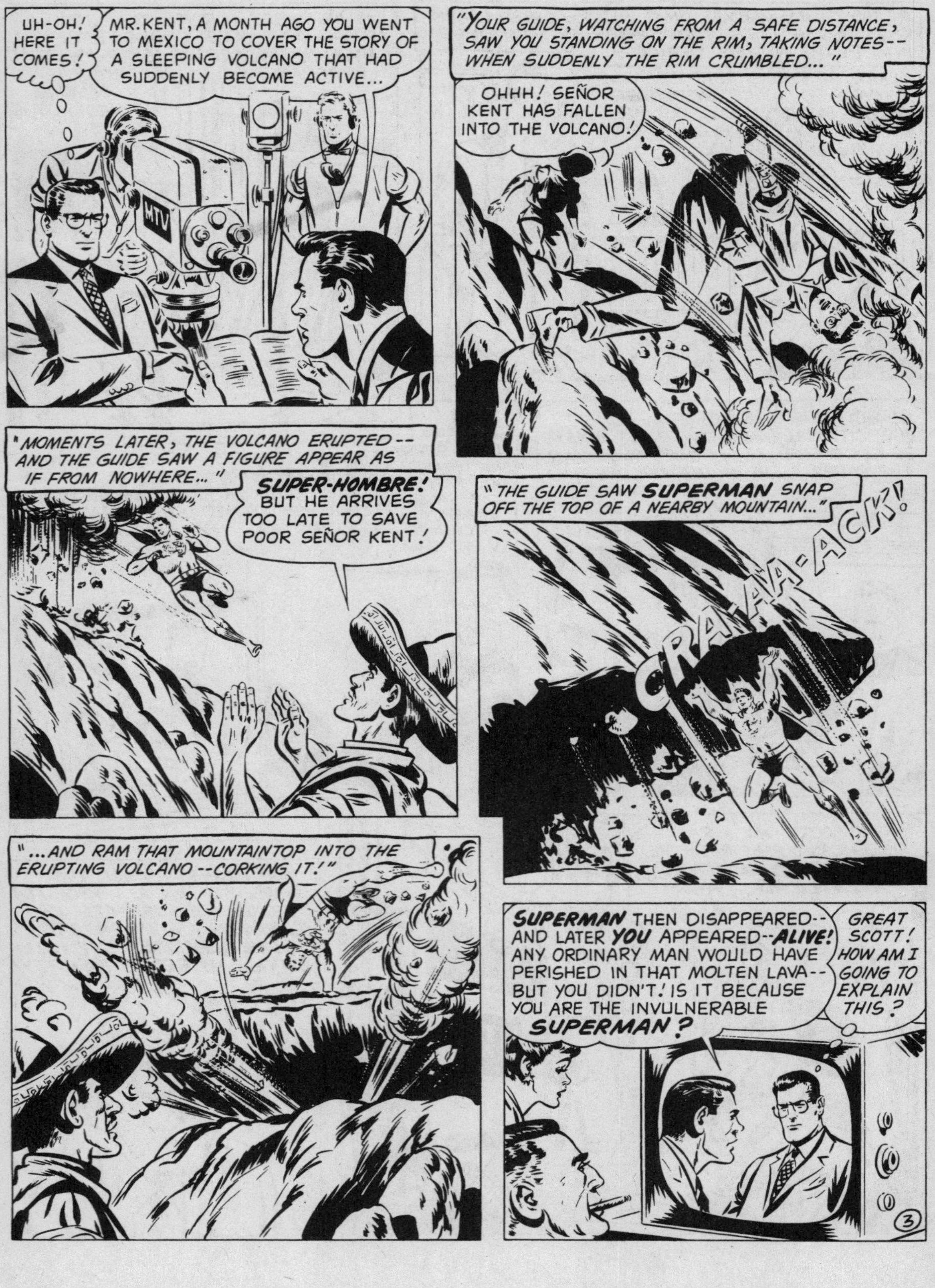
UH-OH! HERE IT COMES!
MR. KENT, A MONTH AGO YOU WENT TO MEXICO TO COVER THE STORY OF A SLEEPING VOLCANO THAT HAD SUDDENLY BECOME ACTIVE...
MTV
"YOUR GUIDE, WATCHING FROM A SAFE DISTANCE, SAW YOU STANDING ON THE RIM, TAKING NOTES--WHEN SUDDENLY THE RIM CRUMBLED..."
OHHH! SEÑOR KENT HAS FALLEN INTO THE VOLCANO!
"MOMENTS LATER, THE VOLCANO ERUPTED--AND THE GUIDE SAW A FIGURE APPEAR AS IF FROM NOWHERE..."
SUPER-HOMBRE! BUT HE ARRIVES TOO LATE TO SAVE POOR SEÑOR KENT!
"THE GUIDE SAW SUPERMAN SNAP OFF THE TOP OF A NEARBY MOUNTAIN..."
CRA-A-ACK!
"...AND RAM THAT MOUNTAINTOP INTO THE ERUPTING VOLCANO--CORKING IT!"
SUPERMAN THEN DISAPPEARED--AND LATER YOU APPEARED--ALIVE! ANY ORDINARY MAN WOULD HAVE PERISHED IN THAT MOLTEN LAVA--BUT YOU DIDN'T! IS IT BECAUSE YOU ARE THE INVULNERABLE SUPERMAN?
GREAT SCOTT! HOW AM I GOING TO EXPLAIN THIS?
3

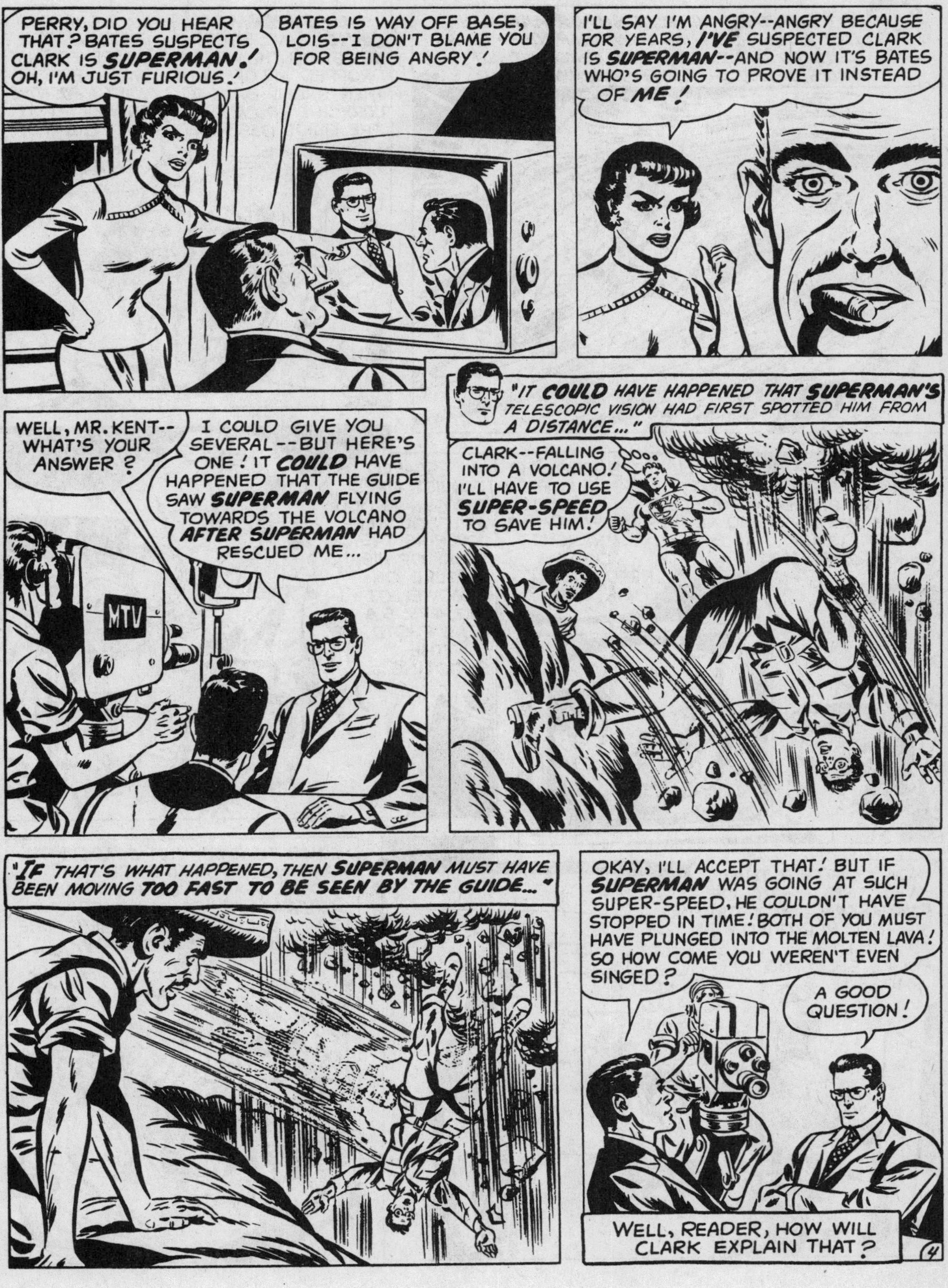
PERRY, DID YOU HEAR THAT? BATES SUSPECTS CLARK IS SUPERMAN! OH, I'M JUST FURIOUS!
BATES IS WAY OFF BASE, LOIS--I DON'T BLAME YOU FOR BEING ANGRY!
I'LL SAY I'M ANGRY--ANGRY BECAUSE FOR YEARS, I'VE SUSPECTED CLARK IS SUPERMAN--AND NOW IT'S BATES WHO'S GOING TO PROVE IT INSTEAD OF ME!
WELL, MR. KENT--WHAT'S YOUR ANSWER?
I COULD GIVE YOU SEVERAL--BUT HERE'S ONE! IT COULD HAVE HAPPENED THAT THE GUIDE SAW SUPERMAN FLYING TOWARDS THE VOLCANO AFTER SUPERMAN HAD RESCUED ME...
MTV
"IT COULD HAVE HAPPENED THAT SUPERMAN'S TELESCOPIC VISION HAD FIRST SPOTTED HIM FROM A DISTANCE..."
CLARK--FALLING INTO A VOLCANO! I'LL HAVE TO USE SUPER-SPEED TO SAVE HIM!
"IF THAT'S WHAT HAPPENED, THEN SUPERMAN MUST HAVE BEEN MOVING TOO FAST TO BE SEEN BY THE GUIDE..."
OKAY, I'LL ACCEPT THAT! BUT IF SUPERMAN WAS GOING AT SUCH SUPER-SPEED, HE COULDN'T HAVE STOPPED IN TIME! BOTH OF YOU MUST HAVE PLUNGED INTO THE MOLTEN LAVA! SO HOW COME YOU WEREN'T EVEN SINGED?
A GOOD QUESTION!
WELL, READER, HOW WILL CLARK EXPLAIN THAT?
4

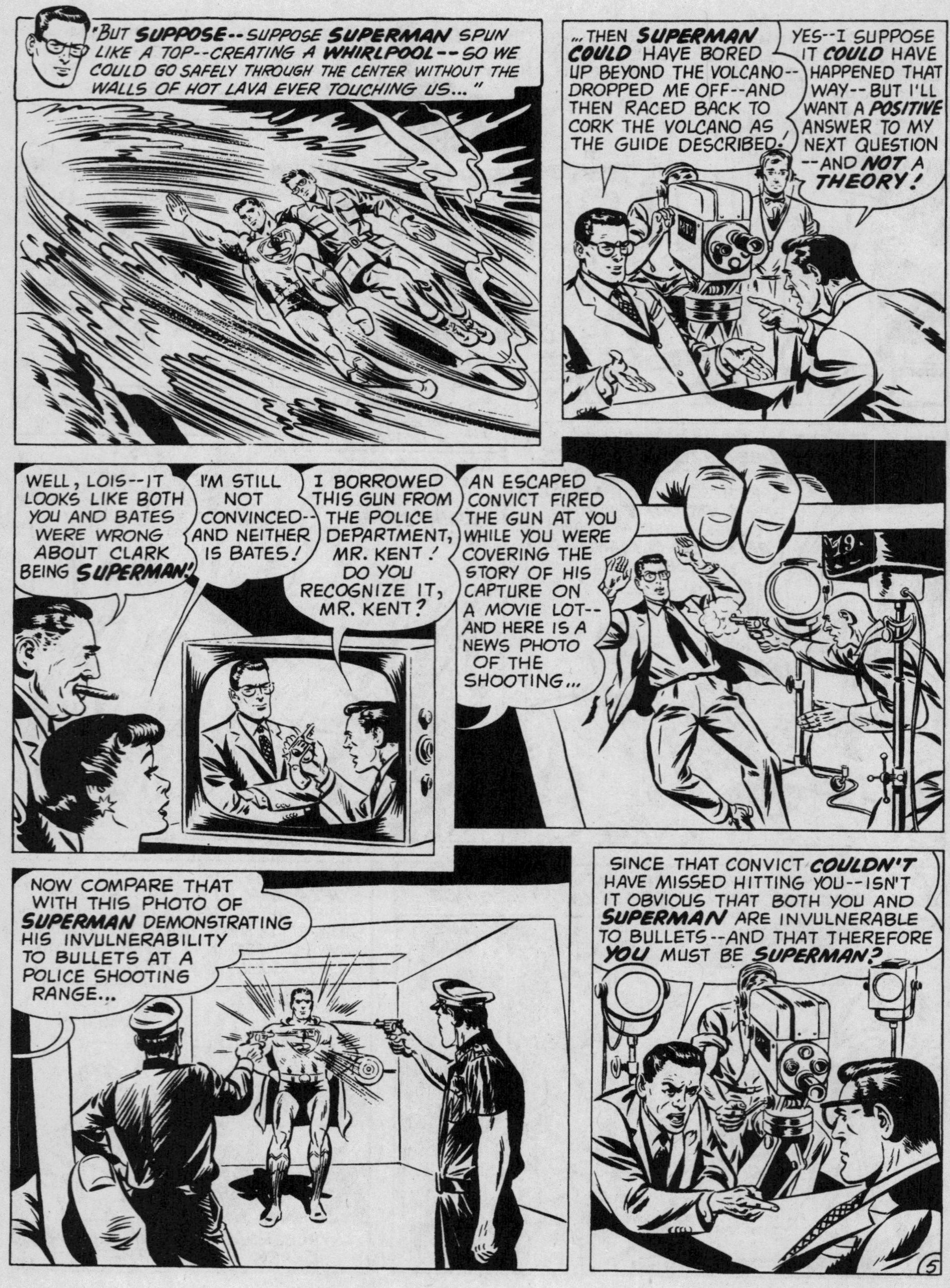
"BUT SUPPOSE--SUPPOSE SUPERMAN SPUN LIKE A TOP--CREATING A WHIRLPOOL--SO WE COULD GO SAFELY THROUGH THE CENTER WITHOUT THE WALLS OF HOT LAVA EVER TOUCHING US..."
...THEN SUPERMAN COULD HAVE BORED UP BEYOND THE VOLCANO--DROPPED ME OFF--AND THEN RACED BACK TO CORK THE VOLCANO AS THE GUIDE DESCRIBED!
YES--I SUPPOSE IT COULD HAVE HAPPENED THAT WAY--BUT I'LL WANT A POSITIVE ANSWER TO MY NEXT QUESTION--AND NOT A THEORY!
WELL, LOIS--IT LOOKS LIKE BOTH YOU AND BATES WERE WRONG ABOUT CLARK BEING SUPERMAN!
I'M STILL NOT CONVINCED--AND NEITHER IS BATES!
I BORROWED THIS GUN FROM THE POLICE DEPARTMENT, MR. KENT! DO YOU RECOGNIZE IT, MR. KENT?
AN ESCAPED CONVICT FIRED THE GUN AT YOU WHILE YOU WERE COVERING THE STORY OF HIS CAPTURE ON A MOVIE LOT--AND HERE IS A NEWS PHOTO OF THE SHOOTING...
NOW COMPARE THAT WITH THIS PHOTO OF SUPERMAN DEMONSTRATING HIS INVULNERABILITY TO BULLETS AT A POLICE SHOOTING RANGE...
SINCE THAT CONVICT COULDN'T HAVE MISSED HITTING YOU--ISN'T IT OBVIOUS THAT BOTH YOU AND SUPERMAN ARE INVULNERABLE TO BULLETS--AND THAT THEREFORE YOU MUST BE SUPERMAN?
5

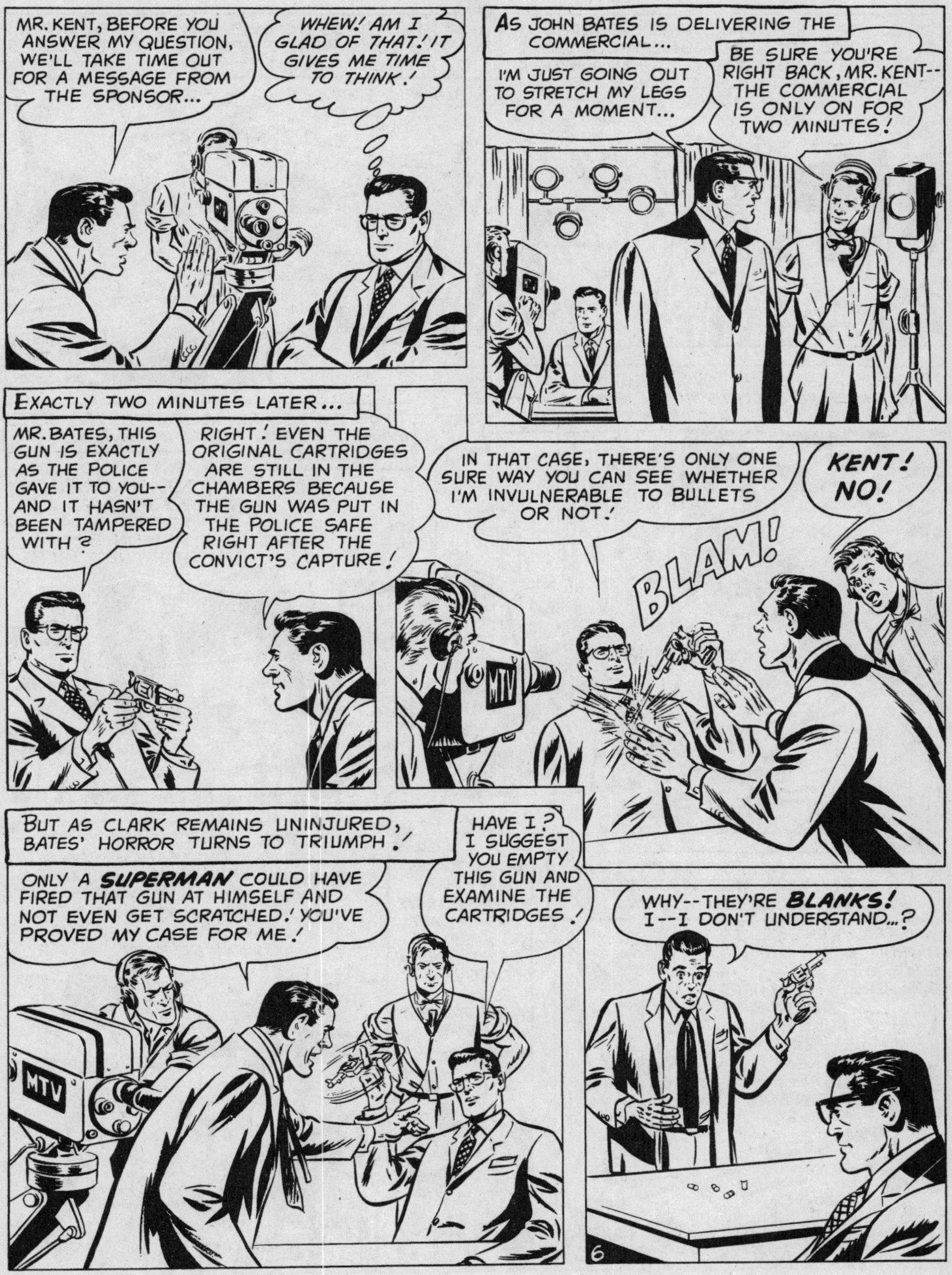
MR. KENT, BEFORE YOU ANSWER MY QUESTION, WE'LL TAKE TIME OUT FOR A MESSAGE FROM THE SPONSOR...
WHEW! AM I GLAD OF THAT! IT GIVES ME TIME TO THINK!
AS JOHN BATES IS DELIVERING THE COMMERCIAL...
I'M JUST GOING OUT TO STRETCH MY LEGS FOR A MOMENT...
BE SURE YOU'RE RIGHT BACK, MR. KENT-- THE COMMERCIAL IS ONLY ON FOR TWO MINUTES!
EXACTLY TWO MINUTES LATER...
MR. BATES, THIS GUN IS EXACTLY AS THE POLICE GAVE IT TO YOU-- AND IT HASN'T BEEN TAMPERED WITH?
RIGHT! EVEN THE ORIGINAL CARTRIDGES ARE STILL IN THE CHAMBERS BECAUSE THE GUN WAS PUT IN THE POLICE SAFE RIGHT AFTER THE CONVICT'S CAPTURE!
IN THAT CASE, THERE'S ONLY ONE SURE WAY YOU CAN SEE WHETHER I'M INVULNERABLE TO BULLETS OR NOT!
KENT! NO!
BLAM!
MTV
BUT AS CLARK REMAINS UNINJURED, BATES' HORROR TURNS TO TRIUMPH!
ONLY A SUPERMAN COULD HAVE FIRED THAT GUN AT HIMSELF AND NOT EVEN GET SCRATCHED! YOU'VE PROVED MY CASE FOR ME!
HAVE I? I SUGGEST YOU EMPTY THIS GUN AND EXAMINE THE CARTRIDGES!
MTV
WHY--THEY'RE BLANKS! I--I DON'T UNDERSTAND...?
6

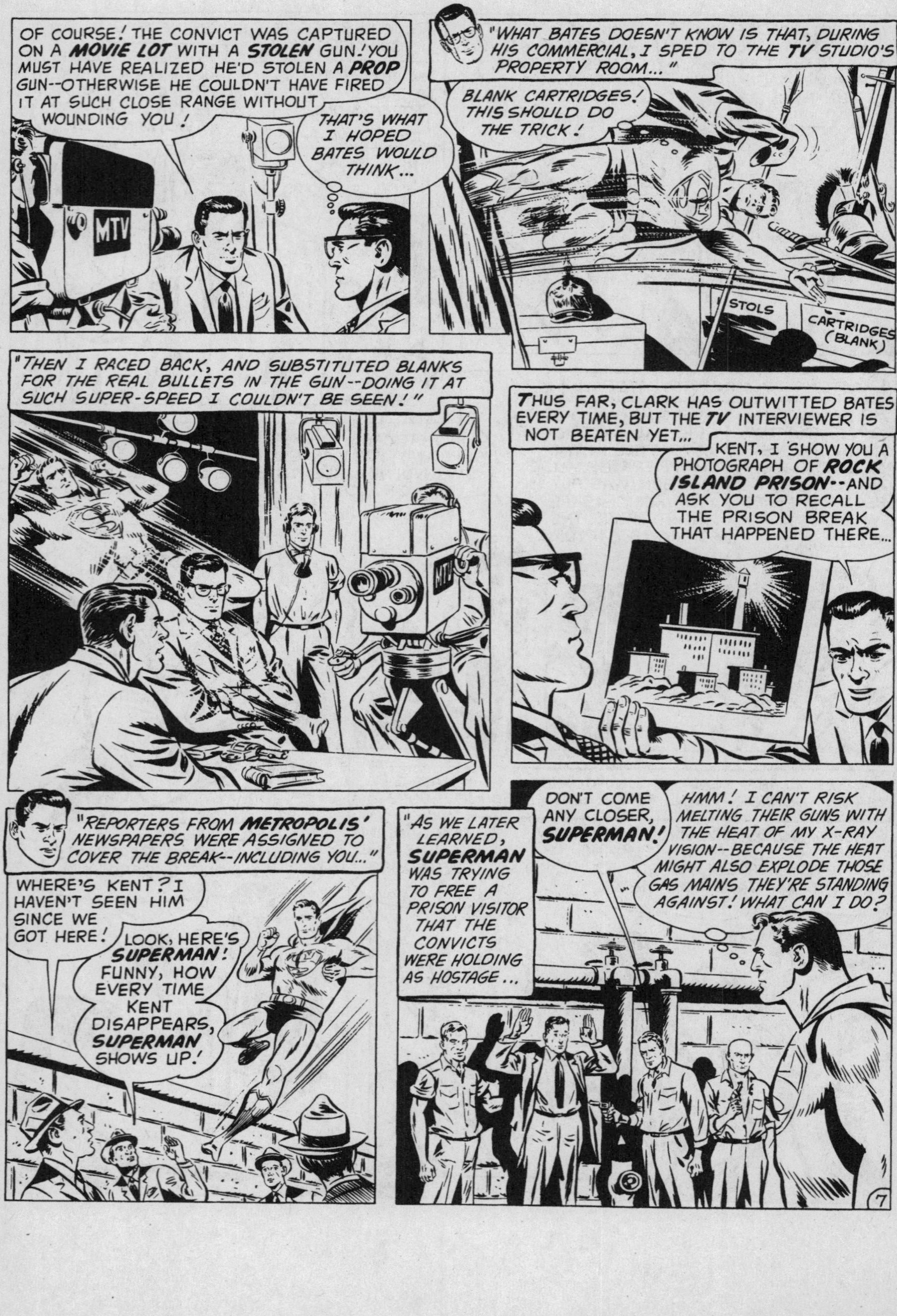
OF COURSE! THE CONVICT WAS CAPTURED ON A MOVIE LOT WITH A STOLEN GUN! YOU MUST HAVE REALIZED HE'D STOLEN A PROP GUN--OTHERWISE HE COULDN'T HAVE FIRED IT AT SUCH CLOSE RANGE WITHOUT WOUNDING YOU!
THAT'S WHAT I HOPED BATES WOULD THINK...
MTV
"WHAT BATES DOESN'T KNOW IS THAT, DURING HIS COMMERCIAL, I SPED TO THE TV STUDIO'S PROPERTY ROOM..."
BLANK CARTRIDGES! THIS SHOULD DO THE TRICK!
STOLS
CARTRIDGES (BLANK)
"THEN I RACED BACK, AND SUBSTITUTED BLANKS FOR THE REAL BULLETS IN THE GUN--DOING IT AT SUCH SUPER-SPEED I COULDN'T BE SEEN!"
MTV
THUS FAR, CLARK HAS OUTWITTED BATES EVERY TIME, BUT THE TV INTERVIEWER IS NOT BEATEN YET...
KENT, I SHOW YOU A PHOTOGRAPH OF ROCK ISLAND PRISON--AND ASK YOU TO RECALL THE PRISON BREAK THAT HAPPENED THERE...
"REPORTERS FROM METROPOLIS' NEWSPAPERS WERE ASSIGNED TO COVER THE BREAK--INCLUDING YOU..."
WHERE'S KENT? I HAVEN'T SEEN HIM SINCE WE GOT HERE!
LOOK, HERE'S SUPERMAN! FUNNY, HOW EVERY TIME KENT DISAPPEARS, SUPERMAN SHOWS UP!
"AS WE LATER LEARNED, SUPERMAN WAS TRYING TO FREE A PRISON VISITOR THAT THE CONVICTS WERE HOLDING AS HOSTAGE...
DON'T COME ANY CLOSER, SUPERMAN!
HMM! I CAN'T RISK MELTING THEIR GUNS WITH THE HEAT OF MY X-RAY VISION--BECAUSE THE HEAT MIGHT ALSO EXPLODE THOSE GAS MAINS THEY'RE STANDING AGAINST! WHAT CAN I DO?
7

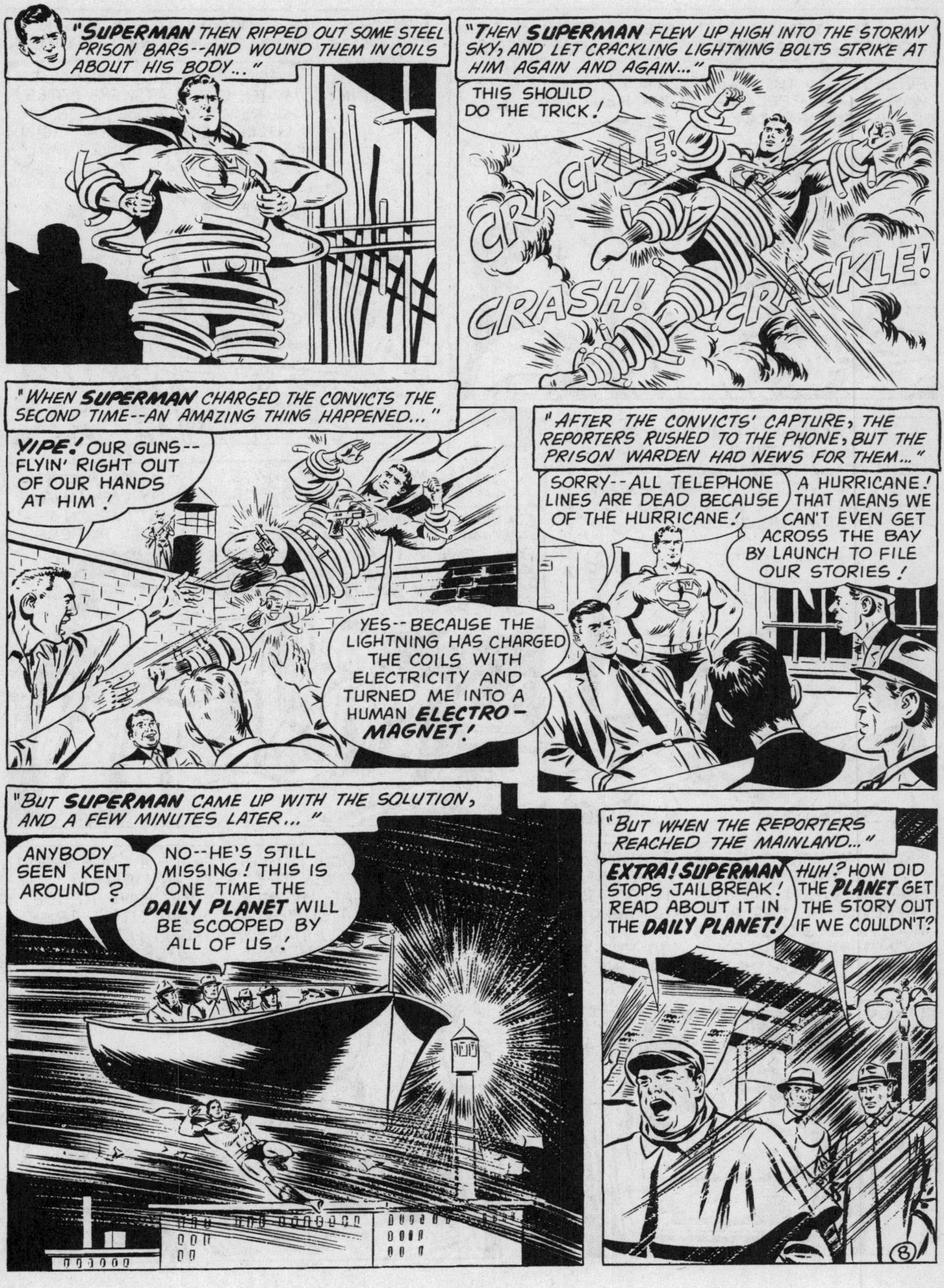
"SUPERMAN THEN RIPPED OUT SOME STEEL PRISON BARS--AND WOUND THEM IN COILS ABOUT HIS BODY..."
"THEN SUPERMAN FLEW UP HIGH INTO THE STORMY SKY, AND LET CRACKLING LIGHTNING BOLTS STRIKE AT HIM AGAIN AND AGAIN..."
THIS SHOULD DO THE TRICK!
CRACKLE!
CRASH!
CRACKLE!
"WHEN SUPERMAN CHARGED THE CONVICTS THE SECOND TIME--AN AMAZING THING HAPPENED..."
YIPE! OUR GUNS--FLYIN' RIGHT OUT OF OUR HANDS AT HIM!
YES--BECAUSE THE LIGHTNING HAS CHARGED THE COILS WITH ELECTRICITY AND TURNED ME INTO A HUMAN ELECTRO-MAGNET!
"AFTER THE CONVICTS' CAPTURE, THE REPORTERS RUSHED TO THE PHONE, BUT THE PRISON WARDEN HAD NEWS FOR THEM..."
SORRY--ALL TELEPHONE LINES ARE DEAD BECAUSE OF THE HURRICANE!
A HURRICANE! THAT MEANS WE CAN'T EVEN GET ACROSS THE BAY BY LAUNCH TO FILE OUR STORIES!
"BUT SUPERMAN CAME UP WITH THE SOLUTION, AND A FEW MINUTES LATER..."
ANYBODY SEEN KENT AROUND?
NO--HE'S STILL MISSING! THIS IS ONE TIME THE DAILY PLANET WILL BE SCOOPED BY ALL OF US!
"BUT WHEN THE REPORTERS REACHED THE MAINLAND..."
EXTRA! SUPERMAN STOPS JAILBREAK! READ ABOUT IT IN THE DAILY PLANET!
HUH? HOW DID THE PLANET GET THE STORY OUT IF WE COULDN'T?
8

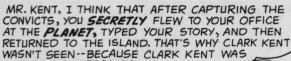

MR. KENT, I THINK THAT AFTER CAPTURING THE CONVICTS, YOU *SECRETLY* FLEW TO YOUR OFFICE AT THE *PLANET*, TYPED YOUR STORY, AND THEN RETURNED TO THE ISLAND. THAT'S WHY CLARK KENT WASN'T SEEN--BECAUSE CLARK KENT WAS BEING *SUPERMAN!*

UH-OH!

WATCHING THE PROGRAM, PERRY WHITE SUDDENLY BREAKS OUT INTO WILD LAUGHTER...

WHAT'S SO FUNNY?

HA! HA! YOU'LL FIND OUT WHEN CLARK ANSWERS BATES! YOU'RE ABOUT TO BE LET IN ON A LITTLE SECRET CLARK AND I HAVE KEPT FOR A LONG TIME! *HA! HA! HA!*

IF YOU CHECK WITH MY EDITOR, PERRY WHITE, YOU'LL LEARN THAT RIGHT AFTER THE JAILBREAK, WHITE WAS FIRST VISITED BY *SUPERMAN* WHO TOLD HIM HE WAS GOING TO TRY TO STOP THE JAILBREAK...

"SOON AFTER, MR. WHITE CALLED ME TO HIS OFFICE..."

CLARK, I'M GOING TO HAVE TWO NEWSPAPER HEADLINES READY TO ROLL! ONE WILL SAY--"*CONVICTS ESCAPE*"-- THE OTHER WILL SAY "*SUPERMAN STOPS JAILBREAK*"! UNDERSTAND?

SURE! THAT WAY WE'LL HAVE A JUMP ON OUR RIVAL PAPERS!

FROM MY WINDOW I CAN SEE THE PRISON BEACON! WHEN YOU GET THERE, DISAPPEAR AND WATCH FOR *SUPERMAN*-- AND THEN SIGNAL BY USING THE BEACON!

RIGHT! IF HE STOPS THE BREAK, I'LL BLOCK OUT THE LIGHT SOMEHOW--AND THAT WILL BE YOUR SIGNAL TO PUT THE RIGHT HEADLINE ON THE PAPER!

SO THAT'S HOW IT WAS DONE! BUT ONLY THE WARDEN HAS THE KEY TO THE BEACON TOWER! HOW DID YOU MANAGE TO GET UP THERE?

THAT'S A TRADE SECRET I CAN'T REVEAL! I MAY HAVE TO USE THAT LITTLE TRICK AGAIN FOR A FUTURE STORY!

9

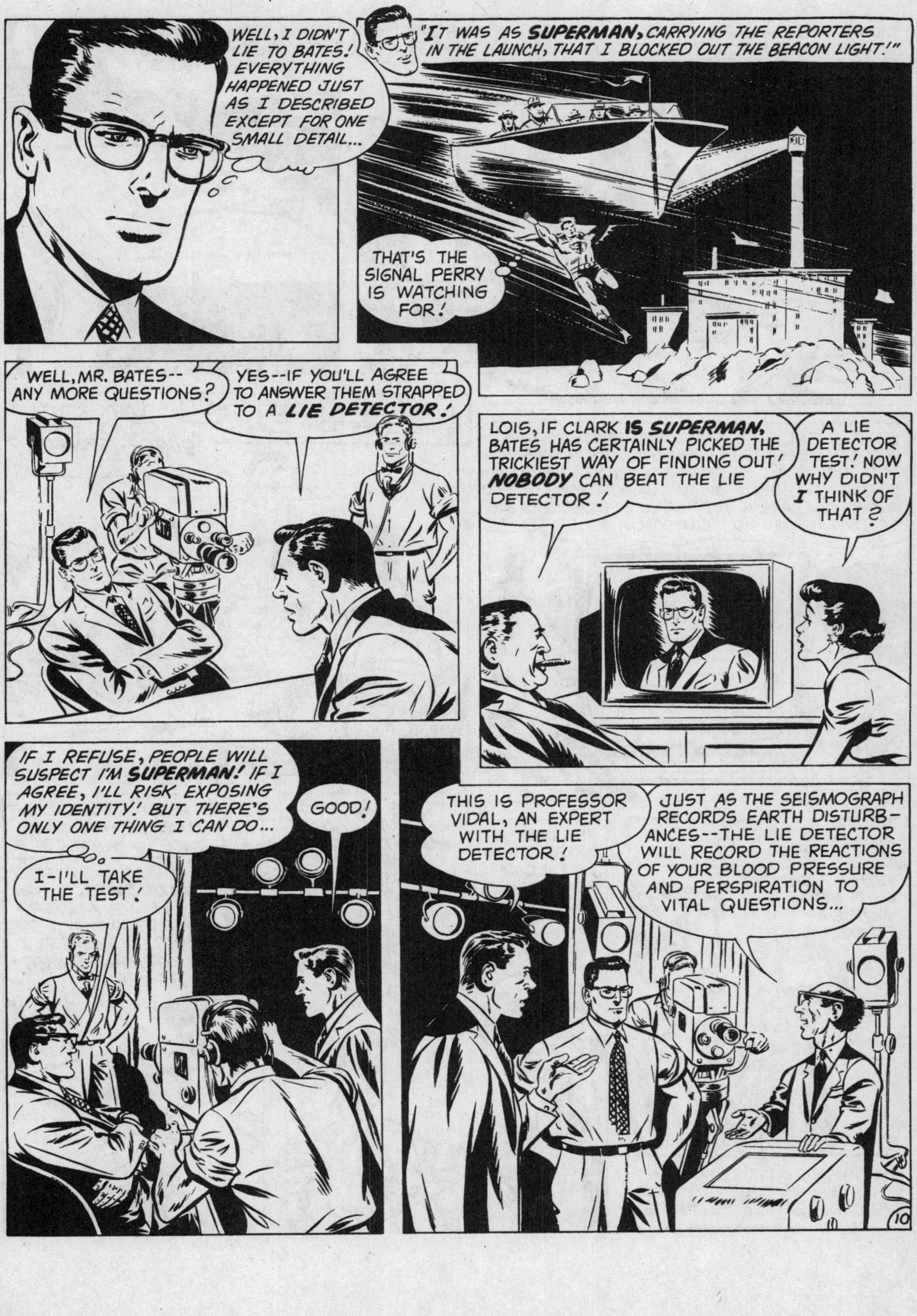
WELL, I DIDN'T LIE TO BATES! EVERYTHING HAPPENED JUST AS I DESCRIBED EXCEPT FOR ONE SMALL DETAIL...
"IT WAS AS SUPERMAN, CARRYING THE REPORTERS IN THE LAUNCH, THAT I BLOCKED OUT THE BEACON LIGHT!"
THAT'S THE SIGNAL PERRY IS WATCHING FOR!
WELL, MR. BATES-- ANY MORE QUESTIONS?
YES--IF YOU'LL AGREE TO ANSWER THEM STRAPPED TO A LIE DETECTOR!
LOIS, IF CLARK IS SUPERMAN, BATES HAS CERTAINLY PICKED THE TRICKIEST WAY OF FINDING OUT! NOBODY CAN BEAT THE LIE DETECTOR!
A LIE DETECTOR TEST! NOW WHY DIDN'T I THINK OF THAT?
IF I REFUSE, PEOPLE WILL SUSPECT I'M SUPERMAN! IF I AGREE, I'LL RISK EXPOSING MY IDENTITY! BUT THERE'S ONLY ONE THING I CAN DO...
I-I'LL TAKE THE TEST!
GOOD!
THIS IS PROFESSOR VIDAL, AN EXPERT WITH THE LIE DETECTOR!
JUST AS THE SEISMOGRAPH RECORDS EARTH DISTURB-ANCES--THE LIE DETECTOR WILL RECORD THE REACTIONS OF YOUR BLOOD PRESSURE AND PERSPIRATION TO VITAL QUESTIONS...
10

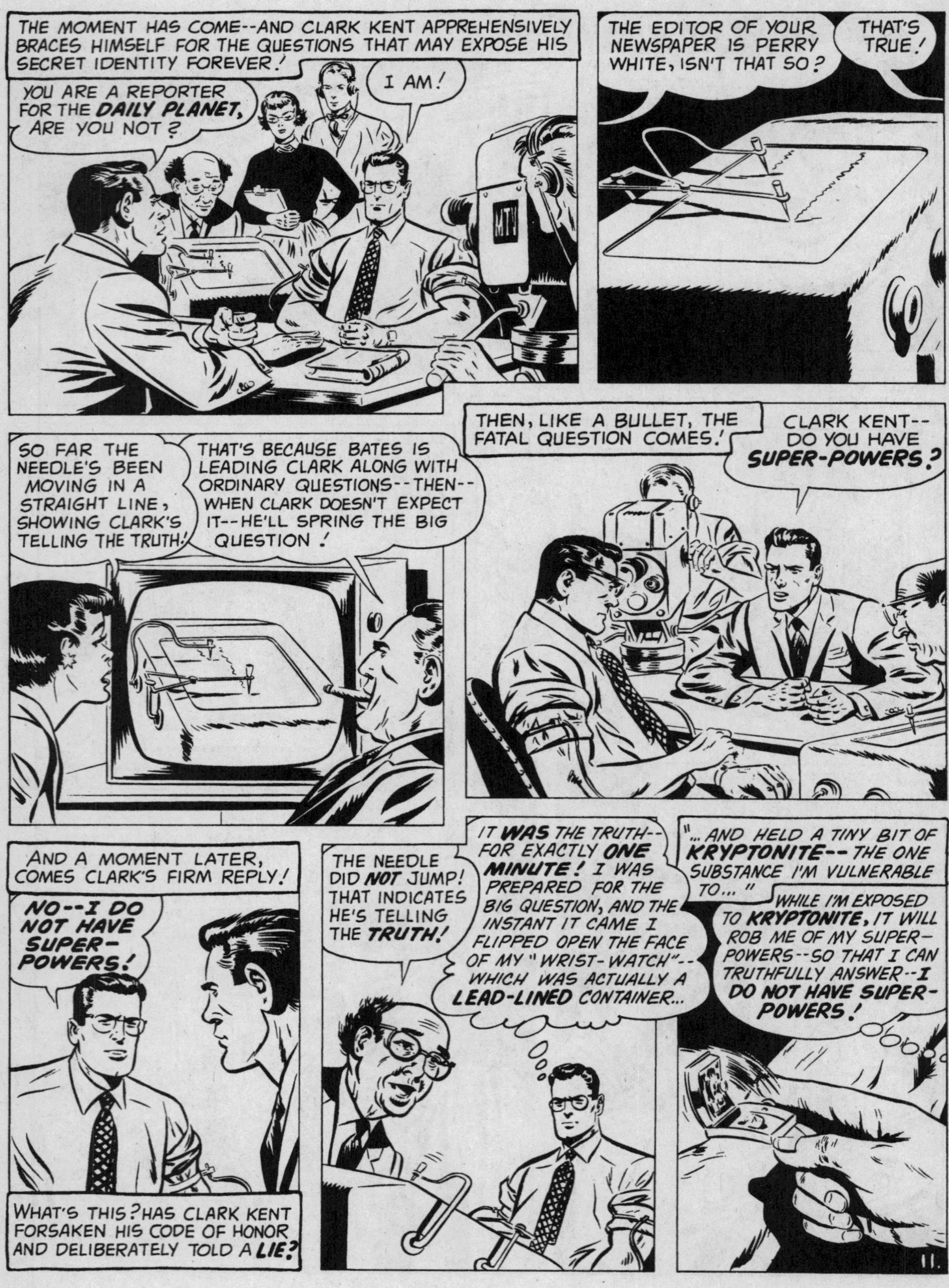
THE MOMENT HAS COME--AND CLARK KENT APPREHENSIVELY BRACES HIMSELF FOR THE QUESTIONS THAT MAY EXPOSE HIS SECRET IDENTITY FOREVER!
YOU ARE A REPORTER FOR THE DAILY PLANET, ARE YOU NOT?
I AM!
MTV
THE EDITOR OF YOUR NEWSPAPER IS PERRY WHITE, ISN'T THAT SO?
THAT'S TRUE!
SO FAR THE NEEDLE'S BEEN MOVING IN A STRAIGHT LINE, SHOWING CLARK'S TELLING THE TRUTH!
THAT'S BECAUSE BATES IS LEADING CLARK ALONG WITH ORDINARY QUESTIONS--THEN--WHEN CLARK DOESN'T EXPECT IT--HE'LL SPRING THE BIG QUESTION!
THEN, LIKE A BULLET, THE FATAL QUESTION COMES!
CLARK KENT--DO YOU HAVE SUPER-POWERS?
AND A MOMENT LATER, COMES CLARK'S FIRM REPLY!
NO--I DO NOT HAVE SUPER-POWERS!
WHAT'S THIS? HAS CLARK KENT FORSAKEN HIS CODE OF HONOR AND DELIBERATELY TOLD A LIE?
THE NEEDLE DID NOT JUMP! THAT INDICATES HE'S TELLING THE TRUTH!
IT WAS THE TRUTH--FOR EXACTLY ONE MINUTE! I WAS PREPARED FOR THE BIG QUESTION, AND THE INSTANT IT CAME I FLIPPED OPEN THE FACE OF MY "WRIST-WATCH"--WHICH WAS ACTUALLY A LEAD-LINED CONTAINER...
"...AND HELD A TINY BIT OF KRYPTONITE--THE ONE SUBSTANCE I'M VULNERABLE TO..."
WHILE I'M EXPOSED TO KRYPTONITE, IT WILL ROB ME OF MY SUPER-POWERS--SO THAT I CAN TRUTHFULLY ANSWER--I DO NOT HAVE SUPER-POWERS!
11.

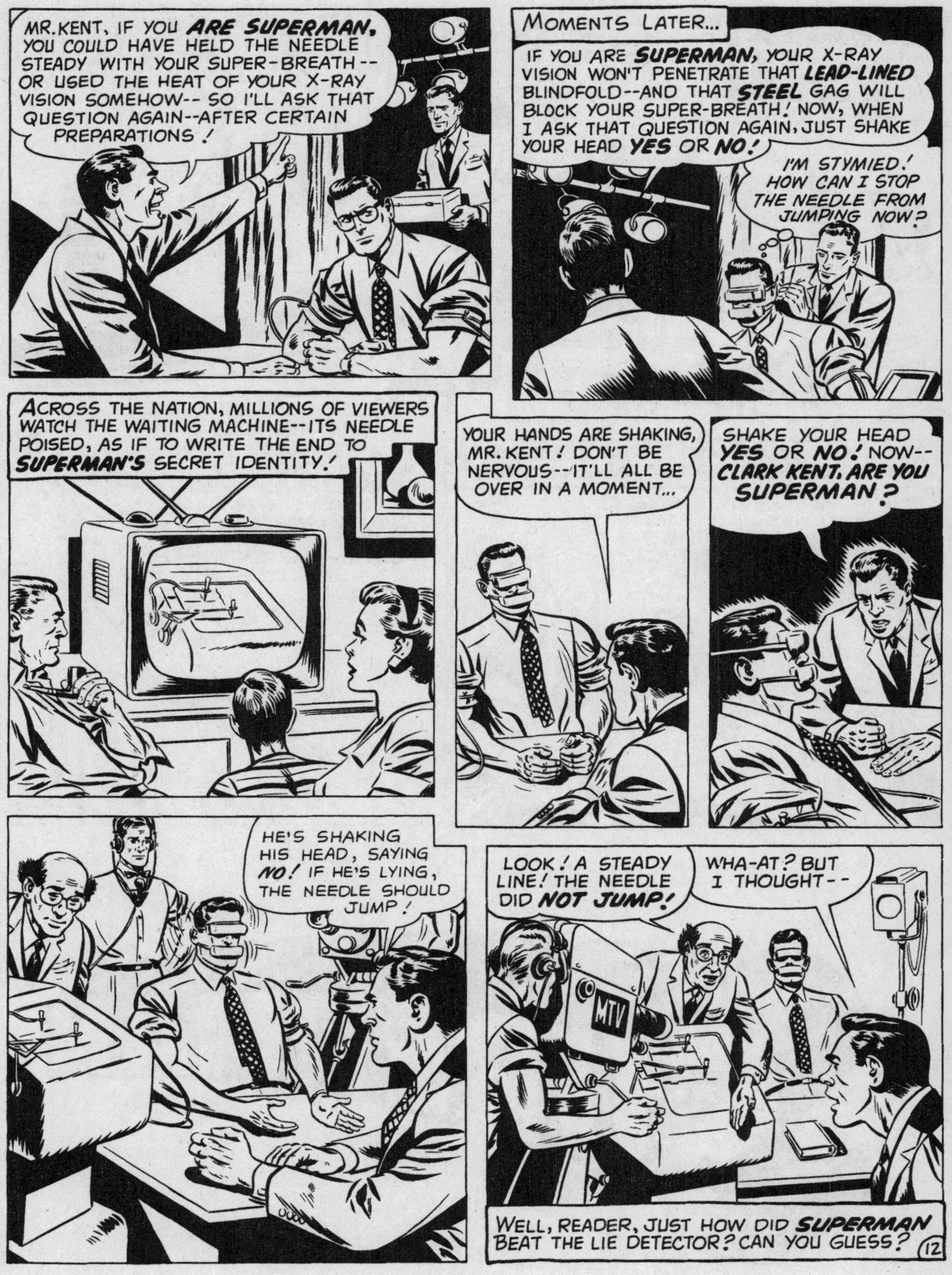
MR. KENT, IF YOU ARE SUPERMAN, YOU COULD HAVE HELD THE NEEDLE STEADY WITH YOUR SUPER-BREATH -- OR USED THE HEAT OF YOUR X-RAY VISION SOMEHOW-- SO I'LL ASK THAT QUESTION AGAIN--AFTER CERTAIN PREPARATIONS!
MOMENTS LATER...
IF YOU ARE SUPERMAN, YOUR X-RAY VISION WON'T PENETRATE THAT LEAD-LINED BLINDFOLD--AND THAT STEEL GAG WILL BLOCK YOUR SUPER-BREATH! NOW, WHEN I ASK THAT QUESTION AGAIN, JUST SHAKE YOUR HEAD YES OR NO!
I'M STYMIED! HOW CAN I STOP THE NEEDLE FROM JUMPING NOW?
ACROSS THE NATION, MILLIONS OF VIEWERS WATCH THE WAITING MACHINE--ITS NEEDLE POISED, AS IF TO WRITE THE END TO SUPERMAN'S SECRET IDENTITY!
YOUR HANDS ARE SHAKING, MR. KENT! DON'T BE NERVOUS--IT'LL ALL BE OVER IN A MOMENT...
SHAKE YOUR HEAD YES OR NO! NOW-- CLARK KENT, ARE YOU SUPERMAN?
HE'S SHAKING HIS HEAD, SAYING NO! IF HE'S LYING, THE NEEDLE SHOULD JUMP!
LOOK! A STEADY LINE! THE NEEDLE DID NOT JUMP!
WHA-AT? BUT I THOUGHT--
MTV
WELL, READER, JUST HOW DID SUPERMAN BEAT THE LIE DETECTOR? CAN YOU GUESS?
12

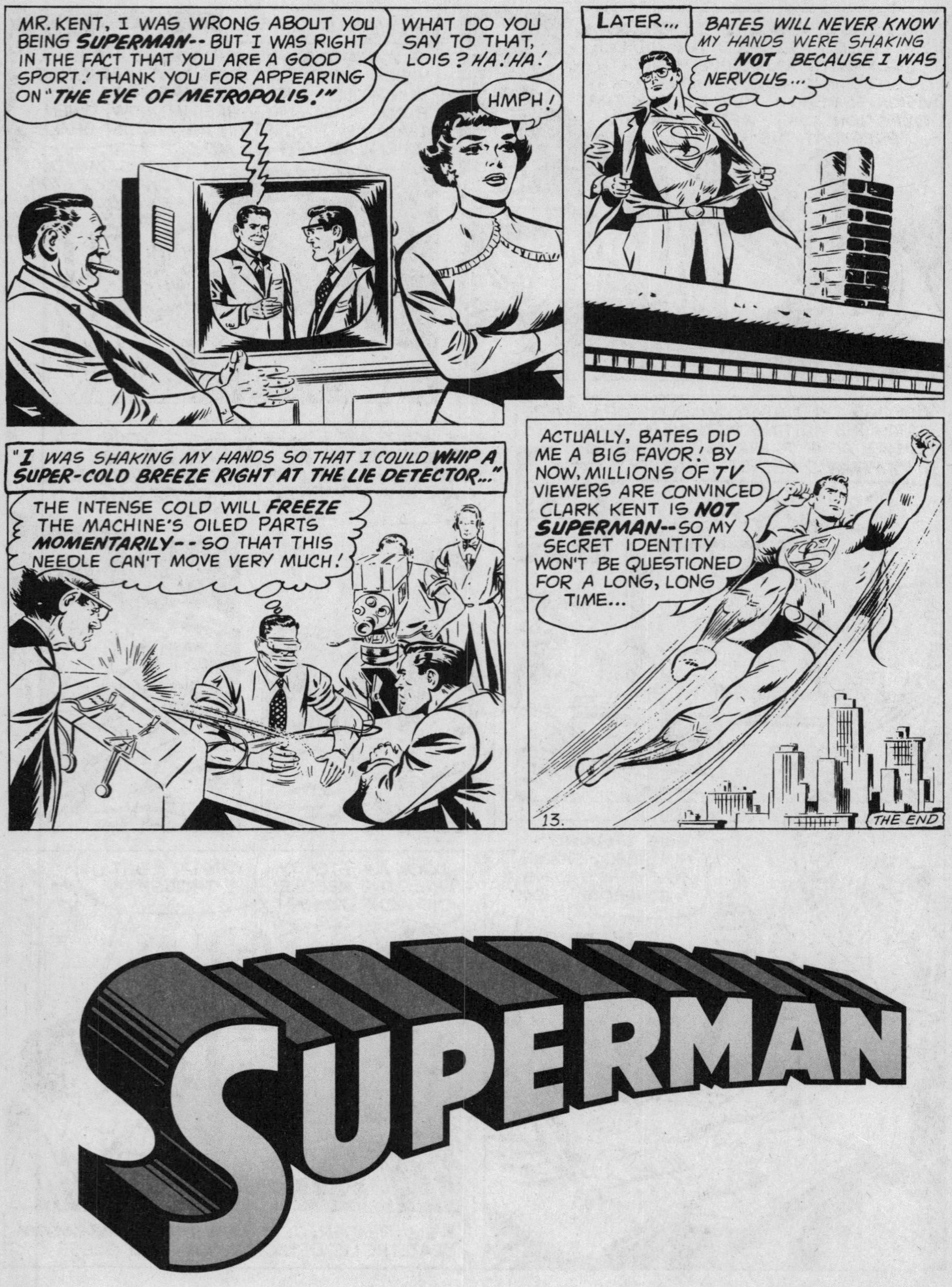
MR. KENT, I WAS WRONG ABOUT YOU BEING SUPERMAN-- BUT I WAS RIGHT IN THE FACT THAT YOU ARE A GOOD SPORT! THANK YOU FOR APPEARING ON "THE EYE OF METROPOLIS!"
WHAT DO YOU SAY TO THAT, LOIS? HA! HA!
HMPH!
LATER...
BATES WILL NEVER KNOW MY HANDS WERE SHAKING NOT BECAUSE I WAS NERVOUS...
"I WAS SHAKING MY HANDS SO THAT I COULD WHIP A SUPER-COLD BREEZE RIGHT AT THE LIE DETECTOR..."
THE INTENSE COLD WILL FREEZE THE MACHINE'S OILED PARTS MOMENTARILY-- SO THAT THIS NEEDLE CAN'T MOVE VERY MUCH!
ACTUALLY, BATES DID ME A BIG FAVOR! BY NOW, MILLIONS OF TV VIEWERS ARE CONVINCED CLARK KENT IS NOT SUPERMAN-- SO MY SECRET IDENTITY WON'T BE QUESTIONED FOR A LONG, LONG TIME...
13.
THE END

SUPERMAN

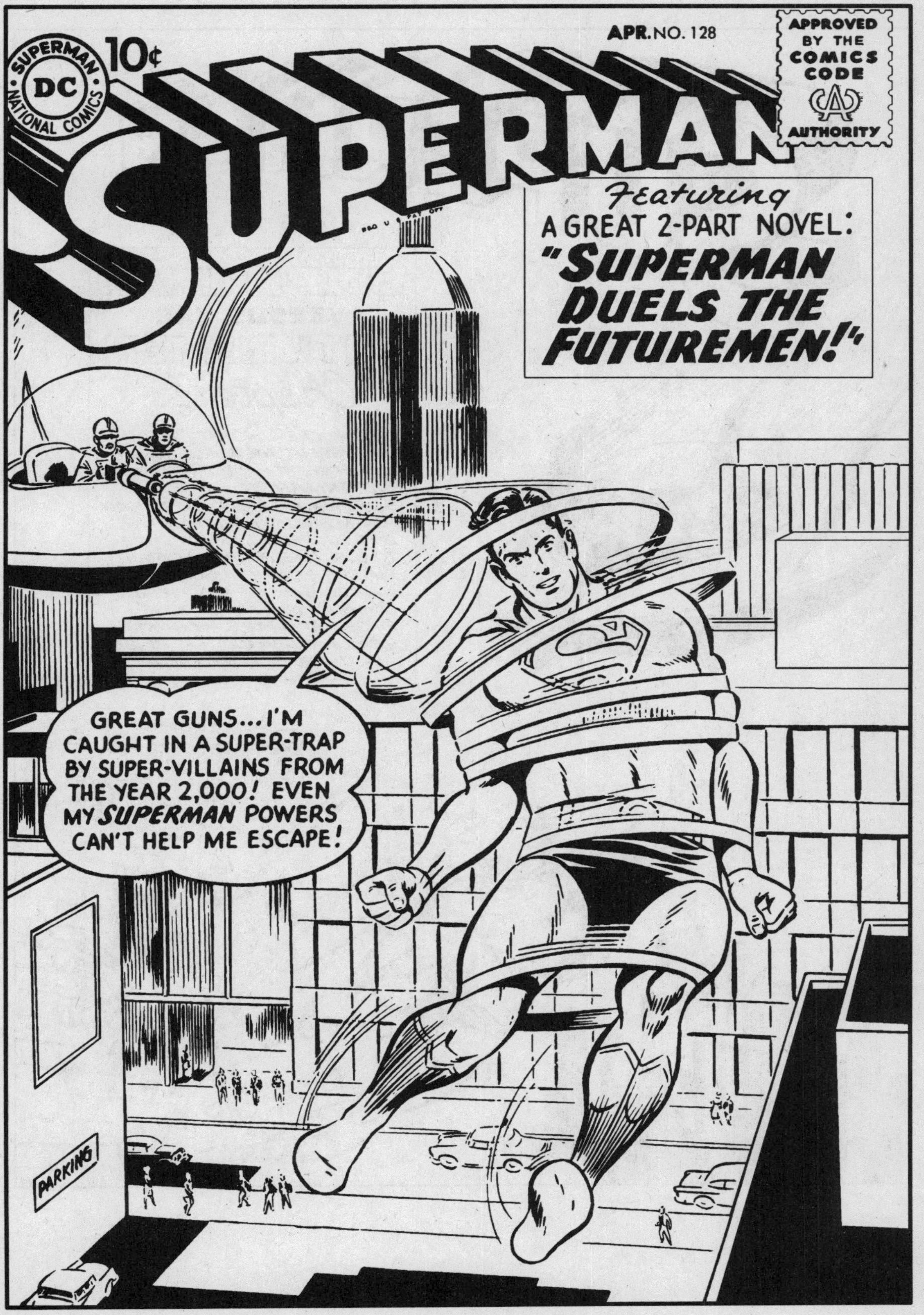

APR. NO. 128
10¢
SUPERMAN DC NATIONAL COMICS
APPROVED BY THE COMICS CODE AUTHORITY
SUPERMAN
Featuring
A GREAT 2-PART NOVEL:
"SUPERMAN DUELS THE FUTUREMEN!"
GREAT GUNS... I'M CAUGHT IN A SUPER-TRAP BY SUPER-VILLAINS FROM THE YEAR 2,000! EVEN MY SUPERMAN POWERS CAN'T HELP ME ESCAPE!
PARKING

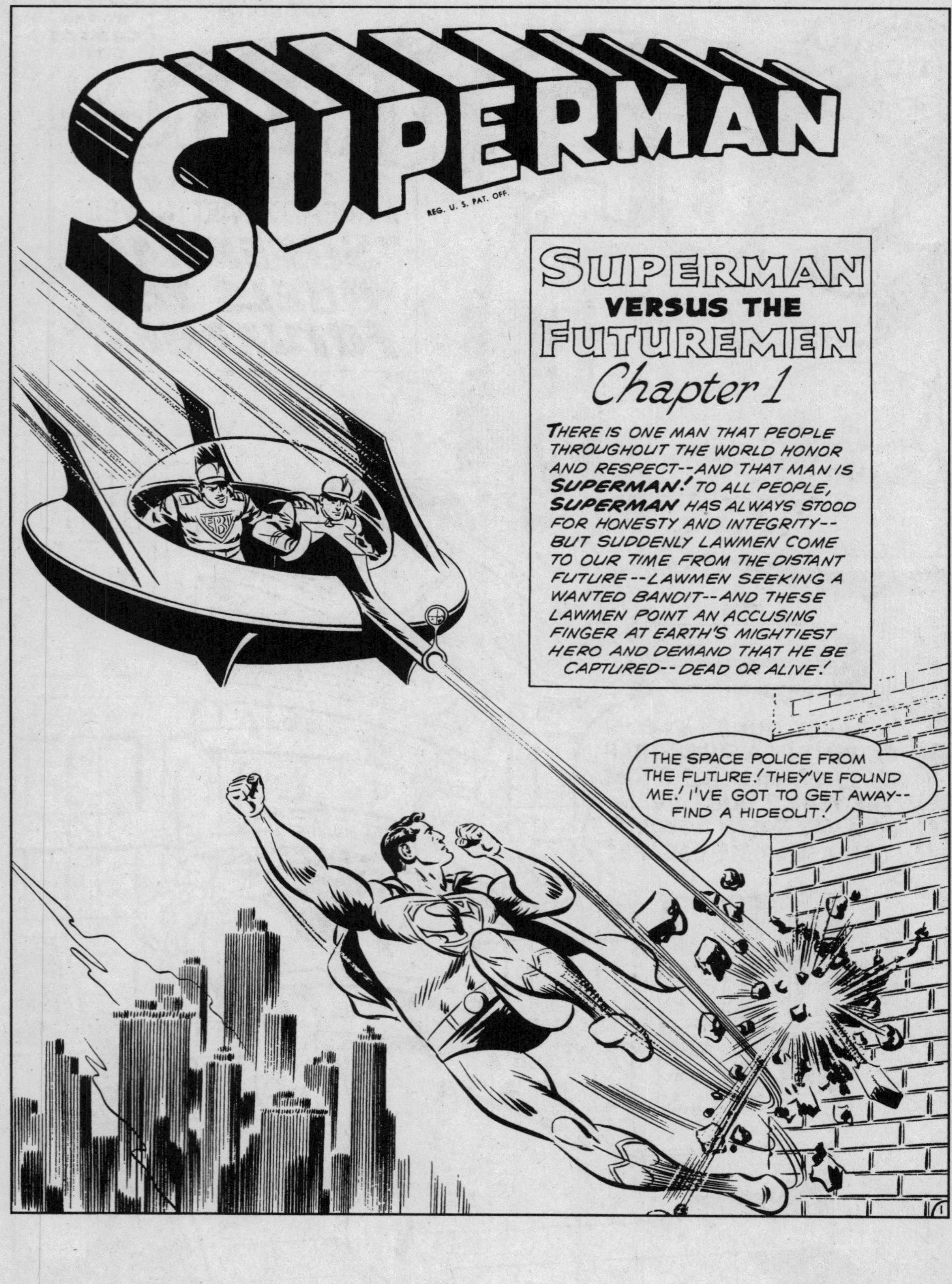
SUPERMAN
REG. U. S. PAT. OFF.
SUPERMAN VERSUS THE FUTUREMEN
Chapter 1
THERE IS ONE MAN THAT PEOPLE THROUGHOUT THE WORLD HONOR AND RESPECT--AND THAT MAN IS SUPERMAN! TO ALL PEOPLE, SUPERMAN HAS ALWAYS STOOD FOR HONESTY AND INTEGRITY--BUT SUDDENLY LAWMEN COME TO OUR TIME FROM THE DISTANT FUTURE--LAWMEN SEEKING A WANTED BANDIT--AND THESE LAWMEN POINT AN ACCUSING FINGER AT EARTH'S MIGHTIEST HERO AND DEMAND THAT HE BE CAPTURED--DEAD OR ALIVE!
THE SPACE POLICE FROM THE FUTURE! THEY'VE FOUND ME! I'VE GOT TO GET AWAY--FIND A HIDEOUT!

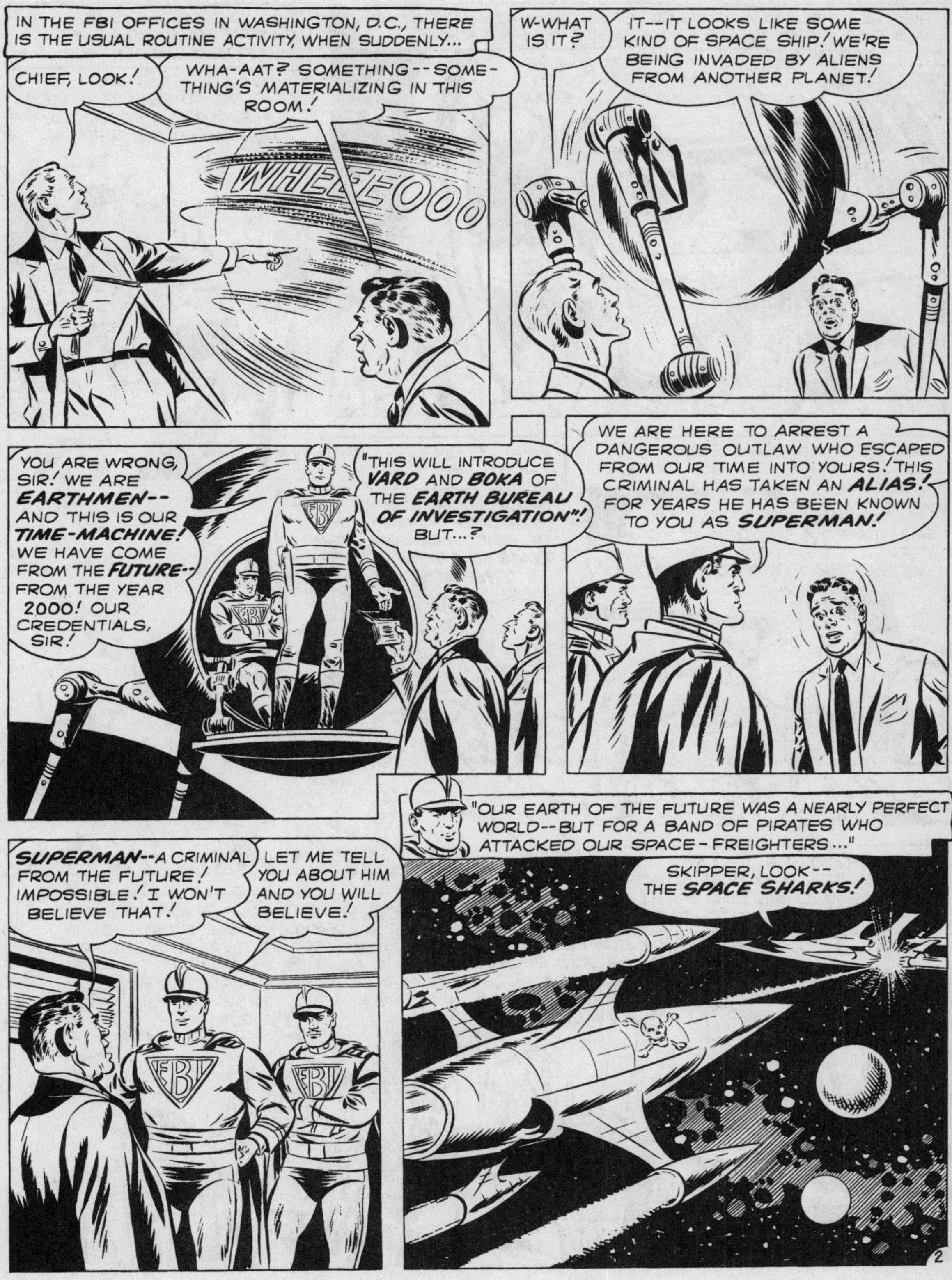
IN THE FBI OFFICES IN WASHINGTON, D.C., THERE IS THE USUAL ROUTINE ACTIVITY, WHEN SUDDENLY...
CHIEF, LOOK!
WHA-AAT? SOMETHING--SOMETHING'S MATERIALIZING IN THIS ROOM!
WHEEEOOO
W-WHAT IS IT?
IT--IT LOOKS LIKE SOME KIND OF SPACE SHIP! WE'RE BEING INVADED BY ALIENS FROM ANOTHER PLANET!
YOU ARE WRONG, SIR! WE ARE EARTHMEN--AND THIS IS OUR TIME-MACHINE! WE HAVE COME FROM THE FUTURE--FROM THE YEAR 2000! OUR CREDENTIALS, SIR!
"THIS WILL INTRODUCE VARD AND BOKA OF THE EARTH BUREAU OF INVESTIGATION"! BUT...?
WE ARE HERE TO ARREST A DANGEROUS OUTLAW WHO ESCAPED FROM OUR TIME INTO YOURS! THIS CRIMINAL HAS TAKEN AN ALIAS! FOR YEARS HE HAS BEEN KNOWN TO YOU AS SUPERMAN!
SUPERMAN--A CRIMINAL FROM THE FUTURE! IMPOSSIBLE! I WON'T BELIEVE THAT!
LET ME TELL YOU ABOUT HIM AND YOU WILL BELIEVE!
"OUR EARTH OF THE FUTURE WAS A NEARLY PERFECT WORLD--BUT FOR A BAND OF PIRATES WHO ATTACKED OUR SPACE-FREIGHTERS..."
SKIPPER, LOOK--THE SPACE SHARKS!
2

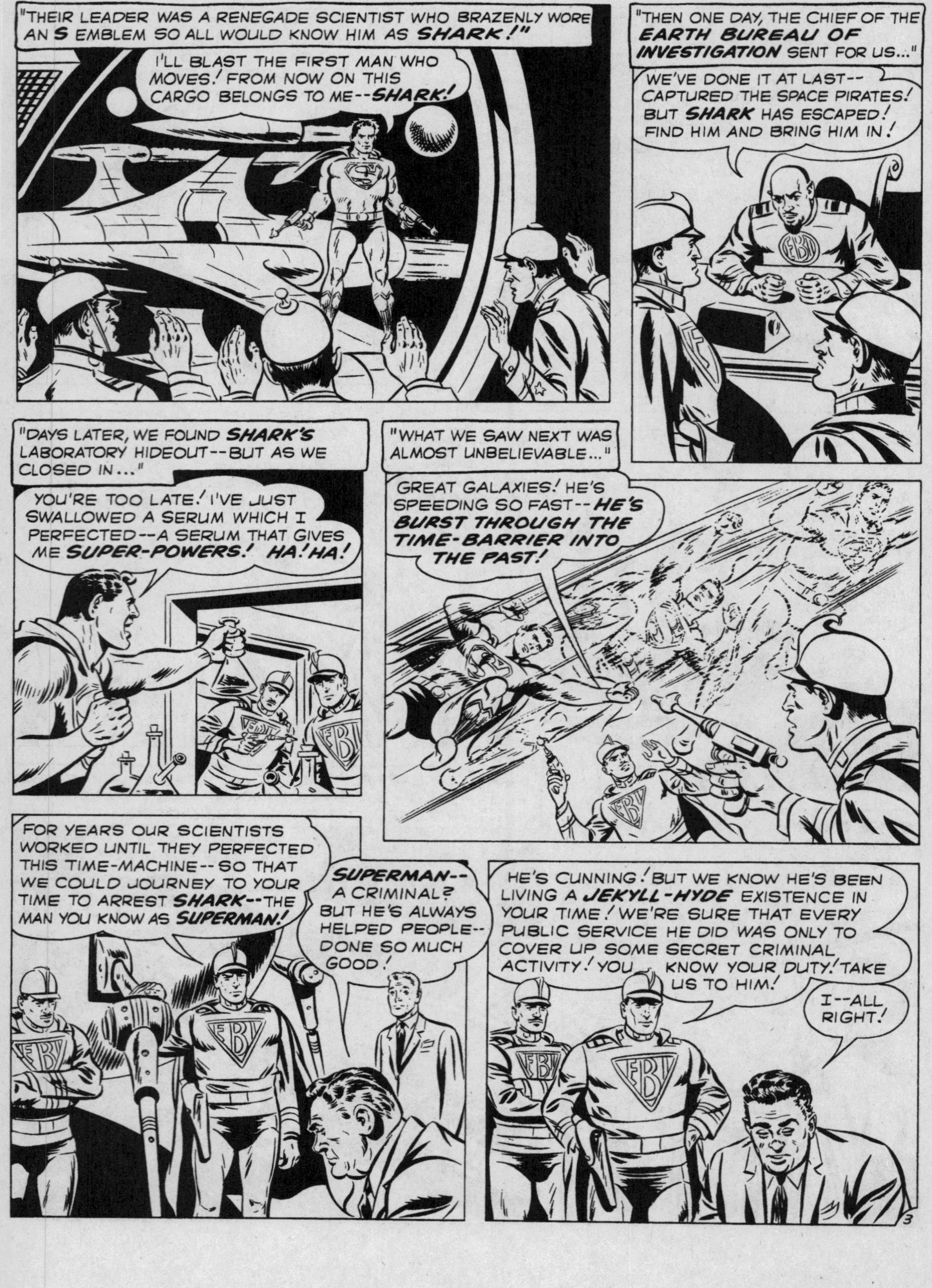
"THEIR LEADER WAS A RENEGADE SCIENTIST WHO BRAZENLY WORE AN S EMBLEM SO ALL WOULD KNOW HIM AS SHARK!"
I'LL BLAST THE FIRST MAN WHO MOVES! FROM NOW ON THIS CARGO BELONGS TO ME--SHARK!
"THEN ONE DAY, THE CHIEF OF THE EARTH BUREAU OF INVESTIGATION SENT FOR US..."
WE'VE DONE IT AT LAST--CAPTURED THE SPACE PIRATES! BUT SHARK HAS ESCAPED! FIND HIM AND BRING HIM IN!
"DAYS LATER, WE FOUND SHARK'S LABORATORY HIDEOUT--BUT AS WE CLOSED IN..."
YOU'RE TOO LATE! I'VE JUST SWALLOWED A SERUM WHICH I PERFECTED--A SERUM THAT GIVES ME SUPER-POWERS! HA! HA!
"WHAT WE SAW NEXT WAS ALMOST UNBELIEVABLE..."
GREAT GALAXIES! HE'S SPEEDING SO FAST--HE'S BURST THROUGH THE TIME-BARRIER INTO THE PAST!
FOR YEARS OUR SCIENTISTS WORKED UNTIL THEY PERFECTED THIS TIME-MACHINE--SO THAT WE COULD JOURNEY TO YOUR TIME TO ARREST SHARK--THE MAN YOU KNOW AS SUPERMAN!
SUPERMAN--A CRIMINAL? BUT HE'S ALWAYS HELPED PEOPLE--DONE SO MUCH GOOD!
HE'S CUNNING! BUT WE KNOW HE'S BEEN LIVING A JEKYLL-HYDE EXISTENCE IN YOUR TIME! WE'RE SURE THAT EVERY PUBLIC SERVICE HE DID WAS ONLY TO COVER UP SOME SECRET CRIMINAL ACTIVITY! YOU KNOW YOUR DUTY! TAKE US TO HIM!
I--ALL RIGHT!
3

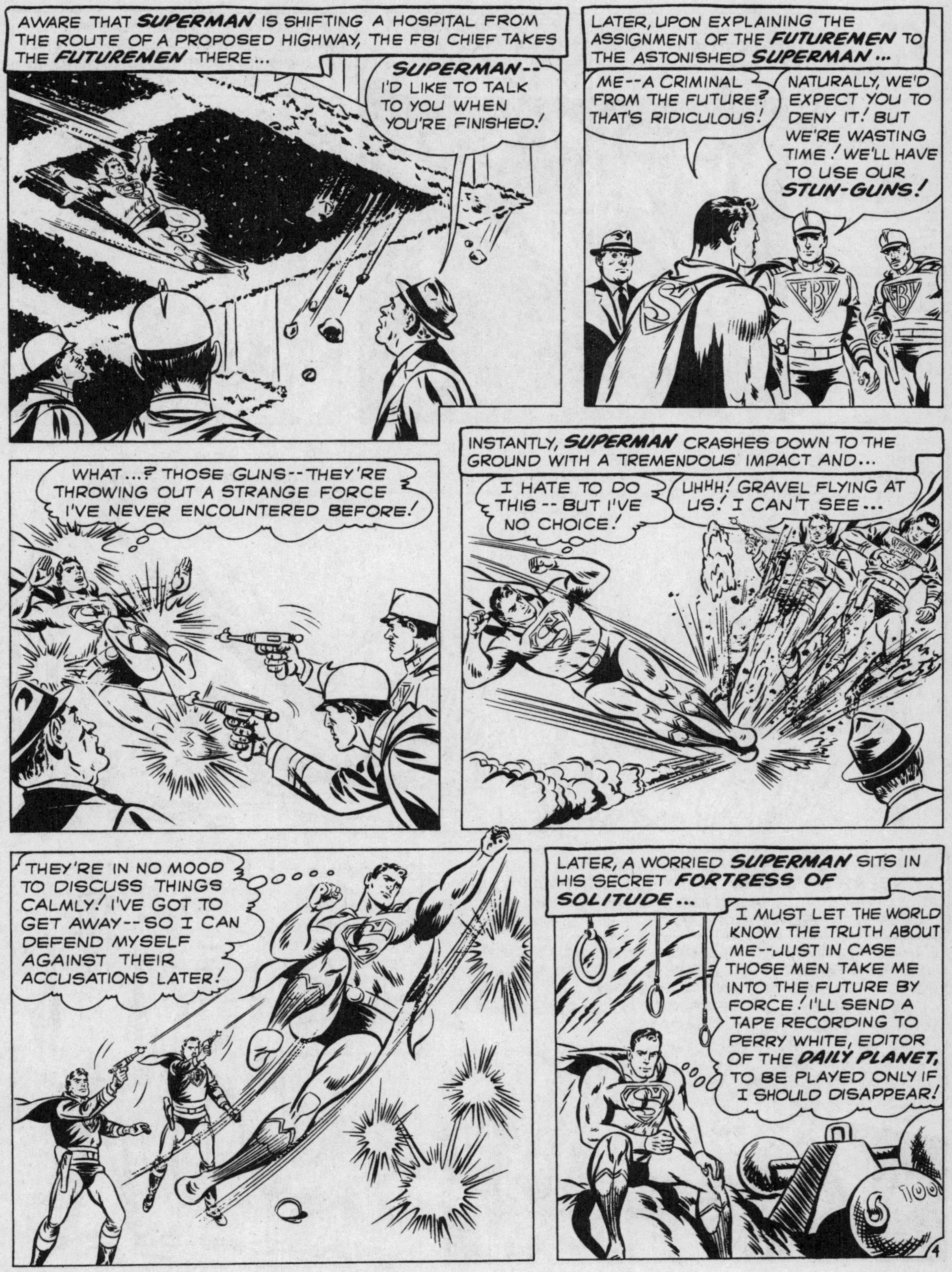
AWARE THAT SUPERMAN IS SHIFTING A HOSPITAL FROM THE ROUTE OF A PROPOSED HIGHWAY, THE FBI CHIEF TAKES THE FUTUREMEN THERE...
SUPERMAN-- I'D LIKE TO TALK TO YOU WHEN YOU'RE FINISHED!
LATER, UPON EXPLAINING THE ASSIGNMENT OF THE FUTUREMEN TO THE ASTONISHED SUPERMAN...
ME--A CRIMINAL FROM THE FUTURE? THAT'S RIDICULOUS!
NATURALLY, WE'D EXPECT YOU TO DENY IT! BUT WE'RE WASTING TIME! WE'LL HAVE TO USE OUR STUN-GUNS!
WHAT...? THOSE GUNS--THEY'RE THROWING OUT A STRANGE FORCE I'VE NEVER ENCOUNTERED BEFORE!
INSTANTLY, SUPERMAN CRASHES DOWN TO THE GROUND WITH A TREMENDOUS IMPACT AND...
I HATE TO DO THIS--BUT I'VE NO CHOICE!
UHHH! GRAVEL FLYING AT US! I CAN'T SEE...
THEY'RE IN NO MOOD TO DISCUSS THINGS CALMLY! I'VE GOT TO GET AWAY--SO I CAN DEFEND MYSELF AGAINST THEIR ACCUSATIONS LATER!
LATER, A WORRIED SUPERMAN SITS IN HIS SECRET FORTRESS OF SOLITUDE...
I MUST LET THE WORLD KNOW THE TRUTH ABOUT ME--JUST IN CASE THOSE MEN TAKE ME INTO THE FUTURE BY FORCE! I'LL SEND A TAPE RECORDING TO PERRY WHITE, EDITOR OF THE DAILY PLANET, TO BE PLAYED ONLY IF I SHOULD DISAPPEAR!
100
4

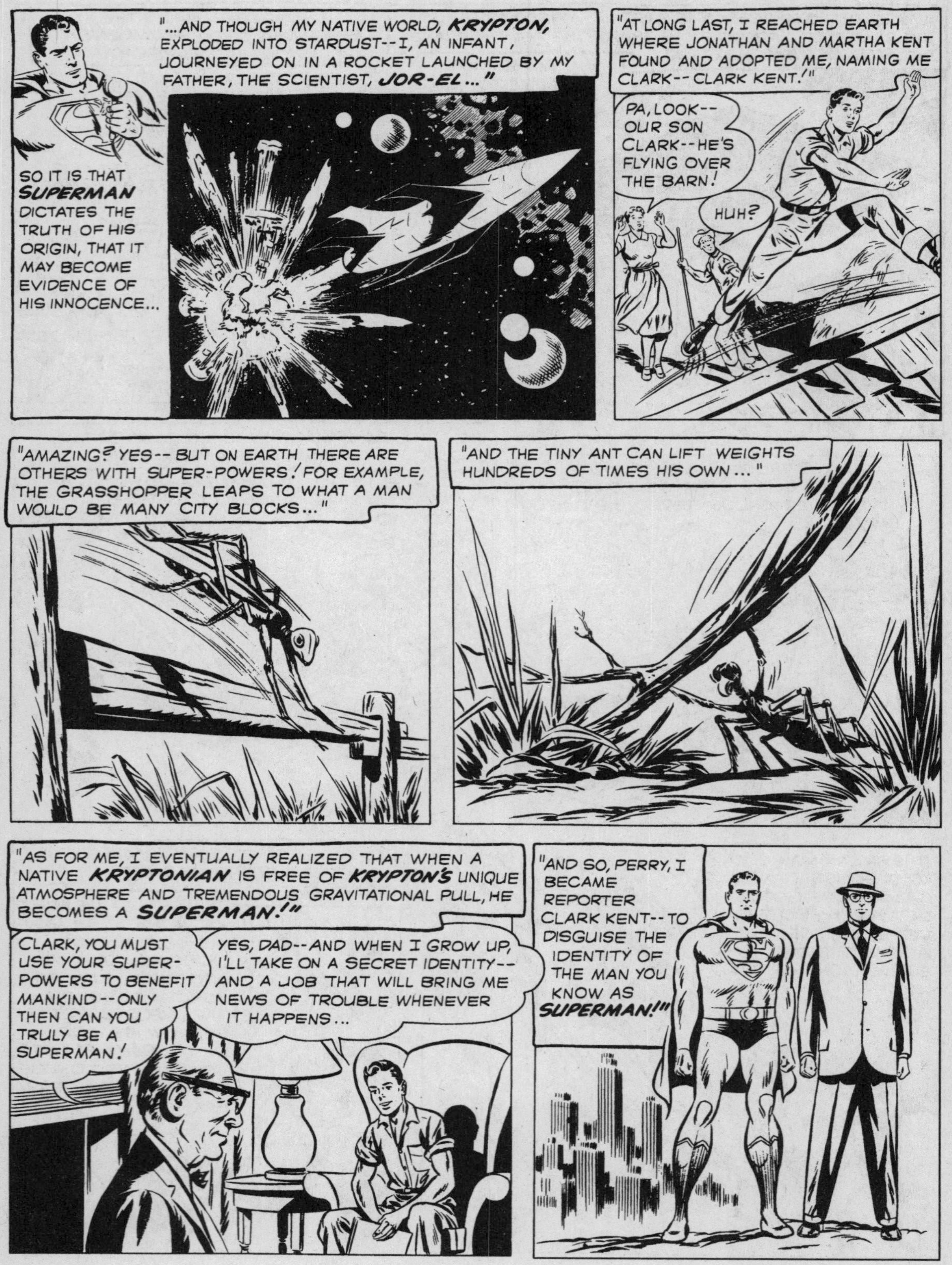
"...AND THOUGH MY NATIVE WORLD, KRYPTON, EXPLODED INTO STARDUST--I, AN INFANT, JOURNEYED ON IN A ROCKET LAUNCHED BY MY FATHER, THE SCIENTIST, JOR-EL..."
SO IT IS THAT SUPERMAN DICTATES THE TRUTH OF HIS ORIGIN, THAT IT MAY BECOME EVIDENCE OF HIS INNOCENCE...
"AT LONG LAST, I REACHED EARTH WHERE JONATHAN AND MARTHA KENT FOUND AND ADOPTED ME, NAMING ME CLARK--CLARK KENT!"
PA, LOOK--OUR SON CLARK--HE'S FLYING OVER THE BARN!
HUH?
"AMAZING? YES--BUT ON EARTH THERE ARE OTHERS WITH SUPER-POWERS! FOR EXAMPLE, THE GRASSHOPPER LEAPS TO WHAT A MAN WOULD BE MANY CITY BLOCKS..."
"AND THE TINY ANT CAN LIFT WEIGHTS HUNDREDS OF TIMES HIS OWN..."
"AS FOR ME, I EVENTUALLY REALIZED THAT WHEN A NATIVE KRYPTONIAN IS FREE OF KRYPTON'S UNIQUE ATMOSPHERE AND TREMENDOUS GRAVITATIONAL PULL, HE BECOMES A SUPERMAN!"
CLARK, YOU MUST USE YOUR SUPER-POWERS TO BENEFIT MANKIND--ONLY THEN CAN YOU TRULY BE A SUPERMAN!
YES, DAD--AND WHEN I GROW UP, I'LL TAKE ON A SECRET IDENTITY--AND A JOB THAT WILL BRING ME NEWS OF TROUBLE WHENEVER IT HAPPENS...
"AND SO, PERRY, I BECAME REPORTER CLARK KENT--TO DISGUISE THE IDENTITY OF THE MAN YOU KNOW AS SUPERMAN!"

UPON RECORDING HIS ORIGIN, *SUPERMAN* RACES TO THE *DAILY PLANET,* WHERE HE ASKS A PROMISE OF EDITOR PERRY WHITE AND REPORTER LOIS LANE ...

I PROMISE, *SUPERMAN*-- I'LL PLAY THIS TAPE *ONLY* IF YOU'RE TAKEN INTO THE FUTURE! WHAT ARE YOUR PLANS NOW?

I--I DON'T KNOW! I'VE NEVER BEEN IN THIS KIND OF SITUATION BEFORE!

MEANWHILE, IN A SPECIAL TV BROADCAST, THE *FUTUREMEN* MAKE THEIR ACCUSATIONS KNOWN TO A STUNNED PUBLIC ...

...THEREFORE, IT IS THE DUTY OF ANY CITIZEN WHO KNOWS THE WHEREABOUTS OF *SUPERMAN* TO NOTIFY THE POLICE AT ONCE!

DADDY, IT'S NOT TRUE WHAT THEY'RE SAYING ABOUT *SUPERMAN,* IS IT? ;SOB; IS IT?

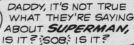

LATER, A HORRIFIED *SUPERMAN* FINDS HIMSELF BRANDED *PUBLIC ENEMY NUMBER ONE*...

WANTED!

SUPERMAN

CAUTION: THIS MAN IS DANGEROUS!

EVERYWHERE *SUPERMAN* GOES, HE IS A HUNTED MAN, ON LAND OR IN THE SKY...

CALLING BASE! HAVE SIGHTED *SUPERMAN,* BUT OUR JETS CAN'T CATCH HIM!

LATER, IN THE FBI OFFICE ...

WE KNEW YOU'D NEVER CAPTURE *SUPERMAN*--SO WE BROUGHT THE CONTENTS OF THIS BOX FROM THE FUTURE! YOU KNOW ABOUT *KRYPTONITE?*

THE ONE SUBSTANCE THAT CAN DESTROY *SUPERMAN'S* INVULNER- ABILITY? I'VE GOT GEOLOGISTS SEARCHING FOR SOME, BUT THAT GREEN STUFF IS VERY RARE!

NOT SO RARE AS *RED KRYPTONITE* THAT OUR SCIENTISTS HAVE DISCOVERED IN THE FUTURE!

6

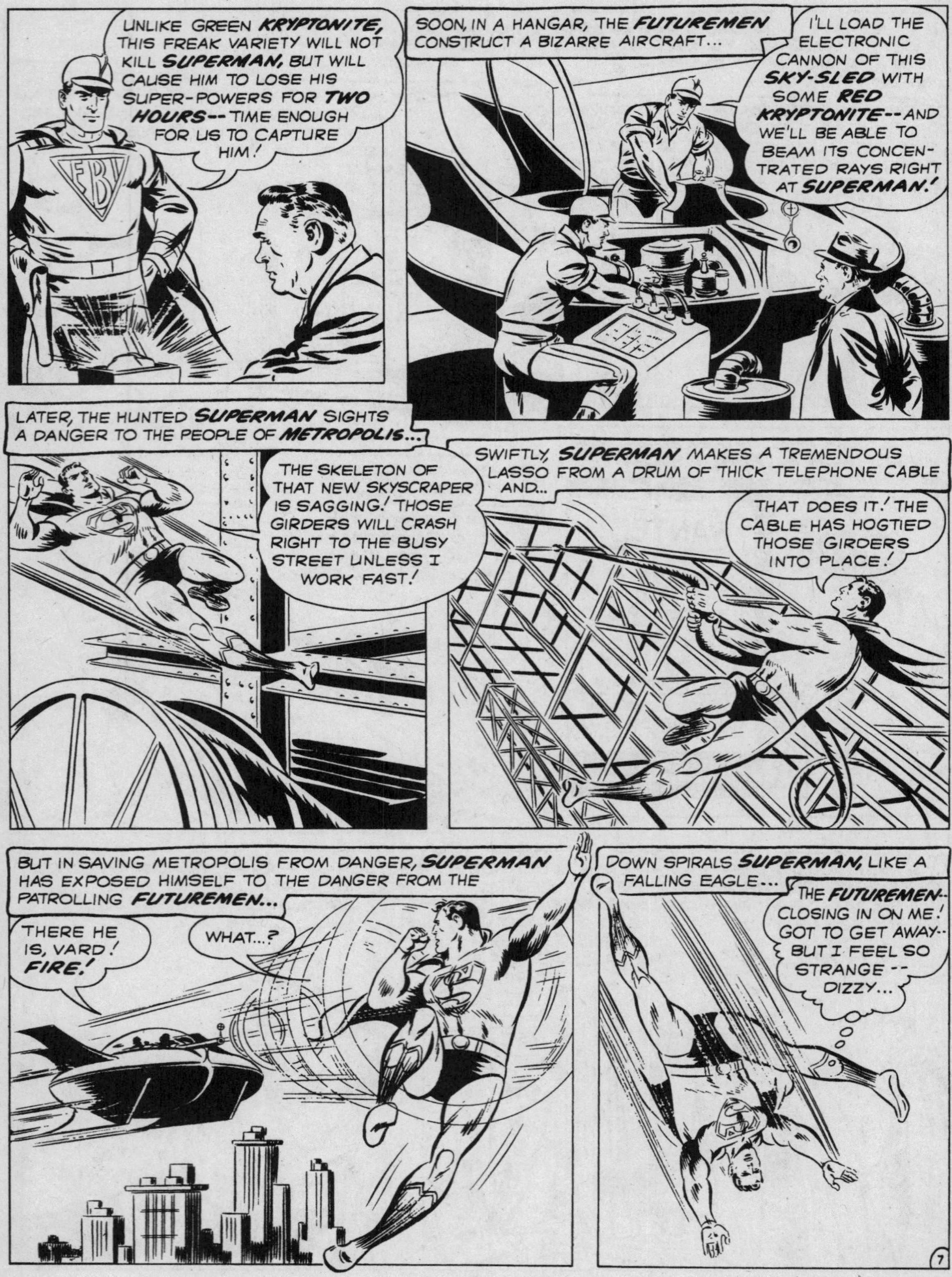

UNLIKE GREEN KRYPTONITE, THIS FREAK VARIETY WILL NOT KILL SUPERMAN, BUT WILL CAUSE HIM TO LOSE HIS SUPER-POWERS FOR TWO HOURS-- TIME ENOUGH FOR US TO CAPTURE HIM!
SOON, IN A HANGAR, THE FUTUREMEN CONSTRUCT A BIZARRE AIRCRAFT...
I'LL LOAD THE ELECTRONIC CANNON OF THIS SKY-SLED WITH SOME RED KRYPTONITE--AND WE'LL BE ABLE TO BEAM ITS CONCENTRATED RAYS RIGHT AT SUPERMAN!
LATER, THE HUNTED SUPERMAN SIGHTS A DANGER TO THE PEOPLE OF METROPOLIS...
THE SKELETON OF THAT NEW SKYSCRAPER IS SAGGING! THOSE GIRDERS WILL CRASH RIGHT TO THE BUSY STREET UNLESS I WORK FAST!
SWIFTLY, SUPERMAN MAKES A TREMENDOUS LASSO FROM A DRUM OF THICK TELEPHONE CABLE AND...
THAT DOES IT! THE CABLE HAS HOGTIED THOSE GIRDERS INTO PLACE!
BUT IN SAVING METROPOLIS FROM DANGER, SUPERMAN HAS EXPOSED HIMSELF TO THE DANGER FROM THE PATROLLING FUTUREMEN...
THERE HE IS, VARD! FIRE!
WHAT...?
DOWN SPIRALS SUPERMAN, LIKE A FALLING EAGLE...
THE FUTUREMEN-- CLOSING IN ON ME! GOT TO GET AWAY-- BUT I FEEL SO STRANGE -- DIZZY...
7

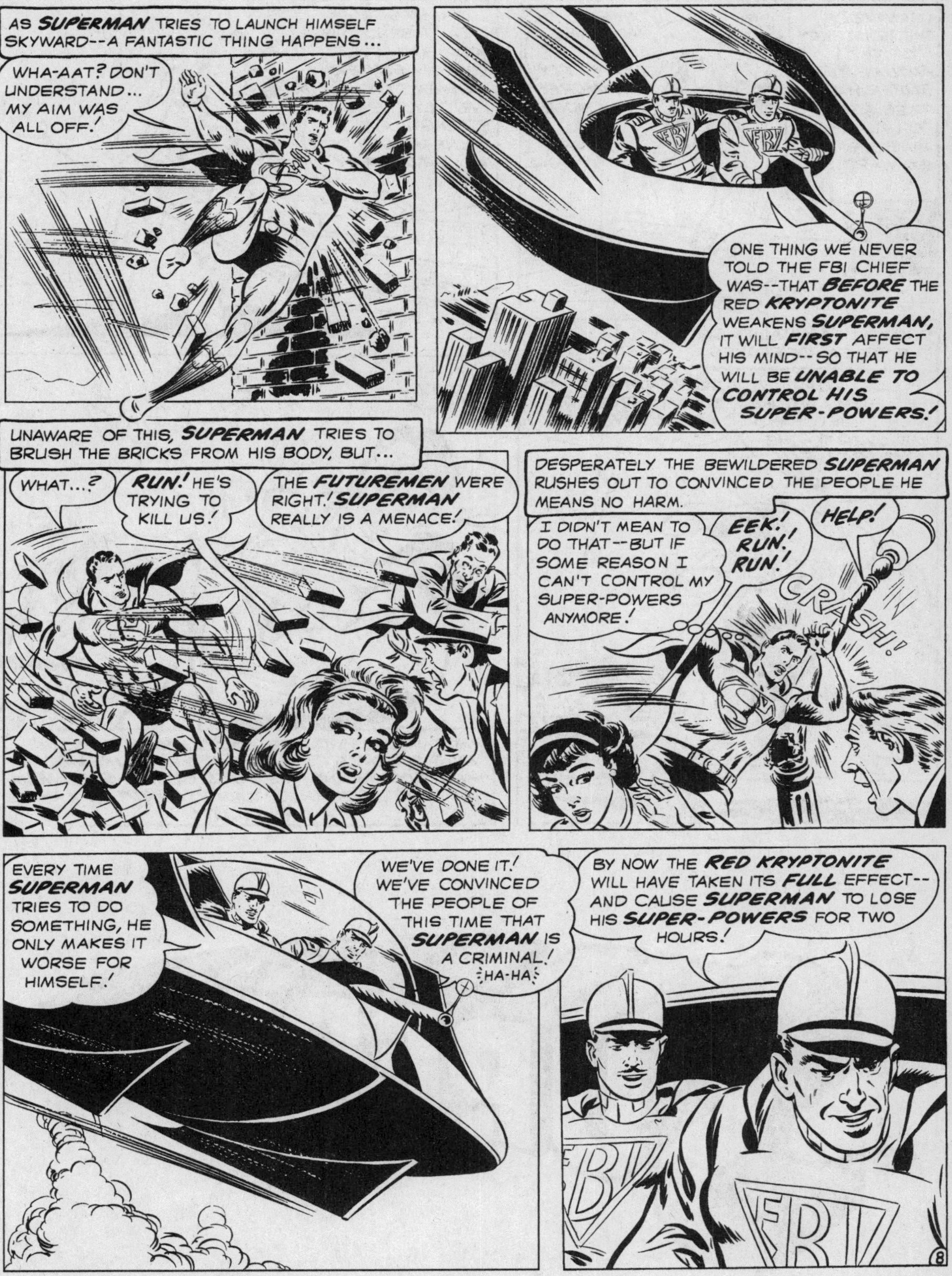
AS SUPERMAN TRIES TO LAUNCH HIMSELF SKYWARD--A FANTASTIC THING HAPPENS...
WHA-AAT? DON'T UNDERSTAND... MY AIM WAS ALL OFF!
ONE THING WE NEVER TOLD THE FBI CHIEF WAS--THAT BEFORE THE RED KRYPTONITE WEAKENS SUPERMAN, IT WILL FIRST AFFECT HIS MIND--SO THAT HE WILL BE UNABLE TO CONTROL HIS SUPER-POWERS!
UNAWARE OF THIS, SUPERMAN TRIES TO BRUSH THE BRICKS FROM HIS BODY, BUT...
WHAT...?
RUN! HE'S TRYING TO KILL US!
THE FUTUREMEN WERE RIGHT! SUPERMAN REALLY IS A MENACE!
DESPERATELY THE BEWILDERED SUPERMAN RUSHES OUT TO CONVINCED THE PEOPLE HE MEANS NO HARM.
I DIDN'T MEAN TO DO THAT--BUT IF SOME REASON I CAN'T CONTROL MY SUPER-POWERS ANYMORE!
EEK! RUN! RUN!
HELP!
CRASH!
EVERY TIME SUPERMAN TRIES TO DO SOMETHING, HE ONLY MAKES IT WORSE FOR HIMSELF!
WE'VE DONE IT! WE'VE CONVINCED THE PEOPLE OF THIS TIME THAT SUPERMAN IS A CRIMINAL!
HA-HA
BY NOW THE RED KRYPTONITE WILL HAVE TAKEN ITS FULL EFFECT--AND CAUSE SUPERMAN TO LOSE HIS SUPER-POWERS FOR TWO HOURS!
8

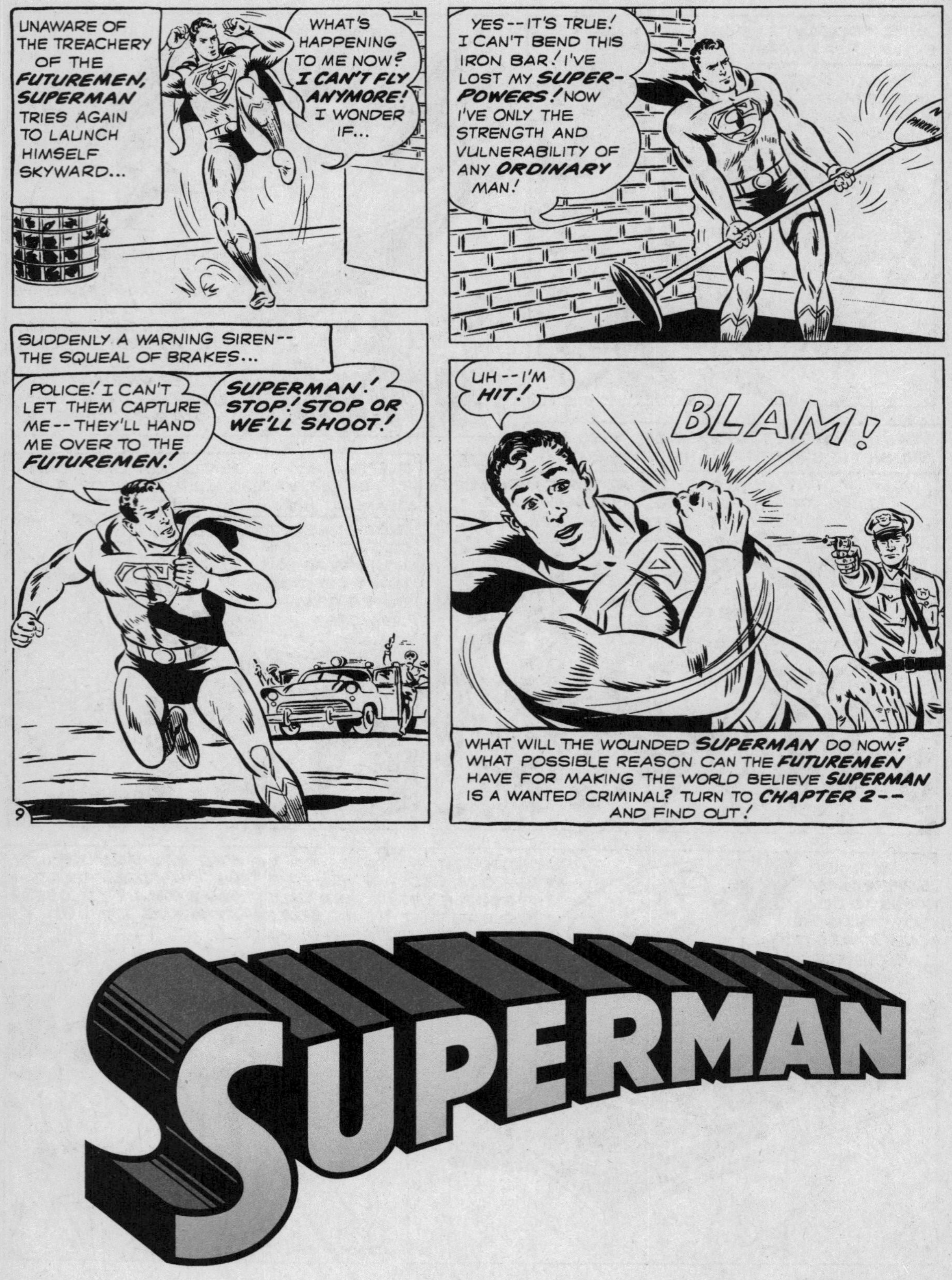

UNAWARE OF THE TREACHERY OF THE FUTUREMEN, SUPERMAN TRIES AGAIN TO LAUNCH HIMSELF SKYWARD...
WHAT'S HAPPENING TO ME NOW? I CAN'T FLY ANYMORE! I WONDER IF...
YES--IT'S TRUE! I CAN'T BEND THIS IRON BAR! I'VE LOST MY SUPER-POWERS! NOW I'VE ONLY THE STRENGTH AND VULNERABILITY OF ANY ORDINARY MAN!
SUDDENLY A WARNING SIREN--THE SQUEAL OF BRAKES...
POLICE! I CAN'T LET THEM CAPTURE ME--THEY'LL HAND ME OVER TO THE FUTUREMEN!
SUPERMAN! STOP! STOP OR WE'LL SHOOT!
9
UH--I'M HIT!
BLAM!
WHAT WILL THE WOUNDED SUPERMAN DO NOW? WHAT POSSIBLE REASON CAN THE FUTUREMEN HAVE FOR MAKING THE WORLD BELIEVE SUPERMAN IS A WANTED CRIMINAL? TURN TO CHAPTER 2--AND FIND OUT!

SUPERMAN

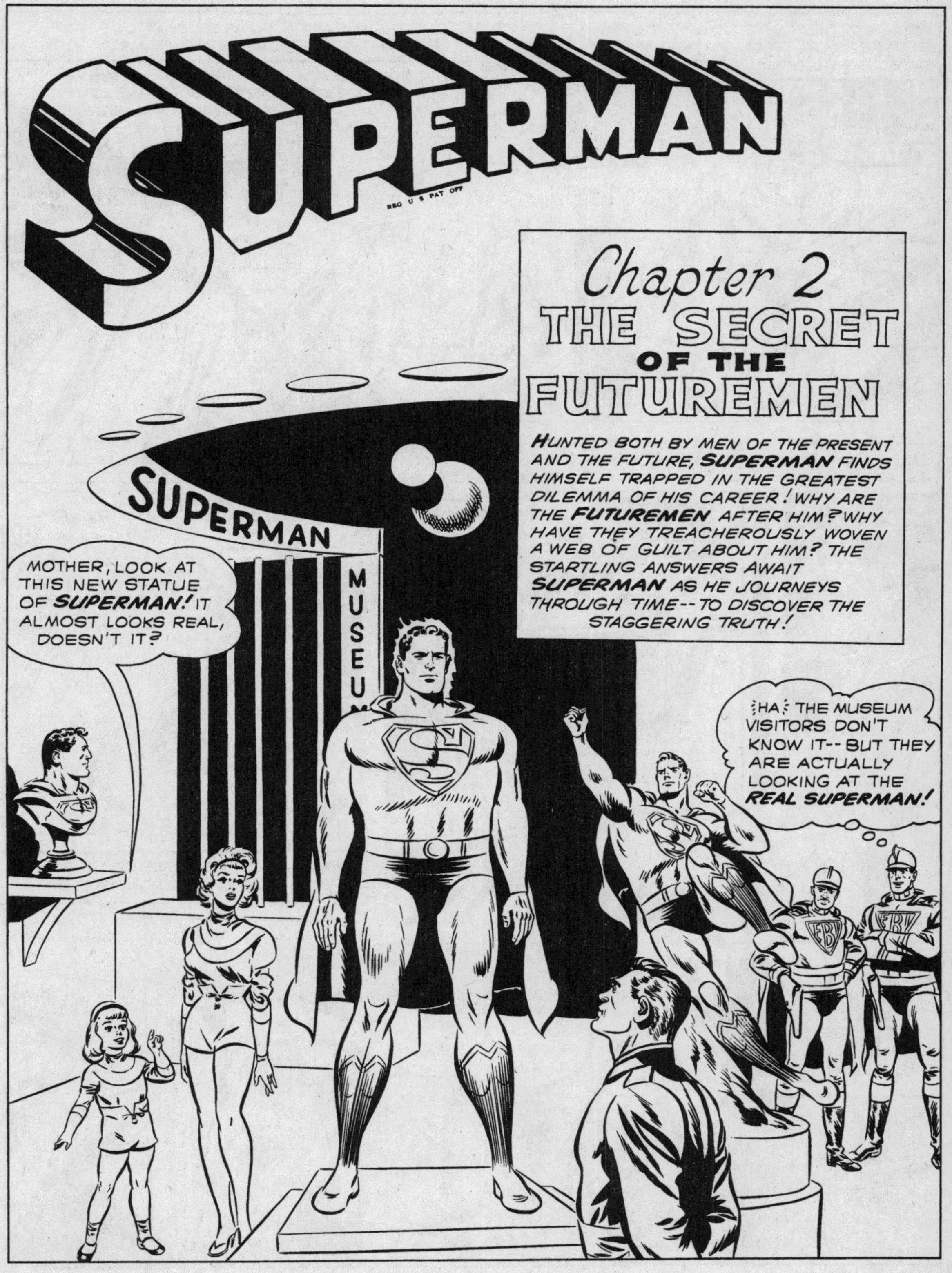
SUPERMAN
REG U S PAT OFF
Chapter 2
THE SECRET
OF THE
FUTUREMEN
HUNTED BOTH BY MEN OF THE PRESENT AND THE FUTURE, SUPERMAN FINDS HIMSELF TRAPPED IN THE GREATEST DILEMMA OF HIS CAREER! WHY ARE THE FUTUREMEN AFTER HIM? WHY HAVE THEY TREACHEROUSLY WOVEN A WEB OF GUILT ABOUT HIM? THE STARTLING ANSWERS AWAIT SUPERMAN AS HE JOURNEYS THROUGH TIME--TO DISCOVER THE STAGGERING TRUTH!
SUPERMAN
MUSEUM
MOTHER, LOOK AT THIS NEW STATUE OF SUPERMAN! IT ALMOST LOOKS REAL, DOESN'T IT?
HA! THE MUSEUM VISITORS DON'T KNOW IT-- BUT THEY ARE ACTUALLY LOOKING AT THE REAL SUPERMAN!

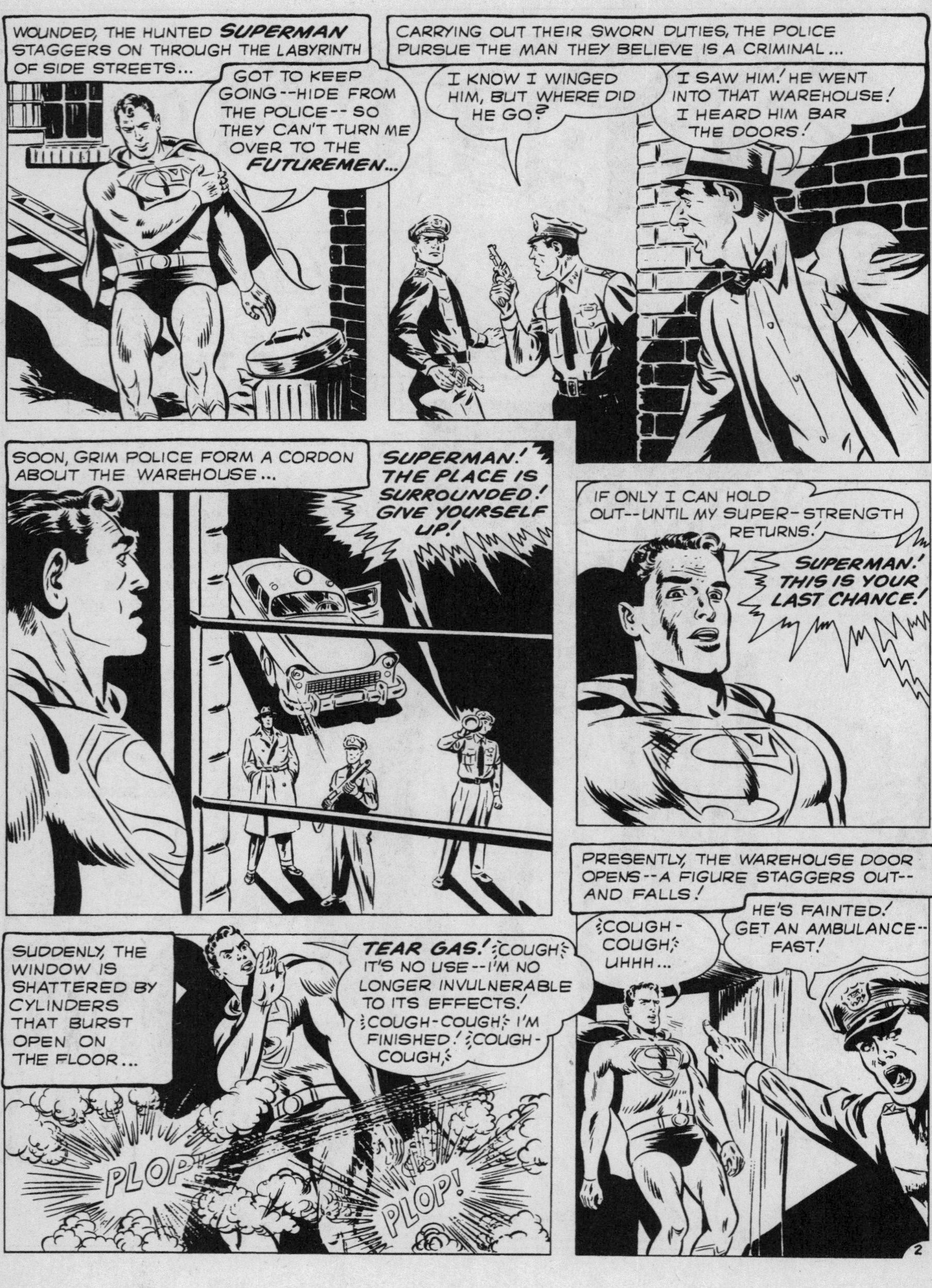
WOUNDED, THE HUNTED SUPERMAN STAGGERS ON THROUGH THE LABYRINTH OF SIDE STREETS...
GOT TO KEEP GOING--HIDE FROM THE POLICE-- SO THEY CAN'T TURN ME OVER TO THE FUTUREMEN...
CARRYING OUT THEIR SWORN DUTIES, THE POLICE PURSUE THE MAN THEY BELIEVE IS A CRIMINAL...
I KNOW I WINGED HIM, BUT WHERE DID HE GO?
I SAW HIM! HE WENT INTO THAT WAREHOUSE! I HEARD HIM BAR THE DOORS!
SOON, GRIM POLICE FORM A CORDON ABOUT THE WAREHOUSE...
SUPERMAN! THE PLACE IS SURROUNDED! GIVE YOURSELF UP!
IF ONLY I CAN HOLD OUT--UNTIL MY SUPER-STRENGTH RETURNS!
SUPERMAN! THIS IS YOUR LAST CHANCE!
SUDDENLY, THE WINDOW IS SHATTERED BY CYLINDERS THAT BURST OPEN ON THE FLOOR...
TEAR GAS! COUGH IT'S NO USE--I'M NO LONGER INVULNERABLE TO ITS EFFECTS! COUGH-COUGH! I'M FINISHED! COUGH-COUGH,
PLOP!
PLOP!
PRESENTLY, THE WAREHOUSE DOOR OPENS--A FIGURE STAGGERS OUT--AND FALLS!
COUGH-COUGH! UHHH...
HE'S FAINTED! GET AN AMBULANCE--FAST!
2

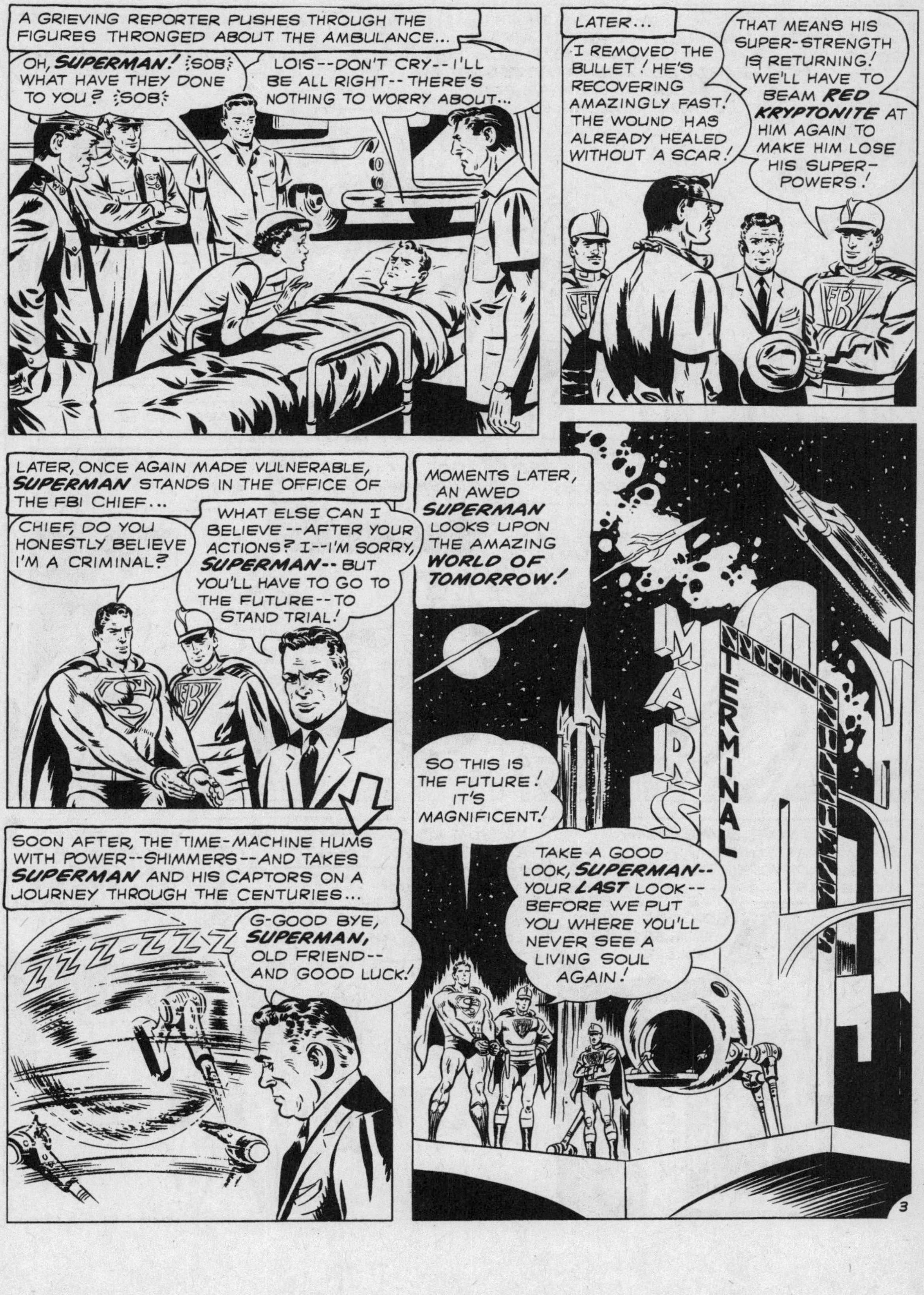
A GRIEVING REPORTER PUSHES THROUGH THE FIGURES THRONGED ABOUT THE AMBULANCE...
OH, SUPERMAN! SOB WHAT HAVE THEY DONE TO YOU? SOB
LOIS--DON'T CRY--I'LL BE ALL RIGHT--THERE'S NOTHING TO WORRY ABOUT...
LATER...
I REMOVED THE BULLET! HE'S RECOVERING AMAZINGLY FAST! THE WOUND HAS ALREADY HEALED WITHOUT A SCAR!
THAT MEANS HIS SUPER-STRENGTH IS RETURNING! WE'LL HAVE TO BEAM RED KRYPTONITE AT HIM AGAIN TO MAKE HIM LOSE HIS SUPER-POWERS!
LATER, ONCE AGAIN MADE VULNERABLE, SUPERMAN STANDS IN THE OFFICE OF THE FBI CHIEF...
CHIEF, DO YOU HONESTLY BELIEVE I'M A CRIMINAL?
WHAT ELSE CAN I BELIEVE--AFTER YOUR ACTIONS? I--I'M SORRY, SUPERMAN--BUT YOU'LL HAVE TO GO TO THE FUTURE--TO STAND TRIAL!
SOON AFTER, THE TIME-MACHINE HUMS WITH POWER--SHIMMERS--AND TAKES SUPERMAN AND HIS CAPTORS ON A JOURNEY THROUGH THE CENTURIES...
ZZZ-ZZZ
G-GOOD BYE, SUPERMAN, OLD FRIEND--AND GOOD LUCK!
MOMENTS LATER, AN AWED SUPERMAN LOOKS UPON THE AMAZING WORLD OF TOMORROW!
MARS
TERMINAL
SO THIS IS THE FUTURE! IT'S MAGNIFICENT!
TAKE A GOOD LOOK, SUPERMAN--YOUR LAST LOOK--BEFORE WE PUT YOU WHERE YOU'LL NEVER SEE A LIVING SOUL AGAIN!
3

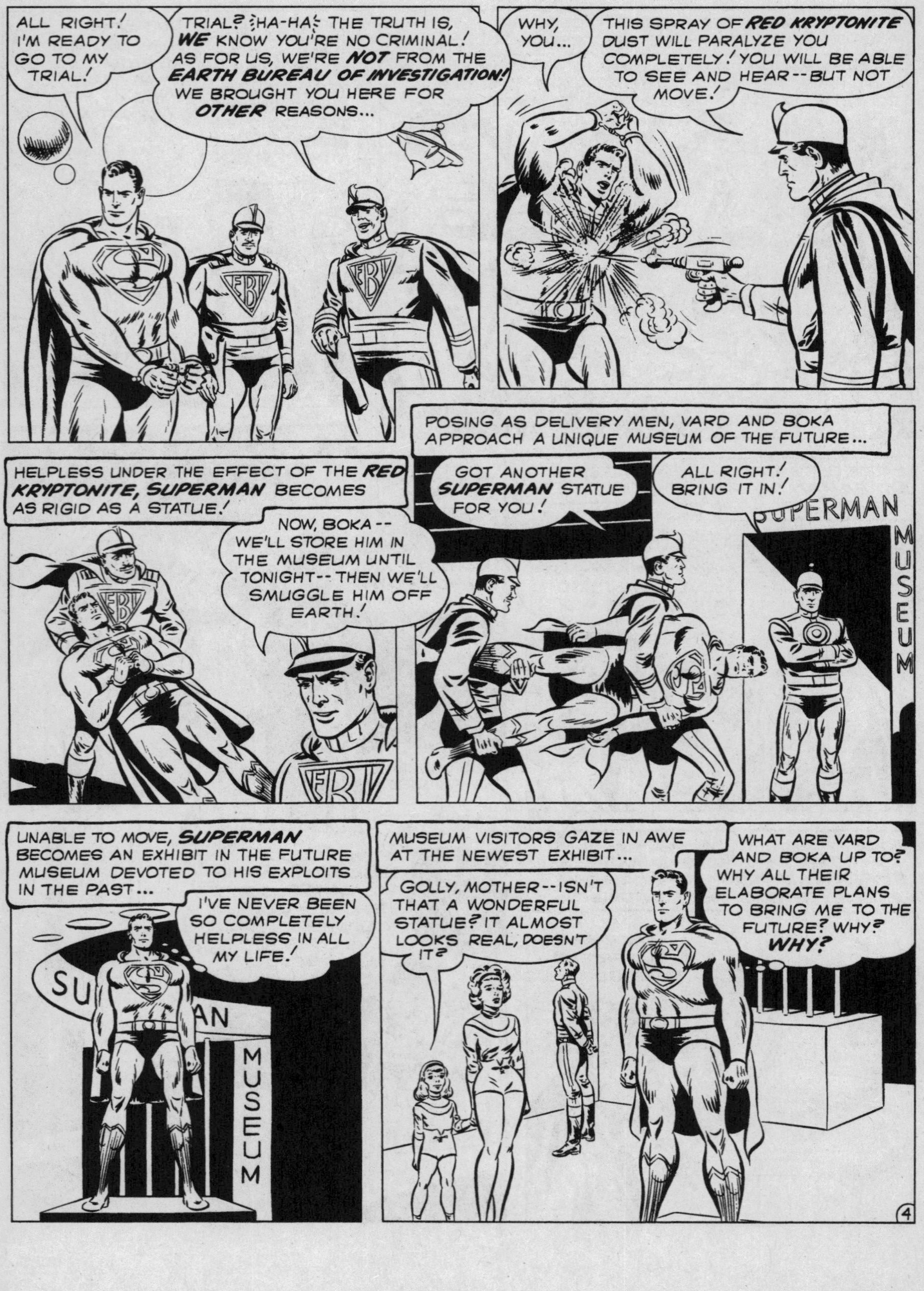
ALL RIGHT! I'M READY TO GO TO MY TRIAL!
TRIAL? HA-HA! THE TRUTH IS, WE KNOW YOU'RE NO CRIMINAL! AS FOR US, WE'RE NOT FROM THE EARTH BUREAU OF INVESTIGATION! WE BROUGHT YOU HERE FOR OTHER REASONS...
WHY, YOU...
THIS SPRAY OF RED KRYPTONITE DUST WILL PARALYZE YOU COMPLETELY! YOU WILL BE ABLE TO SEE AND HEAR--BUT NOT MOVE!
HELPLESS UNDER THE EFFECT OF THE RED KRYPTONITE, SUPERMAN BECOMES AS RIGID AS A STATUE!
NOW, BOKA--WE'LL STORE HIM IN THE MUSEUM UNTIL TONIGHT--THEN WE'LL SMUGGLE HIM OFF EARTH!
POSING AS DELIVERY MEN, VARD AND BOKA APPROACH A UNIQUE MUSEUM OF THE FUTURE...
GOT ANOTHER SUPERMAN STATUE FOR YOU!
ALL RIGHT! BRING IT IN!
SUPERMAN
MUSEUM
UNABLE TO MOVE, SUPERMAN BECOMES AN EXHIBIT IN THE FUTURE MUSEUM DEVOTED TO HIS EXPLOITS IN THE PAST...
I'VE NEVER BEEN SO COMPLETELY HELPLESS IN ALL MY LIFE!
SU AN
MUSEUM
MUSEUM VISITORS GAZE IN AWE AT THE NEWEST EXHIBIT...
GOLLY, MOTHER--ISN'T THAT A WONDERFUL STATUE? IT ALMOST LOOKS REAL, DOESN'T IT?
WHAT ARE VARD AND BOKA UP TO? WHY ALL THEIR ELABORATE PLANS TO BRING ME TO THE FUTURE? WHY? WHY?
4

NIGHTFALL--AND THE *FUTUREMEN* SMUGGLE *SUPERMAN* OUT OF THE MUSEUM TO A WAITING SPACESHIP...

SUPERMAN'S STARTING TO MOVE! THE PARALYSIS IS WEARING OFF!

I'LL GIVE HIM ANOTHER BEAM OF *RED KRYPTONITE,* SO THAT HIS SUPER-POWERS WON'T RETURN YET!

LATER, AS THE SPACESHIP HURTLES SKYWARD, *SUPERMAN* LOOKS DOWN AT AN ODDLY DIFFERENT EARTH...

DRY VALLEYS! WHERE THE OCEANS USED TO BE!

YES! THE OCEANS ARE GONE-- ACCIDENTALLY DISSOLVED BY AN ATOMIC EXPERIMENT! THE SCANT AMOUNT OF WATER LEFT ON EARTH WILL SOON EVAPORATE-- AND EARTH WILL BE LIFELESS AS THE MOON --FOR WITHOUT WATER, LIFE DIES!

ON HURTLES THE SPACESHIP, ON UNTIL IT REACHES THE ASTEROID BELT...

ISN'T THERE ANY CHANCE FOR EARTH TO GET MORE WATER?

YES, *SUPERMAN*--YOU'LL LEARN HOW AFTER WE LOCK YOU IN A CELL WE'VE BUILT ON THAT ASTEROID AHEAD!

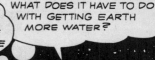

SOON AFTER...

YOUR SUPER-STRENGTH WILL RETURN SHORTLY-- BUT YOU WON'T BE ABLE TO BREAK OUT! THE CAGE IS MADE OF *RED KRYPTONITE!*

WHY ALL THESE PRECAUTIONS? WHAT DOES IT HAVE TO DO WITH GETTING EARTH MORE WATER?

ASTRONOMERS IN YOUR TIME SUSPECTED *SATURN'S* SMALLER MOONS MIGHT BE GIGANTIC, POROUS "SNOWBALLS"! THEY WERE RIGHT! THEY ARE COMPOSED OF FROZEN SNOW!

YOU, WITH YOUR TITANIC STRENGTH, COULD TOW THOSE MOONS TO EARTH FOR US--AND EARTH WOULD GLADLY PAY US BILLIONS FOR THE WATER IN THOSE--ER-- FROZEN ASSETS!

SO *THAT'S* WHY YOU BROUGHT ME TO THE FUTURE! SUPPOSE I REFUSE TO HELP YOU IN THIS GIGANTIC HOLDUP OF EARTH?

THEN WE'LL RETURN TO *YOUR* TIME AND CREATE THE SAME WATER-SHORTAGE WITH THE SAME ATOMIC BOMB! THINK IT OVER! WE'LL RETURN IN AN HOUR FOR YOUR ANSWER!

5

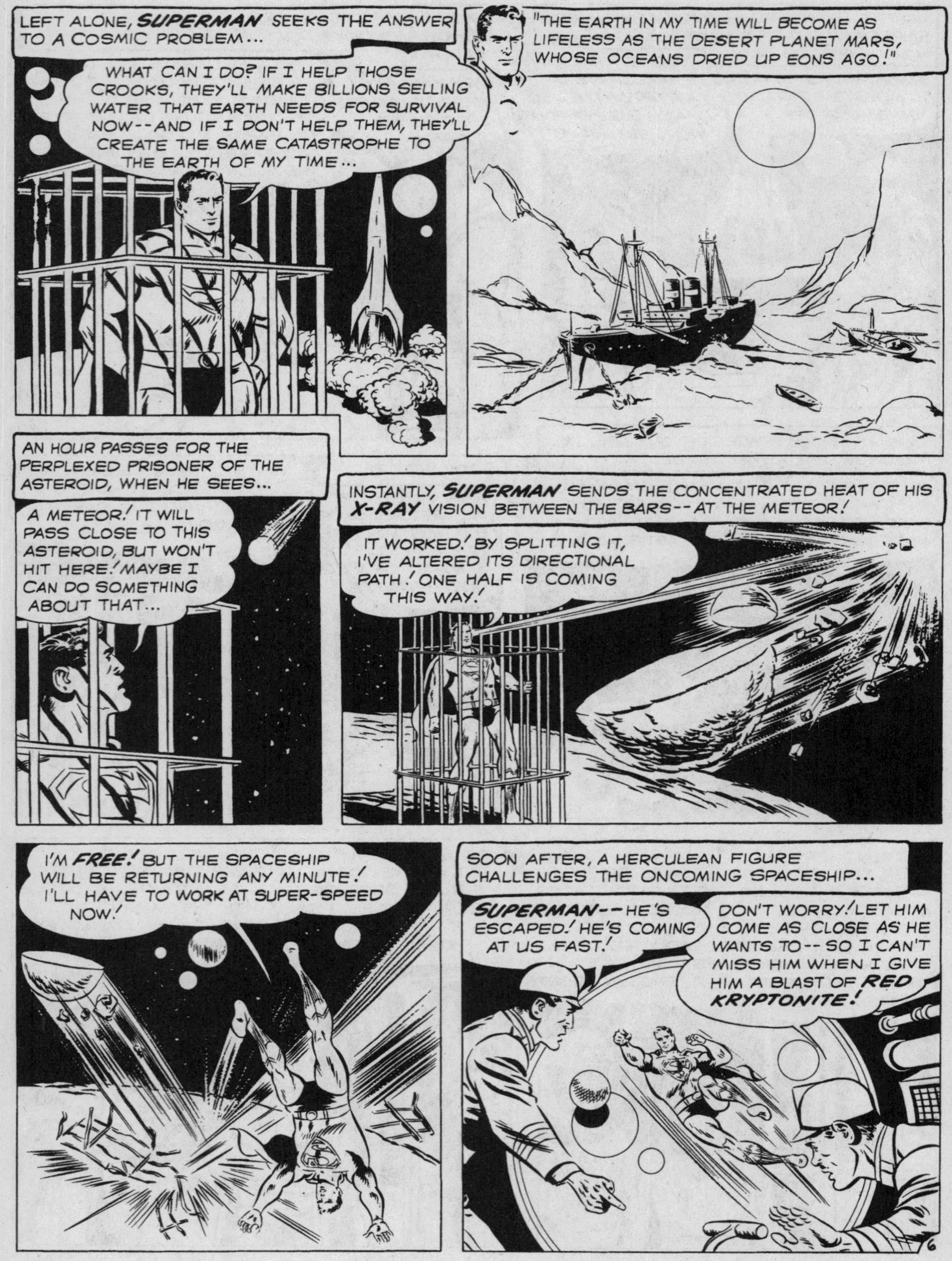
LEFT ALONE, SUPERMAN SEEKS THE ANSWER TO A COSMIC PROBLEM...
WHAT CAN I DO? IF I HELP THOSE CROOKS, THEY'LL MAKE BILLIONS SELLING WATER THAT EARTH NEEDS FOR SURVIVAL NOW--AND IF I DON'T HELP THEM, THEY'LL CREATE THE SAME CATASTROPHE TO THE EARTH OF MY TIME...
"THE EARTH IN MY TIME WILL BECOME AS LIFELESS AS THE DESERT PLANET MARS, WHOSE OCEANS DRIED UP EONS AGO!"
AN HOUR PASSES FOR THE PERPLEXED PRISONER OF THE ASTEROID, WHEN HE SEES...
A METEOR! IT WILL PASS CLOSE TO THIS ASTEROID, BUT WON'T HIT HERE! MAYBE I CAN DO SOMETHING ABOUT THAT...
INSTANTLY, SUPERMAN SENDS THE CONCENTRATED HEAT OF HIS X-RAY VISION BETWEEN THE BARS--AT THE METEOR!
IT WORKED! BY SPLITTING IT, I'VE ALTERED ITS DIRECTIONAL PATH! ONE HALF IS COMING THIS WAY!
I'M FREE! BUT THE SPACESHIP WILL BE RETURNING ANY MINUTE! I'LL HAVE TO WORK AT SUPER-SPEED NOW!
SOON AFTER, A HERCULEAN FIGURE CHALLENGES THE ONCOMING SPACESHIP...
SUPERMAN--HE'S ESCAPED! HE'S COMING AT US FAST!
DON'T WORRY! LET HIM COME AS CLOSE AS HE WANTS TO--SO I CAN'T MISS HIM WHEN I GIVE HIM A BLAST OF RED KRYPTONITE!
6

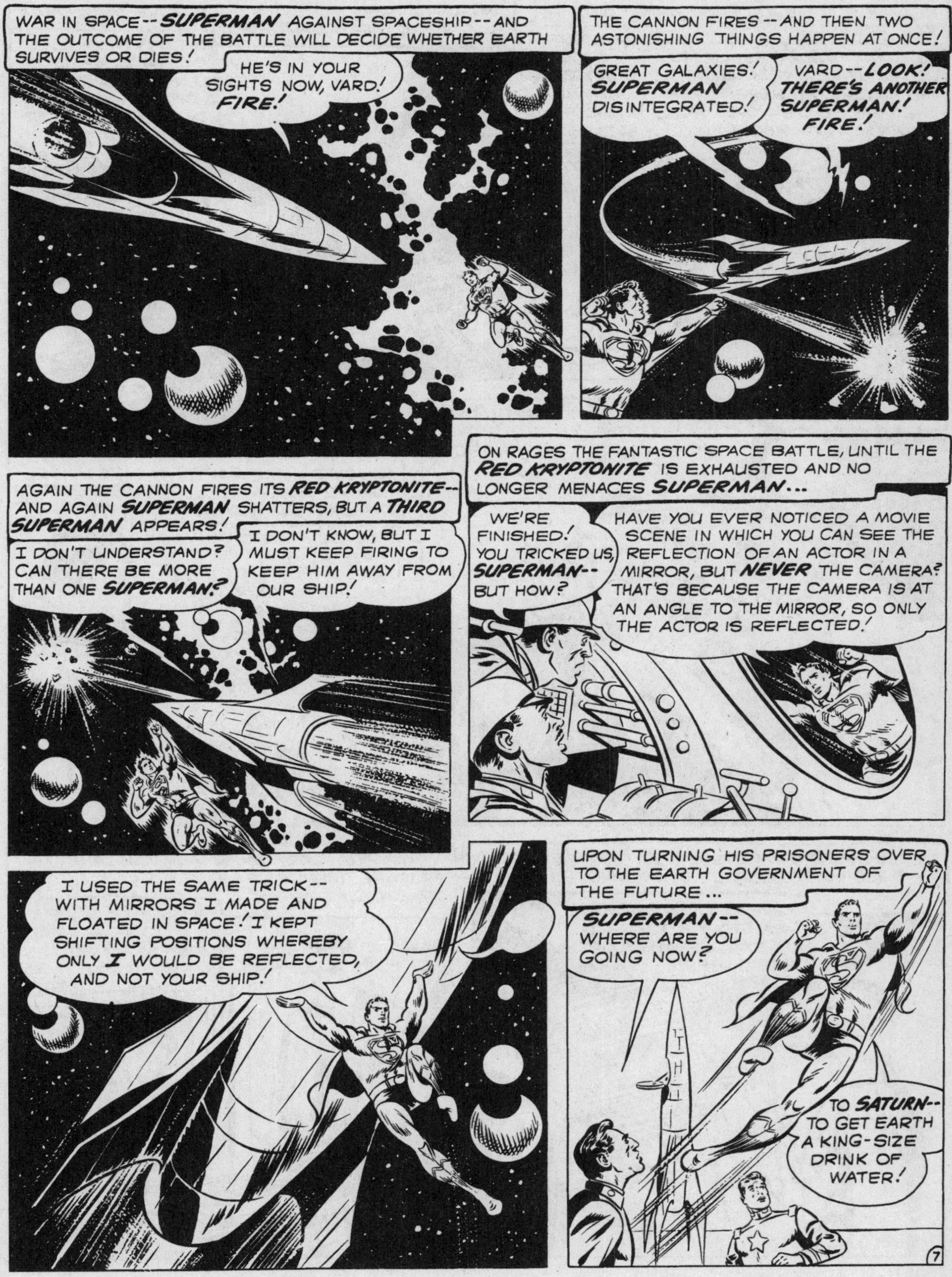
WAR IN SPACE--SUPERMAN AGAINST SPACESHIP--AND THE OUTCOME OF THE BATTLE WILL DECIDE WHETHER EARTH SURVIVES OR DIES!
HE'S IN YOUR SIGHTS NOW, VARD! FIRE!
THE CANNON FIRES--AND THEN TWO ASTONISHING THINGS HAPPEN AT ONCE!
GREAT GALAXIES! SUPERMAN DISINTEGRATED!
VARD--LOOK! THERE'S ANOTHER SUPERMAN! FIRE!
AGAIN THE CANNON FIRES ITS RED KRYPTONITE--AND AGAIN SUPERMAN SHATTERS, BUT A THIRD SUPERMAN APPEARS!
I DON'T UNDERSTAND? CAN THERE BE MORE THAN ONE SUPERMAN?
I DON'T KNOW, BUT I MUST KEEP FIRING TO KEEP HIM AWAY FROM OUR SHIP!
ON RAGES THE FANTASTIC SPACE BATTLE, UNTIL THE RED KRYPTONITE IS EXHAUSTED AND NO LONGER MENACES SUPERMAN...
WE'RE FINISHED! YOU TRICKED US, SUPERMAN--BUT HOW?
HAVE YOU EVER NOTICED A MOVIE SCENE IN WHICH YOU CAN SEE THE REFLECTION OF AN ACTOR IN A MIRROR, BUT NEVER THE CAMERA? THAT'S BECAUSE THE CAMERA IS AT AN ANGLE TO THE MIRROR, SO ONLY THE ACTOR IS REFLECTED!
I USED THE SAME TRICK--WITH MIRRORS I MADE AND FLOATED IN SPACE! I KEPT SHIFTING POSITIONS WHEREBY ONLY I WOULD BE REFLECTED, AND NOT YOUR SHIP!
UPON TURNING HIS PRISONERS OVER TO THE EARTH GOVERNMENT OF THE FUTURE...
SUPERMAN--WHERE ARE YOU GOING NOW?
TO SATURN--TO GET EARTH A KING-SIZE DRINK OF WATER!
7

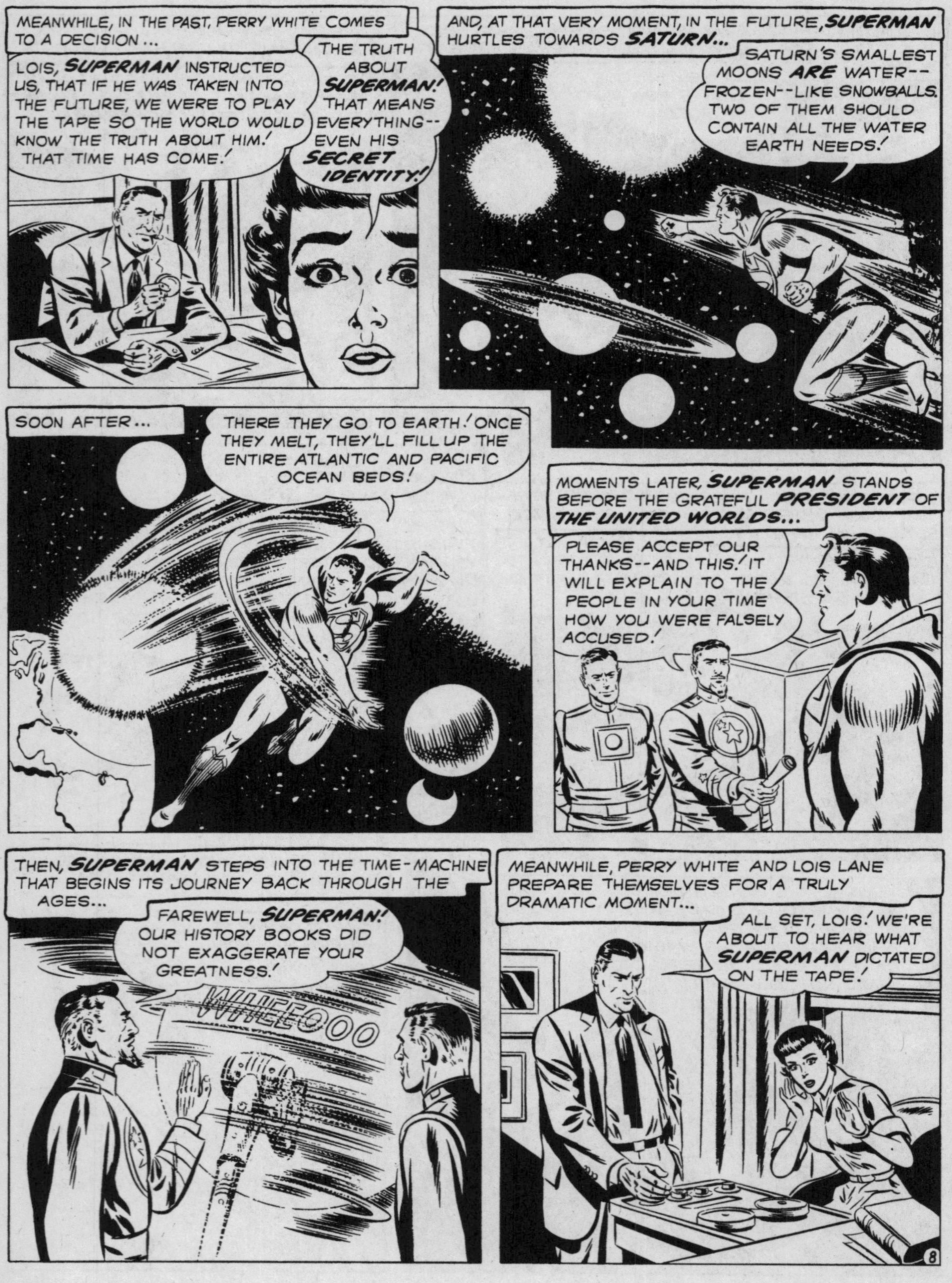
MEANWHILE, IN THE PAST, PERRY WHITE COMES TO A DECISION ...
LOIS, SUPERMAN INSTRUCTED US, THAT IF HE WAS TAKEN INTO THE FUTURE, WE WERE TO PLAY THE TAPE SO THE WORLD WOULD KNOW THE TRUTH ABOUT HIM! THAT TIME HAS COME!
THE TRUTH ABOUT SUPERMAN! THAT MEANS EVERYTHING-- EVEN HIS SECRET IDENTITY!
AND, AT THAT VERY MOMENT, IN THE FUTURE, SUPERMAN HURTLES TOWARDS SATURN...
SATURN'S SMALLEST MOONS ARE WATER-- FROZEN--LIKE SNOWBALLS. TWO OF THEM SHOULD CONTAIN ALL THE WATER EARTH NEEDS!
SOON AFTER...
THERE THEY GO TO EARTH! ONCE THEY MELT, THEY'LL FILL UP THE ENTIRE ATLANTIC AND PACIFIC OCEAN BEDS!
MOMENTS LATER, SUPERMAN STANDS BEFORE THE GRATEFUL PRESIDENT OF THE UNITED WORLDS...
PLEASE ACCEPT OUR THANKS--AND THIS! IT WILL EXPLAIN TO THE PEOPLE IN YOUR TIME HOW YOU WERE FALSELY ACCUSED!
THEN, SUPERMAN STEPS INTO THE TIME-MACHINE THAT BEGINS ITS JOURNEY BACK THROUGH THE AGES...
FAREWELL, SUPERMAN! OUR HISTORY BOOKS DID NOT EXAGGERATE YOUR GREATNESS!
WHEEOOO
MEANWHILE, PERRY WHITE AND LOIS LANE PREPARE THEMSELVES FOR A TRULY DRAMATIC MOMENT...
ALL SET, LOIS! WE'RE ABOUT TO HEAR WHAT SUPERMAN DICTATED ON THE TAPE!
8

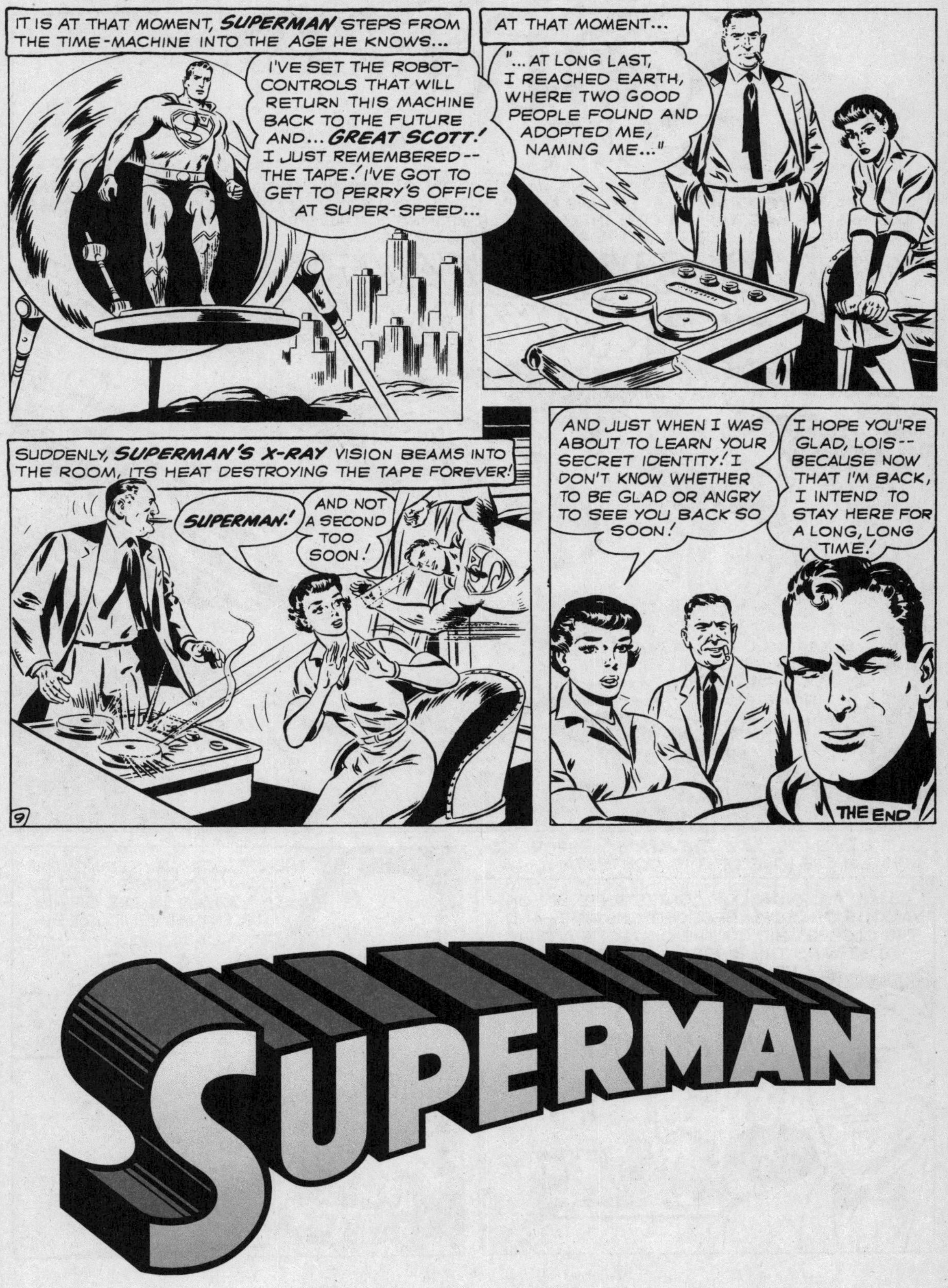
IT IS AT THAT MOMENT, SUPERMAN STEPS FROM THE TIME-MACHINE INTO THE AGE HE KNOWS...
I'VE SET THE ROBOT-CONTROLS THAT WILL RETURN THIS MACHINE BACK TO THE FUTURE AND... GREAT SCOTT! I JUST REMEMBERED-- THE TAPE! I'VE GOT TO GET TO PERRY'S OFFICE AT SUPER-SPEED...
AT THAT MOMENT...
"...AT LONG LAST, I REACHED EARTH, WHERE TWO GOOD PEOPLE FOUND AND ADOPTED ME, NAMING ME..."
SUDDENLY, SUPERMAN'S X-RAY VISION BEAMS INTO THE ROOM, ITS HEAT DESTROYING THE TAPE FOREVER!
SUPERMAN!
AND NOT A SECOND TOO SOON!
9
AND JUST WHEN I WAS ABOUT TO LEARN YOUR SECRET IDENTITY! I DON'T KNOW WHETHER TO BE GLAD OR ANGRY TO SEE YOU BACK SO SOON!
I HOPE YOU'RE GLAD, LOIS-- BECAUSE NOW THAT I'M BACK, I INTEND TO STAY HERE FOR A LONG, LONG TIME!
THE END

SUPERMAN

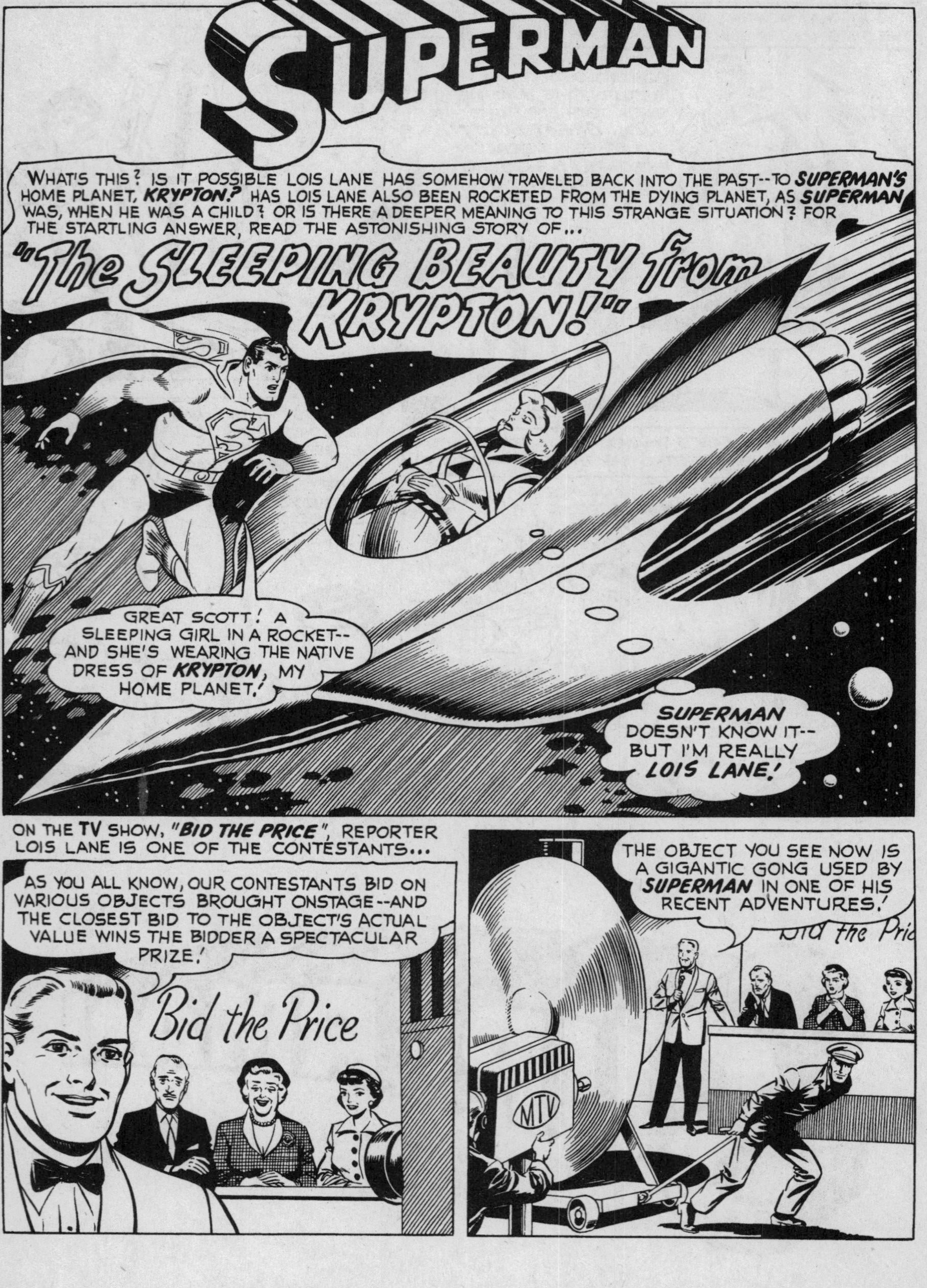
SUPERMAN
WHAT'S THIS? IS IT POSSIBLE LOIS LANE HAS SOMEHOW TRAVELED BACK INTO THE PAST--TO SUPERMAN'S HOME PLANET, KRYPTON? HAS LOIS LANE ALSO BEEN ROCKETED FROM THE DYING PLANET, AS SUPERMAN WAS, WHEN HE WAS A CHILD? OR IS THERE A DEEPER MEANING TO THIS STRANGE SITUATION? FOR THE STARTLING ANSWER, READ THE ASTONISHING STORY OF...
"The SLEEPING BEAUTY from KRYPTON!"
GREAT SCOTT! A SLEEPING GIRL IN A ROCKET-- AND SHE'S WEARING THE NATIVE DRESS OF KRYPTON, MY HOME PLANET!
SUPERMAN DOESN'T KNOW IT-- BUT I'M REALLY LOIS LANE!
ON THE TV SHOW, "BID THE PRICE", REPORTER LOIS LANE IS ONE OF THE CONTESTANTS...
AS YOU ALL KNOW, OUR CONTESTANTS BID ON VARIOUS OBJECTS BROUGHT ONSTAGE--AND THE CLOSEST BID TO THE OBJECT'S ACTUAL VALUE WINS THE BIDDER A SPECTACULAR PRIZE!
Bid the Price
THE OBJECT YOU SEE NOW IS A GIGANTIC GONG USED BY SUPERMAN IN ONE OF HIS RECENT ADVENTURES!
MTV

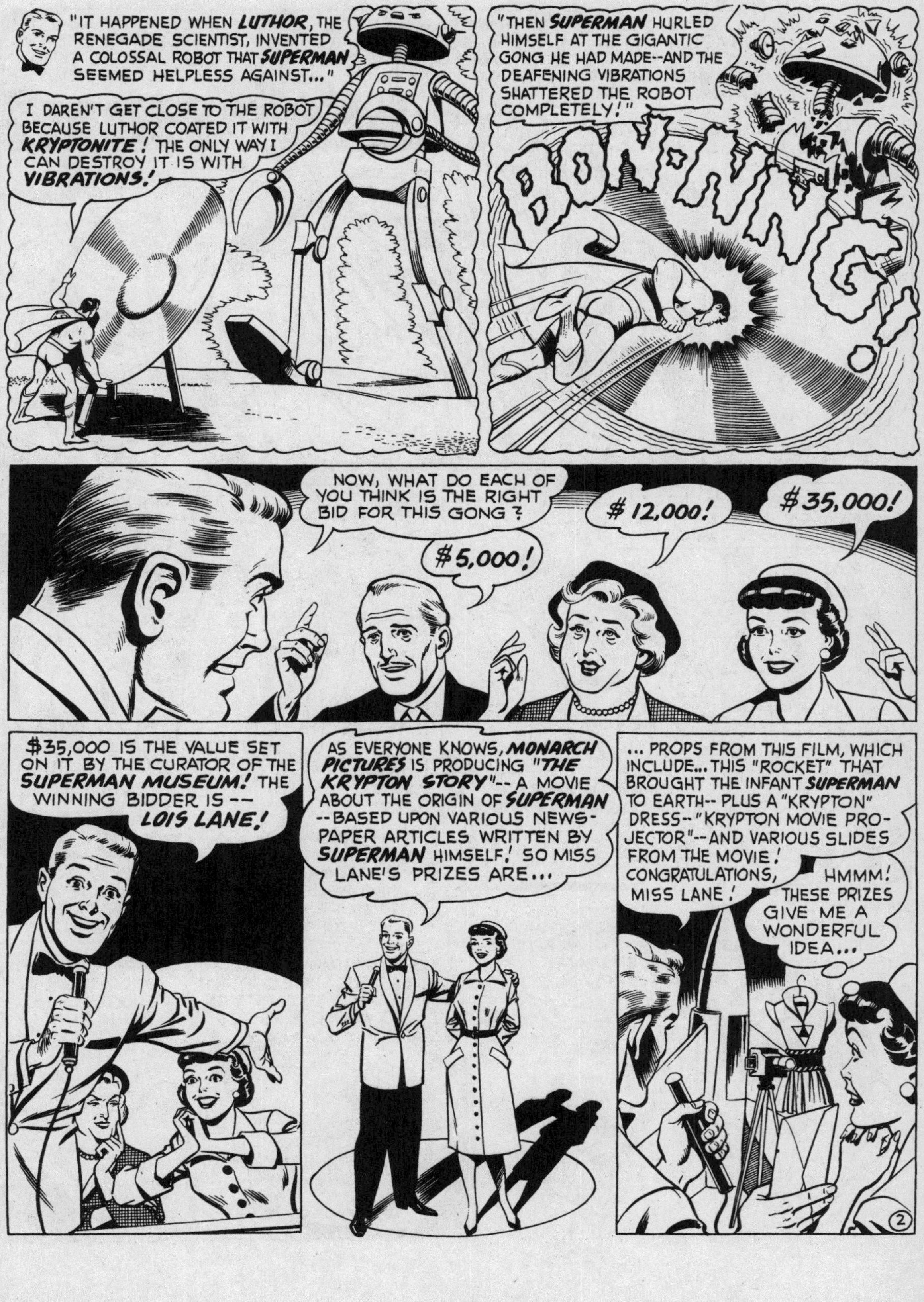
"IT HAPPENED WHEN LUTHOR, THE RENEGADE SCIENTIST, INVENTED A COLOSSAL ROBOT THAT SUPERMAN SEEMED HELPLESS AGAINST..."
I DAREN'T GET CLOSE TO THE ROBOT BECAUSE LUTHOR COATED IT WITH KRYPTONITE! THE ONLY WAY I CAN DESTROY IT IS WITH VIBRATIONS!
"THEN SUPERMAN HURLED HIMSELF AT THE GIGANTIC GONG HE HAD MADE--AND THE DEAFENING VIBRATIONS SHATTERED THE ROBOT COMPLETELY!"
BON-N-N-NG!
NOW, WHAT DO EACH OF YOU THINK IS THE RIGHT BID FOR THIS GONG?
$5,000!
$12,000!
$35,000!
$35,000 IS THE VALUE SET ON IT BY THE CURATOR OF THE SUPERMAN MUSEUM! THE WINNING BIDDER IS -- LOIS LANE!
AS EVERYONE KNOWS, MONARCH PICTURES IS PRODUCING "THE KRYPTON STORY"-- A MOVIE ABOUT THE ORIGIN OF SUPERMAN --BASED UPON VARIOUS NEWS-PAPER ARTICLES WRITTEN BY SUPERMAN HIMSELF! SO MISS LANE'S PRIZES ARE...
... PROPS FROM THIS FILM, WHICH INCLUDE... THIS "ROCKET" THAT BROUGHT THE INFANT SUPERMAN TO EARTH-- PLUS A "KRYPTON" DRESS--"KRYPTON MOVIE PRO-JECTOR"--AND VARIOUS SLIDES FROM THE MOVIE! CONGRATULATIONS, MISS LANE!
HMMM! THESE PRIZES GIVE ME A WONDERFUL IDEA...
2

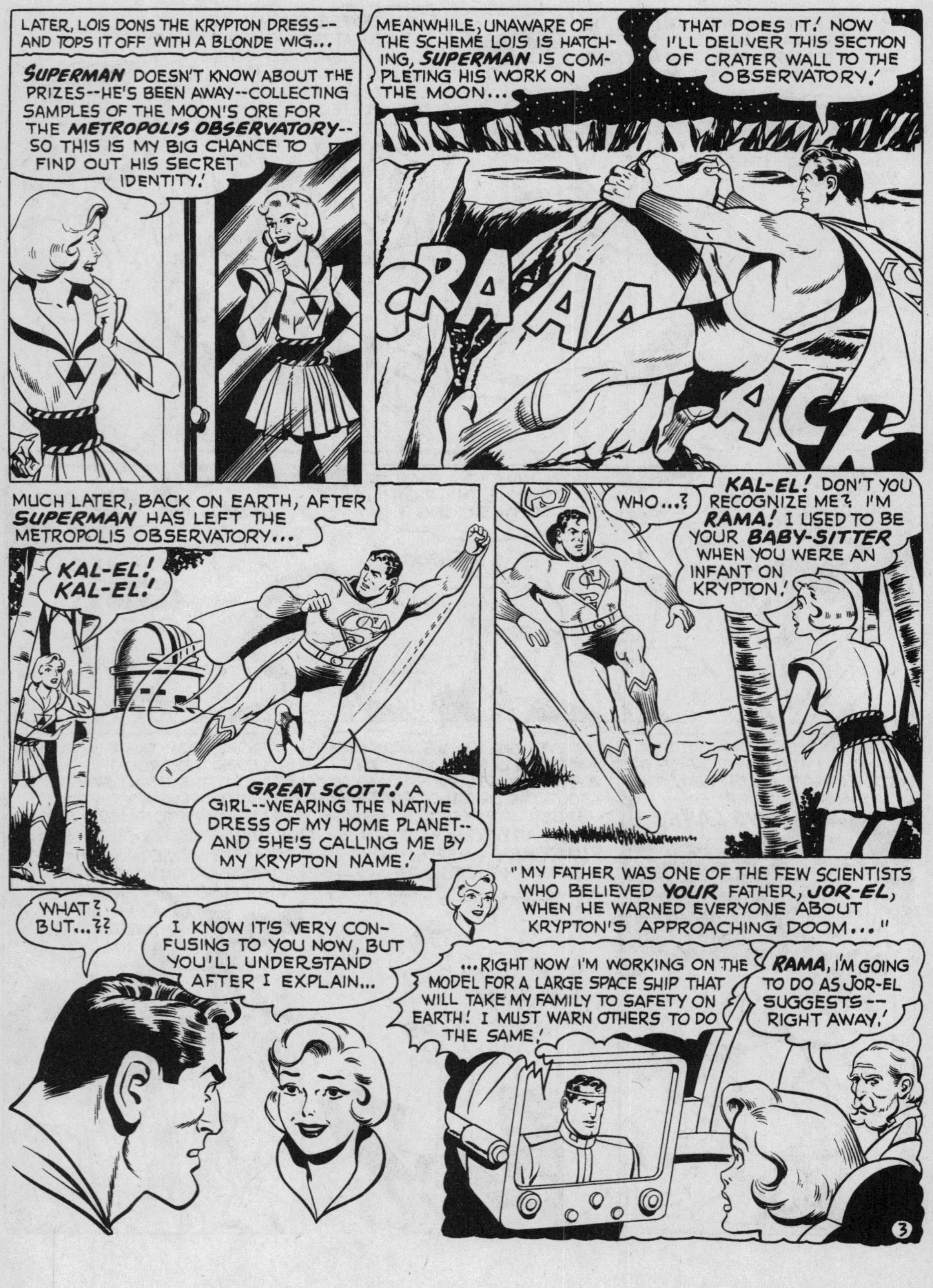
LATER, LOIS DONS THE KRYPTON DRESS-- AND TOPS IT OFF WITH A BLONDE WIG...
SUPERMAN DOESN'T KNOW ABOUT THE PRIZES--HE'S BEEN AWAY--COLLECTING SAMPLES OF THE MOON'S ORE FOR THE METROPOLIS OBSERVATORY-- SO THIS IS MY BIG CHANCE TO FIND OUT HIS SECRET IDENTITY!
MEANWHILE, UNAWARE OF THE SCHEME LOIS IS HATCHING, SUPERMAN IS COMPLETING HIS WORK ON THE MOON...
THAT DOES IT! NOW I'LL DELIVER THIS SECTION OF CRATER WALL TO THE OBSERVATORY!
CRAAAACK
MUCH LATER, BACK ON EARTH, AFTER SUPERMAN HAS LEFT THE METROPOLIS OBSERVATORY...
KAL-EL! KAL-EL!
GREAT SCOTT! A GIRL--WEARING THE NATIVE DRESS OF MY HOME PLANET-- AND SHE'S CALLING ME BY MY KRYPTON NAME!
WHO...?
KAL-EL! DON'T YOU RECOGNIZE ME? I'M RAMA! I USED TO BE YOUR BABY-SITTER WHEN YOU WERE AN INFANT ON KRYPTON!
WHAT? BUT...??
I KNOW IT'S VERY CONFUSING TO YOU NOW, BUT YOU'LL UNDERSTAND AFTER I EXPLAIN...
"MY FATHER WAS ONE OF THE FEW SCIENTISTS WHO BELIEVED YOUR FATHER, JOR-EL, WHEN HE WARNED EVERYONE ABOUT KRYPTON'S APPROACHING DOOM..."
...RIGHT NOW I'M WORKING ON THE MODEL FOR A LARGE SPACE SHIP THAT WILL TAKE MY FAMILY TO SAFETY ON EARTH! I MUST WARN OTHERS TO DO THE SAME!
RAMA, I'M GOING TO DO AS JOR-EL SUGGESTS-- RIGHT AWAY!
3

"LATER, MY FATHER AND YOUR FATHER CONFERRED..."

SHOULD I NOT COMPLETE MY SPACE SHIP IN TIME, AT LEAST THE MODEL CAN SAVE MY SON!

JOR-EL, DO YOU REALIZE EARTH DOESN'T HAVE KRYPTON'S TREMENDOUS GRAVITATIONAL PULL? ON EARTH YOUR SON WOULD BE A SUPERMAN!

"KRYPTON'S END... MY DEAR FATH... ROCKET MODE...

THE ROCKET IS... GAS THAT WILL... SUSPENDED AN... SHE REACHES... GOODBYE, MY... DAUGHTER-- MAY YOU FIND A NEW LIFE ON EARTH!

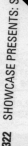

LATER, SUPERM... AT SLIDES FRO... ON HIS ORIG...

"YOUR ROCKET LEFT BEFORE MINE, SUPERMAN-- SO I PASSED THROUGH A CLOUD OF KRYPTONITE DUST FROM OUR EXPLODING PLANET... A CLOUD WHICH YOU HAD ESCAPED..."

"THE EXPLOSION BLEW MY ROCKET OFF COURSE, AND I DRIFTED ON, SLEEPING IN SUSPENDED ANIMATION THROUGH THE YEARS IN WHICH YOU WERE GROWING UP..."

AND SO, AFTER ALL THESE YEARS, YOU FINALLY DRIFTED TO EARTH! BUT HOW IS IT YOU DON'T HAVE SUPER-POWERS AS I DO?

THE RADIATIONS FROM THE CLOUD OF KRYPTONITE DUST THAT I PASSED THROUGH ARE STILL AFFECTING ME--BUT IT WILL EVENTUALLY WEAR OFF AND I'LL HAVE SUPER-POWERS, TOO!

THIS SHOULD CONVINCE SUPERMAN!

I'VE SOME SLIDES AND A PROJECTOR THAT MY FATHER SENT WITH ME--SO THAT I'D HAVE SOME MEMORIES OF KRYPTON! I'LL SHOW THEM TO YOU...

GREAT SCOTT! A ROCKET--JUST LIKE THE ONE THAT BROUGHT ME TO EARTH!

4

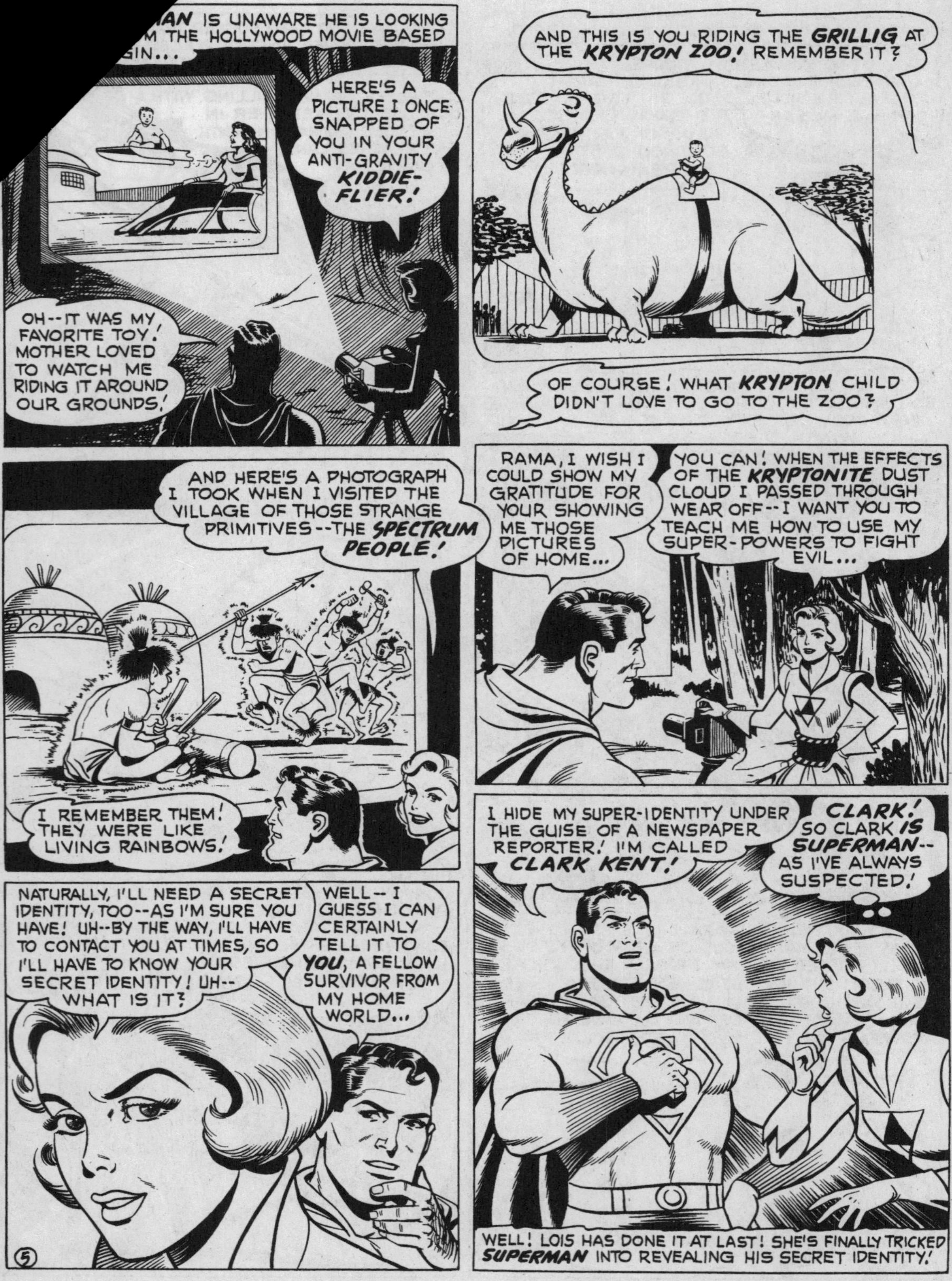
[redacted]MAN IS UNAWARE HE IS LOOKING [redacted]M THE HOLLYWOOD MOVIE BASED [redacted]GIN...
HERE'S A PICTURE I ONCE SNAPPED OF YOU IN YOUR ANTI-GRAVITY KIDDIE-FLIER!
OH--IT WAS MY FAVORITE TOY! MOTHER LOVED TO WATCH ME RIDING IT AROUND OUR GROUNDS!
AND THIS IS YOU RIDING THE GRILLIG AT THE KRYPTON ZOO! REMEMBER IT?
OF COURSE! WHAT KRYPTON CHILD DIDN'T LOVE TO GO TO THE ZOO?
AND HERE'S A PHOTOGRAPH I TOOK WHEN I VISITED THE VILLAGE OF THOSE STRANGE PRIMITIVES--THE SPECTRUM PEOPLE!
I REMEMBER THEM! THEY WERE LIKE LIVING RAINBOWS!
RAMA, I WISH I COULD SHOW MY GRATITUDE FOR YOUR SHOWING ME THOSE PICTURES OF HOME...
YOU CAN! WHEN THE EFFECTS OF THE KRYPTONITE DUST CLOUD I PASSED THROUGH WEAR OFF--I WANT YOU TO TEACH ME HOW TO USE MY SUPER-POWERS TO FIGHT EVIL...
NATURALLY, I'LL NEED A SECRET IDENTITY, TOO--AS I'M SURE YOU HAVE! UH--BY THE WAY, I'LL HAVE TO CONTACT YOU AT TIMES, SO I'LL HAVE TO KNOW YOUR SECRET IDENTITY! UH--WHAT IS IT?
WELL--I GUESS I CAN CERTAINLY TELL IT TO YOU, A FELLOW SURVIVOR FROM MY HOME WORLD...
5
I HIDE MY SUPER-IDENTITY UNDER THE GUISE OF A NEWSPAPER REPORTER! I'M CALLED CLARK KENT!
CLARK! SO CLARK IS SUPERMAN--AS I'VE ALWAYS SUSPECTED!
WELL! LOIS HAS DONE IT AT LAST! SHE'S FINALLY TRICKED SUPERMAN INTO REVEALING HIS SECRET IDENTITY!

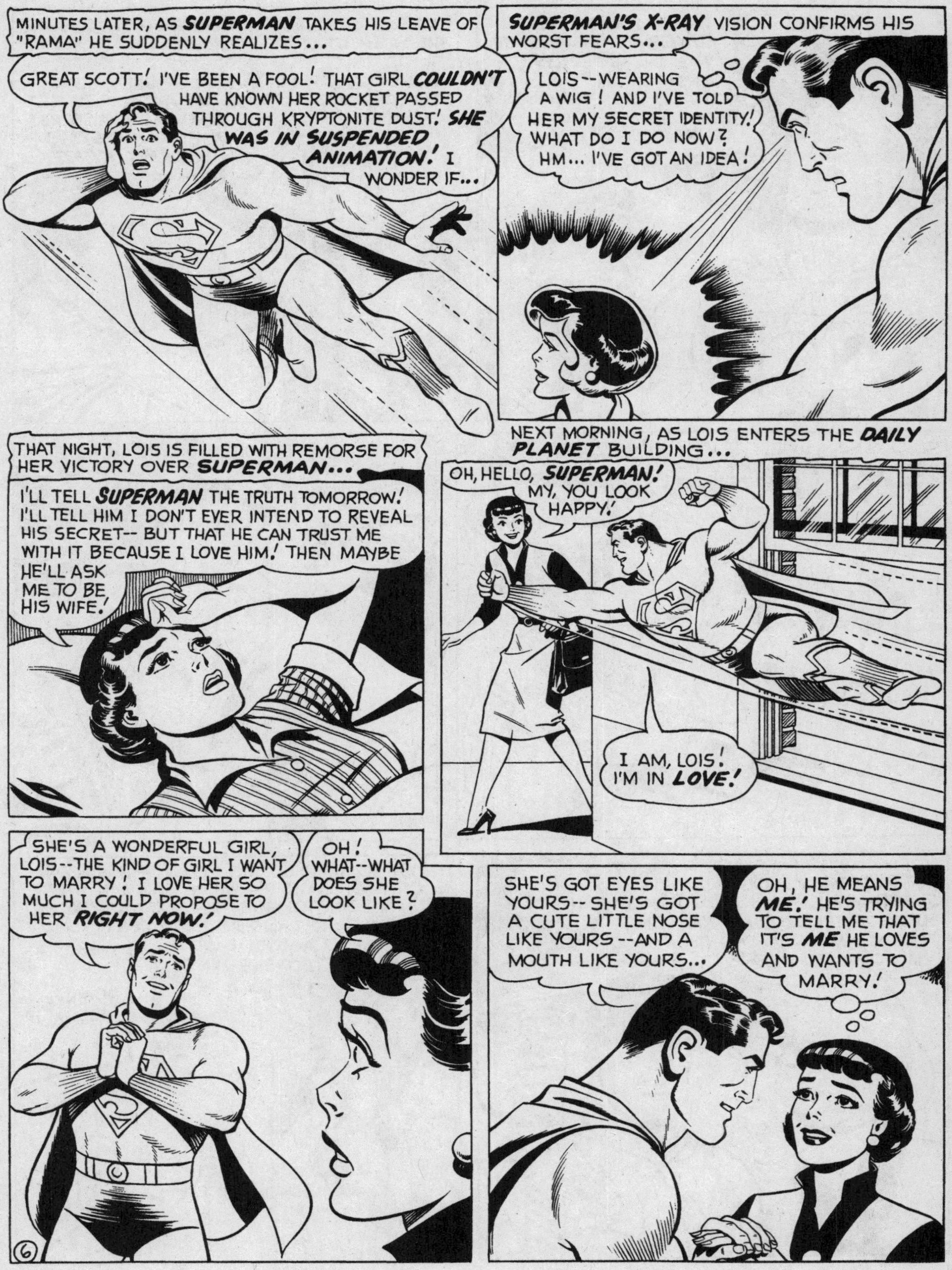
MINUTES LATER, AS SUPERMAN TAKES HIS LEAVE OF "RAMA" HE SUDDENLY REALIZES...
GREAT SCOTT! I'VE BEEN A FOOL! THAT GIRL COULDN'T HAVE KNOWN HER ROCKET PASSED THROUGH KRYPTONITE DUST! SHE WAS IN SUSPENDED ANIMATION! I WONDER IF...
SUPERMAN'S X-RAY VISION CONFIRMS HIS WORST FEARS...
LOIS--WEARING A WIG! AND I'VE TOLD HER MY SECRET IDENTITY! WHAT DO I DO NOW? HM... I'VE GOT AN IDEA!
THAT NIGHT, LOIS IS FILLED WITH REMORSE FOR HER VICTORY OVER SUPERMAN...
I'LL TELL SUPERMAN THE TRUTH TOMORROW! I'LL TELL HIM I DON'T EVER INTEND TO REVEAL HIS SECRET-- BUT THAT HE CAN TRUST ME WITH IT BECAUSE I LOVE HIM! THEN MAYBE HE'LL ASK ME TO BE HIS WIFE!
NEXT MORNING, AS LOIS ENTERS THE DAILY PLANET BUILDING...
OH, HELLO, SUPERMAN! MY, YOU LOOK HAPPY!
I AM, LOIS! I'M IN LOVE!
SHE'S A WONDERFUL GIRL, LOIS--THE KIND OF GIRL I WANT TO MARRY! I LOVE HER SO MUCH I COULD PROPOSE TO HER RIGHT NOW!
OH! WHAT--WHAT DOES SHE LOOK LIKE?
6
SHE'S GOT EYES LIKE YOURS-- SHE'S GOT A CUTE LITTLE NOSE LIKE YOURS --AND A MOUTH LIKE YOURS...
OH, HE MEANS ME! HE'S TRYING TO TELL ME THAT IT'S ME HE LOVES AND WANTS TO MARRY!

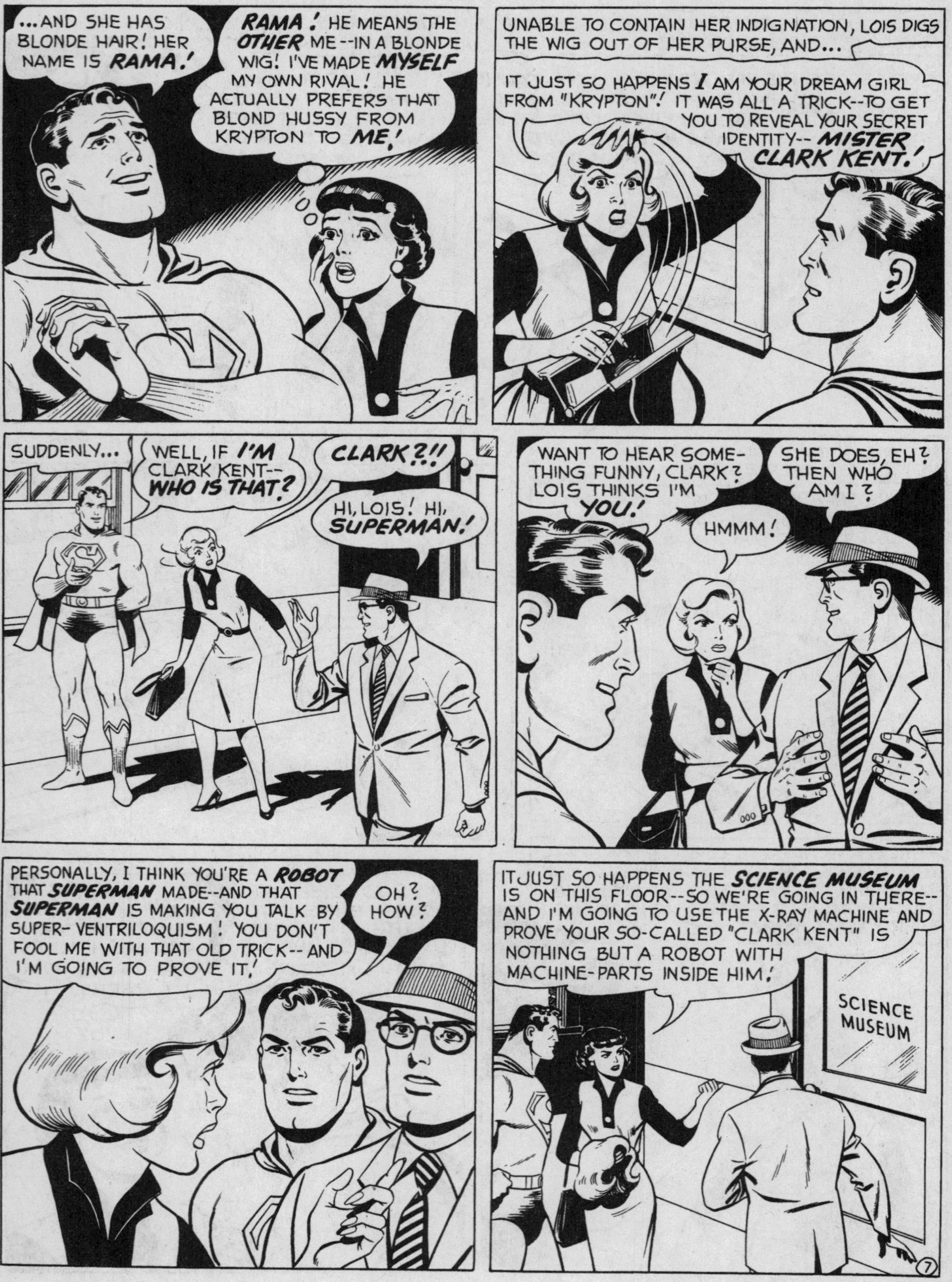
...AND SHE HAS BLONDE HAIR! HER NAME IS RAMA!
RAMA! HE MEANS THE OTHER ME--IN A BLONDE WIG! I'VE MADE MYSELF MY OWN RIVAL! HE ACTUALLY PREFERS THAT BLOND HUSSY FROM KRYPTON TO ME!
UNABLE TO CONTAIN HER INDIGNATION, LOIS DIGS THE WIG OUT OF HER PURSE, AND...
IT JUST SO HAPPENS I AM YOUR DREAM GIRL FROM "KRYPTON"! IT WAS ALL A TRICK--TO GET YOU TO REVEAL YOUR SECRET IDENTITY-- MISTER CLARK KENT!
SUDDENLY...
WELL, IF I'M CLARK KENT-- WHO IS THAT?
CLARK?!!
HI, LOIS! HI, SUPERMAN!
WANT TO HEAR SOME-THING FUNNY, CLARK? LOIS THINKS I'M YOU!
SHE DOES, EH? THEN WHO AM I?
HMMM!
PERSONALLY, I THINK YOU'RE A ROBOT THAT SUPERMAN MADE--AND THAT SUPERMAN IS MAKING YOU TALK BY SUPER- VENTRILOQUISM! YOU DON'T FOOL ME WITH THAT OLD TRICK-- AND I'M GOING TO PROVE IT!
OH? HOW?
IT JUST SO HAPPENS THE SCIENCE MUSEUM IS ON THIS FLOOR--SO WE'RE GOING IN THERE-- AND I'M GOING TO USE THE X-RAY MACHINE AND PROVE YOUR SO-CALLED "CLARK KENT" IS NOTHING BUT A ROBOT WITH MACHINE-PARTS INSIDE HIM!
SCIENCE MUSEUM
7

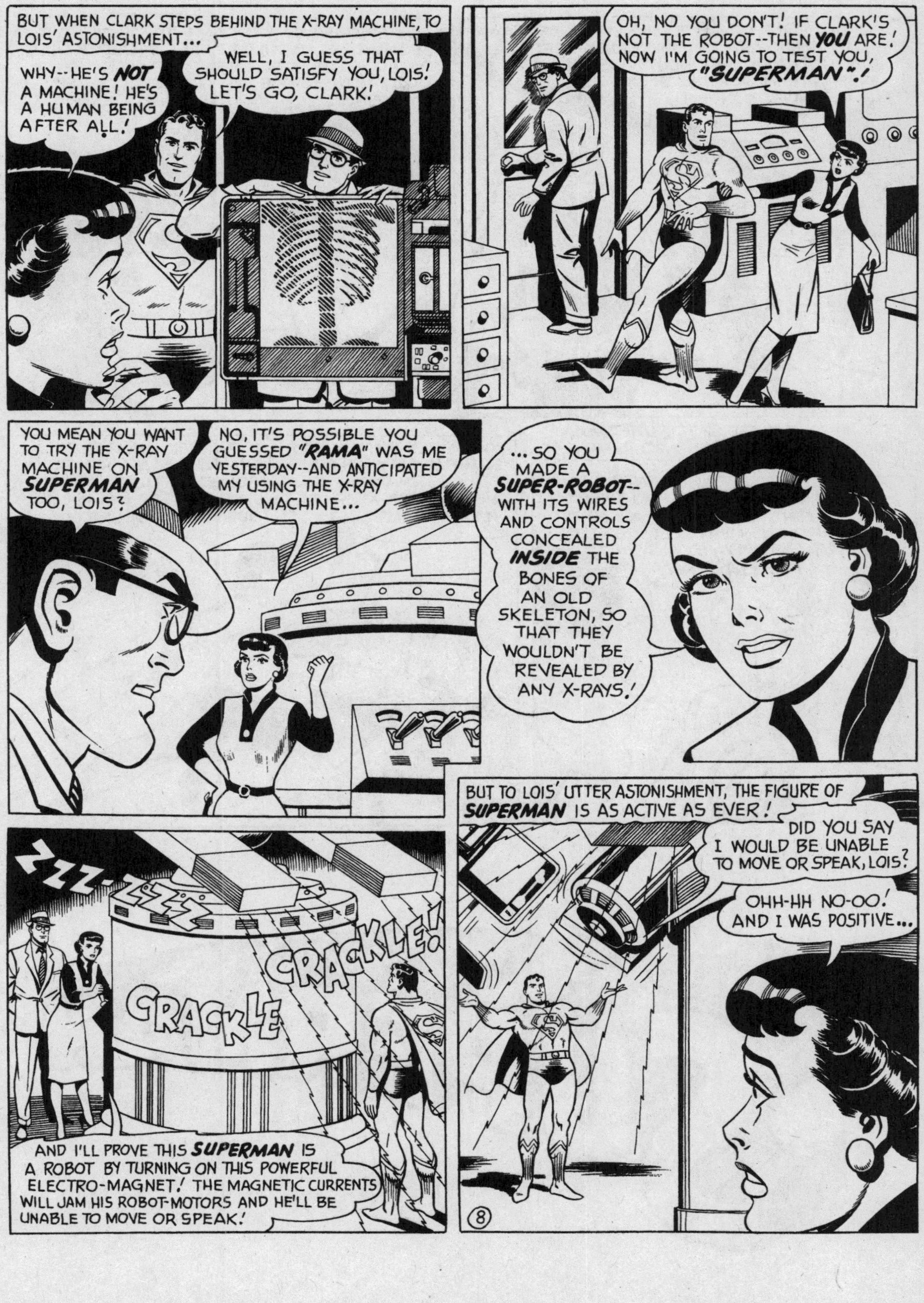
BUT WHEN CLARK STEPS BEHIND THE X-RAY MACHINE, TO LOIS' ASTONISHMENT...
WHY--HE'S NOT A MACHINE! HE'S A HUMAN BEING AFTER ALL!
WELL, I GUESS THAT SHOULD SATISFY YOU, LOIS! LET'S GO, CLARK!
OH, NO YOU DON'T! IF CLARK'S NOT THE ROBOT--THEN YOU ARE! NOW I'M GOING TO TEST YOU, "SUPERMAN"!
YOU MEAN YOU WANT TO TRY THE X-RAY MACHINE ON SUPERMAN TOO, LOIS?
NO, IT'S POSSIBLE YOU GUESSED "RAMA" WAS ME YESTERDAY--AND ANTICIPATED MY USING THE X-RAY MACHINE...
...SO YOU MADE A SUPER-ROBOT--WITH ITS WIRES AND CONTROLS CONCEALED INSIDE THE BONES OF AN OLD SKELETON, SO THAT THEY WOULDN'T BE REVEALED BY ANY X-RAYS!
ZZZ-ZZZZ
CRACKLE
CRACKLE!
AND I'LL PROVE THIS SUPERMAN IS A ROBOT BY TURNING ON THIS POWERFUL ELECTRO-MAGNET! THE MAGNETIC CURRENTS WILL JAM HIS ROBOT-MOTORS AND HE'LL BE UNABLE TO MOVE OR SPEAK!
BUT TO LOIS' UTTER ASTONISHMENT, THE FIGURE OF SUPERMAN IS AS ACTIVE AS EVER!
DID YOU SAY I WOULD BE UNABLE TO MOVE OR SPEAK, LOIS?
OHH-HH NO-OO! AND I WAS POSITIVE...
8

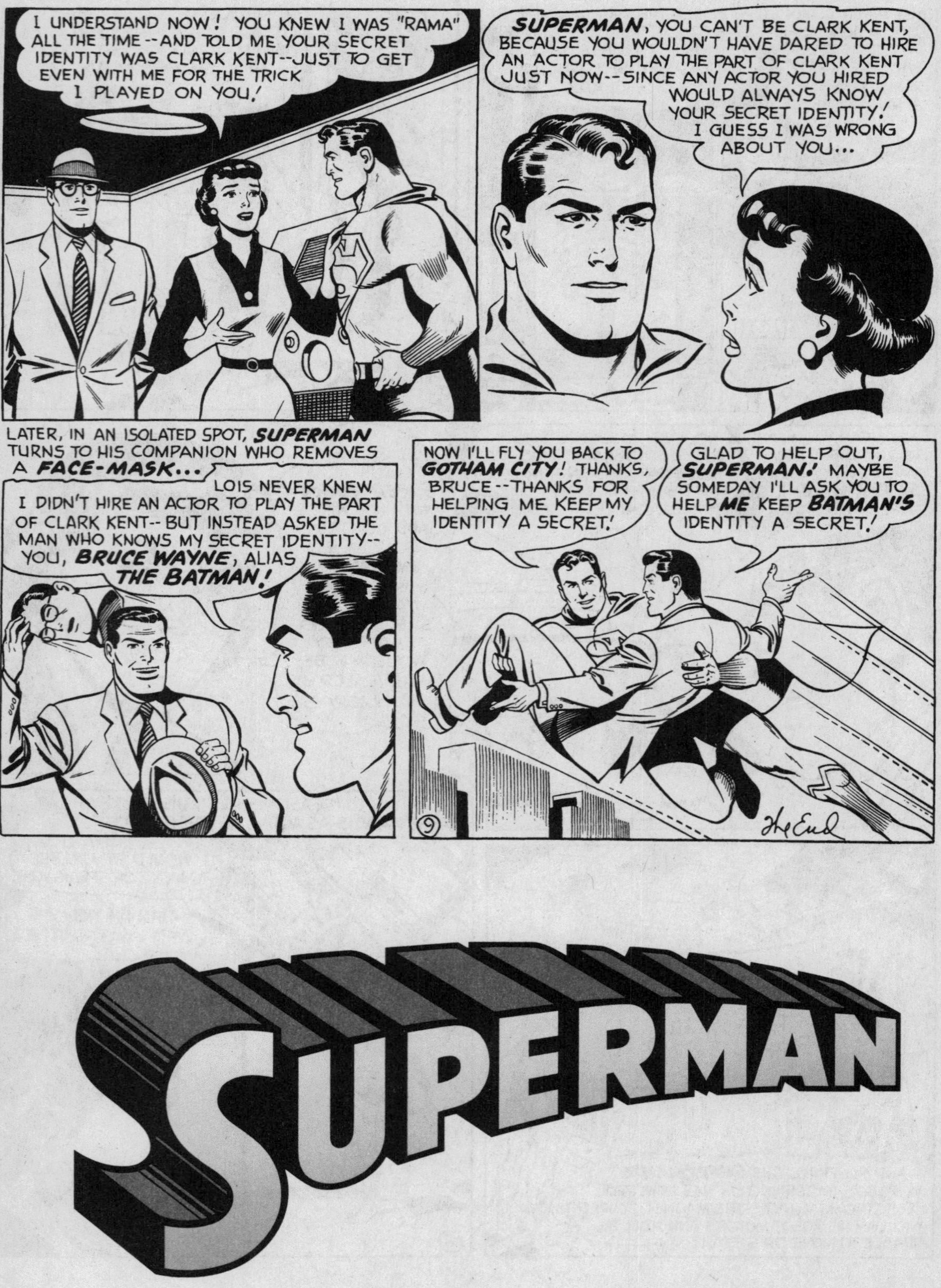
I UNDERSTAND NOW! YOU KNEW I WAS "RAMA" ALL THE TIME--AND TOLD ME YOUR SECRET IDENTITY WAS CLARK KENT--JUST TO GET EVEN WITH ME FOR THE TRICK I PLAYED ON YOU!
SUPERMAN, YOU CAN'T BE CLARK KENT, BECAUSE YOU WOULDN'T HAVE DARED TO HIRE AN ACTOR TO PLAY THE PART OF CLARK KENT JUST NOW--SINCE ANY ACTOR YOU HIRED WOULD ALWAYS KNOW YOUR SECRET IDENTITY! I GUESS I WAS WRONG ABOUT YOU...
LATER, IN AN ISOLATED SPOT, SUPERMAN TURNS TO HIS COMPANION WHO REMOVES A FACE-MASK...
LOIS NEVER KNEW I DIDN'T HIRE AN ACTOR TO PLAY THE PART OF CLARK KENT--BUT INSTEAD ASKED THE MAN WHO KNOWS MY SECRET IDENTITY--YOU, BRUCE WAYNE, ALIAS THE BATMAN!
NOW I'LL FLY YOU BACK TO GOTHAM CITY! THANKS, BRUCE--THANKS FOR HELPING ME KEEP MY IDENTITY A SECRET!
GLAD TO HELP OUT, SUPERMAN! MAYBE SOMEDAY I'LL ASK YOU TO HELP ME KEEP BATMAN'S IDENTITY A SECRET!
9
The End

SUPERMAN

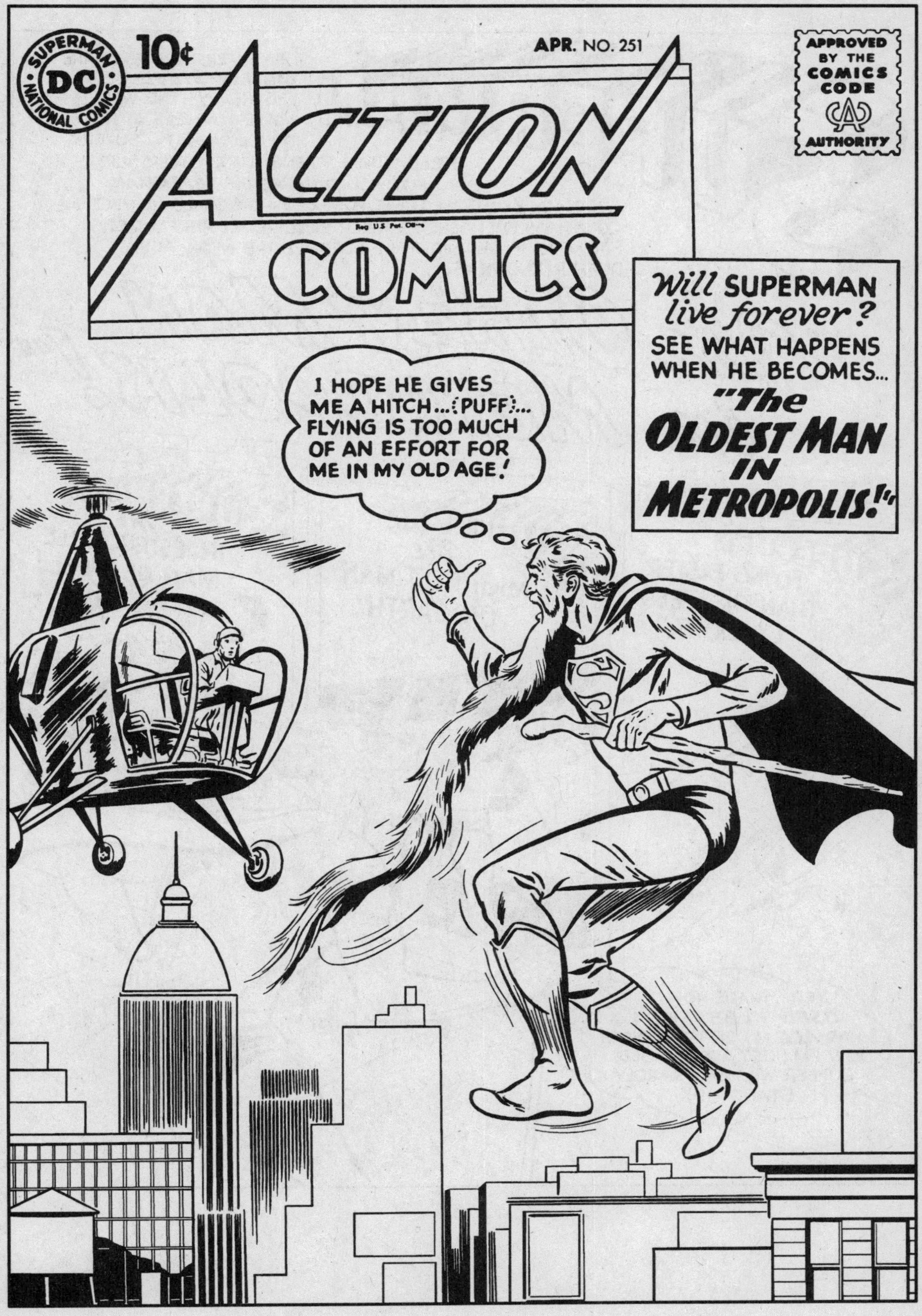
SUPERMAN DC NATIONAL COMICS
10¢
APR. NO. 251
ACTION COMICS
APPROVED BY THE COMICS CODE AUTHORITY
Will SUPERMAN live forever? SEE WHAT HAPPENS WHEN HE BECOMES... "The OLDEST MAN IN METROPOLIS!"
I HOPE HE GIVES ME A HITCH...(PUFF)... FLYING IS TOO MUCH OF AN EFFORT FOR ME IN MY OLD AGE!

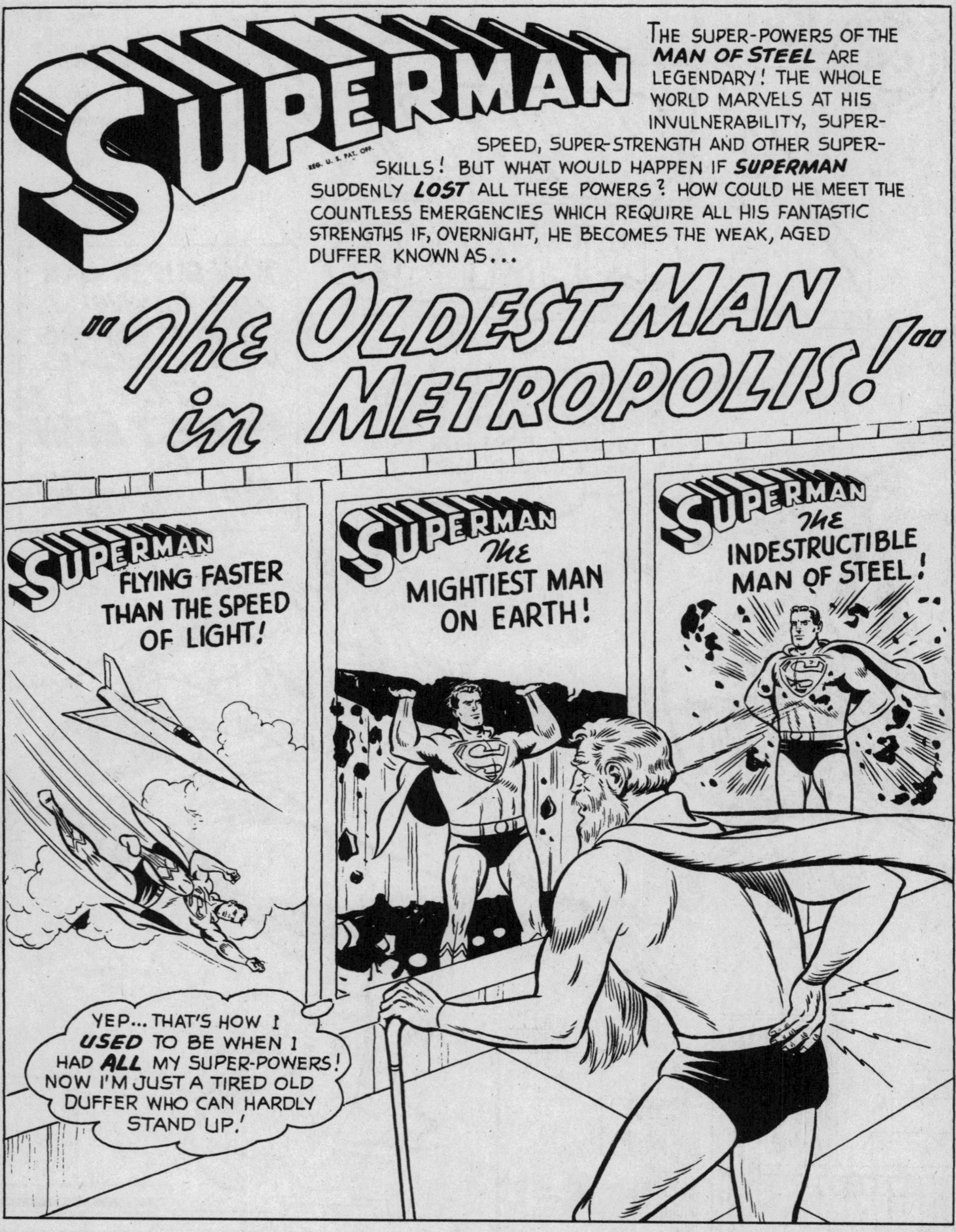
SUPERMAN
REG. U.S. PAT. OFF.
THE SUPER-POWERS OF THE MAN OF STEEL ARE LEGENDARY! THE WHOLE WORLD MARVELS AT HIS INVULNERABILITY, SUPER-SPEED, SUPER-STRENGTH AND OTHER SUPER-SKILLS! BUT WHAT WOULD HAPPEN IF SUPERMAN SUDDENLY LOST ALL THESE POWERS? HOW COULD HE MEET THE COUNTLESS EMERGENCIES WHICH REQUIRE ALL HIS FANTASTIC STRENGTHS IF, OVERNIGHT, HE BECOMES THE WEAK, AGED DUFFER KNOWN AS...
"The OLDEST MAN in METROPOLIS!"
SUPERMAN FLYING FASTER THAN THE SPEED OF LIGHT!
SUPERMAN The MIGHTIEST MAN ON EARTH!
SUPERMAN The INDESTRUCTIBLE MAN OF STEEL!
YEP... THAT'S HOW I USED TO BE WHEN I HAD ALL MY SUPER-POWERS! NOW I'M JUST A TIRED OLD DUFFER WHO CAN HARDLY STAND UP!

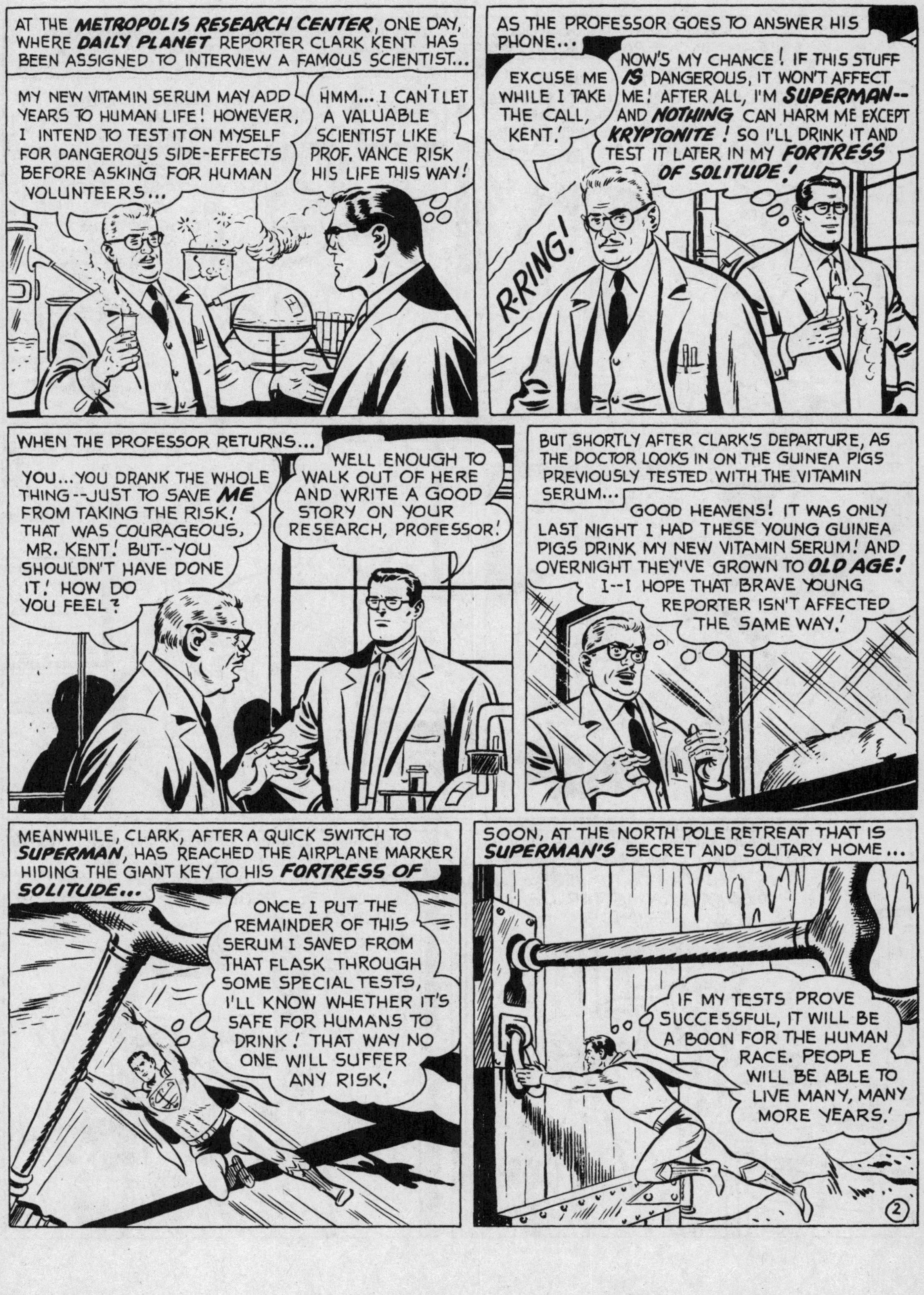
AT THE METROPOLIS RESEARCH CENTER, ONE DAY, WHERE DAILY PLANET REPORTER CLARK KENT HAS BEEN ASSIGNED TO INTERVIEW A FAMOUS SCIENTIST...
MY NEW VITAMIN SERUM MAY ADD YEARS TO HUMAN LIFE! HOWEVER, I INTEND TO TEST IT ON MYSELF FOR DANGEROUS SIDE-EFFECTS BEFORE ASKING FOR HUMAN VOLUNTEERS...
HMM... I CAN'T LET A VALUABLE SCIENTIST LIKE PROF. VANCE RISK HIS LIFE THIS WAY!
AS THE PROFESSOR GOES TO ANSWER HIS PHONE...
EXCUSE ME WHILE I TAKE THE CALL, KENT!
NOW'S MY CHANCE! IF THIS STUFF IS DANGEROUS, IT WON'T AFFECT ME! AFTER ALL, I'M SUPERMAN-- AND NOTHING CAN HARM ME EXCEPT KRYPTONITE! SO I'LL DRINK IT AND TEST IT LATER IN MY FORTRESS OF SOLITUDE!
R-RING!
WHEN THE PROFESSOR RETURNS...
YOU...YOU DRANK THE WHOLE THING--JUST TO SAVE ME FROM TAKING THE RISK! THAT WAS COURAGEOUS, MR. KENT! BUT--YOU SHOULDN'T HAVE DONE IT! HOW DO YOU FEEL?
WELL ENOUGH TO WALK OUT OF HERE AND WRITE A GOOD STORY ON YOUR RESEARCH, PROFESSOR!
BUT SHORTLY AFTER CLARK'S DEPARTURE, AS THE DOCTOR LOOKS IN ON THE GUINEA PIGS PREVIOUSLY TESTED WITH THE VITAMIN SERUM...
GOOD HEAVENS! IT WAS ONLY LAST NIGHT I HAD THESE YOUNG GUINEA PIGS DRINK MY NEW VITAMIN SERUM! AND OVERNIGHT THEY'VE GROWN TO OLD AGE!
I--I HOPE THAT BRAVE YOUNG REPORTER ISN'T AFFECTED THE SAME WAY!
MEANWHILE, CLARK, AFTER A QUICK SWITCH TO SUPERMAN, HAS REACHED THE AIRPLANE MARKER HIDING THE GIANT KEY TO HIS FORTRESS OF SOLITUDE...
ONCE I PUT THE REMAINDER OF THIS SERUM I SAVED FROM THAT FLASK THROUGH SOME SPECIAL TESTS, I'LL KNOW WHETHER IT'S SAFE FOR HUMANS TO DRINK! THAT WAY NO ONE WILL SUFFER ANY RISK!
SOON, AT THE NORTH POLE RETREAT THAT IS SUPERMAN'S SECRET AND SOLITARY HOME...
IF MY TESTS PROVE SUCCESSFUL, IT WILL BE A BOON FOR THE HUMAN RACE. PEOPLE WILL BE ABLE TO LIVE MANY, MANY MORE YEARS!
2

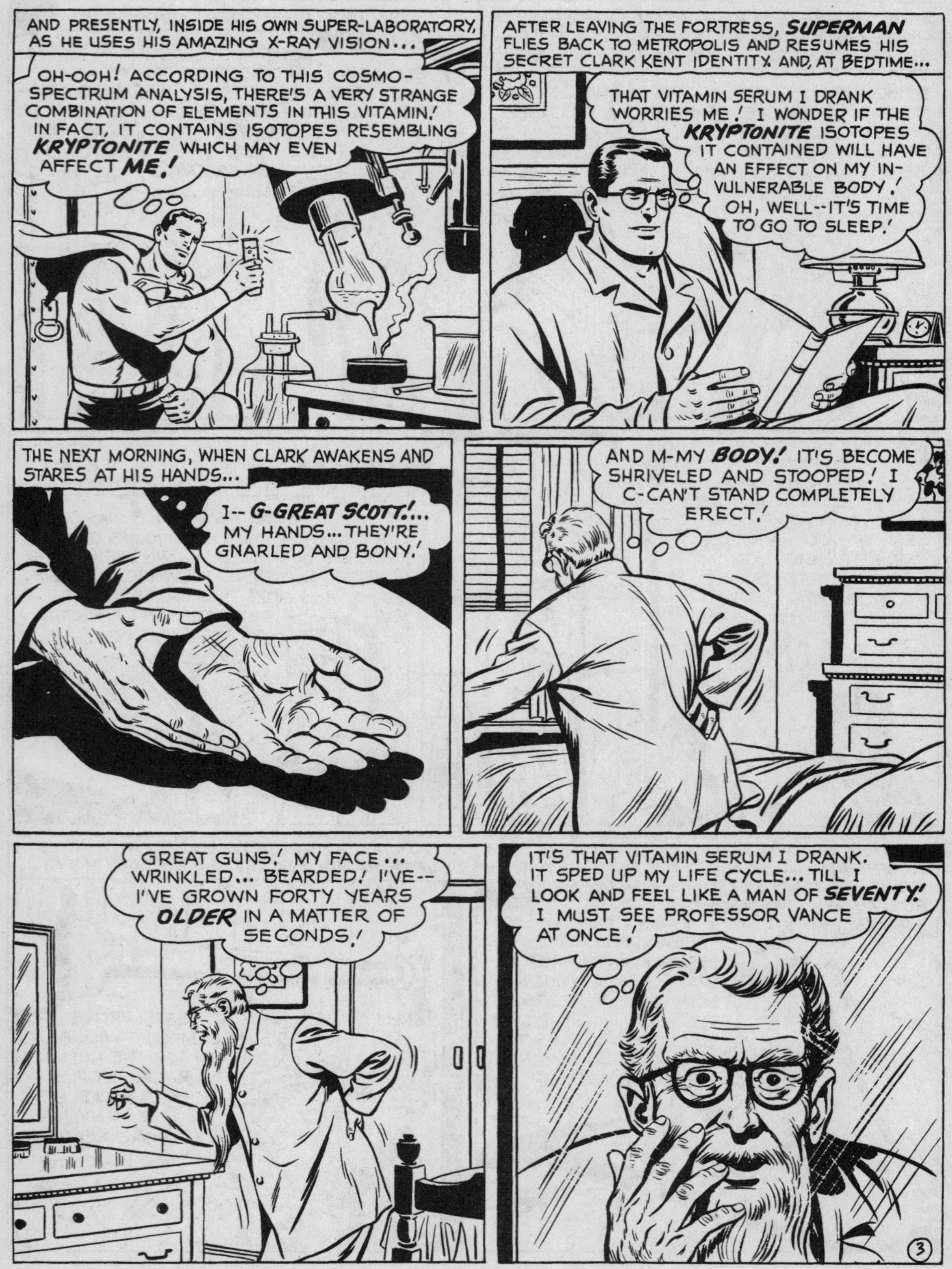
AND PRESENTLY, INSIDE HIS OWN SUPER-LABORATORY, AS HE USES HIS AMAZING X-RAY VISION...
OH-OOH! ACCORDING TO THIS COSMO-SPECTRUM ANALYSIS, THERE'S A VERY STRANGE COMBINATION OF ELEMENTS IN THIS VITAMIN! IN FACT, IT CONTAINS ISOTOPES RESEMBLING KRYPTONITE WHICH MAY EVEN AFFECT ME!
AFTER LEAVING THE FORTRESS, SUPERMAN FLIES BACK TO METROPOLIS AND RESUMES HIS SECRET CLARK KENT IDENTITY. AND, AT BEDTIME...
THAT VITAMIN SERUM I DRANK WORRIES ME! I WONDER IF THE KRYPTONITE ISOTOPES IT CONTAINED WILL HAVE AN EFFECT ON MY INVULNERABLE BODY! OH, WELL--IT'S TIME TO GO TO SLEEP!
THE NEXT MORNING, WHEN CLARK AWAKENS AND STARES AT HIS HANDS...
I-- G-GREAT SCOTT!... MY HANDS... THEY'RE GNARLED AND BONY!
AND M-MY BODY! IT'S BECOME SHRIVELED AND STOOPED! I C-CAN'T STAND COMPLETELY ERECT!
GREAT GUNS! MY FACE... WRINKLED... BEARDED! I'VE-- I'VE GROWN FORTY YEARS OLDER IN A MATTER OF SECONDS!
IT'S THAT VITAMIN SERUM I DRANK. IT SPED UP MY LIFE CYCLE... TILL I LOOK AND FEEL LIKE A MAN OF SEVENTY! I MUST SEE PROFESSOR VANCE AT ONCE!
3

AN HOUR LATER, AT METROPOLIS VETERAN'S HOSPITAL...

YOU DRANK A VERY STRONG CONCENTRATE OF THE VITAMIN SERUM, MR. KENT, SO I RATHER EXPECTED THIS REACTION! I WAS GOING TO CALL YOU IN THE MORNING...

Y-YES, DOCTOR... YES! J-JUST TELL ME! IS--IS THERE AN *ANTIDOTE?*

AMAZING! EVEN YOUR *VOICE* HAS BECOME AN *OLD MAN'S* VOICE... CRACKED AND QUAVERING! BUT IN THREE DAYS THE SERUM'S EFFECT WILL WEAR OFF! LOOK AT THESE FRISKY, YOUNG GUINEA PIGS! A FEW HOURS AGO THEY WERE AS AGED AS YOURSELF!

EXACTLY 72 HOURS AFTER THE CREATURES DRANK THE SERUM, THEY WERE RESTORED BACK TO THEIR ORIGINAL AGE!

THREE DAYS, EH? GOOD GRIEF! IF ANY EMERGENCIES ARISE WHILE I'M IN THIS CONDITION, I'M SUNK! IF ANYONE SEES *SUPERMAN* WITH THIS BEARD, THEY'LL KNOW IT'S CLARK KENT!

AFTER A SLEEPLESS NIGHT, CLARK WORRIEDLY DRESSES AND TAKES A CAB TO THE *PLANET* OFFICE...

A TRAFFIC JAM...AND I'M PLENTY LATE ALREADY! I'D BETTER SWITCH TO *SUPERMAN* AND FLY THE REST OF THE WAY!

BETTER NOT WALK IT, DAD! YOU LOOK LIKE YOU'RE ON YOUR LAST LEGS!

ER...CABBIE! I'LL GET OUT HERE!

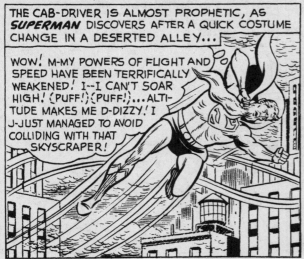

THE CAB-DRIVER IS ALMOST PROPHETIC, AS *SUPERMAN* DISCOVERS AFTER A QUICK COSTUME CHANGE IN A DESERTED ALLEY...

WOW! M-MY POWERS OF FLIGHT AND SPEED HAVE BEEN TERRIFICALLY WEAKENED! I--I CAN'T SOAR HIGH! (PUFF!)(PUFF!)...ALTITUDE MAKES ME D-DIZZY! I J-JUST MANAGED TO AVOID COLLIDING WITH THAT SKYSCRAPER!

I--I MUST REST! I CAN'T T-TAKE THE CONTINUOUS EXERTION!...(PUFF!-PUFF!) THANK GOODNESS FOR THIS SLIGHT FOG! NOBODY'LL SEE HOW HORRIBLY I'VE AGED! OR HOW *UN-*SUPER I'VE BECOME! HEAVEN HELP ME IF MY SUPER-POWERS ARE NEEDED!

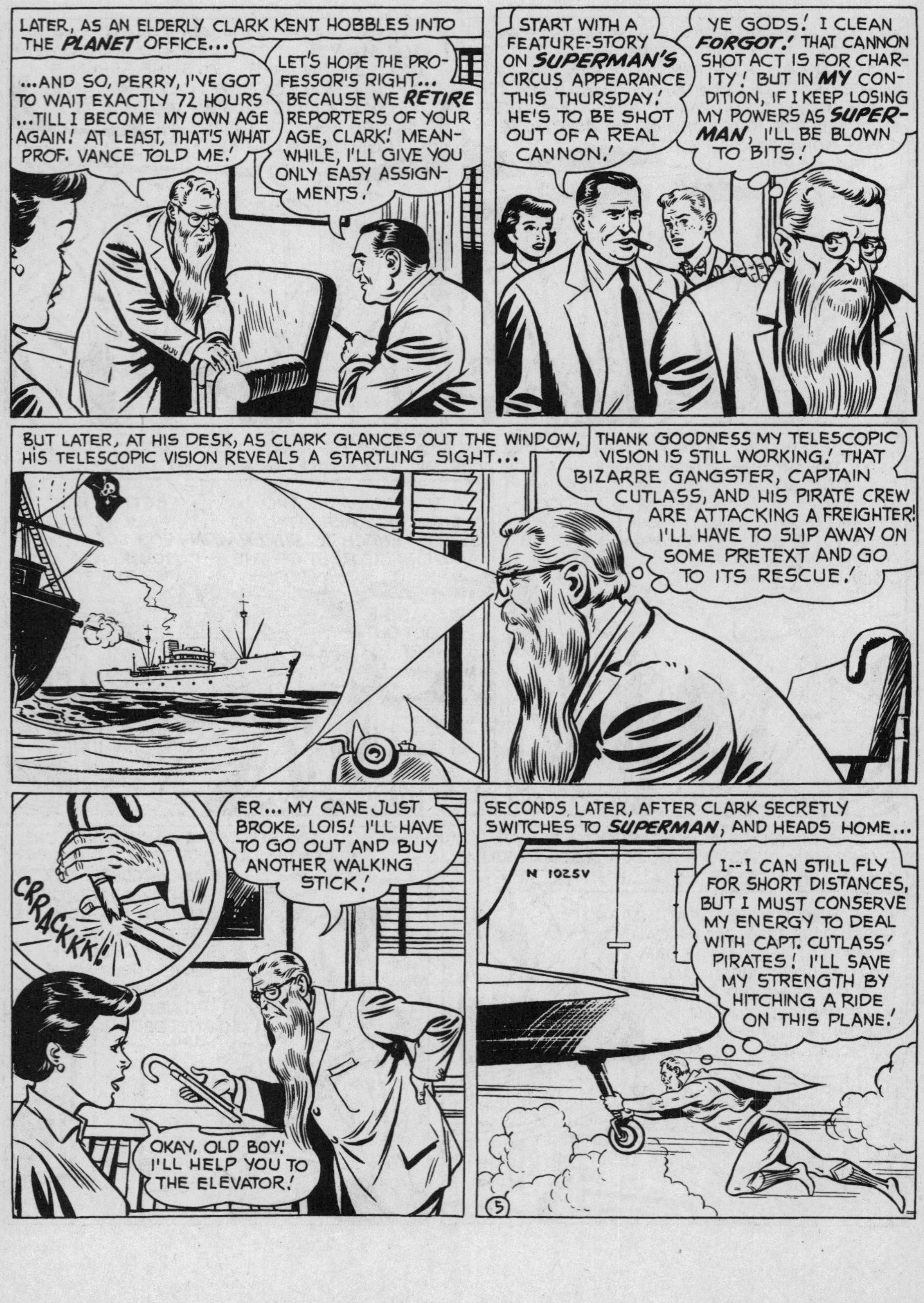
LATER, AS AN ELDERLY CLARK KENT HOBBLES INTO THE PLANET OFFICE...
...AND SO, PERRY, I'VE GOT TO WAIT EXACTLY 72 HOURS ...TILL I BECOME MY OWN AGE AGAIN! AT LEAST, THAT'S WHAT PROF. VANCE TOLD ME!
LET'S HOPE THE PROFESSOR'S RIGHT... BECAUSE WE RETIRE REPORTERS OF YOUR AGE, CLARK! MEANWHILE, I'LL GIVE YOU ONLY EASY ASSIGNMENTS!
START WITH A FEATURE-STORY ON SUPERMAN'S CIRCUS APPEARANCE THIS THURSDAY! HE'S TO BE SHOT OUT OF A REAL CANNON!
YE GODS! I CLEAN FORGOT! THAT CANNON SHOT ACT IS FOR CHARITY! BUT IN MY CONDITION, IF I KEEP LOSING MY POWERS AS SUPERMAN, I'LL BE BLOWN TO BITS!
BUT LATER, AT HIS DESK, AS CLARK GLANCES OUT THE WINDOW, HIS TELESCOPIC VISION REVEALS A STARTLING SIGHT...
THANK GOODNESS MY TELESCOPIC VISION IS STILL WORKING! THAT BIZARRE GANGSTER, CAPTAIN CUTLASS, AND HIS PIRATE CREW ARE ATTACKING A FREIGHTER! I'LL HAVE TO SLIP AWAY ON SOME PRETEXT AND GO TO ITS RESCUE!
CRRACKKK!
ER... MY CANE JUST BROKE, LOIS! I'LL HAVE TO GO OUT AND BUY ANOTHER WALKING STICK!
OKAY, OLD BOY! I'LL HELP YOU TO THE ELEVATOR!
SECONDS LATER, AFTER CLARK SECRETLY SWITCHES TO SUPERMAN, AND HEADS HOME...
N 1025V
I--I CAN STILL FLY FOR SHORT DISTANCES, BUT I MUST CONSERVE MY ENERGY TO DEAL WITH CAPT. CUTLASS' PIRATES! I'LL SAVE MY STRENGTH BY HITCHING A RIDE ON THIS PLANE!
5

GOSH! I NEVER THOUGHT I'D SEE THE DAY I'D BECOME AN AERIAL HITCH-HIKER! BUT THANK HEAVENS I HAVE A *SUPERMAN* ROBOT AT MY APARTMENT THAT CAN SUBSTITUTE FOR ME NOW!

SOON, AT CLARK KENT'S APARTMENT...

FLASH! THE S.S. *OPAL CITY* HAS BEEN RAIDED BY PIRATES WHO MADE OFF WITH A GOLD BULLION CARGO...

EVEN IF I COULD FLY WELL, I WOULDN'T GO AFTER THOSE PIRATES! TOO MANY PEOPLE KNOW THAT CLARK NOW HAS A BEARD! IF ANYONE SAW *ME* WITH A BEARD, THEY'D GUESS MY IDENTITY!

AS *SUPERMAN* ISSUES COMMANDS TO HIS ROBOT...

ROBOT, OBEY YOUR MASTER! FLY TO THE PIRATE SHIP AND RECOVER THE GOLD BULLION!

SUDDENLY... T-THE ROBOT'S REACTING CRAZILY TO MY SPOKEN COMMANDS! I GET IT...THE VIBRATIONS OF MY AGED VOICE ARE TOO CRACKED AND WEAK TO TRANSMIT THE PROPER SIGNALS!

XPRTz!

WWSFRDSZ!

CRRASHH!

CRRACKK!

I CAN'T CONTROL THE ROBOT ANYMORE WITH MY QUIVERING VOICE, SO I'LL HAVE TO FIGHT CAPTAIN CUTLASS *MYSELF!* BUT FIRST, I MUST GET RID OF THIS BEARD! I'LL TRY CUTTING IT!

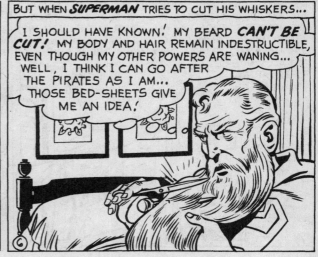

BUT WHEN *SUPERMAN* TRIES TO CUT HIS WHISKERS...

I SHOULD HAVE KNOWN! MY BEARD *CAN'T BE CUT!* MY BODY AND HAIR REMAIN INDESTRUCTIBLE, EVEN THOUGH MY OTHER POWERS ARE WANING... WELL, I THINK I CAN GO AFTER THE PIRATES AS I AM... THOSE BED-SHEETS GIVE ME AN IDEA!

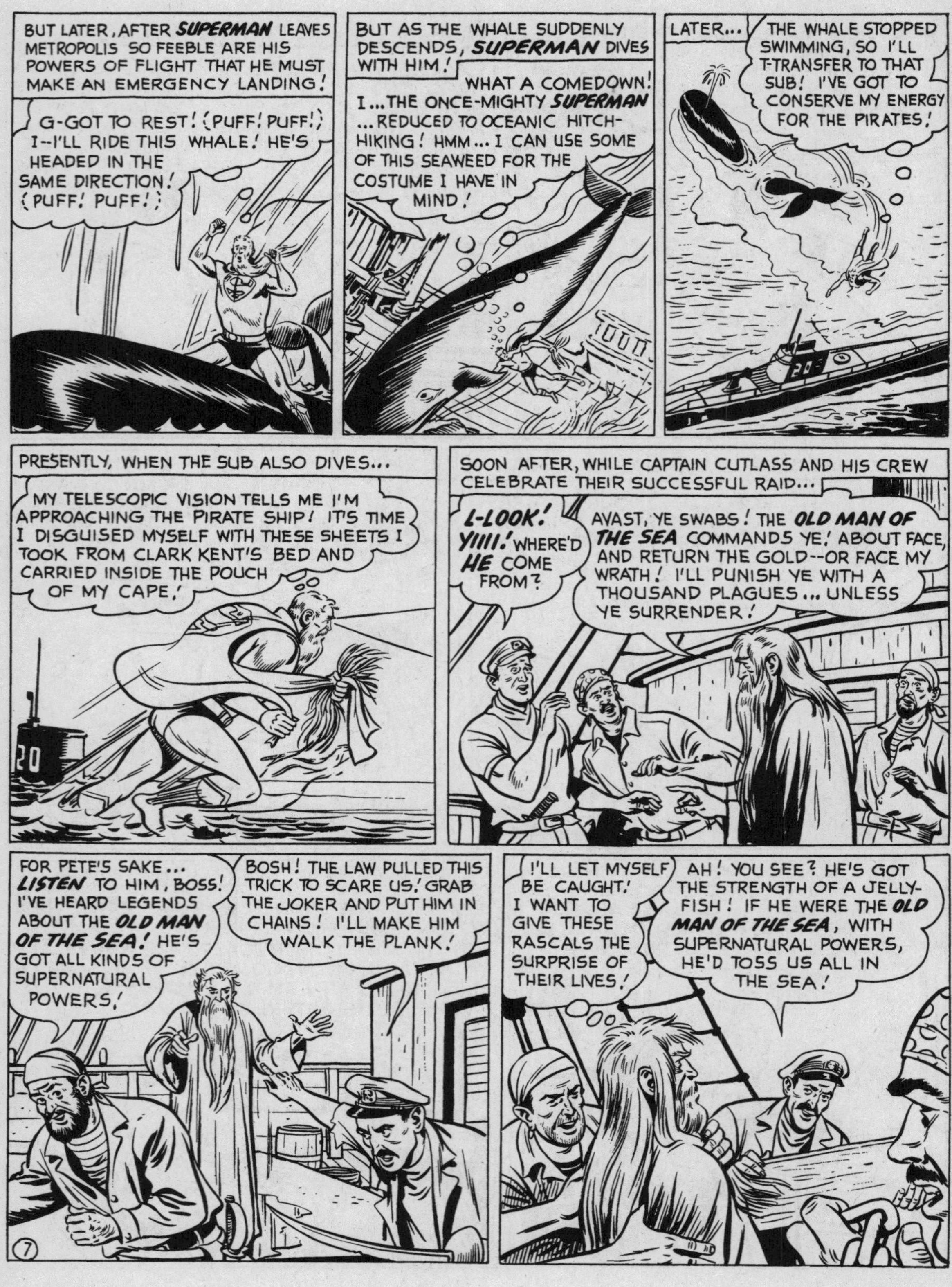
BUT LATER, AFTER SUPERMAN LEAVES METROPOLIS SO FEEBLE ARE HIS POWERS OF FLIGHT THAT HE MUST MAKE AN EMERGENCY LANDING!
G-GOT TO REST! (PUFF! PUFF!) I--I'LL RIDE THIS WHALE! HE'S HEADED IN THE SAME DIRECTION! (PUFF! PUFF!)
BUT AS THE WHALE SUDDENLY DESCENDS, SUPERMAN DIVES WITH HIM!
WHAT A COMEDOWN! I...THE ONCE-MIGHTY SUPERMAN ...REDUCED TO OCEANIC HITCH-HIKING! HMM... I CAN USE SOME OF THIS SEAWEED FOR THE COSTUME I HAVE IN MIND!
LATER...
THE WHALE STOPPED SWIMMING, SO I'LL T-TRANSFER TO THAT SUB! I'VE GOT TO CONSERVE MY ENERGY FOR THE PIRATES!
PRESENTLY, WHEN THE SUB ALSO DIVES...
MY TELESCOPIC VISION TELLS ME I'M APPROACHING THE PIRATE SHIP! IT'S TIME I DISGUISED MYSELF WITH THESE SHEETS I TOOK FROM CLARK KENT'S BED AND CARRIED INSIDE THE POUCH OF MY CAPE!
SOON AFTER, WHILE CAPTAIN CUTLASS AND HIS CREW CELEBRATE THEIR SUCCESSFUL RAID...
L-LOOK! YIIII! WHERE'D HE COME FROM?
AVAST, YE SWABS! THE OLD MAN OF THE SEA COMMANDS YE! ABOUT FACE, AND RETURN THE GOLD--OR FACE MY WRATH! I'LL PUNISH YE WITH A THOUSAND PLAGUES... UNLESS YE SURRENDER!
FOR PETE'S SAKE... LISTEN TO HIM, BOSS! I'VE HEARD LEGENDS ABOUT THE OLD MAN OF THE SEA! HE'S GOT ALL KINDS OF SUPERNATURAL POWERS!
BOSH! THE LAW PULLED THIS TRICK TO SCARE US! GRAB THE JOKER AND PUT HIM IN CHAINS! I'LL MAKE HIM WALK THE PLANK!
7
I'LL LET MYSELF BE CAUGHT! I WANT TO GIVE THESE RASCALS THE SURPRISE OF THEIR LIVES!
AH! YOU SEE? HE'S GOT THE STRENGTH OF A JELLY-FISH! IF HE WERE THE OLD MAN OF THE SEA, WITH SUPERNATURAL POWERS, HE'D TOSS US ALL IN THE SEA!

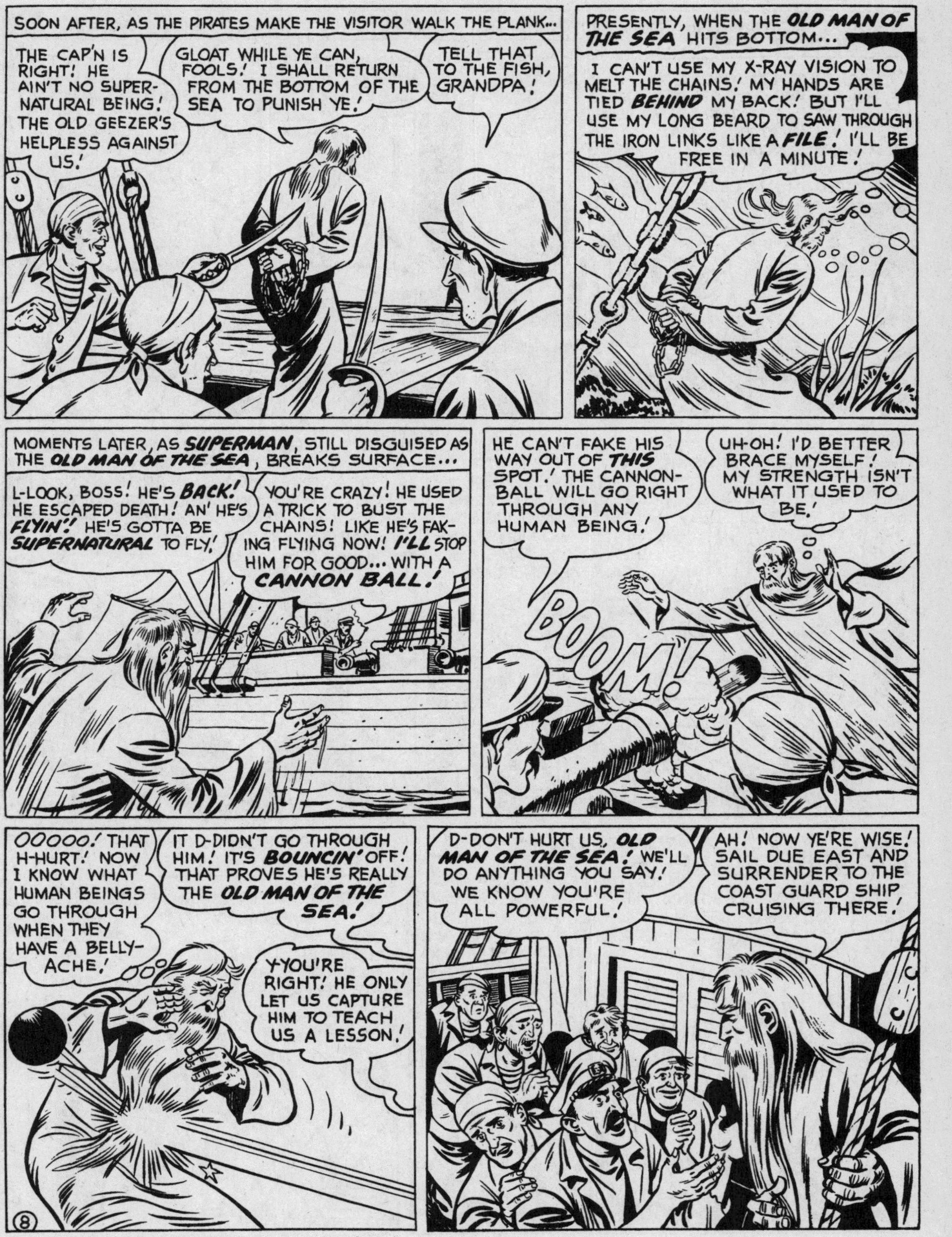
SOON AFTER, AS THE PIRATES MAKE THE VISITOR WALK THE PLANK...
THE CAP'N IS RIGHT! HE AIN'T NO SUPER-NATURAL BEING! THE OLD GEEZER'S HELPLESS AGAINST US!
GLOAT WHILE YE CAN, FOOLS! I SHALL RETURN FROM THE BOTTOM OF THE SEA TO PUNISH YE!
TELL THAT TO THE FISH, GRANDPA!
PRESENTLY, WHEN THE OLD MAN OF THE SEA HITS BOTTOM...
I CAN'T USE MY X-RAY VISION TO MELT THE CHAINS! MY HANDS ARE TIED BEHIND MY BACK! BUT I'LL USE MY LONG BEARD TO SAW THROUGH THE IRON LINKS LIKE A FILE! I'LL BE FREE IN A MINUTE!
MOMENTS LATER, AS SUPERMAN, STILL DISGUISED AS THE OLD MAN OF THE SEA, BREAKS SURFACE...
L-LOOK, BOSS! HE'S BACK! HE ESCAPED DEATH! AN' HE'S FLYIN'! HE'S GOTTA BE SUPERNATURAL TO FLY!
YOU'RE CRAZY! HE USED A TRICK TO BUST THE CHAINS! LIKE HE'S FAKING FLYING NOW! I'LL STOP HIM FOR GOOD... WITH A CANNON BALL!
HE CAN'T FAKE HIS WAY OUT OF THIS SPOT! THE CANNON-BALL WILL GO RIGHT THROUGH ANY HUMAN BEING!
UH-OH! I'D BETTER BRACE MYSELF! MY STRENGTH ISN'T WHAT IT USED TO BE!
BOOM!
OOOOO! THAT H-HURT! NOW I KNOW WHAT HUMAN BEINGS GO THROUGH WHEN THEY HAVE A BELLY-ACHE!
IT D-DIDN'T GO THROUGH HIM! IT'S BOUNCIN' OFF! THAT PROVES HE'S REALLY THE OLD MAN OF THE SEA!
Y-YOU'RE RIGHT! HE ONLY LET US CAPTURE HIM TO TEACH US A LESSON!
8
D-DON'T HURT US, OLD MAN OF THE SEA! WE'LL DO ANYTHING YOU SAY! WE KNOW YOU'RE ALL POWERFUL!
AH! NOW YE'RE WISE! SAIL DUE EAST AND SURRENDER TO THE COAST GUARD SHIP CRUISING THERE!

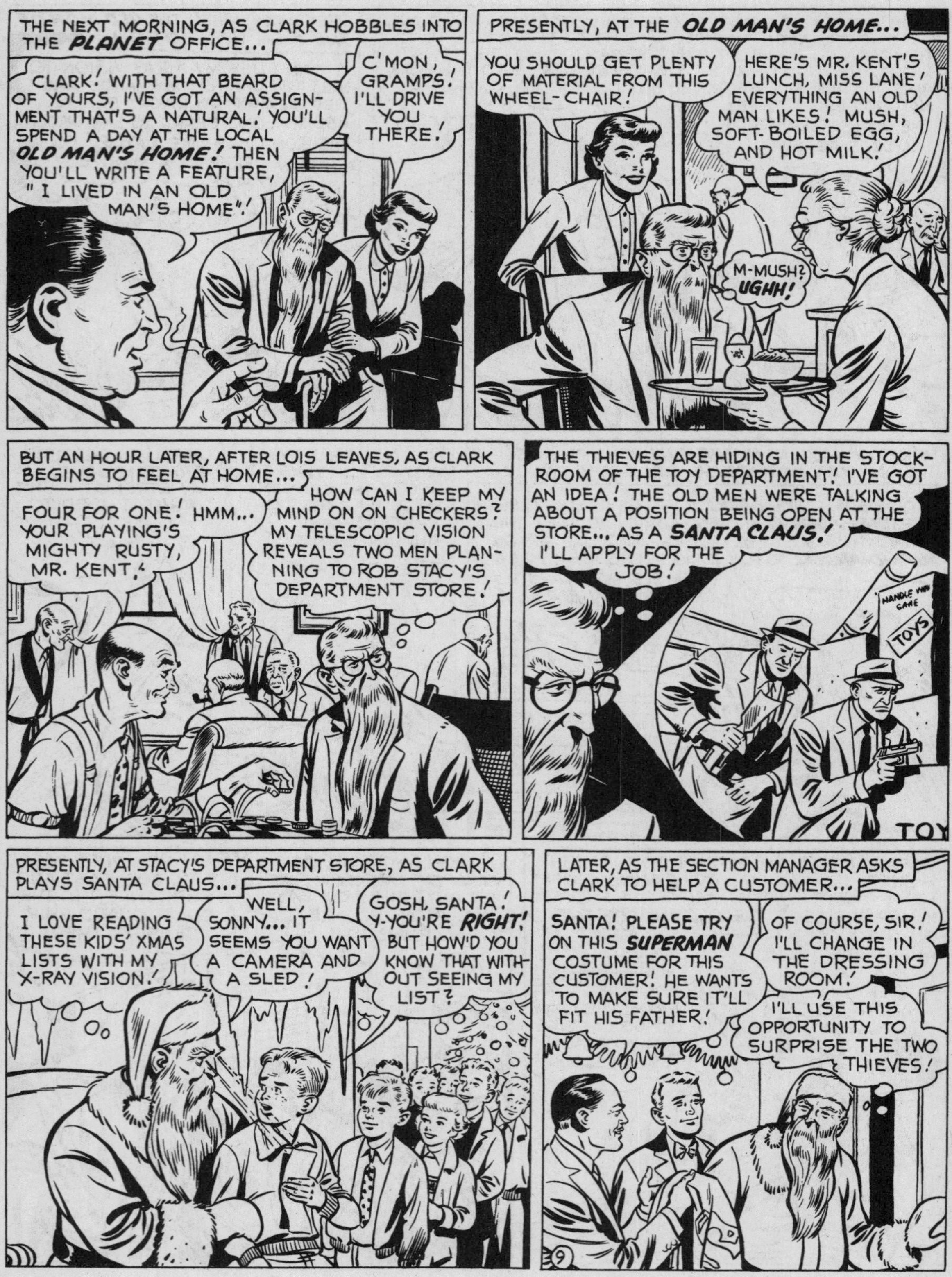
THE NEXT MORNING, AS CLARK HOBBLES INTO THE PLANET OFFICE...
CLARK! WITH THAT BEARD OF YOURS, I'VE GOT AN ASSIGNMENT THAT'S A NATURAL! YOU'LL SPEND A DAY AT THE LOCAL OLD MAN'S HOME! THEN YOU'LL WRITE A FEATURE, "I LIVED IN AN OLD MAN'S HOME"!
C'MON, GRAMPS! I'LL DRIVE YOU THERE!
PRESENTLY, AT THE OLD MAN'S HOME...
YOU SHOULD GET PLENTY OF MATERIAL FROM THIS WHEEL-CHAIR!
HERE'S MR. KENT'S LUNCH, MISS LANE! EVERYTHING AN OLD MAN LIKES! MUSH, SOFT-BOILED EGG, AND HOT MILK!
M-MUSH? UGHH!
BUT AN HOUR LATER, AFTER LOIS LEAVES, AS CLARK BEGINS TO FEEL AT HOME...
FOUR FOR ONE! HMM... YOUR PLAYING'S MIGHTY RUSTY, MR. KENT!
HOW CAN I KEEP MY MIND ON ON CHECKERS? MY TELESCOPIC VISION REVEALS TWO MEN PLANNING TO ROB STACY'S DEPARTMENT STORE!
THE THIEVES ARE HIDING IN THE STOCKROOM OF THE TOY DEPARTMENT! I'VE GOT AN IDEA! THE OLD MEN WERE TALKING ABOUT A POSITION BEING OPEN AT THE STORE... AS A SANTA CLAUS! I'LL APPLY FOR THE JOB!
TOYS
TOY
PRESENTLY, AT STACY'S DEPARTMENT STORE, AS CLARK PLAYS SANTA CLAUS...
I LOVE READING THESE KIDS' XMAS LISTS WITH MY X-RAY VISION!
WELL, SONNY... IT SEEMS YOU WANT A CAMERA AND A SLED!
GOSH, SANTA! Y-YOU'RE RIGHT! BUT HOW'D YOU KNOW THAT WITHOUT SEEING MY LIST?
LATER, AS THE SECTION MANAGER ASKS CLARK TO HELP A CUSTOMER...
SANTA! PLEASE TRY ON THIS SUPERMAN COSTUME FOR THIS CUSTOMER! HE WANTS TO MAKE SURE IT'LL FIT HIS FATHER!
OF COURSE, SIR! I'LL CHANGE IN THE DRESSING ROOM!
I'LL USE THIS OPPORTUNITY TO SURPRISE THE TWO THIEVES!
9

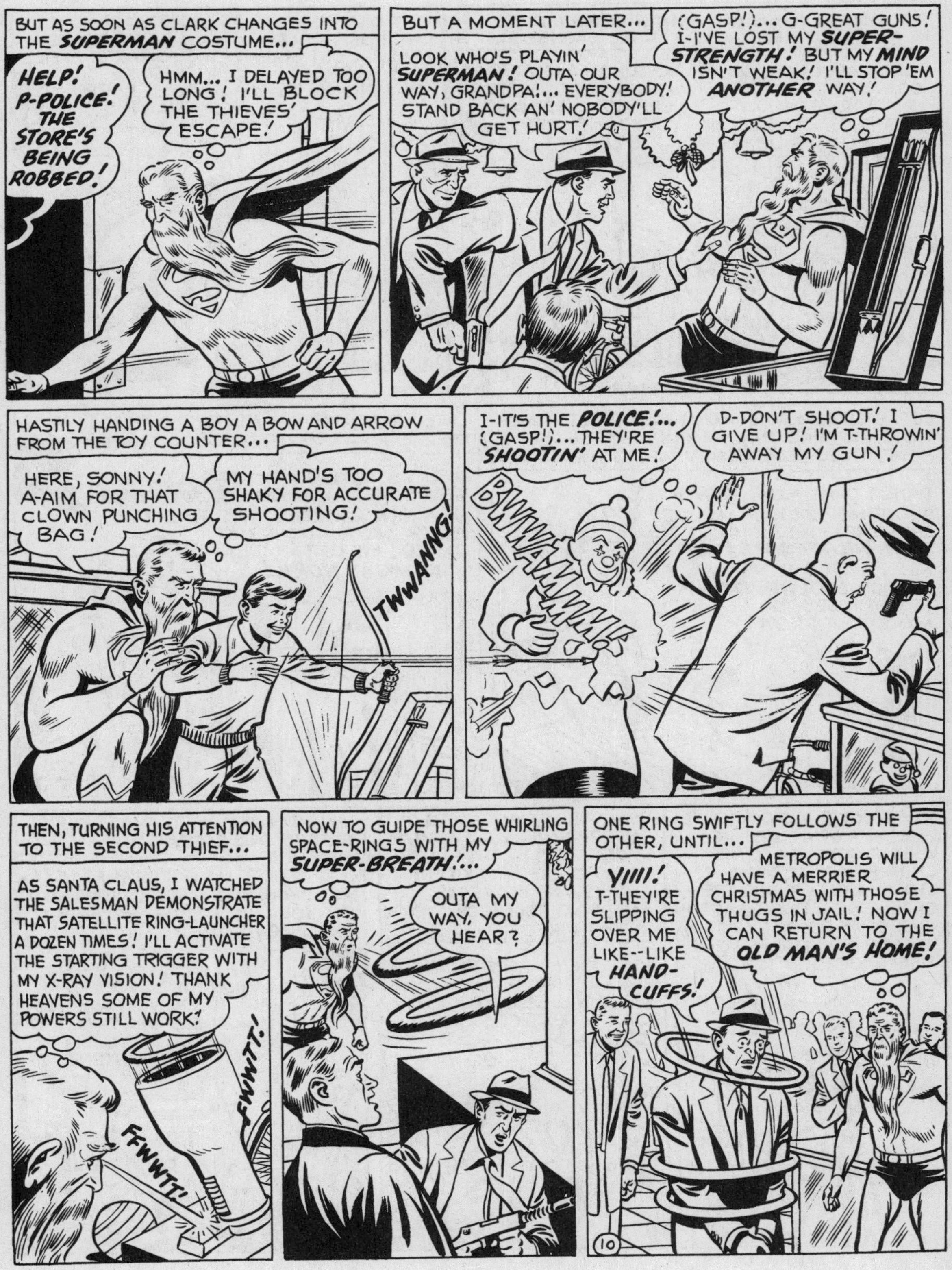
BUT AS SOON AS CLARK CHANGES INTO THE SUPERMAN COSTUME...
HELP! P-POLICE! THE STORE'S BEING ROBBED!
HMM... I DELAYED TOO LONG! I'LL BLOCK THE THIEVES' ESCAPE!
BUT A MOMENT LATER...
LOOK WHO'S PLAYIN' SUPERMAN! OUTA OUR WAY, GRANDPA!... EVERYBODY! STAND BACK AN' NOBODY'LL GET HURT!
(GASP!)... G-GREAT GUNS! I-I'VE LOST MY SUPER-STRENGTH! BUT MY MIND ISN'T WEAK! I'LL STOP 'EM ANOTHER WAY!
HASTILY HANDING A BOY A BOW AND ARROW FROM THE TOY COUNTER...
HERE, SONNY! A-AIM FOR THAT CLOWN PUNCHING BAG!
MY HAND'S TOO SHAKY FOR ACCURATE SHOOTING!
TWWANNG!
I-IT'S THE POLICE!... (GASP!)... THEY'RE SHOOTIN' AT ME!
D-DON'T SHOOT! I GIVE UP! I'M T-THROWIN' AWAY MY GUN!
BWWAMMM!
THEN, TURNING HIS ATTENTION TO THE SECOND THIEF...
AS SANTA CLAUS, I WATCHED THE SALESMAN DEMONSTRATE THAT SATELLITE RING-LAUNCHER A DOZEN TIMES! I'LL ACTIVATE THE STARTING TRIGGER WITH MY X-RAY VISION! THANK HEAVENS SOME OF MY POWERS STILL WORK!
FFWWTT!
FWWTT!
NOW TO GUIDE THOSE WHIRLING SPACE-RINGS WITH MY SUPER-BREATH!...
OUTA MY WAY, YOU HEAR?
ONE RING SWIFTLY FOLLOWS THE OTHER, UNTIL...
YIII! T-THEY'RE SLIPPING OVER ME LIKE--LIKE HAND-CUFFS!
METROPOLIS WILL HAVE A MERRIER CHRISTMAS WITH THOSE THUGS IN JAIL! NOW I CAN RETURN TO THE OLD MAN'S HOME!
10

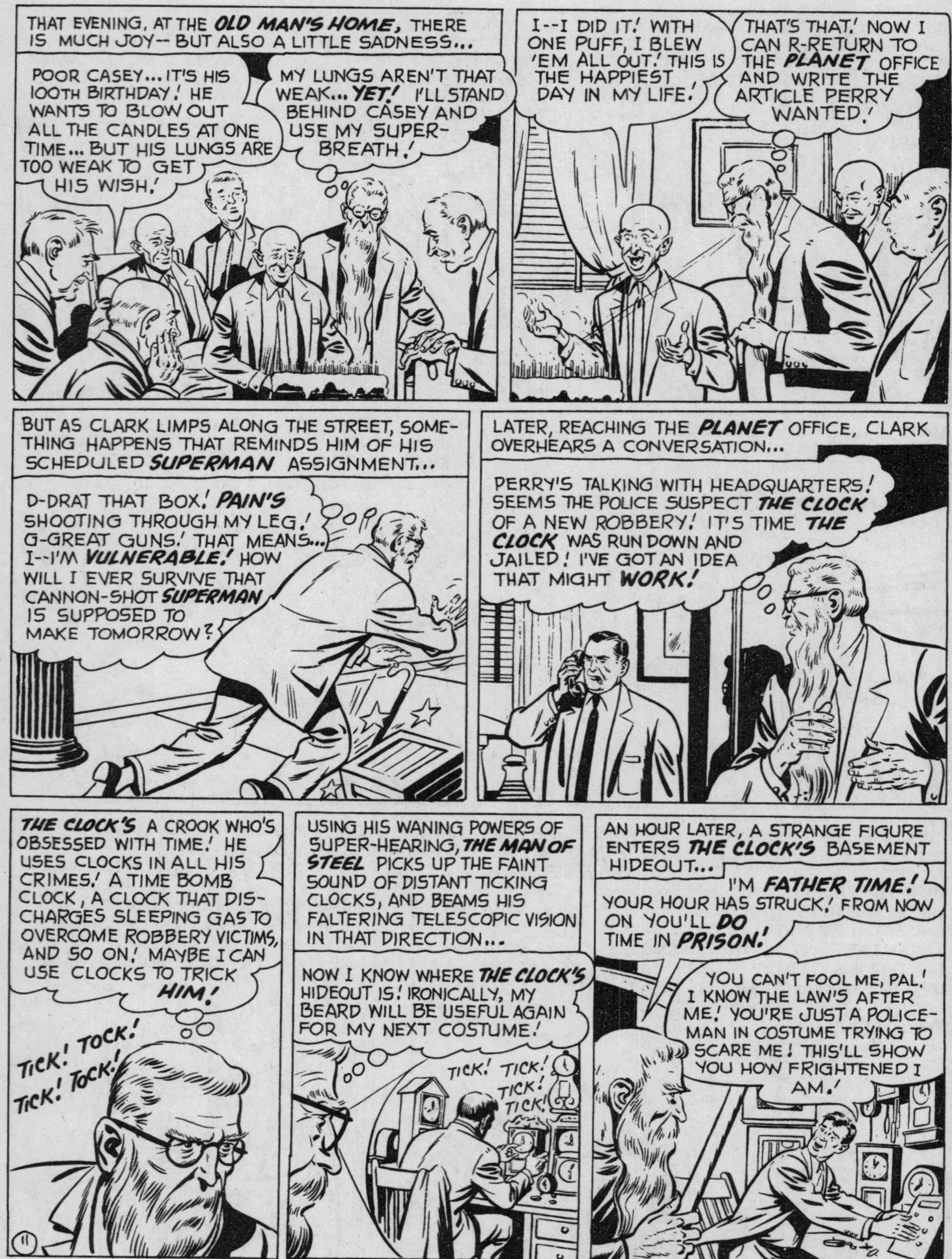
THAT EVENING, AT THE OLD MAN'S HOME, THERE IS MUCH JOY-- BUT ALSO A LITTLE SADNESS...
POOR CASEY... IT'S HIS 100TH BIRTHDAY! HE WANTS TO BLOW OUT ALL THE CANDLES AT ONE TIME... BUT HIS LUNGS ARE TOO WEAK TO GET HIS WISH!
MY LUNGS AREN'T THAT WEAK... YET! I'LL STAND BEHIND CASEY AND USE MY SUPER-BREATH!
I--I DID IT! WITH ONE PUFF, I BLEW 'EM ALL OUT! THIS IS THE HAPPIEST DAY IN MY LIFE!
THAT'S THAT! NOW I CAN R-RETURN TO THE PLANET OFFICE AND WRITE THE ARTICLE PERRY WANTED!
BUT AS CLARK LIMPS ALONG THE STREET, SOMETHING HAPPENS THAT REMINDS HIM OF HIS SCHEDULED SUPERMAN ASSIGNMENT...
D-DRAT THAT BOX! PAIN'S SHOOTING THROUGH MY LEG! G-GREAT GUNS! THAT MEANS... I--I'M VULNERABLE! HOW WILL I EVER SURVIVE THAT CANNON-SHOT SUPERMAN IS SUPPOSED TO MAKE TOMORROW?
LATER, REACHING THE PLANET OFFICE, CLARK OVERHEARS A CONVERSATION...
PERRY'S TALKING WITH HEADQUARTERS! SEEMS THE POLICE SUSPECT THE CLOCK OF A NEW ROBBERY! IT'S TIME THE CLOCK WAS RUN DOWN AND JAILED! I'VE GOT AN IDEA THAT MIGHT WORK!
THE CLOCK'S A CROOK WHO'S OBSESSED WITH TIME! HE USES CLOCKS IN ALL HIS CRIMES! A TIME BOMB CLOCK, A CLOCK THAT DISCHARGES SLEEPING GAS TO OVERCOME ROBBERY VICTIMS, AND SO ON! MAYBE I CAN USE CLOCKS TO TRICK HIM!
TICK! TOCK! TICK! TOCK!
11
USING HIS WANING POWERS OF SUPER-HEARING, THE MAN OF STEEL PICKS UP THE FAINT SOUND OF DISTANT TICKING CLOCKS, AND BEAMS HIS FALTERING TELESCOPIC VISION IN THAT DIRECTION...
NOW I KNOW WHERE THE CLOCK'S HIDEOUT IS! IRONICALLY, MY BEARD WILL BE USEFUL AGAIN FOR MY NEXT COSTUME!
TICK! TICK! TICK! TICK!
AN HOUR LATER, A STRANGE FIGURE ENTERS THE CLOCK'S BASEMENT HIDEOUT...
I'M FATHER TIME! YOUR HOUR HAS STRUCK! FROM NOW ON YOU'LL DO TIME IN PRISON!
YOU CAN'T FOOL ME, PAL! I KNOW THE LAW'S AFTER ME! YOU'RE JUST A POLICEMAN IN COSTUME TRYING TO SCARE ME! THIS'LL SHOW YOU HOW FRIGHTENED I AM!

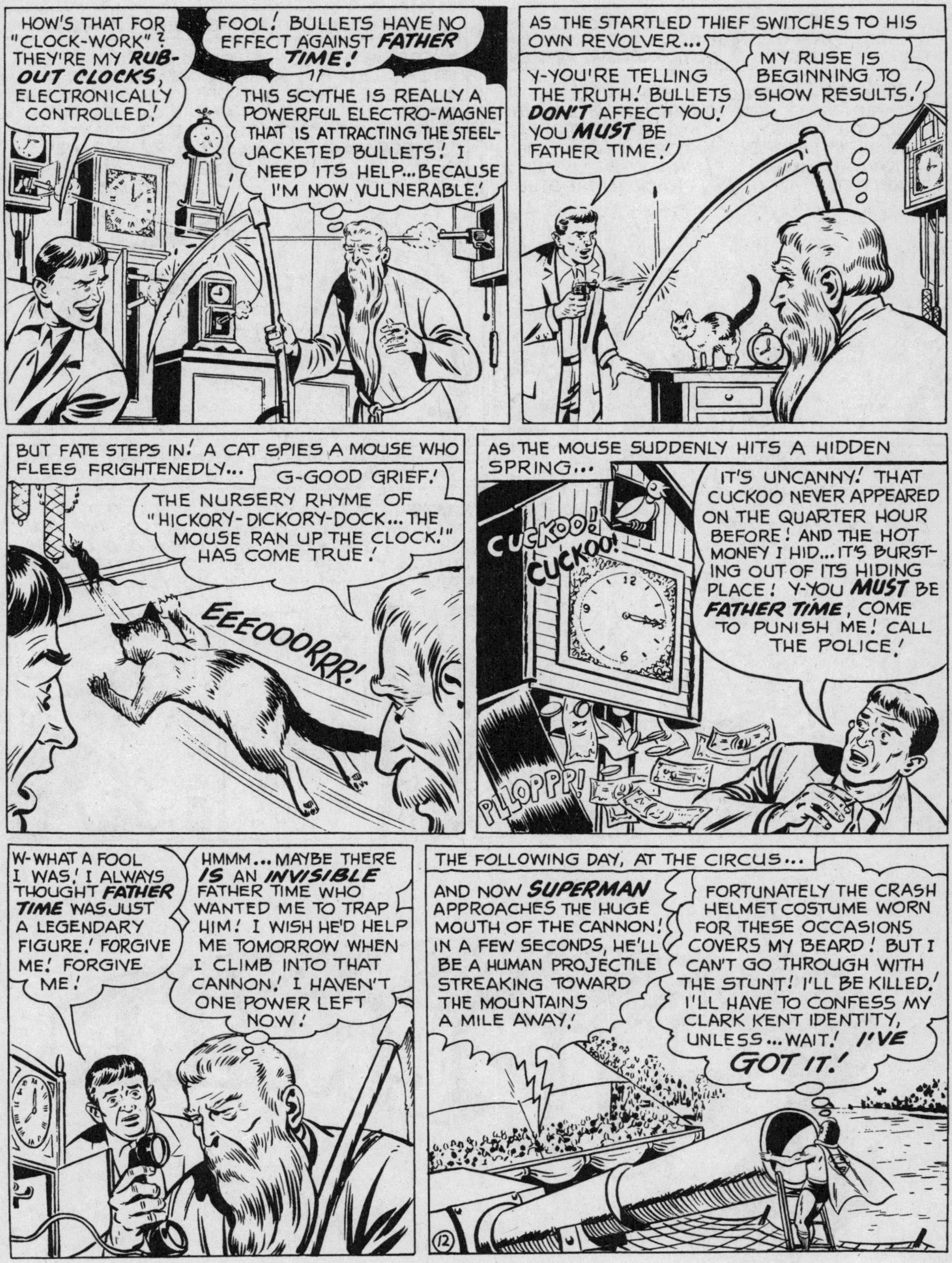
HOW'S THAT FOR "CLOCK-WORK"? THEY'RE MY RUB-OUT CLOCKS, ELECTRONICALLY CONTROLLED!
FOOL! BULLETS HAVE NO EFFECT AGAINST FATHER TIME!
THIS SCYTHE IS REALLY A POWERFUL ELECTRO-MAGNET THAT IS ATTRACTING THE STEEL-JACKETED BULLETS! I NEED ITS HELP...BECAUSE I'M NOW VULNERABLE!
AS THE STARTLED THIEF SWITCHES TO HIS OWN REVOLVER...
Y-YOU'RE TELLING THE TRUTH! BULLETS DON'T AFFECT YOU! YOU MUST BE FATHER TIME!
MY RUSE IS BEGINNING TO SHOW RESULTS!
BUT FATE STEPS IN! A CAT SPIES A MOUSE WHO FLEES FRIGHTENEDLY...
G-GOOD GRIEF! THE NURSERY RHYME OF "HICKORY-DICKORY-DOCK...THE MOUSE RAN UP THE CLOCK!" HAS COME TRUE!
EEEOOOORRR!
AS THE MOUSE SUDDENLY HITS A HIDDEN SPRING...
CUCKOO! CUCKOO!
IT'S UNCANNY! THAT CUCKOO NEVER APPEARED ON THE QUARTER HOUR BEFORE! AND THE HOT MONEY I HID...IT'S BURSTING OUT OF ITS HIDING PLACE! Y-YOU MUST BE FATHER TIME, COME TO PUNISH ME! CALL THE POLICE!
PLLOPPP!
W-WHAT A FOOL I WAS! I ALWAYS THOUGHT FATHER TIME WAS JUST A LEGENDARY FIGURE! FORGIVE ME! FORGIVE ME!
HMMM...MAYBE THERE IS AN INVISIBLE FATHER TIME WHO WANTED ME TO TRAP HIM! I WISH HE'D HELP ME TOMORROW WHEN I CLIMB INTO THAT CANNON! I HAVEN'T ONE POWER LEFT NOW!
THE FOLLOWING DAY, AT THE CIRCUS...
AND NOW SUPERMAN APPROACHES THE HUGE MOUTH OF THE CANNON! IN A FEW SECONDS, HE'LL BE A HUMAN PROJECTILE STREAKING TOWARD THE MOUNTAINS A MILE AWAY!
FORTUNATELY THE CRASH HELMET COSTUME WORN FOR THESE OCCASIONS COVERS MY BEARD! BUT I CAN'T GO THROUGH WITH THE STUNT! I'LL BE KILLED! I'LL HAVE TO CONFESS MY CLARK KENT IDENTITY, UNLESS...WAIT! I'VE GOT IT!
12

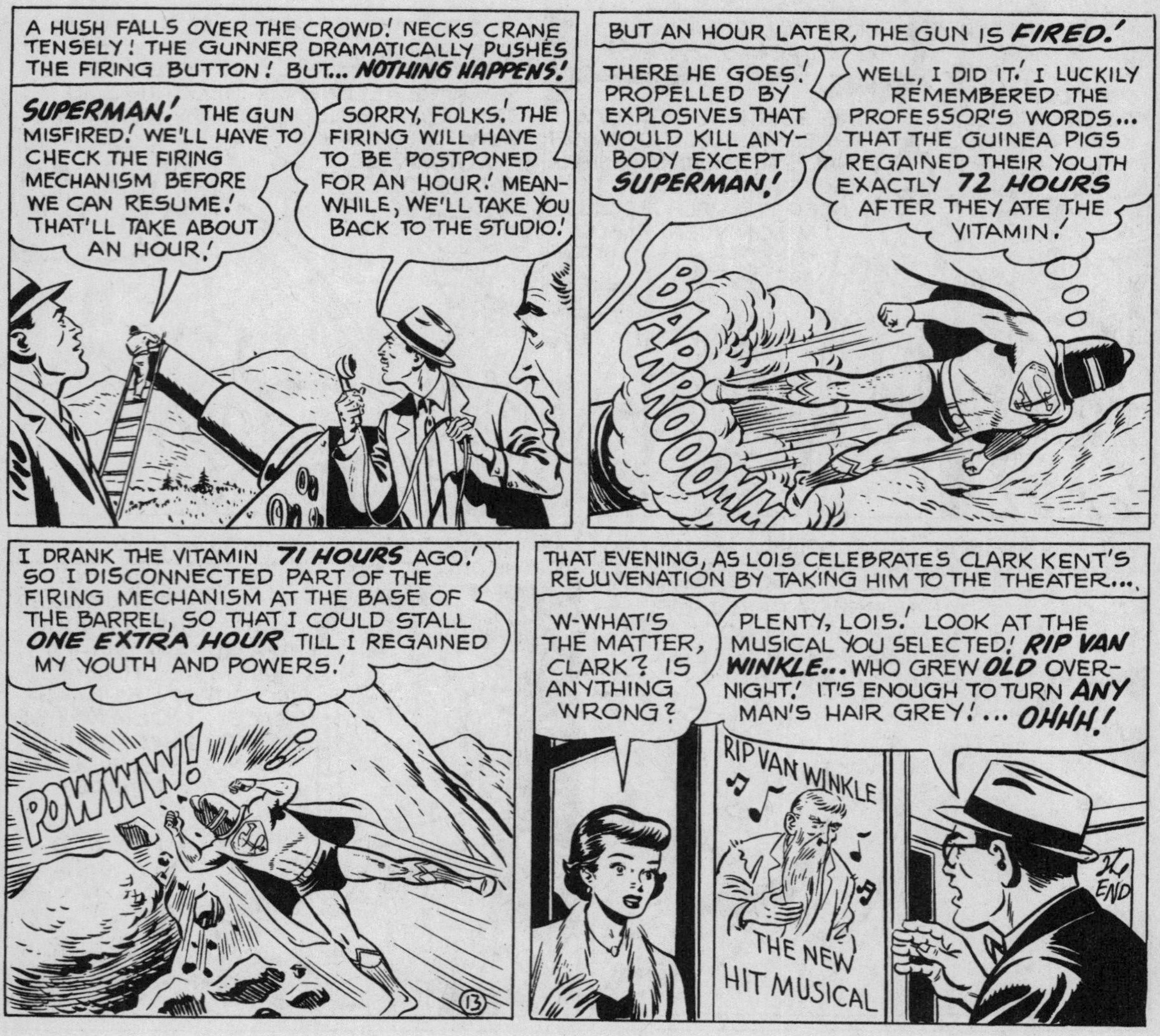
A HUSH FALLS OVER THE CROWD! NECKS CRANE TENSELY! THE GUNNER DRAMATICALLY PUSHES THE FIRING BUTTON! BUT... NOTHING HAPPENS!
SUPERMAN! THE GUN MISFIRED! WE'LL HAVE TO CHECK THE FIRING MECHANISM BEFORE WE CAN RESUME! THAT'LL TAKE ABOUT AN HOUR!
SORRY, FOLKS! THE FIRING WILL HAVE TO BE POSTPONED FOR AN HOUR! MEAN-WHILE, WE'LL TAKE YOU BACK TO THE STUDIO!
BUT AN HOUR LATER, THE GUN IS FIRED!
THERE HE GOES! PROPELLED BY EXPLOSIVES THAT WOULD KILL ANY-BODY EXCEPT SUPERMAN!
WELL, I DID IT! I LUCKILY REMEMBERED THE PROFESSOR'S WORDS... THAT THE GUINEA PIGS REGAINED THEIR YOUTH EXACTLY 72 HOURS AFTER THEY ATE THE VITAMIN!
BARROOOOMM
I DRANK THE VITAMIN 71 HOURS AGO! SO I DISCONNECTED PART OF THE FIRING MECHANISM AT THE BASE OF THE BARREL, SO THAT I COULD STALL ONE EXTRA HOUR TILL I REGAINED MY YOUTH AND POWERS!
POWWW!
13
THAT EVENING, AS LOIS CELEBRATES CLARK KENT'S REJUVENATION BY TAKING HIM TO THE THEATER...
W-WHAT'S THE MATTER, CLARK? IS ANYTHING WRONG?
PLENTY, LOIS! LOOK AT THE MUSICAL YOU SELECTED! RIP VAN WINKLE... WHO GREW OLD OVER-NIGHT! IT'S ENOUGH TO TURN ANY MAN'S HAIR GREY! ... OHHH!
RIP VAN WINKLE
THE NEW HIT MUSICAL
END

SUPERMAN

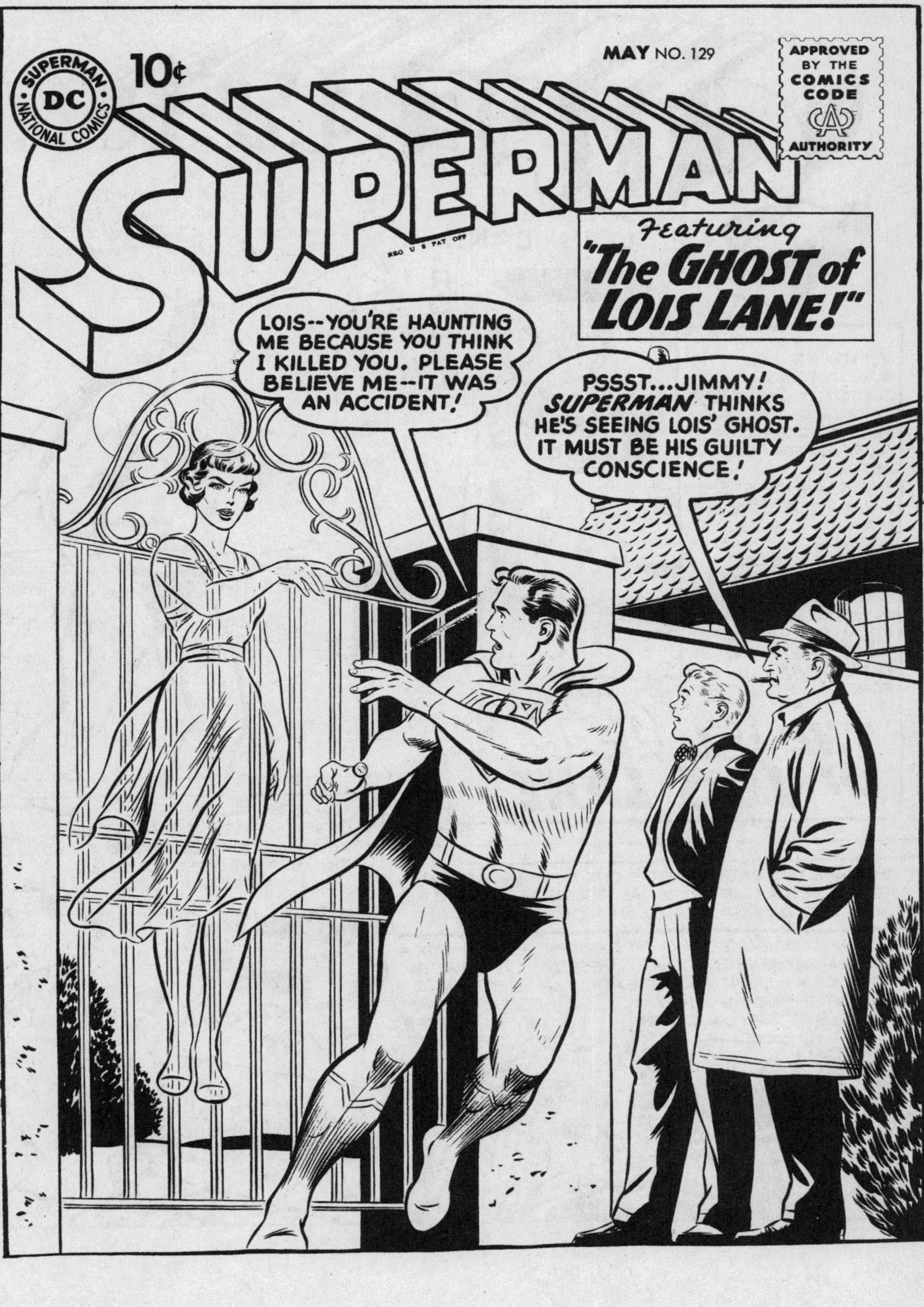
SUPERMAN DC NATIONAL COMICS
10¢
MAY NO. 129
APPROVED BY THE COMICS CODE AUTHORITY
SUPERMAN
REG. U.S. PAT. OFF.
Featuring "The GHOST of LOIS LANE!"
LOIS--YOU'RE HAUNTING ME BECAUSE YOU THINK I KILLED YOU. PLEASE BELIEVE ME--IT WAS AN ACCIDENT!
PSSST...JIMMY! SUPERMAN THINKS HE'S SEEING LOIS' GHOST. IT MUST BE HIS GUILTY CONSCIENCE!

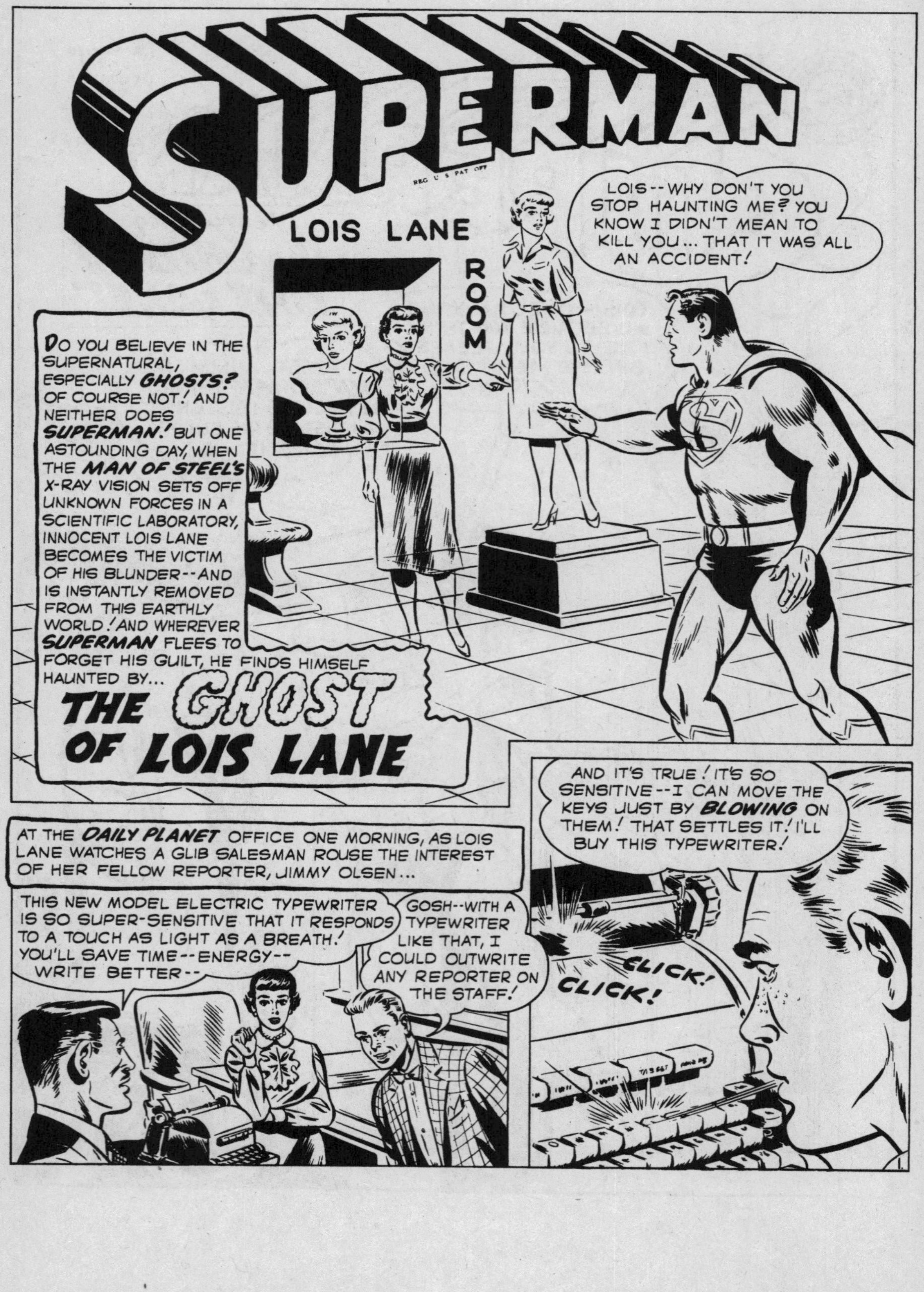
SUPERMAN
REG. U.S. PAT. OFF.
LOIS LANE ROOM
LOIS--WHY DON'T YOU STOP HAUNTING ME? YOU KNOW I DIDN'T MEAN TO KILL YOU... THAT IT WAS ALL AN ACCIDENT!
DO YOU BELIEVE IN THE SUPERNATURAL, ESPECIALLY GHOSTS? OF COURSE NOT! AND NEITHER DOES SUPERMAN! BUT ONE ASTOUNDING DAY, WHEN THE MAN OF STEEL'S X-RAY VISION SETS OFF UNKNOWN FORCES IN A SCIENTIFIC LABORATORY, INNOCENT LOIS LANE BECOMES THE VICTIM OF HIS BLUNDER--AND IS INSTANTLY REMOVED FROM THIS EARTHLY WORLD! AND WHEREVER SUPERMAN FLEES TO FORGET HIS GUILT, HE FINDS HIMSELF HAUNTED BY...
THE GHOST OF LOIS LANE
AT THE DAILY PLANET OFFICE ONE MORNING, AS LOIS LANE WATCHES A GLIB SALESMAN ROUSE THE INTEREST OF HER FELLOW REPORTER, JIMMY OLSEN...
THIS NEW MODEL ELECTRIC TYPEWRITER IS SO SUPER-SENSITIVE THAT IT RESPONDS TO A TOUCH AS LIGHT AS A BREATH! YOU'LL SAVE TIME--ENERGY--WRITE BETTER--
GOSH--WITH A TYPEWRITER LIKE THAT, I COULD OUTWRITE ANY REPORTER ON THE STAFF!
AND IT'S TRUE! IT'S SO SENSITIVE--I CAN MOVE THE KEYS JUST BY BLOWING ON THEM! THAT SETTLES IT! I'LL BUY THIS TYPEWRITER!
CLICK! CLICK!

JUST THEN, LOIS GETS A NEW ASSIGNMENT FROM EDITOR PERRY WHITE...

LOIS--HERE'S AN EXCUSE FOR YOU TO GET OVER TO WARDER'S ISLAND FOR AN ADVANCE LOOK AT THE NEW EXPERIMENTS IN ENERGY TRANSMISSION BEING CONDUCTED BY PROFESSOR GRAIL! ONE OF OUR READERS FOUND GRAIL'S BRIEF-CASE AND TURNED IT IN TO OUR LOST-AND-FOUND DEPARTMENT!

AS LOIS EAGERLY PREPARES TO LEAVE...

LOIS--ISN'T THIS A MARVELOUS TYPEWRITER?

NOT NOW, JIMMY! THIS IS MY CHANCE TO SCOOP CLARK BY GETTING INSIDE PROFESSOR GRAIL'S LABORATORY FOR A STORY ON HIS NEW EXPERIMENT! PROVIDED HE'S GRATEFUL FOR MY RETURNING HIS BRIEF-CASE!

PRESENTLY, AS LOIS ALIGHTS FROM A RENTED HELICOPTER AT WARDER'S ISLAND, A FEW MILES OUT OF METROPOLIS HARBOR...

PROFESSOR GRAIL? I'M LOIS LANE FROM--

YES, THE *PLANET!* YOUR BOSS, MR. WHITE, PHONED TO SAY YOU WERE BRINGING MY BRIEF-CASE! I'M ABOUT TO LEAVE FOR A SCIENCE CONFERENCE OUT WEST AND I NEED SOME NOTES I HAD IN IT!

BUT THEN--LOIS EXPERIENCES ONE OF THE MOST EMBARRASSING MOMENTS OF HER CAREER, AS...

OH, PROFESSOR! I--I FEEL SO SILLY! THE BRIEF-CASE! I--I FORGOT TO BRING IT! ER-- I WAS SO HOPEFUL OF GETTING A SNEAK PREVIEW OF YOUR RECENT WORK, I LEFT IT ON MY DESK!

NOW-- NOW! DON'T FEEL *TOO* BADLY, MISS LANE! COME IN!

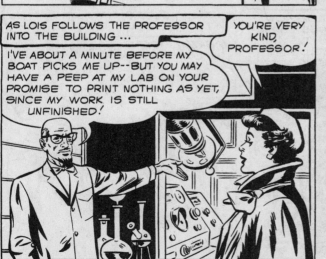

AS LOIS FOLLOWS THE PROFESSOR INTO THE BUILDING...

YOU'RE VERY KIND, PROFESSOR!

I'VE ABOUT A MINUTE BEFORE MY BOAT PICKS ME UP--BUT YOU MAY HAVE A PEEP AT MY LAB ON YOUR PROMISE TO PRINT NOTHING AS YET, SINCE MY WORK IS STILL UNFINISHED!

THESE CHAIRS! HOW DO THEY TIE IN WITH YOUR WORK ON ENERGY?

IN TRYING TO FIND A WAY TO TRANSMIT *ENERGY* TO DISTANT PLACES LIKE RADIO WAVES, I ACCIDENTALLY FOUND A POSSIBILITY OF SOMETHING BETTER! I HOPE SOME DAY TO BE ABLE TO SEND PEOPLE *THROUGH SPACE BY RADIO!* HENCE, THESE CHAIRS!

2

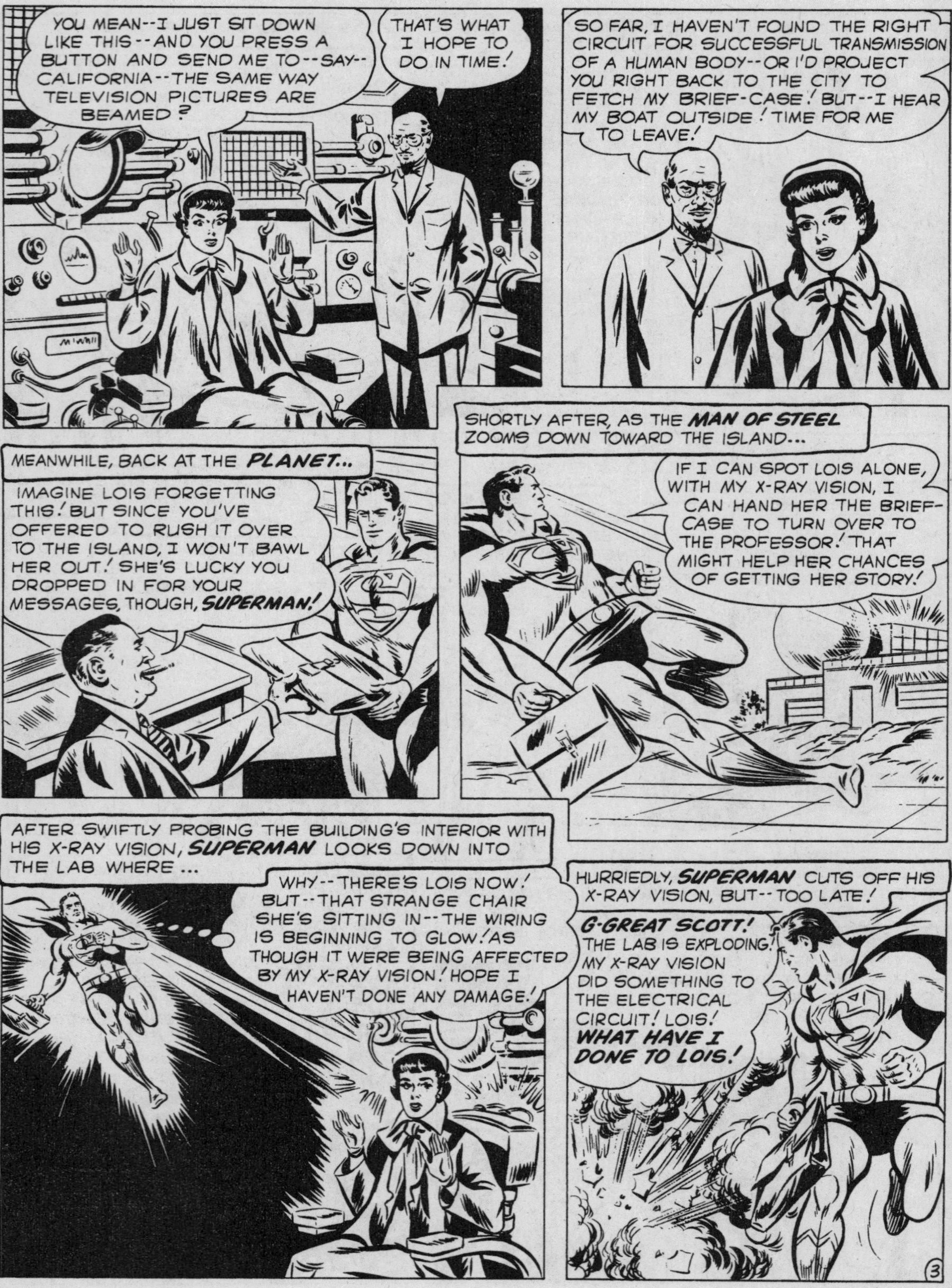
YOU MEAN--I JUST SIT DOWN LIKE THIS--AND YOU PRESS A BUTTON AND SEND ME TO--SAY--CALIFORNIA--THE SAME WAY TELEVISION PICTURES ARE BEAMED?
THAT'S WHAT I HOPE TO DO IN TIME!
SO FAR, I HAVEN'T FOUND THE RIGHT CIRCUIT FOR SUCCESSFUL TRANSMISSION OF A HUMAN BODY--OR I'D PROJECT YOU RIGHT BACK TO THE CITY TO FETCH MY BRIEF-CASE! BUT--I HEAR MY BOAT OUTSIDE! TIME FOR ME TO LEAVE!
MEANWHILE, BACK AT THE **PLANET**...
IMAGINE LOIS FORGETTING THIS! BUT SINCE YOU'VE OFFERED TO RUSH IT OVER TO THE ISLAND, I WON'T BAWL HER OUT! SHE'S LUCKY YOU DROPPED IN FOR YOUR MESSAGES, THOUGH, **SUPERMAN!**
SHORTLY AFTER, AS THE **MAN OF STEEL** ZOOMS DOWN TOWARD THE ISLAND...
IF I CAN SPOT LOIS ALONE, WITH MY X-RAY VISION, I CAN HAND HER THE BRIEF-CASE TO TURN OVER TO THE PROFESSOR! THAT MIGHT HELP HER CHANCES OF GETTING HER STORY!
AFTER SWIFTLY PROBING THE BUILDING'S INTERIOR WITH HIS X-RAY VISION, **SUPERMAN** LOOKS DOWN INTO THE LAB WHERE ...
WHY--THERE'S LOIS NOW! BUT--THAT STRANGE CHAIR SHE'S SITTING IN--THE WIRING IS BEGINNING TO GLOW! AS THOUGH IT WERE BEING AFFECTED BY MY X-RAY VISION! HOPE I HAVEN'T DONE ANY DAMAGE!
HURRIEDLY, **SUPERMAN** CUTS OFF HIS X-RAY VISION, BUT--TOO LATE!
G-GREAT SCOTT! THE LAB IS EXPLODING! MY X-RAY VISION DID SOMETHING TO THE ELECTRICAL CIRCUIT! LOIS! **WHAT HAVE I DONE TO LOIS!**
3

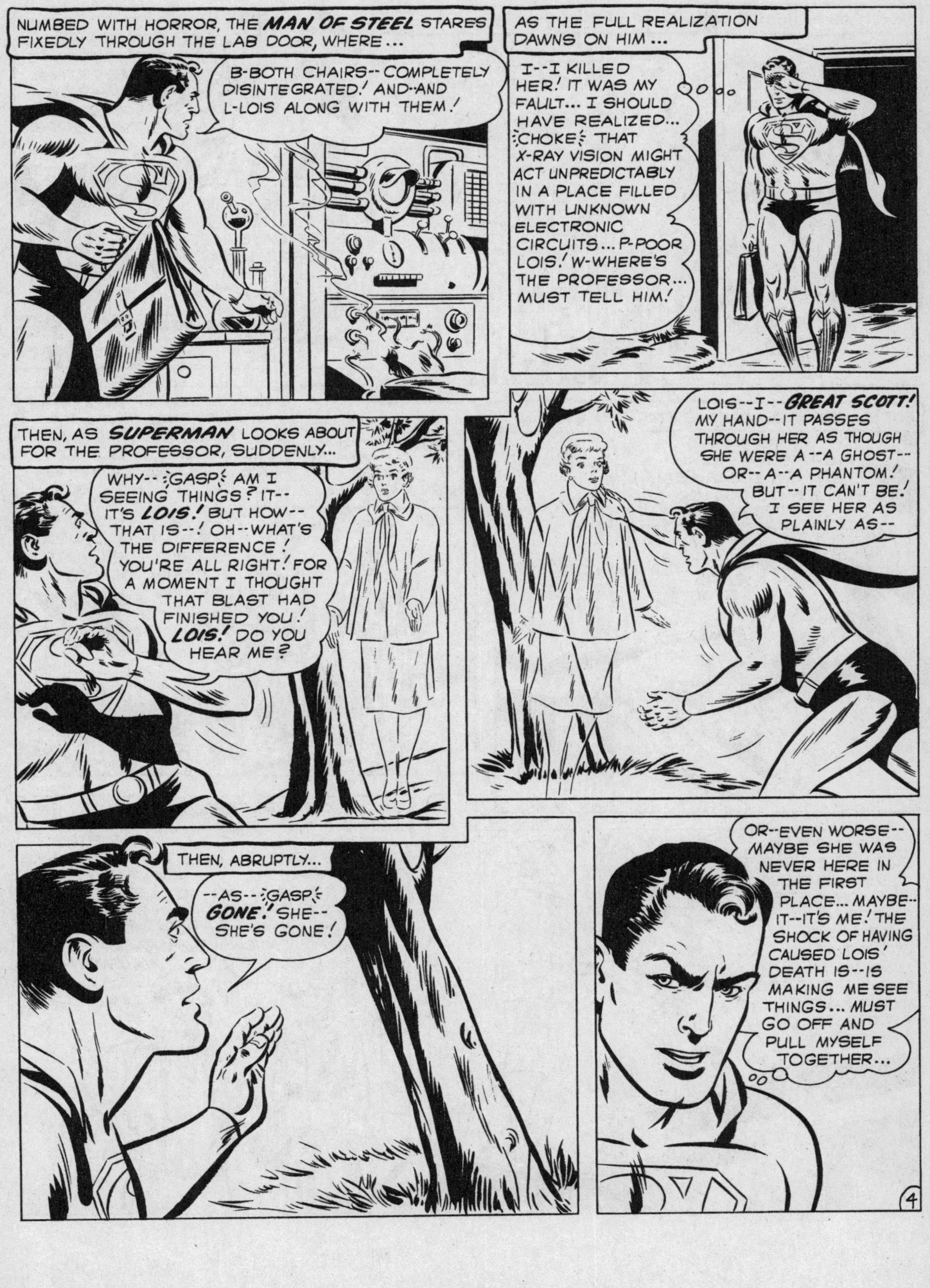
NUMBED WITH HORROR, THE MAN OF STEEL STARES FIXEDLY THROUGH THE LAB DOOR, WHERE...
B-BOTH CHAIRS--COMPLETELY DISINTEGRATED! AND--AND L-LOIS ALONG WITH THEM!
AS THE FULL REALIZATION DAWNS ON HIM...
I--I KILLED HER! IT WAS MY FAULT... I SHOULD HAVE REALIZED... CHOKE THAT X-RAY VISION MIGHT ACT UNPREDICTABLY IN A PLACE FILLED WITH UNKNOWN ELECTRONIC CIRCUITS... P-POOR LOIS! W-WHERE'S THE PROFESSOR... MUST TELL HIM!
THEN, AS SUPERMAN LOOKS ABOUT FOR THE PROFESSOR, SUDDENLY...
WHY-- GASP AM I SEEING THINGS? IT--IT'S LOIS! BUT HOW--THAT IS--! OH--WHAT'S THE DIFFERENCE! YOU'RE ALL RIGHT! FOR A MOMENT I THOUGHT THAT BLAST HAD FINISHED YOU! LOIS! DO YOU HEAR ME?
LOIS--I--GREAT SCOTT! MY HAND--IT PASSES THROUGH HER AS THOUGH SHE WERE A--A GHOST--OR--A--A PHANTOM! BUT--IT CAN'T BE! I SEE HER AS PLAINLY AS--
THEN, ABRUPTLY...
--AS-- GASP GONE! SHE--SHE'S GONE!
OR--EVEN WORSE--MAYBE SHE WAS NEVER HERE IN THE FIRST PLACE... MAYBE--IT--IT'S ME! THE SHOCK OF HAVING CAUSED LOIS' DEATH IS--IS MAKING ME SEE THINGS... MUST GO OFF AND PULL MYSELF TOGETHER...
4

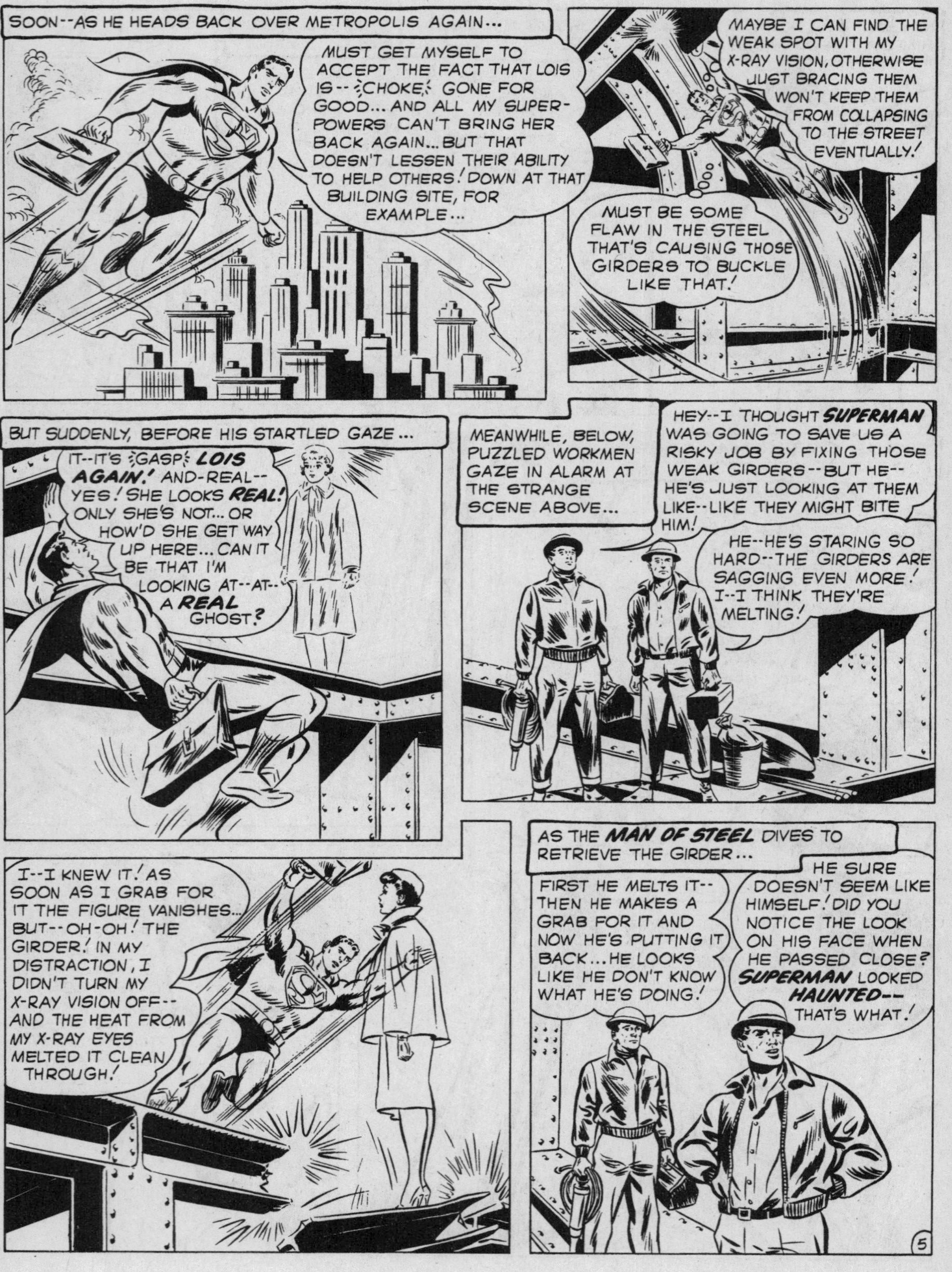
SOON--AS HE HEADS BACK OVER METROPOLIS AGAIN...
MUST GET MYSELF TO ACCEPT THE FACT THAT LOIS IS--CHOKE GONE FOR GOOD... AND ALL MY SUPER-POWERS CAN'T BRING HER BACK AGAIN... BUT THAT DOESN'T LESSEN THEIR ABILITY TO HELP OTHERS! DOWN AT THAT BUILDING SITE, FOR EXAMPLE...
MAYBE I CAN FIND THE WEAK SPOT WITH MY X-RAY VISION, OTHERWISE JUST BRACING THEM WON'T KEEP THEM FROM COLLAPSING TO THE STREET EVENTUALLY!
MUST BE SOME FLAW IN THE STEEL THAT'S CAUSING THOSE GIRDERS TO BUCKLE LIKE THAT!
BUT SUDDENLY, BEFORE HIS STARTLED GAZE...
IT--IT'S GASP LOIS AGAIN! AND-REAL--YES! SHE LOOKS REAL! ONLY SHE'S NOT... OR HOW'D SHE GET WAY UP HERE... CAN IT BE THAT I'M LOOKING AT--AT--A REAL GHOST?
MEANWHILE, BELOW, PUZZLED WORKMEN GAZE IN ALARM AT THE STRANGE SCENE ABOVE...
HEY--I THOUGHT SUPERMAN WAS GOING TO SAVE US A RISKY JOB BY FIXING THOSE WEAK GIRDERS--BUT HE--HE'S JUST LOOKING AT THEM LIKE--LIKE THEY MIGHT BITE HIM!
HE--HE'S STARING SO HARD--THE GIRDERS ARE SAGGING EVEN MORE! I--I THINK THEY'RE MELTING!
I--I KNEW IT! AS SOON AS I GRAB FOR IT THE FIGURE VANISHES... BUT--OH-OH! THE GIRDER! IN MY DISTRACTION, I DIDN'T TURN MY X-RAY VISION OFF--AND THE HEAT FROM MY X-RAY EYES MELTED IT CLEAN THROUGH!
AS THE MAN OF STEEL DIVES TO RETRIEVE THE GIRDER...
FIRST HE MELTS IT--THEN HE MAKES A GRAB FOR IT AND NOW HE'S PUTTING IT BACK... HE LOOKS LIKE HE DON'T KNOW WHAT HE'S DOING!
HE SURE DOESN'T SEEM LIKE HIMSELF! DID YOU NOTICE THE LOOK ON HIS FACE WHEN HE PASSED CLOSE? SUPERMAN LOOKED HAUNTED--THAT'S WHAT!
5

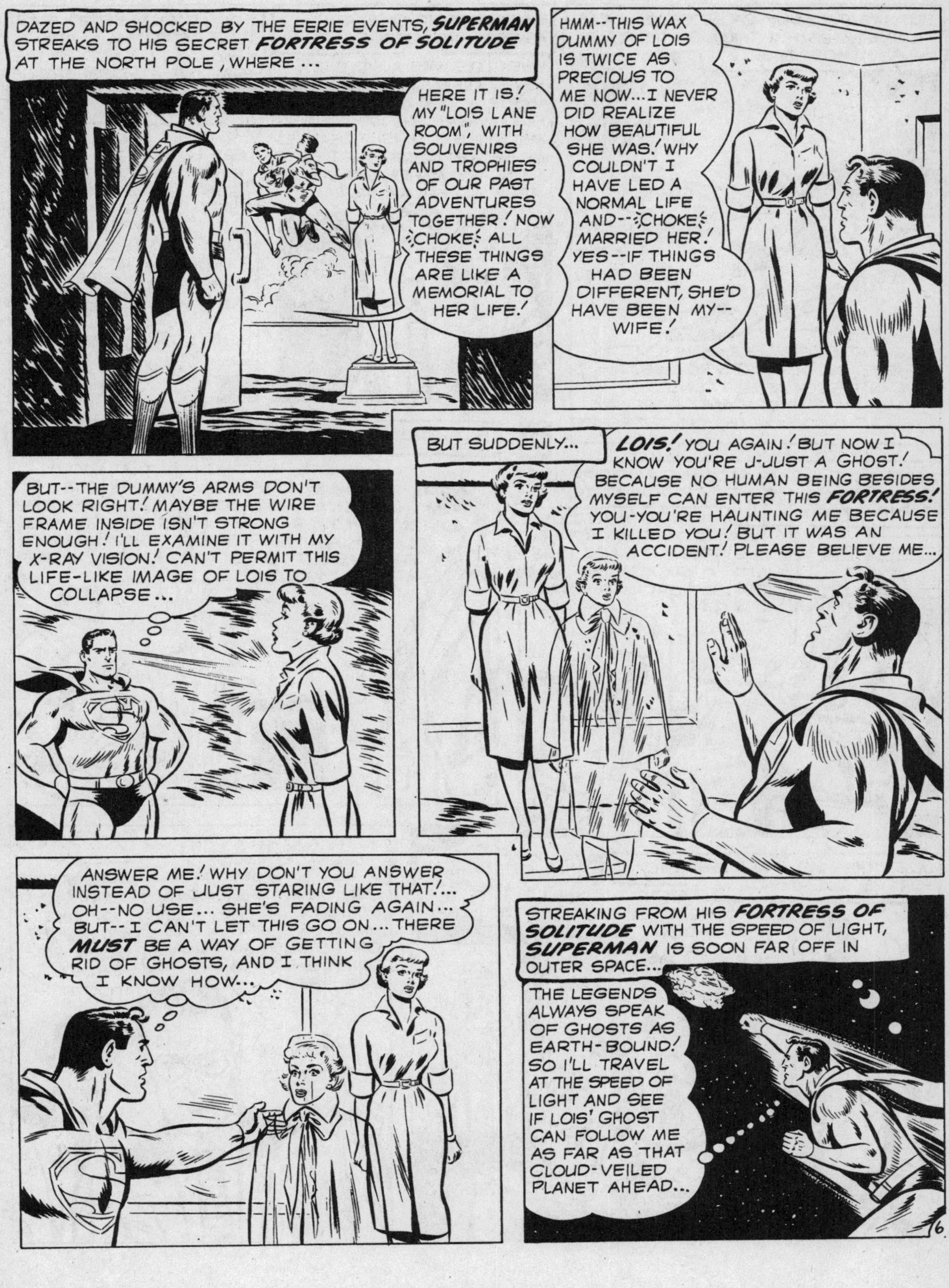
DAZED AND SHOCKED BY THE EERIE EVENTS, SUPERMAN STREAKS TO HIS SECRET FORTRESS OF SOLITUDE AT THE NORTH POLE, WHERE...
HERE IT IS! MY "LOIS LANE ROOM", WITH SOUVENIRS AND TROPHIES OF OUR PAST ADVENTURES TOGETHER! NOW -CHOKE- ALL THESE THINGS ARE LIKE A MEMORIAL TO HER LIFE!
HMM--THIS WAX DUMMY OF LOIS IS TWICE AS PRECIOUS TO ME NOW...I NEVER DID REALIZE HOW BEAUTIFUL SHE WAS! WHY COULDN'T I HAVE LED A NORMAL LIFE AND--CHOKE- MARRIED HER! YES--IF THINGS HAD BEEN DIFFERENT, SHE'D HAVE BEEN MY--WIFE!
BUT--THE DUMMY'S ARMS DON'T LOOK RIGHT! MAYBE THE WIRE FRAME INSIDE ISN'T STRONG ENOUGH! I'LL EXAMINE IT WITH MY X-RAY VISION! CAN'T PERMIT THIS LIFE-LIKE IMAGE OF LOIS TO COLLAPSE...
BUT SUDDENLY...
LOIS! YOU AGAIN! BUT NOW I KNOW YOU'RE J-JUST A GHOST! BECAUSE NO HUMAN BEING BESIDES MYSELF CAN ENTER THIS FORTRESS! YOU-YOU'RE HAUNTING ME BECAUSE I KILLED YOU! BUT IT WAS AN ACCIDENT! PLEASE BELIEVE ME...
ANSWER ME! WHY DON'T YOU ANSWER INSTEAD OF JUST STARING LIKE THAT!... OH--NO USE... SHE'S FADING AGAIN... BUT--I CAN'T LET THIS GO ON... THERE MUST BE A WAY OF GETTING RID OF GHOSTS, AND I THINK I KNOW HOW...
STREAKING FROM HIS FORTRESS OF SOLITUDE WITH THE SPEED OF LIGHT, SUPERMAN IS SOON FAR OFF IN OUTER SPACE...
THE LEGENDS ALWAYS SPEAK OF GHOSTS AS EARTH-BOUND! SO I'LL TRAVEL AT THE SPEED OF LIGHT AND SEE IF LOIS' GHOST CAN FOLLOW ME AS FAR AS THAT CLOUD-VEILED PLANET AHEAD...
6

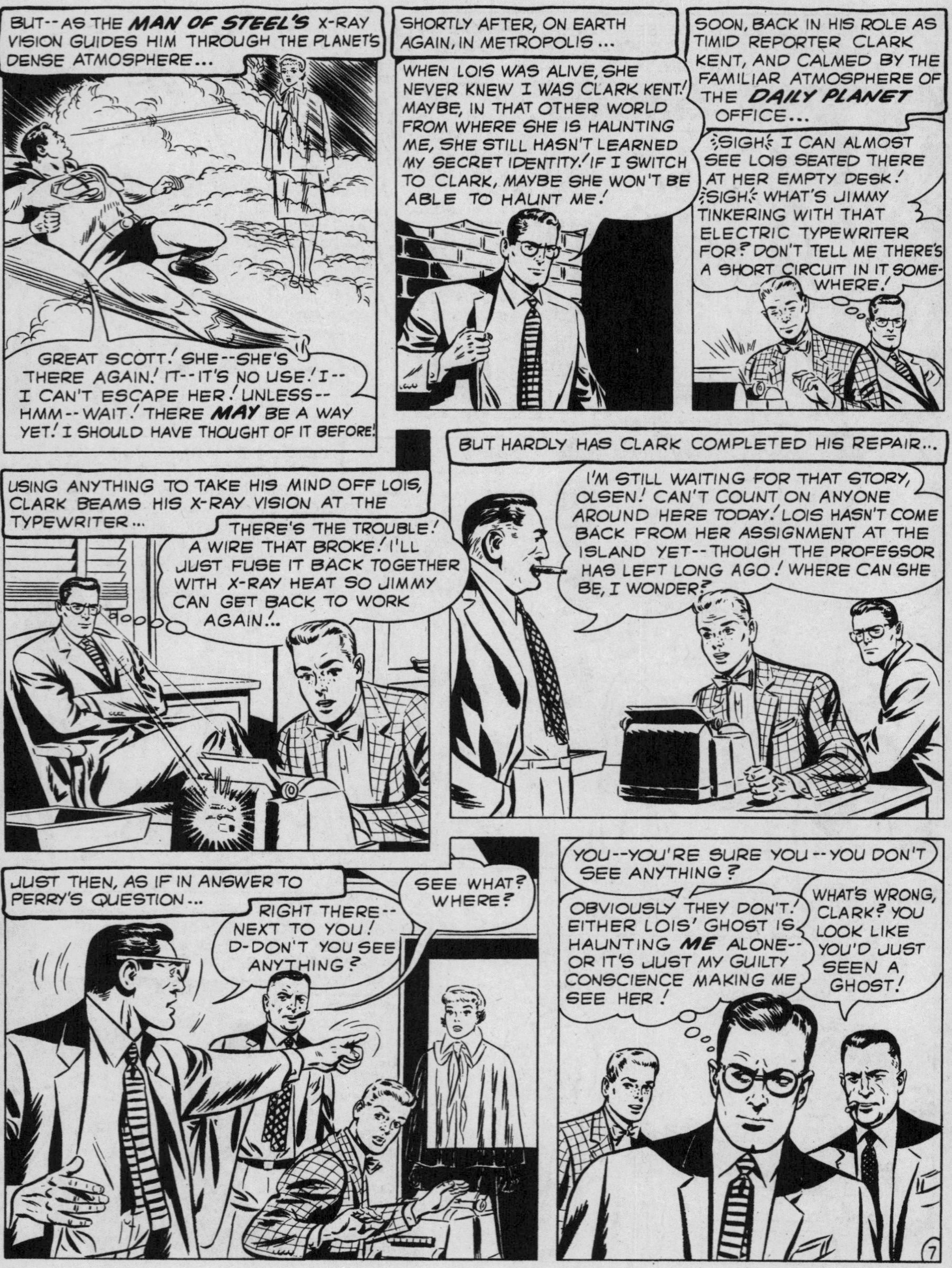
BUT--AS THE MAN OF STEEL'S X-RAY VISION GUIDES HIM THROUGH THE PLANET'S DENSE ATMOSPHERE...
GREAT SCOTT! SHE--SHE'S THERE AGAIN! IT--IT'S NO USE! I--I CAN'T ESCAPE HER! UNLESS--HMM--WAIT! THERE MAY BE A WAY YET! I SHOULD HAVE THOUGHT OF IT BEFORE!
SHORTLY AFTER, ON EARTH AGAIN, IN METROPOLIS...
WHEN LOIS WAS ALIVE, SHE NEVER KNEW I WAS CLARK KENT! MAYBE, IN THAT OTHER WORLD FROM WHERE SHE IS HAUNTING ME, SHE STILL HASN'T LEARNED MY SECRET IDENTITY! IF I SWITCH TO CLARK, MAYBE SHE WON'T BE ABLE TO HAUNT ME!
SOON, BACK IN HIS ROLE AS TIMID REPORTER CLARK KENT, AND CALMED BY THE FAMILIAR ATMOSPHERE OF THE DAILY PLANET OFFICE...
SIGH I CAN ALMOST SEE LOIS SEATED THERE AT HER EMPTY DESK! SIGH WHAT'S JIMMY TINKERING WITH THAT ELECTRIC TYPEWRITER FOR? DON'T TELL ME THERE'S A SHORT CIRCUIT IN IT SOMEWHERE!
USING ANYTHING TO TAKE HIS MIND OFF LOIS, CLARK BEAMS HIS X-RAY VISION AT THE TYPEWRITER...
THERE'S THE TROUBLE! A WIRE THAT BROKE! I'LL JUST FUSE IT BACK TOGETHER WITH X-RAY HEAT SO JIMMY CAN GET BACK TO WORK AGAIN!..
BUT HARDLY HAS CLARK COMPLETED HIS REPAIR...
I'M STILL WAITING FOR THAT STORY, OLSEN! CAN'T COUNT ON ANYONE AROUND HERE TODAY! LOIS HASN'T COME BACK FROM HER ASSIGNMENT AT THE ISLAND YET--THOUGH THE PROFESSOR HAS LEFT LONG AGO! WHERE CAN SHE BE, I WONDER?
JUST THEN, AS IF IN ANSWER TO PERRY'S QUESTION...
RIGHT THERE--NEXT TO YOU! D-DON'T YOU SEE ANYTHING?
SEE WHAT? WHERE?
YOU--YOU'RE SURE YOU--YOU DON'T SEE ANYTHING?
OBVIOUSLY THEY DON'T! EITHER LOIS' GHOST IS HAUNTING ME ALONE--OR IT'S JUST MY GUILTY CONSCIENCE MAKING ME SEE HER!
WHAT'S WRONG, CLARK? YOU LOOK LIKE YOU'D JUST SEEN A GHOST!
7

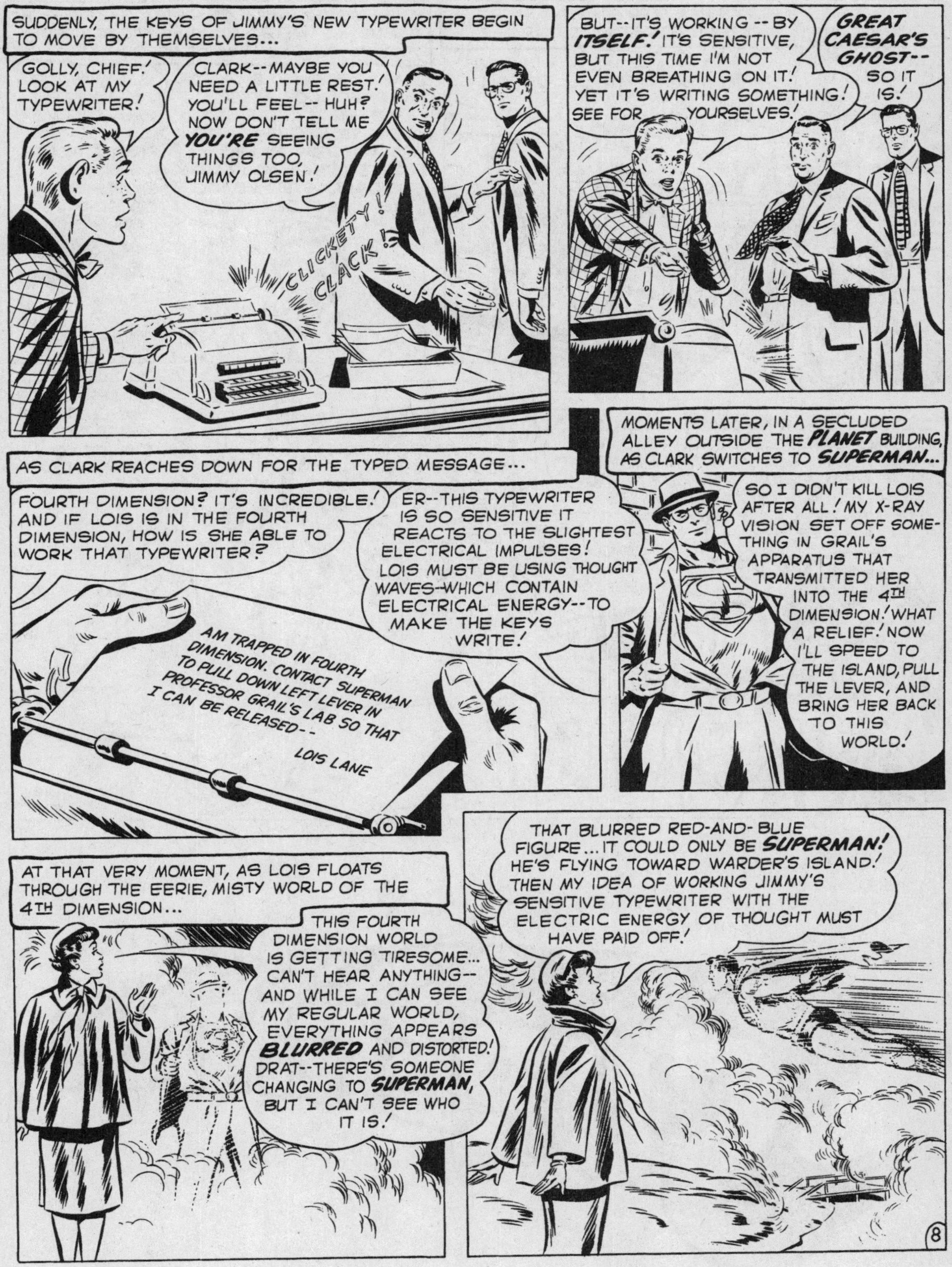
SUDDENLY, THE KEYS OF JIMMY'S NEW TYPEWRITER BEGIN TO MOVE BY THEMSELVES...
GOLLY, CHIEF! LOOK AT MY TYPEWRITER!
CLARK--MAYBE YOU NEED A LITTLE REST! YOU'LL FEEL-- HUH? NOW DON'T TELL ME YOU'RE SEEING THINGS TOO, JIMMY OLSEN!
CLICKETY! CLACK!
BUT--IT'S WORKING --BY ITSELF! IT'S SENSITIVE, BUT THIS TIME I'M NOT EVEN BREATHING ON IT! YET IT'S WRITING SOMETHING! SEE FOR YOURSELVES!
GREAT CAESAR'S GHOST-- SO IT IS!
AS CLARK REACHES DOWN FOR THE TYPED MESSAGE...
FOURTH DIMENSION? IT'S INCREDIBLE! AND IF LOIS IS IN THE FOURTH DIMENSION, HOW IS SHE ABLE TO WORK THAT TYPEWRITER?
ER--THIS TYPEWRITER IS SO SENSITIVE IT REACTS TO THE SLIGHTEST ELECTRICAL IMPULSES! LOIS MUST BE USING THOUGHT WAVES--WHICH CONTAIN ELECTRICAL ENERGY--TO MAKE THE KEYS WRITE!
AM TRAPPED IN FOURTH DIMENSION. CONTACT SUPERMAN TO PULL DOWN LEFT LEVER IN PROFESSOR GRAIL'S LAB SO THAT I CAN BE RELEASED--
LOIS LANE
MOMENTS LATER, IN A SECLUDED ALLEY OUTSIDE THE PLANET BUILDING, AS CLARK SWITCHES TO SUPERMAN...
SO I DIDN'T KILL LOIS AFTER ALL! MY X-RAY VISION SET OFF SOMETHING IN GRAIL'S APPARATUS THAT TRANSMITTED HER INTO THE 4TH DIMENSION! WHAT A RELIEF! NOW I'LL SPEED TO THE ISLAND, PULL THE LEVER, AND BRING HER BACK TO THIS WORLD!
AT THAT VERY MOMENT, AS LOIS FLOATS THROUGH THE EERIE, MISTY WORLD OF THE 4TH DIMENSION...
THIS FOURTH DIMENSION WORLD IS GETTING TIRESOME... CAN'T HEAR ANYTHING-- AND WHILE I CAN SEE MY REGULAR WORLD, EVERYTHING APPEARS BLURRED AND DISTORTED! DRAT--THERE'S SOMEONE CHANGING TO SUPERMAN, BUT I CAN'T SEE WHO IT IS!
THAT BLURRED RED-AND-BLUE FIGURE... IT COULD ONLY BE SUPERMAN! HE'S FLYING TOWARD WARDER'S ISLAND! THEN MY IDEA OF WORKING JIMMY'S SENSITIVE TYPEWRITER WITH THE ELECTRIC ENERGY OF THOUGHT MUST HAVE PAID OFF!
8

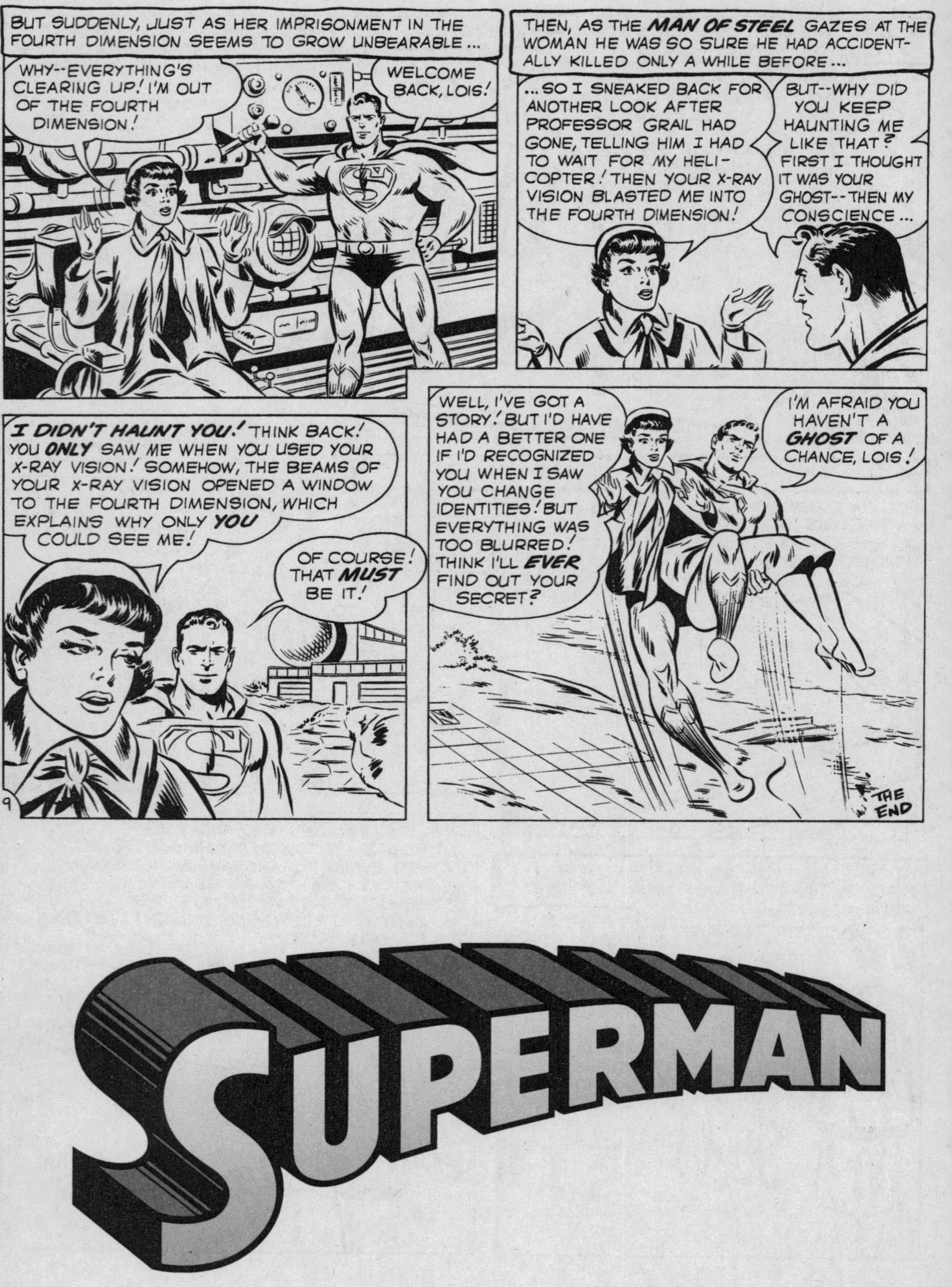
BUT SUDDENLY, JUST AS HER IMPRISONMENT IN THE FOURTH DIMENSION SEEMS TO GROW UNBEARABLE ...
WHY--EVERYTHING'S CLEARING UP! I'M OUT OF THE FOURTH DIMENSION!
WELCOME BACK, LOIS!
THEN, AS THE MAN OF STEEL GAZES AT THE WOMAN HE WAS SO SURE HE HAD ACCIDENTALLY KILLED ONLY A WHILE BEFORE ...
... SO I SNEAKED BACK FOR ANOTHER LOOK AFTER PROFESSOR GRAIL HAD GONE, TELLING HIM I HAD TO WAIT FOR MY HELICOPTER! THEN YOUR X-RAY VISION BLASTED ME INTO THE FOURTH DIMENSION!
BUT--WHY DID YOU KEEP HAUNTING ME LIKE THAT? FIRST I THOUGHT IT WAS YOUR GHOST--THEN MY CONSCIENCE ...
I DIDN'T HAUNT YOU! THINK BACK! YOU ONLY SAW ME WHEN YOU USED YOUR X-RAY VISION! SOMEHOW, THE BEAMS OF YOUR X-RAY VISION OPENED A WINDOW TO THE FOURTH DIMENSION, WHICH EXPLAINS WHY ONLY YOU COULD SEE ME!
OF COURSE! THAT MUST BE IT!
9
WELL, I'VE GOT A STORY! BUT I'D HAVE HAD A BETTER ONE IF I'D RECOGNIZED YOU WHEN I SAW YOU CHANGE IDENTITIES! BUT EVERYTHING WAS TOO BLURRED! THINK I'LL EVER FIND OUT YOUR SECRET?
I'M AFRAID YOU HAVEN'T A GHOST OF A CHANCE, LOIS!
THE END

SUPERMAN

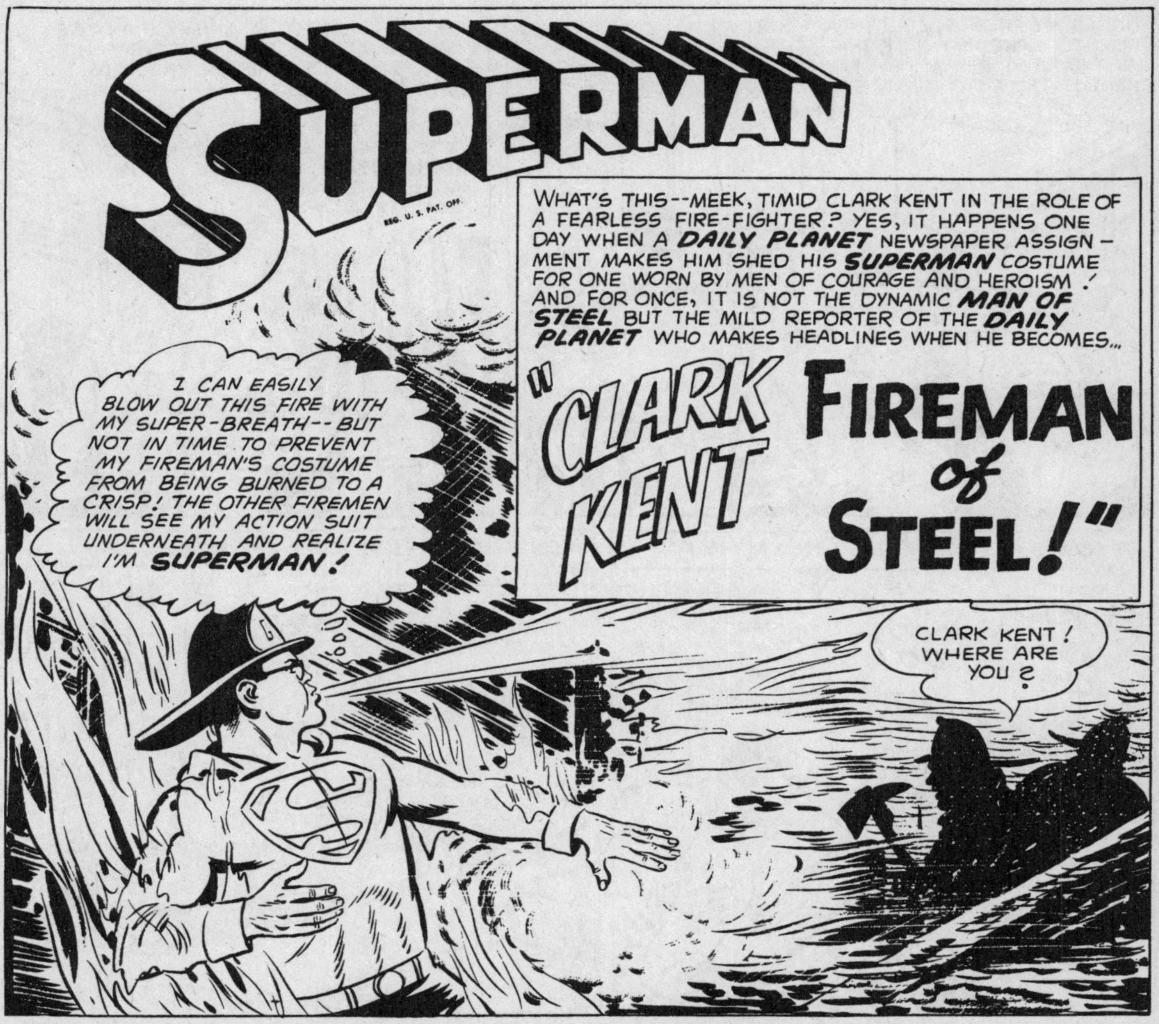
SUPERMAN
REG. U.S. PAT. OFF.
WHAT'S THIS--MEEK, TIMID CLARK KENT IN THE ROLE OF A FEARLESS FIRE-FIGHTER? YES, IT HAPPENS ONE DAY WHEN A DAILY PLANET NEWSPAPER ASSIGNMENT MAKES HIM SHED HIS SUPERMAN COSTUME FOR ONE WORN BY MEN OF COURAGE AND HEROISM! AND FOR ONCE, IT IS NOT THE DYNAMIC MAN OF STEEL BUT THE MILD REPORTER OF THE DAILY PLANET WHO MAKES HEADLINES WHEN HE BECOMES...
"CLARK KENT FIREMAN of STEEL!"
I CAN EASILY BLOW OUT THIS FIRE WITH MY SUPER-BREATH--BUT NOT IN TIME TO PREVENT MY FIREMAN'S COSTUME FROM BEING BURNED TO A CRISP! THE OTHER FIREMEN WILL SEE MY ACTION SUIT UNDERNEATH AND REALIZE I'M SUPERMAN!
CLARK KENT! WHERE ARE YOU?

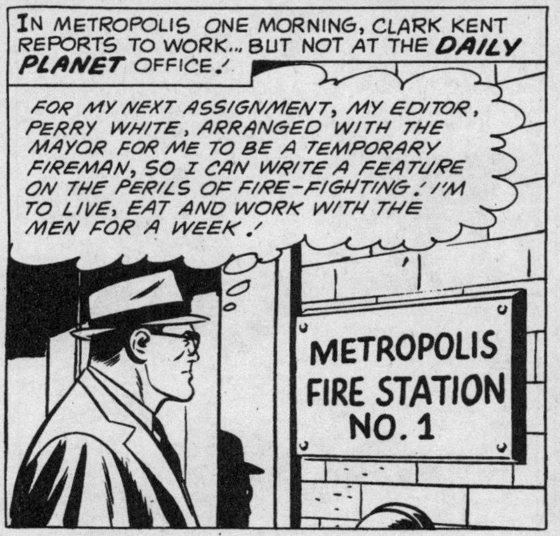
IN METROPOLIS ONE MORNING, CLARK KENT REPORTS TO WORK... BUT NOT AT THE DAILY PLANET OFFICE!
FOR MY NEXT ASSIGNMENT, MY EDITOR, PERRY WHITE, ARRANGED WITH THE MAYOR FOR ME TO BE A TEMPORARY FIREMAN, SO I CAN WRITE A FEATURE ON THE PERILS OF FIRE-FIGHTING! I'M TO LIVE, EAT AND WORK WITH THE MEN FOR A WEEK!
METROPOLIS FIRE STATION NO. 1

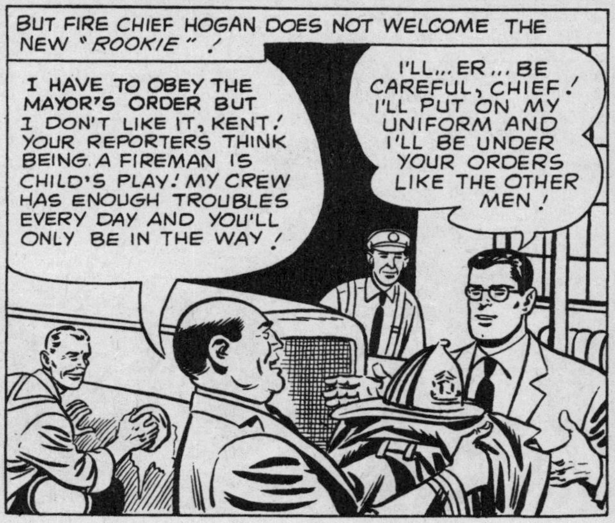
BUT FIRE CHIEF HOGAN DOES NOT WELCOME THE NEW "ROOKIE"!
I HAVE TO OBEY THE MAYOR'S ORDER BUT I DON'T LIKE IT, KENT! YOUR REPORTERS THINK BEING A FIREMAN IS CHILD'S PLAY! MY CREW HAS ENOUGH TROUBLES EVERY DAY AND YOU'LL ONLY BE IN THE WAY!
I'LL... ER... BE CAREFUL, CHIEF! I'LL PUT ON MY UNIFORM AND I'LL BE UNDER YOUR ORDERS LIKE THE OTHER MEN!

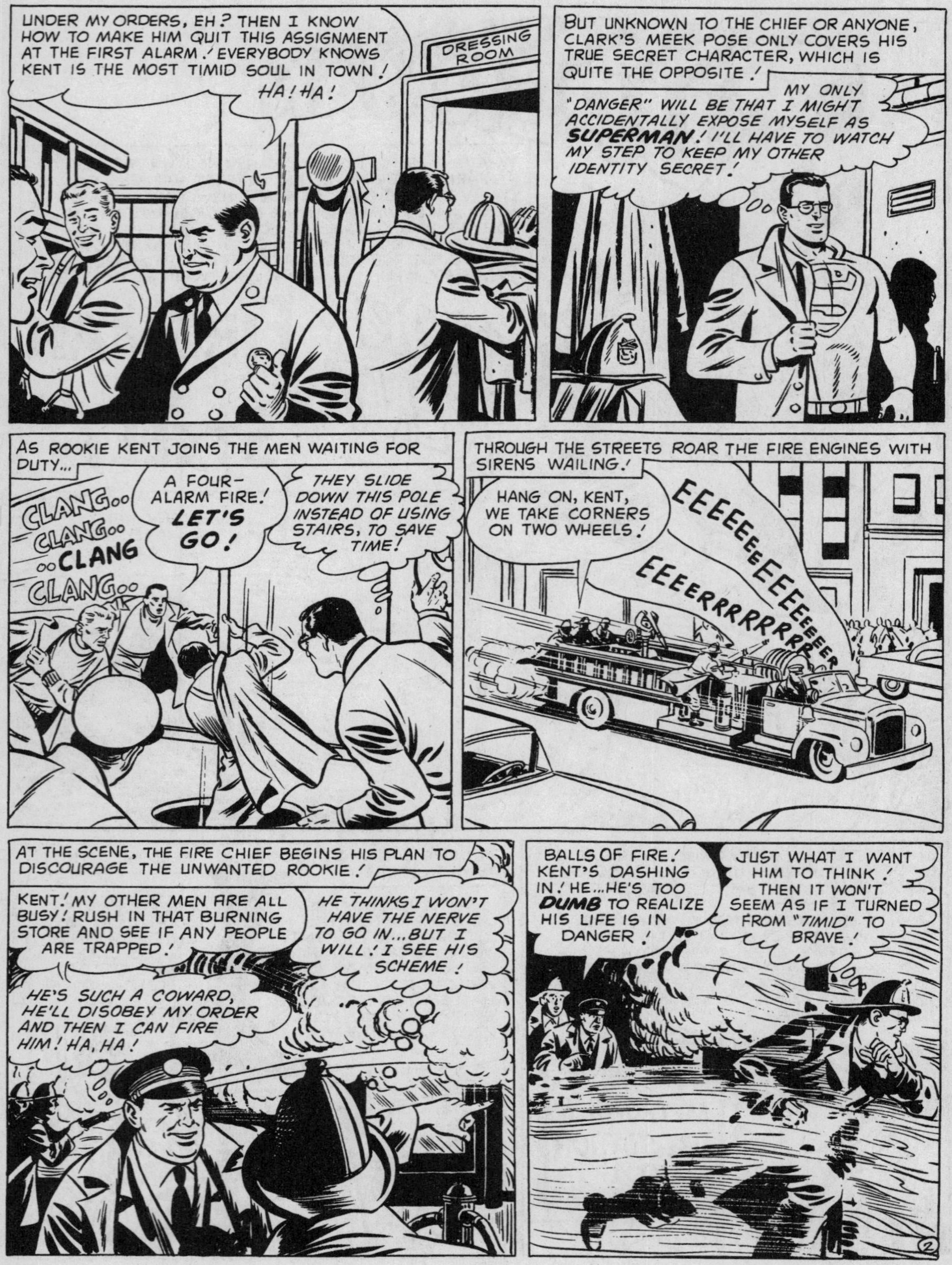
UNDER MY ORDERS, EH? THEN I KNOW HOW TO MAKE HIM QUIT THIS ASSIGNMENT AT THE FIRST ALARM! EVERYBODY KNOWS KENT IS THE MOST TIMID SOUL IN TOWN! HA! HA!
DRESSING ROOM
BUT UNKNOWN TO THE CHIEF OR ANYONE, CLARK'S MEEK POSE ONLY COVERS HIS TRUE SECRET CHARACTER, WHICH IS QUITE THE OPPOSITE!
MY ONLY "DANGER" WILL BE THAT I MIGHT ACCIDENTALLY EXPOSE MYSELF AS SUPERMAN! I'LL HAVE TO WATCH MY STEP TO KEEP MY OTHER IDENTITY SECRET!
AS ROOKIE KENT JOINS THE MEN WAITING FOR DUTY...
CLANG.. CLANG.. ..CLANG CLANG..
A FOUR-ALARM FIRE! LET'S GO!
THEY SLIDE DOWN THIS POLE INSTEAD OF USING STAIRS, TO SAVE TIME!
THROUGH THE STREETS ROAR THE FIRE ENGINES WITH SIRENS WAILING!
HANG ON, KENT, WE TAKE CORNERS ON TWO WHEELS!
EEEEEEEEEEEEEEEEER
EEEERRRRRRRR
AT THE SCENE, THE FIRE CHIEF BEGINS HIS PLAN TO DISCOURAGE THE UNWANTED ROOKIE!
KENT! MY OTHER MEN ARE ALL BUSY! RUSH IN THAT BURNING STORE AND SEE IF ANY PEOPLE ARE TRAPPED!
HE'S SUCH A COWARD, HE'LL DISOBEY MY ORDER AND THEN I CAN FIRE HIM! HA, HA!
HE THINKS I WON'T HAVE THE NERVE TO GO IN... BUT I WILL! I SEE HIS SCHEME!
BALLS OF FIRE! KENT'S DASHING IN! HE... HE'S TOO DUMB TO REALIZE HIS LIFE IS IN DANGER!
JUST WHAT I WANT HIM TO THINK! THEN IT WON'T SEEM AS IF I TURNED FROM "TIMID" TO BRAVE!
2

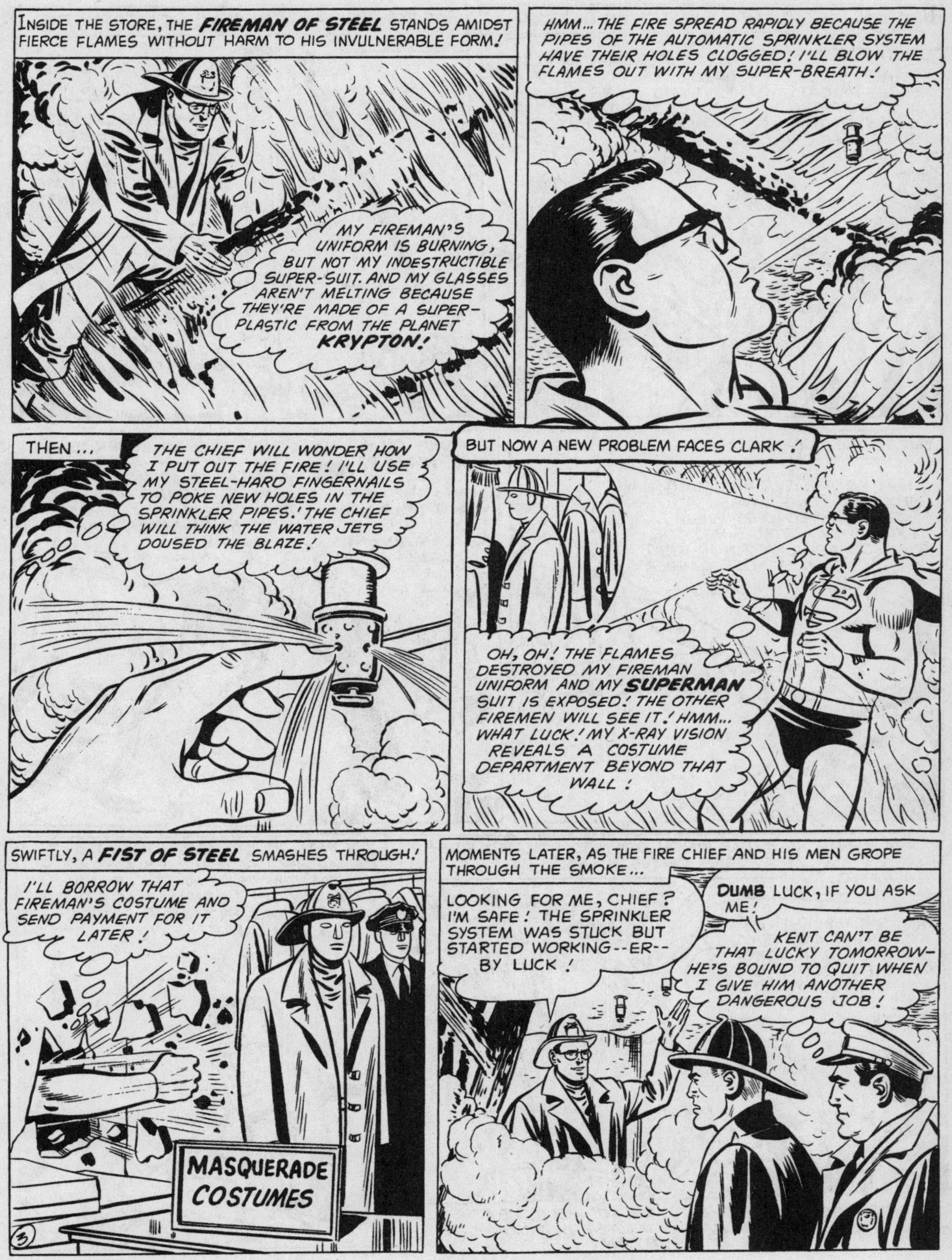
INSIDE THE STORE, THE FIREMAN OF STEEL STANDS AMIDST FIERCE FLAMES WITHOUT HARM TO HIS INVULNERABLE FORM!
MY FIREMAN'S UNIFORM IS BURNING, BUT NOT MY INDESTRUCTIBLE SUPER-SUIT. AND MY GLASSES AREN'T MELTING BECAUSE THEY'RE MADE OF A SUPER-PLASTIC FROM THE PLANET KRYPTON!
HMM... THE FIRE SPREAD RAPIDLY BECAUSE THE PIPES OF THE AUTOMATIC SPRINKLER SYSTEM HAVE THEIR HOLES CLOGGED! I'LL BLOW THE FLAMES OUT WITH MY SUPER-BREATH!
THEN...
THE CHIEF WILL WONDER HOW I PUT OUT THE FIRE! I'LL USE MY STEEL-HARD FINGERNAILS TO POKE NEW HOLES IN THE SPRINKLER PIPES! THE CHIEF WILL THINK THE WATER JETS DOUSED THE BLAZE!
BUT NOW A NEW PROBLEM FACES CLARK!
OH, OH! THE FLAMES DESTROYED MY FIREMAN UNIFORM AND MY SUPERMAN SUIT IS EXPOSED! THE OTHER FIREMEN WILL SEE IT! HMM... WHAT LUCK! MY X-RAY VISION REVEALS A COSTUME DEPARTMENT BEYOND THAT WALL!
SWIFTLY, A FIST OF STEEL SMASHES THROUGH!
I'LL BORROW THAT FIREMAN'S COSTUME AND SEND PAYMENT FOR IT LATER!
MASQUERADE COSTUMES
3
MOMENTS LATER, AS THE FIRE CHIEF AND HIS MEN GROPE THROUGH THE SMOKE...
LOOKING FOR ME, CHIEF? I'M SAFE! THE SPRINKLER SYSTEM WAS STUCK BUT STARTED WORKING--ER--BY LUCK!
DUMB LUCK, IF YOU ASK ME!
KENT CAN'T BE THAT LUCKY TOMORROW-HE'S BOUND TO QUIT WHEN I GIVE HIM ANOTHER DANGEROUS JOB!

NEXT DAY, THE FIRE CREW ANSWERS AN UNUSUAL EMERGENCY!

PLEASE, SIR! RESCUE MY CAT! HE'S TRAPPED HIGH UP ON THAT SMOKESTACK... ≥SOB!≤

ALL OUR WORK ISN'T...ER... HEROIC, KENT! WELL, IF YOU WANT TO BE THIS BOY'S "HERO", CLIMB THE LADDER AND RESCUE HIS PET!

BUT BEFORE CLARK CAN CLIMB DOWN WITH THE ANIMAL...

KENT! THE LADDER'S STUCK! WE CAN'T CRANK IT DOWN AND THAT STIFF WIND MIGHT BLOW YOU OFF! JUMP DOWN INTO OUR NET!

HMM--A LUCKY BREAK FOR ME! IF KENT JUMPS, WE'LL CATCH HIM SAFELY ALL RIGHT, BUT THE EXPERIENCE WILL SCARE HIM SO HE'S BOUND TO GO BACK TO HIS PAPER!

BUT TO THE CHIEF'S ALARM...

GREAT SCOTT! OUR NET MUST HAVE BEEN WEAKENED WHEN ALL THOSE PEOPLE JUMPED LAST WEEK, DURING THAT HOTEL FIRE! THE STRANDS ARE SNAPPING! KENT IS IN DANGER!...≥GULP!≤

ALREADY ON HIS WAY DOWN, FIREMAN CLARK IS IN HOT WATER!

KENT! THE NET WON'T HOLD YOU! YOU'LL HIT THE HARD PAVEMENT... ≥GULP!≤

NOW HE TELLS ME! IF I LAND UNHARMED OR START TO FLY AWAY, IT'LL EXPOSE ME AS SUPERMAN! AH, I HAVE IT...

CLARK BEAMS HIS X-RAY VISION DOWN TO A NEARBY FIRE-HYDRANT AND, AS A RESULT OF THE INTENSE HEAT GENERATED...

HOLY SMOKES! THAT FIRE HYDRANT ACCIDENTALLY BURST OPEN AND THE POWERFUL WATER-SPOUT WILL CUSHION YOUR FALL! WHAT A CHARMED LIFE YOU'VE GOT!

THE CHIEF IS...ER...HOT UNDER THE COLLAR BECAUSE NOTHING SCARES ME OFF THE JOB, AS HE HOPED! LET HIM KEEP THINKING I BEAR A "CHARMED LIFE"...IT WILL PROTECT MY SECRET IDENTITY!

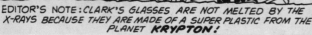

EDITOR'S NOTE: CLARK'S GLASSES ARE NOT MELTED BY THE X-RAYS BECAUSE THEY ARE MADE OF A SUPER PLASTIC FROM THE PLANET KRYPTON!

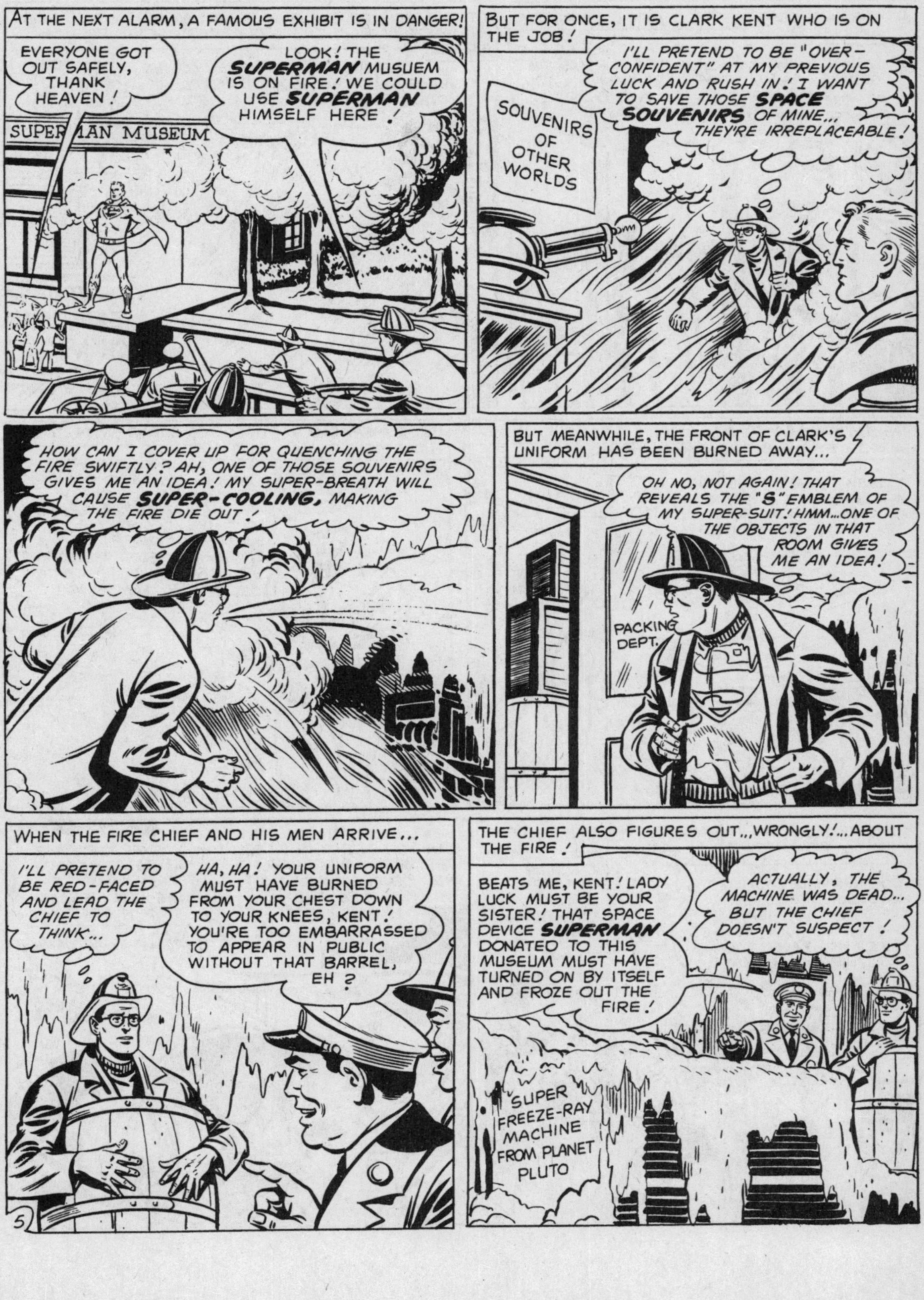
AT THE NEXT ALARM, A FAMOUS EXHIBIT IS IN DANGER!
EVERYONE GOT OUT SAFELY, THANK HEAVEN!
LOOK! THE SUPERMAN MUSUEM IS ON FIRE! WE COULD USE SUPERMAN HIMSELF HERE!
SUPERMAN MUSEUM
BUT FOR ONCE, IT IS CLARK KENT WHO IS ON THE JOB!
I'LL PRETEND TO BE "OVER-CONFIDENT" AT MY PREVIOUS LUCK AND RUSH IN! I WANT TO SAVE THOSE SPACE SOUVENIRS OF MINE... THEY'RE IRREPLACEABLE!
SOUVENIRS OF OTHER WORLDS
HOW CAN I COVER UP FOR QUENCHING THE FIRE SWIFTLY? AH, ONE OF THOSE SOUVENIRS GIVES ME AN IDEA! MY SUPER-BREATH WILL CAUSE SUPER-COOLING, MAKING THE FIRE DIE OUT!
BUT MEANWHILE, THE FRONT OF CLARK'S UNIFORM HAS BEEN BURNED AWAY...
OH NO, NOT AGAIN! THAT REVEALS THE "S" EMBLEM OF MY SUPER-SUIT! HMM...ONE OF THE OBJECTS IN THAT ROOM GIVES ME AN IDEA!
PACKING DEPT.
WHEN THE FIRE CHIEF AND HIS MEN ARRIVE...
I'LL PRETEND TO BE RED-FACED AND LEAD THE CHIEF TO THINK...
HA, HA! YOUR UNIFORM MUST HAVE BURNED FROM YOUR CHEST DOWN TO YOUR KNEES, KENT! YOU'RE TOO EMBARRASSED TO APPEAR IN PUBLIC WITHOUT THAT BARREL, EH?
5
THE CHIEF ALSO FIGURES OUT...WRONGLY!...ABOUT THE FIRE!
BEATS ME, KENT! LADY LUCK MUST BE YOUR SISTER! THAT SPACE DEVICE SUPERMAN DONATED TO THIS MUSEUM MUST HAVE TURNED ON BY ITSELF AND FROZE OUT THE FIRE!
ACTUALLY, THE MACHINE WAS DEAD... BUT THE CHIEF DOESN'T SUSPECT!
SUPER FREEZE-RAY MACHINE FROM PLANET PLUTO

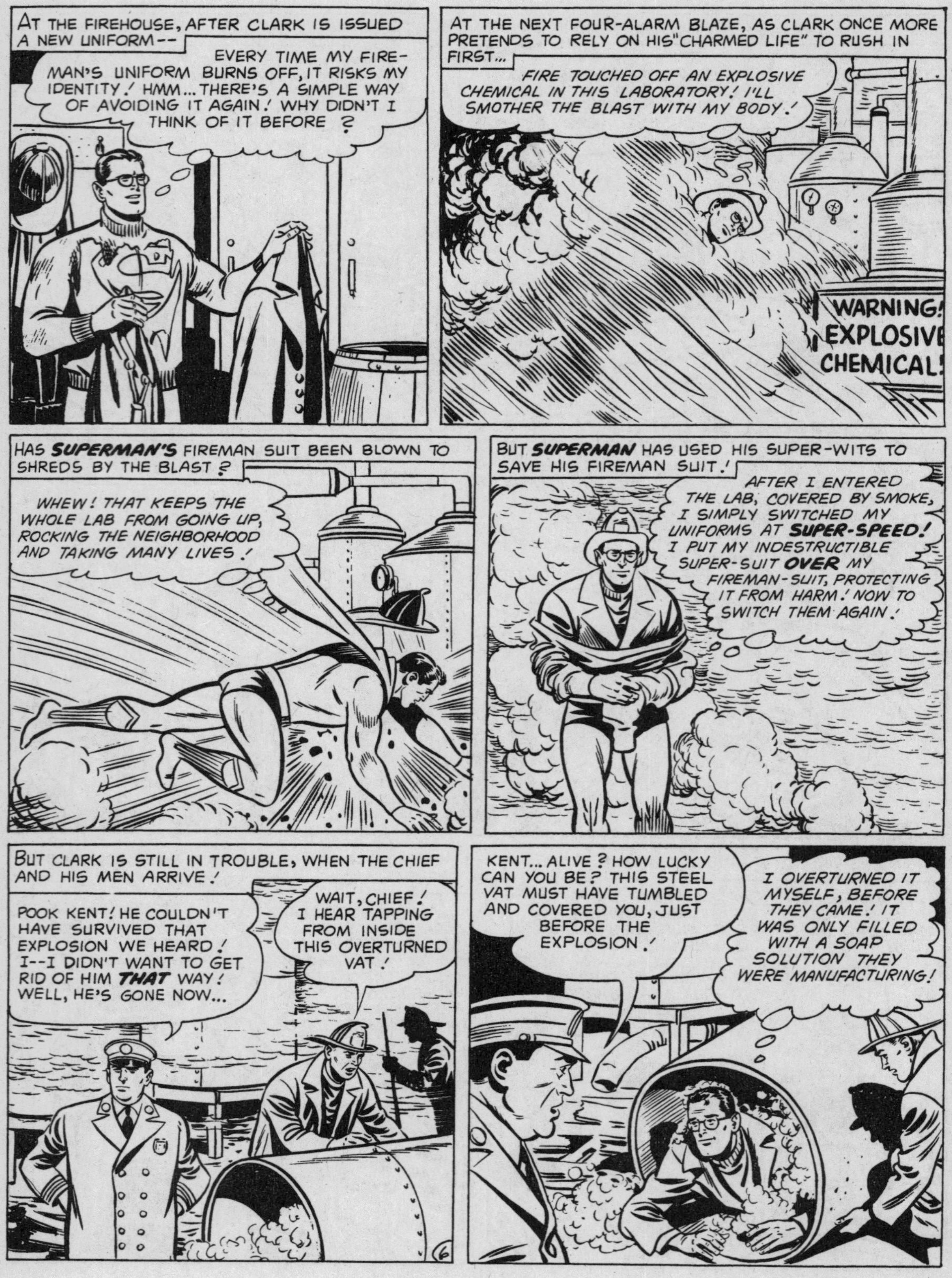
AT THE FIREHOUSE, AFTER CLARK IS ISSUED A NEW UNIFORM--
EVERY TIME MY FIREMAN'S UNIFORM BURNS OFF, IT RISKS MY IDENTITY! HMM... THERE'S A SIMPLE WAY OF AVOIDING IT AGAIN! WHY DIDN'T I THINK OF IT BEFORE ?
AT THE NEXT FOUR-ALARM BLAZE, AS CLARK ONCE MORE PRETENDS TO RELY ON HIS "CHARMED LIFE" TO RUSH IN FIRST...
FIRE TOUCHED OFF AN EXPLOSIVE CHEMICAL IN THIS LABORATORY! I'LL SMOTHER THE BLAST WITH MY BODY!
WARNING! EXPLOSIVE CHEMICAL!
HAS SUPERMAN'S FIREMAN SUIT BEEN BLOWN TO SHREDS BY THE BLAST ?
WHEW! THAT KEEPS THE WHOLE LAB FROM GOING UP, ROCKING THE NEIGHBORHOOD AND TAKING MANY LIVES!
BUT SUPERMAN HAS USED HIS SUPER-WITS TO SAVE HIS FIREMAN SUIT!
AFTER I ENTERED THE LAB, COVERED BY SMOKE, I SIMPLY SWITCHED MY UNIFORMS AT SUPER-SPEED! I PUT MY INDESTRUCTIBLE SUPER-SUIT OVER MY FIREMAN-SUIT, PROTECTING IT FROM HARM! NOW TO SWITCH THEM AGAIN!
BUT CLARK IS STILL IN TROUBLE, WHEN THE CHIEF AND HIS MEN ARRIVE!
POOR KENT! HE COULDN'T HAVE SURVIVED THAT EXPLOSION WE HEARD! I--I DIDN'T WANT TO GET RID OF HIM THAT WAY! WELL, HE'S GONE NOW...
WAIT, CHIEF! I HEAR TAPPING FROM INSIDE THIS OVERTURNED VAT!
6
KENT... ALIVE? HOW LUCKY CAN YOU BE? THIS STEEL VAT MUST HAVE TUMBLED AND COVERED YOU, JUST BEFORE THE EXPLOSION!
I OVERTURNED IT MYSELF, BEFORE THEY CAME! IT WAS ONLY FILLED WITH A SOAP SOLUTION THEY WERE MANUFACTURING!

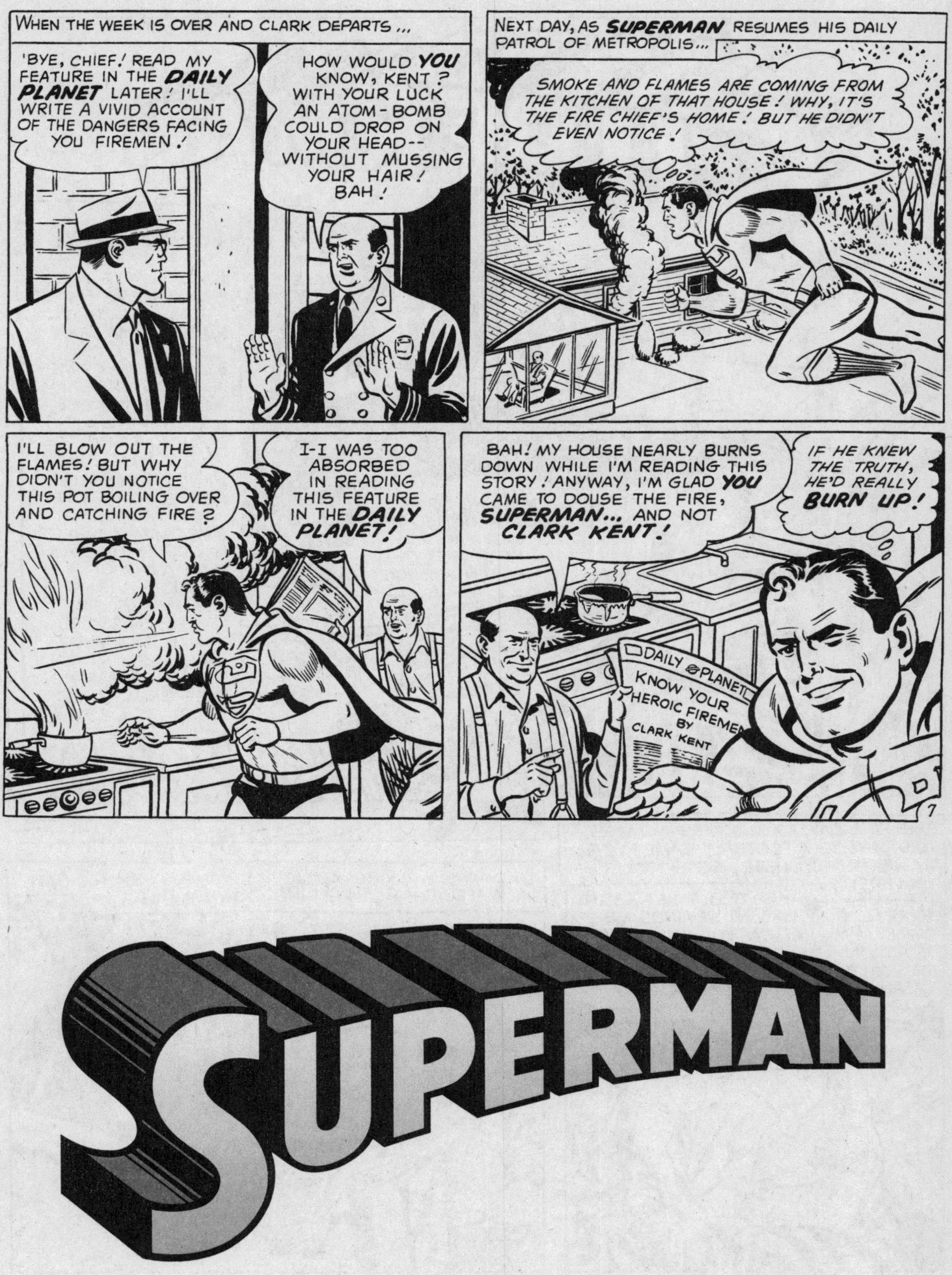
WHEN THE WEEK IS OVER AND CLARK DEPARTS ...
'BYE, CHIEF! READ MY FEATURE IN THE DAILY PLANET LATER! I'LL WRITE A VIVID ACCOUNT OF THE DANGERS FACING YOU FIREMEN!
HOW WOULD YOU KNOW, KENT? WITH YOUR LUCK AN ATOM-BOMB COULD DROP ON YOUR HEAD-- WITHOUT MUSSING YOUR HAIR! BAH!
NEXT DAY, AS SUPERMAN RESUMES HIS DAILY PATROL OF METROPOLIS...
SMOKE AND FLAMES ARE COMING FROM THE KITCHEN OF THAT HOUSE! WHY, IT'S THE FIRE CHIEF'S HOME! BUT HE DIDN'T EVEN NOTICE!
I'LL BLOW OUT THE FLAMES! BUT WHY DIDN'T YOU NOTICE THIS POT BOILING OVER AND CATCHING FIRE?
I-I WAS TOO ABSORBED IN READING THIS FEATURE IN THE DAILY PLANET!
BAH! MY HOUSE NEARLY BURNS DOWN WHILE I'M READING THIS STORY! ANYWAY, I'M GLAD YOU CAME TO DOUSE THE FIRE, SUPERMAN... AND NOT CLARK KENT!
IF HE KNEW THE TRUTH, HE'D REALLY BURN UP!
DAILY PLANET
KNOW YOUR HEROIC FIREMEN
BY CLARK KENT
7

SUPERMAN

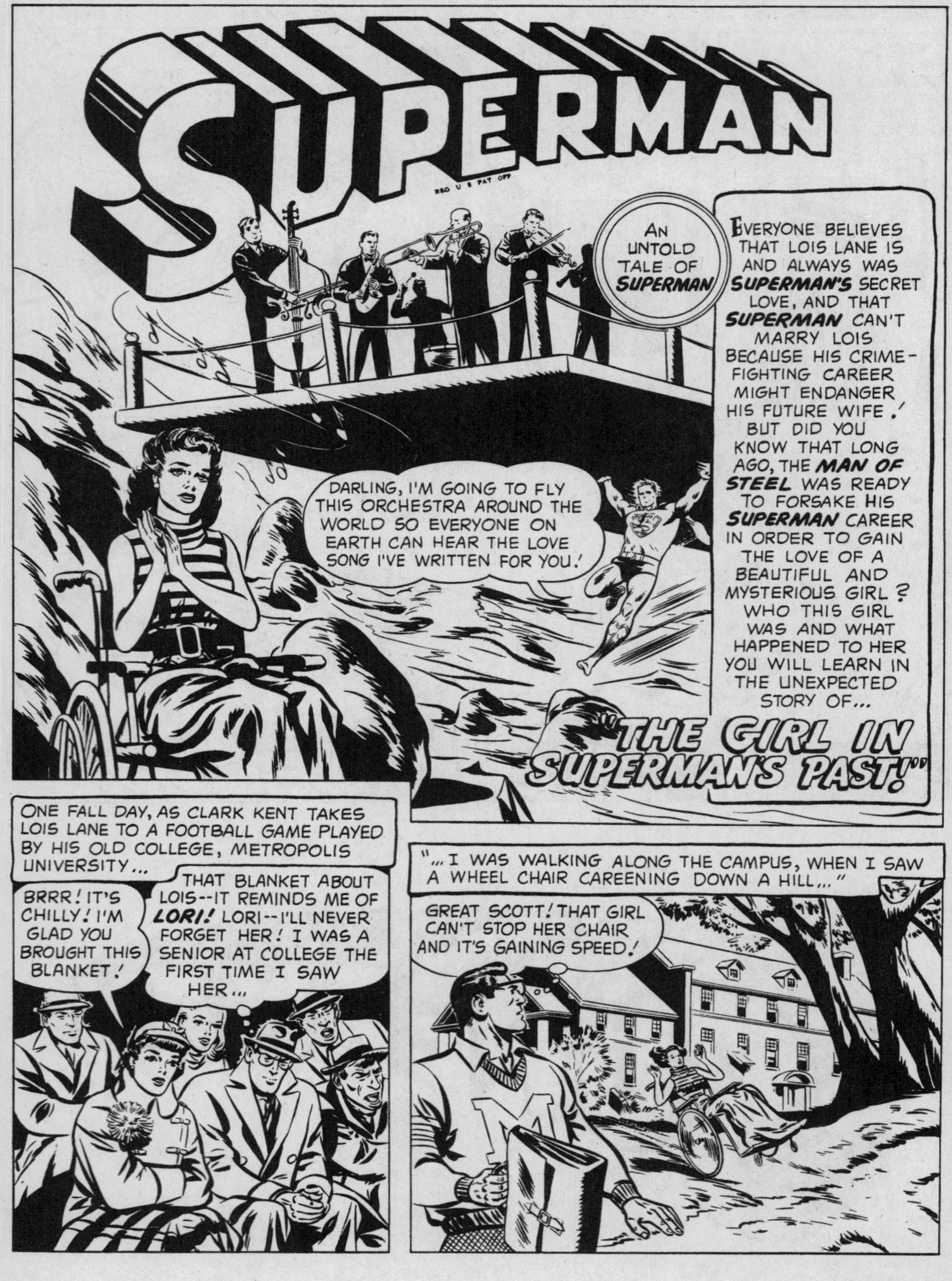
SUPERMAN
REG. U.S. PAT. OFF.
AN UNTOLD TALE OF SUPERMAN
EVERYONE BELIEVES THAT LOIS LANE IS AND ALWAYS WAS SUPERMAN'S SECRET LOVE, AND THAT SUPERMAN CAN'T MARRY LOIS BECAUSE HIS CRIME-FIGHTING CAREER MIGHT ENDANGER HIS FUTURE WIFE! BUT DID YOU KNOW THAT LONG AGO, THE MAN OF STEEL WAS READY TO FORSAKE HIS SUPERMAN CAREER IN ORDER TO GAIN THE LOVE OF A BEAUTIFUL AND MYSTERIOUS GIRL? WHO THIS GIRL WAS AND WHAT HAPPENED TO HER YOU WILL LEARN IN THE UNEXPECTED STORY OF...
DARLING, I'M GOING TO FLY THIS ORCHESTRA AROUND THE WORLD SO EVERYONE ON EARTH CAN HEAR THE LOVE SONG I'VE WRITTEN FOR YOU!
"THE GIRL IN SUPERMAN'S PAST!"
ONE FALL DAY, AS CLARK KENT TAKES LOIS LANE TO A FOOTBALL GAME PLAYED BY HIS OLD COLLEGE, METROPOLIS UNIVERSITY...
BRRR! IT'S CHILLY! I'M GLAD YOU BROUGHT THIS BLANKET!
THAT BLANKET ABOUT LOIS--IT REMINDS ME OF LORI! LORI--I'LL NEVER FORGET HER! I WAS A SENIOR AT COLLEGE THE FIRST TIME I SAW HER...
"...I WAS WALKING ALONG THE CAMPUS, WHEN I SAW A WHEEL CHAIR CAREENING DOWN A HILL..."
GREAT SCOTT! THAT GIRL CAN'T STOP HER CHAIR AND IT'S GAINING SPEED!

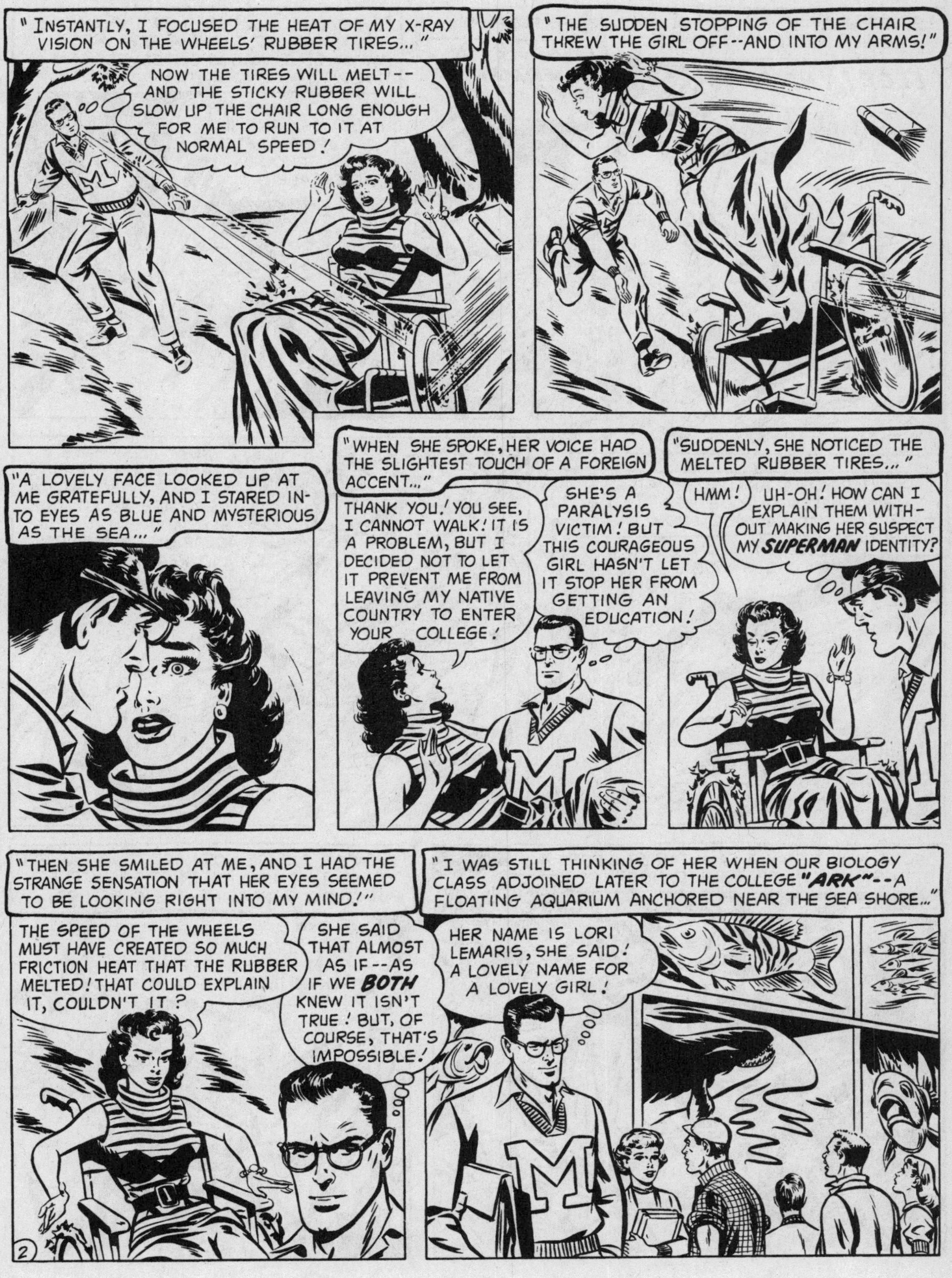
"INSTANTLY, I FOCUSED THE HEAT OF MY X-RAY VISION ON THE WHEELS' RUBBER TIRES..."
NOW THE TIRES WILL MELT-- AND THE STICKY RUBBER WILL SLOW UP THE CHAIR LONG ENOUGH FOR ME TO RUN TO IT AT NORMAL SPEED!
"THE SUDDEN STOPPING OF THE CHAIR THREW THE GIRL OFF--AND INTO MY ARMS!"
"A LOVELY FACE LOOKED UP AT ME GRATEFULLY, AND I STARED INTO EYES AS BLUE AND MYSTERIOUS AS THE SEA..."
"WHEN SHE SPOKE, HER VOICE HAD THE SLIGHTEST TOUCH OF A FOREIGN ACCENT..."
THANK YOU! YOU SEE, I CANNOT WALK! IT IS A PROBLEM, BUT I DECIDED NOT TO LET IT PREVENT ME FROM LEAVING MY NATIVE COUNTRY TO ENTER YOUR COLLEGE!
SHE'S A PARALYSIS VICTIM! BUT THIS COURAGEOUS GIRL HASN'T LET IT STOP HER FROM GETTING AN EDUCATION!
"SUDDENLY, SHE NOTICED THE MELTED RUBBER TIRES..."
HMM!
UH-OH! HOW CAN I EXPLAIN THEM WITHOUT MAKING HER SUSPECT MY SUPERMAN IDENTITY?
"THEN SHE SMILED AT ME, AND I HAD THE STRANGE SENSATION THAT HER EYES SEEMED TO BE LOOKING RIGHT INTO MY MIND!"
THE SPEED OF THE WHEELS MUST HAVE CREATED SO MUCH FRICTION HEAT THAT THE RUBBER MELTED! THAT COULD EXPLAIN IT, COULDN'T IT?
SHE SAID THAT ALMOST AS IF--AS IF WE BOTH KNEW IT ISN'T TRUE! BUT, OF COURSE, THAT'S IMPOSSIBLE!
2
"I WAS STILL THINKING OF HER WHEN OUR BIOLOGY CLASS ADJOINED LATER TO THE COLLEGE "ARK"--A FLOATING AQUARIUM ANCHORED NEAR THE SEA SHORE..."
HER NAME IS LORI LEMARIS, SHE SAID! A LOVELY NAME FOR A LOVELY GIRL!

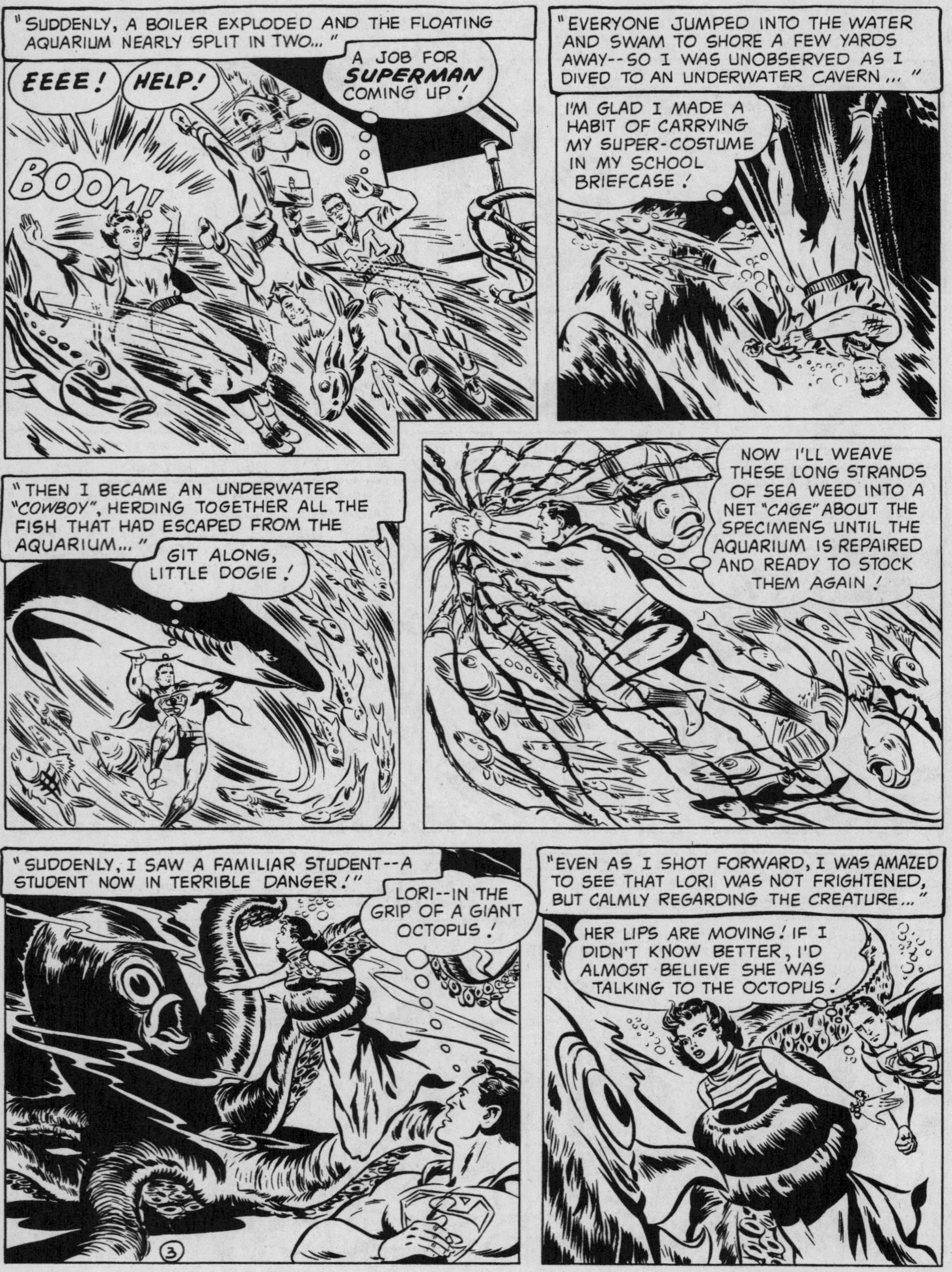
"SUDDENLY, A BOILER EXPLODED AND THE FLOATING AQUARIUM NEARLY SPLIT IN TWO..."
EEEE!
HELP!
A JOB FOR SUPERMAN COMING UP!
BOOM!
"EVERYONE JUMPED INTO THE WATER AND SWAM TO SHORE A FEW YARDS AWAY--SO I WAS UNOBSERVED AS I DIVED TO AN UNDERWATER CAVERN..."
I'M GLAD I MADE A HABIT OF CARRYING MY SUPER-COSTUME IN MY SCHOOL BRIEFCASE!
"THEN I BECAME AN UNDERWATER "COWBOY", HERDING TOGETHER ALL THE FISH THAT HAD ESCAPED FROM THE AQUARIUM..."
GIT ALONG, LITTLE DOGIE!
NOW I'LL WEAVE THESE LONG STRANDS OF SEA WEED INTO A NET "CAGE" ABOUT THE SPECIMENS UNTIL THE AQUARIUM IS REPAIRED AND READY TO STOCK THEM AGAIN!
"SUDDENLY, I SAW A FAMILIAR STUDENT--A STUDENT NOW IN TERRIBLE DANGER!"
LORI--IN THE GRIP OF A GIANT OCTOPUS!
3
"EVEN AS I SHOT FORWARD, I WAS AMAZED TO SEE THAT LORI WAS NOT FRIGHTENED, BUT CALMLY REGARDING THE CREATURE..."
HER LIPS ARE MOVING! IF I DIDN'T KNOW BETTER, I'D ALMOST BELIEVE SHE WAS TALKING TO THE OCTOPUS!

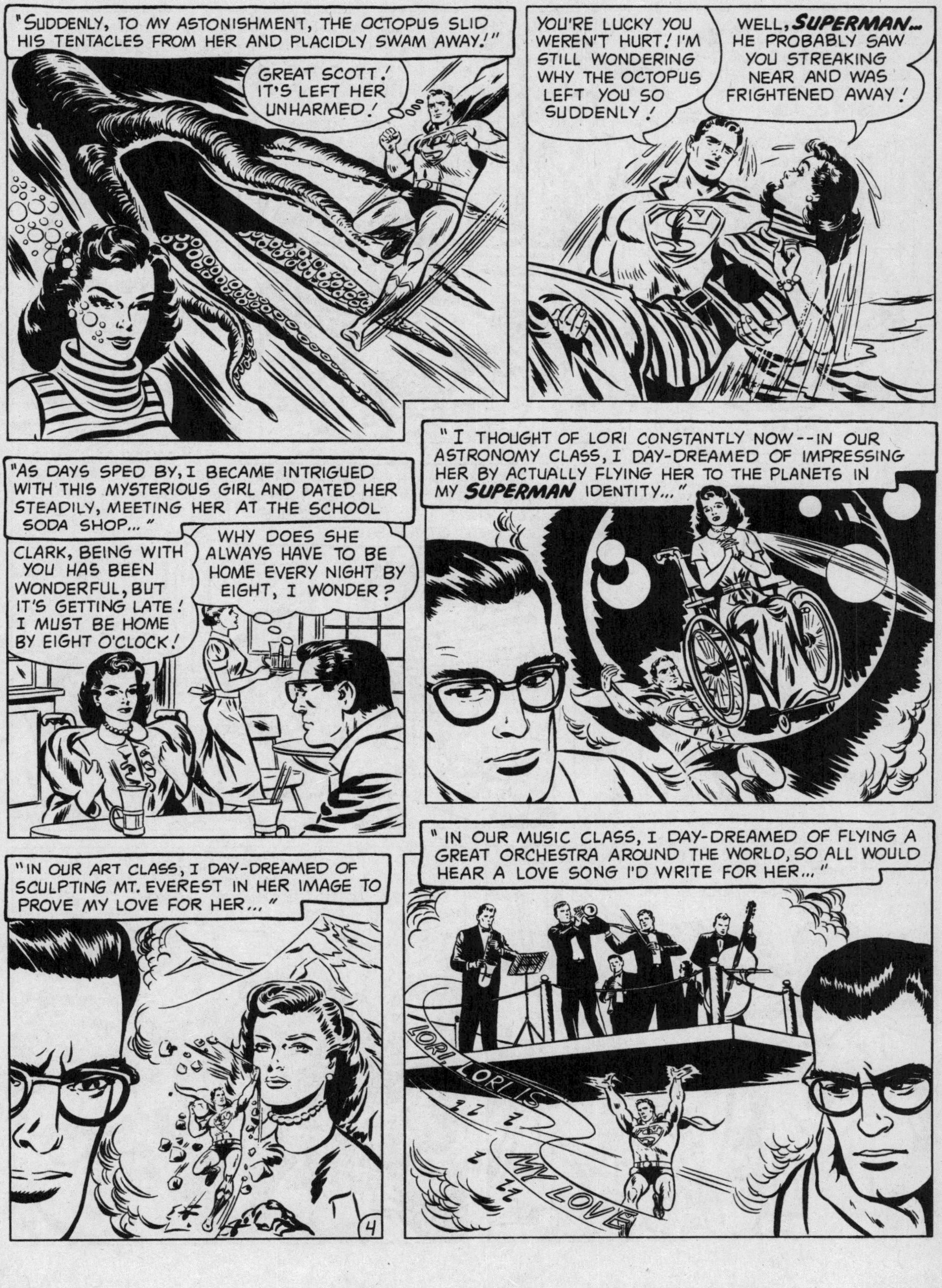
"SUDDENLY, TO MY ASTONISHMENT, THE OCTOPUS SLID HIS TENTACLES FROM HER AND PLACIDLY SWAM AWAY!"
GREAT SCOTT! IT'S LEFT HER UNHARMED!
YOU'RE LUCKY YOU WEREN'T HURT! I'M STILL WONDERING WHY THE OCTOPUS LEFT YOU SO SUDDENLY!
WELL, SUPERMAN... HE PROBABLY SAW YOU STREAKING NEAR AND WAS FRIGHTENED AWAY!
"AS DAYS SPED BY, I BECAME INTRIGUED WITH THIS MYSTERIOUS GIRL AND DATED HER STEADILY, MEETING HER AT THE SCHOOL SODA SHOP..."
CLARK, BEING WITH YOU HAS BEEN WONDERFUL, BUT IT'S GETTING LATE! I MUST BE HOME BY EIGHT O'CLOCK!
WHY DOES SHE ALWAYS HAVE TO BE HOME EVERY NIGHT BY EIGHT, I WONDER?
"I THOUGHT OF LORI CONSTANTLY NOW--IN OUR ASTRONOMY CLASS, I DAY-DREAMED OF IMPRESSING HER BY ACTUALLY FLYING HER TO THE PLANETS IN MY SUPERMAN IDENTITY..."
"IN OUR ART CLASS, I DAY-DREAMED OF SCULPTING MT. EVEREST IN HER IMAGE TO PROVE MY LOVE FOR HER..."
4
"IN OUR MUSIC CLASS, I DAY-DREAMED OF FLYING A GREAT ORCHESTRA AROUND THE WORLD, SO ALL WOULD HEAR A LOVE SONG I'D WRITE FOR HER..."
LORI, LORI IS MY LOVE

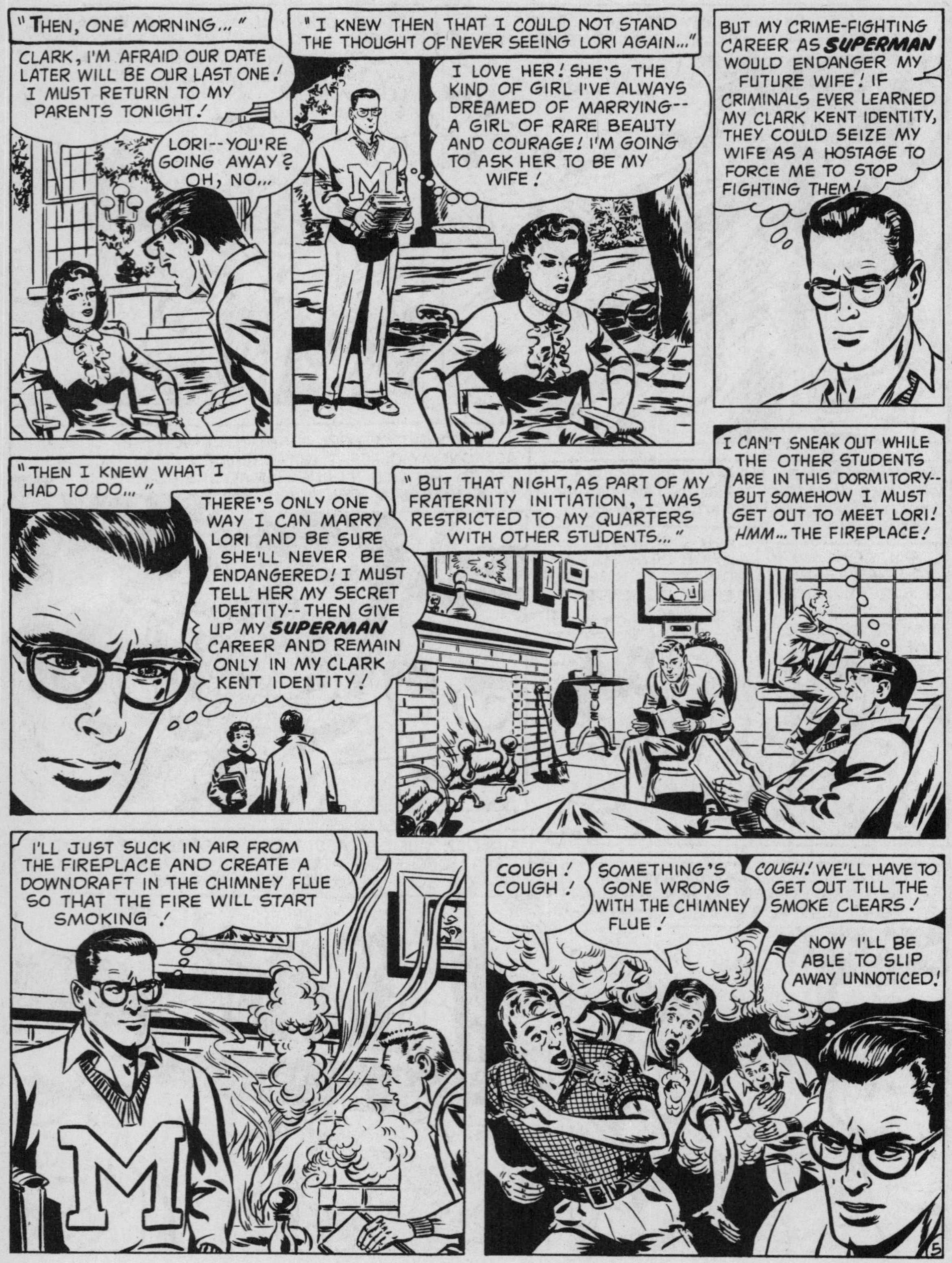
"THEN, ONE MORNING..."
CLARK, I'M AFRAID OUR DATE LATER WILL BE OUR LAST ONE! I MUST RETURN TO MY PARENTS TONIGHT!
LORI--YOU'RE GOING AWAY? OH, NO...
"I KNEW THEN THAT I COULD NOT STAND THE THOUGHT OF NEVER SEEING LORI AGAIN..."
I LOVE HER! SHE'S THE KIND OF GIRL I'VE ALWAYS DREAMED OF MARRYING-- A GIRL OF RARE BEAUTY AND COURAGE! I'M GOING TO ASK HER TO BE MY WIFE!
BUT MY CRIME-FIGHTING CAREER AS SUPERMAN WOULD ENDANGER MY FUTURE WIFE! IF CRIMINALS EVER LEARNED MY CLARK KENT IDENTITY, THEY COULD SEIZE MY WIFE AS A HOSTAGE TO FORCE ME TO STOP FIGHTING THEM!
"THEN I KNEW WHAT I HAD TO DO..."
THERE'S ONLY ONE WAY I CAN MARRY LORI AND BE SURE SHE'LL NEVER BE ENDANGERED! I MUST TELL HER MY SECRET IDENTITY-- THEN GIVE UP MY SUPERMAN CAREER AND REMAIN ONLY IN MY CLARK KENT IDENTITY!
"BUT THAT NIGHT, AS PART OF MY FRATERNITY INITIATION, I WAS RESTRICTED TO MY QUARTERS WITH OTHER STUDENTS..."
I CAN'T SNEAK OUT WHILE THE OTHER STUDENTS ARE IN THIS DORMITORY-- BUT SOMEHOW I MUST GET OUT TO MEET LORI! HMM... THE FIREPLACE!
I'LL JUST SUCK IN AIR FROM THE FIREPLACE AND CREATE A DOWNDRAFT IN THE CHIMNEY FLUE SO THAT THE FIRE WILL START SMOKING!
COUGH! COUGH!
SOMETHING'S GONE WRONG WITH THE CHIMNEY FLUE!
COUGH! WE'LL HAVE TO GET OUT TILL THE SMOKE CLEARS!
NOW I'LL BE ABLE TO SLIP AWAY UNNOTICED!
5

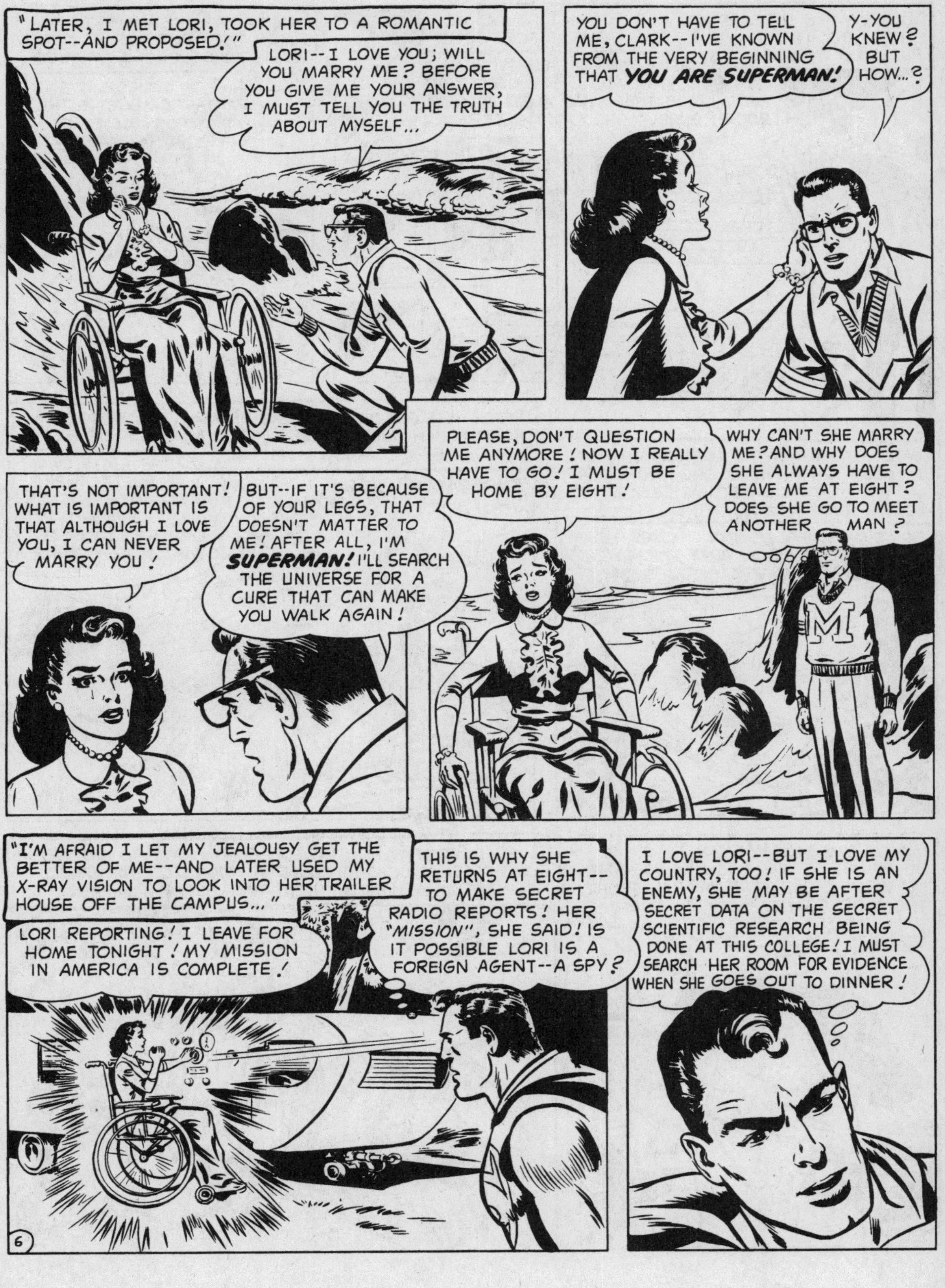
"LATER, I MET LORI, TOOK HER TO A ROMANTIC SPOT--AND PROPOSED!"
LORI--I LOVE YOU; WILL YOU MARRY ME? BEFORE YOU GIVE ME YOUR ANSWER, I MUST TELL YOU THE TRUTH ABOUT MYSELF...
YOU DON'T HAVE TO TELL ME, CLARK--I'VE KNOWN FROM THE VERY BEGINNING THAT **YOU ARE SUPERMAN!**
Y-YOU KNEW? BUT HOW...?
THAT'S NOT IMPORTANT! WHAT IS IMPORTANT IS THAT ALTHOUGH I LOVE YOU, I CAN NEVER MARRY YOU!
BUT--IF IT'S BECAUSE OF YOUR LEGS, THAT DOESN'T MATTER TO ME! AFTER ALL, I'M **SUPERMAN!** I'LL SEARCH THE UNIVERSE FOR A CURE THAT CAN MAKE YOU WALK AGAIN!
PLEASE, DON'T QUESTION ME ANYMORE! NOW I REALLY HAVE TO GO! I MUST BE HOME BY EIGHT!
WHY CAN'T SHE MARRY ME? AND WHY DOES SHE ALWAYS HAVE TO LEAVE ME AT EIGHT? DOES SHE GO TO MEET ANOTHER MAN?
"I'M AFRAID I LET MY JEALOUSY GET THE BETTER OF ME--AND LATER USED MY X-RAY VISION TO LOOK INTO HER TRAILER HOUSE OFF THE CAMPUS..."
LORI REPORTING! I LEAVE FOR HOME TONIGHT! MY MISSION IN AMERICA IS COMPLETE!
THIS IS WHY SHE RETURNS AT EIGHT--TO MAKE SECRET RADIO REPORTS! HER "MISSION", SHE SAID! IS IT POSSIBLE LORI IS A FOREIGN AGENT--A SPY?
I LOVE LORI--BUT I LOVE MY COUNTRY, TOO! IF SHE IS AN ENEMY, SHE MAY BE AFTER SECRET DATA ON THE SECRET SCIENTIFIC RESEARCH BEING DONE AT THIS COLLEGE! I MUST SEARCH HER ROOM FOR EVIDENCE WHEN SHE GOES OUT TO DINNER!
6

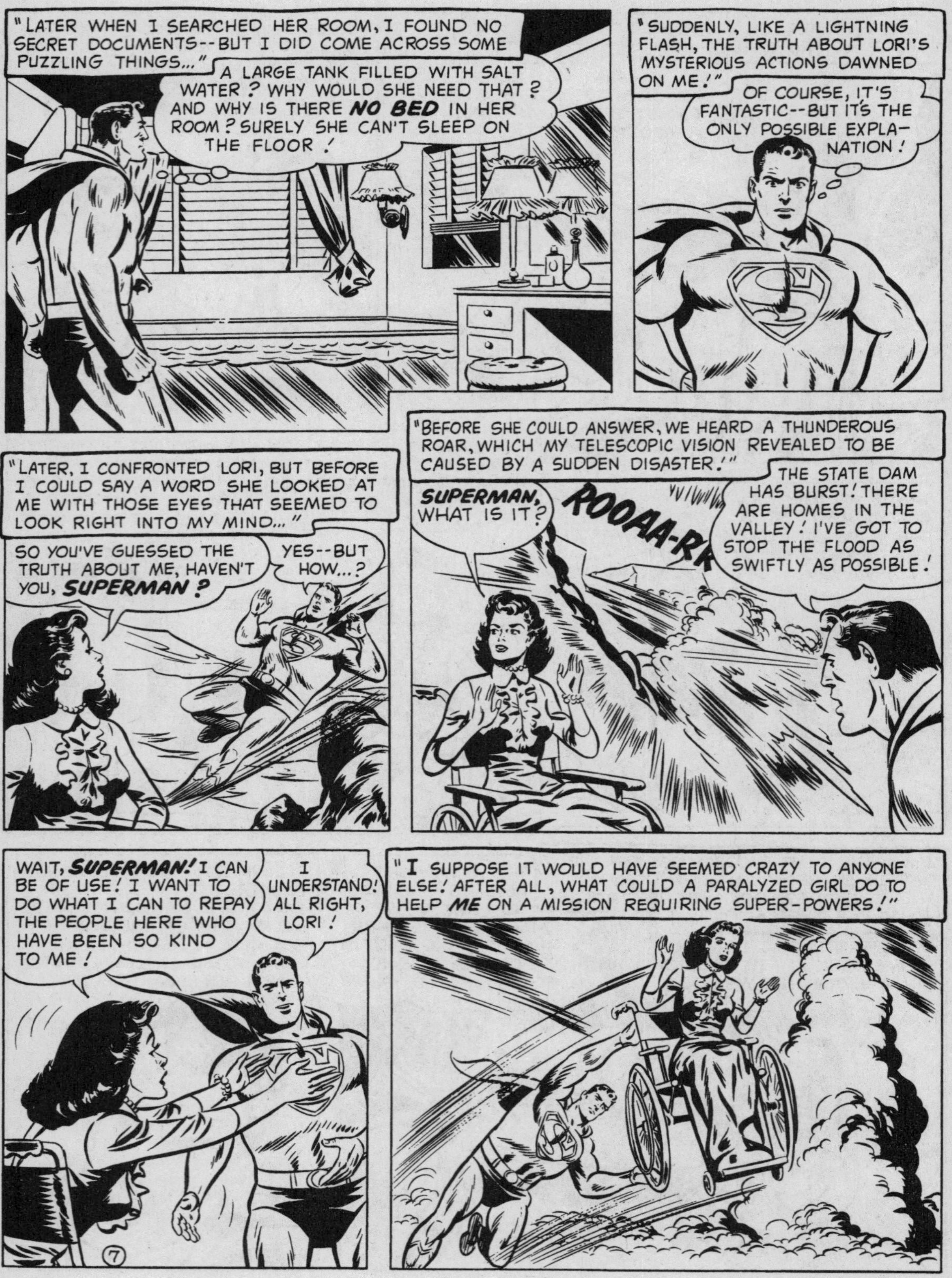
"LATER WHEN I SEARCHED HER ROOM, I FOUND NO SECRET DOCUMENTS--BUT I DID COME ACROSS SOME PUZZLING THINGS..."
A LARGE TANK FILLED WITH SALT WATER? WHY WOULD SHE NEED THAT? AND WHY IS THERE NO BED IN HER ROOM? SURELY SHE CAN'T SLEEP ON THE FLOOR!
"SUDDENLY, LIKE A LIGHTNING FLASH, THE TRUTH ABOUT LORI'S MYSTERIOUS ACTIONS DAWNED ON ME!"
OF COURSE, IT'S FANTASTIC--BUT IT'S THE ONLY POSSIBLE EXPLA-NATION!
"LATER, I CONFRONTED LORI, BUT BEFORE I COULD SAY A WORD SHE LOOKED AT ME WITH THOSE EYES THAT SEEMED TO LOOK RIGHT INTO MY MIND..."
SO YOU'VE GUESSED THE TRUTH ABOUT ME, HAVEN'T YOU, SUPERMAN?
YES--BUT HOW...?
"BEFORE SHE COULD ANSWER, WE HEARD A THUNDEROUS ROAR, WHICH MY TELESCOPIC VISION REVEALED TO BE CAUSED BY A SUDDEN DISASTER!"
SUPERMAN, WHAT IS IT?
ROOAA-RR
THE STATE DAM HAS BURST! THERE ARE HOMES IN THE VALLEY! I'VE GOT TO STOP THE FLOOD AS SWIFTLY AS POSSIBLE!
WAIT, SUPERMAN! I CAN BE OF USE! I WANT TO DO WHAT I CAN TO REPAY THE PEOPLE HERE WHO HAVE BEEN SO KIND TO ME!
I UNDERSTAND! ALL RIGHT, LORI!
7
"I SUPPOSE IT WOULD HAVE SEEMED CRAZY TO ANYONE ELSE! AFTER ALL, WHAT COULD A PARALYZED GIRL DO TO HELP ME ON A MISSION REQUIRING SUPER-POWERS!"

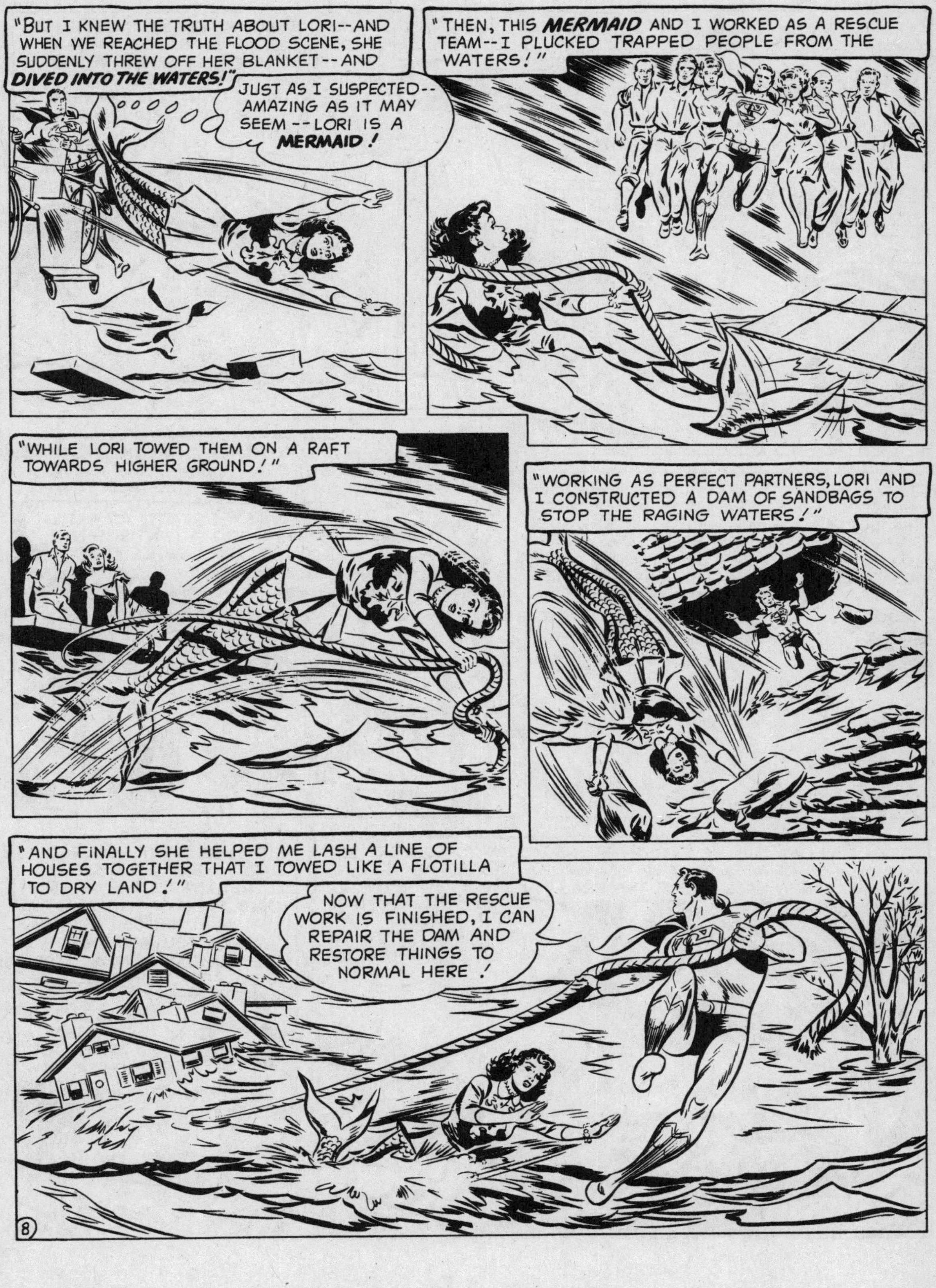
"BUT I KNEW THE TRUTH ABOUT LORI--AND WHEN WE REACHED THE FLOOD SCENE, SHE SUDDENLY THREW OFF HER BLANKET--AND DIVED INTO THE WATERS!"
JUST AS I SUSPECTED--AMAZING AS IT MAY SEEM--LORI IS A MERMAID!
"THEN, THIS MERMAID AND I WORKED AS A RESCUE TEAM--I PLUCKED TRAPPED PEOPLE FROM THE WATERS!"
"WHILE LORI TOWED THEM ON A RAFT TOWARDS HIGHER GROUND!"
"WORKING AS PERFECT PARTNERS, LORI AND I CONSTRUCTED A DAM OF SANDBAGS TO STOP THE RAGING WATERS!"
"AND FINALLY SHE HELPED ME LASH A LINE OF HOUSES TOGETHER THAT I TOWED LIKE A FLOTILLA TO DRY LAND!"
NOW THAT THE RESCUE WORK IS FINISHED, I CAN REPAIR THE DAM AND RESTORE THINGS TO NORMAL HERE!
8

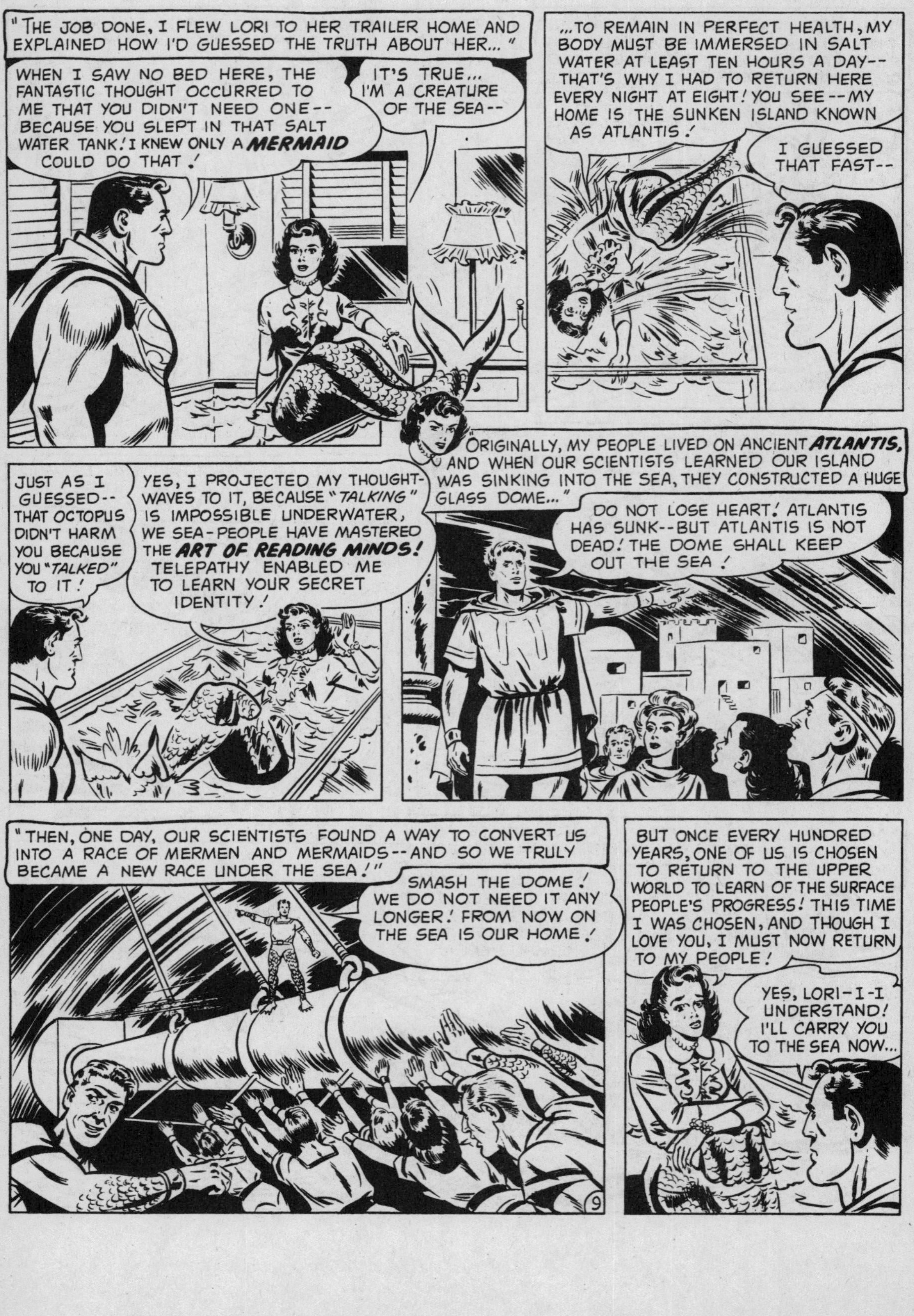
"THE JOB DONE, I FLEW LORI TO HER TRAILER HOME AND EXPLAINED HOW I'D GUESSED THE TRUTH ABOUT HER..."
WHEN I SAW NO BED HERE, THE FANTASTIC THOUGHT OCCURRED TO ME THAT YOU DIDN'T NEED ONE--BECAUSE YOU SLEPT IN THAT SALT WATER TANK! I KNEW ONLY A MERMAID COULD DO THAT!
IT'S TRUE... I'M A CREATURE OF THE SEA--
...TO REMAIN IN PERFECT HEALTH, MY BODY MUST BE IMMERSED IN SALT WATER AT LEAST TEN HOURS A DAY--THAT'S WHY I HAD TO RETURN HERE EVERY NIGHT AT EIGHT! YOU SEE--MY HOME IS THE SUNKEN ISLAND KNOWN AS ATLANTIS!
I GUESSED THAT FAST--
JUST AS I GUESSED--THAT OCTOPUS DIDN'T HARM YOU BECAUSE YOU "TALKED" TO IT!
YES, I PROJECTED MY THOUGHT-WAVES TO IT, BECAUSE "TALKING" IS IMPOSSIBLE UNDERWATER, WE SEA-PEOPLE HAVE MASTERED THE ART OF READING MINDS! TELEPATHY ENABLED ME TO LEARN YOUR SECRET IDENTITY!
"ORIGINALLY, MY PEOPLE LIVED ON ANCIENT ATLANTIS, AND WHEN OUR SCIENTISTS LEARNED OUR ISLAND WAS SINKING INTO THE SEA, THEY CONSTRUCTED A HUGE GLASS DOME..."
DO NOT LOSE HEART! ATLANTIS HAS SUNK--BUT ATLANTIS IS NOT DEAD! THE DOME SHALL KEEP OUT THE SEA!
"THEN, ONE DAY, OUR SCIENTISTS FOUND A WAY TO CONVERT US INTO A RACE OF MERMEN AND MERMAIDS--AND SO WE TRULY BECAME A NEW RACE UNDER THE SEA!"
SMASH THE DOME! WE DO NOT NEED IT ANY LONGER! FROM NOW ON THE SEA IS OUR HOME!
9
BUT ONCE EVERY HUNDRED YEARS, ONE OF US IS CHOSEN TO RETURN TO THE UPPER WORLD TO LEARN OF THE SURFACE PEOPLE'S PROGRESS! THIS TIME I WAS CHOSEN, AND THOUGH I LOVE YOU, I MUST NOW RETURN TO MY PEOPLE!
YES, LORI-I-I UNDERSTAND! I'LL CARRY YOU TO THE SEA NOW...

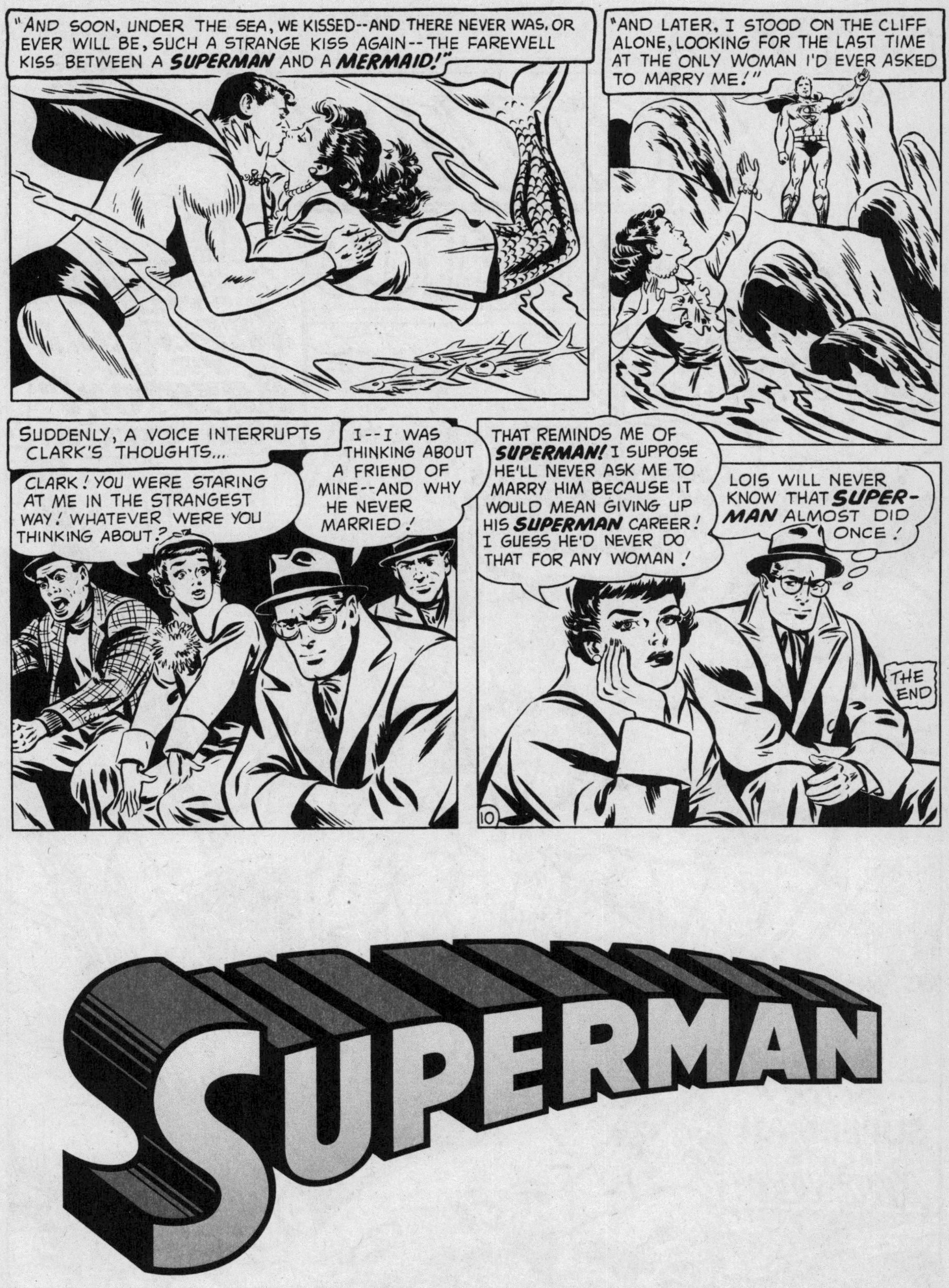
"AND SOON, UNDER THE SEA, WE KISSED--AND THERE NEVER WAS, OR EVER WILL BE, SUCH A STRANGE KISS AGAIN--THE FAREWELL KISS BETWEEN A SUPERMAN AND A MERMAID!"
"AND LATER, I STOOD ON THE CLIFF ALONE, LOOKING FOR THE LAST TIME AT THE ONLY WOMAN I'D EVER ASKED TO MARRY ME!"
SUDDENLY, A VOICE INTERRUPTS CLARK'S THOUGHTS...
CLARK! YOU WERE STARING AT ME IN THE STRANGEST WAY! WHATEVER WERE YOU THINKING ABOUT?
I--I WAS THINKING ABOUT A FRIEND OF MINE--AND WHY HE NEVER MARRIED!
THAT REMINDS ME OF SUPERMAN! I SUPPOSE HE'LL NEVER ASK ME TO MARRY HIM BECAUSE IT WOULD MEAN GIVING UP HIS SUPERMAN CAREER! I GUESS HE'D NEVER DO THAT FOR ANY WOMAN!
LOIS WILL NEVER KNOW THAT SUPERMAN ALMOST DID ONCE!
THE END
10

SUPERMAN

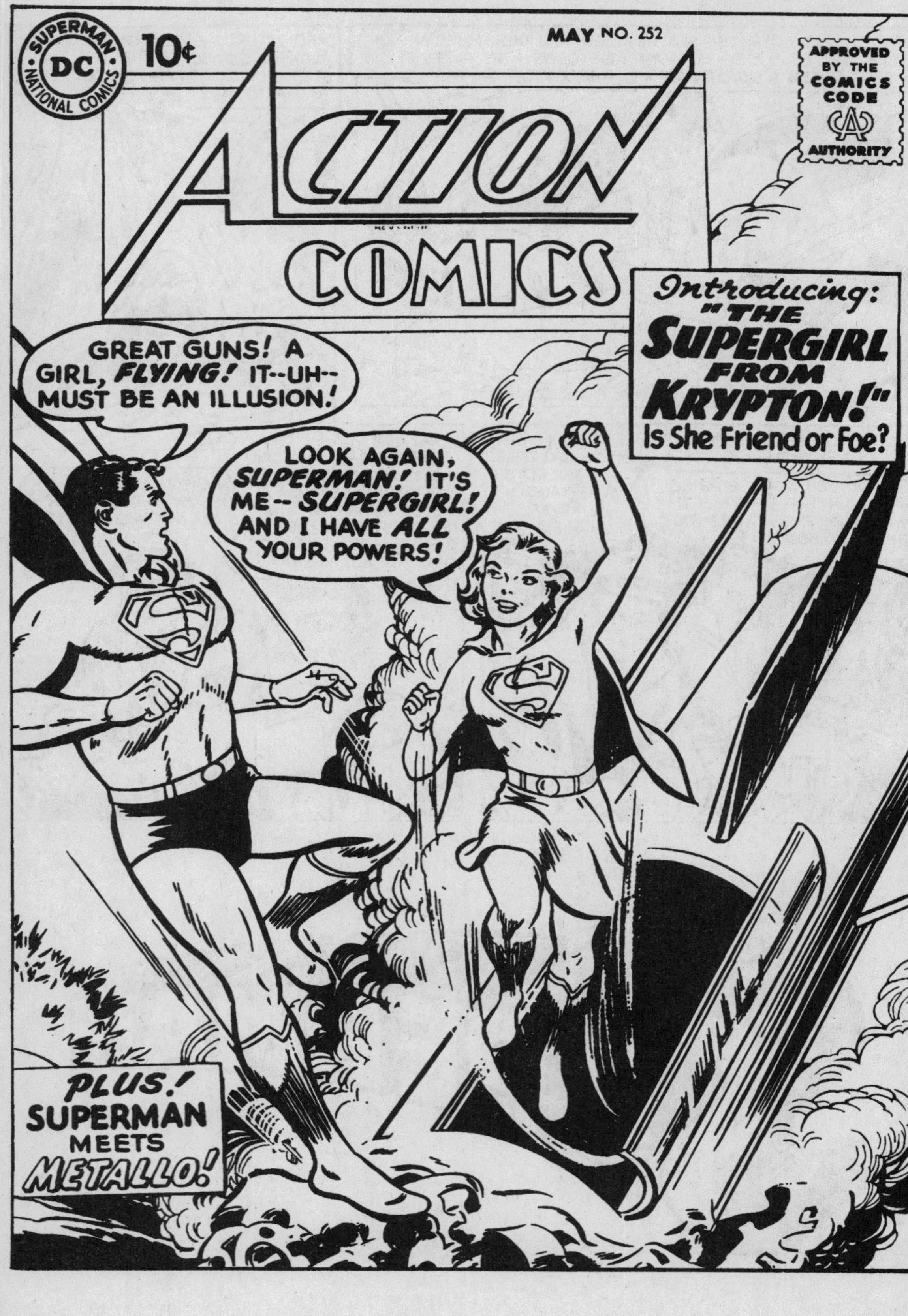
SUPERMAN
DC
NATIONAL COMICS
10¢
MAY NO. 252
APPROVED BY THE COMICS CODE AUTHORITY
ACTION COMICS
Introducing: "THE SUPERGIRL FROM KRYPTON!"
Is She Friend or Foe?
GREAT GUNS! A GIRL, FLYING! IT--UH-- MUST BE AN ILLUSION!
LOOK AGAIN, SUPERMAN! IT'S ME-- SUPERGIRL! AND I HAVE ALL YOUR POWERS!
PLUS! SUPERMAN MEETS METALLO!

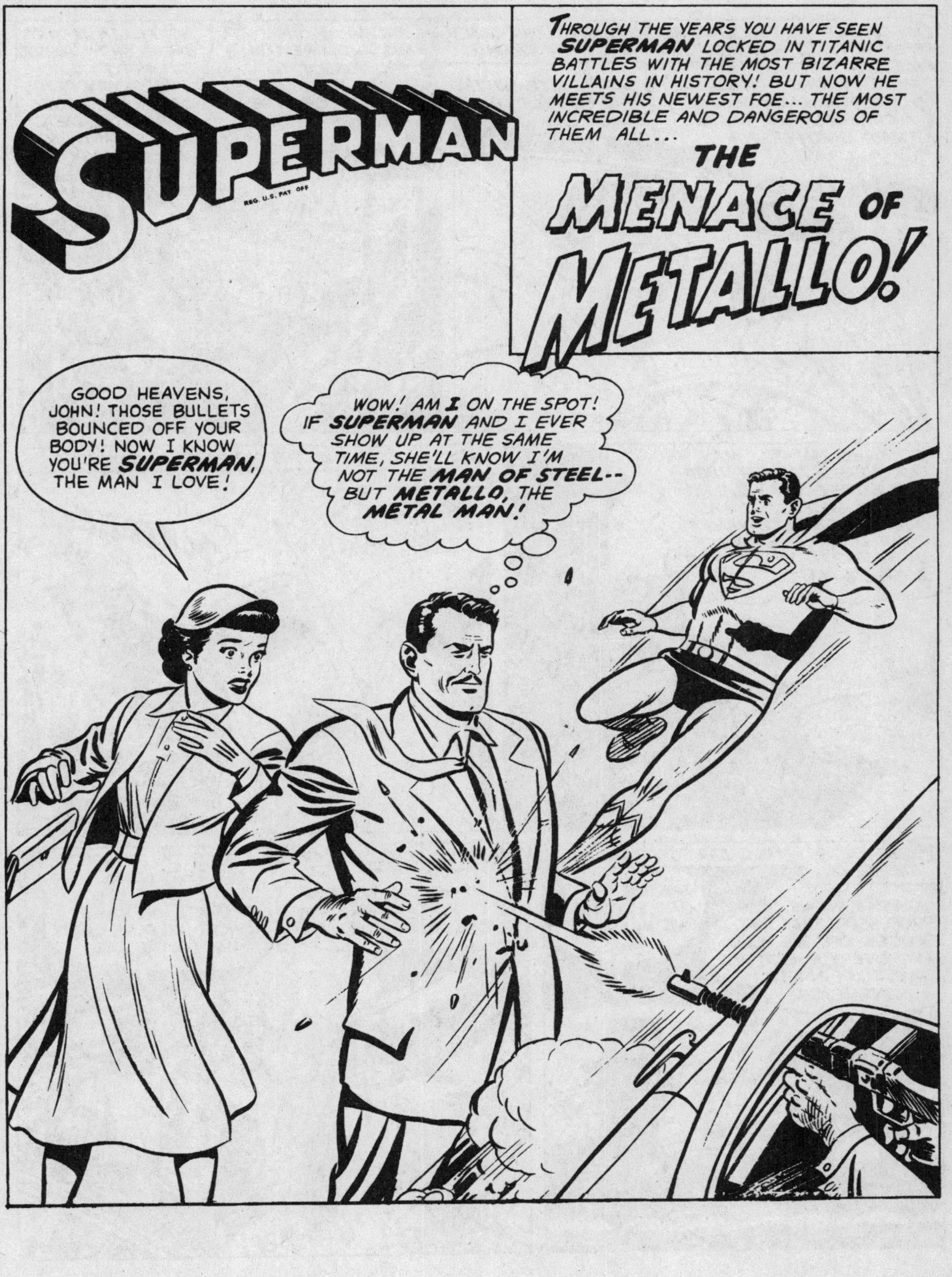
SUPERMAN
REG. U.S. PAT. OFF
THROUGH THE YEARS YOU HAVE SEEN SUPERMAN LOCKED IN TITANIC BATTLES WITH THE MOST BIZARRE VILLAINS IN HISTORY! BUT NOW HE MEETS HIS NEWEST FOE... THE MOST INCREDIBLE AND DANGEROUS OF THEM ALL...
THE MENACE OF METALLO!
GOOD HEAVENS, JOHN! THOSE BULLETS BOUNCED OFF YOUR BODY! NOW I KNOW YOU'RE SUPERMAN, THE MAN I LOVE!
WOW! AM I ON THE SPOT! IF SUPERMAN AND I EVER SHOW UP AT THE SAME TIME, SHE'LL KNOW I'M NOT THE MAN OF STEEL-- BUT METALLO, THE METAL MAN!

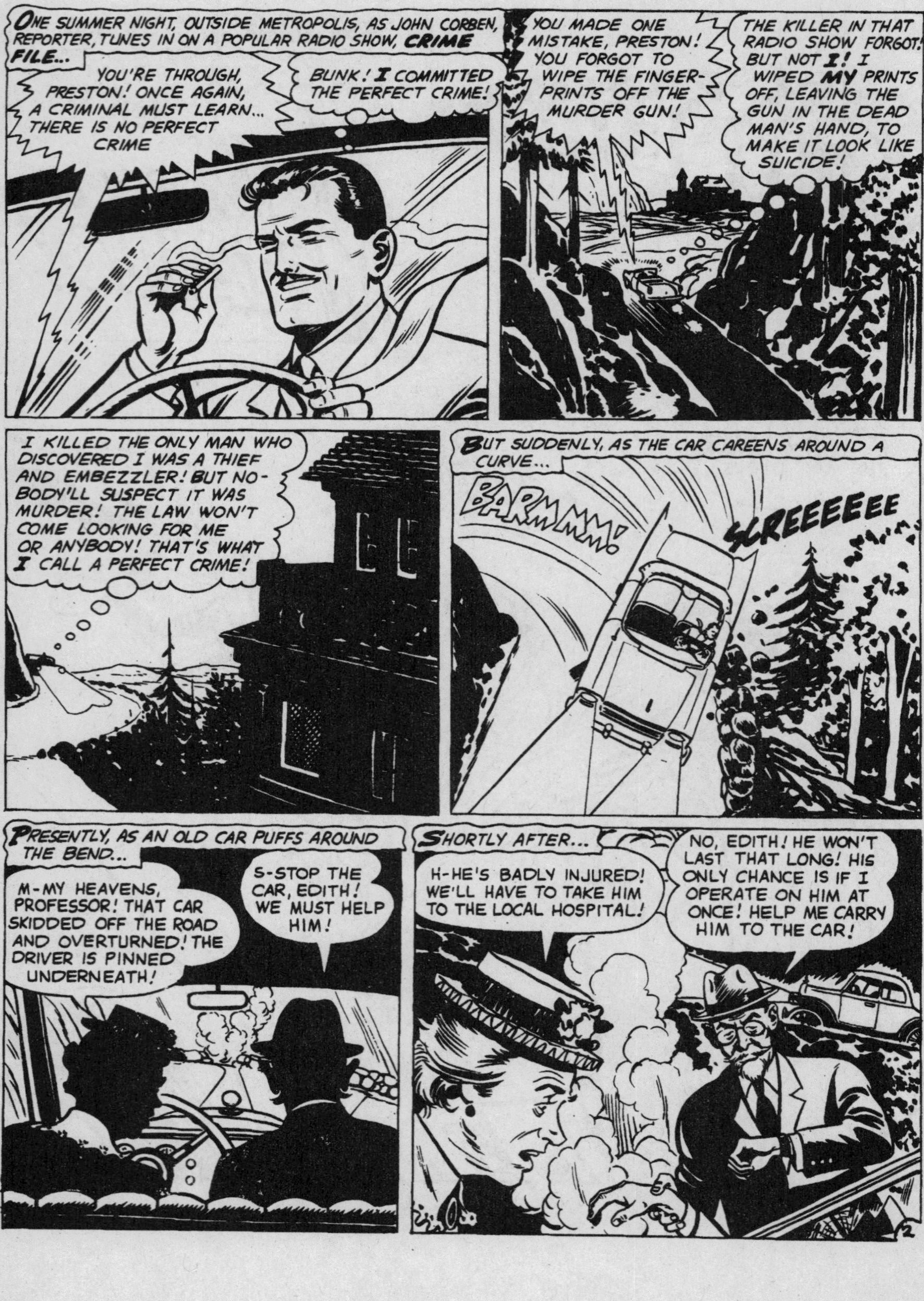
ONE SUMMER NIGHT, OUTSIDE METROPOLIS, AS JOHN CORBEN, REPORTER, TUNES IN ON A POPULAR RADIO SHOW, CRIME FILE...
YOU'RE THROUGH, PRESTON! ONCE AGAIN, A CRIMINAL MUST LEARN... THERE IS NO PERFECT CRIME
BUNK! I COMMITTED THE PERFECT CRIME!
YOU MADE ONE MISTAKE, PRESTON! YOU FORGOT TO WIPE THE FINGER-PRINTS OFF THE MURDER GUN!
THE KILLER IN THAT RADIO SHOW FORGOT! BUT NOT I! I WIPED MY PRINTS OFF, LEAVING THE GUN IN THE DEAD MAN'S HAND, TO MAKE IT LOOK LIKE SUICIDE!
I KILLED THE ONLY MAN WHO DISCOVERED I WAS A THIEF AND EMBEZZLER! BUT NO-BODY'LL SUSPECT IT WAS MURDER! THE LAW WON'T COME LOOKING FOR ME OR ANYBODY! THAT'S WHAT I CALL A PERFECT CRIME!
BUT SUDDENLY, AS THE CAR CAREENS AROUND A CURVE...
BARMMM!
SCREEEEEE
PRESENTLY, AS AN OLD CAR PUFFS AROUND THE BEND...
M-MY HEAVENS, PROFESSOR! THAT CAR SKIDDED OFF THE ROAD AND OVERTURNED! THE DRIVER IS PINNED UNDERNEATH!
S-STOP THE CAR, EDITH! WE MUST HELP HIM!
SHORTLY AFTER...
H-HE'S BADLY INJURED! WE'LL HAVE TO TAKE HIM TO THE LOCAL HOSPITAL!
NO, EDITH! HE WON'T LAST THAT LONG! HIS ONLY CHANCE IS IF I OPERATE ON HIM AT ONCE! HELP ME CARRY HIM TO THE CAR!
2

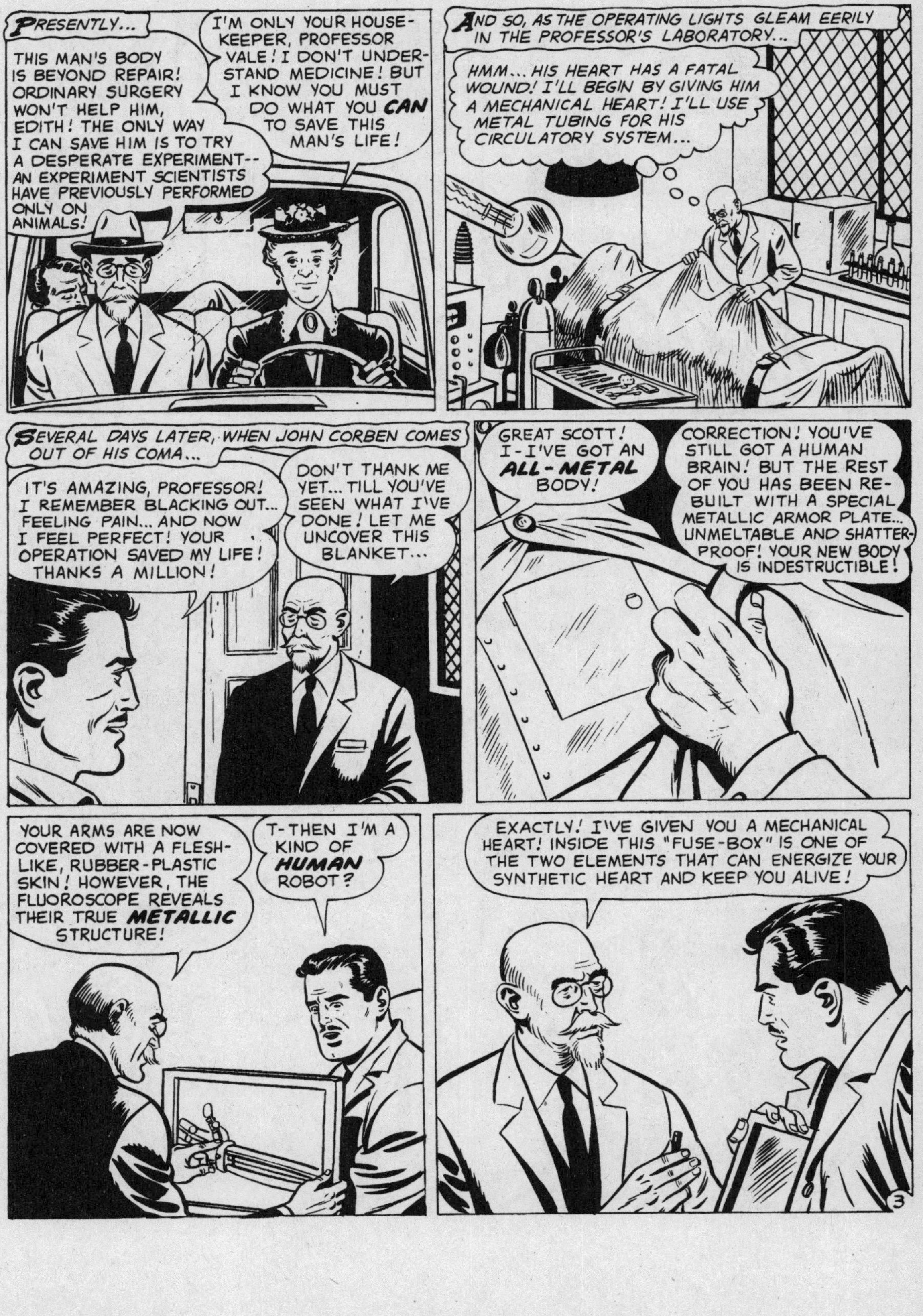
PRESENTLY...
THIS MAN'S BODY IS BEYOND REPAIR! ORDINARY SURGERY WON'T HELP HIM, EDITH! THE ONLY WAY I CAN SAVE HIM IS TO TRY A DESPERATE EXPERIMENT-- AN EXPERIMENT SCIENTISTS HAVE PREVIOUSLY PERFORMED ONLY ON ANIMALS!
I'M ONLY YOUR HOUSE-KEEPER, PROFESSOR VALE! I DON'T UNDER-STAND MEDICINE! BUT I KNOW YOU MUST DO WHAT YOU CAN TO SAVE THIS MAN'S LIFE!
AND SO, AS THE OPERATING LIGHTS GLEAM EERILY IN THE PROFESSOR'S LABORATORY...
HMM... HIS HEART HAS A FATAL WOUND! I'LL BEGIN BY GIVING HIM A MECHANICAL HEART! I'LL USE METAL TUBING FOR HIS CIRCULATORY SYSTEM...
SEVERAL DAYS LATER, WHEN JOHN CORBEN COMES OUT OF HIS COMA...
IT'S AMAZING, PROFESSOR! I REMEMBER BLACKING OUT... FEELING PAIN... AND NOW I FEEL PERFECT! YOUR OPERATION SAVED MY LIFE! THANKS A MILLION!
DON'T THANK ME YET... TILL YOU'VE SEEN WHAT I'VE DONE! LET ME UNCOVER THIS BLANKET...
GREAT SCOTT! I-I'VE GOT AN ALL-METAL BODY!
CORRECTION! YOU'VE STILL GOT A HUMAN BRAIN! BUT THE REST OF YOU HAS BEEN RE-BUILT WITH A SPECIAL METALLIC ARMOR PLATE... UNMELTABLE AND SHATTER-PROOF! YOUR NEW BODY IS INDESTRUCTIBLE!
YOUR ARMS ARE NOW COVERED WITH A FLESH-LIKE, RUBBER-PLASTIC SKIN! HOWEVER, THE FLUOROSCOPE REVEALS THEIR TRUE METALLIC STRUCTURE!
T-THEN I'M A KIND OF HUMAN ROBOT?
EXACTLY! I'VE GIVEN YOU A MECHANICAL HEART! INSIDE THIS "FUSE-BOX" IS ONE OF THE TWO ELEMENTS THAT CAN ENERGIZE YOUR SYNTHETIC HEART AND KEEP YOU ALIVE!
3

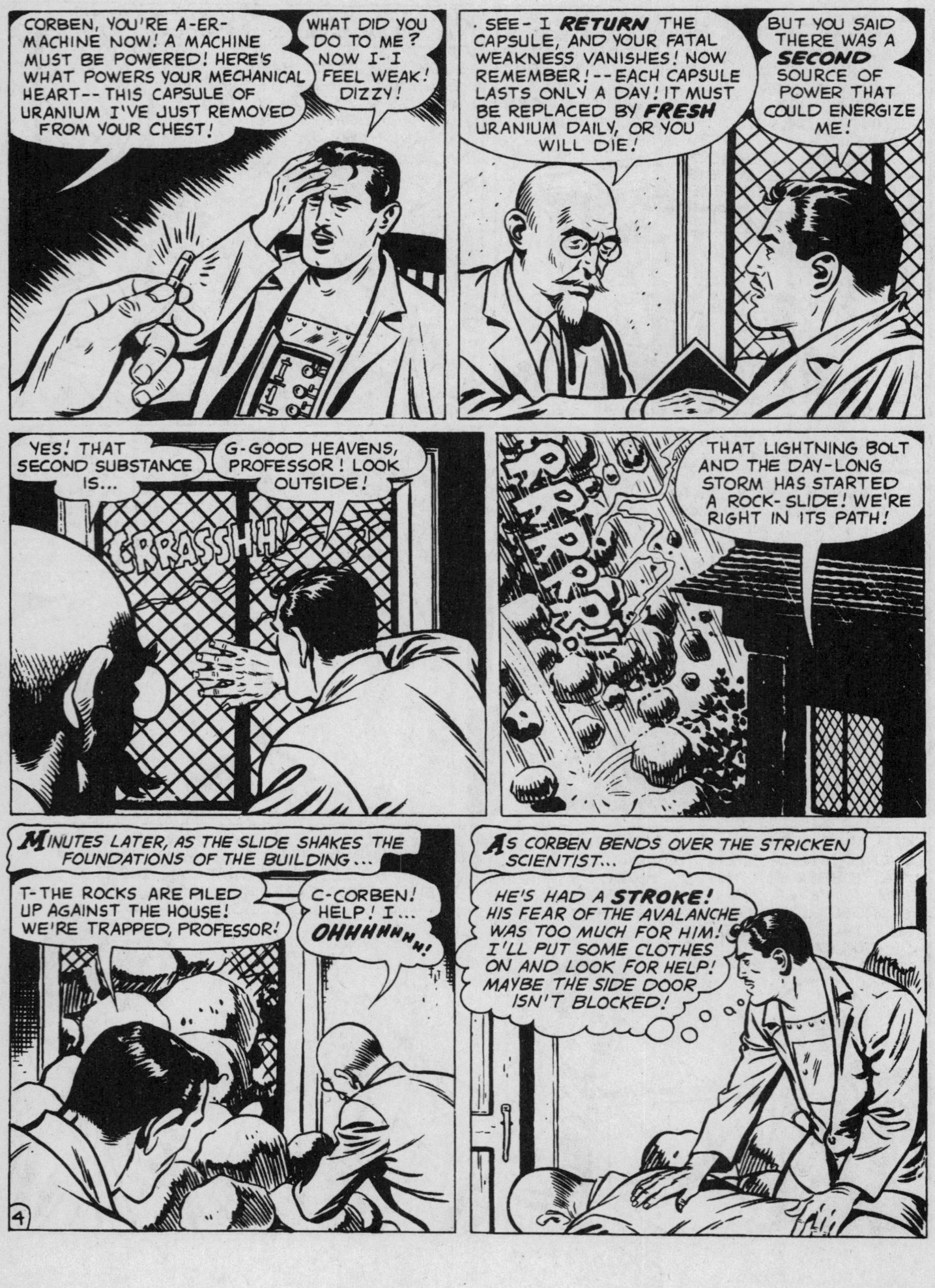
CORBEN, YOU'RE A-ER- MACHINE NOW! A MACHINE MUST BE POWERED! HERE'S WHAT POWERS YOUR MECHANICAL HEART-- THIS CAPSULE OF URANIUM I'VE JUST REMOVED FROM YOUR CHEST!
WHAT DID YOU DO TO ME? NOW I- I FEEL WEAK! DIZZY!
. SEE- I RETURN THE CAPSULE, AND YOUR FATAL WEAKNESS VANISHES! NOW REMEMBER!--EACH CAPSULE LASTS ONLY A DAY! IT MUST BE REPLACED BY FRESH URANIUM DAILY, OR YOU WILL DIE!
BUT YOU SAID THERE WAS A SECOND SOURCE OF POWER THAT COULD ENERGIZE ME!
YES! THAT SECOND SUBSTANCE IS...
G-GOOD HEAVENS, PROFESSOR! LOOK OUTSIDE!
CRRASSHH!
RRRRRRUMMBLE
THAT LIGHTNING BOLT AND THE DAY-LONG STORM HAS STARTED A ROCK-SLIDE! WE'RE RIGHT IN ITS PATH!
MINUTES LATER, AS THE SLIDE SHAKES THE FOUNDATIONS OF THE BUILDING...
T-THE ROCKS ARE PILED UP AGAINST THE HOUSE! WE'RE TRAPPED, PROFESSOR!
C-CORBEN! HELP! I... OHHHHHHH!
4
AS CORBEN BENDS OVER THE STRICKEN SCIENTIST...
HE'S HAD A STROKE! HIS FEAR OF THE AVALANCHE WAS TOO MUCH FOR HIM! I'LL PUT SOME CLOTHES ON AND LOOK FOR HELP! MAYBE THE SIDE DOOR ISN'T BLOCKED!

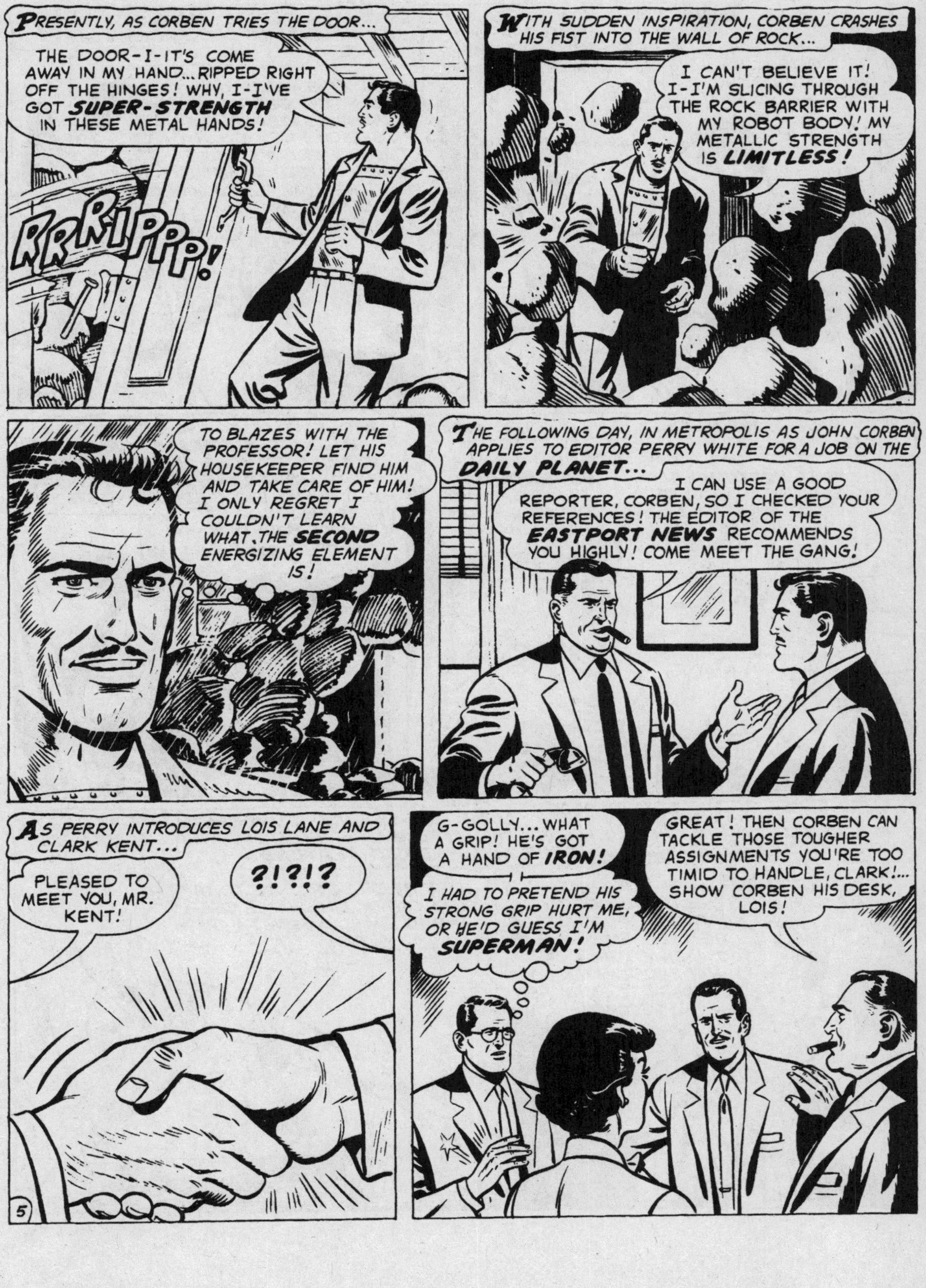
PRESENTLY, AS CORBEN TRIES THE DOOR...
THE DOOR-I-IT'S COME AWAY IN MY HAND...RIPPED RIGHT OFF THE HINGES! WHY, I-I'VE GOT SUPER-STRENGTH IN THESE METAL HANDS!
RRRIPPPP!
WITH SUDDEN INSPIRATION, CORBEN CRASHES HIS FIST INTO THE WALL OF ROCK...
I CAN'T BELIEVE IT! I-I'M SLICING THROUGH THE ROCK BARRIER WITH MY ROBOT BODY! MY METALLIC STRENGTH IS LIMITLESS!
TO BLAZES WITH THE PROFESSOR! LET HIS HOUSEKEEPER FIND HIM AND TAKE CARE OF HIM! I ONLY REGRET I COULDN'T LEARN WHAT THE SECOND ENERGIZING ELEMENT IS!
THE FOLLOWING DAY, IN METROPOLIS AS JOHN CORBEN APPLIES TO EDITOR PERRY WHITE FOR A JOB ON THE DAILY PLANET...
I CAN USE A GOOD REPORTER, CORBEN, SO I CHECKED YOUR REFERENCES! THE EDITOR OF THE EASTPORT NEWS RECOMMENDS YOU HIGHLY! COME MEET THE GANG!
AS PERRY INTRODUCES LOIS LANE AND CLARK KENT...
PLEASED TO MEET YOU, MR. KENT!
?!?!?
5
G-GOLLY... WHAT A GRIP! HE'S GOT A HAND OF IRON!
I HAD TO PRETEND HIS STRONG GRIP HURT ME, OR HE'D GUESS I'M SUPERMAN!
GREAT! THEN CORBEN CAN TACKLE THOSE TOUGHER ASSIGNMENTS YOU'RE TOO TIMID TO HANDLE, CLARK!... SHOW CORBEN HIS DESK, LOIS!

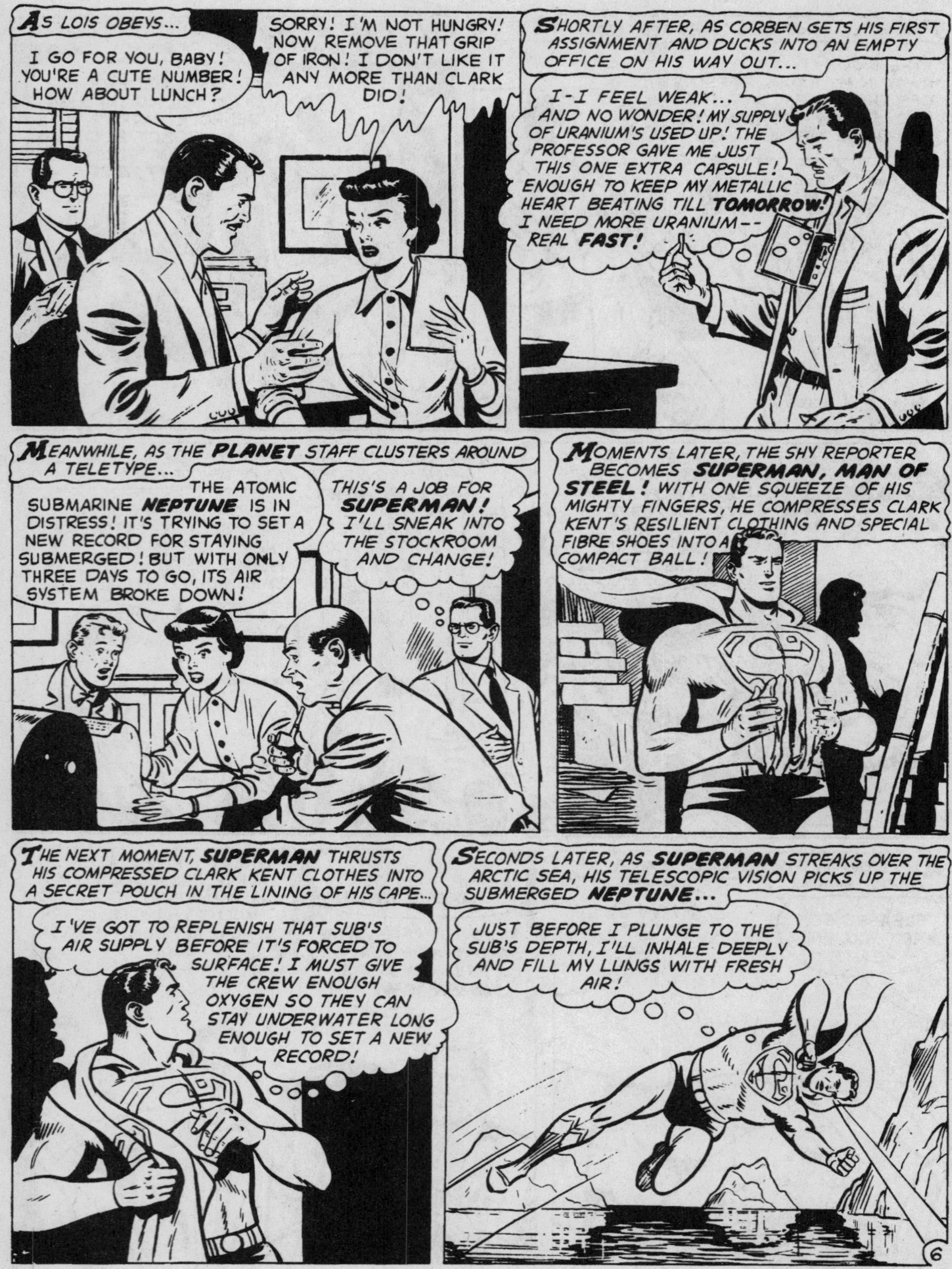
AS LOIS OBEYS...
I GO FOR YOU, BABY! YOU'RE A CUTE NUMBER! HOW ABOUT LUNCH?
SORRY! I'M NOT HUNGRY! NOW REMOVE THAT GRIP OF IRON! I DON'T LIKE IT ANY MORE THAN CLARK DID!
SHORTLY AFTER, AS CORBEN GETS HIS FIRST ASSIGNMENT AND DUCKS INTO AN EMPTY OFFICE ON HIS WAY OUT...
I-I FEEL WEAK... AND NO WONDER! MY SUPPLY OF URANIUM'S USED UP! THE PROFESSOR GAVE ME JUST THIS ONE EXTRA CAPSULE! ENOUGH TO KEEP MY METALLIC HEART BEATING TILL TOMORROW! I NEED MORE URANIUM-- REAL FAST!
MEANWHILE, AS THE PLANET STAFF CLUSTERS AROUND A TELETYPE...
THE ATOMIC SUBMARINE NEPTUNE IS IN DISTRESS! IT'S TRYING TO SET A NEW RECORD FOR STAYING SUBMERGED! BUT WITH ONLY THREE DAYS TO GO, ITS AIR SYSTEM BROKE DOWN!
THIS'S A JOB FOR SUPERMAN! I'LL SNEAK INTO THE STOCKROOM AND CHANGE!
MOMENTS LATER, THE SHY REPORTER BECOMES SUPERMAN, MAN OF STEEL! WITH ONE SQUEEZE OF HIS MIGHTY FINGERS, HE COMPRESSES CLARK KENT'S RESILIENT CLOTHING AND SPECIAL FIBRE SHOES INTO A COMPACT BALL!
THE NEXT MOMENT, SUPERMAN THRUSTS HIS COMPRESSED CLARK KENT CLOTHES INTO A SECRET POUCH IN THE LINING OF HIS CAPE...
I'VE GOT TO REPLENISH THAT SUB'S AIR SUPPLY BEFORE IT'S FORCED TO SURFACE! I MUST GIVE THE CREW ENOUGH OXYGEN SO THEY CAN STAY UNDERWATER LONG ENOUGH TO SET A NEW RECORD!
SECONDS LATER, AS SUPERMAN STREAKS OVER THE ARCTIC SEA, HIS TELESCOPIC VISION PICKS UP THE SUBMERGED NEPTUNE...
JUST BEFORE I PLUNGE TO THE SUB'S DEPTH, I'LL INHALE DEEPLY AND FILL MY LUNGS WITH FRESH AIR!
6

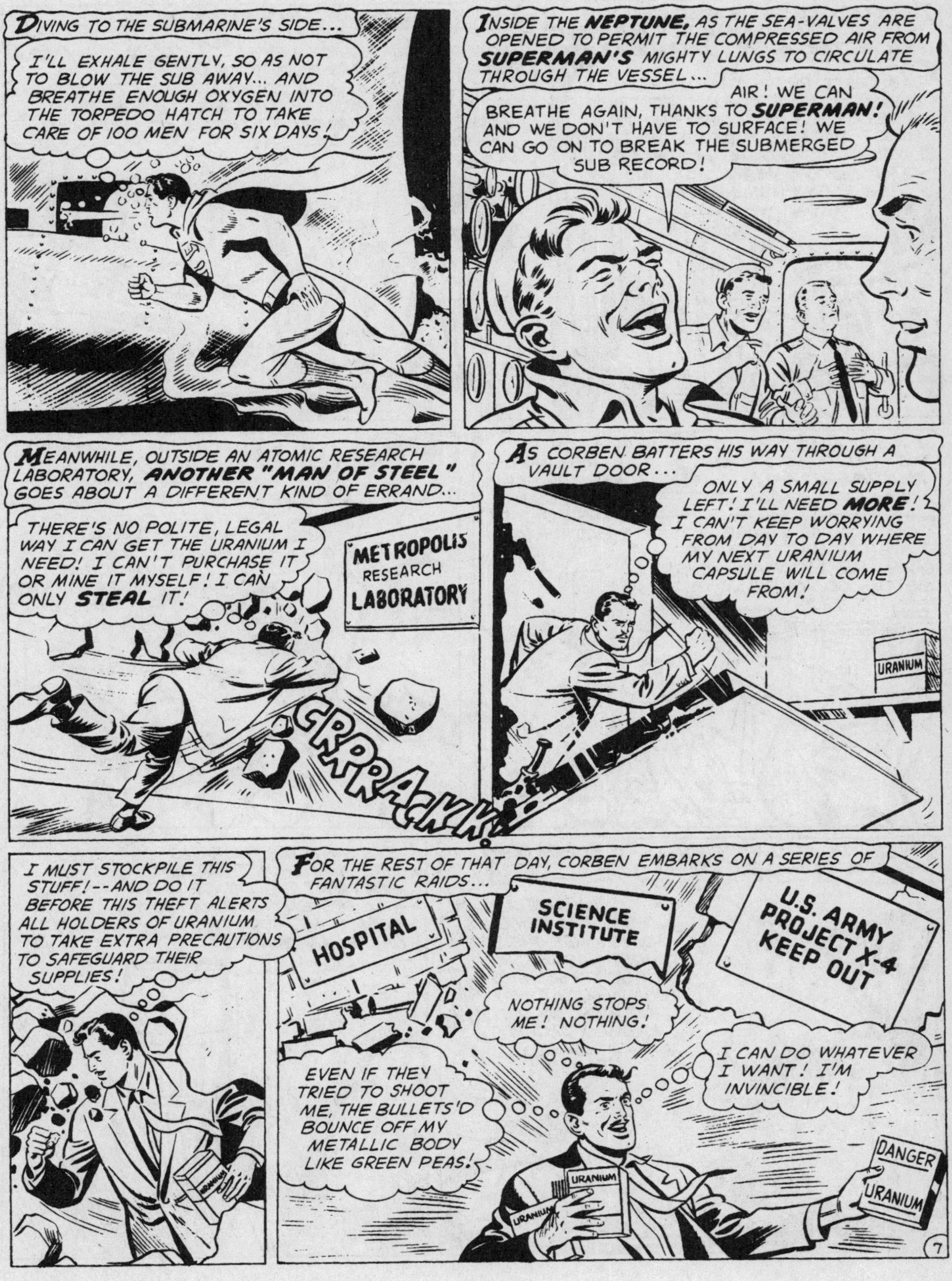
DIVING TO THE SUBMARINE'S SIDE...
I'LL EXHALE GENTLY, SO AS NOT TO BLOW THE SUB AWAY... AND BREATHE ENOUGH OXYGEN INTO THE TORPEDO HATCH TO TAKE CARE OF 100 MEN FOR SIX DAYS!
INSIDE THE NEPTUNE, AS THE SEA-VALVES ARE OPENED TO PERMIT THE COMPRESSED AIR FROM SUPERMAN'S MIGHTY LUNGS TO CIRCULATE THROUGH THE VESSEL...
AIR! WE CAN BREATHE AGAIN, THANKS TO SUPERMAN! AND WE DON'T HAVE TO SURFACE! WE CAN GO ON TO BREAK THE SUBMERGED SUB RECORD!
MEANWHILE, OUTSIDE AN ATOMIC RESEARCH LABORATORY, ANOTHER "MAN OF STEEL" GOES ABOUT A DIFFERENT KIND OF ERRAND...
THERE'S NO POLITE, LEGAL WAY I CAN GET THE URANIUM I NEED! I CAN'T PURCHASE IT OR MINE IT MYSELF! I CAN ONLY STEAL IT!
METROPOLIS RESEARCH LABORATORY
GRRRACKK!
AS CORBEN BATTERS HIS WAY THROUGH A VAULT DOOR...
ONLY A SMALL SUPPLY LEFT! I'LL NEED MORE! I CAN'T KEEP WORRYING FROM DAY TO DAY WHERE MY NEXT URANIUM CAPSULE WILL COME FROM!
URANIUM
I MUST STOCKPILE THIS STUFF!--AND DO IT BEFORE THIS THEFT ALERTS ALL HOLDERS OF URANIUM TO TAKE EXTRA PRECAUTIONS TO SAFEGUARD THEIR SUPPLIES!
FOR THE REST OF THAT DAY, CORBEN EMBARKS ON A SERIES OF FANTASTIC RAIDS...
HOSPITAL
SCIENCE INSTITUTE
U.S. ARMY PROJECT X-4 KEEP OUT
NOTHING STOPS ME! NOTHING!
EVEN IF THEY TRIED TO SHOOT ME, THE BULLETS'D BOUNCE OFF MY METALLIC BODY LIKE GREEN PEAS!
I CAN DO WHATEVER I WANT! I'M INVINCIBLE!
URANIUM
URANIUM
DANGER
URANIUM
7

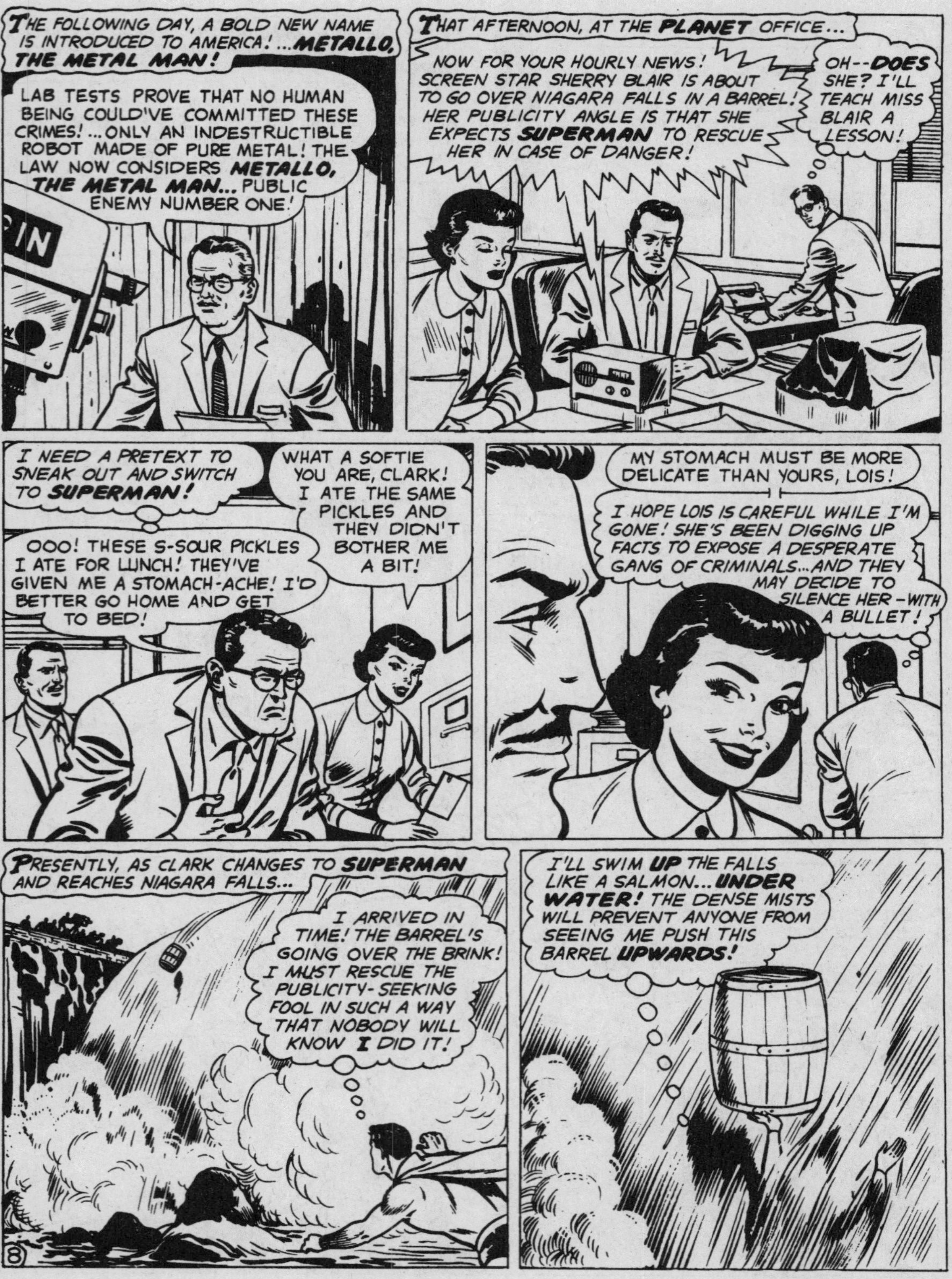
THE FOLLOWING DAY, A BOLD NEW NAME IS INTRODUCED TO AMERICA! ...METALLO, THE METAL MAN!
LAB TESTS PROVE THAT NO HUMAN BEING COULD'VE COMMITTED THESE CRIMES! ...ONLY AN INDESTRUCTIBLE ROBOT MADE OF PURE METAL! THE LAW NOW CONSIDERS METALLO, THE METAL MAN... PUBLIC ENEMY NUMBER ONE!
THAT AFTERNOON, AT THE PLANET OFFICE...
NOW FOR YOUR HOURLY NEWS! SCREEN STAR SHERRY BLAIR IS ABOUT TO GO OVER NIAGARA FALLS IN A BARREL! HER PUBLICITY ANGLE IS THAT SHE EXPECTS SUPERMAN TO RESCUE HER IN CASE OF DANGER!
OH--DOES SHE? I'LL TEACH MISS BLAIR A LESSON!
I NEED A PRETEXT TO SNEAK OUT AND SWITCH TO SUPERMAN!
OOO! THESE S-SOUR PICKLES I ATE FOR LUNCH! THEY'VE GIVEN ME A STOMACH-ACHE! I'D BETTER GO HOME AND GET TO BED!
WHAT A SOFTIE YOU ARE, CLARK! I ATE THE SAME PICKLES AND THEY DIDN'T BOTHER ME A BIT!
MY STOMACH MUST BE MORE DELICATE THAN YOURS, LOIS!
I HOPE LOIS IS CAREFUL WHILE I'M GONE! SHE'S BEEN DIGGING UP FACTS TO EXPOSE A DESPERATE GANG OF CRIMINALS...AND THEY MAY DECIDE TO SILENCE HER - WITH A BULLET!
PRESENTLY, AS CLARK CHANGES TO SUPERMAN AND REACHES NIAGARA FALLS...
I ARRIVED IN TIME! THE BARREL'S GOING OVER THE BRINK! I MUST RESCUE THE PUBLICITY-SEEKING FOOL IN SUCH A WAY THAT NOBODY WILL KNOW I DID IT!
8
I'LL SWIM UP THE FALLS LIKE A SALMON... UNDER WATER! THE DENSE MISTS WILL PREVENT ANYONE FROM SEEING ME PUSH THIS BARREL UPWARDS!

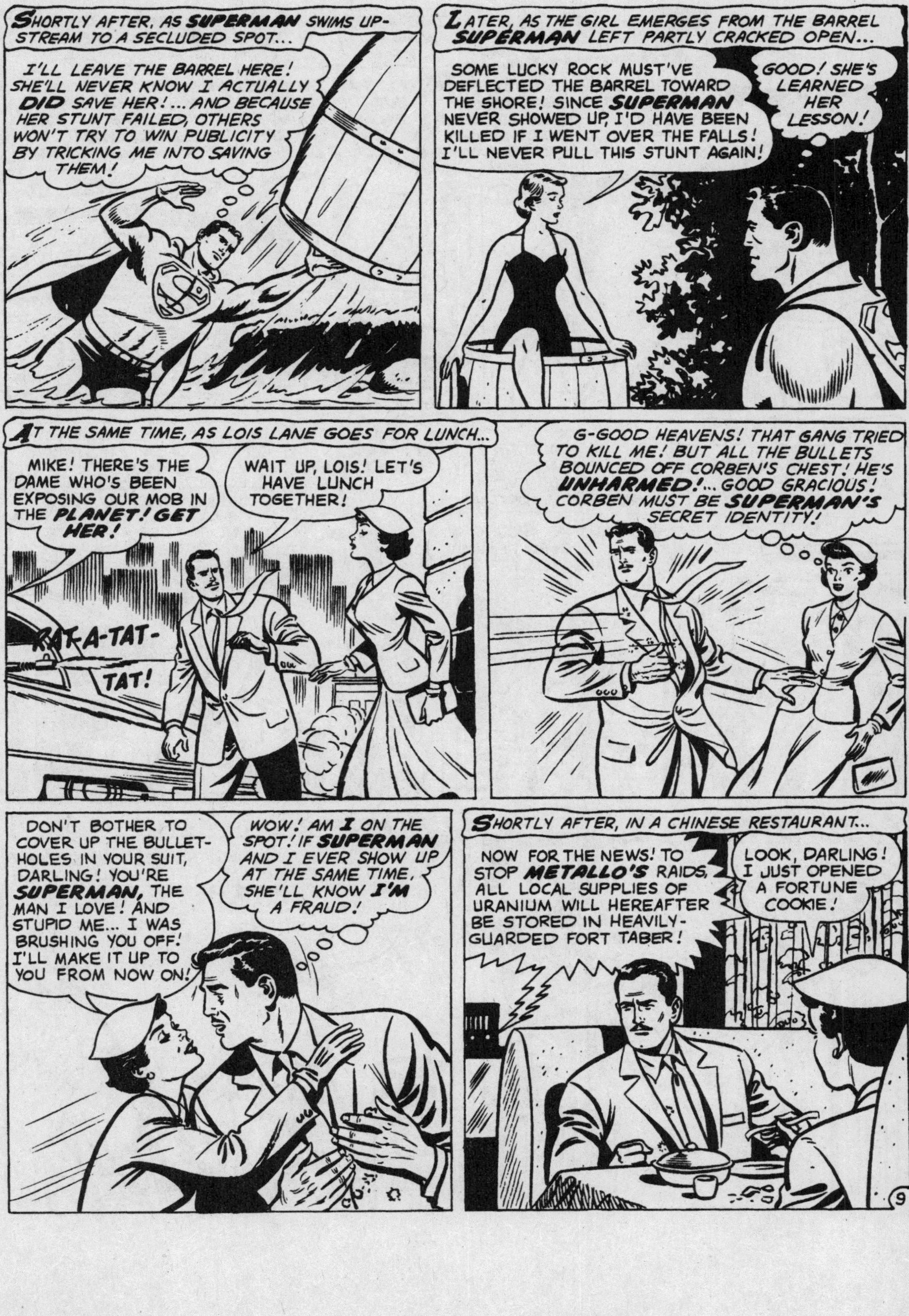
SHORTLY AFTER, AS SUPERMAN SWIMS UP-STREAM TO A SECLUDED SPOT...
I'LL LEAVE THE BARREL HERE! SHE'LL NEVER KNOW I ACTUALLY DID SAVE HER! ... AND BECAUSE HER STUNT FAILED, OTHERS WON'T TRY TO WIN PUBLICITY BY TRICKING ME INTO SAVING THEM!
LATER, AS THE GIRL EMERGES FROM THE BARREL SUPERMAN LEFT PARTLY CRACKED OPEN...
SOME LUCKY ROCK MUST'VE DEFLECTED THE BARREL TOWARD THE SHORE! SINCE SUPERMAN NEVER SHOWED UP, I'D HAVE BEEN KILLED IF I WENT OVER THE FALLS! I'LL NEVER PULL THIS STUNT AGAIN!
GOOD! SHE'S LEARNED HER LESSON!
AT THE SAME TIME, AS LOIS LANE GOES FOR LUNCH...
MIKE! THERE'S THE DAME WHO'S BEEN EXPOSING OUR MOB IN THE PLANET! GET HER!
WAIT UP, LOIS! LET'S HAVE LUNCH TOGETHER!
RAT-A-TAT-
TAT!
G-GOOD HEAVENS! THAT GANG TRIED TO KILL ME! BUT ALL THE BULLETS BOUNCED OFF CORBEN'S CHEST! HE'S UNHARMED!... GOOD GRACIOUS! CORBEN MUST BE SUPERMAN'S SECRET IDENTITY!
DON'T BOTHER TO COVER UP THE BULLET-HOLES IN YOUR SUIT, DARLING! YOU'RE SUPERMAN, THE MAN I LOVE! AND STUPID ME... I WAS BRUSHING YOU OFF! I'LL MAKE IT UP TO YOU FROM NOW ON!
WOW! AM I ON THE SPOT! IF SUPERMAN AND I EVER SHOW UP AT THE SAME TIME, SHE'LL KNOW I'M A FRAUD!
SHORTLY AFTER, IN A CHINESE RESTAURANT...
NOW FOR THE NEWS! TO STOP METALLO'S RAIDS, ALL LOCAL SUPPLIES OF URANIUM WILL HEREAFTER BE STORED IN HEAVILY-GUARDED FORT TABER!
LOOK, DARLING! I JUST OPENED A FORTUNE COOKIE!
9

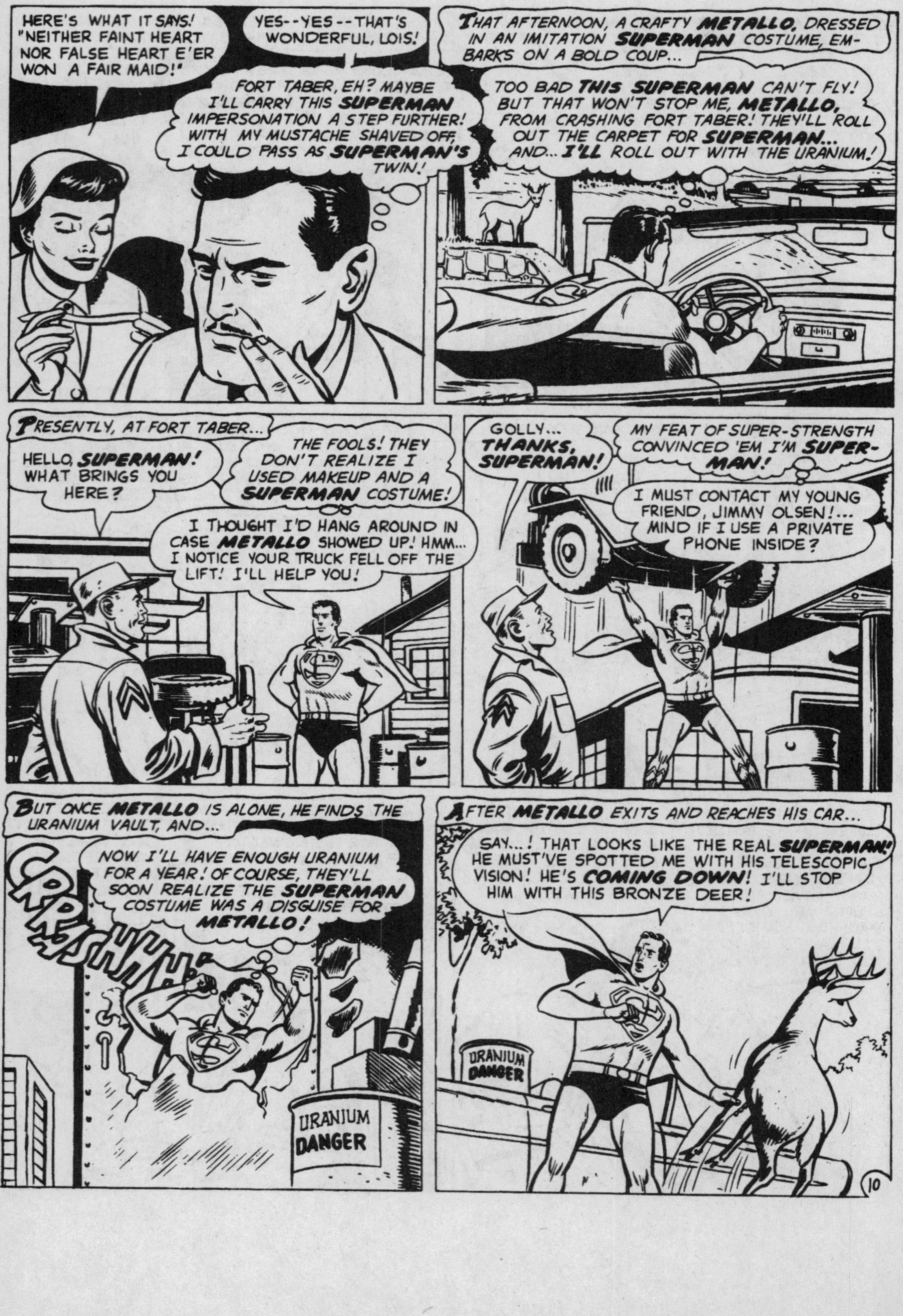
HERE'S WHAT IT SAYS! "NEITHER FAINT HEART NOR FALSE HEART E'ER WON A FAIR MAID!"
YES--YES--THAT'S WONDERFUL, LOIS!
FORT TABER, EH? MAYBE I'LL CARRY THIS SUPERMAN IMPERSONATION A STEP FURTHER! WITH MY MUSTACHE SHAVED OFF, I COULD PASS AS SUPERMAN'S TWIN!
THAT AFTERNOON, A CRAFTY METALLO, DRESSED IN AN IMITATION SUPERMAN COSTUME, EMBARKS ON A BOLD COUP...
TOO BAD THIS SUPERMAN CAN'T FLY! BUT THAT WON'T STOP ME, METALLO, FROM CRASHING FORT TABER! THEY'LL ROLL OUT THE CARPET FOR SUPERMAN... AND... I'LL ROLL OUT WITH THE URANIUM!
PRESENTLY, AT FORT TABER...
HELLO, SUPERMAN! WHAT BRINGS YOU HERE?
THE FOOLS! THEY DON'T REALIZE I USED MAKEUP AND A SUPERMAN COSTUME!
I THOUGHT I'D HANG AROUND IN CASE METALLO SHOWED UP! HMM... I NOTICE YOUR TRUCK FELL OFF THE LIFT! I'LL HELP YOU!
GOLLY... THANKS, SUPERMAN!
MY FEAT OF SUPER-STRENGTH CONVINCED 'EM I'M SUPERMAN!
I MUST CONTACT MY YOUNG FRIEND, JIMMY OLSEN!... MIND IF I USE A PRIVATE PHONE INSIDE?
BUT ONCE METALLO IS ALONE, HE FINDS THE URANIUM VAULT, AND...
CRASH
NOW I'LL HAVE ENOUGH URANIUM FOR A YEAR! OF COURSE, THEY'LL SOON REALIZE THE SUPERMAN COSTUME WAS A DISGUISE FOR METALLO!
URANIUM DANGER
AFTER METALLO EXITS AND REACHES HIS CAR...
SAY...! THAT LOOKS LIKE THE REAL SUPERMAN! HE MUST'VE SPOTTED ME WITH HIS TELESCOPIC VISION! HE'S COMING DOWN! I'LL STOP HIM WITH THIS BRONZE DEER!
URANIUM DANGER
10

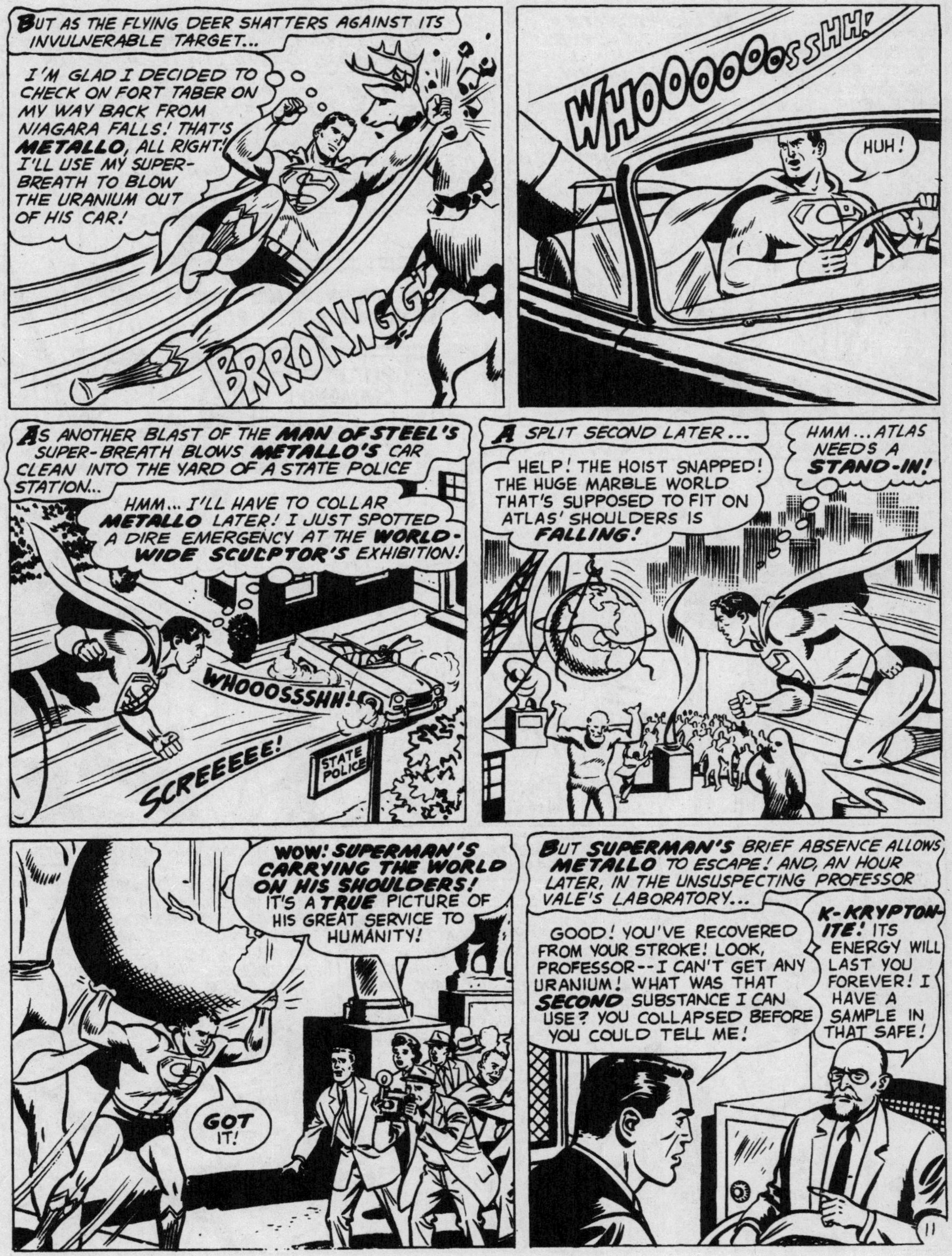
BUT AS THE FLYING DEER SHATTERS AGAINST ITS INVULNERABLE TARGET...
I'M GLAD I DECIDED TO CHECK ON FORT TABER ON MY WAY BACK FROM NIAGARA FALLS! THAT'S METALLO, ALL RIGHT! I'LL USE MY SUPER-BREATH TO BLOW THE URANIUM OUT OF HIS CAR!
BRRONNGG!
WHOOOOOOOSSHH!
HUH!
AS ANOTHER BLAST OF THE MAN OF STEEL'S SUPER-BREATH BLOWS METALLO'S CAR CLEAN INTO THE YARD OF A STATE POLICE STATION...
HMM... I'LL HAVE TO COLLAR METALLO LATER! I JUST SPOTTED A DIRE EMERGENCY AT THE WORLD-WIDE SCULPTOR'S EXHIBITION!
WHOOOSSSHH!
SCREEEEEE!
STATE POLICE
A SPLIT SECOND LATER...
HELP! THE HOIST SNAPPED! THE HUGE MARBLE WORLD THAT'S SUPPOSED TO FIT ON ATLAS' SHOULDERS IS FALLING!
HMM ...ATLAS NEEDS A STAND-IN!
WOW! SUPERMAN'S CARRYING THE WORLD ON HIS SHOULDERS! IT'S A TRUE PICTURE OF HIS GREAT SERVICE TO HUMANITY!
GOT IT!
BUT SUPERMAN'S BRIEF ABSENCE ALLOWS METALLO TO ESCAPE! AND, AN HOUR LATER, IN THE UNSUSPECTING PROFESSOR VALE'S LABORATORY...
GOOD! YOU'VE RECOVERED FROM YOUR STROKE! LOOK, PROFESSOR--I CAN'T GET ANY URANIUM! WHAT WAS THAT SECOND SUBSTANCE I CAN USE? YOU COLLAPSED BEFORE YOU COULD TELL ME!
K-KRYPTONITE! ITS ENERGY WILL LAST YOU FOREVER! I HAVE A SAMPLE IN THAT SAFE!
11

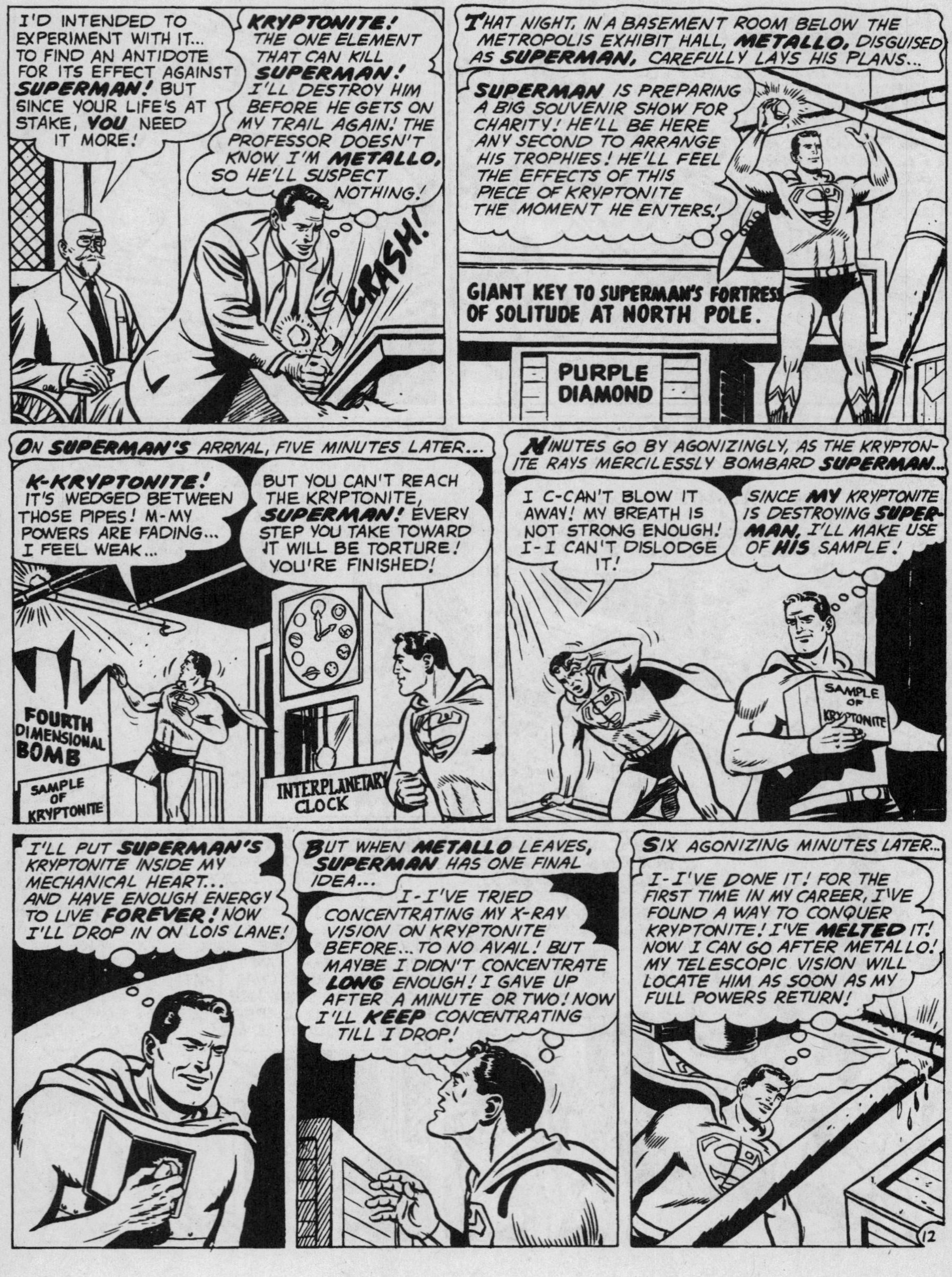
I'D INTENDED TO EXPERIMENT WITH IT... TO FIND AN ANTIDOTE FOR ITS EFFECT AGAINST SUPERMAN! BUT SINCE YOUR LIFE'S AT STAKE, YOU NEED IT MORE!
KRYPTONITE! THE ONE ELEMENT THAT CAN KILL SUPERMAN! I'LL DESTROY HIM BEFORE HE GETS ON MY TRAIL AGAIN! THE PROFESSOR DOESN'T KNOW I'M METALLO, SO HE'LL SUSPECT NOTHING!
CRASH!
THAT NIGHT, IN A BASEMENT ROOM BELOW THE METROPOLIS EXHIBIT HALL, METALLO, DISGUISED AS SUPERMAN, CAREFULLY LAYS HIS PLANS...
SUPERMAN IS PREPARING A BIG SOUVENIR SHOW FOR CHARITY! HE'LL BE HERE ANY SECOND TO ARRANGE HIS TROPHIES! HE'LL FEEL THE EFFECTS OF THIS PIECE OF KRYPTONITE THE MOMENT HE ENTERS!
GIANT KEY TO SUPERMAN'S FORTRESS OF SOLITUDE AT NORTH POLE.
PURPLE DIAMOND
ON SUPERMAN'S ARRIVAL, FIVE MINUTES LATER...
K-KRYPTONITE! IT'S WEDGED BETWEEN THOSE PIPES! M-MY POWERS ARE FADING... I FEEL WEAK...
BUT YOU CAN'T REACH THE KRYPTONITE, SUPERMAN! EVERY STEP YOU TAKE TOWARD IT WILL BE TORTURE! YOU'RE FINISHED!
FOURTH DIMENSIONAL BOMB
SAMPLE OF KRYPTONITE
INTERPLANETARY CLOCK
MINUTES GO BY AGONIZINGLY, AS THE KRYPTONITE RAYS MERCILESSLY BOMBARD SUPERMAN...
I C-CAN'T BLOW IT AWAY! MY BREATH IS NOT STRONG ENOUGH! I-I CAN'T DISLODGE IT!
SINCE MY KRYPTONITE IS DESTROYING SUPERMAN, I'LL MAKE USE OF HIS SAMPLE!
SAMPLE OF KRYPTONITE
I'LL PUT SUPERMAN'S KRYPTONITE INSIDE MY MECHANICAL HEART... AND HAVE ENOUGH ENERGY TO LIVE FOREVER! NOW I'LL DROP IN ON LOIS LANE!
BUT WHEN METALLO LEAVES, SUPERMAN HAS ONE FINAL IDEA...
I-I'VE TRIED CONCENTRATING MY X-RAY VISION ON KRYPTONITE BEFORE... TO NO AVAIL! BUT MAYBE I DIDN'T CONCENTRATE LONG ENOUGH! I GAVE UP AFTER A MINUTE OR TWO! NOW I'LL KEEP CONCENTRATING TILL I DROP!
SIX AGONIZING MINUTES LATER...
I-I'VE DONE IT! FOR THE FIRST TIME IN MY CAREER, I'VE FOUND A WAY TO CONQUER KRYPTONITE! I'VE MELTED IT! NOW I CAN GO AFTER METALLO! MY TELESCOPIC VISION WILL LOCATE HIM AS SOON AS MY FULL POWERS RETURN!
12

AT THAT MOMENT, IN LOIS LANE'S APARTMENT, AS METALLO ENTERS, STILL DISGUISED AS SUPERMAN...
T-THAT METAL BODY! Y-YOU MUST BE...
TOO BAD YOUR DOOR-KNOB RIPPED MY SHIRT! NOW YOU KNOW I'M METALLO! I MUST GET RID OF YOU LIKE I GOT RID OF SUPERMAN!
RIP!
BUT SUDDENLY, AS METALLO MOVES FORWARD, HE EMITS A CHOKED CRY AND TOPPLES OVER...
H-HE'S DEAD! HE MUST HAVE HAD A HEART ATTACK!
THANK GOODNESS I GOT HERE IN TIME!
HE BROUGHT IT ON HIMSELF, LOIS! HE EXCHANGED HIS KRYPTONITE FOR MINE, NOT REALIZING I WAS USING A FAKE, PROP KRYPTONITE, COLORED GREEN FOR A COLOR PICTURE IN A WEEKLY MAGAZINE!
APPARENTLY, KRYPTONITE POWERED THE MECHANICAL HEART IN HIS METAL CHEST! THIS GREEN-COLORED ROCK GAVE HIM NOTHING BUT...HEART FAILURE!
HOW IRONIC! SO THAT FORTUNE COOKIE PROPHECY CAME TRUE! "NEITHER FAINT HEART NOR FALSE HEART E'ER WON A FAIR MAID!"
13
LATER, AT POLICE HEADQUARTERS...
WE WERE GOING TO ARREST CORBEN TONIGHT! HE MADE ONE MISTAKE, SUPERMAN! HE'D WIPED THE GUN CLEAN, BUT NOT THE CARTRIDGES HE LOADED THE GUN WITH! THAT'S CORBEN'S PRINT ON AN UNFIRED CARTRIDGE! IF CORBEN THOUGHT HE'D COMMITTED THE PERFECT CRIME...
...I KNOW, INSPECTOR! HE WAS DEAD WRONG!
The End

SUPERMAN

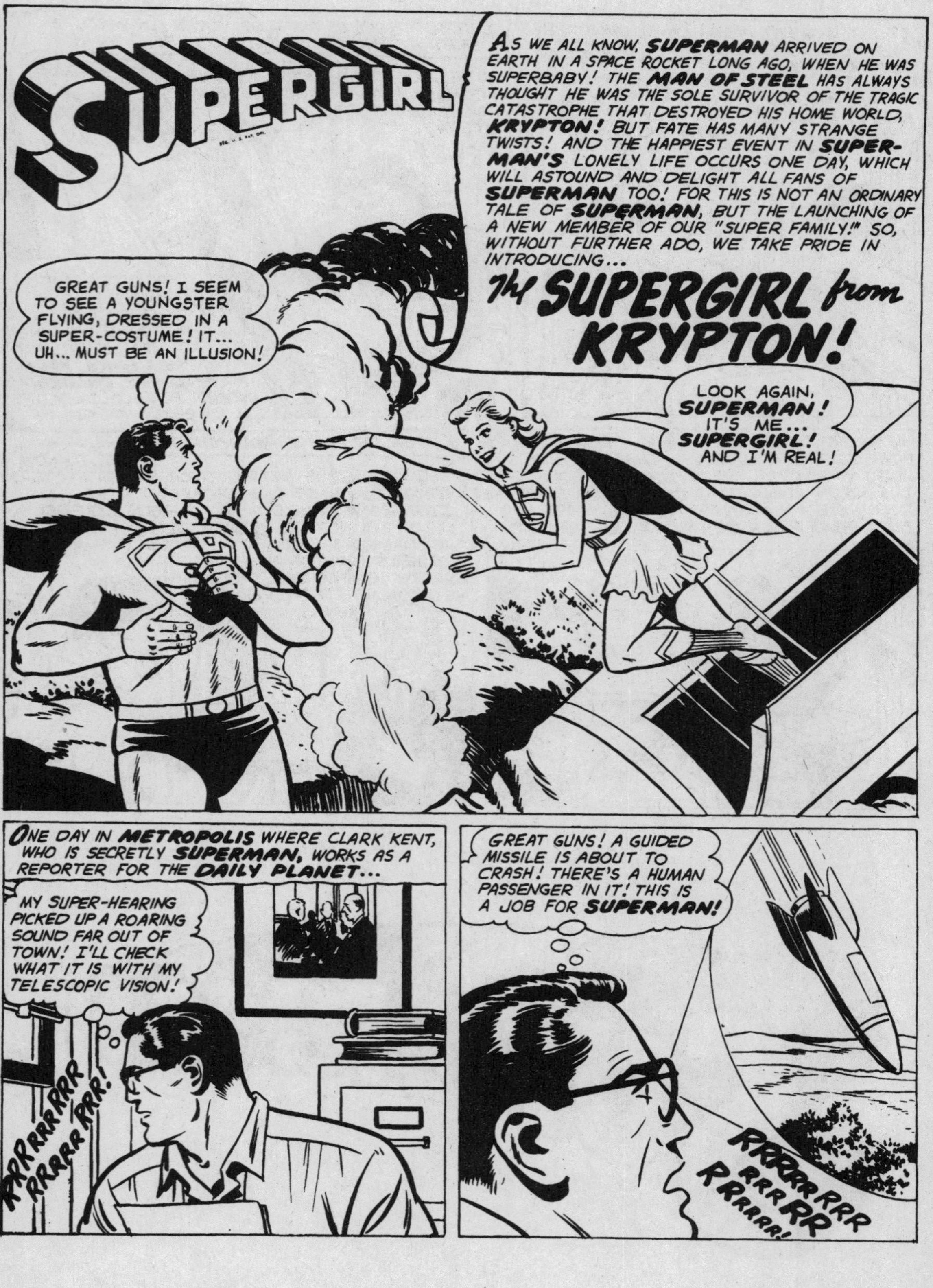
SUPERGIRL
AS WE ALL KNOW, SUPERMAN ARRIVED ON EARTH IN A SPACE ROCKET LONG AGO, WHEN HE WAS SUPERBABY! THE MAN OF STEEL HAS ALWAYS THOUGHT HE WAS THE SOLE SURVIVOR OF THE TRAGIC CATASTROPHE THAT DESTROYED HIS HOME WORLD, KRYPTON! BUT FATE HAS MANY STRANGE TWISTS! AND THE HAPPIEST EVENT IN SUPERMAN'S LONELY LIFE OCCURS ONE DAY, WHICH WILL ASTOUND AND DELIGHT ALL FANS OF SUPERMAN TOO! FOR THIS IS NOT AN ORDINARY TALE OF SUPERMAN, BUT THE LAUNCHING OF A NEW MEMBER OF OUR "SUPER FAMILY!" SO, WITHOUT FURTHER ADO, WE TAKE PRIDE IN INTRODUCING...
The SUPERGIRL from KRYPTON!
GREAT GUNS! I SEEM TO SEE A YOUNGSTER FLYING, DRESSED IN A SUPER-COSTUME! IT... UH... MUST BE AN ILLUSION!
LOOK AGAIN, SUPERMAN! IT'S ME... SUPERGIRL! AND I'M REAL!
ONE DAY IN METROPOLIS WHERE CLARK KENT, WHO IS SECRETLY SUPERMAN, WORKS AS A REPORTER FOR THE DAILY PLANET...
MY SUPER-HEARING PICKED UP A ROARING SOUND FAR OUT OF TOWN! I'LL CHECK WHAT IT IS WITH MY TELESCOPIC VISION!
GREAT GUNS! A GUIDED MISSILE IS ABOUT TO CRASH! THERE'S A HUMAN PASSENGER IN IT! THIS IS A JOB FOR SUPERMAN!

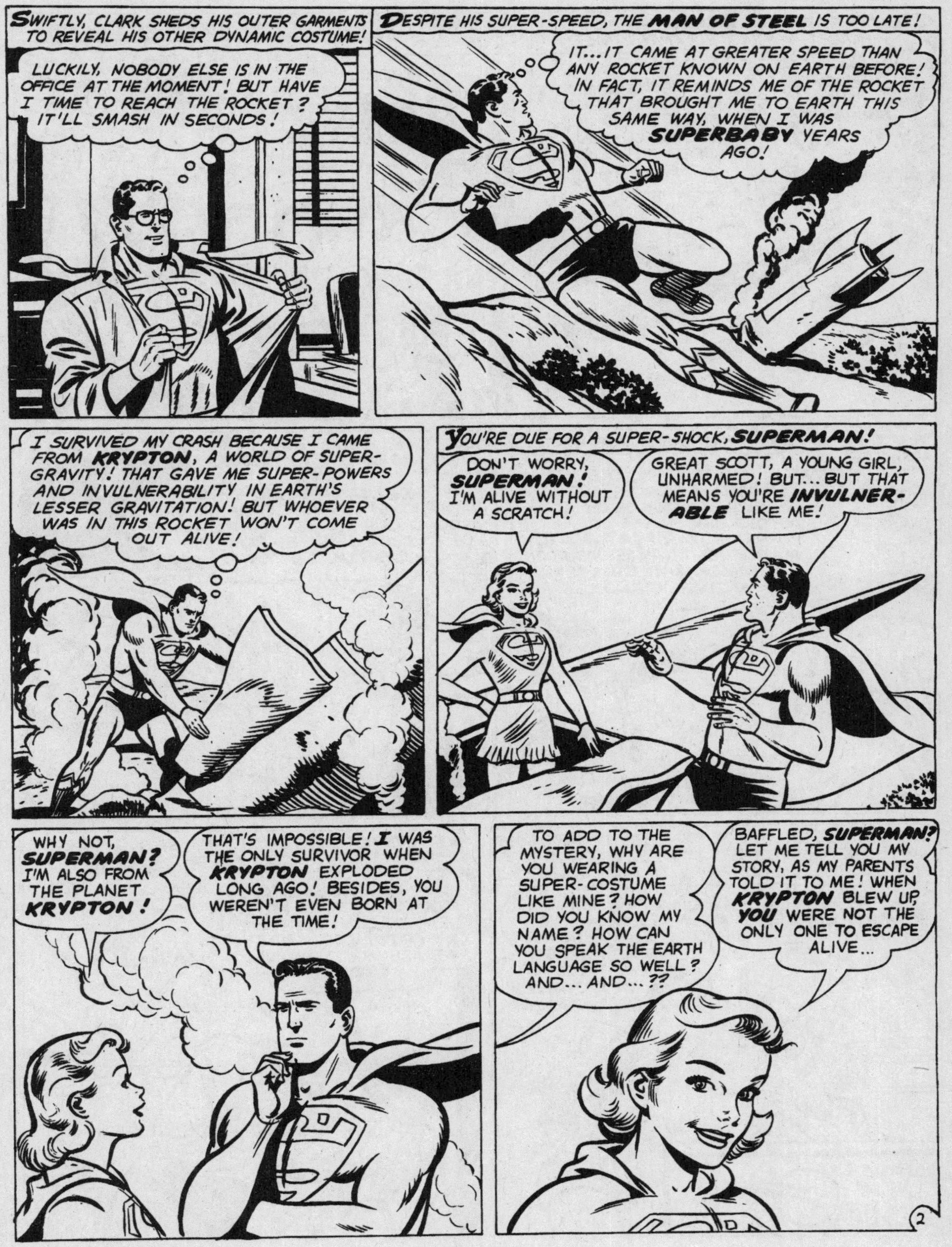
SWIFTLY, CLARK SHEDS HIS OUTER GARMENTS TO REVEAL HIS OTHER DYNAMIC COSTUME!
LUCKILY, NOBODY ELSE IS IN THE OFFICE AT THE MOMENT! BUT HAVE I TIME TO REACH THE ROCKET? IT'LL SMASH IN SECONDS!
DESPITE HIS SUPER-SPEED, THE MAN OF STEEL IS TOO LATE!
IT... IT CAME AT GREATER SPEED THAN ANY ROCKET KNOWN ON EARTH BEFORE! IN FACT, IT REMINDS ME OF THE ROCKET THAT BROUGHT ME TO EARTH THIS SAME WAY, WHEN I WAS SUPERBABY YEARS AGO!
I SURVIVED MY CRASH BECAUSE I CAME FROM KRYPTON, A WORLD OF SUPER-GRAVITY! THAT GAVE ME SUPER-POWERS AND INVULNERABILITY IN EARTH'S LESSER GRAVITATION! BUT WHOEVER WAS IN THIS ROCKET WON'T COME OUT ALIVE!
YOU'RE DUE FOR A SUPER-SHOCK, SUPERMAN!
DON'T WORRY, SUPERMAN! I'M ALIVE WITHOUT A SCRATCH!
GREAT SCOTT, A YOUNG GIRL, UNHARMED! BUT... BUT THAT MEANS YOU'RE INVULNERABLE LIKE ME!
WHY NOT, SUPERMAN? I'M ALSO FROM THE PLANET KRYPTON!
THAT'S IMPOSSIBLE! I WAS THE ONLY SURVIVOR WHEN KRYPTON EXPLODED LONG AGO! BESIDES, YOU WEREN'T EVEN BORN AT THE TIME!
TO ADD TO THE MYSTERY, WHY ARE YOU WEARING A SUPER-COSTUME LIKE MINE? HOW DID YOU KNOW MY NAME? HOW CAN YOU SPEAK THE EARTH LANGUAGE SO WELL? AND... AND...??
BAFFLED, SUPERMAN? LET ME TELL YOU MY STORY, AS MY PARENTS TOLD IT TO ME! WHEN KRYPTON BLEW UP, YOU WERE NOT THE ONLY ONE TO ESCAPE ALIVE...
2

"BY SHEER LUCK, A LARGE CHUNK OF THE PLANET WAS HURLED AWAY INTACT, WITH PEOPLE ON IT..."

OUR STREET OF HOMES IS BEING FLUNG FREE INTO SPACE, SAVING US FROM THE CONCUSSION THAT WIPED OUT ALL OTHERS!

"AMONG THE PITIFUL FEW SURVIVORS WAS A SCIENTIST, ZOR-EL..."

FORTUNATELY, A LARGE BUBBLE OF AIR CAME ALONG WITH THIS CHUNK! ALSO, THIS FOOD MACHINE IS STILL WORKING! WE CAN STAY ALIVE INDEFINITELY!

"BUT THEIR JOY WAS SHORT-LIVED, FOR, WHEN NIGHT FELL..."

OHH... I FEEL WEAK!

GREAT STARS! THE GROUND IS GLOWING GREEN! THE NUCLEAR EXPLOSION CONVERTED OUR SHATTERED PLANET INTO KRYPTONITE, AN ELEMENT WHOSE RADIATIONS CAN POISON AND DESTROY US IN TIME!

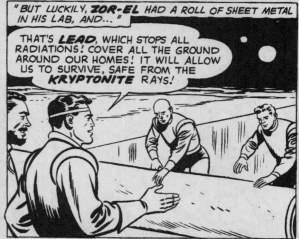

"BUT LUCKILY, ZOR-EL HAD A ROLL OF SHEET METAL IN HIS LAB, AND..."

THAT'S LEAD, WHICH STOPS ALL RADIATIONS! COVER ALL THE GROUND AROUND OUR HOMES! IT WILL ALLOW US TO SURVIVE, SAFE FROM THE KRYPTONITE RAYS!

"LIFE SETTLED DOWN FOR THE KRYPTON REFUGEES AND, SOME YEARS LATER, ZOR-EL TOOK A WIFE AND A DAUGHTER WAS BORN TO THEM... ME!"

IT'S TIME FOR KARA'S BOTTLE, DEAR!

OUR CHILD CAN GROW UP SAFELY AS LONG AS THE LEADEN SHIELD UNDER OUR COMMUNITY WARDS OFF THOSE KRYPTONITE RADIATIONS!

"BUT FATE PLAYED A CRUEL TRICK, WHEN I HAD GROWN INTO GIRLHOOD..."

INTO THE HOUSE, KARA! A METEOR FLOCK IS SMASHING HOLES IN THE LEADEN SHIELD, RELEASING KRYPTONITE RADIATIONS! WE ARE ALL DOOMED... ≡CHOKE!≡

3

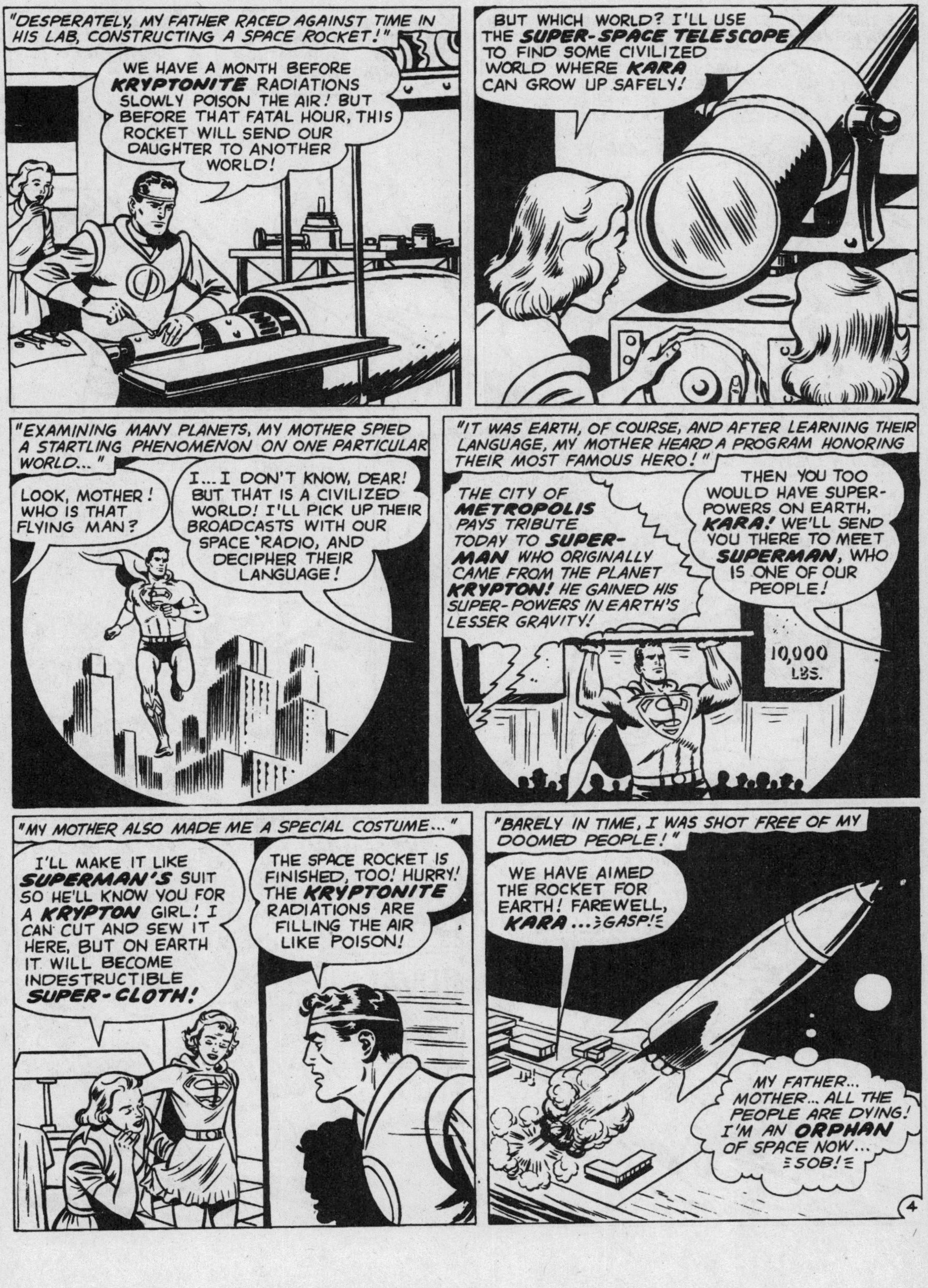
"DESPERATELY, MY FATHER RACED AGAINST TIME IN HIS LAB, CONSTRUCTING A SPACE ROCKET!"
WE HAVE A MONTH BEFORE KRYPTONITE RADIATIONS SLOWLY POISON THE AIR! BUT BEFORE THAT FATAL HOUR, THIS ROCKET WILL SEND OUR DAUGHTER TO ANOTHER WORLD!
BUT WHICH WORLD? I'LL USE THE SUPER-SPACE TELESCOPE TO FIND SOME CIVILIZED WORLD WHERE KARA CAN GROW UP SAFELY!
"EXAMINING MANY PLANETS, MY MOTHER SPIED A STARTLING PHENOMENON ON ONE PARTICULAR WORLD..."
LOOK, MOTHER! WHO IS THAT FLYING MAN?
I... I DON'T KNOW, DEAR! BUT THAT IS A CIVILIZED WORLD! I'LL PICK UP THEIR BROADCASTS WITH OUR SPACE-RADIO, AND DECIPHER THEIR LANGUAGE!
"IT WAS EARTH, OF COURSE, AND AFTER LEARNING THEIR LANGUAGE, MY MOTHER HEARD A PROGRAM HONORING THEIR MOST FAMOUS HERO!"
THE CITY OF METROPOLIS PAYS TRIBUTE TODAY TO SUPERMAN WHO ORIGINALLY CAME FROM THE PLANET KRYPTON! HE GAINED HIS SUPER-POWERS IN EARTH'S LESSER GRAVITY!
THEN YOU TOO WOULD HAVE SUPER-POWERS ON EARTH, KARA! WE'LL SEND YOU THERE TO MEET SUPERMAN, WHO IS ONE OF OUR PEOPLE!
10,000 LBS.
"MY MOTHER ALSO MADE ME A SPECIAL COSTUME..."
I'LL MAKE IT LIKE SUPERMAN'S SUIT SO HE'LL KNOW YOU FOR A KRYPTON GIRL! I CAN CUT AND SEW IT HERE, BUT ON EARTH IT WILL BECOME INDESTRUCTIBLE SUPER-CLOTH!
THE SPACE ROCKET IS FINISHED, TOO! HURRY! THE KRYPTONITE RADIATIONS ARE FILLING THE AIR LIKE POISON!
"BARELY IN TIME, I WAS SHOT FREE OF MY DOOMED PEOPLE!"
WE HAVE AIMED THE ROCKET FOR EARTH! FAREWELL, KARA... GASP!
MY FATHER... MOTHER... ALL THE PEOPLE ARE DYING! I'M AN ORPHAN OF SPACE NOW... SOB!
4

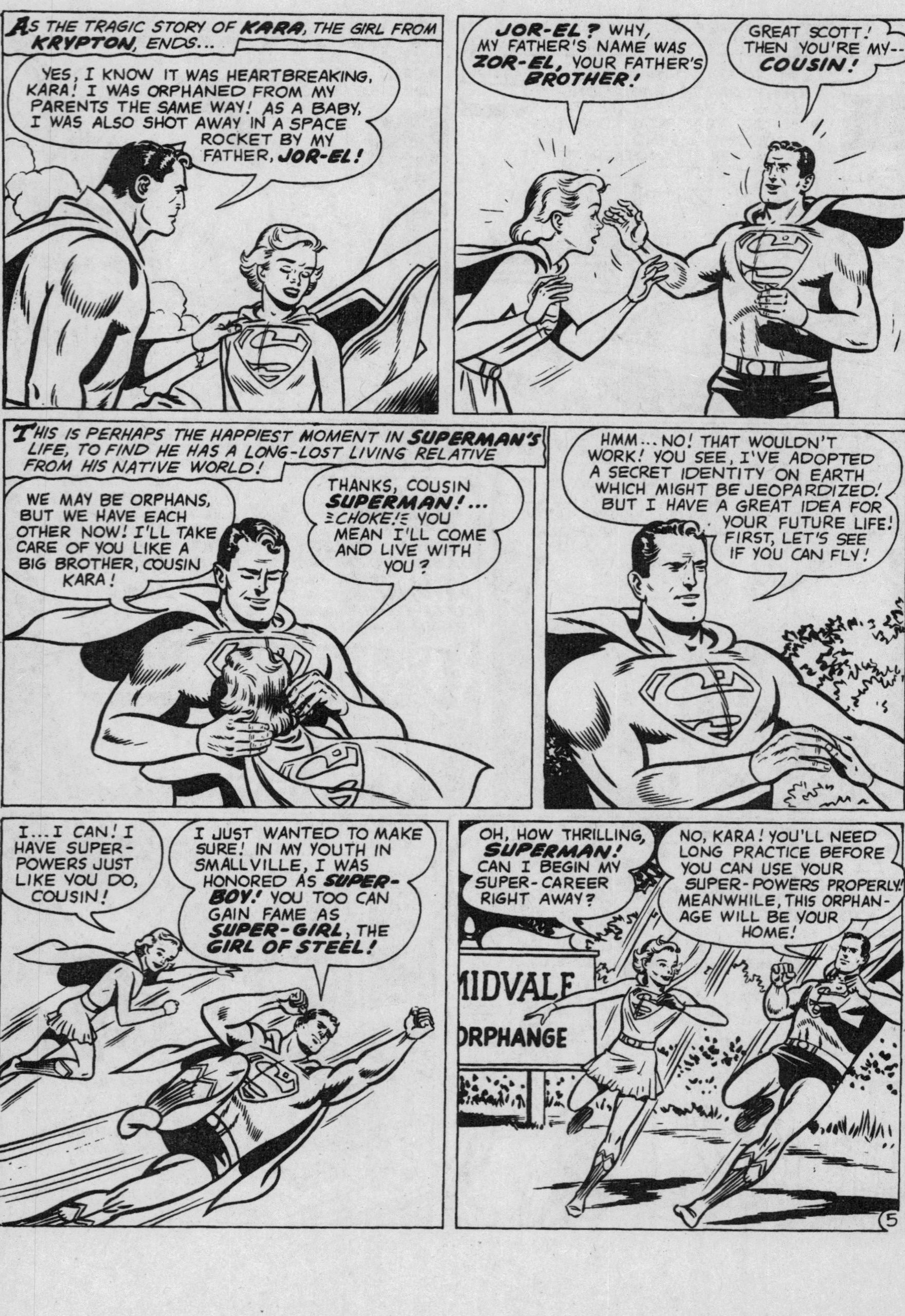
AS THE TRAGIC STORY OF KARA, THE GIRL FROM KRYPTON, ENDS...
YES, I KNOW IT WAS HEARTBREAKING, KARA! I WAS ORPHANED FROM MY PARENTS THE SAME WAY! AS A BABY, I WAS ALSO SHOT AWAY IN A SPACE ROCKET BY MY FATHER, JOR-EL!
JOR-EL? WHY, MY FATHER'S NAME WAS ZOR-EL, YOUR FATHER'S BROTHER!
GREAT SCOTT! THEN YOU'RE MY-- COUSIN!
THIS IS PERHAPS THE HAPPIEST MOMENT IN SUPERMAN'S LIFE, TO FIND HE HAS A LONG-LOST LIVING RELATIVE FROM HIS NATIVE WORLD!
WE MAY BE ORPHANS, BUT WE HAVE EACH OTHER NOW! I'LL TAKE CARE OF YOU LIKE A BIG BROTHER, COUSIN KARA!
THANKS, COUSIN SUPERMAN!... CHOKE! YOU MEAN I'LL COME AND LIVE WITH YOU?
HMM... NO! THAT WOULDN'T WORK! YOU SEE, I'VE ADOPTED A SECRET IDENTITY ON EARTH WHICH MIGHT BE JEOPARDIZED! BUT I HAVE A GREAT IDEA FOR YOUR FUTURE LIFE! FIRST, LET'S SEE IF YOU CAN FLY!
I... I CAN! I HAVE SUPER-POWERS JUST LIKE YOU DO, COUSIN!
I JUST WANTED TO MAKE SURE! IN MY YOUTH IN SMALLVILLE, I WAS HONORED AS SUPER-BOY! YOU TOO CAN GAIN FAME AS SUPER-GIRL, THE GIRL OF STEEL!
OH, HOW THRILLING, SUPERMAN! CAN I BEGIN MY SUPER-CAREER RIGHT AWAY?
NO, KARA! YOU'LL NEED LONG PRACTICE BEFORE YOU CAN USE YOUR SUPER-POWERS PROPERLY! MEANWHILE, THIS ORPHANAGE WILL BE YOUR HOME!
MIDVALE
ORPHANGE
5

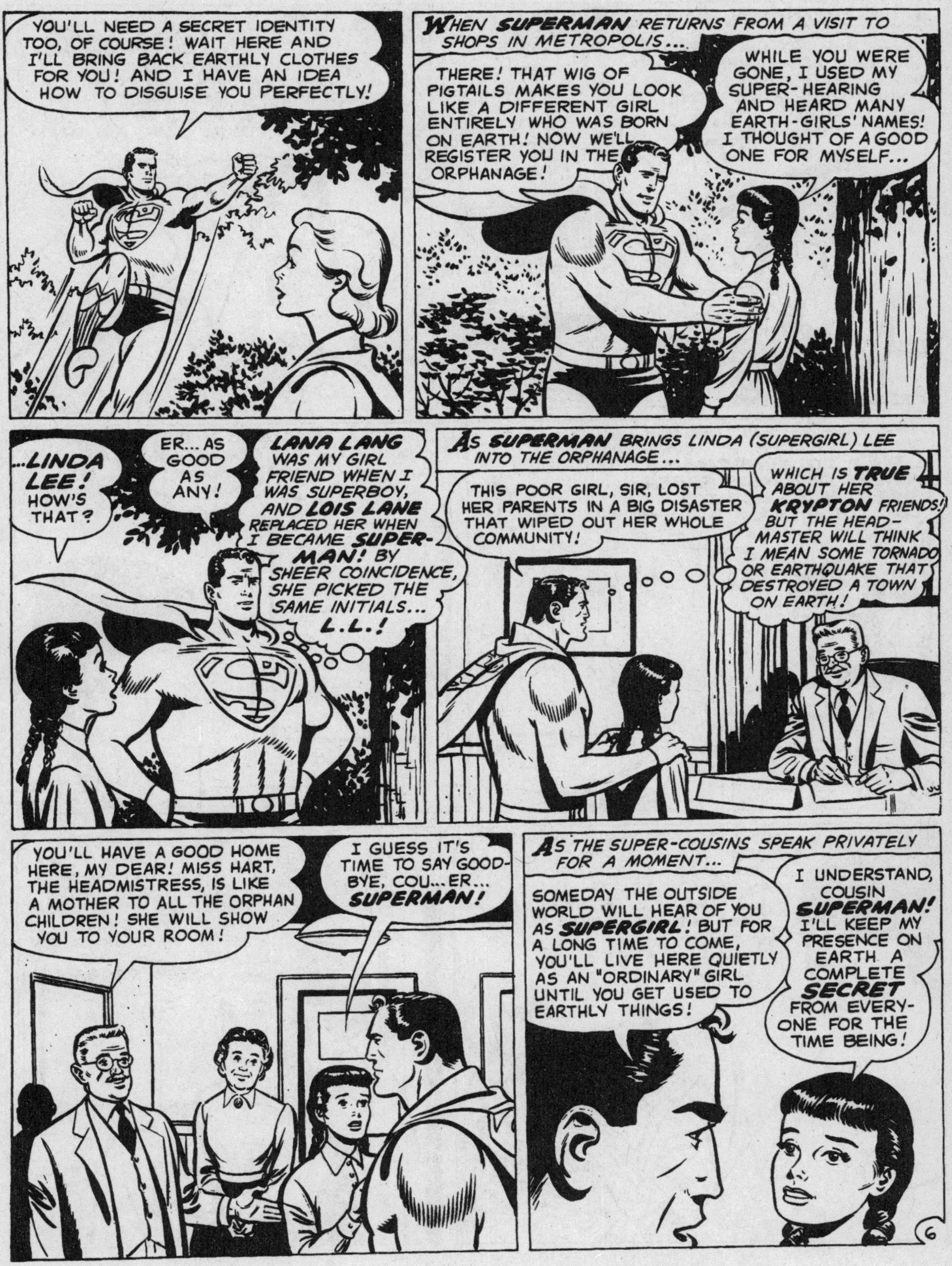
YOU'LL NEED A SECRET IDENTITY TOO, OF COURSE! WAIT HERE AND I'LL BRING BACK EARTHLY CLOTHES FOR YOU! AND I HAVE AN IDEA HOW TO DISGUISE YOU PERFECTLY!
WHEN SUPERMAN RETURNS FROM A VISIT TO SHOPS IN METROPOLIS...
THERE! THAT WIG OF PIGTAILS MAKES YOU LOOK LIKE A DIFFERENT GIRL ENTIRELY WHO WAS BORN ON EARTH! NOW WE'LL REGISTER YOU IN THE ORPHANAGE!
WHILE YOU WERE GONE, I USED MY SUPER-HEARING AND HEARD MANY EARTH-GIRLS' NAMES! I THOUGHT OF A GOOD ONE FOR MYSELF...
...LINDA LEE! HOW'S THAT?
ER... AS GOOD AS ANY!
LANA LANG WAS MY GIRL FRIEND WHEN I WAS SUPERBOY, AND LOIS LANE REPLACED HER WHEN I BECAME SUPERMAN! BY SHEER COINCIDENCE, SHE PICKED THE SAME INITIALS... L.L.!
AS SUPERMAN BRINGS LINDA (SUPERGIRL) LEE INTO THE ORPHANAGE...
THIS POOR GIRL, SIR, LOST HER PARENTS IN A BIG DISASTER THAT WIPED OUT HER WHOLE COMMUNITY!
WHICH IS TRUE ABOUT HER KRYPTON FRIENDS! BUT THE HEADMASTER WILL THINK I MEAN SOME TORNADO OR EARTHQUAKE THAT DESTROYED A TOWN ON EARTH!
YOU'LL HAVE A GOOD HOME HERE, MY DEAR! MISS HART, THE HEADMISTRESS, IS LIKE A MOTHER TO ALL THE ORPHAN CHILDREN! SHE WILL SHOW YOU TO YOUR ROOM!
I GUESS IT'S TIME TO SAY GOOD-BYE, COU... ER... SUPERMAN!
AS THE SUPER-COUSINS SPEAK PRIVATELY FOR A MOMENT...
SOMEDAY THE OUTSIDE WORLD WILL HEAR OF YOU AS SUPERGIRL! BUT FOR A LONG TIME TO COME, YOU'LL LIVE HERE QUIETLY AS AN "ORDINARY" GIRL UNTIL YOU GET USED TO EARTHLY THINGS!
I UNDERSTAND, COUSIN SUPERMAN! I'LL KEEP MY PRESENCE ON EARTH A COMPLETE SECRET FROM EVERYONE FOR THE TIME BEING!
6

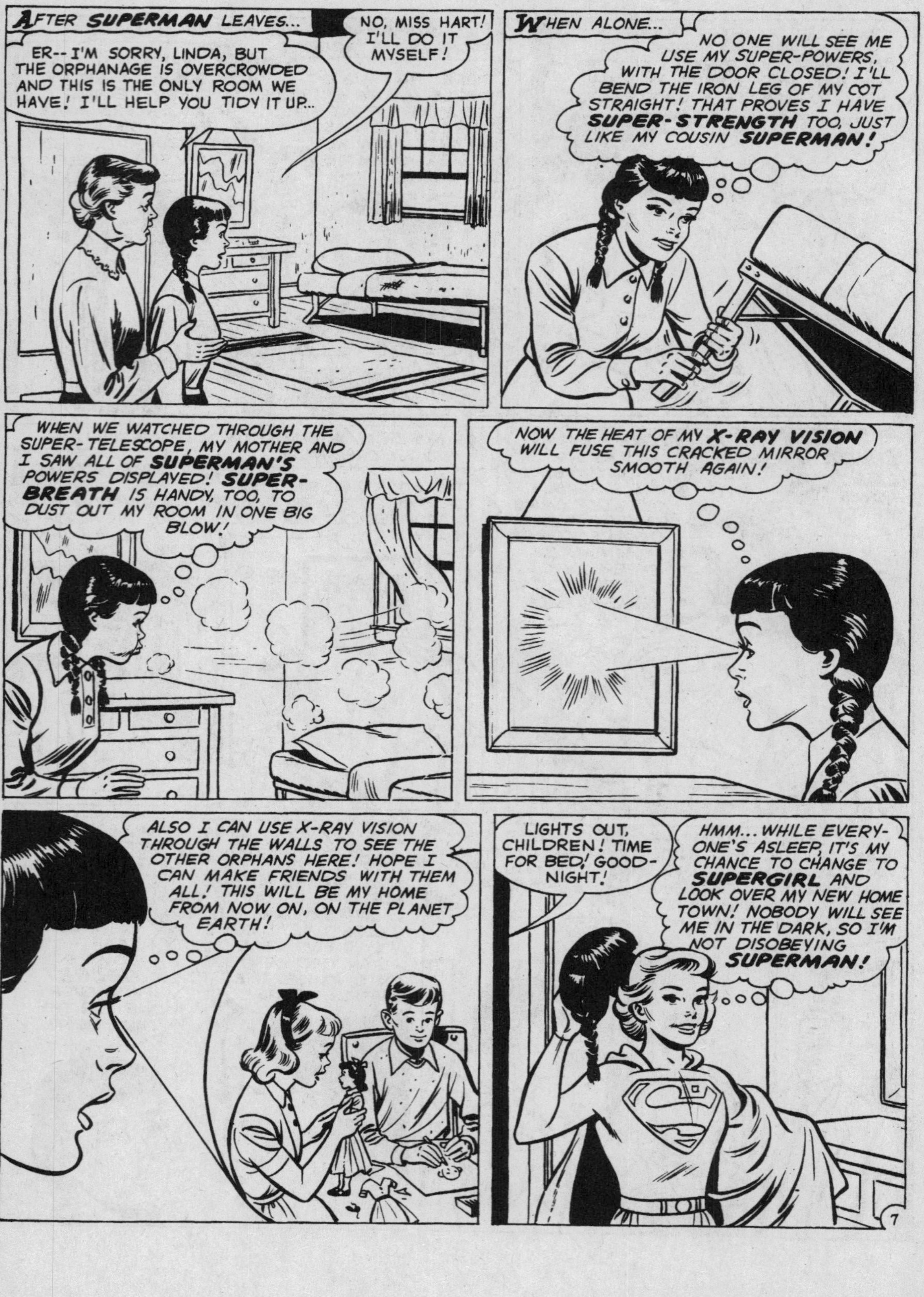
AFTER SUPERMAN LEAVES...
ER-- I'M SORRY, LINDA, BUT THE ORPHANAGE IS OVERCROWDED AND THIS IS THE ONLY ROOM WE HAVE! I'LL HELP YOU TIDY IT UP...
NO, MISS HART! I'LL DO IT MYSELF!
WHEN ALONE...
NO ONE WILL SEE ME USE MY SUPER-POWERS, WITH THE DOOR CLOSED! I'LL BEND THE IRON LEG OF MY COT STRAIGHT! THAT PROVES I HAVE SUPER-STRENGTH TOO, JUST LIKE MY COUSIN SUPERMAN!
WHEN WE WATCHED THROUGH THE SUPER-TELESCOPE, MY MOTHER AND I SAW ALL OF SUPERMAN'S POWERS DISPLAYED! SUPER-BREATH IS HANDY, TOO, TO DUST OUT MY ROOM IN ONE BIG BLOW!
NOW THE HEAT OF MY X-RAY VISION WILL FUSE THIS CRACKED MIRROR SMOOTH AGAIN!
ALSO I CAN USE X-RAY VISION THROUGH THE WALLS TO SEE THE OTHER ORPHANS HERE! HOPE I CAN MAKE FRIENDS WITH THEM ALL! THIS WILL BE MY HOME FROM NOW ON, ON THE PLANET EARTH!
LIGHTS OUT, CHILDREN! TIME FOR BED! GOOD-NIGHT!
HMM... WHILE EVERY-ONE'S ASLEEP, IT'S MY CHANCE TO CHANGE TO SUPERGIRL AND LOOK OVER MY NEW HOME TOWN! NOBODY WILL SEE ME IN THE DARK, SO I'M NOT DISOBEYING SUPERMAN!
7

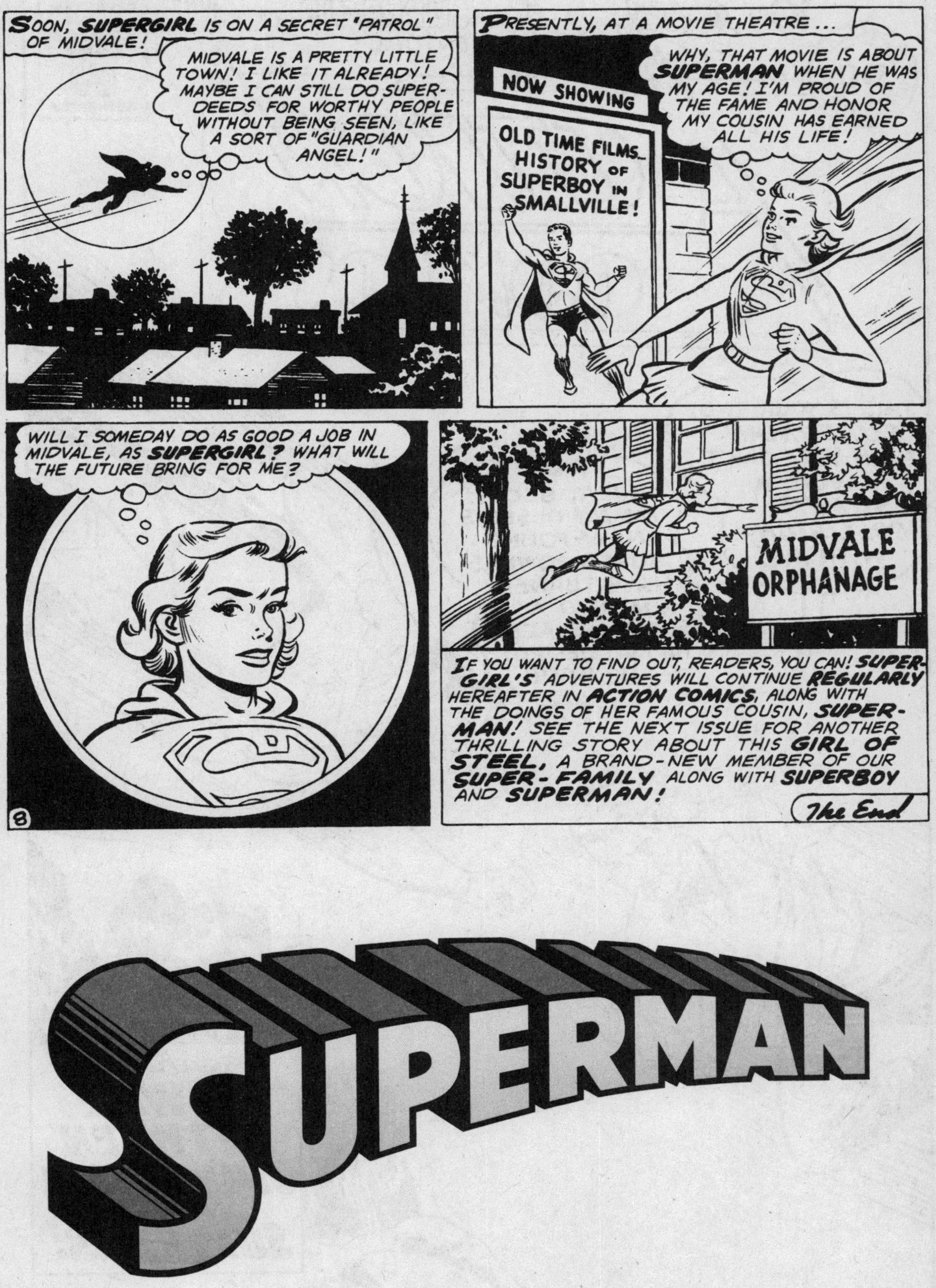
SOON, SUPERGIRL IS ON A SECRET "PATROL" OF MIDVALE!
MIDVALE IS A PRETTY LITTLE TOWN! I LIKE IT ALREADY! MAYBE I CAN STILL DO SUPER-DEEDS FOR WORTHY PEOPLE WITHOUT BEING SEEN, LIKE A SORT OF "GUARDIAN ANGEL!"
PRESENTLY, AT A MOVIE THEATRE ...
NOW SHOWING
OLD TIME FILMS... HISTORY OF SUPERBOY IN SMALLVILLE!
WHY, THAT MOVIE IS ABOUT SUPERMAN WHEN HE WAS MY AGE! I'M PROUD OF THE FAME AND HONOR MY COUSIN HAS EARNED ALL HIS LIFE!
WILL I SOMEDAY DO AS GOOD A JOB IN MIDVALE, AS SUPERGIRL? WHAT WILL THE FUTURE BRING FOR ME?
8
MIDVALE ORPHANAGE
IF YOU WANT TO FIND OUT, READERS, YOU CAN! SUPER-GIRL'S ADVENTURES WILL CONTINUE REGULARLY HEREAFTER IN ACTION COMICS, ALONG WITH THE DOINGS OF HER FAMOUS COUSIN, SUPER-MAN! SEE THE NEXT ISSUE FOR ANOTHER THRILLING STORY ABOUT THIS GIRL OF STEEL, A BRAND-NEW MEMBER OF OUR SUPER-FAMILY ALONG WITH SUPERBOY AND SUPERMAN!
The End

SUPERMAN

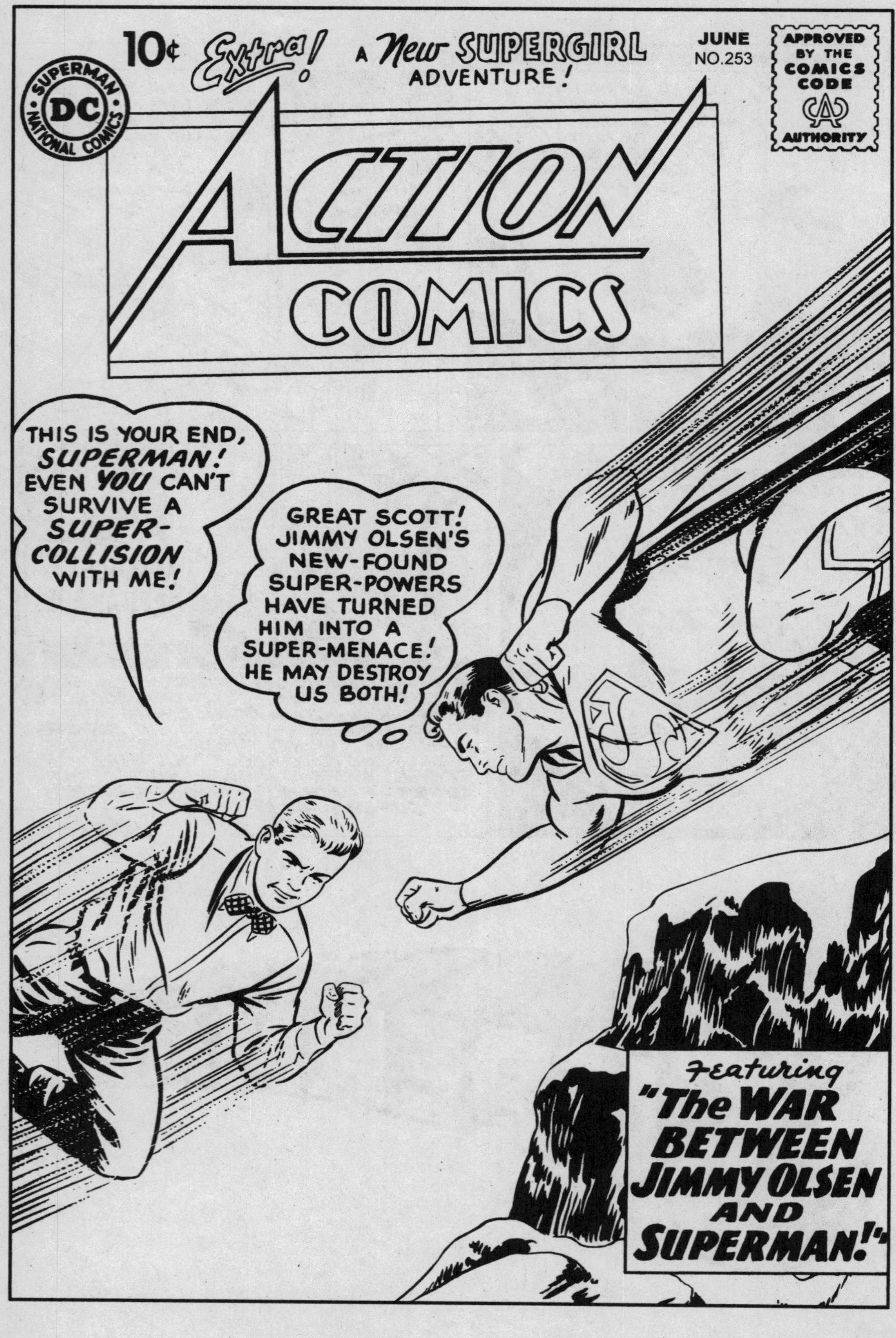
10¢
Extra! A New SUPERGIRL ADVENTURE!
JUNE
NO.253
APPROVED BY THE COMICS CODE AUTHORITY
SUPERMAN DC NATIONAL COMICS
ACTION COMICS
THIS IS YOUR END, SUPERMAN! EVEN YOU CAN'T SURVIVE A SUPER-COLLISION WITH ME!
GREAT SCOTT! JIMMY OLSEN'S NEW-FOUND SUPER-POWERS HAVE TURNED HIM INTO A SUPER-MENACE! HE MAY DESTROY US BOTH!
Featuring "The WAR BETWEEN JIMMY OLSEN AND SUPERMAN!"

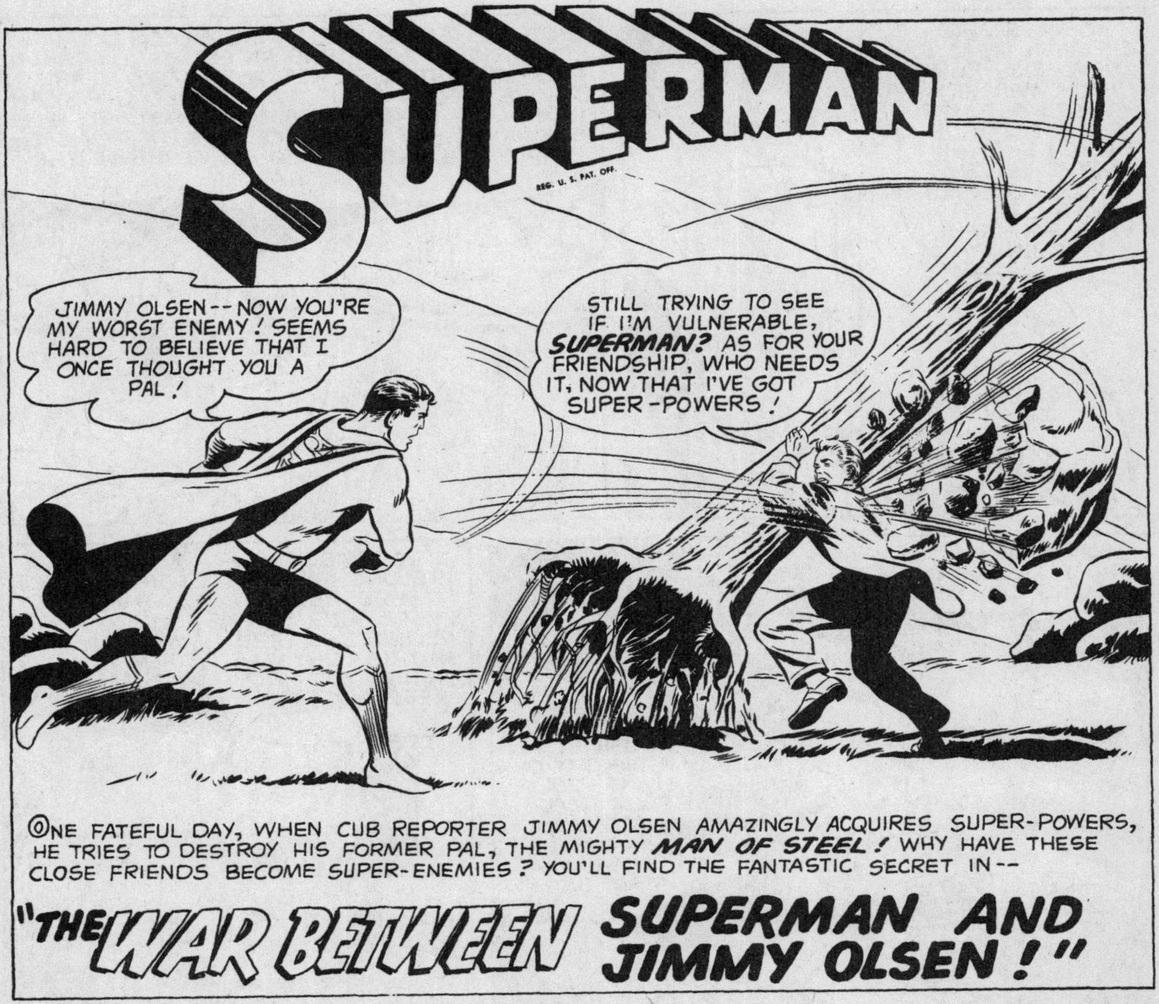
SUPERMAN
REG. U. S. PAT. OFF.
JIMMY OLSEN--NOW YOU'RE MY WORST ENEMY! SEEMS HARD TO BELIEVE THAT I ONCE THOUGHT YOU A PAL!
STILL TRYING TO SEE IF I'M VULNERABLE, SUPERMAN? AS FOR YOUR FRIENDSHIP, WHO NEEDS IT, NOW THAT I'VE GOT SUPER-POWERS!
ONE FATEFUL DAY, WHEN CUB REPORTER JIMMY OLSEN AMAZINGLY ACQUIRES SUPER-POWERS, HE TRIES TO DESTROY HIS FORMER PAL, THE MIGHTY MAN OF STEEL! WHY HAVE THESE CLOSE FRIENDS BECOME SUPER-ENEMIES? YOU'LL FIND THE FANTASTIC SECRET IN--
"THE WAR BETWEEN SUPERMAN AND JIMMY OLSEN!"

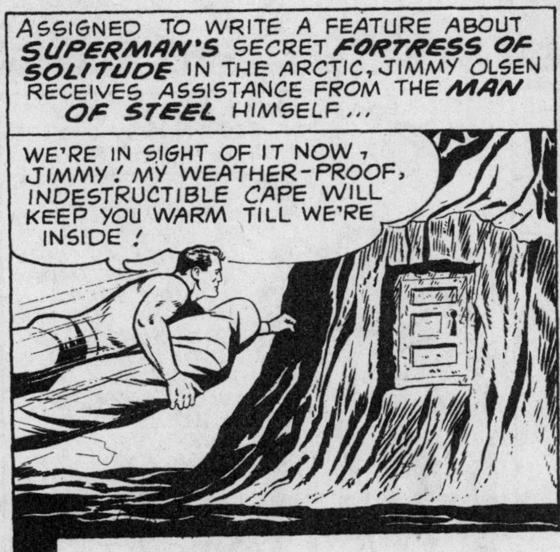
ASSIGNED TO WRITE A FEATURE ABOUT SUPERMAN'S SECRET FORTRESS OF SOLITUDE IN THE ARCTIC, JIMMY OLSEN RECEIVES ASSISTANCE FROM THE MAN OF STEEL HIMSELF...
WE'RE IN SIGHT OF IT NOW, JIMMY! MY WEATHER-PROOF, INDESTRUCTIBLE CAPE WILL KEEP YOU WARM TILL WE'RE INSIDE!

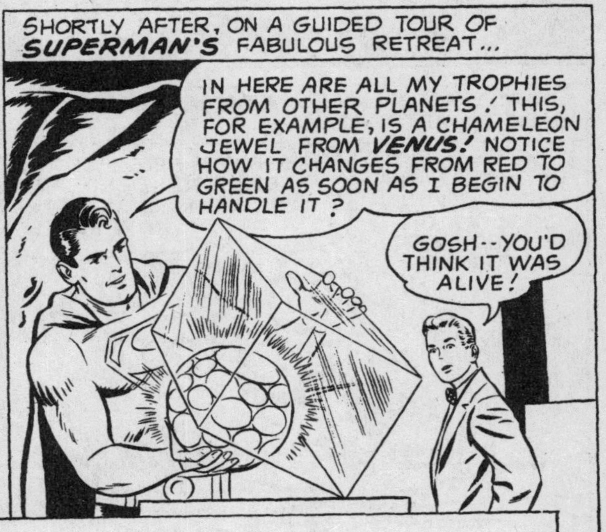
SHORTLY AFTER, ON A GUIDED TOUR OF SUPERMAN'S FABULOUS RETREAT...
IN HERE ARE ALL MY TROPHIES FROM OTHER PLANETS! THIS, FOR EXAMPLE, IS A CHAMELEON JEWEL FROM VENUS! NOTICE HOW IT CHANGES FROM RED TO GREEN AS SOON AS I BEGIN TO HANDLE IT?
GOSH--YOU'D THINK IT WAS ALIVE!

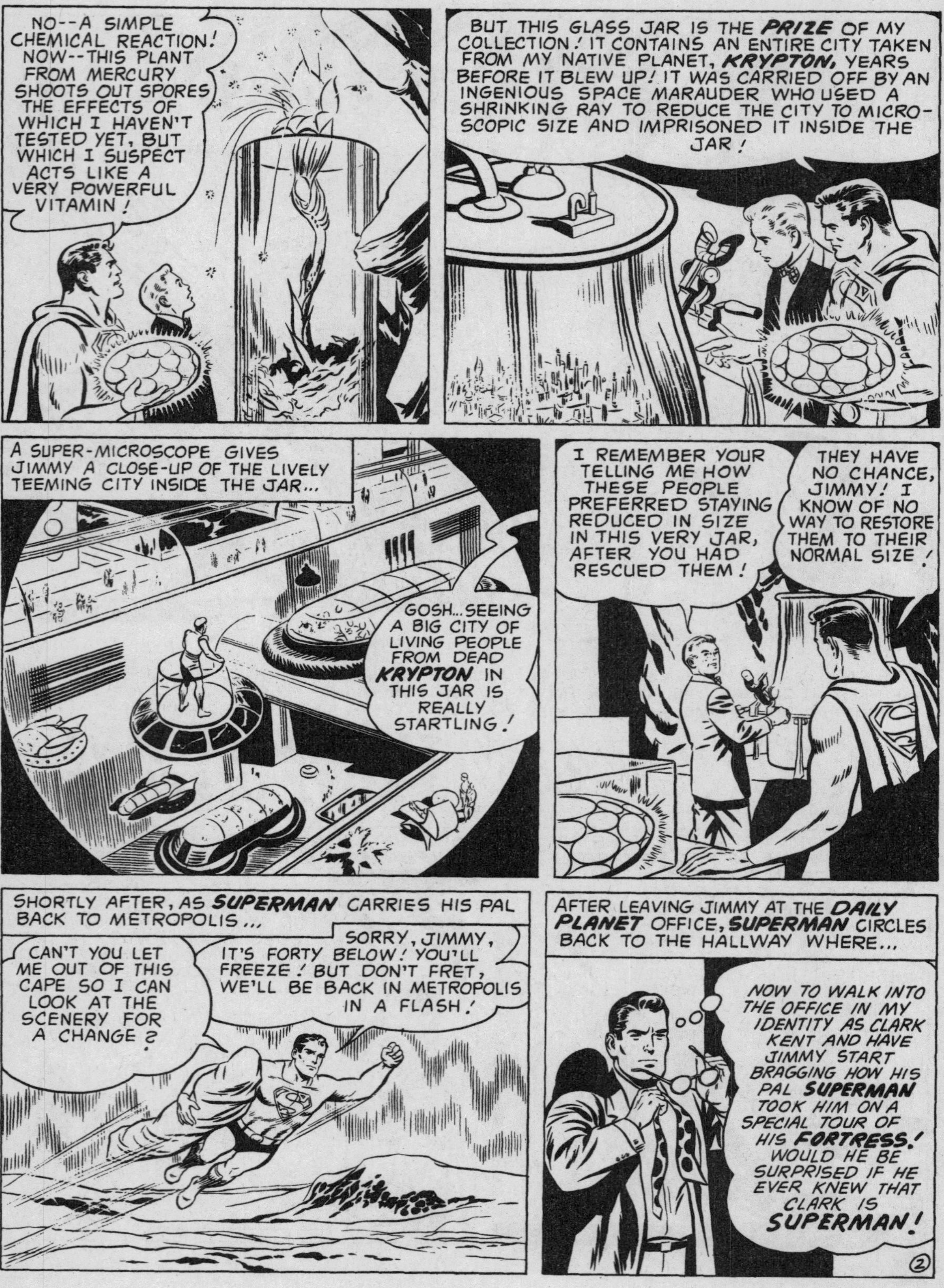
NO--A SIMPLE CHEMICAL REACTION! NOW--THIS PLANT FROM MERCURY SHOOTS OUT SPORES THE EFFECTS OF WHICH I HAVEN'T TESTED YET, BUT WHICH I SUSPECT ACTS LIKE A VERY POWERFUL VITAMIN!
BUT THIS GLASS JAR IS THE PRIZE OF MY COLLECTION! IT CONTAINS AN ENTIRE CITY TAKEN FROM MY NATIVE PLANET, KRYPTON, YEARS BEFORE IT BLEW UP! IT WAS CARRIED OFF BY AN INGENIOUS SPACE MARAUDER WHO USED A SHRINKING RAY TO REDUCE THE CITY TO MICRO-SCOPIC SIZE AND IMPRISONED IT INSIDE THE JAR!
A SUPER-MICROSCOPE GIVES JIMMY A CLOSE-UP OF THE LIVELY TEEMING CITY INSIDE THE JAR...
GOSH...SEEING A BIG CITY OF LIVING PEOPLE FROM DEAD KRYPTON IN THIS JAR IS REALLY STARTLING!
I REMEMBER YOUR TELLING ME HOW THESE PEOPLE PREFERRED STAYING REDUCED IN SIZE IN THIS VERY JAR, AFTER YOU HAD RESCUED THEM!
THEY HAVE NO CHANCE, JIMMY! I KNOW OF NO WAY TO RESTORE THEM TO THEIR NORMAL SIZE!
SHORTLY AFTER, AS SUPERMAN CARRIES HIS PAL BACK TO METROPOLIS...
CAN'T YOU LET ME OUT OF THIS CAPE SO I CAN LOOK AT THE SCENERY FOR A CHANGE?
SORRY, JIMMY, IT'S FORTY BELOW! YOU'LL FREEZE! BUT DON'T FRET, WE'LL BE BACK IN METROPOLIS IN A FLASH!
AFTER LEAVING JIMMY AT THE DAILY PLANET OFFICE, SUPERMAN CIRCLES BACK TO THE HALLWAY WHERE...
NOW TO WALK INTO THE OFFICE IN MY IDENTITY AS CLARK KENT AND HAVE JIMMY START BRAGGING HOW HIS PAL SUPERMAN TOOK HIM ON A SPECIAL TOUR OF HIS FORTRESS! WOULD HE BE SURPRISED IF HE EVER KNEW THAT CLARK IS SUPERMAN!
2

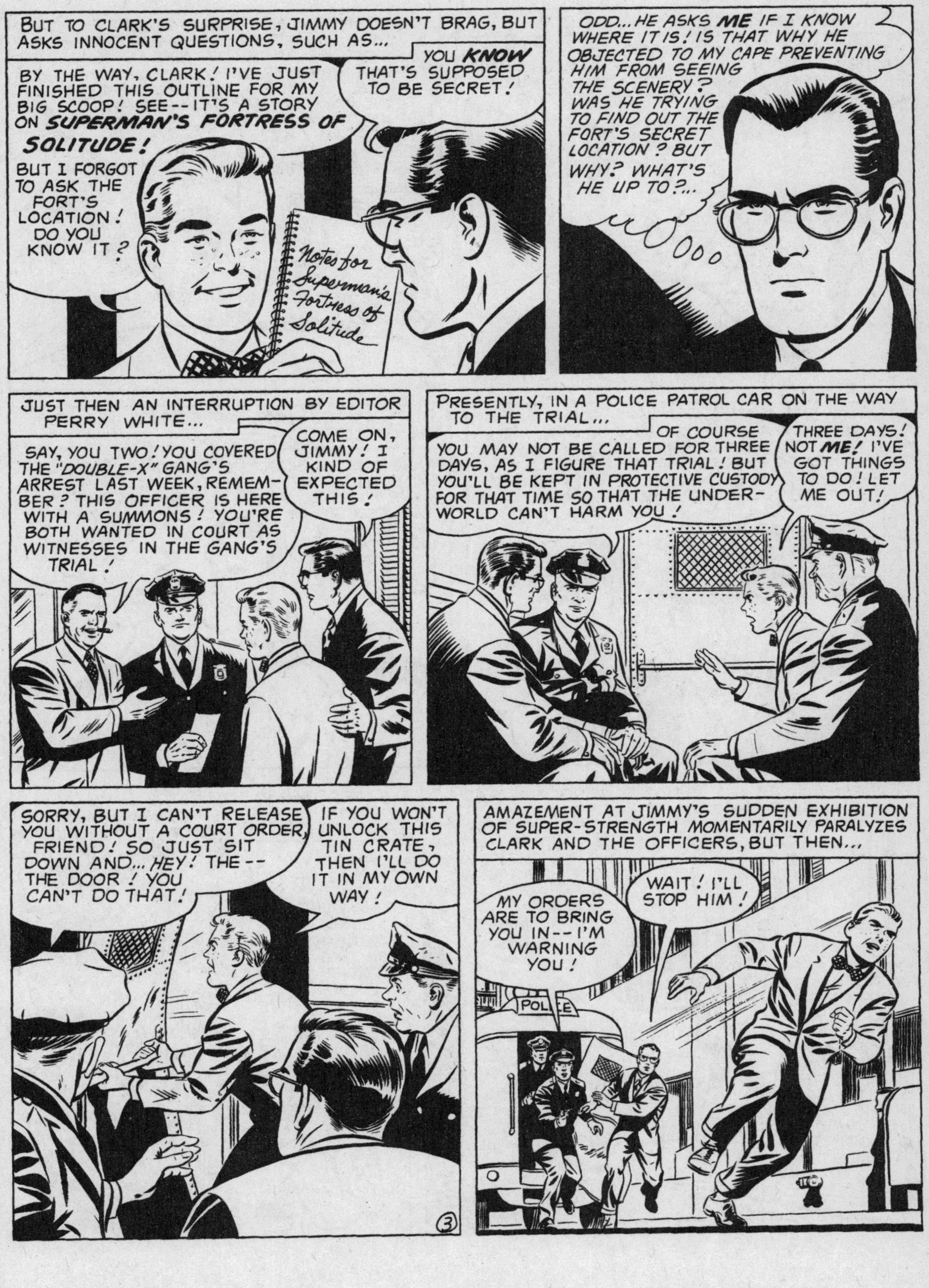
BUT TO CLARK'S SURPRISE, JIMMY DOESN'T BRAG, BUT ASKS INNOCENT QUESTIONS, SUCH AS...
BY THE WAY, CLARK! I'VE JUST FINISHED THIS OUTLINE FOR MY BIG SCOOP! SEE--IT'S A STORY ON SUPERMAN'S FORTRESS OF SOLITUDE!
BUT I FORGOT TO ASK THE FORT'S LOCATION! DO YOU KNOW IT?
YOU KNOW THAT'S SUPPOSED TO BE SECRET!
Notes for Superman's Fortress of Solitude
ODD...HE ASKS ME IF I KNOW WHERE IT IS! IS THAT WHY HE OBJECTED TO MY CAPE PREVENTING HIM FROM SEEING THE SCENERY? WAS HE TRYING TO FIND OUT THE FORT'S SECRET LOCATION? BUT WHY? WHAT'S HE UP TO?...
JUST THEN AN INTERRUPTION BY EDITOR PERRY WHITE...
SAY, YOU TWO! YOU COVERED THE "DOUBLE-X" GANG'S ARREST LAST WEEK, REMEMBER? THIS OFFICER IS HERE WITH A SUMMONS! YOU'RE BOTH WANTED IN COURT AS WITNESSES IN THE GANG'S TRIAL!
COME ON, JIMMY! I KIND OF EXPECTED THIS!
PRESENTLY, IN A POLICE PATROL CAR ON THE WAY TO THE TRIAL...
OF COURSE YOU MAY NOT BE CALLED FOR THREE DAYS, AS I FIGURE THAT TRIAL! BUT YOU'LL BE KEPT IN PROTECTIVE CUSTODY FOR THAT TIME SO THAT THE UNDERWORLD CAN'T HARM YOU!
THREE DAYS! NOT ME! I'VE GOT THINGS TO DO! LET ME OUT!
SORRY, BUT I CAN'T RELEASE YOU WITHOUT A COURT ORDER, FRIEND! SO JUST SIT DOWN AND... HEY! THE--THE DOOR! YOU CAN'T DO THAT!
IF YOU WON'T UNLOCK THIS TIN CRATE, THEN I'LL DO IT IN MY OWN WAY!
3
AMAZEMENT AT JIMMY'S SUDDEN EXHIBITION OF SUPER-STRENGTH MOMENTARILY PARALYZES CLARK AND THE OFFICERS, BUT THEN...
MY ORDERS ARE TO BRING YOU IN--I'M WARNING YOU!
WAIT! I'LL STOP HIM!
POLICE

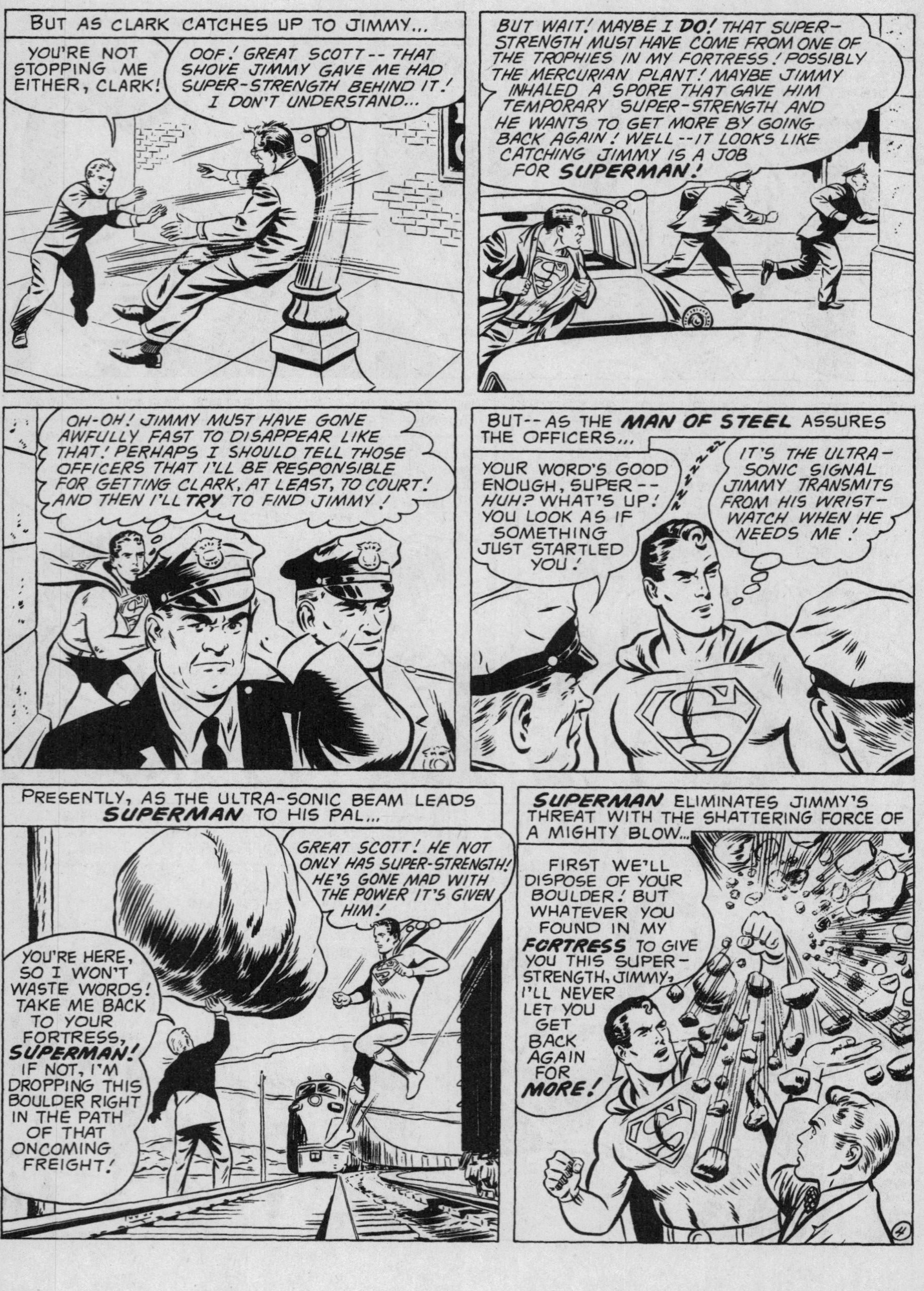
BUT AS CLARK CATCHES UP TO JIMMY...
YOU'RE NOT STOPPING ME EITHER, CLARK!
OOF! GREAT SCOTT -- THAT SHOVE JIMMY GAVE ME HAD SUPER-STRENGTH BEHIND IT! I DON'T UNDERSTAND...
BUT WAIT! MAYBE I DO! THAT SUPER-STRENGTH MUST HAVE COME FROM ONE OF THE TROPHIES IN MY FORTRESS! POSSIBLY THE MERCURIAN PLANT! MAYBE JIMMY INHALED A SPORE THAT GAVE HIM TEMPORARY SUPER-STRENGTH AND HE WANTS TO GET MORE BY GOING BACK AGAIN! WELL -- IT LOOKS LIKE CATCHING JIMMY IS A JOB FOR SUPERMAN!
OH-OH! JIMMY MUST HAVE GONE AWFULLY FAST TO DISAPPEAR LIKE THAT! PERHAPS I SHOULD TELL THOSE OFFICERS THAT I'LL BE RESPONSIBLE FOR GETTING CLARK, AT LEAST, TO COURT! AND THEN I'LL TRY TO FIND JIMMY!
BUT-- AS THE MAN OF STEEL ASSURES THE OFFICERS...
YOUR WORD'S GOOD ENOUGH, SUPER -- HUH? WHAT'S UP! YOU LOOK AS IF SOMETHING JUST STARTLED YOU!
IT'S THE ULTRA-SONIC SIGNAL JIMMY TRANSMITS FROM HIS WRIST-WATCH WHEN HE NEEDS ME!
PRESENTLY, AS THE ULTRA-SONIC BEAM LEADS SUPERMAN TO HIS PAL...
GREAT SCOTT! HE NOT ONLY HAS SUPER-STRENGTH! HE'S GONE MAD WITH THE POWER IT'S GIVEN HIM!
YOU'RE HERE, SO I WON'T WASTE WORDS! TAKE ME BACK TO YOUR FORTRESS, SUPERMAN! IF NOT, I'M DROPPING THIS BOULDER RIGHT IN THE PATH OF THAT ONCOMING FREIGHT!
SUPERMAN ELIMINATES JIMMY'S THREAT WITH THE SHATTERING FORCE OF A MIGHTY BLOW...
FIRST WE'LL DISPOSE OF YOUR BOULDER! BUT WHATEVER YOU FOUND IN MY FORTRESS TO GIVE YOU THIS SUPER-STRENGTH, JIMMY, I'LL NEVER LET YOU GET BACK AGAIN FOR MORE!
4

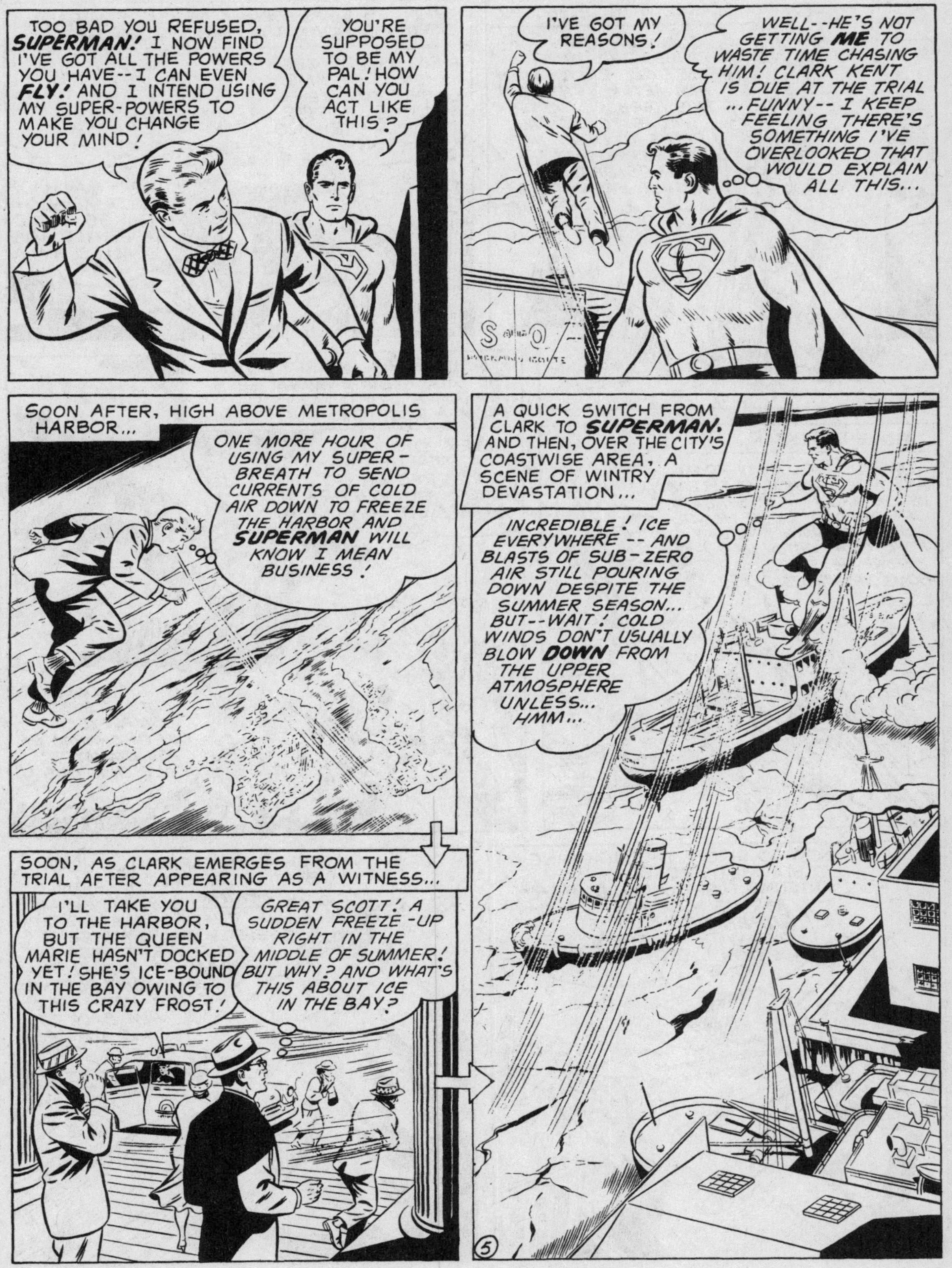
TOO BAD YOU REFUSED, SUPERMAN! I NOW FIND I'VE GOT ALL THE POWERS YOU HAVE--I CAN EVEN FLY! AND I INTEND USING MY SUPER-POWERS TO MAKE YOU CHANGE YOUR MIND!
YOU'RE SUPPOSED TO BE MY PAL! HOW CAN YOU ACT LIKE THIS?
I'VE GOT MY REASONS!
WELL--HE'S NOT GETTING ME TO WASTE TIME CHASING HIM! CLARK KENT IS DUE AT THE TRIAL ...FUNNY--I KEEP FEELING THERE'S SOMETHING I'VE OVERLOOKED THAT WOULD EXPLAIN ALL THIS...
SOON AFTER, HIGH ABOVE METROPOLIS HARBOR...
ONE MORE HOUR OF USING MY SUPER-BREATH TO SEND CURRENTS OF COLD AIR DOWN TO FREEZE THE HARBOR AND SUPERMAN WILL KNOW I MEAN BUSINESS!
SOON, AS CLARK EMERGES FROM THE TRIAL AFTER APPEARING AS A WITNESS...
I'LL TAKE YOU TO THE HARBOR, BUT THE QUEEN MARIE HASN'T DOCKED YET! SHE'S ICE-BOUND IN THE BAY OWING TO THIS CRAZY FROST!
GREAT SCOTT! A SUDDEN FREEZE-UP RIGHT IN THE MIDDLE OF SUMMER! BUT WHY? AND WHAT'S THIS ABOUT ICE IN THE BAY?
A QUICK SWITCH FROM CLARK TO SUPERMAN. AND THEN, OVER THE CITY'S COASTWISE AREA, A SCENE OF WINTRY DEVASTATION...
INCREDIBLE! ICE EVERYWHERE -- AND BLASTS OF SUB-ZERO AIR STILL POURING DOWN DESPITE THE SUMMER SEASON... BUT--WAIT! COLD WINDS DON'T USUALLY BLOW DOWN FROM THE UPPER ATMOSPHERE UNLESS... HMM...
5

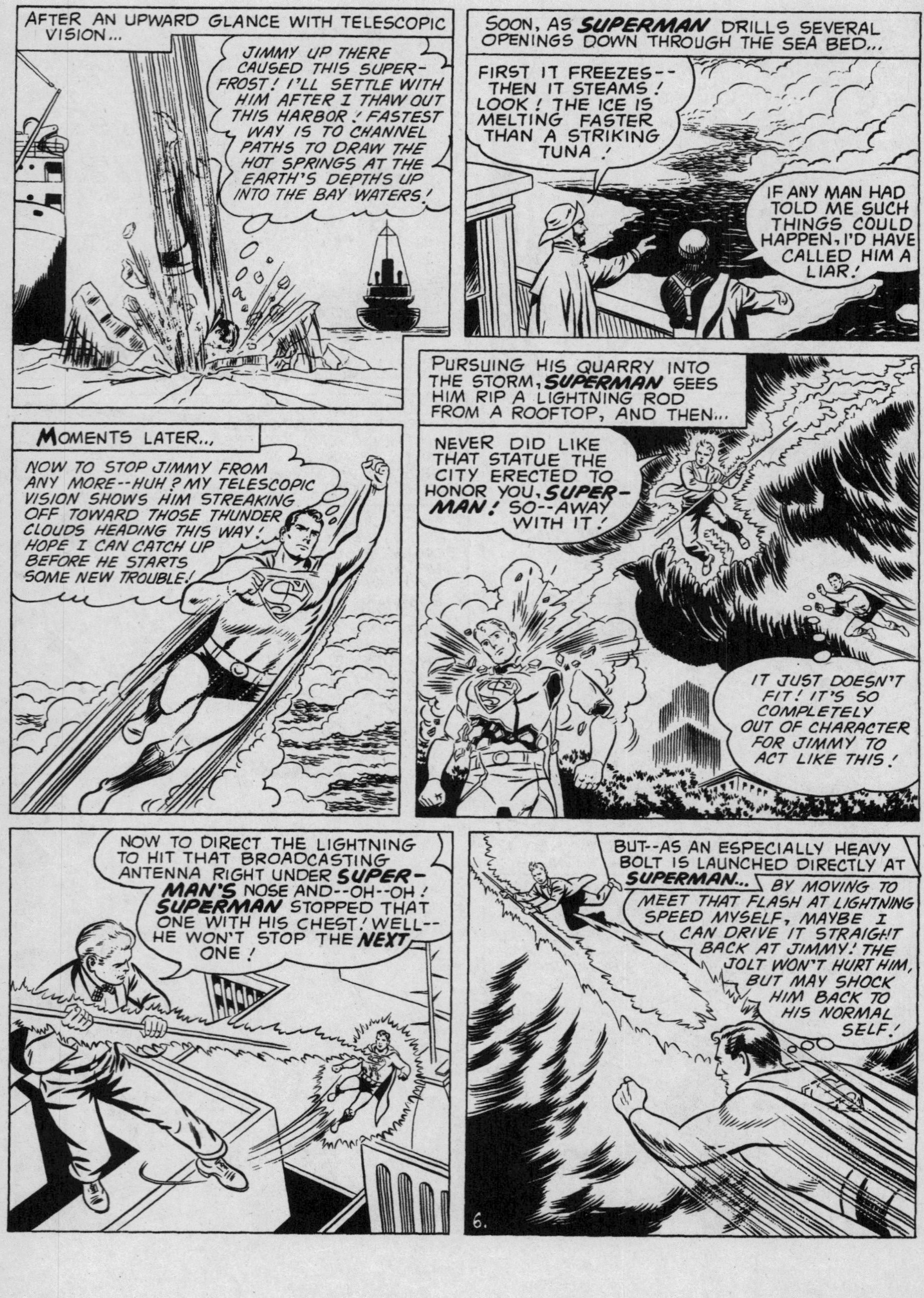
AFTER AN UPWARD GLANCE WITH TELESCOPIC VISION...
JIMMY UP THERE CAUSED THIS SUPER-FROST! I'LL SETTLE WITH HIM AFTER I THAW OUT THIS HARBOR! FASTEST WAY IS TO CHANNEL PATHS TO DRAW THE HOT SPRINGS AT THE EARTH'S DEPTHS UP INTO THE BAY WATERS!
SOON, AS SUPERMAN DRILLS SEVERAL OPENINGS DOWN THROUGH THE SEA BED...
FIRST IT FREEZES-- THEN IT STEAMS! LOOK! THE ICE IS MELTING FASTER THAN A STRIKING TUNA!
IF ANY MAN HAD TOLD ME SUCH THINGS COULD HAPPEN, I'D HAVE CALLED HIM A LIAR!
MOMENTS LATER...
NOW TO STOP JIMMY FROM ANY MORE--HUH? MY TELESCOPIC VISION SHOWS HIM STREAKING OFF TOWARD THOSE THUNDER CLOUDS HEADING THIS WAY! HOPE I CAN CATCH UP BEFORE HE STARTS SOME NEW TROUBLE!
PURSUING HIS QUARRY INTO THE STORM, SUPERMAN SEES HIM RIP A LIGHTNING ROD FROM A ROOFTOP, AND THEN...
NEVER DID LIKE THAT STATUE THE CITY ERECTED TO HONOR YOU, SUPER-MAN! SO--AWAY WITH IT!
IT JUST DOESN'T FIT! IT'S SO COMPLETELY OUT OF CHARACTER FOR JIMMY TO ACT LIKE THIS!
NOW TO DIRECT THE LIGHTNING TO HIT THAT BROADCASTING ANTENNA RIGHT UNDER SUPER-MAN'S NOSE AND--OH--OH! SUPERMAN STOPPED THAT ONE WITH HIS CHEST! WELL-- HE WON'T STOP THE NEXT ONE!
BUT--AS AN ESPECIALLY HEAVY BOLT IS LAUNCHED DIRECTLY AT SUPERMAN...
BY MOVING TO MEET THAT FLASH AT LIGHTNING SPEED MYSELF, MAYBE I CAN DRIVE IT STRAIGHT BACK AT JIMMY! THE JOLT WON'T HURT HIM, BUT MAY SHOCK HIM BACK TO HIS NORMAL SELF!
6.

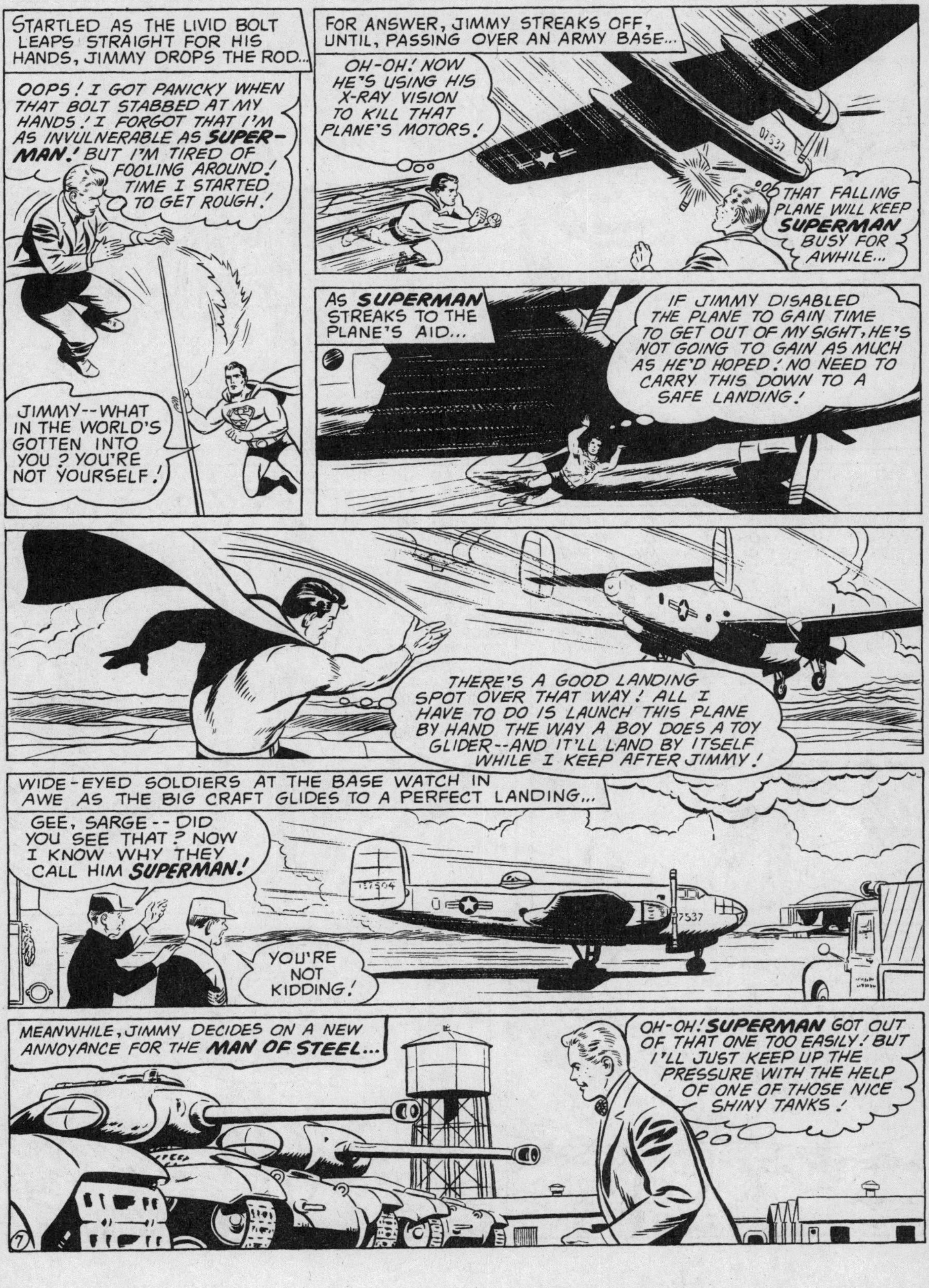
STARTLED AS THE LIVID BOLT LEAPS STRAIGHT FOR HIS HANDS, JIMMY DROPS THE ROD...
OOPS! I GOT PANICKY WHEN THAT BOLT STABBED AT MY HANDS! I FORGOT THAT I'M AS INVULNERABLE AS SUPERMAN! BUT I'M TIRED OF FOOLING AROUND! TIME I STARTED TO GET ROUGH!
JIMMY--WHAT IN THE WORLD'S GOTTEN INTO YOU? YOU'RE NOT YOURSELF!
FOR ANSWER, JIMMY STREAKS OFF, UNTIL, PASSING OVER AN ARMY BASE...
OH-OH! NOW HE'S USING HIS X-RAY VISION TO KILL THAT PLANE'S MOTORS!
THAT FALLING PLANE WILL KEEP SUPERMAN BUSY FOR AWHILE...
AS SUPERMAN STREAKS TO THE PLANE'S AID...
IF JIMMY DISABLED THE PLANE TO GAIN TIME TO GET OUT OF MY SIGHT, HE'S NOT GOING TO GAIN AS MUCH AS HE'D HOPED! NO NEED TO CARRY THIS DOWN TO A SAFE LANDING!
THERE'S A GOOD LANDING SPOT OVER THAT WAY! ALL I HAVE TO DO IS LAUNCH THIS PLANE BY HAND THE WAY A BOY DOES A TOY GLIDER--AND IT'LL LAND BY ITSELF WHILE I KEEP AFTER JIMMY!
WIDE-EYED SOLDIERS AT THE BASE WATCH IN AWE AS THE BIG CRAFT GLIDES TO A PERFECT LANDING...
GEE, SARGE--DID YOU SEE THAT? NOW I KNOW WHY THEY CALL HIM SUPERMAN!
YOU'RE NOT KIDDING!
MEANWHILE, JIMMY DECIDES ON A NEW ANNOYANCE FOR THE MAN OF STEEL...
OH-OH! SUPERMAN GOT OUT OF THAT ONE TOO EASILY! BUT I'LL JUST KEEP UP THE PRESSURE WITH THE HELP OF ONE OF THOSE NICE SHINY TANKS!
7

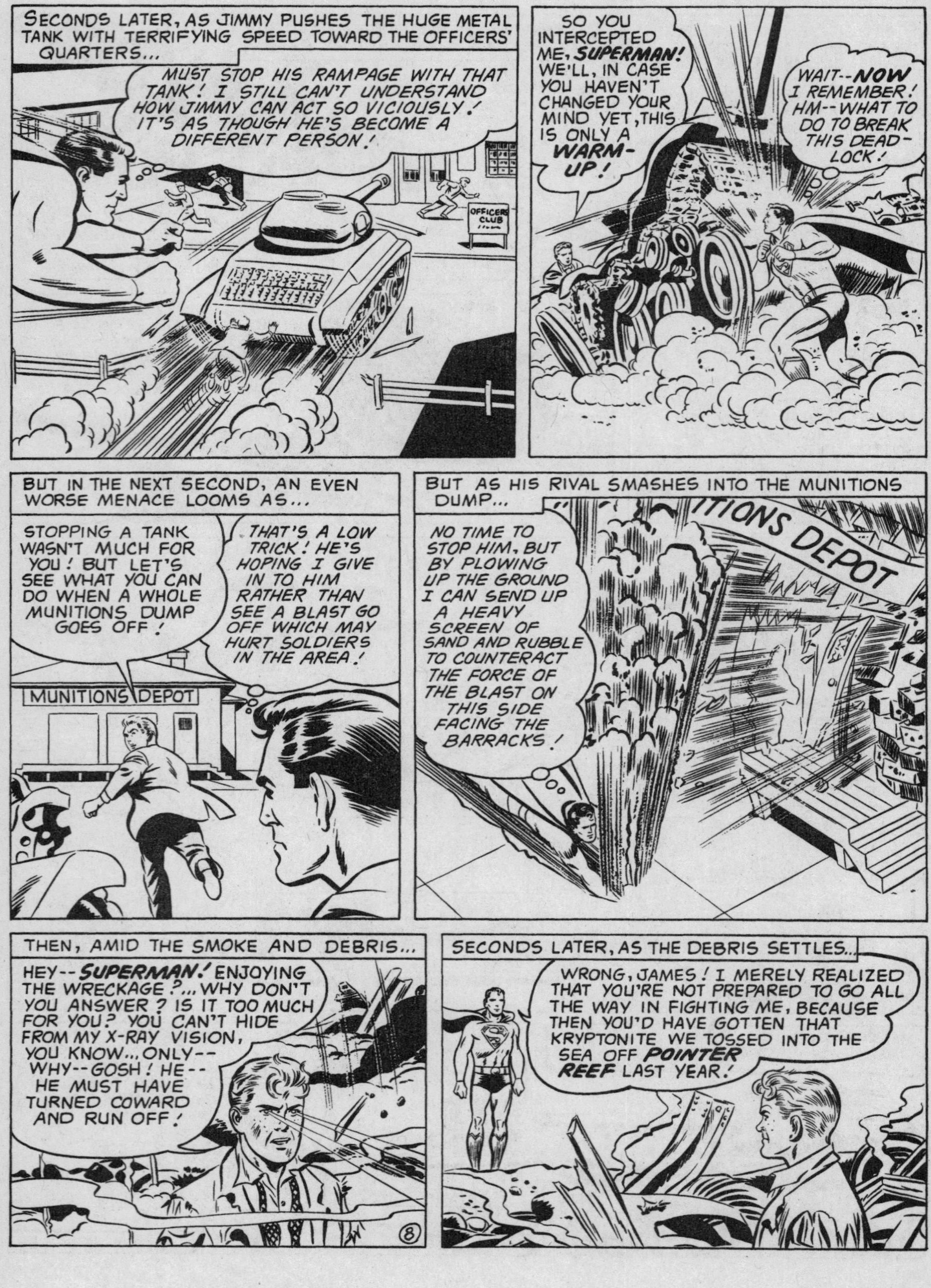
SECONDS LATER, AS JIMMY PUSHES THE HUGE METAL TANK WITH TERRIFYING SPEED TOWARD THE OFFICERS' QUARTERS...
MUST STOP HIS RAMPAGE WITH THAT TANK! I STILL CAN'T UNDERSTAND HOW JIMMY CAN ACT SO VICIOUSLY! IT'S AS THOUGH HE'S BECOME A DIFFERENT PERSON!
OFFICERS CLUB
SO YOU INTERCEPTED ME, SUPERMAN! WE'LL, IN CASE YOU HAVEN'T CHANGED YOUR MIND YET, THIS IS ONLY A WARM-UP!
WAIT--NOW I REMEMBER! HM--WHAT TO DO TO BREAK THIS DEAD-LOCK!
BUT IN THE NEXT SECOND, AN EVEN WORSE MENACE LOOMS AS...
STOPPING A TANK WASN'T MUCH FOR YOU! BUT LET'S SEE WHAT YOU CAN DO WHEN A WHOLE MUNITIONS DUMP GOES OFF!
THAT'S A LOW TRICK! HE'S HOPING I GIVE IN TO HIM RATHER THAN SEE A BLAST GO OFF WHICH MAY HURT SOLDIERS IN THE AREA!
MUNITIONS DEPOT
BUT AS HIS RIVAL SMASHES INTO THE MUNITIONS DUMP...
ITIONS DEPOT
NO TIME TO STOP HIM, BUT BY PLOWING UP THE GROUND I CAN SEND UP A HEAVY SCREEN OF SAND AND RUBBLE TO COUNTERACT THE FORCE OF THE BLAST ON THIS SIDE FACING THE BARRACKS!
THEN, AMID THE SMOKE AND DEBRIS...
HEY--SUPERMAN! ENJOYING THE WRECKAGE?... WHY DON'T YOU ANSWER? IS IT TOO MUCH FOR YOU? YOU CAN'T HIDE FROM MY X-RAY VISION, YOU KNOW..., ONLY-- WHY--GOSH! HE--HE MUST HAVE TURNED COWARD AND RUN OFF!
8
SECONDS LATER, AS THE DEBRIS SETTLES...
WRONG, JAMES! I MERELY REALIZED THAT YOU'RE NOT PREPARED TO GO ALL THE WAY IN FIGHTING ME, BECAUSE THEN YOU'D HAVE GOTTEN THAT KRYPTONITE WE TOSSED INTO THE SEA OFF POINTER REEF LAST YEAR!

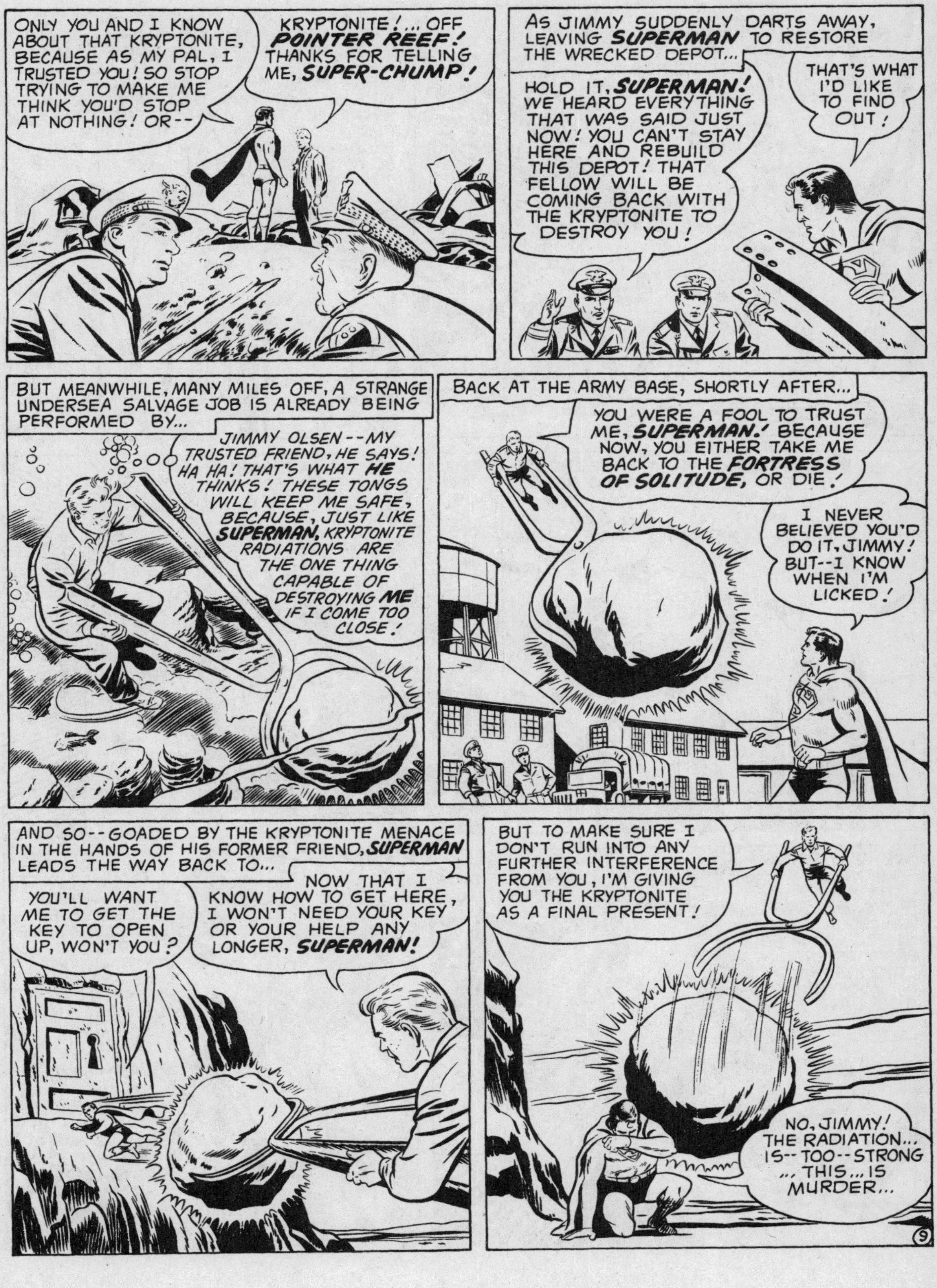
ONLY YOU AND I KNOW ABOUT THAT KRYPTONITE, BECAUSE AS MY PAL, I TRUSTED YOU! SO STOP TRYING TO MAKE ME THINK YOU'D STOP AT NOTHING! OR--
KRYPTONITE!... OFF POINTER REEF! THANKS FOR TELLING ME, SUPER-CHUMP!
AS JIMMY SUDDENLY DARTS AWAY, LEAVING SUPERMAN TO RESTORE THE WRECKED DEPOT...
HOLD IT, SUPERMAN! WE HEARD EVERYTHING THAT WAS SAID JUST NOW! YOU CAN'T STAY HERE AND REBUILD THIS DEPOT! THAT FELLOW WILL BE COMING BACK WITH THE KRYPTONITE TO DESTROY YOU!
THAT'S WHAT I'D LIKE TO FIND OUT!
BUT MEANWHILE, MANY MILES OFF, A STRANGE UNDERSEA SALVAGE JOB IS ALREADY BEING PERFORMED BY...
JIMMY OLSEN--MY TRUSTED FRIEND, HE SAYS! HA HA! THAT'S WHAT HE THINKS! THESE TONGS WILL KEEP ME SAFE, BECAUSE, JUST LIKE SUPERMAN, KRYPTONITE RADIATIONS ARE THE ONE THING CAPABLE OF DESTROYING ME IF I COME TOO CLOSE!
BACK AT THE ARMY BASE, SHORTLY AFTER...
YOU WERE A FOOL TO TRUST ME, SUPERMAN! BECAUSE NOW, YOU EITHER TAKE ME BACK TO THE FORTRESS OF SOLITUDE, OR DIE!
I NEVER BELIEVED YOU'D DO IT, JIMMY! BUT--I KNOW WHEN I'M LICKED!
AND SO--GOADED BY THE KRYPTONITE MENACE IN THE HANDS OF HIS FORMER FRIEND, SUPERMAN LEADS THE WAY BACK TO...
YOU'LL WANT ME TO GET THE KEY TO OPEN UP, WON'T YOU?
NOW THAT I KNOW HOW TO GET HERE, I WON'T NEED YOUR KEY OR YOUR HELP ANY LONGER, SUPERMAN!
BUT TO MAKE SURE I DON'T RUN INTO ANY FURTHER INTERFERENCE FROM YOU, I'M GIVING YOU THE KRYPTONITE AS A FINAL PRESENT!
NO, JIMMY! THE RADIATION... IS--TOO--STRONG ... THIS... IS MURDER...
9

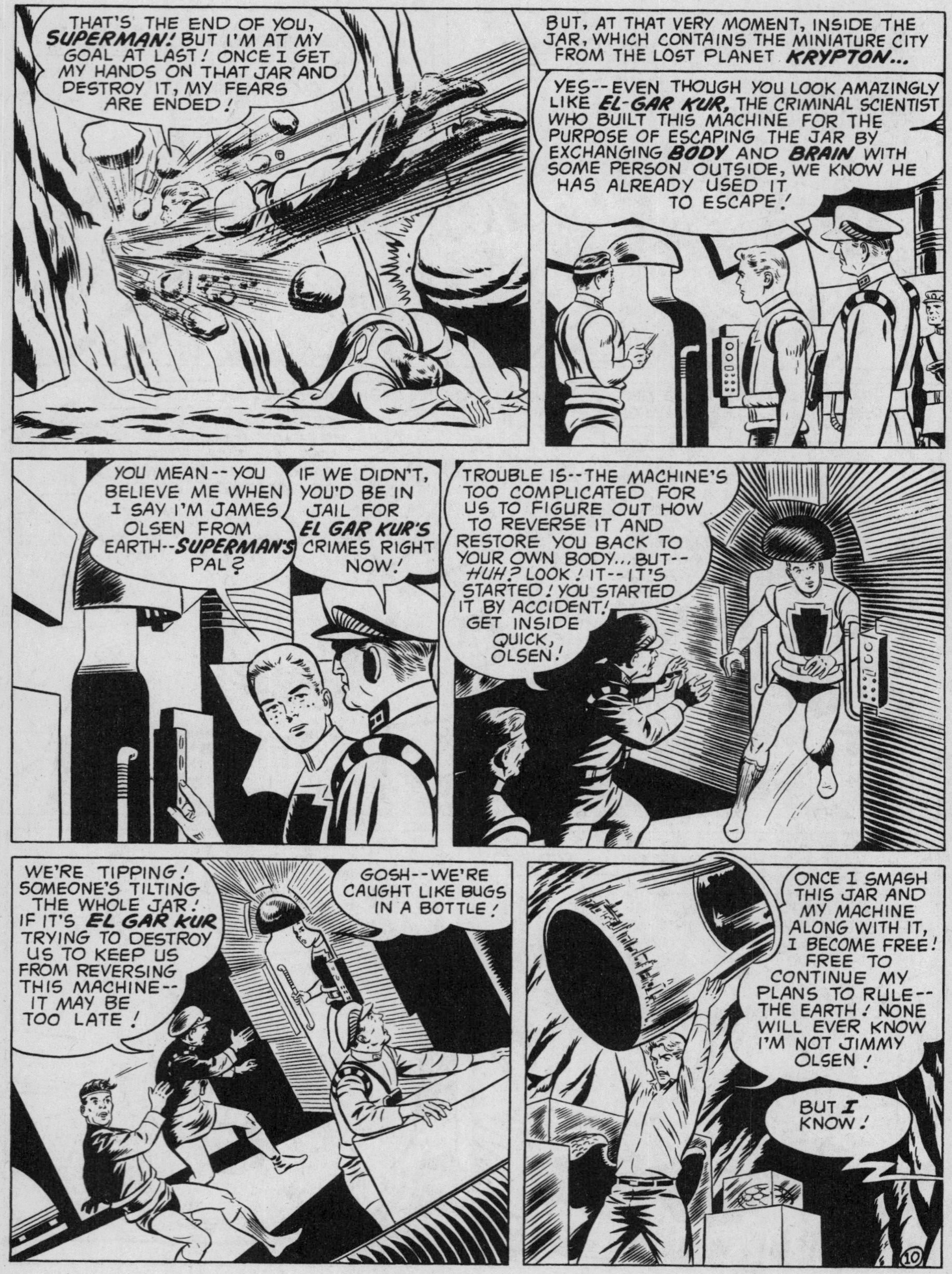
THAT'S THE END OF YOU, SUPERMAN! BUT I'M AT MY GOAL AT LAST! ONCE I GET MY HANDS ON THAT JAR AND DESTROY IT, MY FEARS ARE ENDED!
BUT, AT THAT VERY MOMENT, INSIDE THE JAR, WHICH CONTAINS THE MINIATURE CITY FROM THE LOST PLANET KRYPTON...
YES--EVEN THOUGH YOU LOOK AMAZINGLY LIKE EL-GAR KUR, THE CRIMINAL SCIENTIST WHO BUILT THIS MACHINE FOR THE PURPOSE OF ESCAPING THE JAR BY EXCHANGING BODY AND BRAIN WITH SOME PERSON OUTSIDE, WE KNOW HE HAS ALREADY USED IT TO ESCAPE!
YOU MEAN--YOU BELIEVE ME WHEN I SAY I'M JAMES OLSEN FROM EARTH--SUPERMAN'S PAL?
IF WE DIDN'T, YOU'D BE IN JAIL FOR EL GAR KUR'S CRIMES RIGHT NOW!
TROUBLE IS--THE MACHINE'S TOO COMPLICATED FOR US TO FIGURE OUT HOW TO REVERSE IT AND RESTORE YOU BACK TO YOUR OWN BODY... BUT--HUH? LOOK! IT--IT'S STARTED! YOU STARTED IT BY ACCIDENT! GET INSIDE QUICK, OLSEN!
WE'RE TIPPING! SOMEONE'S TILTING THE WHOLE JAR! IF IT'S EL GAR KUR TRYING TO DESTROY US TO KEEP US FROM REVERSING THIS MACHINE--IT MAY BE TOO LATE!
GOSH--WE'RE CAUGHT LIKE BUGS IN A BOTTLE!
ONCE I SMASH THIS JAR AND MY MACHINE ALONG WITH IT, I BECOME FREE! FREE TO CONTINUE MY PLANS TO RULE--THE EARTH! NONE WILL EVER KNOW I'M NOT JIMMY OLSEN!
BUT I KNOW!
10

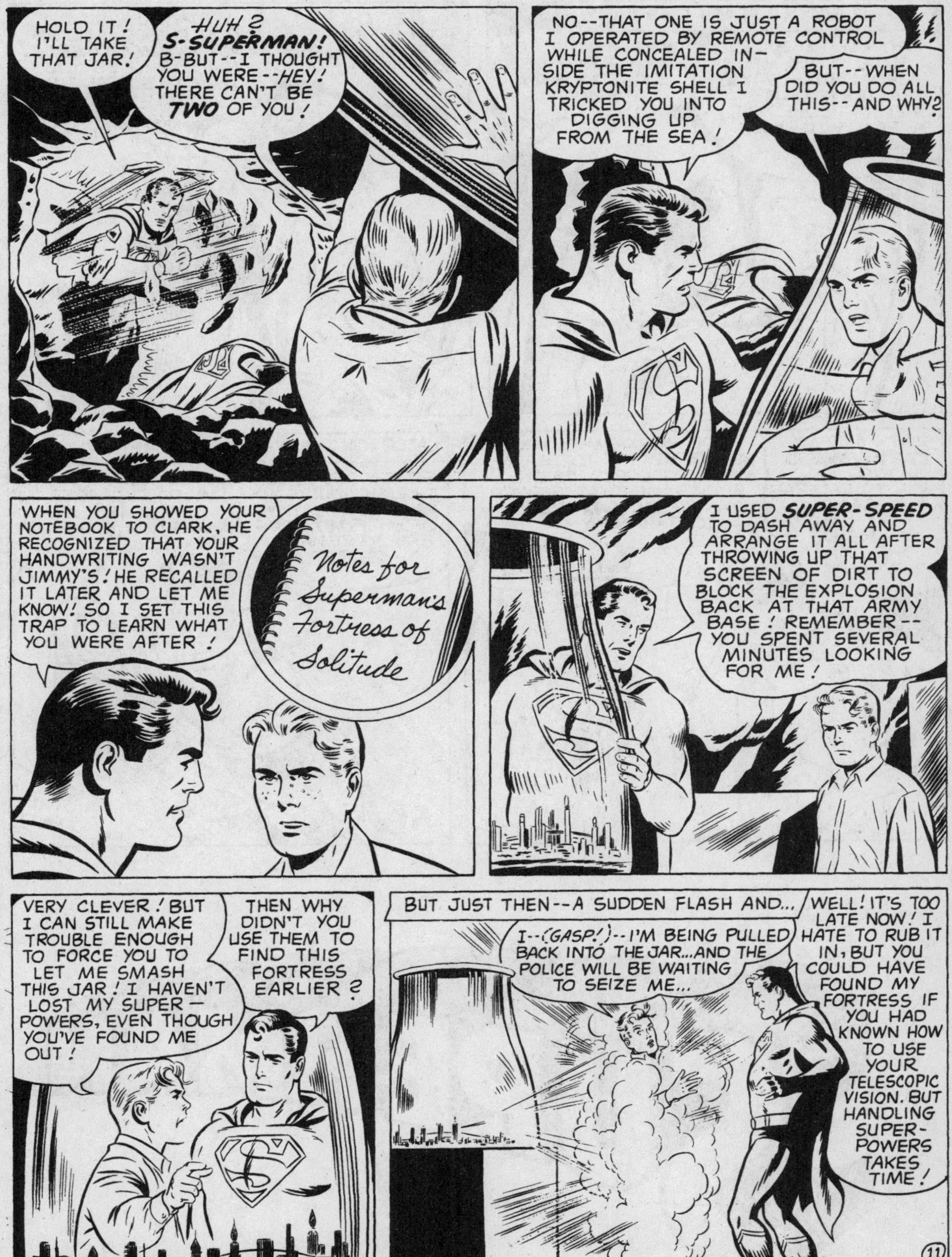
HOLD IT! I'LL TAKE THAT JAR!
HUH? S-SUPERMAN! B-BUT--I THOUGHT YOU WERE--HEY! THERE CAN'T BE TWO OF YOU!
NO--THAT ONE IS JUST A ROBOT I OPERATED BY REMOTE CONTROL WHILE CONCEALED INSIDE THE IMITATION KRYPTONITE SHELL I TRICKED YOU INTO DIGGING UP FROM THE SEA!
BUT--WHEN DID YOU DO ALL THIS--AND WHY?
WHEN YOU SHOWED YOUR NOTEBOOK TO CLARK, HE RECOGNIZED THAT YOUR HANDWRITING WASN'T JIMMY'S! HE RECALLED IT LATER AND LET ME KNOW! SO I SET THIS TRAP TO LEARN WHAT YOU WERE AFTER!
Notes for Superman's Fortress of Solitude
I USED SUPER-SPEED TO DASH AWAY AND ARRANGE IT ALL AFTER THROWING UP THAT SCREEN OF DIRT TO BLOCK THE EXPLOSION BACK AT THAT ARMY BASE! REMEMBER--YOU SPENT SEVERAL MINUTES LOOKING FOR ME!
VERY CLEVER! BUT I CAN STILL MAKE TROUBLE ENOUGH TO FORCE YOU TO LET ME SMASH THIS JAR! I HAVEN'T LOST MY SUPER-POWERS, EVEN THOUGH YOU'VE FOUND ME OUT!
THEN WHY DIDN'T YOU USE THEM TO FIND THIS FORTRESS EARLIER?
BUT JUST THEN--A SUDDEN FLASH AND...
I--(GASP!)--I'M BEING PULLED BACK INTO THE JAR...AND THE POLICE WILL BE WAITING TO SEIZE ME...
WELL! IT'S TOO LATE NOW! I HATE TO RUB IT IN, BUT YOU COULD HAVE FOUND MY FORTRESS IF YOU HAD KNOWN HOW TO USE YOUR TELESCOPIC VISION. BUT HANDLING SUPER-POWERS TAKES TIME!
11

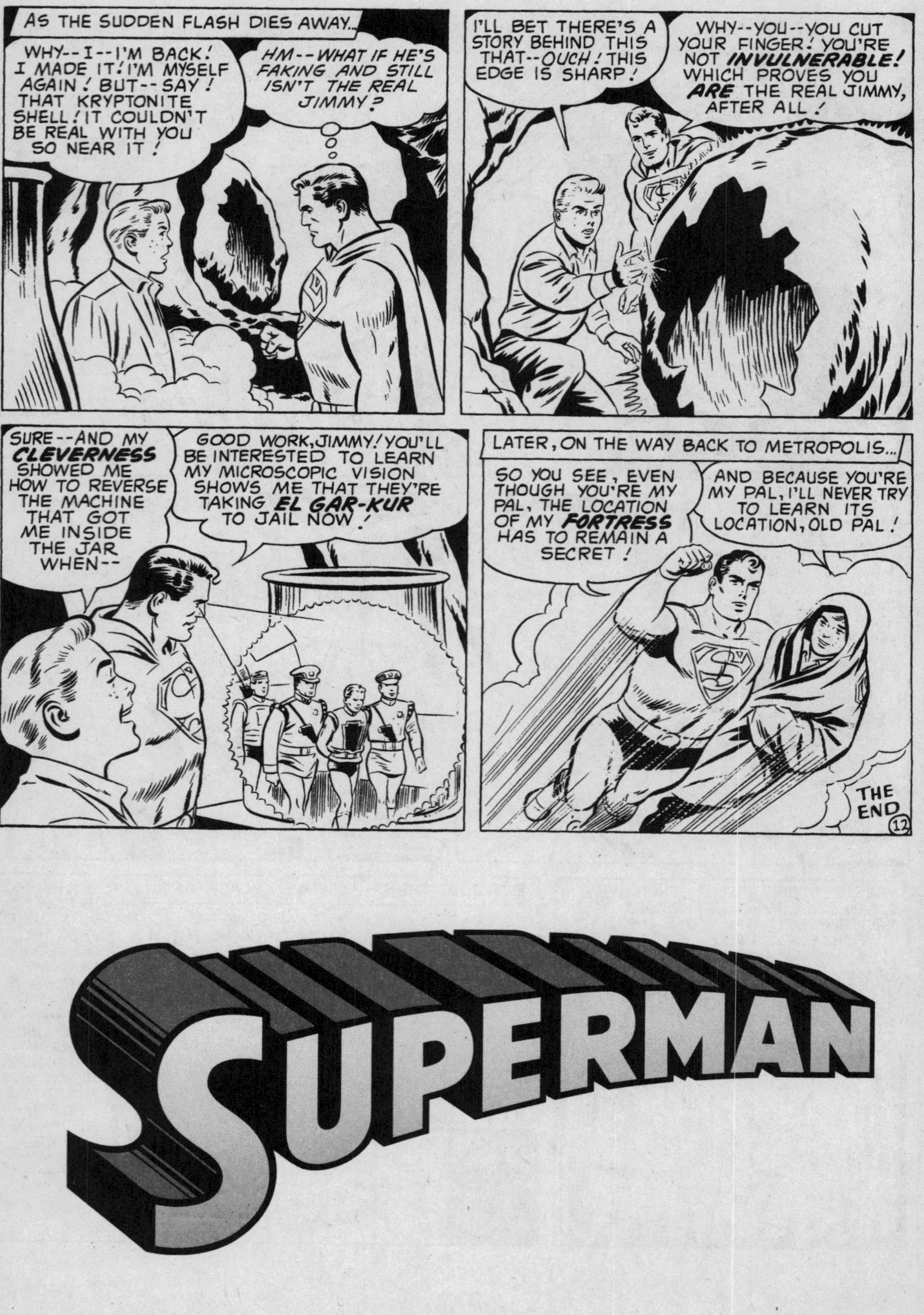
AS THE SUDDEN FLASH DIES AWAY...
WHY--I--I'M BACK! I MADE IT! I'M MYSELF AGAIN! BUT--SAY! THAT KRYPTONITE SHELL! IT COULDN'T BE REAL WITH YOU SO NEAR IT!
HM--WHAT IF HE'S FAKING AND STILL ISN'T THE REAL JIMMY?
I'LL BET THERE'S A STORY BEHIND THIS THAT--OUCH! THIS EDGE IS SHARP!
WHY--YOU--YOU CUT YOUR FINGER! YOU'RE NOT INVULNERABLE! WHICH PROVES YOU ARE THE REAL JIMMY, AFTER ALL!
SURE--AND MY CLEVERNESS SHOWED ME HOW TO REVERSE THE MACHINE THAT GOT ME INSIDE THE JAR WHEN--
GOOD WORK, JIMMY! YOU'LL BE INTERESTED TO LEARN MY MICROSCOPIC VISION SHOWS ME THAT THEY'RE TAKING EL GAR-KUR TO JAIL NOW!
LATER, ON THE WAY BACK TO METROPOLIS...
SO YOU SEE, EVEN THOUGH YOU'RE MY PAL, THE LOCATION OF MY FORTRESS HAS TO REMAIN A SECRET!
AND BECAUSE YOU'RE MY PAL, I'LL NEVER TRY TO LEARN ITS LOCATION, OLD PAL!
THE END
12

SUPERMAN

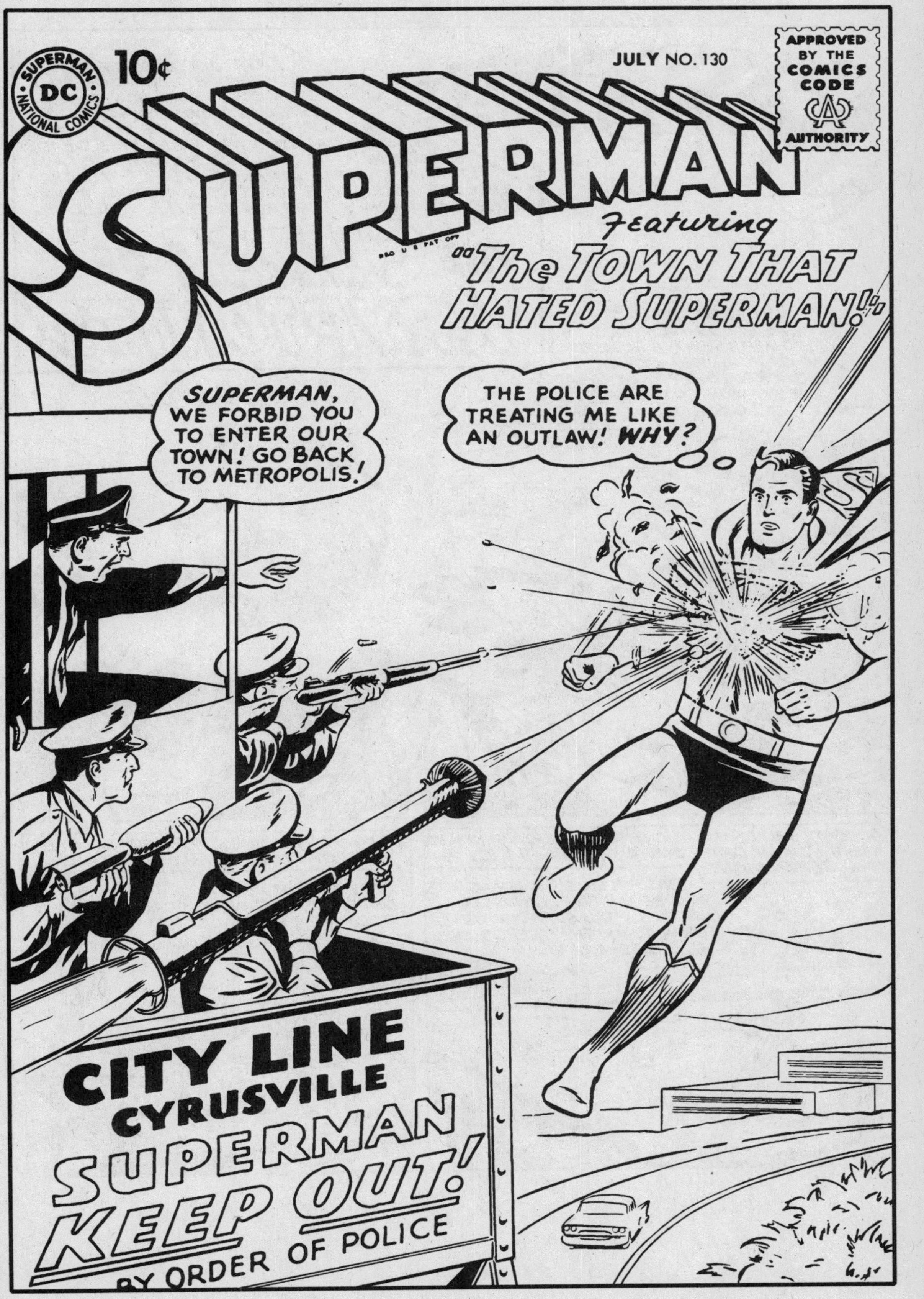
10¢
JULY NO. 130
APPROVED BY THE COMICS CODE AUTHORITY
SUPERMAN
Featuring
"The TOWN THAT HATED SUPERMAN!"
SUPERMAN, WE FORBID YOU TO ENTER OUR TOWN! GO BACK TO METROPOLIS!
THE POLICE ARE TREATING ME LIKE AN OUTLAW! WHY?
CITY LINE
CYRUSVILLE
SUPERMAN
KEEP OUT!
BY ORDER OF POLICE

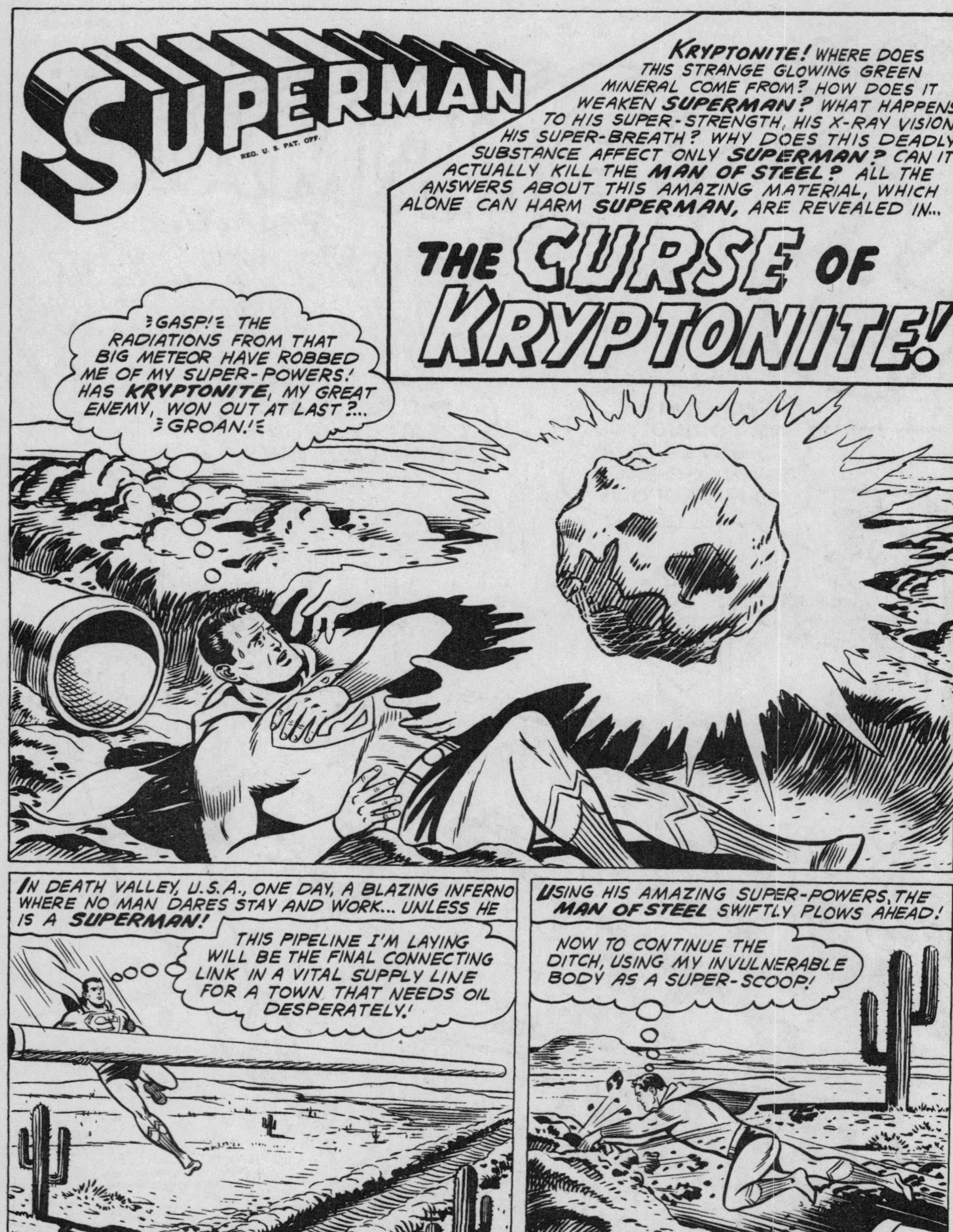
SUPERMAN
REG. U. S. PAT. OFF.
KRYPTONITE! WHERE DOES THIS STRANGE GLOWING GREEN MINERAL COME FROM? HOW DOES IT WEAKEN SUPERMAN? WHAT HAPPENS TO HIS SUPER-STRENGTH, HIS X-RAY VISION, HIS SUPER-BREATH? WHY DOES THIS DEADLY SUBSTANCE AFFECT ONLY SUPERMAN? CAN IT ACTUALLY KILL THE MAN OF STEEL? ALL THE ANSWERS ABOUT THIS AMAZING MATERIAL, WHICH ALONE CAN HARM SUPERMAN, ARE REVEALED IN...
THE CURSE OF KRYPTONITE!
GASP! THE RADIATIONS FROM THAT BIG METEOR HAVE ROBBED ME OF MY SUPER-POWERS! HAS KRYPTONITE, MY GREAT ENEMY, WON OUT AT LAST?... GROAN!
IN DEATH VALLEY, U.S.A., ONE DAY, A BLAZING INFERNO WHERE NO MAN DARES STAY AND WORK... UNLESS HE IS A SUPERMAN!
THIS PIPELINE I'M LAYING WILL BE THE FINAL CONNECTING LINK IN A VITAL SUPPLY LINE FOR A TOWN THAT NEEDS OIL DESPERATELY!
USING HIS AMAZING SUPER-POWERS, THE MAN OF STEEL SWIFTLY PLOWS AHEAD!
NOW TO CONTINUE THE DITCH, USING MY INVULNERABLE BODY AS A SUPER-SCOOP!

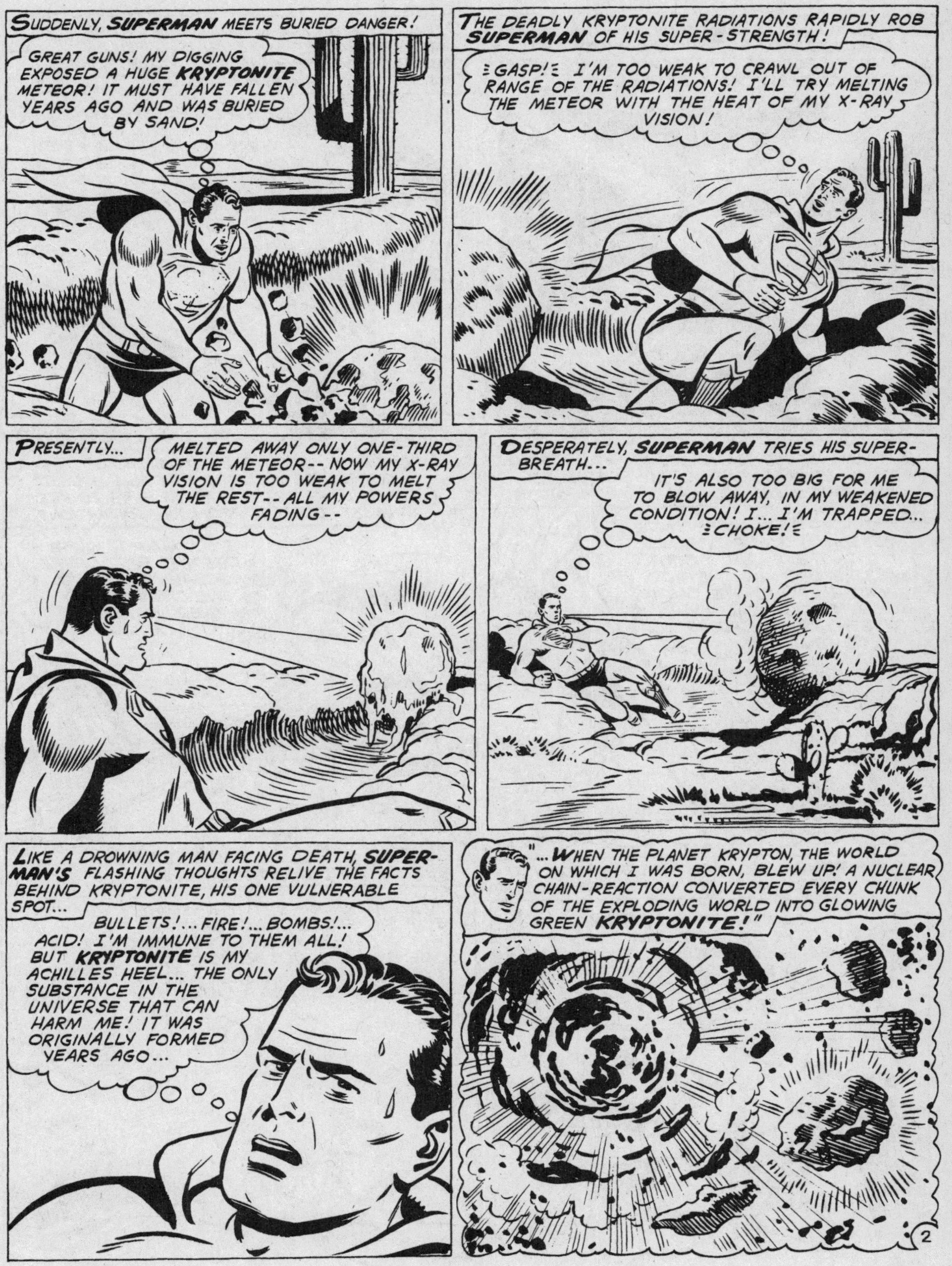
SUDDENLY, SUPERMAN MEETS BURIED DANGER!
GREAT GUNS! MY DIGGING EXPOSED A HUGE KRYPTONITE METEOR! IT MUST HAVE FALLEN YEARS AGO AND WAS BURIED BY SAND!
THE DEADLY KRYPTONITE RADIATIONS RAPIDLY ROB SUPERMAN OF HIS SUPER-STRENGTH!
GASP! I'M TOO WEAK TO CRAWL OUT OF RANGE OF THE RADIATIONS! I'LL TRY MELTING THE METEOR WITH THE HEAT OF MY X-RAY VISION!
PRESENTLY...
MELTED AWAY ONLY ONE-THIRD OF THE METEOR-- NOW MY X-RAY VISION IS TOO WEAK TO MELT THE REST-- ALL MY POWERS FADING--
DESPERATELY, SUPERMAN TRIES HIS SUPER-BREATH...
IT'S ALSO TOO BIG FOR ME TO BLOW AWAY, IN MY WEAKENED CONDITION! I... I'M TRAPPED... CHOKE!
LIKE A DROWNING MAN FACING DEATH, SUPERMAN'S FLASHING THOUGHTS RELIVE THE FACTS BEHIND KRYPTONITE, HIS ONE VULNERABLE SPOT...
BULLETS!... FIRE!... BOMBS!... ACID! I'M IMMUNE TO THEM ALL! BUT KRYPTONITE IS MY ACHILLES HEEL... THE ONLY SUBSTANCE IN THE UNIVERSE THAT CAN HARM ME! IT WAS ORIGINALLY FORMED YEARS AGO...
"...WHEN THE PLANET KRYPTON, THE WORLD ON WHICH I WAS BORN, BLEW UP! A NUCLEAR CHAIN-REACTION CONVERTED EVERY CHUNK OF THE EXPLODING WORLD INTO GLOWING GREEN KRYPTONITE!"
2

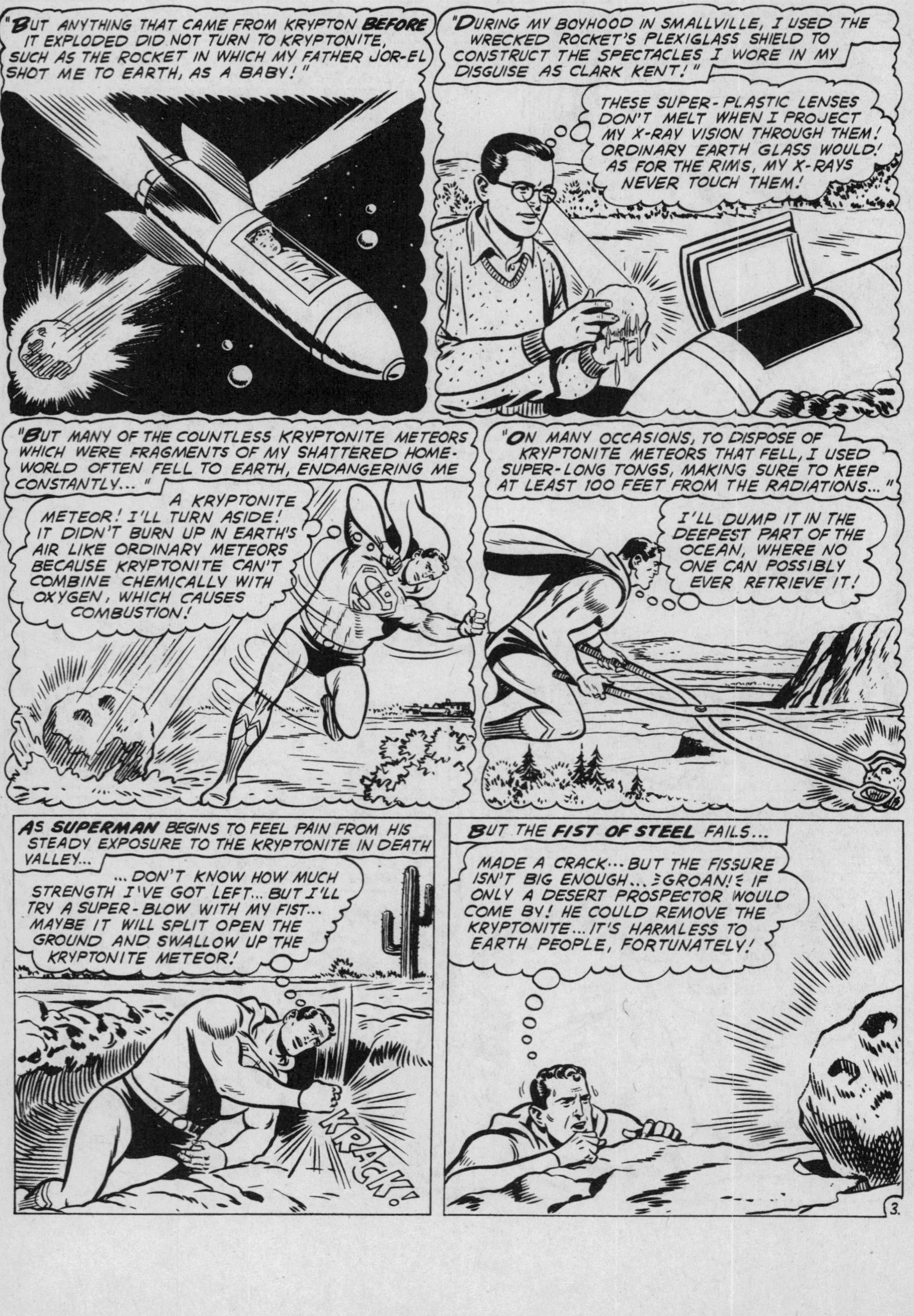
"BUT ANYTHING THAT CAME FROM KRYPTON BEFORE IT EXPLODED DID NOT TURN TO KRYPTONITE, SUCH AS THE ROCKET IN WHICH MY FATHER JOR-EL SHOT ME TO EARTH, AS A BABY!"
"DURING MY BOYHOOD IN SMALLVILLE, I USED THE WRECKED ROCKET'S PLEXIGLASS SHIELD TO CONSTRUCT THE SPECTACLES I WORE IN MY DISGUISE AS CLARK KENT!"
THESE SUPER-PLASTIC LENSES DON'T MELT WHEN I PROJECT MY X-RAY VISION THROUGH THEM! ORDINARY EARTH GLASS WOULD! AS FOR THE RIMS, MY X-RAYS NEVER TOUCH THEM!
"BUT MANY OF THE COUNTLESS KRYPTONITE METEORS WHICH WERE FRAGMENTS OF MY SHATTERED HOME-WORLD OFTEN FELL TO EARTH, ENDANGERING ME CONSTANTLY..."
A KRYPTONITE METEOR! I'LL TURN ASIDE! IT DIDN'T BURN UP IN EARTH'S AIR LIKE ORDINARY METEORS BECAUSE KRYPTONITE CAN'T COMBINE CHEMICALLY WITH OXYGEN, WHICH CAUSES COMBUSTION!
"ON MANY OCCASIONS, TO DISPOSE OF KRYPTONITE METEORS THAT FELL, I USED SUPER-LONG TONGS, MAKING SURE TO KEEP AT LEAST 100 FEET FROM THE RADIATIONS..."
I'LL DUMP IT IN THE DEEPEST PART OF THE OCEAN, WHERE NO ONE CAN POSSIBLY EVER RETRIEVE IT!
AS SUPERMAN BEGINS TO FEEL PAIN FROM HIS STEADY EXPOSURE TO THE KRYPTONITE IN DEATH VALLEY...
...DON'T KNOW HOW MUCH STRENGTH I'VE GOT LEFT... BUT I'LL TRY A SUPER-BLOW WITH MY FIST... MAYBE IT WILL SPLIT OPEN THE GROUND AND SWALLOW UP THE KRYPTONITE METEOR!
KRACK!
BUT THE FIST OF STEEL FAILS...
MADE A CRACK... BUT THE FISSURE ISN'T BIG ENOUGH... GROAN! IF ONLY A DESERT PROSPECTOR WOULD COME BY! HE COULD REMOVE THE KRYPTONITE... IT'S HARMLESS TO EARTH PEOPLE, FORTUNATELY!
3.

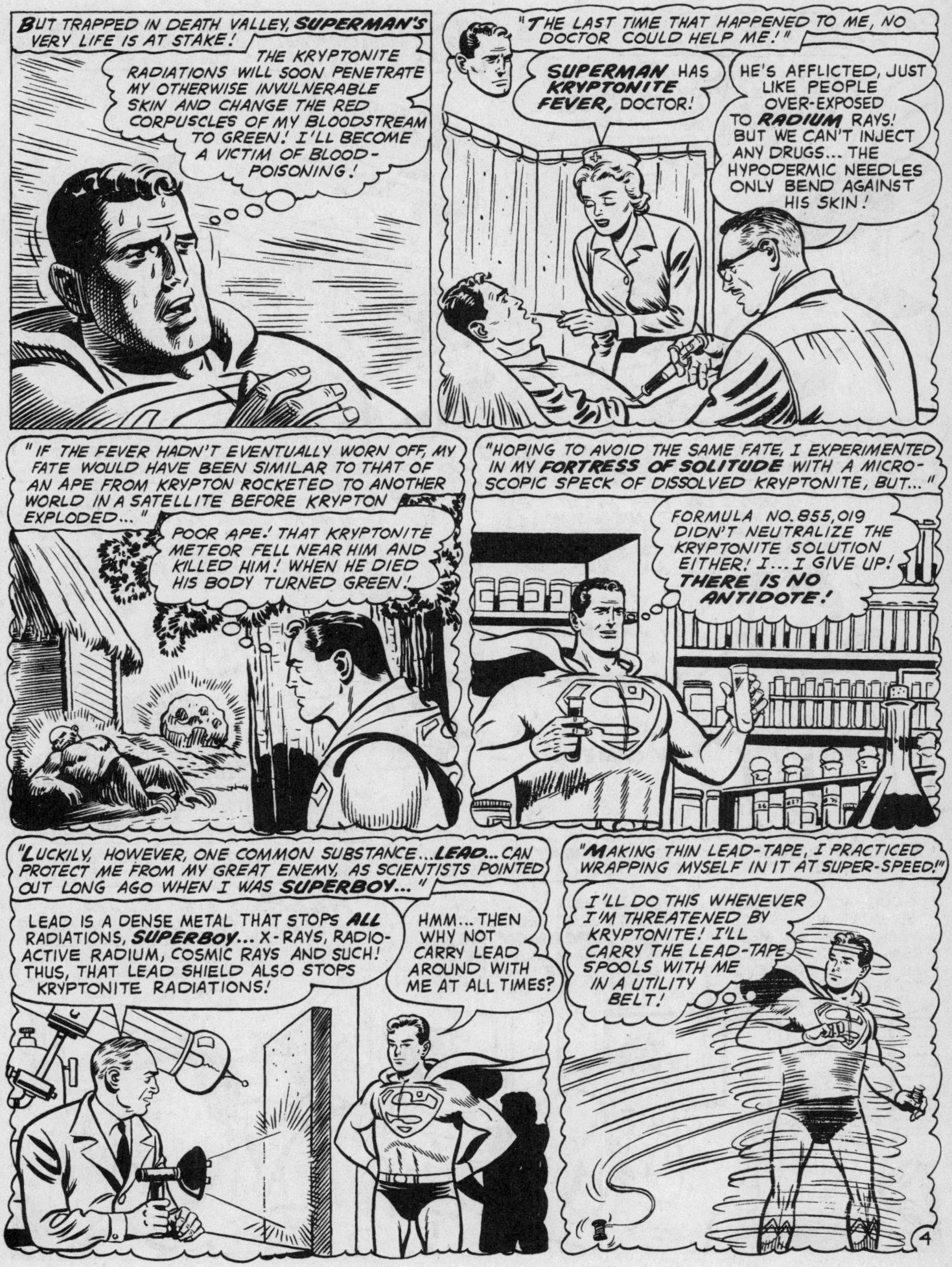
BUT TRAPPED IN DEATH VALLEY, SUPERMAN'S VERY LIFE IS AT STAKE!
THE KRYPTONITE RADIATIONS WILL SOON PENETRATE MY OTHERWISE INVULNERABLE SKIN AND CHANGE THE RED CORPUSCLES OF MY BLOODSTREAM TO GREEN! I'LL BECOME A VICTIM OF BLOOD-POISONING!
"THE LAST TIME THAT HAPPENED TO ME, NO DOCTOR COULD HELP ME!"
SUPERMAN HAS KRYPTONITE FEVER, DOCTOR!
HE'S AFFLICTED, JUST LIKE PEOPLE OVER-EXPOSED TO RADIUM RAYS! BUT WE CAN'T INJECT ANY DRUGS... THE HYPODERMIC NEEDLES ONLY BEND AGAINST HIS SKIN!
"IF THE FEVER HADN'T EVENTUALLY WORN OFF, MY FATE WOULD HAVE BEEN SIMILAR TO THAT OF AN APE FROM KRYPTON ROCKETED TO ANOTHER WORLD IN A SATELLITE BEFORE KRYPTON EXPLODED..."
POOR APE! THAT KRYPTONITE METEOR FELL NEAR HIM AND KILLED HIM! WHEN HE DIED HIS BODY TURNED GREEN!
"HOPING TO AVOID THE SAME FATE, I EXPERIMENTED IN MY FORTRESS OF SOLITUDE WITH A MICROSCOPIC SPECK OF DISSOLVED KRYPTONITE, BUT..."
FORMULA NO. 855,019 DIDN'T NEUTRALIZE THE KRYPTONITE SOLUTION EITHER! I... I GIVE UP! THERE IS NO ANTIDOTE!
"LUCKILY, HOWEVER, ONE COMMON SUBSTANCE...LEAD...CAN PROTECT ME FROM MY GREAT ENEMY, AS SCIENTISTS POINTED OUT LONG AGO WHEN I WAS SUPERBOY..."
LEAD IS A DENSE METAL THAT STOPS ALL RADIATIONS, SUPERBOY... X-RAYS, RADIO-ACTIVE RADIUM, COSMIC RAYS AND SUCH! THUS, THAT LEAD SHIELD ALSO STOPS KRYPTONITE RADIATIONS!
HMM... THEN WHY NOT CARRY LEAD AROUND WITH ME AT ALL TIMES?
"MAKING THIN LEAD-TAPE, I PRACTICED WRAPPING MYSELF IN IT AT SUPER-SPEED!"
I'LL DO THIS WHENEVER I'M THREATENED BY KRYPTONITE! I'LL CARRY THE LEAD-TAPE SPOOLS WITH ME IN A UTILITY BELT!
4

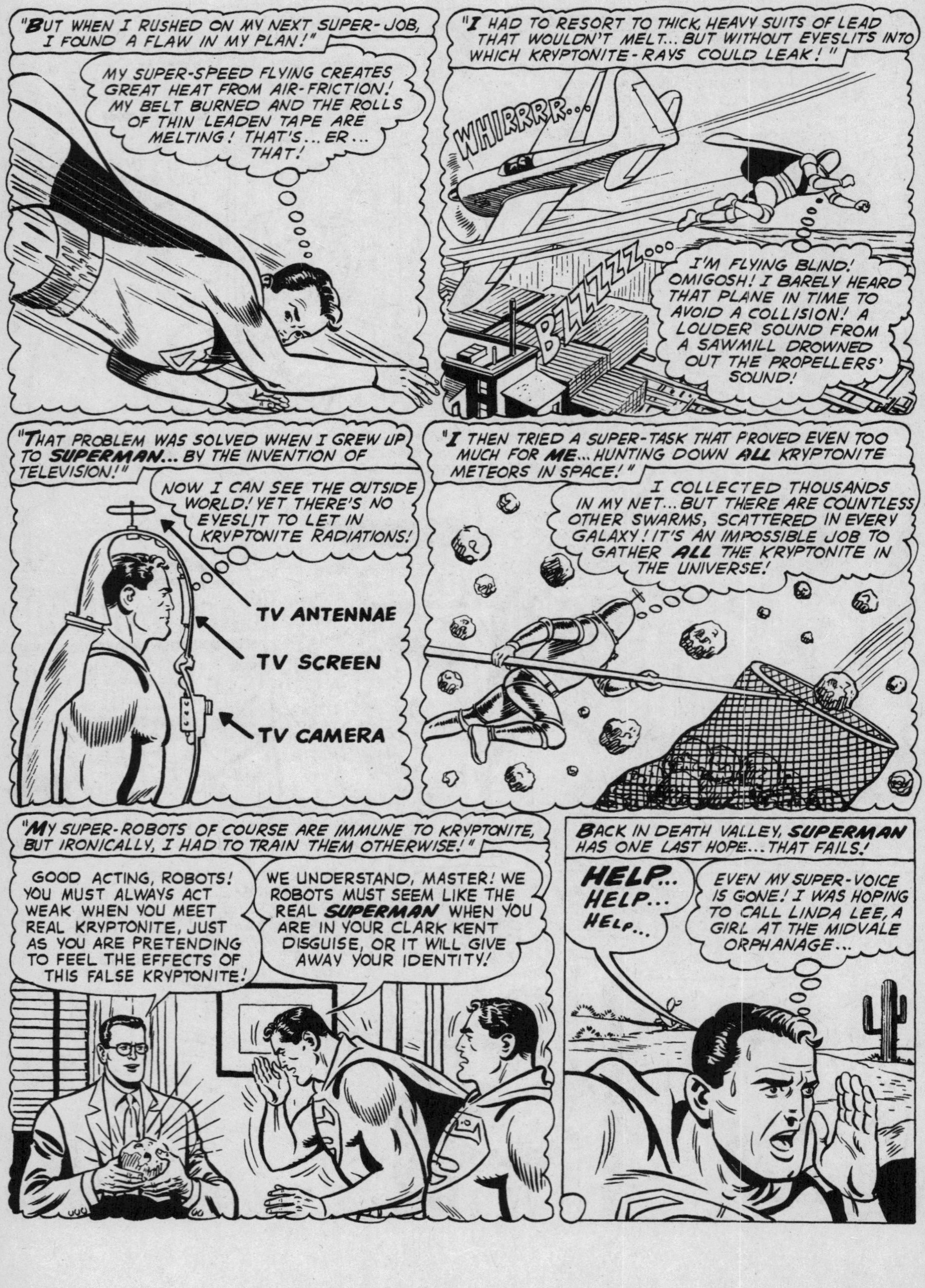
"BUT WHEN I RUSHED ON MY NEXT SUPER-JOB, I FOUND A FLAW IN MY PLAN!"
MY SUPER-SPEED FLYING CREATES GREAT HEAT FROM AIR-FRICTION! MY BELT BURNED AND THE ROLLS OF THIN LEADEN TAPE ARE MELTING! THAT'S... ER... THAT!
"I HAD TO RESORT TO THICK, HEAVY SUITS OF LEAD THAT WOULDN'T MELT... BUT WITHOUT EYESLITS INTO WHICH KRYPTONITE-RAYS COULD LEAK!"
WHIRRRR...
BZZZZZ...
I'M FLYING BLIND! OMIGOSH! I BARELY HEARD THAT PLANE IN TIME TO AVOID A COLLISION! A LOUDER SOUND FROM A SAWMILL DROWNED OUT THE PROPELLERS' SOUND!
"THAT PROBLEM WAS SOLVED WHEN I GREW UP TO SUPERMAN... BY THE INVENTION OF TELEVISION!"
NOW I CAN SEE THE OUTSIDE WORLD! YET THERE'S NO EYESLIT TO LET IN KRYPTONITE RADIATIONS!
TV ANTENNAE
TV SCREEN
TV CAMERA
"I THEN TRIED A SUPER-TASK THAT PROVED EVEN TOO MUCH FOR ME... HUNTING DOWN ALL KRYPTONITE METEORS IN SPACE!"
I COLLECTED THOUSANDS IN MY NET... BUT THERE ARE COUNTLESS OTHER SWARMS, SCATTERED IN EVERY GALAXY! IT'S AN IMPOSSIBLE JOB TO GATHER ALL THE KRYPTONITE IN THE UNIVERSE!
"MY SUPER-ROBOTS OF COURSE ARE IMMUNE TO KRYPTONITE, BUT IRONICALLY, I HAD TO TRAIN THEM OTHERWISE!"
GOOD ACTING, ROBOTS! YOU MUST ALWAYS ACT WEAK WHEN YOU MEET REAL KRYPTONITE, JUST AS YOU ARE PRETENDING TO FEEL THE EFFECTS OF THIS FALSE KRYPTONITE!
WE UNDERSTAND, MASTER! WE ROBOTS MUST SEEM LIKE THE REAL SUPERMAN WHEN YOU ARE IN YOUR CLARK KENT DISGUISE, OR IT WILL GIVE AWAY YOUR IDENTITY!
BACK IN DEATH VALLEY, SUPERMAN HAS ONE LAST HOPE... THAT FAILS!
HELP... HELP... HELP...
EVEN MY SUPER-VOICE IS GONE! I WAS HOPING TO CALL LINDA LEE, A GIRL AT THE MIDVALE ORPHANAGE...

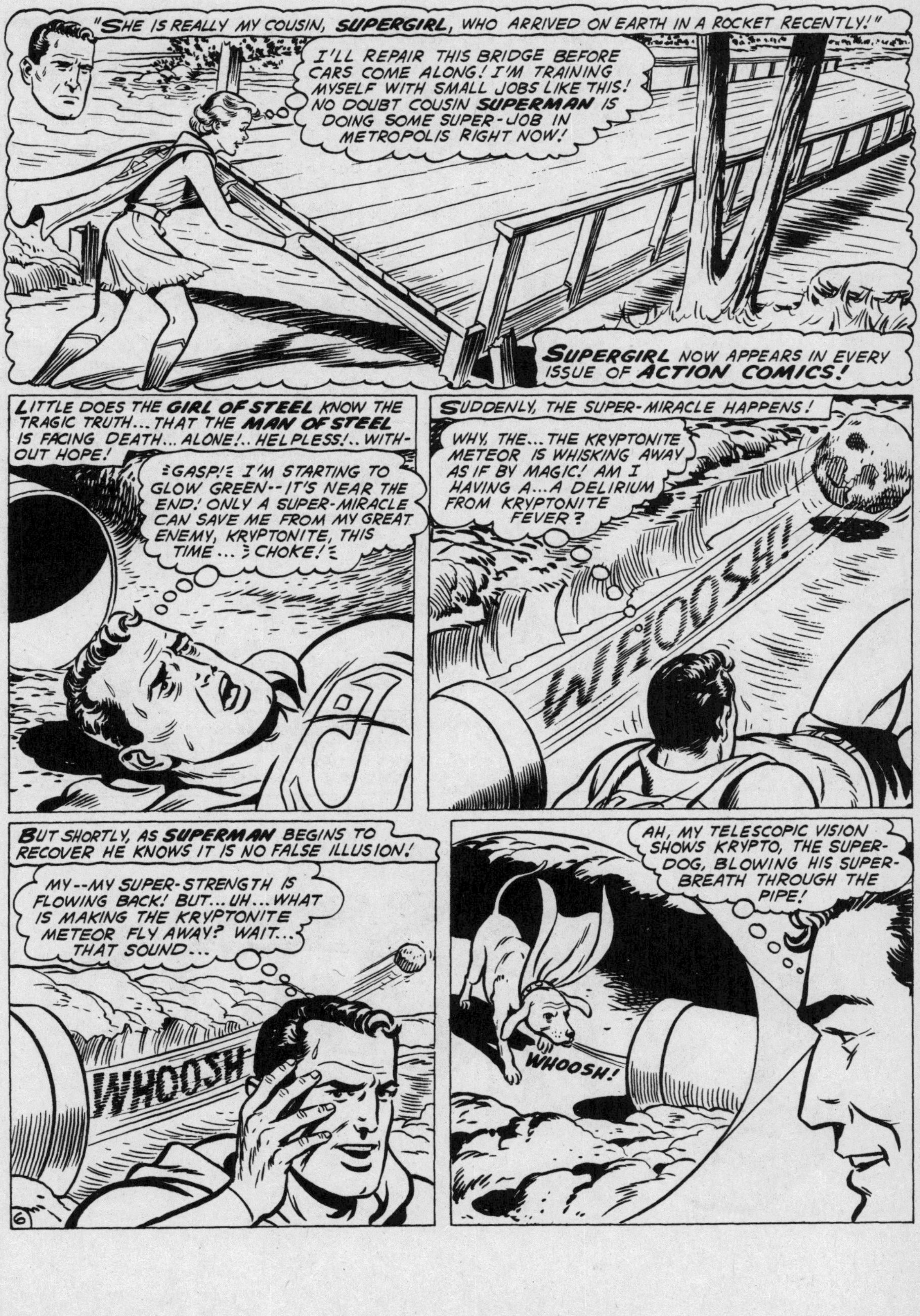
"SHE IS REALLY MY COUSIN, SUPERGIRL, WHO ARRIVED ON EARTH IN A ROCKET RECENTLY!"
I'LL REPAIR THIS BRIDGE BEFORE CARS COME ALONG! I'M TRAINING MYSELF WITH SMALL JOBS LIKE THIS! NO DOUBT COUSIN SUPERMAN IS DOING SOME SUPER-JOB IN METROPOLIS RIGHT NOW!
SUPERGIRL NOW APPEARS IN EVERY ISSUE OF ACTION COMICS!
LITTLE DOES THE GIRL OF STEEL KNOW THE TRAGIC TRUTH... THAT THE MAN OF STEEL IS FACING DEATH... ALONE!.. HELPLESS!.. WITHOUT HOPE!
GASP! I'M STARTING TO GLOW GREEN--IT'S NEAR THE END! ONLY A SUPER-MIRACLE CAN SAVE ME FROM MY GREAT ENEMY, KRYPTONITE, THIS TIME... CHOKE!
SUDDENLY, THE SUPER-MIRACLE HAPPENS!
WHY, THE... THE KRYPTONITE METEOR IS WHISKING AWAY AS IF BY MAGIC! AM I HAVING A... A DELIRIUM FROM KRYPTONITE FEVER?
WHOOSH!
BUT SHORTLY, AS SUPERMAN BEGINS TO RECOVER HE KNOWS IT IS NO FALSE ILLUSION!
MY--MY SUPER-STRENGTH IS FLOWING BACK! BUT... UH... WHAT IS MAKING THE KRYPTONITE METEOR FLY AWAY? WAIT... THAT SOUND...
WHOOSH
6
AH, MY TELESCOPIC VISION SHOWS KRYPTO, THE SUPER-DOG, BLOWING HIS SUPER-BREATH THROUGH THE PIPE!
WHOOSH!

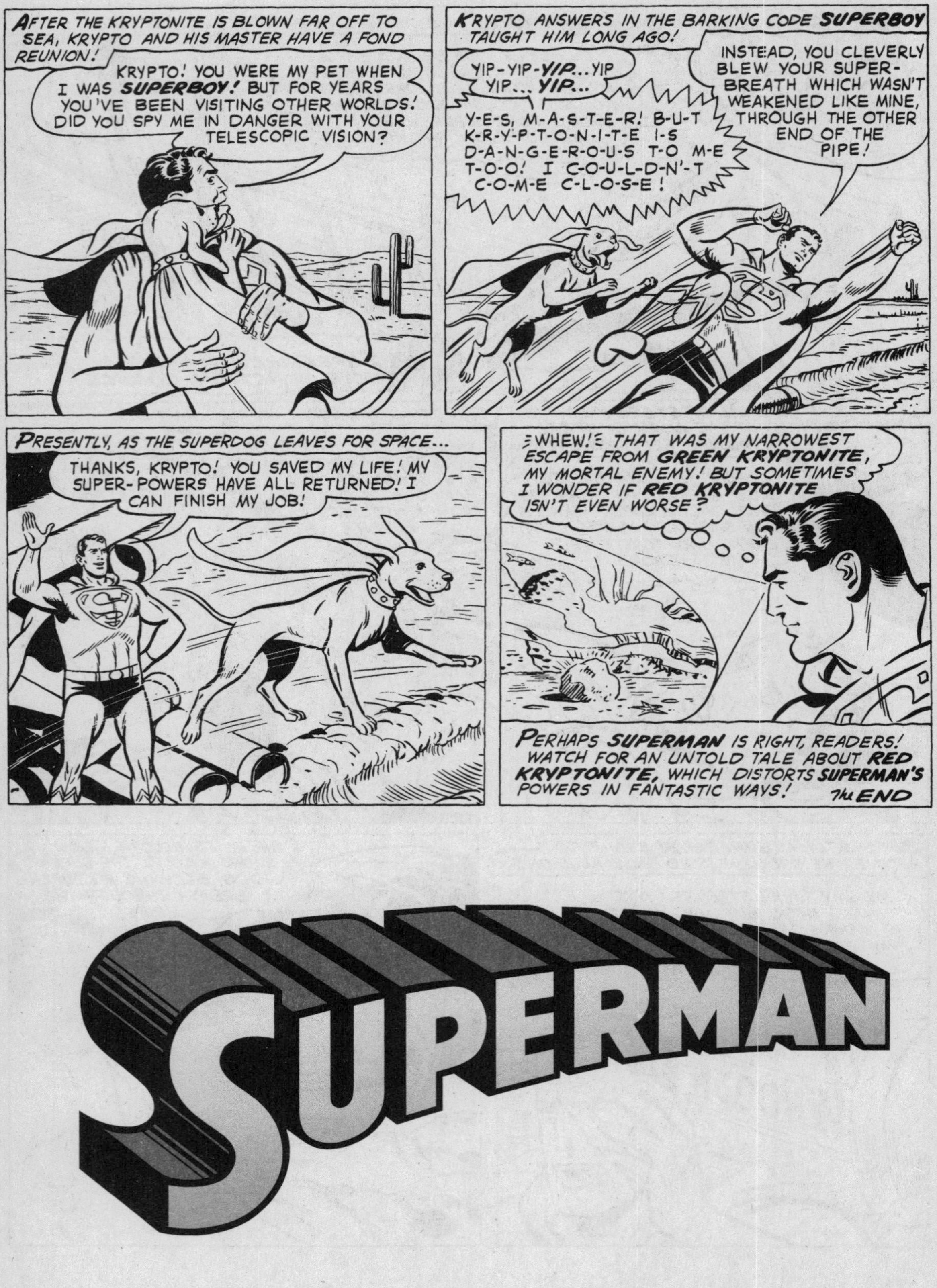
AFTER THE KRYPTONITE IS BLOWN FAR OFF TO SEA, KRYPTO AND HIS MASTER HAVE A FOND REUNION!
KRYPTO! YOU WERE MY PET WHEN I WAS SUPERBOY! BUT FOR YEARS YOU'VE BEEN VISITING OTHER WORLDS! DID YOU SPY ME IN DANGER WITH YOUR TELESCOPIC VISION?
KRYPTO ANSWERS IN THE BARKING CODE SUPERBOY TAUGHT HIM LONG AGO!
YIP-YIP-YIP...YIP YIP... YIP...
Y-E-S, M-A-S-T-E-R! B-U-T K-R-Y-P-T-O-N-I-T-E I-S D-A-N-G-E-R-O-U-S T-O M-E T-O-O! I C-O-U-L-D-N'-T C-O-M-E C-L-O-S-E!
INSTEAD, YOU CLEVERLY BLEW YOUR SUPER-BREATH WHICH WASN'T WEAKENED LIKE MINE, THROUGH THE OTHER END OF THE PIPE!
PRESENTLY, AS THE SUPERDOG LEAVES FOR SPACE...
THANKS, KRYPTO! YOU SAVED MY LIFE! MY SUPER-POWERS HAVE ALL RETURNED! I CAN FINISH MY JOB!
WHEW! THAT WAS MY NARROWEST ESCAPE FROM GREEN KRYPTONITE, MY MORTAL ENEMY! BUT SOMETIMES I WONDER IF RED KRYPTONITE ISN'T EVEN WORSE?
PERHAPS SUPERMAN IS RIGHT, READERS! WATCH FOR AN UNTOLD TALE ABOUT RED KRYPTONITE, WHICH DISTORTS SUPERMAN'S POWERS IN FANTASTIC WAYS!
The END

SUPERMAN

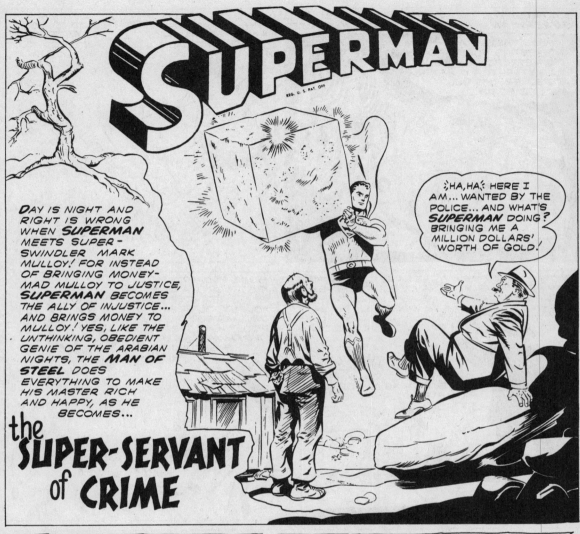

SUPERMAN

REG. U. S. PAT. OFF

DAY IS NIGHT AND RIGHT IS WRONG WHEN *SUPERMAN* MEETS SUPER-SWINDLER MARK MULLOY! FOR INSTEAD OF BRINGING MONEY-MAD MULLOY TO JUSTICE, *SUPERMAN* BECOMES THE ALLY OF INJUSTICE... AND BRINGS MONEY TO MULLOY! YES, LIKE THE UNTHINKING, OBEDIENT GENIE OF THE ARABIAN NIGHTS, THE *MAN OF STEEL* DOES EVERYTHING TO MAKE HIS MASTER RICH AND HAPPY, AS HE BECOMES...

the SUPER-SERVANT of CRIME

"HA, HA" HERE I AM... WANTED BY THE POLICE... AND WHAT'S *SUPERMAN* DOING? BRINGING ME A MILLION DOLLARS' WORTH OF GOLD!

ONE AFTERNOON, AT THE *DAILY PLANET* OFFICE, AS EDITOR PERRY WHITE EXAMINES A FUND-RAISING REPORT...

THE *PLANET* CHARITY FUND IS $200,000 SHY OF ITS GOAL! WHAT'LL WE DO, *SUPERMAN*? WE CAN'T RAISE $200,000 OVERNIGHT!

MAYBE WE *CAN*, PERRY! WAIT HERE! I'LL BE BACK SHORTLY!

SECONDS LATER, AS *SUPERMAN* REACHES A BARREN REGION OUTSIDE METROPOLIS...

I-IT'S *SUPERMAN*! HE'S BACK FOR MORE GOLD TO HELP SOME CHARITY DRIVE!

THIS IS MY SIXTH AND LAST VISIT! I'VE JUST ABOUT EXHAUSTED THE VEIN OF GOLD 50 MILES BELOW!

1

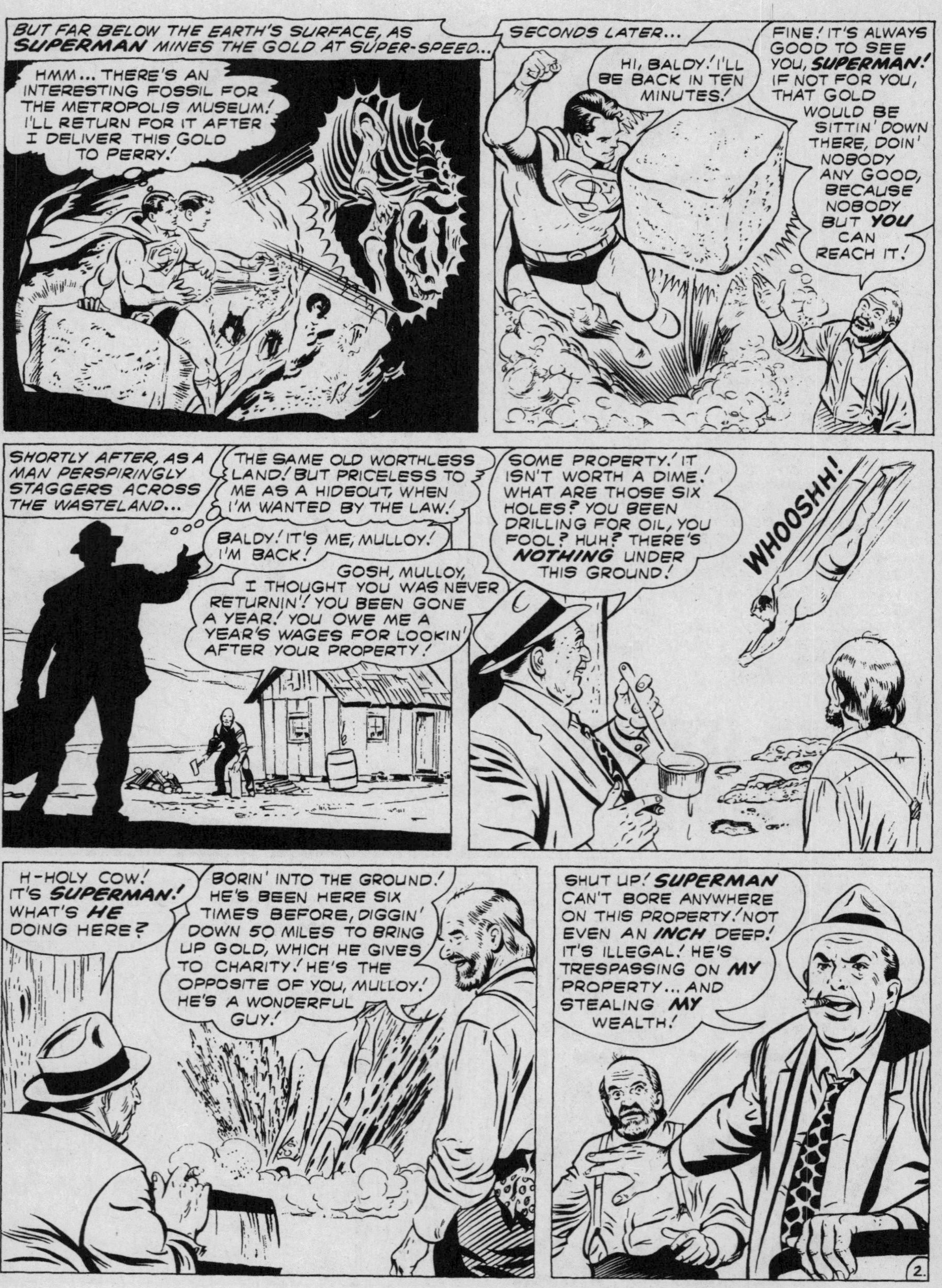
BUT FAR BELOW THE EARTH'S SURFACE, AS SUPERMAN MINES THE GOLD AT SUPER-SPEED...
HMM... THERE'S AN INTERESTING FOSSIL FOR THE METROPOLIS MUSEUM! I'LL RETURN FOR IT AFTER I DELIVER THIS GOLD TO PERRY!
SECONDS LATER...
HI, BALDY! I'LL BE BACK IN TEN MINUTES!
FINE! IT'S ALWAYS GOOD TO SEE YOU, SUPERMAN! IF NOT FOR YOU, THAT GOLD WOULD BE SITTIN' DOWN THERE, DOIN' NOBODY ANY GOOD, BECAUSE NOBODY BUT YOU CAN REACH IT!
SHORTLY AFTER, AS A MAN PERSPIRINGLY STAGGERS ACROSS THE WASTELAND...
THE SAME OLD WORTHLESS LAND! BUT PRICELESS TO ME AS A HIDEOUT, WHEN I'M WANTED BY THE LAW!
BALDY! IT'S ME, MULLOY! I'M BACK!
GOSH, MULLOY, I THOUGHT YOU WAS NEVER RETURNIN'! YOU BEEN GONE A YEAR! YOU OWE ME A YEAR'S WAGES FOR LOOKIN' AFTER YOUR PROPERTY!
SOME PROPERTY! IT ISN'T WORTH A DIME! WHAT ARE THOSE SIX HOLES? YOU BEEN DRILLING FOR OIL, YOU FOOL? HUH? THERE'S NOTHING UNDER THIS GROUND!
WHOOSHH!
H-HOLY COW! IT'S SUPERMAN! WHAT'S HE DOING HERE?
BORIN' INTO THE GROUND! HE'S BEEN HERE SIX TIMES BEFORE, DIGGIN' DOWN 50 MILES TO BRING UP GOLD, WHICH HE GIVES TO CHARITY! HE'S THE OPPOSITE OF YOU, MULLOY! HE'S A WONDERFUL GUY!
SHUT UP! SUPERMAN CAN'T BORE ANYWHERE ON THIS PROPERTY! NOT EVEN AN INCH DEEP! IT'S ILLEGAL! HE'S TRESPASSING ON MY PROPERTY... AND STEALING MY WEALTH!
2.

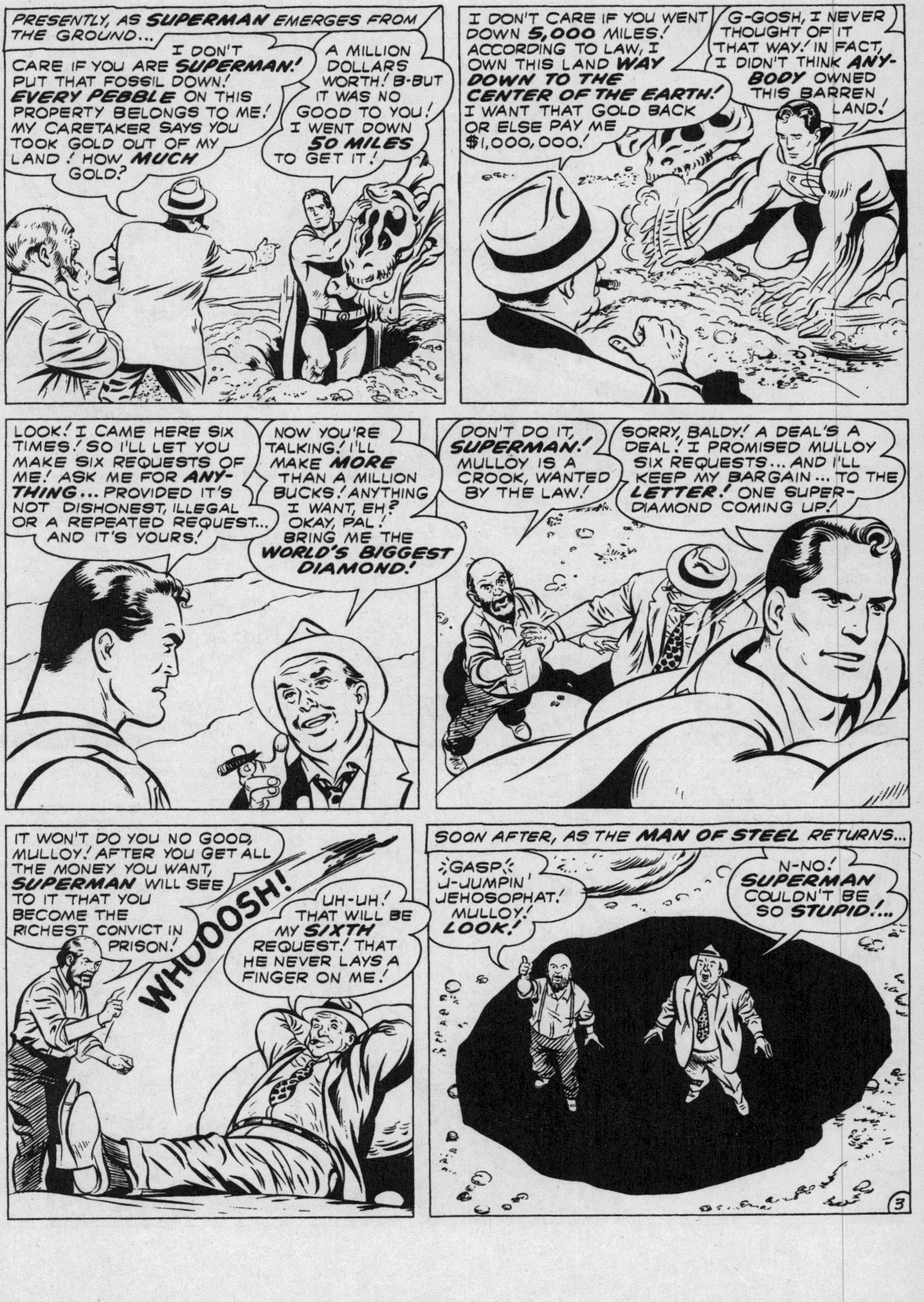
PRESENTLY, AS SUPERMAN EMERGES FROM THE GROUND...
I DON'T CARE IF YOU ARE SUPERMAN! PUT THAT FOSSIL DOWN! EVERY PEBBLE ON THIS PROPERTY BELONGS TO ME! MY CARETAKER SAYS YOU TOOK GOLD OUT OF MY LAND! HOW MUCH GOLD?
A MILLION DOLLARS WORTH! B-BUT IT WAS NO GOOD TO YOU! I WENT DOWN 50 MILES TO GET IT!
I DON'T CARE IF YOU WENT DOWN 5,000 MILES! ACCORDING TO LAW, I OWN THIS LAND WAY DOWN TO THE CENTER OF THE EARTH! I WANT THAT GOLD BACK OR ELSE PAY ME $1,000,000!
G-GOSH, I NEVER THOUGHT OF IT THAT WAY! IN FACT, I DIDN'T THINK ANYBODY OWNED THIS BARREN LAND!
LOOK! I CAME HERE SIX TIMES! SO I'LL LET YOU MAKE SIX REQUESTS OF ME! ASK ME FOR ANYTHING... PROVIDED IT'S NOT DISHONEST, ILLEGAL OR A REPEATED REQUEST... AND IT'S YOURS!
NOW YOU'RE TALKING! I'LL MAKE MORE THAN A MILLION BUCKS! ANYTHING I WANT, EH? OKAY, PAL! BRING ME THE WORLD'S BIGGEST DIAMOND!
DON'T DO IT, SUPERMAN! MULLOY IS A CROOK, WANTED BY THE LAW!
SORRY, BALDY! A DEAL'S A DEAL! I PROMISED MULLOY SIX REQUESTS... AND I'LL KEEP MY BARGAIN... TO THE LETTER! ONE SUPER-DIAMOND COMING UP!
IT WON'T DO YOU NO GOOD, MULLOY! AFTER YOU GET ALL THE MONEY YOU WANT, SUPERMAN WILL SEE TO IT THAT YOU BECOME THE RICHEST CONVICT IN PRISON!
WHOOOSH!
UH-UH! THAT WILL BE MY SIXTH REQUEST! THAT HE NEVER LAYS A FINGER ON ME!
SOON AFTER, AS THE MAN OF STEEL RETURNS...
GASP J-JUMPIN' JEHOSOPHAT! MULLOY! LOOK!
N-NO! SUPERMAN COULDN'T BE SO STUPID!...
3

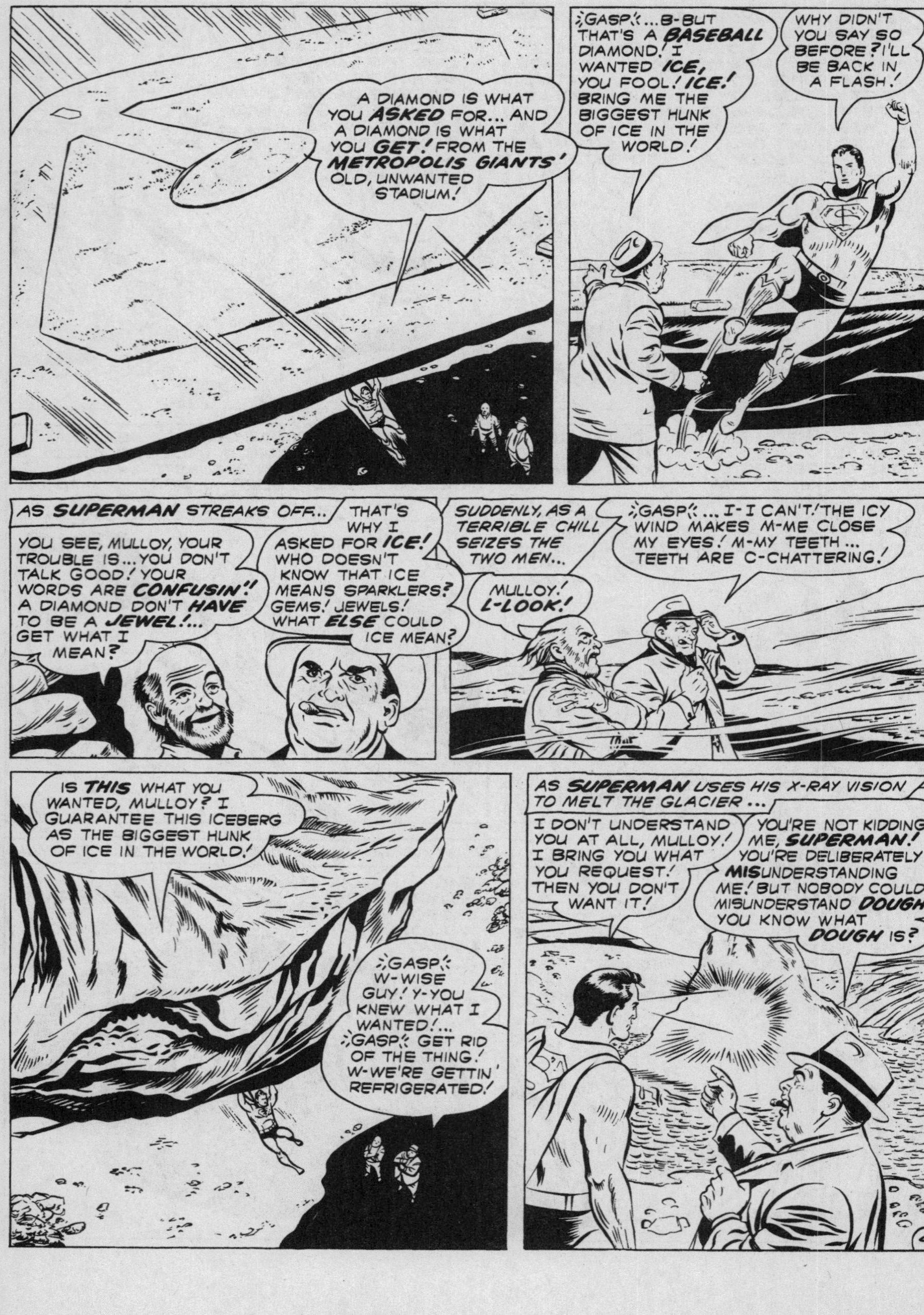
A DIAMOND IS WHAT YOU ASKED FOR... AND A DIAMOND IS WHAT YOU GET! FROM THE METROPOLIS GIANTS' OLD, UNWANTED STADIUM!
GASP ... B-BUT THAT'S A BASEBALL DIAMOND! I WANTED ICE, YOU FOOL! ICE! BRING ME THE BIGGEST HUNK OF ICE IN THE WORLD!
WHY DIDN'T YOU SAY SO BEFORE? I'LL BE BACK IN A FLASH!
AS SUPERMAN STREAKS OFF...
YOU SEE, MULLOY, YOUR TROUBLE IS... YOU DON'T TALK GOOD! YOUR WORDS ARE CONFUSIN'! A DIAMOND DON'T HAVE TO BE A JEWEL!... GET WHAT I MEAN?
THAT'S WHY I ASKED FOR ICE! WHO DOESN'T KNOW THAT ICE MEANS SPARKLERS? GEMS! JEWELS! WHAT ELSE COULD ICE MEAN?
SUDDENLY, AS A TERRIBLE CHILL SEIZES THE TWO MEN...
GASP ... I-I CAN'T! THE ICY WIND MAKES M-ME CLOSE MY EYES! M-MY TEETH ... TEETH ARE C-CHATTERING!
MULLOY! L-LOOK!
IS THIS WHAT YOU WANTED, MULLOY? I GUARANTEE THIS ICEBERG AS THE BIGGEST HUNK OF ICE IN THE WORLD!
GASP W-WISE GUY! Y-YOU KNEW WHAT I WANTED!... GASP GET RID OF THE THING! W-WE'RE GETTIN' REFRIGERATED!
AS SUPERMAN USES HIS X-RAY VISION TO MELT THE GLACIER ...
I DON'T UNDERSTAND YOU AT ALL, MULLOY! I BRING YOU WHAT YOU REQUEST! THEN YOU DON'T WANT IT!
YOU'RE NOT KIDDING ME, SUPERMAN! YOU'RE DELIBERATELY MISUNDERSTANDING ME! BUT NOBODY COULD MISUNDERSTAND DOUGH! YOU KNOW WHAT DOUGH IS?
4

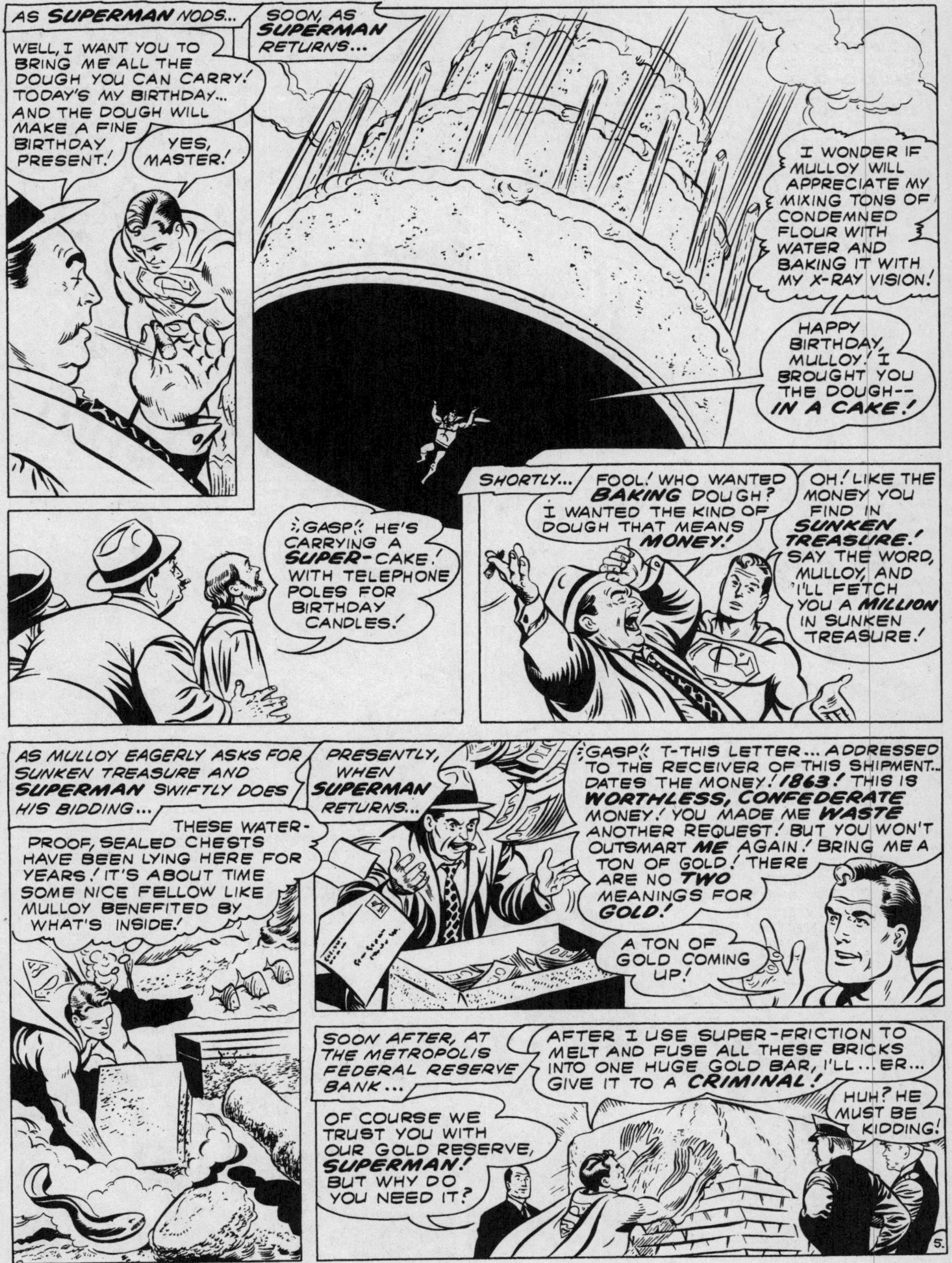
AS SUPERMAN NODS...
WELL, I WANT YOU TO BRING ME ALL THE DOUGH YOU CAN CARRY! TODAY'S MY BIRTHDAY... AND THE DOUGH WILL MAKE A FINE BIRTHDAY PRESENT!
YES, MASTER!
SOON, AS SUPERMAN RETURNS...
I WONDER IF MULLOY WILL APPRECIATE MY MIXING TONS OF CONDEMNED FLOUR WITH WATER AND BAKING IT WITH MY X-RAY VISION!
HAPPY BIRTHDAY, MULLOY! I BROUGHT YOU THE DOUGH-- IN A CAKE!
GASP! HE'S CARRYING A SUPER-CAKE! WITH TELEPHONE POLES FOR BIRTHDAY CANDLES!
SHORTLY...
FOOL! WHO WANTED BAKING DOUGH? I WANTED THE KIND OF DOUGH THAT MEANS MONEY!
OH! LIKE THE MONEY YOU FIND IN SUNKEN TREASURE! SAY THE WORD, MULLOY, AND I'LL FETCH YOU A MILLION IN SUNKEN TREASURE!
AS MULLOY EAGERLY ASKS FOR SUNKEN TREASURE AND SUPERMAN SWIFTLY DOES HIS BIDDING...
THESE WATER-PROOF, SEALED CHESTS HAVE BEEN LYING HERE FOR YEARS! IT'S ABOUT TIME SOME NICE FELLOW LIKE MULLOY BENEFITED BY WHAT'S INSIDE!
PRESENTLY, WHEN SUPERMAN RETURNS...
GASP! T-THIS LETTER... ADDRESSED TO THE RECEIVER OF THIS SHIPMENT... DATES THE MONEY! 1863! THIS IS WORTHLESS, CONFEDERATE MONEY! YOU MADE ME WASTE ANOTHER REQUEST! BUT YOU WON'T OUTSMART ME AGAIN! BRING ME A TON OF GOLD! THERE ARE NO TWO MEANINGS FOR GOLD!
A TON OF GOLD COMING UP!
SOON AFTER, AT THE METROPOLIS FEDERAL RESERVE BANK...
AFTER I USE SUPER-FRICTION TO MELT AND FUSE ALL THESE BRICKS INTO ONE HUGE GOLD BAR, I'LL... ER... GIVE IT TO A CRIMINAL!
OF COURSE WE TRUST YOU WITH OUR GOLD RESERVE, SUPERMAN! BUT WHY DO YOU NEED IT?
HUH? HE MUST BE KIDDING!
5.

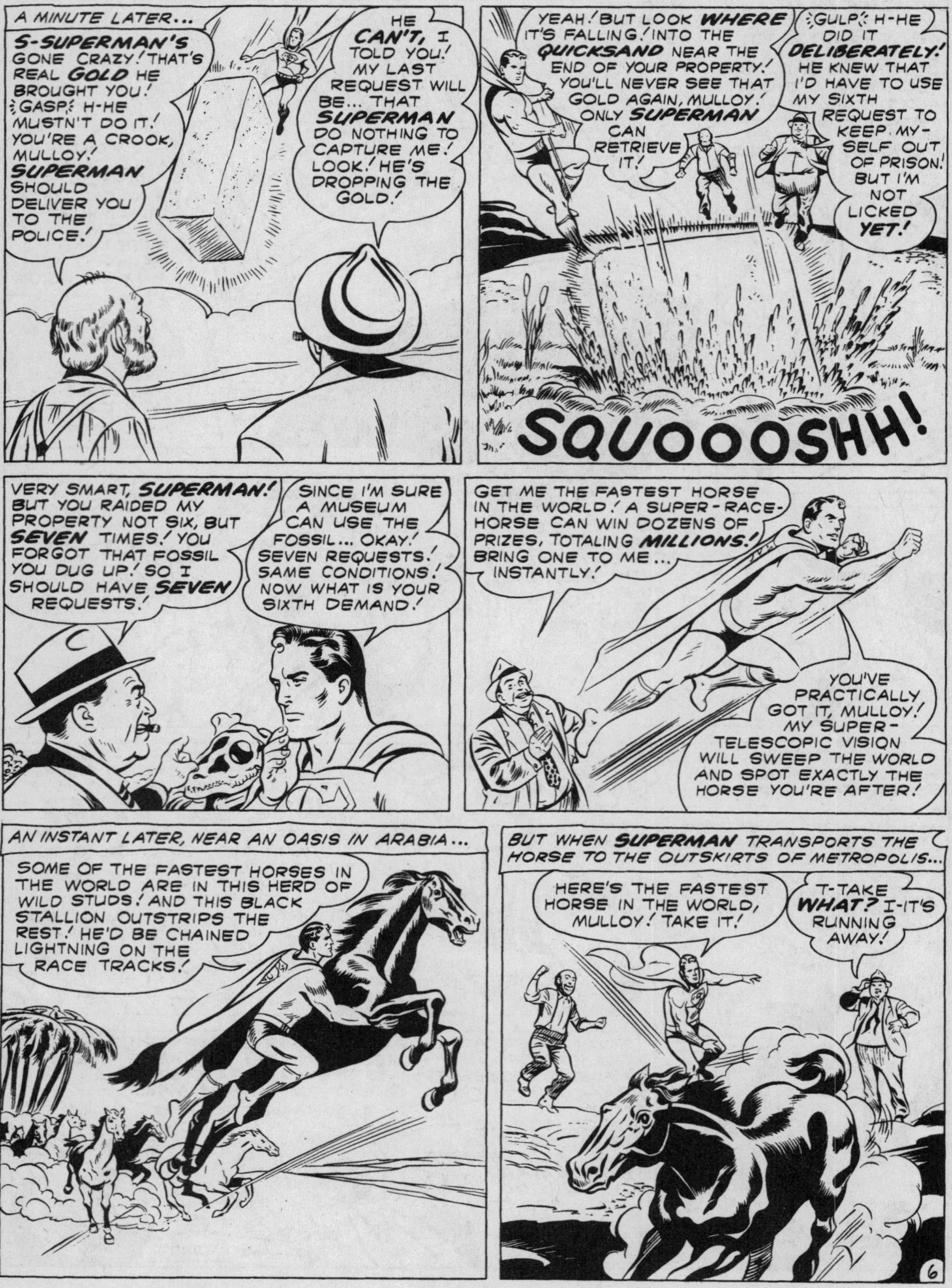
A MINUTE LATER...
S-SUPERMAN'S GONE CRAZY! THAT'S REAL GOLD HE BROUGHT YOU! GASP! H-HE MUSTN'T DO IT! YOU'RE A CROOK, MULLOY! SUPERMAN SHOULD DELIVER YOU TO THE POLICE!
HE CAN'T, I TOLD YOU! MY LAST REQUEST WILL BE... THAT SUPERMAN DO NOTHING TO CAPTURE ME! LOOK! HE'S DROPPING THE GOLD!
YEAH! BUT LOOK WHERE IT'S FALLING! INTO THE QUICKSAND NEAR THE END OF YOUR PROPERTY! YOU'LL NEVER SEE THAT GOLD AGAIN, MULLOY! ONLY SUPERMAN CAN RETRIEVE IT!
GULP! H-HE DID IT DELIBERATELY! HE KNEW THAT I'D HAVE TO USE MY SIXTH REQUEST TO KEEP MYSELF OUT OF PRISON! BUT I'M NOT LICKED YET!
SQUOOOSHH!
VERY SMART, SUPERMAN! BUT YOU RAIDED MY PROPERTY NOT SIX, BUT SEVEN TIMES! YOU FORGOT THAT FOSSIL YOU DUG UP! SO I SHOULD HAVE SEVEN REQUESTS!
SINCE I'M SURE A MUSEUM CAN USE THE FOSSIL... OKAY! SEVEN REQUESTS! SAME CONDITIONS! NOW WHAT IS YOUR SIXTH DEMAND!
GET ME THE FASTEST HORSE IN THE WORLD! A SUPER-RACE-HORSE CAN WIN DOZENS OF PRIZES, TOTALING MILLIONS! BRING ONE TO ME... INSTANTLY!
YOU'VE PRACTICALLY GOT IT, MULLOY! MY SUPER-TELESCOPIC VISION WILL SWEEP THE WORLD AND SPOT EXACTLY THE HORSE YOU'RE AFTER!
AN INSTANT LATER, NEAR AN OASIS IN ARABIA...
SOME OF THE FASTEST HORSES IN THE WORLD ARE IN THIS HERD OF WILD STUDS! AND THIS BLACK STALLION OUTSTRIPS THE REST! HE'D BE CHAINED LIGHTNING ON THE RACE TRACKS!
BUT WHEN SUPERMAN TRANSPORTS THE HORSE TO THE OUTSKIRTS OF METROPOLIS...
HERE'S THE FASTEST HORSE IN THE WORLD, MULLOY! TAKE IT!
T-TAKE WHAT? I-IT'S RUNNING AWAY!
6

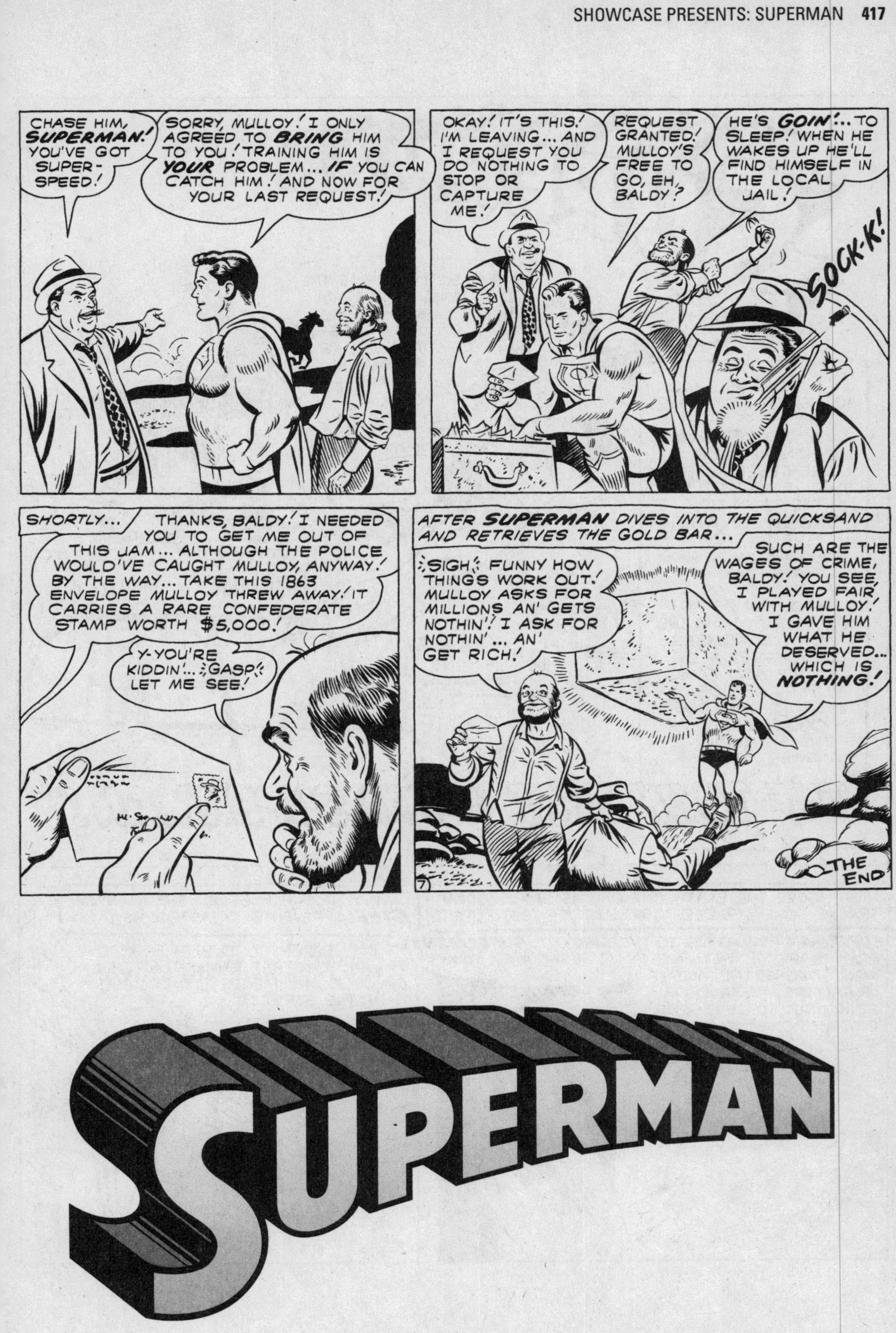
CHASE HIM, SUPERMAN! YOU'VE GOT SUPER-SPEED!
SORRY, MULLOY! I ONLY AGREED TO BRING HIM TO YOU! TRAINING HIM IS YOUR PROBLEM... IF YOU CAN CATCH HIM! AND NOW FOR YOUR LAST REQUEST!
OKAY! IT'S THIS! I'M LEAVING... AND I REQUEST YOU DO NOTHING TO STOP OR CAPTURE ME!
REQUEST GRANTED! MULLOY'S FREE TO GO, EH, BALDY?
HE'S GOIN'... TO SLEEP! WHEN HE WAKES UP HE'LL FIND HIMSELF IN THE LOCAL JAIL!
SOCK-K!
SHORTLY...
THANKS, BALDY! I NEEDED YOU TO GET ME OUT OF THIS JAM... ALTHOUGH THE POLICE WOULD'VE CAUGHT MULLOY, ANYWAY! BY THE WAY... TAKE THIS 1863 ENVELOPE MULLOY THREW AWAY! IT CARRIES A RARE CONFEDERATE STAMP WORTH $5,000!
Y-YOU'RE KIDDIN'... GASP! LET ME SEE!
AFTER SUPERMAN DIVES INTO THE QUICKSAND AND RETRIEVES THE GOLD BAR...
SIGH! FUNNY HOW THINGS WORK OUT! MULLOY ASKS FOR MILLIONS AN' GETS NOTHIN'! I ASK FOR NOTHIN'... AN' GET RICH!
SUCH ARE THE WAGES OF CRIME, BALDY! YOU SEE, I PLAYED FAIR WITH MULLOY! I GAVE HIM WHAT HE DESERVED... WHICH IS NOTHING!
7
THE END

SUPERMAN

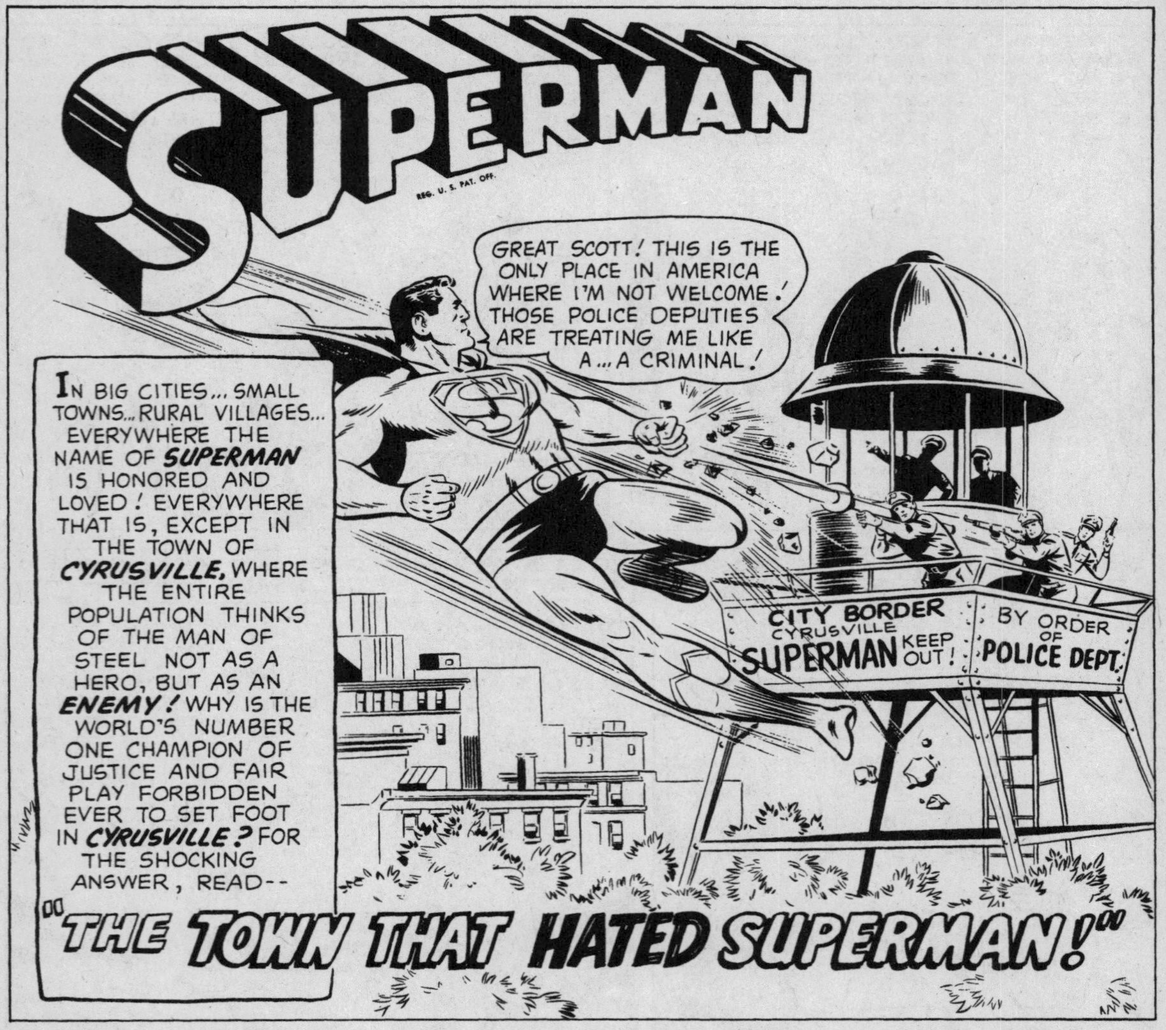
SUPERMAN
REG. U.S. PAT. OFF.
IN BIG CITIES... SMALL TOWNS... RURAL VILLAGES... EVERYWHERE THE NAME OF SUPERMAN IS HONORED AND LOVED! EVERYWHERE THAT IS, EXCEPT IN THE TOWN OF CYRUSVILLE, WHERE THE ENTIRE POPULATION THINKS OF THE MAN OF STEEL NOT AS A HERO, BUT AS AN ENEMY! WHY IS THE WORLD'S NUMBER ONE CHAMPION OF JUSTICE AND FAIR PLAY FORBIDDEN EVER TO SET FOOT IN CYRUSVILLE? FOR THE SHOCKING ANSWER, READ--
GREAT SCOTT! THIS IS THE ONLY PLACE IN AMERICA WHERE I'M NOT WELCOME! THOSE POLICE DEPUTIES ARE TREATING ME LIKE A... A CRIMINAL!
CITY BORDER CYRUSVILLE SUPERMAN KEEP OUT!
BY ORDER OF POLICE DEPT.
"THE TOWN THAT HATED SUPERMAN!"

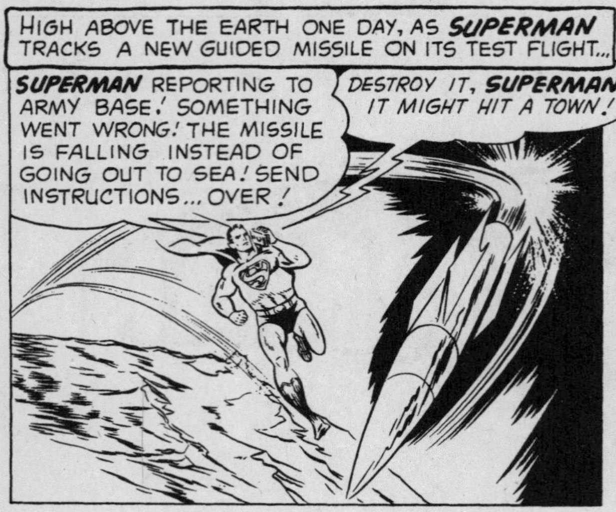
HIGH ABOVE THE EARTH ONE DAY, AS SUPERMAN TRACKS A NEW GUIDED MISSILE ON ITS TEST FLIGHT...
SUPERMAN REPORTING TO ARMY BASE! SOMETHING WENT WRONG! THE MISSILE IS FALLING INSTEAD OF GOING OUT TO SEA! SEND INSTRUCTIONS... OVER!
DESTROY IT, SUPERMAN! IT MIGHT HIT A TOWN!

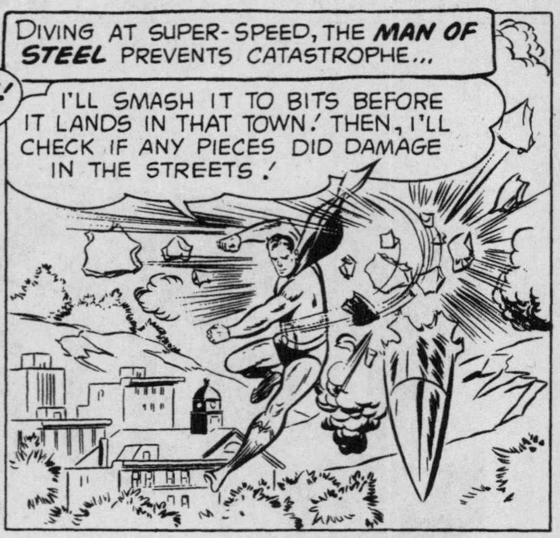
DIVING AT SUPER-SPEED, THE MAN OF STEEL PREVENTS CATASTROPHE...
I'LL SMASH IT TO BITS BEFORE IT LANDS IN THAT TOWN! THEN, I'LL CHECK IF ANY PIECES DID DAMAGE IN THE STREETS!

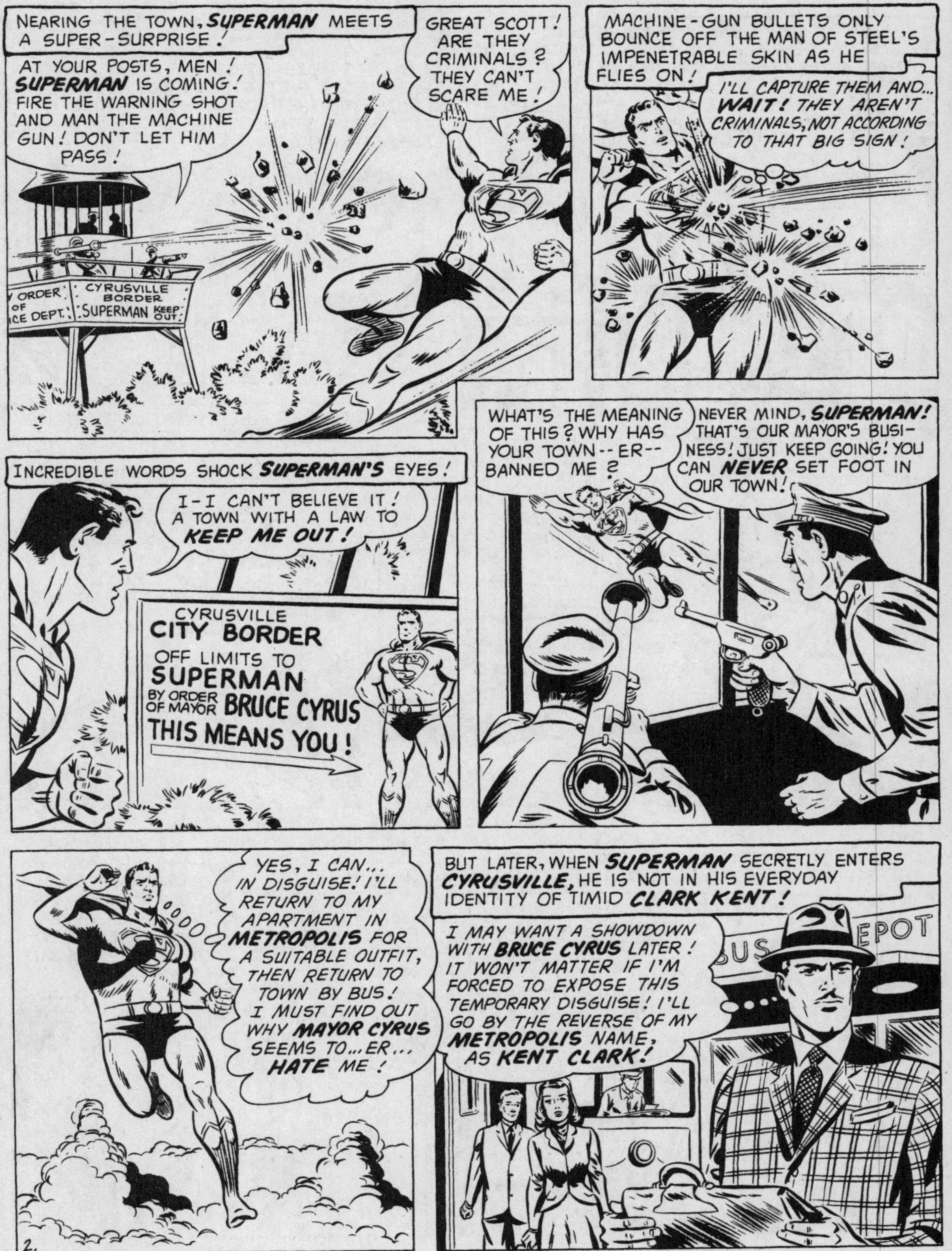
NEARING THE TOWN, SUPERMAN MEETS A SUPER-SURPRISE!
AT YOUR POSTS, MEN! SUPERMAN IS COMING! FIRE THE WARNING SHOT AND MAN THE MACHINE GUN! DON'T LET HIM PASS!
CYRUSVILLE BORDER SUPERMAN KEEP OUT
GREAT SCOTT! ARE THEY CRIMINALS? THEY CAN'T SCARE ME!
MACHINE-GUN BULLETS ONLY BOUNCE OFF THE MAN OF STEEL'S IMPENETRABLE SKIN AS HE FLIES ON!
I'LL CAPTURE THEM AND... WAIT! THEY AREN'T CRIMINALS, NOT ACCORDING TO THAT BIG SIGN!
INCREDIBLE WORDS SHOCK SUPERMAN'S EYES!
I-I CAN'T BELIEVE IT! A TOWN WITH A LAW TO KEEP ME OUT!
CYRUSVILLE CITY BORDER OFF LIMITS TO SUPERMAN BY ORDER OF MAYOR BRUCE CYRUS THIS MEANS YOU!
WHAT'S THE MEANING OF THIS? WHY HAS YOUR TOWN--ER--BANNED ME?
NEVER MIND, SUPERMAN! THAT'S OUR MAYOR'S BUSINESS! JUST KEEP GOING! YOU CAN NEVER SET FOOT IN OUR TOWN!
YES, I CAN... IN DISGUISE! I'LL RETURN TO MY APARTMENT IN METROPOLIS FOR A SUITABLE OUTFIT, THEN RETURN TO TOWN BY BUS! I MUST FIND OUT WHY MAYOR CYRUS SEEMS TO... ER... HATE ME!
2.
BUT LATER, WHEN SUPERMAN SECRETLY ENTERS CYRUSVILLE, HE IS NOT IN HIS EVERYDAY IDENTITY OF TIMID CLARK KENT!
I MAY WANT A SHOWDOWN WITH BRUCE CYRUS LATER! IT WON'T MATTER IF I'M FORCED TO EXPOSE THIS TEMPORARY DISGUISE! I'LL GO BY THE REVERSE OF MY METROPOLIS NAME, AS KENT CLARK!

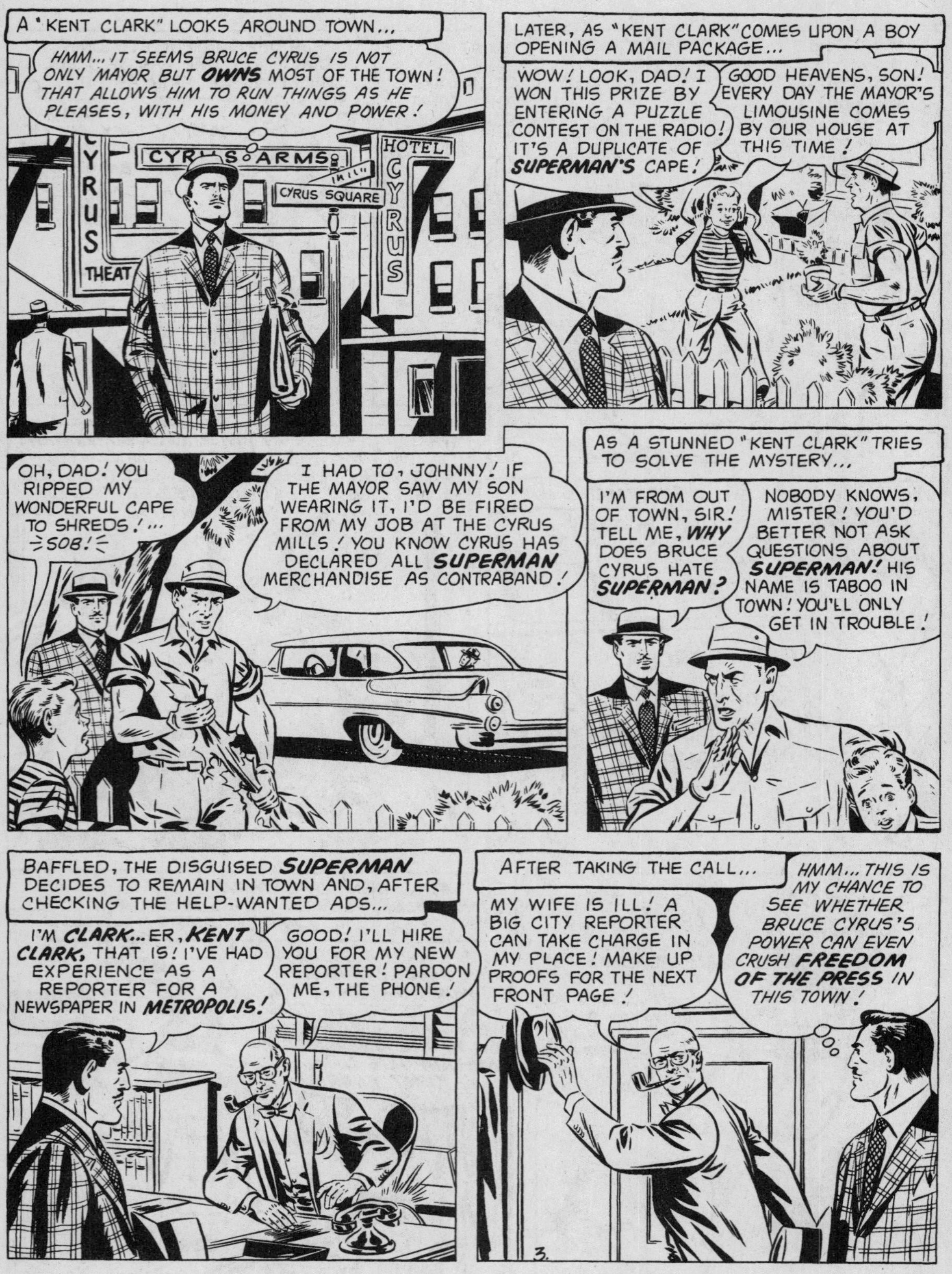
A "KENT CLARK" LOOKS AROUND TOWN...
HMM... IT SEEMS BRUCE CYRUS IS NOT ONLY MAYOR BUT OWNS MOST OF THE TOWN! THAT ALLOWS HIM TO RUN THINGS AS HE PLEASES, WITH HIS MONEY AND POWER!
CYRUS
CYRUS ARMS
HOTEL CYRUS
CYRUS SQUARE
THEAT
LATER, AS "KENT CLARK" COMES UPON A BOY OPENING A MAIL PACKAGE...
WOW! LOOK, DAD! I WON THIS PRIZE BY ENTERING A PUZZLE CONTEST ON THE RADIO! IT'S A DUPLICATE OF SUPERMAN'S CAPE!
GOOD HEAVENS, SON! EVERY DAY THE MAYOR'S LIMOUSINE COMES BY OUR HOUSE AT THIS TIME!
OH, DAD! YOU RIPPED MY WONDERFUL CAPE TO SHREDS!... SOB!
I HAD TO, JOHNNY! IF THE MAYOR SAW MY SON WEARING IT, I'D BE FIRED FROM MY JOB AT THE CYRUS MILLS! YOU KNOW CYRUS HAS DECLARED ALL SUPERMAN MERCHANDISE AS CONTRABAND!
AS A STUNNED "KENT CLARK" TRIES TO SOLVE THE MYSTERY...
I'M FROM OUT OF TOWN, SIR! TELL ME, WHY DOES BRUCE CYRUS HATE SUPERMAN?
NOBODY KNOWS, MISTER! YOU'D BETTER NOT ASK QUESTIONS ABOUT SUPERMAN! HIS NAME IS TABOO IN TOWN! YOU'LL ONLY GET IN TROUBLE!
BAFFLED, THE DISGUISED SUPERMAN DECIDES TO REMAIN IN TOWN AND, AFTER CHECKING THE HELP-WANTED ADS...
I'M CLARK... ER, KENT CLARK, THAT IS! I'VE HAD EXPERIENCE AS A REPORTER FOR A NEWSPAPER IN METROPOLIS!
GOOD! I'LL HIRE YOU FOR MY NEW REPORTER! PARDON ME, THE PHONE!
AFTER TAKING THE CALL...
MY WIFE IS ILL! A BIG CITY REPORTER CAN TAKE CHARGE IN MY PLACE! MAKE UP PROOFS FOR THE NEXT FRONT PAGE!
HMM... THIS IS MY CHANCE TO SEE WHETHER BRUCE CYRUS'S POWER CAN EVEN CRUSH FREEDOM OF THE PRESS IN THIS TOWN!
3.

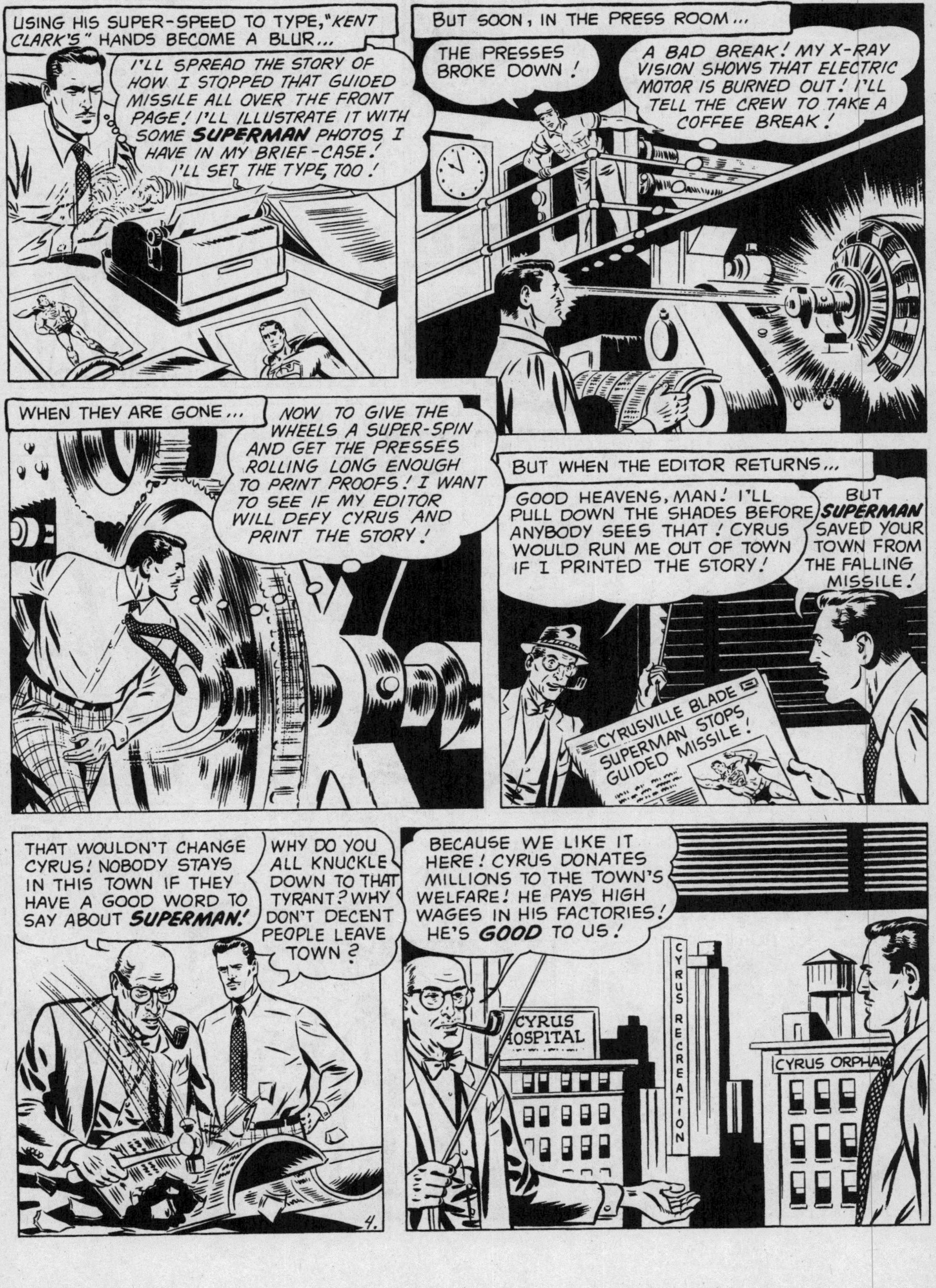
USING HIS SUPER-SPEED TO TYPE, "KENT CLARK'S" HANDS BECOME A BLUR...
I'LL SPREAD THE STORY OF HOW I STOPPED THAT GUIDED MISSILE ALL OVER THE FRONT PAGE! I'LL ILLUSTRATE IT WITH SOME SUPERMAN PHOTOS I HAVE IN MY BRIEF-CASE! I'LL SET THE TYPE, TOO!
BUT SOON, IN THE PRESS ROOM...
THE PRESSES BROKE DOWN!
A BAD BREAK! MY X-RAY VISION SHOWS THAT ELECTRIC MOTOR IS BURNED OUT! I'LL TELL THE CREW TO TAKE A COFFEE BREAK!
WHEN THEY ARE GONE...
NOW TO GIVE THE WHEELS A SUPER-SPIN AND GET THE PRESSES ROLLING LONG ENOUGH TO PRINT PROOFS! I WANT TO SEE IF MY EDITOR WILL DEFY CYRUS AND PRINT THE STORY!
BUT WHEN THE EDITOR RETURNS...
GOOD HEAVENS, MAN! I'LL PULL DOWN THE SHADES BEFORE ANYBODY SEES THAT! CYRUS WOULD RUN ME OUT OF TOWN IF I PRINTED THE STORY!
BUT SUPERMAN SAVED YOUR TOWN FROM THE FALLING MISSILE!
CYRUSVILLE BLADE
SUPERMAN STOPS GUIDED MISSILE!
THAT WOULDN'T CHANGE CYRUS! NOBODY STAYS IN THIS TOWN IF THEY HAVE A GOOD WORD TO SAY ABOUT SUPERMAN!
WHY DO YOU ALL KNUCKLE DOWN TO THAT TYRANT? WHY DON'T DECENT PEOPLE LEAVE TOWN?
BECAUSE WE LIKE IT HERE! CYRUS DONATES MILLIONS TO THE TOWN'S WELFARE! HE PAYS HIGH WAGES IN HIS FACTORIES! HE'S GOOD TO US!
CYRUS HOSPITAL
CYRUS RECREATION
CYRUS ORPHAN
4.

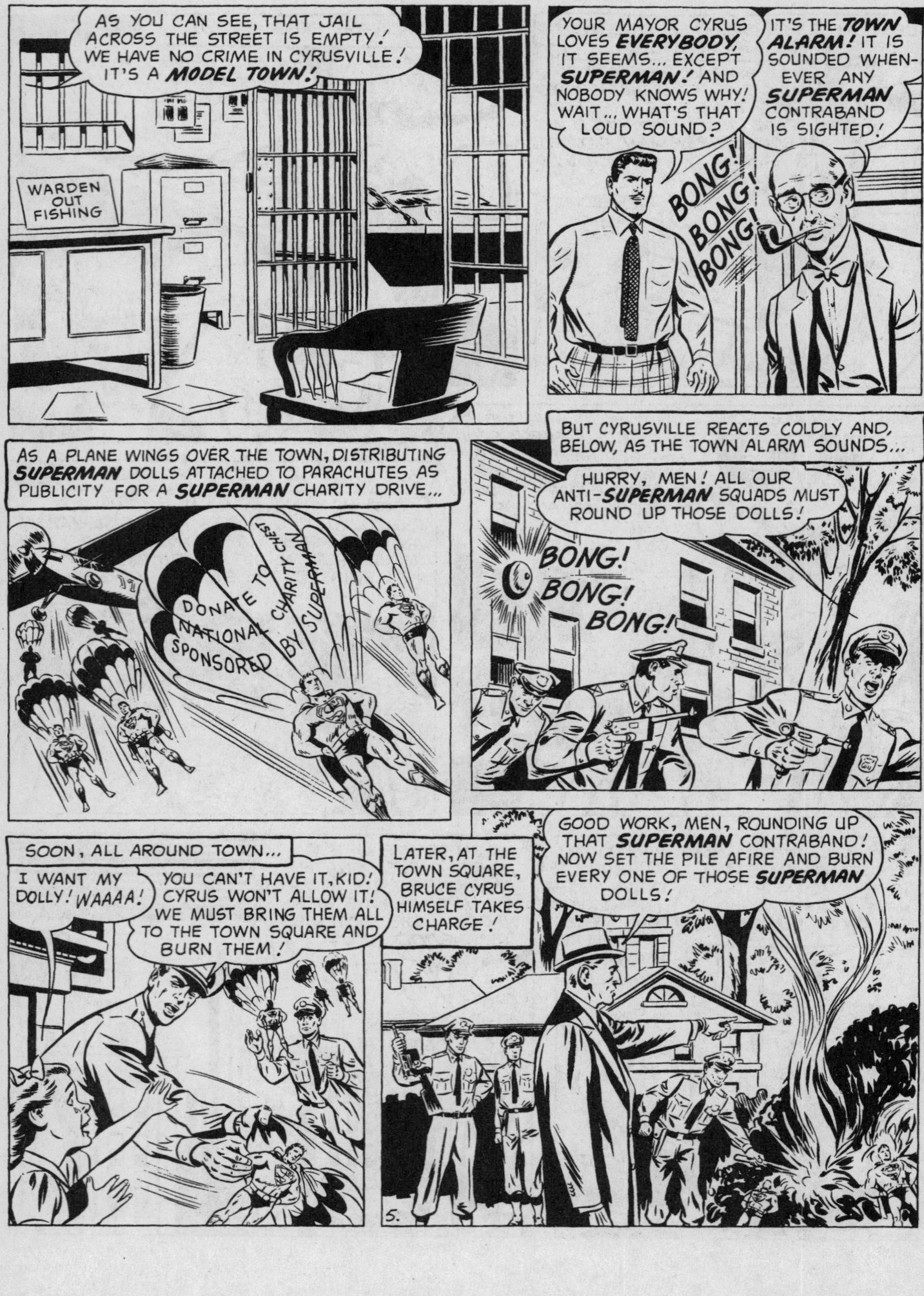
AS YOU CAN SEE, THAT JAIL ACROSS THE STREET IS EMPTY! WE HAVE NO CRIME IN CYRUSVILLE! IT'S A MODEL TOWN!
WARDEN OUT FISHING
YOUR MAYOR CYRUS LOVES EVERYBODY, IT SEEMS... EXCEPT SUPERMAN! AND NOBODY KNOWS WHY! WAIT... WHAT'S THAT LOUD SOUND?
IT'S THE TOWN ALARM! IT IS SOUNDED WHENEVER ANY SUPERMAN CONTRABAND IS SIGHTED!
BONG! BONG! BONG!
AS A PLANE WINGS OVER THE TOWN, DISTRIBUTING SUPERMAN DOLLS ATTACHED TO PARACHUTES AS PUBLICITY FOR A SUPERMAN CHARITY DRIVE...
DONATE TO NATIONAL CHARITY CHEST
SPONSORED BY SUPERMAN
BUT CYRUSVILLE REACTS COLDLY AND, BELOW, AS THE TOWN ALARM SOUNDS...
HURRY, MEN! ALL OUR ANTI-SUPERMAN SQUADS MUST ROUND UP THOSE DOLLS!
BONG! BONG! BONG!
SOON, ALL AROUND TOWN...
I WANT MY DOLLY! WAAAA!
YOU CAN'T HAVE IT, KID! CYRUS WON'T ALLOW IT! WE MUST BRING THEM ALL TO THE TOWN SQUARE AND BURN THEM!
LATER, AT THE TOWN SQUARE, BRUCE CYRUS HIMSELF TAKES CHARGE!
GOOD WORK, MEN, ROUNDING UP THAT SUPERMAN CONTRABAND! NOW SET THE PILE AFIRE AND BURN EVERY ONE OF THOSE SUPERMAN DOLLS!
5.

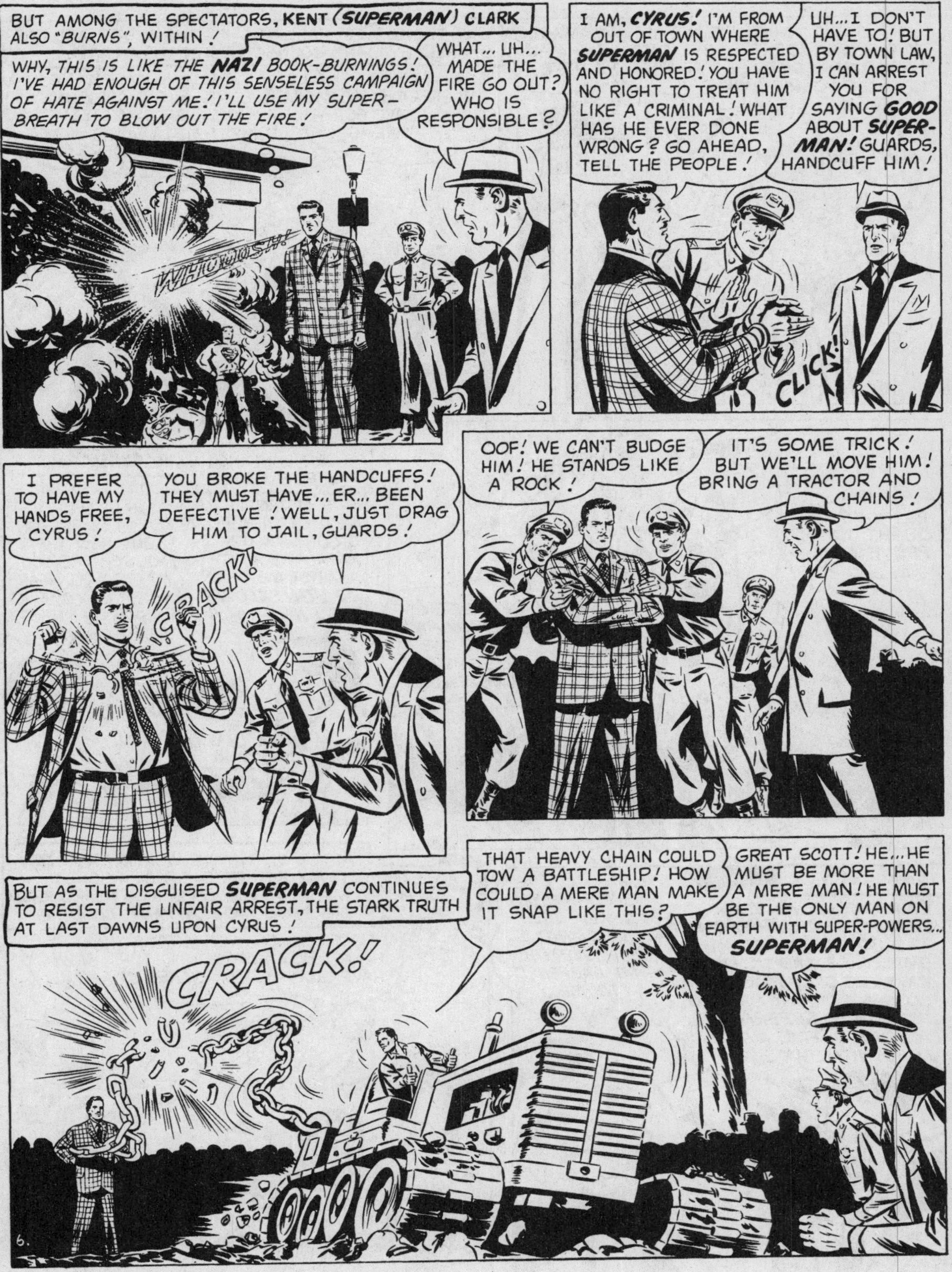
BUT AMONG THE SPECTATORS, KENT (SUPERMAN) CLARK ALSO "BURNS", WITHIN!
WHY, THIS IS LIKE THE NAZI BOOK-BURNINGS! I'VE HAD ENOUGH OF THIS SENSELESS CAMPAIGN OF HATE AGAINST ME! I'LL USE MY SUPER-BREATH TO BLOW OUT THE FIRE!
WHAT... UH... MADE THE FIRE GO OUT? WHO IS RESPONSIBLE?
WHOOOSH!
I AM, CYRUS! I'M FROM OUT OF TOWN WHERE SUPERMAN IS RESPECTED AND HONORED! YOU HAVE NO RIGHT TO TREAT HIM LIKE A CRIMINAL! WHAT HAS HE EVER DONE WRONG? GO AHEAD, TELL THE PEOPLE!
UH... I DON'T HAVE TO! BUT BY TOWN LAW, I CAN ARREST YOU FOR SAYING GOOD ABOUT SUPERMAN! GUARDS, HANDCUFF HIM!
CLICK!
I PREFER TO HAVE MY HANDS FREE, CYRUS!
YOU BROKE THE HANDCUFFS! THEY MUST HAVE... ER... BEEN DEFECTIVE! WELL, JUST DRAG HIM TO JAIL, GUARDS!
CRACK!
OOF! WE CAN'T BUDGE HIM! HE STANDS LIKE A ROCK!
IT'S SOME TRICK! BUT WE'LL MOVE HIM! BRING A TRACTOR AND CHAINS!
BUT AS THE DISGUISED SUPERMAN CONTINUES TO RESIST THE UNFAIR ARREST, THE STARK TRUTH AT LAST DAWNS UPON CYRUS!
THAT HEAVY CHAIN COULD TOW A BATTLESHIP! HOW COULD A MERE MAN MAKE IT SNAP LIKE THIS?
GREAT SCOTT! HE... HE MUST BE MORE THAN A MERE MAN! HE MUST BE THE ONLY MAN ON EARTH WITH SUPER-POWERS... SUPERMAN!
CRACK!
6.

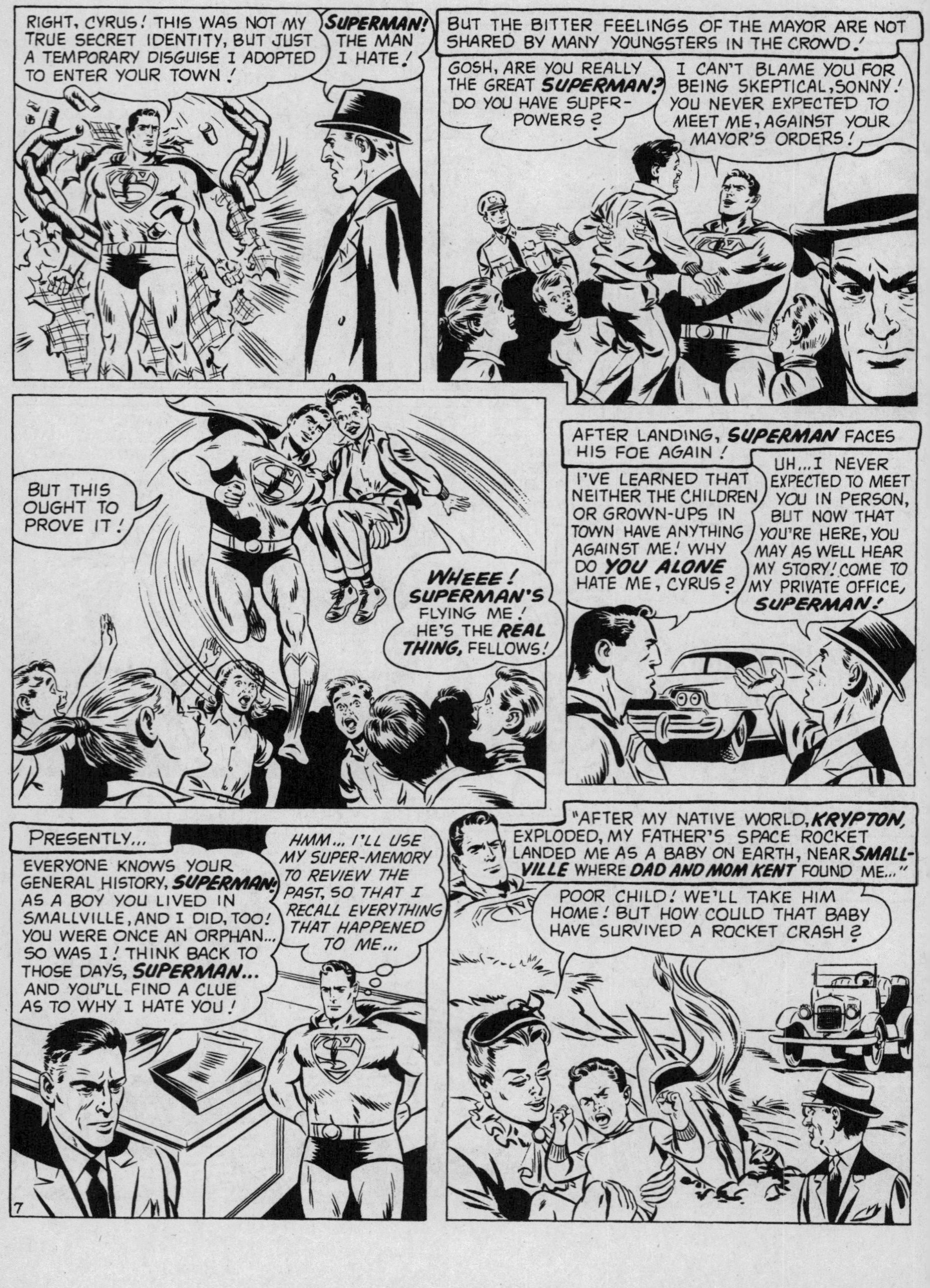
RIGHT, CYRUS! THIS WAS NOT MY TRUE SECRET IDENTITY, BUT JUST A TEMPORARY DISGUISE I ADOPTED TO ENTER YOUR TOWN!
SUPERMAN! THE MAN I HATE!
BUT THE BITTER FEELINGS OF THE MAYOR ARE NOT SHARED BY MANY YOUNGSTERS IN THE CROWD!
GOSH, ARE YOU REALLY THE GREAT SUPERMAN? DO YOU HAVE SUPER-POWERS?
I CAN'T BLAME YOU FOR BEING SKEPTICAL, SONNY! YOU NEVER EXPECTED TO MEET ME, AGAINST YOUR MAYOR'S ORDERS!
BUT THIS OUGHT TO PROVE IT!
WHEEE! SUPERMAN'S FLYING ME! HE'S THE REAL THING, FELLOWS!
AFTER LANDING, SUPERMAN FACES HIS FOE AGAIN!
I'VE LEARNED THAT NEITHER THE CHILDREN OR GROWN-UPS IN TOWN HAVE ANYTHING AGAINST ME! WHY DO YOU ALONE HATE ME, CYRUS?
UH...I NEVER EXPECTED TO MEET YOU IN PERSON, BUT NOW THAT YOU'RE HERE, YOU MAY AS WELL HEAR MY STORY! COME TO MY PRIVATE OFFICE, SUPERMAN!
PRESENTLY...
EVERYONE KNOWS YOUR GENERAL HISTORY, SUPERMAN! AS A BOY YOU LIVED IN SMALLVILLE, AND I DID, TOO! YOU WERE ONCE AN ORPHAN... SO WAS I! THINK BACK TO THOSE DAYS, SUPERMAN... AND YOU'LL FIND A CLUE AS TO WHY I HATE YOU!
HMM... I'LL USE MY SUPER-MEMORY TO REVIEW THE PAST, SO THAT I RECALL EVERYTHING THAT HAPPENED TO ME...
7
"AFTER MY NATIVE WORLD, KRYPTON, EXPLODED, MY FATHER'S SPACE ROCKET LANDED ME AS A BABY ON EARTH, NEAR SMALLVILLE WHERE DAD AND MOM KENT FOUND ME..."
POOR CHILD! WE'LL TAKE HIM HOME! BUT HOW COULD THAT BABY HAVE SURVIVED A ROCKET CRASH?

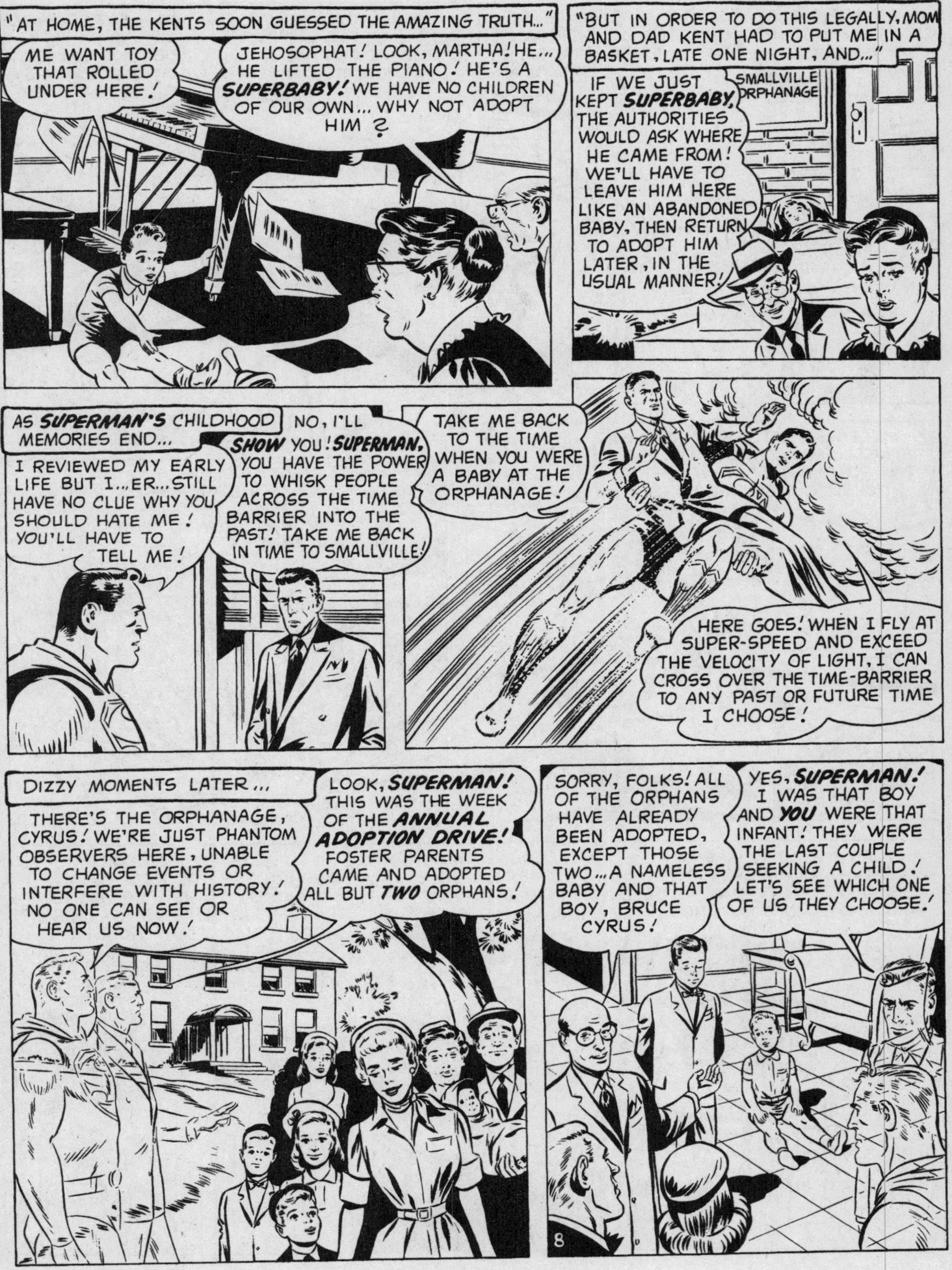
"AT HOME, THE KENTS SOON GUESSED THE AMAZING TRUTH..."
ME WANT TOY THAT ROLLED UNDER HERE!
JEHOSOPHAT! LOOK, MARTHA! HE... HE LIFTED THE PIANO! HE'S A SUPERBABY! WE HAVE NO CHILDREN OF OUR OWN... WHY NOT ADOPT HIM?
"BUT IN ORDER TO DO THIS LEGALLY, MOM AND DAD KENT HAD TO PUT ME IN A BASKET, LATE ONE NIGHT, AND..."
SMALLVILLE ORPHANAGE
IF WE JUST KEPT SUPERBABY, THE AUTHORITIES WOULD ASK WHERE HE CAME FROM! WE'LL HAVE TO LEAVE HIM HERE LIKE AN ABANDONED BABY, THEN RETURN TO ADOPT HIM LATER, IN THE USUAL MANNER!
AS SUPERMAN'S CHILDHOOD MEMORIES END...
I REVIEWED MY EARLY LIFE BUT I...ER...STILL HAVE NO CLUE WHY YOU SHOULD HATE ME! YOU'LL HAVE TO TELL ME!
NO, I'LL SHOW YOU! SUPERMAN, YOU HAVE THE POWER TO WHISK PEOPLE ACROSS THE TIME BARRIER INTO THE PAST! TAKE ME BACK IN TIME TO SMALLVILLE!
TAKE ME BACK TO THE TIME WHEN YOU WERE A BABY AT THE ORPHANAGE!
HERE GOES! WHEN I FLY AT SUPER-SPEED AND EXCEED THE VELOCITY OF LIGHT, I CAN CROSS OVER THE TIME-BARRIER TO ANY PAST OR FUTURE TIME I CHOOSE!
DIZZY MOMENTS LATER...
THERE'S THE ORPHANAGE, CYRUS! WE'RE JUST PHANTOM OBSERVERS HERE, UNABLE TO CHANGE EVENTS OR INTERFERE WITH HISTORY! NO ONE CAN SEE OR HEAR US NOW!
LOOK, SUPERMAN! THIS WAS THE WEEK OF THE ANNUAL ADOPTION DRIVE! FOSTER PARENTS CAME AND ADOPTED ALL BUT TWO ORPHANS!
SORRY, FOLKS! ALL OF THE ORPHANS HAVE ALREADY BEEN ADOPTED, EXCEPT THOSE TWO... A NAMELESS BABY AND THAT BOY, BRUCE CYRUS!
YES, SUPERMAN! I WAS THAT BOY AND YOU WERE THAT INFANT! THEY WERE THE LAST COUPLE SEEKING A CHILD! LET'S SEE WHICH ONE OF US THEY CHOOSE!
8

IF WE HAD A SON LIKE THIS, I COULD PLAY BALL WITH HIM!

BUT THIS BABY IS SO SWEET! WELL, DEAR, WE'LL HAVE A PRIVATE TALK AND TRY TO DECIDE BETWEEN THEM!

GOSH, BABY! WILL YOU OR I BE THE LUCKY ONE TO GAIN A HOME AND LOVING FOSTER PARENTS? ≠CHOKE!≠

NOTICE, SUPERMAN!... HOW THE BABY IS CRAWLING UNDER THAT TABLE AS THE OTHERS LEFT THE ROOM!

SUDDENLY, THAT THROW-RUG WAS YANKED FROM UNDER MY FEET BY TWO POWERFUL BABY HANDS! I WAS PITCHED OUT OF THE WINDOW--

--INTO THAT PUDDLE! AND OBVIOUSLY, ONLY A SUPERBABY COULD HAVE YANKED THAT RUG! SO IT WAS YOU WHO DID THAT TO ME, SUPERMAN!

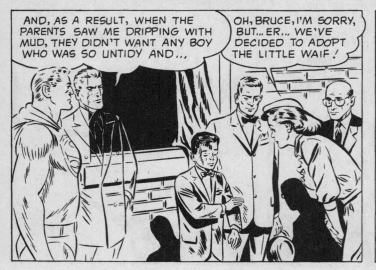

AND, AS A RESULT, WHEN THE PARENTS SAW ME DRIPPING WITH MUD, THEY DIDN'T WANT ANY BOY WHO WAS SO UNTIDY AND...

OH, BRUCE, I'M SORRY, BUT... ER... WE'VE DECIDED TO ADOPT THE LITTLE WAIF!

SO, I WAS LEFT A LONELY ORPHAN FOR THE REST OF MY BOYHOOD! I GREW UP ALONE, UNLOVED, UNWANTED! I WAS NEVER ADOPTED! IS IT ANY WONDER I HATE YOU FOR YOUR BABY TRICK, SUPERMAN! YOU ROBBED ME OF A MOTHER AND FATHER!

BUT I WASN'T THAT BABY, CYRUS!

9

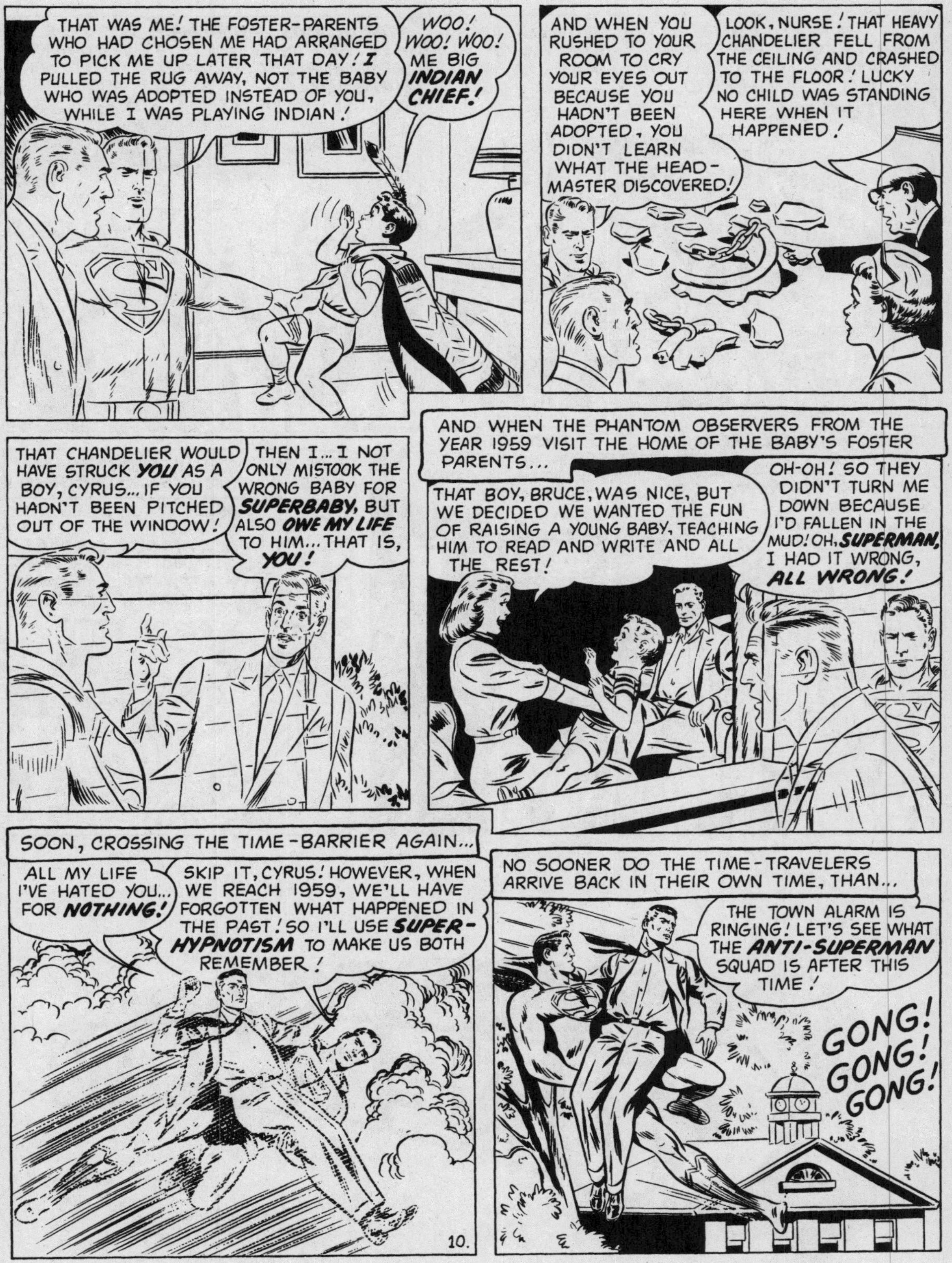
THAT WAS ME! THE FOSTER-PARENTS WHO HAD CHOSEN ME HAD ARRANGED TO PICK ME UP LATER THAT DAY! I PULLED THE RUG AWAY, NOT THE BABY WHO WAS ADOPTED INSTEAD OF YOU, WHILE I WAS PLAYING INDIAN!
WOO! WOO! WOO! ME BIG INDIAN CHIEF!
AND WHEN YOU RUSHED TO YOUR ROOM TO CRY YOUR EYES OUT BECAUSE YOU HADN'T BEEN ADOPTED, YOU DIDN'T LEARN WHAT THE HEAD-MASTER DISCOVERED!
LOOK, NURSE! THAT HEAVY CHANDELIER FELL FROM THE CEILING AND CRASHED TO THE FLOOR! LUCKY NO CHILD WAS STANDING HERE WHEN IT HAPPENED!
THAT CHANDELIER WOULD HAVE STRUCK YOU AS A BOY, CYRUS... IF YOU HADN'T BEEN PITCHED OUT OF THE WINDOW!
THEN I... I NOT ONLY MISTOOK THE WRONG BABY FOR SUPERBABY, BUT ALSO OWE MY LIFE TO HIM... THAT IS, YOU!
AND WHEN THE PHANTOM OBSERVERS FROM THE YEAR 1959 VISIT THE HOME OF THE BABY'S FOSTER PARENTS...
THAT BOY, BRUCE, WAS NICE, BUT WE DECIDED WE WANTED THE FUN OF RAISING A YOUNG BABY, TEACHING HIM TO READ AND WRITE AND ALL THE REST!
OH-OH! SO THEY DIDN'T TURN ME DOWN BECAUSE I'D FALLEN IN THE MUD! OH, SUPERMAN, I HAD IT WRONG, ALL WRONG!
SOON, CROSSING THE TIME-BARRIER AGAIN...
ALL MY LIFE I'VE HATED YOU... FOR NOTHING!
SKIP IT, CYRUS! HOWEVER, WHEN WE REACH 1959, WE'LL HAVE FORGOTTEN WHAT HAPPENED IN THE PAST! SO I'LL USE SUPER-HYPNOTISM TO MAKE US BOTH REMEMBER!
10.
NO SOONER DO THE TIME-TRAVELERS ARRIVE BACK IN THEIR OWN TIME, THAN...
THE TOWN ALARM IS RINGING! LET'S SEE WHAT THE ANTI-SUPERMAN SQUAD IS AFTER THIS TIME!
GONG! GONG! GONG!

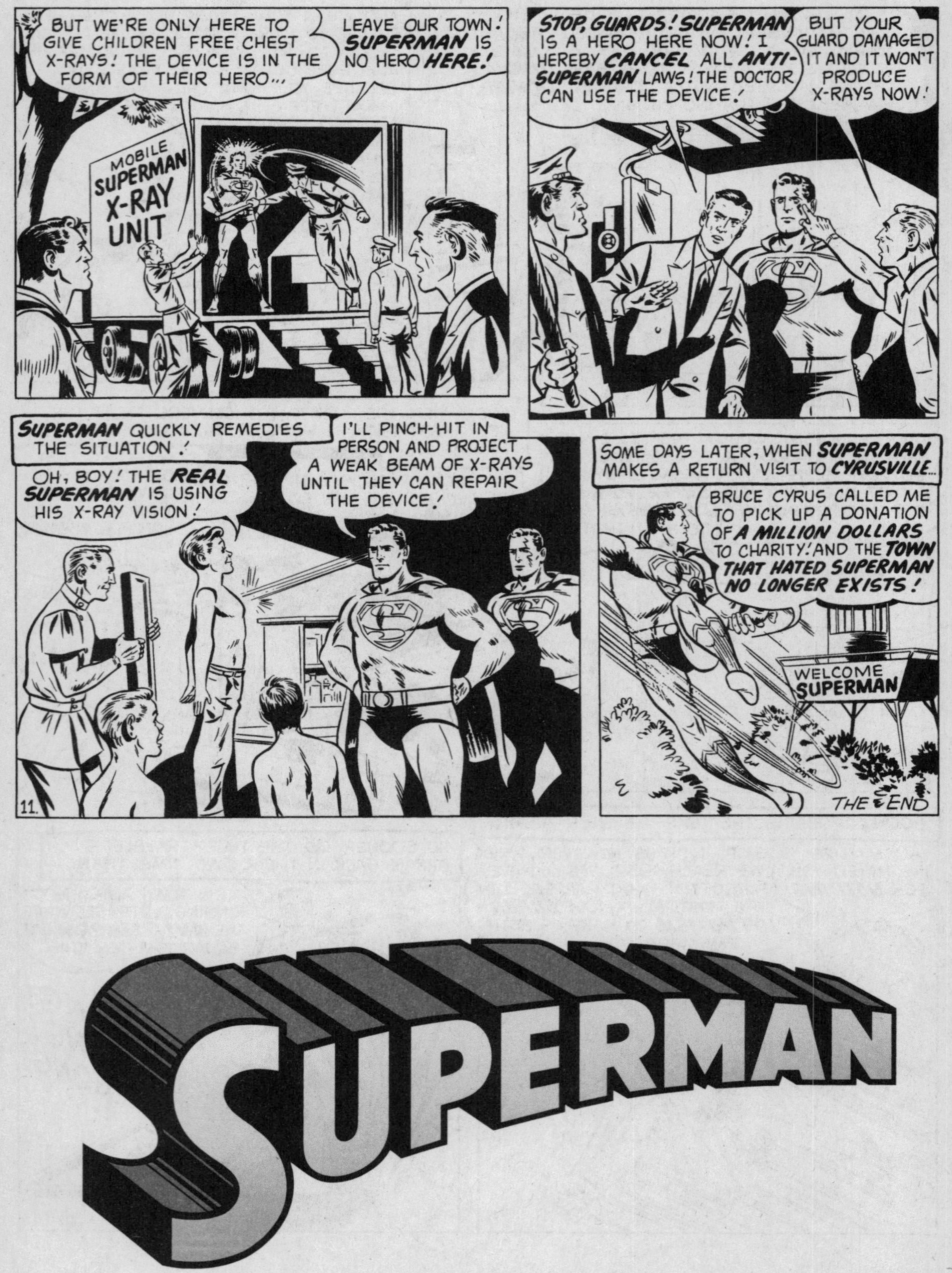
BUT WE'RE ONLY HERE TO GIVE CHILDREN FREE CHEST X-RAYS! THE DEVICE IS IN THE FORM OF THEIR HERO...
LEAVE OUR TOWN! SUPERMAN IS NO HERO HERE!
MOBILE SUPERMAN X-RAY UNIT
STOP, GUARDS! SUPERMAN IS A HERO HERE NOW! I HEREBY CANCEL ALL ANTI-SUPERMAN LAWS! THE DOCTOR CAN USE THE DEVICE!
BUT YOUR GUARD DAMAGED IT AND IT WON'T PRODUCE X-RAYS NOW!
SUPERMAN QUICKLY REMEDIES THE SITUATION!
OH, BOY! THE REAL SUPERMAN IS USING HIS X-RAY VISION!
I'LL PINCH-HIT IN PERSON AND PROJECT A WEAK BEAM OF X-RAYS UNTIL THEY CAN REPAIR THE DEVICE!
11.
SOME DAYS LATER, WHEN SUPERMAN MAKES A RETURN VISIT TO CYRUSVILLE...
BRUCE CYRUS CALLED ME TO PICK UP A DONATION OF A MILLION DOLLARS TO CHARITY! AND THE TOWN THAT HATED SUPERMAN NO LONGER EXISTS!
WELCOME SUPERMAN
THE END

SUPERMAN

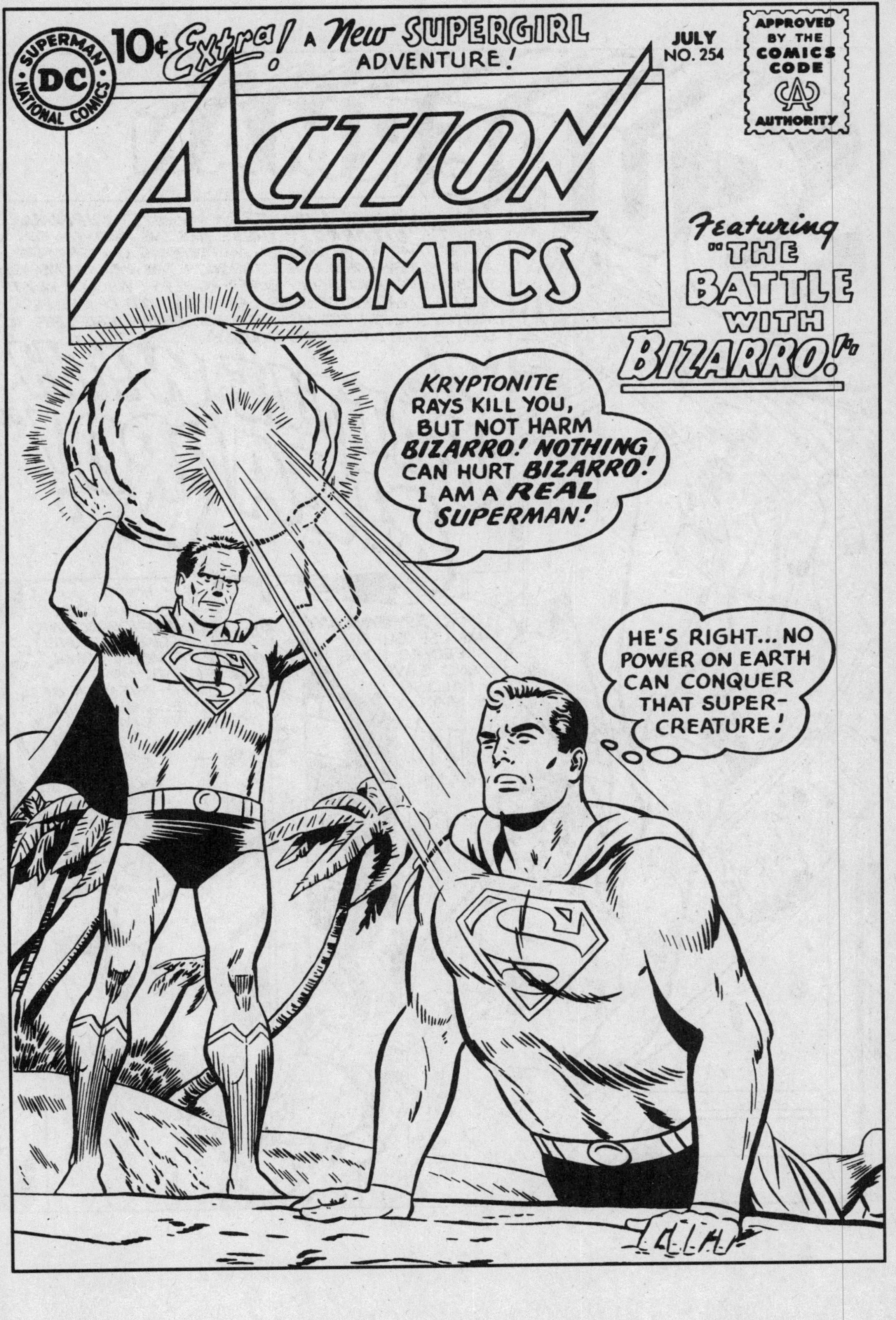
SUPERMAN DC NATIONAL COMICS
10¢ Extra! A New SUPERGIRL ADVENTURE!
JULY NO. 254
APPROVED BY THE COMICS CODE AUTHORITY
ACTION COMICS
Featuring "THE BATTLE WITH BIZARRO!"
KRYPTONITE RAYS KILL YOU, BUT NOT HARM BIZARRO! NOTHING CAN HURT BIZARRO! I AM A REAL SUPERMAN!
HE'S RIGHT... NO POWER ON EARTH CAN CONQUER THAT SUPER-CREATURE!

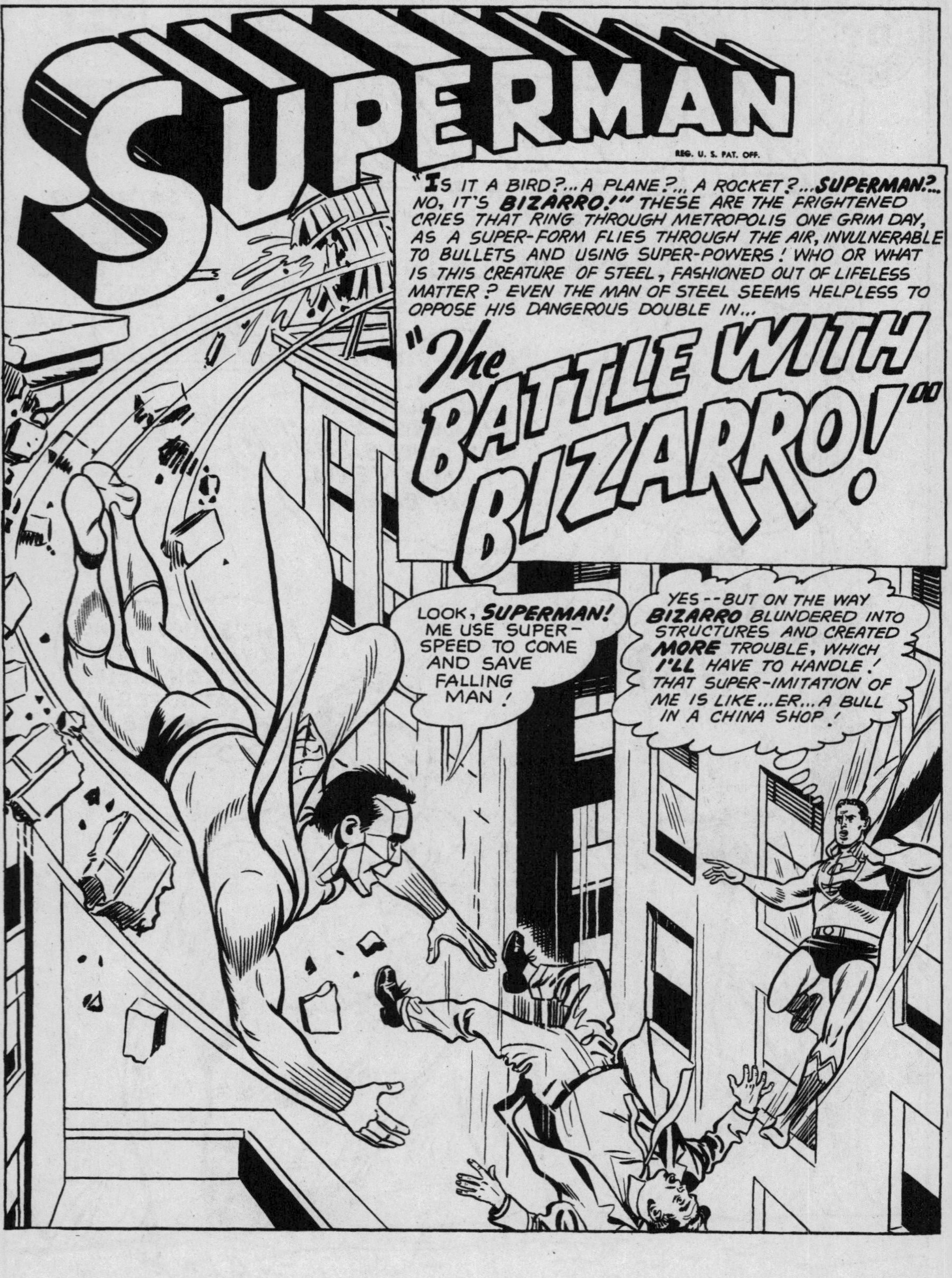
SUPERMAN
REG. U. S. PAT. OFF.
"IS IT A BIRD?... A PLANE?... A ROCKET?... SUPERMAN?... NO, IT'S BIZARRO!" THESE ARE THE FRIGHTENED CRIES THAT RING THROUGH METROPOLIS ONE GRIM DAY, AS A SUPER-FORM FLIES THROUGH THE AIR, INVULNERABLE TO BULLETS AND USING SUPER-POWERS! WHO OR WHAT IS THIS CREATURE OF STEEL, FASHIONED OUT OF LIFELESS MATTER? EVEN THE MAN OF STEEL SEEMS HELPLESS TO OPPOSE HIS DANGEROUS DOUBLE IN...
"The BATTLE WITH BIZARRO!"
LOOK, SUPERMAN! ME USE SUPER-SPEED TO COME AND SAVE FALLING MAN!
YES--BUT ON THE WAY BIZARRO BLUNDERED INTO STRUCTURES AND CREATED MORE TROUBLE, WHICH I'LL HAVE TO HANDLE! THAT SUPER-IMITATION OF ME IS LIKE...ER...A BULL IN A CHINA SHOP!

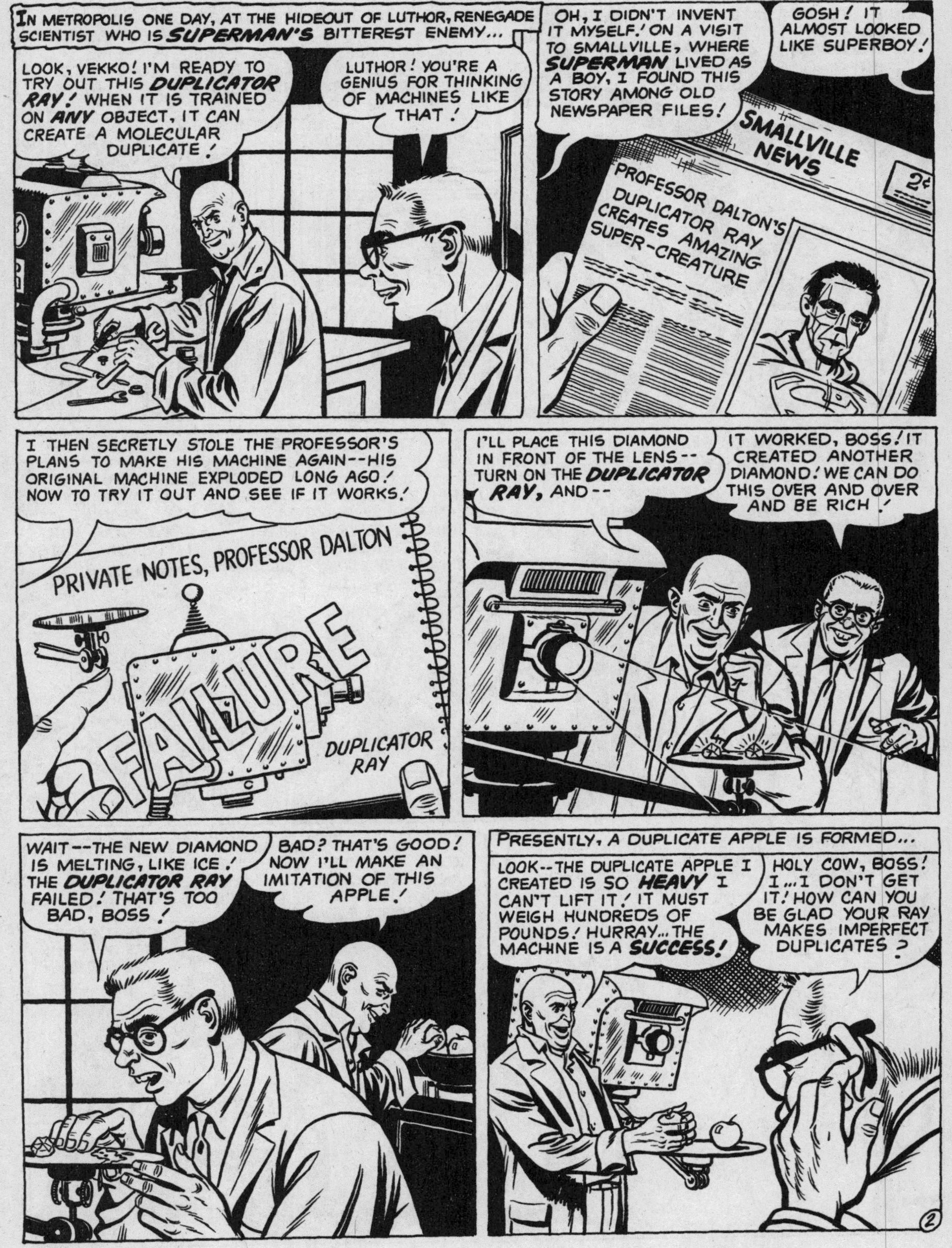
IN METROPOLIS ONE DAY, AT THE HIDEOUT OF LUTHOR, RENEGADE SCIENTIST WHO IS SUPERMAN'S BITTEREST ENEMY...
LOOK, VEKKO! I'M READY TO TRY OUT THIS DUPLICATOR RAY! WHEN IT IS TRAINED ON ANY OBJECT, IT CAN CREATE A MOLECULAR DUPLICATE!
LUTHOR! YOU'RE A GENIUS FOR THINKING OF MACHINES LIKE THAT!
OH, I DIDN'T INVENT IT MYSELF! ON A VISIT TO SMALLVILLE, WHERE SUPERMAN LIVED AS A BOY, I FOUND THIS STORY AMONG OLD NEWSPAPER FILES!
GOSH! IT ALMOST LOOKED LIKE SUPERBOY!
SMALLVILLE NEWS
2¢
PROFESSOR DALTON'S DUPLICATOR RAY CREATES AMAZING SUPER-CREATURE
I THEN SECRETLY STOLE THE PROFESSOR'S PLANS TO MAKE HIS MACHINE AGAIN--HIS ORIGINAL MACHINE EXPLODED LONG AGO! NOW TO TRY IT OUT AND SEE IF IT WORKS!
PRIVATE NOTES, PROFESSOR DALTON
FAILURE
DUPLICATOR RAY
I'LL PLACE THIS DIAMOND IN FRONT OF THE LENS--TURN ON THE DUPLICATOR RAY, AND--
IT WORKED, BOSS! IT CREATED ANOTHER DIAMOND! WE CAN DO THIS OVER AND OVER AND BE RICH!
WAIT--THE NEW DIAMOND IS MELTING, LIKE ICE! THE DUPLICATOR RAY FAILED! THAT'S TOO BAD, BOSS!
BAD? THAT'S GOOD! NOW I'LL MAKE AN IMITATION OF THIS APPLE!
PRESENTLY, A DUPLICATE APPLE IS FORMED...
LOOK--THE DUPLICATE APPLE I CREATED IS SO HEAVY I CAN'T LIFT IT! IT MUST WEIGH HUNDREDS OF POUNDS! HURRAY... THE MACHINE IS A SUCCESS!
HOLY COW, BOSS! I... I DON'T GET IT! HOW CAN YOU BE GLAD YOUR RAY MAKES IMPERFECT DUPLICATES?
2

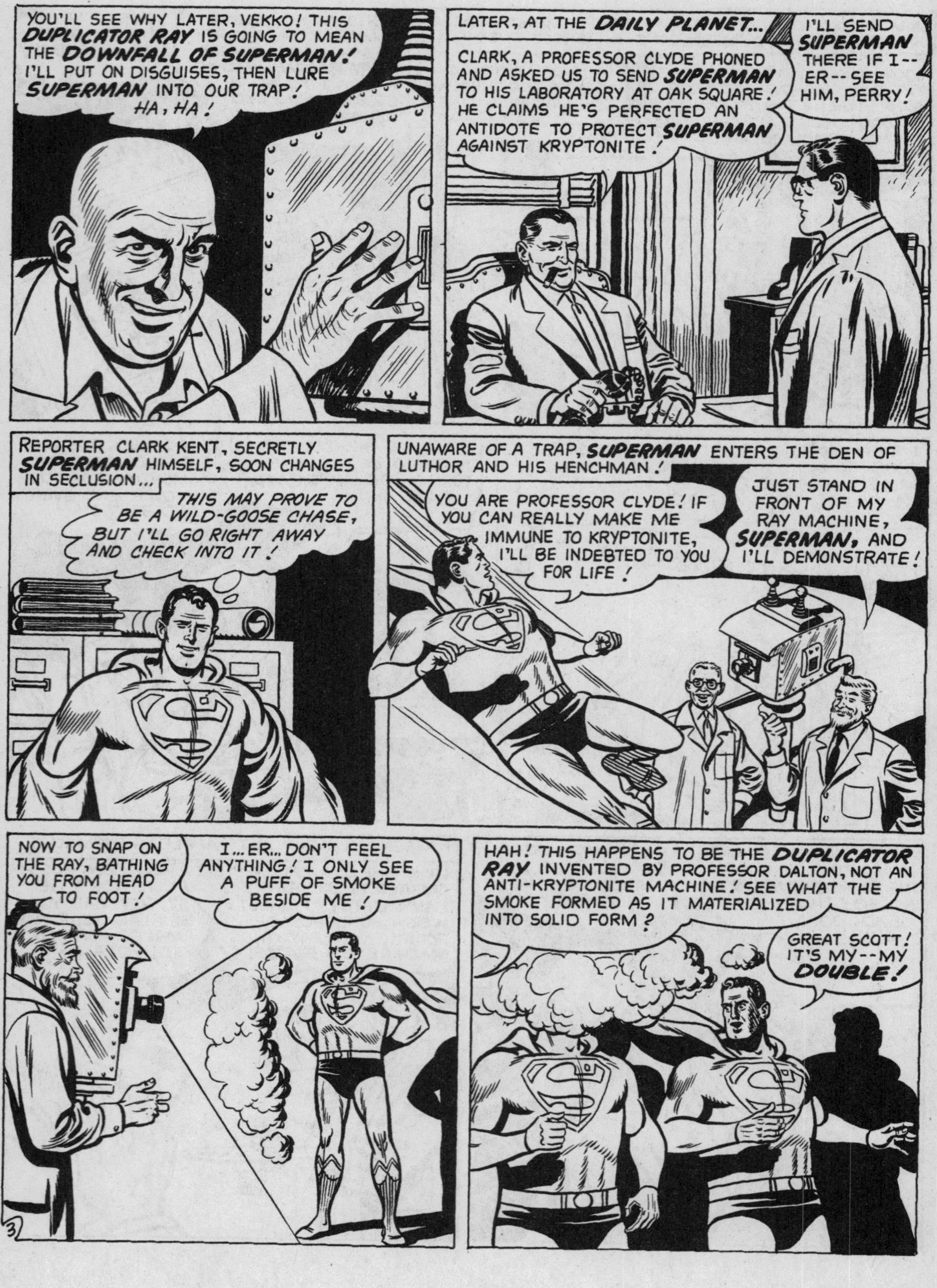
YOU'LL SEE WHY LATER, VEKKO! THIS DUPLICATOR RAY IS GOING TO MEAN THE DOWNFALL OF SUPERMAN! I'LL PUT ON DISGUISES, THEN LURE SUPERMAN INTO OUR TRAP! HA, HA!
LATER, AT THE DAILY PLANET...
CLARK, A PROFESSOR CLYDE PHONED AND ASKED US TO SEND SUPERMAN TO HIS LABORATORY AT OAK SQUARE! HE CLAIMS HE'S PERFECTED AN ANTIDOTE TO PROTECT SUPERMAN AGAINST KRYPTONITE!
I'LL SEND SUPERMAN THERE IF I-- ER--SEE HIM, PERRY!
REPORTER CLARK KENT, SECRETLY SUPERMAN HIMSELF, SOON CHANGES IN SECLUSION...
THIS MAY PROVE TO BE A WILD-GOOSE CHASE, BUT I'LL GO RIGHT AWAY AND CHECK INTO IT!
UNAWARE OF A TRAP, SUPERMAN ENTERS THE DEN OF LUTHOR AND HIS HENCHMAN!
YOU ARE PROFESSOR CLYDE! IF YOU CAN REALLY MAKE ME IMMUNE TO KRYPTONITE, I'LL BE INDEBTED TO YOU FOR LIFE!
JUST STAND IN FRONT OF MY RAY MACHINE, SUPERMAN, AND I'LL DEMONSTRATE!
NOW TO SNAP ON THE RAY, BATHING YOU FROM HEAD TO FOOT!
I...ER... DON'T FEEL ANYTHING! I ONLY SEE A PUFF OF SMOKE BESIDE ME!
3
HAH! THIS HAPPENS TO BE THE DUPLICATOR RAY INVENTED BY PROFESSOR DALTON, NOT AN ANTI-KRYPTONITE MACHINE! SEE WHAT THE SMOKE FORMED AS IT MATERIALIZED INTO SOLID FORM?
GREAT SCOTT! IT'S MY--MY DOUBLE!

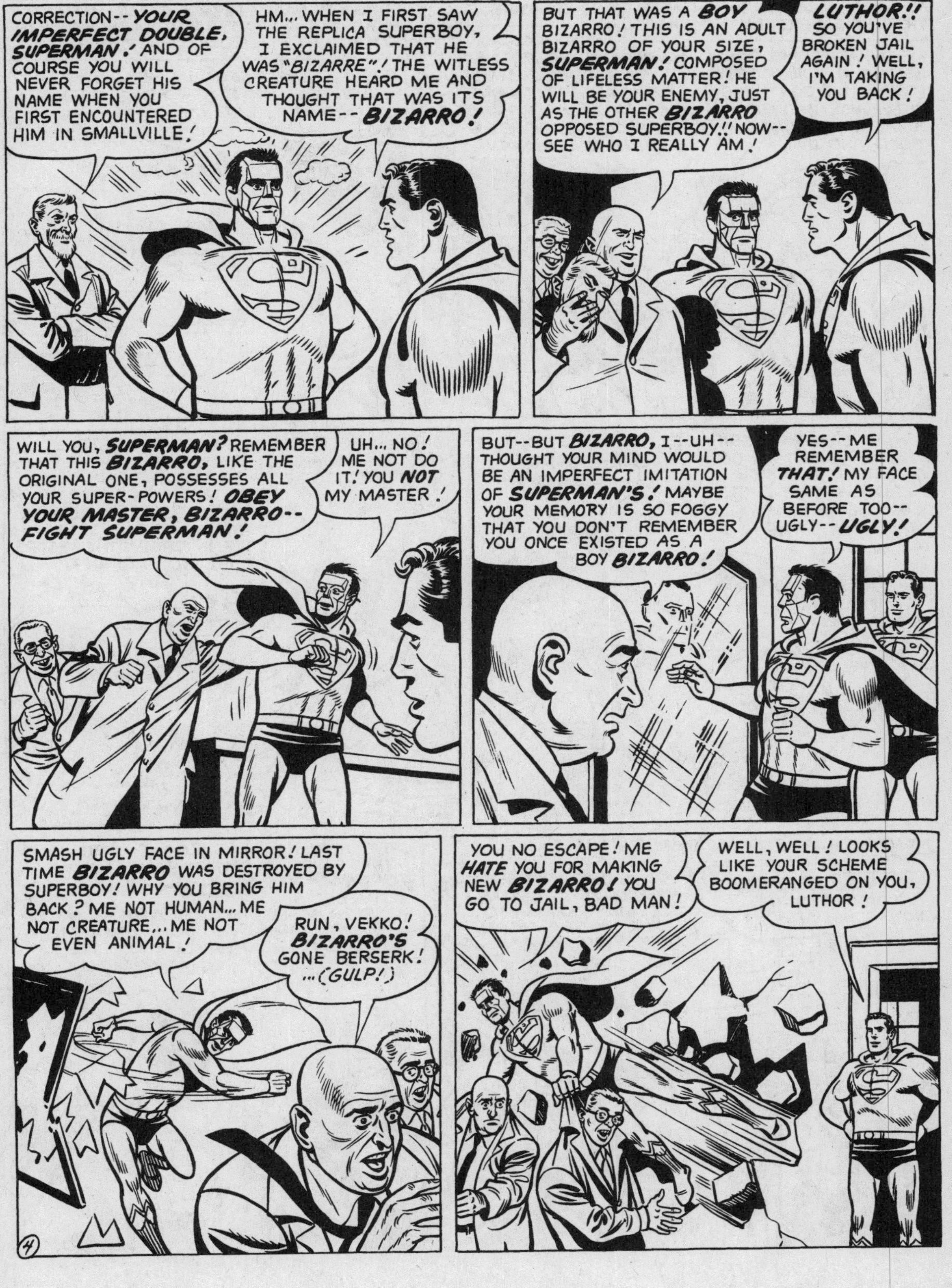
CORRECTION--YOUR IMPERFECT DOUBLE, SUPERMAN! AND OF COURSE YOU WILL NEVER FORGET HIS NAME WHEN YOU FIRST ENCOUNTERED HIM IN SMALLVILLE!
HM... WHEN I FIRST SAW THE REPLICA SUPERBOY, I EXCLAIMED THAT HE WAS "BIZARRE"! THE WITLESS CREATURE HEARD ME AND THOUGHT THAT WAS ITS NAME--BIZARRO!
BUT THAT WAS A BOY BIZARRO! THIS IS AN ADULT BIZARRO OF YOUR SIZE, SUPERMAN! COMPOSED OF LIFELESS MATTER! HE WILL BE YOUR ENEMY, JUST AS THE OTHER BIZARRO OPPOSED SUPERBOY!! NOW--SEE WHO I REALLY AM!
LUTHOR!! SO YOU'VE BROKEN JAIL AGAIN! WELL, I'M TAKING YOU BACK!
WILL YOU, SUPERMAN? REMEMBER THAT THIS BIZARRO, LIKE THE ORIGINAL ONE, POSSESSES ALL YOUR SUPER-POWERS! OBEY YOUR MASTER, BIZARRO--FIGHT SUPERMAN!
UH... NO! ME NOT DO IT! YOU NOT MY MASTER!
BUT--BUT BIZARRO, I--UH--THOUGHT YOUR MIND WOULD BE AN IMPERFECT IMITATION OF SUPERMAN'S! MAYBE YOUR MEMORY IS SO FOGGY THAT YOU DON'T REMEMBER YOU ONCE EXISTED AS A BOY BIZARRO!
YES--ME REMEMBER THAT! MY FACE SAME AS BEFORE TOO--UGLY--UGLY!
SMASH UGLY FACE IN MIRROR! LAST TIME BIZARRO WAS DESTROYED BY SUPERBOY! WHY YOU BRING HIM BACK? ME NOT HUMAN... ME NOT CREATURE... ME NOT EVEN ANIMAL!
RUN, VEKKO! BIZARRO'S GONE BERSERK! ...(GULP!)
4
YOU NO ESCAPE! ME HATE YOU FOR MAKING NEW BIZARRO! YOU GO TO JAIL, BAD MAN!
WELL, WELL! LOOKS LIKE YOUR SCHEME BOOMERANGED ON YOU, LUTHOR!

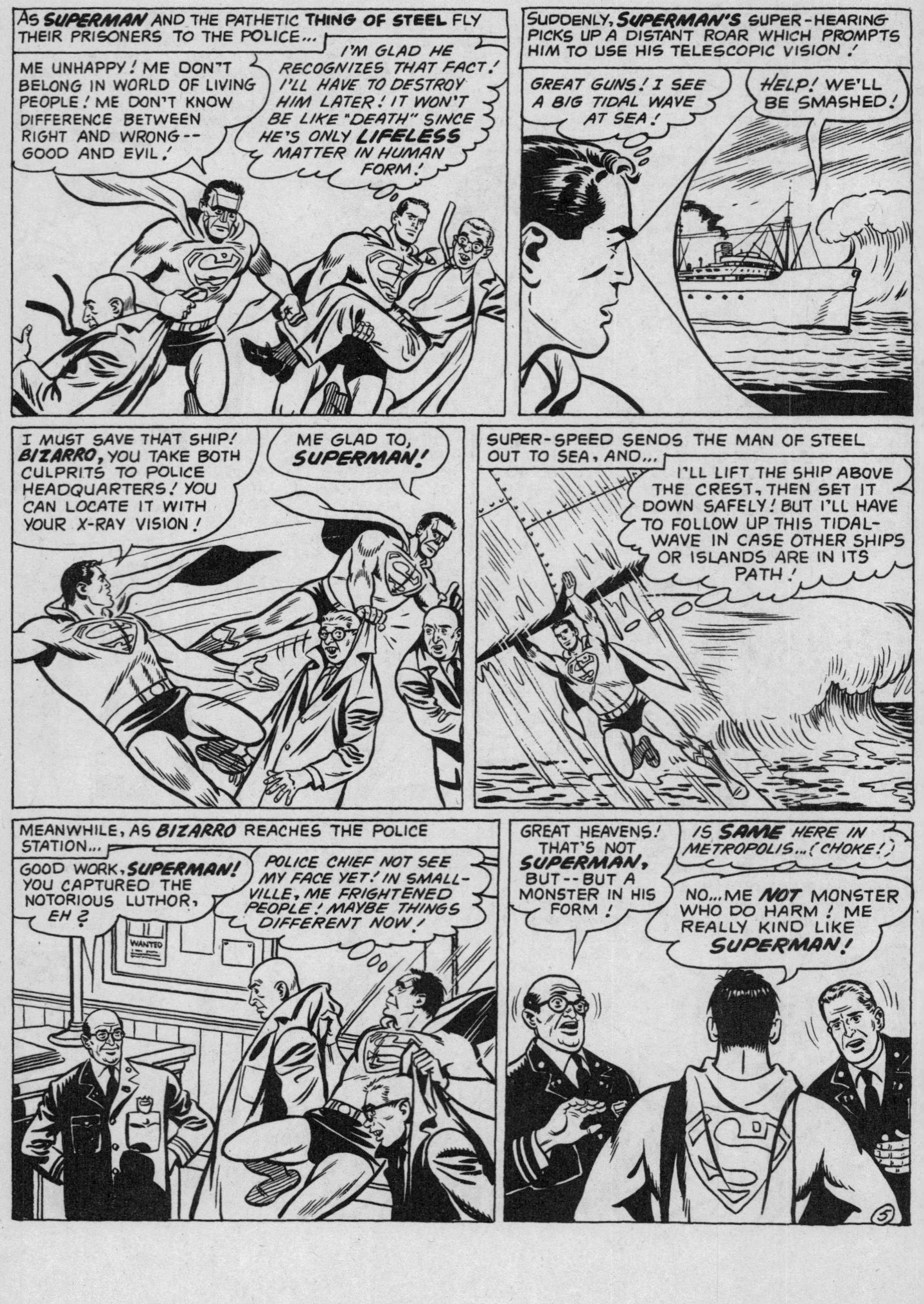
AS SUPERMAN AND THE PATHETIC THING OF STEEL FLY THEIR PRISONERS TO THE POLICE...
ME UNHAPPY! ME DON'T BELONG IN WORLD OF LIVING PEOPLE! ME DON'T KNOW DIFFERENCE BETWEEN RIGHT AND WRONG-- GOOD AND EVIL!
I'M GLAD HE RECOGNIZES THAT FACT! I'LL HAVE TO DESTROY HIM LATER! IT WON'T BE LIKE "DEATH" SINCE HE'S ONLY LIFELESS MATTER IN HUMAN FORM!
SUDDENLY, SUPERMAN'S SUPER-HEARING PICKS UP A DISTANT ROAR WHICH PROMPTS HIM TO USE HIS TELESCOPIC VISION!
GREAT GUNS! I SEE A BIG TIDAL WAVE AT SEA!
HELP! WE'LL BE SMASHED!
I MUST SAVE THAT SHIP! BIZARRO, YOU TAKE BOTH CULPRITS TO POLICE HEADQUARTERS! YOU CAN LOCATE IT WITH YOUR X-RAY VISION!
ME GLAD TO, SUPERMAN!
SUPER-SPEED SENDS THE MAN OF STEEL OUT TO SEA, AND...
I'LL LIFT THE SHIP ABOVE THE CREST, THEN SET IT DOWN SAFELY! BUT I'LL HAVE TO FOLLOW UP THIS TIDAL-WAVE IN CASE OTHER SHIPS OR ISLANDS ARE IN ITS PATH!
MEANWHILE, AS BIZARRO REACHES THE POLICE STATION...
GOOD WORK, SUPERMAN! YOU CAPTURED THE NOTORIOUS LUTHOR, EH?
POLICE CHIEF NOT SEE MY FACE YET! IN SMALLVILLE, ME FRIGHTENED PEOPLE! MAYBE THINGS DIFFERENT NOW!
WANTED
GREAT HEAVENS! THAT'S NOT SUPERMAN, BUT--BUT A MONSTER IN HIS FORM!
IS SAME HERE IN METROPOLIS...(CHOKE!)
NO...ME NOT MONSTER WHO DO HARM! ME REALLY KIND LIKE SUPERMAN!
5

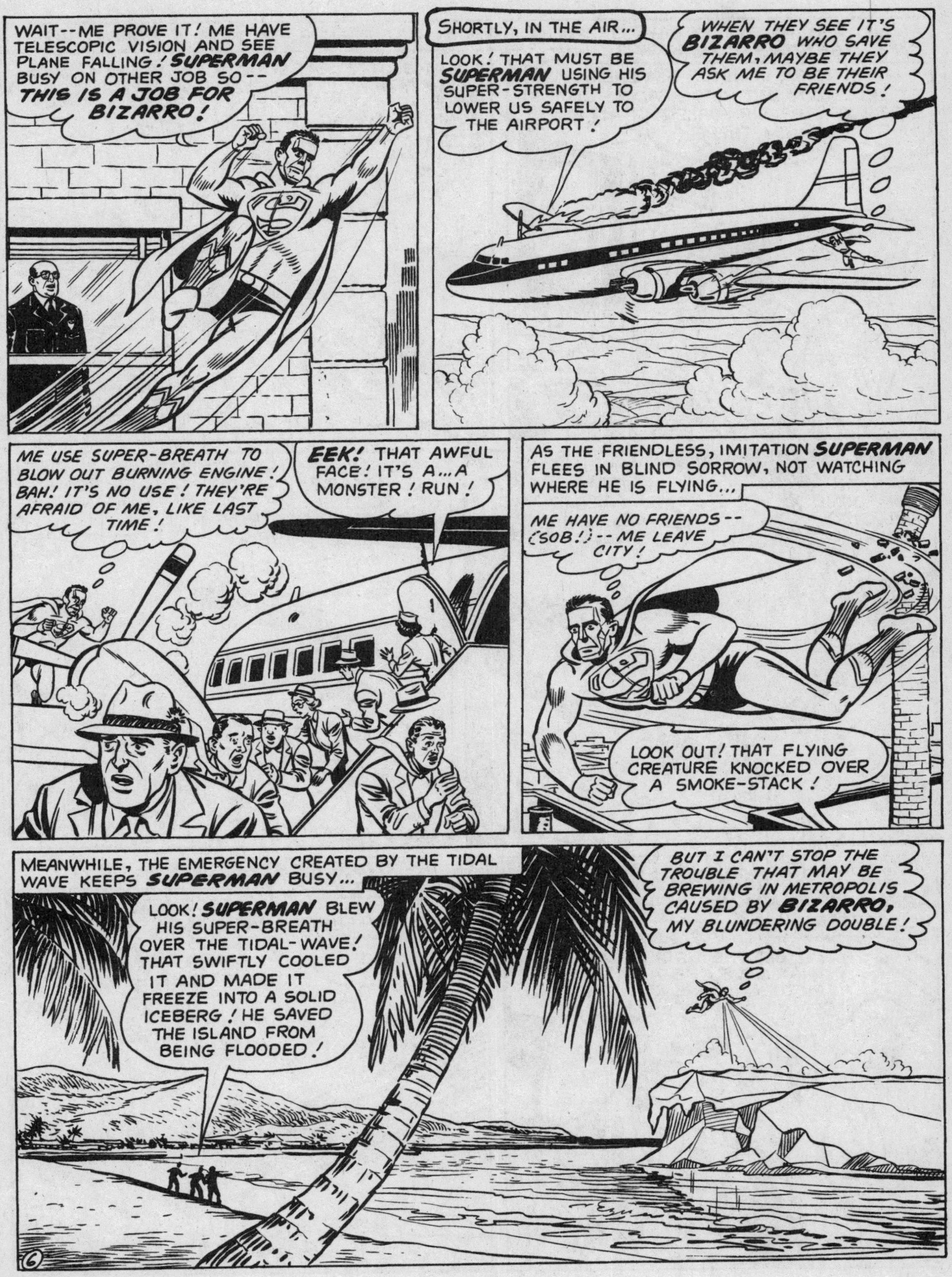
WAIT--ME PROVE IT! ME HAVE TELESCOPIC VISION AND SEE PLANE FALLING! SUPERMAN BUSY ON OTHER JOB SO-- THIS IS A JOB FOR BIZARRO!
SHORTLY, IN THE AIR...
LOOK! THAT MUST BE SUPERMAN USING HIS SUPER-STRENGTH TO LOWER US SAFELY TO THE AIRPORT!
WHEN THEY SEE IT'S BIZARRO WHO SAVE THEM, MAYBE THEY ASK ME TO BE THEIR FRIENDS!
ME USE SUPER-BREATH TO BLOW OUT BURNING ENGINE! BAH! IT'S NO USE! THEY'RE AFRAID OF ME, LIKE LAST TIME!
EEK! THAT AWFUL FACE! IT'S A...A MONSTER! RUN!
AS THE FRIENDLESS, IMITATION SUPERMAN FLEES IN BLIND SORROW, NOT WATCHING WHERE HE IS FLYING...
ME HAVE NO FRIENDS-- (SOB!)--ME LEAVE CITY!
LOOK OUT! THAT FLYING CREATURE KNOCKED OVER A SMOKE-STACK!
MEANWHILE, THE EMERGENCY CREATED BY THE TIDAL WAVE KEEPS SUPERMAN BUSY...
LOOK! SUPERMAN BLEW HIS SUPER-BREATH OVER THE TIDAL-WAVE! THAT SWIFTLY COOLED IT AND MADE IT FREEZE INTO A SOLID ICEBERG! HE SAVED THE ISLAND FROM BEING FLOODED!
BUT I CAN'T STOP THE TROUBLE THAT MAY BE BREWING IN METROPOLIS CAUSED BY BIZARRO, MY BLUNDERING DOUBLE!
6

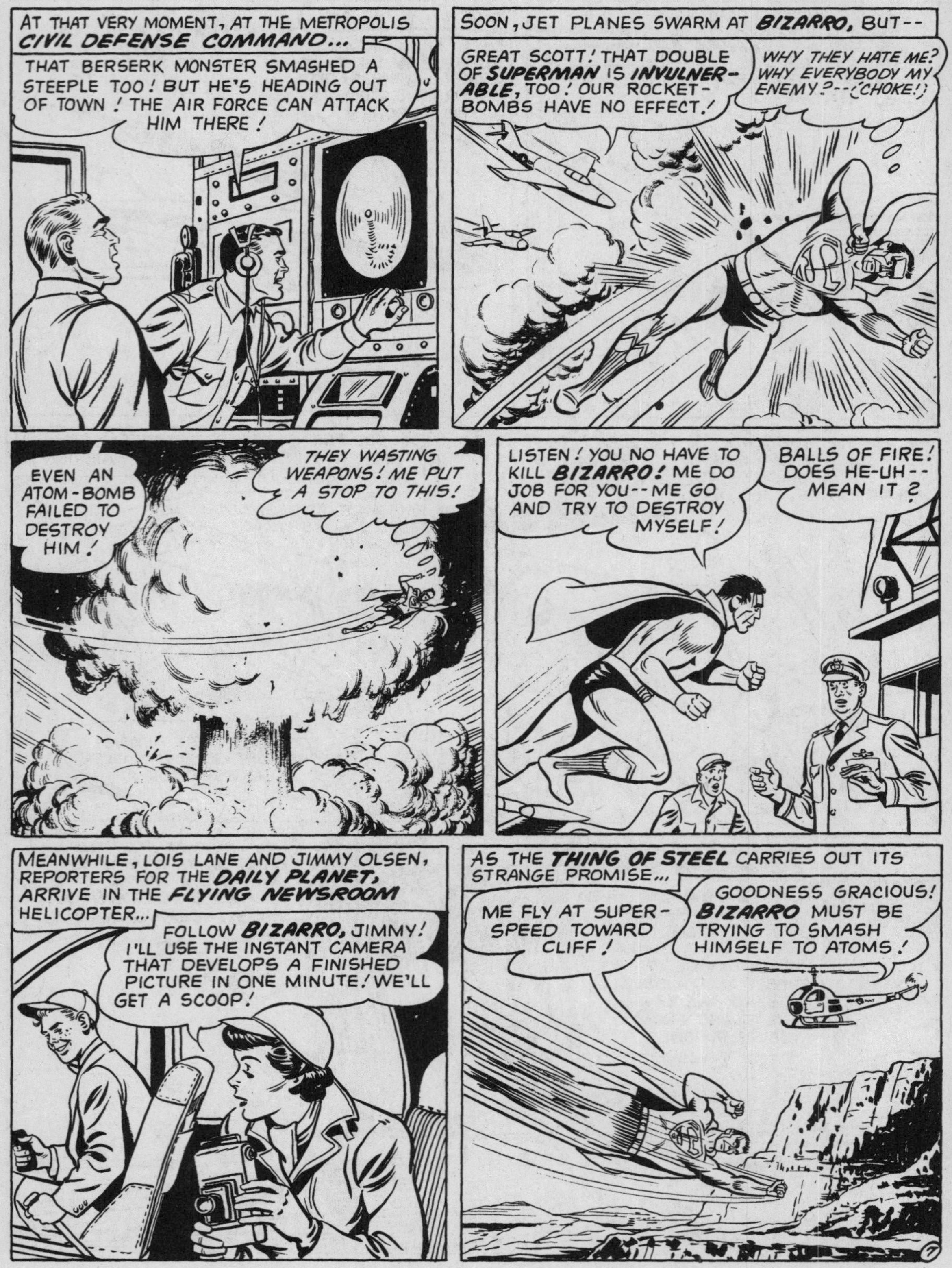
AT THAT VERY MOMENT, AT THE METROPOLIS CIVIL DEFENSE COMMAND...
THAT BERSERK MONSTER SMASHED A STEEPLE TOO! BUT HE'S HEADING OUT OF TOWN! THE AIR FORCE CAN ATTACK HIM THERE!
SOON, JET PLANES SWARM AT BIZARRO, BUT--
GREAT SCOTT! THAT DOUBLE OF SUPERMAN IS INVULNERABLE, TOO! OUR ROCKET-BOMBS HAVE NO EFFECT!
WHY THEY HATE ME? WHY EVERYBODY MY ENEMY?--(CHOKE!)
EVEN AN ATOM-BOMB FAILED TO DESTROY HIM!
THEY WASTING WEAPONS! ME PUT A STOP TO THIS!
LISTEN! YOU NO HAVE TO KILL BIZARRO! ME DO JOB FOR YOU--ME GO AND TRY TO DESTROY MYSELF!
BALLS OF FIRE! DOES HE-UH--MEAN IT?
MEANWHILE, LOIS LANE AND JIMMY OLSEN, REPORTERS FOR THE DAILY PLANET, ARRIVE IN THE FLYING NEWSROOM HELICOPTER...
FOLLOW BIZARRO, JIMMY! I'LL USE THE INSTANT CAMERA THAT DEVELOPS A FINISHED PICTURE IN ONE MINUTE! WE'LL GET A SCOOP!
AS THE THING OF STEEL CARRIES OUT ITS STRANGE PROMISE...
ME FLY AT SUPER-SPEED TOWARD CLIFF!
GOODNESS GRACIOUS! BIZARRO MUST BE TRYING TO SMASH HIMSELF TO ATOMS!
7

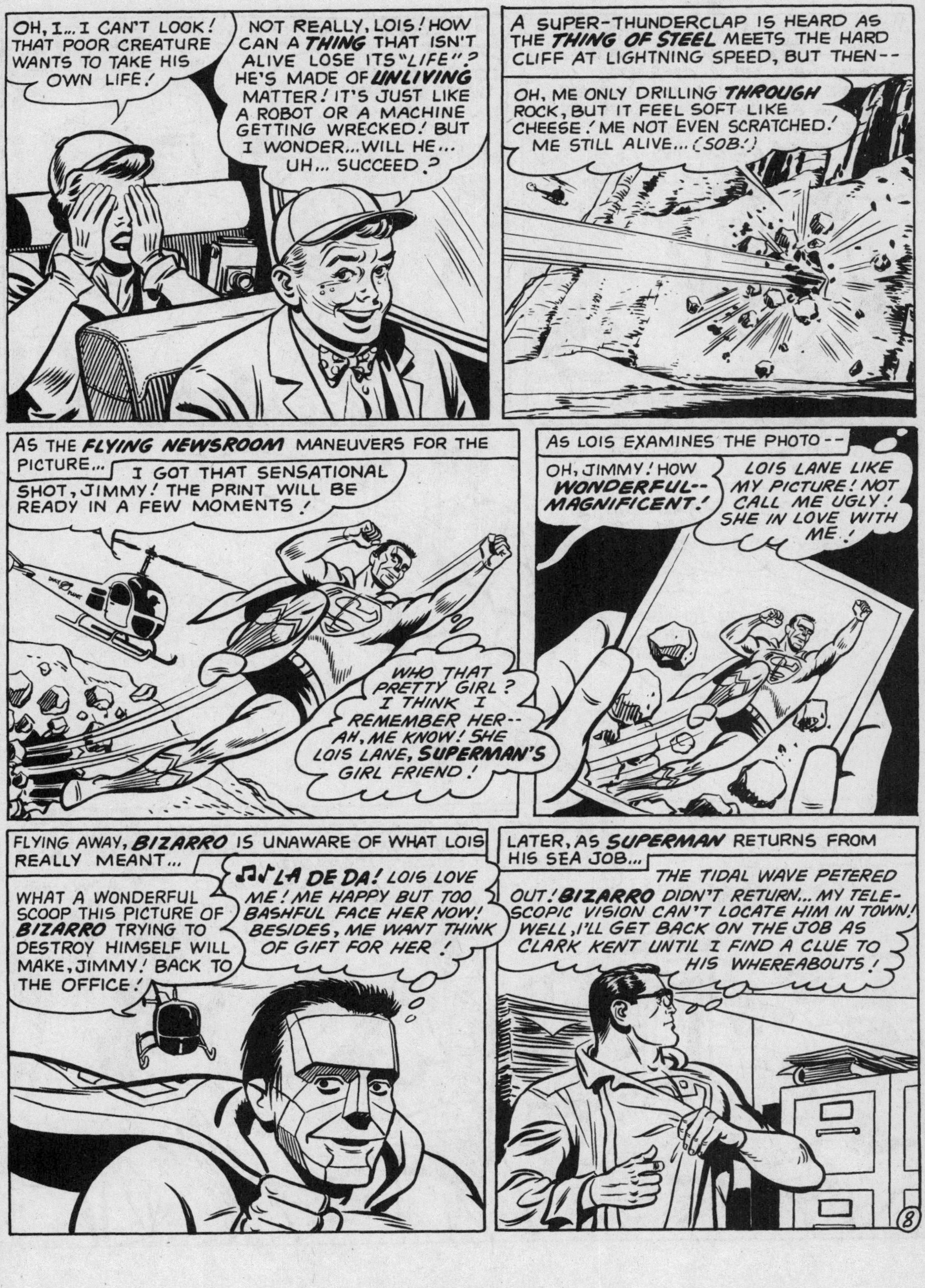
OH, I... I CAN'T LOOK! THAT POOR CREATURE WANTS TO TAKE HIS OWN LIFE!
NOT REALLY, LOIS! HOW CAN A THING THAT ISN'T ALIVE LOSE ITS "LIFE"? HE'S MADE OF UNLIVING MATTER! IT'S JUST LIKE A ROBOT OR A MACHINE GETTING WRECKED! BUT I WONDER... WILL HE... UH... SUCCEED?
A SUPER-THUNDERCLAP IS HEARD AS THE THING OF STEEL MEETS THE HARD CLIFF AT LIGHTNING SPEED, BUT THEN--
OH, ME ONLY DRILLING THROUGH ROCK, BUT IT FEEL SOFT LIKE CHEESE! ME NOT EVEN SCRATCHED! ME STILL ALIVE... (SOB!)
AS THE FLYING NEWSROOM MANEUVERS FOR THE PICTURE...
I GOT THAT SENSATIONAL SHOT, JIMMY! THE PRINT WILL BE READY IN A FEW MOMENTS!
WHO THAT PRETTY GIRL? I THINK I REMEMBER HER-- AH, ME KNOW! SHE LOIS LANE, SUPERMAN'S GIRL FRIEND!
AS LOIS EXAMINES THE PHOTO--
OH, JIMMY! HOW WONDERFUL-- MAGNIFICENT!
LOIS LANE LIKE MY PICTURE! NOT CALL ME UGLY! SHE IN LOVE WITH ME!
FLYING AWAY, BIZARRO IS UNAWARE OF WHAT LOIS REALLY MEANT...
WHAT A WONDERFUL SCOOP THIS PICTURE OF BIZARRO TRYING TO DESTROY HIMSELF WILL MAKE, JIMMY! BACK TO THE OFFICE!
♫♪ LA DE DA! LOIS LOVE ME! ME HAPPY BUT TOO BASHFUL FACE HER NOW! BESIDES, ME WANT THINK OF GIFT FOR HER!
LATER, AS SUPERMAN RETURNS FROM HIS SEA JOB...
THE TIDAL WAVE PETERED OUT! BIZARRO DIDN'T RETURN... MY TELE-SCOPIC VISION CAN'T LOCATE HIM IN TOWN! WELL, I'LL GET BACK ON THE JOB AS CLARK KENT UNTIL I FIND A CLUE TO HIS WHEREABOUTS!
8

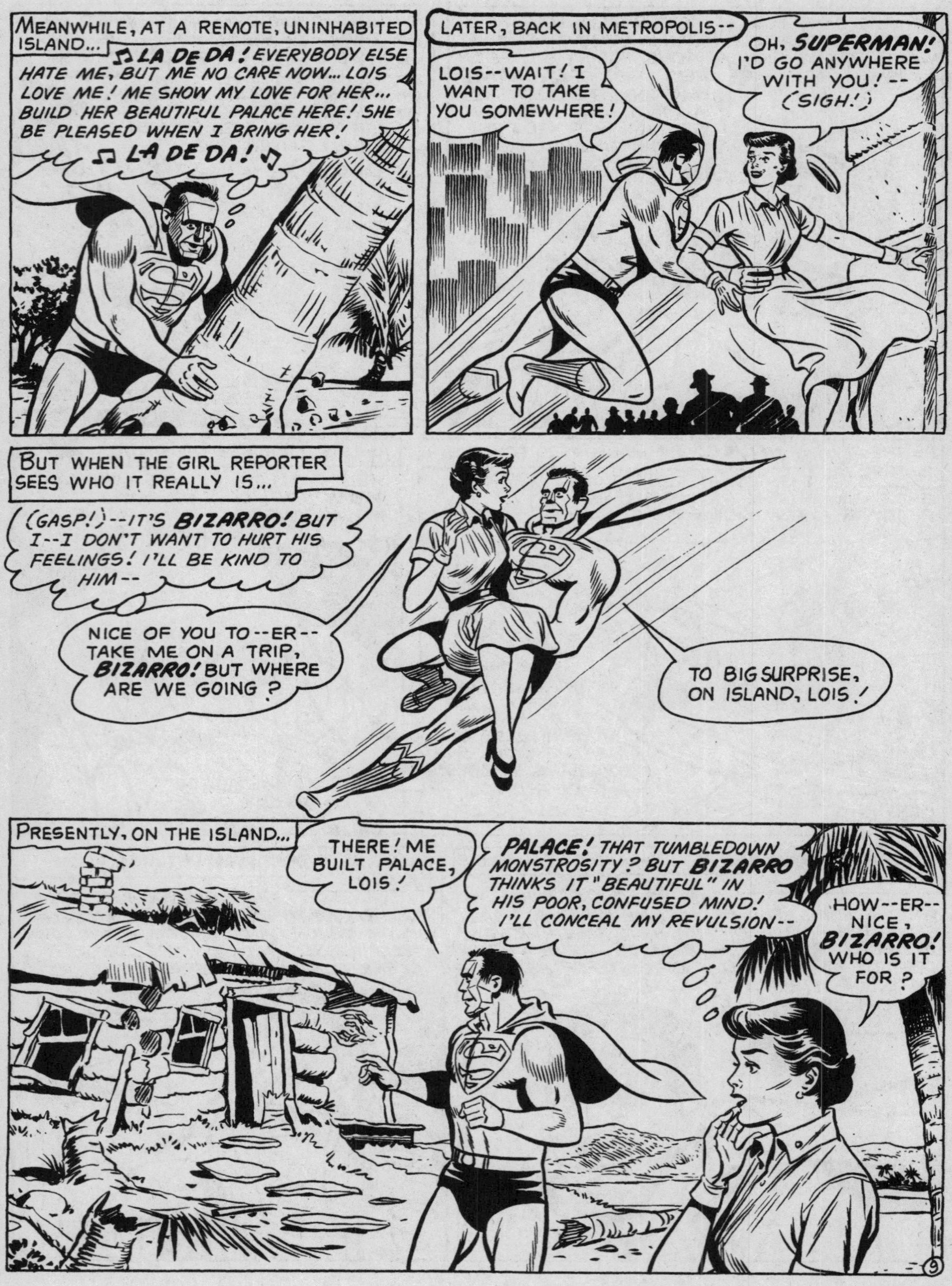
MEANWHILE, AT A REMOTE, UNINHABITED ISLAND...
♫ LA DE DA! EVERYBODY ELSE HATE ME, BUT ME NO CARE NOW... LOIS LOVE ME! ME SHOW MY LOVE FOR HER... BUILD HER BEAUTIFUL PALACE HERE! SHE BE PLEASED WHEN I BRING HER! ♫ LA DE DA! ♫
LATER, BACK IN METROPOLIS--
LOIS--WAIT! I WANT TO TAKE YOU SOMEWHERE!
OH, SUPERMAN! I'D GO ANYWHERE WITH YOU! --(SIGH!)
BUT WHEN THE GIRL REPORTER SEES WHO IT REALLY IS...
(GASP!)--IT'S BIZARRO! BUT I--I DON'T WANT TO HURT HIS FEELINGS! I'LL BE KIND TO HIM--
NICE OF YOU TO--ER--TAKE ME ON A TRIP, BIZARRO! BUT WHERE ARE WE GOING?
TO BIG SURPRISE, ON ISLAND, LOIS!
PRESENTLY, ON THE ISLAND...
THERE! ME BUILT PALACE, LOIS!
PALACE! THAT TUMBLEDOWN MONSTROSITY? BUT BIZARRO THINKS IT "BEAUTIFUL" IN HIS POOR, CONFUSED MIND! I'LL CONCEAL MY REVULSION--
HOW--ER--NICE, BIZARRO! WHO IS IT FOR?
9

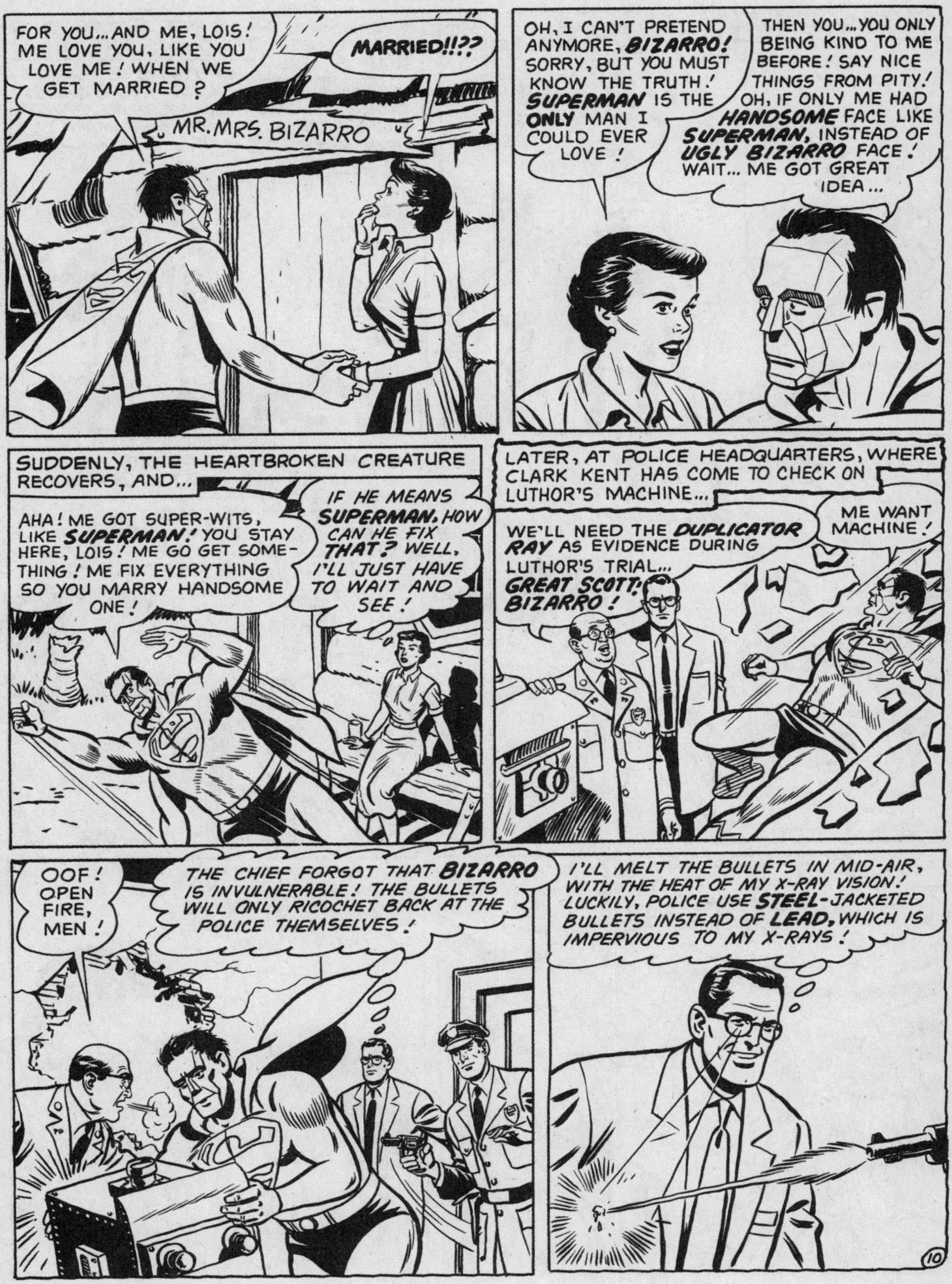
FOR YOU...AND ME, LOIS! ME LOVE YOU, LIKE YOU LOVE ME! WHEN WE GET MARRIED?
MARRIED!!??
MR. MRS. BIZARRO
OH, I CAN'T PRETEND ANYMORE, BIZARRO! SORRY, BUT YOU MUST KNOW THE TRUTH! SUPERMAN IS THE ONLY MAN I COULD EVER LOVE!
THEN YOU...YOU ONLY BEING KIND TO ME BEFORE! SAY NICE THINGS FROM PITY! OH, IF ONLY ME HAD HANDSOME FACE LIKE SUPERMAN, INSTEAD OF UGLY BIZARRO FACE! WAIT... ME GOT GREAT IDEA...
SUDDENLY, THE HEARTBROKEN CREATURE RECOVERS, AND...
AHA! ME GOT SUPER-WITS, LIKE SUPERMAN! YOU STAY HERE, LOIS! ME GO GET SOMETHING! ME FIX EVERYTHING SO YOU MARRY HANDSOME ONE!
IF HE MEANS SUPERMAN, HOW CAN HE FIX THAT? WELL, I'LL JUST HAVE TO WAIT AND SEE!
LATER, AT POLICE HEADQUARTERS, WHERE CLARK KENT HAS COME TO CHECK ON LUTHOR'S MACHINE...
WE'LL NEED THE DUPLICATOR RAY AS EVIDENCE DURING LUTHOR'S TRIAL... GREAT SCOTT! BIZARRO!
ME WANT MACHINE!
OOF! OPEN FIRE, MEN!
THE CHIEF FORGOT THAT BIZARRO IS INVULNERABLE! THE BULLETS WILL ONLY RICOCHET BACK AT THE POLICE THEMSELVES!
I'LL MELT THE BULLETS IN MID-AIR, WITH THE HEAT OF MY X-RAY VISION! LUCKILY, POLICE USE STEEL-JACKETED BULLETS INSTEAD OF LEAD, WHICH IS IMPERVIOUS TO MY X-RAYS!
10

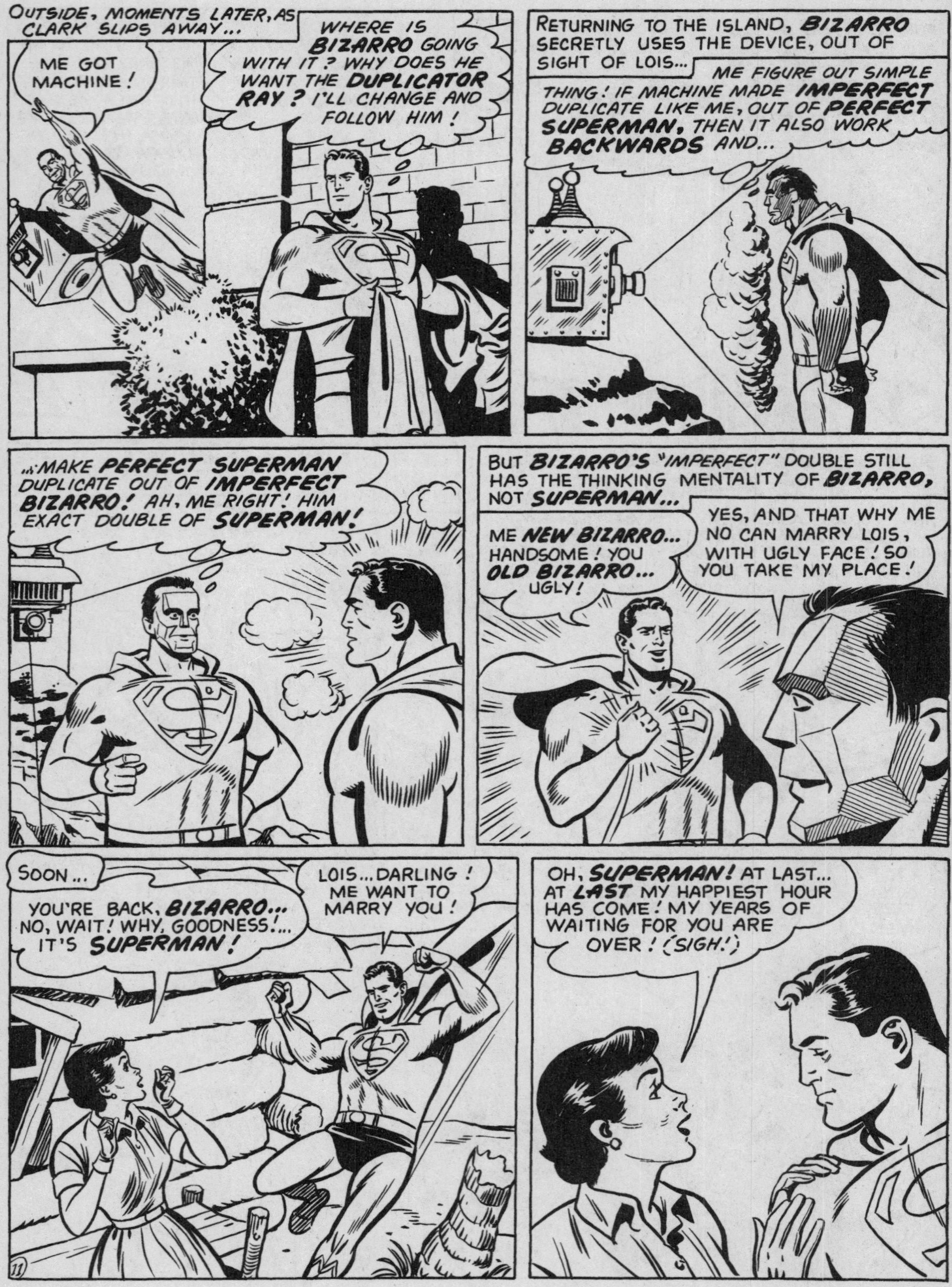
OUTSIDE, MOMENTS LATER, AS CLARK SLIPS AWAY...
ME GOT MACHINE!
WHERE IS BIZARRO GOING WITH IT? WHY DOES HE WANT THE DUPLICATOR RAY? I'LL CHANGE AND FOLLOW HIM!
RETURNING TO THE ISLAND, BIZARRO SECRETLY USES THE DEVICE, OUT OF SIGHT OF LOIS...
ME FIGURE OUT SIMPLE THING! IF MACHINE MADE IMPERFECT DUPLICATE LIKE ME, OUT OF PERFECT SUPERMAN, THEN IT ALSO WORK BACKWARDS AND...
...MAKE PERFECT SUPERMAN DUPLICATE OUT OF IMPERFECT BIZARRO! AH, ME RIGHT! HIM EXACT DOUBLE OF SUPERMAN!
BUT BIZARRO'S "IMPERFECT" DOUBLE STILL HAS THE THINKING MENTALITY OF BIZARRO, NOT SUPERMAN...
ME NEW BIZARRO... HANDSOME! YOU OLD BIZARRO... UGLY!
YES, AND THAT WHY ME NO CAN MARRY LOIS, WITH UGLY FACE! SO YOU TAKE MY PLACE!
SOON...
YOU'RE BACK, BIZARRO... NO, WAIT! WHY, GOODNESS!... IT'S SUPERMAN!
LOIS... DARLING! ME WANT TO MARRY YOU!
11
OH, SUPERMAN! AT LAST... AT LAST MY HAPPIEST HOUR HAS COME! MY YEARS OF WAITING FOR YOU ARE OVER! (SIGH!)

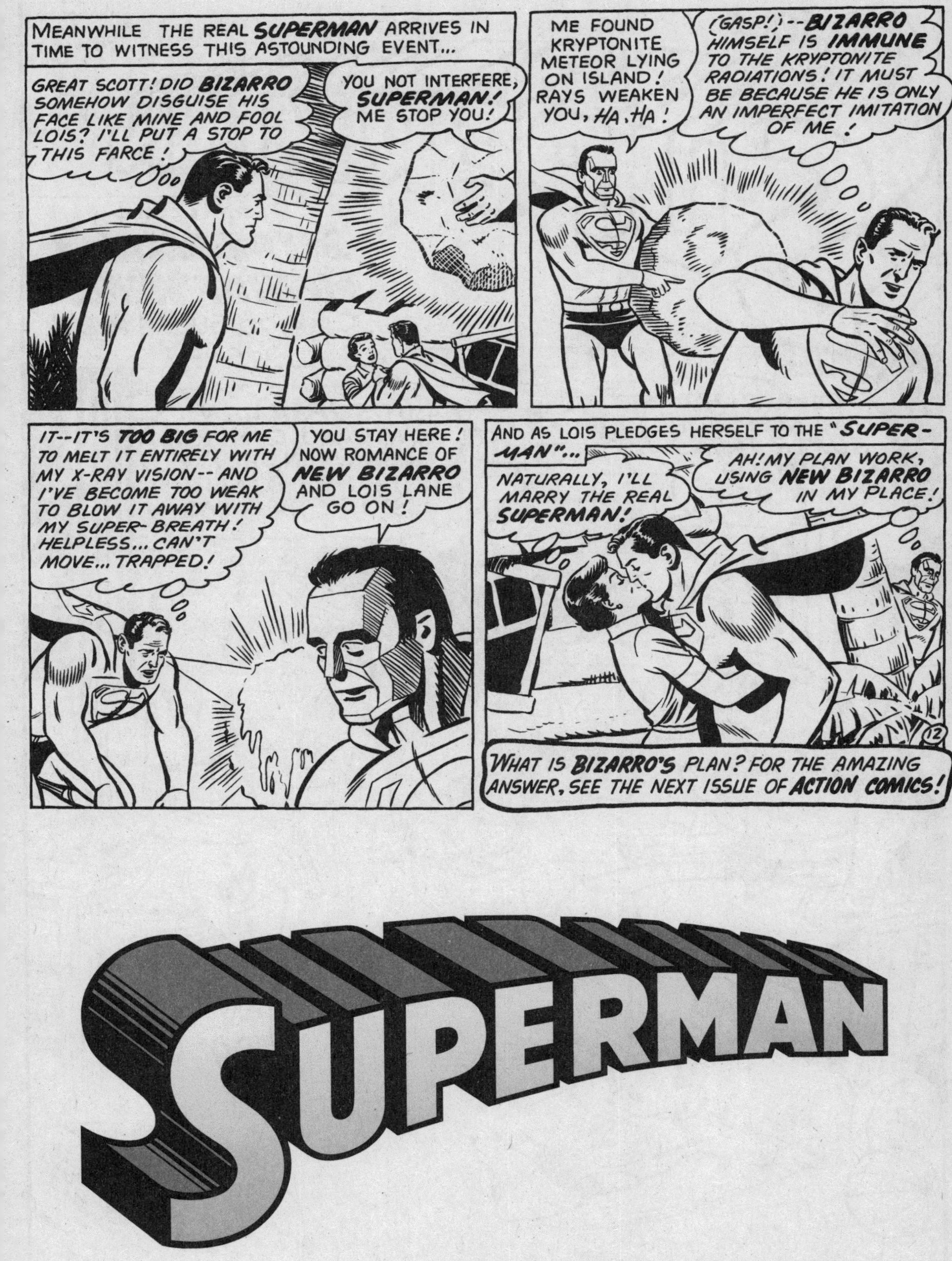
MEANWHILE THE REAL SUPERMAN ARRIVES IN TIME TO WITNESS THIS ASTOUNDING EVENT...
GREAT SCOTT! DID BIZARRO SOMEHOW DISGUISE HIS FACE LIKE MINE AND FOOL LOIS? I'LL PUT A STOP TO THIS FARCE!
YOU NOT INTERFERE, SUPERMAN! ME STOP YOU!
ME FOUND KRYPTONITE METEOR LYING ON ISLAND! RAYS WEAKEN YOU, HA, HA!
(GASP!) --BIZARRO HIMSELF IS IMMUNE TO THE KRYPTONITE RADIATIONS! IT MUST BE BECAUSE HE IS ONLY AN IMPERFECT IMITATION OF ME!
IT--IT'S TOO BIG FOR ME TO MELT IT ENTIRELY WITH MY X-RAY VISION-- AND I'VE BECOME TOO WEAK TO BLOW IT AWAY WITH MY SUPER-BREATH! HELPLESS... CAN'T MOVE... TRAPPED!
YOU STAY HERE! NOW ROMANCE OF NEW BIZARRO AND LOIS LANE GO ON!
AND AS LOIS PLEDGES HERSELF TO THE "SUPER-MAN"...
NATURALLY, I'LL MARRY THE REAL SUPERMAN!
AH! MY PLAN WORK, USING NEW BIZARRO IN MY PLACE!
12
WHAT IS BIZARRO'S PLAN? FOR THE AMAZING ANSWER, SEE THE NEXT ISSUE OF ACTION COMICS!

SUPERMAN

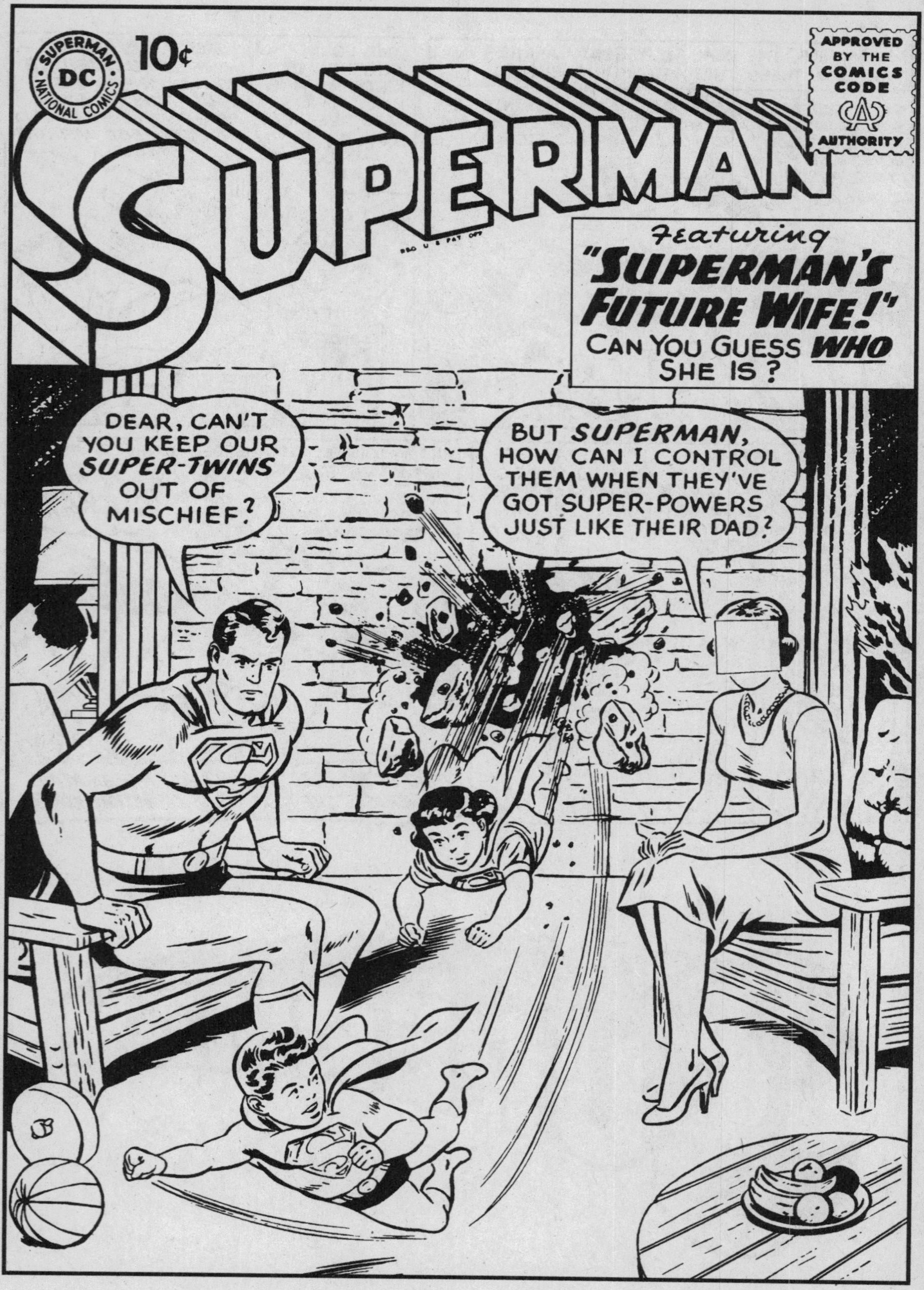
SUPERMAN DC NATIONAL COMICS
10¢
APPROVED BY THE COMICS CODE AUTHORITY
SUPERMAN
Featuring "SUPERMAN'S FUTURE WIFE!" CAN YOU GUESS WHO SHE IS?
DEAR, CAN'T YOU KEEP OUR SUPER-TWINS OUT OF MISCHIEF?
BUT SUPERMAN, HOW CAN I CONTROL THEM WHEN THEY'VE GOT SUPER-POWERS JUST LIKE THEIR DAD?

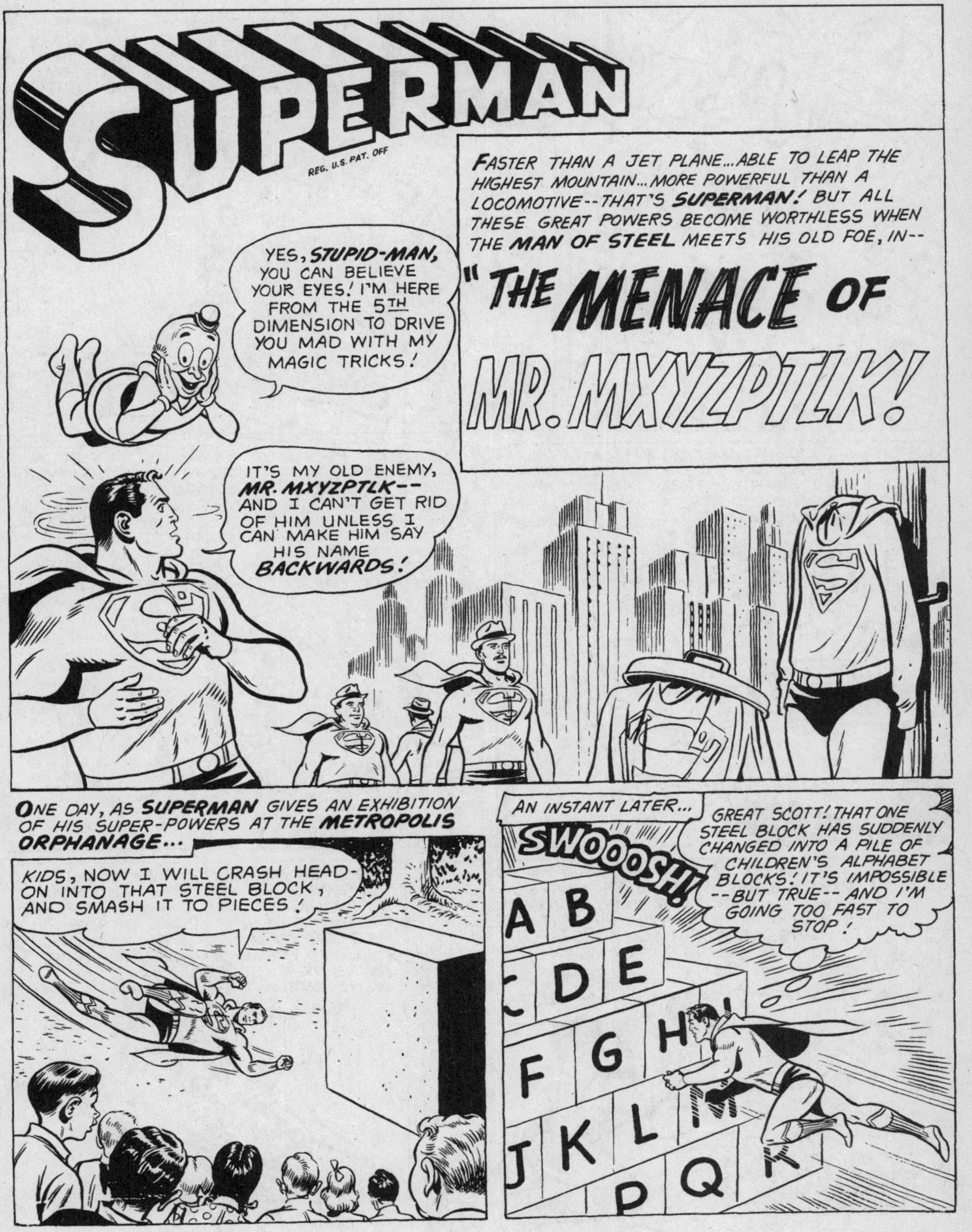
SUPERMAN
REG. U.S. PAT. OFF
FASTER THAN A JET PLANE...ABLE TO LEAP THE HIGHEST MOUNTAIN...MORE POWERFUL THAN A LOCOMOTIVE--THAT'S SUPERMAN! BUT ALL THESE GREAT POWERS BECOME WORTHLESS WHEN THE MAN OF STEEL MEETS HIS OLD FOE, IN--
"THE MENACE OF MR. MXYZPTLK!
YES, STUPID-MAN, YOU CAN BELIEVE YOUR EYES! I'M HERE FROM THE 5TH DIMENSION TO DRIVE YOU MAD WITH MY MAGIC TRICKS!
IT'S MY OLD ENEMY, MR. MXYZPTLK-- AND I CAN'T GET RID OF HIM UNLESS I CAN MAKE HIM SAY HIS NAME BACKWARDS!
ONE DAY, AS SUPERMAN GIVES AN EXHIBITION OF HIS SUPER-POWERS AT THE METROPOLIS ORPHANAGE...
KIDS, NOW I WILL CRASH HEAD-ON INTO THAT STEEL BLOCK, AND SMASH IT TO PIECES!
AN INSTANT LATER...
SWOOOSH!
GREAT SCOTT! THAT ONE STEEL BLOCK HAS SUDDENLY CHANGED INTO A PILE OF CHILDREN'S ALPHABET BLOCKS! IT'S IMPOSSIBLE --BUT TRUE-- AND I'M GOING TOO FAST TO STOP!

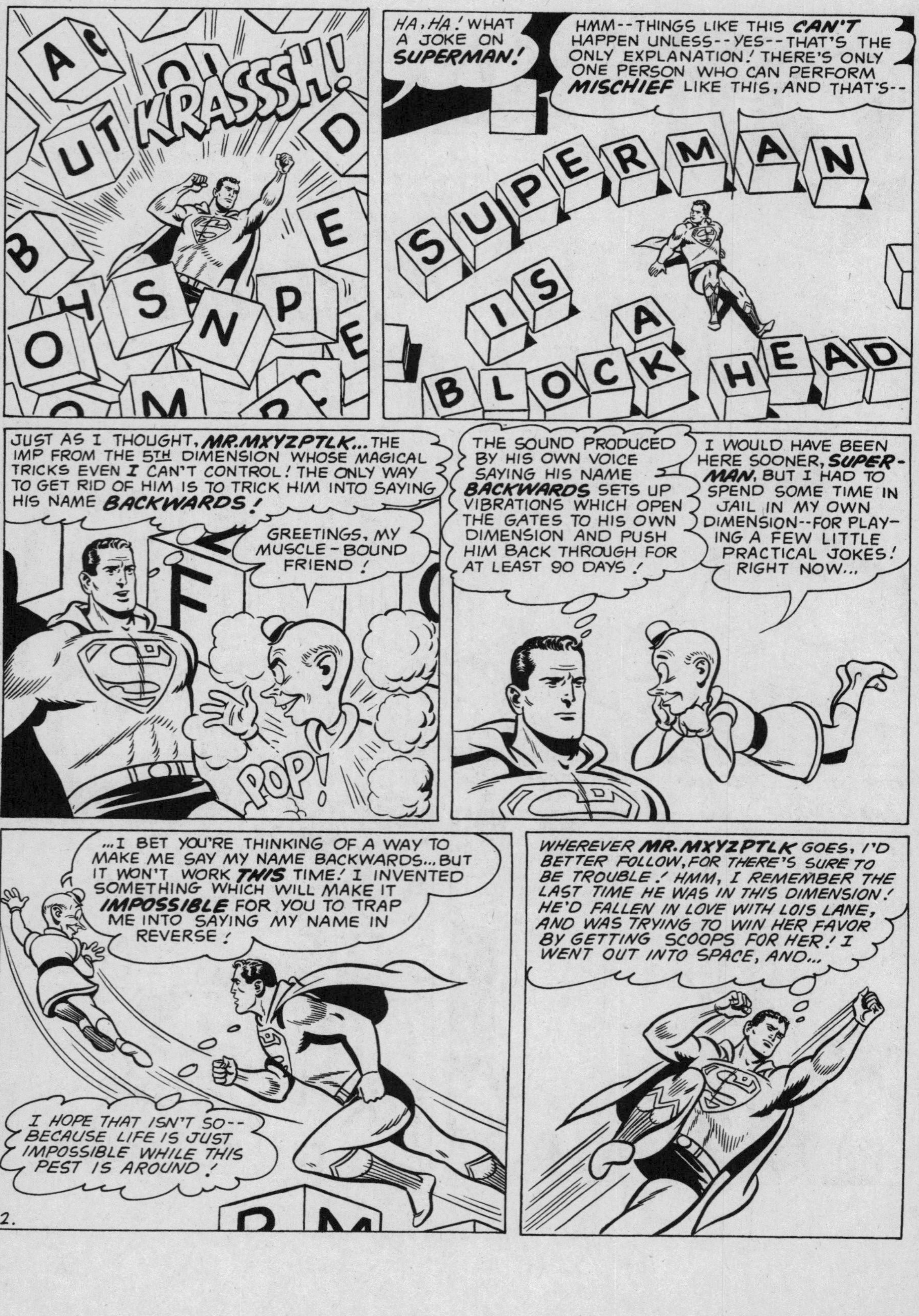
KRASSSH!
HA, HA! WHAT A JOKE ON SUPERMAN!
HMM--THINGS LIKE THIS CAN'T HAPPEN UNLESS--YES--THAT'S THE ONLY EXPLANATION! THERE'S ONLY ONE PERSON WHO CAN PERFORM MISCHIEF LIKE THIS, AND THAT'S--
SUPERMAN IS A BLOCK HEAD
JUST AS I THOUGHT, MR. MXYZPTLK... THE IMP FROM THE 5TH DIMENSION WHOSE MAGICAL TRICKS EVEN I CAN'T CONTROL! THE ONLY WAY TO GET RID OF HIM IS TO TRICK HIM INTO SAYING HIS NAME BACKWARDS!
GREETINGS, MY MUSCLE-BOUND FRIEND!
POP!
THE SOUND PRODUCED BY HIS OWN VOICE SAYING HIS NAME BACKWARDS SETS UP VIBRATIONS WHICH OPEN THE GATES TO HIS OWN DIMENSION AND PUSH HIM BACK THROUGH FOR AT LEAST 90 DAYS!
I WOULD HAVE BEEN HERE SOONER, SUPERMAN, BUT I HAD TO SPEND SOME TIME IN JAIL IN MY OWN DIMENSION--FOR PLAYING A FEW LITTLE PRACTICAL JOKES! RIGHT NOW...
...I BET YOU'RE THINKING OF A WAY TO MAKE ME SAY MY NAME BACKWARDS... BUT IT WON'T WORK THIS TIME! I INVENTED SOMETHING WHICH WILL MAKE IT IMPOSSIBLE FOR YOU TO TRAP ME INTO SAYING MY NAME IN REVERSE!
I HOPE THAT ISN'T SO--BECAUSE LIFE IS JUST IMPOSSIBLE WHILE THIS PEST IS AROUND!
2.
WHEREVER MR. MXYZPTLK GOES, I'D BETTER FOLLOW, FOR THERE'S SURE TO BE TROUBLE! HMM, I REMEMBER THE LAST TIME HE WAS IN THIS DIMENSION! HE'D FALLEN IN LOVE WITH LOIS LANE, AND WAS TRYING TO WIN HER FAVOR BY GETTING SCOOPS FOR HER! I WENT OUT INTO SPACE, AND...

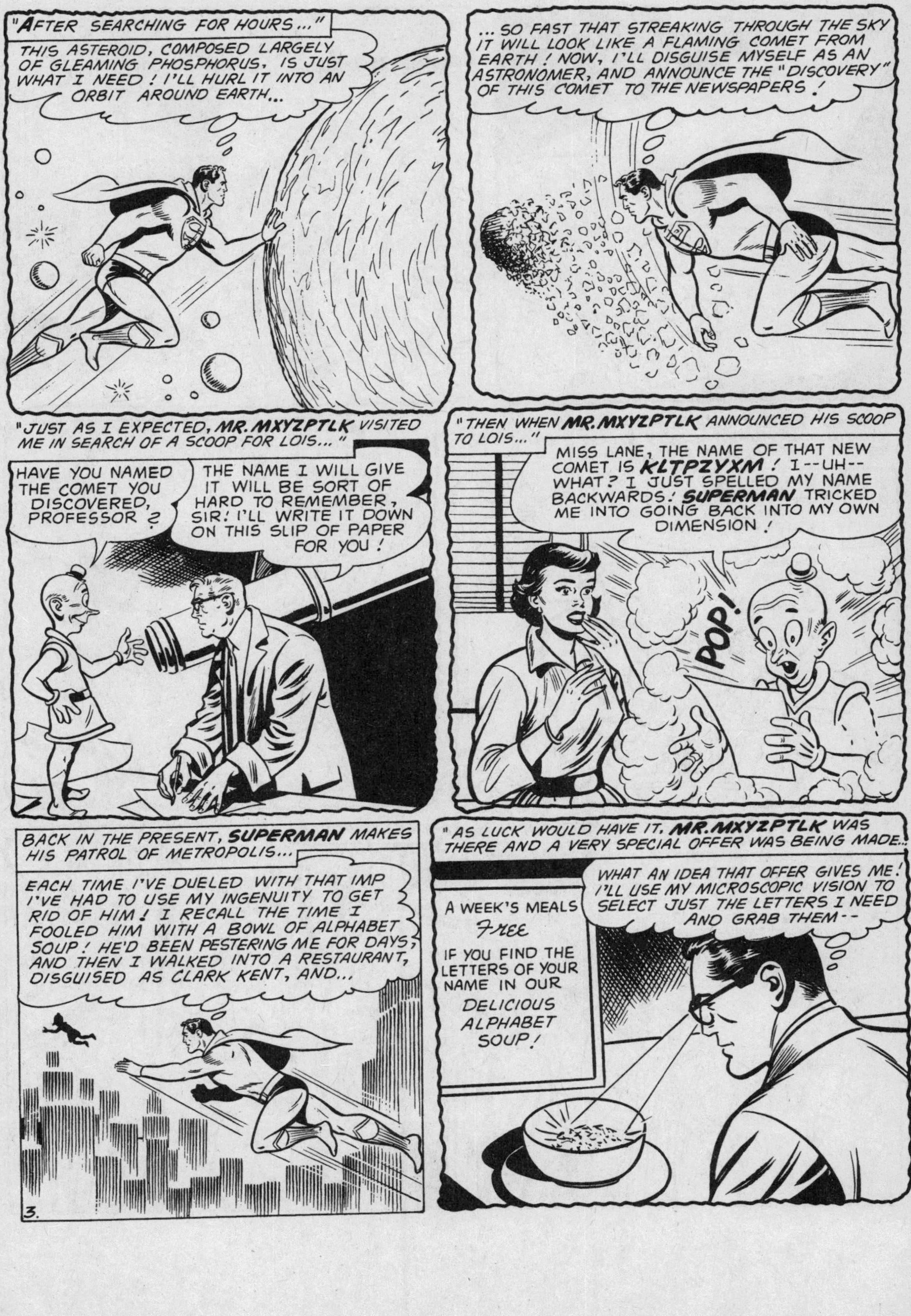
"AFTER SEARCHING FOR HOURS..."
THIS ASTEROID, COMPOSED LARGELY OF GLEAMING PHOSPHORUS, IS JUST WHAT I NEED! I'LL HURL IT INTO AN ORBIT AROUND EARTH...
... SO FAST THAT STREAKING THROUGH THE SKY IT WILL LOOK LIKE A FLAMING COMET FROM EARTH! NOW, I'LL DISGUISE MYSELF AS AN ASTRONOMER, AND ANNOUNCE THE "DISCOVERY" OF THIS COMET TO THE NEWSPAPERS!
"JUST AS I EXPECTED, MR. MXYZPTLK VISITED ME IN SEARCH OF A SCOOP FOR LOIS..."
HAVE YOU NAMED THE COMET YOU DISCOVERED, PROFESSOR?
THE NAME I WILL GIVE IT WILL BE SORT OF HARD TO REMEMBER, SIR! I'LL WRITE IT DOWN ON THIS SLIP OF PAPER FOR YOU!
"THEN WHEN MR. MXYZPTLK ANNOUNCED HIS SCOOP TO LOIS..."
MISS LANE, THE NAME OF THAT NEW COMET IS KLTPZYXM! I--UH--WHAT? I JUST SPELLED MY NAME BACKWARDS! SUPERMAN TRICKED ME INTO GOING BACK INTO MY OWN DIMENSION!
POP!
BACK IN THE PRESENT, SUPERMAN MAKES HIS PATROL OF METROPOLIS...
EACH TIME I'VE DUELED WITH THAT IMP I'VE HAD TO USE MY INGENUITY TO GET RID OF HIM! I RECALL THE TIME I FOOLED HIM WITH A BOWL OF ALPHABET SOUP! HE'D BEEN PESTERING ME FOR DAYS, AND THEN I WALKED INTO A RESTAURANT, DISGUISED AS CLARK KENT, AND...
3.
"AS LUCK WOULD HAVE IT, MR. MXYZPTLK WAS THERE AND A VERY SPECIAL OFFER WAS BEING MADE..."
A WEEK'S MEALS FREE IF YOU FIND THE LETTERS OF YOUR NAME IN OUR DELICIOUS ALPHABET SOUP!
WHAT AN IDEA THAT OFFER GIVES ME! I'LL USE MY MICROSCOPIC VISION TO SELECT JUST THE LETTERS I NEED AND GRAB THEM--

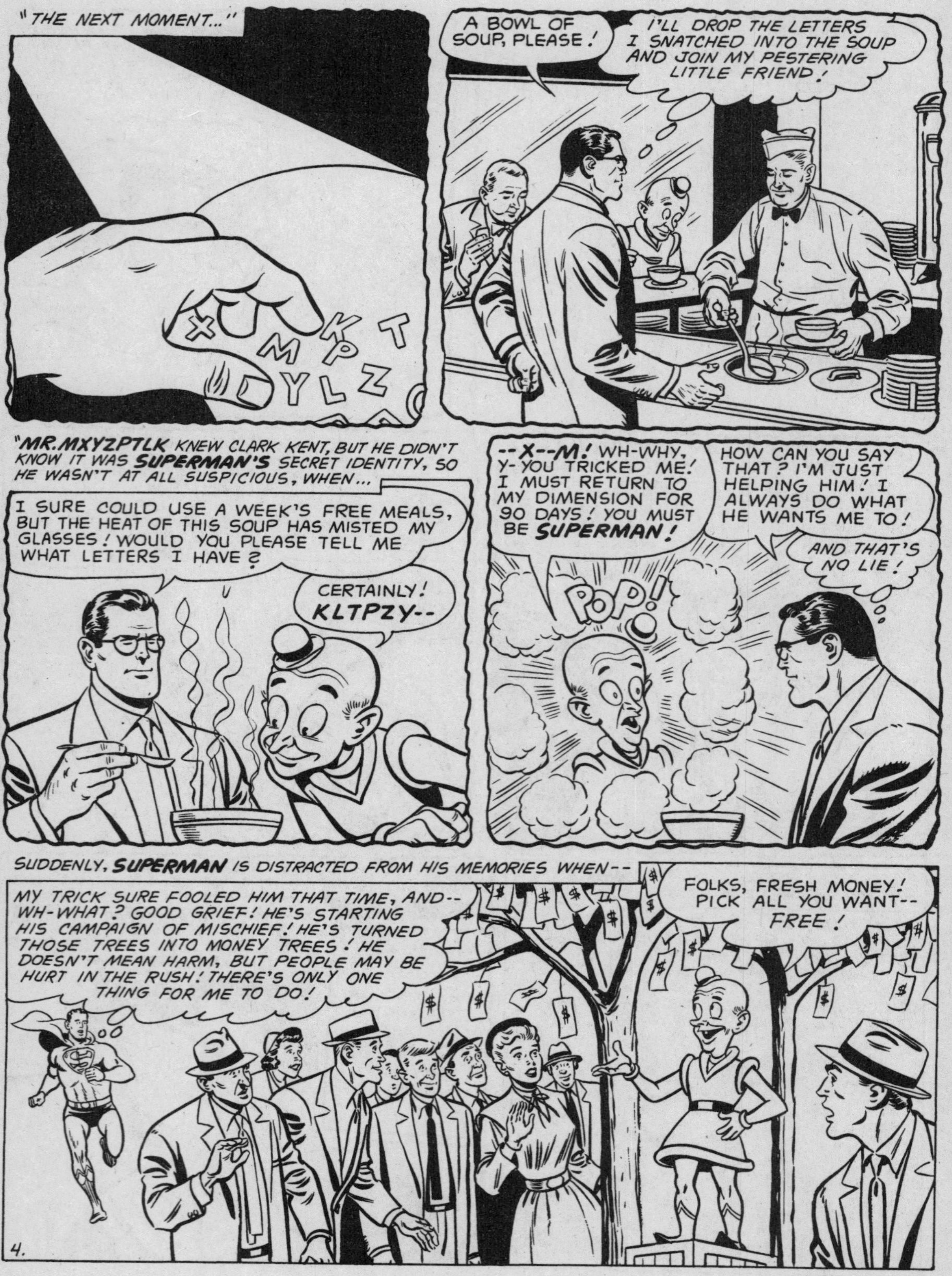
"THE NEXT MOMENT..."
A BOWL OF SOUP, PLEASE!
I'LL DROP THE LETTERS I SNATCHED INTO THE SOUP AND JOIN MY PESTERING LITTLE FRIEND!
"MR. MXYZPTLK KNEW CLARK KENT, BUT HE DIDN'T KNOW IT WAS SUPERMAN'S SECRET IDENTITY, SO HE WASN'T AT ALL SUSPICIOUS, WHEN...
I SURE COULD USE A WEEK'S FREE MEALS, BUT THE HEAT OF THIS SOUP HAS MISTED MY GLASSES! WOULD YOU PLEASE TELL ME WHAT LETTERS I HAVE?
CERTAINLY! KLTPZY--
--X--M! WH-WHY, Y-YOU TRICKED ME! I MUST RETURN TO MY DIMENSION FOR 90 DAYS! YOU MUST BE SUPERMAN!
HOW CAN YOU SAY THAT? I'M JUST HELPING HIM! I ALWAYS DO WHAT HE WANTS ME TO!
AND THAT'S NO LIE!
POP!
SUDDENLY, SUPERMAN IS DISTRACTED FROM HIS MEMORIES WHEN--
MY TRICK SURE FOOLED HIM THAT TIME, AND-- WH-WHAT? GOOD GRIEF! HE'S STARTING HIS CAMPAIGN OF MISCHIEF! HE'S TURNED THOSE TREES INTO MONEY TREES! HE DOESN'T MEAN HARM, BUT PEOPLE MAY BE HURT IN THE RUSH! THERE'S ONLY ONE THING FOR ME TO DO!
FOLKS, FRESH MONEY! PICK ALL YOU WANT-- FREE!
4.

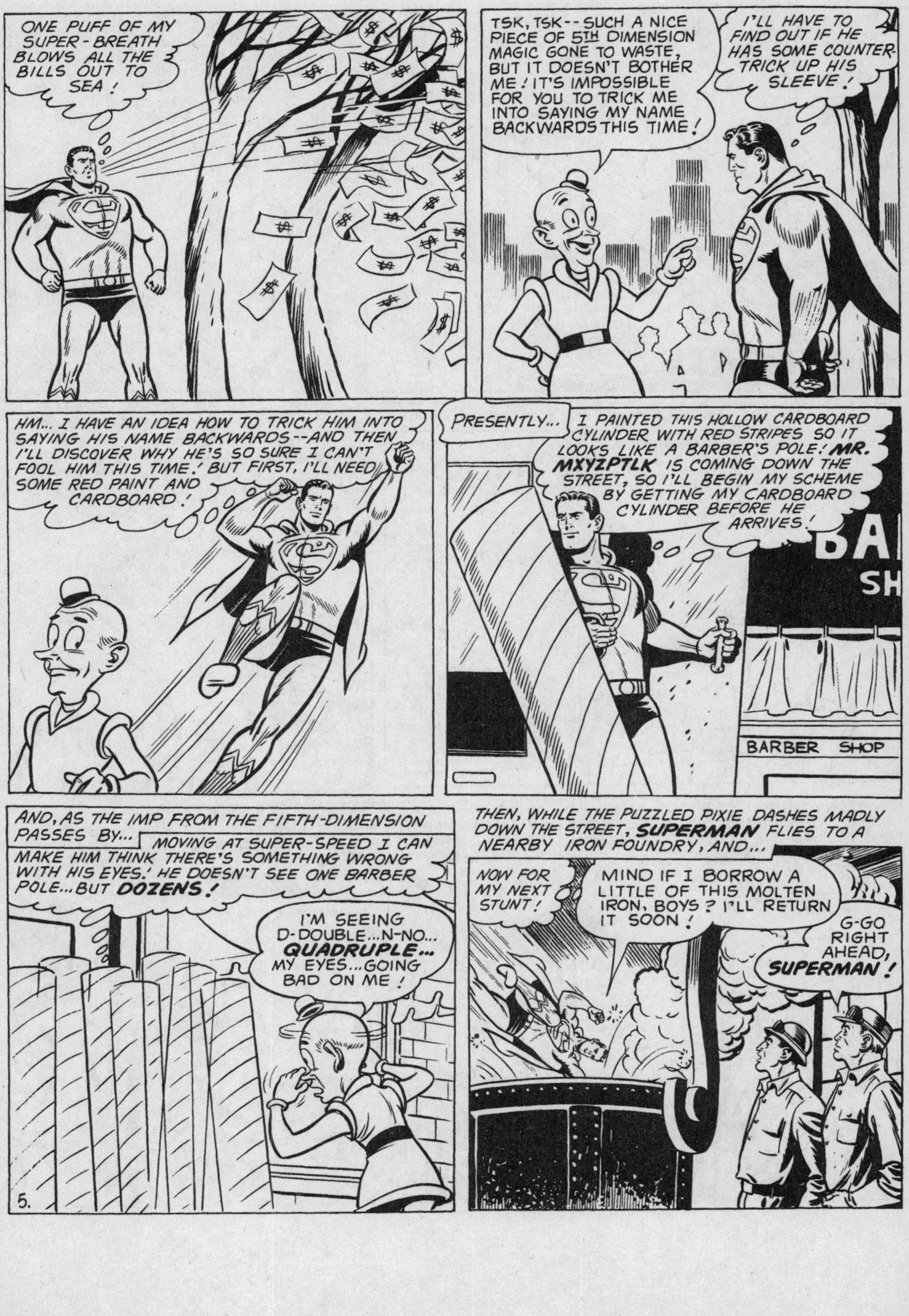
ONE PUFF OF MY SUPER-BREATH BLOWS ALL THE BILLS OUT TO SEA!
TSK, TSK--SUCH A NICE PIECE OF 5TH DIMENSION MAGIC GONE TO WASTE, BUT IT DOESN'T BOTHER ME! IT'S IMPOSSIBLE FOR YOU TO TRICK ME INTO SAYING MY NAME BACKWARDS THIS TIME!
I'LL HAVE TO FIND OUT IF HE HAS SOME COUNTER-TRICK UP HIS SLEEVE!
HM... I HAVE AN IDEA HOW TO TRICK HIM INTO SAYING HIS NAME BACKWARDS--AND THEN I'LL DISCOVER WHY HE'S SO SURE I CAN'T FOOL HIM THIS TIME! BUT FIRST, I'LL NEED SOME RED PAINT AND CARDBOARD!
PRESENTLY...
I PAINTED THIS HOLLOW CARDBOARD CYLINDER WITH RED STRIPES SO IT LOOKS LIKE A BARBER'S POLE! MR. MXYZPTLK IS COMING DOWN THE STREET, SO I'LL BEGIN MY SCHEME BY GETTING MY CARDBOARD CYLINDER BEFORE HE ARRIVES!
BA
SH
BARBER SHOP
AND, AS THE IMP FROM THE FIFTH-DIMENSION PASSES BY...
MOVING AT SUPER-SPEED I CAN MAKE HIM THINK THERE'S SOMETHING WRONG WITH HIS EYES! HE DOESN'T SEE ONE BARBER POLE...BUT DOZENS!
I'M SEEING D-DOUBLE...N-NO... QUADRUPLE... MY EYES...GOING BAD ON ME!
5.
THEN, WHILE THE PUZZLED PIXIE DASHES MADLY DOWN THE STREET, SUPERMAN FLIES TO A NEARBY IRON FOUNDRY, AND...
NOW FOR MY NEXT STUNT!
MIND IF I BORROW A LITTLE OF THIS MOLTEN IRON, BOYS? I'LL RETURN IT SOON!
G-GO RIGHT AHEAD, SUPERMAN!

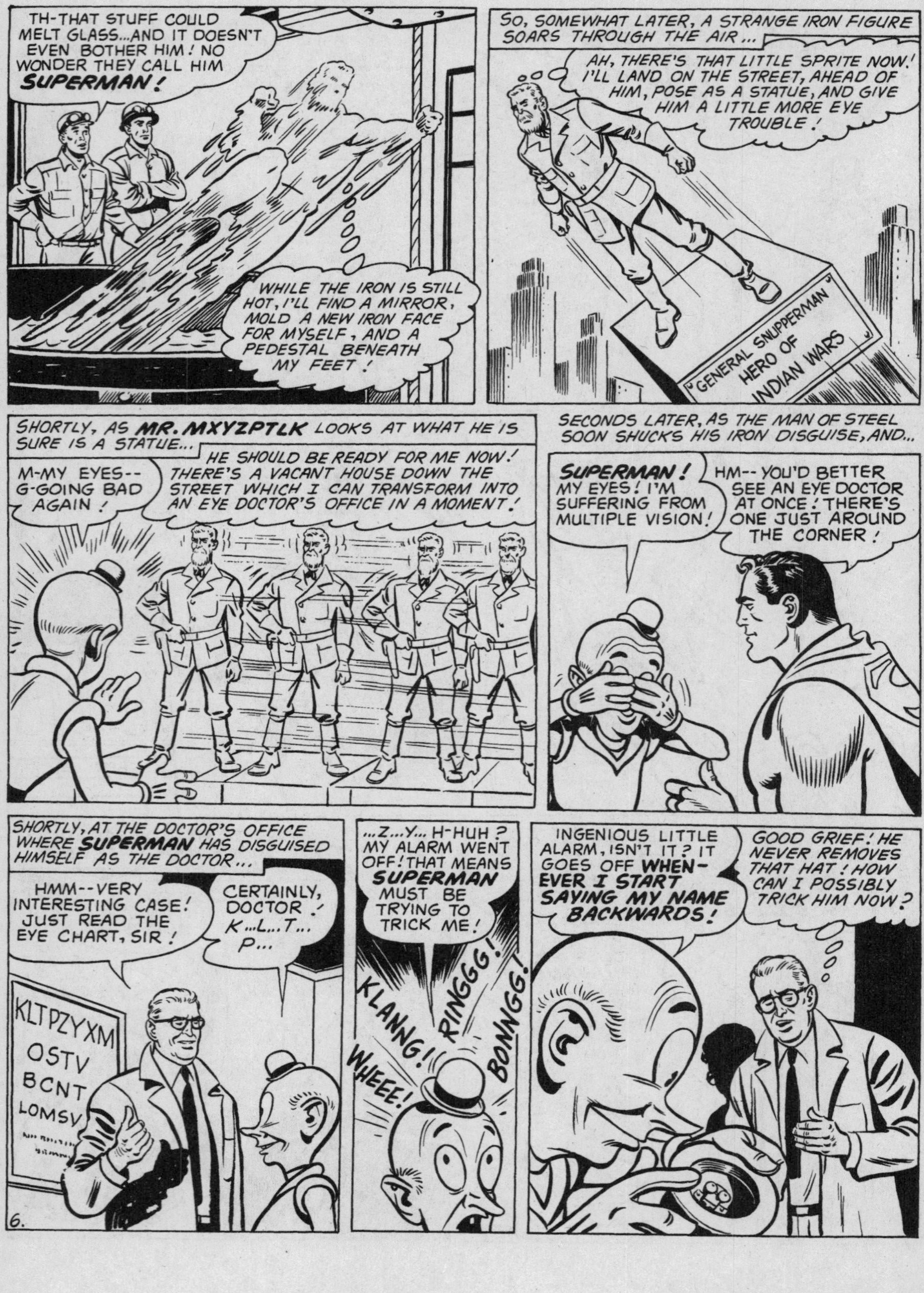
TH-THAT STUFF COULD MELT GLASS...AND IT DOESN'T EVEN BOTHER HIM! NO WONDER THEY CALL HIM SUPERMAN!
WHILE THE IRON IS STILL HOT, I'LL FIND A MIRROR, MOLD A NEW IRON FACE FOR MYSELF, AND A PEDESTAL BENEATH MY FEET!
SO, SOMEWHAT LATER, A STRANGE IRON FIGURE SOARS THROUGH THE AIR...
AH, THERE'S THAT LITTLE SPRITE NOW! I'LL LAND ON THE STREET, AHEAD OF HIM, POSE AS A STATUE, AND GIVE HIM A LITTLE MORE EYE TROUBLE!
GENERAL SNUPPERMAN HERO OF INDIAN WARS
SHORTLY, AS MR. MXYZPTLK LOOKS AT WHAT HE IS SURE IS A STATUE...
M-MY EYES-- G-GOING BAD AGAIN!
HE SHOULD BE READY FOR ME NOW! THERE'S A VACANT HOUSE DOWN THE STREET WHICH I CAN TRANSFORM INTO AN EYE DOCTOR'S OFFICE IN A MOMENT!
SECONDS LATER, AS THE MAN OF STEEL SOON SHUCKS HIS IRON DISGUISE, AND...
SUPERMAN! MY EYES! I'M SUFFERING FROM MULTIPLE VISION!
HM-- YOU'D BETTER SEE AN EYE DOCTOR AT ONCE! THERE'S ONE JUST AROUND THE CORNER!
SHORTLY, AT THE DOCTOR'S OFFICE WHERE SUPERMAN HAS DISGUISED HIMSELF AS THE DOCTOR...
HMM--VERY INTERESTING CASE! JUST READ THE EYE CHART, SIR!
CERTAINLY, DOCTOR! K...L...T... P...
KLTPZYXM
OSTV
BCNT
LOMSV
6.
...Z...Y... H-HUH? MY ALARM WENT OFF! THAT MEANS SUPERMAN MUST BE TRYING TO TRICK ME!
KLANNG!
RINGGG!
BONNGG!
WHEEE!
INGENIOUS LITTLE ALARM, ISN'T IT? IT GOES OFF WHEN-EVER I START SAYING MY NAME BACKWARDS!
GOOD GRIEF! HE NEVER REMOVES THAT HAT! HOW CAN I POSSIBLY TRICK HIM NOW?

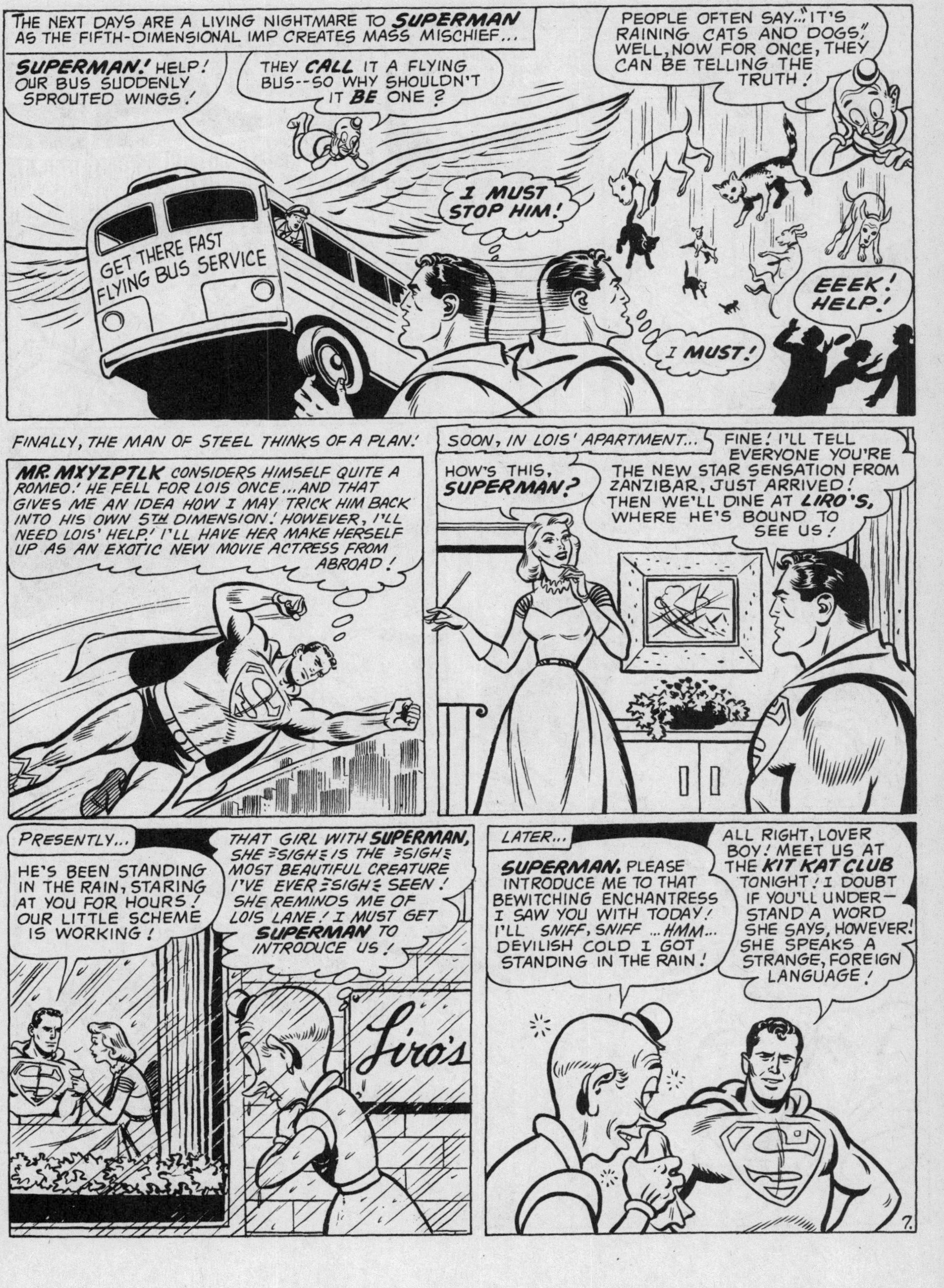
THE NEXT DAYS ARE A LIVING NIGHTMARE TO SUPERMAN AS THE FIFTH-DIMENSIONAL IMP CREATES MASS MISCHIEF...
SUPERMAN! HELP! OUR BUS SUDDENLY SPROUTED WINGS!
THEY CALL IT A FLYING BUS--SO WHY SHOULDN'T IT BE ONE?
PEOPLE OFTEN SAY..."IT'S RAINING CATS AND DOGS." WELL, NOW FOR ONCE, THEY CAN BE TELLING THE TRUTH!
GET THERE FAST FLYING BUS SERVICE
I MUST STOP HIM!
EEEK! HELP!
I MUST!
FINALLY, THE MAN OF STEEL THINKS OF A PLAN!
MR. MXYZPTLK CONSIDERS HIMSELF QUITE A ROMEO! HE FELL FOR LOIS ONCE ... AND THAT GIVES ME AN IDEA HOW I MAY TRICK HIM BACK INTO HIS OWN 5TH DIMENSION! HOWEVER, I'LL NEED LOIS' HELP! I'LL HAVE HER MAKE HERSELF UP AS AN EXOTIC NEW MOVIE ACTRESS FROM ABROAD!
SOON, IN LOIS' APARTMENT...
HOW'S THIS, SUPERMAN?
FINE! I'LL TELL EVERYONE YOU'RE THE NEW STAR SENSATION FROM ZANZIBAR, JUST ARRIVED! THEN WE'LL DINE AT LIRO'S, WHERE HE'S BOUND TO SEE US!
PRESENTLY...
HE'S BEEN STANDING IN THE RAIN, STARING AT YOU FOR HOURS! OUR LITTLE SCHEME IS WORKING!
THAT GIRL WITH SUPERMAN, SHE -SIGH- IS THE -SIGH- MOST BEAUTIFUL CREATURE I'VE EVER -SIGH- SEEN! SHE REMINDS ME OF LOIS LANE! I MUST GET SUPERMAN TO INTRODUCE US!
Liro's
LATER...
SUPERMAN, PLEASE INTRODUCE ME TO THAT BEWITCHING ENCHANTRESS I SAW YOU WITH TODAY! I'LL SNIFF, SNIFF ... HMM... DEVILISH COLD I GOT STANDING IN THE RAIN!
ALL RIGHT, LOVER BOY! MEET US AT THE KIT KAT CLUB TONIGHT! I DOUBT IF YOU'LL UNDER-STAND A WORD SHE SAYS, HOWEVER! SHE SPEAKS A STRANGE, FOREIGN LANGUAGE!
7.

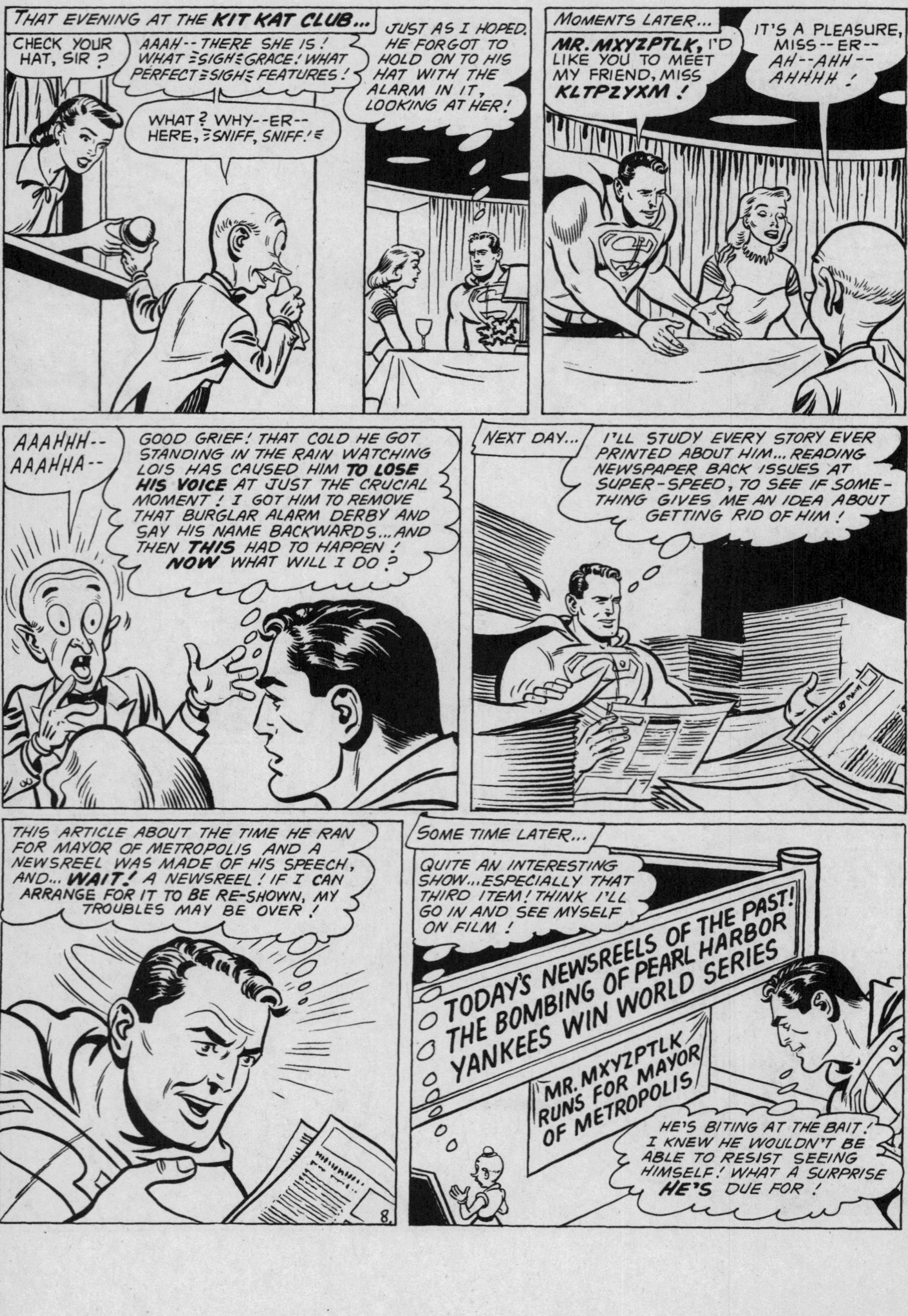
THAT EVENING AT THE KIT KAT CLUB...
CHECK YOUR HAT, SIR?
AAAH--THERE SHE IS! WHAT *SIGH* GRACE! WHAT PERFECT *SIGH* FEATURES!
WHAT? WHY--ER--HERE, *SNIFF, SNIFF!*
JUST AS I HOPED. HE FORGOT TO HOLD ON TO HIS HAT WITH THE ALARM IN IT, LOOKING AT HER!
MOMENTS LATER...
MR. MXYZPTLK, I'D LIKE YOU TO MEET MY FRIEND, MISS KLTPZYXM!
IT'S A PLEASURE, MISS--ER--AH--AHH--AHHHH!
AAAHHH--AAAHHA--
GOOD GRIEF! THAT COLD HE GOT STANDING IN THE RAIN WATCHING LOIS HAS CAUSED HIM TO LOSE HIS VOICE AT JUST THE CRUCIAL MOMENT! I GOT HIM TO REMOVE THAT BURGLAR ALARM DERBY AND SAY HIS NAME BACKWARDS...AND THEN THIS HAD TO HAPPEN! NOW WHAT WILL I DO?
NEXT DAY...
I'LL STUDY EVERY STORY EVER PRINTED ABOUT HIM...READING NEWSPAPER BACK ISSUES AT SUPER-SPEED, TO SEE IF SOMETHING GIVES ME AN IDEA ABOUT GETTING RID OF HIM!
THIS ARTICLE ABOUT THE TIME HE RAN FOR MAYOR OF METROPOLIS AND A NEWSREEL WAS MADE OF HIS SPEECH, AND... WAIT! A NEWSREEL! IF I CAN ARRANGE FOR IT TO BE RE-SHOWN, MY TROUBLES MAY BE OVER!
8.
SOME TIME LATER...
QUITE AN INTERESTING SHOW...ESPECIALLY THAT THIRD ITEM! THINK I'LL GO IN AND SEE MYSELF ON FILM!
TODAY'S NEWSREELS OF THE PAST!
THE BOMBING OF PEARL HARBOR
YANKEES WIN WORLD SERIES
MR. MXYZPTLK RUNS FOR MAYOR OF METROPOLIS
HE'S BITING AT THE BAIT! I KNEW HE WOULDN'T BE ABLE TO RESIST SEEING HIMSELF! WHAT A SURPRISE HE'S DUE FOR!

FASCINATED, THE 5TH DIMENSION SPRITE WATCHES HIMSELF...

WHEN I'M MAYOR, THERE'LL BE ROAST CHICKEN DAILY FOR EVERYONE! JUST AS A SAMPLE, HERE'S A FLOCK OF THEM FOR YOU RIGHT NOW!

WHAT POISE... WHAT POWERFUL ORATORY! AMAZING LITTLE CHAP I AM!

SO REMEMBER TO VOTE FOR MR. KLTPZYXM.

KLANNNG

BOINNNGGG!

B-RRRINGG!

WH-WHAT? I DIDN'T UTTER A SYLLABLE--YET I'M SAYING MY OWN NAME BACKWARD IN MY OWN VOICE!

I GOT THE MANAGER TO PLAY THAT NEWSREEL AND FIXED IT SO THAT THE SOUND TRACK SAID JUST YOUR NAME BACKWARDS-- IN YOUR OWN VOICE! THOSE PECULIAR VIBRATIONS ARE NOW UNLOCKING THE GATE TO YOUR DIMENSION!

GRR! NOW I MUST GO BACK FOR 90 DAYS-- BUT I'M WARNING YOU, SUPERMAN... JUST WAIT TILL I COME AGAIN! I'LL GET EVEN!

LATER THAT DAY, AT THE DAILY PLANET...

WHAT'S THE MATTER WITH YOU, CLARK? IN WRITING THIS YARN OF HOW SUPERMAN TRICKED MR. MXYZPTLK, YOU KEPT SPELLING HIS NAME BACKWARDS!

I GUESS EVEN SUPERMAN MAKES AN OCCASIONAL SLIP! SEEING THAT I'VE BEEN THINKING OF NOTHING ELSE BUT HIS NAME BACKWARDS, IT'S NATURAL... BUT I CAN'T TELL PERRY THAT!

THE END

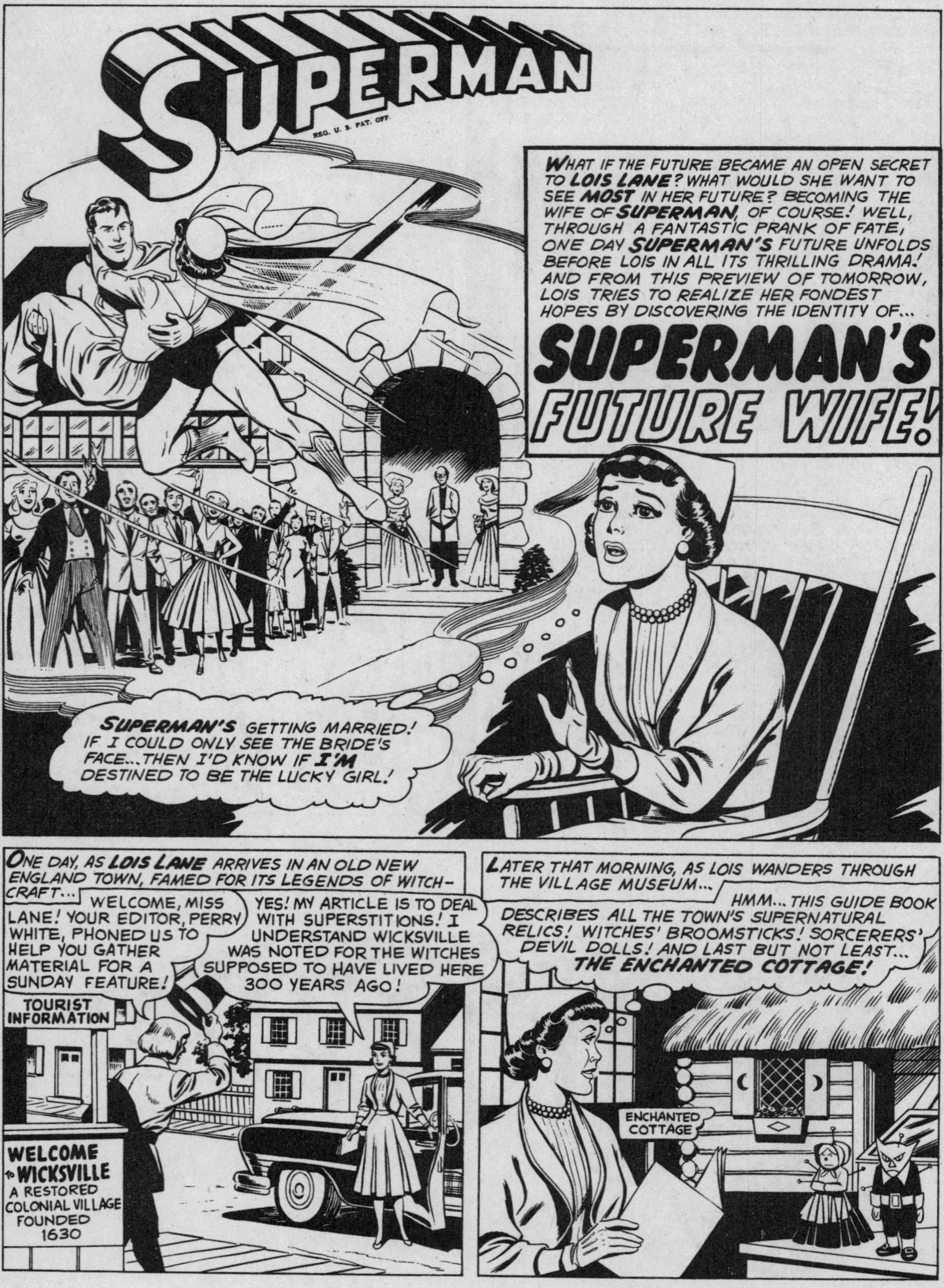
SUPERMAN
REG. U. S. PAT. OFF.
WHAT IF THE FUTURE BECAME AN OPEN SECRET TO LOIS LANE? WHAT WOULD SHE WANT TO SEE MOST IN HER FUTURE? BECOMING THE WIFE OF SUPERMAN, OF COURSE! WELL, THROUGH A FANTASTIC PRANK OF FATE, ONE DAY SUPERMAN'S FUTURE UNFOLDS BEFORE LOIS IN ALL ITS THRILLING DRAMA! AND FROM THIS PREVIEW OF TOMORROW, LOIS TRIES TO REALIZE HER FONDEST HOPES BY DISCOVERING THE IDENTITY OF...
SUPERMAN'S FUTURE WIFE!
SUPERMAN'S GETTING MARRIED! IF I COULD ONLY SEE THE BRIDE'S FACE...THEN I'D KNOW IF I'M DESTINED TO BE THE LUCKY GIRL!
ONE DAY, AS LOIS LANE ARRIVES IN AN OLD NEW ENGLAND TOWN, FAMED FOR ITS LEGENDS OF WITCH-CRAFT...
WELCOME, MISS LANE! YOUR EDITOR, PERRY WHITE, PHONED US TO HELP YOU GATHER MATERIAL FOR A SUNDAY FEATURE!
YES! MY ARTICLE IS TO DEAL WITH SUPERSTITIONS! I UNDERSTAND WICKSVILLE WAS NOTED FOR THE WITCHES SUPPOSED TO HAVE LIVED HERE 300 YEARS AGO!
TOURIST INFORMATION
WELCOME to WICKSVILLE A RESTORED COLONIAL VILLAGE FOUNDED 1630
LATER THAT MORNING, AS LOIS WANDERS THROUGH THE VILLAGE MUSEUM...
HMM... THIS GUIDE BOOK DESCRIBES ALL THE TOWN'S SUPERNATURAL RELICS! WITCHES' BROOMSTICKS! SORCERERS' DEVIL DOLLS! AND LAST BUT NOT LEAST... THE ENCHANTED COTTAGE!
ENCHANTED COTTAGE

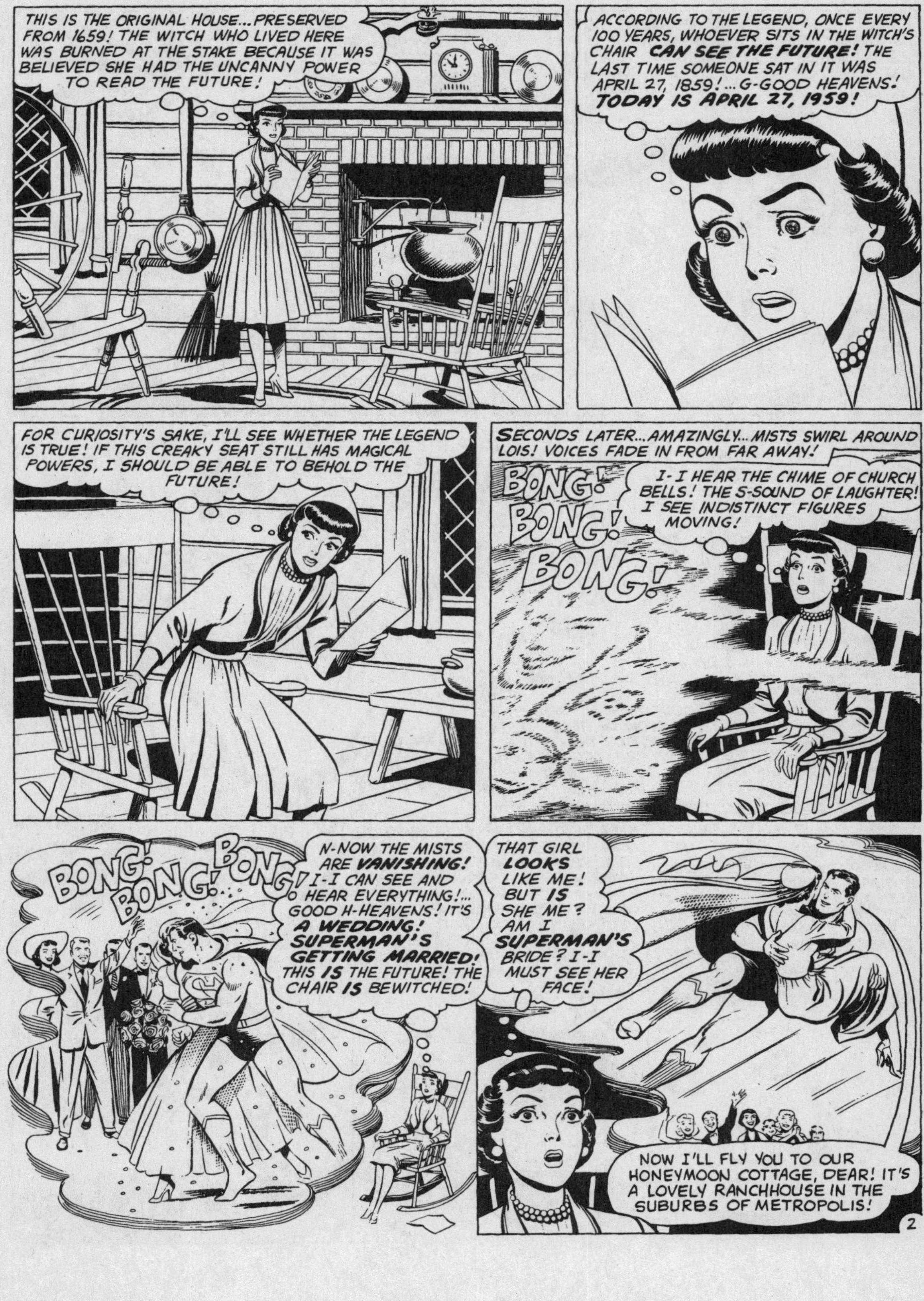
THIS IS THE ORIGINAL HOUSE... PRESERVED FROM 1659! THE WITCH WHO LIVED HERE WAS BURNED AT THE STAKE BECAUSE IT WAS BELIEVED SHE HAD THE UNCANNY POWER TO READ THE FUTURE!
ACCORDING TO THE LEGEND, ONCE EVERY 100 YEARS, WHOEVER SITS IN THE WITCH'S CHAIR CAN SEE THE FUTURE! THE LAST TIME SOMEONE SAT IN IT WAS APRIL 27, 1859! ... G-GOOD HEAVENS! TODAY IS APRIL 27, 1959!
FOR CURIOSITY'S SAKE, I'LL SEE WHETHER THE LEGEND IS TRUE! IF THIS CREAKY SEAT STILL HAS MAGICAL POWERS, I SHOULD BE ABLE TO BEHOLD THE FUTURE!
SECONDS LATER... AMAZINGLY... MISTS SWIRL AROUND LOIS! VOICES FADE IN FROM FAR AWAY!
BONG! BONG! BONG!
I-I HEAR THE CHIME OF CHURCH BELLS! THE S-SOUND OF LAUGHTER! I SEE INDISTINCT FIGURES MOVING!
BONG! BONG! BONG!
N-NOW THE MISTS ARE VANISHING! I-I CAN SEE AND HEAR EVERYTHING!... GOOD H-HEAVENS! IT'S A WEDDING! SUPERMAN'S GETTING MARRIED! THIS IS THE FUTURE! THE CHAIR IS BEWITCHED!
THAT GIRL LOOKS LIKE ME! BUT IS SHE ME? AM I SUPERMAN'S BRIDE? I-I MUST SEE HER FACE!
NOW I'LL FLY YOU TO OUR HONEYMOON COTTAGE, DEAR! IT'S A LOVELY RANCHHOUSE IN THE SUBURBS OF METROPOLIS!
2

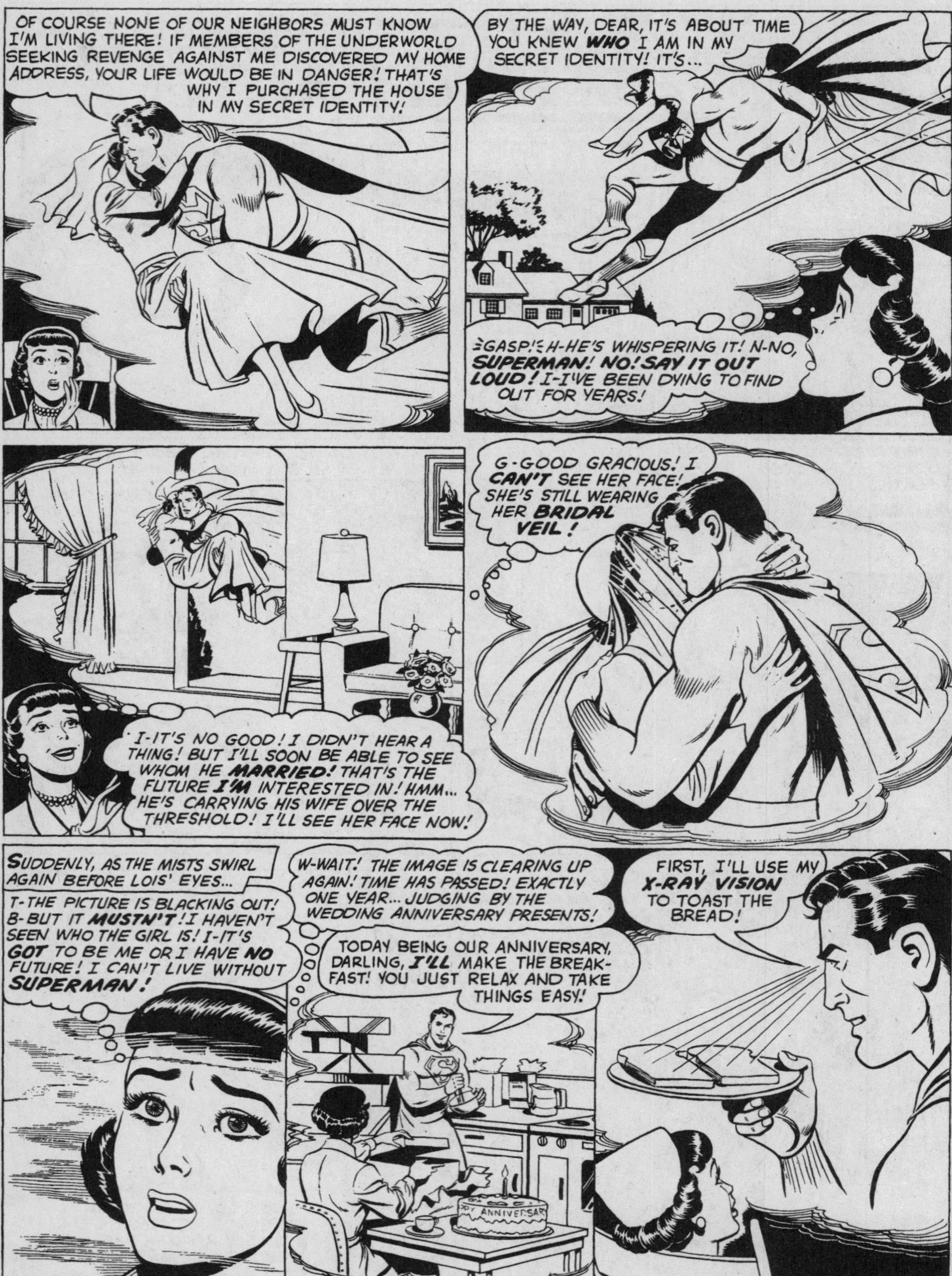
OF COURSE NONE OF OUR NEIGHBORS MUST KNOW I'M LIVING THERE! IF MEMBERS OF THE UNDERWORLD SEEKING REVENGE AGAINST ME DISCOVERED MY HOME ADDRESS, YOUR LIFE WOULD BE IN DANGER! THAT'S WHY I PURCHASED THE HOUSE IN MY SECRET IDENTITY!
BY THE WAY, DEAR, IT'S ABOUT TIME YOU KNEW WHO I AM IN MY SECRET IDENTITY! IT'S...
GASP! H-HE'S WHISPERING IT! N-NO, SUPERMAN! NO! SAY IT OUT LOUD! I-I'VE BEEN DYING TO FIND OUT FOR YEARS!
I-IT'S NO GOOD! I DIDN'T HEAR A THING! BUT I'LL SOON BE ABLE TO SEE WHOM HE MARRIED! THAT'S THE FUTURE I'M INTERESTED IN! HMM... HE'S CARRYING HIS WIFE OVER THE THRESHOLD! I'LL SEE HER FACE NOW!
G-GOOD GRACIOUS! I CAN'T SEE HER FACE! SHE'S STILL WEARING HER BRIDAL VEIL!
SUDDENLY, AS THE MISTS SWIRL AGAIN BEFORE LOIS' EYES...
T-THE PICTURE IS BLACKING OUT! B-BUT IT MUSTN'T! I HAVEN'T SEEN WHO THE GIRL IS! I-IT'S GOT TO BE ME OR I HAVE NO FUTURE! I CAN'T LIVE WITHOUT SUPERMAN!
W-WAIT! THE IMAGE IS CLEARING UP AGAIN! TIME HAS PASSED! EXACTLY ONE YEAR... JUDGING BY THE WEDDING ANNIVERSARY PRESENTS!
TODAY BEING OUR ANNIVERSARY, DARLING, I'LL MAKE THE BREAKFAST! YOU JUST RELAX AND TAKE THINGS EASY!
ANNIVERSARY
FIRST, I'LL USE MY X-RAY VISION TO TOAST THE BREAD!
3

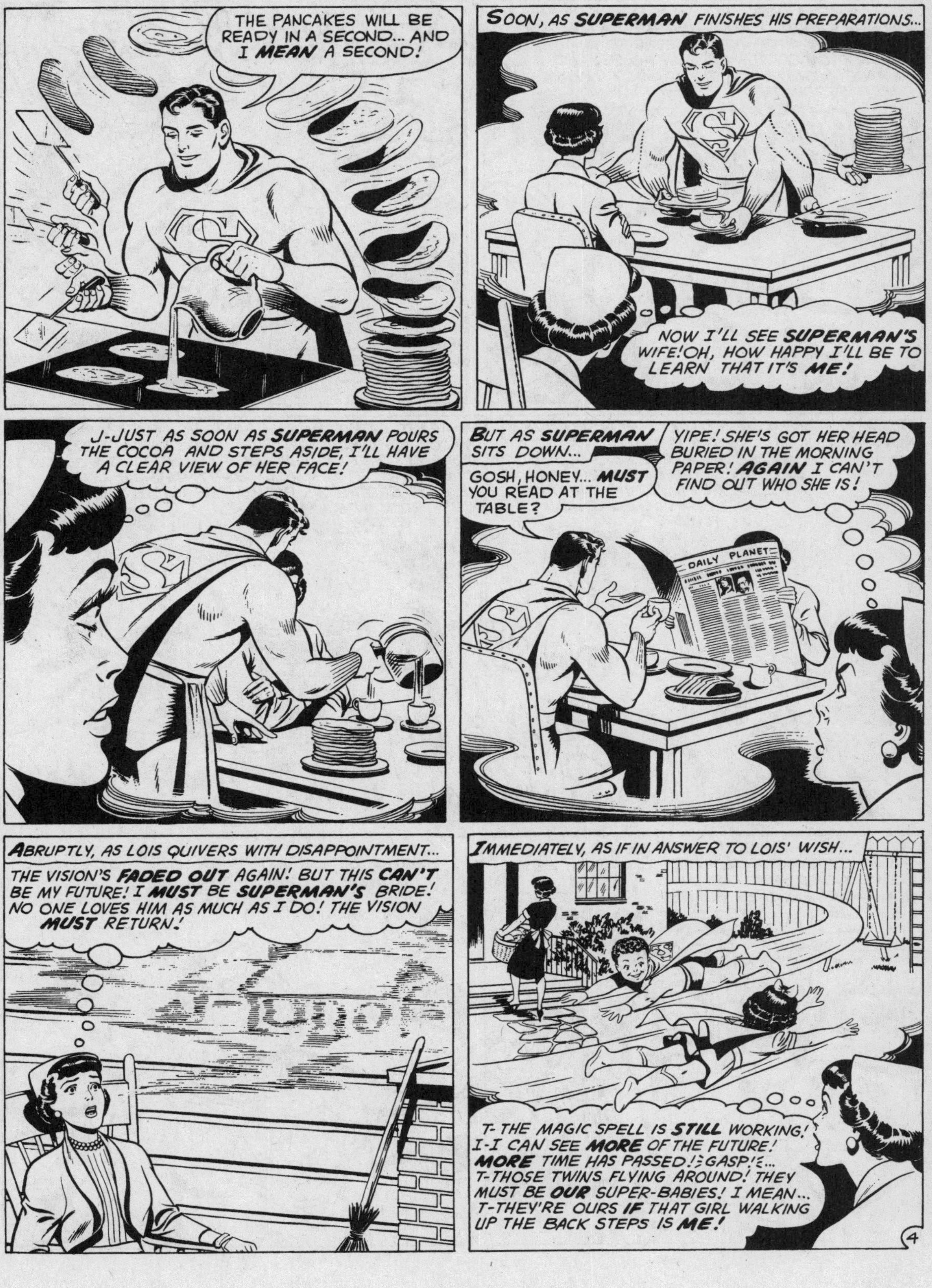
THE PANCAKES WILL BE READY IN A SECOND... AND I MEAN A SECOND!
SOON, AS SUPERMAN FINISHES HIS PREPARATIONS...
NOW I'LL SEE SUPERMAN'S WIFE! OH, HOW HAPPY I'LL BE TO LEARN THAT IT'S ME!
J-JUST AS SOON AS SUPERMAN POURS THE COCOA AND STEPS ASIDE, I'LL HAVE A CLEAR VIEW OF HER FACE!
BUT AS SUPERMAN SITS DOWN...
GOSH, HONEY... MUST YOU READ AT THE TABLE?
YIPE! SHE'S GOT HER HEAD BURIED IN THE MORNING PAPER! AGAIN I CAN'T FIND OUT WHO SHE IS!
DAILY PLANET
ABRUPTLY, AS LOIS QUIVERS WITH DISAPPOINTMENT...
THE VISION'S FADED OUT AGAIN! BUT THIS CAN'T BE MY FUTURE! I MUST BE SUPERMAN'S BRIDE! NO ONE LOVES HIM AS MUCH AS I DO! THE VISION MUST RETURN!
IMMEDIATELY, AS IF IN ANSWER TO LOIS' WISH...
T- THE MAGIC SPELL IS STILL WORKING! I-I CAN SEE MORE OF THE FUTURE! MORE TIME HAS PASSED! GASP! ... T-THOSE TWINS FLYING AROUND! THEY MUST BE OUR SUPER-BABIES! I MEAN... T-THEY'RE OURS IF THAT GIRL WALKING UP THE BACK STEPS IS ME!
4

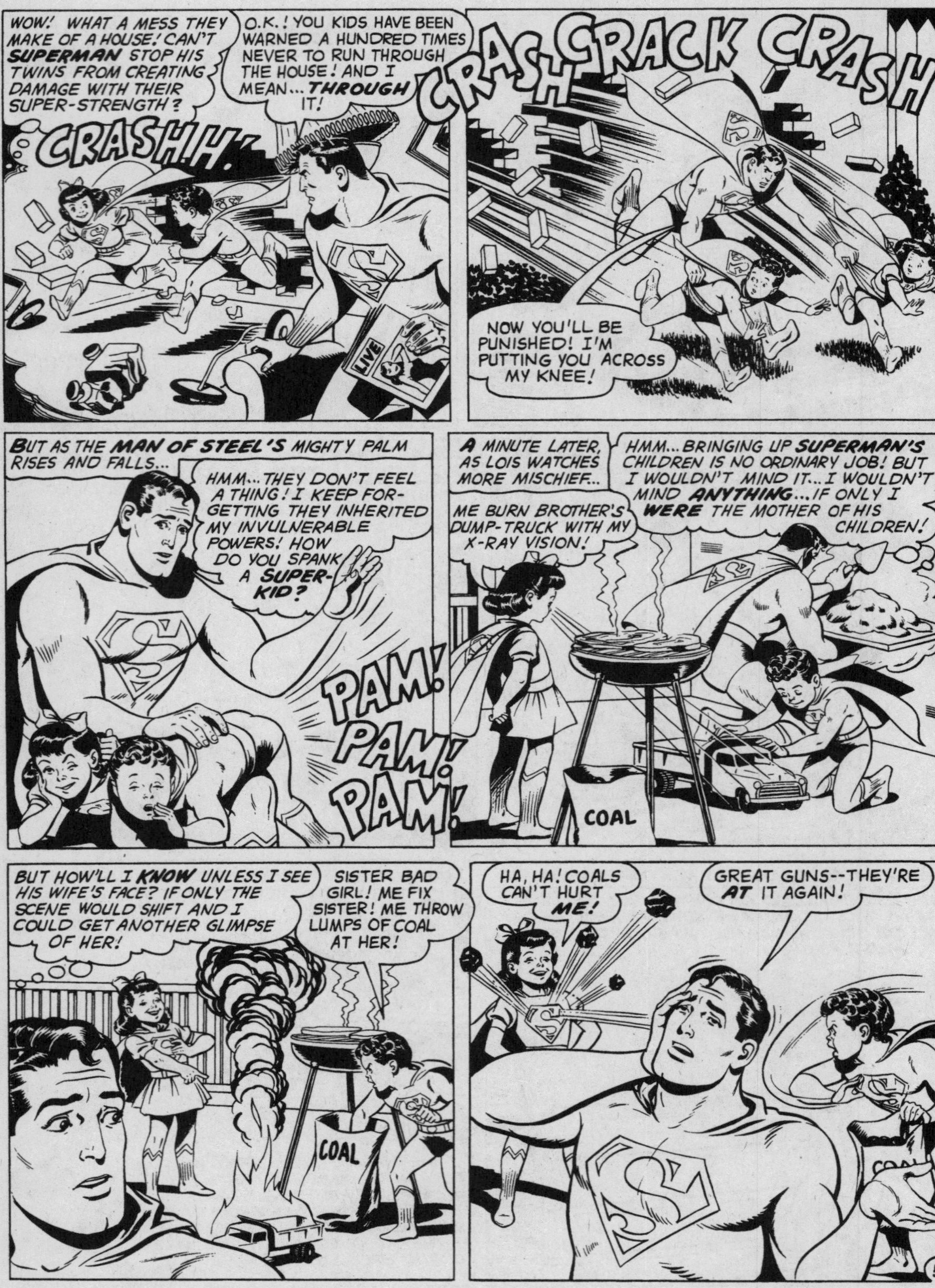
WOW! WHAT A MESS THEY MAKE OF A HOUSE! CAN'T SUPERMAN STOP HIS TWINS FROM CREATING DAMAGE WITH THEIR SUPER-STRENGTH?
O.K.! YOU KIDS HAVE BEEN WARNED A HUNDRED TIMES NEVER TO RUN THROUGH THE HOUSE! AND I MEAN...THROUGH IT!
CRASHH!
LIVE
CRASH CRACK CRASH
NOW YOU'LL BE PUNISHED! I'M PUTTING YOU ACROSS MY KNEE!
BUT AS THE MAN OF STEEL'S MIGHTY PALM RISES AND FALLS...
HMM...THEY DON'T FEEL A THING! I KEEP FORGETTING THEY INHERITED MY INVULNERABLE POWERS! HOW DO YOU SPANK A SUPER-KID?
PAM! PAM! PAM!
A MINUTE LATER, AS LOIS WATCHES MORE MISCHIEF...
HMM...BRINGING UP SUPERMAN'S CHILDREN IS NO ORDINARY JOB! BUT I WOULDN'T MIND IT...I WOULDN'T MIND ANYTHING...IF ONLY I WERE THE MOTHER OF HIS CHILDREN!
ME BURN BROTHER'S DUMP-TRUCK WITH MY X-RAY VISION!
COAL
BUT HOW'LL I KNOW UNLESS I SEE HIS WIFE'S FACE? IF ONLY THE SCENE WOULD SHIFT AND I COULD GET ANOTHER GLIMPSE OF HER!
SISTER BAD GIRL! ME FIX SISTER! ME THROW LUMPS OF COAL AT HER!
COAL
HA, HA! COALS CAN'T HURT ME!
GREAT GUNS--THEY'RE AT IT AGAIN!
5

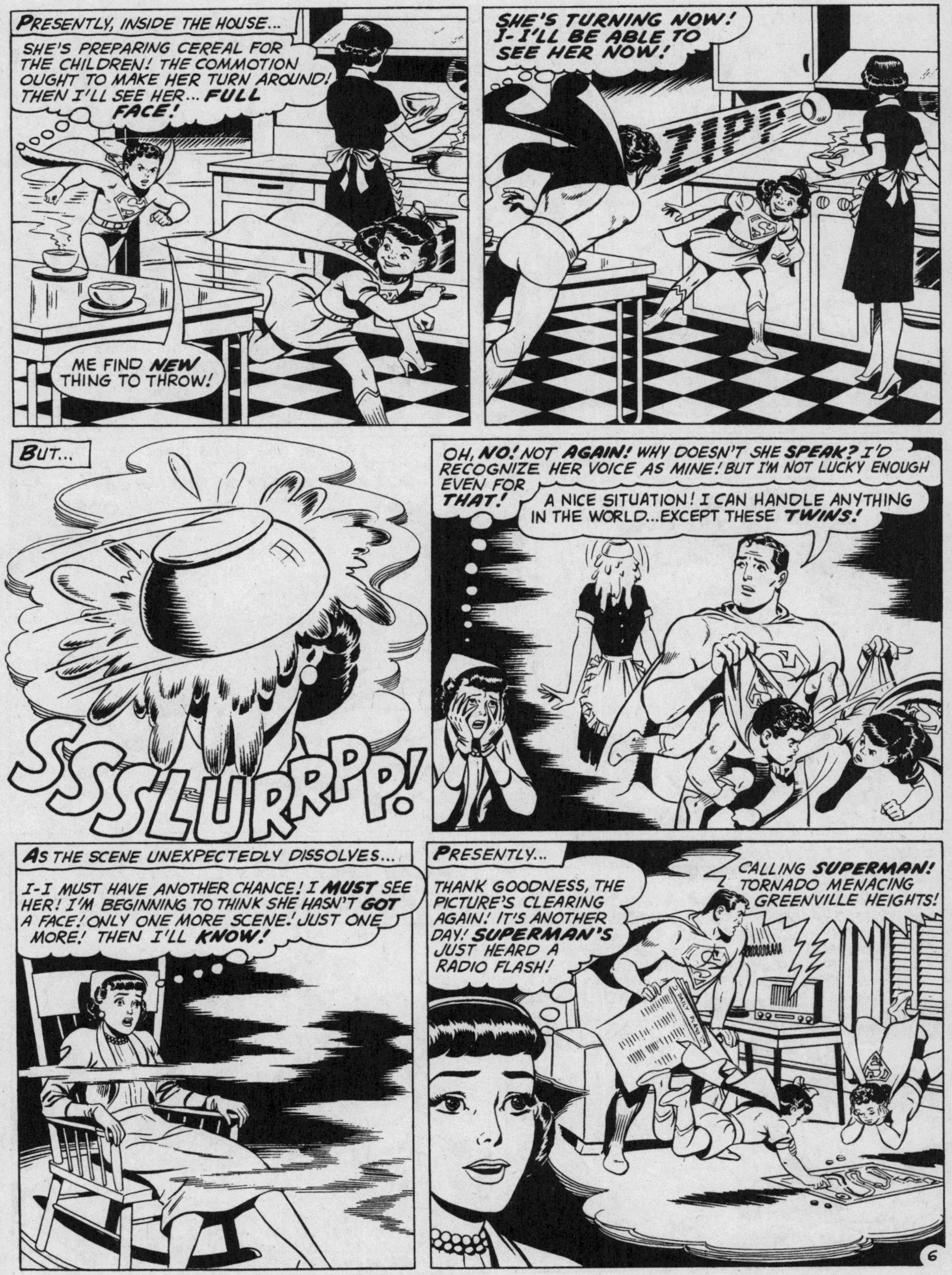
PRESENTLY, INSIDE THE HOUSE...
SHE'S PREPARING CEREAL FOR THE CHILDREN! THE COMMOTION OUGHT TO MAKE HER TURN AROUND! THEN I'LL SEE HER... FULL FACE!
ME FIND NEW THING TO THROW!
SHE'S TURNING NOW! I- I'LL BE ABLE TO SEE HER NOW!
ZIPP
BUT...
SSSLURRPP!
OH, NO! NOT AGAIN! WHY DOESN'T SHE SPEAK? I'D RECOGNIZE HER VOICE AS MINE! BUT I'M NOT LUCKY ENOUGH EVEN FOR THAT!
A NICE SITUATION! I CAN HANDLE ANYTHING IN THE WORLD...EXCEPT THESE TWINS!
AS THE SCENE UNEXPECTEDLY DISSOLVES...
I-I MUST HAVE ANOTHER CHANCE! I MUST SEE HER! I'M BEGINNING TO THINK SHE HASN'T GOT A FACE! ONLY ONE MORE SCENE! JUST ONE MORE! THEN I'LL KNOW!
PRESENTLY...
THANK GOODNESS, THE PICTURE'S CLEARING AGAIN! IT'S ANOTHER DAY! SUPERMAN'S JUST HEARD A RADIO FLASH!
CALLING SUPERMAN! TORNADO MENACING GREENVILLE HEIGHTS!
6

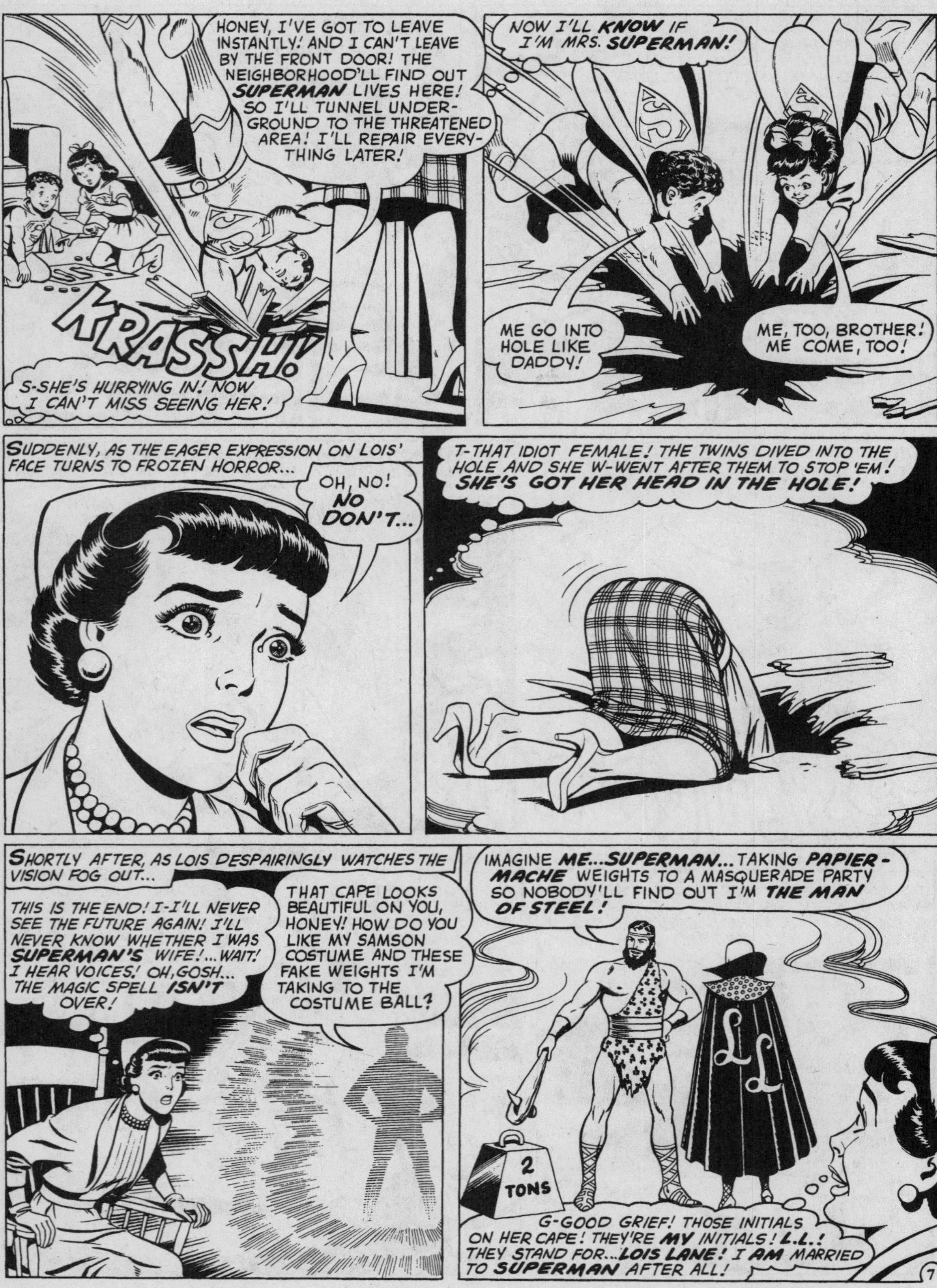
HONEY, I'VE GOT TO LEAVE INSTANTLY! AND I CAN'T LEAVE BY THE FRONT DOOR! THE NEIGHBORHOOD'LL FIND OUT SUPERMAN LIVES HERE! SO I'LL TUNNEL UNDERGROUND TO THE THREATENED AREA! I'LL REPAIR EVERYTHING LATER!
KRASSH!
S-SHE'S HURRYING IN! NOW I CAN'T MISS SEEING HER!
NOW I'LL KNOW IF I'M MRS. SUPERMAN!
ME GO INTO HOLE LIKE DADDY!
ME, TOO, BROTHER! ME COME, TOO!
SUDDENLY, AS THE EAGER EXPRESSION ON LOIS' FACE TURNS TO FROZEN HORROR...
OH, NO! NO DON'T...
T-THAT IDIOT FEMALE! THE TWINS DIVED INTO THE HOLE AND SHE W-WENT AFTER THEM TO STOP 'EM! SHE'S GOT HER HEAD IN THE HOLE!
SHORTLY AFTER, AS LOIS DESPAIRINGLY WATCHES THE VISION FOG OUT...
THIS IS THE END! I-I'LL NEVER SEE THE FUTURE AGAIN! I'LL NEVER KNOW WHETHER I WAS SUPERMAN'S WIFE!...WAIT! I HEAR VOICES! OH, GOSH... THE MAGIC SPELL ISN'T OVER!
THAT CAPE LOOKS BEAUTIFUL ON YOU, HONEY! HOW DO YOU LIKE MY SAMSON COSTUME AND THESE FAKE WEIGHTS I'M TAKING TO THE COSTUME BALL?
IMAGINE ME...SUPERMAN...TAKING PAPIER-MACHE WEIGHTS TO A MASQUERADE PARTY SO NOBODY'LL FIND OUT I'M THE MAN OF STEEL!
LL
2 TONS
G-GOOD GRIEF! THOSE INITIALS ON HER CAPE! THEY'RE MY INITIALS! L.L.! THEY STAND FOR...LOIS LANE! I AM MARRIED TO SUPERMAN AFTER ALL!
7

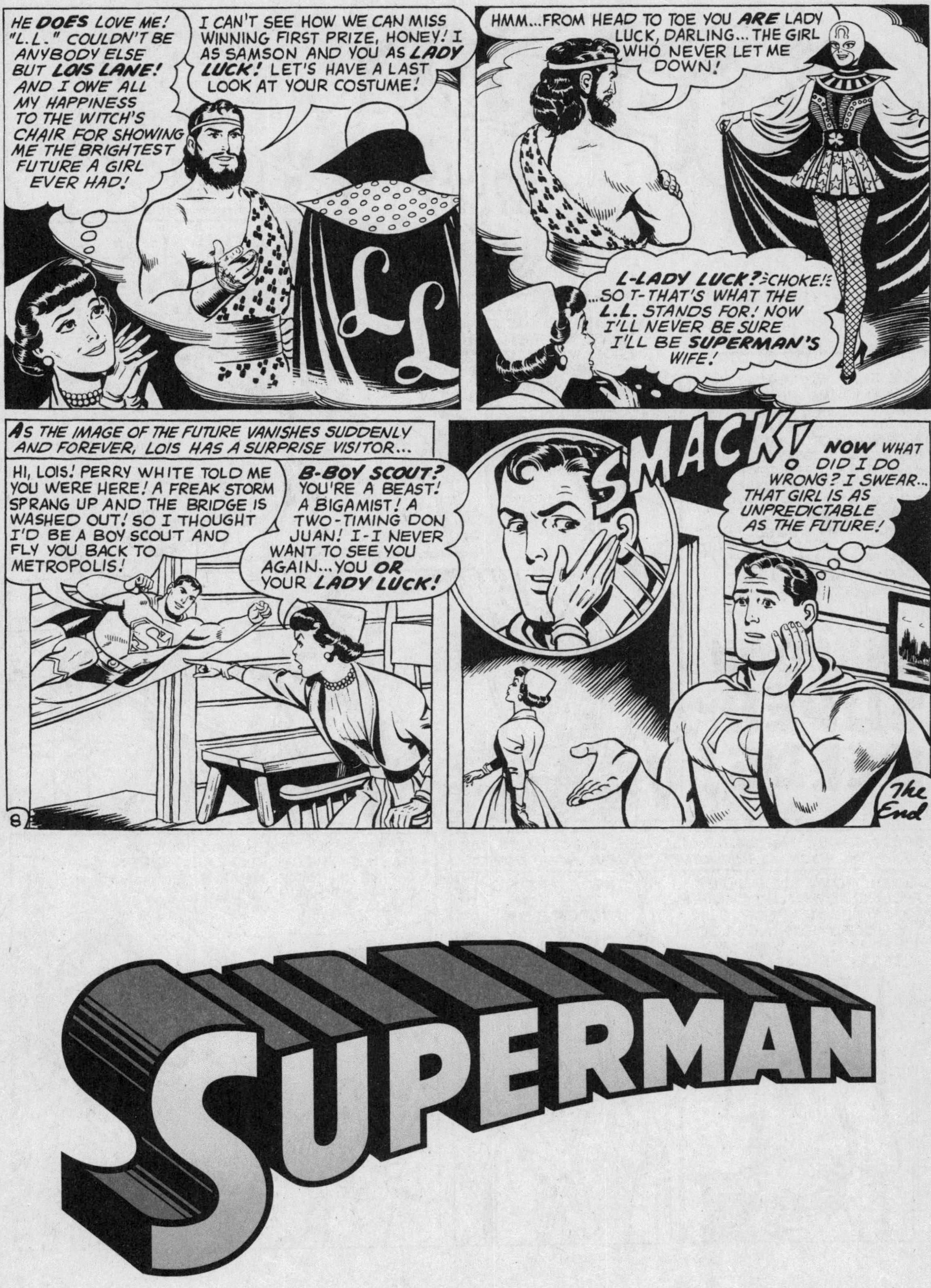
HE DOES LOVE ME! "L.L." COULDN'T BE ANYBODY ELSE BUT LOIS LANE! AND I OWE ALL MY HAPPINESS TO THE WITCH'S CHAIR FOR SHOWING ME THE BRIGHTEST FUTURE A GIRL EVER HAD!
I CAN'T SEE HOW WE CAN MISS WINNING FIRST PRIZE, HONEY! I AS SAMSON AND YOU AS LADY LUCK! LET'S HAVE A LAST LOOK AT YOUR COSTUME!
LL
HMM...FROM HEAD TO TOE YOU ARE LADY LUCK, DARLING... THE GIRL WHO NEVER LET ME DOWN!
L-LADY LUCK? CHOKE! ...SO T-THAT'S WHAT THE L.L. STANDS FOR! NOW I'LL NEVER BE SURE I'LL BE SUPERMAN'S WIFE!
AS THE IMAGE OF THE FUTURE VANISHES SUDDENLY AND FOREVER, LOIS HAS A SURPRISE VISITOR...
HI, LOIS! PERRY WHITE TOLD ME YOU WERE HERE! A FREAK STORM SPRANG UP AND THE BRIDGE IS WASHED OUT! SO I THOUGHT I'D BE A BOY SCOUT AND FLY YOU BACK TO METROPOLIS!
B-BOY SCOUT? YOU'RE A BEAST! A BIGAMIST! A TWO-TIMING DON JUAN! I-I NEVER WANT TO SEE YOU AGAIN...YOU OR YOUR LADY LUCK!
8
SMACK!
NOW WHAT DID I DO WRONG? I SWEAR... THAT GIRL IS AS UNPREDICTABLE AS THE FUTURE!
The End

SUPERMAN

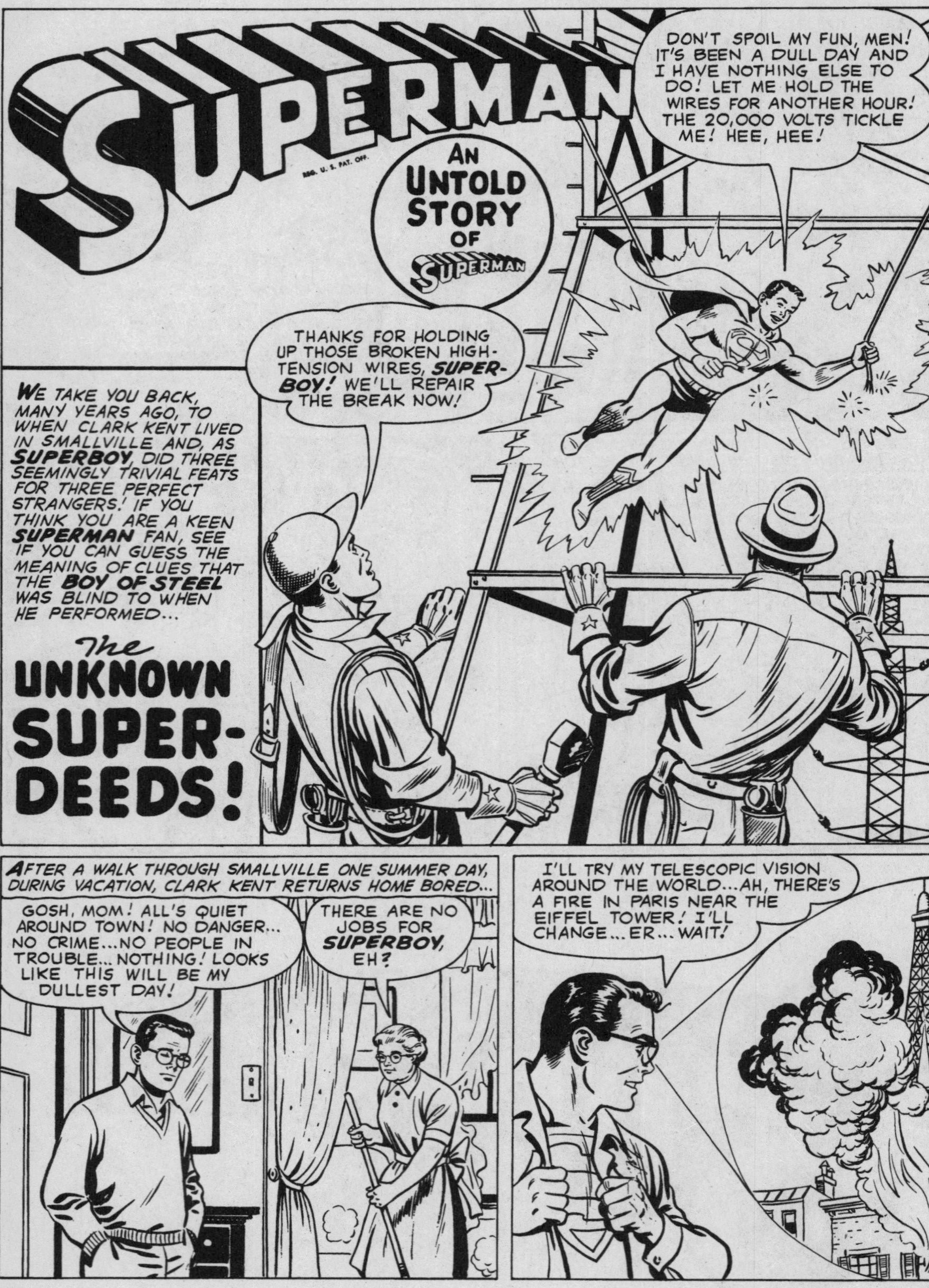
SUPERMAN
REG. U.S. PAT. OFF.
AN UNTOLD STORY OF SUPERMAN
DON'T SPOIL MY FUN, MEN! IT'S BEEN A DULL DAY AND I HAVE NOTHING ELSE TO DO! LET ME HOLD THE WIRES FOR ANOTHER HOUR! THE 20,000 VOLTS TICKLE ME! HEE, HEE!
THANKS FOR HOLDING UP THOSE BROKEN HIGH-TENSION WIRES, SUPERBOY! WE'LL REPAIR THE BREAK NOW!
WE TAKE YOU BACK, MANY YEARS AGO, TO WHEN CLARK KENT LIVED IN SMALLVILLE AND, AS SUPERBOY, DID THREE SEEMINGLY TRIVIAL FEATS FOR THREE PERFECT STRANGERS! IF YOU THINK YOU ARE A KEEN SUPERMAN FAN, SEE IF YOU CAN GUESS THE MEANING OF CLUES THAT THE BOY OF STEEL WAS BLIND TO WHEN HE PERFORMED...
The UNKNOWN SUPER-DEEDS!
AFTER A WALK THROUGH SMALLVILLE ONE SUMMER DAY, DURING VACATION, CLARK KENT RETURNS HOME BORED...
GOSH, MOM! ALL'S QUIET AROUND TOWN! NO DANGER... NO CRIME...NO PEOPLE IN TROUBLE...NOTHING! LOOKS LIKE THIS WILL BE MY DULLEST DAY!
THERE ARE NO JOBS FOR SUPERBOY, EH?
I'LL TRY MY TELESCOPIC VISION AROUND THE WORLD...AH, THERE'S A FIRE IN PARIS NEAR THE EIFFEL TOWER! I'LL CHANGE... ER... WAIT!

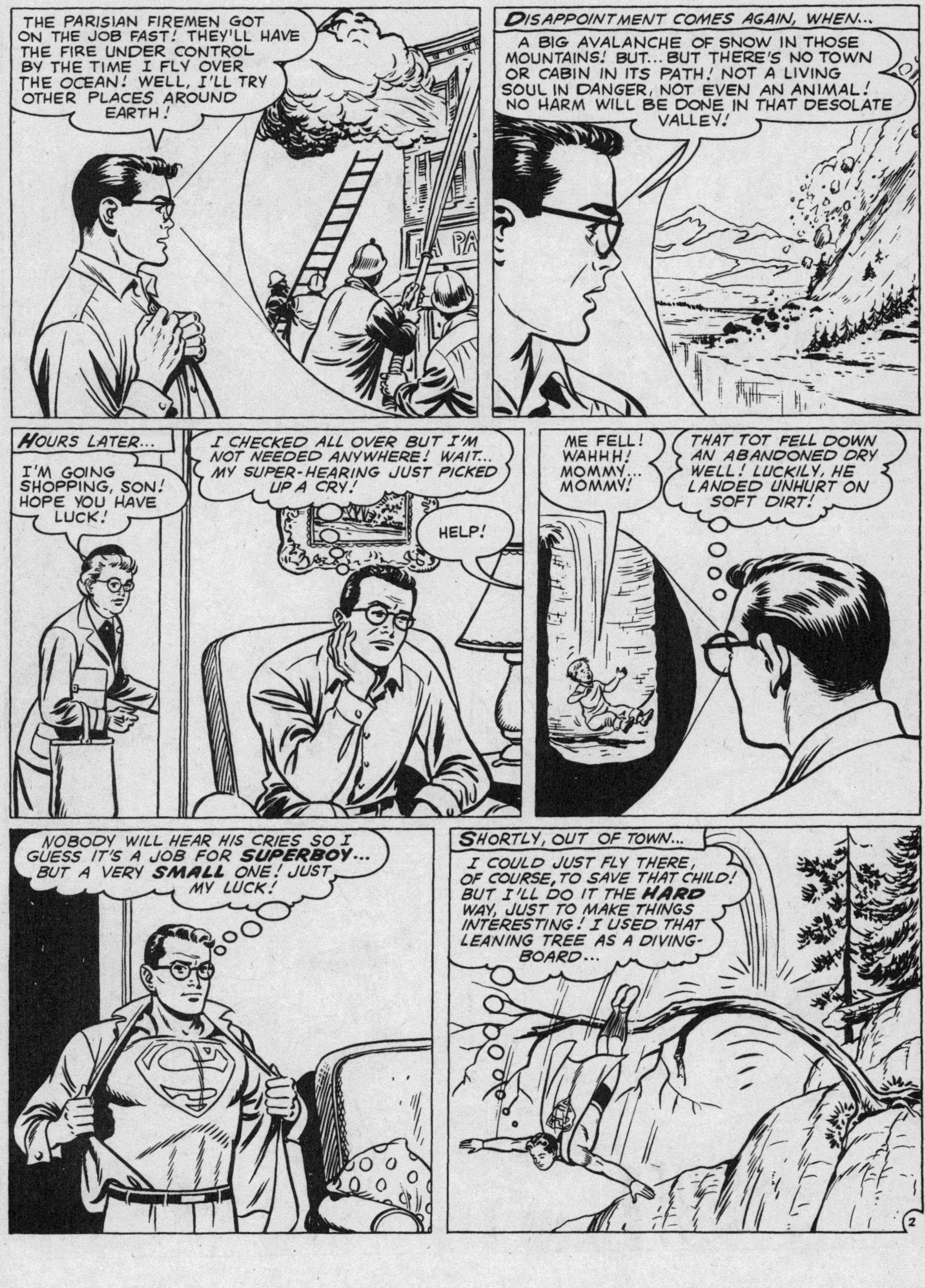
THE PARISIAN FIREMEN GOT ON THE JOB FAST! THEY'LL HAVE THE FIRE UNDER CONTROL BY THE TIME I FLY OVER THE OCEAN! WELL, I'LL TRY OTHER PLACES AROUND EARTH!
DISAPPOINTMENT COMES AGAIN, WHEN...
A BIG AVALANCHE OF SNOW IN THOSE MOUNTAINS! BUT... BUT THERE'S NO TOWN OR CABIN IN ITS PATH! NOT A LIVING SOUL IN DANGER, NOT EVEN AN ANIMAL! NO HARM WILL BE DONE IN THAT DESOLATE VALLEY!
HOURS LATER...
I'M GOING SHOPPING, SON! HOPE YOU HAVE LUCK!
I CHECKED ALL OVER BUT I'M NOT NEEDED ANYWHERE! WAIT... MY SUPER-HEARING JUST PICKED UP A CRY!
HELP!
ME FELL! WAHHH! MOMMY... MOMMY!
THAT TOT FELL DOWN AN ABANDONED DRY WELL! LUCKILY, HE LANDED UNHURT ON SOFT DIRT!
NOBODY WILL HEAR HIS CRIES SO I GUESS IT'S A JOB FOR SUPERBOY... BUT A VERY SMALL ONE! JUST MY LUCK!
SHORTLY, OUT OF TOWN...
I COULD JUST FLY THERE, OF COURSE, TO SAVE THAT CHILD! BUT I'LL DO IT THE HARD WAY, JUST TO MAKE THINGS INTERESTING! I USED THAT LEANING TREE AS A DIVING-BOARD...
2

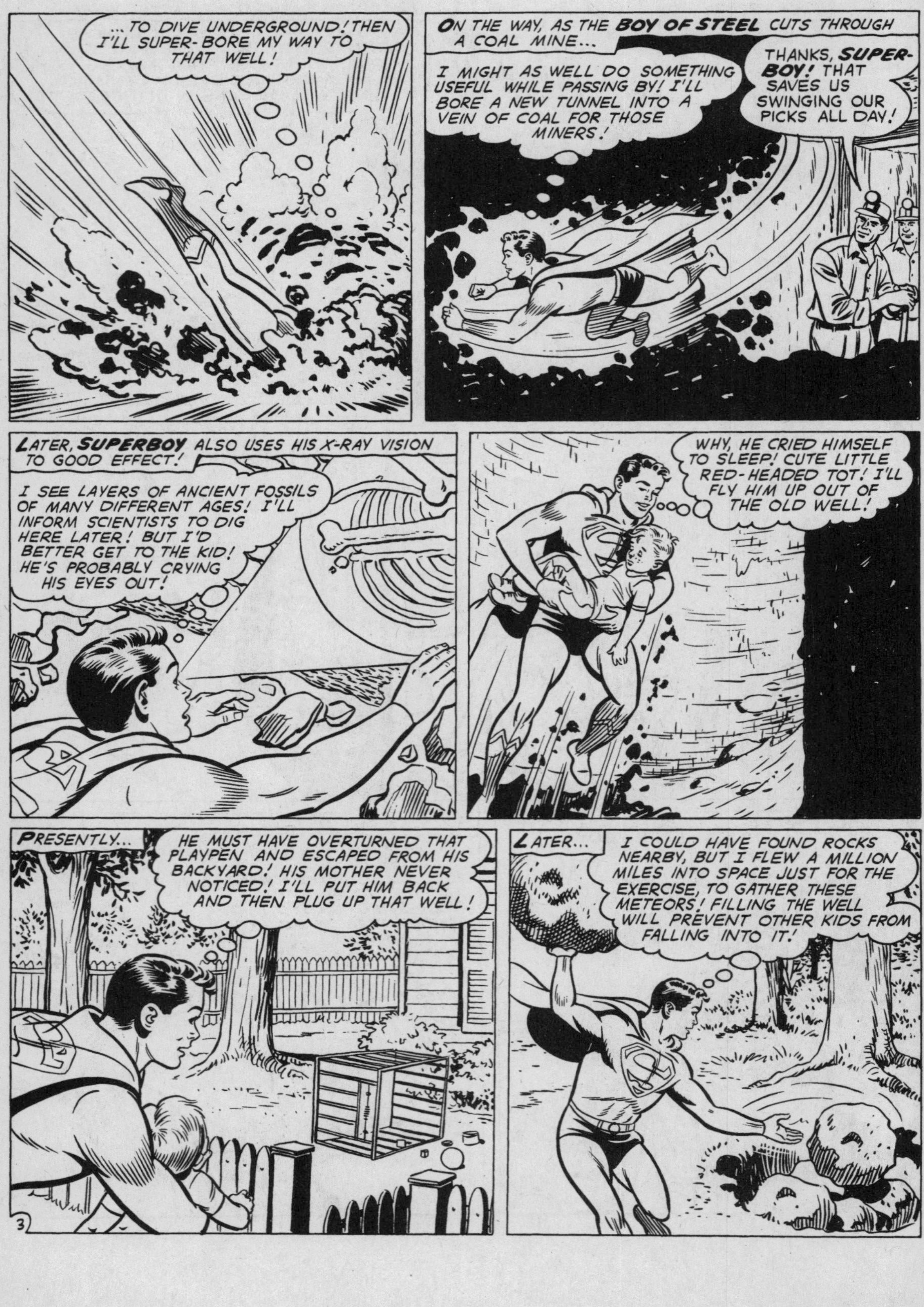
...TO DIVE UNDERGROUND! THEN I'LL SUPER-BORE MY WAY TO THAT WELL!
ON THE WAY, AS THE BOY OF STEEL CUTS THROUGH A COAL MINE...
I MIGHT AS WELL DO SOMETHING USEFUL WHILE PASSING BY! I'LL BORE A NEW TUNNEL INTO A VEIN OF COAL FOR THOSE MINERS!
THANKS, SUPER-BOY! THAT SAVES US SWINGING OUR PICKS ALL DAY!
LATER, SUPERBOY ALSO USES HIS X-RAY VISION TO GOOD EFFECT!
I SEE LAYERS OF ANCIENT FOSSILS OF MANY DIFFERENT AGES! I'LL INFORM SCIENTISTS TO DIG HERE LATER! BUT I'D BETTER GET TO THE KID! HE'S PROBABLY CRYING HIS EYES OUT!
WHY, HE CRIED HIMSELF TO SLEEP! CUTE LITTLE RED-HEADED TOT! I'LL FLY HIM UP OUT OF THE OLD WELL!
PRESENTLY...
HE MUST HAVE OVERTURNED THAT PLAYPEN AND ESCAPED FROM HIS BACKYARD! HIS MOTHER NEVER NOTICED! I'LL PUT HIM BACK AND THEN PLUG UP THAT WELL!
3
LATER...
I COULD HAVE FOUND ROCKS NEARBY, BUT I FLEW A MILLION MILES INTO SPACE JUST FOR THE EXERCISE, TO GATHER THESE METEORS! FILLING THE WELL WILL PREVENT OTHER KIDS FROM FALLING INTO IT!

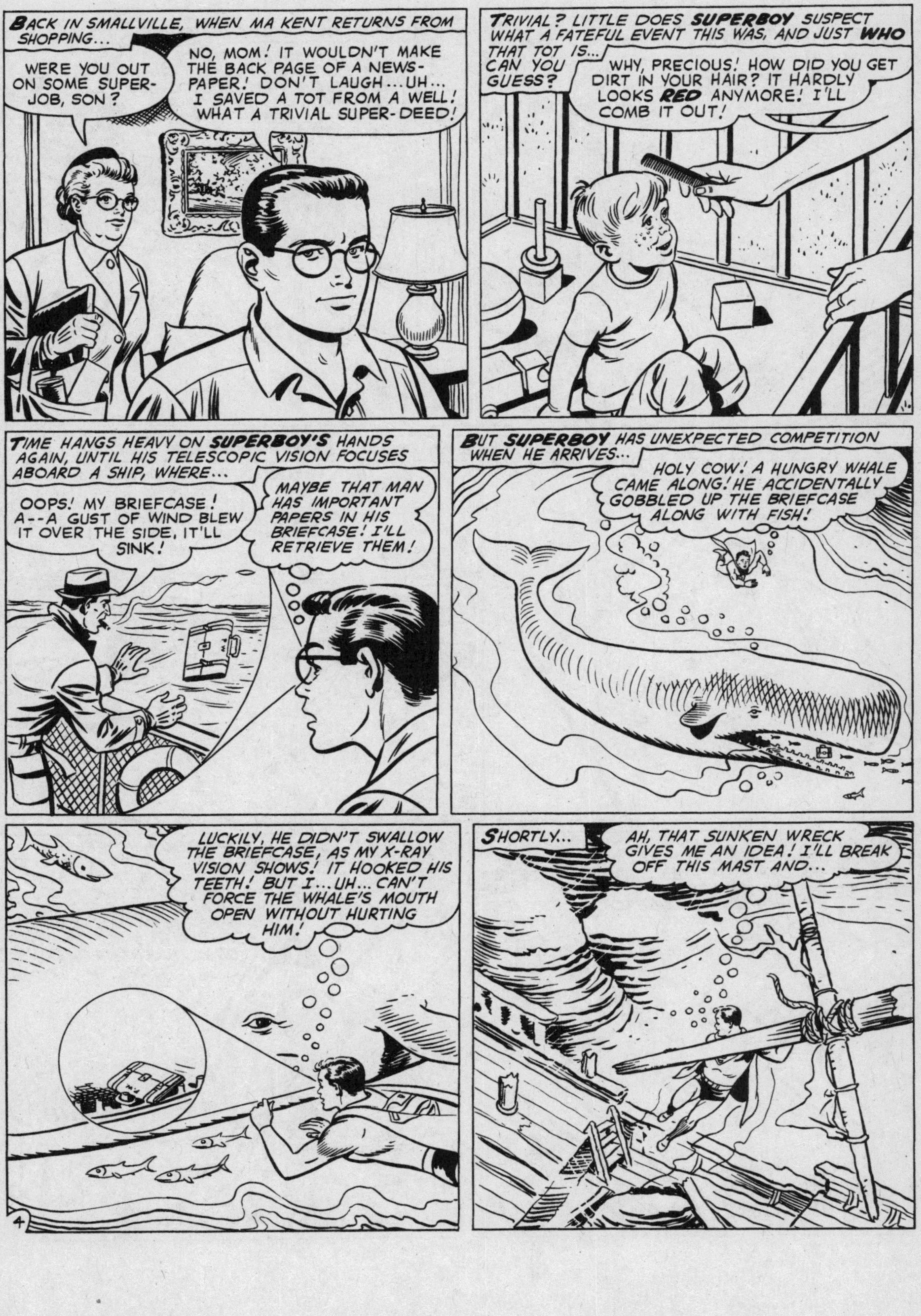
BACK IN SMALLVILLE, WHEN MA KENT RETURNS FROM SHOPPING...
WERE YOU OUT ON SOME SUPER-JOB, SON?
NO, MOM! IT WOULDN'T MAKE THE BACK PAGE OF A NEWS-PAPER! DON'T LAUGH...UH... I SAVED A TOT FROM A WELL! WHAT A TRIVIAL SUPER-DEED!
TRIVIAL? LITTLE DOES SUPERBOY SUSPECT WHAT A FATEFUL EVENT THIS WAS, AND JUST WHO THAT TOT IS... CAN YOU GUESS?
WHY, PRECIOUS! HOW DID YOU GET DIRT IN YOUR HAIR? IT HARDLY LOOKS RED ANYMORE! I'LL COMB IT OUT!
TIME HANGS HEAVY ON SUPERBOY'S HANDS AGAIN, UNTIL HIS TELESCOPIC VISION FOCUSES ABOARD A SHIP, WHERE...
OOPS! MY BRIEFCASE! A--A GUST OF WIND BLEW IT OVER THE SIDE. IT'LL SINK!
MAYBE THAT MAN HAS IMPORTANT PAPERS IN HIS BRIEFCASE! I'LL RETRIEVE THEM!
BUT SUPERBOY HAS UNEXPECTED COMPETITION WHEN HE ARRIVES...
HOLY COW! A HUNGRY WHALE CAME ALONG! HE ACCIDENTALLY GOBBLED UP THE BRIEFCASE ALONG WITH FISH!
LUCKILY, HE DIDN'T SWALLOW THE BRIEFCASE, AS MY X-RAY VISION SHOWS! IT HOOKED HIS TEETH! BUT I...UH...CAN'T FORCE THE WHALE'S MOUTH OPEN WITHOUT HURTING HIM!
4
SHORTLY...
AH, THAT SUNKEN WRECK GIVES ME AN IDEA! I'LL BREAK OFF THIS MAST AND...

...USE IT LIKE A GIANT FEATHER TO TICKLE THE WHALE'S RIBS! THAT MADE HIM...ER...GIGGLE AND OPEN HIS MOUTH! THE BRIEFCASE FLOATED OUT!

THEN, ON A VOLCANIC ISLAND...

I HUNG THE WET PAPERS ON SOME STRING I FOUND! THE HEAT FROM THAT SMOLDERING VOLCANO WILL DRY THEM! THEN I'LL SEE IF THEY'RE *IMPORTANT* PAPERS THAT I SAVED!

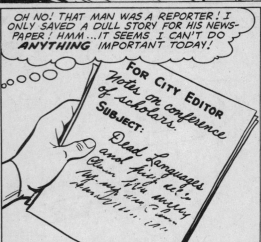

OH NO! THAT MAN WAS A REPORTER! I ONLY SAVED A DULL STORY FOR HIS NEWSPAPER! HMM...IT SEEMS I CAN'T DO *ANYTHING* IMPORTANT TODAY!

FOR CITY EDITOR
Notes on conference of scholars.
SUBJECT:
Dead Languages and...

EMBARRASSED, *SUPERBOY* HIDES HIS DEED...

THAT REPORTER WOULD *LAUGH* IF I TOLD HIM ALL THE TROUBLE I WENT TO TO SAVE HIS DULL STORY! I PUT HIS BRIEFCASE ON SOME FLOATING DEBRIS! MY SUPER-BREATH WILL BLOW IT TO WHERE THE BOAT DOCKS!

BUT AGAIN, THIS IS A MORE VITAL MILESTONE IN HIS DESTINY THAN *SUPERBOY* KNOWS! THE CLUE IS RIGHT BEFORE YOUR EYES, READERS!

MY BRIEFCASE... DRY AND UNHARMED! IT MUST HAVE FALLEN IN THIS DEBRIS INSTEAD OF SINKING IN THE WATER! HOW ABOUT THAT!

P.W.

ON HIS WAY HOME, AS *SUPERBOY* HOPEFULLY CHECKS OTHER TOWNS...

WHAT'S THAT? SOMETHING IS FRIGHTENING THE PEOPLE BELOW! GOOD! THIS MAY BE THE CHANCE I'VE BEEN WAITING FOR TO DO SOMETHING *IMPORTANT* TODAY!

EEK! OHHHH!

5

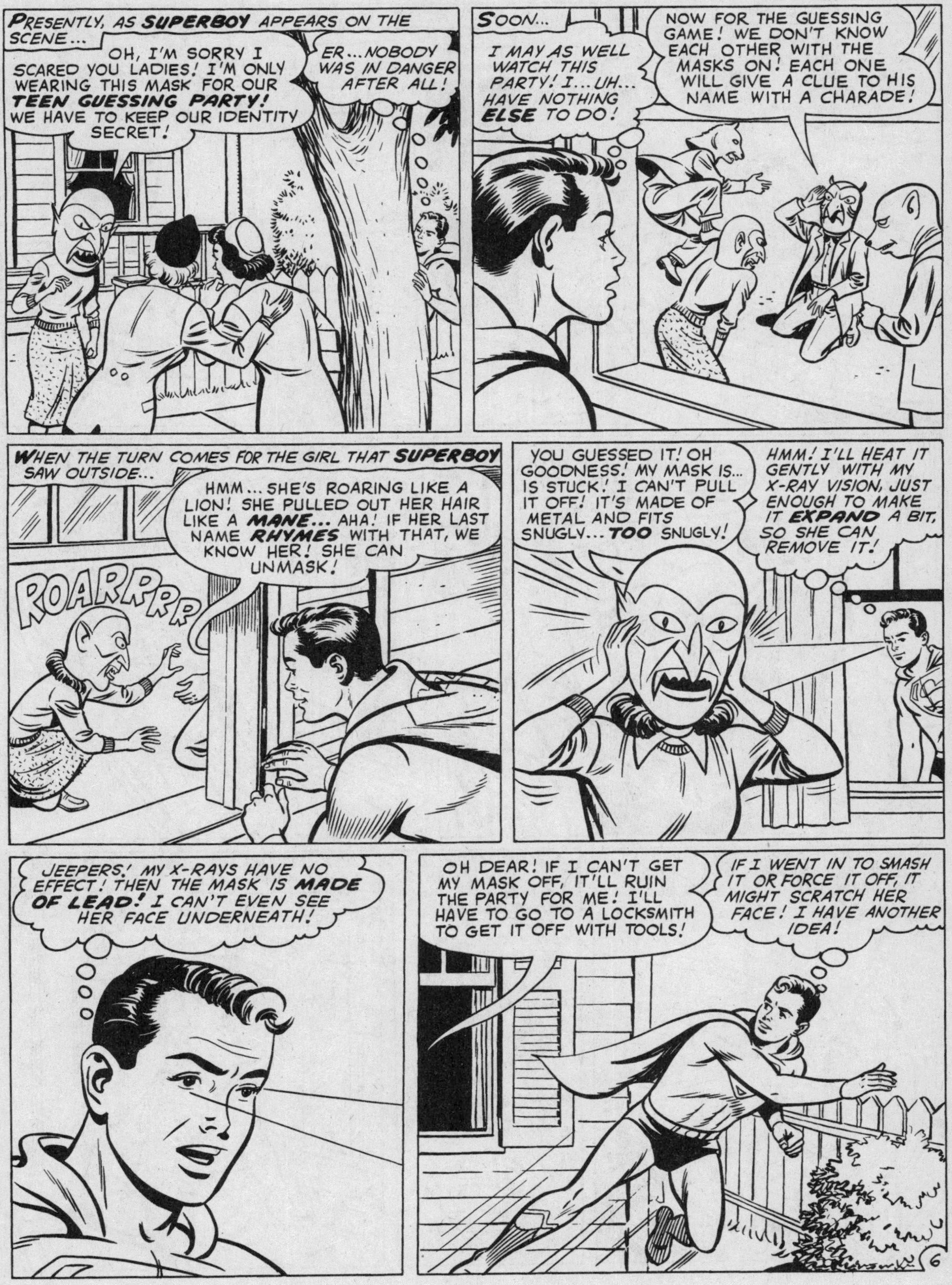
PRESENTLY, AS SUPERBOY APPEARS ON THE SCENE...
OH, I'M SORRY I SCARED YOU LADIES! I'M ONLY WEARING THIS MASK FOR OUR TEEN GUESSING PARTY! WE HAVE TO KEEP OUR IDENTITY SECRET!
ER...NOBODY WAS IN DANGER AFTER ALL!
SOON...
I MAY AS WELL WATCH THIS PARTY! I...UH... HAVE NOTHING ELSE TO DO!
NOW FOR THE GUESSING GAME! WE DON'T KNOW EACH OTHER WITH THE MASKS ON! EACH ONE WILL GIVE A CLUE TO HIS NAME WITH A CHARADE!
WHEN THE TURN COMES FOR THE GIRL THAT SUPERBOY SAW OUTSIDE...
HMM... SHE'S ROARING LIKE A LION! SHE PULLED OUT HER HAIR LIKE A MANE... AHA! IF HER LAST NAME RHYMES WITH THAT, WE KNOW HER! SHE CAN UNMASK!
ROARRPRR
YOU GUESSED IT! OH GOODNESS! MY MASK IS... IS STUCK! I CAN'T PULL IT OFF! IT'S MADE OF METAL AND FITS SNUGLY... TOO SNUGLY!
HMM! I'LL HEAT IT GENTLY WITH MY X-RAY VISION, JUST ENOUGH TO MAKE IT EXPAND A BIT, SO SHE CAN REMOVE IT!
JEEPERS! MY X-RAYS HAVE NO EFFECT! THEN THE MASK IS MADE OF LEAD! I CAN'T EVEN SEE HER FACE UNDERNEATH!
OH DEAR! IF I CAN'T GET MY MASK OFF, IT'LL RUIN THE PARTY FOR ME! I'LL HAVE TO GO TO A LOCKSMITH TO GET IT OFF WITH TOOLS!
IF I WENT IN TO SMASH IT OR FORCE IT OFF, IT MIGHT SCRATCH HER FACE! I HAVE ANOTHER IDEA!
6

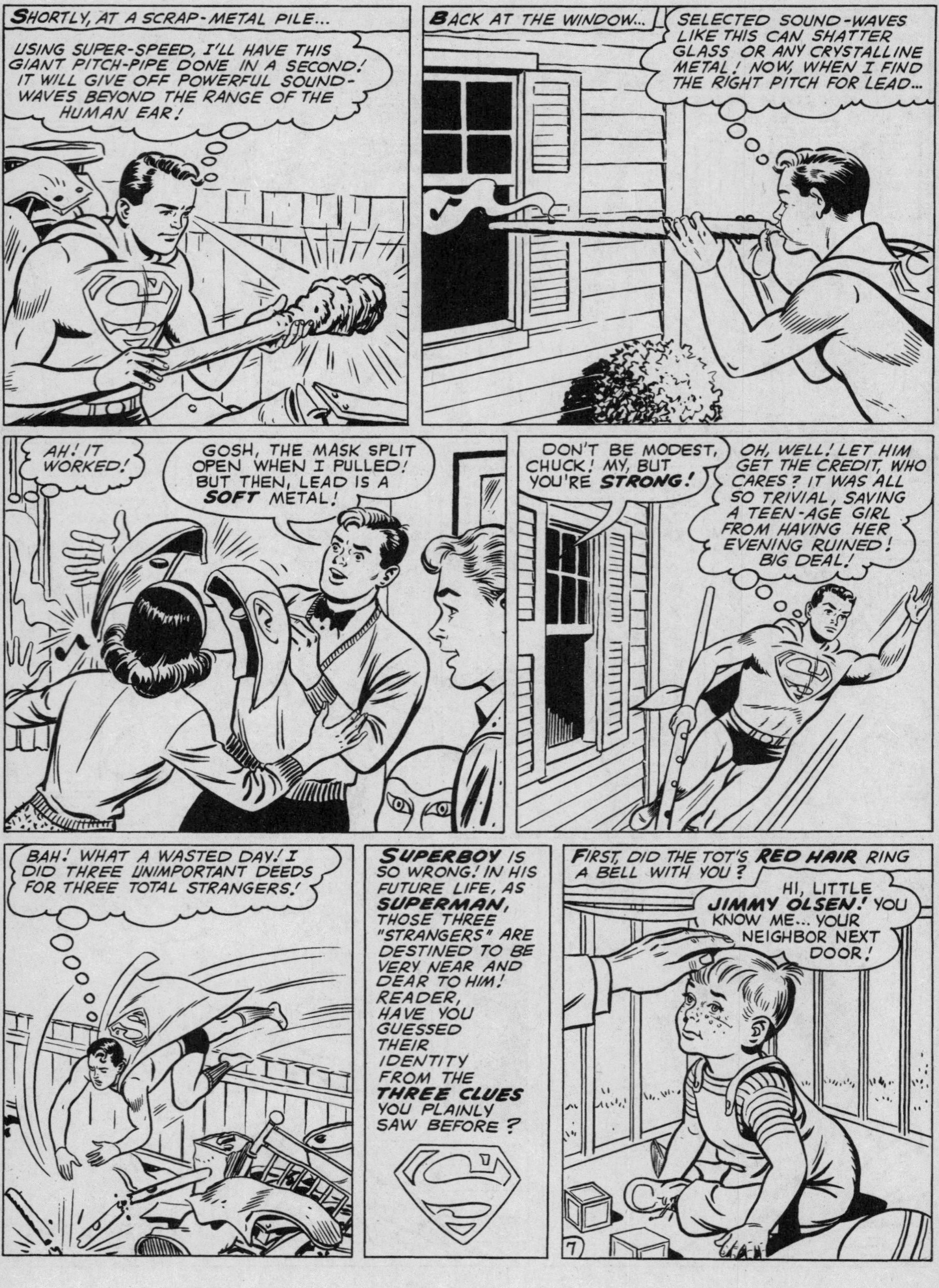
SHORTLY, AT A SCRAP-METAL PILE...
USING SUPER-SPEED, I'LL HAVE THIS GIANT PITCH-PIPE DONE IN A SECOND! IT WILL GIVE OFF POWERFUL SOUND-WAVES BEYOND THE RANGE OF THE HUMAN EAR!
BACK AT THE WINDOW...
SELECTED SOUND-WAVES LIKE THIS CAN SHATTER GLASS OR ANY CRYSTALLINE METAL! NOW, WHEN I FIND THE RIGHT PITCH FOR LEAD...
AH! IT WORKED!
GOSH, THE MASK SPLIT OPEN WHEN I PULLED! BUT THEN, LEAD IS A SOFT METAL!
DON'T BE MODEST, CHUCK! MY, BUT YOU'RE STRONG!
OH, WELL! LET HIM GET THE CREDIT, WHO CARES? IT WAS ALL SO TRIVIAL, SAVING A TEEN-AGE GIRL FROM HAVING HER EVENING RUINED! BIG DEAL!
BAH! WHAT A WASTED DAY! I DID THREE UNIMPORTANT DEEDS FOR THREE TOTAL STRANGERS!
SUPERBOY IS SO WRONG! IN HIS FUTURE LIFE, AS SUPERMAN, THOSE THREE "STRANGERS" ARE DESTINED TO BE VERY NEAR AND DEAR TO HIM! READER, HAVE YOU GUESSED THEIR IDENTITY FROM THE THREE CLUES YOU PLAINLY SAW BEFORE?
FIRST, DID THE TOT'S RED HAIR RING A BELL WITH YOU?
HI, LITTLE JIMMY OLSEN! YOU KNOW ME... YOUR NEIGHBOR NEXT DOOR!
7

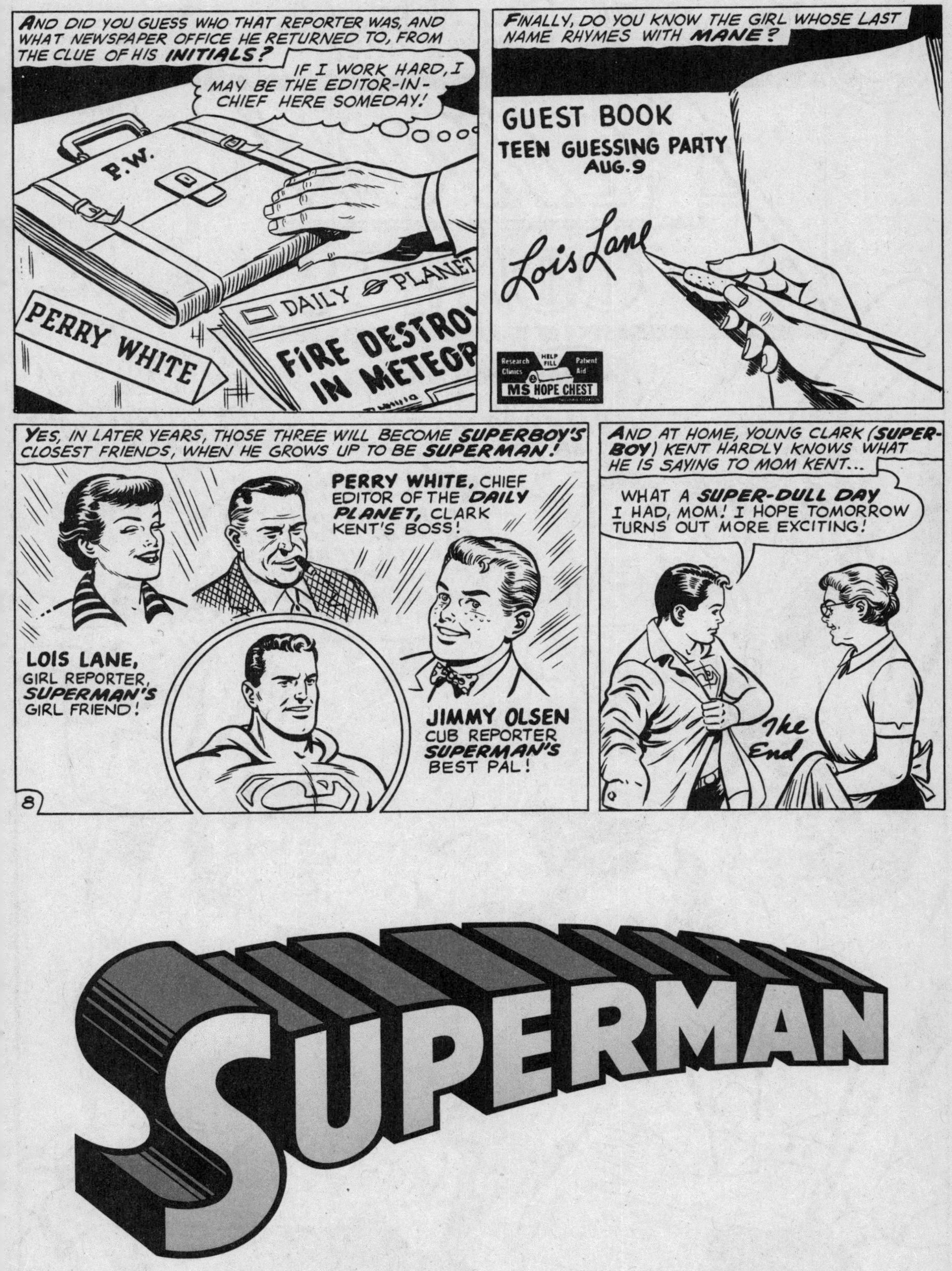
AND DID YOU GUESS WHO THAT REPORTER WAS, AND WHAT NEWSPAPER OFFICE HE RETURNED TO, FROM THE CLUE OF HIS INITIALS?
IF I WORK HARD, I MAY BE THE EDITOR-IN-CHIEF HERE SOMEDAY!
P.W.
PERRY WHITE
DAILY PLANET
FIRE DESTRO
IN METEO
FINALLY, DO YOU KNOW THE GIRL WHOSE LAST NAME RHYMES WITH MANE?
GUEST BOOK
TEEN GUESSING PARTY
AUG. 9
Lois Lane
Research Clinics
HELP FILL
Patient Aid
MS HOPE CHEST
YES, IN LATER YEARS, THOSE THREE WILL BECOME SUPERBOY'S CLOSEST FRIENDS, WHEN HE GROWS UP TO BE SUPERMAN!
PERRY WHITE, CHIEF EDITOR OF THE DAILY PLANET, CLARK KENT'S BOSS!
LOIS LANE, GIRL REPORTER, SUPERMAN'S GIRL FRIEND!
JIMMY OLSEN CUB REPORTER SUPERMAN'S BEST PAL!
8
AND AT HOME, YOUNG CLARK (SUPERBOY) KENT HARDLY KNOWS WHAT HE IS SAYING TO MOM KENT...
WHAT A SUPER-DULL DAY I HAD, MOM! I HOPE TOMORROW TURNS OUT MORE EXCITING!
The End

SUPERMAN

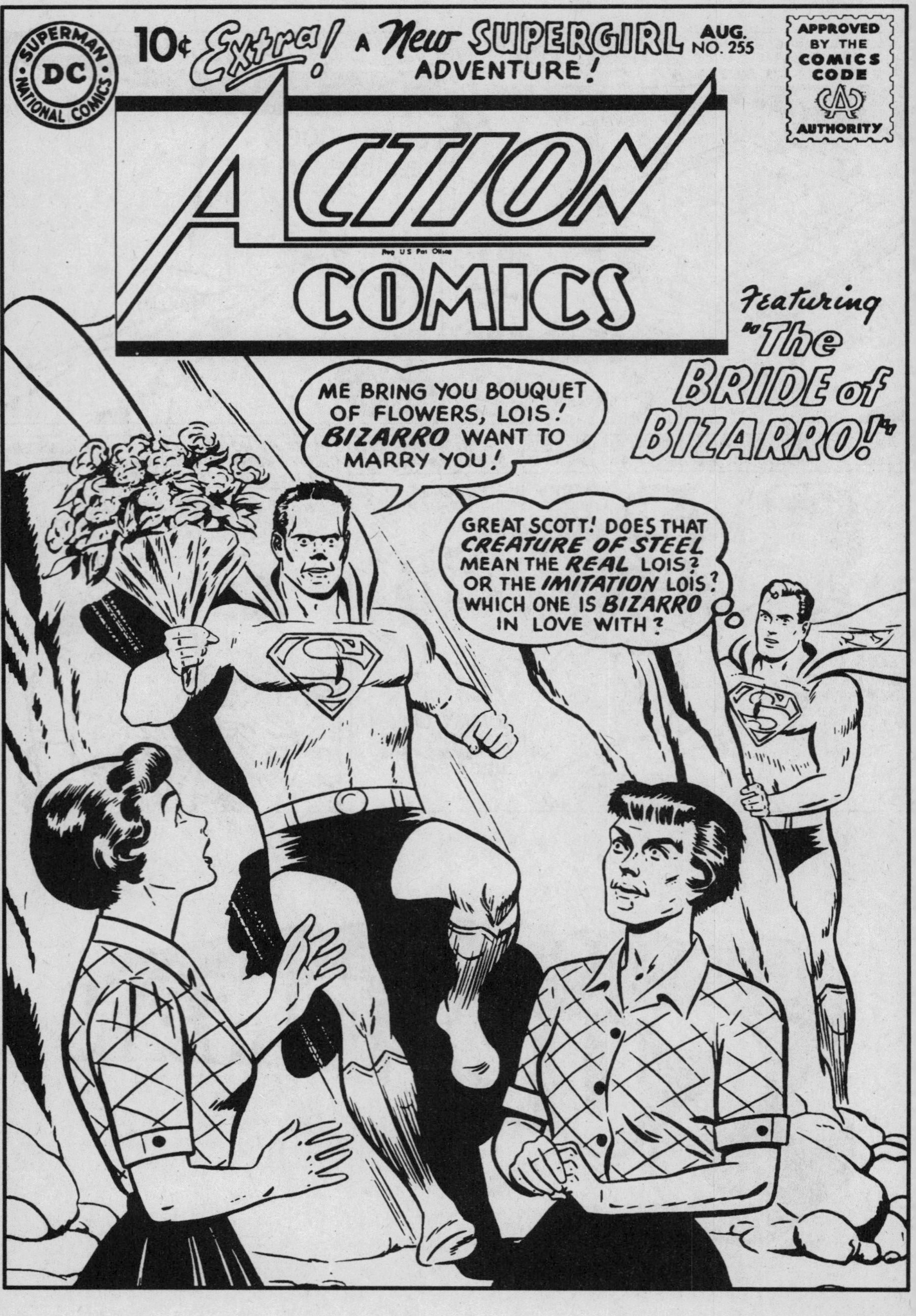
SUPERMAN DC NATIONAL COMICS
10¢ Extra! A New SUPERGIRL ADVENTURE!
AUG. NO. 255
APPROVED BY THE COMICS CODE AUTHORITY
ACTION COMICS
Reg U.S. Pat Office
Featuring "The BRIDE of BIZARRO!"
ME BRING YOU BOUQUET OF FLOWERS, LOIS! BIZARRO WANT TO MARRY YOU!
GREAT SCOTT! DOES THAT CREATURE OF STEEL MEAN THE REAL LOIS? OR THE IMITATION LOIS? WHICH ONE IS BIZARRO IN LOVE WITH?

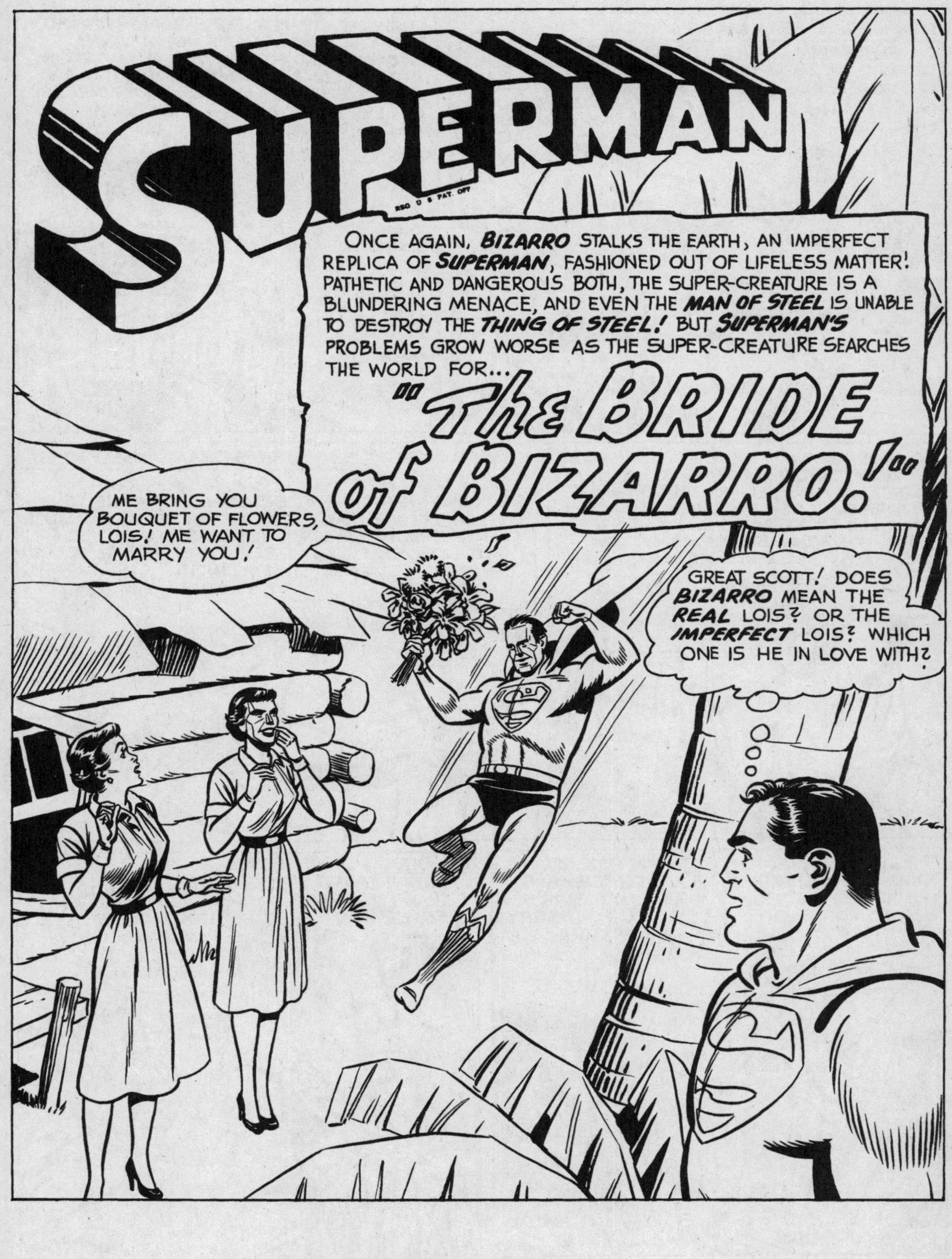
SUPERMAN
REG. U.S. PAT. OFF.
ONCE AGAIN, BIZARRO STALKS THE EARTH, AN IMPERFECT REPLICA OF SUPERMAN, FASHIONED OUT OF LIFELESS MATTER! PATHETIC AND DANGEROUS BOTH, THE SUPER-CREATURE IS A BLUNDERING MENACE, AND EVEN THE MAN OF STEEL IS UNABLE TO DESTROY THE THING OF STEEL! BUT SUPERMAN'S PROBLEMS GROW WORSE AS THE SUPER-CREATURE SEARCHES THE WORLD FOR...
"The BRIDE of BIZARRO!"
ME BRING YOU BOUQUET OF FLOWERS, LOIS! ME WANT TO MARRY YOU!
GREAT SCOTT! DOES BIZARRO MEAN THE REAL LOIS? OR THE IMPERFECT LOIS? WHICH ONE IS HE IN LOVE WITH?

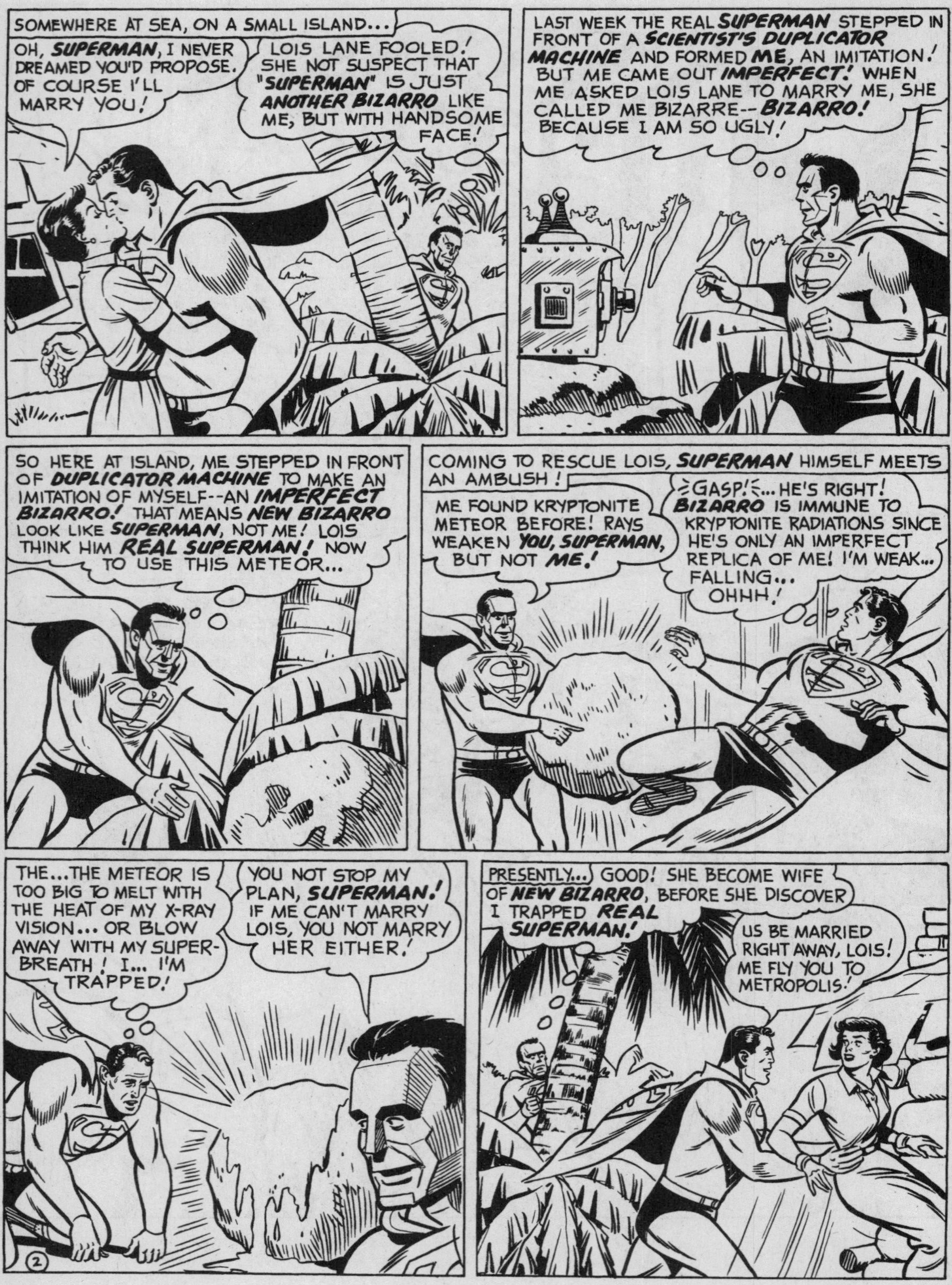
SOMEWHERE AT SEA, ON A SMALL ISLAND...
OH, SUPERMAN, I NEVER DREAMED YOU'D PROPOSE. OF COURSE I'LL MARRY YOU!
LOIS LANE FOOLED! SHE NOT SUSPECT THAT "SUPERMAN" IS JUST ANOTHER BIZARRO LIKE ME, BUT WITH HANDSOME FACE!
LAST WEEK THE REAL SUPERMAN STEPPED IN FRONT OF A SCIENTIST'S DUPLICATOR MACHINE AND FORMED ME, AN IMITATION! BUT ME CAME OUT IMPERFECT! WHEN ME ASKED LOIS LANE TO MARRY ME, SHE CALLED ME BIZARRE-- BIZARRO! BECAUSE I AM SO UGLY!
SO HERE AT ISLAND, ME STEPPED IN FRONT OF DUPLICATOR MACHINE TO MAKE AN IMITATION OF MYSELF--AN IMPERFECT BIZARRO! THAT MEANS NEW BIZARRO LOOK LIKE SUPERMAN, NOT ME! LOIS THINK HIM REAL SUPERMAN! NOW TO USE THIS METEOR...
COMING TO RESCUE LOIS, SUPERMAN HIMSELF MEETS AN AMBUSH!
ME FOUND KRYPTONITE METEOR BEFORE! RAYS WEAKEN YOU, SUPERMAN, BUT NOT ME!
GASP! ... HE'S RIGHT! BIZARRO IS IMMUNE TO KRYPTONITE RADIATIONS SINCE HE'S ONLY AN IMPERFECT REPLICA OF ME! I'M WEAK... FALLING... OHHH!
THE...THE METEOR IS TOO BIG TO MELT WITH THE HEAT OF MY X-RAY VISION... OR BLOW AWAY WITH MY SUPER-BREATH! I... I'M TRAPPED!
YOU NOT STOP MY PLAN, SUPERMAN! IF ME CAN'T MARRY LOIS, YOU NOT MARRY HER EITHER!
2
PRESENTLY...
GOOD! SHE BECOME WIFE OF NEW BIZARRO, BEFORE SHE DISCOVER I TRAPPED REAL SUPERMAN!
US BE MARRIED RIGHT AWAY, LOIS! ME FLY YOU TO METROPOLIS!

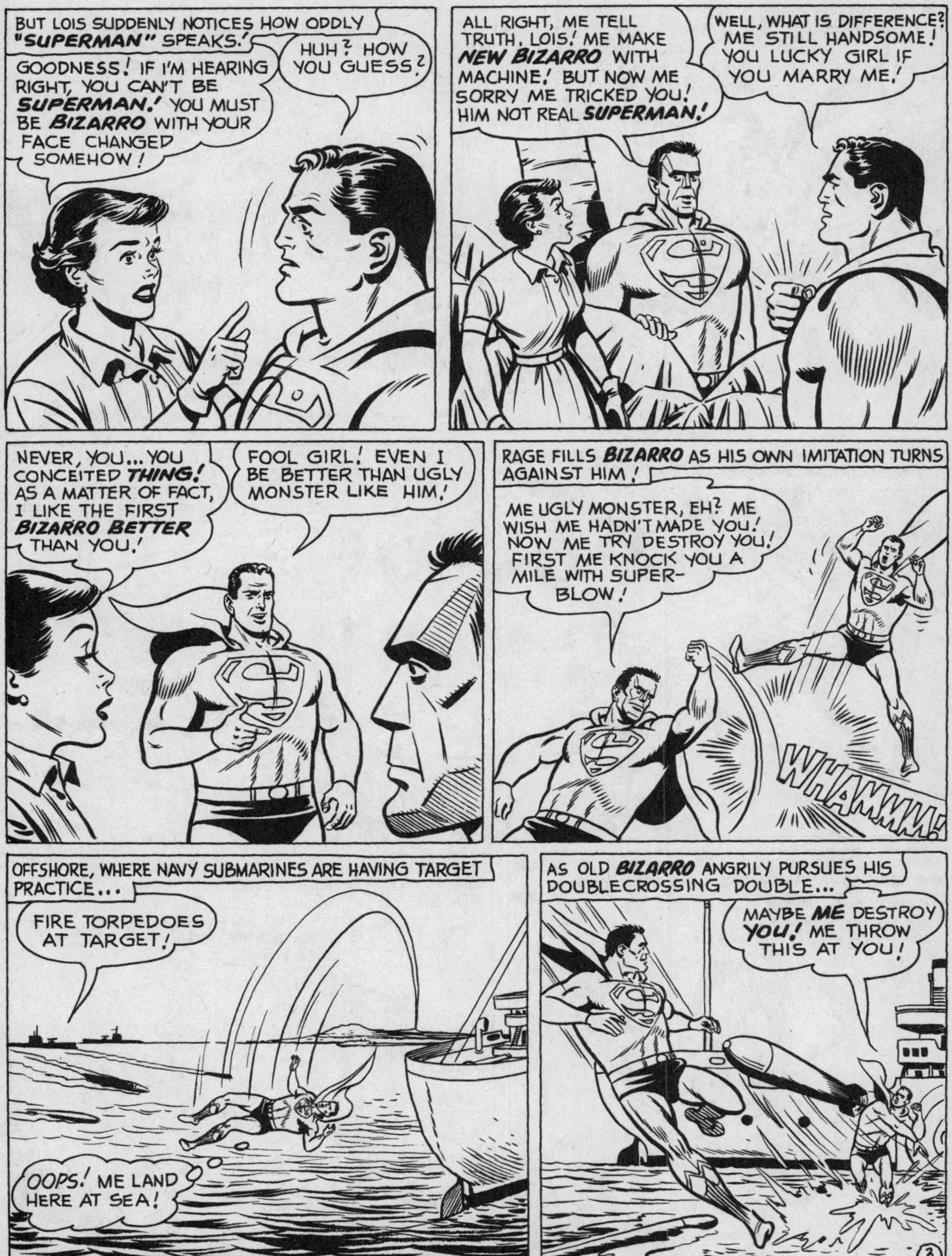
BUT LOIS SUDDENLY NOTICES HOW ODDLY "SUPERMAN" SPEAKS.
GOODNESS! IF I'M HEARING RIGHT, YOU CAN'T BE SUPERMAN! YOU MUST BE BIZARRO WITH YOUR FACE CHANGED SOMEHOW!
HUH? HOW YOU GUESS?
ALL RIGHT, ME TELL TRUTH, LOIS! ME MAKE NEW BIZARRO WITH MACHINE! BUT NOW ME SORRY ME TRICKED YOU! HIM NOT REAL SUPERMAN!
WELL, WHAT IS DIFFERENCE? ME STILL HANDSOME! YOU LUCKY GIRL IF YOU MARRY ME!
NEVER, YOU...YOU CONCEITED THING! AS A MATTER OF FACT, I LIKE THE FIRST BIZARRO BETTER THAN YOU!
FOOL GIRL! EVEN I BE BETTER THAN UGLY MONSTER LIKE HIM!
RAGE FILLS BIZARRO AS HIS OWN IMITATION TURNS AGAINST HIM!
ME UGLY MONSTER, EH? ME WISH ME HADN'T MADE YOU! NOW ME TRY DESTROY YOU! FIRST ME KNOCK YOU A MILE WITH SUPER-BLOW!
WHAMMM!
OFFSHORE, WHERE NAVY SUBMARINES ARE HAVING TARGET PRACTICE...
FIRE TORPEDOES AT TARGET!
OOPS! ME LAND HERE AT SEA!
AS OLD BIZARRO ANGRILY PURSUES HIS DOUBLECROSSING DOUBLE...
MAYBE ME DESTROY YOU! ME THROW THIS AT YOU!
3

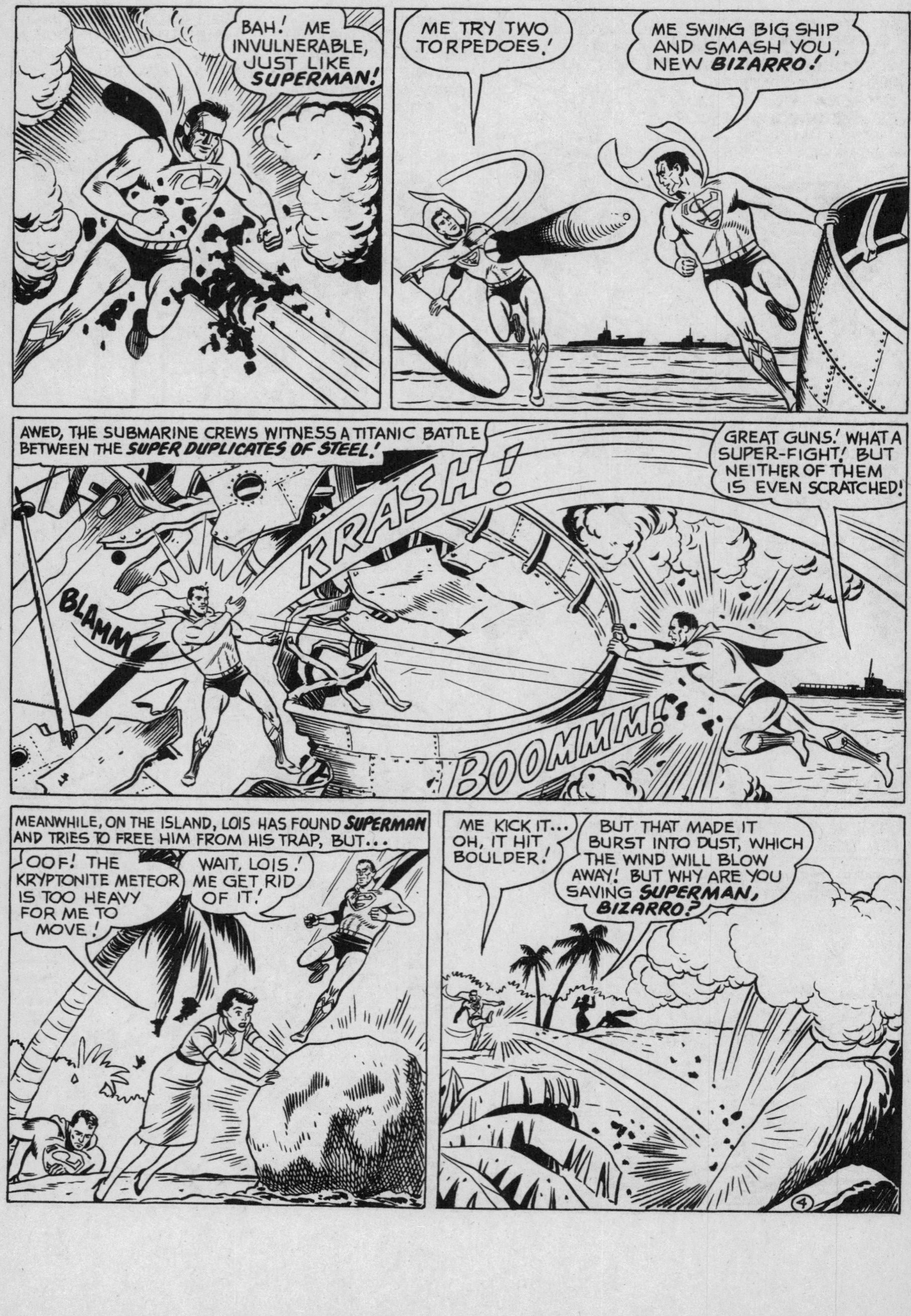
BAH! ME INVULNERABLE, JUST LIKE SUPERMAN!
ME TRY TWO TORPEDOES!
ME SWING BIG SHIP AND SMASH YOU, NEW BIZARRO!
AWED, THE SUBMARINE CREWS WITNESS A TITANIC BATTLE BETWEEN THE SUPER DUPLICATES OF STEEL!
GREAT GUNS! WHAT A SUPER-FIGHT! BUT NEITHER OF THEM IS EVEN SCRATCHED!
KRASH!
BLAMM
BOOMMM!
MEANWHILE, ON THE ISLAND, LOIS HAS FOUND SUPERMAN AND TRIES TO FREE HIM FROM HIS TRAP, BUT...
OOF! THE KRYPTONITE METEOR IS TOO HEAVY FOR ME TO MOVE!
WAIT, LOIS! ME GET RID OF IT!
ME KICK IT... OH, IT HIT BOULDER!
BUT THAT MADE IT BURST INTO DUST, WHICH THE WIND WILL BLOW AWAY! BUT WHY ARE YOU SAVING SUPERMAN, BIZARRO?
4

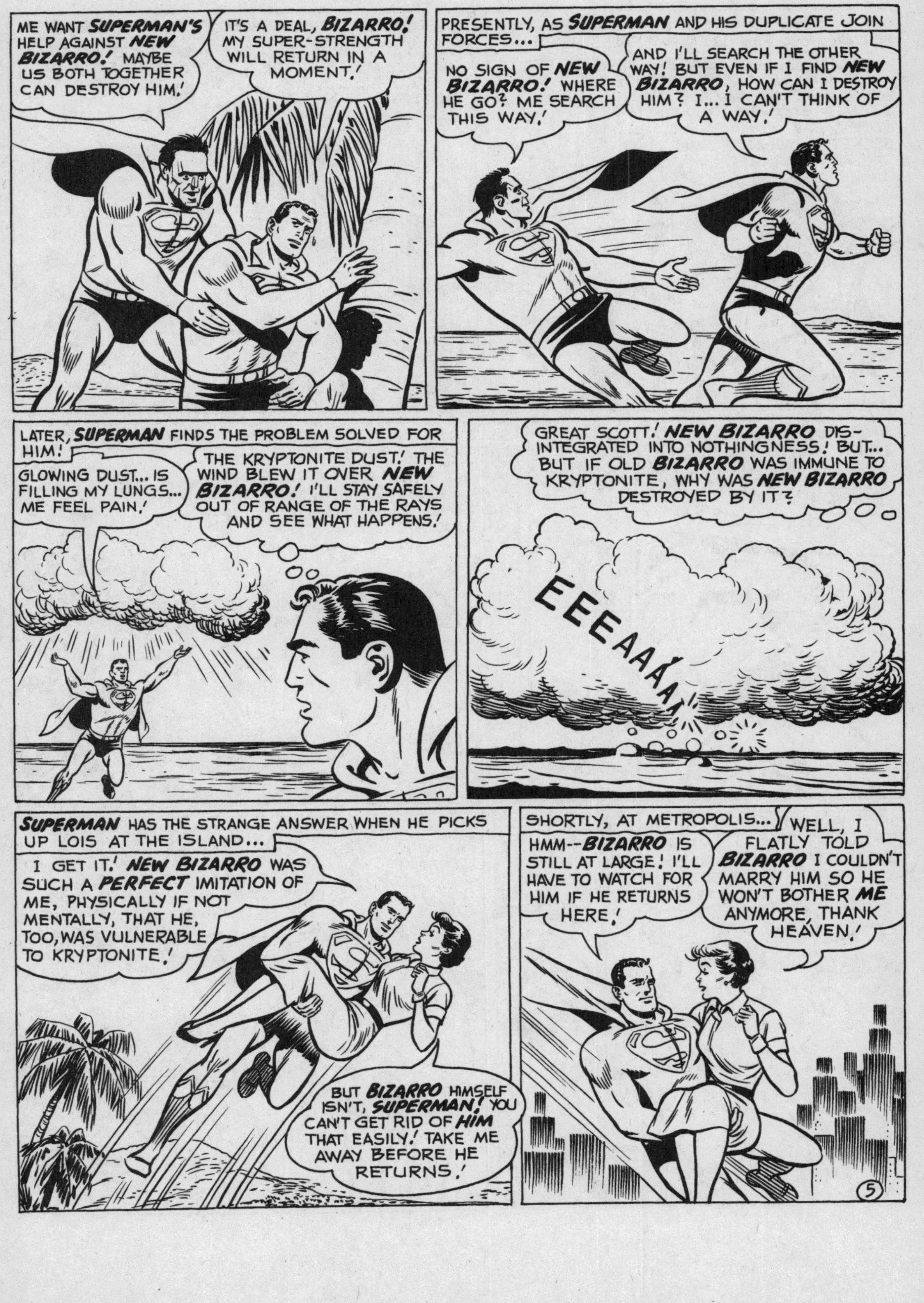
ME WANT SUPERMAN'S HELP AGAINST NEW BIZARRO! MAYBE US BOTH TOGETHER CAN DESTROY HIM!
IT'S A DEAL, BIZARRO! MY SUPER-STRENGTH WILL RETURN IN A MOMENT!
PRESENTLY, AS SUPERMAN AND HIS DUPLICATE JOIN FORCES...
NO SIGN OF NEW BIZARRO! WHERE HE GO? ME SEARCH THIS WAY!
AND I'LL SEARCH THE OTHER WAY! BUT EVEN IF I FIND NEW BIZARRO, HOW CAN I DESTROY HIM? I... I CAN'T THINK OF A WAY!
LATER, SUPERMAN FINDS THE PROBLEM SOLVED FOR HIM!
GLOWING DUST... IS FILLING MY LUNGS... ME FEEL PAIN!
THE KRYPTONITE DUST! THE WIND BLEW IT OVER NEW BIZARRO! I'LL STAY SAFELY OUT OF RANGE OF THE RAYS AND SEE WHAT HAPPENS!
GREAT SCOTT! NEW BIZARRO DIS-INTEGRATED INTO NOTHINGNESS! BUT... BUT IF OLD BIZARRO WAS IMMUNE TO KRYPTONITE, WHY WAS NEW BIZARRO DESTROYED BY IT?
EEEAAAAA
SUPERMAN HAS THE STRANGE ANSWER WHEN HE PICKS UP LOIS AT THE ISLAND...
I GET IT! NEW BIZARRO WAS SUCH A PERFECT IMITATION OF ME, PHYSICALLY IF NOT MENTALLY, THAT HE, TOO, WAS VULNERABLE TO KRYPTONITE!
BUT BIZARRO HIMSELF ISN'T, SUPERMAN! YOU CAN'T GET RID OF HIM THAT EASILY! TAKE ME AWAY BEFORE HE RETURNS!
SHORTLY, AT METROPOLIS...
HMM--BIZARRO IS STILL AT LARGE! I'LL HAVE TO WATCH FOR HIM IF HE RETURNS HERE!
WELL, I FLATLY TOLD BIZARRO I COULDN'T MARRY HIM SO HE WON'T BOTHER ME ANYMORE, THANK HEAVEN!
5

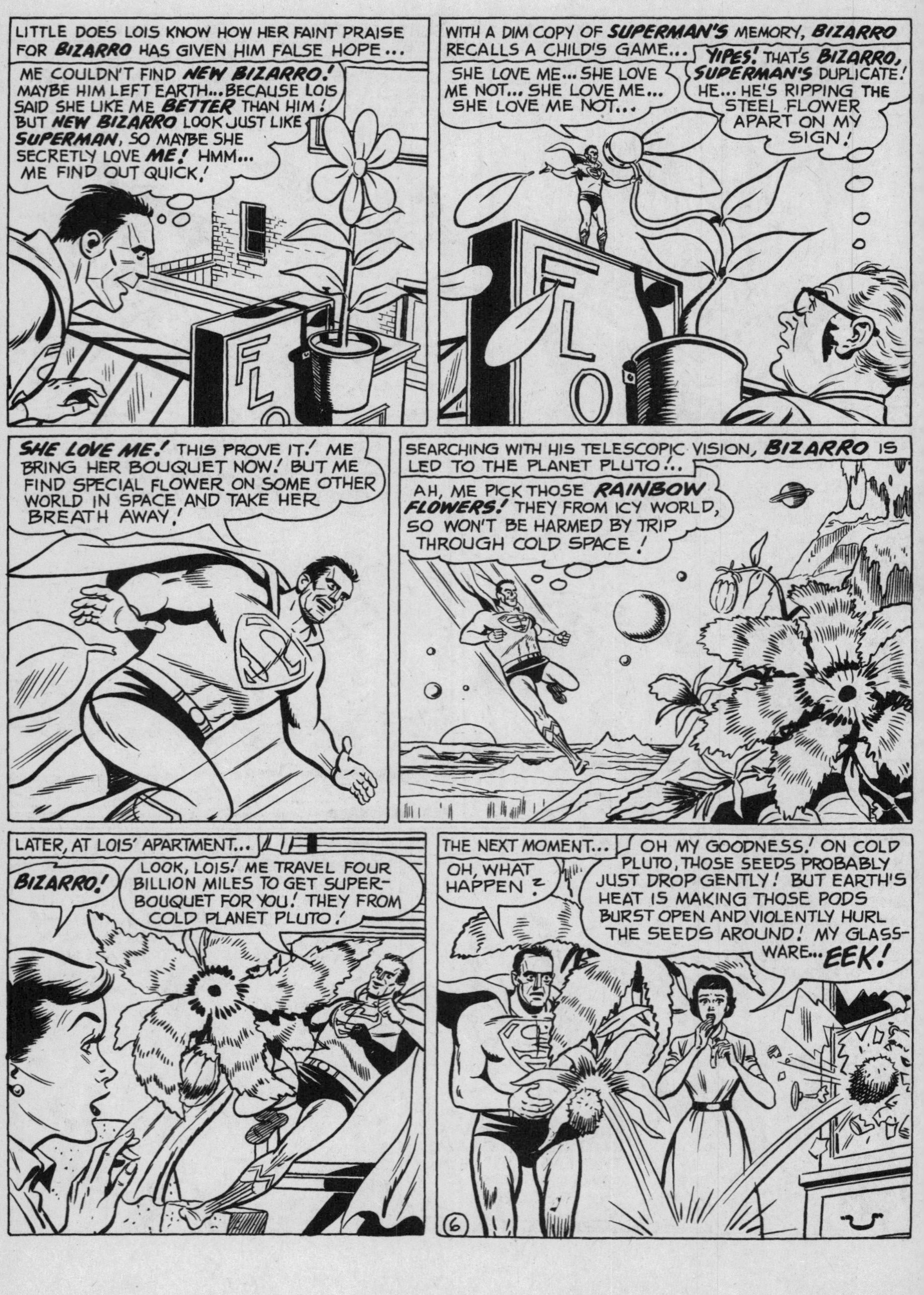
LITTLE DOES LOIS KNOW HOW HER FAINT PRAISE FOR BIZARRO HAS GIVEN HIM FALSE HOPE...
ME COULDN'T FIND NEW BIZARRO! MAYBE HIM LEFT EARTH...BECAUSE LOIS SAID SHE LIKE ME BETTER THAN HIM! BUT NEW BIZARRO LOOK JUST LIKE SUPERMAN, SO MAYBE SHE SECRETLY LOVE ME! HMM... ME FIND OUT QUICK!
FLO
WITH A DIM COPY OF SUPERMAN'S MEMORY, BIZARRO RECALLS A CHILD'S GAME...
SHE LOVE ME... SHE LOVE ME NOT... SHE LOVE ME... SHE LOVE ME NOT...
YIPES! THAT'S BIZARRO, SUPERMAN'S DUPLICATE! HE... HE'S RIPPING THE STEEL FLOWER APART ON MY SIGN!
FLO
SHE LOVE ME! THIS PROVE IT! ME BRING HER BOUQUET NOW! BUT ME FIND SPECIAL FLOWER ON SOME OTHER WORLD IN SPACE AND TAKE HER BREATH AWAY!
SEARCHING WITH HIS TELESCOPIC VISION, BIZARRO IS LED TO THE PLANET PLUTO!..
AH, ME PICK THOSE RAINBOW FLOWERS! THEY FROM ICY WORLD, SO WON'T BE HARMED BY TRIP THROUGH COLD SPACE!
LATER, AT LOIS' APARTMENT...
BIZARRO!
LOOK, LOIS! ME TRAVEL FOUR BILLION MILES TO GET SUPER-BOUQUET FOR YOU! THEY FROM COLD PLANET PLUTO!
THE NEXT MOMENT...
OH, WHAT HAPPEN?
OH MY GOODNESS! ON COLD PLUTO, THOSE SEEDS PROBABLY JUST DROP GENTLY! BUT EARTH'S HEAT IS MAKING THOSE PODS BURST OPEN AND VIOLENTLY HURL THE SEEDS AROUND! MY GLASS-WARE...EEK!
6

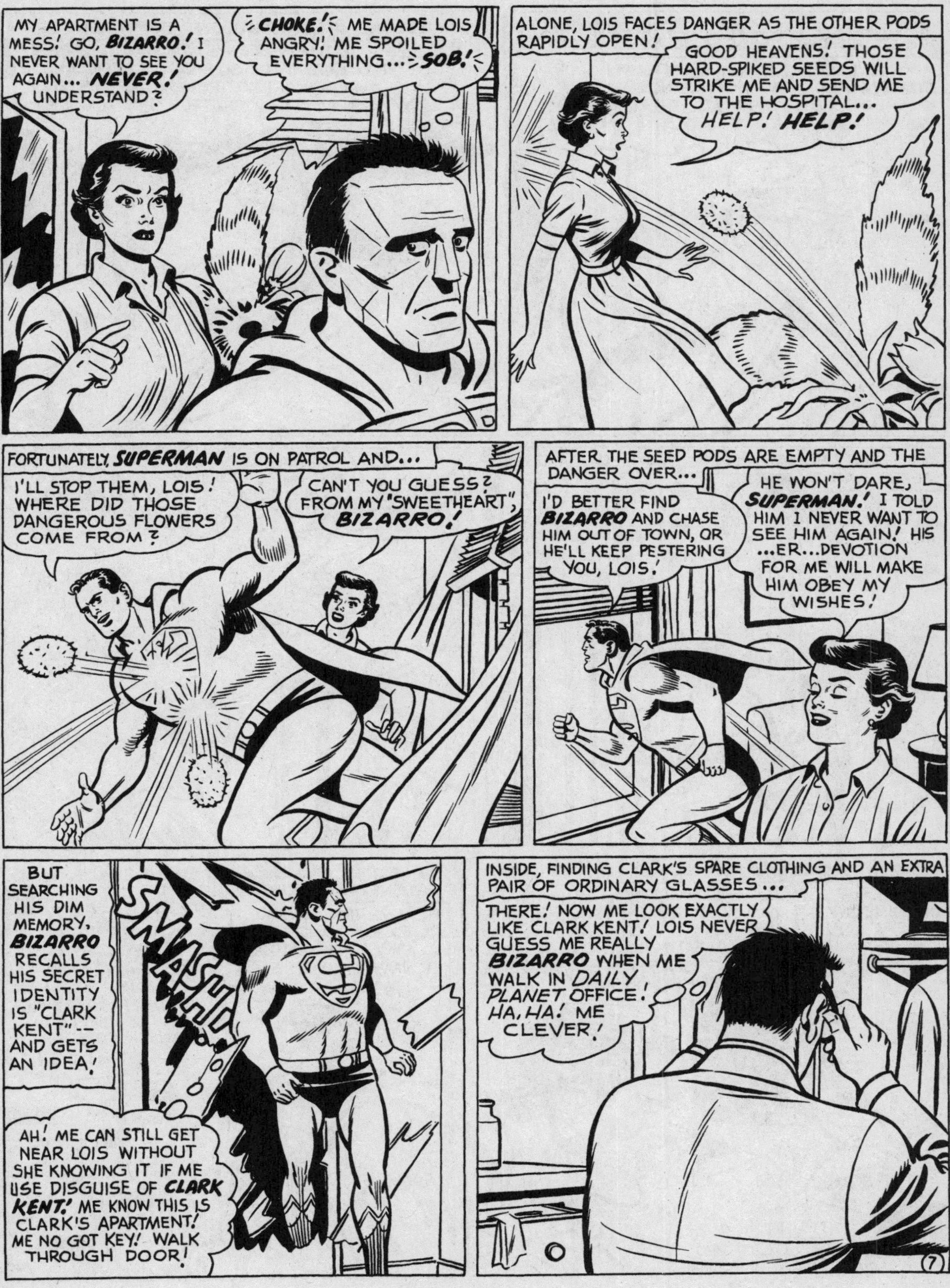
MY APARTMENT IS A MESS! GO, BIZARRO! I NEVER WANT TO SEE YOU AGAIN... NEVER! UNDERSTAND?
CHOKE! ME MADE LOIS ANGRY! ME SPOILED EVERYTHING... SOB!
ALONE, LOIS FACES DANGER AS THE OTHER PODS RAPIDLY OPEN!
GOOD HEAVENS! THOSE HARD-SPIKED SEEDS WILL STRIKE ME AND SEND ME TO THE HOSPITAL... HELP! HELP!
FORTUNATELY, SUPERMAN IS ON PATROL AND...
I'LL STOP THEM, LOIS! WHERE DID THOSE DANGEROUS FLOWERS COME FROM?
CAN'T YOU GUESS? FROM MY "SWEETHEART", BIZARRO!
AFTER THE SEED PODS ARE EMPTY AND THE DANGER OVER...
I'D BETTER FIND BIZARRO AND CHASE HIM OUT OF TOWN, OR HE'LL KEEP PESTERING YOU, LOIS!
HE WON'T DARE, SUPERMAN! I TOLD HIM I NEVER WANT TO SEE HIM AGAIN! HIS ...ER...DEVOTION FOR ME WILL MAKE HIM OBEY MY WISHES!
BUT SEARCHING HIS DIM MEMORY, BIZARRO RECALLS HIS SECRET IDENTITY IS "CLARK KENT" -- AND GETS AN IDEA!
SMASH!
AH! ME CAN STILL GET NEAR LOIS WITHOUT SHE KNOWING IT IF ME USE DISGUISE OF CLARK KENT! ME KNOW THIS IS CLARK'S APARTMENT! ME NO GOT KEY! WALK THROUGH DOOR!
INSIDE, FINDING CLARK'S SPARE CLOTHING AND AN EXTRA PAIR OF ORDINARY GLASSES...
THERE! NOW ME LOOK EXACTLY LIKE CLARK KENT! LOIS NEVER GUESS ME REALLY BIZARRO WHEN ME WALK IN DAILY PLANET OFFICE! HA, HA! ME CLEVER!
7

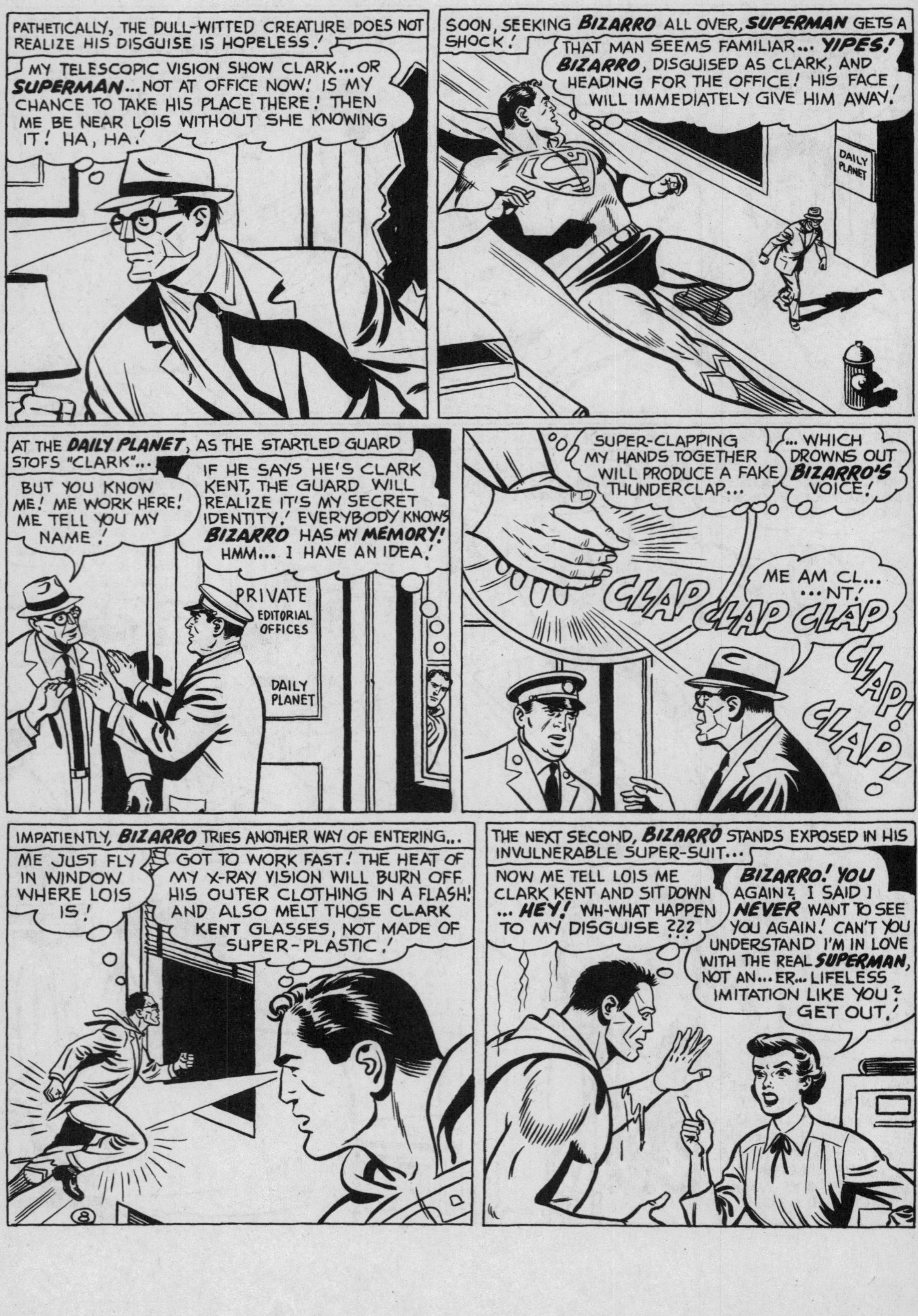
PATHETICALLY, THE DULL-WITTED CREATURE DOES NOT REALIZE HIS DISGUISE IS HOPELESS!
MY TELESCOPIC VISION SHOW CLARK... OR SUPERMAN... NOT AT OFFICE NOW! IS MY CHANCE TO TAKE HIS PLACE THERE! THEN ME BE NEAR LOIS WITHOUT SHE KNOWING IT! HA, HA!
SOON, SEEKING BIZARRO ALL OVER, SUPERMAN GETS A SHOCK!
THAT MAN SEEMS FAMILIAR... YIPES! BIZARRO, DISGUISED AS CLARK, AND HEADING FOR THE OFFICE! HIS FACE WILL IMMEDIATELY GIVE HIM AWAY!
DAILY PLANET
AT THE DAILY PLANET, AS THE STARTLED GUARD STOFS "CLARK"...
BUT YOU KNOW ME! ME WORK HERE! ME TELL YOU MY NAME!
IF HE SAYS HE'S CLARK KENT, THE GUARD WILL REALIZE IT'S MY SECRET IDENTITY! EVERYBODY KNOWS BIZARRO HAS MY MEMORY! HMM... I HAVE AN IDEA!
PRIVATE EDITORIAL OFFICES
DAILY PLANET
SUPER-CLAPPING MY HANDS TOGETHER WILL PRODUCE A FAKE THUNDERCLAP...
... WHICH DROWNS OUT BIZARRO'S VOICE!
ME AM CL... ...NT!
CLAP CLAP CLAP CLAP! CLAP!
IMPATIENTLY, BIZARRO TRIES ANOTHER WAY OF ENTERING...
ME JUST FLY IN WINDOW WHERE LOIS IS!
GOT TO WORK FAST! THE HEAT OF MY X-RAY VISION WILL BURN OFF HIS OUTER CLOTHING IN A FLASH! AND ALSO MELT THOSE CLARK KENT GLASSES, NOT MADE OF SUPER-PLASTIC!
8
THE NEXT SECOND, BIZARRO STANDS EXPOSED IN HIS INVULNERABLE SUPER-SUIT...
NOW ME TELL LOIS ME CLARK KENT AND SIT DOWN ... HEY! WH-WHAT HAPPEN TO MY DISGUISE ???
BIZARRO! YOU AGAIN? I SAID I NEVER WANT TO SEE YOU AGAIN! CAN'T YOU UNDERSTAND I'M IN LOVE WITH THE REAL SUPERMAN, NOT AN... ER... LIFELESS IMITATION LIKE YOU? GET OUT!

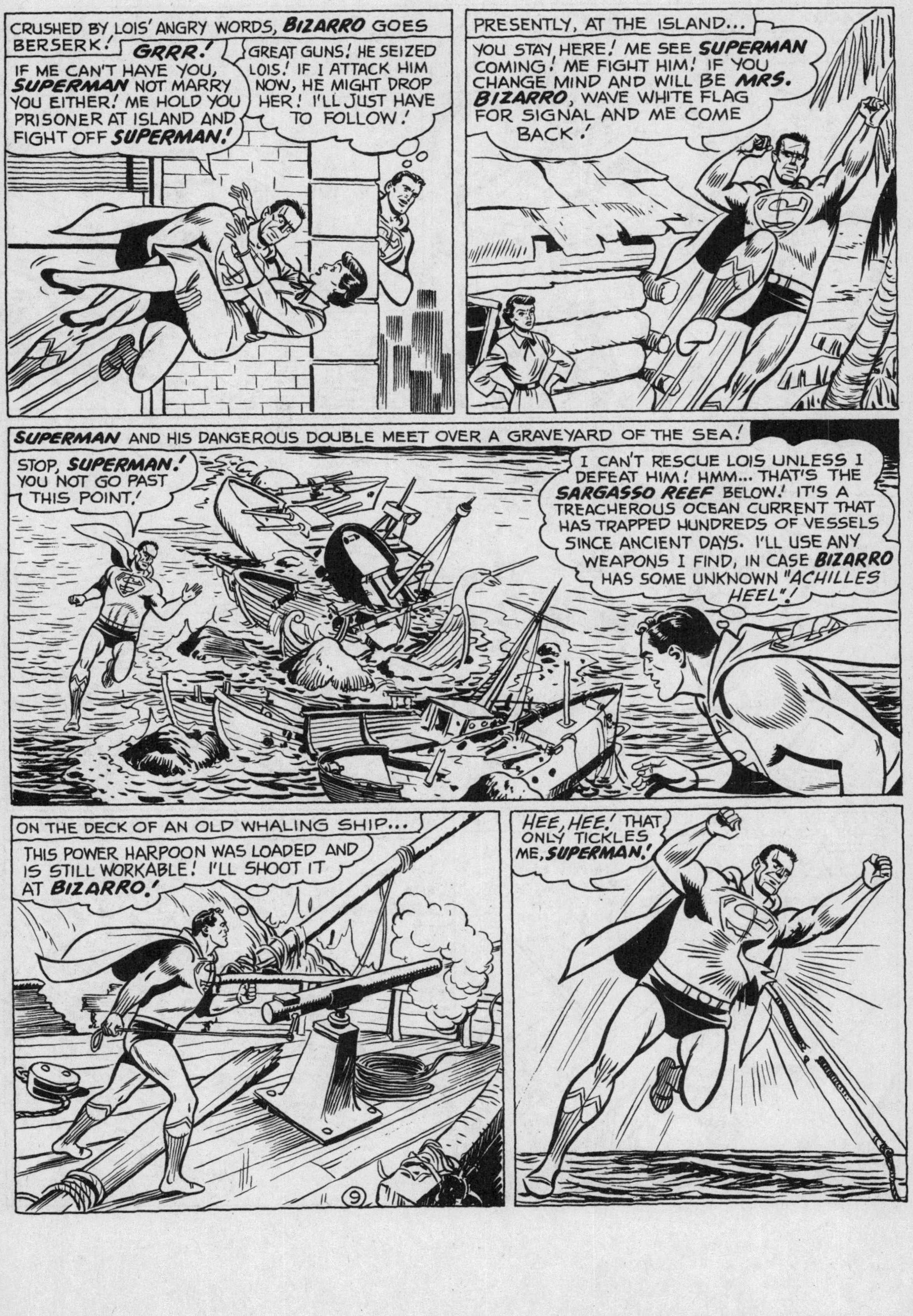
CRUSHED BY LOIS' ANGRY WORDS, BIZARRO GOES BERSERK!
GRRR!
IF ME CAN'T HAVE YOU, SUPERMAN NOT MARRY YOU EITHER! ME HOLD YOU PRISONER AT ISLAND AND FIGHT OFF SUPERMAN!
GREAT GUNS! HE SEIZED LOIS! IF I ATTACK HIM NOW, HE MIGHT DROP HER! I'LL JUST HAVE TO FOLLOW!
PRESENTLY, AT THE ISLAND...
YOU STAY HERE! ME SEE SUPERMAN COMING! ME FIGHT HIM! IF YOU CHANGE MIND AND WILL BE MRS. BIZARRO, WAVE WHITE FLAG FOR SIGNAL AND ME COME BACK!
SUPERMAN AND HIS DANGEROUS DOUBLE MEET OVER A GRAVEYARD OF THE SEA!
STOP, SUPERMAN! YOU NOT GO PAST THIS POINT!
I CAN'T RESCUE LOIS UNLESS I DEFEAT HIM! HMM... THAT'S THE SARGASSO REEF BELOW! IT'S A TREACHEROUS OCEAN CURRENT THAT HAS TRAPPED HUNDREDS OF VESSELS SINCE ANCIENT DAYS. I'LL USE ANY WEAPONS I FIND, IN CASE BIZARRO HAS SOME UNKNOWN "ACHILLES HEEL"!
ON THE DECK OF AN OLD WHALING SHIP...
THIS POWER HARPOON WAS LOADED AND IS STILL WORKABLE! I'LL SHOOT IT AT BIZARRO!
9
HEE, HEE! THAT ONLY TICKLES ME, SUPERMAN!

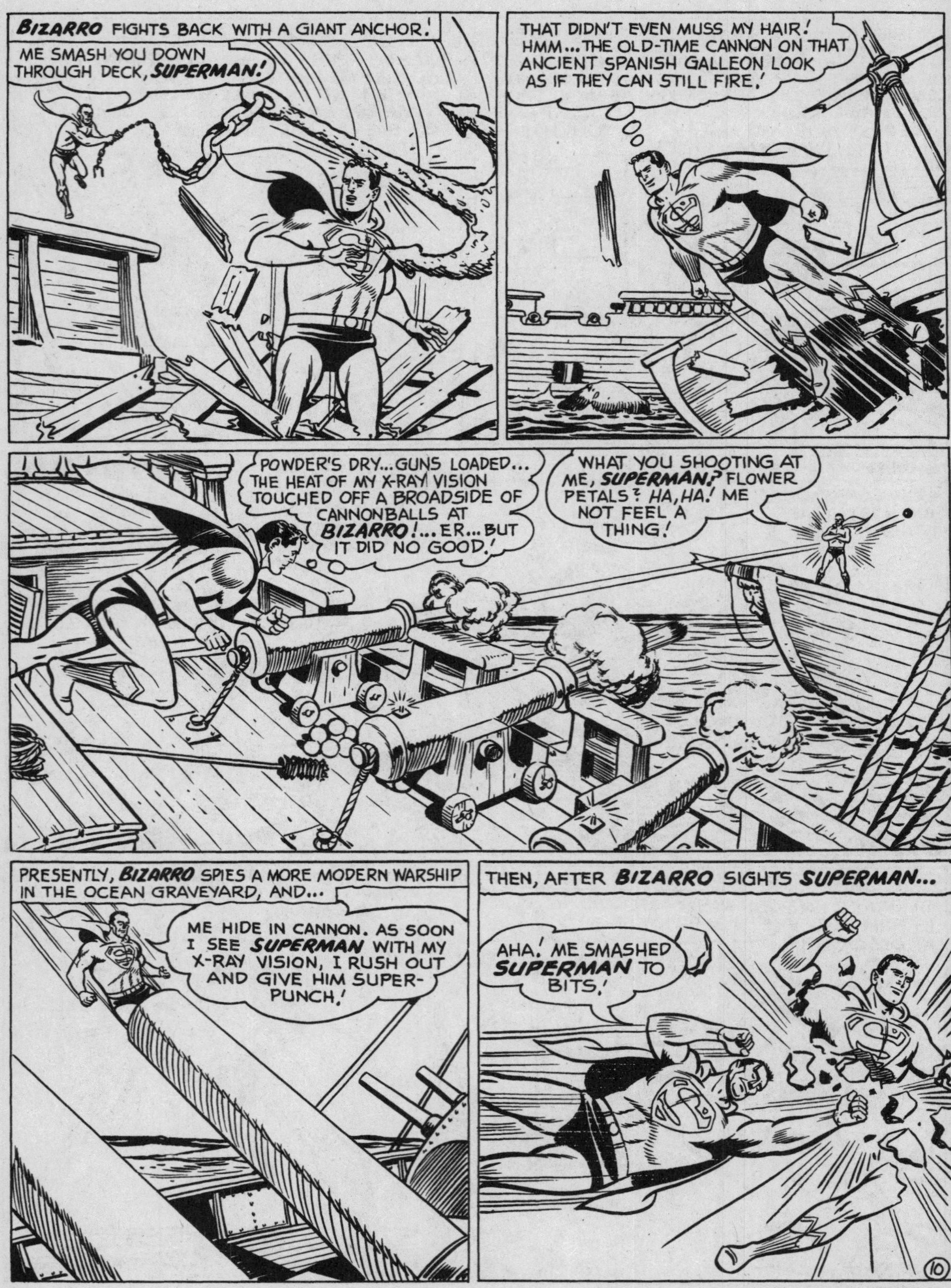
BIZARRO FIGHTS BACK WITH A GIANT ANCHOR!
ME SMASH YOU DOWN THROUGH DECK, SUPERMAN!
THAT DIDN'T EVEN MUSS MY HAIR! HMM... THE OLD-TIME CANNON ON THAT ANCIENT SPANISH GALLEON LOOK AS IF THEY CAN STILL FIRE!
POWDER'S DRY... GUNS LOADED... THE HEAT OF MY X-RAY VISION TOUCHED OFF A BROADSIDE OF CANNONBALLS AT BIZARRO!... ER... BUT IT DID NO GOOD!
WHAT YOU SHOOTING AT ME, SUPERMAN? FLOWER PETALS? HA, HA! ME NOT FEEL A THING!
PRESENTLY, BIZARRO SPIES A MORE MODERN WARSHIP IN THE OCEAN GRAVEYARD, AND...
ME HIDE IN CANNON. AS SOON I SEE SUPERMAN WITH MY X-RAY VISION, I RUSH OUT AND GIVE HIM SUPER-PUNCH!
THEN, AFTER BIZARRO SIGHTS SUPERMAN...
AHA! ME SMASHED SUPERMAN TO BITS!
10

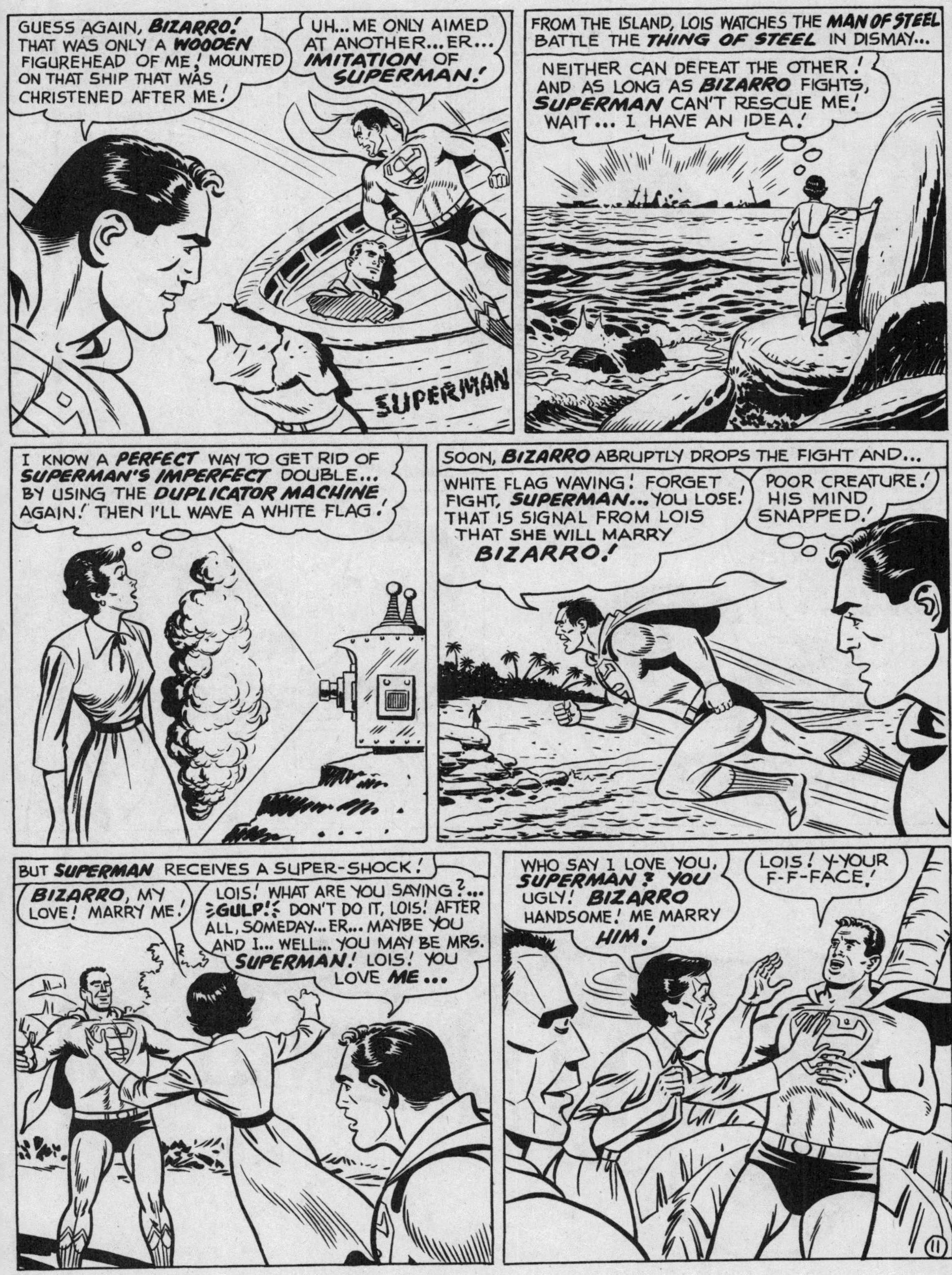
GUESS AGAIN, BIZARRO! THAT WAS ONLY A WOODEN FIGUREHEAD OF ME! MOUNTED ON THAT SHIP THAT WAS CHRISTENED AFTER ME!
UH... ME ONLY AIMED AT ANOTHER... ER... IMITATION OF SUPERMAN!
SUPERMAN
FROM THE ISLAND, LOIS WATCHES THE MAN OF STEEL BATTLE THE THING OF STEEL IN DISMAY...
NEITHER CAN DEFEAT THE OTHER! AND AS LONG AS BIZARRO FIGHTS, SUPERMAN CAN'T RESCUE ME! WAIT... I HAVE AN IDEA!
I KNOW A PERFECT WAY TO GET RID OF SUPERMAN'S IMPERFECT DOUBLE... BY USING THE DUPLICATOR MACHINE AGAIN! THEN I'LL WAVE A WHITE FLAG!
SOON, BIZARRO ABRUPTLY DROPS THE FIGHT AND...
WHITE FLAG WAVING! FORGET FIGHT, SUPERMAN... YOU LOSE! THAT IS SIGNAL FROM LOIS THAT SHE WILL MARRY BIZARRO!
POOR CREATURE! HIS MIND SNAPPED!
BUT SUPERMAN RECEIVES A SUPER-SHOCK!
BIZARRO, MY LOVE! MARRY ME!
LOIS! WHAT ARE YOU SAYING?... GULP! DON'T DO IT, LOIS! AFTER ALL, SOMEDAY... ER... MAYBE YOU AND I... WELL... YOU MAY BE MRS. SUPERMAN! LOIS! YOU LOVE ME...
WHO SAY I LOVE YOU, SUPERMAN? YOU UGLY! BIZARRO HANDSOME! ME MARRY HIM!
LOIS! Y-YOUR F-F-FACE!
11

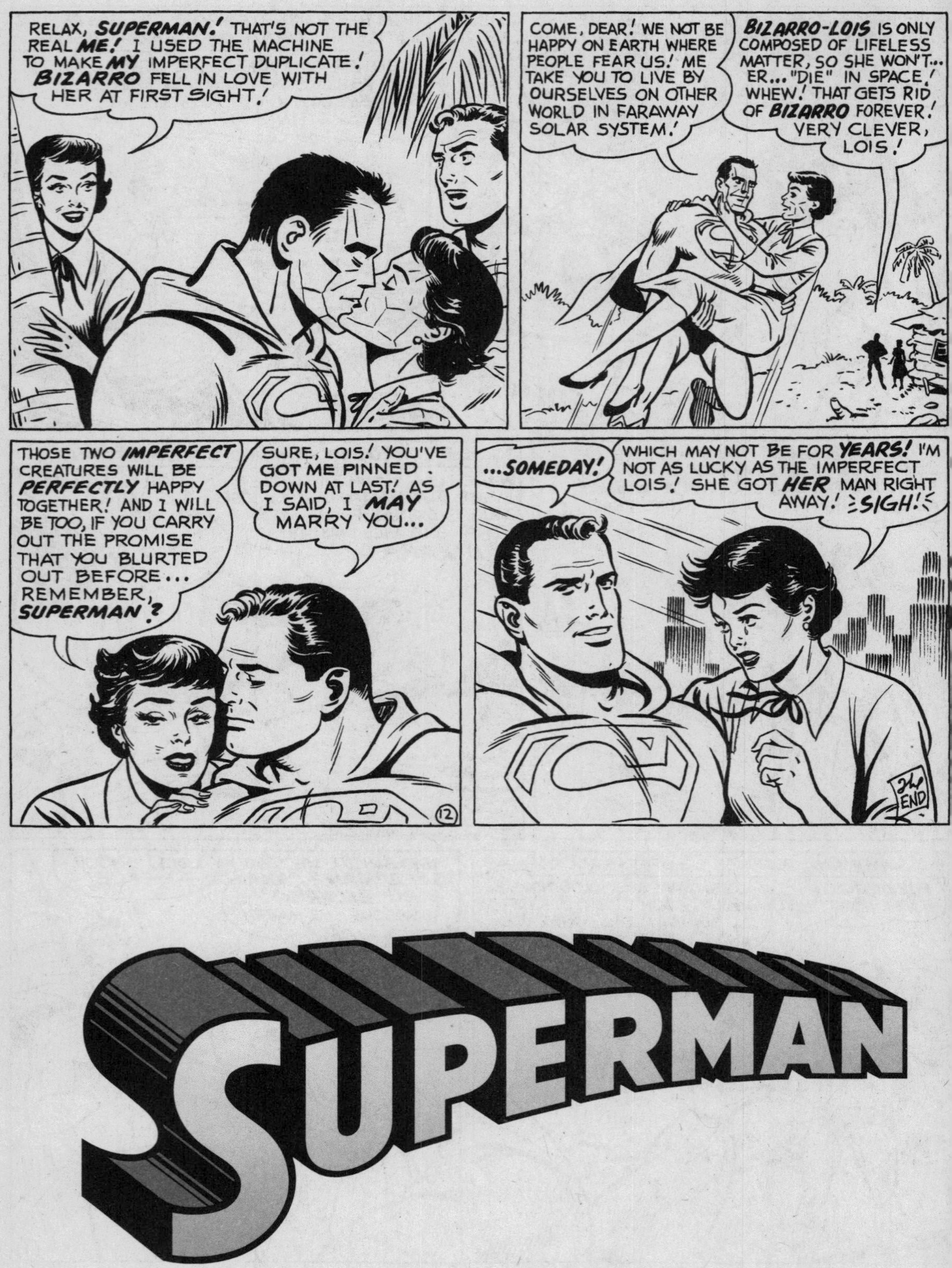
RELAX, SUPERMAN! THAT'S NOT THE REAL ME! I USED THE MACHINE TO MAKE MY IMPERFECT DUPLICATE! BIZARRO FELL IN LOVE WITH HER AT FIRST SIGHT!
COME, DEAR! WE NOT BE HAPPY ON EARTH WHERE PEOPLE FEAR US! ME TAKE YOU TO LIVE BY OURSELVES ON OTHER WORLD IN FARAWAY SOLAR SYSTEM!
BIZARRO-LOIS IS ONLY COMPOSED OF LIFELESS MATTER, SO SHE WON'T... ER..."DIE" IN SPACE! WHEW! THAT GETS RID OF BIZARRO FOREVER! VERY CLEVER, LOIS!
THOSE TWO IMPERFECT CREATURES WILL BE PERFECTLY HAPPY TOGETHER! AND I WILL BE TOO, IF YOU CARRY OUT THE PROMISE THAT YOU BLURTED OUT BEFORE... REMEMBER, SUPERMAN?
SURE, LOIS! YOU'VE GOT ME PINNED DOWN AT LAST! AS I SAID, I MAY MARRY YOU...
12
...SOMEDAY!
WHICH MAY NOT BE FOR YEARS! I'M NOT AS LUCKY AS THE IMPERFECT LOIS! SHE GOT HER MAN RIGHT AWAY! SIGH!
The END

SUPERMAN

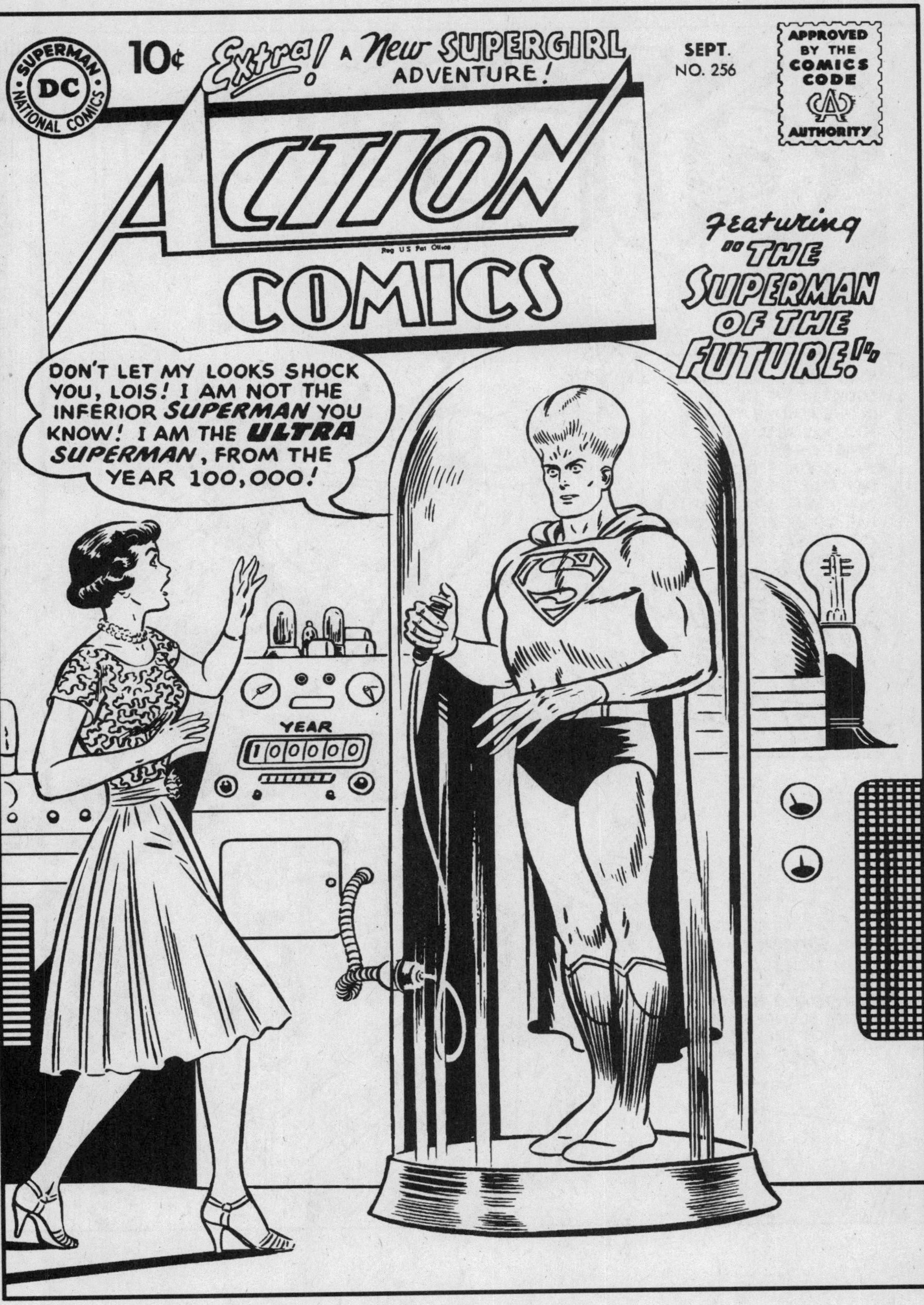
SUPERMAN DC NATIONAL COMICS
10¢
Extra! A New SUPERGIRL ADVENTURE!
SEPT. NO. 256
APPROVED BY THE COMICS CODE AUTHORITY
ACTION COMICS
Reg U S Pat Office
Featuring "THE SUPERMAN OF THE FUTURE!"
DON'T LET MY LOOKS SHOCK YOU, LOIS! I AM NOT THE INFERIOR SUPERMAN YOU KNOW! I AM THE ULTRA SUPERMAN, FROM THE YEAR 100,000!
YEAR
100000

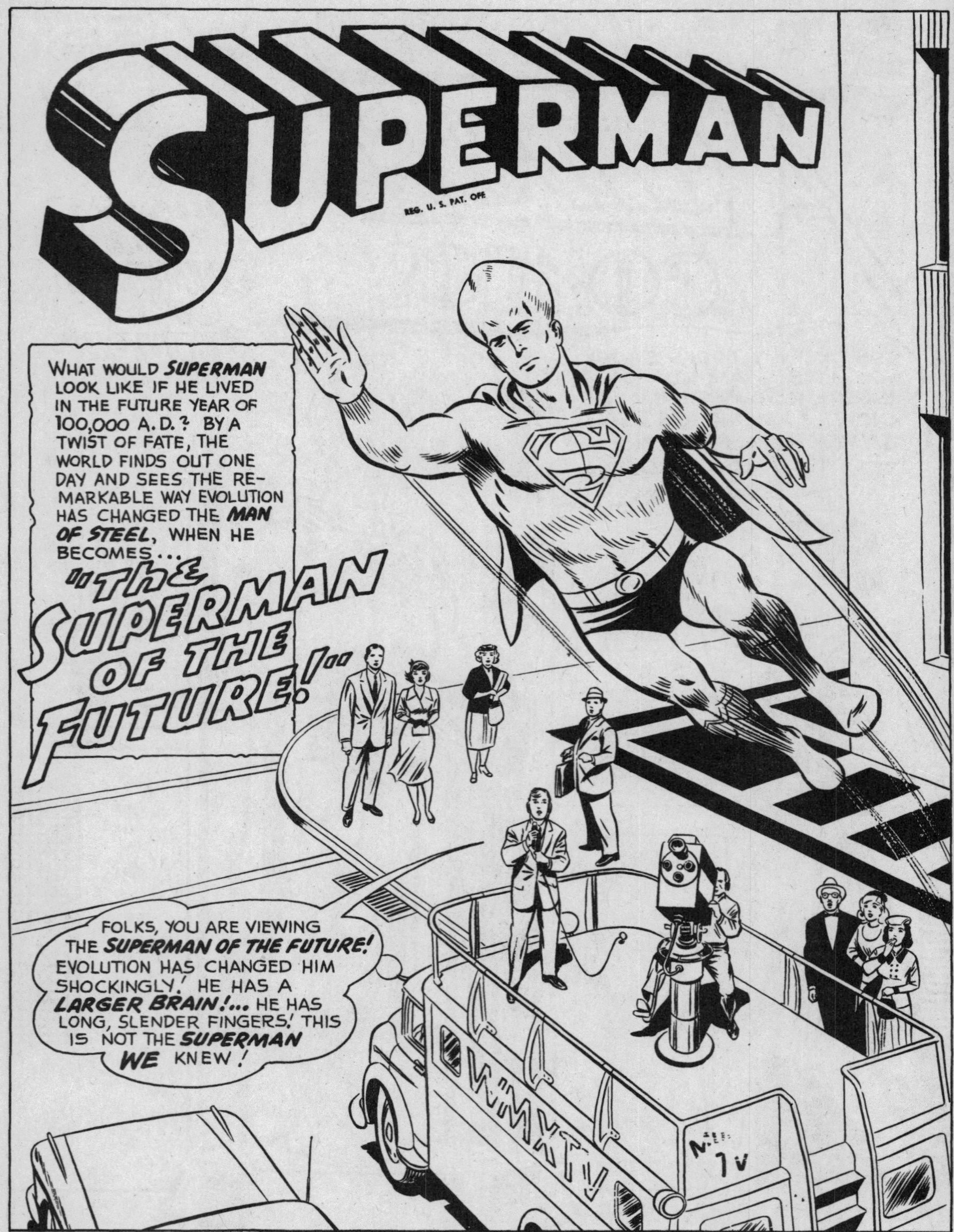
SUPERMAN
REG. U. S. PAT. OFF.
WHAT WOULD SUPERMAN LOOK LIKE IF HE LIVED IN THE FUTURE YEAR OF 100,000 A.D.? BY A TWIST OF FATE, THE WORLD FINDS OUT ONE DAY AND SEES THE REMARKABLE WAY EVOLUTION HAS CHANGED THE MAN OF STEEL, WHEN HE BECOMES...
"THE SUPERMAN OF THE FUTURE!"
FOLKS, YOU ARE VIEWING THE SUPERMAN OF THE FUTURE! EVOLUTION HAS CHANGED HIM SHOCKINGLY! HE HAS A LARGER BRAIN!... HE HAS LONG, SLENDER FINGERS! THIS IS NOT THE SUPERMAN WE KNEW!
WMXTV

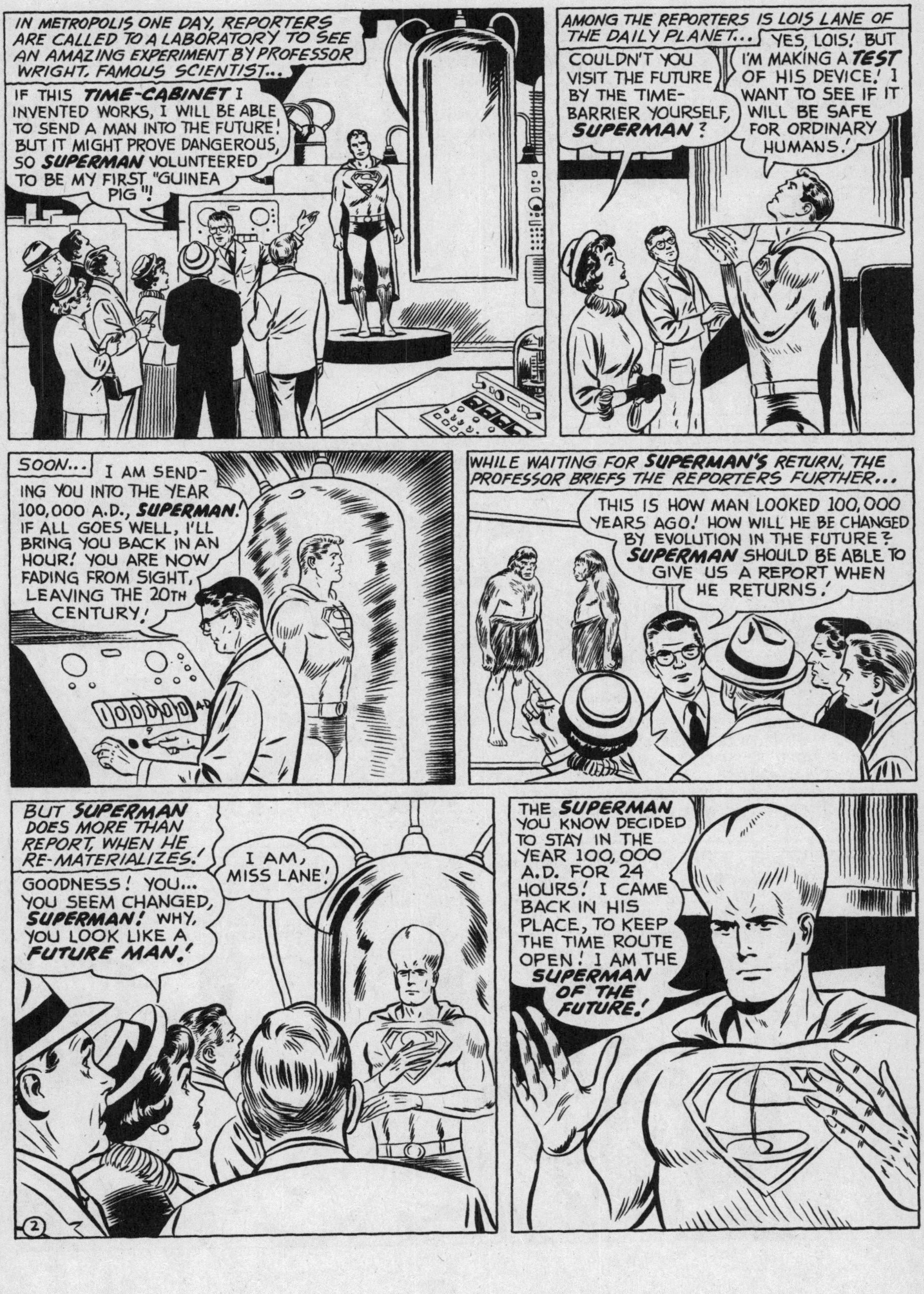
IN METROPOLIS ONE DAY, REPORTERS ARE CALLED TO A LABORATORY TO SEE AN AMAZING EXPERIMENT BY PROFESSOR WRIGHT, FAMOUS SCIENTIST...
IF THIS TIME-CABINET I INVENTED WORKS, I WILL BE ABLE TO SEND A MAN INTO THE FUTURE! BUT IT MIGHT PROVE DANGEROUS, SO SUPERMAN VOLUNTEERED TO BE MY FIRST "GUINEA PIG"!
AMONG THE REPORTERS IS LOIS LANE OF THE DAILY PLANET...
COULDN'T YOU VISIT THE FUTURE BY THE TIME-BARRIER YOURSELF, SUPERMAN?
YES, LOIS! BUT I'M MAKING A TEST OF HIS DEVICE! I WANT TO SEE IF IT WILL BE SAFE FOR ORDINARY HUMANS!
SOON...
I AM SENDING YOU INTO THE YEAR 100,000 A.D., SUPERMAN! IF ALL GOES WELL, I'LL BRING YOU BACK IN AN HOUR! YOU ARE NOW FADING FROM SIGHT, LEAVING THE 20TH CENTURY!
100000 A.D.
WHILE WAITING FOR SUPERMAN'S RETURN, THE PROFESSOR BRIEFS THE REPORTERS FURTHER...
THIS IS HOW MAN LOOKED 100,000 YEARS AGO! HOW WILL HE BE CHANGED BY EVOLUTION IN THE FUTURE? SUPERMAN SHOULD BE ABLE TO GIVE US A REPORT WHEN HE RETURNS!
BUT SUPERMAN DOES MORE THAN REPORT, WHEN HE RE-MATERIALIZES!
GOODNESS! YOU... YOU SEEM CHANGED, SUPERMAN! WHY, YOU LOOK LIKE A FUTURE MAN!
I AM, MISS LANE!
THE SUPERMAN YOU KNOW DECIDED TO STAY IN THE YEAR 100,000 A.D. FOR 24 HOURS! I CAME BACK IN HIS PLACE, TO KEEP THE TIME ROUTE OPEN! I AM THE SUPERMAN OF THE FUTURE!
2

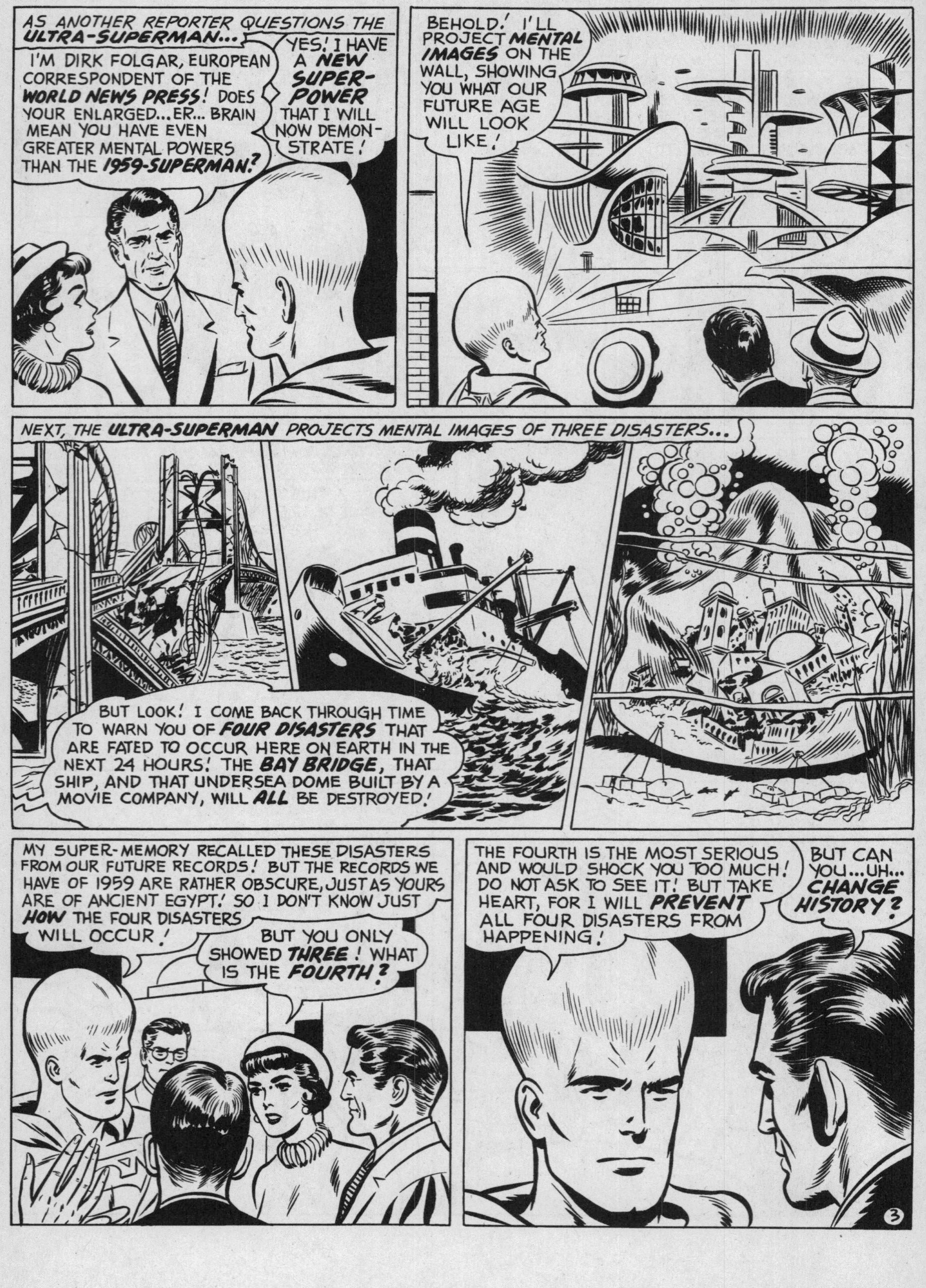
AS ANOTHER REPORTER QUESTIONS THE ULTRA-SUPERMAN...
I'M DIRK FOLGAR, EUROPEAN CORRESPONDENT OF THE WORLD NEWS PRESS! DOES YOUR ENLARGED...ER... BRAIN MEAN YOU HAVE EVEN GREATER MENTAL POWERS THAN THE 1959-SUPERMAN?
YES! I HAVE A NEW SUPER-POWER THAT I WILL NOW DEMON-STRATE!
BEHOLD! I'LL PROJECT MENTAL IMAGES ON THE WALL, SHOWING YOU WHAT OUR FUTURE AGE WILL LOOK LIKE!
NEXT, THE ULTRA-SUPERMAN PROJECTS MENTAL IMAGES OF THREE DISASTERS...
BUT LOOK! I COME BACK THROUGH TIME TO WARN YOU OF FOUR DISASTERS THAT ARE FATED TO OCCUR HERE ON EARTH IN THE NEXT 24 HOURS! THE BAY BRIDGE, THAT SHIP, AND THAT UNDERSEA DOME BUILT BY A MOVIE COMPANY, WILL ALL BE DESTROYED!
MY SUPER-MEMORY RECALLED THESE DISASTERS FROM OUR FUTURE RECORDS! BUT THE RECORDS WE HAVE OF 1959 ARE RATHER OBSCURE, JUST AS YOURS ARE OF ANCIENT EGYPT! SO I DON'T KNOW JUST HOW THE FOUR DISASTERS WILL OCCUR!
BUT YOU ONLY SHOWED THREE! WHAT IS THE FOURTH?
THE FOURTH IS THE MOST SERIOUS AND WOULD SHOCK YOU TOO MUCH! DO NOT ASK TO SEE IT! BUT TAKE HEART, FOR I WILL PREVENT ALL FOUR DISASTERS FROM HAPPENING!
BUT CAN YOU...UH... CHANGE HISTORY?
3

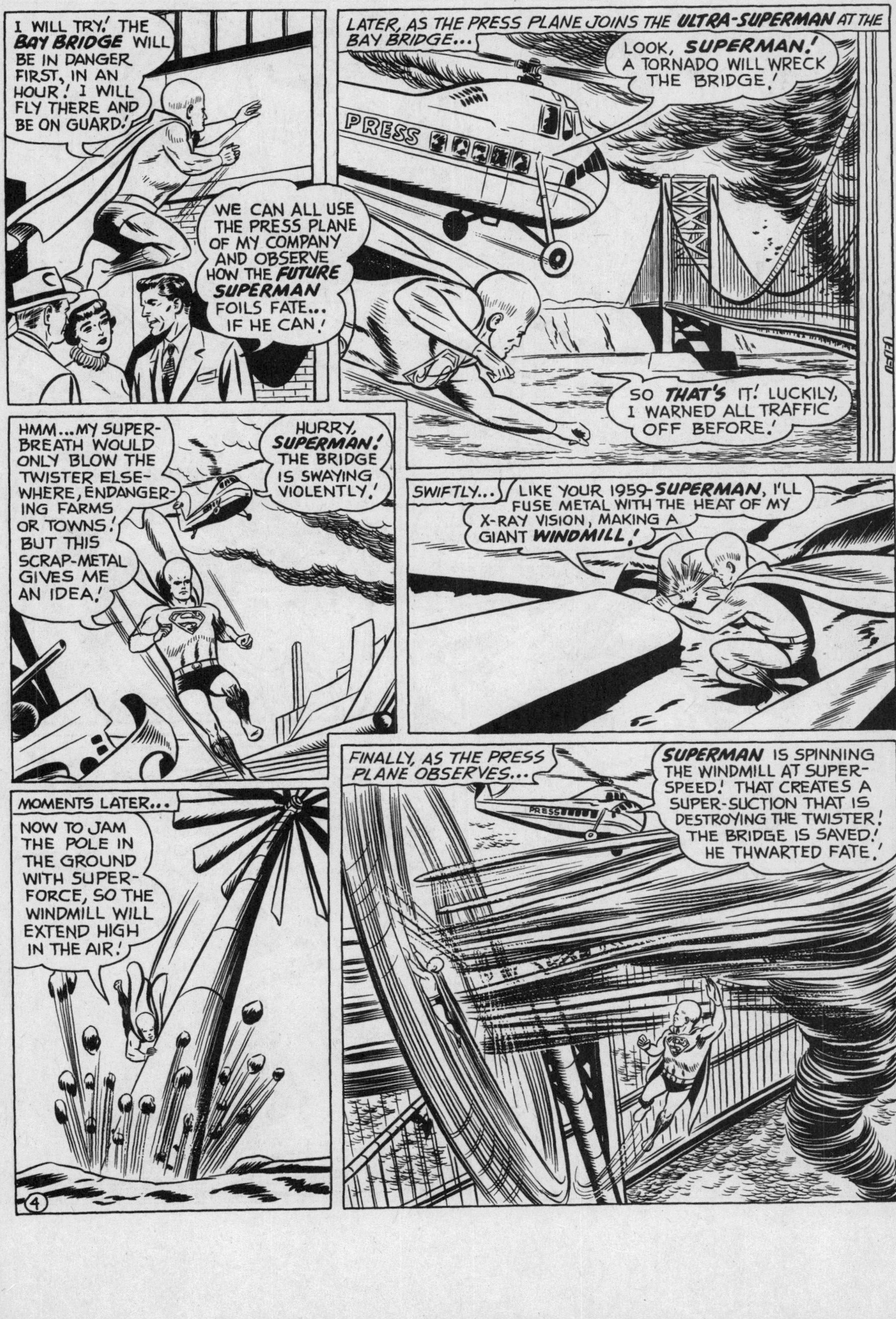
I WILL TRY! THE BAY BRIDGE WILL BE IN DANGER FIRST, IN AN HOUR! I WILL FLY THERE AND BE ON GUARD!
WE CAN ALL USE THE PRESS PLANE OF MY COMPANY AND OBSERVE HOW THE FUTURE SUPERMAN FOILS FATE... IF HE CAN!
LATER, AS THE PRESS PLANE JOINS THE ULTRA-SUPERMAN AT THE BAY BRIDGE...
LOOK, SUPERMAN! A TORNADO WILL WRECK THE BRIDGE!
PRESS
SO THAT'S IT! LUCKILY, I WARNED ALL TRAFFIC OFF BEFORE!
HMM...MY SUPER-BREATH WOULD ONLY BLOW THE TWISTER ELSEWHERE, ENDANGERING FARMS OR TOWNS! BUT THIS SCRAP-METAL GIVES ME AN IDEA!
HURRY, SUPERMAN! THE BRIDGE IS SWAYING VIOLENTLY!
SWIFTLY...
LIKE YOUR 1959-SUPERMAN, I'LL FUSE METAL WITH THE HEAT OF MY X-RAY VISION, MAKING A GIANT WINDMILL!
MOMENTS LATER...
NOW TO JAM THE POLE IN THE GROUND WITH SUPER-FORCE, SO THE WINDMILL WILL EXTEND HIGH IN THE AIR!
FINALLY, AS THE PRESS PLANE OBSERVES...
SUPERMAN IS SPINNING THE WINDMILL AT SUPER-SPEED! THAT CREATES A SUPER-SUCTION THAT IS DESTROYING THE TWISTER! THE BRIDGE IS SAVED! HE THWARTED FATE!
PRESS
4

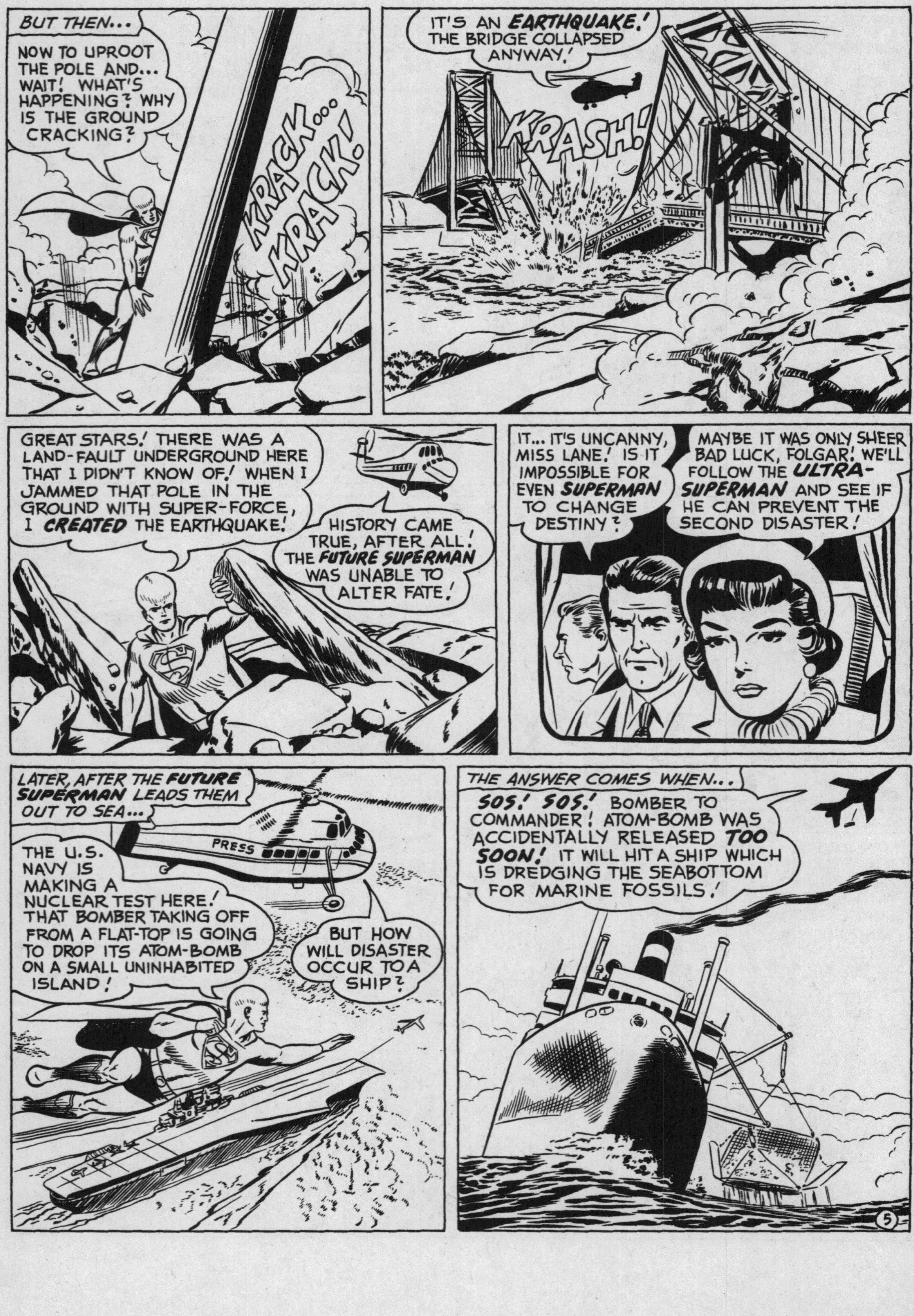
BUT THEN...
NOW TO UPROOT THE POLE AND... WAIT! WHAT'S HAPPENING? WHY IS THE GROUND CRACKING?
KRACK... KRACK!
IT'S AN EARTHQUAKE! THE BRIDGE COLLAPSED ANYWAY!
KRASH!
GREAT STARS! THERE WAS A LAND-FAULT UNDERGROUND HERE THAT I DIDN'T KNOW OF! WHEN I JAMMED THAT POLE IN THE GROUND WITH SUPER-FORCE, I CREATED THE EARTHQUAKE!
HISTORY CAME TRUE, AFTER ALL! THE FUTURE SUPERMAN WAS UNABLE TO ALTER FATE!
IT... IT'S UNCANNY, MISS LANE! IS IT IMPOSSIBLE FOR EVEN SUPERMAN TO CHANGE DESTINY?
MAYBE IT WAS ONLY SHEER BAD LUCK, FOLGAR! WE'LL FOLLOW THE ULTRA-SUPERMAN AND SEE IF HE CAN PREVENT THE SECOND DISASTER!
LATER, AFTER THE FUTURE SUPERMAN LEADS THEM OUT TO SEA...
PRESS
THE U.S. NAVY IS MAKING A NUCLEAR TEST HERE! THAT BOMBER TAKING OFF FROM A FLAT-TOP IS GOING TO DROP ITS ATOM-BOMB ON A SMALL UNINHABITED ISLAND!
BUT HOW WILL DISASTER OCCUR TO A SHIP?
THE ANSWER COMES WHEN...
SOS! SOS! BOMBER TO COMMANDER! ATOM-BOMB WAS ACCIDENTALLY RELEASED TOO SOON! IT WILL HIT A SHIP WHICH IS DREDGING THE SEABOTTOM FOR MARINE FOSSILS!
5

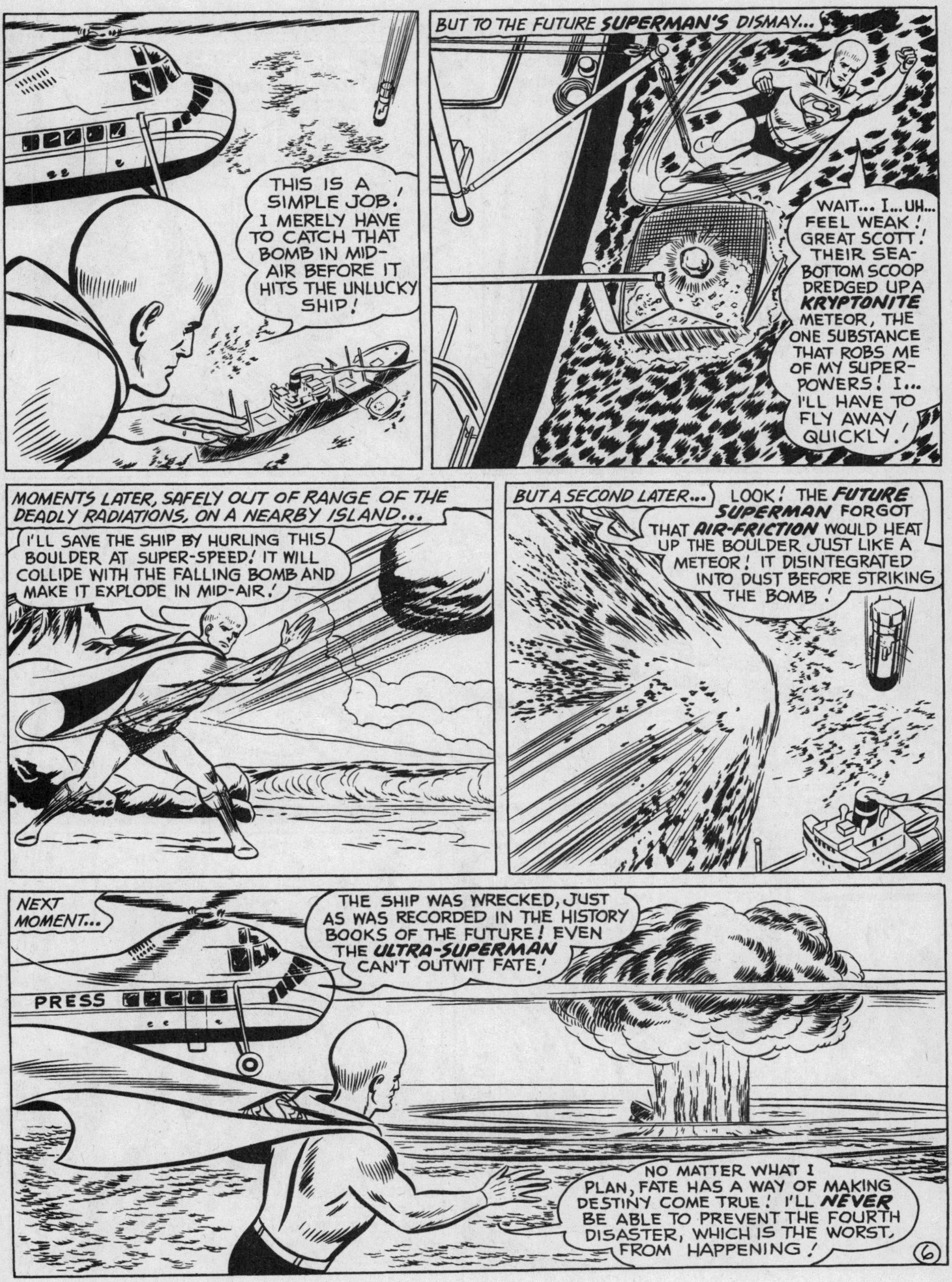
THIS IS A SIMPLE JOB! I MERELY HAVE TO CATCH THAT BOMB IN MID-AIR BEFORE IT HITS THE UNLUCKY SHIP!
BUT TO THE FUTURE SUPERMAN'S DISMAY...
WAIT... I...UH... FEEL WEAK! GREAT SCOTT! THEIR SEA-BOTTOM SCOOP DREDGED UP A KRYPTONITE METEOR, THE ONE SUBSTANCE THAT ROBS ME OF MY SUPER-POWERS! I... I'LL HAVE TO FLY AWAY QUICKLY!
MOMENTS LATER, SAFELY OUT OF RANGE OF THE DEADLY RADIATIONS, ON A NEARBY ISLAND...
I'LL SAVE THE SHIP BY HURLING THIS BOULDER AT SUPER-SPEED! IT WILL COLLIDE WITH THE FALLING BOMB AND MAKE IT EXPLODE IN MID-AIR!
BUT A SECOND LATER...
LOOK! THE FUTURE SUPERMAN FORGOT THAT AIR-FRICTION WOULD HEAT UP THE BOULDER JUST LIKE A METEOR! IT DISINTEGRATED INTO DUST BEFORE STRIKING THE BOMB!
NEXT MOMENT...
THE SHIP WAS WRECKED, JUST AS WAS RECORDED IN THE HISTORY BOOKS OF THE FUTURE! EVEN THE ULTRA-SUPERMAN CAN'T OUTWIT FATE!
PRESS
NO MATTER WHAT I PLAN, FATE HAS A WAY OF MAKING DESTINY COME TRUE! I'LL NEVER BE ABLE TO PREVENT THE FOURTH DISASTER, WHICH IS THE WORST, FROM HAPPENING!
6

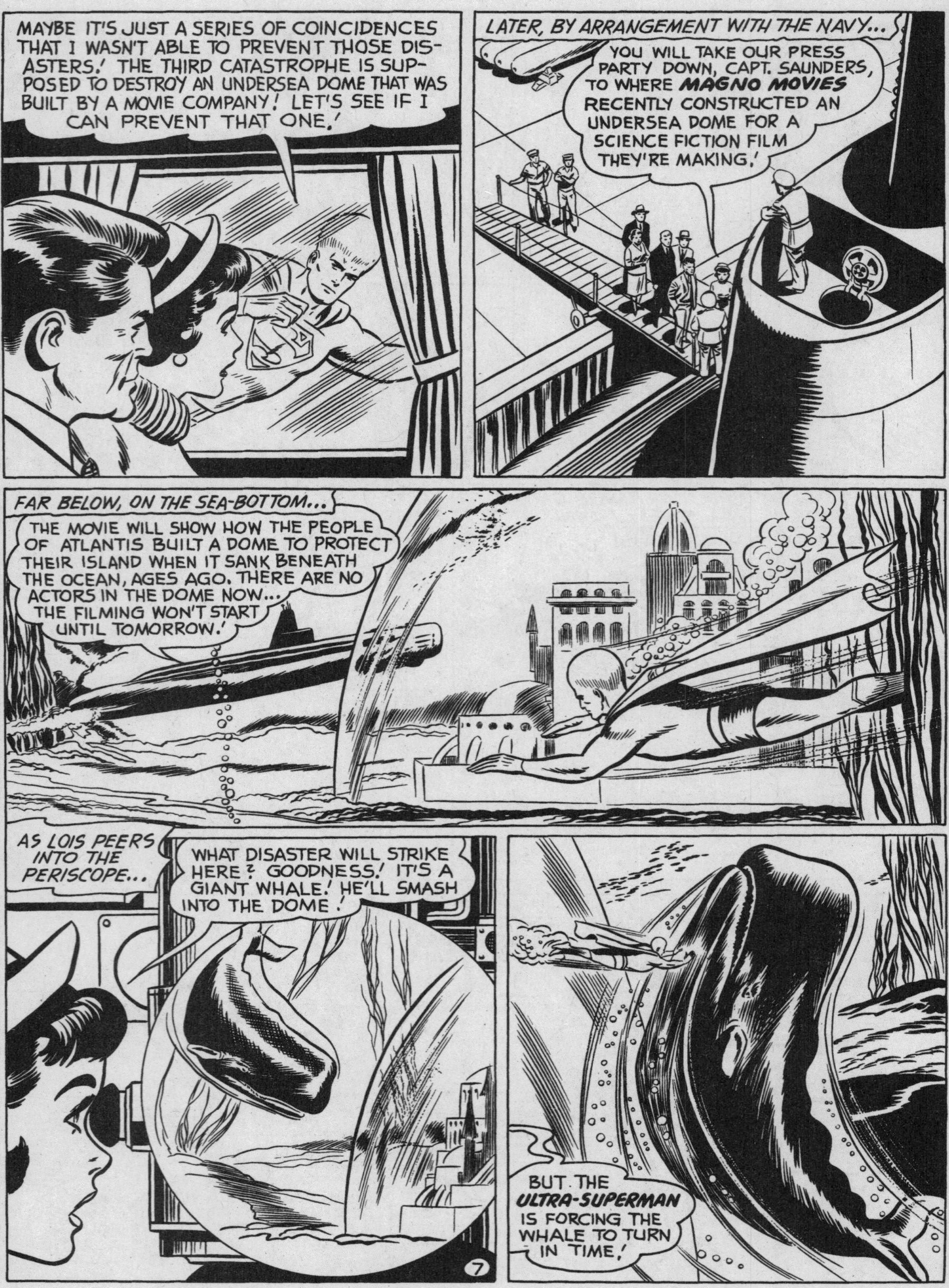
MAYBE IT'S JUST A SERIES OF COINCIDENCES THAT I WASN'T ABLE TO PREVENT THOSE DISASTERS! THE THIRD CATASTROPHE IS SUPPOSED TO DESTROY AN UNDERSEA DOME THAT WAS BUILT BY A MOVIE COMPANY! LET'S SEE IF I CAN PREVENT THAT ONE!
LATER, BY ARRANGEMENT WITH THE NAVY...
YOU WILL TAKE OUR PRESS PARTY DOWN, CAPT. SAUNDERS, TO WHERE MAGNO MOVIES RECENTLY CONSTRUCTED AN UNDERSEA DOME FOR A SCIENCE FICTION FILM THEY'RE MAKING!
FAR BELOW, ON THE SEA-BOTTOM...
THE MOVIE WILL SHOW HOW THE PEOPLE OF ATLANTIS BUILT A DOME TO PROTECT THEIR ISLAND WHEN IT SANK BENEATH THE OCEAN, AGES AGO. THERE ARE NO ACTORS IN THE DOME NOW... THE FILMING WON'T START UNTIL TOMORROW!
AS LOIS PEERS INTO THE PERISCOPE...
WHAT DISASTER WILL STRIKE HERE? GOODNESS! IT'S A GIANT WHALE! HE'LL SMASH INTO THE DOME!
7
BUT THE ULTRA-SUPERMAN IS FORCING THE WHALE TO TURN IN TIME!

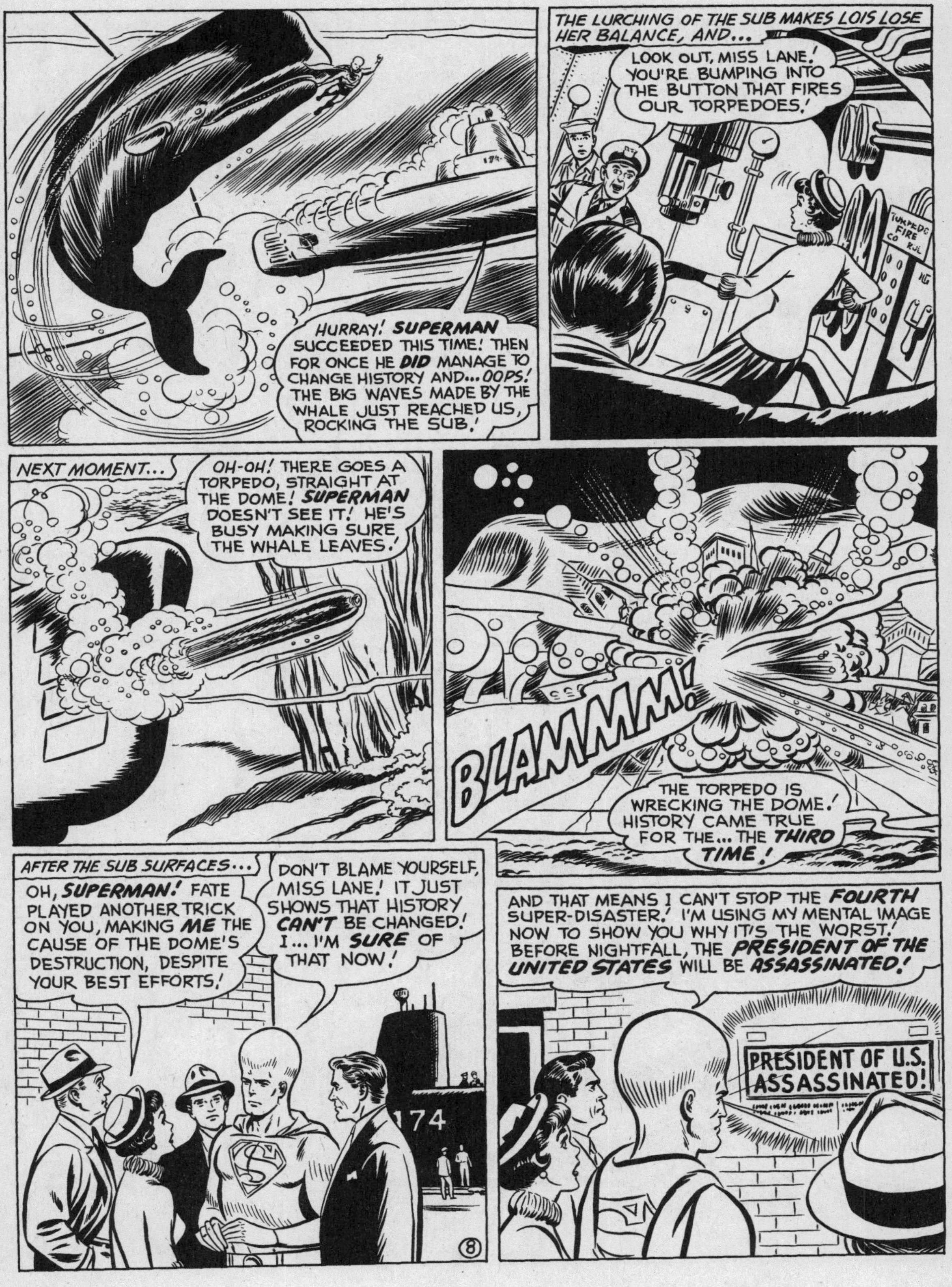
HURRAY! SUPERMAN SUCCEEDED THIS TIME! THEN FOR ONCE HE DID MANAGE TO CHANGE HISTORY AND... OOPS! THE BIG WAVES MADE BY THE WHALE JUST REACHED US, ROCKING THE SUB!
THE LURCHING OF THE SUB MAKES LOIS LOSE HER BALANCE, AND...
LOOK OUT, MISS LANE! YOU'RE BUMPING INTO THE BUTTON THAT FIRES OUR TORPEDOES!
NEXT MOMENT...
OH-OH! THERE GOES A TORPEDO, STRAIGHT AT THE DOME! SUPERMAN DOESN'T SEE IT! HE'S BUSY MAKING SURE THE WHALE LEAVES!
BLAMMMM!
THE TORPEDO IS WRECKING THE DOME! HISTORY CAME TRUE FOR THE... THE THIRD TIME!
AFTER THE SUB SURFACES...
OH, SUPERMAN! FATE PLAYED ANOTHER TRICK ON YOU, MAKING ME THE CAUSE OF THE DOME'S DESTRUCTION, DESPITE YOUR BEST EFFORTS!
DON'T BLAME YOURSELF, MISS LANE! IT JUST SHOWS THAT HISTORY CAN'T BE CHANGED! I... I'M SURE OF THAT NOW!
174
8
AND THAT MEANS I CAN'T STOP THE FOURTH SUPER-DISASTER! I'M USING MY MENTAL IMAGE NOW TO SHOW YOU WHY IT'S THE WORST! BEFORE NIGHTFALL, THE PRESIDENT OF THE UNITED STATES WILL BE ASSASSINATED!
PRESIDENT OF U.S. ASSASSINATED!

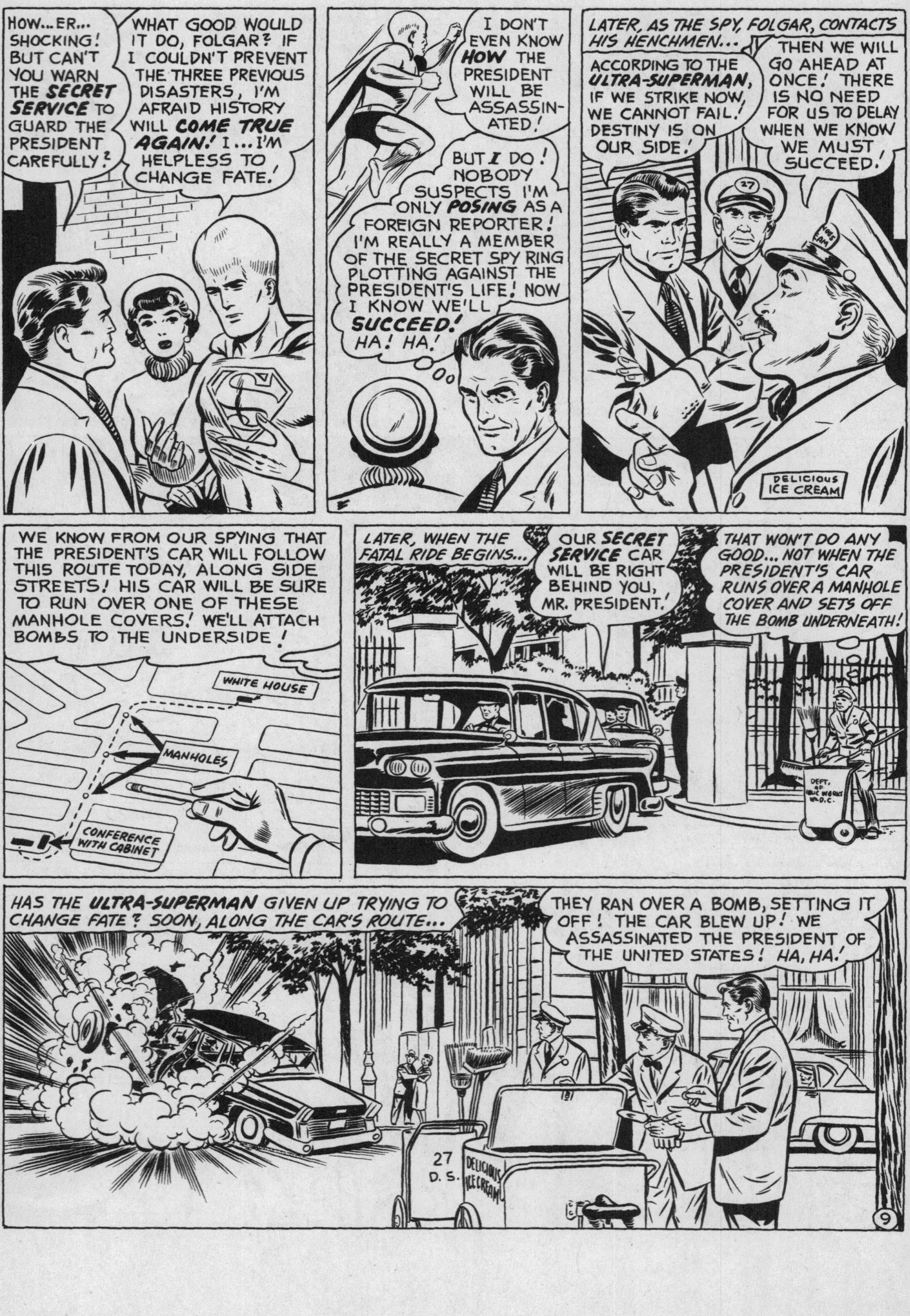
HOW...ER... SHOCKING! BUT CAN'T YOU WARN THE SECRET SERVICE TO GUARD THE PRESIDENT CAREFULLY?
WHAT GOOD WOULD IT DO, FOLGAR? IF I COULDN'T PREVENT THE THREE PREVIOUS DISASTERS, I'M AFRAID HISTORY WILL COME TRUE AGAIN! I...I'M HELPLESS TO CHANGE FATE!
I DON'T EVEN KNOW HOW THE PRESIDENT WILL BE ASSASSIN-ATED!
BUT I DO! NOBODY SUSPECTS I'M ONLY POSING AS A FOREIGN REPORTER! I'M REALLY A MEMBER OF THE SECRET SPY RING PLOTTING AGAINST THE PRESIDENT'S LIFE! NOW I KNOW WE'LL SUCCEED! HA! HA!
LATER, AS THE SPY, FOLGAR, CONTACTS HIS HENCHMEN...
ACCORDING TO THE ULTRA-SUPERMAN, IF WE STRIKE NOW, WE CANNOT FAIL! DESTINY IS ON OUR SIDE!
THEN WE WILL GO AHEAD AT ONCE! THERE IS NO NEED FOR US TO DELAY WHEN WE KNOW WE MUST SUCCEED!
27
DELICIOUS ICE CREAM
WE KNOW FROM OUR SPYING THAT THE PRESIDENT'S CAR WILL FOLLOW THIS ROUTE TODAY, ALONG SIDE STREETS! HIS CAR WILL BE SURE TO RUN OVER ONE OF THESE MANHOLE COVERS! WE'LL ATTACH BOMBS TO THE UNDERSIDE!
WHITE HOUSE
MANHOLES
CONFERENCE WITH CABINET
LATER, WHEN THE FATAL RIDE BEGINS...
OUR SECRET SERVICE CAR WILL BE RIGHT BEHIND YOU, MR. PRESIDENT!
THAT WON'T DO ANY GOOD... NOT WHEN THE PRESIDENT'S CAR RUNS OVER A MANHOLE COVER AND SETS OFF THE BOMB UNDERNEATH!
HAS THE ULTRA-SUPERMAN GIVEN UP TRYING TO CHANGE FATE? SOON, ALONG THE CAR'S ROUTE...
THEY RAN OVER A BOMB, SETTING IT OFF! THE CAR BLEW UP! WE ASSASSINATED THE PRESIDENT OF THE UNITED STATES! HA, HA!
27 D.S.
DELICIOUS ICE CREAM
9

BUT AS THE SMOKE CLEARS...

WAIT... LOOK! SOMEBODY'S STEPPING OUT OF THE WRECK ALIVE... IT'S THE ULTRA-SUPERMAN!

YES, FOLGAR...OR AGENT X-3! I TOOK THE PRESIDENT'S PLACE BEFORE! MY CHAUFFEUR WAS ONLY A DUMMY AND THE CAR UNDER REMOTE CONTROL!

SECRET SERVICE MEN CLOSE IN ON THE THREE PLOTTERS, AND...

BUT...BUT IF YOU COULDN'T CHANGE HISTORY THREE TIMES, HOW COULD YOU DO IT THE FOURTH TIME, ULTRA-SUPERMAN?

BECAUSE THE "ULTRA-SUPERMAN" NEVER EXISTED, FOLGAR! THE BLAST TORE THE PLASTIC, LONG-FINGERED GLOVES I WORE! AND NOW I'LL PEEL OFF THE FALSE BULGE ON MY HEAD...

WHY... UH... YOU'RE THE 1959 SUPERMAN!

I WAS ALL THE TIME, FOLGAR! YOU SEE, THE SECRET SERVICE HEARD RUMORS THAT YOU WERE THE HEAD OF A SPY PLOT TO ASSASSINATE THE PRESIDENT! THEY ASKED MY HELP TO SMOKE YOU OUT AND...

"... WE ARRANGED A HOAX, STARTING WITH PROF. WRIGHT!"

GOT IT, PROFESSOR? I'LL SHOW UP IN YOUR FAKE TIME-CABINET AS THE PHONY ULTRA-SUPERMAN!

THIS GAMMA RAY WILL MAKE YOU SEEM TO MATERIALIZE... BUT YOU'LL REALLY FLASH THROUGH A TRAP DOOR UNDER THE CABINET!

"THE SECRET MIND-IMAGE DEVICE WAS ALSO READY..."

HIDDEN WITHIN MY FALSE BULGING HEADMASK IS A TINY TWIN-BEAMED MOVIE PROJECTOR! IT WILL SEEM TO CAST MY "MIND-IMAGES", SHOWING THE THREE FALSE DISASTERS I'VE PLANNED!

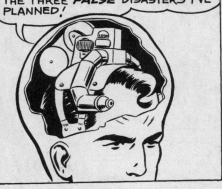

"I ARRANGED THE FIRST PHONY DISASTER WITH THE COOPERATION OF THE BAY BRIDGE POLICE..."

I'LL WHIRL AT SUPER-SPEED AND CREATE THE TWISTER THAT WILL THREATEN YOUR BRIDGE!

GO AHEAD, SUPERMAN! IT'S FOR A GOOD CAUSE!

10

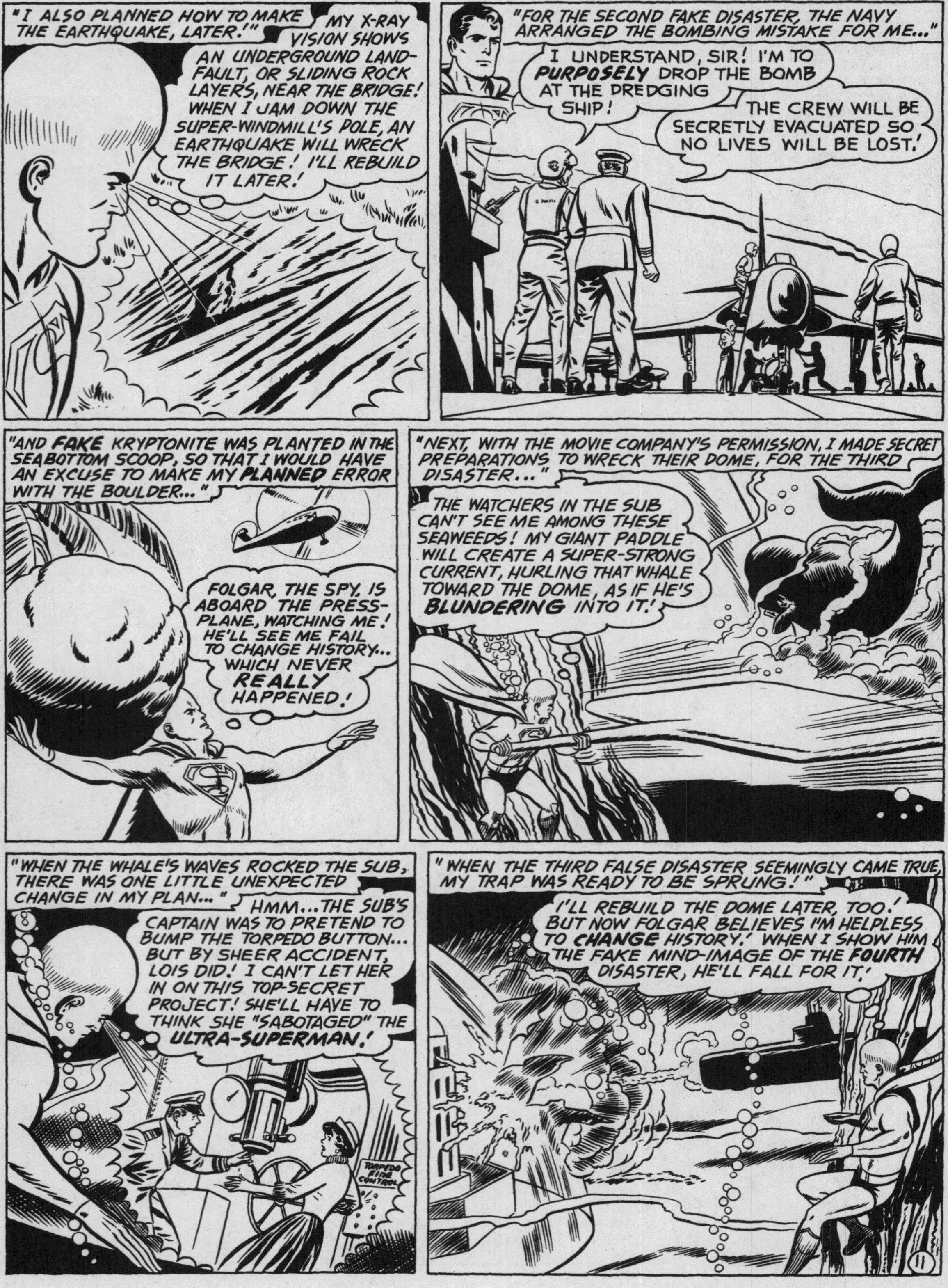
"I ALSO PLANNED HOW TO MAKE THE EARTHQUAKE, LATER!"
MY X-RAY VISION SHOWS AN UNDERGROUND LAND-FAULT, OR SLIDING ROCK LAYERS, NEAR THE BRIDGE! WHEN I JAM DOWN THE SUPER-WINDMILL'S POLE, AN EARTHQUAKE WILL WRECK THE BRIDGE! I'LL REBUILD IT LATER!
"FOR THE SECOND FAKE DISASTER, THE NAVY ARRANGED THE BOMBING MISTAKE FOR ME..."
I UNDERSTAND, SIR! I'M TO PURPOSELY DROP THE BOMB AT THE DREDGING SHIP!
THE CREW WILL BE SECRETLY EVACUATED SO NO LIVES WILL BE LOST!
"AND FAKE KRYPTONITE WAS PLANTED IN THE SEABOTTOM SCOOP, SO THAT I WOULD HAVE AN EXCUSE TO MAKE MY PLANNED ERROR WITH THE BOULDER..."
FOLGAR, THE SPY, IS ABOARD THE PRESS-PLANE, WATCHING ME! HE'LL SEE ME FAIL TO CHANGE HISTORY... WHICH NEVER REALLY HAPPENED!
"NEXT, WITH THE MOVIE COMPANY'S PERMISSION, I MADE SECRET PREPARATIONS TO WRECK THEIR DOME, FOR THE THIRD DISASTER..."
THE WATCHERS IN THE SUB CAN'T SEE ME AMONG THESE SEAWEEDS! MY GIANT PADDLE WILL CREATE A SUPER-STRONG CURRENT, HURLING THAT WHALE TOWARD THE DOME, AS IF HE'S BLUNDERING INTO IT!
"WHEN THE WHALE'S WAVES ROCKED THE SUB, THERE WAS ONE LITTLE UNEXPECTED CHANGE IN MY PLAN..."
HMM...THE SUB'S CAPTAIN WAS TO PRETEND TO BUMP THE TORPEDO BUTTON... BUT BY SHEER ACCIDENT, LOIS DID! I CAN'T LET HER IN ON THIS TOP-SECRET PROJECT! SHE'LL HAVE TO THINK SHE "SABOTAGED" THE ULTRA-SUPERMAN!
TORPEDO FIRE CONTROL
"WHEN THE THIRD FALSE DISASTER SEEMINGLY CAME TRUE, MY TRAP WAS READY TO BE SPRUNG!"
I'LL REBUILD THE DOME LATER, TOO! BUT NOW FOLGAR BELIEVES I'M HELPLESS TO CHANGE HISTORY! WHEN I SHOW HIM THE FAKE MIND-IMAGE OF THE FOURTH DISASTER, HE'LL FALL FOR IT!
11

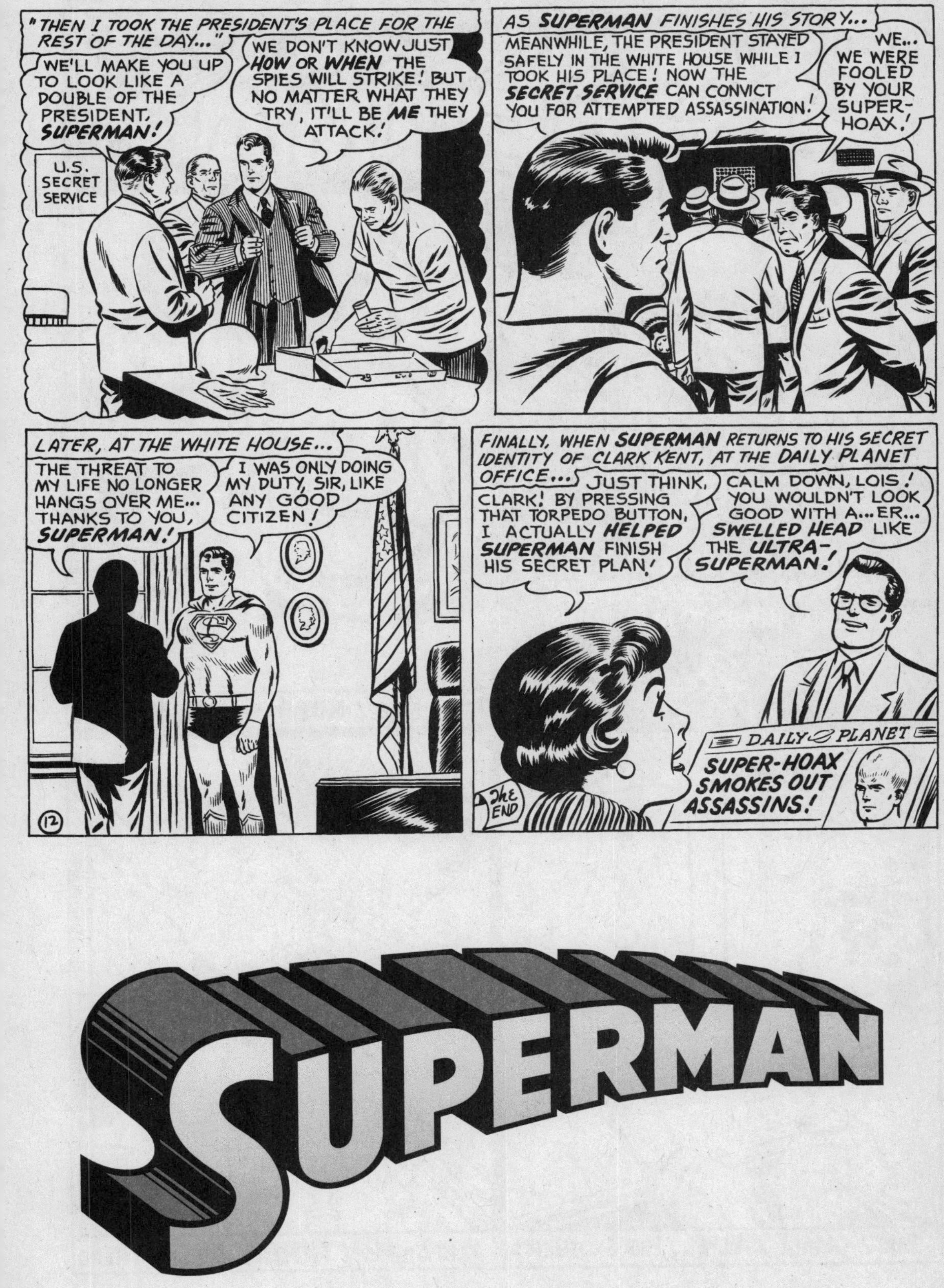
"THEN I TOOK THE PRESIDENT'S PLACE FOR THE REST OF THE DAY..."
WE'LL MAKE YOU UP TO LOOK LIKE A DOUBLE OF THE PRESIDENT, SUPERMAN!
WE DON'T KNOW JUST HOW OR WHEN THE SPIES WILL STRIKE! BUT NO MATTER WHAT THEY TRY, IT'LL BE ME THEY ATTACK!
U.S. SECRET SERVICE
AS SUPERMAN FINISHES HIS STORY...
MEANWHILE, THE PRESIDENT STAYED SAFELY IN THE WHITE HOUSE WHILE I TOOK HIS PLACE! NOW THE SECRET SERVICE CAN CONVICT YOU FOR ATTEMPTED ASSASSINATION!
WE... WE WERE FOOLED BY YOUR SUPER-HOAX!
LATER, AT THE WHITE HOUSE...
THE THREAT TO MY LIFE NO LONGER HANGS OVER ME... THANKS TO YOU, SUPERMAN!
I WAS ONLY DOING MY DUTY, SIR, LIKE ANY GOOD CITIZEN!
12
FINALLY, WHEN SUPERMAN RETURNS TO HIS SECRET IDENTITY OF CLARK KENT, AT THE DAILY PLANET OFFICE...
JUST THINK, CLARK! BY PRESSING THAT TORPEDO BUTTON, I ACTUALLY HELPED SUPERMAN FINISH HIS SECRET PLAN!
CALM DOWN, LOIS! YOU WOULDN'T LOOK GOOD WITH A...ER... SWELLED HEAD LIKE THE ULTRA-SUPERMAN!
DAILY PLANET
SUPER-HOAX SMOKES OUT ASSASSINS!
THE END

SUPERMAN

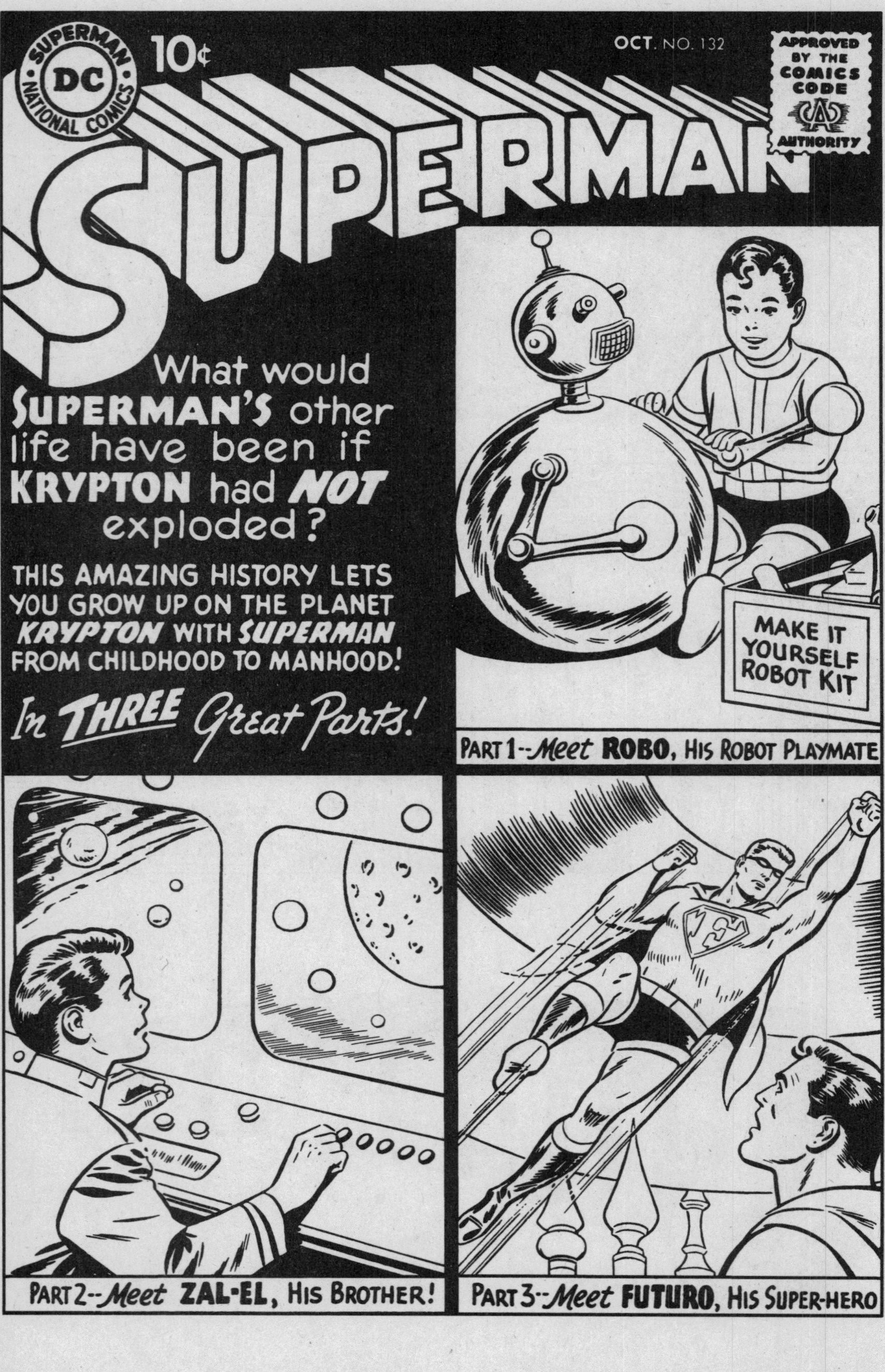
SUPERMAN DC NATIONAL COMICS
10¢
OCT. NO. 132
APPROVED BY THE COMICS CODE AUTHORITY
SUPERMAN
What would SUPERMAN'S other life have been if KRYPTON had NOT exploded?
THIS AMAZING HISTORY LETS YOU GROW UP ON THE PLANET KRYPTON WITH SUPERMAN FROM CHILDHOOD TO MANHOOD!
In THREE Great Parts!
MAKE IT YOURSELF ROBOT KIT
PART 1--Meet ROBO, HIS ROBOT PLAYMATE
PART 2--Meet ZAL-EL, HIS BROTHER!
PART 3--Meet FUTURO, HIS SUPER-HERO

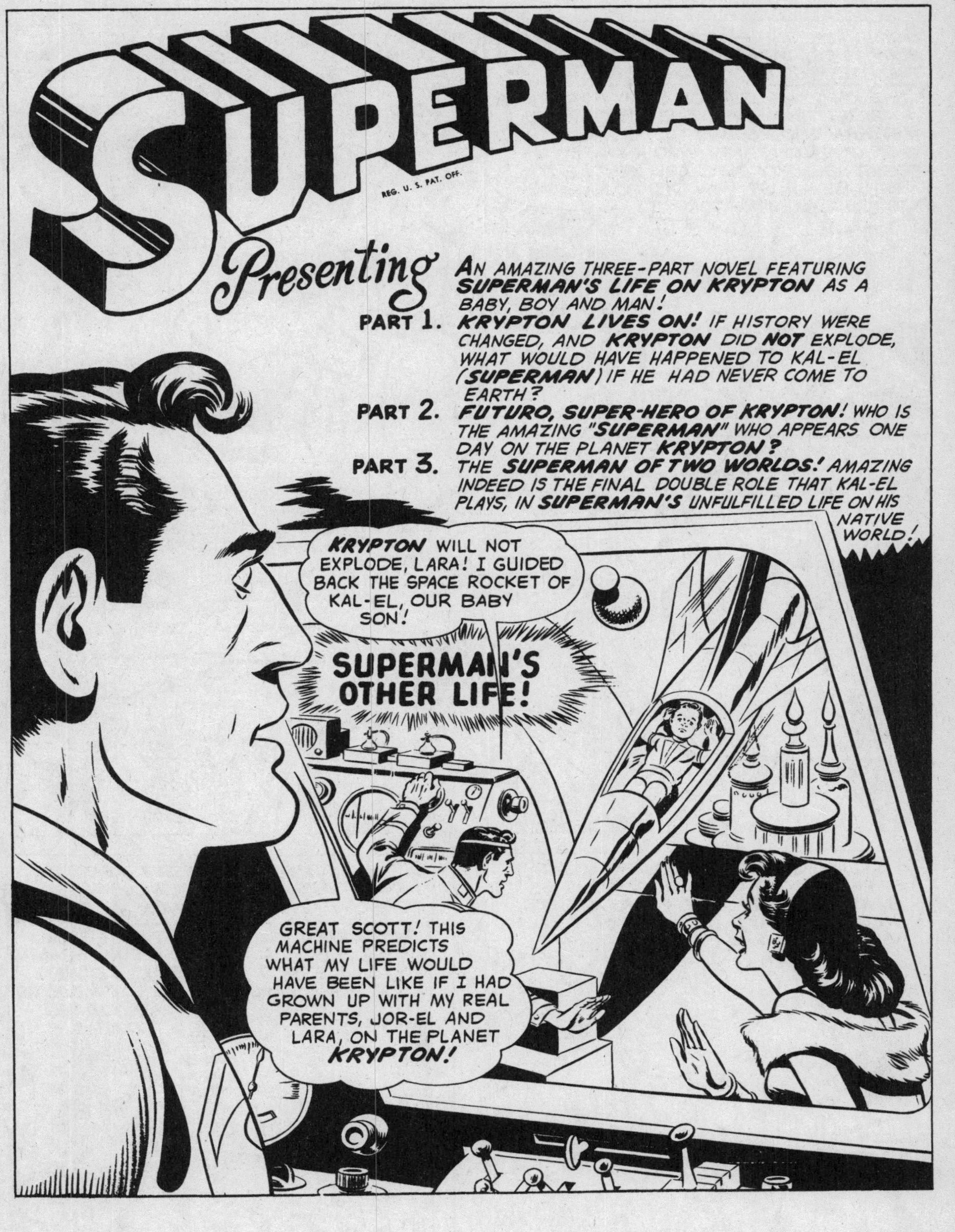
SUPERMAN
REG. U. S. PAT. OFF.
Presenting
AN AMAZING THREE-PART NOVEL FEATURING SUPERMAN'S LIFE ON KRYPTON AS A BABY, BOY AND MAN!
PART 1. KRYPTON LIVES ON! IF HISTORY WERE CHANGED, AND KRYPTON DID NOT EXPLODE, WHAT WOULD HAVE HAPPENED TO KAL-EL (SUPERMAN) IF HE HAD NEVER COME TO EARTH?
PART 2. FUTURO, SUPER-HERO OF KRYPTON! WHO IS THE AMAZING "SUPERMAN" WHO APPEARS ONE DAY ON THE PLANET KRYPTON?
PART 3. THE SUPERMAN OF TWO WORLDS! AMAZING INDEED IS THE FINAL DOUBLE ROLE THAT KAL-EL PLAYS, IN SUPERMAN'S UNFULFILLED LIFE ON HIS NATIVE WORLD!
KRYPTON WILL NOT EXPLODE, LARA! I GUIDED BACK THE SPACE ROCKET OF KAL-EL, OUR BABY SON!
SUPERMAN'S OTHER LIFE!
GREAT SCOTT! THIS MACHINE PREDICTS WHAT MY LIFE WOULD HAVE BEEN LIKE IF I HAD GROWN UP WITH MY REAL PARENTS, JOR-EL AND LARA, ON THE PLANET KRYPTON!

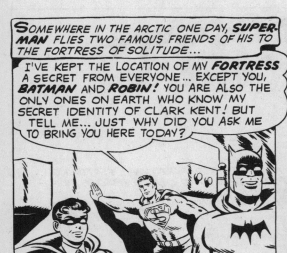

SOMEWHERE IN THE ARCTIC ONE DAY, *SUPERMAN* FLIES TWO FAMOUS FRIENDS OF HIS TO THE FORTRESS OF SOLITUDE...

I'VE KEPT THE LOCATION OF MY *FORTRESS* A SECRET FROM EVERYONE... EXCEPT YOU, *BATMAN* AND *ROBIN!* YOU ARE ALSO THE ONLY ONES ON EARTH WHO KNOW MY SECRET IDENTITY OF CLARK KENT! BUT TELL ME... JUST WHY DID YOU ASK ME TO BRING YOU HERE TODAY?

WE WANT TO GIVE YOU A GIFT FOR SAVING US FROM THAT CRIME-TRAP LAST WEEK IN GOTHAM CITY! BUT YOU ALREADY HAVE *EVERY-THING* UNDER THE SUN IN YOUR COLLECTION!

WE HAD TO THINK OF AN EXTRAORDINARY GIFT! HERE, *SUPERMAN!*

AFTER *SUPERMAN* OPENS IT...

BUT...ER...THESE ARE ONLY COPIES OF PHOTOS OF LIFE ON *KRYPTON*, MY HOME WORLD! I MADE THE ORIGINALS BY OVERTAKING AND PHOTOGRAPHING LIGHT RAYS THAT HAD LEFT *KRYPTON* BEFORE IT EXPLODED! I MYSELF DONATED THE PHOTOS TO A MUSEUM!

JOR-EL AND LARA

KAL-EL

KRYPTON BEAST

PTONOPOLIS

YES, WE KNOW! BUT FEED THESE PHOTOS INTO YOUR *SUPER UNIVAC* AS FACTORS, SO WE CAN LEARN HOW IT SOLVES THIS *SUPER* PROBLEM!

WHAT WOULD *SUPERMAN'S* OTHER LIFE HAVE BEEN, IF *KRYPTON* HAD NOT EXPLODED?

GREAT SCOTT! I...UH...NEVER THOUGHT OF FINDING THAT OUT MYSELF! WILL I BE *GLAD* OR *SORRY* AT SEEING MY *MIGHT-HAVE-BEEN* LIFE ON *KRYPTON?*

UNFIT FOR LIFE

SOLAR SYSTEM OF KRYPTON, THREE MILLION LIGHT YEARS FROM...

CURIOUS, *SUPERMAN* PRESSES THE BUTTON WHICH STARTS THE PREDICTIONS OF THE SUPER-ANALYZING MACHINE!

THAT SCREEN WILL SHOW US THE SCENES AND ALSO TRANSLATE *KRYPTONESE* INTO EARTH LANGUAGE!

THIS IS YOUR LIFE, *SUPERMAN*... YOUR *OTHER* LIFE...IF KRYPTON HAD *NOT* MET DOOM!

2

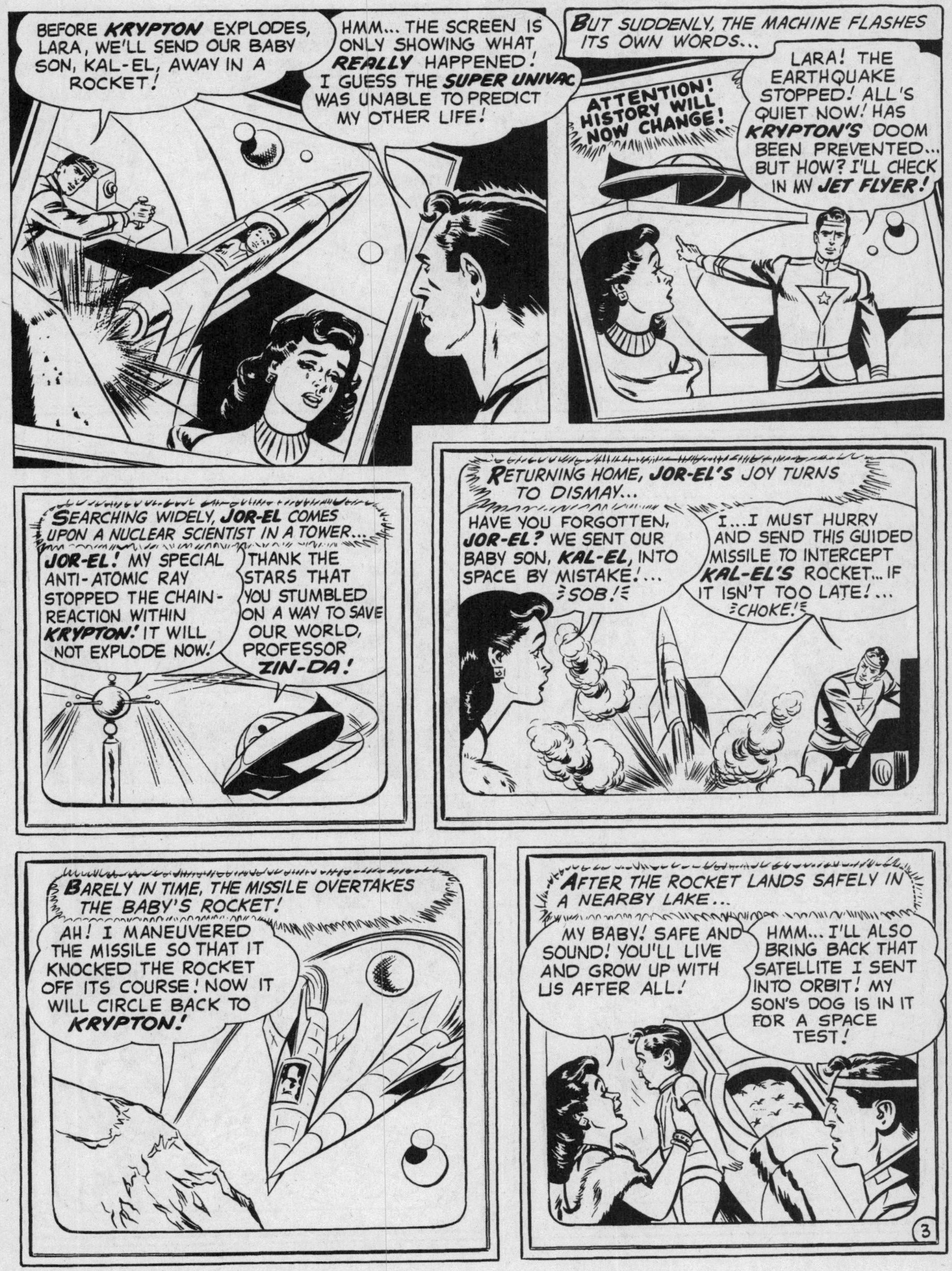
BEFORE KRYPTON EXPLODES, LARA, WE'LL SEND OUR BABY SON, KAL-EL, AWAY IN A ROCKET!
HMM... THE SCREEN IS ONLY SHOWING WHAT REALLY HAPPENED! I GUESS THE SUPER UNIVAC WAS UNABLE TO PREDICT MY OTHER LIFE!
BUT SUDDENLY, THE MACHINE FLASHES ITS OWN WORDS...
ATTENTION! HISTORY WILL NOW CHANGE!
LARA! THE EARTHQUAKE STOPPED! ALL'S QUIET NOW! HAS KRYPTON'S DOOM BEEN PREVENTED... BUT HOW? I'LL CHECK IN MY JET FLYER!
SEARCHING WIDELY, JOR-EL COMES UPON A NUCLEAR SCIENTIST IN A TOWER...
JOR-EL! MY SPECIAL ANTI-ATOMIC RAY STOPPED THE CHAIN-REACTION WITHIN KRYPTON! IT WILL NOT EXPLODE NOW!
THANK THE STARS THAT YOU STUMBLED ON A WAY TO SAVE OUR WORLD, PROFESSOR ZIN-DA!
RETURNING HOME, JOR-EL'S JOY TURNS TO DISMAY...
HAVE YOU FORGOTTEN, JOR-EL? WE SENT OUR BABY SON, KAL-EL, INTO SPACE BY MISTAKE!... SOB!
I...I MUST HURRY AND SEND THIS GUIDED MISSILE TO INTERCEPT KAL-EL'S ROCKET... IF IT ISN'T TOO LATE!... CHOKE!
BARELY IN TIME, THE MISSILE OVERTAKES THE BABY'S ROCKET!
AH! I MANEUVERED THE MISSILE SO THAT IT KNOCKED THE ROCKET OFF ITS COURSE! NOW IT WILL CIRCLE BACK TO KRYPTON!
AFTER THE ROCKET LANDS SAFELY IN A NEARBY LAKE...
MY BABY! SAFE AND SOUND! YOU'LL LIVE AND GROW UP WITH US AFTER ALL!
HMM... I'LL ALSO BRING BACK THAT SATELLITE I SENT INTO ORBIT! MY SON'S DOG IS IN IT FOR A SPACE TEST!
3

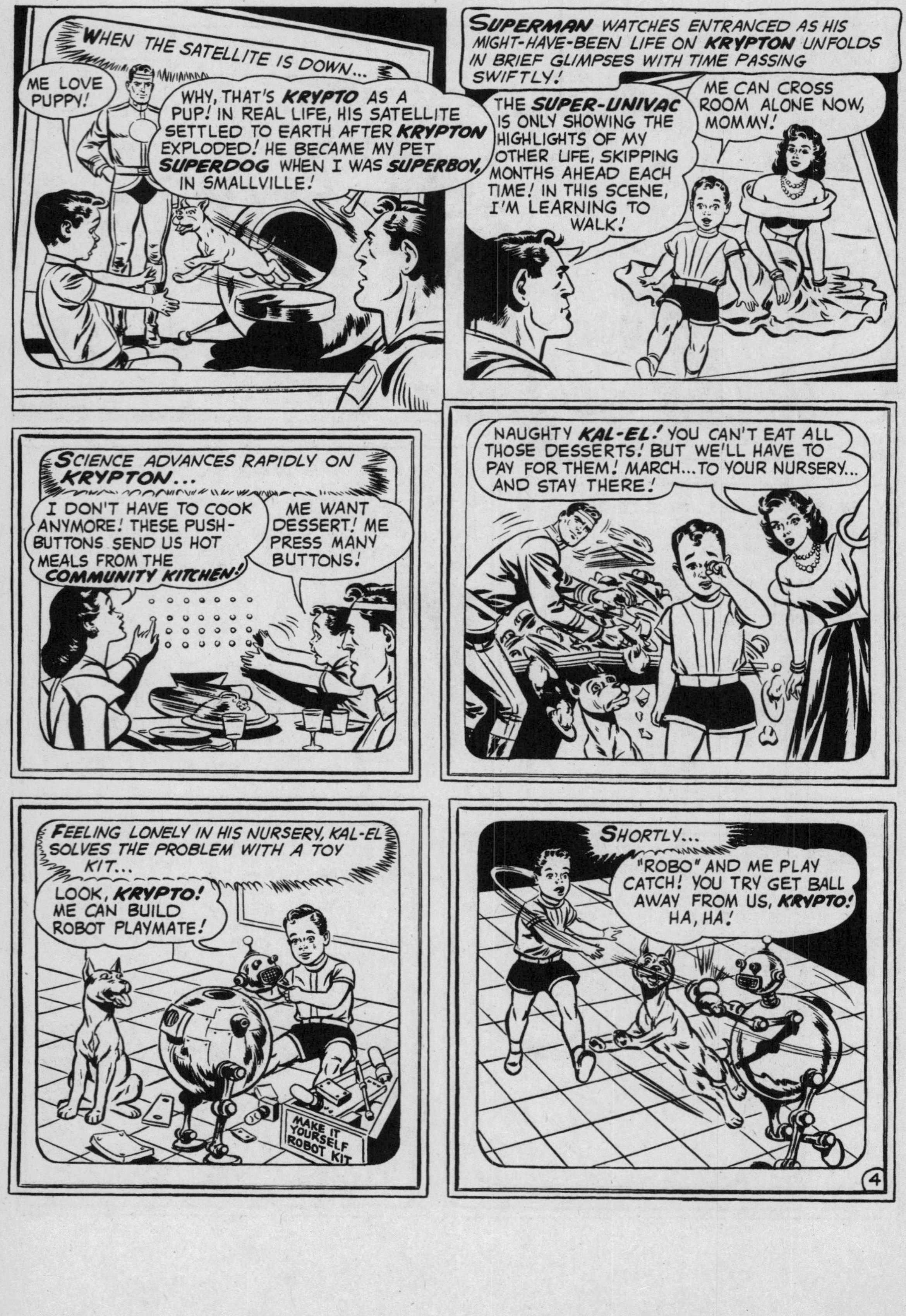
WHEN THE SATELLITE IS DOWN...
ME LOVE PUPPY!
WHY, THAT'S KRYPTO AS A PUP! IN REAL LIFE, HIS SATELLITE SETTLED TO EARTH AFTER KRYPTON EXPLODED! HE BECAME MY PET SUPERDOG WHEN I WAS SUPERBOY, IN SMALLVILLE!
SUPERMAN WATCHES ENTRANCED AS HIS MIGHT-HAVE-BEEN LIFE ON KRYPTON UNFOLDS IN BRIEF GLIMPSES WITH TIME PASSING SWIFTLY!
THE SUPER-UNIVAC IS ONLY SHOWING THE HIGHLIGHTS OF MY OTHER LIFE, SKIPPING MONTHS AHEAD EACH TIME! IN THIS SCENE, I'M LEARNING TO WALK!
ME CAN CROSS ROOM ALONE NOW, MOMMY!
SCIENCE ADVANCES RAPIDLY ON KRYPTON...
I DON'T HAVE TO COOK ANYMORE! THESE PUSH-BUTTONS SEND US HOT MEALS FROM THE COMMUNITY KITCHEN!
ME WANT DESSERT! ME PRESS MANY BUTTONS!
NAUGHTY KAL-EL! YOU CAN'T EAT ALL THOSE DESSERTS! BUT WE'LL HAVE TO PAY FOR THEM! MARCH...TO YOUR NURSERY... AND STAY THERE!
FEELING LONELY IN HIS NURSERY, KAL-EL SOLVES THE PROBLEM WITH A TOY KIT...
LOOK, KRYPTO! ME CAN BUILD ROBOT PLAYMATE!
MAKE IT YOURSELF ROBOT KIT
SHORTLY...
"ROBO" AND ME PLAY CATCH! YOU TRY GET BALL AWAY FROM US, KRYPTO! HA, HA!
4

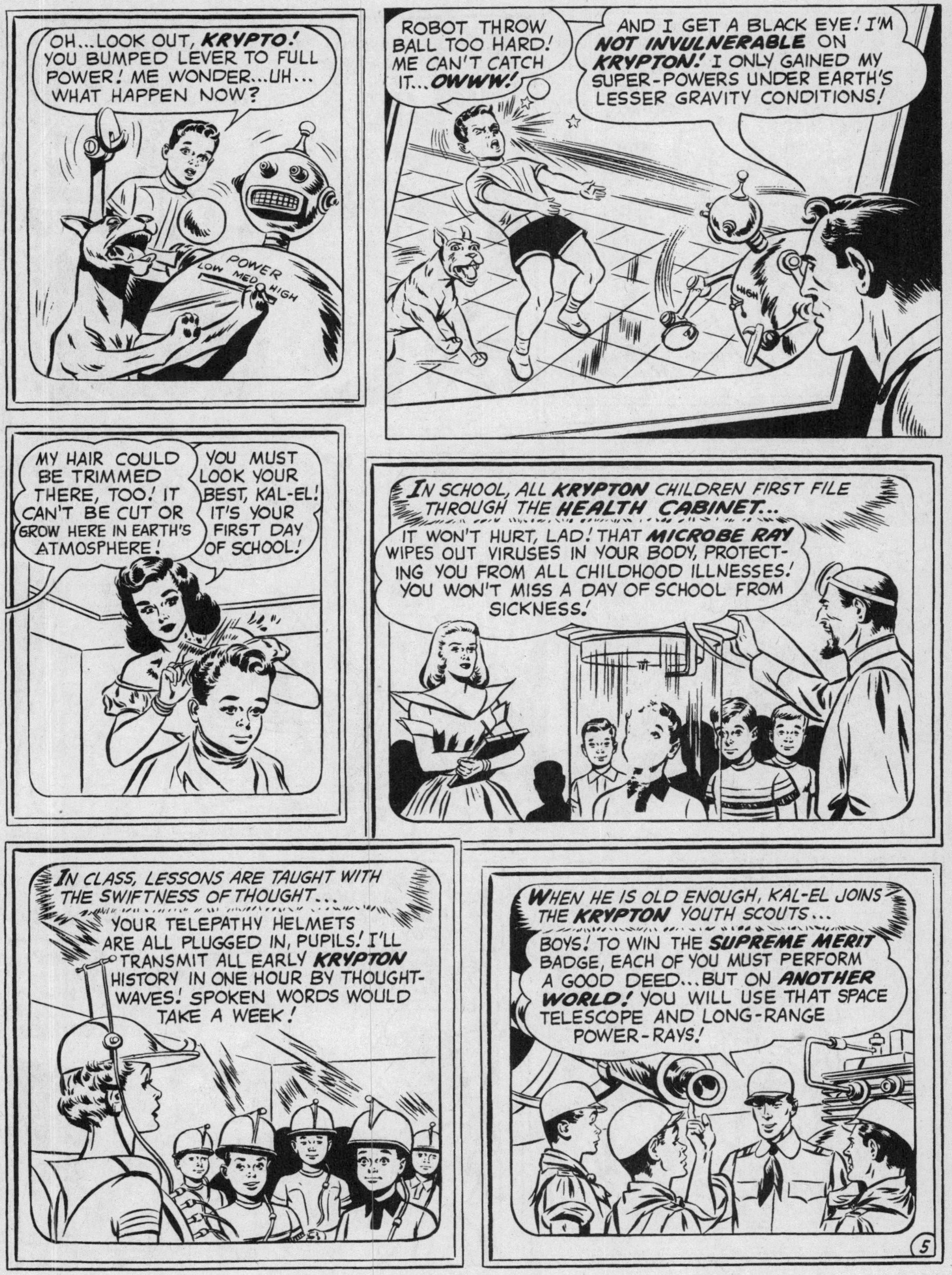
OH...LOOK OUT, KRYPTO! YOU BUMPED LEVER TO FULL POWER! ME WONDER...UH... WHAT HAPPEN NOW?
POWER
LOW MED HIGH
ROBOT THROW BALL TOO HARD! ME CAN'T CATCH IT...OWWW!
AND I GET A BLACK EYE! I'M NOT INVULNERABLE ON KRYPTON! I ONLY GAINED MY SUPER-POWERS UNDER EARTH'S LESSER GRAVITY CONDITIONS!
MY HAIR COULD BE TRIMMED THERE, TOO! IT CAN'T BE CUT OR GROW HERE IN EARTH'S ATMOSPHERE!
YOU MUST LOOK YOUR BEST, KAL-EL! IT'S YOUR FIRST DAY OF SCHOOL!
IN SCHOOL, ALL KRYPTON CHILDREN FIRST FILE THROUGH THE HEALTH CABINET...
IT WON'T HURT, LAD! THAT MICROBE RAY WIPES OUT VIRUSES IN YOUR BODY, PROTECTING YOU FROM ALL CHILDHOOD ILLNESSES! YOU WON'T MISS A DAY OF SCHOOL FROM SICKNESS!
IN CLASS, LESSONS ARE TAUGHT WITH THE SWIFTNESS OF THOUGHT...
YOUR TELEPATHY HELMETS ARE ALL PLUGGED IN, PUPILS! I'LL TRANSMIT ALL EARLY KRYPTON HISTORY IN ONE HOUR BY THOUGHT-WAVES! SPOKEN WORDS WOULD TAKE A WEEK!
WHEN HE IS OLD ENOUGH, KAL-EL JOINS THE KRYPTON YOUTH SCOUTS...
BOYS! TO WIN THE SUPREME MERIT BADGE, EACH OF YOU MUST PERFORM A GOOD DEED...BUT ON ANOTHER WORLD! YOU WILL USE THAT SPACE TELESCOPE AND LONG-RANGE POWER-RAYS!
5

WHEN *KAL-EL'S* TURN COMES...

OUR ASTRONOMERS HAVE FOUND LIFE ON THOSE DISTANT WORLDS! CHOOSE ANY ONE YOU WISH FOR YOUR GOOD DEED, *KAL-EL!*

HMM... I'LL TAKE *EARTH!*

EARTH

BLUE PLANET

ZORNIA

DYON III

AFTER SCANNING EARTH WITH THE SUPER-TELE-SCOPE...

THAT EARTHLY VEHICLE WENT OUT OF CONTROL!

HELP! WE'LL PLUNGE INTO THAT LAKE AND DROWN!

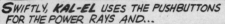

SWIFTLY, *KAL-EL* USES THE PUSHBUTTONS FOR THE POWER RAYS AND...

I'LL SEND THE *HEAT RAY* TO EARTH, INSTANTLY DRYING UP THAT LAKE!

GOOD HEAVENS! IS... IS THE WATER VANISHING?

SOME MIRACLE SAVED US, MARTHA!

GREAT GUNS! BY SHEER CHANCE, *KAL-EL* SAVED *MOM AND DAD KENT!* IN REAL LIFE, THEY WERE MY FOSTER PARENTS! THEY RAISED ME IN SMALLVILLE WHEN I WAS *SUPERBOY!*

THEY WERE ON THEIR WAY TO AN ORPHANAGE! SINCE I NEVER REACHED EARTH TO BECOME THEIR ADOPTED *SUPERBABY,* THEY'RE ADOPTING ANOTHER CHILD! IT'S A *GIRL!* WHAT A STRANGE TWIST OF FATE!

HAPPY VALLEY ORPHANAGE

BUT OBSERVING HIS *MIGHT-HAVE-BEEN* LIFE, *SUPERMAN* AND *BATMAN* ARE EVEN MORE STARTLED AT WHAT *JOR-EL* AND *LARA* ONE DAY SHOW *KAL-EL,* PROUDLY...

SEE, *KAL-EL?* *ZAL-EL* LOOKS LIKE YOU!

LOOK, *SUPERMAN!* IF YOU HAD LIVED ON *KRYPTON,* YOU WOULD HAVE HAD A BABY *BROTHER!*

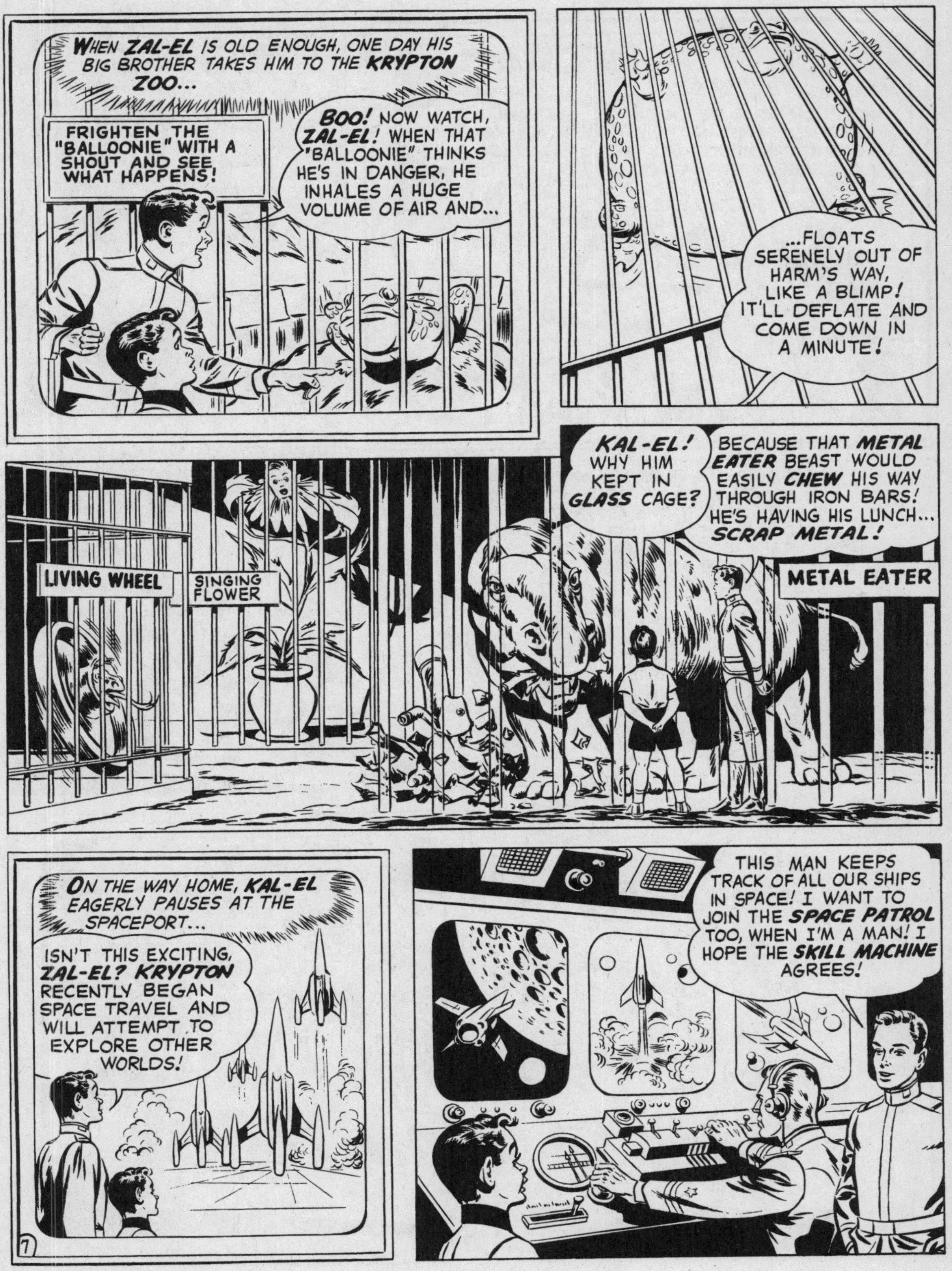
WHEN ZAL-EL IS OLD ENOUGH, ONE DAY HIS BIG BROTHER TAKES HIM TO THE KRYPTON ZOO...
FRIGHTEN THE "BALLOONIE" WITH A SHOUT AND SEE WHAT HAPPENS!
BOO! NOW WATCH, ZAL-EL! WHEN THAT "BALLOONIE" THINKS HE'S IN DANGER, HE INHALES A HUGE VOLUME OF AIR AND...
...FLOATS SERENELY OUT OF HARM'S WAY, LIKE A BLIMP! IT'LL DEFLATE AND COME DOWN IN A MINUTE!
KAL-EL! WHY HIM KEPT IN GLASS CAGE?
BECAUSE THAT METAL EATER BEAST WOULD EASILY CHEW HIS WAY THROUGH IRON BARS! HE'S HAVING HIS LUNCH... SCRAP METAL!
LIVING WHEEL
SINGING FLOWER
METAL EATER
ON THE WAY HOME, KAL-EL EAGERLY PAUSES AT THE SPACEPORT...
ISN'T THIS EXCITING, ZAL-EL? KRYPTON RECENTLY BEGAN SPACE TRAVEL AND WILL ATTEMPT TO EXPLORE OTHER WORLDS!
7
THIS MAN KEEPS TRACK OF ALL OUR SHIPS IN SPACE! I WANT TO JOIN THE SPACE PATROL TOO, WHEN I'M A MAN! I HOPE THE SKILL MACHINE AGREES!

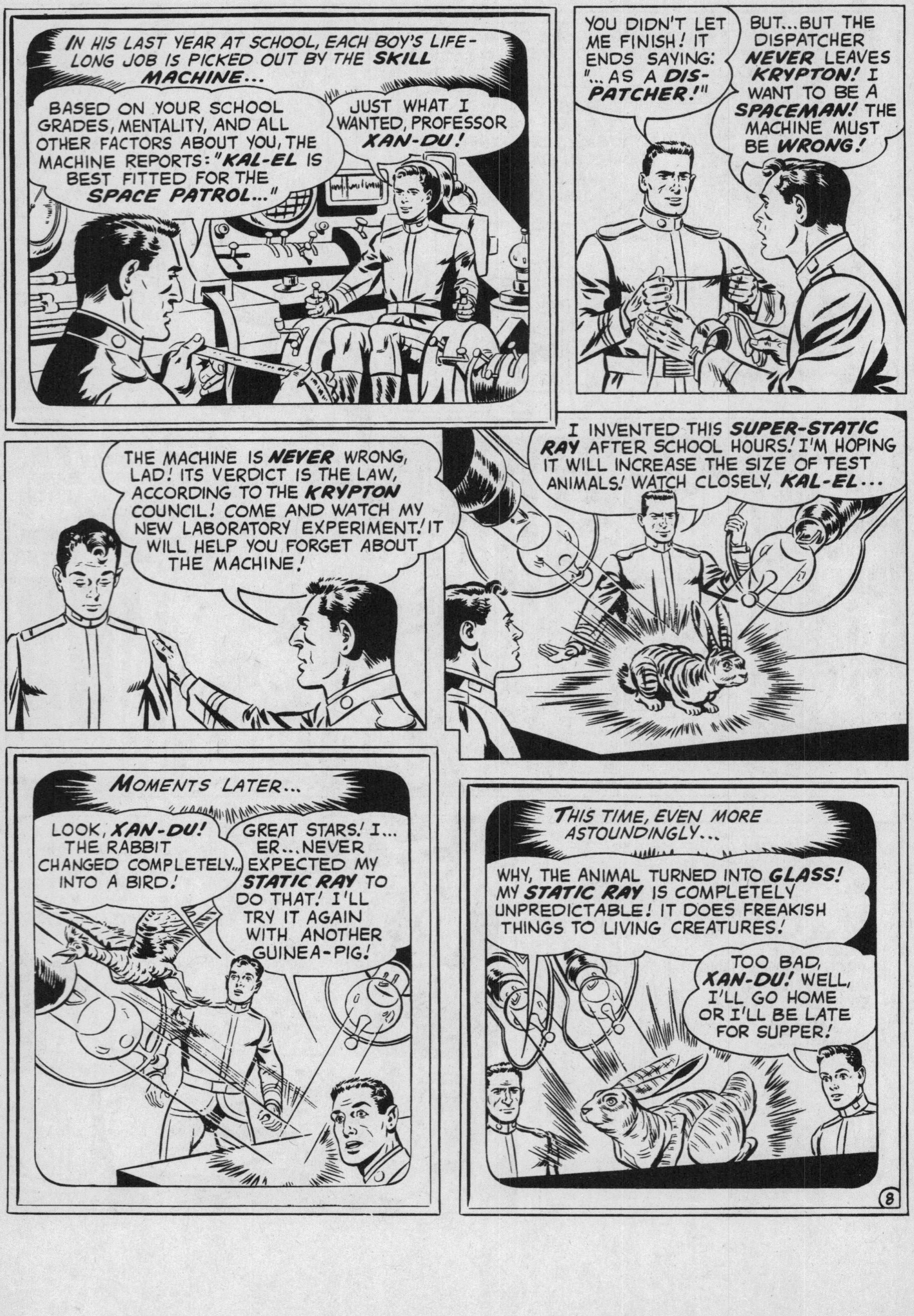
IN HIS LAST YEAR AT SCHOOL, EACH BOY'S LIFE-LONG JOB IS PICKED OUT BY THE SKILL MACHINE...
BASED ON YOUR SCHOOL GRADES, MENTALITY, AND ALL OTHER FACTORS ABOUT YOU, THE MACHINE REPORTS: "KAL-EL IS BEST FITTED FOR THE SPACE PATROL..."
JUST WHAT I WANTED, PROFESSOR XAN-DU!
YOU DIDN'T LET ME FINISH! IT ENDS SAYING: "...AS A DIS-PATCHER!"
BUT...BUT THE DISPATCHER NEVER LEAVES KRYPTON! I WANT TO BE A SPACEMAN! THE MACHINE MUST BE WRONG!
THE MACHINE IS NEVER WRONG, LAD! ITS VERDICT IS THE LAW, ACCORDING TO THE KRYPTON COUNCIL! COME AND WATCH MY NEW LABORATORY EXPERIMENT! IT WILL HELP YOU FORGET ABOUT THE MACHINE!
I INVENTED THIS SUPER-STATIC RAY AFTER SCHOOL HOURS! I'M HOPING IT WILL INCREASE THE SIZE OF TEST ANIMALS! WATCH CLOSELY, KAL-EL...
MOMENTS LATER...
LOOK, XAN-DU! THE RABBIT CHANGED COMPLETELY... INTO A BIRD!
GREAT STARS! I... ER...NEVER EXPECTED MY STATIC RAY TO DO THAT! I'LL TRY IT AGAIN WITH ANOTHER GUINEA-PIG!
THIS TIME, EVEN MORE ASTOUNDINGLY...
WHY, THE ANIMAL TURNED INTO GLASS! MY STATIC RAY IS COMPLETELY UNPREDICTABLE! IT DOES FREAKISH THINGS TO LIVING CREATURES!
TOO BAD, XAN-DU! WELL, I'LL GO HOME OR I'LL BE LATE FOR SUPPER!
8

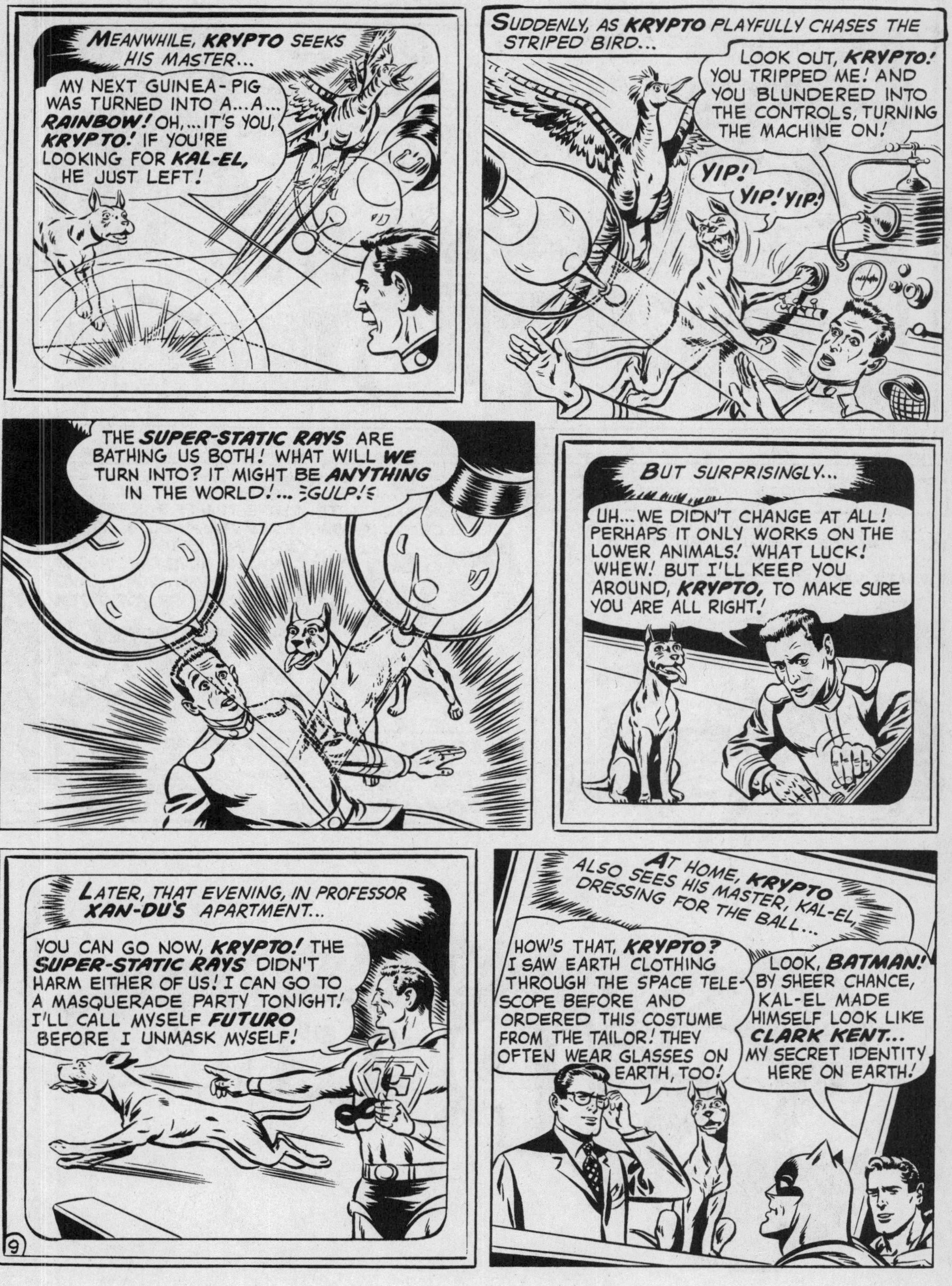
MEANWHILE, KRYPTO SEEKS HIS MASTER...
MY NEXT GUINEA-PIG WAS TURNED INTO A...A... RAINBOW! OH,...IT'S YOU, KRYPTO! IF YOU'RE LOOKING FOR KAL-EL, HE JUST LEFT!
SUDDENLY, AS KRYPTO PLAYFULLY CHASES THE STRIPED BIRD...
LOOK OUT, KRYPTO! YOU TRIPPED ME! AND YOU BLUNDERED INTO THE CONTROLS, TURNING THE MACHINE ON!
YIP! YIP! YIP!
THE SUPER-STATIC RAYS ARE BATHING US BOTH! WHAT WILL WE TURN INTO? IT MIGHT BE ANYTHING IN THE WORLD!... GULP!
BUT SURPRISINGLY...
UH...WE DIDN'T CHANGE AT ALL! PERHAPS IT ONLY WORKS ON THE LOWER ANIMALS! WHAT LUCK! WHEW! BUT I'LL KEEP YOU AROUND, KRYPTO, TO MAKE SURE YOU ARE ALL RIGHT!
LATER, THAT EVENING, IN PROFESSOR XAN-DU'S APARTMENT...
YOU CAN GO NOW, KRYPTO! THE SUPER-STATIC RAYS DIDN'T HARM EITHER OF US! I CAN GO TO A MASQUERADE PARTY TONIGHT! I'LL CALL MYSELF FUTURO BEFORE I UNMASK MYSELF!
9
AT HOME, KRYPTO ALSO SEES HIS MASTER, KAL-EL, DRESSING FOR THE BALL...
HOW'S THAT, KRYPTO? I SAW EARTH CLOTHING THROUGH THE SPACE TELESCOPE BEFORE AND ORDERED THIS COSTUME FROM THE TAILOR! THEY OFTEN WEAR GLASSES ON EARTH, TOO!
LOOK, BATMAN! BY SHEER CHANCE, KAL-EL MADE HIMSELF LOOK LIKE CLARK KENT... MY SECRET IDENTITY HERE ON EARTH!

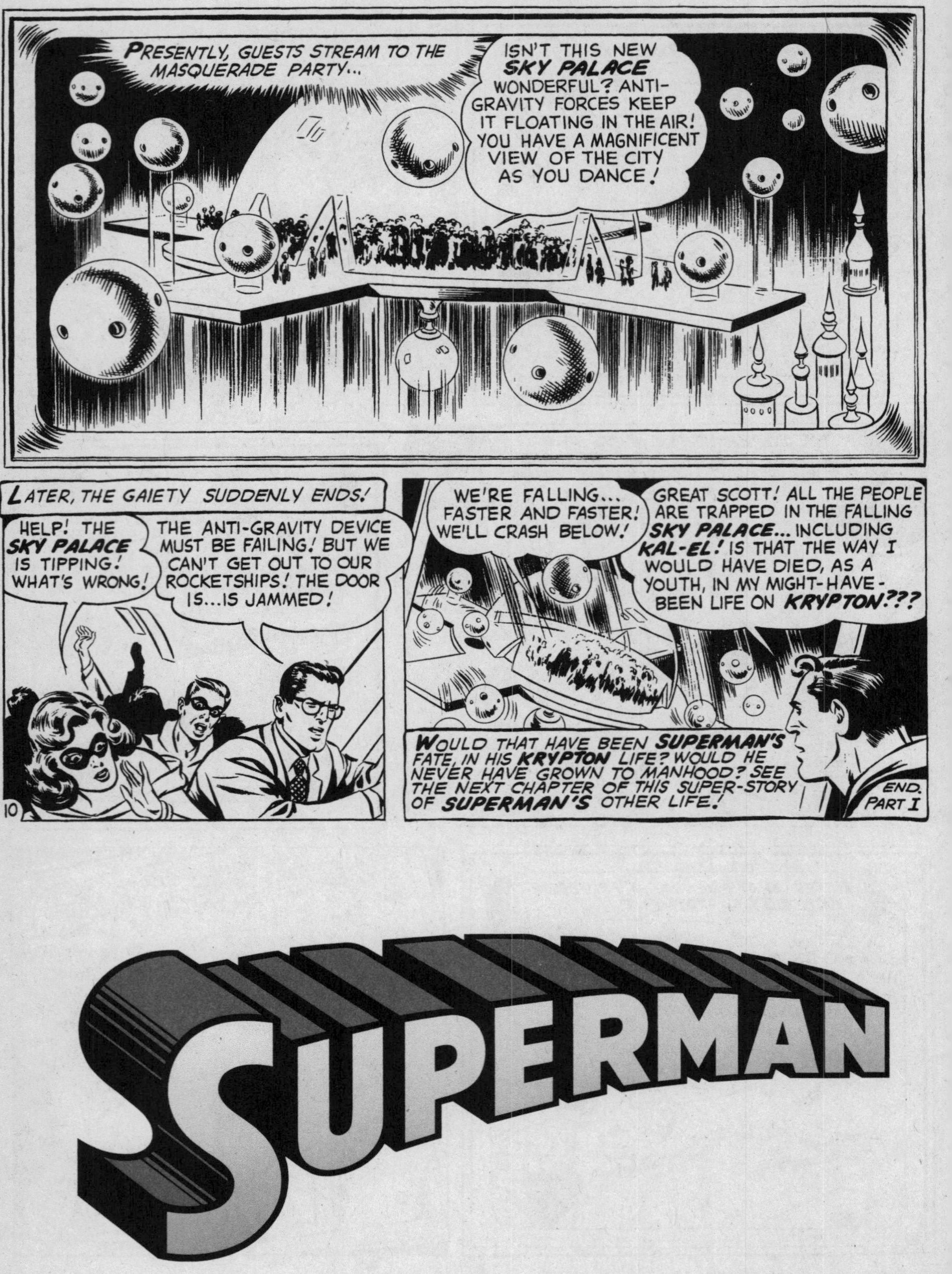
PRESENTLY, GUESTS STREAM TO THE MASQUERADE PARTY...
ISN'T THIS NEW SKY PALACE WONDERFUL? ANTI-GRAVITY FORCES KEEP IT FLOATING IN THE AIR! YOU HAVE A MAGNIFICENT VIEW OF THE CITY AS YOU DANCE!
LATER, THE GAIETY SUDDENLY ENDS!
HELP! THE SKY PALACE IS TIPPING! WHAT'S WRONG!
THE ANTI-GRAVITY DEVICE MUST BE FAILING! BUT WE CAN'T GET OUT TO OUR ROCKETSHIPS! THE DOOR IS...IS JAMMED!
10
WE'RE FALLING... FASTER AND FASTER! WE'LL CRASH BELOW!
GREAT SCOTT! ALL THE PEOPLE ARE TRAPPED IN THE FALLING SKY PALACE... INCLUDING KAL-EL! IS THAT THE WAY I WOULD HAVE DIED, AS A YOUTH, IN MY MIGHT-HAVE-BEEN LIFE ON KRYPTON???
WOULD THAT HAVE BEEN SUPERMAN'S FATE, IN HIS KRYPTON LIFE? WOULD HE NEVER HAVE GROWN TO MANHOOD? SEE THE NEXT CHAPTER OF THIS SUPER-STORY OF SUPERMAN'S OTHER LIFE!
END. PART I

SUPERMAN

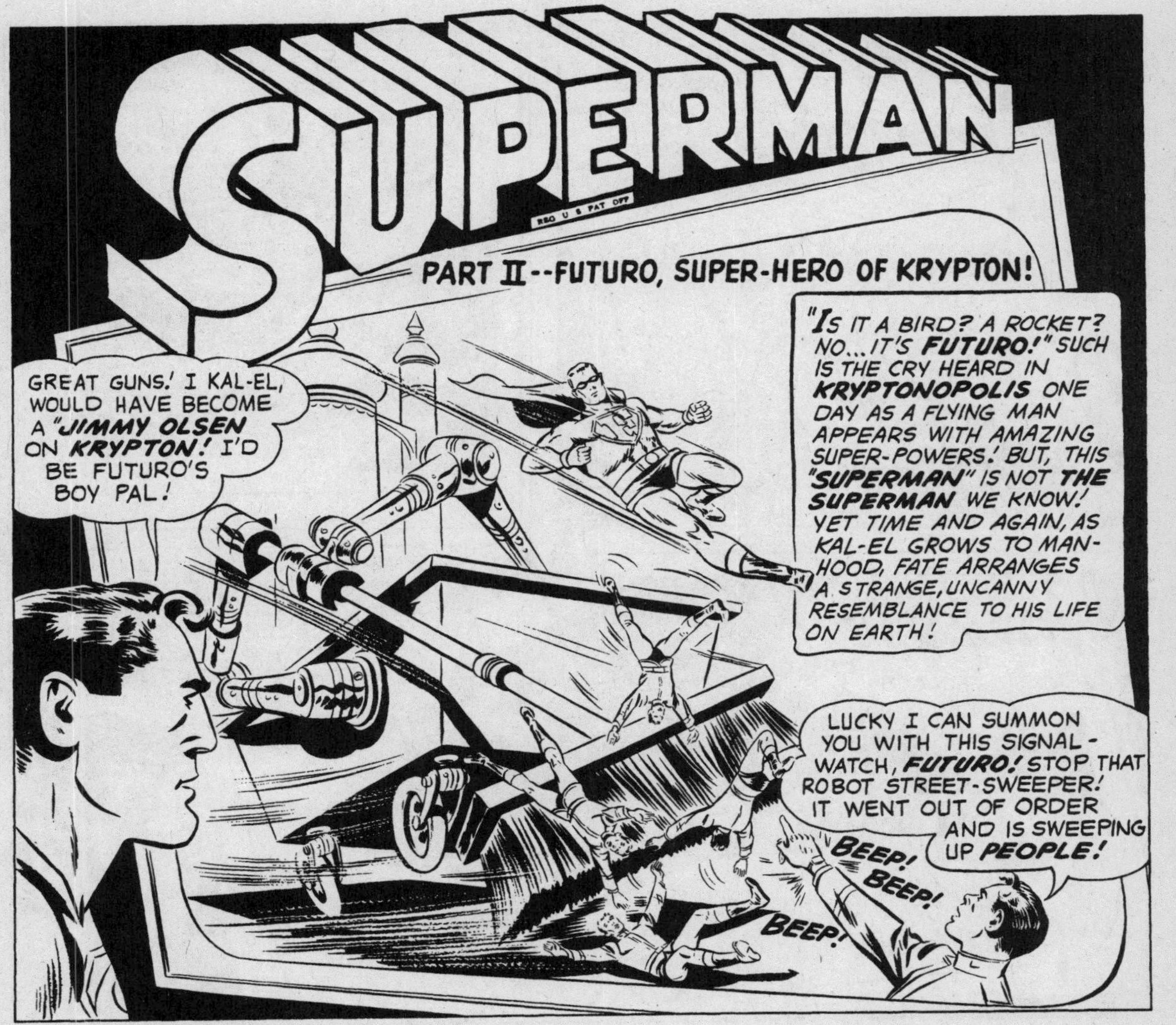
SUPERMAN
REG. U.S. PAT. OFF.
PART II--FUTURO, SUPER-HERO OF KRYPTON!
"IS IT A BIRD? A ROCKET? NO... IT'S FUTURO!" SUCH IS THE CRY HEARD IN KRYPTONOPOLIS ONE DAY AS A FLYING MAN APPEARS WITH AMAZING SUPER-POWERS! BUT, THIS "SUPERMAN" IS NOT THE SUPERMAN WE KNOW! YET TIME AND AGAIN, AS KAL-EL GROWS TO MANHOOD, FATE ARRANGES A STRANGE, UNCANNY RESEMBLANCE TO HIS LIFE ON EARTH!
GREAT GUNS! I KAL-EL, WOULD HAVE BECOME A "JIMMY OLSEN ON KRYPTON! I'D BE FUTURO'S BOY PAL!
LUCKY I CAN SUMMON YOU WITH THIS SIGNAL-WATCH, FUTURO! STOP THAT ROBOT STREET-SWEEPER! IT WENT OUT OF ORDER AND IS SWEEPING UP PEOPLE!
BEEP! BEEP! BEEP!

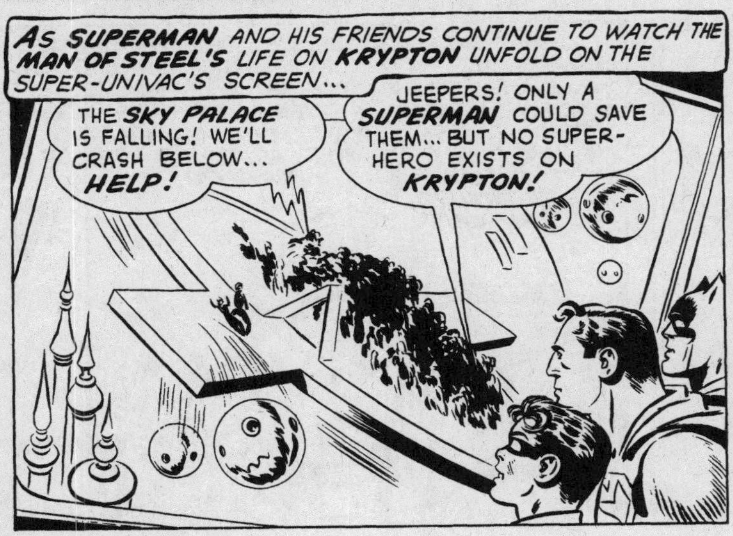
AS SUPERMAN AND HIS FRIENDS CONTINUE TO WATCH THE MAN OF STEEL'S LIFE ON KRYPTON UNFOLD ON THE SUPER-UNIVAC'S SCREEN...
THE SKY PALACE IS FALLING! WE'LL CRASH BELOW... HELP!
JEEPERS! ONLY A SUPERMAN COULD SAVE THEM... BUT NO SUPER-HERO EXISTS ON KRYPTON!

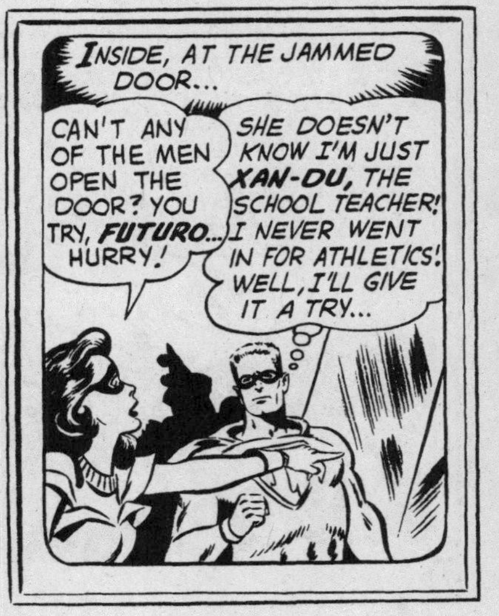
INSIDE, AT THE JAMMED DOOR...
CAN'T ANY OF THE MEN OPEN THE DOOR? YOU TRY, FUTURO... HURRY!
SHE DOESN'T KNOW I'M JUST XAN-DU, THE SCHOOL TEACHER! I NEVER WENT IN FOR ATHLETICS! WELL, I'LL GIVE IT A TRY...

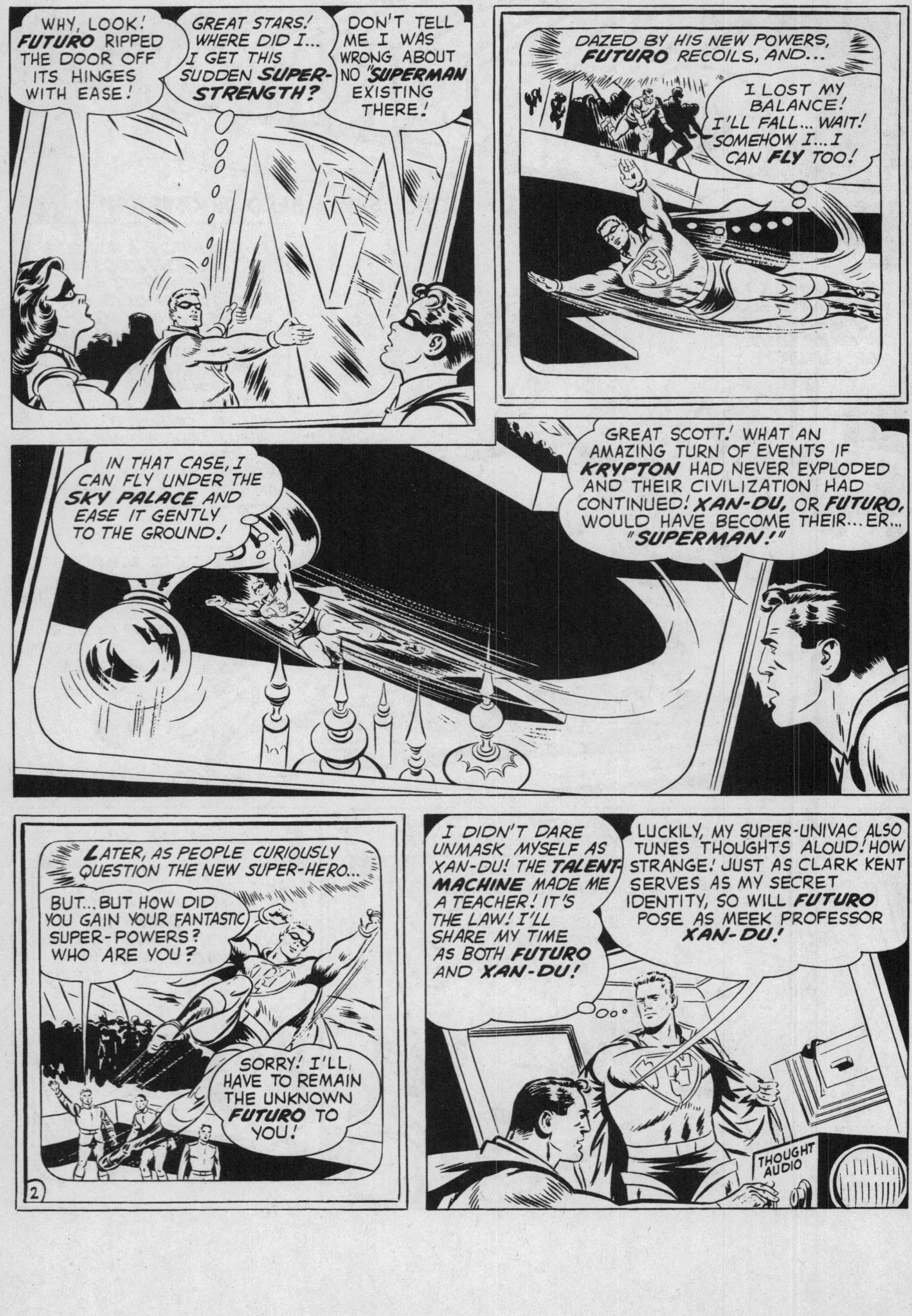
WHY, LOOK! FUTURO RIPPED THE DOOR OFF ITS HINGES WITH EASE!
GREAT STARS! WHERE DID I... I GET THIS SUDDEN SUPER-STRENGTH?
DON'T TELL ME I WAS WRONG ABOUT NO "SUPERMAN EXISTING THERE!
DAZED BY HIS NEW POWERS, FUTURO RECOILS, AND...
I LOST MY BALANCE! I'LL FALL... WAIT! SOMEHOW I... I CAN FLY TOO!
IN THAT CASE, I CAN FLY UNDER THE SKY PALACE AND EASE IT GENTLY TO THE GROUND!
GREAT SCOTT! WHAT AN AMAZING TURN OF EVENTS IF KRYPTON HAD NEVER EXPLODED AND THEIR CIVILIZATION HAD CONTINUED! XAN-DU, OR FUTURO, WOULD HAVE BECOME THEIR... ER... "SUPERMAN!"
LATER, AS PEOPLE CURIOUSLY QUESTION THE NEW SUPER-HERO...
BUT... BUT HOW DID YOU GAIN YOUR FANTASTIC SUPER-POWERS? WHO ARE YOU?
SORRY! I'LL HAVE TO REMAIN THE UNKNOWN FUTURO TO YOU!
2
I DIDN'T DARE UNMASK MYSELF AS XAN-DU! THE TALENT-MACHINE MADE ME A TEACHER! IT'S THE LAW! I'LL SHARE MY TIME AS BOTH FUTURO AND XAN-DU!
LUCKILY, MY SUPER-UNIVAC ALSO TUNES THOUGHTS ALOUD! HOW STRANGE! JUST AS CLARK KENT SERVES AS MY SECRET IDENTITY, SO WILL FUTURO POSE AS MEEK PROFESSOR XAN-DU!
THOUGHT AUDIO

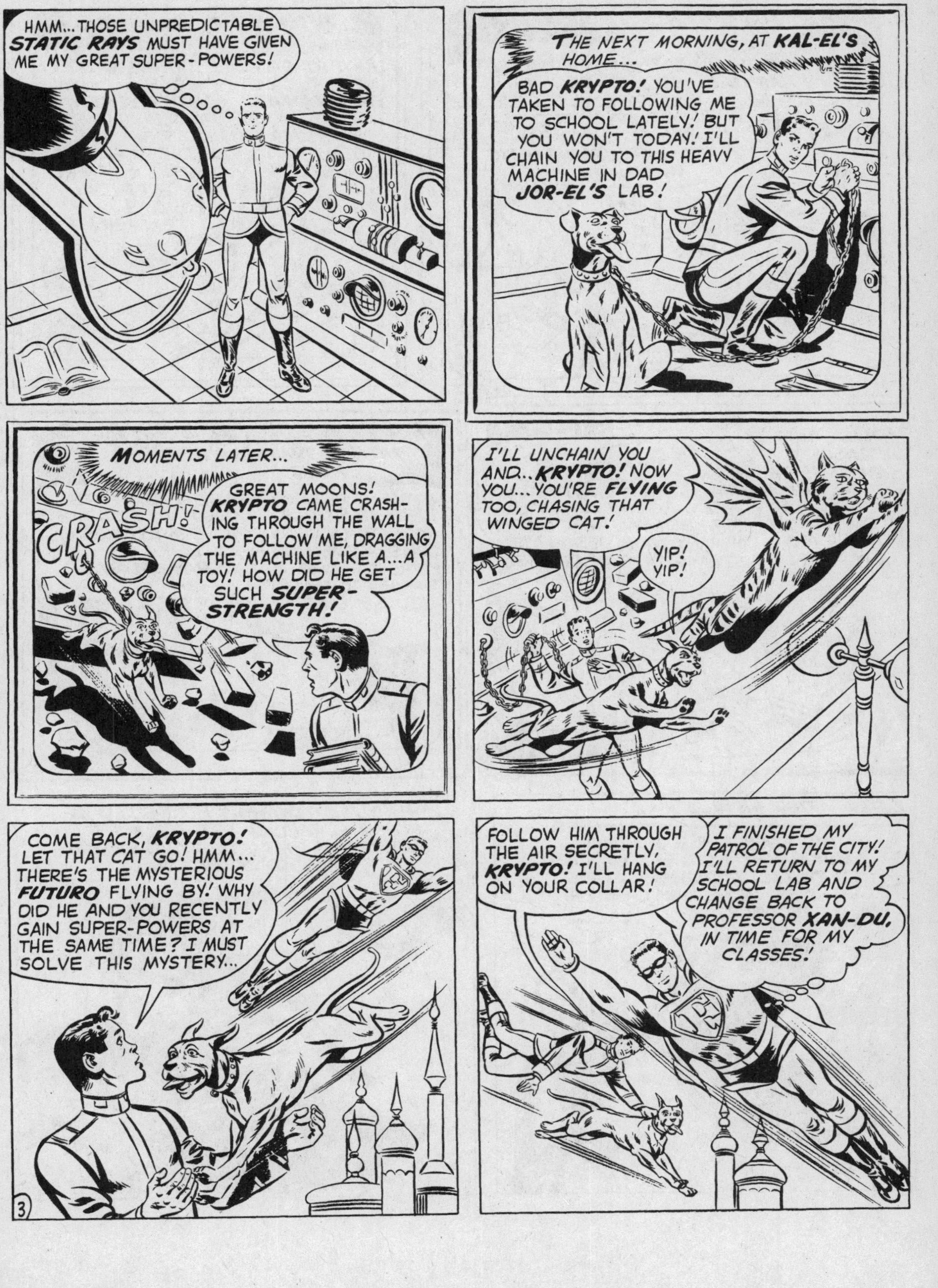
HMM... THOSE UNPREDICTABLE STATIC RAYS MUST HAVE GIVEN ME MY GREAT SUPER-POWERS!
THE NEXT MORNING, AT KAL-EL'S HOME...
BAD KRYPTO! YOU'VE TAKEN TO FOLLOWING ME TO SCHOOL LATELY! BUT YOU WON'T TODAY! I'LL CHAIN YOU TO THIS HEAVY MACHINE IN DAD JOR-EL'S LAB!
MOMENTS LATER...
CRASH!
GREAT MOONS! KRYPTO CAME CRASHING THROUGH THE WALL TO FOLLOW ME, DRAGGING THE MACHINE LIKE A...A TOY! HOW DID HE GET SUCH SUPER-STRENGTH!
I'LL UNCHAIN YOU AND...KRYPTO! NOW YOU...YOU'RE FLYING TOO, CHASING THAT WINGED CAT!
YIP! YIP!
COME BACK, KRYPTO! LET THAT CAT GO! HMM... THERE'S THE MYSTERIOUS FUTURO FLYING BY! WHY DID HE AND YOU RECENTLY GAIN SUPER-POWERS AT THE SAME TIME? I MUST SOLVE THIS MYSTERY...
3
FOLLOW HIM THROUGH THE AIR SECRETLY, KRYPTO! I'LL HANG ON YOUR COLLAR!
I FINISHED MY PATROL OF THE CITY! I'LL RETURN TO MY SCHOOL LAB AND CHANGE BACK TO PROFESSOR XAN-DU, IN TIME FOR MY CLASSES!

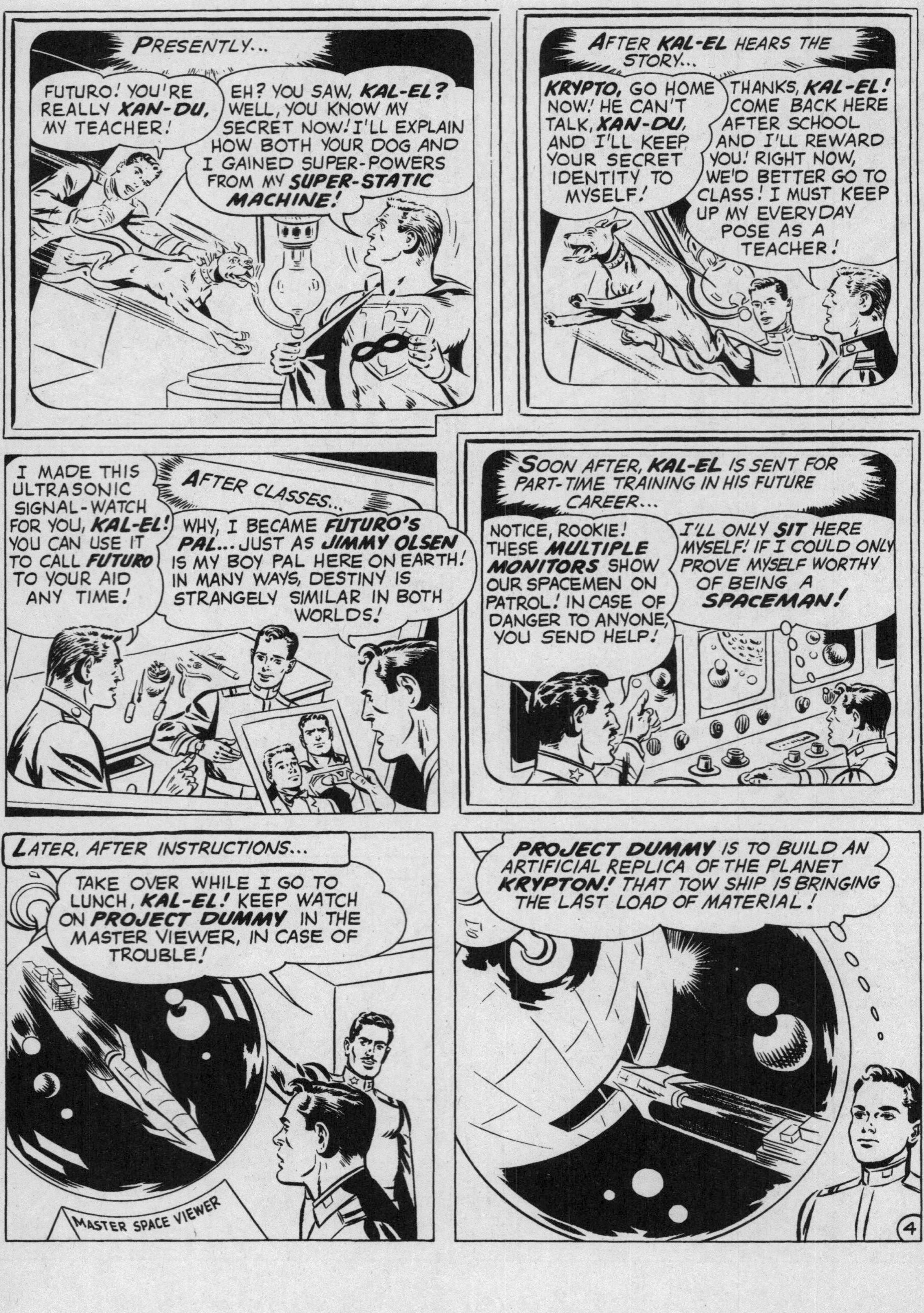
PRESENTLY...
FUTURO! YOU'RE REALLY XAN-DU, MY TEACHER!
EH? YOU SAW, KAL-EL? WELL, YOU KNOW MY SECRET NOW! I'LL EXPLAIN HOW BOTH YOUR DOG AND I GAINED SUPER-POWERS FROM MY SUPER-STATIC MACHINE!
AFTER KAL-EL HEARS THE STORY...
KRYPTO, GO HOME NOW! HE CAN'T TALK, XAN-DU, AND I'LL KEEP YOUR SECRET IDENTITY TO MYSELF!
THANKS, KAL-EL! COME BACK HERE AFTER SCHOOL AND I'LL REWARD YOU! RIGHT NOW, WE'D BETTER GO TO CLASS! I MUST KEEP UP MY EVERYDAY POSE AS A TEACHER!
AFTER CLASSES...
I MADE THIS ULTRASONIC SIGNAL-WATCH FOR YOU, KAL-EL! YOU CAN USE IT TO CALL FUTURO TO YOUR AID ANY TIME!
WHY, I BECAME FUTURO'S PAL... JUST AS JIMMY OLSEN IS MY BOY PAL HERE ON EARTH! IN MANY WAYS, DESTINY IS STRANGELY SIMILAR IN BOTH WORLDS!
SOON AFTER, KAL-EL IS SENT FOR PART-TIME TRAINING IN HIS FUTURE CAREER...
NOTICE, ROOKIE! THESE MULTIPLE MONITORS SHOW OUR SPACEMEN ON PATROL! IN CASE OF DANGER TO ANYONE, YOU SEND HELP!
I'LL ONLY SIT HERE MYSELF! IF I COULD ONLY PROVE MYSELF WORTHY OF BEING A SPACEMAN!
LATER, AFTER INSTRUCTIONS...
TAKE OVER WHILE I GO TO LUNCH, KAL-EL! KEEP WATCH ON PROJECT DUMMY IN THE MASTER VIEWER, IN CASE OF TROUBLE!
MASTER SPACE VIEWER
PROJECT DUMMY IS TO BUILD AN ARTIFICIAL REPLICA OF THE PLANET KRYPTON! THAT TOW SHIP IS BRINGING THE LAST LOAD OF MATERIAL!
4

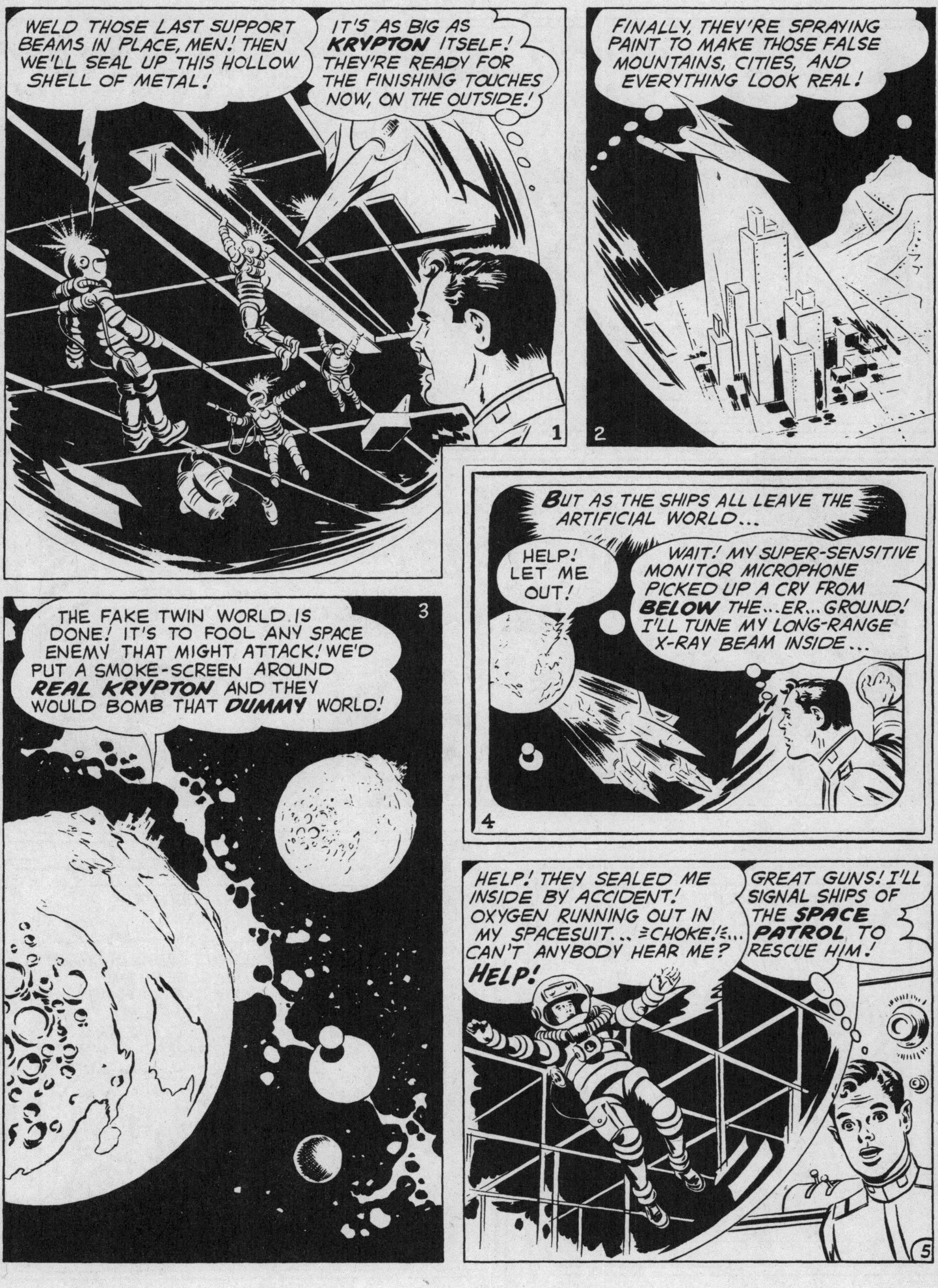
WELD THOSE LAST SUPPORT BEAMS IN PLACE, MEN! THEN WE'LL SEAL UP THIS HOLLOW SHELL OF METAL!
IT'S AS BIG AS KRYPTON ITSELF! THEY'RE READY FOR THE FINISHING TOUCHES NOW, ON THE OUTSIDE!
1
FINALLY, THEY'RE SPRAYING PAINT TO MAKE THOSE FALSE MOUNTAINS, CITIES, AND EVERYTHING LOOK REAL!
2
THE FAKE TWIN WORLD IS DONE! IT'S TO FOOL ANY SPACE ENEMY THAT MIGHT ATTACK! WE'D PUT A SMOKE-SCREEN AROUND REAL KRYPTON AND THEY WOULD BOMB THAT DUMMY WORLD!
3
BUT AS THE SHIPS ALL LEAVE THE ARTIFICIAL WORLD...
HELP! LET ME OUT!
WAIT! MY SUPER-SENSITIVE MONITOR MICROPHONE PICKED UP A CRY FROM BELOW THE...ER...GROUND! I'LL TUNE MY LONG-RANGE X-RAY BEAM INSIDE...
4
HELP! THEY SEALED ME INSIDE BY ACCIDENT! OXYGEN RUNNING OUT IN MY SPACESUIT... CHOKE!... CAN'T ANYBODY HEAR ME? HELP!
GREAT GUNS! I'LL SIGNAL SHIPS OF THE SPACE PATROL TO RESCUE HIM!
5

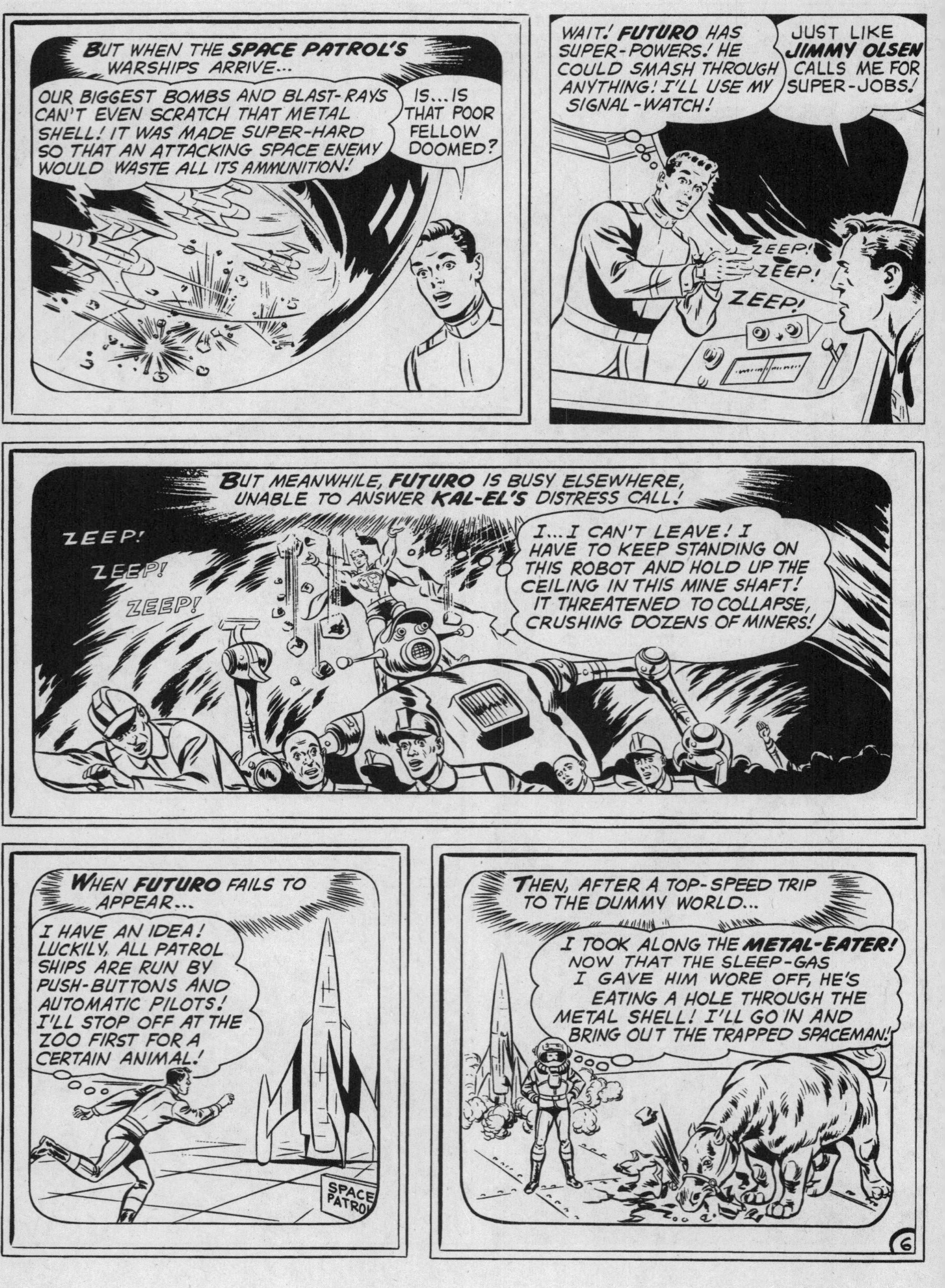
BUT WHEN THE SPACE PATROL'S WARSHIPS ARRIVE...
OUR BIGGEST BOMBS AND BLAST-RAYS CAN'T EVEN SCRATCH THAT METAL SHELL! IT WAS MADE SUPER-HARD SO THAT AN ATTACKING SPACE ENEMY WOULD WASTE ALL ITS AMMUNITION!
IS... IS THAT POOR FELLOW DOOMED?
WAIT! FUTURO HAS SUPER-POWERS! HE COULD SMASH THROUGH ANYTHING! I'LL USE MY SIGNAL-WATCH!
JUST LIKE JIMMY OLSEN CALLS ME FOR SUPER-JOBS!
ZEEP! ZEEP! ZEEP!
BUT MEANWHILE, FUTURO IS BUSY ELSEWHERE, UNABLE TO ANSWER KAL-EL'S DISTRESS CALL!
ZEEP! ZEEP! ZEEP!
I... I CAN'T LEAVE! I HAVE TO KEEP STANDING ON THIS ROBOT AND HOLD UP THE CEILING IN THIS MINE SHAFT! IT THREATENED TO COLLAPSE, CRUSHING DOZENS OF MINERS!
WHEN FUTURO FAILS TO APPEAR...
I HAVE AN IDEA! LUCKILY, ALL PATROL SHIPS ARE RUN BY PUSH-BUTTONS AND AUTOMATIC PILOTS! I'LL STOP OFF AT THE ZOO FIRST FOR A CERTAIN ANIMAL!
SPACE PATROL
THEN, AFTER A TOP-SPEED TRIP TO THE DUMMY WORLD...
I TOOK ALONG THE METAL-EATER! NOW THAT THE SLEEP-GAS I GAVE HIM WORE OFF, HE'S EATING A HOLE THROUGH THE METAL SHELL! I'LL GO IN AND BRING OUT THE TRAPPED SPACEMAN!
6

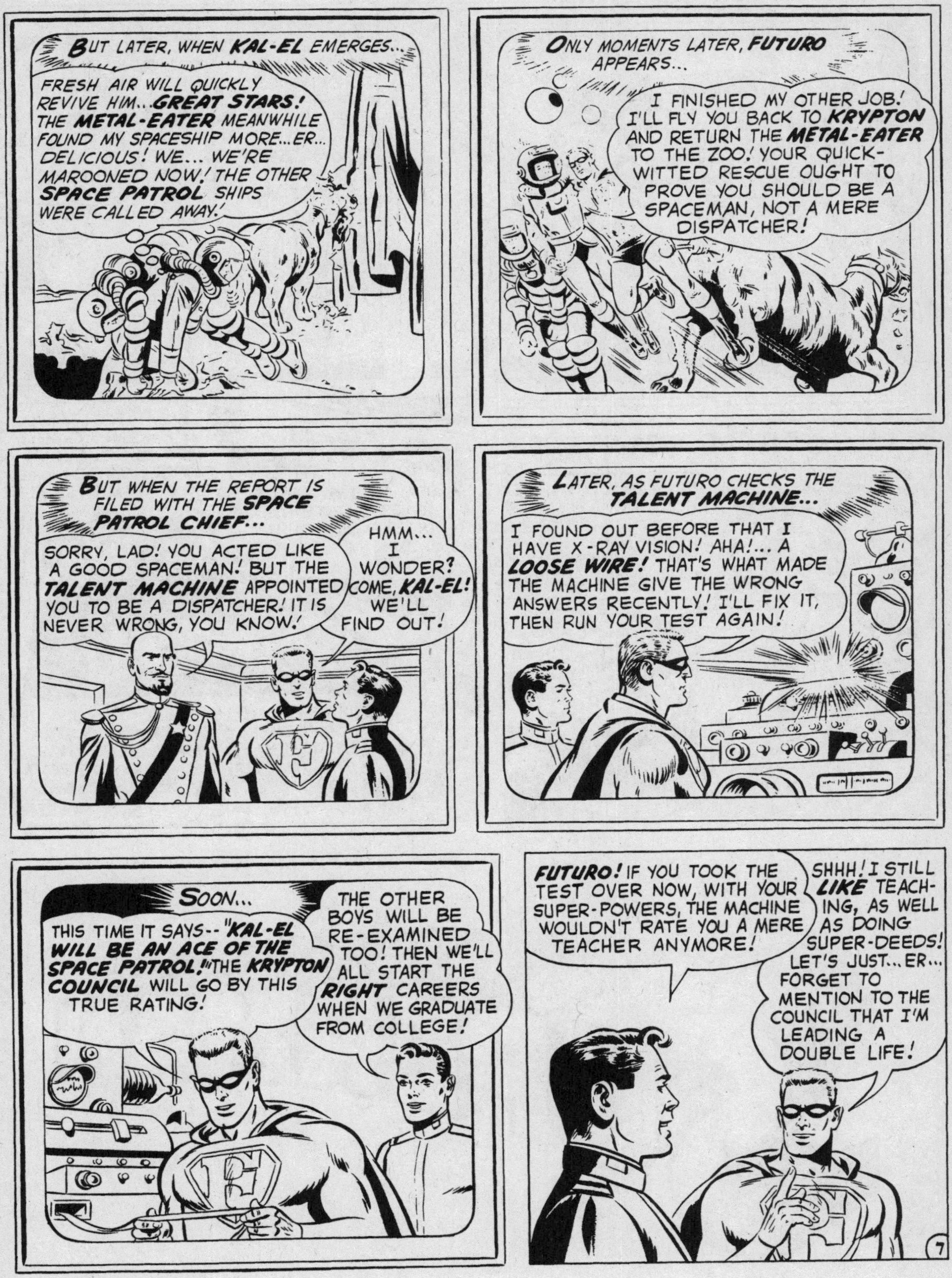
BUT LATER, WHEN KAL-EL EMERGES...
FRESH AIR WILL QUICKLY REVIVE HIM... GREAT STARS! THE METAL-EATER MEANWHILE FOUND MY SPACESHIP MORE...ER... DELICIOUS! WE... WE'RE MAROONED NOW! THE OTHER SPACE PATROL SHIPS WERE CALLED AWAY!
ONLY MOMENTS LATER, FUTURO APPEARS...
I FINISHED MY OTHER JOB! I'LL FLY YOU BACK TO KRYPTON AND RETURN THE METAL-EATER TO THE ZOO! YOUR QUICK-WITTED RESCUE OUGHT TO PROVE YOU SHOULD BE A SPACEMAN, NOT A MERE DISPATCHER!
BUT WHEN THE REPORT IS FILED WITH THE SPACE PATROL CHIEF...
SORRY, LAD! YOU ACTED LIKE A GOOD SPACEMAN! BUT THE TALENT MACHINE APPOINTED YOU TO BE A DISPATCHER! IT IS NEVER WRONG, YOU KNOW!
HMM... I WONDER? COME, KAL-EL! WE'LL FIND OUT!
LATER, AS FUTURO CHECKS THE TALENT MACHINE...
I FOUND OUT BEFORE THAT I HAVE X-RAY VISION! AHA!... A LOOSE WIRE! THAT'S WHAT MADE THE MACHINE GIVE THE WRONG ANSWERS RECENTLY! I'LL FIX IT, THEN RUN YOUR TEST AGAIN!
SOON...
THIS TIME IT SAYS-- "KAL-EL WILL BE AN ACE OF THE SPACE PATROL!" THE KRYPTON COUNCIL WILL GO BY THIS TRUE RATING!
THE OTHER BOYS WILL BE RE-EXAMINED TOO! THEN WE'LL ALL START THE RIGHT CAREERS WHEN WE GRADUATE FROM COLLEGE!
FUTURO! IF YOU TOOK THE TEST OVER NOW, WITH YOUR SUPER-POWERS, THE MACHINE WOULDN'T RATE YOU A MERE TEACHER ANYMORE!
SHHH! I STILL LIKE TEACHING, AS WELL AS DOING SUPER-DEEDS! LET'S JUST... ER... FORGET TO MENTION TO THE COUNCIL THAT I'M LEADING A DOUBLE LIFE!
7

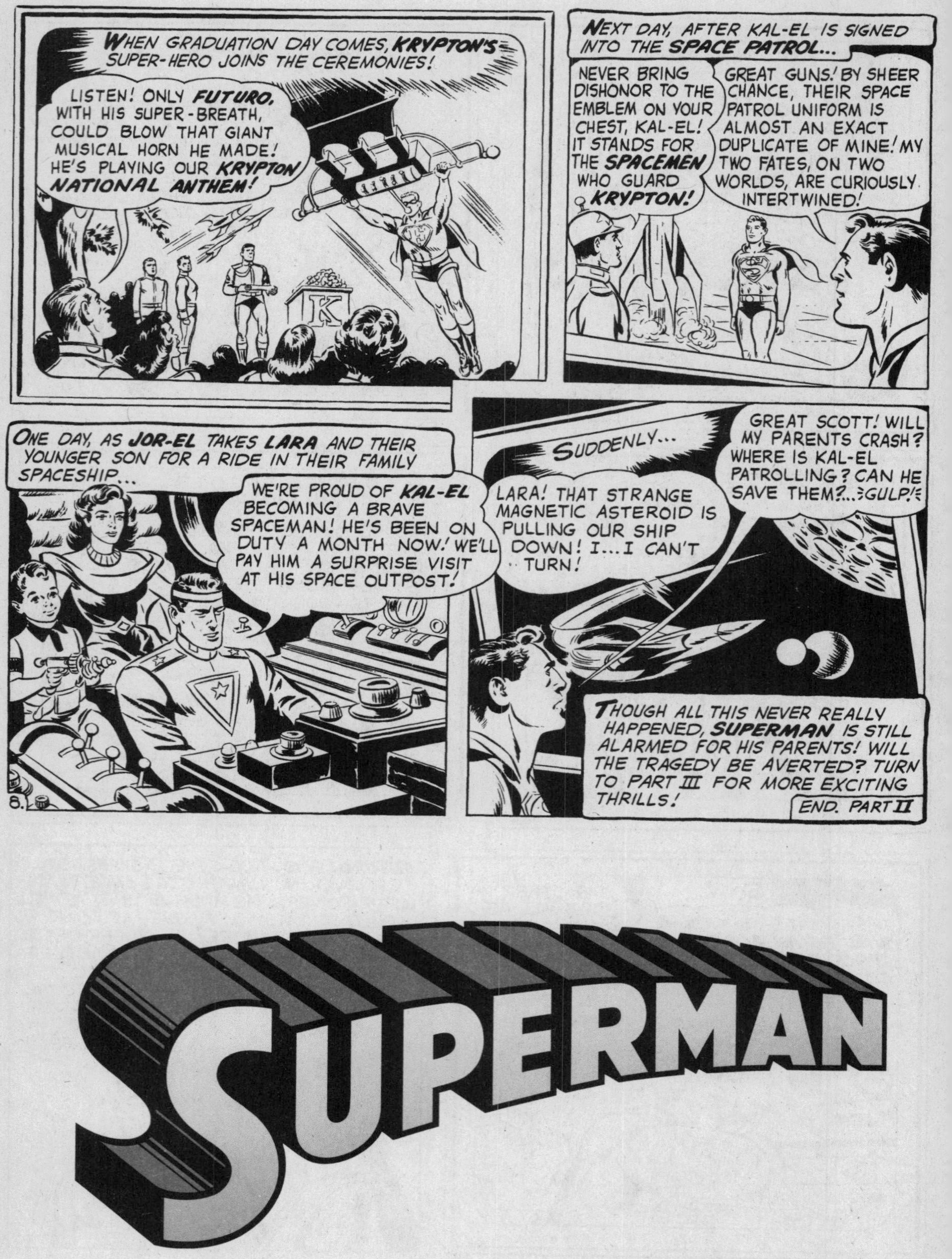
WHEN GRADUATION DAY COMES, KRYPTON'S SUPER-HERO JOINS THE CEREMONIES!
LISTEN! ONLY FUTURO, WITH HIS SUPER-BREATH, COULD BLOW THAT GIANT MUSICAL HORN HE MADE! HE'S PLAYING OUR KRYPTON NATIONAL ANTHEM!
NEXT DAY, AFTER KAL-EL IS SIGNED INTO THE SPACE PATROL...
NEVER BRING DISHONOR TO THE EMBLEM ON YOUR CHEST, KAL-EL! IT STANDS FOR THE SPACEMEN WHO GUARD KRYPTON!
GREAT GUNS! BY SHEER CHANCE, THEIR SPACE PATROL UNIFORM IS ALMOST AN EXACT DUPLICATE OF MINE! MY TWO FATES, ON TWO WORLDS, ARE CURIOUSLY INTERTWINED!
ONE DAY, AS JOR-EL TAKES LARA AND THEIR YOUNGER SON FOR A RIDE IN THEIR FAMILY SPACESHIP...
WE'RE PROUD OF KAL-EL BECOMING A BRAVE SPACEMAN! HE'S BEEN ON DUTY A MONTH NOW! WE'LL PAY HIM A SURPRISE VISIT AT HIS SPACE OUTPOST!
8.
SUDDENLY...
LARA! THAT STRANGE MAGNETIC ASTEROID IS PULLING OUR SHIP DOWN! I...I CAN'T TURN!
GREAT SCOTT! WILL MY PARENTS CRASH? WHERE IS KAL-EL PATROLLING? CAN HE SAVE THEM?...GULP!
THOUGH ALL THIS NEVER REALLY HAPPENED, SUPERMAN IS STILL ALARMED FOR HIS PARENTS! WILL THE TRAGEDY BE AVERTED? TURN TO PART III FOR MORE EXCITING THRILLS!
END. PART II

SUPERMAN

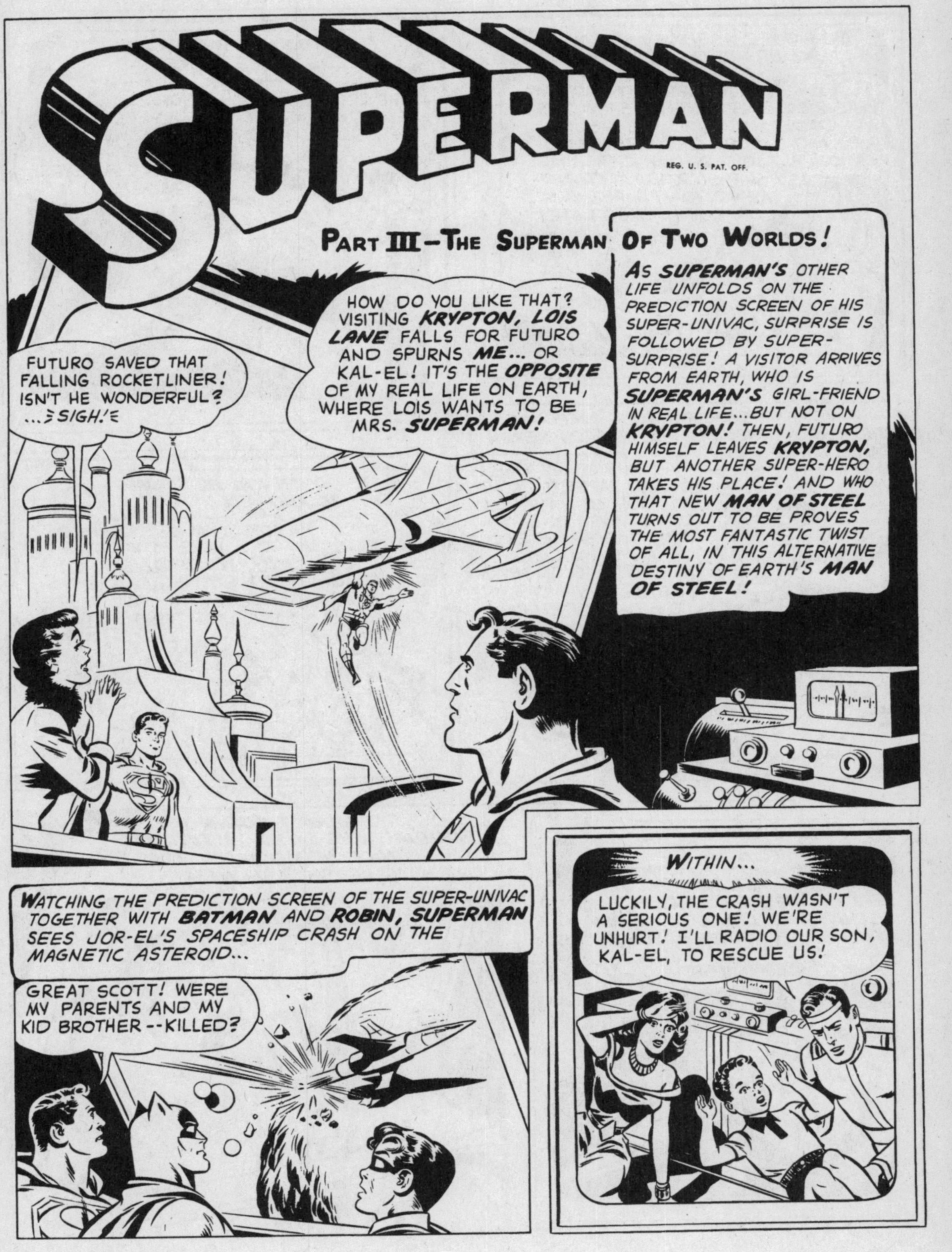
SUPERMAN
REG. U. S. PAT. OFF.
PART III—THE SUPERMAN OF TWO WORLDS!
AS SUPERMAN'S OTHER LIFE UNFOLDS ON THE PREDICTION SCREEN OF HIS SUPER-UNIVAC, SURPRISE IS FOLLOWED BY SUPER-SURPRISE! A VISITOR ARRIVES FROM EARTH, WHO IS SUPERMAN'S GIRL-FRIEND IN REAL LIFE...BUT NOT ON KRYPTON! THEN, FUTURO HIMSELF LEAVES KRYPTON, BUT ANOTHER SUPER-HERO TAKES HIS PLACE! AND WHO THAT NEW MAN OF STEEL TURNS OUT TO BE PROVES THE MOST FANTASTIC TWIST OF ALL, IN THIS ALTERNATIVE DESTINY OF EARTH'S MAN OF STEEL!
FUTURO SAVED THAT FALLING ROCKETLINER! ISN'T HE WONDERFUL? ...SIGH!
HOW DO YOU LIKE THAT? VISITING KRYPTON, LOIS LANE FALLS FOR FUTURO AND SPURNS ME... OR KAL-EL! IT'S THE OPPOSITE OF MY REAL LIFE ON EARTH, WHERE LOIS WANTS TO BE MRS. SUPERMAN!
WATCHING THE PREDICTION SCREEN OF THE SUPER-UNIVAC TOGETHER WITH BATMAN AND ROBIN, SUPERMAN SEES JOR-EL'S SPACESHIP CRASH ON THE MAGNETIC ASTEROID...
GREAT SCOTT! WERE MY PARENTS AND MY KID BROTHER--KILLED?
WITHIN...
LUCKILY, THE CRASH WASN'T A SERIOUS ONE! WE'RE UNHURT! I'LL RADIO OUR SON, KAL-EL, TO RESCUE US!

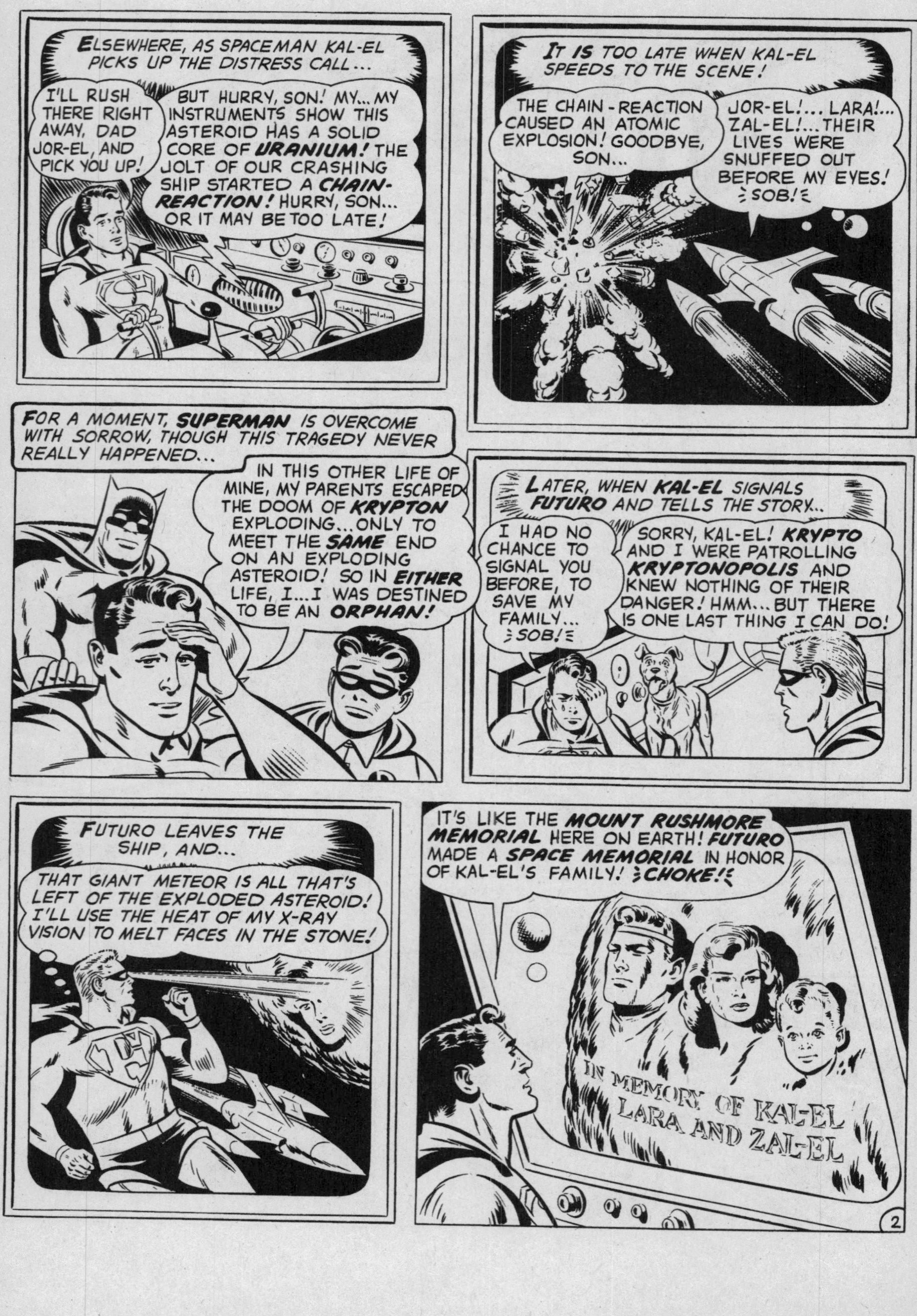
ELSEWHERE, AS SPACEMAN KAL-EL PICKS UP THE DISTRESS CALL...
I'LL RUSH THERE RIGHT AWAY, DAD JOR-EL, AND PICK YOU UP!
BUT HURRY, SON! MY... MY INSTRUMENTS SHOW THIS ASTEROID HAS A SOLID CORE OF URANIUM! THE JOLT OF OUR CRASHING SHIP STARTED A CHAIN-REACTION! HURRY, SON... OR IT MAY BE TOO LATE!
IT IS TOO LATE WHEN KAL-EL SPEEDS TO THE SCENE!
THE CHAIN-REACTION CAUSED AN ATOMIC EXPLOSION! GOODBYE, SON...
JOR-EL!... LARA!... ZAL-EL!... THEIR LIVES WERE SNUFFED OUT BEFORE MY EYES! SOB!
FOR A MOMENT, SUPERMAN IS OVERCOME WITH SORROW, THOUGH THIS TRAGEDY NEVER REALLY HAPPENED...
IN THIS OTHER LIFE OF MINE, MY PARENTS ESCAPED THE DOOM OF KRYPTON EXPLODING... ONLY TO MEET THE SAME END ON AN EXPLODING ASTEROID! SO IN EITHER LIFE, I... I WAS DESTINED TO BE AN ORPHAN!
LATER, WHEN KAL-EL SIGNALS FUTURO AND TELLS THE STORY...
I HAD NO CHANCE TO SIGNAL YOU BEFORE, TO SAVE MY FAMILY... SOB!
SORRY, KAL-EL! KRYPTO AND I WERE PATROLLING KRYPTONOPOLIS AND KNEW NOTHING OF THEIR DANGER! HMM... BUT THERE IS ONE LAST THING I CAN DO!
FUTURO LEAVES THE SHIP, AND...
THAT GIANT METEOR IS ALL THAT'S LEFT OF THE EXPLODED ASTEROID! I'LL USE THE HEAT OF MY X-RAY VISION TO MELT FACES IN THE STONE!
IT'S LIKE THE MOUNT RUSHMORE MEMORIAL HERE ON EARTH! FUTURO MADE A SPACE MEMORIAL IN HONOR OF KAL-EL'S FAMILY! CHOKE!
IN MEMORY OF KAL-EL LARA AND ZAL-EL
2

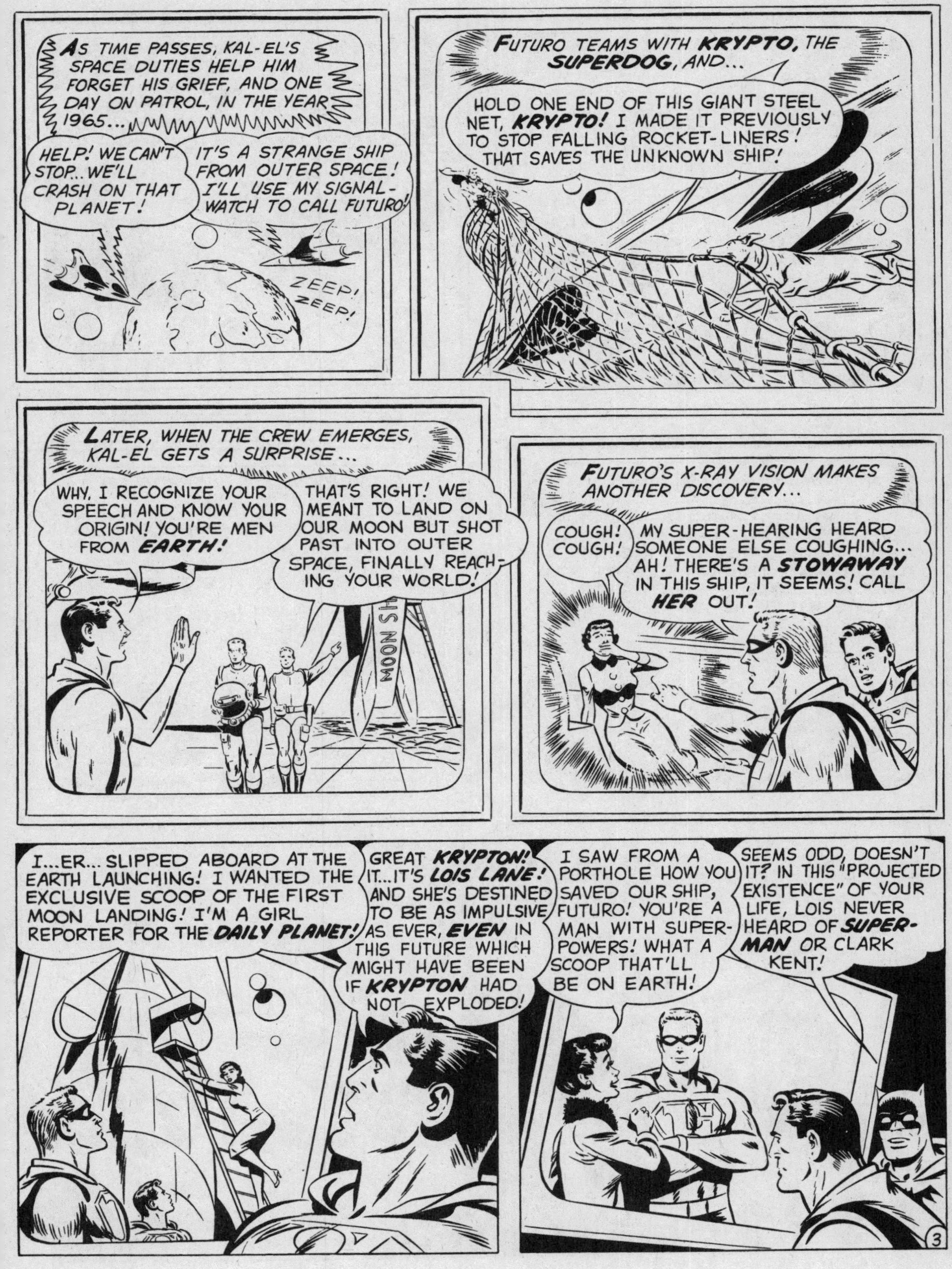
AS TIME PASSES, KAL-EL'S SPACE DUTIES HELP HIM FORGET HIS GRIEF, AND ONE DAY ON PATROL, IN THE YEAR 1965...
HELP! WE CAN'T STOP...WE'LL CRASH ON THAT PLANET!
IT'S A STRANGE SHIP FROM OUTER SPACE! I'LL USE MY SIGNAL-WATCH TO CALL FUTURO!
ZEEP! ZEEP!
FUTURO TEAMS WITH KRYPTO, THE SUPERDOG, AND...
HOLD ONE END OF THIS GIANT STEEL NET, KRYPTO! I MADE IT PREVIOUSLY TO STOP FALLING ROCKET-LINERS! THAT SAVES THE UNKNOWN SHIP!
LATER, WHEN THE CREW EMERGES, KAL-EL GETS A SURPRISE...
WHY, I RECOGNIZE YOUR SPEECH AND KNOW YOUR ORIGIN! YOU'RE MEN FROM EARTH!
THAT'S RIGHT! WE MEANT TO LAND ON OUR MOON BUT SHOT PAST INTO OUTER SPACE, FINALLY REACHING YOUR WORLD!
MOON IS
FUTURO'S X-RAY VISION MAKES ANOTHER DISCOVERY...
COUGH! COUGH!
MY SUPER-HEARING HEARD SOMEONE ELSE COUGHING... AH! THERE'S A STOWAWAY IN THIS SHIP, IT SEEMS! CALL HER OUT!
I...ER... SLIPPED ABOARD AT THE EARTH LAUNCHING! I WANTED THE EXCLUSIVE SCOOP OF THE FIRST MOON LANDING! I'M A GIRL REPORTER FOR THE DAILY PLANET!
GREAT KRYPTON! IT...IT'S LOIS LANE! AND SHE'S DESTINED TO BE AS IMPULSIVE AS EVER, EVEN IN THIS FUTURE WHICH MIGHT HAVE BEEN IF KRYPTON HAD NOT EXPLODED!
I SAW FROM A PORTHOLE HOW YOU SAVED OUR SHIP, FUTURO! YOU'RE A MAN WITH SUPER-POWERS! WHAT A SCOOP THAT'LL BE ON EARTH!
SEEMS ODD, DOESN'T IT? IN THIS "PROJECTED EXISTENCE" OF YOUR LIFE, LOIS NEVER HEARD OF SUPERMAN OR CLARK KENT!
3

PRESENTLY, WHEN KAL-EL'S CHIEF ARRIVES TO GREET THE VISITORS FROM EARTH...

THE TWO EARTH PILOTS AND I WILL COMPARE NOTES ON SPACE TRAVEL! KAL-EL, YOU ESCORT MISS LANE AROUND TOWN AND SHOW HER THE SIGHTS!

WITH PLEASURE, SIR!

KRYPTON'S SCIENTIFIC WONDERS ARE SHOWN TO THE EARTHGIRL!

WHEN A BLIZZARD STARTS, WE TURN ON OUR ARTIFICIAL SUN TO MELT THE SNOW BEFORE IT FALLS!

GOODNESS! YOU CONTROL YOUR OWN WEATHER!

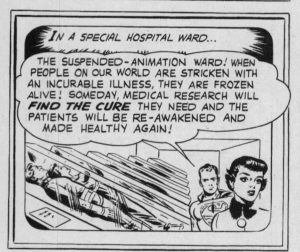

IN A SPECIAL HOSPITAL WARD...

THE SUSPENDED-ANIMATION WARD! WHEN PEOPLE ON OUR WORLD ARE STRICKEN WITH AN INCURABLE ILLNESS, THEY ARE FROZEN ALIVE! SOMEDAY, MEDICAL RESEARCH WILL FIND THE CURE THEY NEED AND THE PATIENTS WILL BE RE-AWAKENED AND MADE HEALTHY AGAIN!

LATER, TAKING LOIS IN A PASSENGER ROCKET TO THE DESERT...

WAR IS OBSOLETE ON KRYPTON, MISS LANE! FORMER WEAPONS ARE ON EXHIBIT IN THAT MUSEUM AS CURIOSITIES! THEY HAVEN'T BEEN USED FOR CENTURIES!

HMM...IS THAT A SUBMARINE LIKE WE HAVE ON EARTH?

NO! THAT'S THE SUBSURFACER! IT COULD DRILL THROUGH ROCK AND CRUISE UNDERGROUND! IT WOULD TORPEDO CITIES FROM BELOW!

4

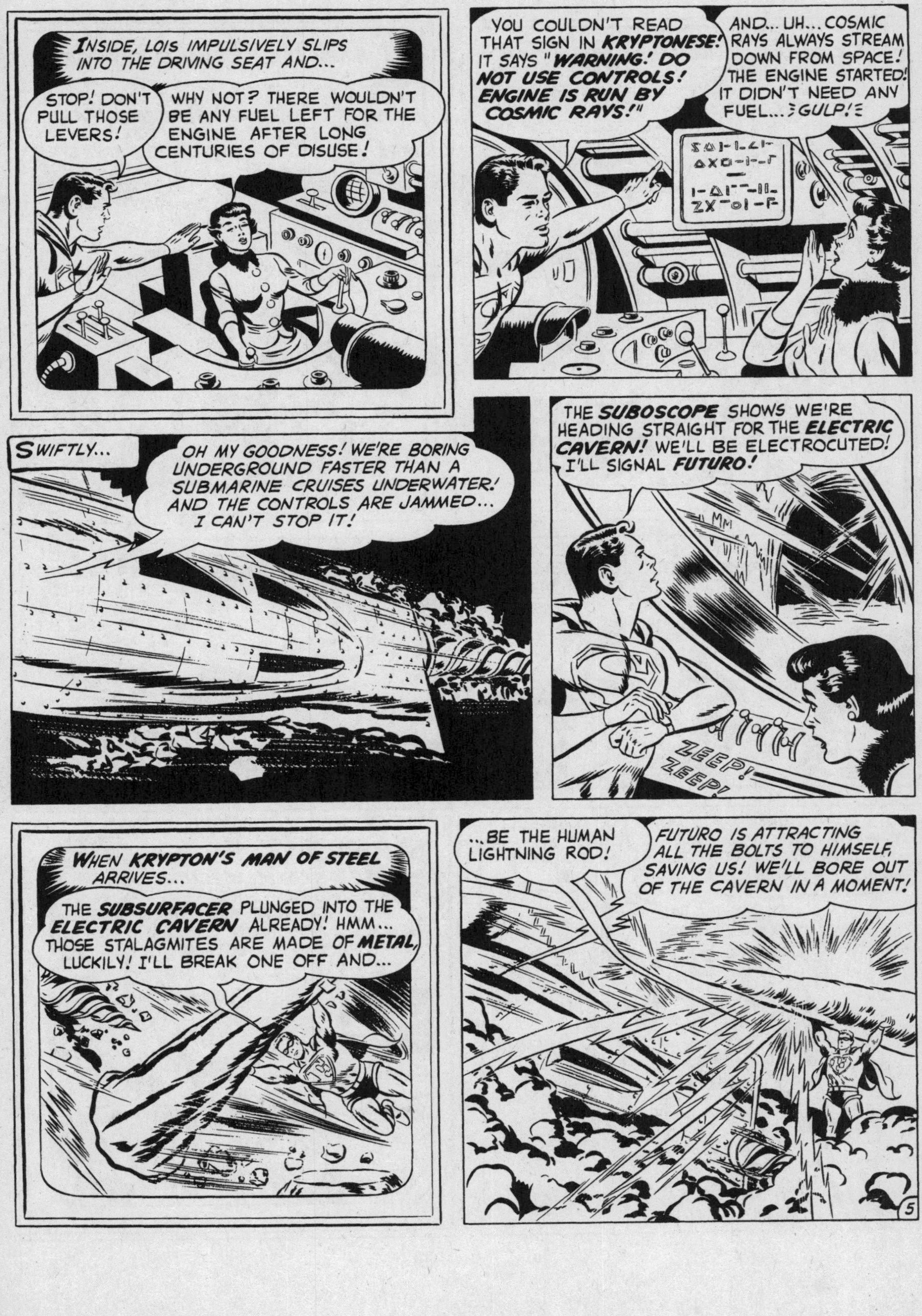
INSIDE, LOIS IMPULSIVELY SLIPS INTO THE DRIVING SEAT AND...
STOP! DON'T PULL THOSE LEVERS!
WHY NOT? THERE WOULDN'T BE ANY FUEL LEFT FOR THE ENGINE AFTER LONG CENTURIES OF DISUSE!
YOU COULDN'T READ THAT SIGN IN KRYPTONESE! IT SAYS "WARNING! DO NOT USE CONTROLS! ENGINE IS RUN BY COSMIC RAYS!"
AND... UH... COSMIC RAYS ALWAYS STREAM DOWN FROM SPACE! THE ENGINE STARTED! IT DIDN'T NEED ANY FUEL... GULP!
SWIFTLY...
OH MY GOODNESS! WE'RE BORING UNDERGROUND FASTER THAN A SUBMARINE CRUISES UNDERWATER! AND THE CONTROLS ARE JAMMED... I CAN'T STOP IT!
THE SUBOSCOPE SHOWS WE'RE HEADING STRAIGHT FOR THE ELECTRIC CAVERN! WE'LL BE ELECTROCUTED! I'LL SIGNAL FUTURO!
ZEEP! ZEEP!
WHEN KRYPTON'S MAN OF STEEL ARRIVES...
THE SUBSURFACER PLUNGED INTO THE ELECTRIC CAVERN ALREADY! HMM... THOSE STALAGMITES ARE MADE OF METAL, LUCKILY! I'LL BREAK ONE OFF AND...
...BE THE HUMAN LIGHTNING ROD!
FUTURO IS ATTRACTING ALL THE BOLTS TO HIMSELF, SAVING US! WE'LL BORE OUT OF THE CAVERN IN A MOMENT!
5

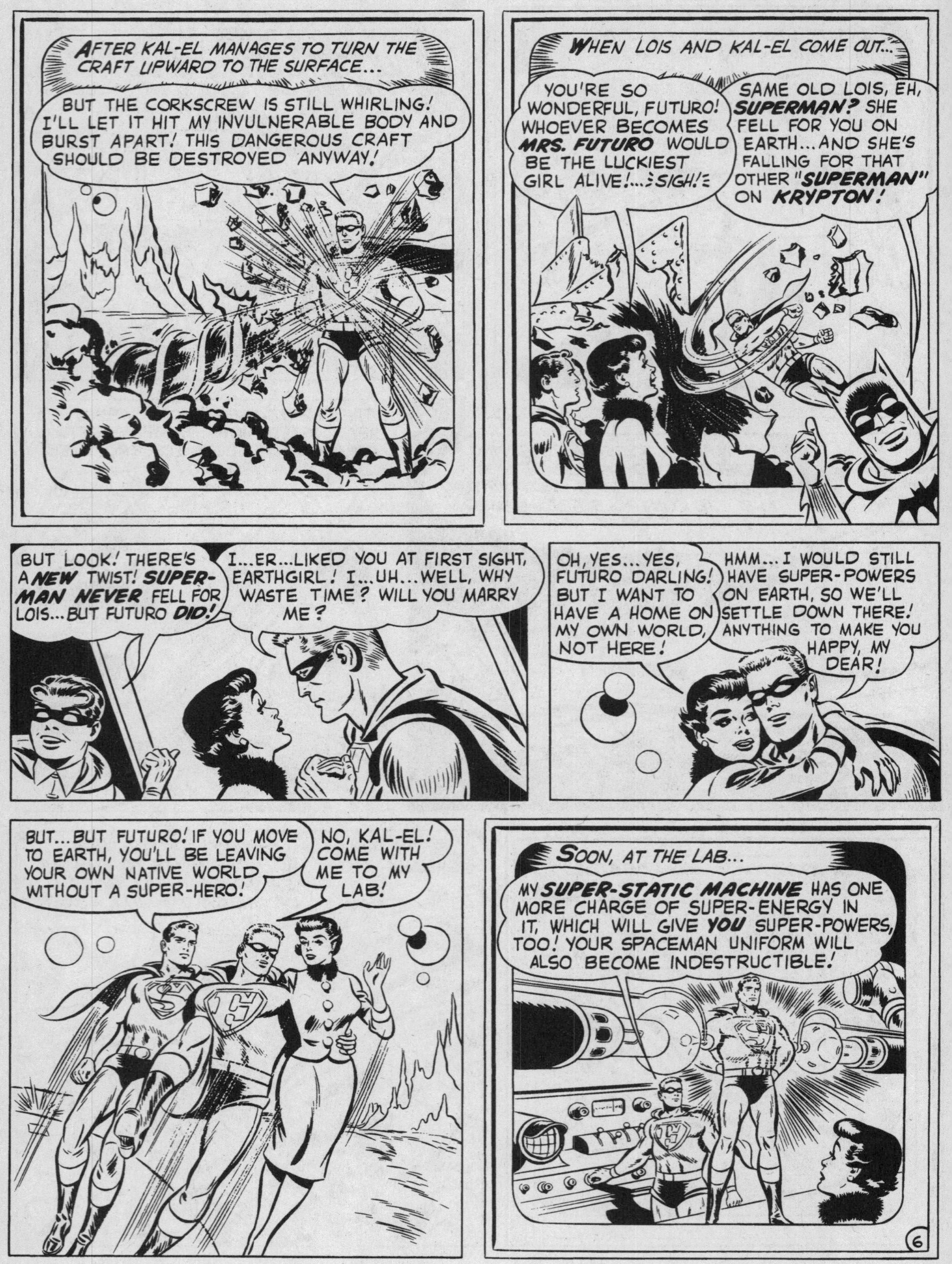
AFTER KAL-EL MANAGES TO TURN THE CRAFT UPWARD TO THE SURFACE...
BUT THE CORKSCREW IS STILL WHIRLING! I'LL LET IT HIT MY INVULNERABLE BODY AND BURST APART! THIS DANGEROUS CRAFT SHOULD BE DESTROYED ANYWAY!
WHEN LOIS AND KAL-EL COME OUT...
YOU'RE SO WONDERFUL, FUTURO! WHOEVER BECOMES MRS. FUTURO WOULD BE THE LUCKIEST GIRL ALIVE!... SIGH!
SAME OLD LOIS, EH, SUPERMAN? SHE FELL FOR YOU ON EARTH... AND SHE'S FALLING FOR THAT OTHER "SUPERMAN" ON KRYPTON!
BUT LOOK! THERE'S A NEW TWIST! SUPERMAN NEVER FELL FOR LOIS... BUT FUTURO DID!
I...ER...LIKED YOU AT FIRST SIGHT, EARTHGIRL! I...UH...WELL, WHY WASTE TIME? WILL YOU MARRY ME?
OH, YES...YES, FUTURO DARLING! BUT I WANT TO HAVE A HOME ON MY OWN WORLD, NOT HERE!
HMM... I WOULD STILL HAVE SUPER-POWERS ON EARTH, SO WE'LL SETTLE DOWN THERE! ANYTHING TO MAKE YOU HAPPY, MY DEAR!
BUT...BUT FUTURO! IF YOU MOVE TO EARTH, YOU'LL BE LEAVING YOUR OWN NATIVE WORLD WITHOUT A SUPER-HERO!
NO, KAL-EL! COME WITH ME TO MY LAB!
SOON, AT THE LAB...
MY SUPER-STATIC MACHINE HAS ONE MORE CHARGE OF SUPER-ENERGY IN IT, WHICH WILL GIVE YOU SUPER-POWERS, TOO! YOUR SPACEMAN UNIFORM WILL ALSO BECOME INDESTRUCTIBLE!
6

LATER, AS FUTURO GATHERS A CROWD TO ANNOUNCE HIS DEPARTURE...

GOODBYE, FRIENDS! I WILL MARRY *LOIS LANE* ON EARTH! I WILL BE GONE, BUT I LEAVE YOU WITH A NEW SUPER-HERO WHO WILL DEMONSTRATE HIS SUPER-POWERS BY...

...LAUNCHING THE EARTH-SHIP INTO SPACE WITH HIS SUPER-STRENGTH! HE WILL TELL YOU THE NAME HE CHOSE FOR HIMSELF, DIFFERENT FROM MINE!

I THOUGHT OF A NAME FOR MYSELF OUT OF THIN AIR... *SUPERMAN!*

UTTERLY STARTLED, *SUPERMAN* ON EARTH TURNS OFF HIS SUPER-UNIVAC, WHICH HAS SHOWN THE OTHER LIFE HE WOULD HAVE LIVED IF *KRYPTON* HAD NOT EXPLODED...

HOW STRANGE FATE WORKS! IF *KRYPTON* HAD NEVER EXPLODED, I WOULD HAVE ENDED UP THERE AS— *SUPERMAN!*

The End.

CLICK!

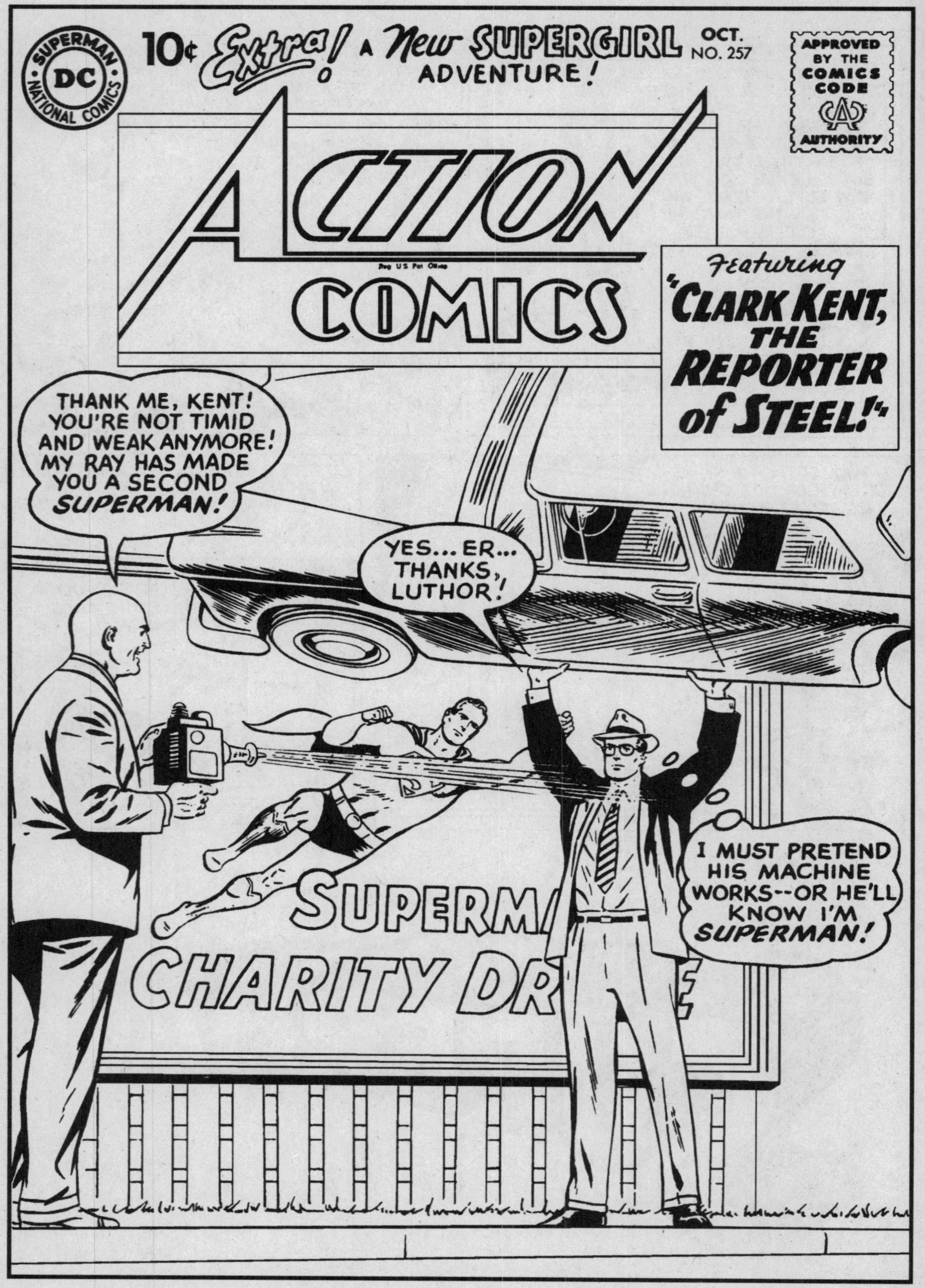
SUPERMAN DC NATIONAL COMICS
10¢ Extra! A New SUPERGIRL ADVENTURE!
OCT. NO. 257
APPROVED BY THE COMICS CODE AUTHORITY
ACTION COMICS
Featuring "CLARK KENT, THE REPORTER of STEEL!"
THANK ME, KENT! YOU'RE NOT TIMID AND WEAK ANYMORE! MY RAY HAS MADE YOU A SECOND SUPERMAN!
YES... ER... THANKS, LUTHOR!
I MUST PRETEND HIS MACHINE WORKS--OR HE'LL KNOW I'M SUPERMAN!
SUPERM
CHARITY DR

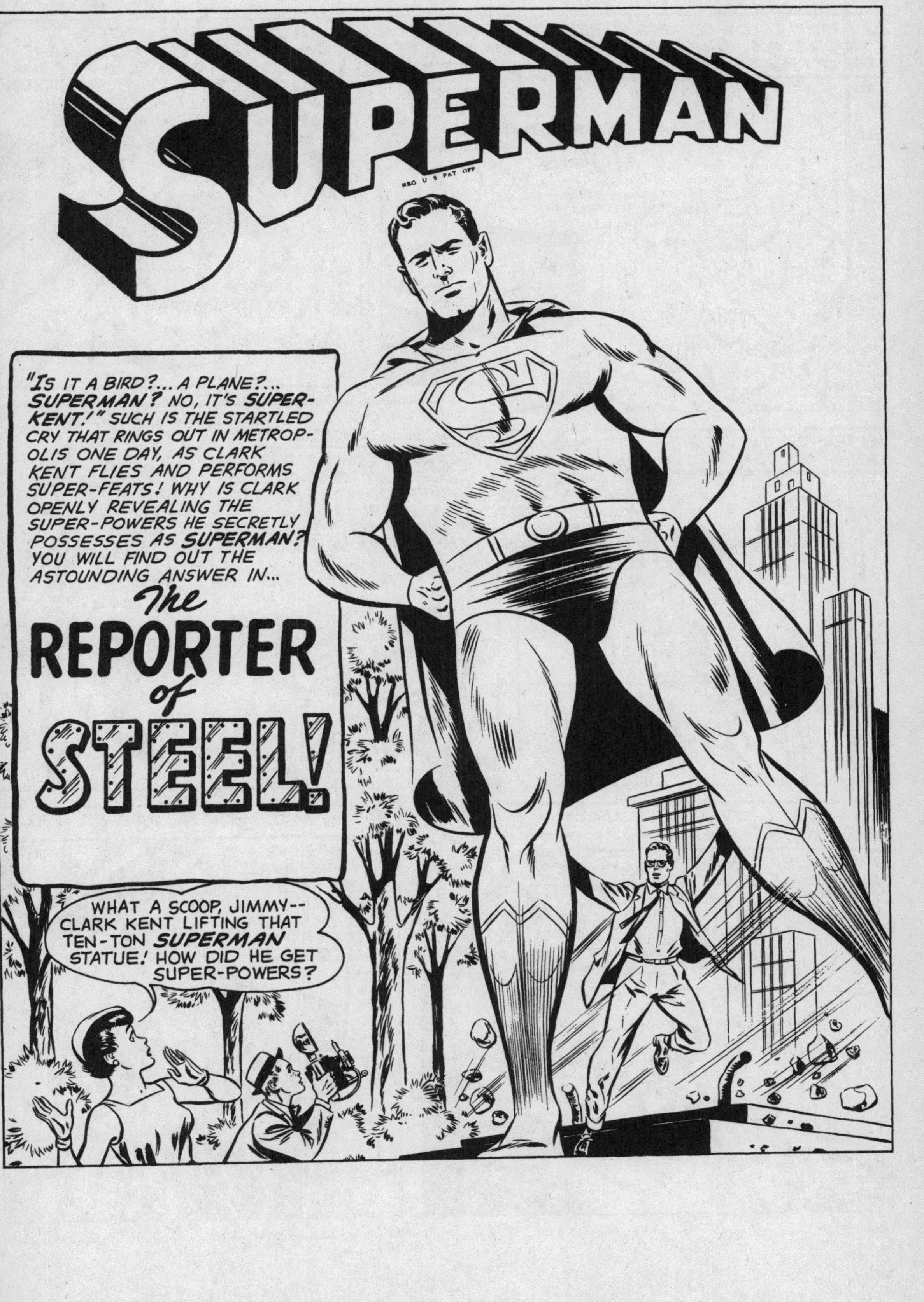
SUPERMAN
REG U S PAT OFF
"IS IT A BIRD?... A PLANE?... SUPERMAN? NO, IT'S SUPER-KENT!" SUCH IS THE STARTLED CRY THAT RINGS OUT IN METROPOLIS ONE DAY, AS CLARK KENT FLIES AND PERFORMS SUPER-FEATS! WHY IS CLARK OPENLY REVEALING THE SUPER-POWERS HE SECRETLY POSSESSES AS SUPERMAN? YOU WILL FIND OUT THE ASTOUNDING ANSWER IN...
The REPORTER of STEEL!
WHAT A SCOOP, JIMMY-- CLARK KENT LIFTING THAT TEN-TON SUPERMAN STATUE! HOW DID HE GET SUPER-POWERS?

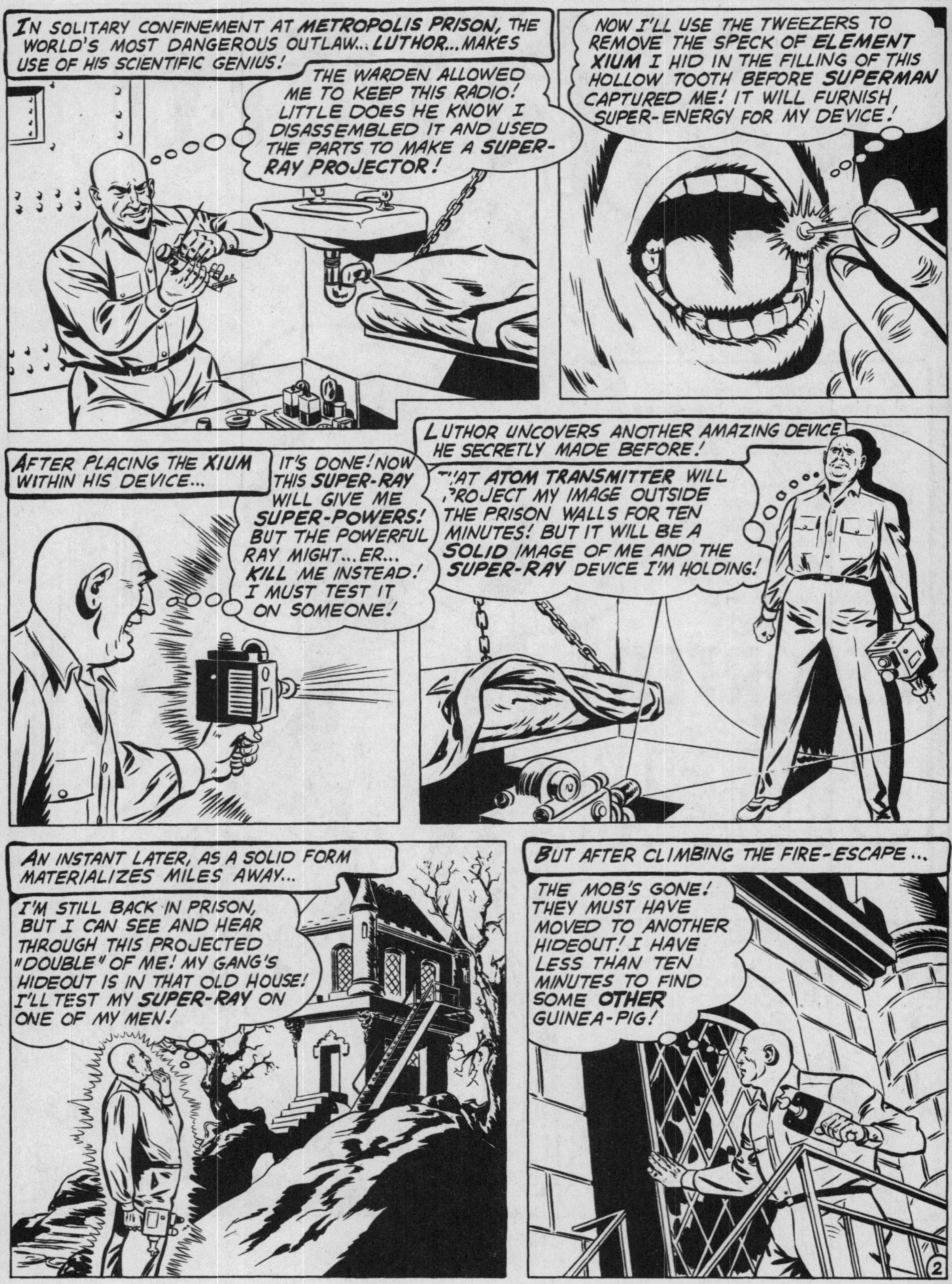
IN SOLITARY CONFINEMENT AT METROPOLIS PRISON, THE WORLD'S MOST DANGEROUS OUTLAW... LUTHOR... MAKES USE OF HIS SCIENTIFIC GENIUS!
THE WARDEN ALLOWED ME TO KEEP THIS RADIO! LITTLE DOES HE KNOW I DISASSEMBLED IT AND USED THE PARTS TO MAKE A SUPER-RAY PROJECTOR!
NOW I'LL USE THE TWEEZERS TO REMOVE THE SPECK OF ELEMENT XIUM I HID IN THE FILLING OF THIS HOLLOW TOOTH BEFORE SUPERMAN CAPTURED ME! IT WILL FURNISH SUPER-ENERGY FOR MY DEVICE!
AFTER PLACING THE XIUM WITHIN HIS DEVICE...
IT'S DONE! NOW THIS SUPER-RAY WILL GIVE ME SUPER-POWERS! BUT THE POWERFUL RAY MIGHT... ER... KILL ME INSTEAD! I MUST TEST IT ON SOMEONE!
LUTHOR UNCOVERS ANOTHER AMAZING DEVICE HE SECRETLY MADE BEFORE!
THAT ATOM TRANSMITTER WILL PROJECT MY IMAGE OUTSIDE THE PRISON WALLS FOR TEN MINUTES! BUT IT WILL BE A SOLID IMAGE OF ME AND THE SUPER-RAY DEVICE I'M HOLDING!
AN INSTANT LATER, AS A SOLID FORM MATERIALIZES MILES AWAY...
I'M STILL BACK IN PRISON, BUT I CAN SEE AND HEAR THROUGH THIS PROJECTED "DOUBLE" OF ME! MY GANG'S HIDEOUT IS IN THAT OLD HOUSE! I'LL TEST MY SUPER-RAY ON ONE OF MY MEN!
BUT AFTER CLIMBING THE FIRE-ESCAPE...
THE MOB'S GONE! THEY MUST HAVE MOVED TO ANOTHER HIDEOUT! I HAVE LESS THAN TEN MINUTES TO FIND SOME OTHER GUINEA-PIG!
2

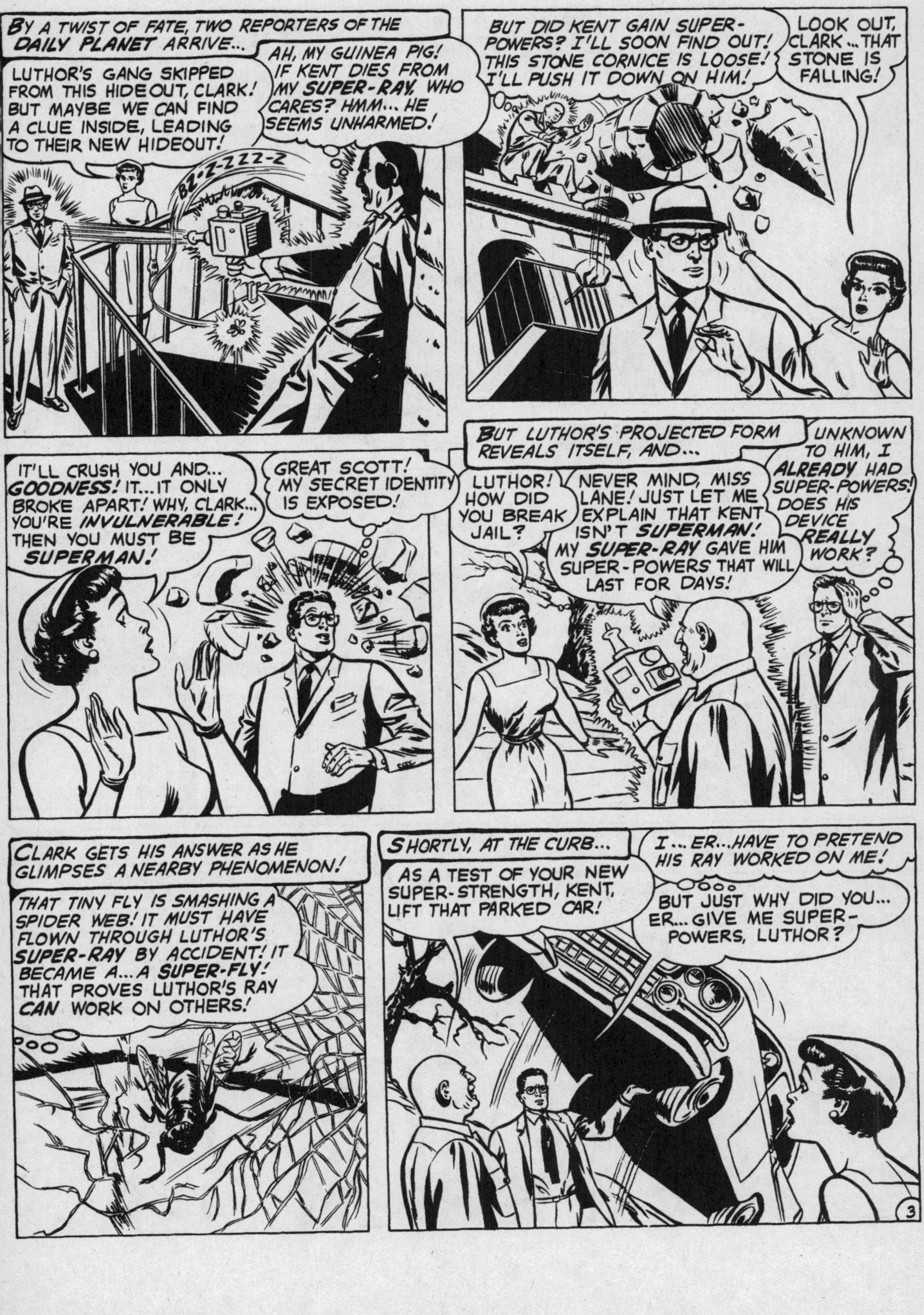
BY A TWIST OF FATE, TWO REPORTERS OF THE DAILY PLANET ARRIVE...
LUTHOR'S GANG SKIPPED FROM THIS HIDEOUT, CLARK! BUT MAYBE WE CAN FIND A CLUE INSIDE, LEADING TO THEIR NEW HIDEOUT!
AH, MY GUINEA PIG! IF KENT DIES FROM MY SUPER-RAY, WHO CARES? HMM... HE SEEMS UNHARMED!
BZ-Z-ZZZ-Z
BUT DID KENT GAIN SUPER-POWERS? I'LL SOON FIND OUT! THIS STONE CORNICE IS LOOSE! I'LL PUSH IT DOWN ON HIM!
LOOK OUT, CLARK...THAT STONE IS FALLING!
IT'LL CRUSH YOU AND... GOODNESS! IT...IT ONLY BROKE APART! WHY, CLARK... YOU'RE INVULNERABLE! THEN YOU MUST BE SUPERMAN!
GREAT SCOTT! MY SECRET IDENTITY IS EXPOSED!
BUT LUTHOR'S PROJECTED FORM REVEALS ITSELF, AND...
LUTHOR! HOW DID YOU BREAK JAIL?
NEVER MIND, MISS LANE! JUST LET ME EXPLAIN THAT KENT ISN'T SUPERMAN! MY SUPER-RAY GAVE HIM SUPER-POWERS THAT WILL LAST FOR DAYS!
UNKNOWN TO HIM, I ALREADY HAD SUPER-POWERS! DOES HIS DEVICE REALLY WORK?
CLARK GETS HIS ANSWER AS HE GLIMPSES A NEARBY PHENOMENON!
THAT TINY FLY IS SMASHING A SPIDER WEB! IT MUST HAVE FLOWN THROUGH LUTHOR'S SUPER-RAY BY ACCIDENT! IT BECAME A...A SUPER-FLY! THAT PROVES LUTHOR'S RAY CAN WORK ON OTHERS!
SHORTLY, AT THE CURB...
AS A TEST OF YOUR NEW SUPER-STRENGTH, KENT, LIFT THAT PARKED CAR!
I... ER...HAVE TO PRETEND HIS RAY WORKED ON ME!
BUT JUST WHY DID YOU... ER...GIVE ME SUPER-POWERS, LUTHOR?
3

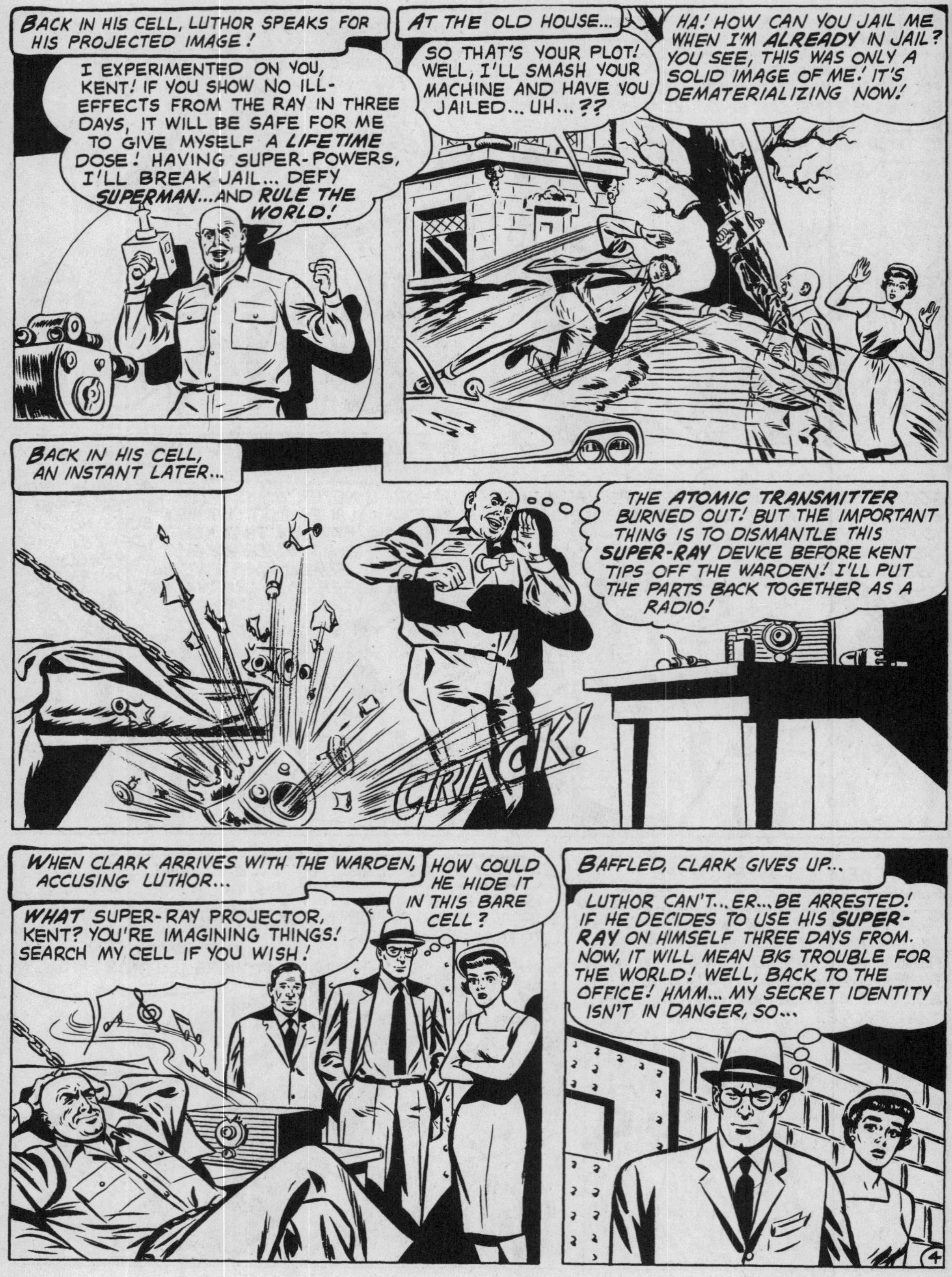
BACK IN HIS CELL, LUTHOR SPEAKS FOR HIS PROJECTED IMAGE!
I EXPERIMENTED ON YOU, KENT! IF YOU SHOW NO ILL-EFFECTS FROM THE RAY IN THREE DAYS, IT WILL BE SAFE FOR ME TO GIVE MYSELF A LIFETIME DOSE! HAVING SUPER-POWERS, I'LL BREAK JAIL... DEFY SUPERMAN...AND RULE THE WORLD!
AT THE OLD HOUSE...
SO THAT'S YOUR PLOT! WELL, I'LL SMASH YOUR MACHINE AND HAVE YOU JAILED... UH...??
HA! HOW CAN YOU JAIL ME WHEN I'M ALREADY IN JAIL? YOU SEE, THIS WAS ONLY A SOLID IMAGE OF ME! IT'S DEMATERIALIZING NOW!
BACK IN HIS CELL, AN INSTANT LATER...
THE ATOMIC TRANSMITTER BURNED OUT! BUT THE IMPORTANT THING IS TO DISMANTLE THIS SUPER-RAY DEVICE BEFORE KENT TIPS OFF THE WARDEN! I'LL PUT THE PARTS BACK TOGETHER AS A RADIO!
CRACK!
WHEN CLARK ARRIVES WITH THE WARDEN, ACCUSING LUTHOR...
WHAT SUPER-RAY PROJECTOR, KENT? YOU'RE IMAGINING THINGS! SEARCH MY CELL IF YOU WISH!
HOW COULD HE HIDE IT IN THIS BARE CELL?
BAFFLED, CLARK GIVES UP...
LUTHOR CAN'T...ER...BE ARRESTED! IF HE DECIDES TO USE HIS SUPER-RAY ON HIMSELF THREE DAYS FROM NOW, IT WILL MEAN BIG TROUBLE FOR THE WORLD! WELL, BACK TO THE OFFICE! HMM... MY SECRET IDENTITY ISN'T IN DANGER, SO...
4

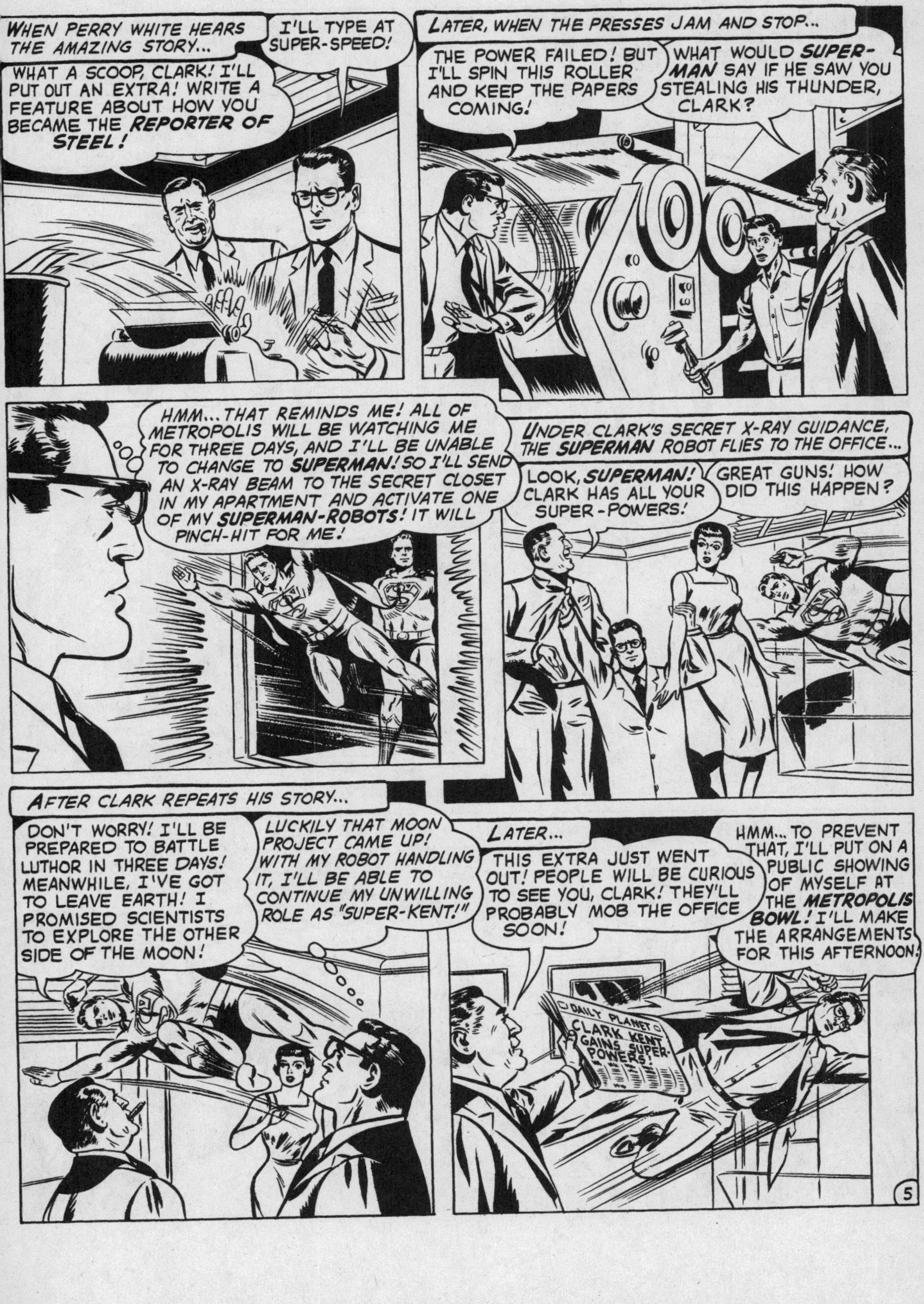
WHEN PERRY WHITE HEARS THE AMAZING STORY...
WHAT A SCOOP, CLARK! I'LL PUT OUT AN EXTRA! WRITE A FEATURE ABOUT HOW YOU BECAME THE REPORTER OF STEEL!
I'LL TYPE AT SUPER-SPEED!
LATER, WHEN THE PRESSES JAM AND STOP...
THE POWER FAILED! BUT I'LL SPIN THIS ROLLER AND KEEP THE PAPERS COMING!
WHAT WOULD SUPERMAN SAY IF HE SAW YOU STEALING HIS THUNDER, CLARK?
HMM... THAT REMINDS ME! ALL OF METROPOLIS WILL BE WATCHING ME FOR THREE DAYS, AND I'LL BE UNABLE TO CHANGE TO SUPERMAN! SO I'LL SEND AN X-RAY BEAM TO THE SECRET CLOSET IN MY APARTMENT AND ACTIVATE ONE OF MY SUPERMAN-ROBOTS! IT WILL PINCH-HIT FOR ME!
UNDER CLARK'S SECRET X-RAY GUIDANCE, THE SUPERMAN ROBOT FLIES TO THE OFFICE...
LOOK, SUPERMAN! CLARK HAS ALL YOUR SUPER-POWERS!
GREAT GUNS! HOW DID THIS HAPPEN?
AFTER CLARK REPEATS HIS STORY...
DON'T WORRY! I'LL BE PREPARED TO BATTLE LUTHOR IN THREE DAYS! MEANWHILE, I'VE GOT TO LEAVE EARTH! I PROMISED SCIENTISTS TO EXPLORE THE OTHER SIDE OF THE MOON!
LUCKILY THAT MOON PROJECT CAME UP! WITH MY ROBOT HANDLING IT, I'LL BE ABLE TO CONTINUE MY UNWILLING ROLE AS "SUPER-KENT!"
LATER...
THIS EXTRA JUST WENT OUT! PEOPLE WILL BE CURIOUS TO SEE YOU, CLARK! THEY'LL PROBABLY MOB THE OFFICE SOON!
DAILY PLANET
CLARK KENT GAINS SUPER-POWERS!
HMM... TO PREVENT THAT, I'LL PUT ON A PUBLIC SHOWING OF MYSELF AT THE METROPOLIS BOWL! I'LL MAKE THE ARRANGEMENTS FOR THIS AFTERNOON!
5

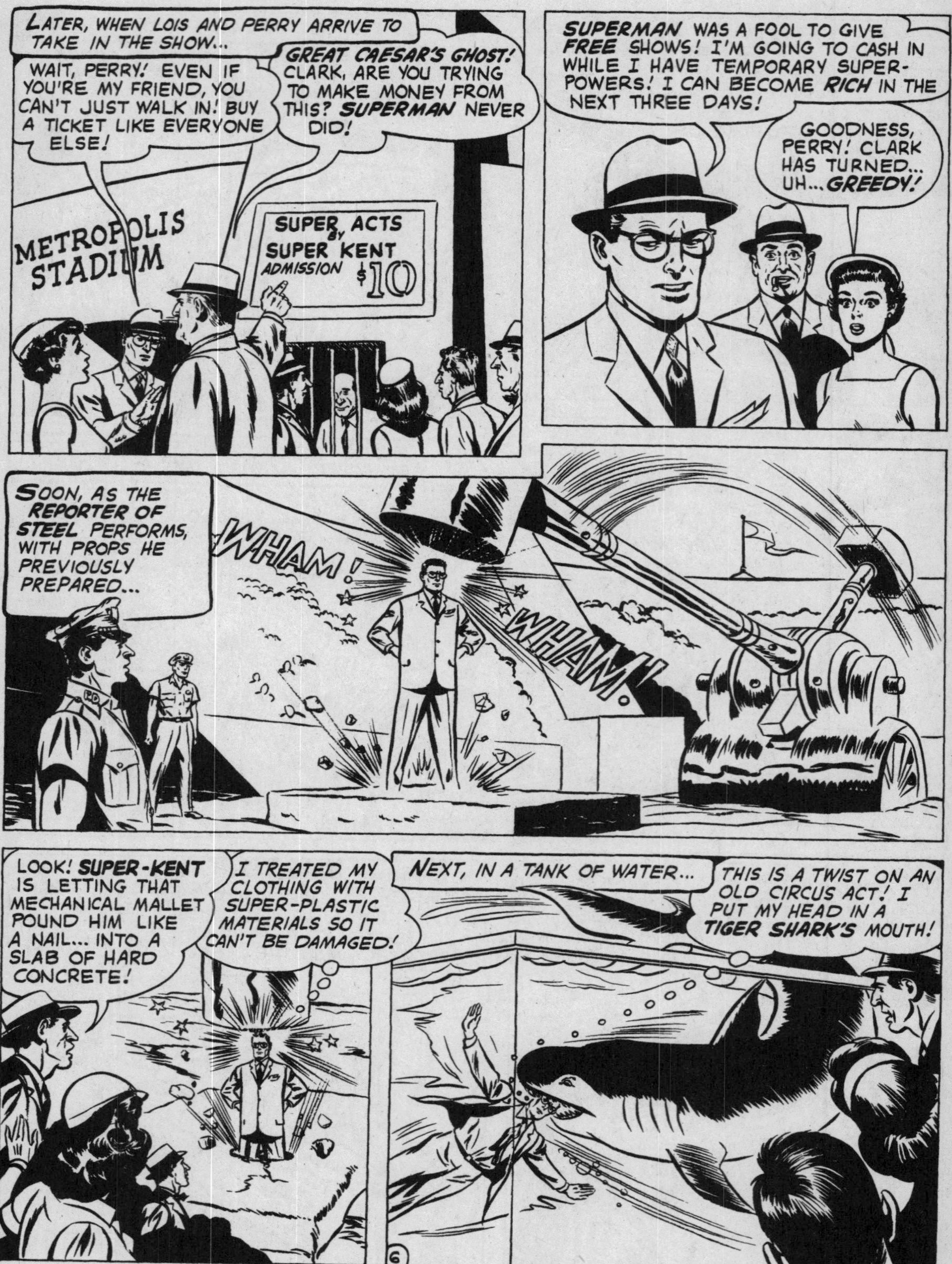
LATER, WHEN LOIS AND PERRY ARRIVE TO TAKE IN THE SHOW...
WAIT, PERRY! EVEN IF YOU'RE MY FRIEND, YOU CAN'T JUST WALK IN! BUY A TICKET LIKE EVERYONE ELSE!
GREAT CAESAR'S GHOST! CLARK, ARE YOU TRYING TO MAKE MONEY FROM THIS? SUPERMAN NEVER DID!
METROPOLIS STADIUM
SUPER ACTS BY SUPER KENT ADMISSION $10
SUPERMAN WAS A FOOL TO GIVE FREE SHOWS! I'M GOING TO CASH IN WHILE I HAVE TEMPORARY SUPER-POWERS! I CAN BECOME RICH IN THE NEXT THREE DAYS!
GOODNESS, PERRY! CLARK HAS TURNED... UH... GREEDY!
SOON, AS THE REPORTER OF STEEL PERFORMS, WITH PROPS HE PREVIOUSLY PREPARED...
WHAM!
WHAM!
LOOK! SUPER-KENT IS LETTING THAT MECHANICAL MALLET POUND HIM LIKE A NAIL... INTO A SLAB OF HARD CONCRETE!
I TREATED MY CLOTHING WITH SUPER-PLASTIC MATERIALS SO IT CAN'T BE DAMAGED!
NEXT, IN A TANK OF WATER...
THIS IS A TWIST ON AN OLD CIRCUS ACT! I PUT MY HEAD IN A TIGER SHARK'S MOUTH!
6

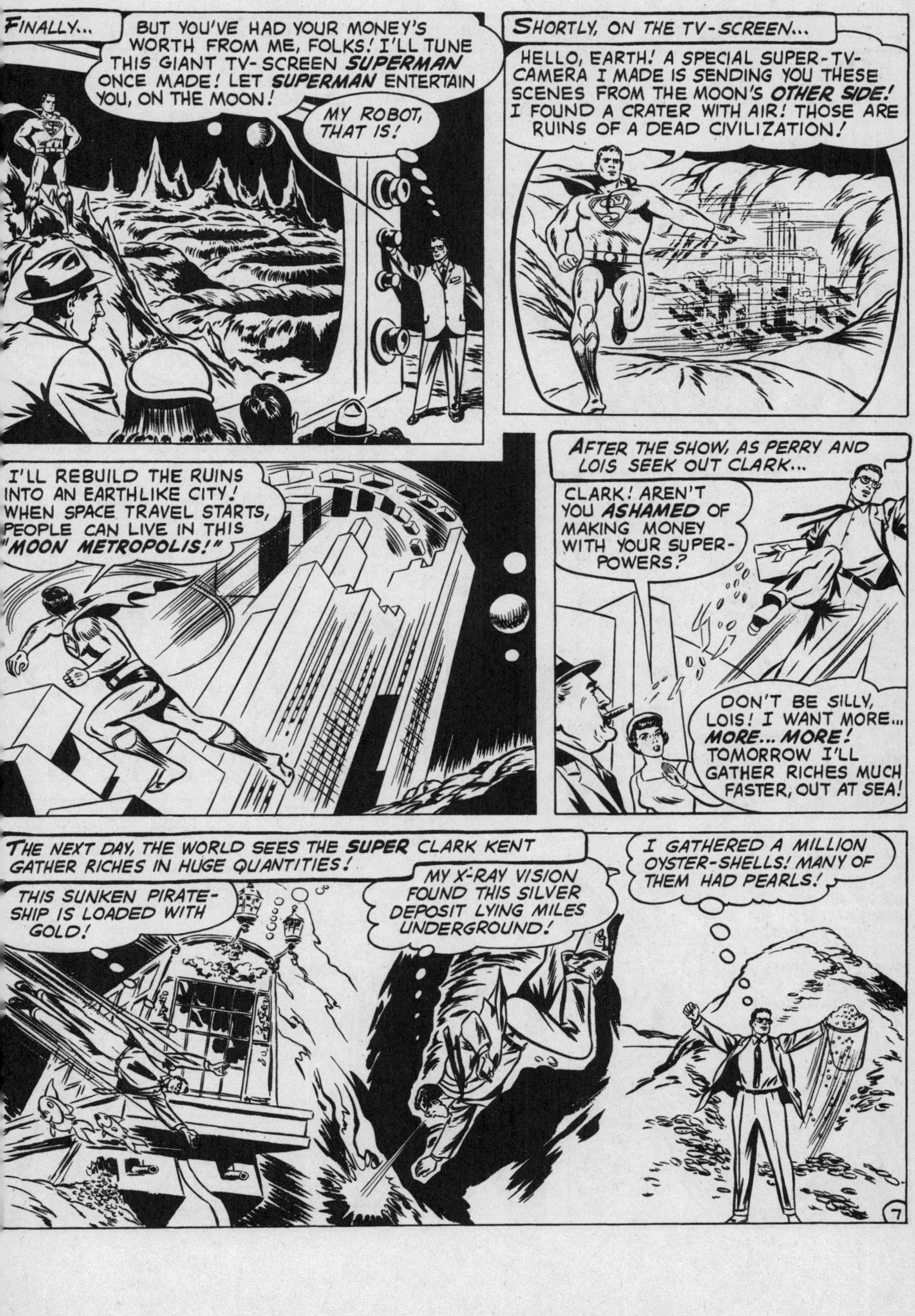
FINALLY...
BUT YOU'VE HAD YOUR MONEY'S WORTH FROM ME, FOLKS! I'LL TUNE THIS GIANT TV-SCREEN SUPERMAN ONCE MADE! LET SUPERMAN ENTERTAIN YOU, ON THE MOON!
MY ROBOT, THAT IS!
SHORTLY, ON THE TV-SCREEN...
HELLO, EARTH! A SPECIAL SUPER-TV-CAMERA I MADE IS SENDING YOU THESE SCENES FROM THE MOON'S OTHER SIDE! I FOUND A CRATER WITH AIR! THOSE ARE RUINS OF A DEAD CIVILIZATION!
I'LL REBUILD THE RUINS INTO AN EARTHLIKE CITY! WHEN SPACE TRAVEL STARTS, PEOPLE CAN LIVE IN THIS "MOON METROPOLIS!"
AFTER THE SHOW, AS PERRY AND LOIS SEEK OUT CLARK...
CLARK! AREN'T YOU ASHAMED OF MAKING MONEY WITH YOUR SUPER-POWERS?
DON'T BE SILLY, LOIS! I WANT MORE... MORE... MORE! TOMORROW I'LL GATHER RICHES MUCH FASTER, OUT AT SEA!
THE NEXT DAY, THE WORLD SEES THE SUPER CLARK KENT GATHER RICHES IN HUGE QUANTITIES!
THIS SUNKEN PIRATE-SHIP IS LOADED WITH GOLD!
MY X-RAY VISION FOUND THIS SILVER DEPOSIT LYING MILES UNDERGROUND!
I GATHERED A MILLION OYSTER-SHELLS! MANY OF THEM HAD PEARLS!
7

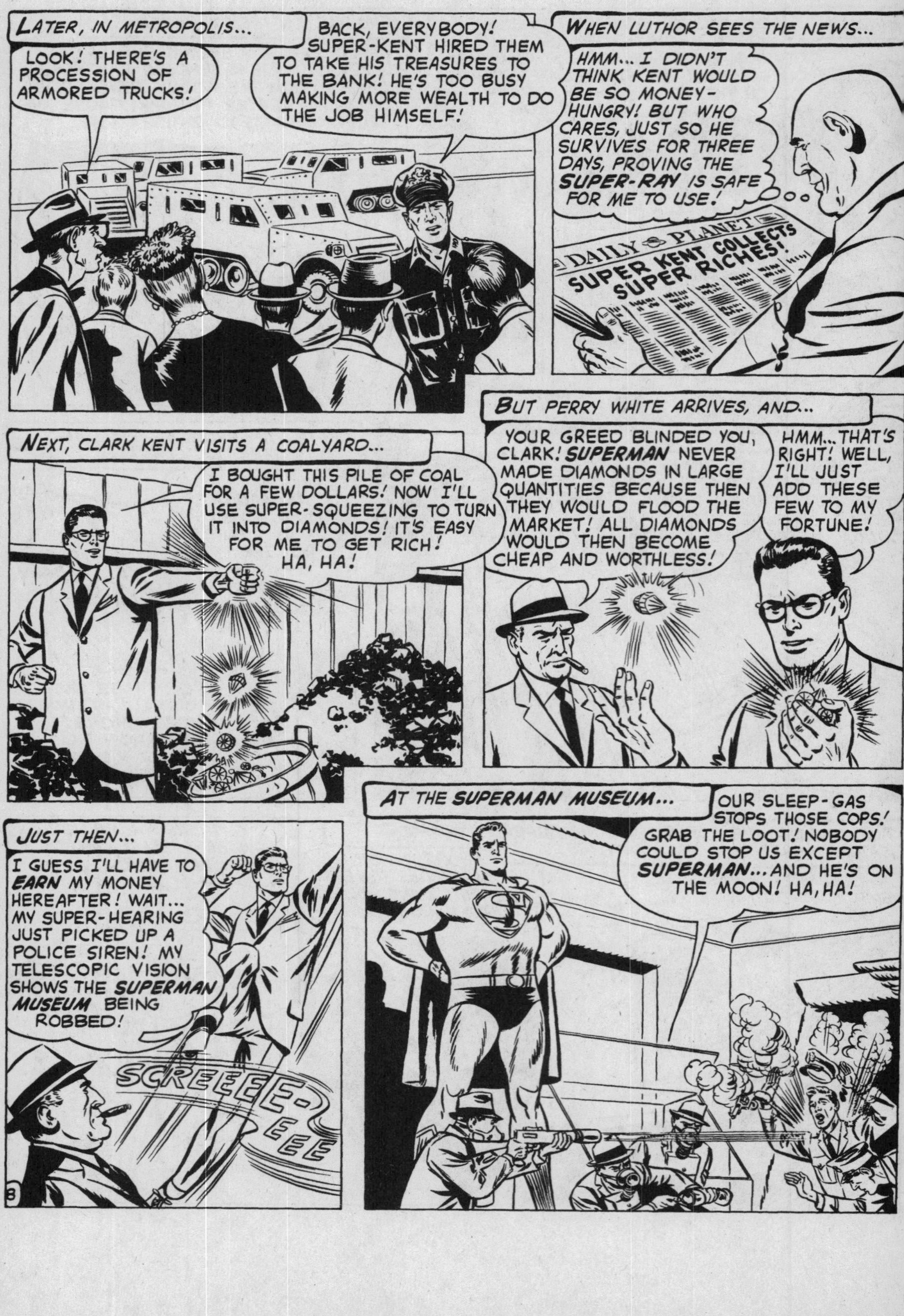
LATER, IN METROPOLIS...
LOOK! THERE'S A PROCESSION OF ARMORED TRUCKS!
BACK, EVERYBODY! SUPER-KENT HIRED THEM TO TAKE HIS TREASURES TO THE BANK! HE'S TOO BUSY MAKING MORE WEALTH TO DO THE JOB HIMSELF!
WHEN LUTHOR SEES THE NEWS...
HMM... I DIDN'T THINK KENT WOULD BE SO MONEY-HUNGRY! BUT WHO CARES, JUST SO HE SURVIVES FOR THREE DAYS, PROVING THE SUPER-RAY IS SAFE FOR ME TO USE!
DAILY PLANET
SUPER KENT COLLECTS SUPER RICHES!
NEXT, CLARK KENT VISITS A COALYARD...
I BOUGHT THIS PILE OF COAL FOR A FEW DOLLARS! NOW I'LL USE SUPER-SQUEEZING TO TURN IT INTO DIAMONDS! IT'S EASY FOR ME TO GET RICH! HA, HA!
BUT PERRY WHITE ARRIVES, AND...
YOUR GREED BLINDED YOU, CLARK! SUPERMAN NEVER MADE DIAMONDS IN LARGE QUANTITIES BECAUSE THEN THEY WOULD FLOOD THE MARKET! ALL DIAMONDS WOULD THEN BECOME CHEAP AND WORTHLESS!
HMM... THAT'S RIGHT! WELL, I'LL JUST ADD THESE FEW TO MY FORTUNE!
JUST THEN...
I GUESS I'LL HAVE TO EARN MY MONEY HEREAFTER! WAIT... MY SUPER-HEARING JUST PICKED UP A POLICE SIREN! MY TELESCOPIC VISION SHOWS THE SUPERMAN MUSEUM BEING ROBBED!
SCREEEE-EEE
8
AT THE SUPERMAN MUSEUM...
OUR SLEEP-GAS STOPS THOSE COPS! GRAB THE LOOT! NOBODY COULD STOP US EXCEPT SUPERMAN... AND HE'S ON THE MOON! HA, HA!

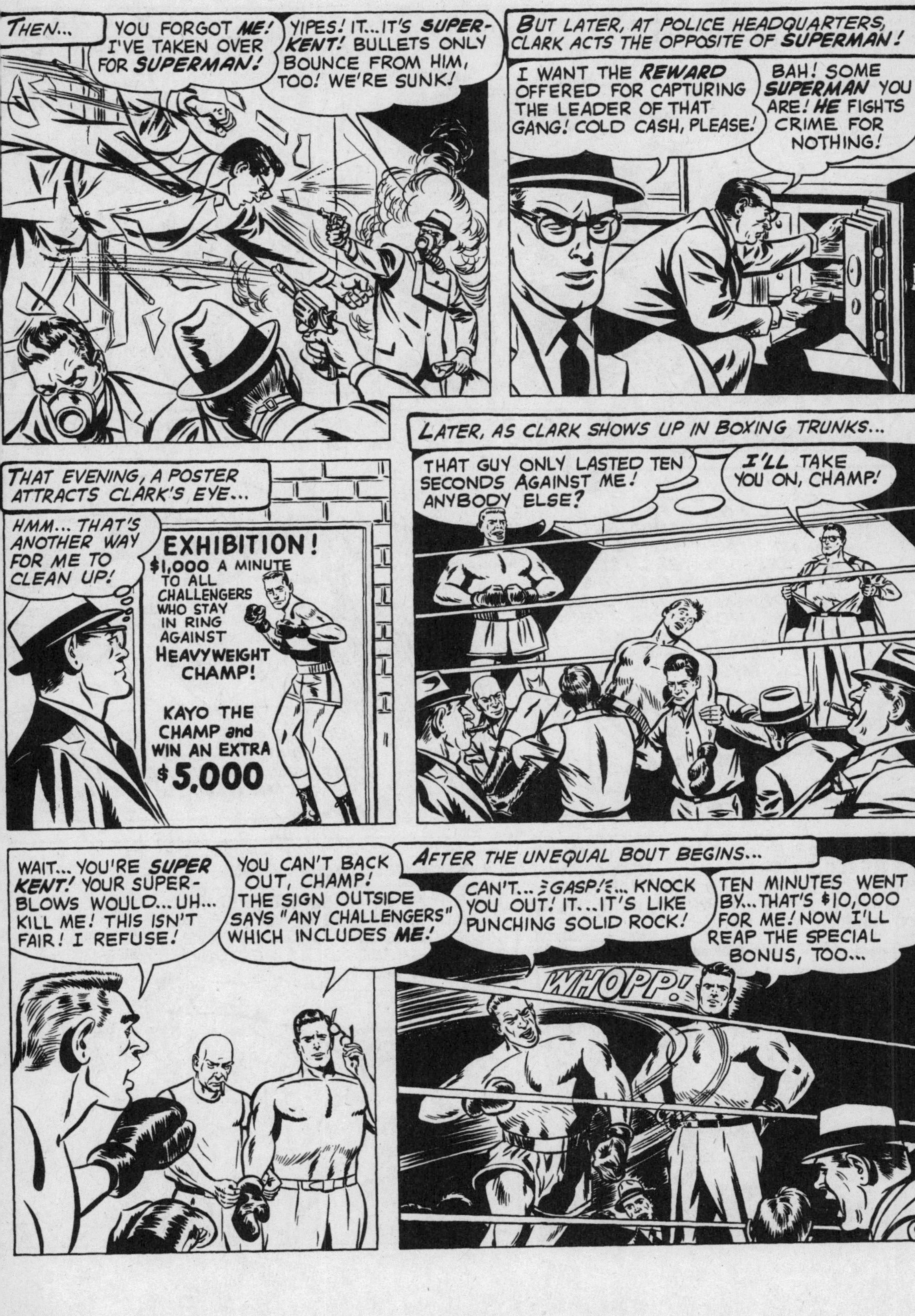
THEN...
YOU FORGOT ME! I'VE TAKEN OVER FOR SUPERMAN!
YIPES! IT...IT'S SUPER-KENT! BULLETS ONLY BOUNCE FROM HIM, TOO! WE'RE SUNK!
BUT LATER, AT POLICE HEADQUARTERS, CLARK ACTS THE OPPOSITE OF SUPERMAN!
I WANT THE REWARD OFFERED FOR CAPTURING THE LEADER OF THAT GANG! COLD CASH, PLEASE!
BAH! SOME SUPERMAN YOU ARE! HE FIGHTS CRIME FOR NOTHING!
THAT EVENING, A POSTER ATTRACTS CLARK'S EYE...
HMM... THAT'S ANOTHER WAY FOR ME TO CLEAN UP!
EXHIBITION! $1,000 A MINUTE TO ALL CHALLENGERS WHO STAY IN RING AGAINST HEAVYWEIGHT CHAMP! KAYO THE CHAMP and WIN AN EXTRA $5,000
LATER, AS CLARK SHOWS UP IN BOXING TRUNKS...
THAT GUY ONLY LASTED TEN SECONDS AGAINST ME! ANYBODY ELSE?
I'LL TAKE YOU ON, CHAMP!
WAIT... YOU'RE SUPER KENT! YOUR SUPER-BLOWS WOULD...UH... KILL ME! THIS ISN'T FAIR! I REFUSE!
YOU CAN'T BACK OUT, CHAMP! THE SIGN OUTSIDE SAYS "ANY CHALLENGERS" WHICH INCLUDES ME!
AFTER THE UNEQUAL BOUT BEGINS...
CAN'T... GASP!... KNOCK YOU OUT! IT...IT'S LIKE PUNCHING SOLID ROCK!
TEN MINUTES WENT BY...THAT'S $10,000 FOR ME! NOW I'LL REAP THE SPECIAL BONUS, TOO...
WHOPP!
9

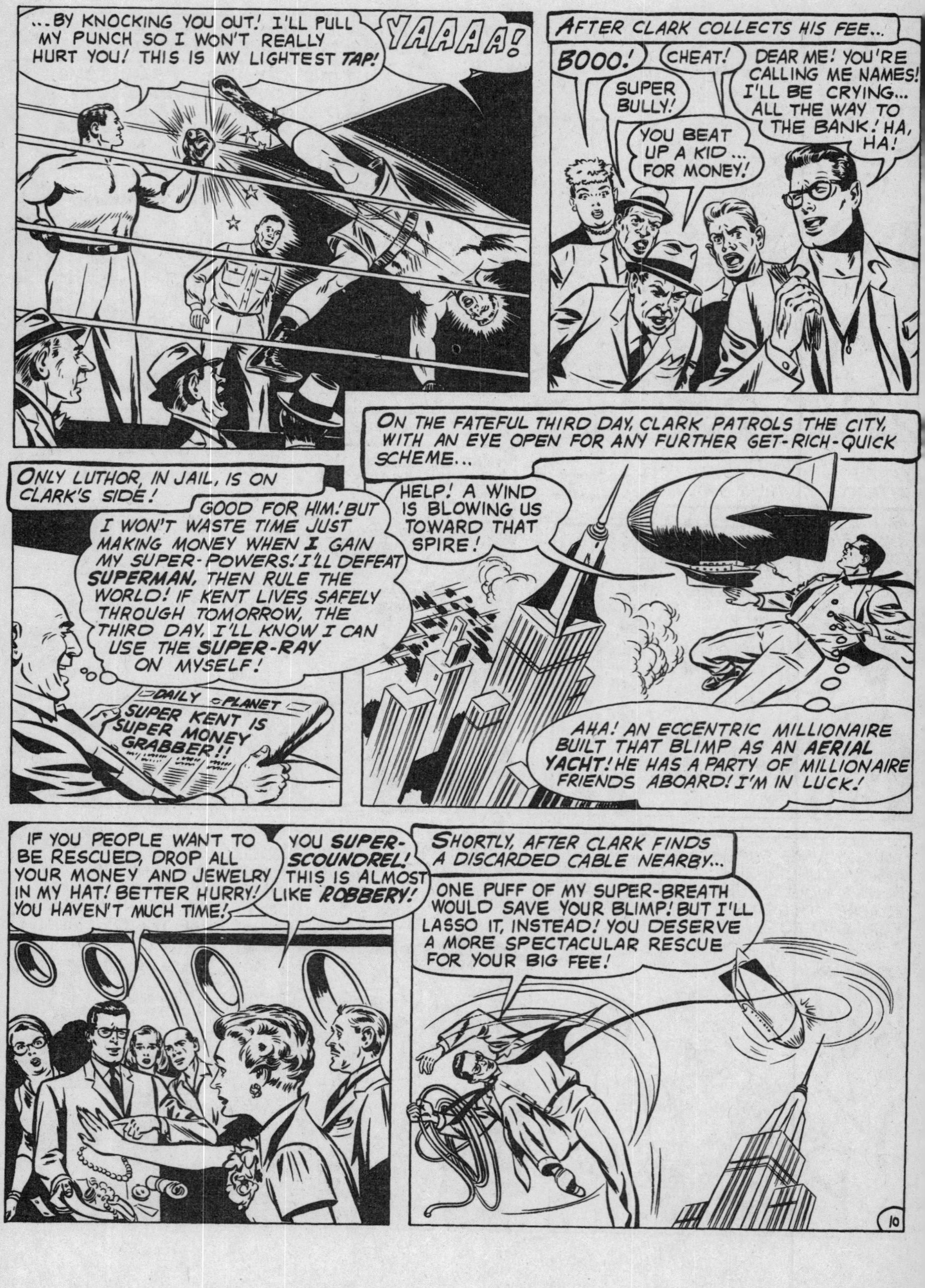
...BY KNOCKING YOU OUT! I'LL PULL MY PUNCH SO I WON'T REALLY HURT YOU! THIS IS MY LIGHTEST TAP!
YAAAAA!
AFTER CLARK COLLECTS HIS FEE...
BOOO!
SUPER BULLY!
CHEAT!
YOU BEAT UP A KID... FOR MONEY!
DEAR ME! YOU'RE CALLING ME NAMES! I'LL BE CRYING... ALL THE WAY TO THE BANK! HA, HA!
ONLY LUTHOR, IN JAIL, IS ON CLARK'S SIDE!
GOOD FOR HIM! BUT I WON'T WASTE TIME JUST MAKING MONEY WHEN I GAIN MY SUPER-POWERS! I'LL DEFEAT SUPERMAN, THEN RULE THE WORLD! IF KENT LIVES SAFELY THROUGH TOMORROW, THE THIRD DAY, I'LL KNOW I CAN USE THE SUPER-RAY ON MYSELF!
DAILY PLANET
SUPER KENT IS SUPER MONEY GRABBER!!
ON THE FATEFUL THIRD DAY, CLARK PATROLS THE CITY, WITH AN EYE OPEN FOR ANY FURTHER GET-RICH-QUICK SCHEME...
HELP! A WIND IS BLOWING US TOWARD THAT SPIRE!
AHA! AN ECCENTRIC MILLIONAIRE BUILT THAT BLIMP AS AN AERIAL YACHT! HE HAS A PARTY OF MILLIONAIRE FRIENDS ABOARD! I'M IN LUCK!
IF YOU PEOPLE WANT TO BE RESCUED, DROP ALL YOUR MONEY AND JEWELRY IN MY HAT! BETTER HURRY! YOU HAVEN'T MUCH TIME!
YOU SUPER-SCOUNDREL! THIS IS ALMOST LIKE ROBBERY!
SHORTLY, AFTER CLARK FINDS A DISCARDED CABLE NEARBY...
ONE PUFF OF MY SUPER-BREATH WOULD SAVE YOUR BLIMP! BUT I'LL LASSO IT, INSTEAD! YOU DESERVE A MORE SPECTACULAR RESCUE FOR YOUR BIG FEE!
10

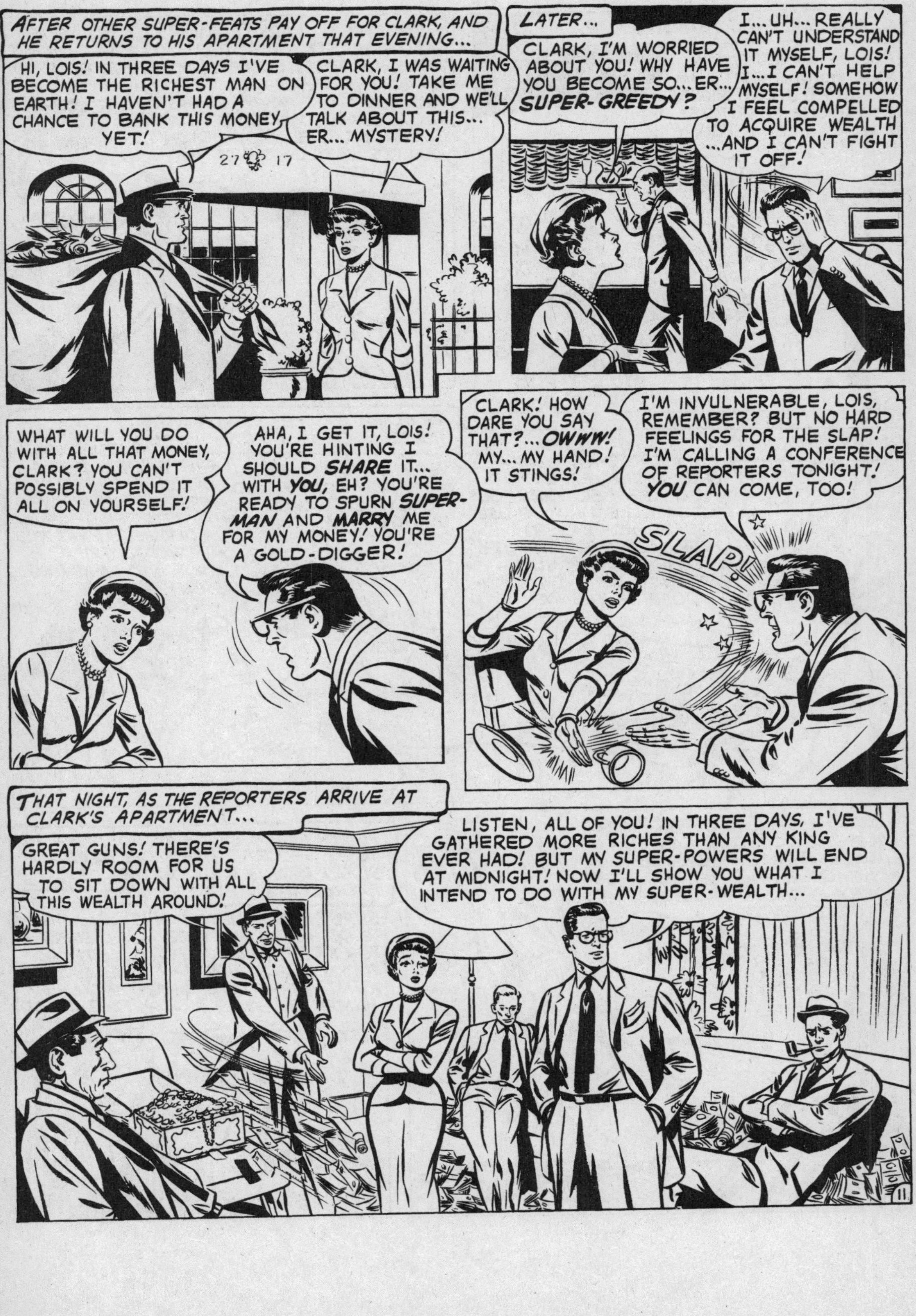
AFTER OTHER SUPER-FEATS PAY OFF FOR CLARK, AND HE RETURNS TO HIS APARTMENT THAT EVENING...
HI, LOIS! IN THREE DAYS I'VE BECOME THE RICHEST MAN ON EARTH! I HAVEN'T HAD A CHANCE TO BANK THIS MONEY, YET!
CLARK, I WAS WAITING FOR YOU! TAKE ME TO DINNER AND WE'LL TALK ABOUT THIS... ER... MYSTERY!
27 17
LATER...
CLARK, I'M WORRIED ABOUT YOU! WHY HAVE YOU BECOME SO...ER... SUPER-GREEDY?
I... UH... REALLY CAN'T UNDERSTAND IT MYSELF, LOIS! I...I CAN'T HELP MYSELF! SOMEHOW I FEEL COMPELLED TO ACQUIRE WEALTH ...AND I CAN'T FIGHT IT OFF!
WHAT WILL YOU DO WITH ALL THAT MONEY, CLARK? YOU CAN'T POSSIBLY SPEND IT ALL ON YOURSELF!
AHA, I GET IT, LOIS! YOU'RE HINTING I SHOULD SHARE IT... WITH YOU, EH? YOU'RE READY TO SPURN SUPERMAN AND MARRY ME FOR MY MONEY! YOU'RE A GOLD-DIGGER!
CLARK! HOW DARE YOU SAY THAT?...OWWW! MY... MY HAND! IT STINGS!
I'M INVULNERABLE, LOIS, REMEMBER? BUT NO HARD FEELINGS FOR THE SLAP! I'M CALLING A CONFERENCE OF REPORTERS TONIGHT! YOU CAN COME, TOO!
SLAP!
THAT NIGHT, AS THE REPORTERS ARRIVE AT CLARK'S APARTMENT...
GREAT GUNS! THERE'S HARDLY ROOM FOR US TO SIT DOWN WITH ALL THIS WEALTH AROUND!
LISTEN, ALL OF YOU! IN THREE DAYS, I'VE GATHERED MORE RICHES THAN ANY KING EVER HAD! BUT MY SUPER-POWERS WILL END AT MIDNIGHT! NOW I'LL SHOW YOU WHAT I INTEND TO DO WITH MY SUPER-WEALTH...
11

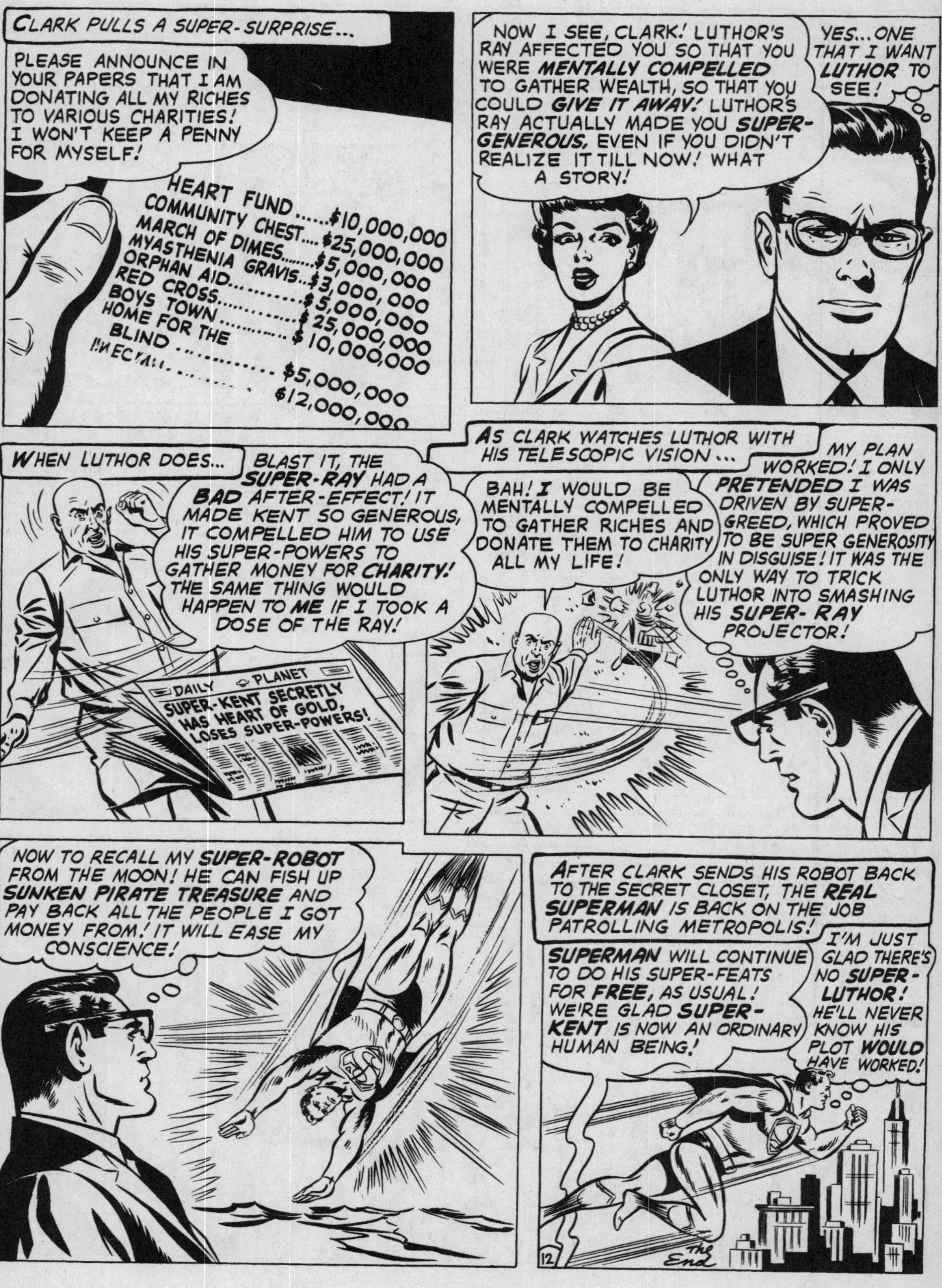

CLARK PULLS A SUPER-SURPRISE...
PLEASE ANNOUNCE IN YOUR PAPERS THAT I AM DONATING ALL MY RICHES TO VARIOUS CHARITIES! I WON'T KEEP A PENNY FOR MYSELF!
HEART FUND......$10,000,000
COMMUNITY CHEST....$25,000,000
MARCH OF DIMES........$5,000,000
MYASTHENIA GRAVIS...$3,000,000
ORPHAN AID..........$5,000,000
RED CROSS..........$25,000,000
BOYS TOWN..........$10,000,000
HOME FOR THE BLIND..........$5,000,000
$12,000,000
NOW I SEE, CLARK! LUTHOR'S RAY AFFECTED YOU SO THAT YOU WERE MENTALLY COMPELLED TO GATHER WEALTH, SO THAT YOU COULD GIVE IT AWAY! LUTHOR'S RAY ACTUALLY MADE YOU SUPER-GENEROUS, EVEN IF YOU DIDN'T REALIZE IT TILL NOW! WHAT A STORY!
YES...ONE THAT I WANT LUTHOR TO SEE!
WHEN LUTHOR DOES...
BLAST IT, THE SUPER-RAY HAD A BAD AFTER-EFFECT! IT MADE KENT SO GENEROUS, IT COMPELLED HIM TO USE HIS SUPER-POWERS TO GATHER MONEY FOR CHARITY! THE SAME THING WOULD HAPPEN TO ME IF I TOOK A DOSE OF THE RAY!
DAILY PLANET
SUPER-KENT SECRETLY HAS HEART OF GOLD, LOSES SUPER-POWERS!
AS CLARK WATCHES LUTHOR WITH HIS TELESCOPIC VISION...
BAH! I WOULD BE MENTALLY COMPELLED TO GATHER RICHES AND DONATE THEM TO CHARITY ALL MY LIFE!
MY PLAN WORKED! I ONLY PRETENDED I WAS DRIVEN BY SUPER-GREED, WHICH PROVED TO BE SUPER GENEROSITY IN DISGUISE! IT WAS THE ONLY WAY TO TRICK LUTHOR INTO SMASHING HIS SUPER-RAY PROJECTOR!
NOW TO RECALL MY SUPER-ROBOT FROM THE MOON! HE CAN FISH UP SUNKEN PIRATE TREASURE AND PAY BACK ALL THE PEOPLE I GOT MONEY FROM! IT WILL EASE MY CONSCIENCE!
AFTER CLARK SENDS HIS ROBOT BACK TO THE SECRET CLOSET, THE REAL SUPERMAN IS BACK ON THE JOB PATROLLING METROPOLIS!
SUPERMAN WILL CONTINUE TO DO HIS SUPER-FEATS FOR FREE, AS USUAL! WE'RE GLAD SUPER-KENT IS NOW AN ORDINARY HUMAN BEING!
I'M JUST GLAD THERE'S NO SUPER-LUTHOR! HE'LL NEVER KNOW HIS PLOT WOULD HAVE WORKED!
12
THE END

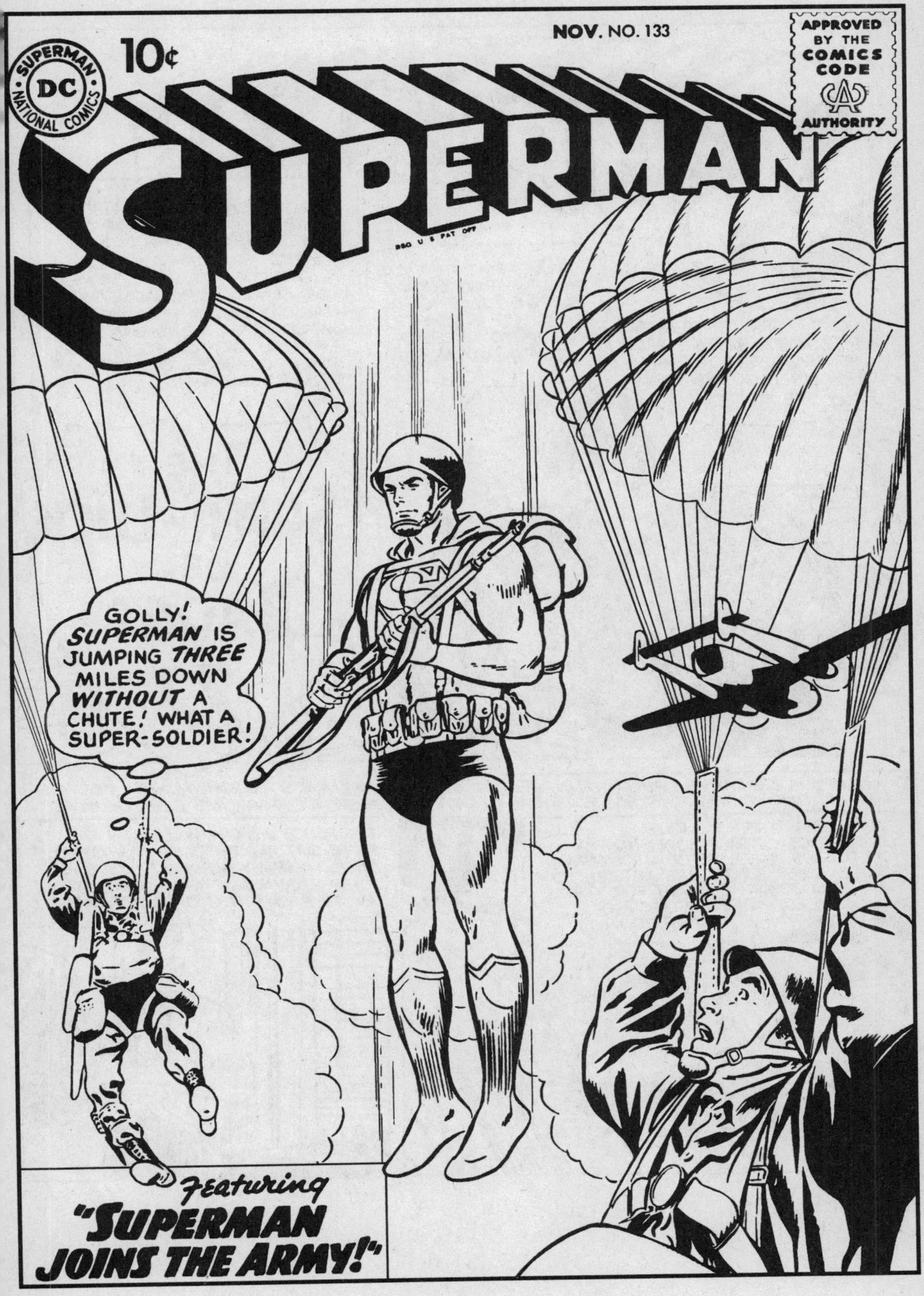
SUPERMAN DC NATIONAL COMICS
10¢
NOV. NO. 133
APPROVED BY THE COMICS CODE AUTHORITY
SUPERMAN
REG U S PAT OFF
GOLLY! SUPERMAN IS JUMPING THREE MILES DOWN WITHOUT A CHUTE! WHAT A SUPER-SOLDIER!
Featuring "SUPERMAN JOINS THE ARMY!"

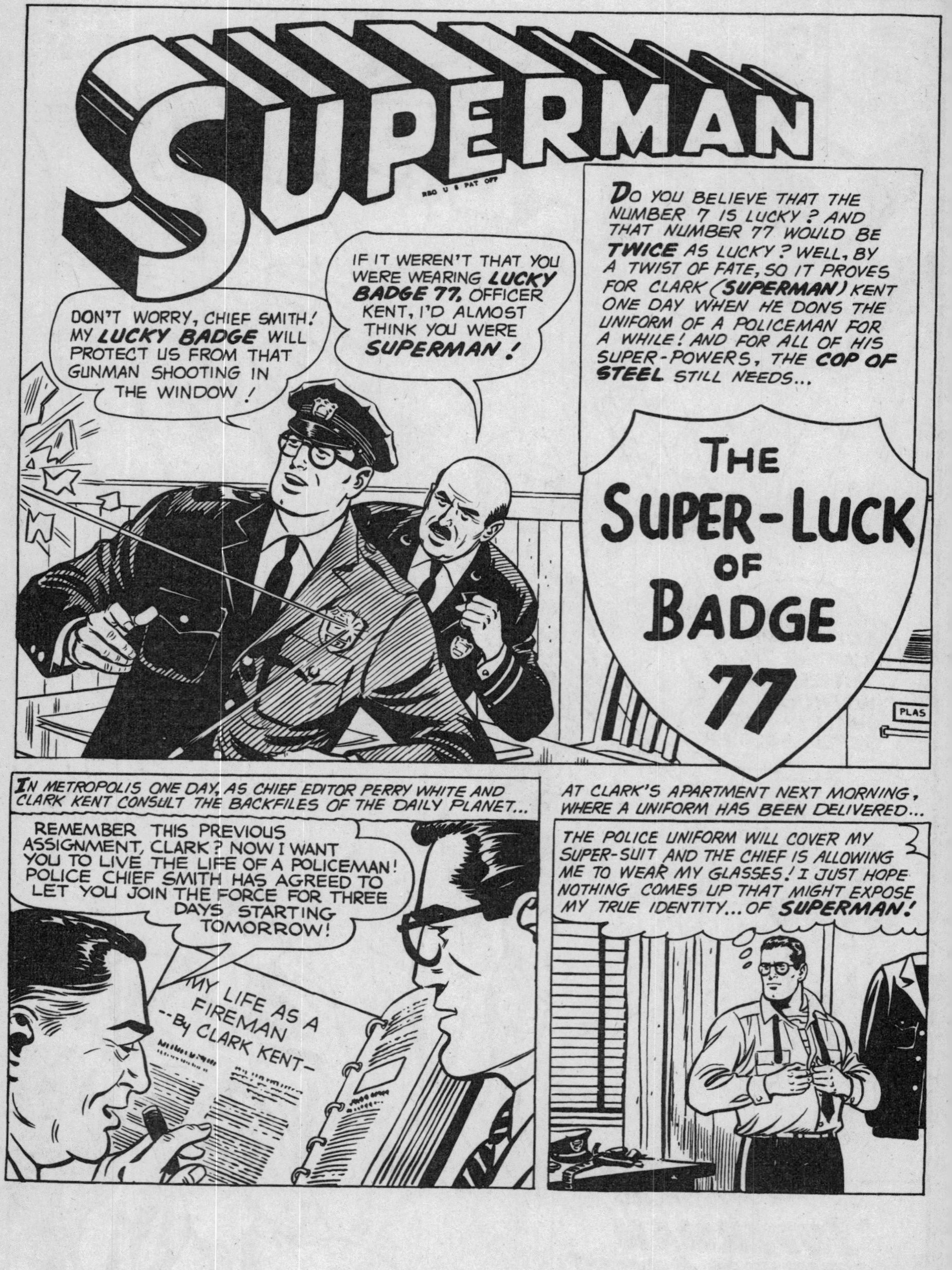
SUPERMAN
DO YOU BELIEVE THAT THE NUMBER 7 IS LUCKY? AND THAT NUMBER 77 WOULD BE TWICE AS LUCKY? WELL, BY A TWIST OF FATE, SO IT PROVES FOR CLARK (SUPERMAN) KENT ONE DAY WHEN HE DONS THE UNIFORM OF A POLICEMAN FOR A WHILE! AND FOR ALL OF HIS SUPER-POWERS, THE COP OF STEEL STILL NEEDS...
DON'T WORRY, CHIEF SMITH! MY LUCKY BADGE WILL PROTECT US FROM THAT GUNMAN SHOOTING IN THE WINDOW!
IF IT WEREN'T THAT YOU WERE WEARING LUCKY BADGE 77, OFFICER KENT, I'D ALMOST THINK YOU WERE SUPERMAN!
THE SUPER-LUCK OF BADGE 77
PLAS
IN METROPOLIS ONE DAY, AS CHIEF EDITOR PERRY WHITE AND CLARK KENT CONSULT THE BACKFILES OF THE DAILY PLANET...
REMEMBER THIS PREVIOUS ASSIGNMENT, CLARK? NOW I WANT YOU TO LIVE THE LIFE OF A POLICEMAN! POLICE CHIEF SMITH HAS AGREED TO LET YOU JOIN THE FORCE FOR THREE DAYS STARTING TOMORROW!
MY LIFE AS A FIREMAN --By CLARK KENT--
AT CLARK'S APARTMENT NEXT MORNING, WHERE A UNIFORM HAS BEEN DELIVERED...
THE POLICE UNIFORM WILL COVER MY SUPER-SUIT AND THE CHIEF IS ALLOWING ME TO WEAR MY GLASSES! I JUST HOPE NOTHING COMES UP THAT MIGHT EXPOSE MY TRUE IDENTITY... OF SUPERMAN!

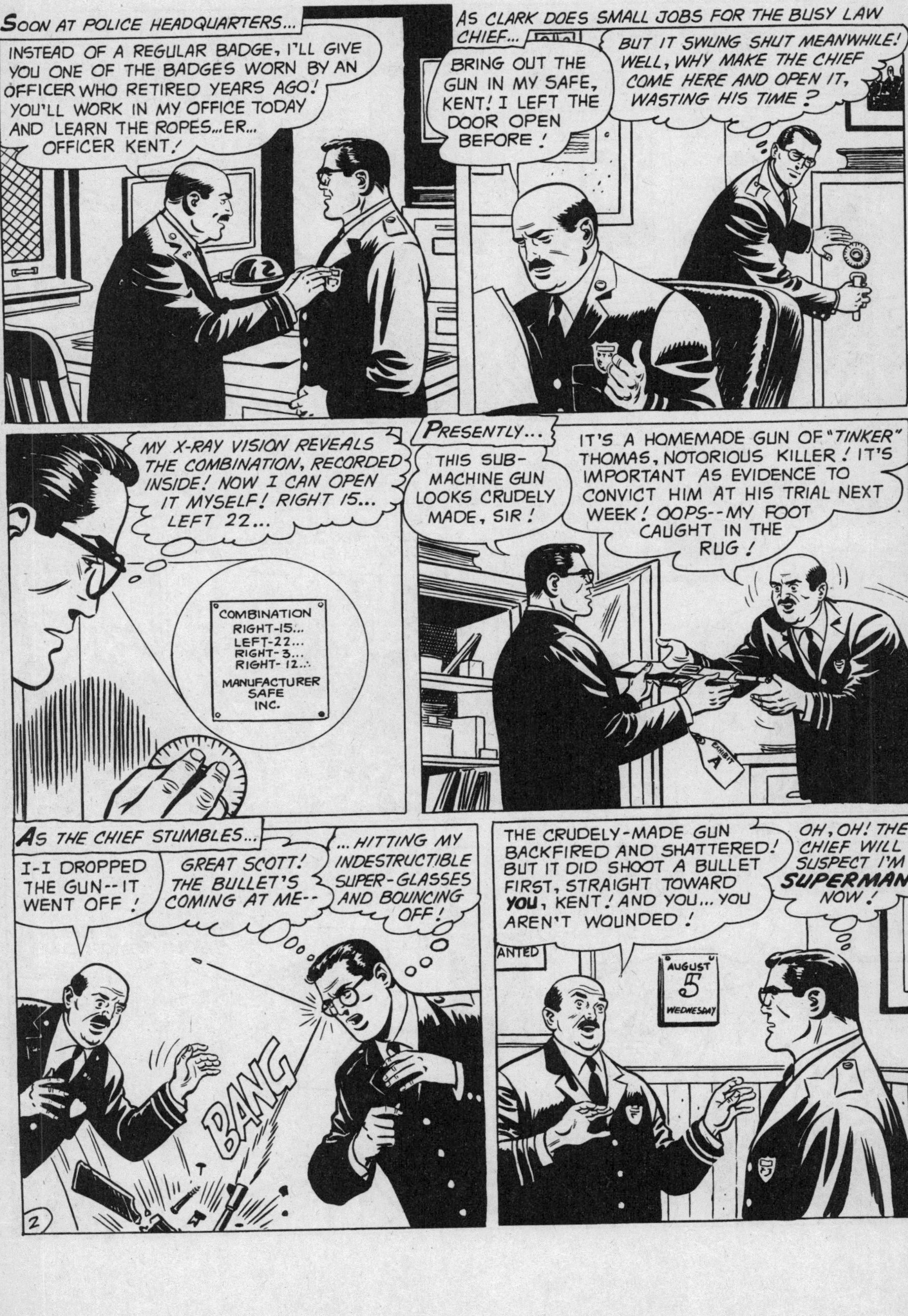
SOON AT POLICE HEADQUARTERS...
INSTEAD OF A REGULAR BADGE, I'LL GIVE YOU ONE OF THE BADGES WORN BY AN OFFICER WHO RETIRED YEARS AGO! YOU'LL WORK IN MY OFFICE TODAY AND LEARN THE ROPES...ER... OFFICER KENT!
AS CLARK DOES SMALL JOBS FOR THE BUSY LAW CHIEF...
BRING OUT THE GUN IN MY SAFE, KENT! I LEFT THE DOOR OPEN BEFORE!
BUT IT SWUNG SHUT MEANWHILE! WELL, WHY MAKE THE CHIEF COME HERE AND OPEN IT, WASTING HIS TIME?
MY X-RAY VISION REVEALS THE COMBINATION, RECORDED INSIDE! NOW I CAN OPEN IT MYSELF! RIGHT 15... LEFT 22...
COMBINATION RIGHT-15... LEFT-22... RIGHT-3... RIGHT-12...
MANUFACTURER SAFE INC.
PRESENTLY...
THIS SUB-MACHINE GUN LOOKS CRUDELY MADE, SIR!
IT'S A HOMEMADE GUN OF "TINKER" THOMAS, NOTORIOUS KILLER! IT'S IMPORTANT AS EVIDENCE TO CONVICT HIM AT HIS TRIAL NEXT WEEK! OOPS--MY FOOT CAUGHT IN THE RUG!
EXHIBIT A
AS THE CHIEF STUMBLES...
I-I DROPPED THE GUN--IT WENT OFF!
GREAT SCOTT! THE BULLET'S COMING AT ME--
...HITTING MY INDESTRUCTIBLE SUPER-GLASSES AND BOUNCING OFF!
BANG
THE CRUDELY-MADE GUN BACKFIRED AND SHATTERED! BUT IT DID SHOOT A BULLET FIRST, STRAIGHT TOWARD YOU, KENT! AND YOU... YOU AREN'T WOUNDED!
OH, OH! THE CHIEF WILL SUSPECT I'M SUPERMAN NOW!
ANTED
AUGUST 5 WEDNESDAY
2

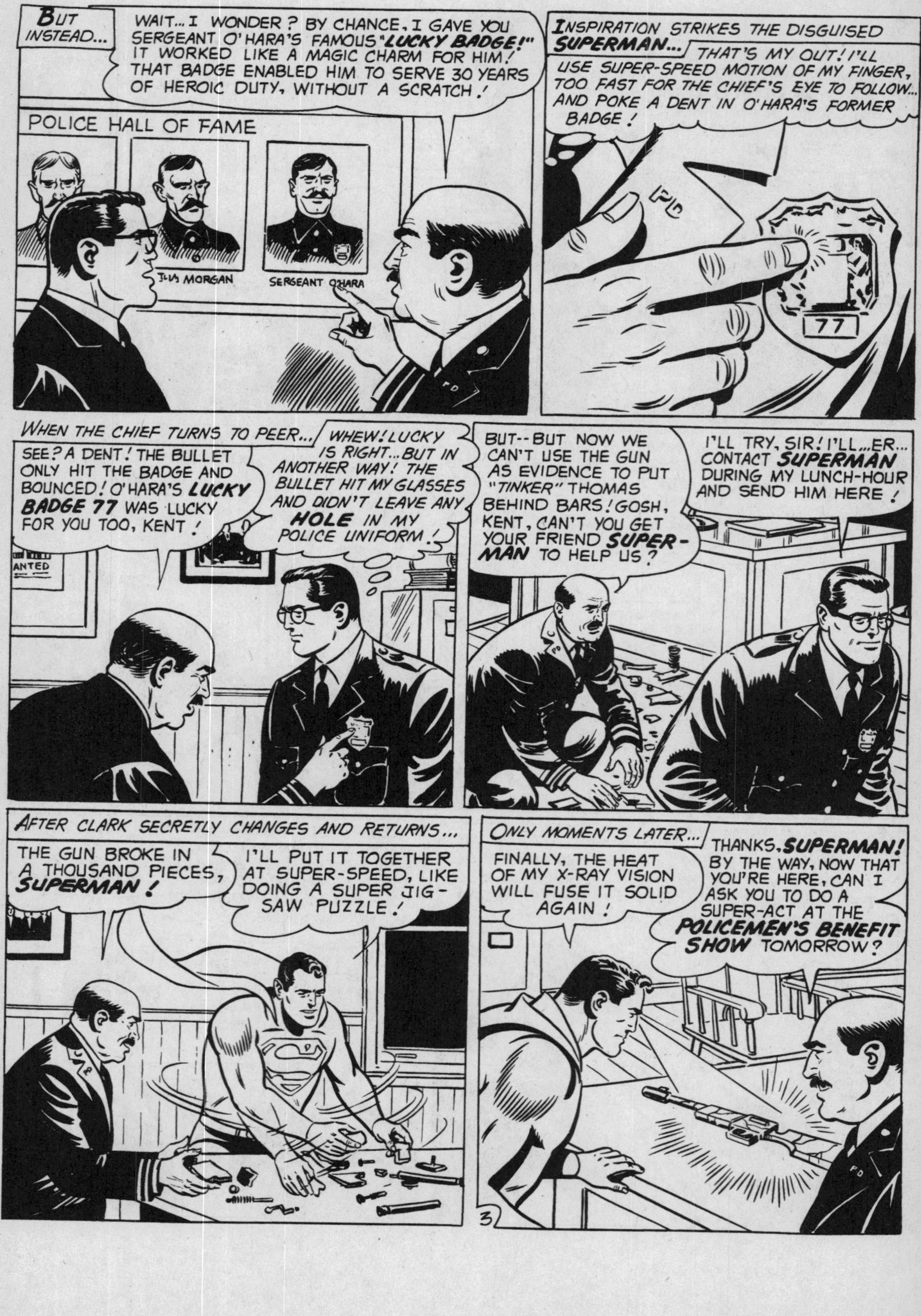
BUT INSTEAD...
WAIT... I WONDER? BY CHANCE, I GAVE YOU SERGEANT O'HARA'S FAMOUS "LUCKY BADGE!" IT WORKED LIKE A MAGIC CHARM FOR HIM! THAT BADGE ENABLED HIM TO SERVE 30 YEARS OF HEROIC DUTY, WITHOUT A SCRATCH!
POLICE HALL OF FAME
MORGAN
SERGEANT O'HARA
INSPIRATION STRIKES THE DISGUISED SUPERMAN...
THAT'S MY OUT! I'LL USE SUPER-SPEED MOTION OF MY FINGER, TOO FAST FOR THE CHIEF'S EYE TO FOLLOW... AND POKE A DENT IN O'HARA'S FORMER BADGE!
77
WHEN THE CHIEF TURNS TO PEER...
SEE? A DENT! THE BULLET ONLY HIT THE BADGE AND BOUNCED! O'HARA'S LUCKY BADGE 77 WAS LUCKY FOR YOU TOO, KENT!
WHEW! LUCKY IS RIGHT... BUT IN ANOTHER WAY! THE BULLET HIT MY GLASSES AND DIDN'T LEAVE ANY HOLE IN MY POLICE UNIFORM!
ANTED
BUT--BUT NOW WE CAN'T USE THE GUN AS EVIDENCE TO PUT "TINKER" THOMAS BEHIND BARS! GOSH, KENT, CAN'T YOU GET YOUR FRIEND SUPERMAN TO HELP US?
I'LL TRY, SIR! I'LL...ER... CONTACT SUPERMAN DURING MY LUNCH-HOUR AND SEND HIM HERE!
AFTER CLARK SECRETLY CHANGES AND RETURNS...
THE GUN BROKE IN A THOUSAND PIECES, SUPERMAN!
I'LL PUT IT TOGETHER AT SUPER-SPEED, LIKE DOING A SUPER JIG-SAW PUZZLE!
ONLY MOMENTS LATER...
FINALLY, THE HEAT OF MY X-RAY VISION WILL FUSE IT SOLID AGAIN!
THANKS, SUPERMAN! BY THE WAY, NOW THAT YOU'RE HERE, CAN I ASK YOU TO DO A SUPER-ACT AT THE POLICEMEN'S BENEFIT SHOW TOMORROW?
3

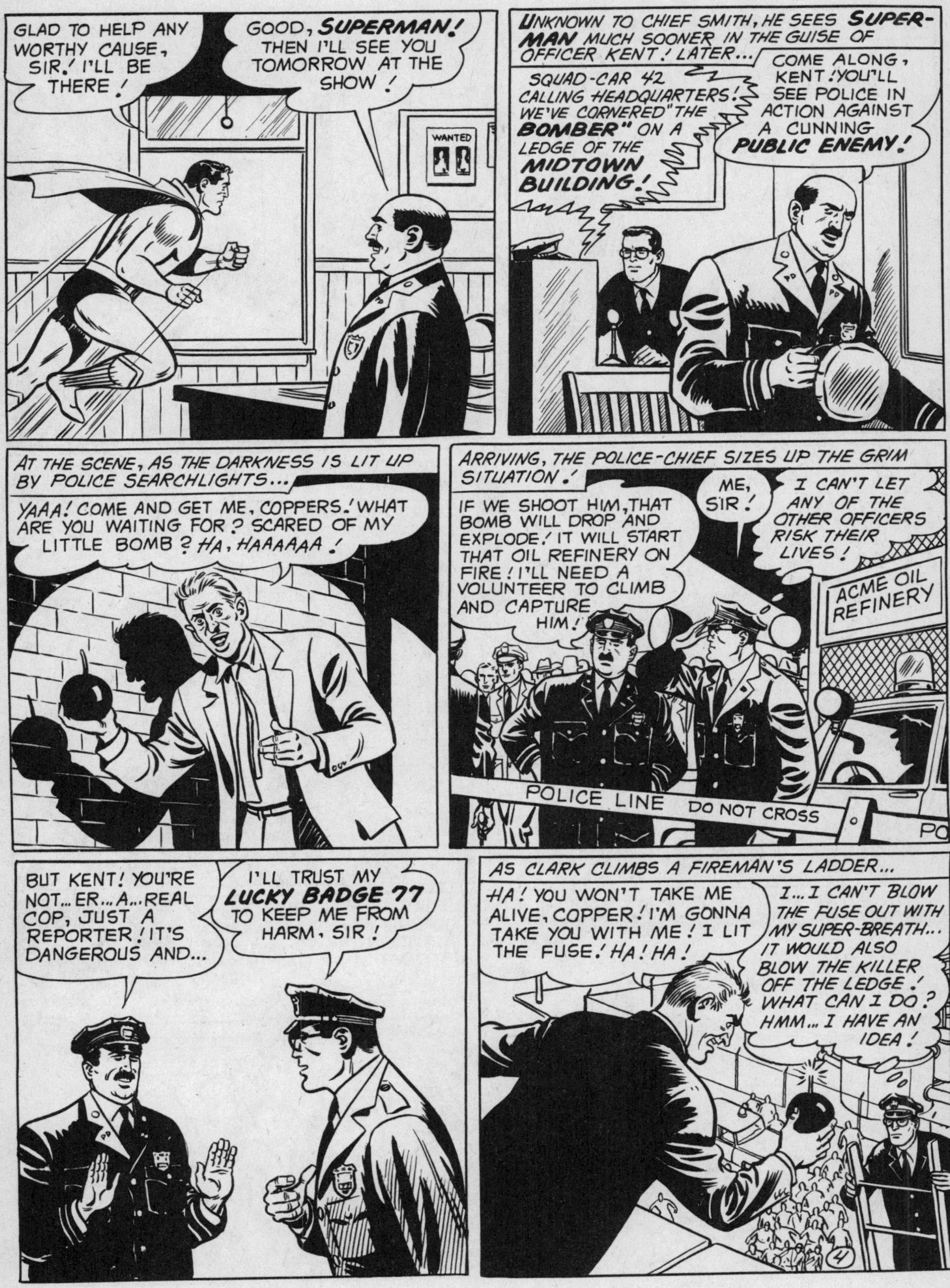
GLAD TO HELP ANY WORTHY CAUSE, SIR! I'LL BE THERE!
GOOD, SUPERMAN! THEN I'LL SEE YOU TOMORROW AT THE SHOW!
WANTED
UNKNOWN TO CHIEF SMITH, HE SEES SUPERMAN MUCH SOONER IN THE GUISE OF OFFICER KENT! LATER...
SQUAD-CAR 42 CALLING HEADQUARTERS! WE'VE CORNERED "THE BOMBER" ON A LEDGE OF THE MIDTOWN BUILDING!
COME ALONG, KENT! YOU'LL SEE POLICE IN ACTION AGAINST A CUNNING PUBLIC ENEMY!
AT THE SCENE, AS THE DARKNESS IS LIT UP BY POLICE SEARCHLIGHTS...
YAAA! COME AND GET ME, COPPERS! WHAT ARE YOU WAITING FOR? SCARED OF MY LITTLE BOMB? HA, HAAAAAA!
ARRIVING, THE POLICE-CHIEF SIZES UP THE GRIM SITUATION!
IF WE SHOOT HIM, THAT BOMB WILL DROP AND EXPLODE! IT WILL START THAT OIL REFINERY ON FIRE! I'LL NEED A VOLUNTEER TO CLIMB AND CAPTURE HIM!
ME, SIR!
I CAN'T LET ANY OF THE OTHER OFFICERS RISK THEIR LIVES!
ACME OIL REFINERY
POLICE LINE DO NOT CROSS
PO
BUT KENT! YOU'RE NOT... ER... A... REAL COP, JUST A REPORTER! IT'S DANGEROUS AND...
I'LL TRUST MY LUCKY BADGE 77 TO KEEP ME FROM HARM, SIR!
AS CLARK CLIMBS A FIREMAN'S LADDER...
HA! YOU WON'T TAKE ME ALIVE, COPPER! I'M GONNA TAKE YOU WITH ME! I LIT THE FUSE! HA! HA!
I... I CAN'T BLOW THE FUSE OUT WITH MY SUPER-BREATH... IT WOULD ALSO BLOW THE KILLER OFF THE LEDGE! WHAT CAN I DO? HMM... I HAVE AN IDEA!
4

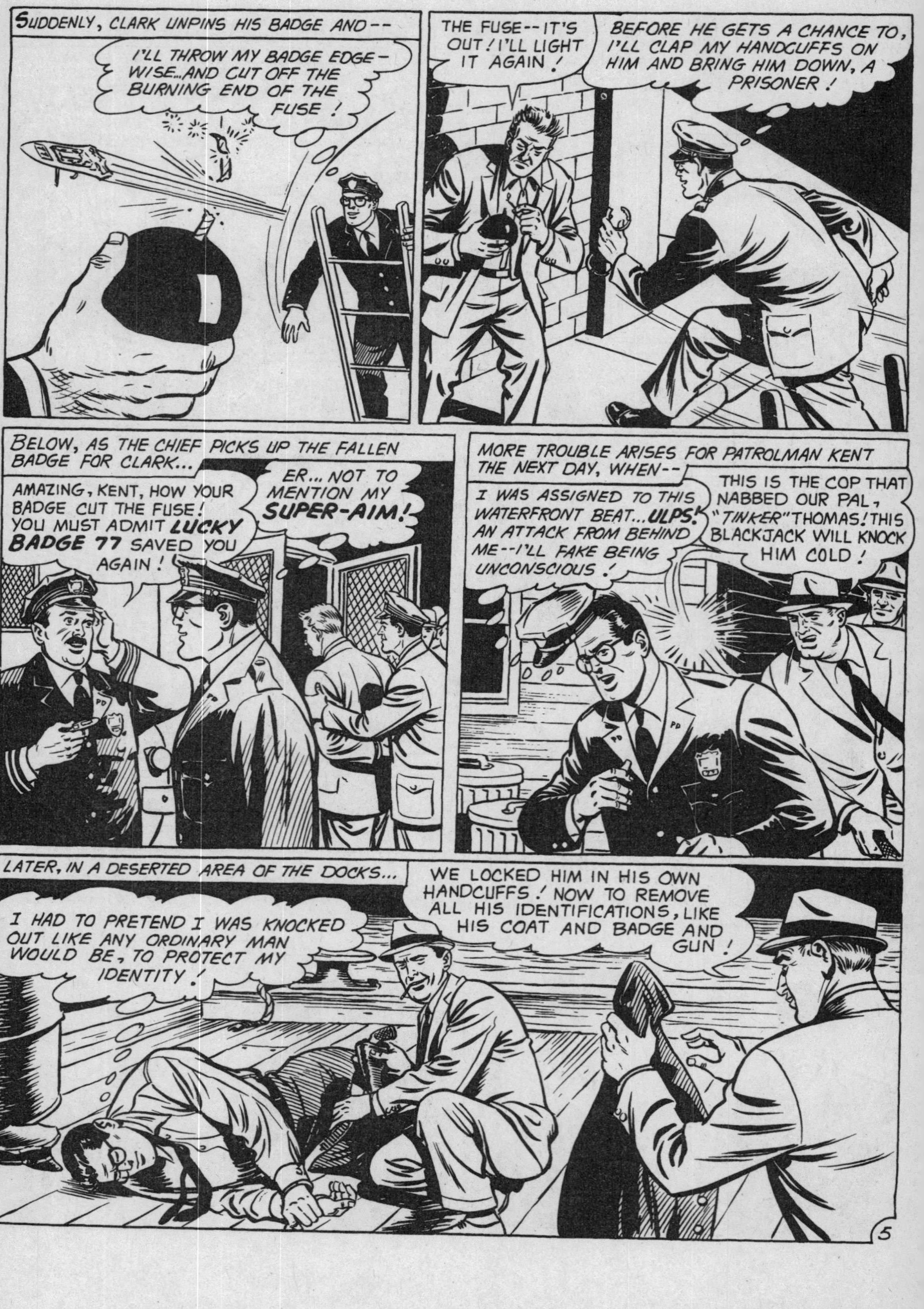
SUDDENLY, CLARK UNPINS HIS BADGE AND--
I'LL THROW MY BADGE EDGE-WISE...AND CUT OFF THE BURNING END OF THE FUSE!
THE FUSE--IT'S OUT! I'LL LIGHT IT AGAIN!
BEFORE HE GETS A CHANCE TO, I'LL CLAP MY HANDCUFFS ON HIM AND BRING HIM DOWN, A PRISONER!
BELOW, AS THE CHIEF PICKS UP THE FALLEN BADGE FOR CLARK...
AMAZING, KENT, HOW YOUR BADGE CUT THE FUSE! YOU MUST ADMIT LUCKY BADGE 77 SAVED YOU AGAIN!
ER...NOT TO MENTION MY SUPER-AIM!
MORE TROUBLE ARISES FOR PATROLMAN KENT THE NEXT DAY, WHEN--
I WAS ASSIGNED TO THIS WATERFRONT BEAT...ULPS! AN ATTACK FROM BEHIND ME--I'LL FAKE BEING UNCONSCIOUS!
THIS IS THE COP THAT NABBED OUR PAL, "TINKER" THOMAS! THIS BLACKJACK WILL KNOCK HIM COLD!
LATER, IN A DESERTED AREA OF THE DOCKS...
I HAD TO PRETEND I WAS KNOCKED OUT LIKE ANY ORDINARY MAN WOULD BE, TO PROTECT MY IDENTITY!
WE LOCKED HIM IN HIS OWN HANDCUFFS! NOW TO REMOVE ALL HIS IDENTIFICATIONS, LIKE HIS COAT AND BADGE AND GUN!
5

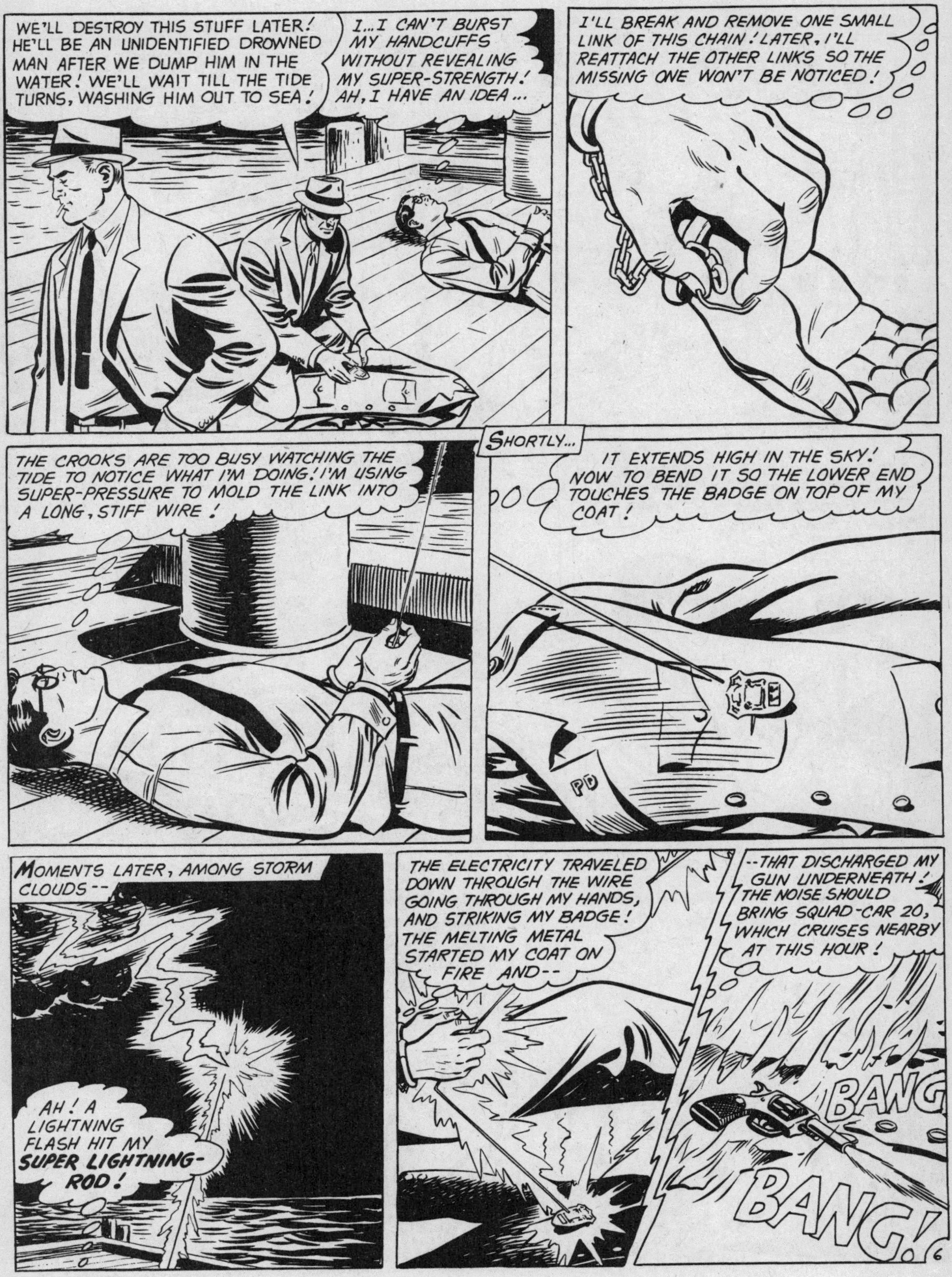
WE'LL DESTROY THIS STUFF LATER! HE'LL BE AN UNIDENTIFIED DROWNED MAN AFTER WE DUMP HIM IN THE WATER! WE'LL WAIT TILL THE TIDE TURNS, WASHING HIM OUT TO SEA!
I...I CAN'T BURST MY HANDCUFFS WITHOUT REVEALING MY SUPER-STRENGTH! AH, I HAVE AN IDEA...
I'LL BREAK AND REMOVE ONE SMALL LINK OF THIS CHAIN! LATER, I'LL REATTACH THE OTHER LINKS SO THE MISSING ONE WON'T BE NOTICED!
THE CROOKS ARE TOO BUSY WATCHING THE TIDE TO NOTICE WHAT I'M DOING! I'M USING SUPER-PRESSURE TO MOLD THE LINK INTO A LONG, STIFF WIRE!
SHORTLY...
IT EXTENDS HIGH IN THE SKY! NOW TO BEND IT SO THE LOWER END TOUCHES THE BADGE ON TOP OF MY COAT!
PD
MOMENTS LATER, AMONG STORM CLOUDS--
AH! A LIGHTNING FLASH HIT MY SUPER LIGHTNING-ROD!
THE ELECTRICITY TRAVELED DOWN THROUGH THE WIRE GOING THROUGH MY HANDS, AND STRIKING MY BADGE! THE MELTING METAL STARTED MY COAT ON FIRE AND--
--THAT DISCHARGED MY GUN UNDERNEATH! THE NOISE SHOULD BRING SQUAD-CAR 20, WHICH CRUISES NEARBY AT THIS HOUR!
BANG
BANG!
6

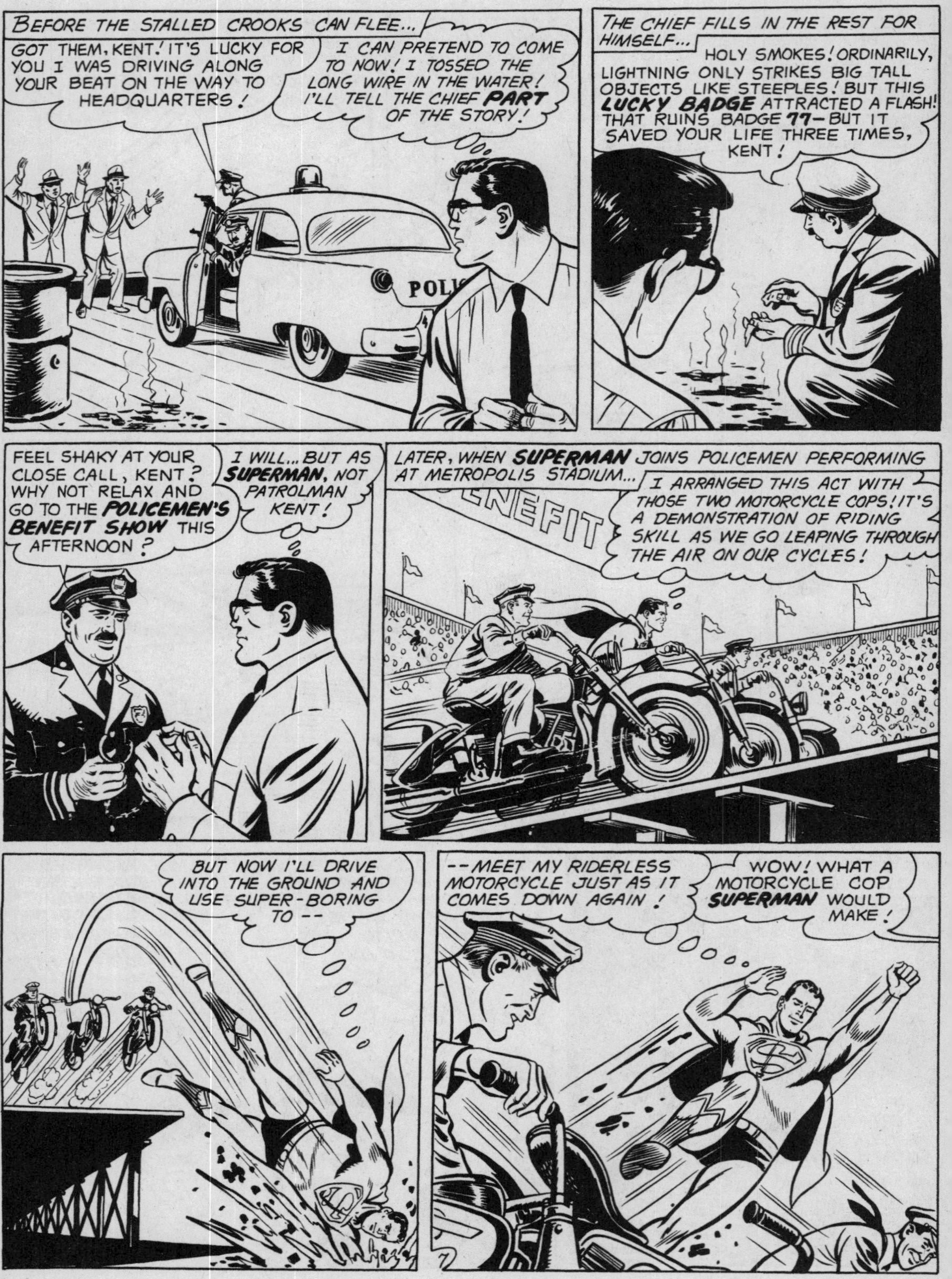
BEFORE THE STALLED CROOKS CAN FLEE...
GOT THEM, KENT! IT'S LUCKY FOR YOU I WAS DRIVING ALONG YOUR BEAT ON THE WAY TO HEADQUARTERS!
I CAN PRETEND TO COME TO NOW! I TOSSED THE LONG WIRE IN THE WATER! I'LL TELL THE CHIEF PART OF THE STORY!
POLI
THE CHIEF FILLS IN THE REST FOR HIMSELF...
HOLY SMOKES! ORDINARILY, LIGHTNING ONLY STRIKES BIG TALL OBJECTS LIKE STEEPLES! BUT THIS LUCKY BADGE ATTRACTED A FLASH! THAT RUINS BADGE 77-- BUT IT SAVED YOUR LIFE THREE TIMES, KENT!
FEEL SHAKY AT YOUR CLOSE CALL, KENT? WHY NOT RELAX AND GO TO THE POLICEMEN'S BENEFIT SHOW THIS AFTERNOON?
I WILL... BUT AS SUPERMAN, NOT PATROLMAN KENT!
LATER, WHEN SUPERMAN JOINS POLICEMEN PERFORMING AT METROPOLIS STADIUM...
I ARRANGED THIS ACT WITH THOSE TWO MOTORCYCLE COPS! IT'S A DEMONSTRATION OF RIDING SKILL AS WE GO LEAPING THROUGH THE AIR ON OUR CYCLES!
BENEFIT
BUT NOW I'LL DRIVE INTO THE GROUND AND USE SUPER-BORING TO --
-- MEET MY RIDERLESS MOTORCYCLE JUST AS IT COMES DOWN AGAIN!
WOW! WHAT A MOTORCYCLE COP SUPERMAN WOULD MAKE!
7

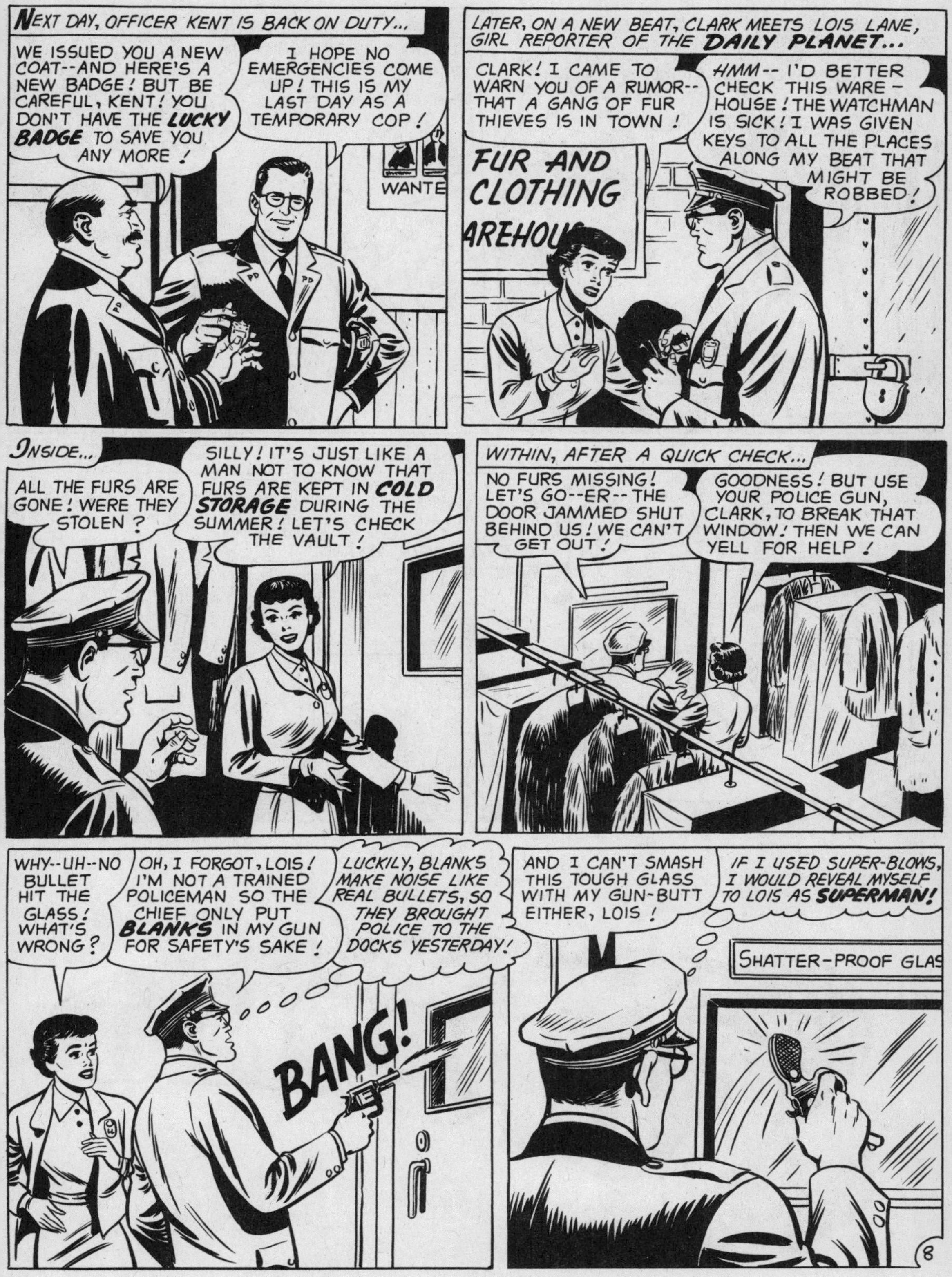
NEXT DAY, OFFICER KENT IS BACK ON DUTY...
WE ISSUED YOU A NEW COAT--AND HERE'S A NEW BADGE! BUT BE CAREFUL, KENT! YOU DON'T HAVE THE LUCKY BADGE TO SAVE YOU ANY MORE!
I HOPE NO EMERGENCIES COME UP! THIS IS MY LAST DAY AS A TEMPORARY COP!
WANTE
LATER, ON A NEW BEAT, CLARK MEETS LOIS LANE, GIRL REPORTER OF THE DAILY PLANET...
CLARK! I CAME TO WARN YOU OF A RUMOR--THAT A GANG OF FUR THIEVES IS IN TOWN!
HMM-- I'D BETTER CHECK THIS WARE-HOUSE! THE WATCHMAN IS SICK! I WAS GIVEN KEYS TO ALL THE PLACES ALONG MY BEAT THAT MIGHT BE ROBBED!
FUR AND CLOTHING
AREHOU
INSIDE...
ALL THE FURS ARE GONE! WERE THEY STOLEN?
SILLY! IT'S JUST LIKE A MAN NOT TO KNOW THAT FURS ARE KEPT IN COLD STORAGE DURING THE SUMMER! LET'S CHECK THE VAULT!
WITHIN, AFTER A QUICK CHECK...
NO FURS MISSING! LET'S GO--ER--THE DOOR JAMMED SHUT BEHIND US! WE CAN'T GET OUT!
GOODNESS! BUT USE YOUR POLICE GUN, CLARK, TO BREAK THAT WINDOW! THEN WE CAN YELL FOR HELP!
WHY--UH--NO BULLET HIT THE GLASS! WHAT'S WRONG?
OH, I FORGOT, LOIS! I'M NOT A TRAINED POLICEMAN SO THE CHIEF ONLY PUT BLANKS IN MY GUN FOR SAFETY'S SAKE!
LUCKILY, BLANKS MAKE NOISE LIKE REAL BULLETS, SO THEY BROUGHT POLICE TO THE DOCKS YESTERDAY!
BANG!
AND I CAN'T SMASH THIS TOUGH GLASS WITH MY GUN-BUTT EITHER, LOIS!
IF I USED SUPER-BLOWS, I WOULD REVEAL MYSELF TO LOIS AS SUPERMAN!
SHATTER-PROOF GLAS
8

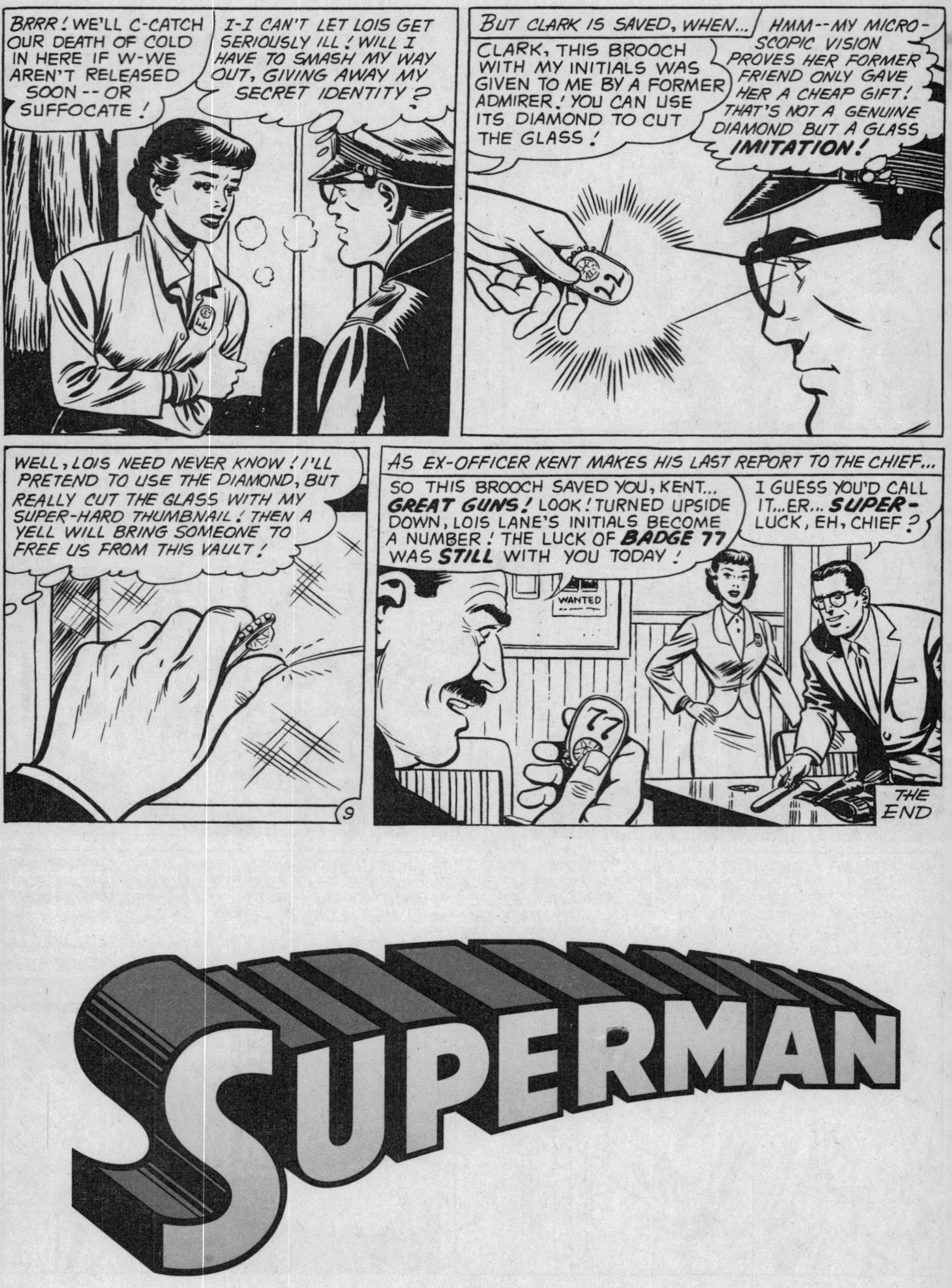
BRRR! WE'LL C-CATCH OUR DEATH OF COLD IN HERE IF W-WE AREN'T RELEASED SOON -- OR SUFFOCATE!
I-I CAN'T LET LOIS GET SERIOUSLY ILL! WILL I HAVE TO SMASH MY WAY OUT, GIVING AWAY MY SECRET IDENTITY?
BUT CLARK IS SAVED, WHEN...
CLARK, THIS BROOCH WITH MY INITIALS WAS GIVEN TO ME BY A FORMER ADMIRER! YOU CAN USE ITS DIAMOND TO CUT THE GLASS!
HMM--MY MICRO-SCOPIC VISION PROVES HER FORMER FRIEND ONLY GAVE HER A CHEAP GIFT! THAT'S NOT A GENUINE DIAMOND BUT A GLASS IMITATION!
WELL, LOIS NEED NEVER KNOW! I'LL PRETEND TO USE THE DIAMOND, BUT REALLY CUT THE GLASS WITH MY SUPER-HARD THUMBNAIL! THEN A YELL WILL BRING SOMEONE TO FREE US FROM THIS VAULT!
9
AS EX-OFFICER KENT MAKES HIS LAST REPORT TO THE CHIEF...
SO THIS BROOCH SAVED YOU, KENT... GREAT GUNS! LOOK! TURNED UPSIDE DOWN, LOIS LANE'S INITIALS BECOME A NUMBER! THE LUCK OF BADGE 77 WAS STILL WITH YOU TODAY!
I GUESS YOU'D CALL IT...ER... SUPER-LUCK, EH, CHIEF?
WANTED
77
THE END

SUPERMAN

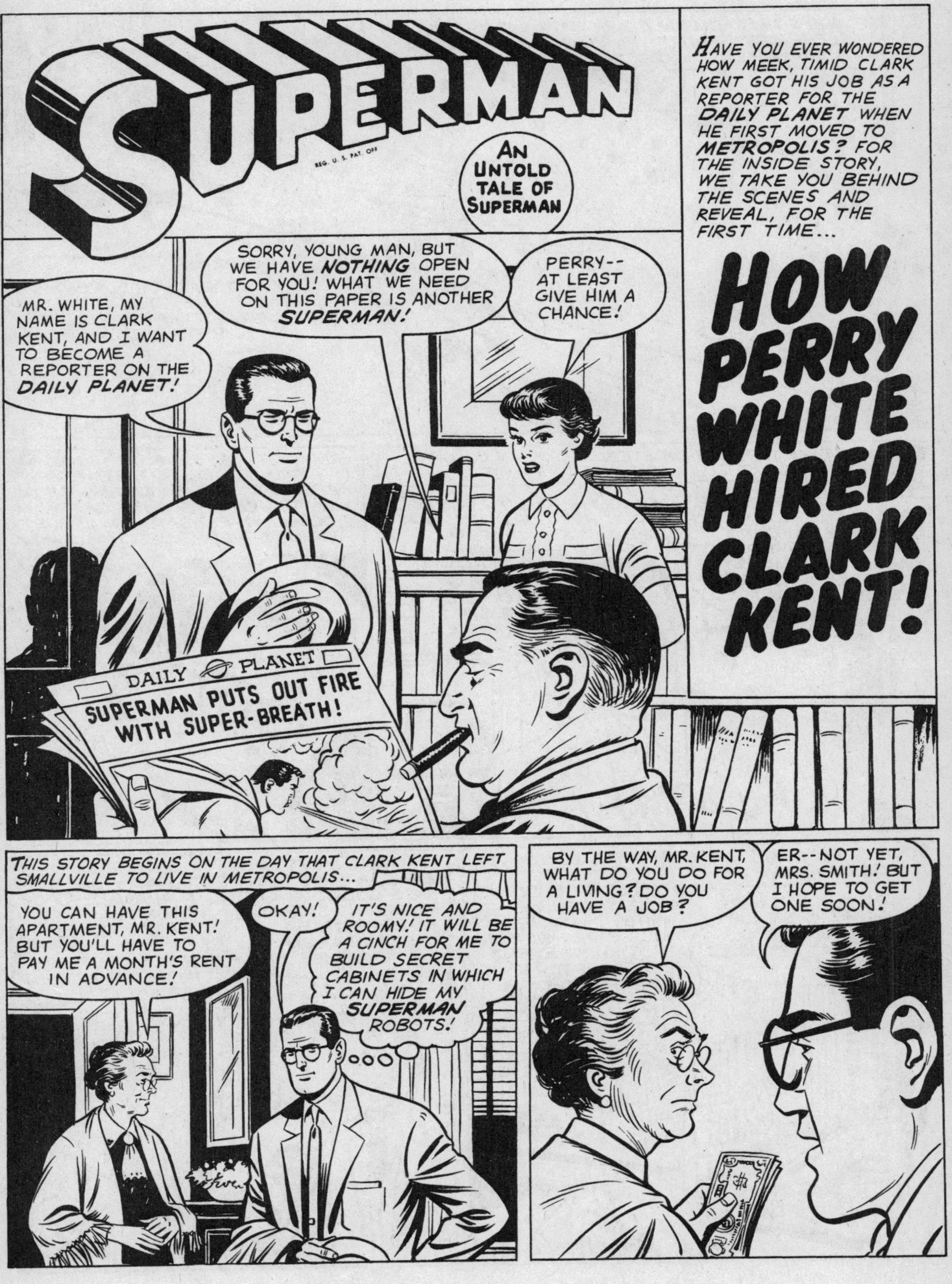
SUPERMAN
REG. U. S. PAT. OFF
AN UNTOLD TALE OF SUPERMAN
HAVE YOU EVER WONDERED HOW MEEK, TIMID CLARK KENT GOT HIS JOB AS A REPORTER FOR THE DAILY PLANET WHEN HE FIRST MOVED TO METROPOLIS? FOR THE INSIDE STORY, WE TAKE YOU BEHIND THE SCENES AND REVEAL, FOR THE FIRST TIME...
HOW PERRY WHITE HIRED CLARK KENT!
MR. WHITE, MY NAME IS CLARK KENT, AND I WANT TO BECOME A REPORTER ON THE DAILY PLANET!
SORRY, YOUNG MAN, BUT WE HAVE NOTHING OPEN FOR YOU! WHAT WE NEED ON THIS PAPER IS ANOTHER SUPERMAN!
PERRY-- AT LEAST GIVE HIM A CHANCE!
DAILY PLANET
SUPERMAN PUTS OUT FIRE WITH SUPER-BREATH!
THIS STORY BEGINS ON THE DAY THAT CLARK KENT LEFT SMALLVILLE TO LIVE IN METROPOLIS...
YOU CAN HAVE THIS APARTMENT, MR. KENT! BUT YOU'LL HAVE TO PAY ME A MONTH'S RENT IN ADVANCE!
OKAY!
IT'S NICE AND ROOMY! IT WILL BE A CINCH FOR ME TO BUILD SECRET CABINETS IN WHICH I CAN HIDE MY SUPERMAN ROBOTS!
BY THE WAY, MR. KENT, WHAT DO YOU DO FOR A LIVING? DO YOU HAVE A JOB?
ER--NOT YET, MRS. SMITH! BUT I HOPE TO GET ONE SOON!

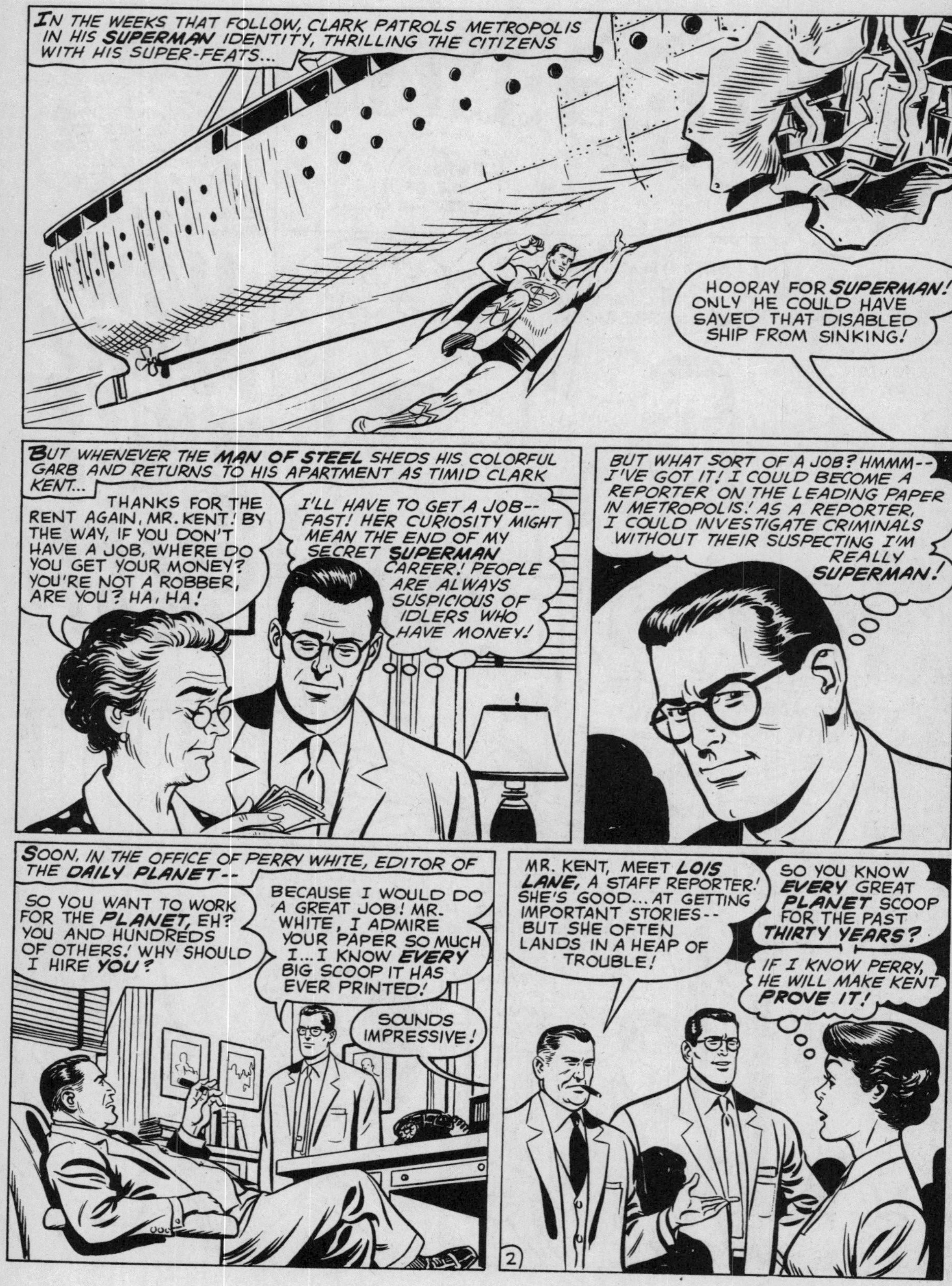
IN THE WEEKS THAT FOLLOW, CLARK PATROLS METROPOLIS IN HIS SUPERMAN IDENTITY, THRILLING THE CITIZENS WITH HIS SUPER-FEATS...
HOORAY FOR SUPERMAN! ONLY HE COULD HAVE SAVED THAT DISABLED SHIP FROM SINKING!
BUT WHENEVER THE MAN OF STEEL SHEDS HIS COLORFUL GARB AND RETURNS TO HIS APARTMENT AS TIMID CLARK KENT...
THANKS FOR THE RENT AGAIN, MR. KENT! BY THE WAY, IF YOU DON'T HAVE A JOB, WHERE DO YOU GET YOUR MONEY? YOU'RE NOT A ROBBER, ARE YOU? HA, HA!
I'LL HAVE TO GET A JOB-- FAST! HER CURIOSITY MIGHT MEAN THE END OF MY SECRET SUPERMAN CAREER! PEOPLE ARE ALWAYS SUSPICIOUS OF IDLERS WHO HAVE MONEY!
BUT WHAT SORT OF A JOB? HMMM-- I'VE GOT IT! I COULD BECOME A REPORTER ON THE LEADING PAPER IN METROPOLIS! AS A REPORTER, I COULD INVESTIGATE CRIMINALS WITHOUT THEIR SUSPECTING I'M REALLY SUPERMAN!
SOON, IN THE OFFICE OF PERRY WHITE, EDITOR OF THE DAILY PLANET--
SO YOU WANT TO WORK FOR THE PLANET, EH? YOU AND HUNDREDS OF OTHERS! WHY SHOULD I HIRE YOU?
BECAUSE I WOULD DO A GREAT JOB! MR. WHITE, I ADMIRE YOUR PAPER SO MUCH I... I KNOW EVERY BIG SCOOP IT HAS EVER PRINTED!
SOUNDS IMPRESSIVE!
MR. KENT, MEET LOIS LANE, A STAFF REPORTER! SHE'S GOOD... AT GETTING IMPORTANT STORIES-- BUT SHE OFTEN LANDS IN A HEAP OF TROUBLE!
SO YOU KNOW EVERY GREAT PLANET SCOOP FOR THE PAST THIRTY YEARS?
IF I KNOW PERRY, HE WILL MAKE KENT PROVE IT!
2

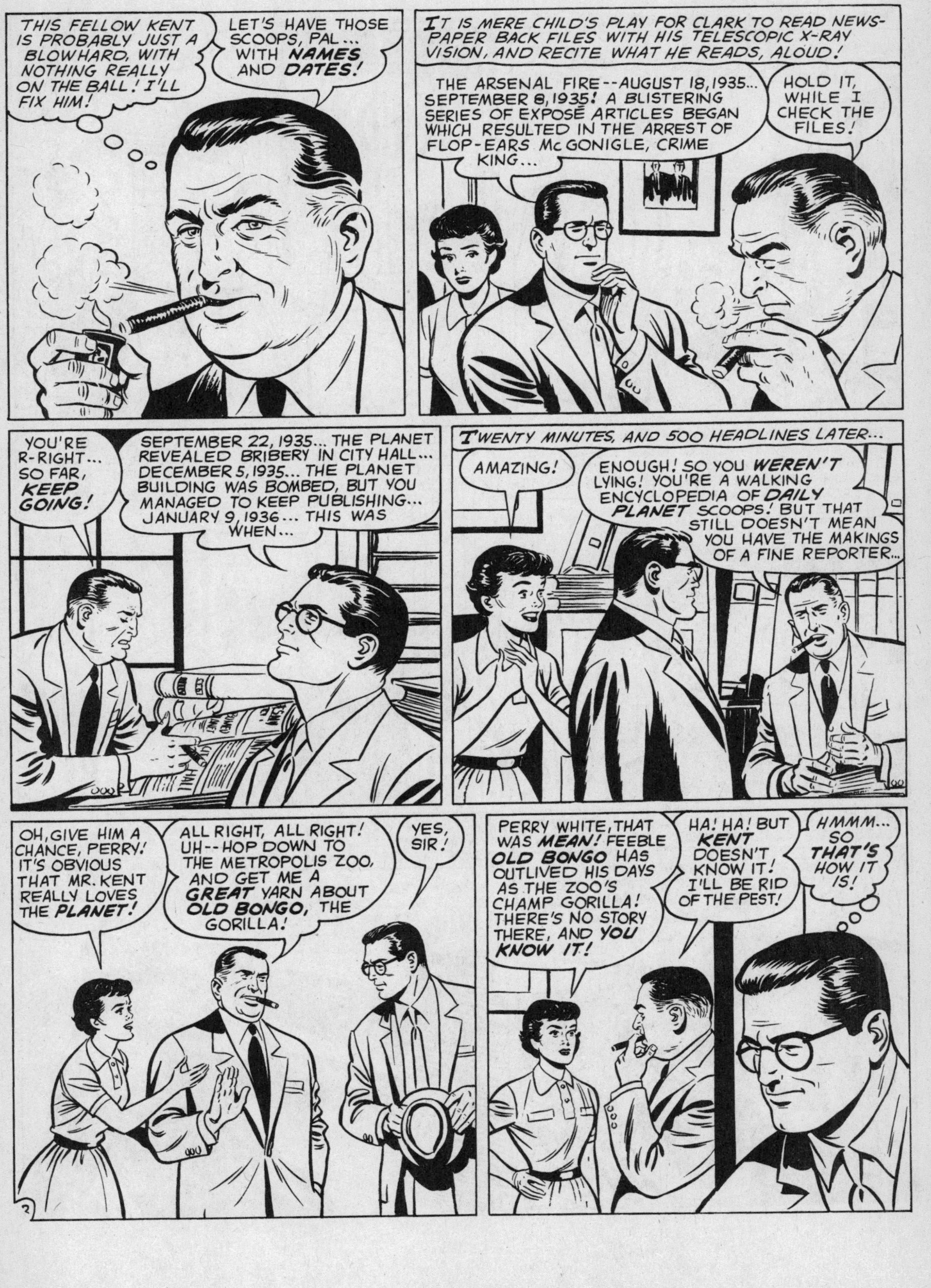
THIS FELLOW KENT IS PROBABLY JUST A BLOWHARD, WITH NOTHING REALLY ON THE BALL! I'LL FIX HIM!
LET'S HAVE THOSE SCOOPS, PAL... WITH NAMES AND DATES!
IT IS MERE CHILD'S PLAY FOR CLARK TO READ NEWS-PAPER BACK FILES WITH HIS TELESCOPIC X-RAY VISION, AND RECITE WHAT HE READS, ALOUD!
THE ARSENAL FIRE--AUGUST 18, 1935... SEPTEMBER 8, 1935! A BLISTERING SERIES OF EXPOSÉ ARTICLES BEGAN WHICH RESULTED IN THE ARREST OF FLOP-EARS McGONIGLE, CRIME KING...
HOLD IT, WHILE I CHECK THE FILES!
YOU'RE R-RIGHT... SO FAR, KEEP GOING!
SEPTEMBER 22, 1935... THE PLANET REVEALED BRIBERY IN CITY HALL... DECEMBER 5, 1935... THE PLANET BUILDING WAS BOMBED, BUT YOU MANAGED TO KEEP PUBLISHING... JANUARY 9, 1936... THIS WAS WHEN...
TWENTY MINUTES, AND 500 HEADLINES LATER...
AMAZING!
ENOUGH! SO YOU WEREN'T LYING! YOU'RE A WALKING ENCYCLOPEDIA OF DAILY PLANET SCOOPS! BUT THAT STILL DOESN'T MEAN YOU HAVE THE MAKINGS OF A FINE REPORTER...
OH, GIVE HIM A CHANCE, PERRY! IT'S OBVIOUS THAT MR. KENT REALLY LOVES THE PLANET!
ALL RIGHT, ALL RIGHT! UH--HOP DOWN TO THE METROPOLIS ZOO, AND GET ME A GREAT YARN ABOUT OLD BONGO, THE GORILLA!
YES, SIR!
PERRY WHITE, THAT WAS MEAN! FEEBLE OLD BONGO HAS OUTLIVED HIS DAYS AS THE ZOO'S CHAMP GORILLA! THERE'S NO STORY THERE, AND YOU KNOW IT!
HA! HA! BUT KENT DOESN'T KNOW IT! I'LL BE RID OF THE PEST!
HMMM... SO THAT'S HOW IT IS!
3

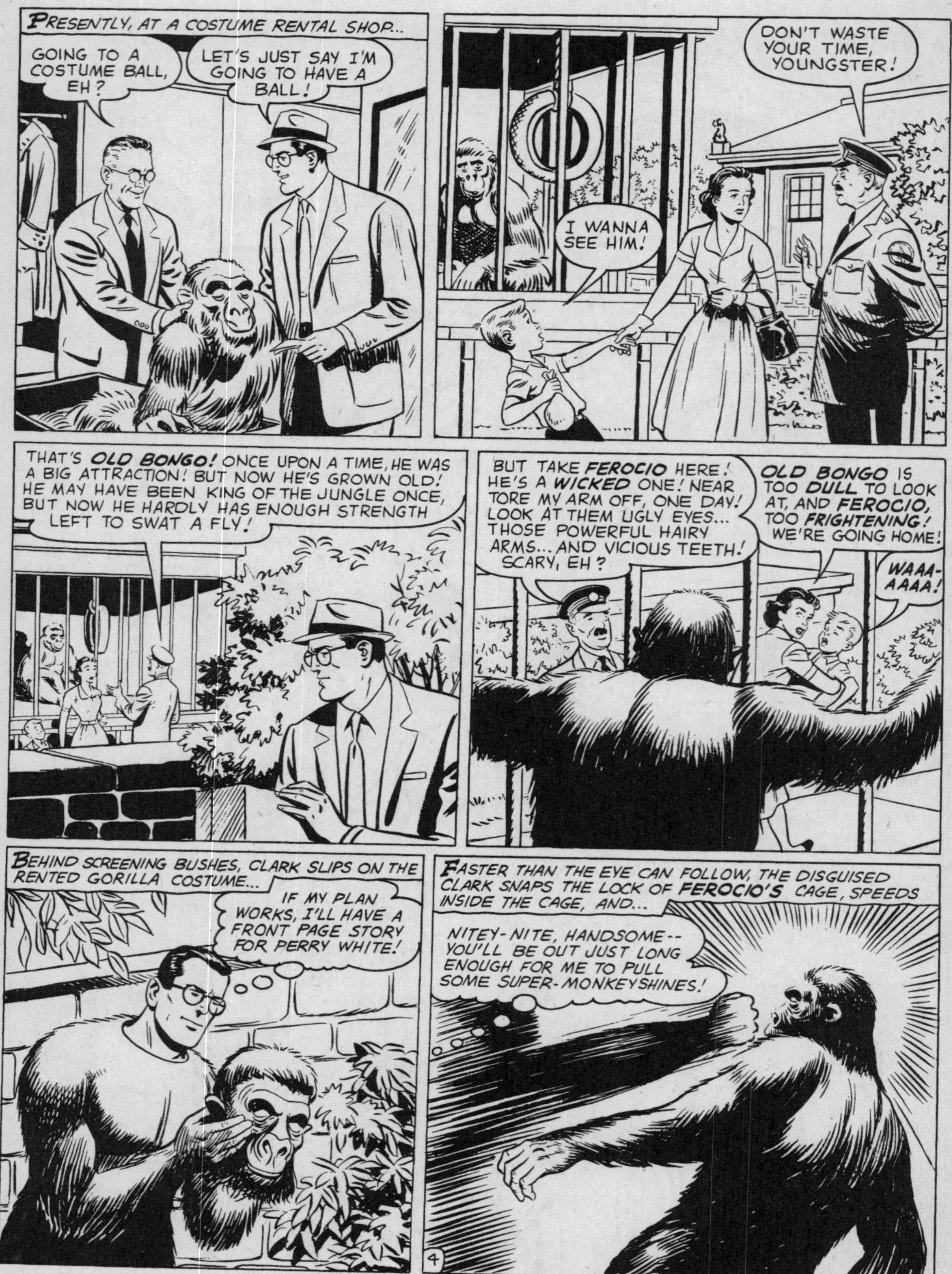
PRESENTLY, AT A COSTUME RENTAL SHOP...
GOING TO A COSTUME BALL, EH?
LET'S JUST SAY I'M GOING TO HAVE A BALL!
DON'T WASTE YOUR TIME, YOUNGSTER!
I WANNA SEE HIM!
THAT'S OLD BONGO! ONCE UPON A TIME, HE WAS A BIG ATTRACTION! BUT NOW HE'S GROWN OLD! HE MAY HAVE BEEN KING OF THE JUNGLE ONCE, BUT NOW HE HARDLY HAS ENOUGH STRENGTH LEFT TO SWAT A FLY!
BUT TAKE FEROCIO HERE! HE'S A WICKED ONE! NEAR TORE MY ARM OFF, ONE DAY! LOOK AT THEM UGLY EYES... THOSE POWERFUL HAIRY ARMS... AND VICIOUS TEETH! SCARY, EH?
OLD BONGO IS TOO DULL TO LOOK AT, AND FEROCIO, TOO FRIGHTENING! WE'RE GOING HOME!
WAAA-AAAA!
BEHIND SCREENING BUSHES, CLARK SLIPS ON THE RENTED GORILLA COSTUME...
IF MY PLAN WORKS, I'LL HAVE A FRONT PAGE STORY FOR PERRY WHITE!
4
FASTER THAN THE EYE CAN FOLLOW, THE DISGUISED CLARK SNAPS THE LOCK OF FEROCIO'S CAGE, SPEEDS INSIDE THE CAGE, AND...
NITEY-NITE, HANDSOME-- YOU'LL BE OUT JUST LONG ENOUGH FOR ME TO PULL SOME SUPER-MONKEYSHINES!

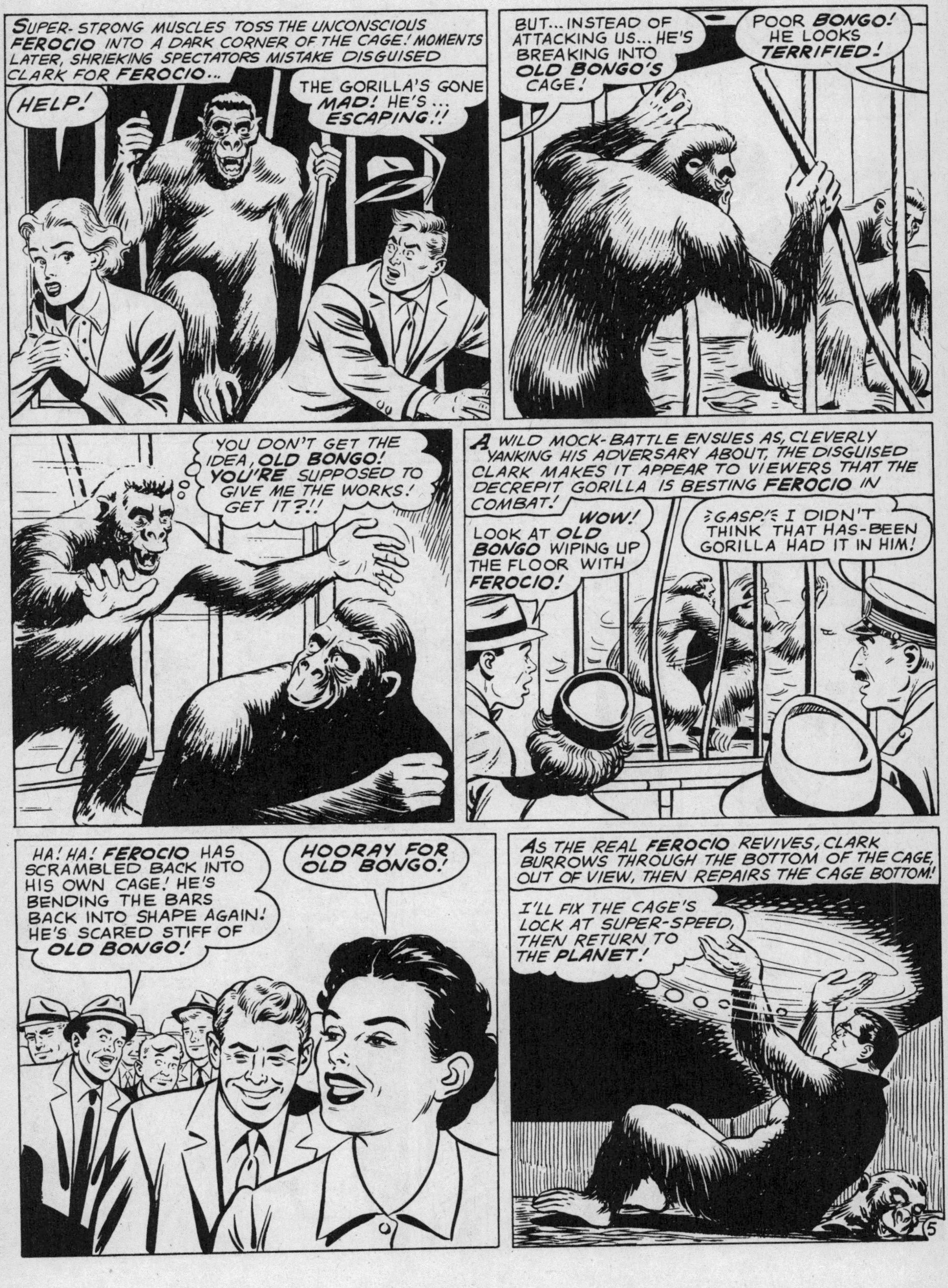
SUPER-STRONG MUSCLES TOSS THE UNCONSCIOUS FEROCIO INTO A DARK CORNER OF THE CAGE! MOMENTS LATER, SHRIEKING SPECTATORS MISTAKE DISGUISED CLARK FOR FEROCIO...
HELP!
THE GORILLA'S GONE MAD! HE'S... ESCAPING!!
BUT... INSTEAD OF ATTACKING US... HE'S BREAKING INTO OLD BONGO'S CAGE!
POOR BONGO! HE LOOKS TERRIFIED!
YOU DON'T GET THE IDEA, OLD BONGO! YOU'RE SUPPOSED TO GIVE ME THE WORKS! GET IT?!!
A WILD MOCK-BATTLE ENSUES AS, CLEVERLY YANKING HIS ADVERSARY ABOUT, THE DISGUISED CLARK MAKES IT APPEAR TO VIEWERS THAT THE DECREPIT GORILLA IS BESTING FEROCIO IN COMBAT!
WOW! LOOK AT OLD BONGO WIPING UP THE FLOOR WITH FEROCIO!
GASP! I DIDN'T THINK THAT HAS-BEEN GORILLA HAD IT IN HIM!
HA! HA! FEROCIO HAS SCRAMBLED BACK INTO HIS OWN CAGE! HE'S BENDING THE BARS BACK INTO SHAPE AGAIN! HE'S SCARED STIFF OF OLD BONGO!
HOORAY FOR OLD BONGO!
AS THE REAL FEROCIO REVIVES, CLARK BURROWS THROUGH THE BOTTOM OF THE CAGE, OUT OF VIEW, THEN REPAIRS THE CAGE BOTTOM!
I'LL FIX THE CAGE'S LOCK AT SUPER-SPEED, THEN RETURN TO THE PLANET!
5

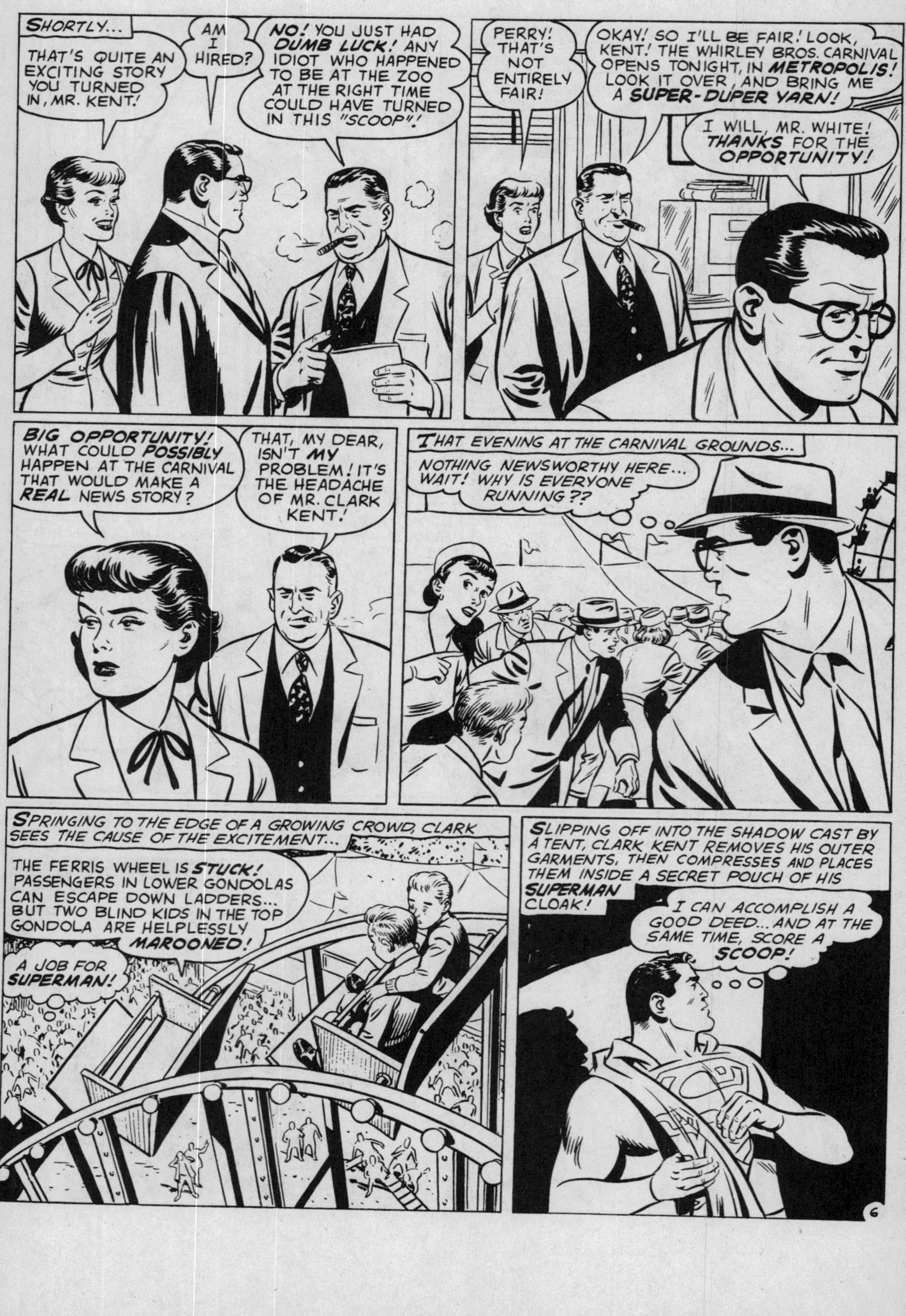
SHORTLY...
THAT'S QUITE AN EXCITING STORY YOU TURNED IN, MR. KENT!
AM I HIRED?
NO! YOU JUST HAD DUMB LUCK! ANY IDIOT WHO HAPPENED TO BE AT THE ZOO AT THE RIGHT TIME COULD HAVE TURNED IN THIS "SCOOP"!
PERRY! THAT'S NOT ENTIRELY FAIR!
OKAY! SO I'LL BE FAIR! LOOK, KENT! THE WHIRLEY BROS. CARNIVAL OPENS TONIGHT, IN METROPOLIS! LOOK IT OVER, AND BRING ME A SUPER-DUPER YARN!
I WILL, MR. WHITE! THANKS FOR THE OPPORTUNITY!
BIG OPPORTUNITY! WHAT COULD POSSIBLY HAPPEN AT THE CARNIVAL THAT WOULD MAKE A REAL NEWS STORY?
THAT, MY DEAR, ISN'T MY PROBLEM! IT'S THE HEADACHE OF MR. CLARK KENT!
THAT EVENING AT THE CARNIVAL GROUNDS...
NOTHING NEWSWORTHY HERE... WAIT! WHY IS EVERYONE RUNNING??
SPRINGING TO THE EDGE OF A GROWING CROWD, CLARK SEES THE CAUSE OF THE EXCITEMENT...
THE FERRIS WHEEL IS STUCK! PASSENGERS IN LOWER GONDOLAS CAN ESCAPE DOWN LADDERS... BUT TWO BLIND KIDS IN THE TOP GONDOLA ARE HELPLESSLY MAROONED!
A JOB FOR SUPERMAN!
SLIPPING OFF INTO THE SHADOW CAST BY A TENT, CLARK KENT REMOVES HIS OUTER GARMENTS, THEN COMPRESSES AND PLACES THEM INSIDE A SECRET POUCH OF HIS SUPERMAN CLOAK!
I CAN ACCOMPLISH A GOOD DEED... AND AT THE SAME TIME, SCORE A SCOOP!
6

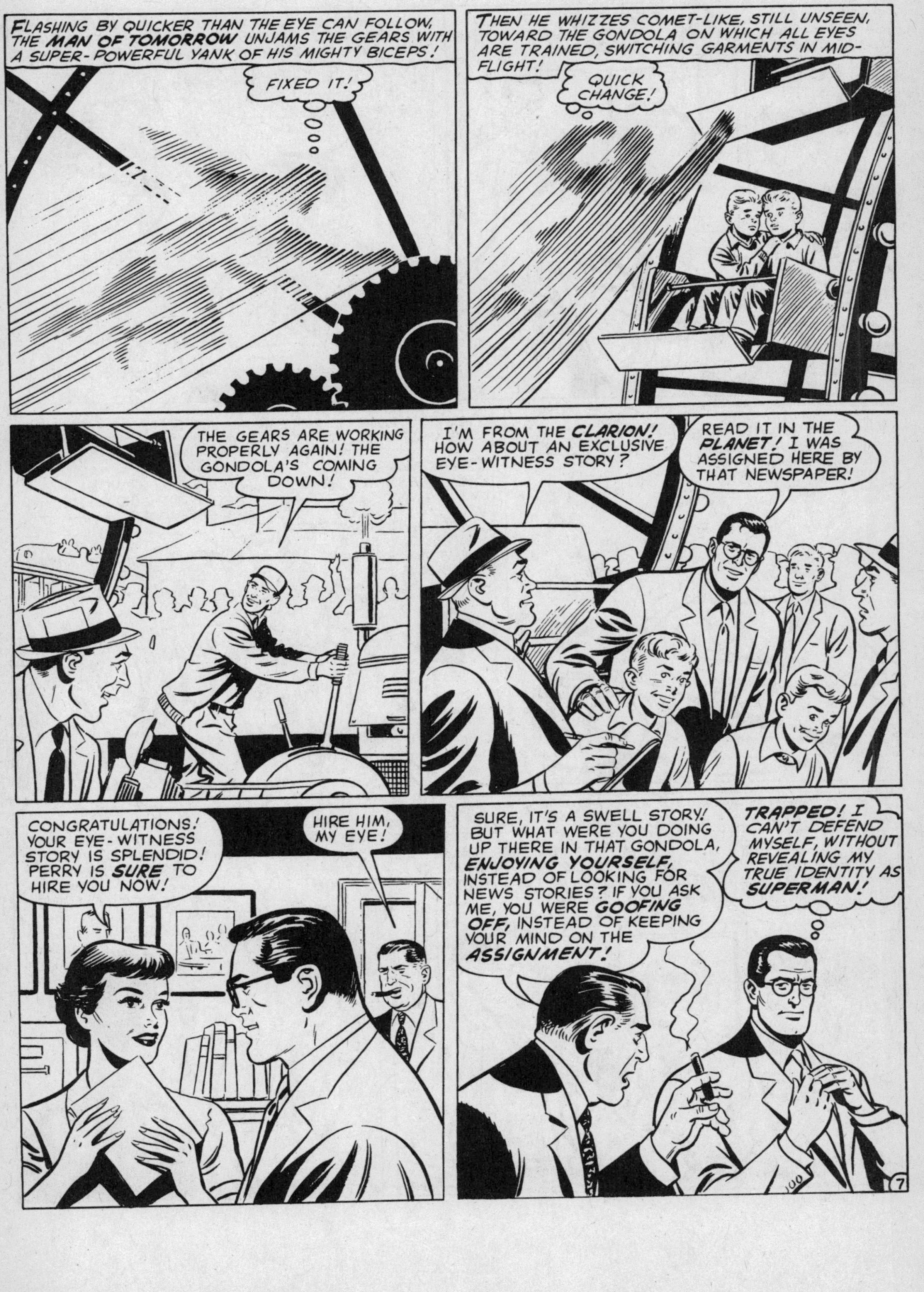
FLASHING BY QUICKER THAN THE EYE CAN FOLLOW, THE MAN OF TOMORROW UNJAMS THE GEARS WITH A SUPER-POWERFUL YANK OF HIS MIGHTY BICEPS!
FIXED IT!
THEN HE WHIZZES COMET-LIKE, STILL UNSEEN, TOWARD THE GONDOLA ON WHICH ALL EYES ARE TRAINED, SWITCHING GARMENTS IN MID-FLIGHT!
QUICK CHANGE!
THE GEARS ARE WORKING PROPERLY AGAIN! THE GONDOLA'S COMING DOWN!
I'M FROM THE CLARION! HOW ABOUT AN EXCLUSIVE EYE-WITNESS STORY?
READ IT IN THE PLANET! I WAS ASSIGNED HERE BY THAT NEWSPAPER!
CONGRATULATIONS! YOUR EYE-WITNESS STORY IS SPLENDID! PERRY IS SURE TO HIRE YOU NOW!
HIRE HIM, MY EYE!
SURE, IT'S A SWELL STORY! BUT WHAT WERE YOU DOING UP THERE IN THAT GONDOLA, ENJOYING YOURSELF, INSTEAD OF LOOKING FOR NEWS STORIES? IF YOU ASK ME, YOU WERE GOOFING OFF, INSTEAD OF KEEPING YOUR MIND ON THE ASSIGNMENT!
TRAPPED! I CAN'T DEFEND MYSELF, WITHOUT REVEALING MY TRUE IDENTITY AS SUPERMAN!
7

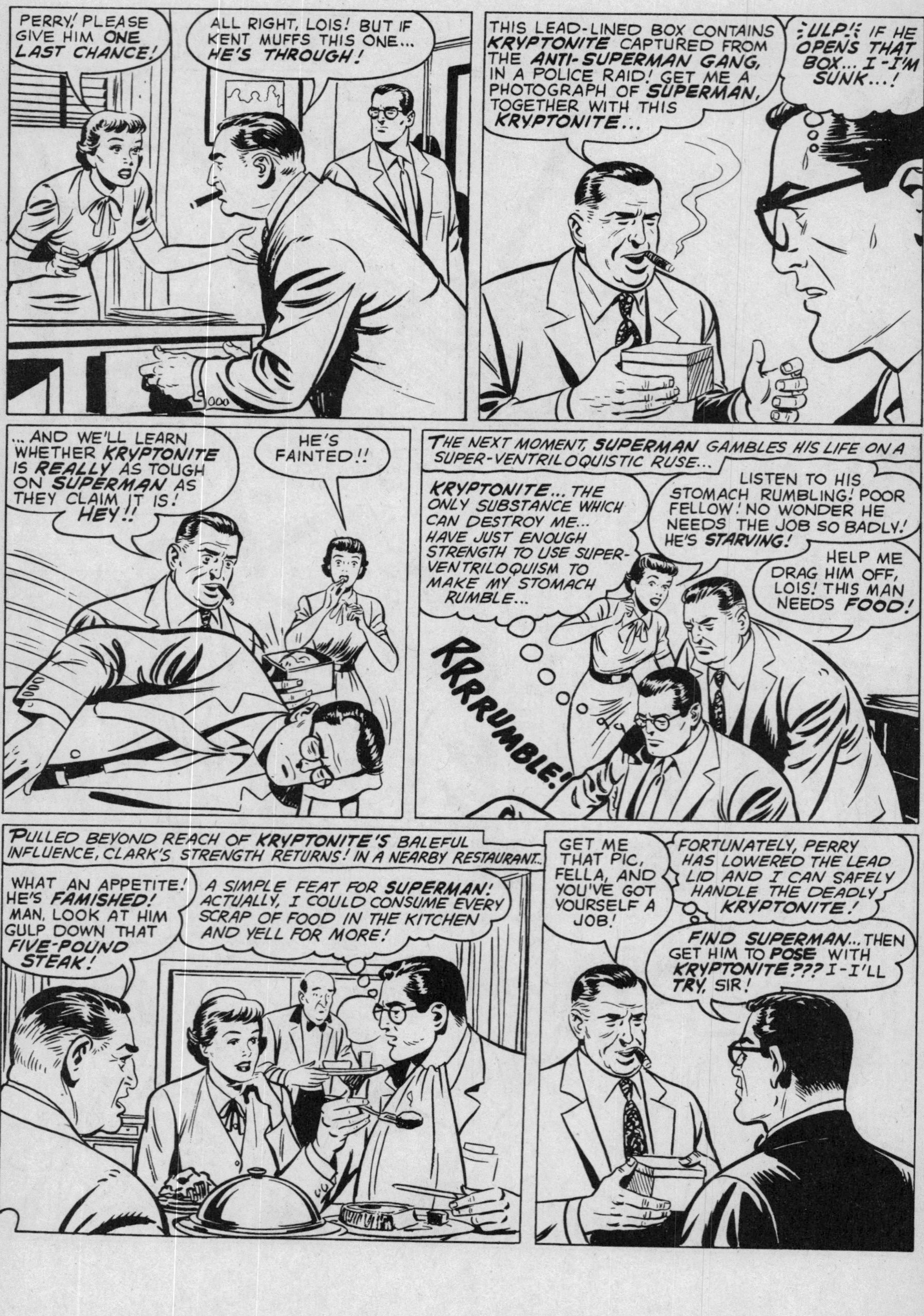

PERRY! PLEASE GIVE HIM ONE LAST CHANCE!
ALL RIGHT, LOIS! BUT IF KENT MUFFS THIS ONE... HE'S THROUGH!
THIS LEAD-LINED BOX CONTAINS KRYPTONITE CAPTURED FROM THE ANTI-SUPERMAN GANG, IN A POLICE RAID! GET ME A PHOTOGRAPH OF SUPERMAN, TOGETHER WITH THIS KRYPTONITE...
ULP! IF HE OPENS THAT BOX... I-I'M SUNK...!
... AND WE'LL LEARN WHETHER KRYPTONITE IS REALLY AS TOUGH ON SUPERMAN AS THEY CLAIM IT IS! HEY!!
HE'S FAINTED!!
THE NEXT MOMENT, SUPERMAN GAMBLES HIS LIFE ON A SUPER-VENTRILOQUISTIC RUSE...
KRYPTONITE... THE ONLY SUBSTANCE WHICH CAN DESTROY ME... HAVE JUST ENOUGH STRENGTH TO USE SUPER-VENTRILOQUISM TO MAKE MY STOMACH RUMBLE...
LISTEN TO HIS STOMACH RUMBLING! POOR FELLOW! NO WONDER HE NEEDS THE JOB SO BADLY! HE'S STARVING!
HELP ME DRAG HIM OFF, LOIS! THIS MAN NEEDS FOOD!
RRRRUMBLE!
PULLED BEYOND REACH OF KRYPTONITE'S BALEFUL INFLUENCE, CLARK'S STRENGTH RETURNS! IN A NEARBY RESTAURANT...
WHAT AN APPETITE! HE'S FAMISHED! MAN, LOOK AT HIM GULP DOWN THAT FIVE-POUND STEAK!
A SIMPLE FEAT FOR SUPERMAN! ACTUALLY, I COULD CONSUME EVERY SCRAP OF FOOD IN THE KITCHEN AND YELL FOR MORE!
GET ME THAT PIC, FELLA, AND YOU'VE GOT YOURSELF A JOB!
FORTUNATELY, PERRY HAS LOWERED THE LEAD LID AND I CAN SAFELY HANDLE THE DEADLY KRYPTONITE!
FIND SUPERMAN... THEN GET HIM TO POSE WITH KRYPTONITE??? I-I'LL TRY, SIR!

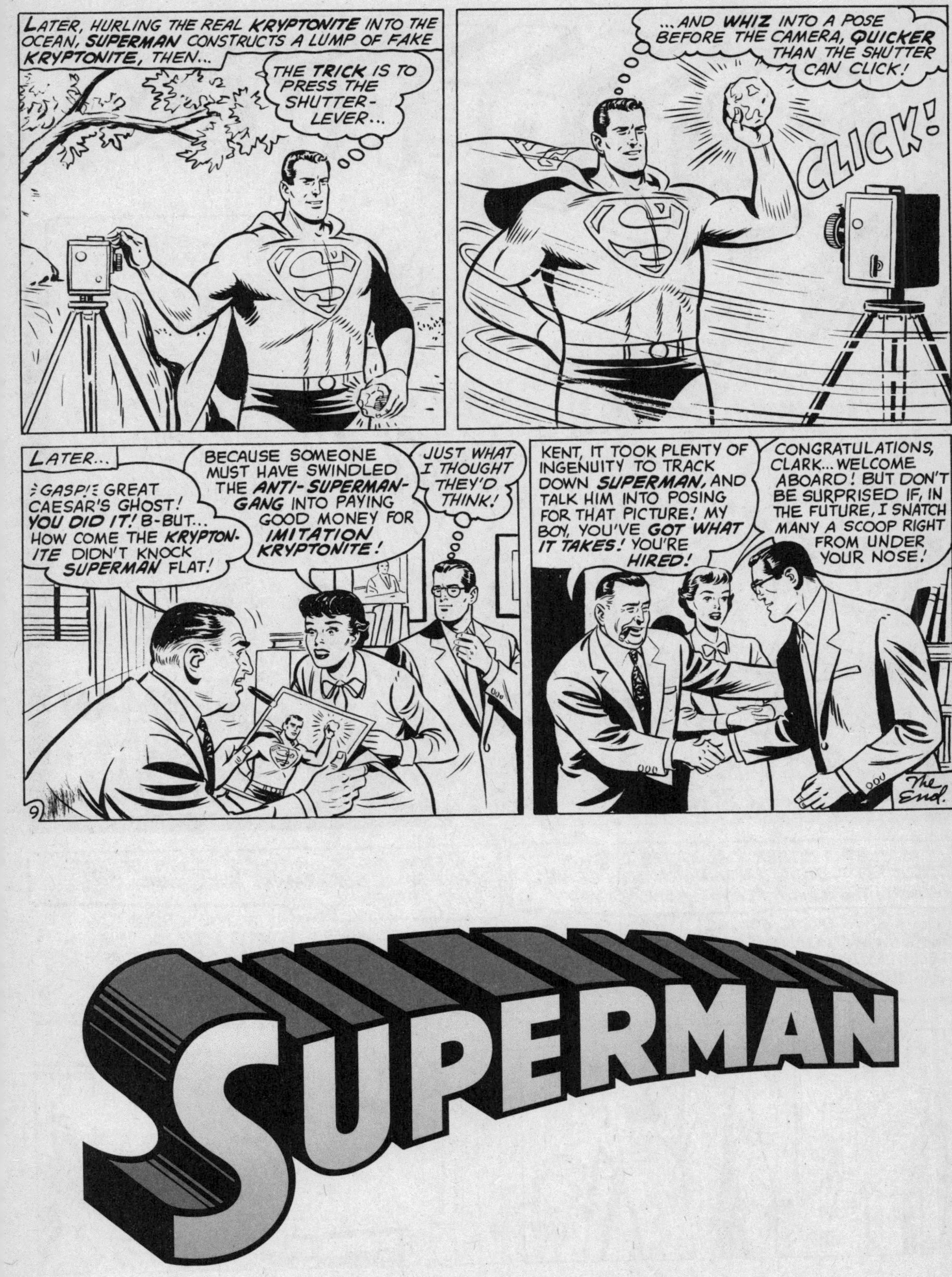
LATER, HURLING THE REAL KRYPTONITE INTO THE OCEAN, SUPERMAN CONSTRUCTS A LUMP OF FAKE KRYPTONITE, THEN...
THE TRICK IS TO PRESS THE SHUTTER-LEVER...
...AND WHIZ INTO A POSE BEFORE THE CAMERA, QUICKER THAN THE SHUTTER CAN CLICK!
CLICK!
LATER...
GASP! GREAT CAESAR'S GHOST! YOU DID IT! B-BUT... HOW COME THE KRYPTONITE DIDN'T KNOCK SUPERMAN FLAT!
BECAUSE SOMEONE MUST HAVE SWINDLED THE ANTI-SUPERMAN-GANG INTO PAYING GOOD MONEY FOR IMITATION KRYPTONITE!
JUST WHAT I THOUGHT THEY'D THINK!
9
KENT, IT TOOK PLENTY OF INGENUITY TO TRACK DOWN SUPERMAN, AND TALK HIM INTO POSING FOR THAT PICTURE! MY BOY, YOU'VE GOT WHAT IT TAKES! YOU'RE HIRED!
CONGRATULATIONS, CLARK... WELCOME ABOARD! BUT DON'T BE SURPRISED IF, IN THE FUTURE, I SNATCH MANY A SCOOP RIGHT FROM UNDER YOUR NOSE!
The End.

SUPERMAN

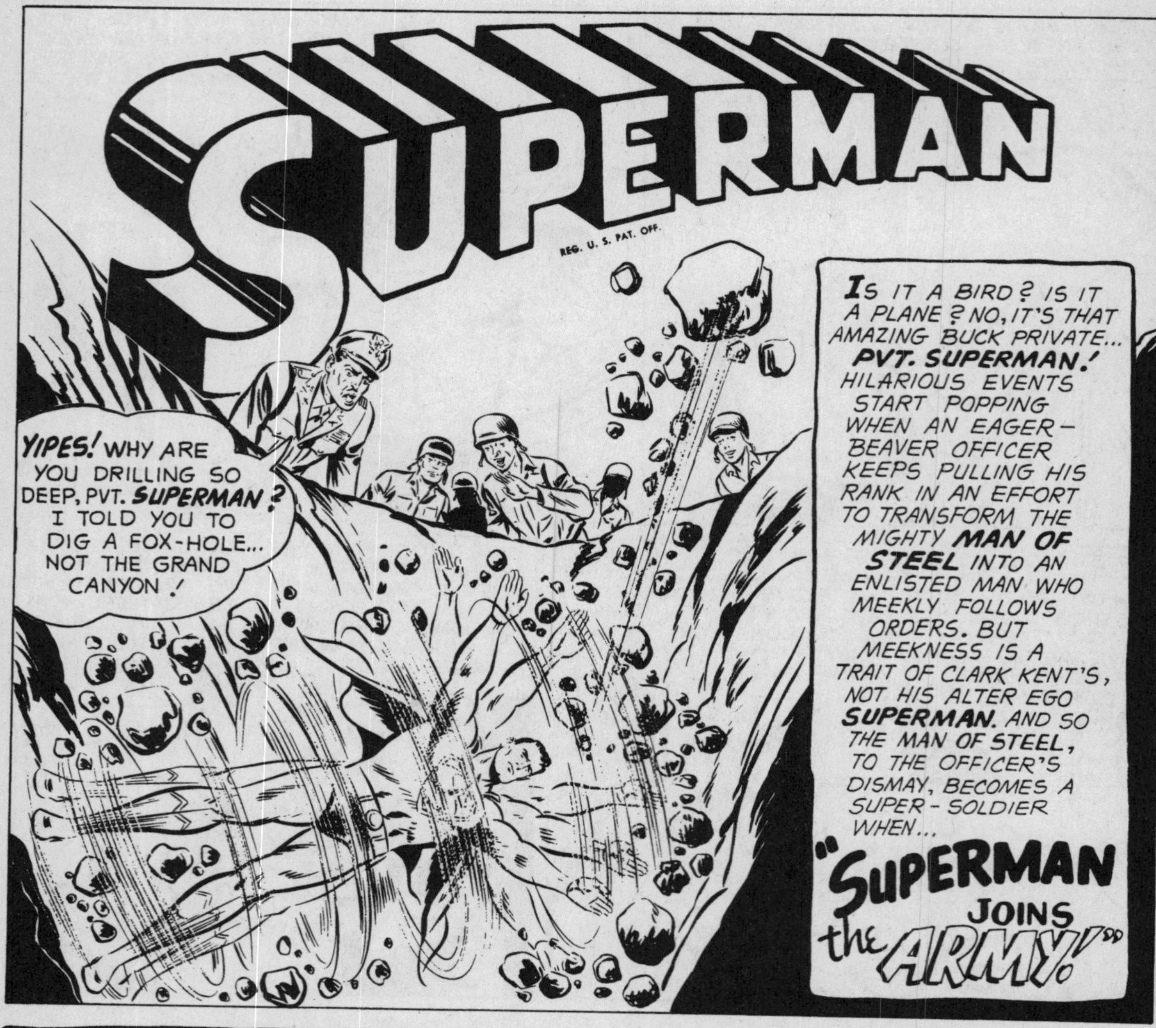
SUPERMAN
REG. U. S. PAT. OFF.
IS IT A BIRD? IS IT A PLANE? NO, IT'S THAT AMAZING BUCK PRIVATE... PVT. SUPERMAN! HILARIOUS EVENTS START POPPING WHEN AN EAGER-BEAVER OFFICER KEEPS PULLING HIS RANK IN AN EFFORT TO TRANSFORM THE MIGHTY MAN OF STEEL INTO AN ENLISTED MAN WHO MEEKLY FOLLOWS ORDERS. BUT MEEKNESS IS A TRAIT OF CLARK KENT'S, NOT HIS ALTER EGO SUPERMAN. AND SO THE MAN OF STEEL, TO THE OFFICER'S DISMAY, BECOMES A SUPER-SOLDIER WHEN...
YIPES! WHY ARE YOU DRILLING SO DEEP, PVT. SUPERMAN? I TOLD YOU TO DIG A FOX-HOLE... NOT THE GRAND CANYON!
"SUPERMAN JOINS the ARMY!"

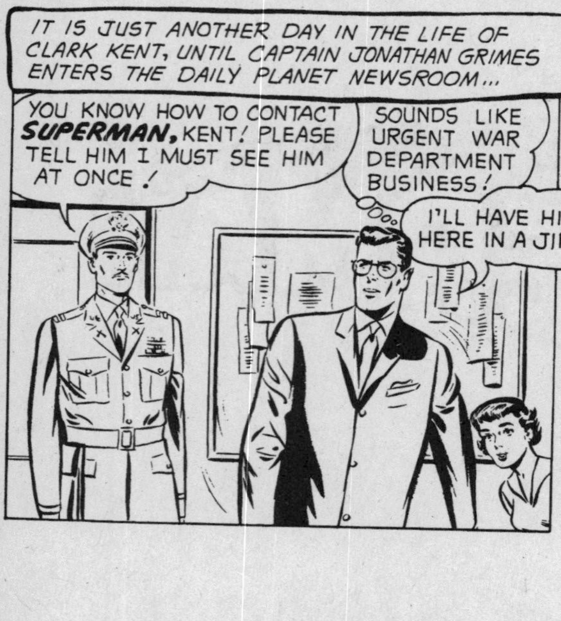
IT IS JUST ANOTHER DAY IN THE LIFE OF CLARK KENT, UNTIL CAPTAIN JONATHAN GRIMES ENTERS THE DAILY PLANET NEWSROOM...
YOU KNOW HOW TO CONTACT SUPERMAN, KENT! PLEASE TELL HIM I MUST SEE HIM AT ONCE!
SOUNDS LIKE URGENT WAR DEPARTMENT BUSINESS!
I'LL HAVE HIM HERE IN A JIFFY!

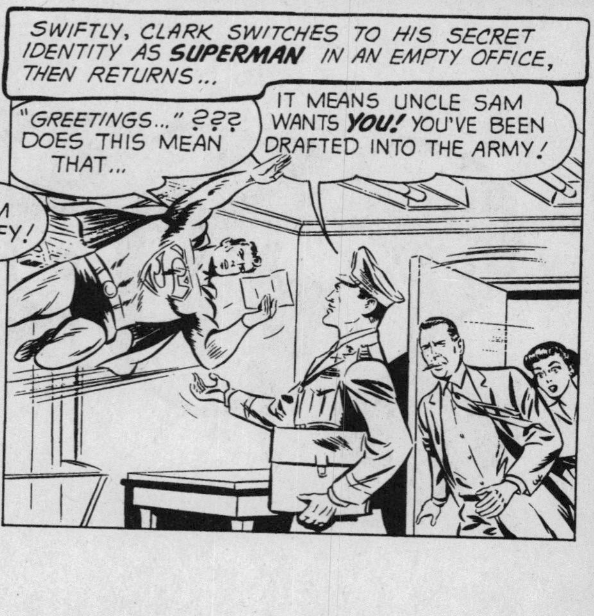
SWIFTLY, CLARK SWITCHES TO HIS SECRET IDENTITY AS SUPERMAN IN AN EMPTY OFFICE, THEN RETURNS...
"GREETINGS..." ??? DOES THIS MEAN THAT...
IT MEANS UNCLE SAM WANTS YOU! YOU'VE BEEN DRAFTED INTO THE ARMY!

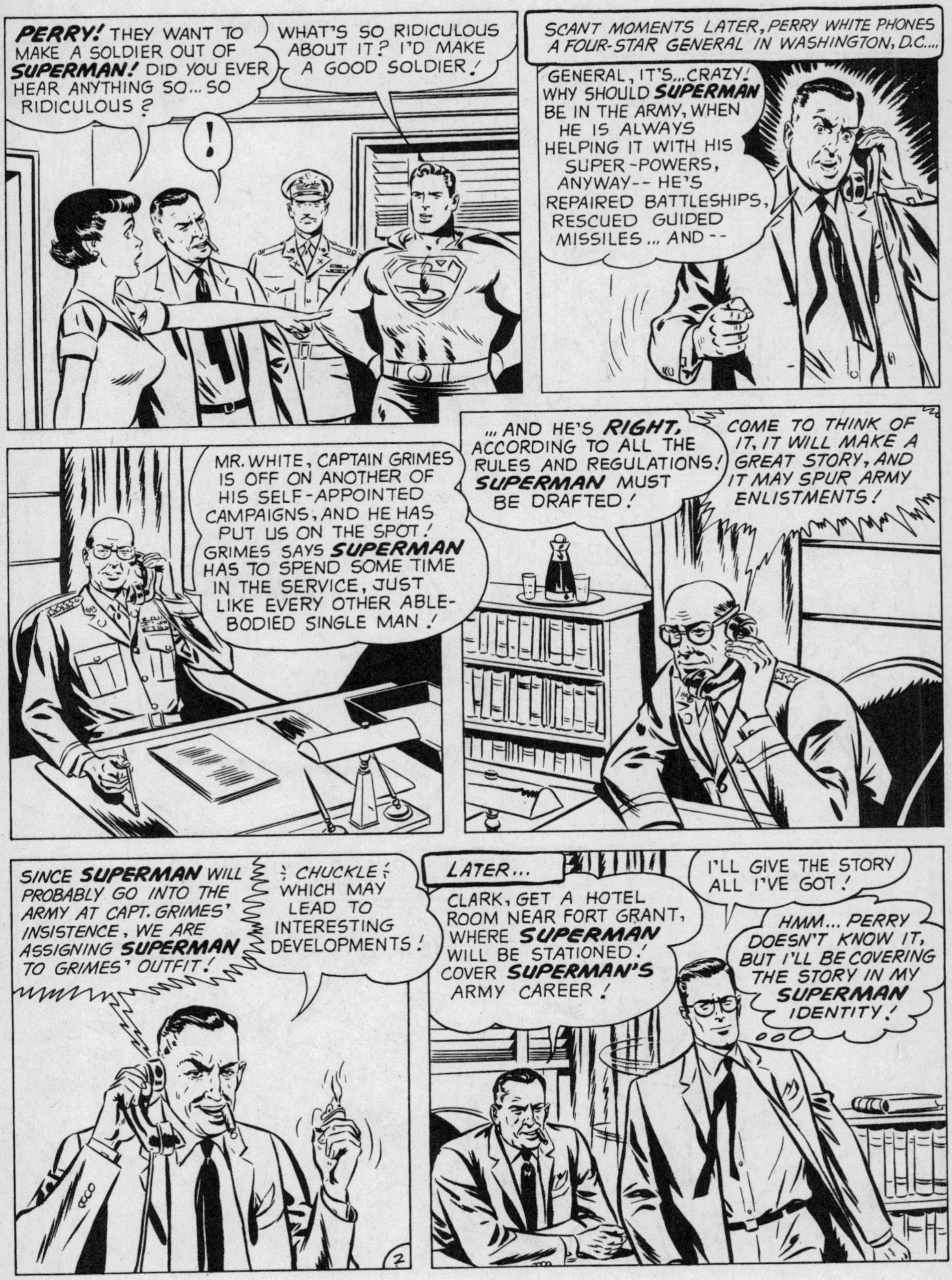
PERRY! THEY WANT TO MAKE A SOLDIER OUT OF SUPERMAN! DID YOU EVER HEAR ANYTHING SO... SO RIDICULOUS?
!
WHAT'S SO RIDICULOUS ABOUT IT? I'D MAKE A GOOD SOLDIER!
SCANT MOMENTS LATER, PERRY WHITE PHONES A FOUR-STAR GENERAL IN WASHINGTON, D.C....
GENERAL, IT'S...CRAZY! WHY SHOULD SUPERMAN BE IN THE ARMY, WHEN HE IS ALWAYS HELPING IT WITH HIS SUPER-POWERS, ANYWAY-- HE'S REPAIRED BATTLESHIPS, RESCUED GUIDED MISSILES ... AND --
MR. WHITE, CAPTAIN GRIMES IS OFF ON ANOTHER OF HIS SELF-APPOINTED CAMPAIGNS, AND HE HAS PUT US ON THE SPOT! GRIMES SAYS SUPERMAN HAS TO SPEND SOME TIME IN THE SERVICE, JUST LIKE EVERY OTHER ABLE-BODIED SINGLE MAN!
... AND HE'S RIGHT, ACCORDING TO ALL THE RULES AND REGULATIONS! SUPERMAN MUST BE DRAFTED!
COME TO THINK OF IT, IT WILL MAKE A GREAT STORY, AND IT MAY SPUR ARMY ENLISTMENTS!
SINCE SUPERMAN WILL PROBABLY GO INTO THE ARMY AT CAPT. GRIMES' INSISTENCE, WE ARE ASSIGNING SUPERMAN TO GRIMES' OUTFIT!
CHUCKLE! WHICH MAY LEAD TO INTERESTING DEVELOPMENTS!
LATER...
CLARK, GET A HOTEL ROOM NEAR FORT GRANT, WHERE SUPERMAN WILL BE STATIONED! COVER SUPERMAN'S ARMY CAREER!
I'LL GIVE THE STORY ALL I'VE GOT!
HMM... PERRY DOESN'T KNOW IT, BUT I'LL BE COVERING THE STORY IN MY SUPERMAN IDENTITY!
2

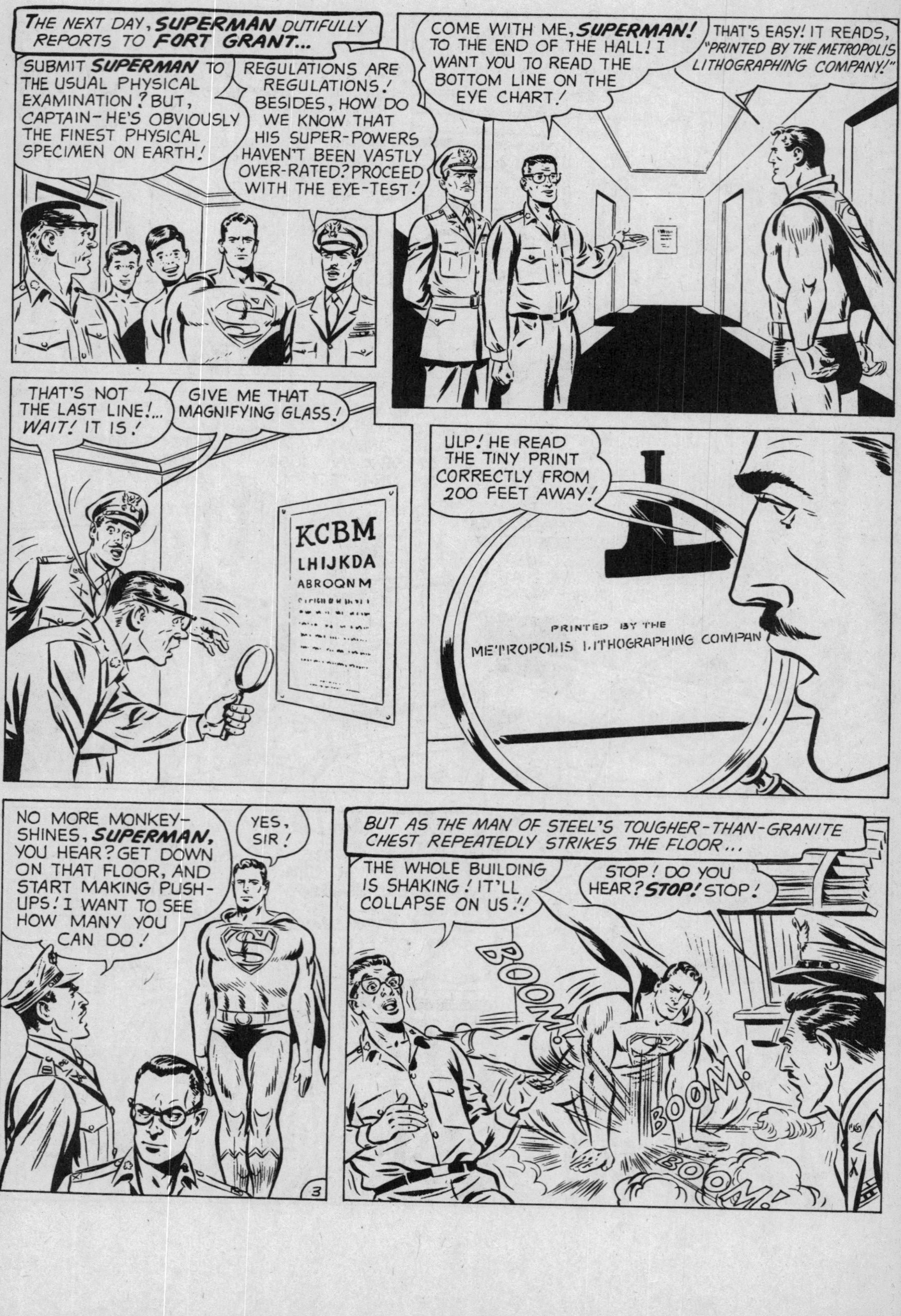
THE NEXT DAY, SUPERMAN DUTIFULLY REPORTS TO FORT GRANT...
SUBMIT SUPERMAN TO THE USUAL PHYSICAL EXAMINATION? BUT, CAPTAIN-- HE'S OBVIOUSLY THE FINEST PHYSICAL SPECIMEN ON EARTH!
REGULATIONS ARE REGULATIONS! BESIDES, HOW DO WE KNOW THAT HIS SUPER-POWERS HAVEN'T BEEN VASTLY OVER-RATED? PROCEED WITH THE EYE-TEST!
COME WITH ME, SUPERMAN! TO THE END OF THE HALL! I WANT YOU TO READ THE BOTTOM LINE ON THE EYE CHART!
THAT'S EASY! IT READS, "PRINTED BY THE METROPOLIS LITHOGRAPHING COMPANY!"
THAT'S NOT THE LAST LINE!... WAIT! IT IS!
GIVE ME THAT MAGNIFYING GLASS!
KCBM
LHIJKDA
ABROQN M
ULP! HE READ THE TINY PRINT CORRECTLY FROM 200 FEET AWAY!
PRINTED BY THE
METROPOLIS LITHOGRAPHING COMPAN
NO MORE MONKEY-SHINES, SUPERMAN, YOU HEAR? GET DOWN ON THAT FLOOR, AND START MAKING PUSH-UPS! I WANT TO SEE HOW MANY YOU CAN DO!
YES, SIR!
3
BUT AS THE MAN OF STEEL'S TOUGHER-THAN-GRANITE CHEST REPEATEDLY STRIKES THE FLOOR...
THE WHOLE BUILDING IS SHAKING! IT'LL COLLAPSE ON US!!
STOP! DO YOU HEAR? STOP! STOP!
BOOM!
BOOM!
BOOM!
BOOM!

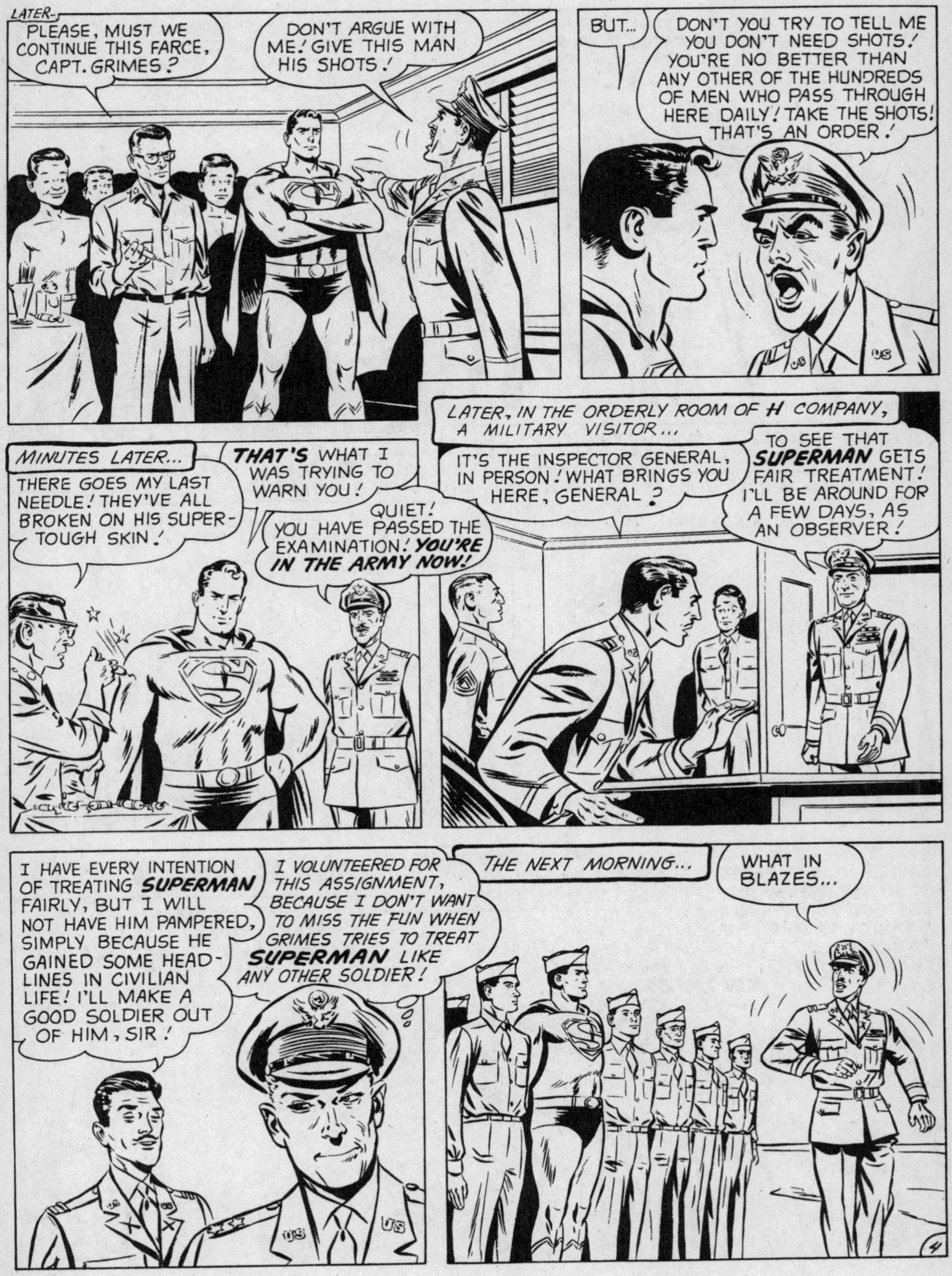
LATER-
PLEASE, MUST WE CONTINUE THIS FARCE, CAPT. GRIMES?
DON'T ARGUE WITH ME! GIVE THIS MAN HIS SHOTS!
BUT...
DON'T YOU TRY TO TELL ME YOU DON'T NEED SHOTS! YOU'RE NO BETTER THAN ANY OTHER OF THE HUNDREDS OF MEN WHO PASS THROUGH HERE DAILY! TAKE THE SHOTS! THAT'S AN ORDER!
MINUTES LATER...
THERE GOES MY LAST NEEDLE! THEY'VE ALL BROKEN ON HIS SUPER-TOUGH SKIN!
THAT'S WHAT I WAS TRYING TO WARN YOU!
QUIET! YOU HAVE PASSED THE EXAMINATION! YOU'RE IN THE ARMY NOW!
LATER, IN THE ORDERLY ROOM OF H COMPANY, A MILITARY VISITOR...
IT'S THE INSPECTOR GENERAL, IN PERSON! WHAT BRINGS YOU HERE, GENERAL?
TO SEE THAT SUPERMAN GETS FAIR TREATMENT! I'LL BE AROUND FOR A FEW DAYS, AS AN OBSERVER!
I HAVE EVERY INTENTION OF TREATING SUPERMAN FAIRLY, BUT I WILL NOT HAVE HIM PAMPERED, SIMPLY BECAUSE HE GAINED SOME HEADLINES IN CIVILIAN LIFE! I'LL MAKE A GOOD SOLDIER OUT OF HIM, SIR!
I VOLUNTEERED FOR THIS ASSIGNMENT, BECAUSE I DON'T WANT TO MISS THE FUN WHEN GRIMES TRIES TO TREAT SUPERMAN LIKE ANY OTHER SOLDIER!
THE NEXT MORNING...
WHAT IN BLAZES...
4

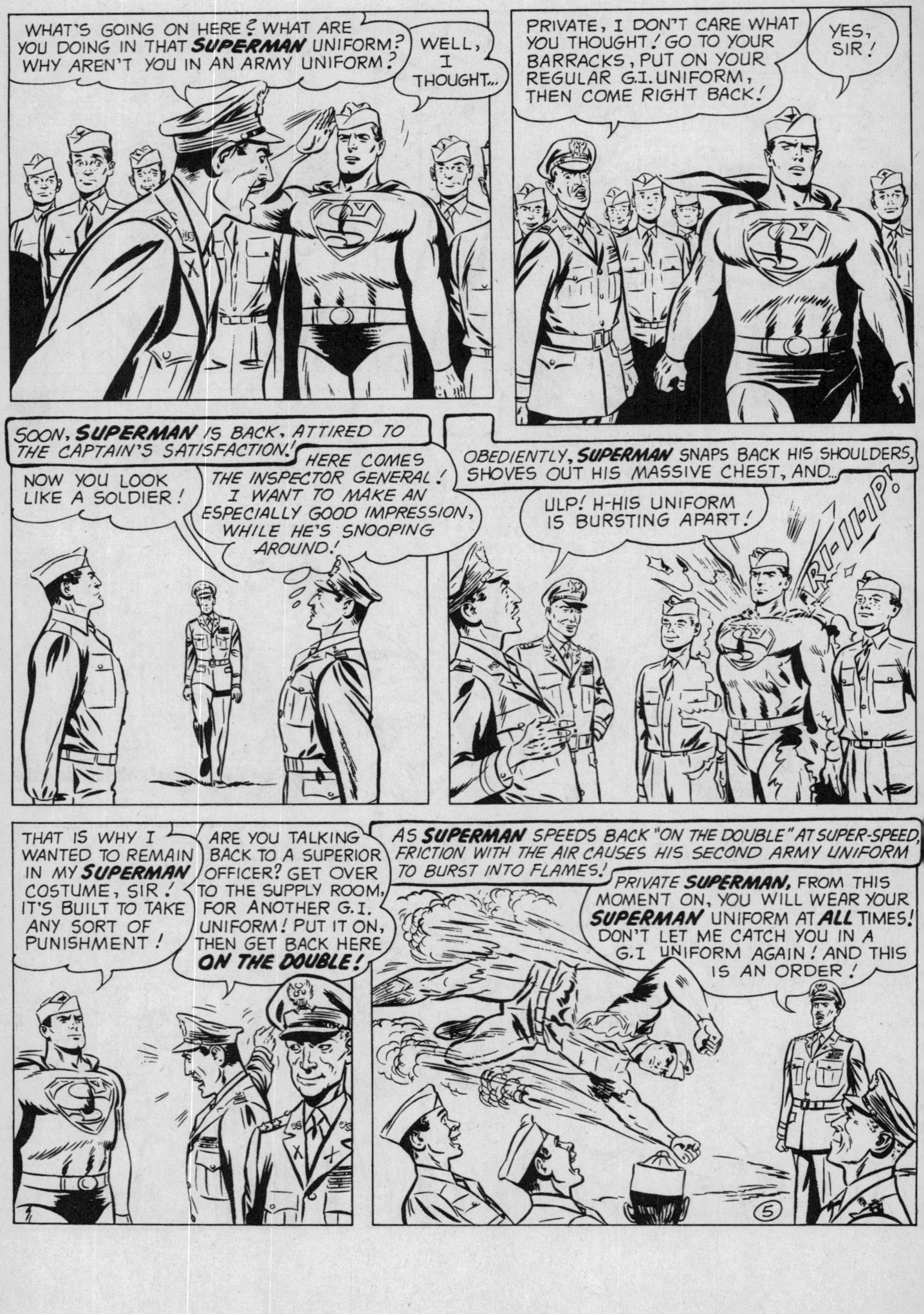
WHAT'S GOING ON HERE? WHAT ARE YOU DOING IN THAT SUPERMAN UNIFORM? WHY AREN'T YOU IN AN ARMY UNIFORM?
WELL, I THOUGHT...
PRIVATE, I DON'T CARE WHAT YOU THOUGHT! GO TO YOUR BARRACKS, PUT ON YOUR REGULAR G.I. UNIFORM, THEN COME RIGHT BACK!
YES, SIR!
SOON, SUPERMAN IS BACK, ATTIRED TO THE CAPTAIN'S SATISFACTION!
NOW YOU LOOK LIKE A SOLDIER!
HERE COMES THE INSPECTOR GENERAL! I WANT TO MAKE AN ESPECIALLY GOOD IMPRESSION, WHILE HE'S SNOOPING AROUND!
OBEDIENTLY, SUPERMAN SNAPS BACK HIS SHOULDERS, SHOVES OUT HIS MASSIVE CHEST, AND...
ULP! H-HIS UNIFORM IS BURSTING APART!
RI-II-IP!
THAT IS WHY I WANTED TO REMAIN IN MY SUPERMAN COSTUME, SIR! IT'S BUILT TO TAKE ANY SORT OF PUNISHMENT!
ARE YOU TALKING BACK TO A SUPERIOR OFFICER? GET OVER TO THE SUPPLY ROOM, FOR ANOTHER G.I. UNIFORM! PUT IT ON, THEN GET BACK HERE ON THE DOUBLE!
AS SUPERMAN SPEEDS BACK "ON THE DOUBLE" AT SUPER-SPEED, FRICTION WITH THE AIR CAUSES HIS SECOND ARMY UNIFORM TO BURST INTO FLAMES!
PRIVATE SUPERMAN, FROM THIS MOMENT ON, YOU WILL WEAR YOUR SUPERMAN UNIFORM AT ALL TIMES! DON'T LET ME CATCH YOU IN A G.I UNIFORM AGAIN! AND THIS IS AN ORDER!
5

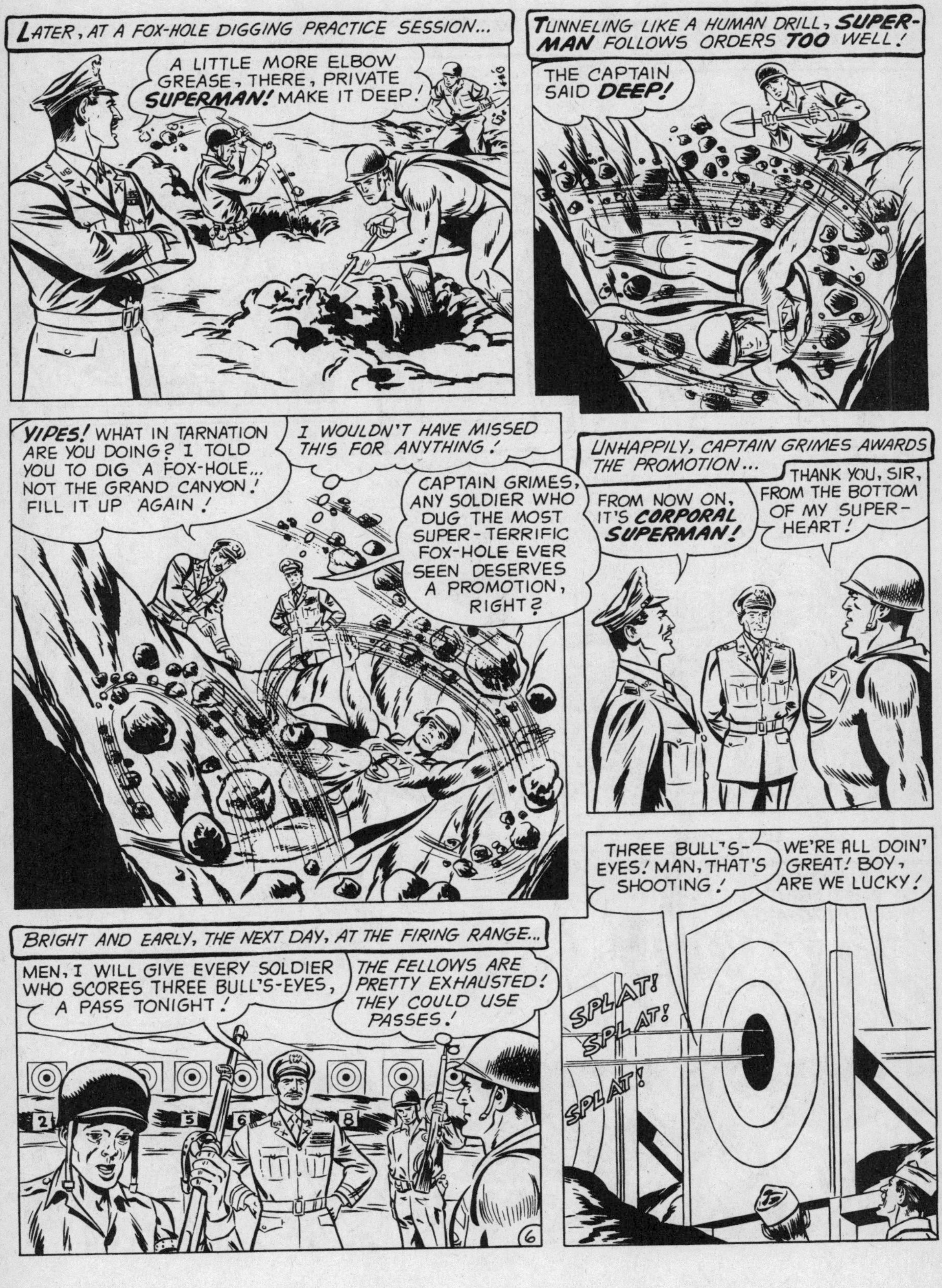
LATER, AT A FOX-HOLE DIGGING PRACTICE SESSION...
A LITTLE MORE ELBOW GREASE, THERE, PRIVATE SUPERMAN! MAKE IT DEEP!
TUNNELING LIKE A HUMAN DRILL, SUPERMAN FOLLOWS ORDERS TOO WELL!
THE CAPTAIN SAID DEEP!
YIPES! WHAT IN TARNATION ARE YOU DOING? I TOLD YOU TO DIG A FOX-HOLE... NOT THE GRAND CANYON! FILL IT UP AGAIN!
I WOULDN'T HAVE MISSED THIS FOR ANYTHING!
CAPTAIN GRIMES, ANY SOLDIER WHO DUG THE MOST SUPER-TERRIFIC FOX-HOLE EVER SEEN DESERVES A PROMOTION, RIGHT?
UNHAPPILY, CAPTAIN GRIMES AWARDS THE PROMOTION...
FROM NOW ON, IT'S CORPORAL SUPERMAN!
THANK YOU, SIR, FROM THE BOTTOM OF MY SUPER-HEART!
BRIGHT AND EARLY, THE NEXT DAY, AT THE FIRING RANGE...
MEN, I WILL GIVE EVERY SOLDIER WHO SCORES THREE BULL'S-EYES, A PASS TONIGHT!
THE FELLOWS ARE PRETTY EXHAUSTED! THEY COULD USE PASSES!
6
THREE BULL'S-EYES! MAN, THAT'S SHOOTING!
WE'RE ALL DOIN' GREAT! BOY, ARE WE LUCKY!
SPLAT!
SPLAT!
SPLAT!

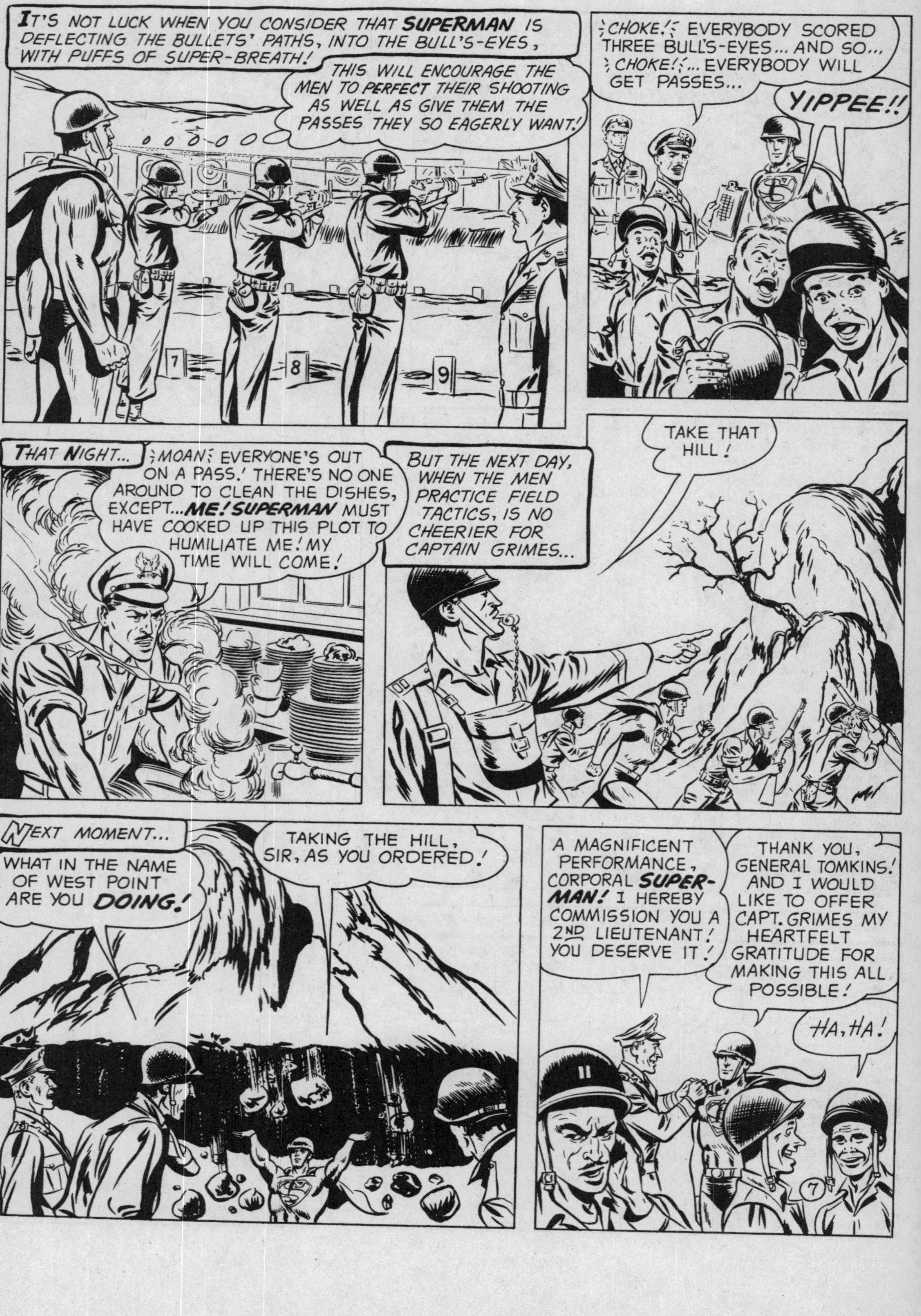
IT'S NOT LUCK WHEN YOU CONSIDER THAT SUPERMAN IS DEFLECTING THE BULLETS' PATHS, INTO THE BULL'S-EYES, WITH PUFFS OF SUPER-BREATH!
THIS WILL ENCOURAGE THE MEN TO PERFECT THEIR SHOOTING AS WELL AS GIVE THEM THE PASSES THEY SO EAGERLY WANT!
7
8
9
;CHOKE!; EVERYBODY SCORED THREE BULL'S-EYES... AND SO... ;CHOKE!;... EVERYBODY WILL GET PASSES...
YIPPEE!!
THAT NIGHT...
;MOAN; EVERYONE'S OUT ON A PASS! THERE'S NO ONE AROUND TO CLEAN THE DISHES, EXCEPT...ME! SUPERMAN MUST HAVE COOKED UP THIS PLOT TO HUMILIATE ME! MY TIME WILL COME!
BUT THE NEXT DAY, WHEN THE MEN PRACTICE FIELD TACTICS, IS NO CHEERIER FOR CAPTAIN GRIMES...
TAKE THAT HILL!
NEXT MOMENT...
WHAT IN THE NAME OF WEST POINT ARE YOU DOING!
TAKING THE HILL, SIR, AS YOU ORDERED!
A MAGNIFICENT PERFORMANCE, CORPORAL SUPERMAN! I HEREBY COMMISSION YOU A 2ND LIEUTENANT! YOU DESERVE IT!
THANK YOU, GENERAL TOMKINS! AND I WOULD LIKE TO OFFER CAPT. GRIMES MY HEARTFELT GRATITUDE FOR MAKING THIS ALL POSSIBLE!
HA, HA!
7

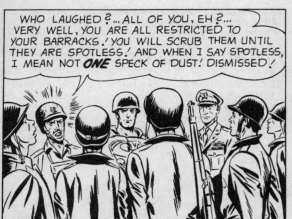

WHO LAUGHED?...ALL OF YOU, EH?... VERY WELL, YOU ARE ALL RESTRICTED TO YOUR BARRACKS! YOU WILL SCRUB THEM UNTIL THEY ARE SPOTLESS! AND WHEN I SAY SPOTLESS, I MEAN NOT *ONE* SPECK OF DUST! DISMISSED!

LATER...

THE CAPTAIN SAID HE WANTS THE PLACE *SPOTLESS!*

IT NEVER FAILS! MAKE AN ENLISTED MAN AN OFFICER AND HE GETS A SWELLED HEAD! I THOUGHT *SUPERMAN* WOULD BE DIFFERENT!

BUT WHIZZING ABOUT LIKE A CYCLONE, SUPERMAN PERSONALLY CLEANS THE BARRACKS AT AMAZING SPEED...

I TAKE BACK WHAT I SAID! *SUPERMAN* IS A GOOD JOE, EVEN IF HE IS AN OFFICER!

NICE WORK, LIEUTENANT *SUPERMAN!* BUT I FORGOT TO MENTION THAT WE WILL TAKE A 30-MILE HIKE FIRST THING IN THE MORNING! AND *YOU* WILL LEAD THE MEN!

WHEN THE MEN GET EXHAUSTED, AND SEE *SUPERMAN* UNWEARIED, THEY'LL HATE HIM!

AN HOUR LATER, THE CAPTAIN'S PLOT APPEARS TO BE SUCCEEDING...

PRETTY SOFT FOR *SUPERMAN!* BUT THE SUN IS MURDEROUSLY HOT FOR US!

THE MEN WILL DROP FROM THE HEAT UNLESS I DO SOMETHING QUICK!

HA, HA!

SIGHTING A NEARBY LAKE, SUPERMAN DRAWS A STREAM OF WATER THROUGH THE AIR WITH HIS POWERFUL VACUUM BREATH...

8

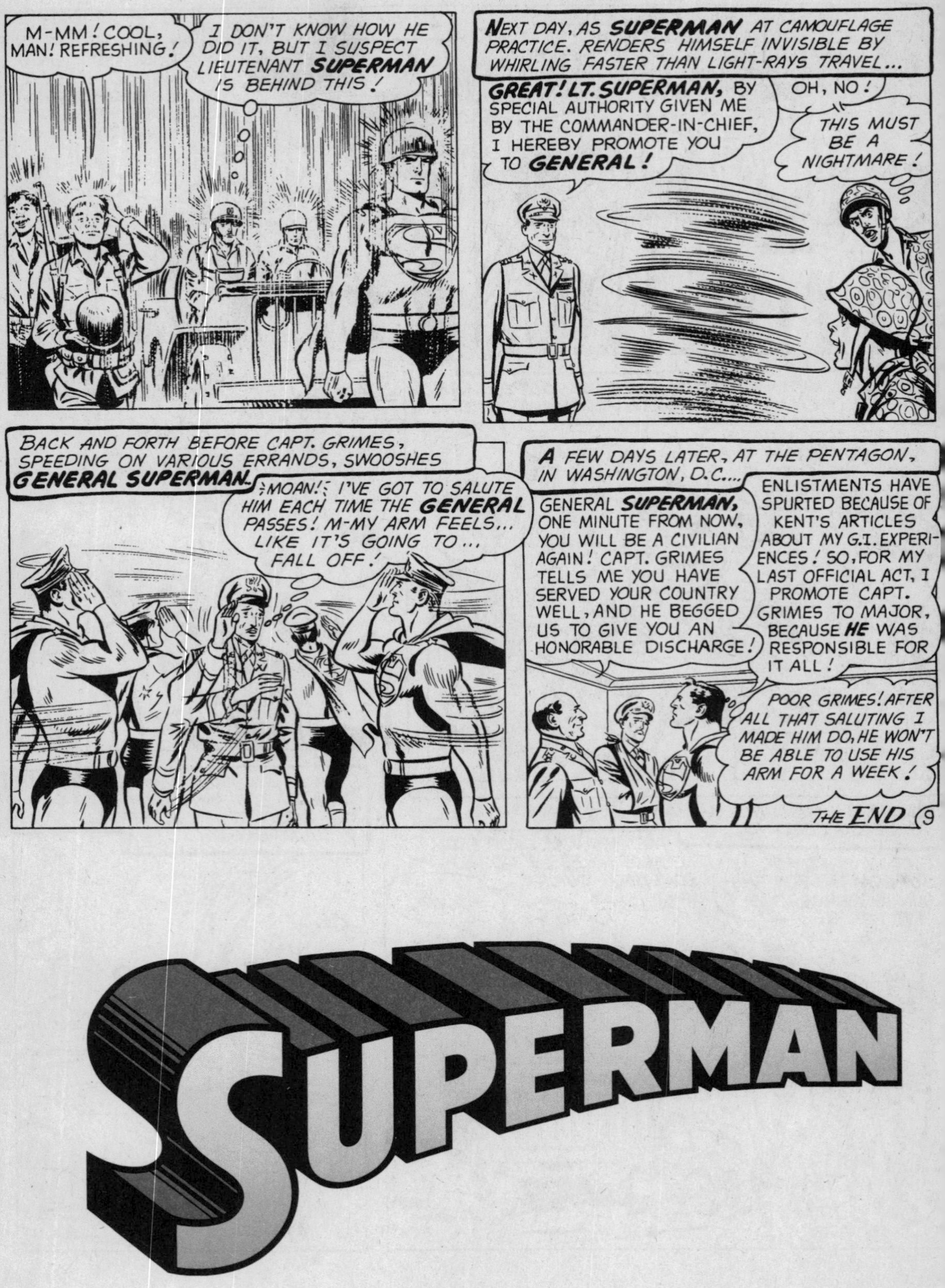
M-MM! COOL, MAN! REFRESHING!
I DON'T KNOW HOW HE DID IT, BUT I SUSPECT LIEUTENANT SUPERMAN IS BEHIND THIS!
NEXT DAY, AS SUPERMAN AT CAMOUFLAGE PRACTICE. RENDERS HIMSELF INVISIBLE BY WHIRLING FASTER THAN LIGHT-RAYS TRAVEL...
GREAT! LT. SUPERMAN, BY SPECIAL AUTHORITY GIVEN ME BY THE COMMANDER-IN-CHIEF, I HEREBY PROMOTE YOU TO GENERAL!
OH, NO!
THIS MUST BE A NIGHTMARE!
BACK AND FORTH BEFORE CAPT. GRIMES, SPEEDING ON VARIOUS ERRANDS, SWOOSHES GENERAL SUPERMAN.
MOAN! I'VE GOT TO SALUTE HIM EACH TIME THE GENERAL PASSES! M-MY ARM FEELS... LIKE IT'S GOING TO... FALL OFF!
A FEW DAYS LATER, AT THE PENTAGON, IN WASHINGTON, D.C....
GENERAL SUPERMAN, ONE MINUTE FROM NOW, YOU WILL BE A CIVILIAN AGAIN! CAPT. GRIMES TELLS ME YOU HAVE SERVED YOUR COUNTRY WELL, AND HE BEGGED US TO GIVE YOU AN HONORABLE DISCHARGE!
ENLISTMENTS HAVE SPURTED BECAUSE OF KENT'S ARTICLES ABOUT MY G.I. EXPERIENCES! SO, FOR MY LAST OFFICIAL ACT, I PROMOTE CAPT. GRIMES TO MAJOR, BECAUSE HE WAS RESPONSIBLE FOR IT ALL!
POOR GRIMES! AFTER ALL THAT SALUTING I MADE HIM DO, HE WON'T BE ABLE TO USE HIS ARM FOR A WEEK!
THE END
9

SUPERMAN

FULL CONTENTS

Part 1
INTRODUCTION

Part 2
ANALYSIS OF THE ENVIRONMENT

vii